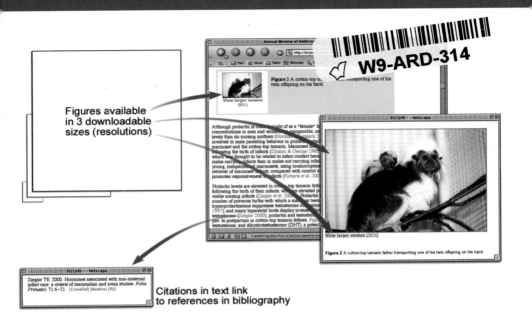

Figures available in 3 downloadable sizes (resolutions)

Figure 2 A cotton-top... transporting one of his twin offspring on his back.

View larger version (80K)

View larger version (241K)

Figure 2 A cotton-top tamarin father transporting one of his twin offspring on his back.

Ziegler TE. 2000. Hormones associated with non-maternal infant care: a review of mammalian and avian studies. *Folia Primatol.* 71:6–21 [CrossRef] [Medline] [ISI]

Citations in text link to references in bibliography

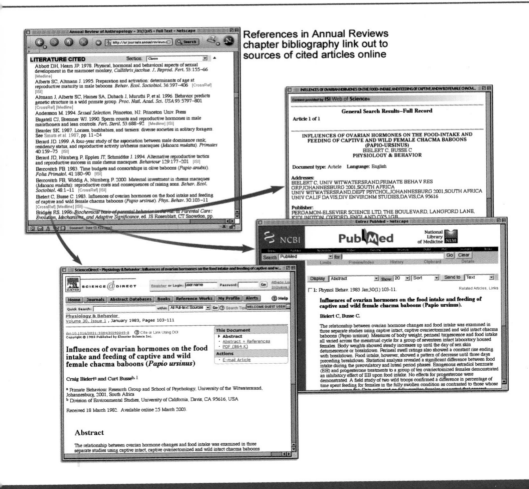

References in Annual Reviews chapter bibliography link out to sources of cited articles online

ANNUAL REVIEW OF ANTHROPOLOGY

ANNUAL REVIEW OF

ANTHROPOLOGY

VOLUME 33, 2004

WILLIAM H. DURHAM, *Editor*
Stanford University

JEAN COMAROFF, *Associate Editor*
University of Chicago

JANE HILL, *Associate Editor*
University of Arizona

www.annualreviews.org   science@annualreviews.org   650-493-4400

ANNUAL REVIEWS
4139 El Camino Way • P.O. Box 10139 • Palo Alto, California 94303-0139

ANNUAL REVIEWS
Palo Alto, California, USA

International Standard Serial Number: 0084-6570
International Standard Book Number: 0-8243-1933-8
Library of Congress Catalog Card Number: 72-821360

TYPESET BY TECHBOOKS, FAIRFAX, VA
PRINTED AND BOUND BY MALLOY INCORPORATED, ANN ARBOR, MI

PREFACE: A "Peer-Invited" Publication

Authors often ask, "Can I list my chapter in the *Annual Review of Anthropology* on my CV as a peer-reviewed article?" Sometimes this question has been provoked because of the careful reading each chapter receives from the Production Editor and at least one member of our Editorial Committee before publication, and the resulting list of suggestions for improvement. And sometimes the question is raised by a junior faculty member, eager to know if his or her contribution will "count" toward a pending tenure review.

There are good reasons why an *ARA* chapter should indeed count in the tenure review process. But it should count (*a*) because it is "peer invited" as explained below, which confers particular distinction and status on a chapter, and (*b*) because it meets the recognized standards of Annual Reviews quality, not because it is peer reviewed in the normal sense. In brief, an *ARA* chapter should count as "peer invited" not "peer reviewed," and we hope that deans and review committees recognize this fact.

"Peer invited" has a special and distinctive meaning. It means that chapters in the *ARA*, or in any Annual Reviews series for that matter, are solicited of those authors who, in the judgment of the full Editorial Committee of eight members (often assisted by two or three additional guest colleagues at the planning meetings), are the very best people in the world to write on a given topic. In our customary practice, an author who is proposed for a particular review topic must be agreed on in advance (i.e., at the planning stage, 20 months or so before publication) by the full set of 8 to 11 colleagues, including scrutinizing scholars from other subfields of the discipline. So where peer review entails selectivity for content once a paper is written, peer invitation entails selectivity for expertise from the start, and often by a larger panel of peers. Even then, each chapter will be later vetted and read carefully to assure that it meets *ARA* standards.

As a result, chapters published in the *ARA* warrant a special status, akin to peer reviewed but of a different kind. Because they are peer invited by an Editorial Committee that selects top experts on specific topics, the resulting reviews form a category distinct from the usual chapter in an edited volume or conference proceeding. The volume before you here is no exception, containing 25 review chapters written by the experts. We hope you find each chapter to be insightful, stimulating, and well worth counting toward tenure reviews as well as other measures of scholarly attainment.

To help with the annual challenge of finding the best authors and topics, we are pleased to welcome to the Editorial Committee Cynthia Beall (of Case Western Reserve), who rotates on for a five-year term as Peter Ellison (of Harvard) rotates off.

We shall all miss Peter's wise words and ecumenical perspective. In like manner, we welcome on board International Correspondent Thomas H. Eriksen (University of Oslo), who steps in for Andre Gingrich (University of Vienna). Again this year, the Editorial Committee is unanimous in its acclaim for our outstanding Production Editor, Jennifer Mann. Thank you, Jennifer, for another smooth and productive year.

William H. Durham
Editor

Annual Review of Anthropology
Volume 33, 2004

CONTENTS

INDEXES

ERRATA

An online log of corrections to *Annual Review of Anthropology*
chapters may be found at http://anthro.annualreviews.org/errata.shtml

RELATED ARTICLES

From the *Annual Review of Ecology and Systematics*, Volume 34 (2003)

Data, Models, and Decisions in US Marine Fisheries Management: Lessons for Ecologists, Kenneth A. Rose and James H. Cowan Jr.

Social Organization and Parasite Risk in Mammals: Integrating Theory and Empirical Studies, Sonia Altizer, Charles L. Nunn, Peter H. Thrall, John L. Gittleman, Janis Antonovics, Andrew A. Cunnningham, Andrew P. Dobson, Vanessa Ezenwa, Kate E. Jones, Amy B. Pedersen, Mary Poss, and Juliet R.C. Pulliam

From the *Annual Review of Genomics and Human Genetics*, Volume 5 (2004)

Africans and Asians Abroad: Genetic Diversity in Europe, Guido Barbujani and David B. Goldstein

Comparative Primate Genomics, Wolfgang Enard and Svante Pääbo

Epigenetics and Human Disease, Yong-Hui Jiang, Jan Bressler, and Arthur L. Beaudet

Medical Genetics in Developing Countries, Arnold Christianson and Bernadette Modell

Population Genetics, History, and Health Patterns in Native Americans, Connie J. Mulligan, Keith Hunley, Suzanne Cole, and Jeffrey C. Long

From the *Annual Review of Nutrition*, Volume 24 (2004)

Vitamin B12 Deficiency as a Worldwide Problem, Sally P. Stabler and Robert H. Allen

From the *Annual Review of Political Science*, Volume 7 (2004)

Global Media and Politics: Transnational Communication Regimes and Civic Cultures, W. Lance Bennett

Actors, Norms, and Impact: Recent International Cooperation Theory and the Influence of the Agent-Structure Debat, Kate O'Neill, Jörg Balsiger, and Stacy D. VanDeveer

What Does Political Economy Tell Us About Economic Development—and Vice Versa? Philip Keefer

Annu. Rev. Anthropol. 2004. 33:1–19
doi: 10.1146/annurev.anthro.33.070203.143928

THE WHOLE PERSON AND ITS ARTIFACTS

Marilyn Strathern

Department of Social Anthropology, University of Cambridge,
Cambridge CB2 3RF, United Kingdom; email ms10026@cam.ac.uk

Key Words sufficient information, personhood, well-being, Papua New Guinea, pharmacogenetics, museums

■ **Abstract** The joint themes of this volume of the *Annual Review of Anthropology*, the body as a public surface and new technologies of communication, are also woven into the design of the new Wellcome Trust Gallery at the British Museum, inspiring the reflections of this chapter. In the museum setting, moreover, an interesting question of scale arises: how particular objects can point sometimes to very particular values and sometimes to very general ones. This museological paradox is explored here. Taking a cue from the Gallery's focus on well-being, we find a parallel in the contrast between particular medicines used for specific complaints and a more general demand made on medicine as a set of organized practices for promoting health. We also find ideas about the whole person. Attending to the whole person requires its own technology, its own artifacts. And looking at artifacts from different times and places compels us to ask, What kind of "whole" is being imagined? The question is posed with materials from early twentieth-century London, mid-century Papua, and turn-of-the-century biomedicine.

Scale plays all kinds of tricks. What, for example, constitutes sufficient information? This question is answerable on its own: One needs as much information as is relevant for the purpose in hand—whether to prove a point, get out of an impasse, or explore a concept. Information is the substance of that proof, solution, or reflection. But when one writes about the process, offers an exposition, the issue becomes what else does the reader need to know. Context cannot be taken for granted: What was implicit as the reason for taking a particular route in the first place must now be made explicit. So information must be added to information, a position that pushes into the foreground the choice of expository mode.

I take advantage of the two themes of this volume, the body as a public surface and new technologies of communication, to dwell on certain enduring moments in social anthropology over the past century. I also exemplify some of the tricks of the trade for handling information in the service of exposition. The materials depicting these particular moments (they come from early twentieth-century London, mid-century Papua, and turn-of-the-century transnational biomedicine) were inspired by a new permanent display at the the Wellcome Trust Gallery in the British

Museum called Living and Dying.[1] The exhibit employs the Museum's extensive ethnographic materials to focus on how people respond to the challenges of life and how they sustain health and well-being. The theme of well-being is not something I would normally address. But one trick of the anthropological trade, being open to the unpredictable, is that one is ever assembling "more" information than one thinks one wants. There ought to be enough in the backpack to make a contribution. I am not saying that anthropologists can write about anything, but rather that disciplines offer resources that can be put to use in unexpected situations. There is a difference between using one's discipline and being an expert, a role that in these interdisciplinary days I find quite troubling.

One effect of the self-avowed knowledge economy has been to turn information into currency. Use value appears to depend on exchange value. Many certainly hold this view of scholarly knowledge. People openly state that there is no point in having such knowledge if one cannot communicate it, and they mean communicate it in the same form, that is, as knowledge. (Arguably, "knowledge" is communicated as "information," but insofar as it is meant to be adding to someone else's knowledge, the terms can be hyphenated.) The fact that knowledge may have contributed to a solution or reflection is beside the point: It is invisible, even useless, unless it can circulate as knowledge-information. The social source of (circulateable, consumable) knowledge-information becomes the expert. Of course there is a huge history behind the formation of the expert in modern times, and again behind the professional; I offer a tiny ethnographic glimpse in the first section. The same person may be both, but the roles are increasingly detached, as (at least in the United Kingdom) professions lose status and knowledge-information experts feed an appetite in public policy for evidence.

Here we have different answers to the question about sufficient information. The expert is like the industrial designer: Everything involved in a situation, any kind of material, must be calibrated for its contribution as evidence. If one provides information on internal migration in order to understand population movement, its sufficiency will be a function of the precision with which the origin of the migrant, economic standing, aspirations, and all other variables can be specified. The values must be unequivocal. Again, apropos marriage arrangements in the absence of registration procedures, deciding on a specific model for calculating a divorce rate, containing a nest of prior decisions such as what constitutes marriage in the first place, means that there is really only one route to collecting data. Development anthropology has long been an arena in which the anthropologist is fashioned as an expert, and a difficult role it is too. I chose London residents (Early Twentieth-Century London, below) to evoke the subjects of much third world development without type-casting such persons as dwellers in the tropics or

---

[1]An earlier version of this text, called "Medicines and Medicines: the Whole Person and its Artefacts," was delivered as the 2003 William Fagg Memorial Lecture, at the opening of the Wellcome Trust Gallery at the British Museum. The Wellcome Trust is a major funder of medical research in the United Kingdom.

the bush or countryside. (The reader also may find an echo with the emergence of "system" as a theoretical object of structural-functionalism.)

The professional, by contrast, closer to practitioners of academic disciplines, is expected to draw on evolving training and experience. A discipline provides ways of thinking to justify taking particular routes. Materials consist of models and theories, and sufficiency pertains to the degree of fit between problem and analytical procedure. Take the comparative method in social anthropology, a paradigmatic trick of the trade. Comparison entails thinking across contexts, juxtaposing values. Knowing what happens elsewhere, one might ask what kind of view of the migrant is preempted by focusing on economic aspirations, or query the relevance of a divorce rate to men's or women's preoccupations. Models for, say, thinking about economics or kinship also follow trajectories of their own. Sufficiency lies in how much one needs to know to satisfy the criteria that make data recognizable, and there may be more than one route to explore. Definitions condense whole debates: "We can refer to a judicial system then," "don't talk of buying women, talk of transferring rights over them," and (a bowdlerized version of David Schneider to Meyer Fortes), "Ah, I get it! *You* mean that conjugal union is *for real*!" Perhaps such condensing of opposing stances is why symbolic anthropology, and its ambivalent relationship to structuralism, remains so influential. The second section, which includes selections from already highly analyzed material from Papua, depends on certain disciplinary traditions of interpretation.

Anthropology is blessed by the rich materials so many people have put at its elbow. I am not an expert on well-being, yet the discipline allows me to tackle issues surrounding it. Cues from the museum display, and familiarity with jumping context, suggest a comparative exercise. Comparison materially enlarges the possibilities of exposition itself, through analogies spoken and unspoken (it does not always matter if communication is uneven). At any rate, and inadvertently, the topic of well-being drew me into the themes of this volume. The first two sections touch on what can be read from bodies, and from body surfaces, strongly so in the Papuan case, in so far as the body regimens described here comprise a technology of communication. The final section is deliberately delocalized. It addresses one of the problems of genetic information, where ethical concerns focus on what should be known and what can be communicated about the body.

EARLY TWENTIETH-CENTURY LONDON

It is coincidence that the year 1914, which witnessed the last major expansion of the British Museum before the present decade, saw another enterprise move premises. There is no comparison with the small Nursery School and Baby Camp that opened in Deptford (South London), unless perhaps in the perception that only changes in scale could meet contemporary needs.

> The teachers stand a little aghast. This nurture is all very well, but it is not their business. Not their business! Then nothing of the greatest things, the removal of disease and vice and dullness is their business! They are not going on to lead us, but only to find a simplified way of spelling?. . . . The teacher of little children is not merely giving them lessons. She is helping to make a brain and nervous system, and this work. . .is going to determine all that comes after. . . . Others are going to teach a big girl history, or a big boy Latin. *She* is going to modify or determine the structure of brain centres. (McMillan 1919, p. 175, quoted by Bradburn 1976, p. 111)

Margaret McMillan had been campaigning since 1897 for reform in the training of elementary and nursery school teachers. At Deptford she experimented with an open-air school for nursery-age children.[2] Need was obvious. Of the first 87 children who entered the camp, all purportedly fit, only nine were found to have no health problems (Stevinson 1927, p. 55). Some of the reasons were clear. Here is a snatch of reported dialogue followed by the author's general comment (Stevinson 1927, p. 12):

"You wouldn't go for to bath them, Miss, now would yer? It wouldn't be right."

"Oh, but, Mrs. Ruffle. . .we always bathe our babies. They love it. Look at them!"

"Ah, Miss," was grandmother's sage reply. "We often like what's bad for us and does us 'arm."

"Many of our mothers put too many clothes on their children. It is hard to make them realize how unhealthy it is. . . . One little boy came to us who suffered from a weak chest. We found he was wrapped round and round in layers of newspaper soaked in camphorated oil. How long this padding had enveloped his poor little body I should not like to say."

McMillan's vision went beyond immediate remedy. "The creation of a nobler human race in a nobler social order" was her ultimate goal but, as her biographer says (Bradburn 1976, p. 50), she realized the children could hardly wait for the new world order. Something needed to be done at once. Poor, in ill health, starved of education, many privations went together. Her expostulation to teachers came from the conviction that children needed nurture in schools.[3] She introduced infants to the rhythm of a well-ordered day, allowed for quiet times, and provided space, fresh air (all year round), wholesome food, and shelters in class-sized units that made up a village of family groups. And why was she concerned to instill professionalism in the teachers? A nursery school teacher needed to be of a higher class than

---

[2]"Margaret envisaged her nursery as providing an environment in which talent would be salvaged and children encouraged to develop the full range of their abilities. Thus the Deptford nursery could be described as an experiment in the manipulation of the environment" (Bradburn 1976, p. 55).

[3]"The real object of our work is 'NURTURE,'" she said, "the organic and natural education which should precede all primary teaching and without which the work of the schools is largely lost" (Bradburn 1976, p. 55).

other teachers so that young children could be "surrounded by young women with cultivated tastes and minds" (Bradburn 1976, p. 113). A nursery school teacher was always dealing "with a brain and soul" even when she seemed to be caring for parts of the outer body such as "a nose and a lip." At any rate, whereas 80% of the new pupils had rickets, none had it a year later; in the influenza epidemic of 1921, many children and adults died in the area but none in the nursery.

A vision of privation and a vision of well-being go together. McMillan put together her school system only by seeing various problems as linked. Deptford was a part of London where the combination of poverty, dirt, and ignorance made good health almost impossible, and without health, the children—some of whom came into the school barely able to articulate words[4]—could not learn. The school was to be a social, as well as educational, establishment. By seven, the upper age limit of the school, children were being introduced to *A Midsummer Night's Dream* and the possibility of play writing.

London a century ago was another time, another culture. But it is as good an example as any of a concern with well-being that bifurcates into two parts. McMillan's analysis has several distinct components. Deficiencies demanded specialist attention: If the school had to provide education, health, and nutrition, then each required a specific technology, specific artifacts. To get the children to rest one needed mats and beds; to get them to work outside in winter one needed coats and hot meals. In contrast, these different remedies all converged in the child: For the three- or four-year-old the diverse experiences will have run together, and that was the idea. One could not do things piecemeal. In the idiom of the time, nurturing the child meant caring for its every aspect. It was being treated, we might say, as a whole person.

If the first approach analyzes, the second synthesizes: The school experiment imagines that it must take a whole regime (of remedy, reform) to bring the whole person into focus. Regime for the system is, of course, regimen for the individual. It should be added that most of the children who were brought to the nursery already were being looked after in their own way. Parents applied both specific remedies (the chest wrapped in newspaper) and general regimens (the care to avoid contact between body surface and water).

The numerous philosophizings of the time on holistic approaches to health or education, with the driving idea that the whole is more than the sum of its parts, had obvious resonance in social science. Holism also has its own history in anthropology and continues to be summoned in appeals to social context. The display in the Wellcome Gallery invites one to consider how the whole is made

---

[4]This was not only because of slovenly ways of upbringing, but from over-respectability, too. Melia and Bella were brought to school beautifully dressed, with silky well-brushed hair, practically mute, totally passive: "Of a morning, after I've washed 'em, I set Melia in one chair and Bella in another, and I've learnt 'em to sit quite still and not get theirselves messed up. They are good children. . .Never say a word, and where you put 'em, there they'll set" (Stevinson 1927, p. 18).

apparent. That it is a display of medical artifacts and issues is highly pertinent. We see both a collection of very specific items and the values or powers to which they point, items simultaneously significant as specifics and keying into wider understandings. This bifurcation is similar to the way persons perceive themselves both as one and as many simultaneously. And this duality in turn has an important bearing on how the efficacy of medicine is communicated.

Medicine, like technology, is only recognized in being efficacious (failed medicine is no such thing, i.e., is not medicine). It works if it achieves results. And those results will of course vary as widely as the subject of treatment. The subject of treatment could be a broken nose, crying at night, or being part of a population with insufficient vitamin D or part of a society in which a child will take home half its bread ration for its family. Treatments must focus on specifics. They entail all kinds of apparatus, artifacts, and specialized technologies, as might be collected in a museum. Medicines—pills, amulets—are such artifacts, particular measures to ward off particular ailments. Often visible and tangible as objects, there are of course other items not so displayable, such as prayers or spells, though these too take a specific form. Various aspects of affliction are identified by the singular treatment they summon. Indeed "specific" was, for long, a colloquialism for a dedicated remedy.

Now ethnographic museums are highly conscious of the nature of specifics, that is, of the tangible qualities of objects that give them singular form. Yet in many cases the curator or ethnographer knows so much more about them than can ever be displayed. Ethnographers are conscious of how interconnected things are. Show a stone axe and most people have some idea of how it will have been used, but show a shaman's drum or a clay figurine and the visitor might not immediately connect these artifacts to a use. What is the museum ethnographer to do? One way is to show how the specific item is part of a larger whole.

Investigators have made several notable attempts in recent years to communicate the whole regime, to convey something of the whole context—the society, the culture—in which artifacts belong. These attempts bear comparison with Miss McMillan's holistic school program. Insofar as there is an educative purpose in a museum display, it is argued, people should be exposed to some sense of the entire combination of circumstances in which an object is produced and used. The displayed object becomes a part of a whole society. Yet it can only be made into a part (that is, part of a whole) if everything known about its circumstances is made explicit—an impossible task. That exegesis has to be in media other than the object itself—wordy explanations, video clips—and there is no limit to the information that can be added. This has been a source of much debate in ethnographic museums and has required ingenious solutions. The new Wellcome Gallery suggests another way of doing things.[5] It offers an alternative approach to the open-ended, never-really-to–be–completed goal of "putting things into context" (Hirsch & Schlecker 2001).

---

[5]I also think of the work of Kuechler, Miller, and Pinney (University College London), O'Hanlon (Oxford), and Henare and Herle (Cambridge).

Because the gallery is dealing with people's perceptions of a world that nourishes and afflicts them, the effects that events and ailments have on their lives, how bodies live and die, it can, museologically speaking, mobilize one highly significant resource; that is, people's own ideas about what a "complete" remedy would be.[6] These ideas may draw on a concept of the whole person, though in many societies that would be a poor translation for the completing or totalizing effects for which people strive. What we do find very often is something similar to the bifurcation encountered earlier in the discussion. Specific treatment for specific conditions accompany occasions on which people enlarge their sense of themselves and attend to well-being through techniques they perceive as encompassing or embracing. Though I use as a short-hand the term holism, recognizing that holism itself has no scale, and that it hardly captures the character of different totalizing practices, modes of holism can bifurcate, too.

On the one hand, all over the world we find systems that echo the kind of programmatic scheme that McMillan promoted, in which numerous distinct and specific items are drawn together, with the sense that nothing less than total enumeration will do. On the other hand, people can use the specifics as such to summon a larger vision of themselves. This idea is a different kind of access to totality: One artifact could be enough to point to the whole.

There is more to such a summoning than metonymy, the convention of parts standing for wholes. An item can remain particular and be animated as a whole entity larger than it appears. There is nothing mysterious about this idea. (An old exercise book may simultaneously recall attempts to write a novel and an entire epoch of aspirations and hopes.) It is a figure seen twice (Riles 2000, pp. 166–70). People understand that an object can both be a specific item and contain the world within itself; it condenses or miniaturizes a wider context. Thus an object may make present powers or forces that affect a person's life, whether imagined as the environment, the cosmos, or the community. Paraphernalia used in seances or ritual performances are an obvious example. The museological outcome is that specific items on display do not have to be crowded around with other objects or other media to make the point about context. The skill is for themselves to point to the concept of wholeness. Not all subjects or themes would be amenable to this approach; well-being happens to be one that does.

In sum, if the relationship between the individual item and the whole world it points to is general in museum displays, the theme of the Wellcome Gallery brings it home by virtue of its focus on well-being and thus on people's own sense of a wider context for their health. I suggested that remedial treatment may bifurcate. Whereas some treatments only seem to minister to body parts or specific afflictions, other treatments will summon a totalizing appreciation of what needs remedy. Here one found another bifurcation, between wholeness imagined as the sum of parts and wholeness summoned in an individual item. But what is part and

---

[6]As in many of these instances, "part" and "whole" are relative, situated conceptions. Thus the specific "whole" identity being claimed may also be construed, merographically, as a "part" of a wider set of identities.

what is whole will depend on where the actor is, the culture he/she belongs to, and the period in history it is! Remedies for human affliction also will depend on what concept of the person is being summoned.

MID-CENTURY PAPUA

If ideas about health and well-being point to ways in which persons can be imagined in a totalizing sense, how is this made known? A few generations and too many wars since 1914, a good example is offered by current debate over the U.K. National Health Service.

Deptford, as was, is gone; the desirability of all-around health care has apparently won. Yet from all sides come accusations of fragmentation affecting health care delivery. We can never keep up with demands to offer a complete service. What is being fragmented now? The same thing—the complaint concerns the failure to treat the patient as a whole person. This is not because the person thinks every aspect of his or her well-being ought to be medicalized; rather the issue is that in addition to the ailment or affliction, the person him- or herself remains. One artifact has become a symbol for the very idea of attending to the whole person; it consists of a specific device—communication with the expert. The momentary conversation between doctor and patient required for passing on information may be sufficient for the patient to feel attended to as some kind of integrated being.

There is a haunting story from old Deptford of a little girl taken by a neighbor to the hospital after a fall to have her face stitched; as soon as the mother saw her, she responded to the girl's hollering and took out the stitches (Stevinson 1927, p. 4). What then was attributed to the patient's ignorance these days would be seen as a failure of communication by the hospital. But there is more than practical medicine here. In present times communication is valued for its own sake because it acknowledges the patient apart from the ailments. Patients may regard themselves as a repository of knowledge (they tell the doctor things) and one who gives knowledge also should receive it, treated not just humanely but also intelligently. Here the whole person makes its appearance as an agent. In short, a rather specific act, sharing information, summons something much more comprehensive—respect for the person as a subject rather than as an object—and that respect in turn (as far as Euro-Americans are concerned) activates the whole person.

If "medicines" depends on the analysis of specific conditions, I wonder if we might use the singular term "medicine" to refer to the synthesis, to the idea that treatment will only be successful in the long run if it also mobilizes procedures dealing with the health of the whole person. The power of medicine is different from the power of medicines. By and large we are happy if people can move between the two, as when the doctor moves from prescription to bedside manner. A small technique itself, that manner acknowledges the person in the patient.

As to information conveyed, the patient adds it to preexisting knowledge. Adding knowledge is what the museum does when it tells you what an artifact is. In the same way as items can become cultural objects or social signifiers through the information attached to them, medicines can become medicine when a little piece of knowledge is shared. Indeed, more generally, many procedures require that you add knowledge, however condensed, to make them effective on a grand scale. But addition may take many forms. Rehearse a spell, demonstrate a connection with someone, show you are the rightful possessor, and the person emerges in full social acknowledgment. Thus knowledge may be evinced in the information that passes between people, or in its retention by the holder who guards his or her rights of use or bestowal. To succeed aesthetically, Australian Aboriginal art requires the authority of ownership; conversely, those with intellectual and spiritual claims are those who enjoy and profit from the efficacy of the art form (Barron 1998). Such connections can be externalized in narrative or song, but that specific possession of knowledge will be enough to signal identity. Embedded knowledge may be added, then, in an artifact. Examples abound; indeed a previous British Museum exhibit on art and memory in world cultures (Mack 2003) showed how objects condense, code, and conserve knowledge of all kinds. Knowledge also may be embodied in small procedures, such as rules and protocols. McMillan's charges did not need to know why they should wash their hands or were being encouraged at water play. All they needed to know was that in addition to their activities there were rules about them. A regime is transformed into a regimen.

If we adopt the term medicine (as opposed to medicines) to connote that well-being demands a totalizing approach (without specifying what that totality could be), I would want it to embrace the two techniques of holism: creating a wider context out of many things, and having one thing summon a wider context. We can think of the two techniques as the difference between a regime to be enacted through numerous rules all of which have to be observed, and a rule that in being observed activates the compulsion of the whole regime.

To make the point I introduce the Papuan North Mekeo studied by Mosko (especially 1985) over the past 30 years; the Mekeo see well-being as a direct outcome of correct bodily management.[7] They take this idea somewhat to extremes and extend it to all manner of activities. A systematic cosmology, and something analogous to the whole person (with important caveats), is summoned by a whole regimen of behaviors, whereas knowledge in the form of rules and protocols means that any one specific rule can enact the power of the regime as a whole.

The North Mekeo have very clear ideas about the difference between well-being and its antithesis. Indeed they ascribe active and passive qualities to the two states: Being "hot" or being able to handle "hot" things means being in the advantageous position of affecting the states of others, productively or malevolently, whereas

---

[7]Mine is a truncated account of an exquisitely elaborated schema, which in the mid-twentieth century existed in many dimensions. I follow Mosko's (1985) "avowedly structuralist" recapture of that schema in the ethnographic present.

being "cold" exposes one to the machinations of others. They divide the world into entities that carry hot influences and those which render the person cold. The schema involves other oppositions as well, between what is sweet and unsweet, dirty and clean, inside and outside; they are not simple. Where to locate the body surface is a case in point. The inside of a Mekeo person's body includes or encompasses an outside. The digestive tract and abdomen is not regarded as the innermost part of a person but, to the contrary, as a passage connected to the outside world, which makes it an appropriate repository of food: The tract is part of the outside that is inside the body. Conversely, wastes from the inside body accumulate in the abdomen and are regarded as the body's interior extruded so its appears on the outside. If this is the Mekeo body, what are the signs of health and illness, and what does it take to attend to the whole person? Here, regimen becomes important.

The body is constantly susceptible to the outside world that flows through it. In a hot, healthy state the interior body (blood and flesh) processes sweet, cooked food, eliminating what remains cold and dirty from the abdomen. But an ill person excretes hot wastes (which may contaminate others; hot dirt is poison), and food remains cold and dirty inside (Mosko 1985, pp. 54–55). Concoctions made from plants such as ginger and chili are normally cold, but when given as medicines to someone who is ill they become sweet and hot and restore the normal functioning of the body. Food is not hot or sweet by itself. What gives ordinary food these qualities is the hot work that goes into its cultivation and preparation. It is not just that food takes work; it requires work (1985, pp. 48, 356), as a hot, bodily activity that renders inedible plants edible. Moreover what is true for food is true for other resources as well: Artifacts such as weapons, charms, pottery, dwellings, canoes are all rendered hot, and available for use, by labor, by the body's heat. Men's work is particularly important here.

Mosko (1985, p. 46) describes what happens when a house begins to get dilapidated and cold, unsweet, to the owner.

> The idea of a fine new house becomes correspondingly sweet. . . .[People] gather building materials from the bush: timber for pilings and frame, palm or bamboo for flooring, split sago branches for walls. . . . These bush things are initially unsweet. Gathering, transporting, trimming, fitting, and binding them are separate skills. By virtue of their planned combination, hot bodily exertions transform the unsweet bush materials into a sweet village resource: the complete dwelling. The tools and other implements the house builders employ in their work are also sweet village resources that have been transformed by the bodily work skills in their manufacture.[8]

We see both analysis and synthesis here. The specific skills are like medicines, each suited to its task. Thus a stone axe is hot for cutting down a tree (and cold

---

[8]As a final comment on how one ensures this state of well-being, he adds, "Thus, the sweet products of work conserve the hot of the active body and are themselves hot for transforming other unsweet bush resources to sweet village ones" (1985, p. 46).

for cooking food), even as fire is hot for cooking food (and cold for cutting down trees) (Mosko 2002, p. 98). Every artifact effects its own type of transformation and thus has its own agency. At the same time, medicine is mobilized in the combination of effort, the knowledge embodied in the coordination of activities, that produces the house as a totalizing object. And the medicine still works after the house is built. This is the twin to the perspective on the whole as a compilation of parts. People's houses remain as singular monuments to their now invisible efforts and indeed are "regarded as extensions of their bodies and persons" (Mosko 2002, p. 100). House building, a specific process, enacts the wider capacity of persons to extend themselves. The specific artifact, the building, recalls that.

Human exertion has cosmological effect, and just as work renders food edible, tools must be rendered usable. Perhaps, after all, the museum visitor referred to earlier could not have immediately deduced what the stone axe was for: If one looks at an axe from Mekeo now, with this added knowledge, one knows it is part of a cycle that sustains human well-being. The axe can be used only at certain times by people in certain states[9]; its efficacy is evidence of the exertion of effort and of the observance of rules. One element of this regime will be sufficient to summon the concept in the future. Indeed wherever the Mekeo look, they see things, occasions, activities that give tangible evidence of their wider aspirations to well-being. A rule about one of these says it about all.

If one rule says it all, no single rule appears in isolation. The same is true of persons. Persons can appear only as part of a nexus of relationships. Note that coordination of the house building involves several people so that a combination of skills is also a combination of persons. But it is not a miscellany. Mekeo have precise notions about the way persons affect one another; one might look here for whole person. As in many Papua New Guinean societies, health depends not just on what the subject does with his or her body but also on protocols that determine what kind of object he or she is to others. People can affect one another by the way they care for their own bodies, widely true in Melanesia through observing rules to mitigate (or enhance) states of pollution or danger. Conversely, well-being entails appropriate beneficial interactions between persons. The analogue to the Euro-American whole person, one could say, is being completed by relationships with others. Though there are as many kinds of completion as there are relationships, this is canonically manifest in interactions between spouses.

So what is medicine? For the Mekeo it lies in managing a body both constitutionally open and closed to others, depending on the phase it is in. In the right situation, and in the right gender, either openness or closure may be healthy or life-threatening. Men put themselves through the most severe regimes of semistarvation in order to render their bodies impervious to the attacks of others. It is virtual attack they fear, sorcery. Whereas an open hot body has the power to

---

[9]Mekeo is not the only area in Papua New Guinea where, in the days of stone axes, tools lost their edge and would not cut properly if used by the wrong people.

enter and receive the bodies of others, a light, dry, closed body renders the sorcery of one's enemies cold.[10] When men are in this second state, ordinary food becomes unsweet, and they avoid their families in order to protect them, purge themselves with medicines, and take pride in a tiny waist, tightening their bodies with belts, in a supermasculine state (Mosko 1985, pp. 86, 91). Rules for behavior and the aesthetics of self-presentation go together. However, men must alternate these states of being because fertility, as well as capacity for work, depends on their bodies being open. Women put themselves through an equally uncomfortable regimen, the proportions reversed. Leading up to and beyond conception, and for the sake of their child's health, they must engorge themselves and, for far longer than men, keep their bodies open and grow the child through the transmission of substance. It is only when her child is weaned that a mother becomes relatively abstemious and closed. Body process is divided into distinct phases; the mutual calibration of husband's and wife's body form communicates their current well-being.

Mekeo people make themselves productive or dangerous to one another, and to themselves, and in corresponding degree seek out fruitful interactions and put remedies in place to overcome the dangers.[11] The idea that harm and adversity can come as much from other people as from anywhere lies behind their remedial strategies. Knowledge is never sufficient: One must keep constant track of the consequences of one's actions, and of the actions of others.

Where people locate their sense of well-being, then, is profoundly relevant for the efficacy they accord to treatment. We encounter several kinds of persons in these few examples. (They are exemplary and not exhaustive.) And the nature of the person indicates what it takes to sustain well-being and remedy affliction in any totalizing way. Following (a) McMillan's children who can be molded by their social and economic environment, I glanced at the whole person revealed through (b) recognition of knowledge-ownership that gives the Australian artist rightful access to intellectual and spiritual creativity and through (c) acknowledgment of agency in the practices of clinical communication. Finally (d) the Mekeo show us

---

[10]The converse of open fertility is exposure to all kinds of other persons, from a man's point of view, including enemies. By closing his body a man hopes to make the sorcery of others cold and ineffective, while his own sorcery is potentially hot to those whose bodies are open and vulnerable. But when they resume sexual relations, they hope to make their wives pregnant as soon as possible (1985, pp. 86–88). Once his wife has conceived and sexual relations are abandoned, it takes a man some six months to "tighten" his body, during which he does as much agricultural work as possible, leaving his wife to continue when he becomes too "cold" for work. The ethnographic present here is the 1970s and before, and much has changed since. In recent publications, Mosko (e.g., 2001) shows how the power of this thinking nowadays works through money and charismatic Christianity.

[11]The open is also the "partible" body (cf. Mosko 2001, 2002); persons grow, have influence, and maintain their own well-being through detaching and attaching parts of themselves from and to others.

instances of persons taking alternate bodily forms that carry them through a life cycle of interaction with others.

Now, what is distributed through these examples may be found by some measure in all of them. I conclude with a single field of practices that yields several different delineations of the person.

TURN-OF-THE-CENTURY BIOMEDICINE

I have created a context of sorts for turning now to a present-day procedure that belonged first to the world of medicine and then more generally to science and technology that is now ubiquitous and has burgeoned over the past generation. In place of rules this procedure offers its own specifics: principles. Any specific principle can summon the whole regime, and the nature of the regime is such that if one observes any of its principles, then one is considering the whole situation. More than that, the field itself acts as a kind of specific in relation to what amounts to a vast area of medical and technological activity. I refer to bioethics.

Bioethics has come to occupy a special place in twenty-first century (Euro-American) governance. Here people talk readily about the whole person. One of the powers of bioethics is the way it can simultaneously stand for the whole person and the whole society. Two sets of materials from research, funded as it happens by the Wellcome Trust, belong to prevalent debates about well-being. One comes from a study of approaches to biomedicine in Sri Lanka (Simpson 2003), and the other is an investigation into pharmacogenetics (Corrigan 2004; O. Corrigan, personal communication).

Given a shift over the past 30 years toward deregulation, an open market economy, and the development of private practice, not to mention acceleration in the scope and diversity of medical treatments, the Sri Lankan medical profession now looks in two directions. On one hand are those who wish to sustain the Western-based medical tradition in which they were trained; on the other are those who think that more account should be taken of indigenous medical practices. Medical ethics dramatizes the split: the Hippocratic tradition and its translation via neoliberal cultural tenets about what constitutes well-being against attempts to introduce Asian religious and philosophical practices. As Simpson depicts this changing and contentious situation, the issue is about how society can be taken into account. People may regard the very action of raising bioethical questions as an index to broaden the context in which to scrutinize particular practices. Thus the Nuffield Report (by the UK-based Nuffield Council on Bioethics) on externally sponsored research in developing countries puts the practice of medical research into the context of economics, politics, and the conditions of primary care that pertain in the developing world. One of the four ethical principles that provides the framework for the Report is "the duty to be sensitive to cultural differences" (Nuffield Counc. 2002, p. xv). The report cannot consider every aspect of these societies, but raising social and cultural questions at all makes society present as a significant reference point.[12] This is one way in which bioethics works as a specific in relation to the whole society.

Sri Lanka is not, of course, the only place where social pluralism raises the obvious question of whose society it is.[13] But the debates there do emphasize the point that worth and well-being are susceptible to local definition, and in any one place there may be several locales (Clark 2002, 2003). First, then, one kind of person who is the subject of bioethical considerations is known by his or her socioeconomic environment and by the cultural inclinations and the values significant to that person's own dignity and self-respect. The specifics are the details of these values, and the whole person is recognized precisely to the extent that the values they hold dear are valued by others in turn.

In another arena all together, it is anticipated that one will be able to take advantage of the specifics of conditions and treatments precisely by considering the whole person. The focus is on diversity between individuals, and from this, on their uniqueness as well. Science offers a particularly powerful way of imagining uniqueness: the person as defined by the genetic body. The genetic body belongs to the person as an individual (give or take a few relatives), and here Western ethics is on its home ground, determining principles for personal good conduct and good conduct toward other individuals. Responsibility for one's own well-being comes into view.

The advantage conferred by specificity belongs, above all, to pharmacogenetics. Pharmacogenetics is a potential solution to the capacity of specifics to proliferate. As far as medicines are concerned, particular ailments, again, call for particular remedies and the more specific the remedy, the more effective the treatment. Yet as our capacity to manufacture medicines increases, the specifics proliferate but never seem specific enough. Too many pills exist for too many diverse conditions and yet are never sufficient because there is no end to the permutations of affliction. Genetically tailored medicine enters with the promise of control that

---

[12]"Individuals live within particular societies, the cultural assumptions and practices of which shape their understanding of themselves and others .... Even when they are in revolt against their cultural upbringing, individuals often tend to think of themselves in the light of the concepts and understandings they have acquired in their society, including their understanding of sickness and health .... As a result, the general duty of respect implies a duty to be sensitive to other cultures" (Nuffield Council 2002, sections 4.14 and 4.25, p. 51).

[13]Simpson writes (2003, p. 15), "At a time when biomedical ethics appears to have begun to take on board the significance of inter-cultural differences, it is therefore appropriate to draw attention to the importance of intra-cultural differences. For the majority of Sri Lankans...the logical place to build a locally informed response to western biomedical ethics is out of Buddhism's own tradition of a virtue-based, consequentialist ethical analysis. However, there are other traditions—Hindu, Christian and Moslem—and other positions—secular, humanist and rationalist—which render 'culture' [ditto, society] far from homogeneous. ..."

works at an ultraspecific level. It addresses the diversity of individual responses to medication by focusing on them. In brief, pharmacogenetics is the application of knowledge about individual genetic variation to the production and administration of medicines. Control comes from being able to specify the needs of the individual patient as known through their genetic make-up. This is a second way of thinking about the person. Insofar as attention is paid to the individual's genome, it summons a whole person of sorts because the genome is imagined as a totalizing or holistic description of the person as a subject of heredity, and persons are held to own these descriptions of themselves.[14]

The promise of pharmacogenetics is to eliminate the hazards of prescribing medicines. In lieu of knowledge gleaned from sampling populations, "a simple and decisive gene test would indicate to the doctor which drug would be optimal for *the specific patient* sitting in front of her" (Melzer et al. 2003, emphasis added). But, Melzer continues, the high levels of precision that people assume would follow genetic information can be seriously questioned. Having access to the whole genome is not in itself informative about the whole patient, given all the external factors (environment) that influence responses to drugs.

When environment is imagined not just as physical but also as social (B. Williams-Jones and O. Corrigan, personal communication), one encounters a third kind of whole person envisioned by bioethics, recalling the National Health Service patient who complains of fragmented treatment. In that case the significant complaint is that the person is not being informed of what is going on. In pharmacogenetics, a crucial issue over conveying information occurs long before the possibility of treatment. Treatment for the person may not even be a long-term prospect. This is the point when trials must be undertaken to establish a match between pharmaceutical remedy and genetic endowment. With the notion of people undergoing genetic testing to assist study of genetic endowment, questions may be asked on behalf of the subject. That is, the person is preconstructed as needing protection from intrusion. General ethical questions arise over the management of genetic information that belongs to the individual and the ownership of knowledge in terms of privacy and disclosure. But pharmacogenetics brings specific questions about consent to medical research, the kind of counseling individuals undergoing testing need, and the relay of information back to the research subject who may also be a patient (Nuffield Council 2003, p. 5, Ch. 3, 5).

Corrigan (2004) shows just what a comprehensive construction of the person is at issue. It is epitomized in the principle of informed consent, the hallmark of the contemporary ethical approach, the one principle that stands for many. Informed consent activates the whole person as a subject or agent. Corrigan's context is the origins of bioethics stimulated by the postwar Nuremberg Code. It is a noble vision:

---

[14]The person here is rendered unique by his or her genetically specifiable body. What is totalizable is the person's entire genetic repertoire (this is not the same as saying that genetics provides a complete description of the person in other dimensions).

> [T]he voluntary consent of the human subject is absolutely essential. . ..The requirement of informed consent [has been] declared a universal human right, grounded in the fundamental dignity and worth of every individual and supported by respect for the liberty and security of the person. (2004)

Liberty in turn includes free will, a force of cosmological proportions in Western thought. More mundanely, rights and obligations are bound up with one another:

> [T]he right to autonomy comes with a concomitant obligation to make a rational choice about whether to consent. . ..And there is a parallel obligation on the part of researchers to provide sufficient information for subjects to make an informed decision. (2004)

As in the case of being attentive to cultural sensibilities, one could not have a greater whole than human dignity compelling ethical action. But the way trials create research subjects draws us back to significant omissions. Corrigan also shows us the outlines of a fourth kind of whole person, the citizen who aspires to self-actualization, and who, in the case of the research subject, knowingly contributes to public welfare for the general good. For all this, she argues, in the field of pharmacogenetics constructing subjects as biological citizens is too narrow a definition of persons and their social environment. One could say, it is not holistic enough. In providing labor and bodily material, for instance, participants in research are coproducers of a particular kind: "representing consenting patients as 'active participants' fails to acknowledge the extent to which they remain objects in the research process" (2004). One might almost say they are divided between being, or occupy the alternating states of, subjects and objects.

Ideas about the person become embedded in these bioethical considerations in diverse modes, of which I have sketched four. The practice of bioethics is the artifact here. As a field of reflection and questioning, bioethics is the tool of a larger quest that seeks medicine beyond the demonstrable effects of medicines.

A PERSONAL NOTE

I conclude with an explicit comment on scale. In her study of the Trobriands, Weiner (1976) struck on a brilliant device for at once including and disposing of Malinowski's cumbersome works. (She had apt quotations from the texts running in parallel to her own and boxed off from it: Malinowski was there but not, so to speak, in her text.) Without suggesting a larger parallel, I borrow from that device and avoid direct reference to my own work. Instead, I draw examples from elsewhere, in a manner some Melanesians would recognize as creating a composite body. Thus the substance comes from other studies; at the same time, the form is necessarily molded by my own disciplinary preoccupations. These preoccupations are, on the surface, a matter of communication (I hope) with those who share them. But perhaps this figure also amounts to what a former student (Crook 2004, Epilogue) would call a "textual person." If so, it is a wholeness with all the limits of the expository mode I have chosen.

At the end of this chapter, the question is what kind of evidence would be sufficient to answer the *Annual Review's* generous invitation to present "personal reflections on the discipline" and thus something of myself. My solution has been to deploy an artifact; this text (apart from the opening and this conclusion) is based on something I had already written for a specific audience and written without the present task in mind. Moreover, it is an artifact that deploys a certain amount of information-knowledge without bringing it in as information-knowledge. To add that information now, to make evident the chapter's basis in past work, and thus the text that is me, one could delineate the person as follows.

Briefly, the opening of the chapter addresses some abiding concerns voiced in *Partial Connections* (Strathern 1991, scale) and the edited *Audit Cultures* (2000, expertise). There also is an allusion to earlier field research in Hagen, Papua New Guinea, apropos divorce in *Women in Between* (1972), and to a study of Hagen migrants in Port Moresby (1975). The Deptford example recalls the class analysis of *Kinship at the Core* (1981) and for me contains the kind of personal associations that inform *After Nature* (1992a) (my mother's sister, Greta Martin, was one of Miss McMillan's teachers). Feminist issues are largely unmarked in this piece, but this example does put a woman in the role of expert. Melanesia has been a constant source of intellectual inspiration. The several contributions to *The Gender of the Gift* (1988) are marked by one, a penetrating work on Mekeo that I did not overtly draw on at the time, though it would have saved me a lot of trouble; others will recognize running through the chapter the figurative/literal construction on which *Gender of the Gift* was partly built. Even more so has inspiration come from many Papua New Guinean acquaintances, among others, and in the final section the Sri Lankan case stands for everything that intellectual interchanges provide [sketched recently in *Property, Substance and Effect* (Strathern 1999) and the joint volume (Hirsch & Strathern 2004). Including the Nuffield Council on Bioethics is a gesture toward other kinds of public arenas (I am a Council member); interests here stem from *Reproducing the Future* (Strathern 1992b) and the joint *Technologies of Procreation* (Edwards et al. 1993). As to artifacts, the also joint *Self-Decoration in Mt Hagen* (Strathern and Strathern 1971) was an early foray. As to museums, I started out as an assistant curator in the Cambridge University Museum of Archaeology and Anthropology.

ACKNOWLEDGMENTS

I am grateful to Oonagh Corrigan and Bob Simpson for permission to use unpublished materials. Of many whom I would thank at the British Museum, Lissant Bolton was crucial as the intellectual architect of the new gallery and as a generous guide to me.

The *Annual Review of Anthropology* is online at http://anthro.annualreviews.org

LITERATURE CITED

Barron A. 1998. No other law? Authority, property and Aboriginal art. In *Intellectual Property and Ethics*, ed. L Bently, S Maniatis, pp. 39–87, London: Sweet & Maxwell

Bradburn E. 1976. *Margaret McMillan: Framework and Expansion of Nursery Education.* Redhill, UK: Denholm House Press. Natl. Christ. Educ. Counc.

Clark D. 2002. Development ethics: a research agenda. *Int. J. Soc. Econ.* 29:830–48

Clark D. 2003. Concepts and perception of human well-being: some evidence from South Africa. *Oxford Dev. Stud.* 31:173–96

Corrigan O. 2004. Informed consent: the contradictory ethical safeguards in pharmacogenetics. In *Donating and Exploiting DNA: Social and Ethical Aspects of Public Participation in Genetic Databases*, ed. R Tutton, O Corrigan, New York: Routledge. In press

Crook T. 2004. *Kim Kurukuru: An Anthropological Exchange with Bolivip, Papua New Guinea*, London: British Academy. In press

Edwards J, Franklin S, Hirsch E, Price F, Strathern M. 1993. *Technologies of Procreation. Kinship in the Age of Assisted Conception.* Manchester, UK: Manchester Univ. Press

Hirsch E, Strathern M. 2004. *Transactions and Creations: Property Debates and the Stimulus of Melanesi.* Oxford: Berghahn

Mack J. 2003. *The Museum of the Mind. Art and Memory in World Cultures.* London: British Mus.

McMillan M. 1919. *The Nursery School.* London: Dent

Melzer D, Raven A, Detmer D, Ling T, Zimmern R, Jillions D. 2003. *My Very Own Medicine: What Must I Know? Information Policy for Pharmacogenetics.* Cambridge: Cambridge Univ. Dept. Public Health Primary Care

Mosko M. 1985. *Quadripartite Structures: Categories, Relations and Homologies in Bush Mekeo Culture.* Cambridge: Cambridge Univ. Press

Mosko M. 2001. Syncretic persons: sociality, agency and personhood in recent charismatic ritual practices among North Mekeo (PNG). *Aust. J. Anthropol.* 12:259–74

Mosko M. 2002. Totem and transaction: the objectification of 'tradition' among North Mekeo. *Oceania* 73:89–109

Nuffield Counc. 2002. *The Ethics of Research Related to Healthcare in Developing Countries.* London: Nuffield Counc. Bioethics

Nuffield Counc. 2003. *Pharmacogenetics: Ethical Issues.* London: Nuffield Counc. Bioethics

Riles A. 2000. *The Network Inside Out.* Ann Arbor: Univ. Mich. Press

Simpson B. 2003. *Between micro realities and macro ethics: What might an anthropology of contemporary biomedical ethics look like?* Presented at ASA Conf., Anthropol. Sci., Manchester

Stevinson E. 1927. *The Open-Air Nursery School.* London/Toronto: Dent

Strathern A, Strathern M. 1971. *Self-Decoration in Mount Hagen.* London: Duckworth

Strathern M. 1972. *Women in Between. Female Roles in a Male World. Mt Hagen, New Guinea.* London: Academic (Seminar)

Strathern M. 1975. *No Money on our Skins. Hagen Migrants in Port Moresby.* Canberra: New Guinea Res. Bull. 61

Strathern M. 1981. *Kinship at the Core: An Anthropology of Elmdon, Essex.* Cambridge: Cambridge Univ. Press

Strathern M. 1988. *The Gender of the Gift. Problems with Women and Problems with Society in Melanesia.* Berkeley/Los Angeles: Univ. Calif. Press

Strathern M. 1991. *Partial Connections.* ASAO Spec. Pub. 3. Savage, MD: Rowman and Littlefield

Strathern M. 1992a. *After Nature. English Kinship in the Late Twentieth Century.* Cambridge: Cambridge Univ. Press

Strathern M. 1992b. *Reproducing the Future.*

Essays on Anthropology, Kinship and the New Reproductive Technologie. Manchester: Manchester Univ. Press

Strathern M. 1999. *Property, Substance and Effect. Anthropological Essays on Persons and Things.* London: Athlone

Strathern M, ed. 2000. *Audit Cultures. Anthropological Studies in Accountability, Ethics and the Academy.* London: Routledge

Weiner A. 1976. *Women of Value, Men of Renown: New Perspectives in Trobriand Exchange.* Austin: Tex. Univ. Press

Annu. Rev. Anthropol. 2004. 33:21–45
doi: 10.1146/annurev.anthro.33.070203.143900

LANGUAGE REVITALIZATION AND NEW TECHNOLOGIES: Cultures of Electronic Mediation and the Refiguring of Communities

Patrick Eisenlohr

*Department of Anthropology, Washington University, Saint Louis,
Missouri 63130; email: peisenlo@wustl.edu*

Key Words language activism, media, computer-mediated communication, information technology, linguistic ideology

■ **Abstract** Recently, language activists and linguists have begun using new technologies in projects aimed at revitalizing the practice of lesser-used languages. This review explores related work, emphasizing how practices of electronic mediation enabled by such technologies both shape and are informed by linguistic ideologies, which in turn crucially influence the possible revived use or abandonment of linguistic varieties. New technologies are treated as part of cultures of electronic mediation, connecting sociocultural valuations to mediated discourse. Their use often has important political implications, given that projects of language revitalization are often linked to claims of ethnolinguistic recognition. Finally, because documentation of lesser-used languages using digital technologies also results in the production of new cultural objects to be stored, displayed, and circulated, attention is also focused on the forms of sociality sustained by the creation and exchange of such electronic artifacts.

INTRODUCTION

New technologies enabling the electronic mediation and mass circulation of discourse have recently become the focus of much interest in activism on behalf of minority or lesser-used languages, which raises the question of how practices of electronic mediation are situated within the sociocultural processes of language obsolescence and revitalization. Generally speaking, there is a striking gap between expert discourses seeking to mobilize Western public awareness of widespread language loss across the world today and the concerns motivating users or former users of a linguistic variety to engage in practices of linguistic revitalization. This difference also has important consequences for a critical evaluation of the use of new technologies of electronic mediation in situations of language revitalization, that is, in "attempts to add new linguistic forms or social functions to an embattled minority language with the aim to increase its uses or users" (King 2001, p. 23).

Recent scholarly concerns about the diminution of linguistic diversity around the world have frequently taken as a model the discourse on biodiversity. Against the background of a long-standing tendency in linguistics to identify languages with organisms dating back to Franz Bopp (Koerner 1983, p. xxix; see also Schleicher 1983 [1863]), the large number of languages reported to be abandoned by their speakers are often explicitly compared to biological species, whose demise would constitute an irreplaceable loss for humanity as a whole (Crystal 2000, p. 32–33; Krauss 1992). Another key theme in recent expert writings on language endangerment is cosmopolitan concerns about the diminishing of human knowledge expected by some linguists as a consequence of language loss (Hale 1992, Nettle & Romaine 2000). Identification of the loss of linguistic diversity with the disappearance of intellectual heritage also has been expressed in terms of popular Whorfianism in writings on language revitalization, according to which "each language reflects a different unique world view and culture complex, mirroring the manner in which a speech community has formulated its thinking and its understanding of the world" (Wurm 1999, p. 163). From this perspective language loss also implies a gradual loss of a comprehensive human view of the world. As other researchers argue, the use of metaphors such as "endangered languages" or "language death" likens languages to organisms attributed with agency, with a tendency to obscure the sociocultural processes ultimately accounting for language maintenance and loss (Gal 1996). The focus on languages as quasi-organisms contributes to the disjuncture between expert discourses and local concerns about language revitalization. Although the combination of cosmopolitan, popular Whorfian and quasiecological concerns in expert discourses has been directed to Western reading publics, as well as funding agencies (Hill 2002), these justifications for language revitalization are much less prominent in the contexts of actual efforts of prominority language activism. In other words, the question "Why bother?" has been answered in different ways by experts and local activists.

An overview of more successful cases of reversing language shift (Fishman 1991, pp. 287–336) in languages such as Hawaiian (No'eau Warner 2001, Warschauer 1998; see also Friedman 2003), Hebrew (Hagège 2000, Kuzar 1999, Spolsky 1996), Welsh (Jones 1998a, Williams 2000), and Catalan (DiGiacomo 2001, Woolard 1989) suggests that ideas about biodiversity or the general impoverishment of human knowledge have had little relevance in these scenarios. In contrast, some ideological link between what is identified as a language to be revitalized and desirable notions of community and identity, often conceived in ethnic terms in a politics of recognition, is vitally important to the creation of these movements of language activism geared toward language renewal and language shift reversal. Situations of language loss are often only widely registered, reported, and experienced as problematic if a set of linguistic practices is (*a*) isolated, a denotational norm established and labeled as a "language" (Silverstein 1998, 2003a), and (*b*) in some way made relevant for processes of identity formation. Local language activists and professional linguists may hold divergent views on what it means to "have" a language and, therefore, of what should be revitalized to begin with, as in the case of the Tolowa of Northern California, where a focus on words as evocative of cultural knowledge and memories of place conflicts with an academic privileging of grammatical structure as the core of what both sides refer to as the Tolowa language (Collins 1998).

Thus, questions of language, community, and identity are central to an investigation of language revitalization processes, including the use of electronic mediation. The issues at stake may certainly be expressed by experts in terms of popular Whorfianism or positively valued diversity of language organisms, when it is in fact more the perceived dangers to the reproduction of ethnic or other forms of groupness that often motivate activism on behalf of a lesser-used language. Therefore, it is necessary to situate practices of electronic mediation in contexts of language activism within linguistic ideologies of community and identity.

ELECTRONIC MEDIATION AND LANGUAGE REVITALIZATION: AREAS OF CONVERGENCE

Scholars often ascribe a key role to mass mediation and circulation of discourse in the creation of communities transcending face-to-face interaction. In this respect, linguistic diversity frequently has been understood as having a key impact on the shape and boundaries of the communities created, as it intervenes in the relationship between mediascapes (Appadurai 1996) and the projection of communities. For example, Anderson's account of nationalism, in its stress on the role of print capitalism, accords differentiation among vernacular languages of Europe a major role in defining the boundaries of national communities (Anderson 1991). Analysts often conceive of modern practices of mass-mediated communication as fostering linguistic change, most notably the spread of unified, nationalized standard languages (Gellner 1983). In this sense, the relationship between cultures of discourse circulation and linguistic change is indeterminate and needs to be grounded in particular sociohistorical contexts.

Studies of language loss and revitalization frequently stress the important role electronic mediation of discourse can play in situations of language shift. In particular radio and television broadcasting in dominant languages has been described as contributing to language shift away from lesser-used or minority languages, making the task of reestablishing the latter as a routine medium of everyday interaction more daunting (Dixon 1991; Dorian 1991; de Graaf 1992; Rouchdy 1989; Grenoble & Whaley 1998, p. 53). Pessimistic perspectives on the relationship between the reproduction of linguistic diversity and electronic mass mediation have even culminated in assessments such as those describing the impact of electronic media on the maintenance of lesser-used languages as "cultural nerve gas" (Krauss 1992, p. 6). Activists have expressed similar views: A production coordinator of the Canadian Inuit Broadcasting Corporation likens the effects of mainstream television to those of a neutron bomb (David 1998, p. 36). In contrast, recent work on minority language broadcasting has stressed the potentially helpful effects of using electronic mediation for the maintenance and renewal of such languages. A central concern of the use of lesser-used languages in electronic mediation is not only encouraging language maintenance and revitalization by providing speakers with opportunities to hear and maintain skills in the language, but also is achieving a transformation of ideological valuations of the language so that the lesser-used language is viewed as part of the contemporary world and as relevant for the future of a particular group (Brandt 1988, McHenry 2002).

Lately there also has been great interest in using computer technology in practices intended to further the maintenance and revitalization of lesser-used languages (Bernard 1992, Darquennes & Weber 2001, Grenoble & Whaley 2002, Kroskrity 2002, Salinas Pedraza 1996, Warschauer 1998). One obvious use of digital technology is that it provides comparatively inexpensive and effective ways of recording linguistic practice in lesser-used languages, especially in situations where language shift is almost complete and the last remaining persons competent in the relevant language are old, and intergenerational transmission of competence in the lesser-used language has failed so far (Bennett 2003, Hinton 2001, Kroskrity 2002, Kroskrity & Reynolds 2001, Parks et al. 1999). Such recordings of sound and image can provide richer and more multidimensional records especially in the fields of phonology and prosody, as well as in performative and interactional contexts of use as compared to print media. These records are then available for future reconstruction of linguistic practices in the lesser-used language at a time when no proficient speakers are living, providing material for the relearning of the linguistic variety in question.

Another area for the use of computer technology is the teaching of lesser-used or minority languages, in particular the search for easier and less costly ways of creating and disseminating teaching materials in endangered languages, such as books, sound recordings, and digital material combining text, sound, and graphics components. Electronic forms of mediation thus become part of techniques of literacy, which are often, though not always (Kroskrity 2000), crucial to obtaining the status of a language valued enough to warrant its reproduction for the variety to be revitalized (Bernard 1996, Errington 2003, Salinas Pedraza 1996, Silverstein 2003a). Developed out of computer-assisted language learning (Chapelle 2002, Levy 1997), telecollaboration in foreign language learning (Warschauer 1996), interactive CD-ROMs, Web sites, and computer networks provide contexts where the computer poses tasks to students, evaluates their responses, and decides on the next task on the basis of their progress. In this respect, the role of the computer as a tutor in language learning may be particularly appropriate in cultural contexts with no role of a formal teacher in society (Auld 2002). Instruction in lesser-used languages using these techniques does not need to be tied to a particular locale anymore and is also accessible, provided computers and the skills for using them are available, to relatively small groups of geographically dispersed language learners, such as Native American groups in North America (Haag & Coston 2002), Hawaiian language learners linked by the *Leoki* computer network (Warschauer 1998, 1999), or Maori in New Zealand (Benton 1996).

Much of the focus in the emerging literature on the use of digital technologies in minority language activism has been on the instrumental advantages for documentation and pedagogical dissemination of discourse in such languages, primarily the ability to record, integrate, and circulate more discourse data across multiple dimensions and the possible economic advantages over previously used technologies. However, the ideological dimensions through which the enabling characteristics of such practices are perceived are crucially important in evaluating the use of digital mediation in these contexts (Kroskrity 2002). To analyze the significance of computer technology for minority language activism, one must understand not only instrumental-technical possibilities but also the sociocultural interpretations of electronic mediation practices; one should analyze cultures of digital mediation analogous to the work carried out on cultures of print (Hall 1996, Warner 1990). After all, any assessment of potential advantages of digital technology is finally mediated by the processes of ideological valuation and interpretation in such cultures of digital mediation. That is, television and radio broadcasting, as well as the creation of digital material in endangered languages for purposes of language revitalization, are informed by ideologies of language (Woolard & Schieffelin 1994) formulating relationships between linguistic practice and modes of social and political belonging and different sociocultural valuations of linguistic forms and varieties (Dorian 1994, 1998). This embeddedness of electronic mediation practices in lesser-used languages in such ideological processes raises the following questions: What assumed relationships between language and community inform practices of electronic mediation intended to promote a lesser-used language? To what extent do local evaluations ascribed to various practices of electronic mediation per se become part of the revitalization process? What relationships of power characterize the multilingual field in which such forms of electronic mediation are located? What are the strategies by which proponents of lesser-used languages seek to achieve a transformation of an ideological field through electronic mediation? What are the limitations imposed by particular technologies on practices of mediation? And finally, how can we account for the ultimate efficacy of such practices, that is changes of potential speakers' attitudes motivating them to engage in regular use of the linguistic variety across generations?

ACCESS, POWER, AND DIGITAL 'LEXICOGRAPHIC REVOLUTION'

Long ago, Fishman distinguished between unmobilized and mobilized modes of language maintenance (Fishman 1972 [1968], pp. 97–98), seeking to draw a distinction between the continued use of a linguistic variety among groups of relatively isolated, marginal speakers and the continued use of a language based on conscious mobilization of material and political resources. The use of electronic forms of mediation for purposes of language revitalization seems to fall mainly into the latter category of language maintenance because it presupposes the intervention of middle classes, state, or nongovernmental institutions with control over resources typically exceeding those of the rural and marginal speakers Fishman had in mind.

Using electronic mediation in language activism implies not only the sheer availability and affordability of access to electronic mass mediation, but also some political and economic control over production and dissemination of electronically mass-mediated discourse. This problem is at the center of debates about whether the spread of digital technology will either support more evenly distributed modes of democratic participation in public discourse and political processes or result in new forms of social inequality and control (Ess & Sudweeks 2001, Loader 1998, Smith & Kollock 1999). Concerns that linguistic differentiation will put many people at a disadvantage in emerging digital public spheres led the European Union, for example, to fund a project to set up digital debating platforms for four minority language groups (Williams 2001). In this respect, access to computer-based electronic mediation in particular implies not only the availability of a material infrastructure of computers, software, appropriate character sets (Godwin-Jones 2002), and Internet connections, but also the skills and attitudes crucial to make successful use of Internet and other computer resources (Wilson & Peterson 2002, p. 457; Villa 2002), such as an understanding of dominant online interaction orders (Kirshenblatt-Gimblett 1996, Crystal 2001) and literacy in dominant languages (Keniston 2001). Such differences regarding interest and attitudes toward digital mediation practices are frequently, but not necessarily, related to divergences in wealth and education (Rey 2001).

Nevertheless, many populations interested in reestablishing the practice of a lesser-used language often are least likely to engage in digital mediation practices (Buszard-Welcher 2001). The use and availability of such technologies often depend on support from state institutions, nongovernmental organizations, or a local middle class willing to use its economic and political resources to protect a language. As a consequence, the use of electronic mass mediation, especially television and digital technology, is often shaped by the power relations between state institutions and populations with an interest in language revitalization or, alternatively, on the ability of such groups to generate the necessary resources independently from state assistance, either through the presence of a middle class (Woolard 1989) or though their ability to attract support from nongovernmental organizations. Also the ideological climate defining the relationships between nation-states and communities associated with lesser-used languages is important. Even those groups of small size with limited resources may gain state support for electronic broadcasting or digital mediation if their cultivation of an ethnolinguistic identity is ideologically compatible or even desirable within the national imaginaries in which they are located, such as in the cases of Sorbian in the former German Democratic Republic (Marti 1990, pp. 54–55) and the lesser-used "autochthonous" languages in the contemporary European Union countries (Arntz 1998, Counc. Eur. 1993, Ó Riagáin 2001, Poche 2000).

Nevertheless, questions of power in language revitalization and new technologies are not just about fighting for access to electronic mediation but also may involve struggles about its restriction. For example, the creation and circulation of interactive CD-ROMs for language learning or the creation of websites with multimedia content in lesser-used languages may face resistance (Villa 2002), questioning the appropriateness of making text or sound in the language available to a wider public beyond what are understood to be the boundaries of the community with an ideological link to the language. Brandt notes that objections to writing and recording discourse among several Native American groups in the Southwest of the United States are often grounded in perspectives that emphasize the cosmologically creative power of speech. Accordingly, speech needs to be properly controlled, something that writing, recording, and mass mediating of discourse does not allow for because it is susceptible to potentially limitless reanimations and recontextualizations (Brandt 1981). Investigators have reported, among the Hopi (K. Hill 2002) and the Western Apache (Adley-SantaMaria 1997), such objections to exposing outsiders to discourse in lesser-used languages. Against the backdrop of such concerns, the wide circulation of discourse in a minority language through mass mediation of any sort can also be viewed as a danger to its value and authenticity and therefore to a central ideological credential as an emblem of community (Dauenhauer & Dauenhauer 1998).

Finally, especially regarding the use of digital technologies as media in language revitalization, questions of access and power are also raised by the fact that digital documentation and collection function as the material equivalent of earlier modern technologies and sites of storage and display, such as the museum and the archive. The latter in turn are closely connected to the rise of nationalism (Anderson 1991). This problem is often overlooked in writings stressing the necessity of "saving" lesser-used languages within discourses of biodiversity, cosmopolitanism, or popular Whorfianism, as outlined earlier in this review. Given that projects of language revitalization and claims for ethnolinguistic recognition often go hand in hand, this link to earlier technologies of the nation-state also puts the linguist-expert's role in a new light. Far from occupying a politically neutral position and concerned only with preserving intellectual assets for "humanity," the processes of selection and collection in documenting "endangered" languages in digital format often end up producing the "heritage" of a people, in a process of "antiquarian curating" (Silverstein 2003b). Because technologies of storage and display of objectualized "heritage" are an important part of what constitutes ethnonational entities in many instances, the linguist and ethnographer as expert may occupy a pivotal role in shaping credentials for ethnolinguistic recognition (Silverstein 2003a). Experts' decisions of inclusion and exclusion of linguistic material in electronic artifacts intended for documentation of lesser-used languages therefore may have profound political consequences in shaping the boundaries and internal setup of communities vying for sociopolitical recognition in a way recalling the activities of nineteenth-century nationalist proponents of a "lexicographic revolution" in Europe, a "golden age of vernacularizing lexicographers, grammarians, philologists and litterateurs" (Anderson 1991, p. 71; see also Hobsbawm 1990, pp. 54–63). Thus, to contextualize the analysis of electronic mediation in lesser-used or minority languages within the history of linguistic ethnonationalism is important, especially because the use of computer media for activism on behalf of lesser-used languages is often centered on the production of the paradigmatic genres of dictionaries, textbooks, and other teaching material, as well as collections of traditional verbal art (Bennett 2003; Benton 1996, p. 194; Cazden 2003; Ka'awa & Hawkins 1997; Kroskrity 2002; Miyashita & Moll 1999; Parks et al. 1999; Salinas Pedraza 1996), which continue to play a ubiquitous role in political regionalisms and nationalisms.

ELECTRONIC MEDIATION, NEW GENRES, AND THE RECONTEXTUALIZATION OF DISCOURSE

One of the consequences of electronic mass mediation is the creation of new genres of linguistic entextualization (Briggs & Bauman 1992, Silverstein 1998, Spitulnik 1996) to which many languages to be revitalized have not before been linked. In numerous instances, this has led to conflicts among speakers regarding the appropriateness of such new genres of linguistic practice. For example, much of radio broadcasting is organized around a set of widely shared generic conventions (Scannell 1991): Programs often start and end in one-hour or half-an-hour intervals, speaker's voices are clearly audible to all, and there are only brief pauses in speaking and turn-taking between speakers, all of which may conflict with the preferred linguistic practices and generic conventions for public linguistic performance among speakers of some lesser-used languages (Browne 1996). The relationship between speech genres in practices of electronic mediation and those otherwise current in local language communities can be understood as the handling of "intertexual gaps" (Briggs & Bauman 1992) that appear when new speech genres linked to electronic mass mediation are viewed as differing from or even as being at odds with those genres of public speaking favored by users of a language considered in need of revitalization. Such a scenario arose from the emergence of a genre of "Broadcast Navajo" in the Southwest of the United States, where radio listeners' expectations derived from the experience of English-language broadcasting enter in conflict with the desire of others to promote "traditional" Navajo linguistic practices (Peterson 1997). In contrast, in his work on Nahua in Mexico Flores Farfán (2002) reminds us that electronic practices of mediation may achieve some continuity with preexisting genres of linguistic entextualization. He describes how a revitalization project in the Nahua Balsas region of Mexico centered on the use of video-taped discourse in Nahua achieves recognizable overlap with locally prized speech genres such as riddles and *amate de historias*, a narrative genre. Similarly, bilingual radio broadcasters in the Mexican state of Chiapas have adopted *spatilab'il sk'ujol*, a traditional face-to-face speech genre of requesting other persons to convey greetings in Tojolab'al Mayan (Brody 2000). Nevertheless, a partial overlap between preelectronic speech genres and new broadcasting genres is not always the goal of minority language activists. With respect to borrowing English-language broadcasting genres by Irish broadcasters, Cotter notes adopting such genres for use in a minority language also can be interpreted as enhancing the authority and ideological valuations of the language to be revitalized by minimizing the intertextual gap between radio discourse in a minority language and prestigious generic models familiar to listeners from mainstream radio broadcasting (Cotter 2001).

COMPETING LINGUISTIC NORMS, AUTHENTICITY, AND EVALUATIONS OF LINGUISTIC CHANGE

Apart from the question of new linguistic genres, linguistic differentiation among users of a lesser-used or minority language, such as dialectal variation and orientation toward multiple linguistic norms, is sometimes an issue of contention once radio or television programs in such languages are broadcast. If purist insistence on a single linguistic norm is used as a model for determining the choice of varieties in broadcasting, the implied hierarchization of linguistic varieties often accentuates conflict among speakers about the value of alternative linguistic norms (Hornberger & King 1999). Such hierarchization may lead to alienation of large numbers of speakers of a lesser-used language, causing the failure of language revitalization as a social movement (Dorian 1994). Researchers have linked the emergence of rival norms of linguistic authenticity, often involving a generational split in situations of language revitalization, to processes of language standardization intended to counter language shift by teaching and producing written material in the lesser-used language. This is the case in activism for Irish (Hindley 1990), Breton (Jones 1998b, McDonald 1990), and Quechua (Hornberger & King 1999), and a similar picture is also developing for Gaelic in Scotland (Dorian 1994, McEwan-Fujita 2003). In these scenarios, a new standard variety explicitly constructed for purposes of language revitalization, such as the linguistic standard decided on by the Irish government in the 1950s and the Breton variety used by urban-based *néo-bretonnants*, is favored by predominantly younger, middle-class speakers who have acquired Irish or Breton as a second language through schooling and cultivate it as an emblem of positively valued ethnic identity. The usage of these standard varieties is often confronted with conservatism by older speakers of various dialectal varieties who tend to be rural and working class in their backgrounds, hold ambivalent perspectives on the value of speaking Irish or Breton, and often consider the new standard artificial and inauthentic. Divergent views about "correct" norms are even at the center of contemporary efforts to reestablish Cornish as a spoken language after a two-century hiatus, pitting two rival factions against each other who base their claims of authenticity on different literary sources (Dorian 1994; Jones 1998a, pp. 338–46).

Conflicts centered around multiple linguistic norms have also been reported from contexts in which the use of a minority language in electronic mass mediation is part of a political process of promoting particular ethnic or national identities through language activism. Already in the 1940s and 1950s the first Breton-language radio broadcasts in France were characterized by the familiar opposition previously mentioned above, pitting the use of a purist, literary standard favored by intellectuals using Breton as a second language against the increased use of dialectal varieties from 1946 onward (Thomas 2001). More recently, conflicting views about the appropriate variety of Catalan for the electronic media also have led to public debate in Catalonia, where protagonists of "heavy" Catalan, a more purist standard showing a greater degree of avoidance of Castilian Spanish lexicon and syntax, have criticized what they see as a growing predominance of "light" Catalan, exhibiting more tolerance toward Spanish linguistic influence in Catalan-language television and radio (Gardner et al. 2000). Here, conflicting views on the appropriate variety of Catalan as "light" or "heavy" are mediated by iconicity, that is stereotypic images of qualitative likeness of the preferred variety (Irvine & Gal 2000). Language policy at state-run Catalan-language television is influenced by a commission of "linguistic normalization," whose recommendations put more emphasis on the usage of "heavy" Catalan (Vallverdú 1995). In contrast, "light" or even "bivalent" usage straddling the boundaries between Castilian and Catalan is found in Catalan radio broadcasting (Woolard 1998), whereas the producers of Welsh television and radio programs also strive for a compromise between the use of the *Cymreg Byw* standard created in the 1970s and various dialectal varieties (Jones 1998a, pp. 273–78). This situation is similar to the case of contemporary Corsican radio stations, which foreground the hybridity and fluidity of linguistic practices on Corsica in a way obviously at odds with the purist ideologies of some Corsican language activists, incorporating both considerable dialectal variation and bilingualism with French (Jaffe 1999).

In contrast, practices of electronic mass mediation also can decisively contribute to a reinforcement of purist ideologies of language and community or even initiate a process of ethnicization of language. The decision to broadcast television programs in a sanskritized variety of Mauritian Bhojpuri, characterized by purist avoidance of otherwise very commonly used Mauritian Creole loans, and intended to reverse language shift to Creole, supports the transformation of Mauritian Bhojpuri from a language of Indo-Mauritians, regardless of religious affiliation, into an ethnic language of Hindus (Eisenlohr 2004). Nevertheless, efforts to highlight the purported link between language and community through electronic mass mediation may have unintended consequences when large numbers of users are ideologically excluded. Such has been the case with Mauritian Bhojpuri, where sanskritizing the language has alienated Muslim speakers (Eisenlohr 2001).

Nevertheless, various language revitalization efforts relying in part on electronic mass mediation find ways to mitigate conflicts surrounding the selection of certain linguistic varieties for broadcasting in the face of great diversity of usage and norms within what has been identified as a language to be revitalized. In Ireland, the programs of the Irish-language *Radió na Gaeltachta* have followed a policy of "scheduled regionalism" (Cotter 2001), rotating broadcasts from the three major dialect regions of the *Gaeltacht* throughout the day, using varieties different from the linguistic standard devised by the Irish government in the 1950s for the compulsory teaching of Irish in schools. In the Andean region, the producers of the Quechua-language satellite radio network *Red Quechua Satelital Continental*, which is explicitly dedicated to language revival, similarly have avoided institutionalizing one variety as broadcast standard in this area of vast dialectal variation. While maintaining shared production facilities, broadcasting centers rotate on a yearly basis between Peru, Bolivia, and Ecuador, thereby avoiding the privileging of one particular regional variety (Luykx 2001). Basque-language radio broadcasters in France try to counter what they see as the downside of a trend toward a "more or less standardized Basque" by sending correspondents' reports five times a week from five different areas within the French Basque region to accommodate dialectal variation (Browne 1990, p. 40). Another way to avoid the potential pitfalls of inducing hierarchization among linguistic varieties of lesser-used languages with regional affiliations through broadcasting preference and selection is to observe a principle of "strict locality," as reported by Hale (2001), with regard to television and radio broadcasts in Australian aboriginal languages such as Warlpiri. A similar approach is followed by *francophonie*-funded rural radio networks broadcasting in local minority languages in the Democratic Republic of the Congo (Edema 2000) and by the *Société de communication Atikamek^w— Montagnais* in northeast Canada, which runs a network of 14 local radio stations broadcasting in Innu (Montagnais) and Atikamekw across a large region with a widely dispersed population (Hervieux 2001).

Views about the appropriate linguistic norms in practices of minority language electronic mass mediation are part of wider ideologies of linguistic differentiation and authenticity, which shape concepts of community and identity in the ethnic minority contexts mentioned above. These ideologies of authenticity also include evaluations of how broadcasting influences linguistic change. Broadcasters may be tempted to impose changes, such as lexical innovations in the field of "modern" terminology, for media broadcasts without regard to whether such changes may be accepted by the people among whom broadcasters seek to promote the use of the language to be revitalized. Broadcasters of *Radió na Gaeltachta* following a strict Irish-only policy cannot rely exclusively on the recommendations of official boards producing new Irish terminology when confronted with the exigencies of live news broadcasting, but also must develop Irish terms "on the spot." They also have resorted to asking listeners for suggestions, such as in the case when a department store in Western Ireland installed the first escalator in the region and finally adopted the lexical innovation for the technical device most frequently suggested by listeners who called in (Browne 1992, p. 425). This is an example showing how radio broadcasters make use of the new genre of call-in shows to seek compromise and flexibility in questions of linguistic diversity and change, thereby avoiding ideological pitfalls of purism for projects of language revitalization.

These studies commonly show the range of stances on authenticity, purism, and compromise in electronic mediation practices in lesser-used languages as contesting language ideologies (Woolard & Schieffelin 1994) of community and identity. Because of their exemplary status as media often indexing ideas of power, status, and modernity, electronic practices of mediation have become a salient field of struggle and production of ethnolinguistic identity and community. As the studies reviewed here show, even if compromises are made, often revitalization activities involve some degree of linguistic unification and standardization of the variety to be promoted. Consequently, a crucial issue for the success or failure of such movements is whether speakers' allegiances shift toward such new standards used in broadcasting or are predominantly attached to local varieties, perceiving no need for a new standard that they associate with middle-class activists and second-language learners, in other words whether "they perceive themselves as parochial communities rather than a national unit" (Jones 1998a, p. 326).

ELECTRONIC MEDIATION AND THE REFUTATION OF LANGUAGE IDEOLOGIES OF CONTEMPT

Linguistic ideologies devaluing the use of minority languages, whether in the guise of a national standard language ideology, doubts whether the continued use of such languages finds divine favor, as reported from some users of Tlingit and Haida in Alaska (Dauenhauer & Dauenhauer 1998) and speakers of other Native American languages in the Southwest of the United States (Zepeda & Hill 1991), or the portrayal of bi- and multilingualism as onerous or unnatural and casting a dominant language as the more sophisticated and naturally adapted vehicle for representing reality (Dorian 1998) are reported to play a key role in many situations of language loss. The question posed here is how new practices of circulating discourse in lesser-used languages using postprint technologies articulate with dominant linguistic ideologies unfavorable to the maintenance and revitalization of such languages.

One of the reasons for the enthusiasm with which such forms of electronic mediation are often initially adopted is that such recontexualization of the practice of a lesser-used language in an electronic medium is frequently interpreted as a refutation of prevalent "ideologies of contempt" (Dorian 1998, Grillo 1989), suggesting that a lesser-used language and the people indexed by it are backward, inferior, or otherwise unfit for modernity (McEwan-Fujita 2003). Stereotypes portraying a language and its associated people as unmodern often involve processes of iconicity, the images of modernity and backwardness thus created frequently constituting key components of language ideologies (Irvine & Gal 2000). Also, ideologies of language directed against the practice of using lesser-used languages frequently work through chronotopes (Bakhtin 1981) of distancing and removal (Kuter 1989), indexically relegating such linguistic varieties to spatially and temporally dislocated and distant positions, away from geographical centers and the temporal present.

By counteracting this spatiotemporal "lag" (Dorian 1980) ascribed by dominant ideologies of language, the existence of radio and television broadcasting (Browne 1996, Cotter 2001) or computer-based mediation (Brandt 1988, Cazden 2003, Kroskrity 2002, Miyashita & Moll 1999, Ouakrime 2001, Warschauer 1998, Williams 2000) in a lesser-used language is often expected to raise valuations of the linguistic variety in question, associating it with notions of prestige and modernity. The valuation-enhancing effect of practices of electronic mediation common to these situations is that they often contribute to a transformation of the ideological field, previously putting the continued use of a lesser-used language at a disadvantage by denying the temporal coevalness (Cotter 2001) and spatial centricity of lesser-used languages and the populations indexed by them. This strategy of combating allochrony (Fabian 1983) through associating values of modernity and orientation to the future (McHenry 2002) with a lesser-used or minority language by circulating discourse through electronic mass mediation can also be seen as a departure from or even contradicting earlier ideological strategies of language revitalization. This applies particularly to the use of Romantic imagery, as in the case of Irish in electronic media, which in some ways only reinforced the semiotics of spatiotemporal removal of ideologies of contempt (Ó Riagáin 1991). The production of a contemporary television soap opera in Gaelic for broadcast in Scotland (Cormack 1994), the production of a CD-ROM for adolescents about ice hockey in Ojibwa (Williams 2002), the creation of a Frisian-language internet portal and news service (Falkena 2001), the creation of internet and CD-ROM-based courses in Welsh (Jones 1998a, p. 20), and the dubbing of the movie *Bambi* into Arapaho (Greymorning 2001) can be considered attempts to counter linguistic ideologies of contempt by transforming the temporal and spatial indexicality working through them. Here it seems that much of the appeal of electronic mediation practices, in particular in their digital forms, lies precisely in their potential to minimize experiences of spatiotemporal distanciation in a way not afforded by the circulation of print (Harvey 1989, Tomlinson 1999). That is, the reindexing of such varieties by ideologically moving them away from peripheral, rural, and obsolete positions in space and time through the use of electronic mediation is a way to contest ideologies of contempt and to formulate alternative ways of ideologically mapping linguistic differentiation on time and space.

Therefore, temporal and spatial indexicality plays a central role in such conscious attempts to reestablish use of a lesser-used language involving the practice of electronic mediation. In particular, proponents of digital technology in lesser-used languages see an opportunity to integrate the use of such languages with the lifestyles and consumer preferences of younger generations, even drawing on an ideology of "coolness" as important for enhancing the attractiveness of using a language to be revitalized among younger speakers (Buszard-Welcher 2001, pp. 337–38; Guardado 1997, p. 58).

INDIGENOUS MEDIA AND ETHNOLINGUISTIC RECOGNITION

Recent anthropological investigations of indigenous media have described such media as an area of political struggle in which indigenous media producers seek visibility and legitimacy for ethnic identities and the political concerns of indigenous groups vis-à-vis the larger national imaginaries in which they are located (Ginsburg 1993). By appropriating technologies of electronic mediation previously monopolized by the nation-state and powerful corporations in order to "talk back," projecting alternative representations of indigenous groups and their concerns, indigenous media producers are also engaged in a social process of constantly refashioning indigenous identities. As Ginsburg notes, such media makers simultaneously address members of their own communities as well as a larger nonindigenous public while fashioning and negotiating images of indigenous ethnic identity and the political concerns of such groups across multiple cultural boundaries not only regarding group membership of producers and audiences, but also regarding aesthetic regimes and conventions of media consumption and valuation (Ginsburg 1994). Although from an analytical perspective the concept of "indigenous" remains elusive, such as that concerning indigenous qualities of media practitioners and content of indigenous media (Spitulnik 1993), it is clear that claims to indigenous identities have powerful political implications and that media strategies foregrounding ethnic identity and cultural difference from the dominant mainstream societies of the respective nation-states can also revolve around questions of linguistic differentiation.

The renewal and highlighting of linguistic difference can constitute a central component in such strategies of ethnic activism in a politics of recognition (Silverstein 2003a), given that many indigenous media producers are explicitly committed to the promotion of indigenous cultural and linguistic traditions and have established transnational support networks for the realization of these goals (Ginsburg 1994). Also, because the reproduction of linguistic difference often supports claims of indigenous alterity and authenticity, which are often central in such forms of cultural activism executed through indigenous media, language revitalization can be a key element of such electronically mediated struggles of recognition vis-à-vis the nation-state and its institutions. Such has been the case with the use of minority languages in indigenous electronic media networks in Canada (David 1998, Meadows 1996), Greenland (Stenbaek 1992), Australia (Hale 2001), New Zealand (Browne 1996), and Morocco (Almasude 1999). In the contemporary European Union, claims of indigenous status for a minority language are a crucial mechanism of exclusion and inclusion and a precondition for obtaining official support, including media broadcasting rights, which in contrast is largely denied to widely used immigrant minority languages such as Arabic, Gujarati, and Turkish (outside Greece) (Cheesman 2001, Cormack 1998, Counc. Eur. 1993). In this way electronic mediation practices aimed at the reproduction of linguistic difference in situations of advanced language shift can be part of struggles of recognition of ethnic groups vis-à-vis national and transnational publics primarily conducted through electronic media production and circulation.

TECHNOLOGY AS IDEOLOGY: REVITALIZATION AND THE MEDIATION OF COMMUNITIES

The changed economics of publishing material in a lesser-used language made possible by using computer technology are accorded supreme importance by some authors assessing the consequences for language revitalization (Bernard 1992,

1996; St. Clair et al. 1999). Nevertheless, as others have argued, an increase in teaching material or otherwise published discourse alone does not necessarily lead to language revitalization in the sense of increased use of a lesser-used language in everyday contexts (Fishman 1991, King 2001). To reverse language shift, the new avenues for publishing and circulating discourse also must be linked to an ideological transformation among speakers, inducing them to reestablish routine use of a language especially when interacting with children and adolescents.

One of the ways in which practices of electronic mediation may support such ideological transformations is through promoting what Henze & Davis (1999, p. 4) call the "ownership" of revitalization efforts by the speakers themselves. Digital technology provides relatively easy possibilities to include local voices and viewpoints in the production of electronically mediated discourse in these languages for purposes of education (Hornberger 1996, Salinas Pedraza 1996); that is, the lower cost and changing modes of access to publishing using digital technology in a lesser-used language may facilitate local input in the production of such material (Warschauer 1998), providing the possibility of authorship to a potentially larger circle of people than is often the case with nonelectronic publishing. This potentially expanded participation may also be the case when compared with the production of most radio and television broadcasting, with the notable exception of the call-in/talk-back genre of radio broadcasting, which can be regarded as a model for "interactive" modes of computer-mediated communication such as chat rooms and email lists. For example, Fabula, a computer software program funded by the Multimedia Software Program of the European Union for the creation of bilingual books in Welsh/English, Irish/English, Basque/French, and Catalan/Spanish, is designed to enable children to take part in the writing process (Edwards et al. 2002). Thus, the teaching and promotion of lesser-used languages can be more easily supported by locally produced material; this may possibly result in ways of teaching such languages that are more attractive and relevant to learners, a goal also targeted by community-based education in indigenous languages using multimedia technology (Hornberger 1996b). By facilitating local participation in designing material to promote the language, proponents of digital technology hope to encourage identification not only with language revitalization efforts but also with the language to be revitalized. Nevertheless, so far there has been little investigation of the ways in which the introduction of these forms of electronic mediation relates to the use of language to be revitalized outside formal learning situations.

However, reframing discourse in an endangered language through digital forms of mediation is often intended to establish an indexical relationship between the notions of power and prestige frequently ascribed to forms of electronic mediation, that is to technology per se, which may for example be experienced by the display of technological objects in homes and other living spaces (Silverstone et al. 1992, Spitulnik 2000), and a lesser-used language (Brandt 1988; Edwards et al. 2002, p. 59). As mentioned previously, this shift frequently is based on a renegotiating of temporal and spatial indexicality, highlighting the relevance of the linguistic variety in question to the present and future constitution of an ethnicized community. However, the question remains how precisely this reindexing of a linguistic variety in the process of being abandoned by its speakers actually results in a greater measure of everyday interaction in the lesser-used language. Taking a skeptical perspective, some researchers have reported a fetishization of technology among speakers of lesser-used languages, who locate the agency to "save" their language in technology instead of in themselves, thereby further undermining revitalization efforts (Dauenhauer & Dauenhauer 1998).

Nevertheless, hopes often are placed on the link between language and community as in the case of indigenous education, where promotion of a language is part of a larger project of empowerment that "confirms indigenous identity, language, and culture," whereas promotion of indigenous languages is reported to have "helped indigenous communities to identify themselves as indigenous communities, supporting their self-definition and self-valuation" (Hornberger 1996b, pp. 361–62). Digital mediation may convey greater ideological value for the language being used, which also would be linked to a greater willingness to highlight an indexical link between this linguistic variety and positively valued ethnic groupness (Salinas Pedraza 1996), possibly resulting in a greater motivation to reestablish its use. In contrast, as studies of language and community show, there is no necessary relationship defined between the valuation of a language as an emblem of group identity and its use as a predominant medium of interaction (Eisenlohr 2004, Gal 1995, Urla 1988), although such a relationship is often presupposed in European linguistic ideologies of the "Andersonian" variety (Silverstein 2000). An important issue here is that it is entirely possible for members of a language community to highly value and identify with a language without actually knowing it well and without using it in routine interaction, something already suggested in Joshua Fishman's early remarks about an "attitudinal halo-ization" of heritage languages among descendants of non-English-speaking immigrants to the United States (Fishman 1966, p. 397). Thus, whether any boost in valuation through practices of digital mediation will actually result in increased use of a lesser-used language in everyday conversation crucially depends on its articulation with linguistic ideologies about languages of group identification current within a particular context.

Another advantage often stressed by proponents of the use of digital forms of mediation in situations of language revitalization is that their use facilitates networking and community building among people interested in the language. Computer technology is indeed a widely used means of interaction among language activists, whether in the form of email lists (http://www.u.arizona.edu/~cashcash/ILAT.html) or in the sharing of knowledge and concerns through Web pages across different groups (Almasude 1999, McClure 2001, Warschauer 1998). Assuming an interest in language revitalization, here also is the question of whether the forms of community that such modes of interaction support are linked to an increase in everyday linguistic practice in the lesser-used language (Villa 2002, Hinton 2001). Recent anthropological studies in the formation of communities through online interaction have conceptualized such forms of sociality as communities of exchange of treasured electronic artifacts with prestige values (Lysloff 2003, Miller & Slater 2000, Slater 2000). Miller & Slater, for example, draw a direct parallel between the pride felt by Trinidadian users of the Internet about the perceived popularity of electronic items signifying Trinidad, measured, among others, in terms of the number of "hits" a Web site receives, and the "fame" constituted through the possession and circulation of prestige objects in earlier anthropological studies of systems of exchange (Miller & Slater 2000, pp. 20–21). This example raises the possibility that the exchange and circulation of valued electronic artifacts in a lesser-used language may become the prominent modes in the formation of communities based on an allegiance to a respective language. Such a scenario contrasts with a dynamic more familiar to studies of language and community—the establishment of a new mass-mediated public in which a language of ethnonational identification is also the medium of communication presumably uniting the community and separating them from others (Anderson 1991). That is, the use of electronic mediation in reversing language shift points to well-established anthropological concerns such as systems of exchange and prestige economies.

From such a perspective, practices of electronic mediation in language revitalization involve the production of new cultural artifacts, which, by virtue of their circulation and a sense of shared consumption and appreciation of these objects, can emerge as a focus of community. However, such communities of exchange do not necessarily imply the actual (re)learning and adoption of the lesser-used language as a means of everyday interaction. Nevertheless, they may introduce a new dimension of objectification on the basis of which elements of endangered languages, in particular lexical items, actually can be treated like valued antiques (Silverstein 1984) or " 'objectualized' as things of value" (Moore 1988, p. 467), or can interact with neoliberal attempts of commodification and "branding" of minority cultures and languages (McEwan-Fujita 2003). Again, the predominant ideological formulations of the link between language and community play a crucial role in determining whether practices of digital mediation in a lesser-used language will promote off-line or off-screen routine use of the language. Especially in those cases where language and processes of group identification are centered on the idea of an ancestral or heritage language (Moore 1988, Eisenlohr 2001) the separation between languages of group identification and languages of everyday interaction may not be challenged by practices of digital mediation.

This perspective on digital mediation practices in language revitalization also may be reinforced by formal properties of some electronic objects and artifacts in lesser-used languages. Many Web sites and CD-ROMs featuring text and sound content in lesser-used languages often use English or another dominant language as a framing device, distinguishing the parts of the Web page or CD-ROM needed to gain basic information and understanding about the artifact and how to navigate through its components from its actual texts or sounds in the lesser-used language to be revitalized (Cotter 2002, Dyck 2002, Kroskrity & Reynolds 2001, Parks et al. 1999). That is, in their often necessarily bilingual setup frequently a formal division exists between contextualizing discourse needed to interpret the electronic artifact using English or another dominant language and the digitally mediated text and discourse in a lesser-used language. It is therefore possible to meaningfully circulate and appreciate such electronic artifacts without actually knowing much of the lesser-used language. The way different linguistic varieties are thus mapped on the distinction between text and discourse with different functions in the setup of these electronic artifacts, whose circulation is intended to foster language revitalization, may well interact with local ideologies of language and group identification in such a way that it reinforces a conceptual separation between linguistic varieties relevant for purposes of group identification and those predominant in everyday interaction so widespread in situations of advanced language shift and language obsolescence.

CONCLUSION

In this review I treat new technologies as enabling practices of electronic mediation, which both intervene in and become part of ideological constructions drawing links between linguistic practice, social identities, and sociocultural valuations. In analyzing how such practices become both constitutive and transformative of linguistically indexed valuations, especially those concerned with the projection of communities, it also is important to note that such electronic mediation results in the creation of artifacts, as in the storing and documenting of elements of lesser-used languages, which themselves may become objects of value. That is, new technologies in language revitalization not only mediate linguistic practice but also may bring about new sites of cultural materiality and objectification with properties independent from those of mediated discourse (Keane 2003). Also, as the discussion of communities created through digital mediation shows, the circulation and exchange of such electronic objects and artifacts may give rise to forms of sociality of their own, independent from those sustained by any empirical revival of a lesser-used language. Whether the use of new technologies in language revitalization results in reversal of language shift away from lesser-used languages can only be answered by considering both the practices of discourse mediation and the production of new cultural objects the use of new technologies engenders as it becomes part of ideological processes establishing links between language and sociocultural values.

ACKNOWLEDGMENTS

I am grateful to Joseph Errington, Susan Gal, Faye Ginsburg, Emily McEwan-Fujita, Bambi Schieffelin, Michael Silverstein, Daniel Suslak, and Kathryn Woolard for their encouragement and for reading and commenting on earlier drafts of this review. I greatly benefited from their astute and eloquent observations. Any shortcomings are of course my responsibility. I also thank Sonal Shah for research assistance.

The *Annual Review of Anthropology* is online at http://anthro.annualreviews.org

LITERATURE CITED

Adley-SantaMaria B. 1997. White Mountain Apache language: issues in language shift, textbook development, and native speaker–university collaboration. See Reyhner 1997, pp. 129–43

Almasude A. 1999. The new mass media and the shaping of Amazigh identity. See Reyhner et al. 1999, pp. 117–28

Anderson B. 1991. *Imagined Communities: Reflections on the Origin and Spread of Nationalism.* London: Verso

Appadurai A. 1996. *Modernity at Large: Cultural Dimensions of Globalization.* Minneapolis: Univ. Minn. Press

Arntz R. 1998. *Das vielsprachige Europa: Eine Herausforderung für Sprachpolitik und Sprachplanung.* Hildesheim: Universitätsbibliothek Hildesheim

Auld G. 2002. The role of the computer in learning Ndj Bbana. *Lang. Learn. Technol.* 6:41–58

Bakhtin MM. 1981. *The Dialogic Imagination: Four Essays.* Austin: Univ. Texas Press

Bennett R. 2003. Saving a language with computers, tape recorders, and radio. See Reyhner et al. 2003, pp. 59–77

Benton R. 1996. Making the medium the message: using an electronic bulletin board system for promoting and revitalizing Maori. In *Telecollaboration in Foreign Language Learning,* ed. M Warschauer, pp. 187–204. Honolulu: Univ. Hawai'i Press

Bernard H. 1992. Preserving language diversity. *Hum. Organ.* 51:82–88

Bernard H. 1996. Language preservation and publishing. See Hornberger 1996a, pp. 139–56

Brandt E. 1981. Native American attitudes toward literacy and recording in the southwest. *J. Ling. Assoc. Southwest* 4:185–95

Brandt E. 1988. Applied linguistic anthropology and American Indian language renewal. *Hum. Organ.* 47:322–29

Briggs CL, Bauman R. 1992. Genre, intertextuality and social power. *J. Ling. Anthropol.* 2:131–72

Brody J. 2000. *spatilab'il sk'ujol* 'tell them "hey" for me': traditional Mayan speech genre goes multimedia. *Texas Ling. Forum* 43:1–14

Browne DR. 1990. Finding a Basque radio voice: the French experience. *Intermedia* 18:39–42

Browne DR. 1992. Radió na Gaeltachta: reviver, preserver or swan song of the Irish language? *Eur. J. Commun.* 7:415–33

Browne DR. 1996. *Electronic Media and Indigenous Peoples: A Voice of Our Own?* Ames: Iowa State Univ. Press

Burnaby B, Reyhner J. 2002. *Indigenous Languages Across the Community.* Flagstaff: North Ariz. Univ.

Buszard-Welcher L. 2001. Can the Web help save my language? See Hinton & Hale 2001, pp. 331–45

Cazden CB. 2003. Sustaining indigenous languages in cyberspace. See Reyhner et al. 2003, pp. 53–57

Chapelle C. 2002. Computer-assisted language learning. In *The Oxford Handbook of Applied Linguistics,* ed. R Kaplan, pp. 498–508. Oxford: Oxford Univ. Press

Cheesman T. 2001. 'Old' and 'new' lesser-used languages of Europe: common cause? In *Language, Ethnicity and the State: Volume 1: Minority Languages in the European Union,* ed. CC O' Reilly, pp. 147–68. Houndmills, UK: Palgrave

Collins J. 1998. Our ideologies and theirs. In *Language Ideologies: Practice and Theory,* ed. B Schieffelin, K Woolard, P Kroskrity, pp. 256–70. Oxford: Oxford Univ. Press

Cormack M. 1994. Programming for cultural defence: the expansion of Gaelic television. *Scott. Aff.* 6:114–31

Cormack M. 1998. Minority language media in Western Europe: preliminary considerations. *Eur. J. Commun.* 13:33–52

Cotter C. 2001. Continuity and vitality: expanding domains through Irish-language radio. See Hinton & Hale 2001, pp. 301–12

Cotter C. 2002. Review of *Irish Now! Lang. Learn. Technol.* 6:34–40

Counc. Eur. 1993. *European Charter for Regional or Minority Languages. Explanatory Report.* Strasbourg, France: Counc. Eur. Press

Crystal D. 2000. *Language Death.* Cambridge, UK: Cambridge Univ. Press

Crystal D. 2001. *Language and the Internet.* Cambridge, UK: Cambridge Univ. Press

Darquennes J, Weber P. 2001. Streiflichter zur Sprachrevitalisierung im europäischen Kontext. In *Minorities and Language Policy/Minderheiten und Sprachpolitik/ Minorités et l'Aménagement Linguistique,* ed. PH Nelde, R Rindler Schjerve, pp. 103–12. St. Augustin, Germany: Asgard

Dauenhauer N, Dauenhauer R. 1998. Technical, emotional, and ideological issues in reversing language shift: examples from Southeast Alaska. In *Endangered Languages: Language Loss and Community Response,* ed. LA Grenoble, LJ Whaley, pp. 57–98. Cambridge, UK: Cambridge Univ. Press

David J. 1998. Seeing ourselves, being ourselves: broadcasting aboriginal television in Canada. *Cult. Surviv. Q.* 22:36–39

de Graaf T. 1992. The small languages of Sakhalin. *Int. J. Soc. Lang.* 94:185–200

DiGiacomo S. 2001. 'Catalan is everyone's thing': normalizing a nation. In *Language, Ethnicity and the State: Volume 1: Minority Languages in the European Union,* ed. CC O'Reilly, pp. 56–77. Houndmills, UK: Palgrave

Dixon R. 1991. The endangered languages of Australia, Indonesia and Oceania. In *Endangered Languages,* ed. RH Robins, EM Uhlenbeck, pp. 229–56. Oxford: Berg

Dorian N. 1980. Linguistic lag as an ethnic marker. *Lang. Soc.* 9:33–41

Dorian N. 1991. Surviving the broadcast media in small language communities. *Educ. Media Int.* 28:134–37

Dorian N. 1994. Purism vs. compromise in language revitalization and language renewal. *Lang. Soc.* 23:479–94

Dorian N. 1998. Western language ideologies and small-language prospects. In *Endangered Languages: Language Loss and Community Response,* ed. LA Grenoble, LJ Whaley, pp. 3–21. Cambridge, UK: Cambridge Univ. Press

Dorian NC, ed. 1989. *Investigating Obsolescence: Studies in Language Contraction and Death.* Cambridge, UK: Cambridge Univ. Press. 445 pp.

Dyck C. 2002. Review of *Tsi Karhakta*: at the edge of the woods. *Lang. Learn. Technol.* 6: 27–33

Edema AB. 2000. Glottoculture et glottophagie en République Démocratique du Congo. In *Les Langues en Danger. Mémoires de la Société de Linguistique de Paris, Nouvelle Série, Tome VIII,* pp. 57–78. Leuven, Belgium: Peeters

Edwards V, Pemberton L, Knight J, Monaghan F. 2002. Fabula: a bilingual multimedia authoring environment for children exploring minority languages. *Lang. Learn. Technol.* 6: 59–69

Eisenlohr P. 2001. *Language ideology and imaginations of Indianness in Mauritius.* PhD thesis, Dept. of Anthropol., Univ. Chicago

Eisenlohr P. 2004. Register-levels of ethnonational purity: the ethnicization of language and community in Mauritius. *Lang. Soc.* 33: 59–80

Errington J. 2003. Getting language rights: the rhetorics of language endangerment and loss. *Am. Anthropol.* 105:723–32

Ess C, Sudweeks F, eds. 2001. *Culture, Technology, Communication: Towards an Intercultural Global Village.* Albany: State Univ. NY Press. 355 pp.

Fabian J. 1983. *Time and the Other: How Anthropology Makes its Object.* New York: Columbia Univ. Press

Falkena O. 2001. Frisian all over the world: the unique experience of one year. See Moseley et al. 2001, pp. 76–80

Fishman JA. 1966. *Language Loyalty in the*

United States: The Maintenance and Perpetuation of Non-English Mother Tongues by American Ethnic and Religious Groups. The Hague: Mouton

Fishman JA. 1972 [1968]. Language maintenance and language shift as a field of inquiry: revisited. In *Language in Sociocultural Change: Essays by Joshua A. Fishman*, ed. A Dil, pp. 76–132. Stanford, CA: Stanford Univ. Press

Fishman JA. 1991. *Reversing Language Shift: Theoretical and Empirical Foundations of Assistance to Threatened Languages.* Clevedon: Multiling. Matters

Flores Farfán J. 2002. The use of multimedia and the arts in language revitalization, maintenance and development: the case of Balsas Nahuas of Guerrero, Mexico. See Burnaby & Reyhner 2002, pp. 225–36

Friedman J. 2003. Globalizing languages: ideologies and realities of the contemporary world system. *Am. Anthropol.* 105:744–52

Gal S. 1995. Lost in a Slavic sea: linguistic theories and expert knowledge in 19th century Hungary. *Pragmatics* 5:155–66

Gal S. 1996. Language shift. In *Kontaktlinguistik/Contact Linguistics/Linguistique de contact*, ed. H Goebl, PH Nelde, Z Starý, W Wölck, pp. 586–93. Berlin: Walter de Gruyter

Gardner N, Puigdevall i Serralvo M, Williams CH. 2000. Language revitalization in comparative context: Ireland, the Basque country and Catalonia. In *Language Revitalization: Policy and Planning in Wales*, ed. CH Williams, pp. 311–61. Cardiff, UK: Univ. Wales Press

Gellner E. 1983. *Nations and Nationalism.* Ithaca, NY: Cornell Univ. Press

Ginsburg F. 1993. Aboriginal media and the Australian imaginary. *Public Cult.* 5:557–78

Ginsburg F. 1994. Embedded aesthetics: creating a discursive space for indigenous media. *Cult. Anthropol.* 9:365–82

Godwin-Jones R. 2002. Emerging technologies: multilingual computing. *Lang. Learn. Technol.* 6:6–11

Grenoble LA, Whaley LJ. 1998. Toward a typology of language endangerment. In *Endangered Languages: Language Loss and Community Response*, ed. LA Grenoble, LJ Whaley, pp. 22–54. Cambridge, UK: Cambridge Univ. Press

Grenoble LA, Whaley LJ. 2002. What does Yaghan have to do with digital technology? *Ling. Discov.* 1. http://linguistic-discovery.dartmouth.edu

Greymorning S. 2001. Reflections on the Arapaho language project, or when Bambi spoke Arapaho and other tales of Arapaho language revitalization efforts. See Hinton & Hale 2001, pp. 287–98

Grillo RD. 1989. *Dominant Languages: Language and Hierarchy in Britain and France.* Cambridge, UK/New York: Cambridge Univ. Press. ix, 261 pp.

Guardado D. 1997. Asturia—a head-start for Asturian on the Internet. *Mercator Media Forum* 3:52–59

Haag M, Coston F. 2002. Early effects of technology on the Oklahoma Choctaw language community. *Lang. Learn. Technol.* 6:70–82

Hagège C. 2000. *Halte à la Mort des Langues.* Paris: Odile Jacob

Hale K. 1992. Language endangerment and the human value of linguistic diversity. *Language* 68:35–41

Hale K. 2001. Strict locality in local language media: an Australian example. See Hinton & Hale 2001, pp. 277–82

Hall DD. 1996. *Cultures of Print: Essays in the History of the Book.* Amherst: Univ. Mass. Press

Harvey D. 1989. *The Condition of Postmodernity.* Oxford: Blackwell

Henze R, Davis KA. 1999. Authenticity and identity: lessons from Indigenous language and education. *Anthropol. Educ. Q.* 30:3–21

Hervieux B. 2001. The new vibrations of the traditional "teueikan." See Moseley et al. 2001, pp. 93–97

Hill J. 2002. "Expert rhetorics" in advocacy for endangered languages: Who is listening and what do they hear? *J. Ling. Anthropol.* 12:119–33

Hill KC. 2002. On publishing the Hopi dictionary. In *Making Dictionaries: Preserving Indigenous Languages of the Americas*, ed. W Frawley, KC Hill, P Munro, pp. 299–311. Berkeley: Univ. Calif. Press

Hindley R. 1990. *The Death of the Irish Language: A Qualified Obituary*. London: Routledge

Hinton L. 2001. Audio-video documentation. See Hinton & Hale 2001, pp. 265–72

Hinton L, Hale K, eds. 2001. *The Green Book of Language Revitalization in Practice*. San Diego: Academic. 450 pp.

Hobsbawm EJ. 1990. *Nations and Nationalism Since 1780: Programme, Myth, Reality*. Cambridge, UK: Cambridge Univ. Press

Hornberger NH, ed. 1996a. *Indigenous Literacies in the Americas: Language Planning from the Bottom Up*. Berlin: Mouton de Gruyter. 393 pp.

Hornberger NH. 1996b. Language planning from the bottom up. See Hornberger 1996a, pp. 357–66

Hornberger NH, King KA. 1999. Authenticity and unification in Quechua language planning. In *Indigenous Community-Based Education*, ed. S May, pp. 160–80. Clevedon: Multiling. Matters

Irvine JT, Gal S. 2000. Language ideology and linguistic differentiation. See Kroskrity 2000, pp. 35–84

Jaffe AM. 1999. *Ideologies in Action: Language Politics on Corsica*. Berlin: Mouton de Gruyter

Jones MC. 1998a. *Language Obsolescence and Revitalization: Linguistic Change in Two Sociolinguistically Contrasting Welsh Communities*. Oxford: Clarendon

Jones MC. 1998b. Death of a language, birth of an identity: Brittany and the Bretons. *Lang. Probl. Lang. Plan.* 22:129–42

Ka'awa M, Hawkins E. 1997. Incorporating technology into a Hawaiian language curriculum. See Reyhner 1997, pp. 151–57

Keane W. 2003. Semiotics and the social analysis of material things. *Lang. Commun.* 23:409–25

Keniston K. 2001. Language, power, and software. See Ess & Sudweeks 2001, pp. 283–306

King KA. 2001. *Language Revitalization Processes and Prospects: Quichua in the Ecuadorian Andes*. Clevedon, UK: Multiling. Matters

Kirshenblatt-Gimblett B. 1996. The electronic vernacular. In *Connected: Engagements with Media*, ed. G Marcus, pp. 21–65. Chicago: Univ. Chicago Press

Koerner K, ed. 1983. *Linguistics and Evolutionary Theory: Three Essays by August Schleicher, Ernst Haeckel and Wilhelm Bleek*. Amsterdam: Benjamins

Krauss M. 1992. The world's languages in crisis. *Language* 68:4–10

Kroskrity P. 2000. Language ideologies in the expression and representation of Arizona Tewa ethnic identity. See Kroskrity 2000, pp. 329–60

Kroskrity P. 2000. *Regimes of Language: Ideologies, Polities and Identities*. Santa Fe, NM: School Am. Res. Press

Kroskrity P. 2002. Language renewal and the technologies of literacy and postliteracy: reflections from Western Mono. In *Making Dictionaries: Preserving Indigenous Languages in the Americas*, ed. W Frawley, KC Hill, P Munro, p. 171–94. Berkeley: Univ. Calif. Press

Kroskrity P, Reynolds J. 2001. On using multimedia in language renewal: observations from making the CD-ROM *Taitaduhaan*. See Hinton & Hale 2001, pp. 317–30

Kuter L. 1989. Breton vs. French: language and the opposition of political, economic, social and cultural values. See Dorian 1989, pp. 75–90

Kuzar R. 1999. Linguistic and political attitudes towards Israeli Hebrew: ongoing revival versus normalcy. In *Language Ideological Debates*, ed. J Blommaert, pp. 267–306. Berlin: Mouton de Gruyter

Levy M. 1997. *Computer-Assisted Language Learning: Context and Conceptualization*. Oxford: Clarendon

Loader B. 1998. *Cyberspace Divide: Equality,*

Agency, and Policy in the Information Society. London: Routledge

Luykx A. 2001. Across the Andean airwaves: satellite radio broadcasting in Quechua. See Moseley et al. 2001, pp. 115–19

Lysloff R. 2003. Musical community on the internet: an on-line ethnography. *Cult. Anthropol.* 18:233–63

Marti R. 1990. *Probleme europäischer Kleinsprachen: Sorbisch und Bündnerromanisch.* München, Germany: Otto Sagner

McClure E. 2001. The role of language in the construction of ethnic identity on the Internet: the case of Assyrian activists in Diaspora. See Moseley et al. 2001, pp. 68–75

McDonald M. 1990. *"We Are Not French!": Language, Culture, and Identity in Brittany.* London: Routledge

McEwan-Fujita E. 2003. *Gaelic in Scotland, Scotland in Europe: minority language revitalization in the age of neoliberalism.* PhD thesis, Dept. Anthropology, Univ. Chicago

McHenry T. 2002. Words as big as the screen: Native American languages and the Internet. *Lang. Learn. Technol.* 6:102–15

Meadows M. 1996. Indigenous cultural diversity: Television Northern Canada. *Cult. Policy* 7:25–44

Miller D, Slater D. 2000. *The Internet: An Ethnographic Approach.* Oxford: Berg

Miyashita M, Moll LA. 1999. Enhancing language material availability using computers. See Reyhner et al. 1999, pp. 113–16

Moore RE. 1988. Lexicalization versus lexical loss in Wasco-Wishram language obsolescence. *Int. J. Am. Ling.* 54:453–68

Moseley C, Ostler N, Ouzzate H, eds. 2001. *Endangered Languages and the Media Proceedings of the Fifth FEL Conf. Agadir, Morocco 20–23 September 2001.* Bath, UK: Found. Endanger. Lang. 131 pp.

Nettle D, Romaine S. 2000. *Vanishing Voices: The Extinction of the World's Languages.* Oxford: Oxford Univ. Press

No'eau Warner S. 2001. The movement to revitalize Hawaiian language and culture. See Hinton & Hale 2001, pp. 133–46

Ó Riagáin D. 1991. State broadcasting and minority languages: the case of Irish in Ireland. *Educ. Media Int.* 28:113–18

Ó Riagáin D. 2001. Many tongues but one voice: a personal overview of the role of the European Bureau for Lesser-Used Languages in promoting Europe's regional and minority languages. In *Language, Ethnicity and the State: Volume 1: Minority Languages in the European Union*, ed. CC O' Reilly, pp. 20–39. Houndmills, UK: Palgrave

Ouakrime M. 2001. Promoting the maintenance of endangered languages through the Internet: the case of Tamazight. See Moseley et al. 2001, pp. 61–67

Parks DR, Kushner J, Hooper W, Francis F, Yellow Bird D, Ditmar S. 1999. Documenting and maintaining Native American languages for the 21st century: the Indiana University model. See Reyhner et al. 1999, pp. 59–83

Peterson LC. 1997. Tuning in to Navajo: the role of radio in native language maintenance. See Reyhner 1997, pp. 214–21

Poche B. 2000. *Les Langues Minoritaires en Europe.* Grenoble, France: Presses Univ. Grenoble

Rey L. 2001. Cultural attitudes toward technology and communication: a study in the "multi-cultural" environment of Switzerland. See Ess & Sudweeks 2001, pp. 151–60

Reyhner J, ed. 1997. *Teaching Indigenous Languages.* Flagstaff: North. Ariz. Univ.

Reyhner J, Cantoni G, St. Clair R, Yazzie E, eds. 1999. *Revitalizing Indigenous Languages.* Flagstaff: North. Ariz. Univ. 140 pp.

Reyhner J, Trujillo O, Carrasco RL, Lockhard L, eds. 2003. *Nurturing Native Languages.* Flagstaff: North. Ariz. Univ. 182 pp.

Rouchdy A. 1989. "Persistence" or "tip" in Egyptian Nubian. See Dorian 1989, pp. 91–102

Salinas Pedraza J. 1996. Saving and strengthening indigenous Mexican languages: the CELIAC experience. See Hornberger 1996a, pp. 171–88

Scannell P, ed. 1991. *Brodcast Talk.* London: Sage. 231 pp.

Schleicher A. 1983 [1863]. The Darwinian

theory and the science of language. See Koerner 1983, pp. 1–69

Silverstein M. 1984. *The "value" of objectual language.* Presented at Annu. Meet. Am. Anthropol. Assoc., 83rd, Denver

Silverstein M. 1998. Contemporary transformations of local linguistic communities. *Annu. Rev. Anthropol.* 27:401–26

Silverstein M. 2000. Whorfianism and the linguistic imagination of nationality. See Kroskrity 2000, pp. 85–138

Silverstein M. 2003a. The whens and wheres—as well as hows—of ethnolinguistic recognition. *Public Cult.* 15:531–58

Silverstein M. 2003b. *From glottoprospecting to antiquarian curating: dilemmas of reflexivity in the linguistics of local language communities.* Presented at Annu. Meet. Am. Anthropol. Assoc., 102nd, Chicago

Silverstone R, Hirsch E, Morley D. 1992. Information and communication technologies and the moral economy of the household. In *Consuming Technologies: Media and Information in Domestic Spaces*, ed. R Silverstone, E Hirsch, pp. 15–31. London: Routledge

Slater D. 2000. Consumption without scarcity: exchange and normativity in an Internet setting. In *Commercial Cultures: Economies, Practices, Spaces*, ed. P Jackson, M Lowe, D Miller, pp. 123–44. Oxford: Berg

Smith MA, Kollock P, eds. 1999. *Communities in Cyberspace.* London: Routledge. 323 pp.

Spitulnik D. 1993. Anthropology and mass media. *Annu. Rev. Anthropol.* 22:293–315

Spitulnik D. 1996. The social circulation of media discourse and the mediation of communities. *J. Ling. Anthropol.* 6:161–87

Spitulnik D. 2000. Documenting radio culture as lived experience: reception studies and the mobile machine in Zambia. In *African Broadcast Cultures: Radio in Transition*, ed. R Fardon, G Furnis, pp. 144–63. Oxford: Currey

Spolsky B. 1996. Conditions for Language Revitalization: A Comparison of the Cases of Hebrew and Maori. In *Language and the State: Revitalization and Revival in Israel*

and Eire, ed. S Wright, pp. 5–29. Clevedon: Multiling. Matters

St. Clair R, Busch J, Webb B. 1999. Self-publishing indigenous language materials. See Reyhner et al. 1999, pp. 129–37

Stenbaek MA. 1992. Mass media in Greenland: the politics of survival. In *Ethnic Minority Media*, ed. SH Riggins, pp. 44–62. Newbury Park, CA: Sage

Thomas N. 2001. Two Breton voices on radio. *Mercator Media Forum* 5:107–14

Tomlinson J. 1999. *Globalization and Culture.* Chicago: Univ. Chicago Press

Urla J. 1988. Ethnic protest and social planning: a look at Basque language revival. *Cult. Anthropol.* 3:379–94

Vallverdú F. 1995. The Catalan used on television. *Mercator Media Forum* 1:65–76

Villa DJ. 2002. Integrating technology into minority language preservation and teaching efforts: an inside job. *Lang. Learn. Technol.* 6:92–101

Warner M. 1990. *The Letters of the Republic: Publication and the Public Sphere in Eighteenth-Century America.* Cambridge, MA: Harvard Univ. Press

Warschauer M, ed. 1996. *Telecollaboration in Foreign Language Learning.* Honolulu: Univ. Hawai'i Press. 235 pp.

Warschauer M. 1998. Technology and indigenous language revitalization: analyzing the experience of Hawai'i. *Can. Mod. Lang. Rev./Rev. Can. Langues Vivantes* 55:139–59

Warschauer M. 1999. *Electronic Literacies: Language, Culture and Power.* Mahwah, NJ: Erlbaum

Williams C, ed. 2000. *Language Revitalization: Policy and Planning in Wales.* Cardiff: Univ. Wales Press

Williams G. 2001. Developing digital democracy. In *Minorities and Language Policy/Minderheiten und Sprachpolitik/Minoritiés et l'Aménagement Linguistique*, ed. PH Nelde, R Rindler Schjerve, pp. 123–33. St. Augustin, Germany: Asgard

Williams S. 2002. Ojibway hockey CD ROM in the making. See Burnaby & Reyhner 2002, pp. 219–23

Wilson S, Peterson LC. 2002. The anthropology of online communities. *Annu. Rev. Anthropol.* 31:449–67

Woolard KA. 1989. *Double Talk: Bilingualism and the Politics of Ethnicity in Catalonia.* Stanford, CA: Stanford Univ. Press

Woolard KA. 1998. Simultaneity and bivalency as strategies in bilingualism. *J. Ling. Anthropol.* 8:3–29

Woolard KA, Schieffelin BB. 1994. Language ideology. *Annu. Rev. Anthropol.* 23:55–82

Wurm S. 1999. Language revivalism and revitalization in Pacific and Asian Areas. *Int. J. Soc. Lang.* 137:163–72

Zepeda O, Hill JH. 1991. The condition of Native American languages in the United States. In *Endangered Languages*, ed. RH Robins, EM Uhlenbeck, pp. 135–55. Oxford: Berg

Annu. Rev. Anthropol. 2004. 33:47–72
doi: 10.1146/annurev.anthro.33.070203.143916
First published online as a Review in Advance on April 27, 2004

MUSIC AND THE GLOBAL ORDER

Martin Stokes

*Music Department, The University of Chicago, Chicago, Illinois 60637;
email: mhstokes@midway.uchicago.edu*

Key Words   globalization, world music, music industry, hybridity, migrancy

■ **Abstract**   Often music is used as a metaphor of global social and cultural processes; it also constitutes an enduring process by and through which people interact within and across cultures. The review explores these processes with reference to an anthropological and ethnomusicological account of globalization that has gathered pace over the last decade. It outlines some of the main ethnographic and historical modes of engagement with persistent neoliberal and other music industry–inspired global myth making (particularly that associated with world music), and argues for an approach to musical globalization that contextualizes those genres, styles, and practices that circulate across cultural borders in specific institutional sites and histories.

INTRODUCTION

The diverse musics prominent in the mass-mediated spaces of urban Western Europe and North America over the last two decades have challenged habits of thinking about global modernity in terms of westernization, modernization, urbanization, and "cultural gray-out" (Lomax 1968). The critical challenge has been complicated by the more expansive claims emanating from the music industry and music press about world music, anxious, in the late 1980s, to inject energy into record sales and attentive to newly exploitable markets outside their traditional zones of operation. World music, according to these claims, testified to a radically new political moment and more equitable cultural relations between the West and the rest. Defining the proper relationship between the critical agenda and the rhetoric of those promoting global music commerce has been a major issue. The problem is not, of course, exclusive to the study of music (see Appadurai 2002, Ferguson 2002, Tsing 2002).

Globalization implies notions of change and social transformation. The critical questions have been, For whom, For whose benefit, How, and When? Some researchers consider such questions within a relatively recent time frame. Small media technologies[1] permit easy dissemination of and access to previously unknown,

---

[1]I follow Sreberni-Mohamedi's (1994) definition of small media to refer primarily to those posttransistor and postmicrochip technologies that have transformed global media space.

remote, or socially exclusive musical styles (Manuel 1993). The accelerated transnational movements of people, capital, commodities, and information energized and crossfertilized music making in the diasporas in the major urban centers of Western Europe and North America and elsewhere (Slobin 2003). The permeability of nationstate borders partially erased by regionalization focused attention on border zones as encounter and creativity sites (Simonett 2001). The approaching (Christian) millennium stimulated musical exchange in (and "as") pilgrimage in anticipation of a dawning new era (Bohlman 1996, 2002). Musical practices heralded general social, political, and epistemic shifts from a modern- to a late- or postmodern order. For others writers, more could be gained by stressing underlying continuities: long histories of musical exchange in colonial and missionary encounter (Bohlman 2003, Radano & Bohlman 2000a); deepening patterns of dependence on metropolitan markets and tastes in music-industry production on the peripheries (Guilbault 1993); the reinscription in new media and its discursive apparatus of colonial conceptions of otherness and difference (Erlmann 1999; Feld 1994, 2000); processes of musical appropriation that both maintain and disguise Western high-modernist aesthetic hierarchies (Born & Hesmondhalgh 2000a); and the reproduction of the hegemonic relationships between centers and peripheries (Taylor 1997).

To tease out shifts in theoretical direction and emphasis in anthropological, ethnomusicological, and other writing on music in the global order is difficult. The period covered in this review (from the late 1980s to 2004) is relatively short. Individual writers, as the paragraph above indicates, can be hard to pin down. Publication dates do not relate simply to the circulation and development of ideas in the field. The dynamics of discussion across rigid disciplinary and subdisciplinary boundaries are complex. Some broad shifts can be detected, though. Critical caution has replaced the highly polarized theoretical positions and millennial anxieties that previously characterized the field. An interdisciplinary frame of reference predominates. Finer-grained historical and ethnographic approaches to global music circulation, with reference to specific genres and sites of intercultural encounter, predominate.

Recent scholarly work may be seen as an attempt to mediate some of the sharply opposed viewpoints of the early 1990s, particularly those of Erlmann and Slobin. Erlmann's vision of music in the global order draws partly on Jameson's analysis of late capitalism, a system geared, in Jameson's view, toward the orderly production and consumption of difference (Erlmann 1994, 1996, 1999; see also Jameson 1991). His view is also rooted in postcolonial critique, in which a colonial global imagination symbolically acknowledges the entangled cultural and historical destinies of the West and the rest, yet mystifies the violently exploitative relations between the two (Moore-Gilbert 1997). Erlmann points to long-term continuities that date back to the 1870s, in which contemporary world music and world beat can be understood in terms of the colonial contexts in which European, Black South African, and Black North American musics circulated and crossfertilized.

Erlmann argues that the period between 1870 and 1920, the high point of European imperial expansion, was a moment of take-off for globalization, after which it took a "single, inexorable form" (Erlmann 1999, p. 15), a mode of representation constituting the dominant narrative of modernity. The late nineteenth century, for Erlmann, was characterized by the panorama, the fetish, and the spectacle, a representational regime defining colonial selves in relation to colonized others in which "the lives and thinking of large numbers were beginning to be wholly enclosed, structured, and even governed by the images they had created for themselves" (Erlmann 1999, p. 176). The late twentieth century was, by contrast, characterized by an increasing tendency toward the presentational and the mimetic. First world aesthetic production, as characterized by world music and world beat, came to seek the "real presence" of the Other rather than a represented abstraction, an intimate entanglement of sounds and bodies in music and dance underpinned at the ideological level by an "all out relationism" and "empathetic sociality" (Erlmann 1999, p. 177). The signs of crisis are evident, but as Erlmann emphasizes, these are simply the currently visible aspects of a systemic crisis that has been integral to colonial modernity from the outset.

Slobin's methods and conclusions stand diametrically opposed (Slobin 1992, 1993). Where Erlmann sees the expanding and totalizing reach of global capitalism, Slobin sees "no overall sense to the system, no hidden agency which controls the flow of culture in a global world" (Slobin 1992, p. 5). He adopts Appadurai's well-known language of "-scapes," exploring the ways in which they articulate particular translocal musical contexts. He develops and nuances a notion of interacting and mutually defining "sub-," "super-," and "intercultures." Intercultures are further nuanced; Slobin distinguishes "industrial," "diasporic," and "affinity" intercultures, shaped by music industries operating outside of their home base, population movements across nation-state boundaries, and consumer choice, respectively. Developing an array of analytic terms that enable anthropologists or ethnomusicologists to shift and link scales in their analysis, Slobin focuses firmly on local projects, on "micromusical" scenes in which musicians and listeners across Europe and North America (the "West" of his subtitle) learn to code switch, negotiate levels, and give shape, form, and meaning to new musical scenes in a global context.

Slobin is reluctant to see "system" at work at the current moment of globalization and is consequently resistant to building a systemic theoretical language to describe it. He wonders whether "any simple analytical system will capture the pathos and the power of music in today's world of rapid deterritorialization and redrawing of boundaries, constant threat of terrorism or armed conflict, and simultaneity of marketing systems" (1993, p. 10). The analytical terms he proposes (the "-scapes," "inter-," "sub-," and "supercultures") are cautiously qualified as steps toward clarification and description but no more. Both musically and theoretically, all is in flux in Slobin's vision of globalization. Its only consistently organizing force is consumer choice, which, in Slobin's account, offers modern subjects more-or-less limitless opportunities for self-fashioning.

To identify Erlmann and Slobin in terms of a pessimistic Marxian critique on the one hand and an optimistic radical liberalism on the other would be somewhat reductive. Marxian critique often has enthused on the topic of musical globalization. Lipsitz, for instance, saw in globalized electronic media a displacement of the "lost" public sphere of the industrial city (Lipsitz 1994). Swedenburg, Back, and others consider the emancipatory potential of "globalization from below" within a specifically Marxian framework, focusing on the global circulation of Black (Back 1995–1996) or Middle Eastern (Swedenburg 2001) sounds and styles. But Erlmann and Slobin did exchange views, and these exchanges gave shape to a certain theoretical polarization in ethnomusicology in the early 1990s. Erlmann (1996) questioned Slobin's gravitation to the local as the site of resistance, self-fashioning, and transformation and as the appropriate focus of ethnographic research. Slobin, for his part, was reluctant to interpret globalization as a systemic and totalizing system of difference production, and these comments were at least partly directed at Erlmann and the traditions of Marxian critique on which he draws. An opposition between global and local, system and agency, pessimism and optimism, top-down and bottom-up approaches to globalization, and Marxian and liberal has thus been inscribed firmly in the ethnomusicological approach to globalization from the beginning.

Much of that written in recent years may be a mediation of these two positions. The top-down perspective has been localized: Specific global projects are understood in specific institutional contexts. Their capacity to shape the world exactly as they intend has been questioned and their world-shaping rhetoric socially, culturally, and historically contextualized. The major recording corporations no longer are considered the only site of agency in the global circulation of musical style. A number of analyses stress the importance of state, civic, and other institutional sponsors of world music scenes, radio and television broadcasting, small independent record labels, academic ethnomusicology programs, civic arts exchanges, and concert-promoting organizations (see, for example, Brusila 2003, Stokes 1994b). Efforts to understand the relationships, emerging convergences, and conflicts of interest, cultural style, and reckonings of scale in such contexts are well underway.

The bottom-up perspective has been broadened theoretically. The production of locality and place is no longer considered the inevitable and benign result of small-scale, face-to-face interaction, but instead a project in which many actors have an interest and a stake. Locality, as many investigators have stressed, is constructed, enacted, and rhetorically defended with an eye (and ear) on others, both near and far. The millennial anxieties that hovered around the topic of globalization and fed some of the more extreme theoretical pronouncements in the 1990s has given way to a more tempered and phlegmatic tone and a renewed commitment to detailed ethnographic and historical descriptions.

The mediation of top-down and bottom-up perspectives being described here relates in significant ways to Tsing's agenda for an anthropology of globalization (Tsing 2002). Tsing suggests the study of globalization is complicated both by its neoliberal propagandists and by some of its Marxian critics, notably Harvey (see, in particular, Harvey 1989). For both neoliberals and Marxian critics, according to Tsing, culture dresses up underlying economic processes. If global culture for neoliberals is simply a pleasurable by-product of a world with no borders or boundaries, for Harvey and other Marxian theorists it is an anxiety-ridden space in which subjects struggle to cope with poorly grasped perceptions of economically driven global space-time compression. For Tsing, critics in both traditions problematically put globalization beyond the bounds of human agency, dissent, and resistance, albeit for very different reasons.

Tsing suggests, instead, a grasp of globalization as a set of projects with cultural and institutional specificities; projects that construct, refer to, dream of, and fantasize of, in very diverse ways, a world as their zone of operation. Globalization in this sense is nothing new. What the modern period has added is a certain self-consciousness, a certain obsession with units and scales. She sees "global" and "local" not as places or processes, but as key discursive elements in world-making projects, around which intensifying self-consciousness and anxiety hovers. The institutional and discursive elements of such world-making projects are the focus of her proposal for a critical ethnography of globalization, one that focuses on the "located specificity of globalist dreams" but that also attends to their hegemonic dynamics and the complex processes by which they interact.

What, though, does the subject of music and dance add to such discussions of globalization? In what ways do practices of world making in and through music and dance differ from those that work in and through medical science, religion, film, environmental politics, or computer games? And how have ethnomusicologists, anthropologists, and others responded to this specificity? The field of globalization study is dominated by social science, which often gives the impression of being ill-equipped, or disinclined, to consider issues specific to music and dance. Academic musicology, for its part, has not always welcomed the insights, methods, and technical vocabularies of social science. Many ethnomusicologists, anthropologists, and popular music scholars writing on musical globalization are conscious of a gap and seek to overcome it, with various consequences. These questions are addressed in this review.

GLOBALIZATION THEORY AND WORLD MUSIC

The histories and trajectories of globalization theory in the social sciences and Western neoliberal economic theory are related, rendering particularly difficult the development of an appropriately critical theory of globalization. A characteristic reflex of those writing about music from various disciplinary perspectives is to critique world music, where some of the most pernicious neoliberal myth-making may, indeed, be identified (Brusila 2003, Feld 1994, Frith 2000, Schade-Poulsen 1999, Stokes 2003, Taylor 1997, Théberge 2003, Turino 2000). In effect, these studies are critiques of neoliberal globalization discourse, though one may argue that they are fed by the peculiar energies and anxieties that emerge when the most deeply naturalized and most pleasure-imbued ideologies are confronted critically.

The term world music is not, of course, remotely adequate for descriptive or critical purposes. The term dates from 1987, when independent record company executives and enthusiasts met in London to determine ways to market to British-based consumers already-circulating commercial recordings of popular musics from many parts of the world. For broadly similar reasons, comparable terms, such as *weltbeat* and *musique mondiale*, emerged elsewhere in Europe at roughly the same time and in Australia a little later (Brusila 2003, Mitchell 1993, Taylor 1997). The term world music was heavily promoted by the music press in the United Kingdom, and later in the United States, and eventually stuck. Billboard began a world music chart and a Grammy category for world music was devised in 1991 (Taylor 1997). The category incorporated various Asian, Latin, African, and Caribbean mass-mediated genres previously well-known in New York, Chicago, Los Angeles, London, Paris, and Berlin, both within and outside the diasporic enclaves in which they originally circulated. Also, some ethnographic classics were revived as a result (such as Colin Turnbull's 1957 central African recordings; see Feld 2000). Recording companies and festival organizations such as womad promoted musicians such as Youssou N'Dour, Fela Kuti, Manu Dibangu, Khaled, Aminah, Nusret Fatah Ali Khan, and many others as "world music artists," a definition many would come to understand and accept (if at all) rather slowly (see Dibangu 1994 for an exceptionally self-aware account of the process; see also N'Dour 1992 and Veal 2000, on Fela Kuti).

The expression world music also incorporated the work of rock musicians such as Brian Eno, Peter Gabriel, Robert Fripp, and David Byrne, and later, Sting, Bjork, and others, who incorporate non-Western sounds through multitracking, sampling, and live performance. This rock-oriented musical exoticism was distinguished as world beat in the United States (Feld 1994), though the distinction was not so carefully maintained in Europe. In England, world dance fusion, ethnic techno, radical global pop, and other such terms marked further subcultural distinctions later in the 1990s (Hesmondhalgh 2000). A complex discourse emerged, intended primarily to energize and enthuse compact disk (CD) buyers, and is living its own unruly life in music journalism (*Songlines, The Rough Guide to World Music* publications, *Folk Roots*) and on the fringes of academia in conferences, artist-in-residence programs, concert tours, workshops, and academic publications.

An early and persistent critical response to world music, by and large, has been to ignore the pervasive promotional discourse and concentrate ethnographically on musical practices in basic contexts of production, circulation, and consumption (Guilbault 1993, Schade-Poulsen 1999). Guilbault's study of Zouk in the French Antilles described a local industry increasingly transformed by its engagement with the French metropolitan market. Zouk is a popular Caribbean hybrid genre that has an underlying kinship with the complexly Africanized forms of the European quadrille, which have circulated in the Caribbean for over a century, and is thus closely connected to the popular musics of Haiti, Cuba, Dominica, and other Caribbean islands (see Aparicio 2000, Austerlitz 1997, Averill 1997, Pacini-Hernandez 1995). It was appreciated in the Antilles, however, for its peculiarly local flavor. This local flavor, as Guilbault (1997) describes, developed in a complex interaction with Caribbean and other diasporas in the French capital, with an emerging White liberal taste for *musique mondiale*, and with Parisian recording studios (then heavily subsidized by the French state) ready to experiment with these new creative forces and potential markets.

Local production in the Antilles thus responded to metropolitan demands for a carefully packaged otherness: clean (i.e., Western art music-derived) tonalities, vocal qualities, and instrumental textures with carefully foregrounded symbols of identifiable otherness. Zouk became a significant source of pride for the local government, particularly when a zouk singer and song were eventually chosen to represent a multicultural France in the Eurovision Song Contest. Zouk production was heavily encouraged through subsidies by the local state for export, though Guilbault carefully notes how the promotion of local industry and local identity deepens cultural and economic dependence on metropolitan France.

The fetishization of the local flavor is most intense in the cultural work taking place in and surrounding recording studios, an important site in which world music practices recently have been explored (Langlois 1996, Meintjes 2003, Schade-Poulsen 1999). Indeed, studio workers are often explicitly charged by their owners with the production of a local sound for global consumption, though the "locality" in question must be produced under extraordinarily dispersed and fragmented conditions of production. Gallo's Down Town studio was charged with producing distinctively Zulu sounds of mbaqanga, as Meintjes describes, though it did so with the aid of expensively imported, studio-technology expertise and ideas about African music (Meintjes 2003). Studios specializing in rai, whether in Algeria, Morocco, or France, blend local and global sounds at the mixing board to produce the mystique of Oran, the fabled birthplace of the genre in western Algeria. Studio engineers here, as in South Africa, devise elaborate techniques to elicit manipulable and appropriately local sounds from musicians often profoundly alienated by the conditions of production in studios (Langlois 1996, Schade-Poulsen 1999).

The global dimensions of the local product are often understood in different ways by record companies, studio managers, technicians, and musicians. For many struggling musicians, it would appear that the global stage is a fantasy, shaped by Khaled, Ladysmith Black Mambazo, and other local talents that have improbably disappeared into global space. Studio managers and record companies, by all accounts, easily manipulate such fantasies. Studio managers, such as those described by Meintjes (2003) in the context of mbaqanga and Langlois (1996) in the context of rai, have cultivated significant influence as gatekeepers, though their grasp of the global market for their products and protégées is limited to the networks they themselves have cultivated. Many studio managers, such as the rai *editeurs* in Oujda, Morocco, discussed by Langlois (1996), see themselves quite clearly as part of a structured hierarchy comprising other such gatekeepers, both within the world of rai and elsewhere. Oujda's *editeurs*, for example, produce rai as world music but aim for a niche at the lower end of the North African and Beur (French Maghrebi) cassette market, as a gap in rai develops and widens between North African–based cassette production and French-based CD production for a broader European and North American audience.

Global strategies, visions, fantasies, and exercises in self-promotion on the part of record companies also should be understood ethnographically, and more research (following Negus 1992) could be done in this area. Working notions of "the world" in recording companies are the outcome of often quite complex conflicts and boardroom discussion, of institutional histories connecting those companies to particular parts of the world, and, it would seem, of a certain element of chance. For example, Barclay was a small Paris-based independent recording company that developed some expertise in marketing French immigrant musics to a broader public alongside its jazz and French chanson operations. They became a subsidiary of PolyGram, a Dutch-German transnational developing a portfolio of small recording companies with experience in European immigrant markets and audiences. Shortly after, Barclay recorded and distributed Khaled's 1992 CD *Didi*, which turned out to be a major commercial success, not only in the Arab world but also across Europe and North America. Its success in Europe and North America was not anticipated by Barclay, judging by the fact that the original 1992 CD only contained transcriptions of the song lyrics in Modern Standard Arabic. Barclay was clearly imagining and prioritizing a mainstream Arab audience, rather than a significant Anglophone or Francophone listenership. If the global visions of companies such as Barclay emerge rather haphazardly, they do so as a result of situated, specific institutional outlooks, cultures, and histories that are amenable to ethnographic description and discussion.

WORLD MUSIC AND CULTURAL IMPERIALISM

The cultural imperialism hypothesis is clearly a poor guide to understanding the global circulation of music today, whether as world music or anything else. Certainly, the six large, transnational, music-recording companies, the so-called big six[2] (see Burnett 1996), have secured a significant degree of control over and profit from the circulation of music in recorded form across much of the planet (see also Laing 2003). Their own mechanisms for understanding the situation, though, are self-serving and provide, at best, an extremely partial vantage point on the issue of global music circulation (Harker 1997). To consider only the circulation of

---

[2]The big six are Time-Warner, Thorn-EMI, Bertelsmann, Sony, PolyGram, and Matsushita. Their efforts to control the global circulation of music recordings have traditionally focused on lobbying for copyright legislation in parts of the world in which cassette and CD piracy is endemic, and on partnerships with local firms to establish local dominance and monopolize retail outlets. For a brief discussion of Raks and PolyGram in Turkey, in many ways typifying the transnationals' strategies in the third world, see Stokes 2003.

recordings, the major players in the industry, despite their best efforts, have little control over copying and piracy endemic across much of the planet or over illegal internet sharing in their own backyards. They certainly have no control over the meanings, practices, and pleasures of listening, dancing, and partying at the site of consumption or the countless local forms of rock, pop, country, rap, and hip-hop to which they give rise (Regev 1997, Mitchell 2001). Even where a clear threat to their business is detected, as in copying, pirating, and illegal web sharing, their efforts to intervene have had relatively little success.

It is not so easy, however, to dismiss the charge of cultural imperialism. Fundamental asymmetries and dependencies in musical exchange have deepened all too evidently. European and North American rock and pop superstars are prominent in charts, music stores, and cassette stands across much of the third world; the reverse is not true. The large majority of these are White North American men: Electronic public space in the global era is increasingly male dominated (Taylor 1997). As Virolle (1995) notes of rai's global success, a genre entirely dominated by female singers such as Cheikha Rimitti in the 1940s and 1950s was almost entirely taken over by men, led by Cheb Khaled, in a few brief years of globalization in the 1980s (Virolle 1995). North African patriarchy failed to keep women quiet. But, Virolle wonders, "will the market system of the major record and entertainment companies manage to accomplish such an aim? Will these women be reduced to silence once again. . .?" (Virolle 2003, p. 229)[3]. Aparicio points to the tendencies of producers, musicians and consumers acting within a global frame of reference to consider music cultures in hierarchical relationships with one another and to configure these hierarchies in gendered and quasi-domestic terms. The femininity of various Latin genres is constantly stressed in their commodified circulation in North America, in promotional language, and in visual iconography. It is also reproduced in the language of local nationalist ideologues in many Caribbean and Latin American contexts to idealize certain kinds of cultural interaction (particularly Anglo-Saxon/Latin) and to marginalize others (particularly Latin/African) (Aparicio 2000). The globalization of music cements the hegemony of significant racial and gendered hierarchies in many parts of the world.

International copyright law and music-industry practice ensure that sounds from the peripheries can be exploited with impunity, whether songs, samples, or keyboard sound patches (Théberge 2003). World music discourse wraps in a warm language of mutually beneficial, politically benign exchange the exploitation of non-Western sounds. This discourse has strategic dimensions when questions of appropriation come to the fore. Paul Simon's promotion of Graceland as part of the struggle against apartheid certainly fell on receptive ears, of both Black and White audiences, upon its release in South Africa (Meintjes 1990), deflecting significant

---

[3]Counterexamples can be adduced, of course. Bithell remarks that the success of the Mystere des Voix Bulgares tour in Corsica facilitated the entry of women into previously male-dominated polyphonic genres and the commercial success of Corsican mixed-gender ensembles in the world music market (Bithell 2003).

criticism directed at Thorn-EMI's profits and Simon's paternalistic attitude toward South African musicians. Lip service to the politics of unequal exchange has been deeply internalized in world music production. The liner notes to Martin Cradick's *Spirit of the Forest* CD (1993), which makes extensive use of samples of Cameroonian Baka polyphony, indicate that royalties for the CD will be given to the Baka to "protect their forest and to develop it in a sustainable way without losing their knowledge and their culture" (cited in Feld 2000, p. 271). Pseudo-radical arguments abound that justify appropriation on racial grounds or via poststructuralist arguments about the death of the author. Such gestures are common, although basic music-industry business practices and habits ensure that exchanges between North and South remain profoundly asymmetrical.

Many discussions of musical globalization stress that processes of extraction, commodification, appropriation, and exploitation seldom are entirely straightforward. Recorded samples of non-Western music often pass through different hands for different purposes. Two case studies bear consideration in this regard (examples taken from Taylor 2003 and Hesmondhalgh 2000). *Polyphonies Vocales des Aborigénes de Taiwan*, an ethnographic CD released in France, features recordings originally made by various Taiwanese aboriginal groups during a European tour promoted and funded by the French and Taiwanese cultural ministries in 1988. In 1992, Michel Cretu, a Romanian-German musician, and his band Enigma added dance grooves to unlikely samples and other sound sources (e.g., Gregorian chant). He licensed the vocals from Maison des Cultures du Monde, sampled the "Jubilant Drinking Song," the CD's first track, originally sung by Ami people, and produced a CD, *The Cross of Changes*. This CD enjoyed extraordinary success in the United Kingdom, the United States, Australia, and Europe, selling some 5 million copies. In 1996, a song from the CD, *The Return to Innocence*, was made one of the official songs for the Atlanta Olympics, along with a number of other previously released world music recordings. Television stations CNN and NBC subsequently used the song to publicize their coverage of the Olympics.

The band Transglobal Underground sampled a Tahitian women's gospel choir on *Temple Head*, their first CD, in 1991. This band made much of their radical cultural politics and aimed, unlike Cretu, for subcultural rather than mainstream success. As Hesmondhalgh describes, "Temple Head," the title track, involved a looped dance beat throughout, live tabla playing, acid house-style piano chords, world music samples, and rapping "on the familiar theme of global unity via music" (Hesmondhalgh 2000, p. 283). In a deal struck between Nation Records, their distributors, and publishers, Coca Cola gained the rights to use a fragment of the song (combining rapping and the Tahitian gospel singers) to advertise their sponsorship of the 1996 Atlanta Olympic Games, and "Temple Head," like "Return to Innocence," became an official Olympic song.

Clearly these songs were worth a great deal for media corporations such as CNN, NBC, and Coca Cola, as well as the other official sponsors of the Olympics, though it is hard to estimate exactly how much. The women of the Tahitian gospel choir received nothing (Hesmondhalgh 2000). The Ami people originally sampled on *The Return to Innocence* apparently received a pittance (Taylor 2003). They were paid $15 a day for their original touring duties and received an unknown sum from a licensing deal struck between Cretu and the Maison du Cultures du Monde, 30,000 FF of which was passed on to the Chinese Arts Foundation in Taiwan. Kuo Ying-nan, one of the original singers in the recording, sued unsuccessfully for a violation of not only his intellectual property but also his human rights. Thorn-EMI defended its use of the sampled material and eventually agreed on an out-of-court settlement in which money was paid to an Ami community trust fund. The principle of Cretu's "ownership" of *The Return to Innocence*, in which he is defined as the "arranger" of "traditional" material, was carefully maintained.

These examples may appear to instantiate a stage-by-stage, unilinear process in which sounds, singers, and samples move from simple, traditional, local contexts to complex, modern, global contexts. This view emphasizes the different global frames, scales, fantasies, and ambitions of very different institutions (village festivities, Pentecostal churches, academic ethnomusicology and museum work, bohemian countercultures, global sports events, transnational corporations) and what happens when people and commodities move between them.[4] It also stresses the power differentials between the many spheres of exchange. But such a view also can reinscribe a crude version both of modernization theory and of cultural imperialism. "The global" can take the place formerly occupied by "the modern" in earlier theoretical paradigms. Like the modern, the global is perceived as being more encompassing in range if not depth, as conforming to capitalist disciplines of labor and commodity exchange, and as being tied to notions of development, civilization, and universality.

Hesmondhalgh and Taylor's examples suggest, by contrast, the multidimensionality of musical globalization. Samples, copies, and appropriations are unruly and unpredictable commodities, inviting further samples, copies, appropriations, and reappropriations in dialogue with the "originals." In some cases, the initiated dialogue is resistive, an act of reclaiming by the locally situated actors. To return briefly to the Ami example, the Enigma recording spawned imitations. Sony's world music supergroup, Deep Forest, sampled Yami (another Taiwanese aboriginal community) on their second CD, *Bohème*. Several Taiwanese bands also made their own versions, closely modeled from the Enigma recording. The Taiwanese bands made pointed efforts to credit and recompense the Ami (and other Taiwanese aboriginal groups) fairly and appropriately, drawing attention to the failure of international copyright and intellectual property legislation to protect Ami musical culture.

This circulation of ethnographic recordings, the serial copying of copies, the appropriation of recorded sounds by people more or less able to make money and

---

[4]The title of Virolle's study of rai implies a certain unidirectionality, "from deepest Algeria to the world stage," though much in the book presents a more complicated and nuanced picture (Virolle 1995). The same could be said of Neunfeldt's (1997) study of the didjeridu "From Arnhem Land to the Internet."

assign more-or-less broadly shared meanings to them has been dubbed schizo-phonic mimesis by Feld (1994, 2000). Feld is particularly interested in the appro-priations in European and North American jazz, pop, rock, dance, and ambient music of the well-known Turnbull and Arom ethnographic recordings of Central African "pygmy" polyphony. Feld borrows Schaefer's term schizophonia to refer to the separation of a recording from its original context of production, shifting an account of global music industry appropriation and exploitation to a more nuanced consideration of "the social life of things" (Appadurai 1988), in this case, sound recordings. Copies elicit other copies in a mutually defining and differentiating process that simultaneously disperses and fetishizes the original. This "original" becomes the site of multiple yet intensifying fantasies of otherness whose racial currents, as in the case of pygmy pop, merit careful attention (Feld 2000).

WORLD MUSIC DISCOURSE ANALYSIS

World music and its subgenres emerged as marketing categories surrounded by a great deal of promotional material in the form of music journalism (both in main-stream music and in such specialist publications as *Folk Roots* and *Songlines*), consumer guides (the *Virgin* and *Rough* guides to world music), liner notes on CDs, and websites. This promotional material quickly solidified into an identifi-able, if complex and unruly, body of discourse, which, in turn, became the object of critical attention. Brusila, Frith, and Théberge's accounts of world music specif-ically are accounts of world music discourse (Brusila 2003, Frith 2000, Théberge 2003), though many others have been interested in the discursive aspects of world music commerce. This critical tack differs from Guilbault's and Schade-Poulsen's mentioned above, which either ignore the discourse to concentrate on "what is really going on" on the ground or specifically criticizes it for misrepresentation (Schade-Poulsen 1999). Arguably it assumes too much homogeneity in world music discourse[5] but traces unacknowledged continuities, stress lines, and contra-dictions in ways that shed much light on the dynamics of world music as a social, cultural, and political field.

As Frith emphasizes, world music discourse did not emerge ab nihilo (Frith 2000). Those involved in its early formulation in London in 1987 were involved

---

[5]Friths' suggestion that world music discourse is significantly coauthored by journalists and academic ethnomusicologists requires some comment. The first edition of the *Rough Guide to World Music* contained the contribution of very few ethnomusicologists, and those were people with significant nonacademic experience in media (such as Jan Fairley, Banning Eyre, and Lucy Duran). Ethnomusicologists have, on the whole, been defensive in response to such publications. Only a few have chosen to connect with, for example, the *Rough Guide* project and did so for varied reasons [the list includes Steven Feld, Laudan Nooshin, Judith Cohen, Martin Stokes, Werner Graebner, Helen Rees, Carole Pegg, Carol Tingey, and Mark Trewin. The two volumes of the second edition, Broughton et al. (1999), total approximately 1400 pages].

in Greater London Council–sponsored multicultural events, independent record labels, and journals specializing in folk and "roots" rock. In many ways the values associated with these activities were smoothly adapted to the new discursive environment of world music. World music genres were validated for their authenticity and their locality. Authenticity was conferred in a language of functionality, political oppositionality, and by analogy with Black American musics. Algerian rai is described as Islamic rock and roll and as Thursday night fever, South African kwela as township jive, Greek amanes as Greek blues, and so forth. Locality was conferred in a language of place, roots, and opposition to the global, each emphasized by metaphors of musical exploration and of the consumer as traveler (as opposed to tourist) on a journey of personal discovery. World music discourse itself bears the mark of its contradictory struggles to secure the meaning of key notions such as authenticity, roots, hybridity, and the local. Many of these contradictions can be seen as somewhat magnified forms of those at work in Western rock discourse, complicated by increasing self-consciousness about hybridity and the increasingly dispersed nature of global music production.

The prominence of the idea of hybridity in world music discourse has attracted considerable attention (Frith 2000, Erlmann 2003, Taylor 1997), particularly because it is opposed to ideas about authenticity. The situation is complex because popular and academic handling of both terms are often entangled—one necessarily has to move between the two to grasp their discursive dynamics. Each (though in diverse ways) prioritize hybridity aesthetically, ethnographically, and politically and are skeptical about, if not openly hostile to, the ideas and practices associated with authenticity.

Study of musical hybridity in the past decade provides evidence of diasporic cultural and political strategies in which migrants, refugees, and diaspora populations detatched from nation-states situate themselves in global flows and build new homes for themselves (see Erlmann 2003). The privileged status of music in these kinds of analyses is connected to its perceived capacities for simultaneity and heterophony (and thus, pastiche, irony, multivocality, and the embrace of contradictions), its collective nature (and thus, imbrication with everyday lives), and its capacity to signify beyond the linguistic domain (and its binary "either/or" codes). From this theoretical perspective, music enables a "politics of the multiple" (Back 1995–1996; see also Gilroy 1993) and provides a unique key to the diasporic condition. The specificity of musical techniques (for example, Gilroy's antiphony) in the articulation of Diasporic consciousness and political practice is often evoked, but evoked in ways that are frustratingly short on detail and concreteness. Normative models of diasporic consciousness and cultural strategy are proposed, which do justice to the musical lives of some diasporas but not others (Slobin 2003).

Although, from a critical perspective, the language of hybridity and diaspora is conceived in opposition to the theory and practice of authenticity, authenticity and hybridity are, from a discursive point of view, more complexly entangled concepts. Popular world music discourse reveals the links between the two terms and betrays their ideological dimensions. In world music circles, as Frith wryly comments, hybridity is "the new authenticity" (Frith 2000). The identification of authentic elements ideologically justifies, naturalizes, and cements the hierarchical and exploitative relationships that (continue to) pertain between centers and peripheries, dominant and subaltern groups. The perpetuation of notions of authenticity through an authenticating discourse of hybridity is one of the means by which world music discourse continues to mediate Northern metropolitan hegemony.

When the Afro-Celt Sound System, a well-known London-based world dance fusion group of the late 1990s, samples and blends African and Celtic musical elements, such elements are portrayed as authentically primordial expressions of local musical identities. Such interpretations, at least, are either supplied or heavily implied by the musicians involved (Vallely 2003). The complex histories of mediation, exchange, and interaction of which they are, in fact, the product are discursively erased. African and Celtic musics are configured as the simple, relatively unmediated products of simple people, attaining global value only when transformed technologically in the industrial centers or by musical technologies associated with them.

Another way in which world music discourse and, according to some critics, much recent ethnomusicology confer on hybrid music a certain kind of authenticity is to stress that that all music is, of its very nature, hybrid. In this view, all music bears the mark of interactions and exchanges between as well as within groups, and to declare otherwise is absurd. Purity of musical expression is not possible. Even in societies in which extraordinarily strenuous efforts are made to disavow their social, cultural, and historical entanglement with others, an exception often is made for music. Across Eastern Europe, for example, nationalist regimes vilified their neighbors to the east, tainted in various ways by their Turkishness. Turkish sounding or Turkish-derived musical genres were of enduring popularity throughout the period, however ambivalently regarded by the nationalist intelligentsia. Such genres exploded into public prominence when these regimes collapsed in the late 1980s (see the various contributions to Slobin 1996). Those determined to see hybridity as a defining mark of the postmodern are thus confronted by the fact that the building blocks of every mixed style are themselves hybrids.

What then is categorized inauthentic in hybridity-valorizing discourses (since a contrast is necessary) is the heavy hand of anti-hybrid nationalist ideologues and their media and education apparatus, whose task is specifically the erasure of others in popular cultural pleasures such as music and dance. The editors of the *Rough Guide to World Music* are more-or-less united in their hostility to such invented national traditions. Ethnomusicologists and popular music scholars also betray either ambivalence, and occasionally outright hostility, to invented traditions perceived as acts of bureaucratic cerebration or thinly veiled bourgeois efforts to control working-class culture (Harker 1985, Manuel 1993, Rice 1994).

This stance is not without problems. First, it tends to reinscribe a simplistic opposition of authentic and inauthentic, merely reversing the conventional polarities. If anything is authentic now, it is hybrid genres, organically connected to the social life and cultural aspirations of particular localities. If anything can be truly described as inauthentic, in this view, it is state-promoted efforts to install authentic national traditions. This is, of course, a crude and ahistorical distinction that reproduces the worst aspects of the colonial fascination for the colonized "real" that resulted in entire streets from Cairo, for example, being transported to European capitals in the nineteenth century as exhibits in world fairs (Mitchell 1991).

Second, it loads onto the authentic complex tasks of resistance, which may be entirely inappropriate to describe basic conditions of production, listening, and circulation. Rai is consistently, and incoherently, characterized in world music discourse as a "music of resistance" simultaneously to the Algerian (secular) state, to the French colonial apparatus, and most recently, to the Islamist political and paramilitary groups in Algeria. Rai musicians, whether in the past or present, have in fact been extraordinarily careful in their self-positioning vis-à-vis Islam and the state; so too have their listeners (see Virolle 1995, Gross et al. 2003, Schade-Poulsen 1999). The romance of resistance in world music discourse leads world music celebrities to stress their antiestablishment credentials, feeding a variety of misleading views of how specific genres emerged and circulated.

Third, such a view of hybridity equates the inauthentic with the nation-building project and sees it as an act of ideological cerebration devoid of pleasure, meaning, or significance for everyday folk. This understanding of inauthenticity, again, provides a poor, ahistorical lens for considering the complex social and cultural life of state-invented traditions, many of which, such as Philip Kutev's Bulgarian folk music ensemble, have actually found an avid world music listenership in North America and Western Europe (Buchanan 1997).

The celebration of hybridity evident in world music discourse, but shared in certain areas of the anthropological and ethnomusicological literature, also erodes important and necessary aesthetic, political, and social distinctions. Aesthetically speaking, one must distinguish between a variety of different ways in which styles, genres, instruments, and sounds perceived as different are brought together: Which constitute foreground, which background? Which subordinate which other musical elements to it? Which are deformed to fit a new musical environment? Which elements mark cultural difference, and which signify or engage with modernity? Which elements blend seamlessly, and which generate a frisson of difference? The variety of different musical techniques employed by avant-garde performers such as the Kronos Quartet, by high-concept rock musicians such as Brian Eno, by Mexican musicians in Los Angeles, or by recording engineers in Bollywood cinema studios too easily can be obscured by blanket terms such as hybridity, cultural creolism, and mestizaje.

Politically, one must distinguish the hybridizing cosmopolitanism (c.f. Turino 2000) of the relatively powerful from the relatively powerless. One needs to be attentive to the diverse positions of power, prestige, and influence from which people make musical alliances and forge musically cosmopolitan selves. Hybridizing strategies often have an elite, rather than subaltern, dynamic. Cultural nationalist traditions, particularly in the Caribbean and Latin America, have been deeply and self-consciously invested in certain forms of hybridity (see, for example, Reily 1994). These forms are characteristically constructed at an ideological level in ways that enable, for example, the alliance between a local and a European or Euro-American cultural self, but that systematically denigrate African elements deemed polluting, primitive, and out of place in the desired national mix. (See Savigliano 1995 on tango; Austerlitz 1997 on merengue; Pacini-Hernandez 1995 on bachata; and Aparicio 2000 on Puerto Rican bugalu.) The hybridizing strategies of subaltern classes affect musical alignments and alliances across nation-state borders for different reasons. Sometimes these strategies imply, especially at moments of festivity and celebration, deep and enduring cultural continuities within regions or former imperiums (see, e.g., Keil et al. 2002 on the circulation of Middle Eastern and Rom musics in the Balkans). Sometimes such moves enable people struggling with minoritarian status in particular nation-states to effect broader identifications. Black musics, as Lipsitz points out, transform the experience of African diaspora minorities across the Caribbean and the Americas into that of a global majority (Lipsitz 1994). Sometimes such moves are simply designed to snub elite culture in situations of overt or covert class antagonism (such is the case, to a certain extent, in Turkish habits of listening to Arab popular musics; see Stokes 1992).

Socially, it is important not to assume a direct relationship between aesthetic strategies (i.e., those operating in texts and performances of various kinds) and those of everyday life, particular among migrants and others living lives of enforced, rather than chosen, cultural fragmentation and hybridity. Artistic production (i.e., to follow the conventional definition, music, dance, and visual and literary work) of migrants and Diaspora communities must be seen in relationship to everyday lives outside of such privileged spaces and privileged art producers, as many anthropologists have stressed (Rouse 2002). This relationship can take various forms. At a general level, the fantasies characteristic of migrant music, film and dance, modernity, cosmopolitanism, upwardly mobile romance, and technological mastery must be understood in relationship to the limited life chances and the endless and humiliating accommodations for the bureaucracies and work routines of host societies that characterize migrant everyday life. The cosmopolitanism of the rich thus must be clearly distinguished from the cosmopolitanism of the poor, even when the techniques and imaginaries of such cosmopolitanisms have common elements. Tsing (2002, p. 469) states bluntly: "[P]oor migrants need to fit into the worlds of others; cosmopolitans want more of the world to be theirs." Terms that blur such crucial distinctions must be handled cautiously.

PERSISTENT STATES AND GLOBAL CITIES

Neoliberal globalization discourse portrays nationalism in decline, state efforts to control national economies and distribute welfare on the wane, and borders increasingly irrelevant. In recent years much social science has, by contrast, been concerned with understanding the global contexts in which they continue to thrive as sites of cultural production. Three brief case studies illustrate some of the related critical directions in music study.

Turino's *Nationalists, Cosmopolitans and Popular Music in Zimbabwe* (2000) focuses on chimurenga and jit, Zimbabwean popular musics that were significantly popular across Europe and North America as world music in the 1980s and 1990s. He is concerned with the continuities in Zimbabwean national musical culture at three contrasting moments: the colonial, the postcolonial, and the global. In all of these moments, national musical identity was forged by local cosmopolitans intent on situating Zimbabwean traditional musics in some broader cultural alignment. In the colonial period, and notably in the relatively liberal climate of the 1950s and early 1960s, the Rhodesian Broadcasting Corporation did much to promote Shona mbira music as an authentic national culture. National culture was thus firmly rooted in the cosmopolitan cultural dispositions of White liberals, horizons that embraced not only Britain, but also Malawi and Zambia, with which Rhodesia was briefly federated.

During and after decolonization, Shona mbira music remained central as national expression. A new generation of well-traveled and musically eclectic Zimbabwean cosmopolitans, such as Thomas Mapfumo, mixed Shona mbira music with rumba-derived Congolese guitar styles and vocal protest music from the period of anticolonial struggle (chimurenga). As jit, this music was popular and obtained degree-of-state support in Zimbabwe. Long-standing fascination for the mbira in America and Europe (in the wake of Paul Berliner's well-known book and recordings; Berliner 1981) enabled Mapfumo to develop a significant market outside Zimbabwe. Turino sees globalization and nationalism as mutually constructing and reinforcing processes, with the activities of local cosmopolitans at heart.

Though some apologists for the new global order consider nation-state borders to be on the wane, social scientists beg to differ and stress the imperative of local-level study (Wilson & Donnan 1998). Specific and localized discussions of how musicians, musical instruments, and musical styles and sounds circulate in and around border zones are still few and far between. The cultural dynamics of border life have however been well described in accounts of a number of Mexican American genres (see for instance Peña 1985 on conjunto and Simonett 2001 on banda). Both genres have been animated by the small but cumulative transformations that take place as musicians and sounds cross and recross the border. In both cases, the relatively free movement of sounds (and other commodities) across the border contrasts with the relatively restricted movement of musicians and their audiences (and other laborers). Small differentials cause significantly different effects north and south of the border, as well as complex interactions.

As a musical genre, banda was one of a number of border-zone hybrids developed in recording studios in Guadalajara in the 1990s. It built on ranchero-style ballad singing (often focused on the Robin Hood–like exploits of drug smugglers), on North West Mexican brass–band playing, and on the polka-based social dance forms of nineteenth- and twentieth-century central European migrants settled in northern Mexico, Texas, and the Midwest United States. The energetic traffic in musical styles that gave birth to banda contrasts markedly with the increasingly restricted traffic in human beings. As a consequence, banda has had complex and somewhat separate ramifications north and south of the border. In the United States it marks an emerging sense of Mexicano identity (as distinct from Hispano/Latino/Chicano identifications); in Mexico itself it dislodged previously privileged forms of national music, such as mariachi, and oriented Mexican public culture northwards.

For many anthropologists and sociologists, global cities are new sites of multicultural energy and creativity significantly freed from the dictates of the nation-states to which they were formerly attached. From a critical point of view, however, the opposition between global cities and nation-states is not so clear. Indeed, states invest significantly in such cities to attract the flow of global capital and attract transnational corporations to them as bases (Keyder 1999, Sassen 1998). Municipalities fund public multicultural arts programs and promote ethnic neighborhoods, cuisines, popular music, dance, and nightlife in order to cultivate a global profile; the managerial rhetoric and practice of globalization in world cities is somewhat uniform, regardless of what each specifically has to sell. From a historical perspective, the recent moment of self-conscious globalization elides complex and varied histories in which such cities have been pulled in and out of the swim of regional and transregional cultural, demographic, and economic flows over centuries. The question then is how state-produced global city rhetoric (and associated administrative practice) articulates with the diverse social forms and practices of cities whose inhabitants have always been attuned, though to greater and lesser extents, to their regional and transnational spheres of influence.

Music understood in the context of a global city, as in studies based in New York, can testify to the processes by which diasporas and migrant populations from nearly everywhere on the planet interact in neighborhood festivities and religious practices, in local media, and in multicultural civic institutions (see Allen & Wilken 1998). In these accounts, processes of globalization have produced a global city with minimal state intervention. In Istanbul, by contrast, the state's orchestration of the city's global identity in the mid-1990s was striking (Keyder 1999). Import-substituting policies in the mid-twentieth century decades of nation-state building in Turkey and political hostility toward mercantile elites resulted in a nationally rather than internationally oriented Istanbul, a city increasingly shorn of its cultural connections with wider regional worlds. The cosmopolitan musical forms (kanto, operetta, fasil) patronized by such elites dwindled. A half century later, though, they were available for nostalgic reappropriation in a variety of new media and live performance venues restored or otherwise enabled by the state. Çicek Pasaji, a major site of informal urban music making and socializing was restored for tourists[6]; media deregulation dismantled the cultural stranglehold

---

[6]Tourism here as in many other places is as much about disciplining locals as entertaining outsiders. For a broader musical perspective, see De Witt 1999 and Rees 2000.

of the nationally oriented Turkish Radio and Television corporation. Digitally remastered CDs fueled the traffic in nostalgia, and new forms of popular music emerged that echoed their cosmopolitanism with a certain self-consciously global twist (Stokes 1999).

Yang (2002) describes a somewhat similar process in Shanghai in the 1990s as recosmopolitanism, a nostalgia for a cosmopolitanism and urbanity erased in an earlier period of nation building and a consumer-driven embrace of music, film, and cuisine signifying broader dimensions of transnational Chinese-ness and Shanghai's much vaunted status as a global city. Narrow cultural nationalism in both contexts is no longer a concern and perhaps is something of a liability, at least to both the Chinese and Turkish state's new managers. Many such "market-state" elites, to use Balakrishnan's (2003) useful formulation, are anxious to distance themselves from narrowly parsed nationalisms that are clearly unappealing to foreign corporations and are entangled with concepts of social welfarism with which such elites no longer wish to be burdened. Yang's term usefully enables a distinction between the ongoing small-media processes that make it increasingly difficult for states such as Turkey and China to control national culture and the ideological production of new cosmopolitanisms by municipalities striving to attract global capital. Civic musical policies may be understood as a small but significant aspect of neocosmopolitanism in cities whose global status is thought about a great deal by their managers.

THE MUSICAL DYNAMICS OF INTERCULTURE

How and why do particular musical forms, styles, processes, sounds, rhythms, and metrical practices traverse national cultural boundaries? How are we to grasp the seemingly contagious movements of certain musical practices when they are clearly grasped and understood very differently by the different groups involved in their exchange and transmission? Monson (1999), in an important article, suggests a specifically musical focus on the processes of cultural interaction across the African diaspora, specifically practices of riffing. This, she suggests, will do something to restore a sense of human agency to discussions of globalization absorbed by systemic thinking and some sense of the collective dimensions of global culture to discussions that emphasize its fragmentation and atomism. But the specific challenge she issues is how we are to grasp the extremely fluid circulation of certain musical practices through and across significantly different cultural spaces.

Monson contributes to a long discussion in ethnomusicology that primarily has been concerned with the global circulation of the musical practices of European art musics (particularly in the context of colonization, Westernization, and missionary activity) and African Diasporic musics (in the context of slavery and the middle passage). Regarding the former, some ethnomusicologists express anxiety about cultural gray out and consider as a contagion to be resisted the spread of Western art and popular music techniques and technologies (for example, Lomax 1968).

Other ethnomusicologists saw it as an opportunity to observe and theorize the role of music in cultural contact and encounter. For example, Nettl (1978), in an early and influential volume, carefully distinguished musical Westernization (the copying or imposition of specific techniques designed to draw its non-Western practitioners into Western religious, cultural, and political space) from musical modernization (the adoption of techniques that conferred modernity but preserved essential national traits).

Mission choirs, military bands, and Western-style music educators in the colonized world contributed to the extraordinary spread of a variety of practices and habits associated with Western art music by the mid-twentieth century: functional harmony; counterpoint; regular metric structures; equally tempered scales; clean instrumental and vocal timbres; large functionally differentiated ensembles and conductors; and discrete, single-authored works, pieces, or songs. Radio broadcasting and sound recording swiftly added the practices associated with amplified voices and studio multitracking, guitars, keyboards and drumkits, three-minute songs that alternate verses and choruses, sound systems, and breakbeats. Such practices have been incorporated into more localized sound worlds in various and complex ways, a matter of perennial interest to ethnomusicologists and others interested in tracking the global movements of genres such as rumba, tango, salsa, American country music, marching bands, rock, blues, jazz, rap, and trance (Averill 1997; Collins 1992; Mitchell 1996, 2001; Regev 1997; Savigliano 1995; Waxer 2002) or in the adaptation of techniques associated with lammelophones and musical bows to instruments such as the guitar in many parts of Africa (Charry 1994, 2000; Eyre 1988, 2000; Turino 2000; Waksman et al. 2003).

Reverse flows are as much a feature of the globalized landscape, however. Musical forms, styles, practices, and instruments associated with the African Diaspora dominate the global landscape at the beginning of the twenty-first century. The global circulation of African Diasporic styles has a long history and complex dynamics. The circulation of rumba, tango, rock, blues, jazz, and various other forms of Western-hemisphere popular music has, among other things, returned techniques developed in the African diaspora to Africa. This fact has not been lost on many West- and North African musicians keen to expand their own horizons and develop audiences elsewhere. West African griots and North African gnawa musicians develop innovative ways of imagining African Diasporic musical relations, partly extending indigenous ideologies of contact, exchange, and movement (particularly as they involve spirits) and partly reflecting the presence in their lives of French or American world music entrepreneurs, concert organizers, and other musicians (Eyre 2000, Kapchan 2002).

The great ease with which African Diaspora sounds and practices travel is often taken for granted even by ethnomusicologists. Late twentieth century North American cultural hegemony is only part of the answer. As Monson (1999) suggests, careful consideration of the musical practices as music could do much to help understand the extraordinary energy with which such important musical devices as the riff circulate. Riffs, for Monson, operate as melodies, as ostinatos functioning as grounds for improvization, or they can be utilized in antiphonal figures or combined in layers. Other techniques have emerged and developed in the long history of musical interactions between Africa and the African Diasporas. Interlocking rhythmic processes and thick, complex, buzzy musical textures are just two; the list is potentially long. Of interest is not only the fact that such techniques circulate but also that this circulation is accompanied by such speedy recognition of musical intimacies and kinships by those involved. As Martin Scorsese's (2003) film about the blues demonstrates, American blues musicians and Malian griot singers have little difficulty getting together and producing a musical experience that is palpably coherent in contexts in which very little else (for example, spoken language) is shared. A naïve afrocentrism is an often insistent discursive accompaniment to such events, often drowning out all else (particularly the music). But diverse riffing practices can be accommodated and negotiated in musical performance with speed and facility.

The cultural hegemony of the United States has thrown certain American popular musics under the spotlight in discussions of musical globalization, but many other socio-musical practices, both in America and elsewhere, may be considered in similar terms. How and why do Italian bel canto singing, Anglo-Celtic jigging and reeling, Latin dance forms from the tango to the Macarena, modal (maqam) improvization in the Middle East and the Balkans, toasting and rapping in the Caribbean and the United States, Central European polka, the bell-patterns of West African drumming, the timbre-rich droning of Australian aboriginal music, and the colotomic processes of Javanese gamelan cross so many cultural boundaries with such energy, boundaries at which so much else comes to an abrupt halt? In many cases, a partial answer may be given if one considers some of the obvious vectors of circulation: mass media and concert life in the contexts of empire and nation building; prestige instruments associated with political, spiritual, educational, and economic hegemonies; instruments and musical practices associated with subaltern religiosity and other forms of heightened sociality (trancing, possession); and political solidarities across borders. Such explanations are partial because reductive, musical practices are perceived simply as filling global spaces shaped and structured by other things. Music, clearly enough, plays an active role in creating and shaping global spaces that otherwise would not have "happened." To take just one example, the prevalence of jigging and reeling in sessions across Europe (Vallely 2003) and elsewhere (Smith 2003) created Irish bars as a global phenomenon, and not the reverse.

How, though, does this creating and shaping of global spaces happen? Keil's (1994) notion of participatory discrepancies, the microfluctuations in groove that bond participants in the musical event, accounts for something significant to all of the practices mentioned above. However, other genres that are described in the same terms enjoy little global circulation. Concepts such as repetition and antiphony are useful to a point, though it is hard to think of any music in which repetition is not a significant feature, and, again, many globalized musical practices are not strictly antiphonal. Concepts and vocabulary for describing intercultural musical processes will require greater sharpness and descriptive focus if broader theorizations are to emerge.

We are left with some general questions, however. First is the question of how such intercultural musical practices retain their identities as recognizable musical processes in such diverse musical environments. How do such intercultural musical practices retain their identities as recognizable musical processes in such diverse musical environments? Bell patterns do different things in salsa, samba, and West African ensembles. They interact with different styles of dancing and movement in performance, they relate to harmonic processes in one context but not another, and they do different symbolic and expressive work. Yet they can be extrapolated and inserted into different socio-musical contexts with a certain facility. One factor may be their cognitive "graspability" within certain broadly shared cultural formations. Music analysis demonstrates that the relationships between a bell pattern and what is happening elsewhere in a West African drumming ensemble are enormously complex (Locke 1987). Yet the generative potential of a twelve-pulse figure that never fully settles on a duple or a triple gestalt appears to be easily grasped and communicated across significant cultural borders. One factor may be their indexical or iconic "groupiness" (Lomax 1968). Many such socio-musical practices quickly communicate to listeners, observers, and dancers the very processes of intense social interaction and physical activity through which they come into being, as a consequence of either visual or aural cues in transmission: interlocking, phrase marking, call and response, droning, simultaneous group improvizations, varied repetitions, etc. What is heard implies forms and processes of embodied social interaction. While such forms and processes may not be highly valued at the level of sanctioned cultural discourse, they may be broadly recognizable in the more submerged repertoires of fantasy, play, and pleasure, and it is this recognition that facilitates their cultural mobility. This is not to argue for a culture-free picture of global music interactions. It is, however, to stress that musical, as well as political, social, and economic, explanations exist as to why particular practices circulate, and to suggest that any properly cultural analysis of the global music order should consider them.

ACKNOWLEDGMENTS

The article was completed during a year's residence at the Franke Institute for the Humanities at the University of Chicago, enabled by a Franke Institute faculty fellowship and the Howard Foundation.

The *Annual Review of Anthropology* is online at http://anthro.annualreviews.org

LITERATURE CITED

Allen R, Wilken L, eds. 1998. *Island Sounds in the Global City: Caribbean Popular Music and Identity in New York*. New York: NY Folklore Soc.

Aparicio F. 2000. Ethnifying rhythms, feminizing cultures. See Radano & Bohlman 2000b, pp. 95–112

Appadurai A, ed. 1988. The Social Life of

Things: Commodities in Cultural Perspective. Cambridge: Cambridge Univ. Press

Appadurai A. 2002. Disjuncture and difference in the global cultural economy. See Inda & Rosaldo 2003, pp. 46–64

Austerlitz P. 1997. *Merengue: Dominican Music and Dominican Identity.* Philadelphia: Temple Univ. Press

Averill G. 1997. *A Day for the Hunter, a Day for the Prey: Popular Music and Power in Haiti.* Chicago: Chicago Univ. Press

Back L. 1995–1996. X amount of Sat Siri Akal! Apache Indian reggae music and the cultural intermezzo. *New Form.* 27:128–47

Balakrishnan G. 2003. Algorhythms of war. *New Left Rev.* 23:5–33

Berliner P. 1981. *The Soul of Mbira: Music and Traditions of the Shona People of Zimbabwe.* Chicago, IL: Univ. Chicago Press

Bithell C. 2003. A man's game? Engendered song and the changing dynamics of musical activity in Corsica. See Magrini 2003, pp. 33–66

Bohlman PV. 1996. Pilgrimage, politics, and the musical remapping of the New Europe. *Ethnomusicology* 40(3):375–412

Bohlman PV. 2002. World music at the end of history. *Ethnomusicology* 46(1):1–32

Bohlman PV. 2003. *A Very Short Introduction to World Music.* Oxford: Oxford Univ. Press

Born G, Hesmondhalgh D. 2000a. Introduction: on difference, representation and appropriation in music. See Born & Hesmondhalgh 2000b, pp. 1–58

Born G, Hesmondhalgh D, eds. 2000b. *Western Music and its Others: Difference, Representation and Appropriation in Music.* Berkeley: Univ. Calif. Press. 360 pp.

Broughton S, Ellingham M, Muddyman D, Trillo R, eds. 1994. *World Music: The Rough Guide.* London: Rough Guides

Broughton S, Ellingham M, Trillo R, eds. 1999. *World Music: The Rough Guide, Volumes 1 and 2 of the New Edition.* London: Rough Guides

Brusila J. 2003. *'Local Music, Not From Here': The Discourse of World Music Examined Through Three Zimbabwean Case Studies: The Bhundhu Boys, Virginia Mukwesha and Sunduza.* Helsinki: Finnish Soc. Ethnomusicol. Publ. 10

Burnett R. 1996. *The Global Jukebox: The International Music Industry.* London: Routledge

Buchanan D. 1997. Bulgaria's Magical Mystère tour: postmodernism, world music marketing, and political change in Eastern Europe. *Ethnomusicology* 41(1):131–58

Charry E. 1994. The Grand Mande guitar tradition of the western Sahel and the Savannah. *World Music* 36(2):21–61

Charry E. 2000. *Mande Music: Traditional and Modern Music of the Maninka and Mandinka of Western Africa.* Chicago, IL: Univ. Chicago Press

Clayton M, Herbert T, Middleton R, eds. 2003. *The Cultural Study of Music: A Critical Introduction.* London: Routledge. 359 pp.

Collins J. 1992. *West African Pop Roots.* Philadelphia: Temple Univ. Press

De Witt M, ed. 1999. Music travel and tourism. *World Music* 41(Spec. Issue 3):155

Dibangu M (with Rouard D). 1994. *Three Kilos of Coffee: An Autobiography.* Chicago, IL: Univ. Chicago Press

Erlmann V. 1994. Africa civilized, Africa uncivilized: local culture, world system and South African music. *J. South. Afr. Stud.* 20(7):165–79

Erlmann V. 1996. The aesthetics of the global imagination: reflections on world music in the 1990s. *Public Cult.* 8(3):467–87

Erlmann V. 1999. *Music, Modernity and the Global Imagination.* Oxford. Oxford Univ. Press

Erlmann V. 2003. Hybridity and globalization (intercultural exchange, acculturation). In *The Continuum Encyclopaedia of Popular Music of the World,* ed. J Shepherd, D Horn, P Oliver, P Wicke, pp. 279–90. New York: Continuum. Vol. 1

Eyre B. 1988. Soukous, Chimurenga, Mbaqanga, and more: new sounds from Africa. *Guitar Play.* 22(10):80–88

Eyre B. 2000. *In Griot Time: An American*

Guitarist in Mali. Philadelphia: Temple Univ. Press

Feld S. 1994. From schizophonia to schismogenesis: on the discourses and commodification practices of 'world music' and 'world beat'. See Keil & Feld 1994, pp. 257–89

Feld S. 2000. The poetics and politics of Pygmy Pop. See Born & Hesmondhalgh 2000b, pp. 280–304

Ferguson J. 2002. Global disconnect: abjection and the aftermath of modernism. See Inda & Rosaldo 2003, pp. 136–53

Frith S. 2000. The discourse of world music. See Born & Hesmondhalgh 2000b, pp. 305–22

Gilroy P. 1993. *The Black Atlantic: Modernity and Double Consciousness*. London: Verso

Gross J, McMurray D, Swedenburg T. 2003. Arab noise and Ramadan nights. Rai, rap and Franco-Maghrebi identities. See Inda & Rosaldo 2003, pp. 198–230

Guilbault J (with Averill G, Benoit E, Rabess G). 1993. *Zouk: World Music in the West Indies*. Chicago, IL: Univ. Chicago Press

Harker D. 1985. *Fakesong: The Manufacture of British 'Folksong'*. Milton Keynes, UK: Open Univ. Press.

Harker D. 1997. The wonderful world of the IFPI: music industry rhetoric, the critics, and the classical Marxist critique. *Pop. Music* 16(1):45–80

Harvey D. 1989. *The Condition of Postmodernity*. Cambridge MA: Blackwell

Hesmondhalgh D. 2000. International times: fusions, exoticisms and anti-racism in electronic dance music. See Born & Hesmondhalgh 2000b, pp. 280–304

Inda J, Rosaldo R, eds. 2002. *The Anthropology of Globalization*. Oxford: Blackwell. 498 pp.

Jameson F. 1991. *Postmodernism, or the Cultural Logic of Late Capitalism*. Durham, NC: Duke Univ. Press

Kapchan D. 2002. Possessing Gnawa culture: displaying sound, creating history in an unofficial museum. *Music Anthropol.* 7:http://www.muspe.unibo.it/period/ma/index/number7/ma_ind7.htm

Keil C. 1994. Participatory discrepancies and the power of music. See Keil & Feld 1994, pp. 96–108

Keil C, Feld S, eds. 1994. *Music Grooves*. Chicago, IL: Univ. Chicago Press. 402 pp.

Keil C, Feld S, Blau D. 2002. *Bright Balkan Morning: Romani Lives and the Power of Music in Greek Macedonia*. Middleton, CT: Wesleyan Univ. Press

Keyder C, ed. 1999. *Istanbul: Between Global and Local*. Lanham, MA: Rowman & Littlefield

Laing D. 2003. Music and the market: the economics of music in the modern world. See Clayton et al. 2003, pp. 309–20

Langlois T. 1996. The local and global in North African popular music. *Pop. Music* 15(3):259–73

Lipsitz G. 1994. *Dangerous Crossroads: Popular Music, Postmodernism and the Poetics of Place*. London: Verso

Locke D. 1987. *Drum Gahu: The Rhythms of West Africa*. Crown Point, NV: White Cliffs Media

Lomax A. 1968. *Folk Song Style and Culture*. Washington, DC: Am. Assoc. Adv. Sci.

Lysloff R, Gay L Jr, eds. 2003. *Music and Technoculture*. Middletown, CT: Wesleyan Univ. Press. 395 pp.

Magrini T, ed. 2003. *Music and Gender: Perspectives from the Mediterranean*. Chicago, IL: Univ. Chicago Press. 371 pp.

Manuel P. 1993. *Cassette Culture: Popular Music and Technology in West India*. Chicago, IL: Univ. Chicago Press

Meintjes L. 1990. Paul Simon's Graceland, South Africa, and the mediation of musical meaning. *Ethnomusicology* 34(1):37–73

Meintjes L. 2003. *Sound of Africa! Making Music Zulu in a South African Studio*. Durham, NC: Duke Univ. Press

Mitchell T. 1991. *Colonising Egypt*. Berkeley: Univ. Calif. Press

Mitchell T. 1993. World music and the popular music industry: an Australian view. *Ethnomusicology* 37(3):309–38

Mitchell T. 1996. *Popular Music and Local Identity: Rock, Pop and Rap in*

Europe and Oceania. London: Leicester Univ. Press

Mitchell T, ed. 2001. *Global Noise: Rap and Hip-Hop Outside the USA*. Middletown, CT: Wesleyan Univ. Press

Monson I. 1999. Riffs, repetition and globalization. *Ethnomusicology* 43(1):31–65

Moore-Gilbert B. 1997. *Postcolonial Theory: Contexts, Practices, Politics*. London: Verso

N'Dour Y. 1992. 'World music' or a world of musics? An African perspective. In *Worldwide: Ten Years of WOMAD*, ed. F Parker. London: WOMAD Commun. Virgin Rec.

Negus K. 1992. *Producing Pop: Culture and Conflict in the Popular Music Industry*. London: Arnold

Nettl, B, ed. 1978. *Eight Urban Musical Cultures: Tradition and Change*. Urbana: Univ. Ill. Press

Neuenfeldt K, ed. 1997. *The Didjeridu: From Arnhem Land to Internet*. Sydney: Perfect Beat

Pacini-Hernandez D. 1995 *Bachata: A Social History of a Dominican Popular Music*. Philadelphia: Temple Univ. Press

Peña M. 1985. *The Texas-Mexican Conjunto: History of a Working Class Music*. Austin: Univ. Tex. Press

Radano R, Bohlman PV, eds. 2000a. Introduction: music and race, their past, their presence. See Radano & Bohlman 2000b, pp. 1–53

Radano R, Bohlman PV, eds. 2000b. *Music and the Racial Imagination*. Chicago, IL: Univ. Chicago Press. 703 pp.

Rees H. 2000. *Echoes of History: Naxi Music in Modern China*. Oxford: Oxford Univ. Press

Regev M. 1997. Rock aesthetics and musics of the world. *Theory Cult. Soc.* 14(3):125–42

Reily S. 1994. Macunaima's music: national identity and ethnomusicological research in Brazil. See Stokes 1994a, pp. 71–96

Rice T. 1994. *May It Fill Your Soul: Experiencing Bulgarian Music*. Chicago, IL: Univ. Chicago Press

Rouse R. 2002. Mexican migration and the social space of postmodernism. See Inda & Rosaldo 2003, pp. 157–71

Sassen S. 1998. *Globalization and its Discontents*. New York: New Press

Savigliano M. 1995. *Tango and the Political Economy of Passion*. Boulder: Westview

Schade-Poulsen M. 1999. *Men and Popular Music in Algeria: The Social Significance of Rai*. Austin: Univ. Tex. Press

Scorsese M. 1993. *Feel Like Going Home*. Seattle: Vulcan Prod. Film

Shepherd J, Horn D, Oliver D, Wicke P, eds. 2003. *The Continuum Encyclopaedia of Popular Music of the World*. New York: Continuum. Vol. 2

Simonett H. 2001. *Banda: Mexican Musical Life Across Borders*. Hanover, CT: Wesleyan Univ. Press

Slobin M. 1992. Micromusics of the West: a comparative approach. *Ethnomusicology* 36(1):1–87

Slobin M. 1993. *Subcultural Sounds: Micromusics of the West*. Hanover, CT: Univ. Wesleyan Press

Slobin M, ed. 1996. *Retuning Culture: Musical Changes in Central and Eastern Europe*. Durham, NC: Duke Univ. Press

Slobin M. 2003. The destiny of 'diaspora' in ethnomusicology. See Clayton et al. 2003, pp. 284–96

Smith G. 2003. Celtic Australia: bush bands, Irish music, folk music, and the new nationalism. See Stokes & Bohlman 2003, pp. 73–91

Sreberni-Mohamedi A. 1994. *Small Media, Big Revolution. Communication, Culture and the Iranian Revolution*. Minneapolis: Univ. Minn. Press

Stokes M. 1992. *The Arabesk Debate: Music and Musicians in Modern Turkey*. Oxford: Clarendon

Stokes M, ed. 1994a. *Ethnicity, Identity and Music: The Musical Construction of Place*. Oxford: Berg. 212 pp.

Stokes M. 1994b. Place, exchange and meaning: Black Sea musicians in the West of Ireland. See Stokes 1994a, pp. 97–115

Stokes M. 1999. Sounding out: the culture industries and the globalization of Istanbul. See Keyder 1999, pp. 121–39

Stokes M. 2003. Globalization and the politics of world music. See Clayton et al. 2003, pp. 297–308

Stokes M, Bohlman P, eds. 2003. *Celtic Modern: Music at the Global Fringe*. Lanham, MA: Scarecrow. 293 pp.

Swedenburg T. 2001. Islamic Hip-Hop vs. Islamophobia: Aki Nawaz, Natacha Atlas, Akhenaton. See Mitchell 2001, pp. 57–85

Taylor T. 1997. *Global Pop: World Music, World Markets*. London: Routledge

Taylor T. 2003. A riddle wrapped in a mystery: transnational music sampling and Enigma's "Return to Innocence". See Lysloff & Gay 2003, pp. 64–92

Théberge, P. 2003. "Ethnic sounds": the economy and discourse of world music sampling. See Lysloff & Gay 2003, pp. 93–108

Tsing A. 2002. Conclusion: the global situation. See Inda & Rosaldo 2002, pp. 453–82

Turino T. 2000. *Nationalists, Cosmopolitans, and Popular Music in Zimbabwe*. Chicago: Univ. Chicago Press

Vallely F. 2003. The apollos of shamrockery: traditional music in the modern age. See Stokes & Bohlman 2003, pp. 201–17

Veal M. 2000. *Fela: The Life and Times of an African Musical Icon*. Philadelphia: Temple Univ. Press

Virolle M. 1995. *La Chanson Rai: De L'Algérie Profonde à la Scène Internationale*. Paris: Karthala

Virolle M. 2003. Representations and female roles in the rai songs. See Magrini 2003, pp. 215–31

Waksman S, Corrado O, Sauvalle S. 2003. Guitar. See Shepherd et al. 2003, pp. 279–90

Waxer L, ed. 2002. *Situating Salsa: Global Markets and Local Meanings in Latin Popular Music*. New York: Routledge

Wilson T, Donnan H, eds. 1998. *Border Identities: Nation and State at International Frontiers*. Cambridge: Cambridge Univ. Press

Yang MM-H. 2002. Mass media and transnational subjectivity in Shanghai: notes on (re)cosmopolitanization in a Chinese metropolis. See Inda & Rosaldo 2003, pp. 325–49

Annu. Rev. Anthropol. 2004. 33:73–102
doi: 10.1146/annurev.anthro.33.070203.144016
First published online as a Review in Advance on April 16, 2004

THE ARCHAEOLOGY OF ANCIENT STATE ECONOMIES

Michael E. Smith

Department of Anthropology, University at Albany, State University of New York, Albany, New York 12222; email: mesmith@albany.edu

Key Words economic anthropology, exchange, commercialization, states

■ **Abstract** This review addresses methods and theories for the archaeological study of ancient state economies, from the earliest states through the Classical period and beyond. Research on this topic within anthropological archaeology has been held back by reliance on simple concepts and an impoverished notion of the extent of variation in ancient state economies. First I review a long-standing debate between scholars who see similarities with modern capitalist economies (modernists and formalists) and those who see ancient economies as radically different from their modern counterparts (primitivists and substantivists). I suggest that the concept of the level of commercialization provides an avenue for transcending this debate and moving research in more productive directions. Next I review work on the traditional archaeological topics of production and exchange. A discussion of the scale of the economy (households, temple and palace institutions, state finance, cities and regional systems, and international economies) reveals considerable variation between and within ancient states. I review key topics in current archaeological political economy, including commercial exchange, money, property, labor, and the nature of economic change, and close with suggestions for future research.

INTRODUCTION

The comparative study of ancient state economies is a topic that has slipped between the disciplinary cracks. Although numerous scholars have researched individual aspects of this subject, few comprehensive syntheses or comparative analyses exist. Economists and economic historians from Karl Marx to Douglass North have applied powerful models to precapitalist economies, but they rarely consider archaeological data; for most economists, Rome (or perhaps Greece) is as "ancient" as they are willing to study. Economic anthropologists ignore ancient states. Historians working in the Near East and the Classical world have rich and detailed economic data, but most of their work remains highly particularistic. Anthropological archaeologists have much relevant data and a comparative anthropological perspective, but interest in the economy has waned since the 1980s;

the reader should note the avoidance of economic topics in recent comparative collections on early states (Feinman & Marcus 1998, Manzanilla 1997). Consequently, most anthropological archaeologists today have an impoverished view of economic variation in ancient states.

The time is ripe for a new synthesis of ancient state economies. This chapter asks what archaeology can contribute to such a synthesis. My category of ancient states includes complex societies prior to the industrial revolution. I focus primarily on the early states studied by anthropological archaeologists (Trigger 2003), and on the Bronze Age, Greek and Roman states studied by Classical archaeologists and Old World prehistorians; nevertheless, the roster of relevant states extends to the Medieval period and other late preindustrial states throughout the world.[1] I adopt the "substantive definition" of the economy as the provisioning of society (entailing production, exchange, and consumption) rather than the "formal definition" of the economy as the allocation of scarce resources among alternative ends (Polanyi 1957). Although not without its ambiguities and difficulties (Wilk 1996, pp. 28–34), the substantive definition has greater applicability in cross-cultural analyses.

Greene's (1986) book, *The Archaeology of the Roman Economy*, the best archaeological study of an ancient state economy yet published, is a good starting point. Greene situates his work within the long-standing debate between the primitivist and the modernist views of the Roman economy (see below). He begins with historian Keith Hopkins' (1983) model of economic growth during the Late Republic and Early Empire periods. Hopkins expressed his model in terms of seven propositions, and Greene (1986) shows that "archaeology has a major part to play in the analysis of at least five out of Hopkins' seven clauses" (pp. 14–15) (increases in agricultural production; population growth; expansion of craft production; increased regional exchange; and a series of changes resulting from taxation in money, including intensified long-distance commerce, expansion of coinage, and urbanization). To these traditional archaeological strengths in production and exchange, anthropological archaeology adds another dimension: the analysis of domestic contexts as loci of consumption. Archaeology also expands the roster of ancient state economies far beyond those documented in the historical record.

CONCEPTUAL FRAMEWORKS

"Same or Other?" Polanyi, Finley, and the Ancient Economy

Some of the longest-running debates about ancient economies involve polarizing tendencies "to see the past as Same (a primitive version of our present, which

---

[1]Given the wide scope of this article, I cannot cite all of the relevant literature. I make an effort to cite syntheses, review articles, and important collections of papers in which the reader can find citations to the literature. I have prepared supplemental bibliographies organized by topic. Follow the Supplemental Material link from the Annual Reviews home page at http://www.annualreviews.org.

teleologically evolves into it) or as Other (as a remote, alien, fundamentally *different* world)" (Moreland 2000, p. 2, emphasis in original). Although it is easy to criticize these debates today as simplistic and outdated, they retain importance for two reasons. First, much archaeological and historical scholarship on early state economies was (and still is) executed within the terms of these debates. Second, they bring into focus a number of important issues in the conceptualization and study of ancient economies today. The most prominent debate of this type focuses on the economies of Classical Greece and Rome.

Early "modernists" argued that the Greek and Roman economies did not differ greatly from the modern economy, whereas the "primitivists" emphasized the small-scale, agrarian orientation, and stagnant nature of the ancient economy compared to modern capitalism (Morris 1999). Finley's (1999) eloquent primitivist views dominated scholarship for several decades. In the late 1980s, however, historians and archaeologists began documenting higher levels of economic activity in ancient Greece and Rome than Finley posited (Greene 1986, Harris 1993, Mattingly & Salmon 2001). The same debate between modernists and primitivists exists in research on the Bronze Age Mediterranean (Sherratt & Sherratt 1991) and early medieval economies (Moreland 2000), and it is a major theme in current research by world systems scholars, who divide themselves into "continuationists" and "transformationists" over the relationship of ancient and modern world systems (Denemark et al. 2000). In these cases, to transcend the dichotomy to achieve a more adequate understanding of ancient economies is problematic for scholars.

The modernist/primitivist debate shares the "Same/Other" dichotomy with the formalist/substantivist debate in economic anthropology. The formalists argued that ancient and non-Western economies differ from capitalist economies only in degree, not in kind, whereas the substantivists argued that noncapitalist economies are fundamentally different from modern capitalism (Wilk 1996). The leading substantivist was Karl Polanyi, many of whose concepts—e.g., the notion that the economy is embedded in society—have been extremely fruitful. One of his central tenets, however—the view that capitalism is fundamentally different from other economic systems—proved quite harmful to the study of ancient state economies.

Anthropological archaeologists were strongly influenced by the major substantivist tracts of Polanyi et al. (1957) and Sahlins (1972), both of whom argue against the application of capitalist notions to noncapitalist societies. According to Polanyi (1957), noncapitalist economies are organized around the exchange mechanisms of reciprocity and redistribution, whereas capitalism is based on market exchange. The problem with this classification—which has been enormously influential in archaeology—is that it leaves no room for noncapitalist commercial exchange. To Polanyi, early state economies were not capitalist, so therefore they must have been based on reciprocity and redistribution. Polanyi did not understand the operation of ancient commercial economies.

When confronted with evidence of ancient commercial activity (in the Near East, Greece, and Rome), Polanyi devised interpretations that ruled out precapitalist commercialism by distorting historical evidence. He claimed that there were no true markets or "prices" (exchange values that rose and fell in response to changes in supply and demand) in the ancient world, but rather "equivalencies" that were set by the king and did not change except by royal decree (1957). These ideas have now been thoroughly refuted (Snell 1997) and Polanyi's views labeled as "dogmatic misconceptions" (Trigger 2003, p. 59); only a few scholars still accept Polanyi's ideas about ancient Old World economies (e.g., Renger 1995). Nevertheless, two generations of anthropological archaeologists were raised on the writings of Polanyi, and his work continues to cast a long shadow over archaeological research on ancient state economies.

Anthropological Archaeology: Adaptationist, Commercial, and Political Approaches

Although ancient state economies played a central role in Polanyi's research, they lost importance in economic anthropology as scholars moved beyond the formalist/substantivist debate. Most textbooks in economic anthropology are written by ethnologists who ignore archaeology and early states (e.g., Wilk 1996). Archaeologists therefore have assumed the task of theorizing ancient state economies largely independently of mainstream economic anthropology. In an influential paper, Brumfiel & Earle (1987b) identified three theoretical approaches to the issue of elite control of craft production: the adaptationist, commercial, and political approaches. Their discussion, however, serves as a useful summary of archaeological thinking on ancient state economies more generally.

The adaptationist approach focuses on the adaptation of human groups to their environment (e.g., Redman 1978). These scholars undertook regional settlement pattern surveys in many areas, and their reconstructions of regional demography and agricultural practices remain fundamental contributions to the economic study of ancient states (Sanders et al. 1979). By focusing on local adaptations, however, adaptationist scholars minimized the importance of long-distance exchanges and interactions (Feinman & Nicholas 1991). Their functionalist notion that political elites assumed control to manage the economy more efficiently for everyone's benefit conflicted with more sophisticated social theories. In their effort to discredit the adaptationist approach theoretically, however, some scholars may have thrown out the baby with the bathwater. Adaptationist theories that the rise of states was caused by population pressure (Cohen 1977) were easy to debunk (Cowgill 1975), but many archaeologists then turned away from demography as an important economic variable, thereby ignoring the essential role of population pressure in generating agricultural change (Netting 1993).

In Brumfiel & Earle's (1987b) description of the commercial development model, "increases in specialization and exchange are seen as an integral part of the spontaneous process of economic growth" (p. 1). They provide two unconvincing reasons for dismissing this approach. First, they claim that few cases existed in which social complexity originated through commercial development. Although such cases may be rare among the earliest states (Trigger 2003), in many more recent cases (e.g., the Swahili and Silk Road economies), commercialization did indeed generate social complexity. Their second objection to the commercial model is the odd notion that the model requires that "sizable profits accumulate in private hands" and that this "rarely happened" (p. 2). Instead of viewing commercial development as a general theoretical approach, however, it is more useful to conceptualize this process as an empirical phenomenon. Just as to talk of commercial development in a state-controlled economy like the Inka or Egyptians would be misleading, to reject commercial development as an active economic force in the Roman or Greek economies also would be absurd. The level of commercialization is, in fact, one of the key dimensions of variation in ancient state economies, a topic explored more fully below.

Clearly Brumfiel & Earle (1987b) favor the political model. Local elites assume control of the economy, but unlike in the adaptationist approach, elites take a more self-centered stance by strategically controlling aspects of the economy for their own economic and political ends. Since 1987, the political model has developed in two directions. One approach has emphasized the role of the individual actor, elevating "agency" and "practice" to central concerns of archaeological research. Although this literature includes some valuable contributions, economics has been pushed aside by political strategizing, prestige, emulation, identity, and gender as major foci of empirical research and theorizing (Pauketat 2001, Stein 2002). This approach (well represented in the new *Journal of Social Archaeology*) typically emphasizes theory-driven speculation over empirical research, and it as yet contributes little to the study of ancient economies. The second research direction to emerge from Brumfiel & Earle's political model is archaeological political economy.

Archaeological Political Economy

"Archaeological political economy" is not yet an integrated theoretical movement. I use this term to identify those materialist approaches to ancient state economies, that are empirically grounded and share a concern with variability in the relationship between politics and economics. Archaeological political economy is described in several recent syntheses (Cobb 2000; Earle 2002b; Hirth 1996; Muller 1997, pp. 1–53; Yoffee 1995). This work is characterized by several broad themes: a global perspective on economies as open systems; attention to the economic dimensions and implications of political behavior and institutions; a concern with inequality and social classes; and a focus on processes of local historical change rather than broad processes of cultural evolution. Archaeological political economy is related to work in anthropological political economy by scholars like Wolf (1982) and Roseberry (1988). Gil Stein (2001, p. 356) recently characterized political economy research on Old World states as emphasizing four themes: (*a*) a shift from models of states as highly centralized to notions of variability and limits of state power; (*b*) a focus on the economic organization of states; (*c*) research on rural areas and center-hinterland interactions; and (*d*) attention to interregional interaction at diverse spatial scales. To these I add the importance of the household perspective for understanding early state economies (see below).

Earle promotes an unfortunate alternative definition of the phrase "political economy." In place of the long-established definition as a theoretical approach to economics (Muller 1997, pp. 1–53; Roseberry 1988), Earle defines political economy as a sector or type of economic realm, "the political economy," which he contrasts with the domestic economy (Earle 2002a; Johnson & Earle 2000, pp. 22–27). Although Earle is a leading contributor to the study of archaeological political economy (as a theoretical and empirical approach), this usage only causes confusion, as witnessed in recent works that switch back and forth between the two definitions without explanation (Feinman & Nicholas 2004, Hirth 1996, Masson & Freidel 2002).

Earle (2002b, p. 7) suggests that the new institutional economics offers an "exceptional opportunity" to understand the economies of ancient states and chiefdoms (North 1981). This school of economics explores the relationships between individual actions and institutions, focusing on concepts of property rights and transaction costs (Acheson 1994; North 1981, 1991). Most applications of this model, including those by anthropologists (Acheson 1994), simply assume a high level of commercialization (Ankarloo 2002), and the work of adapting the new institutional economics approach to uncommercialized or partially commercialized economies barely has begun (Jones 1993). Economist Morris Silver (1995) applies North's concept of transaction costs to ancient Near Eastern economies. Silver repeatedly asserts that particular social practices and institutions lowered transaction costs (thereby contributing to commercial activity), but this statement does not clarify greatly our understanding. Although there are some promising exploratory studies by archaeologists and ancient historians (Manning & Morris 2004, Morris 2004), to date little progress is reported. Economists working in other traditions have published some highly insightful analyses (Allen 1997, Henry 2004, Temin 2001), but these remain isolated contributions.

VARIATION IN ANCIENT STATE ECONOMIES

Most anthropological archaeologists avoid the Classical world, and most Classicists ignore other early state economies, but these biases have little theoretical or comparative justification. One way that Greece and Rome stand out in relation to many early states is their high level of commercialization. These were not, however, the only early states with money, entrepreneurial merchants, and other commercial institutions. In fact, the degree of commercialization is one of the crucial axes of variation in ancient state economies; the type of political organization is another. In the following sections I review these two variables, and in the remainder of the chapter I relate them to the economic processes and institutions of early states.

The Degree of Commercialization

"Commercialization" is a synthetic concept that includes several related aspects of economic process: the extent to which a price-making market allocates

TABLE 1   Classification of ancient state economies by commercialization and political system

	Political system			
Commercial level	**Weak states**	**City-States**	**Territorial states**	**Empires**
Uncommercialized			Egypt, Tiwanaku	Inka
Low commercialization	Angkor	Classic Maya	Shang, Great Zimbabwe	Teotihuacan
Intermediate commercialization	Indus	Sumerian, Mixtec, Aztec		Tarascan, Assyria, Vijayanagara
Advanced precapitalist commercialization		Old Assyrian, Swahili, Classical Greece		Rome

commodities and the factors of production; the prominence of entrepreneurial activity; and the pervasiveness of institutions such as money, marketplaces, credit, and banking (Neale 1971, Smith 1976a, pp. 313–15). Here I focus on internal commercialization as the role of commercial institutions within an economy. External commercialization, which describes exchange between states, is a separate domain described in other sections below. In Table 1 I classify some of the better-known ancient economies according to their levels of internal commercialization. This scheme is adapted from Carol Smith's (1976a) discussion of the level of commercialization in regional peasant economies. I employ a four-class ordinal scale of commercialization; the first three levels correspond roughly to Smith's uncommercialized, partially commercialized, and fully commercialized categories.

Uncommercialized state economies lack marketplaces, independent entrepreneurial merchants, general-purpose money, and other institutions associated with commercial exchange. Full-time craft specialists work for the state or state-connected temple institutions, and agents of the state carry out long-distance transfers and exchanges. Historical descriptions of Egyptian and Inka society, supported by archaeological data, make clear the strong state control of most sectors of these economies and the accompanying proliferation of bureaucratic institutions and practices for management of the economy.

Economies with low commercialization have limited marketplace distribution of goods and services, but land and labor are not commodities. Government control of many sectors of the economy is strong, but typically a small independent commercial sector of merchants and marketplaces does exist. These economies are often of limited spatial scale. Smith includes solar and dendritic marketing systems in this category. Economies with intermediate commercialization correspond approximately to Smith's "fully commercialized" type (1976a). These economies are characterized by interlocking central place market systems for goods and services, and they have commercial institutions such as money and professional entrepreneurial merchants. Land and labor, in contrast, are typically under state or elite control, with only limited occurrence of private property in land. Of the commercial economies listed in Table 1, the Aztec and Sumerian are the best-documented examples. The highest level of commercialization for premodern economies is labeled advanced precapitalist commercialization; this category is not included in Smith's account. Societies at this level of commercialization had dynamic precapitalist economies with extensive markets in goods and land, limited labor markets, and the presence of numerous commercial institutions like banking, credit, and merchant partnerships (Larsen 1976, Temin 2001). The archaeological identification of commercial exchange is discussed below.

Because commercialization is an ordinal scale, my classification is, by necessity, somewhat artificial. I present the categories to illustrate the scale, and they should not be reified. Scholars debate issues such as the roles of banking and credit or the influence of money in many of these economies, and there is much room for disagreement over the classification of individual economies in Table 1.

Types of States

Most anthropological archaeologists view the state more as an evolutionary stage than as a political institution. This view leads to a homogenizing approach that assumes a basic uniformity of ancient states. Categories like "archaic states" (Feinman & Marcus 1998) and "the early state" (Claessen & Skalnik 1978) have a long history in anthropology. This unitary approach to states has been criticized by McGuire (2002, pp. 161–67) and Trigger (2003, pp. 26–28), who argue for greater attention to variability. At the other extreme, splitters argue that particular states were utterly unique (Higham 2002, Murra 1980). I propose a four-class typology of ancient state political forms as a compromise between these extremes (Table 1). I present these types for the purpose of discussing economic patterns and institutions and their relationship to state organization; like the commercial categories presented above, these types should not be reified or taken too seriously.

The category of weak states includes types such as the segmentary state and the galactic polity. Many applications of these states to ancient polities have not succeeded under close scrutiny (Morrison 1997). The Khmer polity of Angkor, however, is a good candidate for an ancient segmentary state. I include the Indus civilization in the weak state category, acknowledging the inconclusive debate between those who view the Indus polity as a state (Kenoyer 1998, pp. 81–83) and those who claim that power was not sufficiently centralized for the Indus polity to be considered a state (Possehl 1998). Although I do not address most of the chiefdom literature in this review for reasons of space, the economies of chiefdoms can be quite difficult to distinguish—conceptually and empirically—from those of weak states (Earle 2002b, Muller 1997).

The category of city-states describes groups of small polities centered on a single urban capital that are linked to regional systems by cultural bonds and extensive interaction. Hansen (2000, 2002) proposes definitions of city-state and city-state culture and assembles 36 examples that fit his criteria. In his introductions and conclusions to these important volumes, Hansen effectively answers critics who reject the city-state concept outside of Greece (Marcus & Feinman 1998), as well as those who take an overly broad definition of this category (Nichols & Charlton 1997). One variation of Hansen's model occurs when a city-state conquers its neighbors to become the seat of an empire, leaving the governments and rulers of subordinate city-states in power; in Table 1, the Aztec and Classical Greece cases include episodes of city-state-based empires.

Large territorial states are one of two political forms (the other being city-states) in Trigger's (2003) masterful comparative analysis. Ancient Egypt is the best-known and best-studied example of this category. The Tiwanaku, Shang, and Great Zimbabwe polities are not documented as extensively as Ancient Egypt, but they fit this category as well. Of all ancient polity types, empires have received the most systematic and comparative attention in recent years (Alcock et al. 2001). The best-documented ancient empires are the Roman, Assyrian, Achaemenid, and Inka polities, as well as the Aztec and Athenian cases included above as city-state-based empires. Table 1 illustrates one of the relationships between commercialization and state power: Large territorial states fall at the low end of the commercialization scale, whereas city-states fall at the high end. Empires, in contrast, cover the entire range of commercialization, from the uncommercialized Inka to the heavily commercialized Roman economy.

PRODUCTION AND EXCHANGE

Demography and Agriculture

Archaeological field survey research has made its greatest contributions to economic analysis in the realms of regional demography and agricultural systems. Even for Classical Greece, with its extensive written documentation, archaeological surveys have "transformed our picture of the settled countryside" (Cartledge 1998, p. 11; Jameson et al. 1994). Similarly, the discovery of surprisingly dense rural settlement in the lowland Classical Maya tropical forest (Culbert & Rice 1990) generated a fundamental transformation in our understanding of that society and its economic organization (Masson & Freidel 2002).

The excavation and mapping of field walls, irrigation canals, terraces, raised fields, and other agricultural features have become major foci of fieldwork for many ancient states, with a large literature of their own (Denevan 2001, Jameson et al. 1994, Whitmore & Turner 2001). Archaeologists have focused most attention on evidence for intensive agricultural practices. The existence of a strong cross-cultural association between intensive agriculture and state societies is not in doubt (Trigger 2003), but the nature and implications of intensive agriculture in specific cases is the topic of considerable debate.

In some cases the functions of ancient water-control systems cannot be determined easily. For example, were the canals and reservoirs at Angkor—which obviously had a symbolic role in urban planning—used to irrigate rice fields?

Scholars have yet to resolve this basic, low-level question (Acker 1998, Stott 1992). More commonly, however, researchers agree on the uses of ancient field systems but not on their social implications. Recent fieldwork on raised fields along the margins of Lake Titicaca in the Andes illustrates the situation. The relationship of this extensive field system with the nearby urban center of Tiwanaku (AD 100–1000) is a topic of debate. Kolata (1991) interprets the raised fields as a large-scale construction effort organized by the Tiwanaku state, whereas Erickson (2000) argues that individual households most likely constructed their own fields without the controlling arm of the state; this debate has yet to be resolved.

Butzer (1996, p. 200) notes that "the Wittfogel model, like Elvis, refuses to die," and archaeologists are still arguing about the state's role in ancient irrigation systems (Billman 2002, Lees 1994, Scarborough 2003). Rather than make grand pronouncements for and against Wittfogel or other simple models (Isaac 1993), however, archaeologists should focus on lower-level issues. The forms of field systems, for example, can provide information about state control. The impressive agricultural terraces of the Inka, with their great regularity and coordination of walls over large areas (Denevan 2001, pp. 170–201), suggest state control, whereas the smaller, irregular forms of Maya and Aztec terraces suggest organization at the household level with little state interference (Dunning & Beach 1994, Smith & Price 1994); these hypotheses are supported by archaeological and documentary accounts of the two economies.

Craft Production

Craft production in ancient states is an active area of current archaeological research. The technologies of many ancient crafts are now relatively well understood thanks to experimental, technical, and comparative studies (David & Kramer 2001), and research addresses the social organization and contexts of production practices. Unfortunately, conceptual advances have been held back by inappropriate use of the concept of specialization, a term that has outlived its usefulness in this area and should be abandoned. Specialization was a major part of Childe's influential model of cultural evolution (Wailes 1996), and no one doubts that states have more specialists than do other kinds of societies (Clark & Parry 1990). But within anthropological archaeology the term specialization came to be used as a synonym for craft production, leading to fruitless arguments about the meaning of the term (Clark 1995); archaeologists working in other traditions, however, apparently were not sidetracked this way (Greene 1986).

In an important paper, Costin (1991) clarifies the issue by identifying four independent variables or dimensions of craft production that she labels intensity, concentration, scale, and context. Although she calls these variables aspects of "specialization," in a later study she recognizes that the relevant overall category is craft production systems (Costin 2001a), not specialization. "Intensity" refers to the full-time versus part-time nature of craftwork. This is the only aspect of craft production systems that can be usefully labeled "specialization." In many ancient states, much production was done by crafters who practiced their trades part-time, not full-time (Trigger 2003, pp. 358–73). "Concentration" describes the location and density of facilities (e.g., rural versus urban, degree of nucleation).

Costin's "scale" describes the size and organization of production facilities. The most influential scheme is Peacock's (1982, pp. 6–11; see also van der Leeuw 1976, pp. 402–3) typology: household production (part-time domestic production for domestic use); household industry (part-time domestic production for exchange); individual workshops (full-time workers in dedicated facilities); nucleated workshops (clusters of workshops); manufactories (large-scale production requiring capital investment); estate production (attached producers working on rural estates); and institutional production (attached producers working for a state or official institution). In many states, most craft production was done within or around the house (household industry) or in workshops connected to the house (Feinman & Nicholas 2000). The loose use of the term workshop for any production location causes confusion, however (for discussion see Moholy-Nagy 1990). Costin's final dimension, "context," describes the social affiliation of producers. Most discussion of this topic focuses on the categories of "independent artisans," who work on their own and distribute their products individually, and "attached artisans," who work for patrons, typically producing luxury goods for elites (Brumfiel 1987, Clark 1995). Two other concepts have been added to this scheme, both called "embedded specialization" (of course, the authors really mean "embedded production"). Ames (1995) uses this term to refer to production of luxury goods by elites themselves (Inomata 2001). Later, Janusek (1999) uses this same term to describe production organized by corporate groups. Other aspects of craft production include recruitment patterns and the social identities and roles of crafters, raw materials and technology, and the standardization of products (Costin 2001b, Costin & Wright 1998, Sinopoli 2003).

High levels of craft intensity and scale tend to be found in highly commercialized economies and in state-controlled institutional settings in uncommercialized economies. Independent and attached producers are found in all states, but with varying contexts. The notion of specialization is difficult to discard; even authors critical of the notion cannot avoid using it (Costin 2001a, Stein 2001). But archaeologists should note that economic historians working on preindustrial craft production carry out rich and detailed analyses without having to use the term specialization in their research (Braudel 1982, Thirsk 1961). Specialization is more usefully limited to a high-level concept describing the division of labor in society, not the organization of craft production.

Trade and Exchange

In the 1980s a curious thing happened to the archaeological study of trade in ancient states. After a period of enormous empirical and conceptual productivity, archaeologists lost interest and moved away from trade studies; this action was part of the overall retreat from economic analysis mentioned above. The previous decade saw fundamental advances in the study of transport systems (Drennan 1984, Greene 1986, pp. 17–43), quantitative artifact distributions (Hodder 1974), and methods to distinguish various types of exchange with artifactual data (Renfrew 1975). A whole suite of techniques for chemical and petrographic artifact sourcing achieved new levels of accuracy and availability. The discipline seemed poised to make major conceptual and empirical advances when interest in these topics suddenly waned. Archaeometry continued to move ahead (Brothwell & Pollard 2001), resulting in an explosion of new scientific data on the sources of artifacts. Unfortunately, archaeologists still do not have the conceptual tools to make sense of the new data. Many recent advances in trade research—such as studies of Roman amphorae and Mesoamerican obsidian—owe more to the sheer accumulation of data than to any conceptual sophistication. The application of new economic models (e.g., Temin 2003) to rich archaeological datasets (Mediterranean shipwrecks in this case, e.g., Ballard et al. 2002, Pulak 1998) holds great promise.

For decades archaeologists have limited their analyses of exchange to Polanyi's simplistic triad of reciprocity, redistribution, and market exchange (Polanyi et al. 1957), a trend that continues unabated (Earle 2002b; Feinman & Nicholas 2004; Masson & Freidel 2002; Stanish 2003, pp. 20–21). Polanyi's classification has serious limitations, however: First, it fails to distinguish exchanges (two-way transactions) from transfers (one-way transactions; see Pryor 1977, pp. 26–31); second, it lumps forms of exchange (e.g., reciprocity) with exchange institutions (e.g., redistribution); and third, it suffers from Polanyi's commercial myopia discussed above. At the risk of sounding overly typological, I present several classifications that illustrate the range of variation that archaeologists should consider in analyzing ancient state exchange systems. I rework insights from several authors, particularly Pryor (1977), Sahlins (1972), Earle (1977), Temin (2001), Smith (1976a), Trigger (2003), and Braudel (1982). At least five relevant categories of transfers exist: allocation within the unit of production (Sahlins's generalized reciprocity); gift, without expectation of return (from the family level to international diplomacy); taxes (obligatory transfers from individuals to the state); tribute (wealth transfers between states); and theft and plunder. In several research traditions, including Mesoamerica and the chiefdom literature, taxes and tribute are lumped together under the label of tribute. Although these categories can be difficult to distinguish archaeologically, it is useful analytically to keep the concepts separate. Exchanges also exist in several alternatives: reciprocal exchange (Sahlins's balanced reciprocity, in which supply and demand forces are weak); market exchange (where supply and demand are important); and unequal exchange (rents, fees, sharecropping arrangements, and other market-type exchanges based on the threat of coercion).

Exchange within and between states is typically organized in a variety of institutional arrangements, of which the following are some of the major categories: reciprocal trade institutions (trade partners, "down-the-line" trade); periodic marketing systems (solar, dendritic, and interlocking forms); redistribution (both voluntary and involuntary forms, including leveling institutions, rationing, and feasting);

state finance (discussed below); internal commercial institutions (merchants, money, credit, banking, accounting systems, etc.); and international exchange institutions (e.g., long-distance merchants, administered trade, ports of trade). I present these lists not as rigid typologies but as examples of the kinds of concepts needed to advance the comparative analysis of ancient state exchange systems. We need to move far beyond Polanyi's simplistic triad; noteworthy recent forays in the correct direction include Knapp & Cherry (1994), Earle (2001), and Stark (1990).

THE SCALE OF THE ECONOMY

Households

As the primary social unit of production, consumption, and reproduction in most agrarian societies, households occupy an important place in the study of ancient state economies. Archaeologists commonly acknowledge houses and their associated artifacts and features as among the best archaeological sources of economic and social data. The development of household archaeology as a distinctive method in the early 1980s included an explicit focus on domestic craft production (Wilk & Rathje 1982), a topic that remains an important area of archaeological research (Feinman & Nicholas 2000, Hendon 1996). By the late 1990s archaeologists working in domestic contexts were devoting more attention to patterns of consumption (Allison 1999), following broader trends in anthropology.

Archaeological research on domestic consumption now covers a variety of topics. The first task usually is to determine the probable uses of artifacts found in and around the house or house compound. Then archaeologists can address consumption-related topics like luxuries versus necessities, or gifts versus commodities (Sherratt & Sherratt 1991; Smith & Berdan 2003, Ch. 18). Feasting has become an important topic of analysis for ancient states (Bray 2003), along with studies of the consumption of alcohol and other special food and drink (Dietler 1990).

Some notable recent findings about ancient household economics concern the nature of variability at a number of scales. In some cases archaeologists have found a high level of variation among houses, often within the same community, in factors like wealth, access to imports, and economic activities (Cahill 2001, Hendon 1996). Several recent books on Latin American states address variation in the integration of past households into wider political and economic systems (Bermann 1994, D'Altroy & Hastorf 2001, Smith & Berdan 2003). Household-level data are crucial for the archaeological analysis of ancient economies, and this area is ripe for significant advances in the future.

Temple and Palace Institutions

In some ancient states, temples and/or palaces were major economic institutions that controlled considerable land and labor and processed large volumes of goods and services. Most of our information about temple institutions comes from written sources, but archaeology is starting to play a larger role in the study of these institutions. Mesopotamian temple economies, once erroneously believed to be coterminous with the entire economies of states, are particularly well documented in cuneiform sources (Van De Mieroop 1999, Zettler 1992); temples owned land and herds, controlled attached farmers and crafters producing textiles and other goods, and even leased land to private individuals. Some temples were located in large walled precincts. Excavations of examples like the Khafajah temple oval or the temple of Innana at Nippur reveal numerous rooms and courtyards outside the temple proper that may have had economic functions, but there is surprisingly little artifactual evidence of economic activities (Delougaz 1940, Zettler 1992). It is sobering to think that without the cuneiform texts we would have little idea that these and other temples were major economic institutions.

A similar situation—written records of major temple-based economic institutions with little archaeological evidence—holds in other ancient states like Egypt, Angkor, and the Inka. Temples without associated complexes of storage rooms and workshops were the norm in societies whose documentary records do not suggest major economic institutions centered on temples, from Greece and Rome to the Aztecs and Mayas.

Royal palaces in virtually all ancient states were the setting for numerous types of activity, from public assemblies to rituals, and most hosted a variety of economic activities focused on the king and royal family (Sheehy 1996). Of particular concern, however, are cases in which the palace was a major locus for craft production for export and a base for international exchange. Such palace economies are well known for the Bronze Age Minoan and Mycenaean societies (Hägg & Marinatos 1987, Voutsaki & Killen 2001) and several other Mediterranean cities like Ebla (Archi 1993) and Amathus in Crete (Aupert 1996). Excavations have uncovered numerous storage facilities and workshops in these palaces, and the interpretation of these data in conjunction with rich economic texts recovered from the palaces has generated sophisticated debates over the precise local and regional economic roles of the palaces. For the Bronze Age Aegean examples much of the palace-based economy was not described in palace archives, giving archaeology a crucial role in the reconstruction of these systems.

State Finance

Although ancient states used a wide variety of methods to finance their activities and enrich their rulers, most archaeologists limit themselves to a few simple models. Within anthropological archaeology the concepts of "staple finance" and "wealth finance" (D'Altroy & Earle 1985) are influential. In systems based on staple finance, rulers extract payments in food and utilitarian items from subjects and use the material to reward state personnel. Wealth finance, in contrast, is based on payments of wealth objects (high-value, low-bulk goods) that are more efficient for rewarding and controlling followers at greater distances. Although useful for the analysis of chiefdoms or uncommercialized states, these concepts are inadequate (by themselves) for understanding government finance in most ancient states.

Lindkvist (1991) suggests the useful concepts of external and internal exploitation. External exploitation, the acquisition of wealth from outside the local society or polity, includes pillage and plunder, taxes on mercantile activity by foreigners, imperial taxes on foreign provinces, and tribute. Forms of internal exploitation include various types of taxes and rent charged to local subjects. Studies of highly commercialized states with extensive historical documentation focus on variation in the type of taxes (labor versus goods versus money) and on the relationship between taxes and rent (Greene 1986, Hopkins 1983).

The sources cited above can be synthesized to identify a variety of forms of ancient state finance: plunder; staple finance; tribute in luxury goods (included in wealth finance; often phrased in ancient texts as gifts between rulers); taxation in goods or money (also a type of wealth finance); rental of state lands; commercial investment (state investment in production or exchange enterprises); and taxation in labor. The first six categories form an ordinal scale of increasing complexity, stability, and volume of transfers, and this scale is strongly associated with the degree of commercialization and the power of the state. Plunder and staple finance, for example, are most common in uncommercialized chiefdoms and weak states, whereas rental of state lands and commercial investment by the government are most common in highly commercialized economies. Taxation in labor (corvée, slavery, and other labor transfers) is a form of finance that typically supplements other mechanisms. The uncommercialized Inka imperial economy is unique in that taxation in labor was the only kind of state finance (Murra 1980).

Apart from some discussions of staple finance and wealth finance (D'Altroy 1992, D'Altroy & Hastorf 2001), there is little systematic research on the archaeological expressions of different forms of state finance. One active area is the use of archaeological data to evaluate documentary accounts of Roman imperial taxation (Greene 1986). For many economies, however, archaeologists cannot even distinguish trade from taxes, much less analyze the type of state finance system; clearly this topic needs greater conceptual sophistication and considerable methodological attention.

Cities and Regional Systems

The most fundamental component of urban economics in antiquity was the provision of food to cities (Smith 2003). Although specific archaeological evidence of the movement of food from rural to urban contexts is elusive, regional-scale reconstructions of demography and agricultural practices provide indirect evidence for urban food provision (Wilkinson 2003). Without documents, however, it is difficult to identify the specific mechanisms (rents, taxes, market exchange) of such provisioning. The large size of two of the earliest cities (Uruk and Teotihuacan), coupled with an unpopulated countryside, indicates that urban farmers must have walked out to their fields, perhaps staying in temporary field shelters (Adams

1981, Cowgill 1997). Among the lowland Maya, in Africa, and perhaps in other areas with low-density cities, intensive farming took place within the urban zone (Isendahl 2002), although the output of such gardening was insufficient to meet urban food needs.

The provisioning of a city with food from its hinterland establishes a regional economic system (in the sense of Smith 1976b), and few cities can be understood economically outside of their regional context (Cowgill 2004, this volume). Most archaeological studies of regional economies are based on survey data (Kowalewski 1990, Wilkinson 2003), and thus their level of coverage of craft production and specific exchange mechanisms is limited. The use of residential excavations to provide more-detailed data on regional exchange and rural-urban interaction is starting to make contributions in many regions (Bermann 1997, Schwartz & Falconer 1994).

Max Weber's (1958) concept of the "consumer city" is one of the major components of the modernist/primitivist debate. Finley and other primitivists promoted Weber's model of ancient cities that had low levels of production and exchange and were drains on society's resources. Recent scholarship indicates levels of urban-based production and commercial exchange in Roman cities higher than Finley described, and archaeology has played a major role in refuting the consumer city model (Mattingly & Salmon 2001, Parkins 1997). For Greek cities, Morris (n.d.) still finds the consumer city model useful.

International Economies

The economics of empires, world systems, merchant diasporas, and other international phenomena have received considerable recent attention from archaeologists, and there are many excellent recent review articles and edited volumes with extensive citations to the literature. From a materialist perspective, economic gain is the primary motive for imperial expansion. Archaeologists have focused on forms of imperial control (direct versus indirect), imperial involvement in agricultural and craft production, the relationship between merchants and the state, and economic transformations at the household level effected by imperial conquest (Alcock et al. 2001, D'Altroy & Hastorf 2001, Greene 1986, Sinopoli 2003, Wells 1999). Variation in imperial economies, both within and among ancient empires, is a major focus of this research.

Several archaeologists working on ancient states employ an amorphous world-systems approach that uses concepts modified from Wallerstein's world systems theory to analyze ancient multistate economies (Algaze 1993, Peregrine & Feinman 1996, Smith & Berdan 2003). Concepts such as cores and peripheries, long-distance commercial exchange, and elite networks are useful to model international systems where cross-polity trade had major social, political, and economic impacts. The phrase world systems has been polarizing within archaeology, however; some scholars exhibit strong negative reactions to any use of the concept. In several strongly worded critiques, for example, Stein (1999, 2002) attacks archaeological world systems research. Unfortunately he chooses to attack Wallerstein's model—rarely used by archaeologists—and not the actual research by archaeologists who work within the various world systems approaches.

Other international models receiving attention include merchant diasporas, prestige-goods systems, and ports of trade. Stein (1999, 2002) focuses archaeological attention on merchant diasporas (Curtin 1984), developing useful archaeological methods for their identification and analysis. Although he presents this notion as an alternative to world systems theory, it actually fits quite nicely into the collection of concepts that compose the world systems perspective. Another international exchange model employed by archaeologists is the prestige-goods exchange system in which elites derive power from their control over the production, exchange, and consumption of luxury goods (Friedman & Rowlands 1978, Junker 1999). This model, sometimes confused with the universal practice of luxury goods exchange among elites, best fits chiefdoms and perhaps partially commercialized weak states. It is incompatible with high levels of commercialization because commercial exchange erodes elite control of the production, exchange, and consumption of luxury goods.

Several ancient polities with internally uncommercialized economies engaged in commercial-type exchange with other polities (external commercial exchange). Polanyi (1963) developed his influential port-of-trade model to account for such cases. Ports of trade were insulated centers located on international borders or coasts where merchants working for various states could gather to exchange goods in a setting of protected neutrality. In Polanyi's model, exchange in ports of trade was politically dominated—not entrepreneurial—and it was carried out in isolation from local exchange systems. Unfortunately, Polanyi's rabid anticommercial views led him and his colleagues to overstate the occurrence and importance of ports of trade (Polanyi et al. 1957), perhaps because the concept allowed Polanyi to explain away evidence for entrepreneurial behavior of professional merchants. Empirical and conceptual advances led to a series of critiques and refutations of the model (Figueira 1984; Knapp & Cherry 1994, pp. 134–42; Pearson 1991, pp. 73–74; Smith & Berdan 2003, Ch. 17), resulting in the reclassification of former "ports of trade" as emporia, trading centers, and other kinds of settlements where commerce took place without the political domination posited by Polanyi. Nevertheless, recent research indicates that some Polanyi-esque ports of trade did exist in the ancient world; the Iron Age port of Naukratis in the Nile Delta probably is the best example (Möller 2000).

TOPICS IN POLITICAL ECONOMY

The Identification of Commercial Exchange

Identification of commercial institutions and practices at the high end of the scale—credit, banking, bills of exchange, merchant partnerships, etc.—requires written records. But other institutions and practices associated with internal commercialization leave material traces that can be studied archaeologically. Coins are the most obvious artifact category here (Greene 1986), but noncoinage money is also important (see discussion below). The physical infrastructure of commercial exchange—marketplaces, warehouses, and port facilities—also may be recoverable archaeologically (Leong 1990), and the presence of shops in urban neighborhoods (Cahill 2001, pp. 112–13) also suggests commercial activity.

Study of the effects of exchange systems on the contexts and spatial distributions of artifacts is a promising approach to the documentation of commercial exchange. Hirth (1998), for example, proposed that administered exchange results in a stronger association between high-value goods and elite contexts than does commercial exchange. The widespread presence of valuable goods in nonelite domestic contexts—typically in lower frequencies than in elite contexts—thus suggests the operation of commercial exchange. Although this sounds plausible, household distribution patterns matching Hirth's predictions for market economies are reported for both the commercialized Aztec economy (Smith 1999) and the uncommercialized Inka economy (D'Altroy & Hastorf 2001, Ch. 10, 11). Additional comparative research is needed to evaluate Hirth's model and its implications. At the regional level, some artifact distribution patterns, such as widespread regional uniformity of imported goods, suggest the operation of market systems (Braswell & Glascock 2002, Nichols et al. 2002). These approaches are important in regions like Mesoamerica where most forms of money were perishable (see below) and evidence of commercial infrastructure is difficult to identify archaeologically.

External commercial exchange in the Mediterranean area has received considerable archaeological attention. Hafford (2001, p. 258), for example, proposes a suite of material correlates of international merchant activity in the Bronze Age—including weights and balances, cylinder seals, scrap metal, and abundant trade goods—and there has been considerable fieldwork on harbors and port facilities (Swiny et al. 1997). Unfortunately, one of the most promising lines of evidence (weights and measures) has contributed little to our understanding of international economic processes. Scholars have been so preoccupied with quantitative metrology (Pare 2000) that they have failed to explore the economic implications of their data beyond some simple inferences (Hafford 2001).

Money

Money can be defined as objects that serve as both a medium of exchange and a unit of account (Grierson 1977, Wray 1998). Within economics there are two fundamental, opposing views of money: the orthodox, neo-Classical metallist view and the minority chartalist approach. These views have ramifications for the analysis of modern capitalist economies; for present purposes I limit consideration to their quite different accounts of the origins of money. Metallists hold that "money enters the picture only in the modest role of a technical device that has been adopted in order to facilitate transactions" (Schumpeter 1954, p. 277). They emphasize the function of money as a medium of exchange and argue that it developed initially within barter economies to facilitate personal purchases because it lowered trans-action costs (i.e., it was more efficient than barter). Once a medium of exchange came into general use, it took on the function of a unit of account (Samuelson 1973, pp. 274–76).

The chartalists give the state a much larger role in the analysis of money and emphasize the function of money as a unit of account. For them, money originated with the rulers of states. States started to keep track of finances using a standard unit. In some cases this unit of account developed into a medium of exchange when rulers demanded tax payments in the particular item (Wray 1998). This led to more widespread use of the item as money (subjects had to exchange goods or services to acquire the item to pay their taxes), contributing to the commercialization of the economy. In other cases early units of account did not develop into media of exchange; examples include oxen in Homeric Greece (Grierson 1977), the *deben* in Pharaonic Egypt (Henry 2004), and perhaps some unit tracked on Inkan *khipus* (Urton 2003). These uncommercialized economies needed accounting standards (because of the extensive bureaucratization of their state-run economies), but they did not need, or did not develop, media of exchange.

The findings of economic anthropology support the chartalist view because barter economies (required in the metallist account) probably never existed (Dalton 1982). The chartalist account fits the origins of coinage quite well; the earliest coins (from Lydia, sixth century BC) were of large denominations and were issued by states to pay public debts (Hudson 2004). Money long predates coinage, however. The earliest money (in Mesopotamia) consisted of irregular pieces of silver (referred to by the German term *hacksilber*), and its origins are far less clear (Balmuth 2001). In other regions with indigenous money—such as Mesoamerica, where cacao beans and cotton textiles served as money—there is little archaeological evidence for the origins of money. Archaeologists have made important contributions to the study of early coinage, but they have been less suc-cessful in documenting or analyzing other types of ancient money. Neither have economic anthropologists contributed much to this topic, probably because most of their work on money consists of either ethnographic descriptions of primitive valuables (media of exchange that do not serve as units of account) or else studies of the impact of capitalist money on non-Western economies. Most economic anthro-pologists have ignored units of account and archaeological data on early money.

Property, Labor, and Other Difficult Topics

Property and labor, as major economic relations, are fundamentally important in any state economy. But because they largely consist of jural relations, they are extremely difficult to analyze with archaeological data. Studies of property sys-tems in ancient states rely almost exclusively on textual data (Haring & de Maijer 1998, Hudson & Levine 1999). Property is the subject of several recent method-ological papers by archaeologists (Earle 2000, Gilman 1998), but these writings serve mainly to confirm that the ability of archaeologists to reconstruct property relations or systems of property is quite limited without written information. The archaeology of labor organization is similar to property relations. Documentary data provide good information on some ancient state labor systems (Powell 1987), and archaeologists have made comparative and conceptual advances (Dietler & Herbich 2001); but the use of archaeological data to analyze labor organization is quite difficult.

Fortunately, the cumulative effects of labor, however organized, do leave clear material remains. This topic has been pursued, particularly in the New World, under the rubric of energetics. Archaeologists have reconstructed the labor and material inputs for stone architecture (Abrams 1994) and the production of ceramics and other crafts (Feinman et al. 1981). Theoretical treatments have addressed the implications of energetics data for political power (Trigger 1990) and urbanization (Sanders & Santley 1983).

Labor input provides the best archaeological approach to the calculation of economic value, both for its theoretical pedigree (Marx 1967) and for the feasibility of energetic reconstructions. The alternative approach to value in modern economics—on the basis of scarcity—is difficult to apply archaeologically because of the interference of formation processes and sampling problems (Smith 1987). As a complement to analyses of economic value and wealth, archaeologists also have considered social or cultural value and their relationship to status and prestige (Bailey 1998). Unfortunately, research on energetics declined in the 1990s, another victim of the retreat from economic analysis at that time.

Economic Change

Much theorizing about change by economists, including North (1981, 1991) and other new institutional economists, is naive and inapplicable to many ancient states because a high level of commercialization is simply assumed (Ankarloo 2002, Jones 1993). Even when discussing ancient commercial economies, economists need to do more than just suggest that particular practices were adopted because they lowered transaction costs (North 1981, Silver 1995). In contrast, much theorizing by anthropological archaeologists, based on the literature of cultural evolution and the substantivist economic anthropology of Polanyi, errs in the opposite direction by denying or downplaying commercial institutions and practices in ancient states (Brumfiel & Earle 1987b, Manzanilla 1997). Useful theories of change must be able to handle ancient economies at all levels of commercialization without the blinders of either the promarket mentality or the antimarket mentality.

Agricultural intensification is a type of economic change that has seen considerable archaeological research and debate (see above). Archaeologists have drawn inspiration (both positive and negative) from the intensification literature (Netting 1993), and the study of agricultural features and methods is an active and productive line of empirical archaeological research on economic change (Johnston 2003, Morrison 1996). An important variable in the literature on agricultural intensification is the ratio of labor to land in a given area. Rough estimates of these parameters are relatively easy to obtain from regional survey data, and a body of comparative and theoretical research discusses the importance of land/labor ratios for processes of economic change (Allen 1997, North 1981). Conditions of abundant land but limited labor tend to generate population growth, colonization of new zones, urbanization, the growth of trade, and economic prosperity. Sustained growth of this sort often transforms the economy into one of abundant labor but limited land, which leads to intensification, greater exploitation of labor, contraction of exchange, and declining standards of living (Smith & Heath-Smith 1994).

The relationship between state power and commercial level is generally inverse (Blanton et al. 1993, Hansen 2000, Trigger 2003, pp. 342–55). Archaeologists apply this generalization dynamically in cases where powerful states with low levels of commercialization give rise over time to smaller states with more commercialized economies. This change has been marked in several cases by the spatial expansion of the economy into an international system, a growing regional economic diversification, and the conversion of former luxury goods into commodities (Blanton et al. 1993, pp. 212–19, Hudson & Levine 1996, Sherratt & Sherratt 1991, Smith & Berdan 2003). In an important series of collections, Hudson and colleagues (in the International Scholars Conference on Ancient Near Eastern Economies) show that commercial institutions and practices in the Near East developed initially within the context of temple and palace institutions and only later took on an independent existence outside the state and other institutions (Hudson & Levine 1996, Hudson & Van de Mieroop 2002). The chartalist view that money originated with states fits well with this notion.

Archaeological research ties into several broader areas of social scientific and historical scholarship on economic change in precapitalist states, including world systems, complexity theory, long-term change, and preindustrial economic growth. Archaeological interaction with the wider world-systems community has a long history (see discussion above), and archaeological contributions are included in an important recent state-of-the-art assessment (Denemark et al. 2000). Complexity theory is starting to make inroads into archaeology. The formal modeling associated with the Santa Fe Institute holds great promise, but most applications focus on egalitarian groups, not states (Bowles & Choi 2003, Kohler & Gumerman 2000). Informal systems approaches so far have been more useful than formal modeling for ancient state economies (Algaze 2001, Jacobs 2000).

Some work in the emerging field of long-term change studies includes serious engagement with archaeology (Dark 1998, Denemark et al. 2000). Also noteworthy is a trend in the analysis of comparative preindustrial economic growth that moves the field far beyond earlier capitalist-centered and Western-centered biases (de Vries 2001, Goldstone 2002). Goldstone and other scholars explore several types of economic growth and work to document and analyze specific episodes of growth throughout history and even prehistory. Morris (2004) is now applying this approach to archaeological data, using architectural, artifactual, and osteological evidence for changing standards of living in Archaic and Classical Greece; this is a promising avenue for continuing research.

FUTURE DIRECTIONS

Archaeologists have made numerous contributions to scholarly understanding of ancient state economies, both those that are documented in textual sources and those lacking documentary data. The literature reviewed above suggests several topics that need increased attention (beyond basic fieldwork and analytical research directed at economic topics). First, we need better material culture models of economic practices and institutions. What do processes like commercial exchange, attached production, temple economies, or economic growth look like in the archaeological record? Second, we need to move beyond the "Same/Other" debate to produce more sophisticated conceptual and theoretical frameworks. Third, we need far more comparative research on ancient state economies. This research should include targeted comparisons of limited domains (e.g., agricultural terracing, gift exchange, or feasting), broader comparisons of whole economies and societies (Trigger 2003), and controlled theory-based economic comparisons like those of Angresano (1996).

Work with economic historians should be a high priority. Unfortunately most economic historians avoid ancient states and archaeology, as shown by the dearth of relevant entries in the recent five-volume *Oxford Encyclopedia of Economic History* (Mokyr 2003). Archaeologists need to interact more closely with those economic historians who do study ancient states. Hudson's collaborative project on ancient Near Eastern economies (Hudson & Levine 1996, 1999; Hudson & Van De Mieroop 2002) has been important and productive, yet these volumes include only three contributions by archaeologists. There is a pervasive bias toward documentary sources, leading historians to ignore archaeology and archaeologists themselves to attribute too much importance to the documentary record (see discussion in Moreland 2001). This bias is particularly pernicious and ironic for economic analysis because archaeology surpasses the documentary record in the quality and quantity of numerous types of economic data for many periods. The topic would also benefit from increased interaction between archaeologists and economists, particularly political economists and economic anthropologists. Finally, archaeologists need to rise above the isolating tendencies of existing regional and disciplinary traditions to enlarge the comparative scope of their analyses of ancient states and their economies.

ACKNOWLEDGMENTS

I am grateful to a number of colleagues for their input during the preparation of this paper. For responding to my request for citations and suggestions early in the process, I thank Kevin Greene, John Henry, John Moreland, Ian Morris, Monica Smith, and Charles Stanish. The following people provided helpful comments on earlier drafts of the manuscript: Guillermo Algaze, George Cowgill, Timothy Earle, Gary Feinman, Jeffrey Frieden, Kevin Greene, John Henry, Kenneth Hirth, Bernard Knapp, Marilyn Masson, Ian Morris, Monica Smith, Glenn Storey, Stuart

Swiny, Peter Temin, and Marc Van De Mieroop. I also acknowledge the value of a simple question Jeff Frieden asked me several years ago about the evidence for commercial exchange in Mesoamerica.

The *Annual Review of Anthropology* is online at http://anthro.annualreviews.org

LITERATURE CITED

Abrams EM. 1994. *How the Maya Built Their World: Energetics and Ancient Architecture.* Austin: Univ. Tex. Press

Acheson JM, ed. 1994. *Anthropology and Institutional Economics.* Lanham, MD: Univ. Press Am.

Acker R. 1998. New geographical tests of the hydraulic thesis at Angkor. *S.E. Asia Res.* 6:5–47

Adams RM. 1981. *Heartland of Cities: Surveys of Ancient Settlement and Land Use on the Central Floodplain of the Euphrates.* Chicago: Univ. Chicago Press

Alcock SE, D'Altroy TN, Morrison KD, Sinopoli CM, eds. 2001. *Empires: Perspectives from Archaeology and History.* New York: Cambridge Univ. Press

Algaze G. 1993. *The Uruk World System: The Dynamics of Expansion of Early Mesopotamian Civilization.* Chicago: Univ. Chicago Press

Algaze G. 2001. Initial social complexity in Southwestern Asia: the Mesopotamian advantage. *Curr. Anthropol.* 42:199–233

Allen R. 1997. Agriculture and the origins of the state in Ancient Egypt. *Expl. Econ. Hist.* 34:134–54

Allison PM, ed. 1999. *The Archaeology of Household Activities.* New York: Routledge

Ames KM. 1995. Chiefly power and household production on the Northwest Coast. In *Foundations of Social Inequality*, ed. TD Price, GM Feinman, pp. 155–87. New York: Plenum

Angresano J. 1996. *Comparative Economics.* Englewood Cliffs, NJ: Prentice-Hall. 2nd ed.

Ankarloo D. 2002. New institutional economics and economic history. *Cap. Class* 78:9–36

Archi A. 1993. Trade and administrative practice: the case of Ebla. *Altorientalische Forschungen* 20:43–58

Aupert P, ed. 1996. *Guide D'Amathonte.* Paris: École Fr. d'Athens, Fond. AG Leventis. Vol. 15

Bailey D. 1998. *The Archaeology of Value: Essays on Prestige and the Process of Valuation.* Oxford: Br. Archaeol. Rep.

Ballard RD, Stager LE, Master D, Yoerger D, Mindell D, et al. 2002. Iron Age shipwrecks in deep water off Ashkelon, Israel. *Am. J. Archaeol.* 106:161–68

Balmuth MS, ed. 2001. *Hacksilber to Coinage: New Insights into the Monetary History of the Near East and Greece.* New York: Am. Numismatic Soc. Vol. 24

Bermann M. 1994. *Lukurmata: Household Archaeology in Prehispanic Bolivia.* Princeton, NJ: Princeton Univ. Press

Bermann M. 1997. Domestic life and vertical integration in the Tiwanaku Hinterland. *Lat. Am. Antiq.* 8:93–112

Billman BR. 2002. Irrigation and the origins of the Southern Moche State on the north coast of Peru. *Lat. Am. Antiq.* 13:371–400

Blanton RE, Kowalewski SA, Feinman GM, Finsten LM. 1993. *Ancient Mesoamerica: A Comparison of Change in Three Regions.* New York: Cambridge Univ. Press. 2nd ed.

Bowles S, Choi J-K. 2003. *The first property rights revolution.* Presented at Workshop on the Co-Evolution of Behaviors and Institutions. Santa Fe Inst., Santa Fe

Braswell GE, Glascock MD. 2002. The emergence of market economies in the Ancient Maya world: obsidian exchange in terminal Classic Yucatán, Mexico. In *Geochemical Evidence for Long-Distance Exchange,* ed. MD Glascock, pp. 33–52. Westport, CT: Bergin & Garvey

Braudel F. 1982. *The Wheels of Commerce*. New York: Harper and Row

Bray T, ed. 2003. *The Archaeology and Politics of Food and Feasting in Early States and Empires*. New York: Kluwer

Brothwell DR, Pollard AM, eds. 2001. *Handbook of Archaeological Sciences*. New York: Wiley

Brumfiel EM. 1987. Elite and utilitarian crafts in the Aztec State. See Brumfiel & Earle 1987a, pp. 102–18

Brumfiel EM, Earle TK, eds. 1987a. *Specialization, Exchange, and Complex Societies*. New York: Cambridge Univ. Press

Brumfiel EM, Earle TK. 1987b. Specialization, exchange, and complex societies: an introduction. See Brumfiel & Earle 1987a, pp. 1–9

Butzer KW. 1996. Irrigation, raised fields and state management: Wittfogel redux? *Antiquity* 70:200–4

Cahill N. 2001. *Household and City Organization at Olynthus*. New Haven, CT: Yale Univ. Press

Cartledge PA. 1998. The economy (economies) of Ancient Greece. *Dialogos* 5:4–24

Claessen HJM, Skalnik P, eds. 1978. *The Early State*. The Hague: Mouton

Clark JE. 1995. Craft specialization as an archaeological category. *Res. Econ. Anthropol.* 16:267–94

Clark JE, Parry WJ. 1990. Craft specialization and cultural complexity. *Res. Econ. Anthropol.* 12:289–346

Cobb CR. 2000. Specialization, exchange, and power in small-scale societies and chiefdoms. In *From Quarry to Cornfield: The Political Economy of Mississippian Hoe Production*, ed. CR Cobb, pp. 19–46. Tuscaloosa: Univ. Ala. Press

Cohen MN. 1977. *The Food Crisis in Prehistory: Overpopulation and the Origins of Agriculture*. New Haven, CT: Yale Univ. Press

Costin CL. 1991. Craft specialization: issues in defining, documenting, and explaining the organization of production. *Archaeol. Method Theory* 3:1–56

Costin CL. 2001a. Craft production systems. See Feinman & Price 2001, pp. 273–328

Costin CL. 2001b. Production and exchange of ceramics. See D'Altroy & Hastorf 2001, pp. 203–42

Costin CL, Wright RP, eds. 1998. *Craft and Social Identity*. Washington, DC: Am. Anthropol. Assoc. Archaeol. Pap., Vol. 8

Cowgill GL. 1975. On causes and consequences of ancient and modern population changes. *Am. Anthropol.* 77:505–25

Cowgill GL. 1997. State and society at Teotihuacan, Mexico. *Annu. Rev. Anthropol.* 26:129–61

Cowgill GL. 2004. Origins and development of urbanism: archaeological perspectives. *Annu. Rev. Anthropol.* 33:525–49

Culbert TP, Rice DS, eds. 1990. *Precolombian Population History in the Maya Lowlands*. Albuquerque: Univ. New Mexico Press

Curtin PD. 1984. *Cross-Cultural Trade in World History*. New York: Cambridge Univ. Press

Dalton G. 1982. Barter. *J. Econ. Issues* 16:181–90

D'Altroy TN. 1992. *Provincial Power in the Inka Empire*. Washington, DC: Smithsonian Inst. Press

D'Altroy TN, Earle T. 1985. Staple finance, wealth finance, and storage in the Inka political economy. *Curr. Anthropol.* 26:187–206

D'Altroy TN, Hastorf CA, eds. 2001. *Empire and Domestic Economy*. New York: Plenum

Dark KR. 1998. *The Waves of Time: Long-Term Change and International Relations*. New York: Continuum

David N, Kramer C. 2001. *Ethnoarchaeology in Action*. New York: Cambridge Univ. Press

de Vries J. 2001. Economic growth before and after the industrial revolution: a modest proposal. In *Early Modern Capitalism*, ed. M Prak, pp. 177–94. New York: Routledge

Delougaz P. 1940. *The Temple Oval at Khafajah*. Chicago: Univ. Chicago Press

Denemark RA, Friedman J, Gills BK, Modelski G, eds. 2000. *World System History: The*

Social Science of Long-Term Change. New York: Routledge

Denevan WM. 2001. *Cultivated Landscapes of Native Amazonia and the Andes: Triumph Over the Soil.* New York: Oxford Univ. Press

Dietler M. 1990. Driven by drink: the role of drinking in the political economy and the case of Iron Age France. *J. Anthropol. Archaeol.* 9:352–406

Dietler M, Herbich I. 2001. Feasts and labor mobilization: dissecting a fundamental economic practice. In *Feasts: Archaeological and Ethnographic Perspectives on Food, Politics, and Power*, ed. M Dietler, B Hayden, pp. 240–64. Washington, DC: Smithsonian Inst. Press

Drennan RD. 1984. Long-distance transport costs in pre-hispanic Mesoamerica. *Am. Anthropol.* 86:105–12

Dunning NP, Beach T. 1994. Soil erosion, slope management, and ancient terracing in the Maya lowlands. *Lat. Am. Antiq.* 5:51–69

Earle T. 1977. A reappraisal of redistribution: complex Hawaiian chiefdoms. In *Exchange Systems in Prehistory*, ed. TK Earle, JE Ericson, pp. 213–29. New York: Academic

Earle T. 2000. Archaeology, property, and prehistory. *Annu. Rev. Anthropol.* 29:39–60

Earle T. 2001. Exchange and social stratification in the Andes: the Xauxa case. See D'Altroy & Hastorf 2001, pp. 297–314

Earle T. 2002a. *Bronze Age Economics: The Beginnings of Political Economies.* Boulder, CO: Westview

Earle T. 2002b. Political economies of chiefdoms and agrarian states. See Earle 2002a, pp. 1–18

Erickson CL. 2000. The Lake Titicaca Basin: a Precolumbian built landscape. In *Imperfect Balance: Landscape Transformations in the Precolumbian Americas*, ed. DL Lentz, pp. 311–56. New York: Columbia Univ. Press

Feinman GM, Marcus J, eds. 1998. *Archaic States.* Santa Fe, NM: Sch. Am. Res.

Feinman GM, Nicholas LM. 1991. New perspectives on prehispanic highland Mesoamerica: a macroregional approach. *Comp. Civiliz. Rev.* 24:13–33

Feinman GM, Nicholas LM. 2000. High-intensity household-scale production in Ancient Mesoamerica: a perspective from Ejutla, Oaxaca. In *Cultural Evolution: Contemporary Viewpoints*, ed. GM Feinman, L Manzanilla, pp. 119–44. New York: Kluwer

Feinman GM, Nicholas LM, eds. 2004. *Archaeological Perspectives on Political Economies.* Salt Lake City: Univ. Utah Press

Feinman GM, Price TD, eds. 2001. *Archaeology at the Millennium: A Sourcebook.* New York: Kluwer

Feinman GM, Upham S, Lightfoot KG. 1981. The production step measure: an ordinal index of labor input in ceramic manufacture. *Am. Antiq.* 46:871–85

Figueira TJ. 1984. Karl Polanyi and Ancient Greek trade: the port of trade. *Anc. World* 10:15–30

Finley MI. 1999 [1977]. *The Ancient Economy.* Berkeley: Univ. Calif. Press

Friedman J, Rowlands MJ. 1978. Notes towards an epigenetic model of the evolution of 'civilisation.' In *The Evolution of Social Systems*, ed. J Friedman, MJ Rowlands, pp. 201–76. Pittsburgh, PA: Univ. Pittsburgh Press

Gilman A. 1998. Reconstructing property systems from archaeological evidence. In *Property in Economic Context*, ed. RC Hunt, A Gilman, pp. 215–33. Lanham, MD: Univ. Press Am.

Goldstone JA. 2002. Efflorescences and economic growth in world history: rethinking the rise of the West and the British industrial revolution. *J. World Hist.* 13:323–89

Greene K. 1986. *The Archaeology of the Roman Economy.* Berkeley: Univ. Calif. Press

Grierson P. 1977. *The Origins of Money.* London: Athlone

Hafford WB. 2001. *Merchants in the Late Bronze Age Eastern Mediterranean: tools, texts, and trade.* PhD thesis. Univ. Penn., Phila.

Hägg R, Marinatos N, eds. 1987. *The Function of the Minoan Palaces.* Stockholm: Svenska Institutet i Athen. Vol. 35

Hansen MH, ed. 2000. *A Comparative Study of*

Thirty City-State Cultures. Copenhagen: R. Dan. Acad. Sci. Lett.

Hansen MH, ed. 2002. *A Comparative Study of Six City-State Cultures.* Copenhagen: R. Dan. Acad. Sci. Lett.

Haring B, de Maijer R, eds. 1998. *Landless and Hungry? Access to Land in Early and Traditional Societies.* Leiden: CNWS

Harris WV. 1993. Between archaic and modern: some current problems in the history of the Roman economy. In *The Inscribed Economy: Production and Distribution in the Roman Empire in Light of Instrumentum Domesticum,* ed. WV Harris, pp. 11–29. Ann Arbor: J. Rom. Archaeol., Suppl. Ser. Vol. 6

Hendon JA. 1996. Archaeological approaches to the organization of domestic labor: household practices and domestic relations. *Annu. Rev. Anthropol.* 25:45–61

Henry JF. 2004. The social origins of money: the case of Egypt. See Wray 2004, pp. 79–98

Higham C. 2002. *The Civilization of Angkor.* Berkeley: Univ. Calif. Press

Hirth KG. 1996. Political economy and archaeology: perspectives on exchange and production. *J. Archaeol. Res.* 4:203–40

Hirth KG. 1998. The distributional approach: a new way to identify marketplace exchange in the archaeological record. *Curr. Anthropol.* 39:451–76

Hodder I. 1974. A regression analysis of some trade and marketing patterns. *W. Archaeol.* 6:172–89

Hopkins K. 1983. Introduction. In *Trade in the Ancient Economy,* ed. P Garnsey, K Hopkins, CR Whittaker, pp. ix–xxv. London: Chatto and Windes

Hudson M. 2004. The archaeology of money. See Wray 2004, pp. 99–127

Hudson M, Levine BA, eds. 1996. *Privatization in the Ancient Near East and Classical World.* Cambridge, MA: Peabody Mus. Archaeol. Ethnol., Harvard Univ.

Hudson M, Levine BA, eds. 1999. *Urbanization and Land Ownership in the Ancient Near East.* Cambridge, MA: Peabody Mus. Archaeol. Ethnol., Harvard Univ.

Hudson M, Van De Mieroop M, eds. 2002. *Debt and Economic Renewal in the Ancient Near East.* Bethesda, MD: CDL

Inomata T. 2001. The power and ideology of artistic creation: elite craft specialists in Classic Maya society. *Curr. Anthropol.* 42:321–49

Isaac BL. 1993. AMP, HH, and OD: some comments. In *Economic Aspects of Water Management in the Prehispanic New World,* ed. VL Scarborough, BL Isaac, pp. 429–71. Greenwich, CT: JAI

Isendahl C. 2002. *Common Knowledge: Lowland Maya Urban Farming at Xuch.* Uppsala: Univ. Uppsala, Dep. Archaeol. Anc. Hist.

Jacobs J. 2000. *The Nature of Economies.* New York: Mod. Libr.

Jameson MH, Runnels CN, van Andel TH. 1994. *A Greek Countryside: The Southern Argolid From Prehistory to the Present.* Stanford, CA: Stanford Univ. Press

Janusek JW. 1999. Craft and local power: embedded specialization in Tiwanaku cities. *Lat. Am. Antiq.* 10:107–31

Johnson AW, Earle TK. 2000. *The Evolution of Human Societies: From Foraging Group to Agrarian State.* Stanford, CA: Stanford Univ. Press. 2nd ed.

Johnston KJ. 2003. The intensification of preindustrial cereal agriculture in the tropics: Boserup, cultivation lengthening, and the Classic Maya. *J. Anthropol. Archaeol.* 22:126–61

Jones SRH. 1993. Transaction costs, institutional change, and the emergence of a market economy in later Anglo-Saxon England. *Econ. Hist. Rev.* 46:658–78

Junker LL. 1999. *Raiding, Trading, and Feasting: The Political Economy of Philippine Chiefdoms.* Honolulu: Univ. Hawaii Press

Kenoyer JM. 1998. *Ancient Cities of the Indus Valley Civilization.* Karachi/New York: Oxford Univ. Press

Knapp AB, Cherry JF. 1994. *Provenience Studies and Bronze Age Cyprus: Production, Exchange, and Politico-Economic Change.* Madison, WI: Prehistory Press

Kohler TA, Gumerman GJ, eds. 2000. *Dynamics in Human and Primate Societies:*

Agent-Based Modeling of Social and Spatial Processes. New York: Oxford Univ. Press

Kolata AL. 1991. The technology and organization of agricultural production in the Tiwanaku state. *Lat. Am. Antiq.* 2:99–125

Kowalewski SA. 1990. The evolution of complexity in the Valley of Oaxaca. *Annu. Rev. Anthropol.* 19:39–58

Larsen MT. 1976. *The Old Assyrian City-State and its Colonies.* Copenhagen: Akademisk Forlag

Lees SH. 1994. Irrigation and society. *J. Archaeol. Res.* 2:361–78

Leong SH. 1990. Collecting centres, feeder points and entrepôts in the Malay Peninsula, 1000 B.C.–A.D. 1400. In *The Southeast Asian Port and Polity: Rise and Demise*, ed. J Kathirithamby-Wells, J Villiers, pp. 17–38. Singapore: Singapore Univ. Press

Lindkvist T. 1991. Social and political power in Sweden, 1000–1300: predatory incursions, royal taxation, and the formation of a feudal state. In *Social Approaches to Viking Studies*, ed. R Samson, pp. 137–45. Glasgow, Scotland: Cruithne Press

Manning JG, Morris I, eds. 2004. *The Ancient Economy: Evidence and Models.* Stanford, CA: Stanford Univ. Press. In press

Manzanilla L, ed. 1997. *Emergence and Change in Early Urban Societies.* New York: Plenum

Marcus J, Feinman GM. 1998. Introduction. See Feinman & Marcus 1998, pp. 3–13

Marx K. 1967. *Capital: A Critique of Political Economy. Volume 1: The Process of Capitalist Production.* New York: Int. Publ.

Masson MA, Freidel DA, eds. 2002. *Ancient Maya Political Economies.* Walnut Creek, CA: Altamira

Mattingly DJ, Salmon J, eds. 2001. *Economies Beyond Agriculture in the Classical World.* New York: Routledge

McGuire RH. 2002. *A Marxist Archaeology.* New York: Percheron Press

Moholy-Nagy H. 1990. The misidentification of Mesoamerican lithic workshops. *Lat. Am. Antiq.* 1:268–79

Mokyr J, ed. 2003. *The Oxford Encyclopedia of Economic History.* New York: Oxford Univ. Press. 5 vols.

Möller A. 2000. *Naukratis: Trade in Archaic Greece.* Oxford: Oxford Univ. Press

Moreland J. 2000. Concepts in the Early Medieval Economy. In *The Long Eighth Century*, ed. IL Hansen, C Wickham, pp. 1–34. Leiden: Brill

Moreland J. 2001. *Archaeology and Text.* London: Duckworth

Morris I. 1999. Foreward. See Finley 1999, pp. ix–xxxvi. Berkeley: Univ. Calif. Press

Morris I. 2004. Economic growth in Ancient Greece. *J. Inst. Theoretical Econ.* 31:In press

Morris I. n.d. The growth of Greek cities in the First Millennium BC. In *From "Giant Villages" to "Giant Towns": A Cross-Cultural Sampling of Preindustrial Urban Issues*, ed. G Storey. Tuscaloosa: Univ. Ala. Press. In press

Morrison KD. 1996. Typological schemes and agricultural change: beyond Boserup in Precolonial South India. *Curr. Anthropol.* 37:583–608

Morrison KD. 1997. Commerce and culture in South Asia: perspectives from archaeology and history. *Annu. Rev. Anthropol.* 26:87–108

Muller J. 1997. *Mississippian Political Economy.* New York: Plenum

Murra JV. 1980. *The Economic Organization of the Inka State.* Greenwich, CT: JAI

Neale WC. 1971. Monetization, commercialization, market orientation, and market dependence. In *Studies in Economic Anthropology*, ed. G Dalton, pp. 25–29. Washington, DC: Am. Anthropol. Assoc.

Netting RM. 1993. *Smallholders, Householders: Farm Families and the Ecology of Intensive, Sustainable Agriculture.* Stanford, CA: Stanford Univ. Press

Nichols DL, Brumfiel EM, Neff H, Hodge M, Charlton TH, Glascock MD. 2002. Neutrons, markets, cities, and empires: a 1000-year perspective on ceramic production and distribution in the Postclassic Basin of Mexico. *J. Anthropol. Archaeol.* 21:25–82

Nichols DL, Charlton TH, eds. 1997. *The Archaeology of City-States: Cross-Cultural*

Approaches. Washington, DC: Smithsonian Inst. Press

North DC. 1981. *Structure and Change in Economic History*. New York: Norton

North DC. 1991. Institutions. *J. Econ. Perspec.* 5:97–112

Pare CFE, ed. 2000. *Metals Make the World Go Round: The Supply and Circulation of Metals in Bronze Age Europe*. Oxford: Oxbow

Parkins HM, ed. 1997. *Roman Urbanism: Beyond the Consumer City*. New York: Routledge

Peacock DPS. 1982. *Pottery in the Roman World: An Ethnoarchaeological Approach*. New York: Longman

Pearson MN. 1991. Merchants and states. In *The Political Economy of Merchant Empires*, ed. JD Tracy, pp. 41–116. New York: Cambridge Univ. Press

Peregrine PN, Feinman GM, eds. 1996. *Pre-Columbian World Systems*. Madison, WI: Prehistory Press

Polanyi K. 1957. The economy as instituted process. See Polanyi et al. 1957, pp. 243–70

Polanyi K. 1963. Ports of trade in early societies. *J. Econ. Hist.* 23:30–45

Polanyi K, Arensburg CM, Pearson HW, eds. 1957. *Trade and Market in the Early Empires*. Chicago: Regnery

Possehl GL. 1998. Sociocultural complexity without the state: the Indus civilization. See Feinman & Marcus 1998, pp. 261–92

Powell MA, ed. 1987. *Labor in the Ancient Near East*. New York: Am. Orient. Soc.

Pryor FL. 1977. *Origins of the Economy: A Comparative Study of Distribution in Primitive and Peasant Economies*. New York: Academic

Pulak C. 1998. The Uluburun shipwreck: an overview. *Int. J. Naut. Archaeol.* 27:188–224

Redman CL. 1978. *The Rise of Civilization*. San Francisco: Freeman

Renfrew C. 1975. Trade as action at a distance: questions of integration and communication. In *Ancient Civilization and Trade*, ed. JA

Sabloff, CC Lamberg-Karlovsky, pp. 3–59. Albuquerque: Univ. New Mexico Press

Renger J. 1995. On economic structures in Ancient Mesopotamia. *Orientalia* 63:157–208

Roseberry W. 1988. Political Economy. *Annu. Rev. Anthropol.* 17:161–85

Sahlins M. 1972. *Stone-Age Economics*. Chicago: Aldine

Samuelson P. 1973. *Economics*. New York: McGraw-Hill. 9th ed.

Sanders WT, Parsons JR, Santley RS. 1979. *The Basin of Mexico: Ecological Processes in the Evolution of a Civilization*. New York: Academic

Sanders WT, Santley RS. 1983. A tale of three cities: energetics and urbanization in prehispanic central Mexico. In *Prehistoric Settlement Patterns: Essays in Honor of Gordon R. Willey*, ed. EZ Vogt, R Leventhal, pp. 243–91. Albuquerque: Univ. New Mexico Press

Scarborough VL. 2003. *The Flow of Power: Ancient Water Systems and Landscapes*. Santa Fe, NM: Sch. Am. Res.

Schumpeter JA. 1954. *History of Economic Analysis*. New York: Oxford Univ. Press

Schwartz GM, Falconer SE, eds. 1994. *Archaeological Views from the Countryside: Village Communities in Early Complex Societies*. Washington, DC: Smithsonian Inst. Press

Sheehy JJ. 1996. Ethnographic analogy and the royal household in 8th century Copan. In *Arqueología Mesoamericana: Homenaje a William T. Sanders*, ed. AG Mastache, JR Parsons, RS Santley, MC Serra Puche, pp. 253–76. Mexico City: Inst. Nac. Antropolog. Histor.

Sherratt A, Sherratt S. 1991. From luxuries to commodities: the nature of Mediterranean Bronze Age trading systems. In *Bronze Age Trade in the Mediterranean*, ed. NH Gale, pp. 351–86. Jonsered: Paul Åströms Förlag

Silver M. 1995. *Economic Structures of Antiquity*. Westport, CT: Greenwood

Sinopoli CM. 2003. *The Political Economy of Craft Production: Crafting Empire in South India, c. 1350–1650*. New York: Cambridge Univ. Press

Smith CA. 1976a. Exchange systems and the

spatial distribution of elites: the organization of stratification in agrarian societies. In *Regional Analysis, Volume 2, Social Systems*, ed. CA Smith, pp. 309–74. New York: Academic

Smith CA, ed. 1976b. *Regional Analysis*. New York: Academic

Smith ME. 1987. Household possessions and wealth in agrarian states: implications for archaeology. *J. Anthropol. Archaeol.* 6:297–335

Smith ME. 1999. Comment on Hirth's "distribution approach." *Curr. Anthropol.* 40:528–30

Smith ME, Berdan FF, eds. 2003. *The Postclassic Mesoamerican World*. Salt Lake City: Univ. Utah Press

Smith ME, Heath-Smith C. 1994. Rural economy in late postclassic Morelos: an archaeological study. In *Economies and Polities in the Aztec Realm*, ed. MG Hodge, ME Smith, pp. 349–76. Albany, NY: Inst. Mesoam. Stud.

Smith ME, Price TJ. 1994. Aztec-period agricultural terraces in Morelos, Mexico: evidence for household-level agricultural intensification. *J. Field Archaeol.* 21:169–79

Smith ML, ed. 2003. *The Social Construction of Ancient Cities*. Washington, DC: Smithsonian Inst. Press

Snell DC. 1997. Appendix: theories of ancient economies and societies. In *Life in the Ancient Near East, 3100–332 BCE*, ed. DC Snell, pp. 145–58. New Haven, CT: Yale Univ. Press

Stanish C. 2003. *Ancient Titicaca: The Evolution of Complex Society in Southern Peru and Northern Bolivia*. Berkeley: Univ. Calif. Press

Stark BL. 1990. The gulf coast and the central highlands of Mexico: alternative models for interaction. *Res. Econ. Anthropol.* 12:243–85

Stein GJ. 1999. *Rethinking World-Systems: Diasporas, Colonies, and Interaction in Uruk Mesopotamia*. Tucson: Univ. Ariz. Press

Stein GJ. 2001. Understanding ancient state societies in the Old World. See Feinman & Price 2001, pp. 353–80

Stein GJ. 2002. From passive periphery to active agents: emerging perspectives in the archaeology of interregional interaction. *Am. Anthropol.* 104:903–16

Stott P. 1992. Angkor: shifting the hydraulic paradigm. In *The Gift of Water: Water Management, Cosmology and the State in South East Asia*, ed. J Rigg, pp. 47–58. London: Sch. Orient. Afr. Stud., Univ. London

Swiny S, Hohlfelder RL, Swiny HW, eds. 1997. *Res Maritimae: Cyprus and the Eastern Mediterranean from Prehistory to Late Antiquity*. Proc. Int. Symp. "Cities on the Sea," 2nd, Nicosia, Cyprus, October 18–22, 1994. Atlanta: Scholars Press. Vol. 4

Temin P. 2001. A market economy in the early Roman Empire. *J. Roman Stud.* 91:169–81

Temin P. 2003. *Mediterranean trade in Biblical times*. Work. Pap. No. 03-12, MIT Dep. Econ.

Thirsk J. 1961. Industries in the countryside. In *Essays in the Economic and Social History of Tudor and Stuart England, in Honor of R. H. Tawney*, ed. FJ Fisher, pp. 70–88. Cambridge: Cambridge Univ. Press

Trigger BG. 1990. Monumental architecture: a thermodynamic explanation of behavior. *W. Archaeol.* 22:119–32

Trigger BG. 2003. *Understanding Early Civilizations: A Comparative Study*. New York: Cambridge Univ. Press

Urton G. 2003. *Signs of the Inka Khipu*. Austin: Univ. Tex. Press

Van De Mieroop M. 1999. *Cuneiform Texts and the Writing of History*. New York: Routledge

van der Leeuw SE. 1976. *Studies in the Technology of Ancient Pottery*. Amsterdam: Univ. Amsterdam

Voutsaki S, Killen J, eds. 2001. *Economy and Politics in the Mycenaean Palace States*. Cambridge: Cambridge Philolog. Soc.

Wailes B, ed. 1996. *Craft Specialization and Social Evolution: In Memory of V. Gordon Childe*. Philadelphia: Univ. Mus.

Weber M. 1958. *The City*. New York: Free Press

Wells PS. 1999. *The Barbarians Speak: How the Conquered Peoples Shaped Roman Europe*. Princeton, NJ: Princeton Univ. Press

Whitmore TM, Turner BL II. 2001. *Cultivated*

Landscapes of Middle America on the Eve of Conquest. New York: Oxford Univ. Press

Wilk RR. 1996. *Economies and Cultures: Foundations of Economic Anthropology.* Boulder, CO: Westview

Wilk RR, Rathje WL, eds. 1982. Archaeology of the household: building a prehistory of domestic life. *Am. Behav. Sci.* 25(6):617–39

Wilkinson TJ. 2003. *Archaeological Landscapes of the Near East.* Tucson: Univ. Ariz. Press

Wolf ER. 1982. *Europe and the People Without History.* Berkeley: Univ. Calif. Press

Wray LR. 1998. *Understanding Modern Money: The Key to Full Employment and Price Stability.* Northampton, MA: Elgar

Wray LR, ed. 2004. *Credit and State Theories of Money: The Contributions of A. Mitchell Innes.* Northampton, MA: Elgar

Yoffee N. 1995. Political economy in early Mesopotamian states. *Annu. Rev. Anthropol.* 24:281–311

Zettler R. 1992. *The Ur III Temple of Inanna at Nippur: The Operation and Organization of Urban Religious Institutions in Mesopotamia in the Late Third Millennium B.C.* Berlin: Dietrich Reimer Verlag

Annu. Rev. Anthropol. 2004. 33:103–15
doi: 10.1146/annurev.anthro.33.070203.143921
Copyright © 2004 by Annual Reviews. All rights reserved
First published online as a Review in Advance on April 30, 2004

NEW TECHNOLOGIES AND LANGUAGE CHANGE:
Toward an Anthropology of Linguistic Frontiers

Susan E. Cook

Department of Anthropology, University of Pretoria, Pretoria, 0002,
South Africa; email: sue.cook@up.ac.za

Key Words   global hip hop, youth culture, global English, urban hybrids, globalization

■ **Abstract**   Research to date on the relationship between new communications technologies and language emphasizes linguistic and social differences between online and off-line interactions and the impact of global English on the non-English-speaking world. These studies conclude, for the most part, that computer-mediated communication reproduces the social, political, and economic relations that exist in the real world. Related areas of research, including ethnographies of global hip hop and studies of urban hybrid language varieties, offer important models for using anthropological approaches to advance our understanding of the interconnections and situated-ness, of language, new technologies, global media, and social change.

INTRODUCTION

How, as anthropologists, do we conceptualize the relationship between conventional forms of verbal interaction and those mediated by new technologies such as the Internet, satellite transmissions, and cell phones? If Crystal is correct in saying that the Internet constitutes a new frontier in human social interaction on par with the inventions of the telephone and telegraph, and even print and broadcast technologies (Crystal 2001), then those scholars of language use, language change, and ideologies of language must surely explore and interrogate the effects of these technologies on traditional modes of communication, the impact of our new capacity to communicate instantly anywhere in the world, and the meaning of language contact as it is taking place in cyberspace. Most of these technologies, notwithstanding constant new advances in computer-mediated graphics, are text or voice based. To say "[i]f the Internet is a revolution, therefore, it is likely to be a linguistic revolution" may not be an exaggeration (Crystal 2001, p. viii). The "if" in that statement bears closer scrutiny, and, as some have suggested, anthropologists are in a strong position to do this work (Wilson & Peterson 2002). It is surprising, therefore, that relatively few ethnographic studies of the impact of new technologies on language use have been published. Whether because

0084-6570/04/1021-0103$14.00

anthropologists cleave too tightly to "notions of community, fieldwork, the body, nature, vision, the subject, identity, and writing," which are insufficient for understanding and analyzing "cyberculture" (Escobar 1994), or because it is not easy to site such inquiry, determine its boundaries, and relinquish the "romance of spatial confinement" (Gupta & Ferguson 2001), (linguistic) anthropology has produced few empirically grounded examinations of the relationship between language use, language status, or language ideologies and new technologies. This chapter thus approaches in two ways the task of reviewing the current state of the art of knowledge about new technologies and language change. First, I expand the scope of inquiry to provide a brief overview of scholarship from other fields and disciplines that attempt to understand the chicken/egg question about language and technology: Do communication technologies change the way people speak/write, or do these media reflect established patterns and norms of verbal interaction? Certain limitations of these approaches suggest important avenues for future anthropological study. Second, I look to related areas of ethnographic study to point the way toward a more creative, contemporary, yet still solidly anthropological approach to the issue of language, technology, and change: studies of cultural and linguistic frontiers as they relate to youth cultures and global media. By insisting that any examination of new technologies be situated within the economic, social, and political contexts where the information and images they convey are consumed, circulated, and signified, these studies demonstrate that anthropology is particularly well suited to investigate the social (and symbolic) dimensions of new technology.

COMMUNICATION TECHNOLOGIES AND LANGUAGE USE

Scholars from a wide range of fields, including psychology, applied linguistics, computer sciences, sociology, and cultural studies, to name a few, have begun to explore the social and linguistic dimensions of technologies such as email and the Internet. Much of the recent scholarship is focused on the promise of new communications technologies to subvert social boundaries such as race, gender, and ethnicity through text-based media that withold certain identity markers. Others have considered the role of communications technology in promoting social justice, economic equality, and democratization. However much new communications technologies alter our ability to represent ourselves, develop new hybrid forms of interaction, or increase the speed at which we exchange information, much that is old exists in new technologies. Not quite a broken promise, the notion of cyberspace as an emancipatory sphere has been updated by many scholars to reflect the fact that by changing the way we do things, we do not necessarily change the things we do (Wilson & Peterson 2002).

The previous statement is not meant to reassure those who lack up-to-the-minute knowledge of the latest communications technologies that they are not missing anything. In fact, email and the Internet represent a whole range of linguistic innovations, from a substantial lexicon that needs constant updating (Glowka et al. 2003) to new styles, conventions, and modes of written expression (Crystal 2001, Baron 2002) and entire new language varieties, such as Netspeak (Crystal 2001, p. 92). From an anthropological perspective, though, the more interesting question lies in the ways that computer-mediated communication actually alters the way we interact as social beings. Are the constraints placed on conventional modes of interaction—rules of discourse, identity markers, conventions of use—significantly altered in cyberspace (Paolillo 2001)? What types of social relations result from these computer-mediated interactions? Can new communications technologies change the way we interact and see ourselves in the real world (Richardson 2001)? Scholars approach these questions from various angles, an overview of which follows.

Sociolinguists interested in the social aspects of computer-mediated communication have investigated this sphere of interaction with reference to conventional social divisions, such as gender, race, and class. Studies of the gendered aspects of Internet communication include an examination of (gender) accommodation theory in email (Thomson et al. 2001) and studies of male-versus-female approaches to Internet communication (Dickerson 2003, Shaw & Gant 2002). Other scholars adopt a more overtly feminist stance toward the gendered aspects of new communications technologies. Examinations of gender in Internet discourse (Smith & Balka 1991, Herring 1993, Herring et al. 1995) and textual (as well as visual) representations of the body via new technologies (Cutting Edge Women's Res. Group 2000) have followed claims that the Internet is a male-dominated space [on the basis of user profiles as well as Web site content descriptions (Dickerson 2003)].

The role of language in computer-mediated identity construction is the focus of numerous studies (Waskul & Douglass 1997, Warschauer 2000, Jacobs-Huey 2004). Similar to gender studies, most studies of race and computer-mediated communications take as their starting point "the cyberself as embedded in language" (Kolko et al. 2000, p. 6), and the Internet is as fraught with problems and issues of race as is face-to-face communication, despite the fact that it is an environment where visual and aural identity markers are absent. In their volume *Race in Cyberspace*, Kolko and her colleagues note that, unlike in the real world, race is either turned on or turned off in cyberspace; that is, it is either the direct focus of discourse and debate or completely invisible (p. 1). Where it is on, expressions of race on the Internet can assume different or exaggerated forms of what could occur in face-to-face interactions, such as "passing" (Nakamura 1999), "crossing," (for example, "those gansta-talking websites . . . being run by rebellious, back-talking, suburban white kids looking for some model, any model") (Lockard 2000, p. 178) and overt racism (Ronkin & Karn 1999). But in the end, there is little evidence that the Internet, or other forms of computer-mediated communication, serves to mitigate the pernicious effects of racism. Kolko and her coeditors put it thus: ". . .the virtual reality that is cyberspace has often been construed as something that exists in binary opposition to 'the real world,' but when it comes to questions of power, politics, and structural relations, cyberspace is as real as it gets" (Kolko et al. 2000, p. 4).

This conclusion also emerges from studies of other social and political aspects of computer-mediated communication. Although scholars note the democratic aspects of email and the Internet (Nelson 1974, Herring 1993, Ess 1994, Baron 1998) and the possibilities of creating ethnicity-neutral chat spaces (Kadende-Kaiser 1999), a broader view of these new technologies in society reveals that access to the language, hardware, and technological cultures of new communication technologies remains inaccessible to many. The digital divide in the United States finds Blacks, Hispanics, and those with household incomes under $30,000 per year underrepresented among Internet users (Lenhart 2003). The worldwide divide is predictably much more stark. This finding may be, in part, a result of specific language issues such as the status of English as the predominant language of the Internet (Crystal 2001, Lockard 2000).

LANGUAGE CONTACT IN CYBERSPACE

Nearly all of the above-mentioned studies that deal with how communications technologies alter our social interactions, both online and off-line, are based on, and in, Western, English-speaking societies. If we broaden the scope to consider the impact of these technologies on language and communication in other parts of the world, the question of global English quickly emerges. The literature on new technologies and language revitalization is reviewed separately in this volume (Eisenlohr 2004, in this volume), but the inverse of the revitalization process is also a subject of study and debate: the spread of English throughout the world, often at the expense of other languages. (I do not review related literature on "new Englishes.") Although non–English language Web sites are rapidly increasing in number (Crystal 2001, p. 216), most of the Web's contents are in English (Lockard 2000, p. 178). This is certainly not the only reason for the rise of global English, which is seen by many as a threat (Tsuda 1997) and by others as an inevitable by-product of globalization or just plain being "in the right place at the right time" (Crystal 1997, p. 110). As Judy points out, the rise of global English must be attributed not only to the fact that membership in the cyber community is based on competence in English, but also to "the complex relationship between the organization of knowledge, economic and political forces, and ideology" (Judy 1999, p. 5). In countries like Tunisia (Judy 1999), Malaysia and Algeria (Judy 1997), and Switzerland (Economist 2000), where English is not a natively spoken or officially sanctioned language, it meets Crystal's definition(s) of a global language: one that "develops a special role that is recognized in every country" (Crystal 1997, p. 2) and one whose "usage is not restricted by countries or . . . by governing bodies" (p. 130). The shift in Crystal's criteria for global language from those "recognized in every country" to those "not restricted by countries or . . . by governing bodies" is telling; state sovereignty and national-level language policies are increasingly irrelevant to implications of the language of the Internet (i.e., English) on societies around the world.

The problem with analyzing this impact in any kind of empirically grounded way is, of course, that mentioned at the beginning of this review: how to site global information flows, how to participate in the process of computer-mediated interaction, and how to observe the new means and modes of deploying global English. One study considers the way consumer magazines in South Africa deploy English together with indigenous forms of African auriture/orality to index contemporary Black middle-class sensibilities. Though fascinating as literary criticism, the study lacks data about readers' responses to these magazines that would ground the authors' conclusions in lived experience (Laden 2001). Conversely, a study of the displacement of English among native speakers in Argentina concludes that the language is losing ground, except for instrumental purposes such as workplace interactions and international communication. Drawing conclusions based solely on attitude surveys, this study can only be regarded as suggestive, rather than empirically sound (Cortes-Conde 1994). A final example concerns a global mega trend of language change, i.e., the spread of the "be like" quotatative system from the United States to the United Kingdom and Canada (Tagliamonte & Hudson 1999). After describing this linguistic feature as it occurs in the three countries, the authors stop short of even speculating about the mechanisms by which the process of international diffusion occurs. This study, like the other two, speaks to local instances of the globalization of English without offering much insight into how, precisely, "the global" and "the local" intersect to produce change and what role new technologies play in the process.

THE WAY FORWARD: PUTTING LANGUAGE AND NEW TECHNOLOGIES INTO CONTEXT

With a few notable exceptions, the scholarship reviewed above focuses either on the linguistic patterns that characterize new technologies or the effects of increasingly globalized communications on whole languages. From an anthropological perspective, most of this scholarship fails to provide either (*a*) an empirically grounded picture of individual experience of these technologies, understood in reference to our entire range of communicative acts, or (*b*) the broader social impacts of these phenomena. The scarcity of studies on the relationship between new technologies and changes in language use, status, and distribution does not, however, mean that ethnographic methods are inadequate for exploring this subject. On the contrary, recent work in related areas, such as the anthropology of global pop culture, exemplifies ethnographic study that is at once fine-grained and attentive to wider transnational issues, trends, and dilemmas.

Studies of global hip hop are a case in point. Tasked with the challenge of understanding the worldwide spread of a musical aesthetic rooted in 1970s urban America (Dimitriadis 1996, Smitherman 1997), ethnographers of global hip hop have confronted a range of methodological and analytic challenges similar to those facing scholars of new technologies. From deciding what the object of study is (an art form? a political ideology? a generational movement?) to deciding the best way to conceptualize the local and global dimensions of hip hop in any particular context, the study of hip hop and rap around the world has produced some ground-breaking work. Condry (2000), for example, understands Japanese hip hop as being inspired by American urban Black music but not bound by its defining ideologies, specifically those related to race, class, and gender. His study of the performers, fans, venues, and producers of Japanese hip hop around Tokyo convince him that this "generational protest" is a reaction to local sociopolitical realities and bears little resemblance, beyond some common compositional features, to American hip hop (Condry 1999). "Global pop culture," as a concept and an experience, then, ceases to have meaning when "all cultural politics is local" (Condry 2000, p. 181). Other work on European rap (Mitchell 2003), Columbian rap (Wade 1999), Gabonese rap (Auzanneau 2002), and hip hop in Sydney, Australia (Maxwell 1997), also demonstrates the possibility of describing and analyzing contemporary global trends without sacrificing either the "situated-ness" of everyday life or the "out-of-sited-ness" of media flows.

Scholars of global hip hop must resist the tendency to essentialize "local," "foreign," or "global" culture (Condry 2000, Mitchell 2001). By understanding hip hop as originating (symbolically, at least) elsewhere, mediated by global communications (including satellite, film, and the Internet, in addition to print media), but produced and signified locally (with room for variation there as well), these scholars are meeting Gupta & Ferguson's (1992) challenge to explore "the processes of production of difference in a world of culturally, socially, and economically interdependent spaces" (p. 14). The implications for the study of new technologies and language change are three. First, studying technologies with global reach and global impact does not require or justify foregoing attentiveness to situated practice and localized meaning. The term global should be understood in the sense that new communication technologies are notable for the speed with which they can transmit information around the globe. Ethnography reveals that the information itself, or the cultures it conveys, does not permeate all societies simultaneously, nor is it consumed in an identical fashion everywhere (or anywhere). The impact on language and communication of these technologies, then, is necessarily context-specific, with comparison across contexts being not only appropriate but desirable.

Second, global hip hop is not the sum total of its products: its songs, dances, and graffiti images. Focusing only on the linguistic patterns, trends, and artifacts of new technologies does little to inform us about the lived experience of communicating via these new modes. The physical, material, economic, ideological, social, and cognitive dimensions of reading, writing, speaking, and listening in technologically mediated ways are highly relevant to our emerging understanding of how these technologies affect our interactions.

Third, young is as young does. One can infer from the studies of hip hop around the world that global flows of aesthetic forms, cultural movements, and political stances (especially those mediated in some way by new technologies) are centered around youth. This seems both logical and obvious. Youth are more willing to explore new technologies, and they are prone to experimentation with the new and resistance to the conventional. But studies of global hip hop (and other aspects of global media) suggest that the social significance of these cultural phenomena need not be seen only in terms of generational issues (Ginsburg et al. 2002). This is important to bear in mind with reference to language and new technologies.

YOUTH CULTURE AND LINGUISTIC FRONTIERS

The idea of "youth" as a social category and "youth culture" as somehow distinct from the surrounding society's practices, understandings, and beliefs dates to the 1960s when North American and British social scientists became interested in drawing distinctions between cultures, subcultures, and "contracultures" (Yinger 1960, Schwartz & Merten 1967, Dorn 1969, Lewis 1976). Over time, the link between media, language, youth, and social change has become a taken-for-granted social fact (Bucholtz 2002). It stands to reason, then, that youth are the vanguard of linguistic changes resulting from new technologies (Bucholtz 2000). This assumption unfolds in the literature. For example, in discussing the language of virtual worlds on the Internet, also known as multiuser domains, Crystal notes that most users are males between the ages of 19 and 25 (Crystal 2001, p. 174). Youth identity construction through language is inextricably tied to mass media, for girls as well (Barker 1997, Currie 1997). Many other studies point to the convergence of youth, media, and linguistic change, including examinations of linguistic innovation (Roth-Gordon 2002), identity construction through "crossing" (Rampton 1995, cf. Hill 1999), slang (Sornig 1981, De Klerk 1990), and in-group codes (Eble 1996, Bucholtz 2000).

The perception that youth are on the frontier of language change could obscure other social, economic, or political fault lines that are equally important to understanding technology's impact on human interaction. One particular group of studies exemplifies both the pitfalls and the promise of exploring language change and youth: studies of hybrid language varieties in Africa. Recent studies of language change in African cities place youth—most often young men—at the center of attempts to document and analyze language varieties that can loosely be termed urban hybrids. These language varieties are best known for their incorporation of lexical material from different languages, extensive code-switching, and a young, urban orientation. Though not a vast or necessarily cohesive literature, these studies nevertheless make an important contribution to our understanding of the role youth play in linguistic change and are especially suggestive of the sometimes overlooked role of media/technology in language change.

Sociolinguistic phenomena such as language contact, creolization, and code-switching have been studied in reference to historical factors such as labor migration, racial segregation, and urbanization in different parts of Africa. Owing to South Africa's particular political and economic history, as well as to the specific contours of its academic sector, many of these studies have been based in, and on, South African language varieties. Studies of African urban hybrid languages can be divided roughly between those that are more sociolinguistic in approach and those that are more anthropological. Many studies in the first category are concerned either with classifying hybrid varieties according to established sociolinguistic categories (Janson 1984, Makhudu 1995, Ntshangase 1995, Childs 1997) or with exploring the implications of these varieties for debates related to multilingualism, such as code-switching (Myers-Scotton 1993, Slabbert & Myers-Scotton 1996, Finlayson & Slabbert 1997; see also Slabbert & Finlayson 1999 for an excellent overview), accommodation theory (Slabbert & Finlayson 2000), and diglossia (Abdulaziz & Osinde 1997).

Although these sociolinguistic studies of urban hybrids in Africa have successfully (and not without controversy) subverted the neocolonial tendency to study only the structural elements of African languages (in which languages are presumed to exist in isolation from one another), they have not given adequate attention to the social, economic, and political dynamics that underlie, and may even be driven by, these language varieties. Often short on data based on naturally occurring speech, and consequently heavily reliant on information derived from self-reported language behavior or "staged" speech, most of these studies reproduce as empirical fact the ideological assumption that urban hybrids are primarily youth-oriented codes. From an analytic perspective, this finding may point to the importance of young people's speech as the vanguard of linguistic change; from another perspective, however, it renders these language varieties irrelevant to language policy debates because they amount to little more than "kids' street slang" (McWhorter 1998).

Conversely, anthropological studies have begun considering more closely the relationship of hybrid language varieties to broader social, political, and economic shifts in urban(izing) contexts in Africa. Spitulnik's work (1996, 1998a) on language, media, and urbanization in Zambia combines analysis of the origins, uses, and characteristics of Town Bemba, an urban hybrid emanating from the capital, Lusaka, with ethnographic accounts of the media's role—specifically radio broadcasting—in altering the linguistic and communicative repertoires of Zambians. If radio is viewed as a new technology in parts of the world where it has only become prevalent in the past 50 years or so, then Spitulnik's work stands as an important example of ethnographic work on new technologies and language change that measures not only the linguistic impact of these innovations, but also the social-symbolic and political-economic aspects of new modes of communication (Spitulnik 1998b, 1998/1999, 2002).

Studies of Senagalese urban language varieties also address important theoretical issues: for instance, calling into question the theoretical premises of the code-switching debate (the presence of distinct codes versus the emergence of hybrid identities expressed in wholly new codes) (McLaughlin 2001, see also Woolard 1999), as well as pointing to the important role of global pop culture in the spread and legitimization of urban hybrids (Swigart 2001). Given the prominence of Senagalese rap on the African continent [an estimated 3000 rap crews are based in the capital Dakar alone (Kwaku 2000)], the convergence of global communications technologies, youth culture, and hybrid language varieties in Dakar offer rich grounds for ethnographic exploration. South Africa, which produces the largest number of African hip hop artists and recordings (in a form known locally—and now internationally—as *kwaito*), also offers opportunities to document the relationship between language change, generational cultures, and new means and modes of communication. Work on similar phenomena in Kenya (Samper 2002) already is beginning to document these connections and draw parallels with other parts of Africa.

Most of the above-mentioned studies of African urban hybrid languages draw a connection between these language varieties and young, usually male, speakers. Whether based on selective observations, reliance on self-reported data, or pure conjecture, this widespread assumption bears closer examination. Ethnographic approaches to communications technologies may prove useful in this regard.

Urban hybrids may be urban in an ideological, more than a geographical, sense (Cook 2002). Similarly, these varieties' relationship to maleness and youth may reflect a social, political, or economic orientation (or aspiration) more than a description of (s)he who uses them (Cook 1999). In the quest to achieve a state of modernness, "urban," "young," and "male" are often aligned in contrast to "rural," "old," and "female" (Appalraju & de Kadt 2002). Although this has important implications for understanding the significance of certain symbolic behaviors, we should not stop observing closely who is really doing what, as distinct from what people think or say they are doing. In the context of urban Africa, attention to the growth of global media and new communications technologies will likely reveal that foreign TV, film, pop music, advertising, and video games, in addition to cell phones, email, and the Internet, are implicated in the growth and spread of hybrid language varieties as much as discourses of "the street," to which much of the emergence and popularization of urban varieties has been attributed to date (McWhorter 1998, Cook 1999; see also Crane 2000, p. 92). Or perhaps there is not as radical a distinction between global media and the cultures emanating from the streets of local cities, townships, and even villages of Africa as these (often racist) discourses would have us imagine (Hill 1999).

CONCLUSION

Anthropologists have ample opportunities to investigate the ways global media, new communications technologies, and language figure into the construction of identities, advancement of political agendas, and emergence of new interactive modes. On the basis of this necessarily incomplete overview of work in related fields and disciplines, the challenge for anthropologists of language and technology clearly is, first, to adopt the broadest possible understanding of "new technologies" in order to examine not only the linguistic aspects of the techniques themselves (computers, email, World Wide Web), but also the impact of the information flows and mediascapes (Appadurai 1996) conveyed by them. Second, anthropological principles such as observing lived experience, combining different data-gathering techniques, and juxtaposing practice and ideology are important tools in the quest to achieve a multidimensional understanding of the mutually constituting relationship between technological innovation and symbolic interaction. Situated, empirically rich ethnography placed on a broad conceptual canvas can produce a deeper and more detailed picture than we have to date of the complex world of language, technology, and social change.

The *Annual Review of Anthropology* is online at http://anthro.annualreviews.org

LITERATURE CITED

Abdulaziz MH, Osinde K. 1997. Sheng and Engsh: development of mixed codes among the urban youth of Kenya. *Int. J. Soc. Lang.* 125:43–63

Appadurai A. 1996. *Modernity at Large: Cultural Dimensions of Globalization.* Minneapolis: Univ. Minn. Press

Appalraju D, de Kadt E. 2002. Gender aspects of bilingualism: language choice patterns of Zulu-speaking rural youth. *South. Afr. Ling. Appl. Lang. Stud.* 20:135–45

Auzanneau M. 2002. Rap in Libreville, Gabon: an urban sociocultural space. In *Black, Blanc, Beur: Rap Music and Hip-Hop Culture in the Francophone World*, ed. AP Durand, pp. 106–23. Latham, MD: Scarecrow

Barker C. 1997. Television and the reflexive project of the self: soaps, teenage talk and hybrid identities. *Brit. J. Sociol.* 48.4:611–28

Baron NS. 1998. Letters by phone or speech by other means: the linguistics of email. *Lang. Commun.* 18:133–70

Baron NS. 2002. Who sets e-mail style? Prescriptivism, coping strategies, and democratising communication access. *Inf. Soc.* 18: 403–13

Bucholtz M. 2000. Language and youth culture. *Am. Speech* 75.3:61–63

Bucholtz M. 2002. Youth and cultural practice. *Annu. Rev. Anthropol.* 31:525–52

Childs GT. 1997. The status of Isicamtho, an Nguni-based urban variety of Soweto. In *Pidgins and Creoles: Structure and Status*, ed.

AK Spears, D Winford, pp. 341–70. Amsterdam/Philadephia: J. Benjamins

Condry I. 1999. *Japanese rap music: an ethnography of globalization in popular culture.* PhD thesis. Yale Univ. 296 pp.

Condry I. 2000. The social production of difference: imitation and authenticity in Japanese rap music. In *Transactions, Transgressions, and Transformations*, ed. H Fehrenbach, UG Poiger, pp. 166–84. New York: Berghan Books

Cook SE. 1999. *Street Setswana: language, identity, and ideology in post-apartheid South Africa.* PhD thesis. Yale Univ. 248 pp.

Cook SE. 2002. Urban language in a rural setting: the case of Phokeng, South Africa. In *Urban Life: Readings in the Anthropology of the City*, ed. G Gmelch, WP Zenner, pp. 106–14. Prospect Heights, IL: Waveland. 4th ed.

Cortes-Conde F. 1994. English as an instrumental language: language displacement in the Anglo-Argentine community. *Biling. Rev.* 19.1:25–39

Crane D. 2000. *In medias* race: filmic representation, networked communication, and racial intermediation. See Kolko et al. 2000, pp. 87–115

Crystal D. 1997. *English as a Global Language.* Cambridge: Cambridge Univ. Press

Crystal D. 2001. *Language and the Internet.* Cambridge: Cambridge Univ. Press

Currie DH. 1997. Decoding femininity:

advertisements and their teenage readers. *Gender Soc.* 11.4:453–77

Cutting Edge Women's Res. Group, ed. 2000. *Digital Desires: Language, Identity and New Technologies.* New York: St. Martin's. 249 pp.

De Klerk V. 1990. Slang: a male domain? *Sex Roles* 22(9/10):589–606

Dickerson S. 2003. Gender differences in stories of everyday Internet use. *Health Care Women Int.* 24:434–51

Dimitriadis G. 1996. Hip hop: from live performance to mediated narrative. *Popul. Music* 15(2):179–94

Dorn DS. 1969. A partial test of the delinquency continuum typology: contracultures and subcultures. *Soc. Forces* 47.3:305–14

Eble C. 1996. *Slang and Sociability: In-Group Language Among College Students.* Chapel Hill: Univ. North Carolina Press

Economist. 2000. Fifth tongue, fifth column? Nov. 18:61

Eisenlohr P. 2004. Language revitalization and new technologies: cultures of electronic mediation and the refiguring of communities. *Annu. Rev. Anthropol.* 33:21–45

Escobar A. 1994. Welcome to Cyberia. *Curr. Anthropol.* 35(3):211–31

Ess C. 1994. The political computer: hypertext, democracy, and Habermas. In *Hyper/Text/Theory*, ed. GP Landow, pp. 225–67. Baltimore, MD: Johns Hopkins Univ. Press

Finlayson R, Slabbert S. 1997. "We just mix": code switching in a South African township. *Int. J. Soc. Lang.* 125:99–130

Ginsburg F, Abu-Lughod L, Larkin B, eds. 2002. *Media Worlds: Anthropology on New Terrain.* Berkeley: Univ. Calif. Press

Glowka AW, Melancon M, Wyckoff DC. 2003. Among the new words. *Am. Speech* 78(2):228–32

Gupta A, Ferguson J. 1992. Beyond 'culture': space, identity, and the politics of difference. *Cult. Anthropol.* 7(1):14

Gupta A, Ferguson J. 2001. Culture, power, place: ethnography at the end of an era. In *Culture, Power, Place: Explorations in Crit-ical Anthropology*, ed. A Gupta, J Ferguson, pp. 1–29. Durham: Duke Univ. Press. 3rd ed.

Herring SC. 1993. Gender and democracy in computer-mediated communication. *Commun. Inst. Online Scholarsh.* comserve@cios.org

Herring SC, Johnson D, DiBenedetto T. 1995. "This discussion is going too far!": Male resistance to female participation on the Internet. In *Gender Articulated: Language and the Socially Constructed Self*, ed. K Hall, M Bucholtz, pp. 67–96. New York: Routledge. 512 pp.

Hill J. 1999. Styling locally, styling globally: What does it mean? *J. Socioling.* 3/4:542–56

Jacobs-Huey L. 2004. BTW, How do YOU wear your hair: establishing racial identity, consciousness and community in an African American listserv group. In *Computer-Mediated Conversation*, ed. S. Herring. Cresskill, NJ: Hampton press. In press

Janson T. 1984. *A language of Sophiatown, Alexandra, and Soweto.* York Creole Conf., York Pap. Ling. 11, Dep. Lang., Univ. York

Judy RAT. 1997. On the politics of global language, or unfungible local value. *Boundary 2* 24(2):101–43

Judy RAT. 1999. Some notes on the status of global English in Tunisia. *Boundary 2.* 26(2):3–29

Kadende-Kaiser RM. 1999. Interpreting language and cultural discourse: Internet communication among Burundians in the diaspora. *Afr. Today* 47(2):121–48

Kolko BE, Nakamura L, Rodman GB, eds. 2000. *Race in Cyberspace.* New York: Routledge. 248 pp.

Kwaku. 2000. African hip-hop getting web exposure. *Billboard* Dec. 23:23

Laden S. 2001. "Making the paper speak well," or, the pace of change in consumer magazines for black South Africans. *Poetics Today* 22(2):515–47

Lenhart A. 2003. The ever-shifting Internet population: a new look at Internet access and the digital divide. *Pew Internet Am. Life Proj.* http://www.pewinternet.org

Lewis GH. 1976. The structure of support in social movements: an analysis of organization and resources mobilization in the youth contra-culture. *Br. J. Sociol.* 27.2:184–96

Lockard J. 2000. Babel machines and electronic universalism. See Kolko et al. 2000, pp. 171–89

Makhudu KDP. 1995. An introduction to Flaaitaal. See Mesthrie 1995, pp. 298–305

Maxwell I. 1997. Hip hop aesthetics and the will to culture. *Aust. J. Anthropol.* 8(1):50–71

McLaughlin F. 2001. Dakar Wolof and the configuration of an urban identity. *J. Afr. Cult. Stud.* 14(2):153–72

McWhorter J. 1998. *The Word on the Street: Fact and Fable About American English.* New York: Plenum Trade

Mesthrie R, ed. 1995. *Language and Social History: Studies in South African Sociolinguistics.* Cape Town: David Philip

Mitchell T, ed. 2001. *Global Noise: Rap and Hip-Hop Outside the USA.* Middletown, CT: Wesleyan Univ. Press. 336 pp.

Mitchell T. 2003. Doin' damage in my native language: the use of "resistance vernaculars" in hip hop in France, Italy, and Aotearoa/New Zealand. In *Global Pop, Local Language*, ed. HM Berger, MT Carroll, pp. 3–18. Jackson: Univ. Press Miss. 352 pp.

Myers-Scotton C. 1993. *Social Motivations for Codeswitching: Evidence from Africa.* Oxford: Clarendon Press

Nakamura L. 1999. Race in/for cyberspace: identity tourism and racial passing on the Internet. In *CyberReader*, ed. V Vitanza. Boston: Allyn and Bacon. 2nd ed.

Nelson TH. 1974. Dream machines: new freedoms through computer screens—a minority report. In *Computer Lib: You Can and Must Understand Computers Now.* Chicago: Hugo's Book Service

Ntshangase DK. 1995. Indaba yami I-straight: language and language practices in Soweto. See Mesthrie 1995, pp. 291–97

Paolillo J. 2001. Language variation on Internet relay chat: a social network approach. *J. Socioling.* 5(2):180–213

Rampton B. 1995. *Crossing: Language and Identity Among Adolescents.* London: Longman

Richardson K. 2001. Risk news in the world of Internet newsgroups. *J. Socioling.* 5(1):50–72

Ronkin M, Karn H. 1999. Mock Ebonics: linguistic racism in parodies of Ebonics on the Internet. *J. Socioling.* 3:360–79

Roth-Gordon J. 2002. *Slang and the struggle over meaning: race, language, and power in Brazil.* PhD thesis, Stanford Univ.

Samper DA. 2002. *Talking Sheng: the role of a hybrid language in the construction of identity and youth culture in Nairobi, Kenya.* PhD thesis, Univ. Penn.

Schwartz G, Merten D. 1967. The language of adolescence: an anthropological approach to the youth culture. *Am. J. Sociol.* 72(5):453–68

Shaw LH, Gant LM. 2002. Users divided? Exploring the gender gap in Internet use. *CyberPsychol. Behav.* 5(6):517–28

Slabbert S, Finlayson R. 1999. A sociohistorical overview of codeswitching studies in the African languages. *S. Afr. J. Afr. Lang.* 19.1:60–73

Slabbert S, Finlayson R. 2000. "I'm a cleva!": the linguistic makeup of identity in a South African urban environment. *Int. J. Soc. Lang.* 144:119–35

Slabbert S, Myers-Scotton C. 1996. The structure of Tsotsitaal and Iscamtho: code switching and in-group identity in South African townships. *Linguistics* 34:317–42

Smith J, Balka E. 1991. Chatting on a feminist computer network. In *Technology and Women's Voices*, ed. C Kramerae, pp. 82–97. New York: Routledge & Kegan Paul

Smitherman G. 1997. "The chain remain the same": communicative practices in the hip hop nation. *J. Black Stud.* 28.1:3–25

Sornig K. 1981. *Lexical Innovation: A Study of Slang, Colloquialisms and Casual Speech.* Amsterdam: Benjamins B.V.

Spitulnik D. 1996. The social circulation of media discourse and the mediation of communities. *J. Ling. Anthropol.* 6(2):161–87

Spitulnik D. 1998a. The language of the city: Town Bemba as urban hybridity. *J. Ling. Anthropol.* 8(1):30–59

Spitulnik D. 1998b. Mediating unity and diversity: the production of language ideologies in Zambian broadcasting. In *Language Ideologies: Practice and Theory*, ed. B Schieffelin, K Woolard, P Kroskrity, pp. 163–88. Oxford: Oxford Univ. Press

Spitulnik D. 1998/1999. Mediated modernities: encounters with the electronic in Zambia. *Vis. Anthropol. Rev.* 14(2):63–84

Spitulnik D. 2002. Mobile machines and fluid audiences: rethinking reception through Zambian radio culture. In *Media Worlds: Anthropology on New Terrain*, ed. F Ginsburg, L Abu-Lughod, B Larkin, pp. 337–54. Berkeley/Los Angeles: Univ. Calif. Press

Swigart L. 2001. The limits of legitimacy: language ideology and shift in contemporary Senegal. *J. Ling. Anthropol.* 10(1):90–130

Tagliamonte S, Hudson R. 1999. Be like et al. beyond America: the quotatative system in British and Canadian Youth (N1). *J. Socioling.* 3(2):147–72

Thomson R, Murachver T, Green J. 2001. Where is the gender in gendered language? *Psychol. Sci.* 12.2:171–75

Tsuda Y. 1997. Hegemony of English versus ecology of language: building equality in international communication. In *World Englishes 2000*, ed. LE Smith, ML Forman, pp. 21–31. Honolulu: Coll. Lang., Ling., Lit., Univ. Hawaii

Wade P. 1999. Working culture: making cultural identities in Cali, Colombia. *Curr. Anthropol.* 40.4:449–71

Warschauer M. 2000. Language, identity, and the Internet. See Kolko et al. 2000, pp. 151–70

Waskul D, Douglass M. 1997. Cyberself: the emergence of self in on-line chat. *Inf. Soc.* 13(4):375–98

Wilson SM, Peterson LC. 2002. The anthropology of online communities. *Annu. Rev. Anthropol.* 31:449–60

Woolard K. 1999. Simultaneity and bivalency as strategies in bilingualism. *J. Ling. Anthropol.* 8:3–29

Yinger JM. 1960. Contraculture and subculture. *Am. Sociol. Rev.* 25(5):625–35

Annu. Rev. Anthropol. 2004. 33:117–43
doi: 10.1146/annurev.anthro.32.061002.093421

THE GLOBALIZATION OF PENTECOSTAL AND CHARISMATIC CHRISTIANITY

Joel Robbins

Department of Anthropology, University of California, San Diego, La Jolla, California 92093-0532; email: jrobbins@weber.ucsd.edu

Key Words Pentecostalism, religion, cultural change, modernity

■ **Abstract** Pentecostal-charismatic Christianity (P/c), the form of Christianity in which believers receive the gifts of the Holy Spirit, is rapidly spreading and can be counted as one of the great success stories of the current era of cultural globalization. Literature on P/c presents a paradoxical picture of the cultural dynamics accompanying its spread. Many scholars argue that P/c is markedly successful in replicating itself in canonical form everywhere it spreads, whereas others stress its ability to adapt itself to the cultures into which it is introduced. Authors thus use P/c to support both theories that construe globalization as a process of Westernizing homogenization and those that understand it as a process of indigenizing differentiation. This review argues that approaches to P/c globalization need to recognize that P/c posesses cultural features that allow it, in most cases, to work in both ways at once. After considering definitional and historical issues and explanations for P/c's spread, the review examines how P/c culture at once preserves its distinctness from the cultures into which it comes into contact and engages those cultures on their own terms. Also discussed are the conceptions that allow P/c to establish locally run and supported institutions in a wide range of settings. A final section considers the nature of the culture P/c, in its homogenizing guise, introduces, examining that culture's relation to modernity and its effects on converts' ideas about gender, politics, and economics.

INTRODUCTION

The form of Christianity in which believers receive the gifts of the Holy Spirit and have ecstatic experiences such as speaking in tongues, healing, and prophesying is one of the great success stories of the current era of cultural globalization. Commonly called Pentecostal-charismatic Christianity (P/c), its origin can be traced to early twentieth-century developments within Christianity in the West, particularly in North America. Yet despite its originally Western provenience, just a hundred years after its birth two thirds of P/c's 523 million adherents live outside the West in areas such as Africa, Latin America, Asia, and Oceania, as do most of the nine million people who convert to it each year (Barrett & Johnson 2002,

0084-6570/04/1021-0117$14.00 **117**

p. 284). Although some question these statistics (Corten 1997, p. 313; Levine 1995, p. 157; Stoll 1990, p. 6), even conservative estimates see the P/c movement as having at least 250 million adherents worldwide, and all agree that its most explosive growth has occurred in the southern hemisphere (Martin 2002, p. xvii). This growth has made P/c the "the most dynamic and fastest growing sector of Protestant Christianity worldwide" and one that many predict will soon surpass Catholicism "to become the predominant global form of Christianity of the 21st century" (Casanova 2001, p. 435).

P/c's success as a globalizing movement is attested to not only by its rapid growth, but also by the range of social contexts to which it has spread. Appearing throughout the world in urban and rural areas, among emerging middle classes and, most spectacularly, among the poor, it has been deeply engaged by many populations that otherwise remain only peripherally or tenuously involved with other global cultural forms. As such, P/c represents a paradigm case of a global cultural flow that starts historically in the West and expands to cover the globe.

In recent decades anthropologists and other scholars have begun to register the global impact of P/c. A number of edited volumes taking regional or comparative approaches have appeared (Boudewijnse et al. 1998, Cleary & Stewart-Gambino 1997, Coleman 2002a, Corten & Marshall-Fratani 2001b, Dow & Sandstrom 2001, Garrard-Burnett & Stoll 1993, Glazier 1980, Hunt et al. 1997b, Poewe 1994, Robbins et al. 2001), as have several widely read synthetic accounts (Brouwer et al. 1996; Cox 1995; Hollenweger 1972, 1997; Jenkins 2002; Martin 1990, 2002). All of these works make the global spread of P/c central to their discussions. What is striking, however, is the apparently paradoxical picture these and other works present of the spread of P/c as a cultural process. On the one hand, many argue that P/c consistently replicates its doctrines, organizational features, and rituals in canonical, Western form wherever it is introduced. Lehmann (2003, p. 121), for example, notes that P/c churches are "notoriously uniform across the globe" and that they display a "radical similarity of practice" despite the radical "dissimilarity" of the contexts in which they appear (see also Berger 1990, p. vii; Brouwer et al. 1996, p. 179; Coleman 2000, p. 67; d'Epinay 1969, p. xxxii; Lehmann 1996, p. 8; Lyon 2000, p. 102; Meyer 1999a, p. 159; Olson 2001, p. 24; Robbins 2001a; Smilde 1997, p. 347). On the other hand, many authors, including many of those who remark on P/c's ability to replicate itself successfully in different cultures, stress that converts are quick to indigenize P/c forms of Christianity, and they credit these churches with a remarkable ability to adapt themselves to the cultures into which they are introduced (Bastian 1993, Manning 1980). In terms of debates on cultural globalization, then, P/c appears to weigh in both for theories that stress processes of Western cultural domination and homogenization and those that emphasize the transformative power of indigenous appropriation and differentiation (Robbins 2003).

In response to such seemingly contradictory assertions, it is hard to dispute Corten's (1997) claim that the study of the cultural processes underlying P/c's spread has been beset by a "lack of precision" (p. 321). As an initial remedy, one might be tempted to refuse the distinction between indigenizing differentiation and globalizing homogenization and instead construe the globalization of Pentecostalism as a prime example of a widespread kind of cultural hybridization poorly captured by either of these alternatives. Yet, in reviewing the P/c literature, it is more productive to note how important these two frameworks of interpretation have been and ask what about P/c Christianity leads it to globalize in a way that appears to fit both of them (cf. Casanova 2001). Following Droogers' (2001) call that scholars attend to the "specific characteristics of Pentecostalism" (p. 41) in discussing its globalization, I assume that specific elements of P/c culture have steered its globalization in this paradoxical direction. After a section defining P/c and briefly recounting its history, and another considering explanations for its growth, I focus on issues of globalization in three sections: one on world-breaking that examines how P/c introduces its own cultural logics while also preserving those of people's traditional cultures; a second on world-making that considers how P/c's globally diffused cultural form establishes churches that are organizationally local and responsive to local cultural concerns; and a third that takes up the relation of P/c to the globalization of modernity by examining its impact in the three well-studied spheres of gender relations, political engagement, and economic behavior.

HISTORICAL AND DEFINITIONAL ISSUES

There is little standardization in social scientific usages of terms such as Pentecostal and charismatic, and several scholars have worried that these terms have become so broad as to be meaningless (Corten & Marshall-Fratani 2001b, p. 4; Droogers 2001, p. 46; Kamsteeg 1998, pp. 10–11). The problem stems from at least two sources. First, all of the terms social scientists use as analytic categories (Pentecostalism, charismatic Christianity, fundamentalism, evangelicalism, etc.) are also folk terms possessed of a wide range of meanings (Kamsteeg 1998, pp. 9–10). Scholars often employ the folk terms used by the groups they study, mistakenly assuming that local meanings will be widely understood by those working elsewhere. In the literature on Spanish-speaking Latin America, for example, scholars often translate the folk term *evangélico* as "evangelical" even when it is clear that the groups they are discussing are best understood, for comparative purposes, as P/c (Annis 1987, p. 76; Brusco 1995, pp. 14–15; Kamsteeg 1998, pp. 9–10; Smilde 1998, p. 287).

A second reason for terminological confusion among social scientists is their lack of attention to P/c's history. Although a basic historical sketch cannot solve all definitional problems, it can establish some useful terminological parameters.

Pentecostalism's roots lie in the Protestant evangelical tradition that grew out of the eighteenth–century, Anglo-American revival movement known as the Great Awakening. Evangelical Christianity, which includes such denominations as Methodists and Baptists, is marked by its emphasis on conversion. People are not born into the evangelical faith but must "voluntarily" choose it on the basis of powerful conversion experiences (often glossed as being "born again"). Because evangelicals believe this experience is available to everyone, they strongly emphasize the importance of evangelistic efforts to convert others. They also hold the Bible in high regard as a text possessed of the highest religious authority and often endeavor to read it in what they take to be literal terms (Noll 2001).

During the nineteenth century, Methodism was the most important evangelical denomination in North America. It was distinguished from others by its doctrine of "Christian perfection" or "sanctification." This doctrine holds that the saved will experience a "second blessing" or "second work of grace" after that of conversion during which the inbred sin people carry, owing to Adam's fall, is removed. In the second half of the nineteenth century, a largely Methodist Holiness movement arose around groups that experimented with different understandings of the nature and number of postconversion experiences that affected a person's salvation. Some Holiness groups understood sanctification, often referred to as "baptism in the Holy Spirit," as the removal of sin, though others saw it as giving converts an "endeument of power" for Christian service, particularly for evangelism. To these ideas, Holiness followers added a commitment to a form of Christian millenarianism known as dispensational premillennialism and an emphasis on faith healing (Anderson 1979; Synan 1997; Wacker 1988, pp. 935–36).

Pentecostalism was born from the ferment of Holiness efforts to work out a stable form of frankly supernatural and experientially robust Christianity around the notion of the second blessing of the Spirit. Its primary innovation was to see speaking in tongues as the necessary "initial physical evidence" of Spirit baptism. Credit for this innovation belongs to Charles Fox Parham, a Holiness preacher who made it central to his teaching from 1900 on. William Seymour, an African American itinerant holiness preacher from Louisiana, was one of his students. After a brief period of study, Seymour moved to Los Angles in 1906, where he eventually opened a ministry in an abandoned African Methodist Episcopal Church on Azusa Street. The revival his Asuza Street preaching initiated is widely recognized as the birth of Pentecostalism.

The Asuza Street revival lasted from 1906 to 1909. Along with the doctrine of tongues, Seymour and others promoted a model of ecstatic Christian life based on the experience of the Apostles during the original Pentecost as reported in Acts 2. Synan (1997, p. 98) describes the scene at Asuza Street:

> Men and women would shout, weep, dance, fall into trances, speak and sing in tongues, and interpret their messages into English. In true Quaker fashion, anyone who felt "moved by the Spirit" would preach or sing. There was no robed choir, no hymnals, no order of services, but there was an abundance of religious enthusiasm.

This pattern of enthusiastic worship, relatively unscripted and egalitarian in offering the floor to all those who the Spirit calls, is the one observers would find all over the world by the end of the twentieth century.

Aside from its emphasis on tongues, Pentecostal doctrine bears much in common with that of the Holiness tradition from which it developed. Sometimes described as the fourfold, foursquare, or "full gospel" pattern of Pentecostal theology, it stresses that (*a*) Jesus offers salvation; (*b*) Jesus heals; (*c*) Jesus baptizes with the Holy Spirit; (*d*) Jesus is coming again (Dayton 1987, pp. 19–23). Along with a strict moralism, these are the core Pentecostal doctrines, and they are the elements of the religion that have proved immensely portable, seemingly able to enter any number of cultural contexts without losing their basic shape.[1]

From the beginning of the revival, Pentecostalism rapidly spread throughout the world and in time established such major denominations as the Assemblies of God (AOG), the Church of God in Christ, and the Church of God (Cleveland), as well as such para-church organizations as the Full Gospel Business Men's Fellowship International. The most momentous event in the history of P/c after Asuza Street came around 1960 with the opening up of the mainline Protestant churches to the gifts of the Spirit. Prior to this time, members of non-Pentecostal churches who experienced Spirit baptism, spoke in tongues, or received other gifts of the Spirit were usually compelled to leave their churches and join Pentecostal ones. But once what became known as the neo-Pentecostal or charismatic movement began to spread, those who had received gifts of the Spirit retained membership in mainline churches and often formed charismatic subgroups within them. By 1970, it was estimated that 10% of clergy and one million lay members of mainline Protestant churches had received the baptism of the Spirit (Synan 1997, p. 233). And in 1967, the charismatic movement also entered Catholicism, and Catholics who received the gifts of the Spirit began staying in their churches and calling themselves Pentecostal or charismatic Catholics (Csordas 1994, McGuire 1982). In keeping with this history, the term charismatic Christian has come to refer to members of non-Pentecostal denominations who believe the gifts of the Spirit are available to contemporary believers.

Since 1970, the charismatic movement has spawned a large number of what many call third-wave or neo-charismatic churches (Miller 1997; Synan 1997, pp. 271–72). Often independent of larger denominations, these churches affirm the availability of the gifts of the Spirit but refuse either the Pentecostal or charismatic label.

The charismatic and neo-charismatic movements differ in several ways from what has come to be called classical Pentecostalism. They often drop the requirement that one speak in tongues to prove one's Spirit baptism and moderate the ascetic moralism of the classical Pentecostal churches, some even allowing members to drink wine or wear jewelry (Synan 1997, pp. 253–54). Both changes are

---

[1]Of the core doctrines, millenarianism is the most variable in its presence in different historical and cultural milieus (Dayton 1987, p. 33). In some places, such as Oceania (Douglas 2001), it is very prominent, whereas in other places, such as Africa and Latin America, it is less so. Finding explanations for the pattern of its presence and absence both historically and cross-culturally is an outstanding issue in Pentecostal studies.

correlated with a generally higher-social-class location, as these movements draw primarily from the established or emerging middle classes of the societies in which they are located (Freston 1997, pp. 187–88; Hallum 2002, p. 227; Hunt et al. 1997b, p. 7; Ojo 1988).

Possessed of middle-class leadership with the educational and financial resources to formulate and project their own visions, the charismatic and neo-charismatic movements have proven to be hotbeds for doctrinal innovation, and many new ideas generated within them play important roles in the contemporary globalization of P/c. For example, the Faith Movement, which promotes the "health and wealth" or "prosperity" gospel, has spread a set of doctrines promising believers both physical health and material success on earth (Coleman 2000, 2002b). North American in origin, the movement has had striking success in parts of Europe, Africa, and Latin America (Corten & Marshall-Fratani 2001b, Gifford 2001, Hunt 2000). Another neo-Charismatic doctrine enjoying worldwide popularity is that of spiritual warfare, which encourages believers to view daily life as dominated by an ongoing struggle between God and local, demonic "territorial spirits," and which often promotes rituals of "deliverance" designed to rid believers of demonic influence (DeBernardi 1999, Gifford 2001, Stritecky 2001).

This historical account has barely touched on the wide variation in aspects of P/c church structure, doctrine, and practice. The great range of churches grouped under the P/c rubric needs to be remembered when evaluating statistics on the size of the P/c movement. It also raises the question of whether it makes analytic sense to lump all of these churches together. Many scholars assume that it does make sense on the basis of their common features, most notably their shared emphasis on ecstatic experiences that are available to all believers. This review takes this tack and tests the value of treating P/c churches as members of a single category for the purpose of examining how they have globalized. Yet as Willems (1967, p. 257) noted long ago, there is also room for work that looks comparatively at what distinguishes churches within the movement, and systematic social scientific (as opposed to theological) work in this area has hardly begun (see Chesnut 1997; Englund 2001; Kamsteeg 1998, p. 234; Lehmann 2001; Marshall 1993).

As broad a category as P/c is, it should be distinguished from Christian fundamentalism. Pentecostalism and fundamentalism both are elements of the broader evangelical movement and both emerged in the early twentieth century. As such, they share general evangelical features such as conversionism, respect for the Bible, and ascetic tendencies. These similarities sometimes lead even well-informed scholars to treat Pentecostalism as a branch of fundamentalism (e.g., Stoll 1990, p. 49). But even as it makes sense in some analytic contexts for scholars to group P/c and Christian Fundamentalism together as brands of conservative Christianity (Woodberry & Smith 1998), it is both a historical and an analytic mistake to assume they are the same (Cox 1997; Freston 2001, p. 288; Hackett 1995, p. 200; Spittler 1994).

On the historical side, fundamentalists, relying on the widespread doctrine that the gifts of the Spirit ceased to be available to people after they were given to the Apostles during the original Pentecost, from the outset firmly rejected Pentecostalism (Cox 1995, pp. 74–76; Spittler 1994, pp. 108–10). Fundamentalists today cling to this rejection (e.g., Harding 2000, pp. 19, 140–41). Less concerned with boundary maintenance, Pentecostals are not as vociferous in their rejection of fundamentalism, but they too recognize the distinction.

Scholars have yet to determine the precise historical reasons for the fundamentalist rejection of Pentecostalism (Riesebrodt 1993). However, several analysts point to cultural differences between the two movements that suggest reasons for their incompatibility and indicate the analytic reasons it is useful to distinguish them. Cox (1995) distinguishes between "fundamentalist" religions focused on doctrinal purity and "experientialist" ones that stress the ability of followers to experience the transcendent. Although he argues that these two tendencies struggle for dominance in contemporary P/c, he admits that historically P/c has been experientialist, and others have used this distinction to distinguish P/c from fundamentalist Christianity (Corten 1997, p. 312; Corten & Marshal-Fratani 2001b, p. 5; Cox 1995, pp. 310, 319). Riesebrodt (1993, pp. 45–46) offers a second distinction, noting that fundamentalists take as the sign of their salvation their ability to live by a strict ethical code, a stance challenged by P/c Christians who find their assurance in ecstatic experience (see also Ammerman 1987). Finally, Martin (1990, 2002) notes that fundamentalists aim to remake the political sphere along religious lines, whereas P/c Christians tend to withdraw from politics and thus to respect the modern separation of church and state. For Martin, this is part of a broader argument that fundamentalists react against modernity, whereas P/c Christians find ways to work within it.

EXPLAINING P/c GROWTH: BEYOND DEPRIVATION AND DISORGANIZATION

The rapid growth and worldwide spread of P/c regularly inspire scholars to ask why it attracts so many converts. Their answers routinely deploy broad sociological arguments about the role of deprivation and anomie in fostering the growth of ecstatic, sectarian, and millenarian religious movements. This section focuses on what such explanations overlook, suggesting that those who use them ignore important aspects of P/c culture and that their narrow emphasis on explaining the *why* of conversion leads them to disregard the question of *how* P/c transforms the cultures into which it is introduced.

This is not to say that deprivation and disorganization arguments are without value. The majority of Azusa Street converts, like the majority of converts in Latin America, Africa, and elsewhere, have been rural migrants to cities, people at the lower end of the social class scale, or rural stay-at-homes displaced from the center of their own worlds by social change (Martin 1990, pp. 190–91). To displaced people, unsure of their social links and morally adrift, P/c's formation of tight communities around a high-intensity, time-consuming ritual life (services in these churches rarely last less that two hours and sometimes go most of the night) and a collectively policed ascetic moral code surely provides a social foundation and sense of direction. To the deprived, those who feel they are not getting their lot in life, P/c offers ecstatic escape, hope for millennial redress, and an egalitarian environment in which everyone is eligible for the highest religious rewards (i.e., salvation and the gifts of the Spirit). Many of the early classics in P/c history and ethnography convincingly deployed these kinds of disorganization and deprivation arguments (e.g., Anderson 1979, d'Epinay 1969, Willems 1967), and these arguments have become so much the common sense of the P/c literature that most works draw on them at least implicitly.

Yet even as deprivation and disorganization arguments are regularly used, they are widely criticized in the P/c literature, and beyond, for attempting to explain a narrower phenomenon (conversion) with a wider one (absolute or felt deprivation or anomie) and for the tautological ways scholars often deploy them (making the fact of conversion the proof of prior experiences of deprivation or anomie) (Chesnut 1997; Gerlach & Hine 1970; Hine 1974; Heelas & Haglund-Heelas 1988; Holston 1999; Hunt 2002a,b; Wacker 1982). Scholars also have taken these arguments to task for failing to give a place to native models of the conversion process (Brodwin 2003, 87; Levine 1995, p. 166; Wacker 2001, p. 60). Even in the face of such criticisms, no one denies that these explanations do tell part of the conversion story in many cases. Yet these criticisms do reveal that there are aspects of P/c Christianity other than those highlighted by deprivation and disorganization arguments, and they suggest that in many cases these neglected aspects of P/c Christianity are important for understanding its growth and global development.

Foremost among these neglected aspects is the paramount importance P/c churches place on evangelization, encouraging all members to act as evangelists working to convert others. The emphasis on outreach was apparent from the start of the movement, with visitors to Asuza Street carrying the message all over North America and the world almost from the outset of the revival (Cox 1995, pp. 101–2, McGee 2001, p. 73). The P/c emphasis on evangelism is also a mainstay of the cross-cultural literature, in which reports of recent converts becoming evangelists are common, and a pattern has been well established in which the movement spreads by indigenous channels (e.g., local evangelists, street-corner preaching, returning labor migrants) as soon as a first group has converted (Annis 1987, pp. 77, 106; Bowen 1996, p. 41; Chesnut 1997, pp. 138–39; Kamsteeg 1998, p. 68; d'Epinay 1969, p. 55; Lehmann 2001, p. 63; Stoll 1990; Martin 1990, p. 121).

Given that evangelization is the most important activity in P/c culture, as d'Epinay (1969, p. 55) and Blumhofer (1993, pp. 208–9) argue, one can say that the culture is rationalized around the value accorded to it. On the level of doctrine, such rationalization in evident in the belief that anyone inspired by the Spirit can evangelize regardless of educational qualifications, a belief that encourages all converts to see themselves as evangelists (Willems 1967). The Spirit is also expected to sustain evangelists, and all over the world people "go out on faith" as missionaries and evangelists, asking for no funding from their home congregations and assuming that if they are truly inspired they will succeed in building churches whose tithes will sustain them (Blumhofer 1993; Stoll 1990, p. 127; Wacker 2001, pp. 130–31).

The egalitarianism of P/c doctrine also supports evangelical efforts as it aids evangelists in attracting a following. Led by an African American preacher and attended by many whites, Asians, and Latinos the Azusa Street mission was, at its outset, strikingly integrated, and on the assumption that all are equal when used by the Spirit it was notable for its openness to letting African Americans and women speak at services (Anderson 1979, p. 69; Synan 1997, p. 99; Wacker 2001, pp. 103–5, 144). Although racial divisions were reinstated in North America as the Pentecostal church grew, P/c has continued to feature its egalitarian inspirational logic both in its outreach, which is often to the poor or otherwise marginalized, and in the life it offers its converts, who are encouraged to see their most important identity not as one of class, race, gender, or ethnicity, but as children of God (Burdick 1998, p. 123; Freston 1998, p. 81; Robbins 1998). Burdick (1993, p. 172) highlights the force of P/c egalitarianism as an evangelistic tool, noting that in Brazil *negros* are flattered when light-skinned evangelists speak to them on the street, and if they attend church they are further impressed by the number of negros in the congregation, some serving as preachers. From the point of view of evangelism, P/c egalitarianism both makes the field of potential converts truly universal and serves as an important ground for appealing to the unconverted.

To the doctrinal factors that fit P/c for evangelization must be added the contribution of P/c's distinctive social organization. P/c Christians are a far-flung network of people held together by their publications and other media productions, conferences, revival meetings, and constant travel. Gerlach & Hine (1970), the first to give this point due emphasis, describe the organization of global P/c as decentralized, segmentary, and reticulate. It is characterized both by a lack of centralized authority able to question the propriety of local evangelical efforts and by a web-like structure of personal connections that allows members to easily find support in new locales they enter for evangelical purposes. Histories of early Pentecostalism are rich in data on how these networks functioned to promote evangelism (e.g., Blumhofer 1993, Synan 1997), and similar networks today support the globe-trotting efforts of well-known evangelists and the more limited but equally important evangelizing circuits of countless lesser-known P/c Christians operating at all scales throughout the world. Coleman (2000) examines in detail the shape of one of these networks and the conferences, media productions, and ideas about language and exchange that underpin it (see also Csordas 1992). Further work is needed on how such networks function and particularly on the role P/c uses of media have played and continue to play within them (Anderson 1979, Hackett 1998).

Turning from evangelism, another factor in P/c's success often underplayed in deprivation and disorganization accounts is the appeal of its ritual life. As Brouwer et al. (1996) state, "one of the greatest appeals of the new Pentecostal groups is the manner of worship. Services appear spontaneous, experiential and exuberant" (p. 179). They have an eventful quality, with people waiting to see what the Spirit will do (Corten 1999, pp. 42–43; d'Epinay 1969, pp. 52–53), and they often erase older boundaries between worship and leisure (Burdick 1993, p. 87). Many people are compelled to attend services, revivals, and other ritualized gatherings by a "spiritual acquisitiveness" generated in them that presses believers "relentlessly on to the next experience" (Blumhofer 1993, pp. 210–11). These ecstatic rituals clearly are, in part, a counterpoint to the ascetic lives converts are enjoined to live outside of religious contexts, and their structures frequently reiterate the alternation of control and release (Kiernan 1976; McGuire 1982; Robbins 2004; Stringer 1999, p. 159; cf. Thompson 1966, pp. 368–69). Further examination of P/c ritual life focused on the ways it engages issues of the management liberation and constraint in the face of modernizing cultural change would be valuable. Yet despite its widely acknowledged importance, detailed study of P/c ritual is notably scarce in the literature. From an anthropological perspective, it represents probably the greatest lacuna in the work done thus far.

A final explanation for the rapid global spread of P/c Christianity neglected in deprivation and disorganization accounts begins with the argument that African religious elements, as mediated through African American culture, have been part of P/c's composition from the outset (MacRobert 1988). Hollenweger (1984, p. 405), the dean of Pentecostal historians, singles out the "black roots" of P/c as the most important reason for P/c's growth. These roots show in P/c's "orality of liturgy," "narrativity of theology and witness," emphasis on participation, use of dreams and visions in worship, and model of mind/body correspondence that promotes healing by prayer. Other influential scholars have developed related ideas to suggest that P/c Christianity expands because it is connected to "a kind of primal spirituality" made up of "archetypal modes of worship, elements that lie close to the surface in some cultures but are buried more deeply in others" (Cox 1995, pp. 101–2; Martin 1990). From an anthropological perspective, these arguments skate close to a kind of generic primitivism and at least implicitly invoke binaries the discipline no longer charters.

Yet even as most anthropologists step back from the "mythic" framings of these arguments (Corten 1997, pp. 313, 321), it is important to recognize that many of them promulgate similar forms of cultural explanation when they assert that P/c proves attractive to people around the world because it embraces enchanted and ecstatic cultural forms very much like their own. Such claims underwrite much of the work that sees P/c as highly malleable and quick to localize because it is extraordinarily open to syncretizing with indigenous forms of worship.

On close inspection, however, these more anthropologically acceptable arguments often prove to be as troublesomely broad and insensitive to the nuances of cultural dynamics as their less acceptable cousins. To begin with, they assume ecstatic experience is generic, such that, for example, possession is possession regardless of its cultural framings. They also overlook the very conscious antisyncretism of most P/c adherents, who are quick to point out that any resemblance between P/c and traditional practice is illusory (Corten 1997, p. 312; Dombrowski 2001, p. 153). Finally, they fail to register the sense in which P/c accepts local enchanted cosmologies only to attack them, thus profoundly altering the way they are understood (e.g., Maxwell 1999, pp. 195–96; Robbins 2003, p. 223). These and related cultural dynamics, dynamics that arguments for easy local cultural assimilation based on similarity often overlook, are precisely what give P/c cultural globalization its distinct profile, and they are the focus of the next section.

WORLD-BREAKING: DUALISM, ASCETICISM, AND ONTOLOGICAL PRESERVATION

Martin (1990) argues that the P/c symbolic world is "integrated around the key notion of transformation" (p. 163). True in almost all cases,[2] the kind of transformation involved is a radical one that separates people both from their pasts and from the surrounding social world. This is why Burdick (1993) calls P/c not just a "cult of transformation" but also one of "discontinuity" (p. 224). Converts are routinely enjoined, as Meyer (1998) found in Ghana, to make a complete break with their pasts, and as Gill (1990, p. 714) reports from Bolivia they sharply distinguish between their pre- and postconversion lives. Similarly, once they make the break, they keep themselves separate from the surrounding social world by adhering to an ascetic moral code that prohibits most of its pleasures and figures it as a realm governed by Satan.

P/c discourse is littered with images of rupture and discontinuity. This emphasis on discontinuity is an important part of how P/c globalizes. Its commitment to schemes of discontinuous transformation effectively makes it, as Dombrowski (2001) aptly puts it, a culture "against culture." All conversionist religions share this concern for transformation to some extent. But the literature suggests four ways the P/c approach to transformation is distinctive: P/c elaborately ritualizes discontinuity; it maintains discontinuity through an ascetic code embedded in a thoroughgoing dualism of great hermeneutic force; it preserves that which it breaks from; and its dualism provides a flexible language of satanic influence that is very sensitive to local social concerns. I address each of these topics in turn.

Baptism is an important ritual of discontinuity in Christian traditions that emphasize adult conversion, and it is in P/c as well (Maxwell 1999, p. 68). Yet P/c also offers a host of postconversion rituals aimed at deepening the break made at conversion. Thoroughgoing in their emphasis on disjunction, these varied rites

---

[2]Though not discussed in detail here, the one exception would be charismatic Catholicism, for which McGuire (1982, p. 50) notes an emphasis on continuity in the rhetoric of conversion, and Csordas (1994) offers accounts of rituals for healing memories and healing ancestry that recuperate the past. In this emphasis on continuity, charismatic Catholicism is likely influenced by a tendency in this direction in Catholicism more generally (Burdick 1993, p. 151; Lester 2003).

can be grouped as "rituals of rupture" that ground the P/c concern with discontinuity in ritually effective action (Robbins 2003, pp. 224–27). The baptism of the Spirit, understood as annulling the influence of Adam's sin, is perhaps the prototype. Other examples of formal techniques P/c has developed to help people break with their pasts include the deliverance rituals by which Ewe Pentecostals in Ghana seek to rid themselves of the demonic influences brought upon them by the traditional ritual practices of their unconverted kin (Meyer 1998, 1999b), and the ritualized practices of "spiritual warfare" by which communities attempt to rid themselves of territorial spirits they engaged with in the past (DeBernardi 1999, p. 86; Robbins 2003, p. 226). There are also rituals of rupture that drive a wedge between converts and the contemporary social world. Sessions aimed at Spiritual "in-filling" and tongue speaking that aim to "seal off" Malawian Pentecostals from the society around them and the evil forces that it harbors (e.g., witchcraft) are a good example (van Dijk 1998), as are in a mundane way the numerous lengthy church services and prayer group meetings that P/c Christians everywhere attend in lieu of participating in their communities' non-P/c social lives.

These rituals of rupture must be understood in the context of the dualistic schemes P/c regularly establishes to define the ruptures it produces. In the first instance, P/c dualism divides the world into those whose lives are directed by God and those who follow the devil (Droogers 2001, p. 46). But the divine and the satanic operate in this scheme as symbols with an open-ended range of referents so that in some places or contexts their opposition comes to figure the opposition between the past and the present (Meyer 1998, Robbins 2004, Tuzin 1997), whereas in others it provides an understanding of the differences between the church and the world, or the public and private realms (Brusco 1995; Chesnut 1997, p. 125). P/c dualism also brings itself to bear on action through its moral codes, which ban contact with the satanic world by forbidding drinking and drug use, extramarital sexuality, fighting and aggressive displays, gambling, ostentatious dress, and participation in secular entertainments such as cinema and dancing (Brodwin 2003, p. 88; Wacker 2001, p. 122). The asceticism these codes enjoin provides people with guides for living with the ruptures P/c ritual and dualism create. Some analysts suggest that their reorientations of people's moral fields are one of the most important aspects of P/c cultural transformation (Austin-Broos 1997; Brodwin 2003; Levine 1995, pp. 171–72; Mariz 1994, p. 8, 1998; Marshall 1993, p. 234; Robbins 2004).

P/c dualism also brings about what is perhaps P/c's most distinctive quality in comparison with other forces for cultural change: its tendency to preserve peoples' beliefs concerning the reality and power of the spiritual worlds from which they have broken. P/c preserves these beliefs in the sense of accepting their cognitive claims concerning the existence of spiritual forces, but it does not retain the "normative presuppositions" about the moral value of the spiritual world that often accompany them (Mariz 1994, p. 68; Csordas 1992, p. 6). By a process of demonization, P/c makes indigenous spirits representatives of the devil (Meyer 1999b). Having demonized the indigenous spirit world, P/c dualism then leads people to devote much of their energy to struggling against it, an activity that has the effect of further proving its existence and demonstrating its relevance to postconversion life (Casanova 2001, pp. 437–38; Corten 1999, p. 36; van Dijk 1997; Werbner 1998a, pp. 11–14).

P/c's preservation of indigenous spiritual ontologies and, most importantly, its continued ritual engagement with the spirits that populate them distinguishes it from other forms of Christianity (Casanova 2001, pp. 437–38; Meyer 1999b) and from other sorts of globalizing projects, such as development (Marshall-Fratani 1998, p. 291). Through such preservation, P/c avails itself of locally meaningful idioms for talking about the past and about current social problems—for spirits always are a language for talking about broader concerns. This openness to local spiritual languages allows P/c dualism to operate differently and mean different things in different places (cf. Corten & Marshall-Fratani 2001b, p. 10). Among the Ewe of Ghana it is an idiom for breaking from kin relations (Meyer 1999b). Among young urban preachers in Malawi, it is the gerontocratic power structure and the witchcraft it controls against which one must struggle (van Dijk 1992, 1995, 1998; see also Maxwell 1999 on Zimbabwe). In many parts of Latin America, it is the male prestige sphere of drink, adultery, and popular Catholic ritual investment that represents the realm of Satan (Annis 1987; Brusco 1995; Burdick 1993, 114; Chesnut 1997), though in others, Satan's domain is also represented for young people by the demonic attractions of a youth culture focused on sexuality and status competition (Burdick 1993), the lures of the drug trade (Lehmann 2001, p. 65), or the domination of traditional elites (Bastian 1993, pp. 46–47). Among the Tlingit and Haida of Southeast Alaska, the demonization of traditional culture provides an idiom for contesting emerging socio-conomic differences (Dombrowski 2001). In these and other cases, the demonized content shows great variation as P/c followers construct it out of local social concerns. Yet even as it absorbs local content, P/c dualism also maintains its globally recognizable shape as a struggle between the divine and the demonic (Barker 2001, 107).

Understanding that this struggle, although similar in form everywhere, is so diverse in content, we can appreciate why investigators often say of P/c that it is both "radically antisyncretic" and "profoundly localized" (DeBernardi 1999, p. 77); that it "is often most indigenous when inveighing against the local most strongly" (Gifford 2001, p. 74); or, finally, that regarding P/c churches "it is in their very struggle against local culture that they prove how locally rooted they are" (Casanova 2001, p. 438). P/c localizes not by fitting into indigenous cultures via some sort of syncretic melding prepared by its "primal" qualities, but by accepting as real local spirit worlds and the problems they represent. This allows P/c converts to turn their new religion immediately to addressing local issues in locally comprehensible terms.

This section has picked apart the tangle that has developed around discussions of P/c globalization that represent it both as a prime example of a homogenizing cultural force and as one of the Western cultural forms most susceptible to localization. If read carefully, the literature shows that P/c's homogenizing force is in large part based on its emphasis on rupture, dualism, and moral asceticism. These features encourage believers to distinguish P/c from what they come to see as their traditional culture and to work to keep the two separate, thus leading believers to maintain relatively canonical versions of P/c itself. Its localization is also a product of its dualism. Although that dualism is antisyncretic, it does lead to the preservation of local ontologies and the social concerns they reflect, albeit as resituated within P/c as an aspect of the demonic world. The resulting cultural formation is a particular kind of hybrid in which the parts of the mixture are kept distinct despite the relations that exist between them (Robbins 2004). The nature of this hybrid accounts for why global and local features appear with equal intensity within P/c cultures.

WORLD-MAKING: INSTITUTIONAL PRODUCTIVITY AND THE LOCALIZATION OF RELIGIOUS AUTHORITY

When scholars refer to P/c as localized, they often have in mind its engagement with local ontologies. Yet frequently they are also making a point about the way the governance of P/c churches tends to be in local hands. P/c churches are often local from the start, having been created by evangelists with local roots. Even when they are part of major Pentecostal denominations such as the AOG, local churches tend to be run by local people. Where the church is dominated by foreign missionaries from non-P/c groups, charismatic revivals often provide "a handy and effective means for local indigenous Christian leaders to break free of domination by missions" and make their churches effectively local regardless of their denominational embeddedness (Bays 1993, p. 175; Robbins 2001b). In most cases, then, P/c churches are staffed from top to bottom with locals who constitute them as institutions responsive to local situations. The question this raises is that of how P/c lends itself so readily to generating locally constructed and operated institutions.

The answer is rooted in the cultural assumptions that make P/c a tool for producing institutions inexpensively and with local materials. One of these assumptions, previously mentioned, is that believers do not need special education to preach or run a church; only Spiritual inspiration is required (d'Epinay 1969, p. 75; Stoll 1990, p. 13; Willems 1967, p. 136). The lack of prerequisite credentials for leadership gives nascent P/c churches a large pool of potential local talent from which to draw. And most converts are given an opportunity to serve in some capacity, since P/c churches sport numerous lay preachers, deacons, and leaders of various men's, women's, and youth groups (D'Epinay 1969, p. 49). Blacking (1981) writes of the South African Zionist church, "the general principle seemed to be that as many members as possible should have an opportunity of holding positions . . ." (p. 45), and even in the large, highly structured AOG church studied by Chesnut (1997, p. 135) in Brazil, 79.5% of the people he interviewed had held church office. By letting so many members occupy formal roles, P/c churches mobilize large numbers of local people in their institution-building efforts.

P/c churches also successfully demand heavy participation from members, who attend church services, meetings, and home Bible studies and participate in evangelization efforts. Chesnut's (1997, p. 141) quantitative data again is telling: the Brazilians he studied participated in an average of 4.7 church activities per week. Such high involvement keeps local P/c institutions active and stable (Gill 1990; Willems 1967, p. 168).

The requirement to tithe and give offerings is another aspect of P/c culture that fosters its ability to create local institutions (Mariz 1994, p. 73). d'Epinay (1969, p. 54) claims that tithing maintains the local autonomy of P/c churches in Chile. Other researchers argue that poor members find in tithing a way to experience the power of occupying the donor role, thereby furthering their sense of involvement in the church (Chesnut 1997, p. 119; Corten 1999, p. 59).

These features of P/c culture give "the tools of association to everyone" and create local social worlds possessed of strong institutional grounding (Levine 1995, p. 169). This institutional productivity is crucial to P/c's value because many of the places where it flourishes are, as Martin (1998, pp. 117–18, after Lash & Urry 1994) puts it, experiencing an "institutional deficit." Comaroff & Comaroff (2003) similarly suggest that P/c-like movements flourish where "neoliberal forces have eroded the capacity of liberal democratic states to provide education, health and welfare. . ." (p. 121). In such situations, P/c can quickly establish locally run and funded institutions that provide their own manner of health, job placement, and educational services (Chesnut 1997; Marshall 1993, p. 225; Willems 1967). The community-building success of P/c churches is of course a mainstay of deprivation and disorganization accounts of its appeal. But it is also important to note that this success is rooted in ideas of Spiritual empowerment, institutional commitment, and religious generosity, which distinguish P/c from other globalizing cultural forms.

P/c FORMATIONS OF GENDER, POLITICS, AND ECONOMICS

This review has focused thus far on aspects of P/c culture that allow it to engage local cultures and establish local institutions. But P/c's other tendency—to establish its own cultural frameworks wherever it travels—raises the issue of the nature of the culture it carries. Taking into account P/c's Western origins and looking back to Weber (1946, 1958) and sometimes to Halévy's (1937) and Thompson's (1966) work on Methodism, scholars speculate on the extent to which P/c culture can be seen as initiating converts into modernity, introducing them to individualism and preparing them for lives in the global capitalist economy (Martin 1990, Martin 2001). Debates on this issue are not well developed or close to consensus. Indeed, they indicate difficulties with any argument that would simply equate P/c with modernity or gloss it merely as an enchanted version thereof. P/c is far from Weber's Calvinism (Cox 1995, p. 230; see also Thompson 1966, p. 363 on Methodism); its evident inner-worldly asceticism is tempered by an equally evident mysticism (Weber 1946, pp. 325–26). And Pentecostalism was developed not by the bourgeoisie but by people whose own relationships to early twentieth-century modernity were contradictory and complex (Comaroff 1985). The ambiguously modern culture their efforts bequeathed to global P/c is best seen in the literature on P/c constructions of gender, political engagement, and economic behavior.

A consistent finding in studies of P/c churches worldwide is that more women than men are active members. Martin (2001, p. 56) reports that 75% of adult evangelicals are women, and studies more narrowly focused on P/c churches report similar percentages (Chesnut 1997, p. 22; Comaroff 1985, p. 204; Cucchiari 1990, p. 698; Gill 1990, p. 712; Hunt 2002c, pp. 159–60). In general women outnumber men in Christianity (Woodhead 2001, p. 73). But P/c's strong commitment to Pauline notions of patriarchy in which women are expected to subordinate themselves to men and participate in churches formally run by men has stimulated much research aimed at determining why P/c Christianity appeals to women.

Discussions of this issue focus either on the openness of P/c institutions to women's involvement and leadership or on the distinctiveness of P/c patriarchy. In looking at the scope P/c churches provide for women's involvement, many investigators note that these churches recognize two bases of authority: inspirational and institutional (Corten 1999, pp. 27–28; Cucchiari 1990, pp. 693–94; Ireland 1991, p. 96). Whereas men monopolize formal institutional positions such as pastor or missionary, women are routinely seen as receiving more gifts of the Spirit, and these gifts underwrite their work as lay preachers, healers, evangelists, and prophets whose voices are often heard in church and other public settings (Chesnut 1997, p. 99, 2003, pp. 141–43; Cucchiari 1990, pp. 689–94; d'Epinay 1969, p. 202; Hunt 2002c, pp. 159–60; Mariz & Machado 1997, pp. 43, 49; Martin 2001, p. 54). P/c churches also foster the creation of all or predominantly female services and prayer groups. These settings provide opportunities for women to develop public leadership skills and are often the one place in patriarchal societies where women can forge new relations outside their kin networks without exposing themselves to charges of immorality (Brusco 1995, pp. 133, 138; Chesnut 1997, p. 139, 2003, p. 145; Dombrowski 2001, pp. 36, 60; Gill 1990, p. 712; Hunt 2002c, p. 159; Stewart & Strathern 2001).

Studies of the nature of P/c patriarchy examine how, despite its support for male domination, it manages to enhance "women's autonomy and equality" and improve relations within their households (Smilde 1997, p. 343; Brusco 1995; Chesnut 1997; Cucchiari 1990; Martin 2001, p. 54). The solution to this "paradox" lies in the way P/c dualism and asceticism contribute to its construction of gender relations. Many of the behaviors P/c asceticism prohibits (e.g., adultery, gambling, drinking, and fighting) were valued primarily by men in preconversion culture (Austin-Broos 1997, p. 123; Chesnut 2003, p. 136; Kiernan 1994, 1997, p. 250; Mariz & Machado 1997, p. 50; Willems 1967, p. 49). In prohibiting these behaviors, converts demonize traditional patriarchy and the public sphere of male prestige competition (Burdick 1993, p. 114; Chesnut 1997, p. 112; Maxwell 1999, p. 106). At the same time, P/c dualism enjoins respect for the marital bond and the household, realms defined as female in many preconversion cultures (Brusco 1995, p. 123; Burdick 1993; Mariz & Machado 1997, pp. 42–43; Marshall 1993; Ojo 1997). By promoting the household while condemning traditional male activities, P/c dualism "domesticates" men by turning their attention and resources to traditionally female concerns (Brusco 1995, pp. 5, 125; Burdick 1993, p. 114; Gill 1990, p. 717; Mariz & Machado 1997, p. 42; Willems 1967, pp. 169–73). Because of the domestic cooperation it demands of men, P/c gender models are only a "patriarchy in the last instance," according to Stacey & Gerard (1990, p. 108).

P/c patriarchy also reconfigures women's understanding of their own positions. Women converts see themselves as obedient primarily to God (Burdick 1993, p. 11). Their submission to men is legitimate only when men fulfill their tasks as God's chosen leaders and do not make demands women would have to sin to fulfill (Smilde 1997, pp. 345, 348). On this basis, observant women feel comfortable criticizing men who sin (Burdick 1993, pp. 112–13) and can draw on divinely given dreams and visions of male misbehavior to lend authority to their criticisms (Chesnut 1997, p. 101). They can also invoke their commitment to God and P/c morality to resist unwanted male sexual advances and regain control of their sexuality (Marshall 1993, pp. 231–32).

Pointing to the scope P/c gives women to limit men's claims to authority, Smilde (1997) says P/c establishes a distinct "religiously bounded patriarchy" (pp. 354–55). Yet it also appeals to men because it does not publicly question their authority and even solidifies it within the household by taking the antagonistic edge off of marital relations (Burdick 1993, p. 114; Mariz & Machado 1997, p. 46; Martin 2001, p. 55). As Chesnut (1997:112) puts it for the Brazilian case, male converts go from being "king of the street" to being "master of the household" (Chesnut 1997, pp. 112). And beyond the household, male converts also can rebuild their identities by taking up leading roles in the church (Austin-Broos 1997, p. 126).

Several classic works suggest that P/c constructions of gender find their value in modernizing situations. Willems (1967, pp. 169–73) argues that P/c constructions of gender render meaningful changes in women's roles caused by industrialization and urbanization in Brazil and Chile. Looking at the Colombian case, Brusco (1995) argues that P/c rearticulates men's and women's values after capitalism has sundered their relative conjunction within the peasant household. Cucchiari (1990, pp. 699–70) and Austin-Broos (1997) offer similarly rich historical analyses for the Italian and Jamaican cases, respectively. There is, however, little discussion in the cross-cultural literature of how P/c gender constructions relate to those of secular modernity. Discussions of women's involvement in churches and their use of church institutions to forge new social networks suggest that in many places P/c churches serve as hybrid public/private spaces (Cucchiari 1990) that, like the department store in Western history (Felski 1995), facilitate women's efforts to construct public social lives for themselves as modernity develops. But Mariz & Machado (1997, pp. 49–52; Mariz 1998, p. 206) argue that scholars working on P/c gender constructions, at least in Brazil, understand them only partially and evaluate them only poorly if they insist on viewing them through the lens of modern liberal political thought. They note that P/c models of oppression and liberation are grounded in ideas about demonic influence and freedom as the ability to choose to follow P/c's ascetic moral codes that are distinct from canonical modern formulations in the West (cf. Mahmood 2001).

Much of the literature on P/c political culture focuses on its potential contribution to movements toward democratization. The two primary positions on this issue were staked out early and are based on judgments of the relative novelty of P/c church organization in relation to the political structures of the surrounding society. Willems (1967, p. 157), writing on Chile and Brazil, argued that the emphasis on egalitarianism and lay control in Pentecostal congregational church structures was a "symbolic subversion of the traditional social order" organized by notions of hierarchy. In response, d'Epinay (1969), also writing on Chile, claimed that Pentecostal churches, centered as they are on the authority of their founding pastors, restored the authoritarian patron/client structure of the collapsed hacienda system and thus failed to transform traditional constructions of political relations.

Bastian (1993) and Martin (1990, 2002) revived this debate in the 1990s. Bastian (1993, pp. 35, 50) picked up d'Epinay's line of argument and claimed that P/c embraced the authoritarianism of traditional popular religion, becoming a "Catholicism without priests" that supported corporatist political structures. Martin (1990, 2002), by contrast, embedded Willems' claims in a sweeping and influential argument that P/c in Latin America (and elsewhere outside the West) is destined to play the politically (and economically) modernizing role its Methodist progenitor played in England and the United States. The core of his argument claims that P/c's dualistic rejection of the secular world allows its members to withdraw into churches that constitute a "free space," a "protective social capsule," in which they can innovate new social forms without challenging elites (Martin 1990, pp. 187–89, 202; cf. Comaroff 1985, p. 213). Within this space, they experiment with voluntaristic and egalitarian social relations and develop new skills in leadership, literacy, public speaking, organization, and self-help (Burdick 1993, p. 226; Dodson 1997, p. 34; Marshall 1993, pp. 224–25; Martin 1990, pp. 108, 234, 284; Stoll 1990, p. 117). Through these experiments, Martin and others suggest, P/c introduces radical changes in the structures that traditionally governed social and political life in Latin America and elsewhere, preparing people for democratic participation.

Ireland's (1991) finding that, in terms of the classic church/sect dichotomy, institutionalized P/c churches operate differently at different levels suggests a way out of the impasse that marks the debate on P/c organizational structure. In their hierarchies, Sunday services, and Sunday schools, P/c churches operate like churches, but in their small-group prayer meetings and home services, they function as sects (Ireland 1991, pp. 89–93). Members tend to emphasize only one of these sets of activities; some are, in effect, church members, whereas others belong to a sect. Willems' and Martin's arguments about P/c transformations of traditional political culture are correct for sect members, but arguments for continued authoritarianism better represent the situation of those who attend church (Ireland 1991, pp. 214–15, 221–22).

Ireland's thesis is supported by Dodson's (1997, p. 32) claim that Bastian extrapolates from the experience of large P/c denominations, as do other exponents of the authoritarian position (e.g., Chesnut 1997). By contrast, those asserting P/c's transformative potential stress its sectarian and schismatic character, arguing that by keeping churches small it maintains their participatory, egalitarian features (Brusco 1995, p. 143; Willems 1967, pp. 113–16).

Ireland's argument indicates the complexity of the empirical situation. P/c church organization is very flexible, and generalizations about organizational experience need to be based on a range of careful ethnographic reports (Kamsteeg 1998, p. 6). Making a related point, Gifford (1998, p. 37) and Freston (1998, p. 45) assert that arguments in favor of P/c's democratizing force are generally speculative. Martin's (1990, pp. 267–68) argument, for example, is ultimately couched in subjunctive terms; he suggests that the political changes P/c makes within the free space of its churches exist in a latent state, waiting to emerge as full-fledged democratization movements when political conditions allow. Those who have done the most far-reaching empirical studies prefer to adopt a neutral stance, neither pessimistic nor optimistic, on the question of P/c's potential contributions to democratization, and they counsel caution when trying to read from what Martin (1990, p. 6) calls P/c's "cultural logic" to its socially modernizing effects (Freston 2001, p. 310; Steigenga 2001, pp. 145–46).

Another common observation about P/c political culture is that it leads to conservatism. What Stoll (1990, p. 327) labels the conspiracy theory view—that P/c churches are largely funded and ideologically shaped by the North American new right—has met with little scholarly support and critics stress that P/c churches are usually run by local leaders whose own agendas resist cooptation (Bastian 1993, p. 51; Coleman 2002b, pp. 12–13; Corten & Marshall-Fratani 2001b, p. 6; Englund 2003; Freston 2001, p. 289; d'Epinay 1969, pp. 87–88; Marshall 1993, pp. 213–15; Steigenga 2001, p. 140). Empirical studies of voting behavior also challenge claims of P/c conservatism, generally finding that church members tend to vote the way others of their social class do (Gill 2002, p. 214; Martin 1990, p. 240; Smilde 1998, pp. 299–30).

Yet several aspects of P/c culture can sometimes foster kinds of conservatism that may not come out in election surveys. For example, the P/c tendency toward withdrawal from public life, even as it may create Martin's free space, can encourage conservatism or at least political quietism. Many authors find that although P/c Christians vote, they tend to shy away from "hard" political acts that they consider immoral, such as working for parties, criticizing public officials, or running for office (Steigenga 2001, p. 141). But other researchers point to the political complexity of P/c withdrawal, noting that it can be a way of maintaining political autonomy (Stoll 1990, p. 319), avoiding the depoliticizing blandishments of mass culture (Freston 2001, p. 302) or building associations that may contribute to the construction of civil society (Dodson 1997, p. 33). P/c withdrawal's embeddedness in narratives of the struggle between God and Satan also makes it sometimes capable of generating radical critiques of the existing order

(Burdick 1993, pp. 218–19; Englund 2003, p. 96; Kamsteeg 1998; Marshall 1993, p. 234).

Another aspect of P/c culture that lends it a conservative caste is its individualism (Smilde 1998, p. 288; Martin 1990, p. 266). By emphasizing evangelization as the remedy for all ills, P/c promotes individual as opposed to structural solutions for social problems and leaves its followers without models of an ideal earthly society on which to base political action (Martin 1990, p. 266; Robbins 2002). As with withdrawal, scholars temper this view by stressing that P/c individualism should not be seen in all cases as apolitical and as hindering a concern for collective well-being (Mariz 1998, p. 215; Martin 1990, p. 234; Stoll 1990, p. 310). In particular, some argue that it is tempered by the moral links the religion fosters between converts and by the way it locates converts within their families (Chordas 1980; van Dijk 1998, p. 176; Martin 2001, p. 95).

Finally, there is a widespread pattern of P/c Christians construing themselves as leaping over their immediate political environment to identify with and recruit real or imagined support from distant P/c sources (Martin 2002, p. 26; Englund 2003). Via such distant identifications, people can resist identifying themselves in ethnic or national terms (Corten & Marshall-Fratani 2001b, p. 3; Robbins 1998); claim formal powers, such as the ability to conduct marriage ceremonies, usually denied them by local authorities (Austin-Broos 1997, pp. 111–12); and connect with members of socially distant classes (Csordas 1992, p. 12; Gifford 1998, p. 341). These identifications may at times appear quixotic—if withdrawal leads to too great a narrowing of the political domain, leaping over sometimes expands the political domain beyond workable limits. Yet it remains true that these distant identifications transform the local political field in ways not captured by common models of political modernization.

The key debate in discussions of P/c economic culture concerns the extent to which P/c plays a role in establishing the "Protestant ethic" in today's converts similar to the one played by Calvinism in Weber's (1958) account of the development of capitalism. Empirical studies of the effect of conversion on economic status are inconclusive (Martin 1990), with some arguing that the status of converts rises (Annis 1987) and others arguing that it does not (Brouwer et al. 1996, pp. 235–36). Analyses of P/c cultural conceptions of the economic domain present a similarly complicated picture. P/c asceticism renders members trustworthy and reliable workers who employers often seek out (Chesnut 1997, p. 166; d'Epinay 1969, p. 133; Martin 1995; Maxwell 1998, p. 354). By hiring P/c Christians to fill lightly supervised positions in the postfordist service economy, employers can, in effect, outsource the task of work discipline to the churches (Martin 1995, p. 111, cf. Thompson 1966). Disciplined though they are, however, P/c Christians' first commitment is to the church. On account of their dualism, they do not sacralize earthly work, may not focus on it as they execute it, and sometimes may quit to pursue evangelical goals (Chesnut 1997, p. 116; d'Epinay 1969, pp. 151–52). Their attitudes toward accumulation also are mixed. Forgoing investment in traditional ritual and male prestige pursuits, and often cutting their ties with their extended families, the way is open for P/c Christians to keep what they earn, but the requirement that they give generously to their churches can prevent substantial accumulation (Maxwell 1998, p. 369). Considering this mixed picture, many scholars settle on characterizing the P/c economic ethos as one that stresses "coping," the avoidance of extreme poverty and ill health, but does not aim to produce great prosperity—and they have found that P/c asceticism often allows converts to meet these goals even in difficult circumstances (Brusco 1995, pp. 144–46; Chesnut 1997, p. 117; Mariz 1994; Maxwell 1998). Some researchers may see this ethos as an adjustment to converts' life chances. But it is more than just resignation; its disregard for prosperity is anchored in P/c's demonization of the world and its pleasures and can, in some cases, issue in partial criticisms of capitalist cultural models of individualism, accumulation, and desire (Burdick 1993, pp. 119–23; Meyer 1995, 1999a).

The discussion has thus far focused on the traditional P/c economic ethos. This ethos has been significantly transformed in the teachings of Faith churches that recently have become popular. The prosperity gospel preached in these churches holds that health and wealth are the believer's due and that illness and poverty are caused by sin and demonic influence (Coleman 2002b, Gifford 2001). Converts are encouraged to give generously with the promise that their gifts will be returned lavishly. With the donations this doctrine generates, Faith churches have grown quickly and heavily invested in media technology to further spread their message (Coleman 2000; Freston 1995, p. 132; Hackett 1995, p. 202). Although Faith churches encourage accumulation, individualism, and entrepreneurship in a way the traditional P/c ethos does not, their "magical" approach to wealth and heavy emphasis on tithing ensures that they too do not promote the classic Protestant ethic but instead represent "an advanced stage of. . .[its] decline" (Freston 1995, p. 131; see also Eves 2003; Gifford 1998, p. 337; Hunt 1998). Although the ultimate scope of Faith churches' popularity remains to be seen, it is interesting to note that members of more traditional P/c churches draw on their own economic ideas to formulate criticisms of these churches, even participating in riots aimed at Faith church members who flaunt their wealth and disregard community obligations (Maxwell 1998, p. 367; Smith 2001).

CONCLUSION

Several years before the booms in anthropological writing on both P/c and globalization, Comaroff (1985) wrote that the charismatic Zionist church she studied was "part of a second global culture. . .lying in the shadow of the first" (p. 254). This review examines what the literature tells us about the dynamics of this second global culture. Its gender, political, and economic constructions suggest that it would be a mistake to reduce it to a mere reflex of the modern as defined by the secular market and political ideas of the first global culture. At the same time, P/c's complex relationship with the traditional cultures it encounters—a relationship of both rejection and preservation—indicate that to see it as a simple force for indigenizing cultural localization is equally wide of the mark. Further studies of the mechanics of P/c's spread promise to enrich not only our understanding of P/c but also of the range of dynamics that mark cultural globalization more generally.

ACKNOWLEDGMENTS

I thank Brian Brazeal, James Holston, Keith McNeal, Alejandro Paz, and Richard Werbner for supplying references and for conversations that helped me develop some of these ideas. I am especially grateful to Jon Bialecki, Simon Coleman, Bruce Knauft, Bruce Koplin, Tanya Luhrmann, Bambi Schieffelin, and Rupert Stasch for their comments on drafts and for extensive discussions that helped shape this review.

The *Annual Review of Anthropology* is online at http://anthro.annualreviews.org

LITERATURE CITED

Ammerman NT. 1987. *Bible Believers: Fundamentalists in the Modern World*. New Brunswick, NJ: Rutgers Univ. Press

Anderson RM. 1979. *Vision of the Disinherited: The Making of American Pentecostalism*. Peabody, MA: Hendrickson

Annis S. 1987. *God and Production in a Guatemalan Town*. Austin: Univ. Texas Press

Austin-Broos DJ. 1997. *Jamaica Genesis: Religion and the Politics of Moral Orders*. Chicago: Univ. Chicago Press

Barker J. 2001. Afterword. *J. Ritual. Stud.* 15(2):105–8

Barrett DB, Johnson TM. 2002. Global statistics. In *The New International Dictionary of Pentecostal and Charismatic Movements*, ed. SM Burgess, EM van der Maas, pp. 283–302. Grand Rapids, MI: Zondervan

Bastian J-P. 1993. The metamorphosis of Latin American Protestant groups: a sociohistorical perspective. *Lat. Am. Res. Rev.* 28:33–61

Bays DH. 1993. Christian revivals in China, 1900–1937. In *Modern Christian Revivals*, ed. EL Blumhofer, R Balmer, pp. 161–79. Urbana: Univ. Ill. Press

Berger P. 1990. Forward. See Martin 1990, pp. vii–x

Blacking J. 1981. Political and musical freedom in the music of some black South African churches. In *The Structure of Folk Models*, ed. L Holy, M Stuchlik, pp. 35–62. London: Academic

Blumhofer EL. 1993. *Aimee Semple McPherson: Everybody's Sister*. Grand Rapids, MI: Eerdmans

Boudewijnse B, Droogers A, Kamsteeg F, eds. 1998. *More Than Opium: An Anthropological Approach to Latin American and Caribbean Pentecostal Praxis*. Lanham: Scarecrow

Bowen K. 1996. *Evangelism and Apostasy: the Evolution and Impact of Evangelicals in Modern Mexico*. Montreal: McGill-Queen's Univ. Press

Brodwin P. 2003. Pentecostalism in translation: religion and the production of community in the Haitian diaspora. *Am. Ethnol.* 30:85–101

Brouwer S, Gifford P, Rose SD. 1996. *Exporting the American Gospel: Global Christian Fundamentalism*. New York: Routledge

Brusco EE. 1995. *The Reformation of Machismo: Evangelical Conversion and Gender in Colombia*. Austin: Univ. Texas Press

Burdick J. 1993. *Looking for God in Brazil: The Progressive Catholic Church in Urban Brazil's Religious Arena*. Berkeley: Univ. Calif. Press

Burdick J. 1998. *Blessed Anastácia: Women,*

Race, and Popular Christianity in Brazil. New York: Routledge

Casanova J. 2001. Religion, the new millennium, and globalization. *Soc. Relig.* 62:415–41

Chesnut RA. 1997. *Born Again in Brazil: The Pentecostal Boom and the Pathogens of Poverty.* New Brunswick, NJ: Rutgers

Chesnut RA. 2003. *Competitive Spirits: Latin America's New Religious Economy.* Oxford: Oxford Univ. Press

Chordas TJ. 1980. Catholic Pentecostalism: a new word in a new world. See Glazier 1980, pp. 143–75

Cleary El, Stewart-Gambino HW, eds. 1997. *Power, Politics, and Pentecostals in Latin America.* Boulder, CO: Westview

Coleman S. 2000. *The Globalisation of Charismatic Christianity: Spreading the Gospel of Prosperity.* Cambridge: Cambridge Univ. Press

Coleman S, ed. 2002a. The Faith Movement: a global religious culture? *Cult. Relig.* 3(1):Spec. issue

Coleman S. 2002b. The Faith Movement: a global religious culture? *Cult. Relig.* 3:3–19

Comaroff J. 1985. *Body of Power, Spirit of Resistance: The Culture and History of a South African People.* Chicago: Univ. Chicago Press

Comaroff J, Comaroff J. 2003. Second comings: neo-Protestant ethics and millennial capitalism in Africa, and elsewhere. In *2000 Years and Beyond: Faith, Identity and the 'Common Era'*, ed. P Gifford, D Archard, TA Hart, N Rapport, pp. 106–26. London: Routledge

Corten A. 1997. The growth of the literature on Afro-American, Latin American and African Pentecostalism. *J. Contemp. Relig.* 12:311–34

Corten A. 1999. *Pentecostalism in Brazil: Emotion of the Poor and Theological Romanticism.* New York: St. Martin's

Corten A, Marshall-Fratani R, eds. 2001a. *Between Babel and Pentecost: Transnational Pentecostalism in Africa and Latin America.* Bloomington: Ind. Univ. Press

Corten A, Marshall-Fratani R. 2001b. Introduction. See Corten & Marshall-Fratani 2001a, pp. 1–21

Cox H. 1995. *Fire From Heaven: The Rise of Pentecostal Spirituality and the Reshaping of Religion in the Twenty-First Century.* Reading, MA.: Addison-Wesley

Cox H. 1997. Into the age of miracles: culture, religion, and the market revolution. *World Policy J.* 14:87–95

Csordas TJ. 1992. Religion and the world system: the Pentecostal ethic and the spirit of monopoly capital. *Dialect. Anthropol.* 17:3–24

Csordas TJ. 1994. *The Sacred Self: A Cultural Phenomenology of Charismatic Healing.* Berkeley: Univ. Calif. Press

Cucchiari S. 1990. Between shame and sanctification: patriarchy and its transformation in Sicilian Pentecostalism. *Am. Ethnol.* 17:687–707

Dayton DW. 1987. *Theological Roots of Pentecostalism.* Peabody, MA: Hendrickson

DeBernardi J. 1999. Spiritual warfare and territorial spirits: the globalization and localisation of a 'practical theology'. *Relig. Stud. Theol.* 18:66–96

D'Epinay CL. 1969. *Haven of the Masses: A Study of the Pentecostal Movement in Chile.* London: Lutterworth

Dodson M. 1997. Pentecostals, politics, and public space in Latin America. See Cleary & Stewart-Gambino 1997, pp. 25–40

Dombrowski K. 2001. *Against Culture: Development, Politics, and Religion in Indian Alaska.* Lincoln: Univ. Neb. Press

Douglas B. 2001. From invisible Christians to gothic theatre: the romance of the millennial in Melanesian anthropology. *Curr. Anthropol.* 42:615–50

Dow JW, Sandstrom AR, eds. 2001. *Holy Saints and Fiery Preachers.* Westport, CT: Praeger

Droogers A. 2001. Globalisation and Pentecostal studies. See Corten & Marshall-Fratani 2001a, pp. 41–61

Englund H. 2001. The quest for missionaries: transnationalism and township

Pentecostalism in Malawi. See Corten & Marshall-Fratani 2001a, pp. 235–55

Englund H. 2003. Christian independency and global membership: Pentecostal extraversions in Malawi. *J. Relig. Afr.* 33:83–111

Eves R. 2003. Money, mayhem and the beast: narratives of the world's end from New Ireland (Papua New Guinea). *J. R. Anthropol. Inst.* 9:527–47

Felski R. 1995. *The Gender of Modernity*. Cambridge, MA: Harvard Univ. Press

Freston P. 1995. Pentecostalism in Brazil: a brief history. *Religion* 25:119–33

Freston P. 1997. Charismatic evangelicals in Latin America: mission and politics on the frontiers of Protestant growth. See Hunt et al. 1997a, pp. 184–204

Freston P. 1998. Evangelicalism and globalization: general observations and some Latin American dimensions. In *A Global Faith: Essays on Evangelicalism and Globalization*, ed. M Hutchinson, O Kalu, pp. 69–88. Sydney: Cent. Study Aust. Christ.

Freston P. 2001. *Evangelicals and Politics in Asia, Africa and Latin America*. Cambridge: Cambridge Univ. Press

Gerlach LP, Hine VH. 1970. *People, Power, Change: Movements of Social Transformation*. Indianapolis: Bobbs-Merrill

Garrard-Burnett V, Stoll D, eds. 1993. *Rethinking Protestantism in Latin America*. Philadelphia: Temple Univ. Press

Gifford P. 1998. *African Christianity: Its Public Role*. Bloomington: Ind. Univ. Press

Gifford P. 2001. The complex provenance of some elements of African Pentecostal theology. See Corten & Marshall-Fratani 2001a, pp. 62–79

Gill A. 2002. Religion and democracy in South America: challenges and opportunities. In *Religion and Politics in Comparative Perspective: The One, The Few, The Many*, ed. TG Jelen, C Wilcox, pp. 195–221. New York: Cambridge Univ. Press

Gill L. 1990. 'Like a veil to cover them': women and the Pentecostal movement in La Paz. *Am. Ethnol.* 17:708–21

Glazier S, ed. 1980. *Perspectives on Pentecostalism: Case Studies from the Caribbean and Latin America*. Lanham: Univ. Press Am.

Hackett RIJ. 1995. The gospel of prosperity in West Africa. In *Religion and the Transformations of Capitalism: Comparative Approaches*, ed. RH Roberts, pp. 199–214. London: Routledge

Hackett RIJ. 1998. Charismatic/Pentecostal appropriation of media technologies in Nigeria and Ghana. *J. Relig. Afr.* 28:258–77

Halévy E. 1937. *A History of the English People in 1815*. London: Penguin

Hallum AM. 2002. Looking for hope in Central America: the Pentecostal movement. See Jelen & Wilcox 2002, pp. 225–39

Harding SF. 2000. *The Book of Jerry Falwell: Fundamentalist Language and Politics*. Princeton, NJ: Princeton Univ. Press

Heelas P, Haglund-Heelas AM. 1988. The inadequacy of 'deprivation' as a theory of conversion. In *Vernacular Christianity: Essays in Social Anthropology of Religion Presented to Godfrey Lienhardt*, ed. W James, DH Johnson, pp. 112–19. Oxford: J. Anthropol. Soc. Oxford Occas. Pap.

Hine VH. 1974. The deprivation and disorganization theories of social movements. In *Religious Movements in Contemporary America*, ed. II Zaretsky, MP Leone, pp. 646–61. Princeton, NJ: Princeton Univ. Press

Hollenweger WJ. 1972. *The Pentecostals*. Minneapolis, MN: Augsburg

Hollenweger WJ. 1984. After twenty years' research on Pentecostalism. *Theology* 87:403–12

Hollenweger WJ. 1997. *Pentecostalism: Origins and Development Worldwide*. Peabody, MA: Hendrickson

Holston J. 1999. Alternative modernities: statecraft and religious imagination in the Valley of the Dawn. *Am. Ethnol.* 26:605–31

Hunt S. 1998. Magical moments: an intellectualist approach to the neo-Pentecostal faith ministries. *Religion* 28:271–80

Hunt S. 2000. 'Winning ways': globalisation and the impact of the health and wealth gospel. *J. Contemp. Relig.* 15:331–47

Hunt S. 2002a. Deprivation and western Pentecostalism revisited: the case of 'classical' Pentecostalism. *PentecoStudies* 1(1):1–32

Hunt S. 2002b. Deprivation and western Pentecostalism revisited: neo-Pentecostalism. *PentecoStudies* 1(2):1–29

Hunt S. 2002c. 'Neither here nor there': the construction of identities and boundary maintenance of West African Pentecostals. *Sociology* 36:146–69

Hunt S, Hamilton M, Walter T, eds. 1997a. *Charismatic Christianity: Sociological Perspectives*. New York: St. Martin's

Hunt S, Hamilton M, Walter T. 1997b. Tongues, Toronto and the millennium. See Hunt et al. 1997a, pp. 1–16

Ireland R. 1991. *Kingdom's Come: Religion and Politics in Brazil*. Pittsburgh, PA: Univ. Pittsburgh Press

Jelen TG, Wilcox C, eds. 2002. *Religion and Politics in Comparative Perspective: The One, The Few, The Many*. New York: Cambridge Univ. Press

Jenkins P. 2002. *The Next Christendom: The Coming of Global Christianity*. Oxford: Oxford Univ. Press

Kamsteeg FH. 1998. *Prophetic Pentecostalism in Chile: A Case Study on Religion and Development Policy*. Lanham: Scarecrow

Kiernan JP. 1976. The work of Zion: an analysis of an African Zionist ritual. *Africa* 46:340–56

Kiernan JP. 1994. Variation on a Christian theme: the healing synthesis of Zulu Zionism. In *Syncretism/Anti-Syncretism: The Politics of Religious Synthesis*, ed. C Stewart, R Shaw, pp. 69–84. London: Routledge

Kiernan JP. 1997. Images of rejection in the construction of morality: Satan and sorcerer as moral signposts in the social landscape of urban Zionists. *Soc. Anthropol.* 5:243–54

Lash S, Urry J. 1994. *Economies of Signs and Space*. London: Sage

Lehmann D. 1996. *Struggle for the Spirit: Religious Transformation and Popular Culture in Brazil and Latin America*. Cambridge: Blackwell

Lehmann D. 2001. Charisma and possession in Africa and Brazil. *Theory Cult. Soc.* 18:45–74

Lehmann D. 2003. Review of D. Martin, Pentecostalism: The World Their Parish. *J. Relig. Afr.* 33:120–22

Lester RJ. 2003. The immediacy of eternity: time and transformation in a Roman Catholic convent. *Relig.* 33:201–19

Levine DH. 1995. Protestants and Catholics in Latin America: a family portrait. In *Fundamentalisms Comprehended*, ed. ME Marty, RS Appleby, pp. 155–78. Chicago: Univ. Chicago Press

Lyon D. 2000. *Jesus in Disneyland: Religion in Postmodern Times*. Cambridge: Polity

MacRobert I. 1988. *The Black Roots and White Racism of Early Pentecostalism in the USA*. London: Macmillan

Mahmood S. 2001. Feminist theory, embodiment, and the docile agent: some reflections on the Egyptian Islamic revival. *Cult. Anthropol.* 16:202–36

Manning FE. 1980. Pentecostalism: Christianity and reputation. See Glazier 1980, pp. 177–87

Mariz CL. 1994. *Coping With Poverty: Pentecostals and Base Communities in Brazil*. Philadelphia: Temple Univ. Press

Mariz CL. 1998. Deliverance and ethics: an analysis of the discourse of Pentecostals who have recovered from alcoholism. See Boudewijnse et al. 1998, pp. 203–23

Mariz CL, Machado MdDC. 1997. Pentecostalism and women in Brazil. See Cleary & Stewart-Gambino 1997, pp. 41–54

Marshall R. 1993. 'Power in the name of Jesus': social transformation and Pentecostalism in western Nigeria 'revisited'. In *Legitimacy and the State in Twentieth-Century Africa: Essays in Honour of A.H.M. Kirk-Greene*, ed. T Ranger, O Vaughan, pp. 213–46. London: Macmillian

Marshall-Fratani R. 1998. Mediating the global and the local in Nigerian Pentecostalism. *J. Relig. Afr.* 28:278–315

Martin D. 1990. *Tongues of Fire: The Explosion of Protestantism in Latin America*. Oxford: Basil Blackwell

Martin B. 1995. New mutations of the Protestant ethic among Latin American Pentecostals. *Religion* 25:101–17

Martin B. 1998. From pre- to postmodernity in Latin America: the case of Pentecostalism. In *Religion, Modernity and Postmodernity*, ed. P Heelas, D Martin, P Morris, pp. 102–46. Oxford: Blackwell

Martin B. 2001. The Pentecostal gender paradox: a cautionary tale for the sociology of religion. In *The Blackwell Companion to Sociology of Religion*, ed. RK Fenn, pp. 52–66. Oxford: Blackwell

Martin D. 2002. *Pentecostalism: The World Their Parish*. Oxford: Blackwell

Maxwell D. 1998. 'Delivered from the spirit of poverty?': Pentecostalism, prosperity and modernity in Zimbabwe. *J. Relig. Afr.* 28: 350–73

Maxwell D. 1999. *Christians and Chiefs in Zimbabwe: A Social History of the Hwesa People*. Westport, CT: Praeger

McGee GB. 2001. To the regions beyond: the global expansion of Pentecostalism. In *The Century of the Holy Spirit: 100 Years of Pentecostal and Charismatic Renewal*, ed. V Synan, pp. 69–95. Nashville, TN: Nelson

McGuire MB. 1982. *Pentecostal Catholics: Power, Charisma, and Order in a Religious Movement*. Philadelphia: Temple Univ. Press

Meyer B. 1995. 'Delivered from the powers of darkness': confessions of satanic riches in Christian Ghana. *Africa* 65:236–55

Meyer B. 1998. 'Make a complete break with the past': memory and postcolonial modernity in Ghanaian Pentecostal discourse. See Werbner 1998b, pp. 182–208

Meyer B. 1999a. Commodities and the power of prayer: Pentecostalist attitudes towards consumption in contemporary Ghana. In *Globalization and Identity: Dialectics of Flow and Closure*, ed. B Meyer, P Geschiere, pp. 151–76. Oxford: Blackwell

Meyer B. 1999b. *Translating the Devil: Religion and Modernity among the Ewe in Ghana*. Trenton, NJ: Africa World Press

Miller DE. 1997. *Reinventing American Protestantism*. Berkeley: Univ. Calif. Press

Noll MA. 2001. *American Evangelical Christianity: An Introduction*. Oxford: Blackwell

Ojo MA. 1988. The contextual significance of the charismatic movements in independent Nigeria. *Africa* 58:175–92

Ojo MA. 1997. Sexuality, marriage and piety among charismatics in Nigeria. *Religion* 27:65–79

Olson E. 2001. Signs of conversion, spirit of commitment: the Pentecostal church in the Kingdom of Tonga. *J. Ritual Stud.* 15:13–26

Poewe K, ed. 1994. *Charismatic Christianity as a Global Culture*. Columbia: Univ. South Carolina Press

Rieseordt M. 1993. *Pious Passion: The Emergence of Modern Fundamentalism in the United States and Iran*. Berkeley: Univ. Calif. Press

Robbins J. 1998. On reading 'world news': apocalyptic narrative, negative nationalism, and transnational Christianity in a Papua New Guinea Society. *Soc. Anal.* 42:103–30

Robbins J. 2001a. Introduction: global religions, Pacific island transformations. *J. Ritual Stud.* 15:7–12

Robbins J. 2001b. Whatever became of revival: from charismatic movement to charismatic church in a Papua New Guinea society. *J. Ritual Stud.* 15:79–90

Robbins J. 2002. 'My wife can't break off part of her belief and give it to me:' apocalyptic interrogations of Christian individualism among the Urapmin of Papua New Guinea. *Paideuma* 48:189–206

Robbins J. 2003. On the paradoxes of global Pentecostalism and the perils of continuity thinking. *Religion* 33:221–31

Robbins J. 2004. *Becoming Sinners: Christianity and Moral Torment in a Papua New Guinea Society*. Berkeley: Univ. Calif. Press

Robbins J, Stewart PJ, Strathern A, eds. 2001. Charismatic and Pentecostal Christianity in Oceania. *J. Ritual Stud.* 15(2):Spec. Issue

Smilde DA. 1997. The fundamental unity of the conservative and revolutionary tendencies in Venezuelan evangelicalism: the case of conjugal relations. *Religion* 27:343–59

Smilde DA. 1998. 'Letting God govern': supernatural agency in the Venezuelan Pentecostal approach to social change. *Soc. Relig.* 59:287–303

Smith DJ. 2001. 'The arrow of God': Pentecostalism, inequality, and the supernatural in south-eastern Nigeria. *Africa* 71:587–613

Spittler RP. 1994. Are Pentecostals and charismatics fundamentalists? A review of American uses of these categories. See Poewe 1994, pp. 103–16

Stacey J, Gerard SE. 1990. 'We are not doormats': the influence of feminism on contemporary evangelicals in the United States. In *Uncertain Terms: Negotiating Gender in American Culture*, ed. F Ginsburg, AL Tsing, pp. 98–117. Boston: Beacon

Steigenga TJ. 2001. *The Politics of the Spirit: The Political Implications of Pentecostalized Religion in Costa Rica and Guatemala*. Lanham, MD: Lexington

Stewart PJ, Strathern A. 2001. The great exchange: moka with God. *J. Ritual Stud.* 15(2):91–104

Stoll D. 1990. *Is Latin America Turning Protestant? The Politics of Evangelical Growth*. Berkeley: Univ. Calif. Press

Stringer MD. 1999. *On the Perception of Worship: the Ethnography of Worship in Four Christian Congregations in Manchester*. Birmingham, AL: Univ. Birmingham Press

Stritecky JM. 2001. Israel, America, and the ancestors: narratives of spiritual warfare in a Pentecostal denomination in Solomon Islands. *J. Ritual Stud.* 15:62–78

Synan V. 1997. *The Holiness-Pentecostal Tradition: Charismatic Movements in the Twentieth Century*. Grand Rapids, MI: Eerdmans

Thompson EP. 1966. *The Making of the English Working Class*. New York: Vintage

Tuzin D. 1997. *The Cassowary's Revenge: The Life and Death of Masculinity in a New Guinea Society*. Chicago: Univ. Chicago Press

van Dijk R. 1992. Young Puritan preachers in post-independence Malawi. *Africa* 62:159–81

van Dijk R. 1995. Fundamentalism and its moral geography in Malawi: the representation of the diasporic and the diabolical. *Crit. Anthropol.* 15:171–91

van Dijk R. 1998. Pentecostalism, cultural memory and the state: contested representations of time in Pentecostal Malawi. See Werbner 1998b, pp. 155–81

van Dijk RA. 1997. From camp to encompassment: discourses of transsubjectivity in the Ghanaian Pentecostal Diaspora. *J. Relig. Afr.* 27:135–59

Wacker G. 1982. Taking another look at the Vision of the Disinherited. *Relig. Stud. Rev.* 8: 15–22

Wacker G. 1988. Pentecostalism. In *Encyclopedia of the American Religious Experience: Studies of Traditions and Movements, Vol. II*, ed. CH Lippy, PW Williams, pp. 933–45. New York: Scribner

Wacker G. 2001. *Heaven Below: Early Pentecostals and American Culture*. Cambridge, MA: Harvard Univ. Press

Weber M. 1946. *From Max Weber: Essays in Sociology*. New York: Oxford Univ. Press

Weber M. 1958. *The Protestant Ethic and the Spirit of Capitalism*. New York: Scribner

Werbner R. 1998a. Beyond oblivion: confronting memory crisis. See Werbner 1998b, pp. 1–17

Werbner R, ed. 1998b. *Memory and the Postcolony: African Anthropology and the Critique of Power*. London: Zed Books

Willems E. 1967. *Followers of the New Faith: Culture Change and the Rise of Protestantism in Brazil and Chile*. Nashville, TN: Vanderbilt Univ. Press

Woodberry RD, Smith CS. 1998. Fundamentalism et al: conservative protestants in America. *Annu. Rev. Sociol.* 24:25–56

Woodhead L. 2001. Feminism and the sociology of religion: from gender-blindness to gendered difference. In *The Blackwell Companion to Sociology of Religion*, ed. RK Fenn, pp. 67–84. Oxford: Blackwell

Annu. Rev. Anthropol. 2004. 33:145–72
doi: 10.1146/annurev.anthro.33.070203.143841

POLITICAL ECONOMIC MOSAICS: Archaeology of the Last Two Millennia in Tropical Sub-Saharan Africa

Ann Brower Stahl

*Department of Anthropology, State University of New York at Binghamton,
Binghamton, New York 13902-6000; email: astahl@binghamton.edu*

Key Words political economy, regional interaction, sub-Saharan Africa, archaeology, Iron Age

■ **Abstract** This review explores recent research that moves away from conventional preoccupations with origins and independent innovation in African Iron Age archaeology. Critiques of cultural evolutionary formulations and empirically robust case studies combine to shape new concerns with the following: the variable expressions of complexity in time and space; the mosaic quality of social, political economic, and technological landscapes; and the effects of global entanglements over the last millennium. Ongoing research in western and eastern Africa highlights the dynamism of political economic arrangements over the last two millennia and reminds us that configurations enshrined in twentieth-century ethnography represent but a moment in the dynamic history of African societies.

INTRODUCTION

The last two thousand years of sub-Saharan Africa's past falls within the so-called Iron Age, which in standard formulations began with the advent of iron production (~500 BC to AD 500) and saw expanding reliance on agricultural production (through the first millennium AD) and emerging complex societies (from ~500 AD). These have been key topics in Iron Age research, which also has been shaped by a concern to construct culture-historical sequences, counter images of Africa as dependent on external stimuli for innovations, and demonstrate the dynamic qualities of Africa's later past (Connah 1998, Robertshaw 1990, Sinclair et al. 1993a, Stahl 1999b). Research often has been underwritten by a cultural evolutionary logic that focused attention on issues of origins and complexity and therefore on sites deemed early or likely to yield evidence of innovation and independent cultural dynamism. Iron Age research also was shaped by its interdisciplinary character, particularly because scenarios derived from comparative ethnography, historical linguistics, and documentary sources often preceded significant

0084-6570/04/1021-0145$14.00

145

archaeological research (e.g., Greenberg 1955, Murdock 1959), though archaeo-logical evidence more often than not has proved these sources wrong (Childs & Herbert 2005; Eggert 2005; LaViolette 2004; LaViolette & Fleisher 2005; Pikirayi 2001, pp. 1–36; Robertshaw 2000, 2003; Schmidt 1990).

These concerns remain important today, and the past 2000 years continues to be subsumed within an "Iron Age" rubric (though perhaps more out of convenience than conviction). Yet the term has been critiqued on several grounds: (*a*) By fo-cusing attention on metallurgy and agricultural production as emblematic of Iron Age societies, it diverts attention away from the complex mosaic of technologies, productive strategies, and political forms that characterized the continent over the past 2000 years (Kusimba 2003, Stahl 1999b); (*b*) it focuses attention on complex societies, diverting attention from the interconnections among societies of different scale (Amselle 1998, LaViolette & Fleisher 2005, Sharpe 1986); and (*c*) it creates a rupture between the "prehistoric" archaeology of "Iron Age" societies and the "historic" archaeology of settlements associated with European colonial activity (LaViolette 2004; Lightfoot 1995, pp. 202–4; Robertshaw 2004, pp. 380–82).

This review highlights recent research that moves away from conventional en-closures of Iron Age archaeology and explores three emerging themes: the com-plexity of complexity; the mosaic character of African social, political economic, and technological landscapes; and how global entanglements shaped African so-cieties of the past millennium. I explore these themes through examples drawn from western and eastern Africa. They are amply illustrated in the archaeology of southern Africa as well, though limitations of space preclude a discussion (see Hall 1990, 1993; Hall & Markell 1993; Kent 2002; Pwiti 2005; Reid 2005; Schrire 1995). Although less well known, limited findings in central Africa resonate with these themes, as well (de Maret 1994/1995, 1999, 2005; Eggert 1994/1995; Mercador et al. 2000).

COMPLEXITY, POLITICAL ECONOMIC MOSAICS, AND ENTANGLEMENTS

Complex societies are an important focus in Anglophone archaeology, and ar-chaeological evidence has been central to assessing anthropological theories on the origins and development of social, political economic complexity. Complexity in its various guises often has been perceived as the culmination of an evolution-ary trajectory whether cast in a neoevolutionary or Marxist light (Rowlands 1989; Shennan 1993, p. 53). Through the 1980s a preoccupation with state-level societies gave way to a growing concern with so-called middle-range societies thought to represent precursors of the state (Earle 1987). Other investigators worked to unhook the components of complexity, for example, the presumed connections between forms of inequality and specific productive systems (Feinman & Neitzel 1984; Haas 2001, pp. 16–17). Still others urged a more fundamental rethinking of evo-lutionary models (Paynter 1989, Yoffee 1993). A preoccupation with hierarchical organizational forms yielded in the 1990s a concern with alternative logics, particularly heterarchy (Ehrenreich et al. 1995). Yet as S. McIntosh observed (1999c), African examples were largely absent from comparative theoretical discussions (e.g. Haas 2001; cf. Bacus & Lucero 1999; also see Lane 2001, p. 793), while archaeologists working in Africa were hampered by a reliance on models of complexity derived from other world areas. S. McIntosh (1999c, p. 4) pointed particularly to the hegemony of Oceanic models, and other contributors to her edited volume highlighted other "statejackets" (David & Sterner 1999, p. 99) into which our understandings of ancient African states have been forced (Asombang 1999, RJ McIntosh 1999). Contributors to that volume called for a renewed engagement with the practices and character of African complex societies past and present, arguing that more nuanced understandings of African social, political economic complexity should play an important role in retheorizing complexity more generally.

Francophone archaeologists have been less concerned with theorizing complexity or relating their studies of West African states to broader anthropological debates; they focus instead on contingency and specificity and particularly on the relationship between historical landscapes and human action (see, e.g., Devisse 1993, Vansina 1995, pp. 374–77; cf. Robertshaw 2000, p. 264). Yet whether informed by social scientific or more particularist historical concerns (McIntosh 2001, p. 15), archaeological research has cast considerable doubt on the received wisdom about the Sudanic states derived from Arab documents, and as outlined below, recent research in western and eastern Africa is beginning to illuminate the variable expressions of complexity and its contexts over the past two millennia.

Though archaeologists who work in Africa are increasingly attuned to the variable expressions of complexity over the past two millennia, investigations have tended to focus on the centers of complexity (LaViolette & Fleisher 2005). This focus has obscured the mosaic quality of African social, political economic, and technological landscapes, mosaics in which foragers interacted with agriculturalists, peripatetic herders passed through the courts of kings, and so-called tribal societies formed on the margins of complex polities. Of course scholars have long recognized the diversity of African societies; however, they have framed this diversity in terms of ethnic-linguistic groupings distinguished by techno-economic differences endowed with evolutionary significance (Murdock 1959; see Kusimba & Kusimba 2005). Despite indictments against early efforts to link language, race, and economy, a notion endures that foraging, cultivation, and pastoralism were indelibly associated with distinct groups. As Sharpe (1986) argues, the conceptual mapping of distinct state and tribal entities by colonial officials severed the necessary connections among societies of "different scales" (also Amselle 1998, pp. 1–24), a separation reinforced by the evolutionary narrative in standard archaeological texts that treat foraging as related to the Late Stone Age, pastoralism and cultivation as related to "neolithic" processes, and complex societies as an Iron Age phenomenon (cf. Stahl 2005). Yet recent archaeological research is beginning to highlight the interactions among societies of different scales, economies and sometimes technologies.

Though these interrelations perhaps have had greatest visibility in relation to the "revisionist" debate in the Kalahari (see Reid 2005 for an overview; also Kent 2002, Sadr 1997, Thorp 1997), archaeologists working in diverse areas are beginning to make substantial progress in illuminating this second theme—the mosaic and interconnected quality of African social, political economic, and technological landscapes. Whereas ethnic-linguistic mosaics were previously viewed as relatively fixed, recognition of their fluidity in time and space is growing. Kopytoff's (1987) concept of the "internal African frontier" has proved influential in analyzing this dynamic quality. New societies were continuously formed in the interstices between established ones through processes of migration. Where political control was weak frontier societies were developed (Amselle 1998, p. 14; Kopytoff 1987, p. 9) by migrants prompted to move through accusations of wrong-doing, successional struggles, or perceived opportunities. Migrants derived from a variety of ethnic-linguistic and political groups, and the societies they forged had a hybrid quality (Amselle 1998), drawing as they did on the cultural practices of surrounding areas and creating new ones in the process. Practices of kinship, religion, political organization, and identity were continuously negotiated (Amselle 1998, pp. 32–35). Boundaries were not fixed but existed in relation to a "chain of societies" (Amselle 1998, pp. xiii) on a landscape at any given time (Kopytoff 1987, p. 12).

The growing emphasis on fluidity and mobility has implications for relationships between rulers and the ruled. When people can "vote with their feet," those "in power" must gain the allegiance of followers through multiple strategies, which resonates with an emphasis in Africa on "wealth in people" (Guyer 1995). A focus on wealth in people emerged in contexts where land was abundant and extensive land use patterns prevailed (e.g., Vansina 1990, p. 251). Under these conditions, attracting followers was the central problem for leaders. Wealth in goods was transformed in varying ways to wealth in followers, which Marxist scholars saw as a crucial source of labor (Meillassoux 1972, Rey 1975). Yet their diverse knowledges were an equally important resource (Guyer & Belinga 1995). Guyer & Belinga posit compositional strategies of leadership that brought together people with diverse, complexly organized knowledges (of crafts, the supernatural, diverse ecologies, and economic opportunities). Compositional strategies resonate with notions of heterarchy and are "quite different from the models of hierarchical gradations of esoteric knowledge as a social control mechanism" (p. 112). This perspective may serve as a means to complicate hierarchy by pointing to its varied forms, an issue that usefully may be explored in relation to what Blanton et al. (1996) term corporate and network modes of power (see below).

The complexity of these social, political, and economic mosaics was further complicated by our third theme—entanglements (Thomas 1991) that ensued from Africa's involvement in emerging world systems. Global entanglements were intimately bound up in expanding systems of exchange, altered frameworks of value, and shifting topologies of power, though we should not assume the priority of external dominance and metropolitan processes over local autonomy and regional dynamics (Thomas 1991, p. 186). Though emphasis often has been placed on the period of the Atlantic trade and the modern world system, global connections run deep—from at least the tenth century with the emerging trans-Saharan trade, and possibly even earlier in western Africa (Magnavita 2003), and from the early centuries AD in eastern Africa with the Indian Ocean trade (LaViolette 2004). Intercontinental connections had wide-ranging implications for production, consumption, demography, and sociopolitical configurations. The character of these connections varied over time and in space and involved diasporic populations whose presence further complicated the mosaic quality of African societies. Whereas some investigators envision these entanglements in terms of "cores" and "peripheries" (e.g., Wallerstein 1986, p. 102), the assumed dominance of the core, the unidirectional emphasis that situates agency within the core, and the assumed primacy of long-distance connections in shaping the political economy of "peripheries" has proved unsatisfactory (Stein 2002, pp. 904–5; Thomas 1991, p. 207). This dissatisfaction has prompted new approaches to the study of interregional interaction that stress local agency, practice, and the variegated quality and multiple effects of these entanglements (Dietler 1998, Lightfoot et al. 1998, Pauketat 2001, Stein 2002), and I explore how these concerns have been incorporated into the study of global entanglements in Africa.

WESTERN AFRICA

Recent research in West Africa (Figure 1) highlights the complexity of African complex societies, illustrated particularly by discussions concerning heterarchy and hierarchy in the Sudanic belt. We also are gaining appreciation for the complex

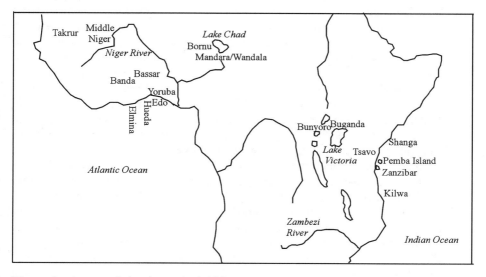

Figure 1   Areas and sites in tropical Africa.

and dynamic relations among societies of different scales and how these mosaics were reshaped through their changing involvement in the trans-Saharan and later Atlantic exchange systems (MacEachern 2005).

Heterarchy in the Middle Niger

The Inland Niger Delta (IND) is a rich interior floodplain inserted into arid surroundings on the southern margins of the Sahara. A series of dry basins (including the Méma) attests to the vast expanse of the Middle Niger in earlier millennia (McIntosh 1998, pp. 34–80). Ecological diversity of the IND contributed to the emergence of regional exchange networks, and historically (from the early second millennium AD) the Middle Niger played a key role in the trans-Saharan trade that linked the forested hinterlands of the Guinea coast (rich in gold and kola nut) with the Mediterranean world. Competition over the Saharan trade fueled a succession of historically known empires: Ghana, Mali, and Songhay.

Both the active and dry basins of the Middle Niger have been subject to extensive survey and variably intensive subsurface testing of sites of varying size over the past quarter century (e.g., Baloian 2002; Bedaux & van der Waals 1994; Bedaux et al. 1978, 2001; Devisse 1993; Haaland 1980; Insoll 1997; McIntosh 1995, 1998, 1999a, 1999b; McIntosh & McIntosh 1993; Raimbault & Sanogo 1991; Togola 1996). The McIntoshes' early work concentrated on large mound sites in a settlement complex associated with the ancient commercial town of Jenné. Historians had long assumed that urban settlements in West Africa were a product of the "golden trade of the Moors" (Bovill 1958); however, excavations at the largest of these mounds, Jenné-jeno, demonstrated that the precursor of the early second millennium city described by Arab chroniclers predated the emergence of trans-Saharan exchange networks and was sustained by exchange among societies ranging from southern forested regions to the Sahara. A concern of early research was to demonstrate the independent origins of African complex societies and to highlight how criteria from other world areas drew a curtain across our understanding of the distinctive qualities of African urbanism (McIntosh & McIntosh 1993; also Connah 2001, Fletcher 1998, MacDonald 1998, LaViolette & Fleisher 2005).

More recent publications emphasize the distinctive organizational features of Middle Niger societies which the McIntoshes envision as heterarchically organized (McIntosh 1998, 1999b). They pose a model of "deep time plurality" in which ethnically and economically diverse populations resisted centralizing tendencies, maintaining instead a form of "articulated specialization" that offered flexibility in the face of short-term climatic change (Magnavita & Magnavita 2001; McIntosh 1993, 1998, pp. 55–57). Fostered by the patchy distribution of resources and scheduling conflicts, such specialization characterized the earliest IND settlements and persisted through rapid population growth into the second millennium AD without notable intensification (McIntosh 1999a, pp. 155, 160, 1999b, pp. 68, 74). This specialization underlay a long-standing resistance to monopolized power and contributed to the durability of heterarchical arrangements in the IND.

In the early centuries of the second millennium AD an indigenously developed heterarchical society gave way to increasing hierarchy under combined pressures of environmental change, disease, and growing involvement in exchange with Islamic North Africa. An evolving "imperial tradition" reinvented extant social relations and culminated in "three and a half centuries of warrior-state chaos" (McIntosh 1998, p. 295). Yet despite a trend toward hierarchy and a coercive political economy, McIntosh (1998, pp. 297–303) argues that deep-time heterarchical relations rooted in ecological diversity and pluralism endowed Middle Niger society with a cultural resiliency not seen in neighboring regions.

Though provocative, the model of articulated specialization is based primarily on varying concentrations of iron-working debris and other artifact categories on site surfaces, particularly at smaller satellite sites surrounding major mounds. MacDonald's excavations at sites in the Méma suggested different economic orientations among neighboring sites (summarized in McIntosh 1998, pp. 61–63), and there is similar clustering of sites as existed around Jenné-jeno (McIntosh 1999b, p. 68); however, Togola (1996, p. 104) observes that the scarcity of surface remains from clustered sites in the Méma does not permit an extension of the hypothesis of articulated specialization to the Méma sites. Baloian's (2002) research partly confirms the specialized character of iron production in the Jenné vicinity; yet documentation of subsistence specialization remains limited. Although the hypothesis of counterpoised power relations rooted in articulated specialization requires further empirical support, it offers an important correction to the presumption that hierarchy necessarily characterizes complex societies. We should be cautious, however, in assuming an ethnic dimension to specialization. Though McIntosh (1998, pp. 295–96) recognizes potential malleability in ethnicity, his model of articulated specialization draws on twentieth-century sources (Gallais 1984) without accounting for how ethnic differentiation was reshaped through the tumultuous conditions of recent centuries (e.g., Gronenborn 1998, p. 254; Holl 2001, p. 153; Lentz 1995).

Hierarchy in the Sudanic Belt

Whereas work in the IND emphasizes the heterarchical character of Middle Niger societies, research in other areas of the Sudanic belt extending from Senegal through the Chad Basin suggests that hierarchically organized polities were common as well, particularly from the late first millennium AD (e.g., Gronenborn 1998), though a paucity of evidence from early first millennium contexts limits our understanding of the circumstances in which these polities emerged (e.g., MacEachern 2001, pp. 135–37; cf. McIntosh & Bocoum 2000). The trans-Saharan trade may not have sparked the development of the earliest complex societies; however, the shift from regional exchange in the first millennium AD toward growing involvement of Sudanic societies in the Saharan trade from the eighth or ninth century AD was associated with a distinctive and recurrent pattern of hierarchically organized predatory states whose power was based on control over the flow of prestige goods (cloth, beads, copper alloys), access to what Goody (1971) termed the means of destruction (firearms, horses; Holl 1994, pp. 141–42; MacEachern 2001, p. 139), and access to enslavable populations (Gronenborn 1998, pp. 251–54, Holl 1995).

Though commonalities in the contexts and expressions of second millennium polities are apparent, expressions vary in several empirically robust case studies. This variation implies that we must probe the content of "hierarchy" to avoid assimilating variability to narrowly conceived models. The expression of hierarchical principles was at times strategic and partial, as in the case of Sukur in the Mandara Highlands of Nigeria. Though public works were associated with the historic Sukur polity and the Sukur sovereign maintained the appearance of a Sudanic ruler, David (1996) argues that "Sukur's institutional complexity was in fact largely a facade, a veil thrown over a reasonably egalitarian society that presented two faces to the world" (p. 599). The external face, directed at Sukur's trading partners, stressed the power of the sovereign; yet internal limits on the sovereign's power were consistent with an egalitarian society. This finding suggests a "type of classless society and a political form hitherto unknown" (p. 599) that has broader implications for our imaginings of past complexity (David & Sterner 1999).

Archaeologists are only beginning to understand the contexts and processes that gave rise to polities like Kanem-Borno (Gronenborn 1998, 2001), Wandala (MacEachern 2001), or Takrur (McIntosh 1999a). Though counterintuitive in relation to narratives of world prehistory, subsistence practices remained extensive and wild resources were important to subsistence through the first millennium AD (and often into the present) (Gronenborn 1998, pp. 248–50; Neumann 2005). Polity boundaries were fluid, and in some instances seats of power were not geographically fixed. For example, the capitol of Kanem-Borno shifted in response to resistance from local populations (Gronenborn 2001, p. 103). These shifts, combined with the likelihood that dwellings were constructed in part from perishable materials, have frustrated attempts to locate ancient capitols (Gronenborn 2001, pp. 103–8). Fluidity and mobility flowed in part from the fact that people, rather than land, were a crucial source of power for African political leaders.

From the late first millennium AD captives became an important means by which polities accessed luxury goods, first via trans-Saharan networks and later via Atlantic trade. Though state revenues flowed from a variety of economic activities (MacEachern 2001, p. 138), access to prestige goods that materially distinguished the powerful depended in part on a state's access to enslavable populations. Though in some cases production for exchange was managed through household labor (David 1996, p. 598), captives provided labor to produce exchangeable goods (e.g., cloth; Gronenborn 2001, p. 111; Roberts 1984). Other captives were "high-value exports that could be traded for exotic products" (MacEachern 2001, p. 138). Thus access to enslavable populations was crucial to maintain hegemony—in some instances as a source of labor, in others as an exchangeable commodity, and in still others as a source of personnel to offset demographic losses. Demographic variables were, therefore, highly salient though robust evidence on demographic implications is scant and remains a topic in need of archaeological investigation.

The importance of people as a crucial state resource trains our attention on the interconnections that existed among societies of different scales across West Africa over the past 2000 years. Second millennium states were part of a mosaic political landscape composed of societies of varying scales partially shaped by the demand for captives. Societies on the margins of states were subject to predation. Vulnerable peoples embraced several strategies to resist enslavement, and these strategies carried implications for demography and ethnogenesis: Some people fought, whereas others sought refuge in neighboring areas, joining the pool of followers crucial to emerging polities (Stahl 2001a); some groups withdrew to remote and/or defendable areas (de Barros 2001; Holl 1994, p. 168; MacEachern 2001, pp. 143–44); and still others built structural defenses (Connah 1981, p. 167; Holl 2001, p. 172; MacEachern 2001, p. 140; Usman 1999, 2003b, 2004). For others, conversion to Islam offered a measure of protection (Alexander 2001, Insoll 2003).

Though the broad features of societal chains were perhaps stable over time (links between states and predation zones; MacEachern 2001, p. 137; Usman 2003b), their manifestations varied in time and space. Intensive raiding of peripheral populations created frontier niches (Kopytoff 1987). Small polities gained advantage as powerful neighbors succumbed to internal fractures. Other societies gained power as intermediaries in the slave trade when the frontier of vulnerable societies receded under pressures of slave raiding [MacEachern's (2001, pp. 141–43) "subcontractors"; see Alexander 2001]. Thus, a key feature of African complex societies is their ramifying character and the changing contours of ramifying networks over time.

Several pioneering archaeological projects provide insight into the implications of these transformations for production, consumption, and exchange (Stahl 2004). de Barros (2001) explores the dynamic history of iron and pottery production in relation to changing interregional political economic contexts in Bassar (northern Togo). Iron production intensified from the fifteenth century with escalating demands for weapons, horse paraphernalia, and protective gear by neighboring cavalry states (Dagomba, Mamprusi, Gonja). Dagomba's incorporation into the expansionist Asante state led to increased demand for slaves, prompting more intensive raiding of Bassar populations and concomitant shifts in settlement and production sites. Sites in the open plains were abandoned and new settlements founded in hilly refuge areas. Comparable shifts occurred farther west in the Mandara Region of northern Cameroon. The Mandara Mountains initially were occupied in the mid-second millennium AD by plains-dwelling groups seeking refuge from Wandala slave raiding. Yet Wandala depended on Montagnard populations in the Mandara Mountains for iron supplies, which the Wandala traded to states like Kanem and Borno in exchange for horses, guns, chain mail, cloth, and salt (MacEachern 1993, p. 256). Montagnard populations depended on Wandala connections to access salt and dried fish; however, the Wandala also posed a threat to them through slave raiding. Thus, the Bassar and Mandara examples show commonalities, particularly in a counterpoised dependent relationship among societies of different scales fraught with considerable tension.

The Atlantic World System

Though West Africa was long enmeshed in international trade, the Portuguese presence at Elmina on the Gold Coast from 1482 marked the beginnings of new exchange relations. The trans-Saharan trade never ceased; however, expanding coastal exchange provided alternative trade outlets, led to the demand for new export products, and created new tastes among West African populations for imports. European powers competed for preeminence, and African polities proliferated along the coast and in forested hinterlands. European interest in West African gold was eclipsed by the discovery of New World reserves, and trade shifted to slaves to supply New World plantation economies. Slaves were the primary export from the sixteenth to eighteenth centuries, a period marked by expanding European involvement on the West African coast. British abolition of the slave trade in 1807 coupled with expanding industrialization in Europe gave rise to the "legitimate" trade in which African raw materials were exchanged for European manufactures.

Historical archaeological research at coastal sites in Ghana and Benin contributes important insights into the varied nature of European/African interactions. DeCorse's (1998, 2001) research on the African settlement adjacent to the European fort Elmina focuses on the effects of culture contact. Despite evidence for the existence of new construction techniques and a wealth of imported objects, DeCorse questions the common assumption made by historical archaeologists that changing material assemblages signal assimilation or acculturation, arguing that change in the material record at Elmina is underwritten by significant continuities in world view. Ritual and burial practices show continuities, as do the layout of houses and foodways despite the adoption of new construction techniques and ceramics. Thus despite sustained involvement of Elmina peoples in international exchange and the wealth that Elmina merchants accrued, townspeople retained central aspects of African beliefs and identity (DeCorse 1998, pp. 369–72, 2001, pp. 178–190).

Kelly (1997, 2001, 2002, 2004) has conducted excavations at Savi, capitol of Hueda from the seventeenth through nineteenth centuries. The Bight of Benin was a major source, and Hueda was a major supplier of slaves to the Atlantic trade. Whereas early European/African interaction is often envisioned anachronistically through the lens of twentieth-century colonialism (Kelly 2002, pp. 96, 102), Kelly emphasizes the agency of Hueda elite in managing the European presence. European trading lodges were located not on the coast but instead 10 km inland in the Hueda capitol of Savi, and indeed within the palace precinct where traders would have been subject to constant surveillance (Kelly 2002, p. 105). Coursed earth construction characterized both Hueda elite and European residences at Savi; however, imported bricks paved public rooms in the palace, whereas residences of

European traders were not so distinguished (Kelly 1997, pp. 363–64). Imported goods were recovered from across the site; however, they were not found in significant quantities nor were they evenly distributed, and Kelly (1997, pp. 362–63) emphasizes the need to investigate rather than assume the significance of these goods within a local cultural context.

These studies underscore the variability of European/African relations on the West African coast. Whereas Europeans controlled trade at Elmina and the African population incorporated a wide array of imported goods into their daily routines, Hueda elite maintained control of trade, and locally produced material culture dominated (Kelly 2002, pp. 97–98). Whereas processes of creolization occurred in some contexts (e.g., Elmina), evidence for material change is far less pronounced in other contexts (e.g., Hueda), outcomes that may have been shaped by the degree of control that Africans exercised over the European presence (Kelly 2002, pp. 115–16).

Though not in direct contact with European traders, the lives and livelihoods of interior peoples also were affected by new economic pressures and changing political alignments. Several archaeological projects have begun to explore the implications of these entanglements for interior societies using a direct historical approach in which investigators use multiple sources (ethnographic, oral historical, and archaeological) to investigate continuity and change over the last 500–700 years. Ogundiran's (2001a, 2001b, 2002a, 2002b) research in the Yoruba-Edo region of Nigeria focuses on issues of social memory and political economic transformations in relation to the changing character of Atlantic commerce. His work stresses the fluid character of social groups and the centrality of ritual and royal ceremony in forging social memory and group identity (Ogundiran 2001b, p. 222). Cross-cutting styles and ritual practices across the region attest the linked trajectory of polities with implications for our understanding of the dynamics of ethnogenesis in the area (Ogundiran 2002b). Ogundiran's work is distinguished by a concern with the social valuation of imports, with how imported objects were recontextualized and shaped new forms of accumulation (Ogundiran 2002a). In similar fashion, Banda Research Project investigations have focused on the effects of global entanglements on the character of daily life in west central Ghana (Stahl 1999a, 2001b; Stahl & Cruz 1998). Banda was home to a historic chieftaincy that emerged in a frontier setting in the late seventeenth to early eighteenth century when the Atlantic trade disrupted long-standing Sudanic and Saharan trade networks. Banda was incorporated into the expansionist Asante state in the late eighteenth century and was subjected to the British at the end of the nineteenth century. Excavations at village sites occupied through this period document changes in the production and consumption of ceramics (Cruz 2003), iron, and cloth (Stahl & Cruz 1998); the character of subsistence (reshaped by New World crops and changing hunting patterns); and settlement and exchange relations associated with shifting political allegiances, warfare, and the upheavals created by the slave trade through the nineteenth century (Stahl 2001a). Ongoing investigations at earlier sites offer insight into the deeper trajectories of these practices in the period of the trans-Saharan trade, paying particular attention to the implications of global entanglements for the reconfiguration of local tastes and daily practices (Stahl 2002). Both projects underscore the dynamic quality of daily life over the last six centuries, a dynamism that is obscured when we assimilate such societies to the "Iron Age" rubric conventionally applied to sites of the last two millennia.

EASTERN AFRICA

The past 2000 years in eastern Africa saw innovations in food production though foraging remained important; metallurgy was embraced but stone tool technologies persisted; and societies of varying scale became enmeshed in the Indian Ocean trade, which varied in character over time (Kusimba & Kusimba 2005). The themes of complexity, societal mosaics, and global entanglements are exemplified by recent research in the Interlacustrine region of the Great Lakes, the Swahili coast, and adjacent hinterlands of eastern Africa (Figure 1).

Interlacustrine Mosaics

Nineteenth-century European accounts attested a bewildering array of states and smaller polities occupying diverse ecological settings in the Great Lakes region. Notable among these were the bordering, rival states Buganda and Bunyoro, each occupying distinct ecological settings and being characterized by different political economic strategies. The centralized Buganda polity bordered the northwest shores of Lake Victoria in forested, rolling hills. Banana and sweet potato cultivation was supplemented by fish from Lake Victoria. The less-centralized Bunyoro polity in the dry grasslands to the northwest supplemented finger millet with other crops. Though cattle were not common in the nineteenth century, traditions stressed their importance in the precolonial period (Robertshaw 1999b, p. 53).

The complex polities of the Interlacustrine region were long presumed to have been imposed on an indigenous population by "civilizing" outsiders (Reid 1996, p. 621; Robertshaw 2003, p. 150). Early archaeological investigations were driven by oral traditions of dynasties presumed to be ancestral to these historic kingdoms (Robertshaw & Taylor 2000, pp. 2–4). Efforts were made in the 1950s-1960s to link these traditions to Bigo, one of several large earthwork sites comprising mounds and trenches in the western part of historic Buganda; however, critical analysis of these traditions suggested that they had been reworked in relation to colonial demands (Schmidt 1990, pp. 256–64; Sutton 1993). Yet the impressive scale of these earthworks suggests considerable labor inputs and is assumed to reflect a stratified political hierarchy (Reid 1996, p. 621).

Recent regional surveys and systematic testing of archaeological sites lend new insights into the character of settlement and political economic arrangements over the past 2000 years (Connah 1997; Reid 1996; Robertshaw 1999a,b; Robertshaw & Taylor 2000). Surveys indicate that substantial occupation of the Interlacustrine area began from the ninth century AD in a period of elevated rainfall (Reid 1996, p. 623; Robertshaw 1994, pp. 114–15; Robertshaw & Taylor 2000, p. 25). Scattered Late Stone Age material and occasional Urewe (Early Iron Age) pottery suggest that early second millennium AD occupations colonized an unoccupied landscape (Reid 1996, p. 625). Geographically distinct subsistence patterns developed in the centuries following early occupation (~800–1300 AD) including specialized pastoralism and intensive banana farming associated with forest clearance and grassland expansion (Schoenbrun 1998, pp. 36–37, 1999, pp. 136–37).

Deep midden accumulations at Ntusi from the eleventh century AD predate the Bigo earthworks by several centuries and were associated with the pioneering occupation of the dry grasslands. Reid (1996, pp. 623–25) argues that cattle were central to the colonization of grassland areas, as were changing technologies of plant food storage. Cultivation and cattle production were practiced within the same households, a pattern that diverges from historical contexts in which these practices were associated with class divisions (Reid 1996, pp. 624–25). Artifact diversity and site size suggests a two-tiered settlement hierarchy in the period of Ntusi's occupation (eleventh through fifteenth centuries AD) with evidence for ivory and iron production at Ntusi. Regional trade with the contemporary salt-producing site of Kiboro on Lake Albert (Connah 1997) seems likely, and links to the East African coast are attested by several glass and cowrie shell beads (Robertshaw 1999a, p. 130). The emerging hierarchy represented by Ntusi may have been linked to the emergence of new terms for leadership, an explosion of cattle terminologies, and a redefinition of gender roles as traced through Schoenbrun's historical linguistic analyses (Robertshaw & Taylor 2000, pp. 14; Schoenbrun 1998, 1999).

Labor rather than land, as in West Africa, would have been a primary concern for the early colonizers of this "internal frontier" (Kopytoff 1987; Robertshaw 1999a, p. 126), and how first settlers attracted followers is a central problem in studying these early second millennium societies (Robertshaw 1999b, p. 58; Schoenbrun 1998, p. 100, 1999, p. 137). Emergent elites likely consolidated power through control of prestige goods, iron production, and ritual authority suggested by hilltop burials accompanied by imported beads, the placement of iron furnaces on site centers, and the association of thirteenth- to fourteenth-century shrine sites (Mubende Hill, Kasunga) with numerous storage pits that imply control of staple resources (Robertshaw 1999b, pp. 58–59; Robertshaw & Taylor 2000, p. 16). According to investigators, increases in vessel size and the large middens at Ntusi suggest involvement in feasting as a means for attracting followers (Robertshaw & Taylor 2000, p. 15). Robertshaw (2003, p. 160) sees evidence for exotics and craft specialization (in ivory production) as consistent with a prestige-goods system associated with what Blanton et al. (1996, pp. 2–5) term exclusionary or network strategies in which external ties that facilitate access to exotic goods, knowledge, and allegiances are translated into local leadership. This pattern is consistent with a frontier setting in which low population densities and mobility limited the potential for appropriation of agricultural surpluses (so-called staple finance; D'Altroy & Earle 1985).

Ntusi was abandoned during a time of declining precipitation in the 1400s when Gwezi shrine sites like Mubende Hill were founded. Grain storage at these sites suggests the importance of cultivation, and the emergence of shrines may have been linked to efforts to control rainfall (Robertshaw & Taylor 2000, pp. 6, 24–25). Higher rainfall levels in the 1400–1500s were correlated with an abandonment of shrine sites and the construction of earthworks in the late fifteenth or sixteenth century (Robertshaw & Taylor 2000, pp. 24–25) and several changes probably relate to a "closing" of the frontier period (Schoenbrun 1999, p. 146). Long-distance exchange diminished from the late fifteenth century (Robertshaw 1999a:130), while earthworks were constructed around hills on which earlier-period burials with glass beads occurred (Robertshaw 1997). This pattern, combined with the communal effort involved in earthwork construction, led Robertshaw (1999b, pp. 60–61, 2003, pp. 160–62) to posit a shift from exclusionary power (associated with an individual leader) toward a corporate strategy (Blanton et al. 1996, pp. 5–7) on the basis of elite appropriation of surplus and associated with labor mobilization directed at monument construction and perhaps raiding and warfare directed at the capture of women and cattle.

Earthworks were abandoned after the mid-seventeenth century for reasons that remain unclear; however, Robertshaw & Taylor (2000, p. 19) suggest that major political economic and social changes occurred across the region from around 1700 AD. Nucleated villages gave way to a pattern of dispersed homesteads, and "capitals appear to have become more peripatetic as their rulers put more emphasis on the size and health of their herds" (p. 19). A correlation with declining rainfall levels coinciding with the Little Ice Age of northern latitudes may have contributed to changing political economic strategies (pp. 25–27). The historic stratification between a pastoral nobility and agricultural peasantry likely developed from this period and was associated with the Bito dynasty of Bunyoro. Increasing contacts with Sudanese and Zanzibari slave traders shaped the political economies of historic Bunyoro and Buganda whose wealth and power flowed from exchange in salt, iron, ivory, slaves, and weapons (Reid 1999, p. 44). Competition and warfare among these states shaped the mobility of settlements. According to Reid (2001/2002, p. 56) the Ganda capitol was relocated on a regular basis and only became a more permanent urban center from the mid-nineteenth century as military pressures relaxed.

Recent interdisciplinary collaboration has enhanced our understanding of Interlacustrine political economic mosaics. Schoenbrun's (1998, 1999) historical linguistic reconstructions enriched analytical possibilities by exploring the changing configuration of social space and cognitive systems within Great Lakes societies. Changing social terminologies corresponded to altered patterns of subsistence and land availability and suggest modifications in the social relations of clanship over time. When land was abundant, families enlarged by allocating land to outsiders, facilitated by ideologies of inclusiveness that enabled "wholesale incorporation of newcomers around a longer-established firstcomer group" (Schoenbrun 1998, p. 124, 1999, p. 144). With time, demographic increase, decreasing land availability, and increased environmental uncertainty, a new social calculus emerged with a patrifocal emphasis associated with hereditary access to title and land (Schoenbrun 1998, p. 125). This shaped new exclusions on the basis of descent, altered the gendered division of labor, and marginalized women from the public sphere (Schoenbrun 1999, p. 146; also Robertshaw 1999b). Frontier egalitarianism was "replaced by innovations in contracts, superior-subordinate relations, and bridewealth exchanges for women" in a new calculus that "now revolved around discriminating and limiting access to productive property" (Schoenbrun 1998, p. 139).

Recent Interlacustrine research underscores that the complex mosaic of historical societies in the region does not mirror the variegated social, political economic forms of the past (see also David & Sterner 1999). Archaeological research is beginning to reveal temporal and spatial variability in the topography of complexity over time. Although healthy skepticism of linguistic dating techniques is in order (Schoenbrun 1998, pp. 38–41, 46–48), Schoenbrun's rich semantic history provides insight into the changing calculus of social group membership and organization. This calculus departs markedly from the tendency to argue for enduring structures of kinship, wealth, and leadership in other parts of Bantu Africa (e.g., Huffman 1996; cf. Beach 1998). Research also shows that, despite a tendency toward increasing political scale over time, "it is also true that its centers were precarious and fleeting" (Schoenbrun 1999, p. 137). To capture the mosaic quality and shifting dimensions of these configurations, we must coordinate research across broad regions and expand systematic survey and testing of sites of varying scales across regions and over time.

East African Coast

The East African coast and associated islands from Somalia to Mozambique were home to an array of historically documented Swahili towns from ~800 AD (Robertshaw 2003, p. 153). As in West Africa, scholars long assumed that these urban centers were foreign-inspired if not -founded, a view conditioned by the assumption that Swahili populations were more Arab than African (Kusimba 1999, pp. 21–31, 43–66; LaViolette & Fleisher 2005; Sutton 1998, p. 119). Coastal settlements were viewed as sea-facing, separated from the interior by a harsh, resource-poor zone in the immediate hinterland (Abungu & Mutoro 1993, p. 695); however, more recent research demonstrates the indigenous character of these societies, the deep antiquity of their involvement in oceanic trade, and the systemic links between interior and coastal societies of different scales.

Early research on Swahili towns centered on stonetowns like Kilwa, an island site off the southern coast of Tanzania associated with ruins of multistoried domestic buildings, ornate mosques, and above-ground tombs. Excavations focused on the fluorescence of these urban centers early in the second millennium AD, interpreted as Islamic trading outposts with few cultural links to their African hinterland (e.g., Chittick 1974, Kirkman 1964). Oral traditions of some ruling families who trace their origins to Arabia or the Persian Gulf seem to support this view (Sutton 1998, p. 118). In the early independence period a reaction against the presumed external origins of Swahili society animated historiographical debates and led to renewed archaeological research directed at the question of Swahili origins (LaViolette & Fleisher 2005; Sutton 1998, pp. 165–66). Horton's (1996) documentation of pre-Islamic levels at Shanga, an early Swahili site on Pate Island off the north coast of Kenya, is particularly important.

The origins of stonetowns like Shanga were rooted in early coastal settlements occupied by people pursuing a mixed economy of fishing, herding, and farming (Horton & Mudida 1993; Wright 1993, pp. 660–61). As in the West African and Interlacustrine contexts discussed above, we have a poor understanding of the centuries before about 800 AD (Kusimba 1999, pp. 33–35, 90–97; Wright 1993, p. 659). Though Greek and Roman documentary sources from the early centuries AD described trade with the East African or "Azanian" coast, material evidence of this trade was confined until recently to occasional finds of Greek and Roman coins (Chami & Msemwa 1997, p. 673). Though Early Iron Age settlements were known in interior areas, evidence for coastal settlement was limited. However, recent research documents settlements of iron-producing peoples near the south Kenyan and Tanzanian coasts from the last century BC to the fifth century AD. By the third century AD some sites (e.g., Limbo; Schmidt 1995, p. 142) were producing iron in significantly greater quantities than were contemporary sites in the interior, presumably for exchange. Other sites (e.g., Kivinja; Chami 2003, Chami & Msemwa 1997) yielded third-century Near Eastern imports (pottery, glass) that attest oceanic exchange; however, there is no evidence for social differentiation in this early period despite the presence of imports (Kusimba 1999, p. 94). A more substantial quantity of imports drawn from a wider catchment is evident at Chibuene in southern Mozambique (occupied from the mid-first millennium AD; Sinclair et al. 1993b, p. 419) and included ivory and copper that likely came from emerging centers in the Limpopo Valley to the south and west (e.g., Mapungubwe; Pwiti 2005). Thus mounting evidence implies the participation of East African coastal and adjacent hinterland regions in oceanic trade from the mid-first millennium AD (Chami & Msemwa 1997, p. 675).

By the ninth century AD there is more substantial evidence for interior and coastal trade (Horton 1996; Kusimba 1999, pp. 60–64). Settlements expanded considerably in size over the course of the ninth and tenth centuries (Wright 1993, p. 663), and iron working and bead manufacture indicate craft specialization (Kessy 2003, pp. 129, 131). By the tenth century similar ceramics were distributed from the Lamu archipelago on the northern Kenyan coast to the southern coast of Mozambique, "2200 km of difficult sailing away" (Wright 1993, p. 660; also Sutton 1998, pp. 120–21), whereas the presence of similar ceramics extending to the Taita hills suggests interior connections (Abungu & Mutoro 1993, p. 695).

The products exported from the Swahili coast after the ninth century likely included iron tools, shell beads, turtle shells, amber, gold and ivory, and perhaps deep water fish (Kusimba 1999, pp. 100, 126–27). Kilwa served as the conduit for Zimbabwean gold into the world system, and its fluorescence in the thirteenth century coincided with the adoption of gold coinage in Europe (Sutton 1998, p. 113). Fuel shortages in Arabia and India contributed to a demand for East African iron; imported iron could be melted down there to make crucible steel (which was exported in substantial quantities to Europe and the Middle East from the late first millennium AD; Kusimba 1999, pp. 103, 106). Though archaeologists have not found large-scale smelting sites on the coast, they have recovered slag, iron-working tools, and forging debris (Kusimba & Killick 2003, p. 113). The importance of iron as an export undermines the image of East Africa as merely a source of natural products (Schmidt 1995, pp. 142–43). The range of imports is better known and included Near Eastern and Chinese ceramics. Larger vessels may have arrived with valuable oils or other liquids. Cloth is another likely import, which is consistent with the rarity of spindle whorls on early coastal sites (Wright 1993, p. 664), though their presence in later contexts attest involvement in cloth production at centers like Kilwa (Sutton 1998, p. 123).

At least some stonetowns were strategically positioned in relation to interior routes or natural harbors (Abungu & Mutoro 1993, p. 701; Kusimba 1999, pp. 123–25). Occupation at Ungwana spanned the period 950–1600 AD, and at its peak it was a prosperous center, as evidenced by abundant prestige goods and substantial residences that were likely home to successful traders (Abungu & Mutoro 1993, pp. 701–2). Links to the interior along the ecologically diverse Tana River drainage are witnessed in the ceramic similarities between river basin settlements and coastal settlements like Ungwana and Shanga.

Swahili towns of the second millennium AD were characterized by durable elite residences constructed from coral-rag that drew the attention of early archaeologists. Less visible but ubiquitous were the earthen and organic structures that housed non-elites. Growing attention to these non-elite structures provided a crucial link between later stonetowns and their earlier indigenous progenitors (Fleisher & LaViolette 1999, p. 88; e.g., Horton 1996, p. 234). Though Swahili towns often have been characterized as residentially segregated on the basis of wealth and social position (Kusimba 1999, p. 151), recent research suggests a more variegated pattern. For example, Sheriff (2001/2002) argues that such segregation emerged in Zanzibar only through colonial policies that attempted to fix differences between residential areas on the basis of building type.

The eleventh through thirteenth centuries witnessed fundamental changes in the organization of society and its ideological basis (Kusimba 1999, pp. 117–54; Wright 1993, pp. 665–70). Underlying productive systems were changed little; however, hierarchical patterning among settlements became more pronounced with town sites (10 ha or larger) dominating local settlement hierarchies that included walled villages, compact and dispersed villages, and hamlets (Kusimba 1999, pp. 119–23). Settlement expanded into sparsely occupied areas of the Kenya coast, and reliance on domestic animals increased at some sites (Horton 1996, p. 397). Islam likely was widely adopted in this period, as indicated by the growing number of mosques and evidence for Islamic burial practices. Though the earliest mosque at

Shanga dates to before the tenth century, there is no evidence of "communities of the faithful" in areas to the south before the eleventh or twelfth centuries (Wright 1993, p. 664). Islam was embraced relatively simultaneously across a 1500-km stretch of coast, with no evidence for its adoption by interior peoples. The growing number of settlements and towns contributed to an increase in instability and conflict that perhaps encouraged conversion to Islam as a means of stabilizing relations with both traders and competing elites (Wright 1993; also LaViolette & Fleisher 2005).

Over time coastal towns became more oriented to mercantile activity than to production as indicated by the declining evidence for smelting and weaving in coastal centers (Kusimba 1999, p. 134). Swahili elite increasingly distinguished themselves from commoners through their embrace of exotic goods. They enforced their distinction through dress, proprietary rules restricting commoner access to imports and rights to build stone houses, and the maintenance of separate burial places and practices (Kusimba 1999, pp. 145–47). Focus on the sea trade was marked by settlement shifts to the seaward side of Pemba Island from the fourteenth century (Kessy 2003, p. 123).

Robertshaw (2003, pp. 163–65) argues that coastal Swahili society was built on exclusionary power strategies in which elites controlled access to prestige goods and differentiated themselves with an "international style" that built on a foundation of Islam and Asian material culture (ceramics, architectural styles). Consistent with a "network strategy" (Blanton et al. 1996, pp. 4–5), there likely was considerable competition among coastal stonetowns (Robertshaw 2003, p. 164; Wright 1993). Yet Kusimba (1999, pp. 180–83) highlights the intermingled character of these strategies in the early coastal contexts, arguing that elites drew on corporate assets and organizational forms to pursue network strategies. With time, however, the limited availability of arable land contributed to a growing reliance on network strategies to offset risks associated with a restricted productive base and contributed to investment in surpluses created by iron production and ivory exchange. Increased importation of exotics over time likely signals the growing importance of prestige-goods-based network strategies; however, the embrace of Islam as a mark of corporate identity and the growing investment in public architecture (particularly mosques) suggests a continued reliance on corporate strategies. "What is seen is a combination of both, with the modes alternating in significance through time" (Kusimba 1999, p. 182). In Kusimba's view, network strategies dominated only after the fourteenth century with the growing emphasis on the extractive ivory and slave trades and the declining importance of craft production. We also must be attuned to spatial variability in the relative reliance on these strategies because, as LaViolette & Fleisher (2005) indicate, evidence for stone buildings is diminished along the southern coast where earth-and-thatch construction was more common. This led them to suggest that power may have been more horizontally differentiated with a variety of leaders vying for "first among equals" (and see LaViolette & Fleisher 2005 on relationships among rural and urban settlements).

When the Portuguese arrived on the East African coast in the early sixteenth century long-standing trade routes connected the interior regions of modern

Zimbabwe with the Swahili coast. The Portuguese, determined to capture control of the gold trade, attacked Kilwa in 1505 (Sutton 1998, p. 116; see also Fleisher 2004) and forcibly imposed a tributary system on conquered coastal societies to extract gold, ivory, and slaves with reverberations for interior areas. Though archaeological research on sites of this period is limited (Kusimba 1999, p. 155), we know that several local industries (iron, textiles) collapsed under the pressure of Portuguese attacks and occupation, and Portuguese control of trade undermined Swahili elites. Population levels on the coast declined as coastal peoples sought refuge in the interior and set up fortified settlements in highland areas. Exchange networks and subsistence production were disrupted. The imposition of Omani Arab rule from the second half of the seventeenth century strengthened the Islamic dimensions of Swahili culture and contributed to growing divisions between interior and coastal regions fueled by an intensified slave trade (Kusimba 1999, pp. 164, 167, 172–73). The establishment of clove and sugar plantations on Pemba and Zanzibar supplied an expanding international market, and production intensified following abolition of the slave trade as captive peoples were burdened with the production of exports (Kessy 2003, pp. 126–27).

We should not proceed from the assumption that international trade was the primary factor driving social change over the past 1500 years in eastern Africa; however, the growing evidence for East Africa's long-term entanglements in oceanic trade draws attention to how they shaped the mosaic quality of production, technology, and societal scale across East Africa. Recent research highlights the interconnections that existed between foragers, pastoralists, and cultivators of interior East Africa, and the ways those interconnections and links with coastal societies altered over the course of the past two millennia. Pioneering archaeological and oral historical work in the Tsavo-Taita area of Kenya, roughly 100 km from the coast, highlights the complicated and enmeshed societal chains that linked interior foragers with coastal city states (Kusimba & Kusimba 2005). The area comprises an ecological mosaic of relatively well-watered hills and lower-lying areas characterized by arid grass- and bushland that produced valuable resources for international trade: animal skins, ivory, rhinoceros horn, and rock crystal. Oral historical research suggests a complicated pattern of migration and intermarriage and alliance among foragers, nomadic pastoralists, and cultivators in the region. Sources of wealth and authority varied, and a mosaic of contemporaneous site types demonstrates the diversity of productive strategies including specialized pastoralism, iron smelting, and foraging activities (Kusimba & Kusimba 2005). Archaeological evidence from rockshelter sites in Tsavo National Park suggests forager involvement in the ivory trade and may signal the development of specialized hunting in response to external demands for ivory (Kusimba 2003, pp. 220–21). Though this research is in an early phase, it emphasizes that we should expect the mosaic of productive strategies, technologies, and social arrangements over the past 2000 years to shift. Emerging relationships between pastoralists, cultivators, and foragers probably led to novel forms of interaction based on relationships ranging from fictive kin and trading partners to clientship, changes in productive strategies and gendered divisions of labor, and new patterns of residence and mobility (Kusimba 2003, pp. 223–24), all of which were complicated by changing involvement in oceanic trade.

East Africa's long-standing global entanglements were reshaped by the extension of Omani Arab control over the Swahili coast associated with intensified slave and ivory trades in the eighteenth and nineteenth centuries. Both slaves and ivory came from interior regions of East Africa, and, as in West Africa, the intensification of the slave trade led to changes in settlement strategies. The proliferation of defensive settlements in upland settings of the Kasigau area (immediately south of Tsavo National Park) occurred as village sites in lower lying areas were abandoned. The substantial dry rock fortifications around rock shelter sites were constructed during the seventeenth and eighteenth centuries in a period when slave raiding was intensifying and attest how the slave trade transformed East African cultural mosaics (Kusimba & Kusimba 2005). Similarly, interior areas further south (Tanzania and Malawi) saw defensive concentrations of settlement from the early eighteenth century, which intensified from the mid-nineteenth century in part owing to the incursion of Ngoni people spurred by the *difaqane* in southern Africa (Burton 2001/2002, p. 14; see Reid 2001/2002 on war and urbanization); however, Pikirayi (2004, p. 258) cautions against assimilating all sites of this period in Zimbabwe to a "refuge culture." Though archaeological research on the past several centuries is limited, it has considerable potential to illuminate the effects of these entanglements on the character of East African societies enshrined in twentieth-century ethnography.

CONCLUSION

Massive partialities are inevitable in a brief review covering 2000 years in a continent three times the size of the United States. Yet select examples highlight new concerns with the variable character of complexity in time and space, the mosaic quality of African political economic landscapes, and the implications of global entanglements, all of which complicate received understandings of "Iron Age" Africa. A key feature of recent research is attention to contextuality and specificity without losing sight of larger scale, often global, political economic processes that affected African societies over the past 2000 years. A focus on the variable strategies pursued by emergent elites (e.g., Blanton et al. 1996) draws attention to issues of social agency, power, and ideology in the process of African state formation, which was long viewed merely as a reflex of external trade relations (Mitchell 2003, p. 177). Though they provide a framework for analyzing variable heterarchical and hierarchical arrangements, these models draw considerably on nineteenth- and twentieth-century sources, and we need to remain attuned to possibilities beyond these sources (David & Sterner 1999, Guyer & Belinga 1995). Similarly our appreciation of the ramifying networks that connected societies of varying scale was prompted in part by the work of historically oriented anthropologists (Amselle 1998, Kopytoff 1987), but whether the sorts of linkages among historical societies adequately capture the character of connections among more ancient ones remains an empirical question.

Long-term projects directed at working through the regional histories of social and political economic forms over *la longue durée* are creating a platform for comparative regional studies of these issues. These projects require considerable investment in basic research—for example, in creating a robust spatiotemporal framework for studying variation in time and space (e.g., Connah 1996, Connah & Daniels 2003, Ogundiran 2002b, Usman 2003a, Wesler 1999, Wotzka & Goedicke 2001)—and we should anticipate that it may take another decade for some of these projects to yield definitive results. Yet as this review demonstrates, these projects significantly complicate historical and ethnographic understandings, and their results often counter entrenched presumptions drawn from broader narratives of world prehistory.

Archaeology also can contribute significantly to our understanding of how changing global entanglements complicated social political economic mosaics in the period "covered" by historical and ethnographic sources. There is a pressing need for sustained and coordinated research on implications of the slave trade. Important work has begun in coastal contexts, but this subject needs to be augmented by an understanding of the implications and responses of interior populations (Kelly 2002, p. 99), and here we need to be aware of how distinctions between "historical" and "Iron Age" archaeology divert attention from the sustained and systemic relations among coastal and interior societies (see Reid & Lane 2004 for debates over the use of the term historical archaeology in Africa). Empirically robust studies of transformations and continuities in later second millennium AD African societies provide a crucial comparative platform for exploring commonalities and differences with more ancient societies, as well (Stahl 2004). This is a central enterprise if we wish to overcome the limitations and partialities of ethnographic and historic models. The results remind us that the "traditional" African societies enshrined by twentieth-century ethnography represent but a moment in the dynamic history of African societies.

The *Annual Review of Anthropology* is online at http://anthro.annualreviews.org

LITERATURE CITED

Abungu GHO, Mutoro HW. 1993. Coast-interior settlements and social relations in the Kenya coastal hinterland. See Shaw et al. 1993, pp. 694–704

Alexander J. 2001. Islam, archaeology and slavery in Africa. *World Archaeol.* 33:44–60

Amselle J-L. 1998. *Mestizo Logics. Anthropology of Identity in Africa and Elsewhere.* Transl. C Royal. Stanford: Stanford Univ. Press. 207 pp.

Asombang RN. 1999. Sacred centers and urbanization in West Central Africa. See SK McIntosh 1999d, pp. 80–87

Bacus EA, Lucero LJ, eds. 1999. *Complex Polities in the Ancient Tropical World.* Archeol. Pap. 9. Arlington, VA: Am. Anthropol. Assoc. 201 pp.

Baloian MC. 2002. Reading complexity from the periphery: a spatial analytic approach to understanding settlement organization represented by nucleated site clusters, Inland Niger Delta, Mali. Presented at Bienn. Meet. Soc. Afr. Archaeol., 16th, Tucson

Beach D. 1998. Cognitive archaeology and imaginary history at Great Zimbabwe. *Curr. Anthropol.* 39:47–72

Bedaux RM, MacDonald K, Person A, Polet H, Sanogo K, et al. 2001. The Dia archaeological project: rescuing cultural heritage in the Inland Niger Delta (Mali). *Antiquity* 75:837–48

Bedaux RM, van de Waals JD, eds. 1994. *Djenne: une Ville Millénaire au Mali.* Leiden: Rijksmuseum voor Volkenkunde. 186 pp.

Bedaux RMA, Constandse-Westermann TS, Hacquebord L, Lange AG, van der Waals JD. 1978. Recherches archeologiques dans le Delta interieur du Niger (Mali). *Palaeohistoria* 20:91–220

Blanton RE, Feinman GM, Kowalewski SA, Peregrine PN. 1996. A dual-processual theory for the evolution of Mesoamerican civilization. *Curr. Anthropol.* 37:1–14

Bovill EW. 1958. *The Golden Trade of the Moors.* London: Oxford Univ. Press. 293 pp.

Burton A. 2001/2002. Introduction. Urbanisation in Eastern Africa: an historical overview, c. 1750–2000. *Azania* 36/37:1–28

Chami F. 2003. Early iron working communities on the East African Coast: excavations at Kivinja, Tanzania. See Kusimba & Kusimba 2003, pp. 87–97

Chami FA, Msemwa P. 1997. A new look at culture and trade on the Azanian coast. *Curr. Anthropol.* 38:673–77

Childs ST, Herbert EW. 2005. Metallurgy and its consequences. See Stahl 2005, 276–300

Chittick N. 1974. *Kilwa: An Islamic Trading City on the East African Coast.* Mem. 5. Nairobi: Br. Inst. East. Afr. 514 pp. 2 vols.

Connah G. 1981. *Three Thousand Years in Africa: Man and His Environment in the Lake Chad Region of Nigeria.* Cambridge: Cambridge Univ. Press. 268 pp.

Connah G. 1996. A chronological sequence for the Ugandan shores of Lake Albert. See Pwiti & Soper 1996, pp. 533–41

Connah G. 1997. The cultural and chronological context of Kibiro, Uganda. *Afr. Archaeol. Rev.* 14:25–67

Connah G, ed. 1998. *Transformations in Africa. Essays on Africa's Later Past.* London: Leicester Univ. Press. 255 pp.

Connah G. 2001. *African Civilizations: An Archaeological Perspective.* Cambridge: Cambridge Univ. Press. 340 pp. 2nd ed.

Connah G, Daniels SGH. 2003. Mining the archives: a pottery sequence for Borno, Nigeria. *J. Afr. Archaeol.* 1:39–76

Cruz MDG. 2003. Shaping quotidian worlds: ceramic production and consumption in Banda, Ghana c. 1780–1994. PhD thesis. State Univ. NY, Binghamton

Cusick JG, ed. 1998. *Studies in Culture Contact. Interaction, Culture Change, and Archaeology.* Occas. Pap. 25. Carbondale: Cent. Archaeol. Invest., South. Ill. Univ. 501 pp.

D'Altroy TN, Earle T. 1985. Staple finance, wealth finance, and storage in the Inka political economy. *Curr. Anthropol.* 26:187–206

David N. 1996. A new political form? The classless industrial society of Sukur (Nigeria). See Pwiti & Soper 1996, pp. 593–600

David N, Sterner J. 1999. Wonderful society: the Burgess Shale creatures, Mandara polities and the nature of prehistory. See McIntosh 1999d, pp. 97–109

de Barros P. 2001. The effects of the slave trade on the Bassar ironworking society of Togo. See DeCorse 2001b, pp. 59–80

DeCorse CR. 1998. Culture contact and change in West Africa. See Cusick 1998, pp. 358–77

DeCorse CR. 2001a. *An Archaeology of Elmina. Africans and Europeans on the Gold Coast, 1400–1900.* Washington, DC: Smithsonian Inst. Press. 286 pp.

DeCorse CR, ed. 2001b. *West Africa During the Atlantic Slave Trade. Archaeological Perspectives.* Leicester, UK: Leicester Univ. Press. 194 pp.

de Maret P. 1994/1995. Pits, pots and the

far-west streams. See Sutton 1994/1995, pp. 318–23

de Maret P. 1999. The power of symbols and the symbols of power through time: probing the Luba past. See McIntosh 1999d, pp. 151–65

de Maret P. 2005. From pottery groups to ethnic groups in Central Africa. See Stahl 2005, 420–40

Devisse J, ed. 1993. *Vallées du Niger*. Paris: Réunion de Musées nationaux

Dietler M. 1998. Consumption, agency and cultural entanglement: theoretical implications of a Mediterranean colonial encounter. See Cusick 1998, pp. 288–315

Earle T. 1987. Chiefdoms in archaeological and ethnohistorical perspective. *Annu. Rev. Anthropol.* 16:279–308

Eggert MKH. 1994/1995. Pots, farming and analogy: early ceramics in the equatorial rainforest. See Sutton 1994/1995, pp. 332–38

Eggert MKH. 2005. The Bantu problem and African archaeology. See Stahl 2005, 301–26

Ehrenreich R, Crumley C, Levy J, eds. 1995. *Heterarchy and the Analysis of Complex Societies*. Archaeol. Pap. 6. Washington, DC: Am. Anthropol. Assoc. 131 pp.

Feinman G, Neitzel J. 1984. Too many types: an overview of sedentary prestate societies in the Americas. *Adv. Archaeol. Methods Theory* 7:39–102

Fleisher J. 2004. Behind the Sultan of Kilwa's "rebellious conduct": local perspectives on an international East African town. See Reid & Lane 2004, pp. 91–123

Fleisher J, LaViolette A. 1999. Elusive wattle-and-daub: finding the hidden majority in the archaeology of the Swahili. *Azania* 34:87–108

Fletcher R. 1998. African urbanism: scale, mobility and transformations. See Connah 1998, pp. 104–38

Gallais J. 1984. *Hommes du Sahel: espaces, temps et pouvoirs: le delta intérieur du Niger, 1960–1980*. Paris: Flammarion. 289 pp.

Goody JR. 1971. *Technology, Tradition and the State in Africa*. Cambridge: Cambridge Univ. Press. 88 pp.

Greenberg JH. 1955. *Studies in African Linguistic Classification*. New Haven, CT: Compass. 116 pp.

Gronenborn D. 1998. Archaeological and ethnohistorical investigations along the southern fringes of Lake Chad, 1993–1996. *Afr. Archaeol. Rev.* 15:225–59

Gronenborn D. 2001. Kanem-Borno: a brief summary of the history and archaeology of an empire of the central *bilad al-sudan*. See DeCorse 2001b, pp. 101–30

Guyer JI. 1995. Wealth in people, wealth in things–introduction. *J. Afr. Hist.* 36:83–90

Guyer JI, Belinga SME. 1995. Wealth in people as wealth in knowledge: accumulation and composition in equatorial Africa. *J. Afr. Hist.* 36:91–120

Haaland R. 1980. Man's role in the changing habitat of the Méma during the period of the old Kingdom of Ghana. *Norweg. Archaeol. Rev.* 13:31–46

Haas J, ed. 2001. *From Leaders to Rulers*. New York: Kluwer. 286 pp.

Hall M. 1990. *Farmers, Kings, and Traders. The People of Southern Africa 200–1860*. Chicago: Univ. Chicago Press. 161 pp.

Hall M. 1993. The archaeology of colonial settlement in southern Africa. *Annu. Rev. Anthropol.* 22:177–200

Hall M, Markell A, eds. 1993. *Historical Archaeology in the Western Cape*. S. Afr. Archaeol. Soc. Goodwin Ser. 7. 103 pp.

Holl AFC. 1994. The cemetery of Houlouf in northern Cameroon (AD 1500-1600): fragments of a past social system. *Afr. Archaeol. Rev.* 12:133–70

Holl AFC. 1995. Réseaux d'échanges préhistoriques dans la plaine tchadienne. *Sahara* 7:17–28

Holl AFC. 2001. 500 years in the Cameroons: making sense of the archaeological record. See DeCorse 2001b, pp. 152–78

Horton MC. 1996. *Shanga. The Archaeology of a Muslim Trading Community on the Coast of East Africa*. Br. Inst. East. Afr. Mem. 14. London: BIEA. 458 pp.

Horton M, Mudida N. 1993. Exploitation of marine resources: evidence for the origin of the Swahili communities of east Africa. See Shaw et al. 1993, pp. 673–93

Huffman TN. 1996. *Snakes and Crocodiles. Power and Symbolism in Ancient Zimbabwe.* Witwatersrand, Africa: Univ. Witwatersrand Press. 228 pp.

Insoll T. 1997. Iron Age Gao: an archaeological contribution. *J. Afr. Hist.* 38:1–30

Insoll T. 2003. *The Archaeology of Islam in Sub-Saharan Africa.* Cambridge: Cambridge Univ. Press. 470 pp.

Kelly KG. 1997. The archaeology of African-European interaction: investigating the social roles of trade, traders, and the use of space in the seventeenth- and eighteenth-century *Hueda* Kingdom, Republic of Bénin. *World Archaeol.* 28:351–69

Kelly KG. 2001. Change and continuity in coastal Bénin. See DeCorse 2001b, pp. 81–100

Kelly KG. 2002. Indigenous responses to colonial encounters on the West African coast: Hueda and Dahomey from the seventeenth through nineteenth century. In *The Archaeology of Colonialism,* ed. CL Lyons, JK Papadopoulos, pp. 96–120. Los Angeles: Getty Res. Inst.

Kelly KG. 2004. The African diaspora starts here: historical archaeology of coastal West Africa. See Reid & Lane 2004, pp. 219–41

Kent S, ed. 2002. *Ethnicity, Hunter-Gatherers and the "Other." Association or Assimilation in Africa.* Washington, DC: Smithsonian Inst. Press. 350 pp.

Kessy ET. 2003. Iron Age settlement patterns and economic change on Zanzibar and Pemba Islands. See Kusimba & Kusimba 2003, pp. 117–31

Kirkman JS. 1964. *Men and Monuments on the East African Coast.* London: Butterworth

Kopytoff I. 1987. The internal African frontier: the making of African political culture. In *The African Frontier: The Reproduction of Traditional African Societies,* ed. I Kopytoff,

pp. 3–84. Bloomington: Indiana Univ. Press. 288 pp.

Kusimba CM. 1999. *The Rise and Fall of Swahili States.* Walnut Creek, CA: AltaMira. 236 pp.

Kusimba CM, Killick D. 2003. Ironworking on the Swahili Coast of Kenya. See Kusimba & Kusimba 2003, pp. 99–115

Kusimba CM, Kusimba SB, eds. 2003. *East African Archaeology. Foragers, Potters, Smiths and Traders.* Philadelphia: Univ. Penn. Mus. Archaeol. Anthropol. 226 pp.

Kusimba CM, Kusimba SB. 2005. Mosaics and interactions: East Africa, 2000 BP to the present. See Stahl 2005, 392–419

Kusimba SB. 2003. *African Foragers: Environment, Technology, Interactions.* Walnut Creek, CA: AltaMira. 284 pp.

Lane P. 2001. African archaeology today. Spec. sect. *Antiquity* 75:793–96

LaViolette A. 2004. Swahili archaeology and history on Pemba Island, Tanzania: a critique and case study of the use of written and oral sources in archaeology. See Reid & Lane 2004, pp. 125–62

LaViolette A, Fleisher J. 2005. The archaeology of sub-Saharan urbanism: cities and their countrysides. See Stahl 2005, 327–52

Lentz C. 1995. 'Tribalism' and ethnicity in Africa: a review of four decades of Anglophone research. *Cah. Sci. Hum.* 31(2):303–28

Lightfoot K, Martinez A, Schiff A. 1998. Daily practice and material culture in pluralistic social settings: an archaeological study of culture change and persistence from Fort Ross, California. *Am. Antiq.* 63:199–222

Lightfoot KG. 1995. Culture contact studies: redefining the relationship between prehistoric and historical archaeology. *Am. Antiq.* 60:199–217

MacDonald KC. 1998. Before the empire of Ghana: pastoralism and the origins of cultural complexity in the Sahel. See Connah 1998, pp. 71–103

MacEachern S. 1993. Selling the iron for their shackles: Wandala-Montagnard interaction in northern Cameroon. *J. Afr. Hist.* 33:241–70

MacEachern S. 2001. State formation and enslavement in the southern Lake Chad basin. See DeCorse 2001b, pp. 131–51

MacEachern S. 2005. Two thousand years of West African history. See Stahl 2005, 441–66

Magnavita C, Magnavita S. 2001. New evidence of proto-urban settlements in the Lake Chad area. *Nyame Akuma* 55:46–50

Magnavita S. 2003. The beads of Kissi, Burkina Faso. *J. Afr. Archaeol.* 1:127–38

McIntosh RJ. 1993. The pulse model. Genesis and accommodation of specialization in the Middle Niger. *J. Afr. Hist.* 34:181–212

McIntosh RJ. 1998. *The Peoples of the Middle Niger.* Oxford: Blackwell. 346 pp.

McIntosh RJ. 1999. Western representations of urbanism and invisible African towns. See McIntosh 1999d, pp. 56–65

McIntosh SK, ed. 1995. *Excavations at Jenné-Jeno, Hambarketolo, and Kaniana (Inland Niger Delta, Mali), the 1981 Season.* Berkeley: Univ. Calif. Press. 605 pp.

McIntosh SK, ed. 1999d. *Beyond Chiefdoms. Pathways to Complexity in Africa.* Cambridge: Cambridge Univ. Press. 176 pp.

McIntosh SK. 1999a. Floodplains and the development of complex society: comparative perspectives from the West African semi-arid tropics. See Bacus & Lucero 1999, pp. 151–65

McIntosh SK. 1999b. Modeling political organization in large-scale settlement clusters: a case study from the Inland Niger Delta. See McIntosh 1999d, pp. 66–79

McIntosh SK. 1999c. Pathways to complexity: an African perspective. See McIntosh 1999d, pp. 1–30

McIntosh SK. 2001. Tools for understanding transformation and continuity in Senegambian society: 1500–1900. See DeCorse 2001b, pp. 14–37

McIntosh SK, Bocoum H. 2000. New perspectives on Sincu Bara, a first millennium site in the Senegal Valley. *Afr. Archaeol. Rev.* 17:1–43

McIntosh SK, McIntosh RJ. 1993. Cities without citadels: understanding urban origins along the middle Niger. See Shaw et al. 1993, pp. 622–41

Meillassoux C. 1972. From reproduction to production: a Marxist approach to Economic Anthropology. *Econ. Soc.* 1:93–103

Mercader J, Rovira S, Gómez-Ramos P. 2000. Shared technologies. Forager-farmer interaction and ancient iron metallurgy in the Ituri rainforest, Democratic Republic of Congo. *Azania* 35:107–22

Mitchell P. 2003. East African archaeology: a southern African perspective. See Kusimba & Kusimba 2003, pp. 167–81

Murdock GP. 1959. *Africa. Its Peoples and their Culture History.* New York: McGraw-Hill. 456 pp.

Neumann K. 2005. The romance of farming—plant cultivation and domestication in Africa. See Stahl 2005, 249–75

Ogundiran AO. 2001a. Ceramic spheres and regional networks in the Yoruba-Edo region, Nigeria, 13th–19th centuries A.C. *J. Field Archaeol.* 28:27–43

Ogundiran AO. 2001b. Factional competition, sociopolitical development, and settlement cycling in Ìlàrè District (*ca.* 1200–1900): oral traditions of historical experience in a Yorùbá community. *Hist. Afr.* 28:203–23

Ogundiran AO. 2002a. Beads, cowries and cultural translations of the Atlantic experience in Yorubaland, 1600–1850. Discuss. Pap. Afr. Humanit. AH 36. Boston: Boston Univ. Afr. Stud. Cent.

Ogundiran AO. 2002b. Filling a gap in the Ife-Benin interaction field (thirteenth–sixteenth centuries AD): excavations in Iloyi Settlement, Ijesaland. *Afr. Archaeol. Rev.* 19:27–60

Pauketat TR, ed. 2001. *The Archaeology of Traditions. Agency and History Before and After Columbus.* Gainesville: Univ. Press Florida. 351 pp.

Paynter R. 1989. The archaeology of equality and inequality. *Annu. Rev. Anthropol.* 18:369–99

Pikirayi I. 2001. *The Zimbabwe Culture. Origins and Decline of Southern Zambezian*

States. Walnut Creek, CA: AltaMira. 303 pp.

Pikirayi I. 2004. Less implicit historical archaeologies: oral traditions and later Karanga settlement in south-central Zimbabwe. See Reid & Lane 2004, pp. 243–67

Pwiti G. 2005. Southern Africa and the East African Coast. See Stahl 2005, 378–91

Pwiti G, Soper R, eds. 1996. *Aspects of African Archaeology*. Pap. from 10th Congr. PanAfrican Assoc. Prehistory Relat. Stud. Harare: Univ. Zimb. Publ. 857 pp.

Raimbault M, Sanogo K, eds. 1991. *Recherches Archéologiques au Mali. Prospections et Inventaire, Fouilles et Études Analytiques en Zone Lacustre*. Paris: Éditions Karthala

Reid A. 2005. Interaction, marginalization and the archaeology of the Kalahari. See Stahl 2005, 353–77

Reid AM, Lane PJ, eds. 2004. *African Historical Archaeologies*. New York: Kluwer Academic/Plenum. 408 pp.

Reid DAM. 1996. Ntusi and the development of social complexity in southern Uganda. See Pwiti & Soper 1996, pp. 621–27

Reid R. 1999. War and militarism in precolonial Buganda. *Azania* 34:45–60

Reid R. 2001/2002. Warfare and urbanisation: the relationship between town and conflict in pre-colonial eastern Africa. *Azania* 36/37:46–62

Rey P-P. 1975. The lineage mode of production. *Crit. Anthropol.* 3:27–29

Roberts R. 1984. Women's work and women's property: household social relations in the Maraka textile industry of the nineteenth century. *Comp. Stud. Soc. Hist.* 26:229–50

Robertshaw P, ed. 1990. *A History of African Archaeology*. London: Currey. 378 pp.

Robertshaw P. 1994. Archaeological survey, ceramic analysis, and site formation in western Uganda. *Afr. Archaeol. Rev.* 12:105–31

Robertshaw P. 1997. Munsa earthworks. A preliminary report on recent excavations. *Azania* 32:1–20

Robertshaw P. 1999a. Seeking and keeping power in Bunyoro-Kitara, Uganda. See McIntosh 1999d, pp. 124–35

Robertshaw P. 1999b. Women, labor, and state formation in western Uganda. See Bacus & Lucero 1999, pp. 51–65

Robertshaw P. 2000. Sibling rivalry? The intersection of archeology and history. *Hist. Afr.* 27:261–86

Robertshaw P. 2003. The origins of the state in East Africa. See Kusimba & Kusimba 2003, pp. 149–66

Robertshaw P. 2004. African historical archaeology(ies): past, present and a possible future. See Reid & Lane 2004, pp. 375–91

Robertshaw P, Taylor D. 2000. Climatic change and the rise of political complexity in western Uganda. *Jr. Afr. Hist.* 41:1–28

Rowlands M. 1989. A question of complexity. In *Domination and Resistance*, ed. D Miller, M Rowlands, C Tilley, pp. 29–40. London: Unwin Hyman. 332 pp.

Sadr K. 1997. Kalahari archaeology and the Bushman debate. *Curr. Anthropol.* 38:104–12

Schmidt PR. 1990. Oral traditions, archaeology and history: a short reflective history. See Robertshaw 1990, pp. 252–70

Schmidt PR. 1995. Using archaeology to remake history in Africa. In *Making Alternative Histories*, ed. P Schmidt, TC Patterson, pp. 119–47. Sante Fe: School Am. Res. Press

Schoenbrun DL. 1998. *A Green Place, a Good Place. Agrarian Change, Gender, and Social Identity in the Great Lakes Region to the 15th Century*. Portsmouth, NH: Heinemann

Schoenbrun DL. 1999. The (in)visible roots of Bunyoro-Kitara and Buganda in the Lakes region: AD 800–1300. See McIntosh 1999d, pp. 136–50

Schrire C. 1995. *Digging Through Darkness. Chronicles of an Archaeologist*. Charlottesville: Univ. Va. Press. 276 pp.

Sharpe B. 1986. Ethnography and a regional system: mental maps and the myth of states and tribe in north-central Nigeria. *Crit. Anthropol.* 6(3):22–65

Shaw T, Sinclair P, Andah B, Okpoko A, eds. 1993. *The Archaeology of Africa. Food, Metals and Towns*. London: Routledge. 857 pp.

Shennan S. 1993. After social evolution: a new

archaeological agenda? See Yoffee & Sherratt 1993, pp. 53–59

Sheriff A. 2001/2002. The spatial dichotomy of Swahili towns: the case of Zanzibar in the nineteenth century. *Azania* 2001/2002:63–81

Sinclair PJJ, Morais JMF, Adamowicz L, Duarte RT. 1993b. A perspective on archaeological research in Mozambique. See Shaw et al. 1993, pp. 409–31

Sinclair PJJ, Shaw T, Andah B. 1993a. Introduction. See Shaw et al. 1993, pp. 1–31

Stahl AB. 1999a. The archaeology of global encounters viewed from Banda, Ghana. *Afr. Archaeol. Rev.* 16:5–81

Stahl AB. 1999b. Perceiving variability in time and space: the evolutionary mapping of African societies. See McIntosh 1999d, pp. 39–55

Stahl AB. 2001a. Historical process and the impact of the Atlantic trade on Banda, Ghana, c. 1800–1920. See DeCorse 2001b, pp. 38–58

Stahl AB. 2001b. *Making History in Banda. Anthropological Visions of Africa's Past.* Cambridge: Cambridge Univ. Press. 268 pp.

Stahl AB. 2002. Colonial entanglements and the practices of taste: an alternative to logocentric approaches. *Am. Anthropol.* 104:827–45

Stahl AB. 2004. Comparative insights into the ancient political economies of West Africa. In *Archaeological Perspectives on Political Economies*, ed. G Feinman, L Nicholas, pp. 253–70. Salt Lake City: Univ. Utah Press

Stahl AB, ed. 2005. *African Archaeology. A Critical Introduction.* Oxford: Blackwell

Stahl AB, Cruz MD. 1998. Men and women in a market economy: gender and craft production in west central Ghana c. 1775–1995. In *Gender in African Prehistory*, ed. S Kent, pp. 205–26. Walnut Creek, CA: AltaMira

Stein GJ. 2002. From passive periphery to active agents: emerging perspectives in the archaeology of interregional interaction. *Am. Anthropol.* 104:903–16

Sutton JEG. 1993. The antecedents of the Interlacustrine kingdoms. *J. Afr. Hist.* 34:33–64

Sutton JEG. 1998. Kilwa. A history of the ancient Swahili town with a guide to the monuments of Kilwa Kisiwani and adjacent islands. *Azania* 33:113–69

Sutton JEG, ed. 1994/1995. *The Growth of Farming Communities in Africa from the Equator Southwards. Azania* 29/30:1–338

Thomas N. 1991. *Entangled Objects. Exchange, Material Culture, and Colonialism in the Pacific.* Cambridge, MA: Harvard Univ. Press. 259 pp.

Thorp C. 1997. Evidence for interaction from recent hunter-gatherer sites in the Caledon Valley. *Afr. Archaeol. Rev.* 14:231–56

Togola T. 1996. Iron age occupation in the Méma region, Mali. *Afr. Archaeol. Rev.* 13:91–110

Usman A. 1999. Fortifications in the northern periphery of Oyo: a report of 1994–95 archaeological research in north central Yorubaland, Nigeria. *Nyame Akuma* 51:45–54

Usman A. 2003a. Ceramic seriation, sites chronology, and Old Oyo factor in northcentral Yorubaland, Nigeria. *Afr. Archaeol. Rev.* 20:149–69

Usman A. 2003b. The ethnohistory and archaeology of warfare in northern Yoruba. *J. Afr. Archaeol.* 1:201–14

Usman A. 2004. On the frontier of empire: understanding the enclosed walls in northern Yoruba, Nigeria. *J. Anthropol. Archaeol.* 23:119–32

Vansina J. 1990. *Paths in the Rainforest. Toward a History of Political Tradition in Equatorial Africa.* Madison: Univ. Wis. Press. 428 pp.

Vansina J. 1995. Historians, are archeologists your siblings? *Hist. Afr.* 22:369–408

Wallerstein I. 1986. *Africa and the Modern World.* Trenton, NJ: Afr. World Press. 209 pp.

Wesler KW. 1999. Chronological sequences in Nigerian ceramics. *Afr. Archaeol. Rev.* 16:239–58

Wotzka H-P, Goedicke C. 2001. Thermoluminescence dates on Late Stone Age and later ceramics from Tapoa Province (southeastern Burkina Faso) and Konduga (Borno, northeastern Nigeria). *Beiträge zur Allgemeinen und Vergleichenden Archäologie* 21:75–126

Wright HT. 1993. Trade and politics on the eastern littoral of Africa, AD 800–1300. See Shaw et al. 1993, pp. 658–72

Yoffee N. 1993. Too many chiefs? (or, safe texts for the '90s). See Yoffee & Sherratt 1993, pp. 60–78

Yoffee N, Sherratt A, eds. 1993. *Archaeological Theory: Who Sets the Agenda?* Cambridge: Cambridge Univ. Press. 139 pp.

Annu. Rev. Anthropol. 2004. 33:173–99
doi: 10.1146/annurev.anthro.33.070203.143823
Copyright © 2004 by Annual Reviews. All rights reserved

PRIMARY STATE FORMATION IN MESOAMERICA

Charles S. Spencer and Elsa M. Redmond

Division of Anthropology, American Museum of Natural History, Central Park West at 79th Street, New York, NY 10024-5192; email: cspencer@amnh.org, eredmond@amnh.org

Key Words political evolution, settlement hierarchy, palace, temple, conquest, chiefdom, Oaxaca, Monte Albán

■ **Abstract** In this review, we examine the earliest states in Mesoamerica and how they developed. We present a definition of the state and explain why first-generation or primary states have special significance in anthropology and archaeology; we also discuss how anthropological archaeologists can detect the emergence of state organization in the archaeological record. We review the archaeological data bearing on early state formation in Oaxaca, the Southern Gulf Coast, the Southeastern Lowlands, and the Basin of Mexico. Although we acknowledge that more data are needed from all regions, we conclude that Oaxaca currently provides the most compelling evidence of primary state formation in Mesoamerica.

INTRODUCTION

Today nearly all people live in state societies, but for most of humanity's time on this planet nobody did. It is hardly surprising that the nature and origin of the state have been of enduring concern in anthropology. Archaeologists, in particular, have long been fascinated by the state; the earliest cases of state formation occurred before detailed written records were kept and can only be studied archaeologically. A quarter-century ago in this series, Wright (1977, p. 383) characterized the state as a society with a centralized and also internally specialized administrative organization. He contrasted the state and the chiefdom, which he considered to be a society with a centralized but not internally specialized administration (Wright 1977, p. 381). Not all chiefdoms evolve into states, but some researchers argue that all first-generation states evolved from preexisting chiefdoms (Carneiro 1981, Earle 1987, Flannery 1995, Marcus 1992, Spencer 1990).

A state administration, from this perspective, is inherently bureaucratic (Cohen 1978, p. 36; Flannery 1972, p. 403). Wright (1977, p. 384) argues that states characteristically have at least four tiers of decision making. Because internal administrative specialization is compatible with the effective delegation of partial authority, subsidiary centers of administration can be established at strategic locations within the state's domain, enabling the state to intervene directly in local affairs. Such subsidiary outposts may be distributed in a nested lattice

0084-6570/04/1021-0173$14.00

of secondary, tertiary, and even quaternary centers. Population distribution usually follows this administrative hierarchy, so well-functioning states often exhibit four or more tiers of settlements according to both administrative functions and population size, whereas chiefdoms exhibit no more than three tiers. Investigators can detect such hierarchies in the archaeological record through the analysis of site-size distributions (Flannery 1998, Wright & Johnson 1975).

Palaces and standardized temples also are features of state organization that can be detected archaeologically (Flannery 1998, Sanders 1974). Royal palaces often have a residential component, where the ruler and his family live, as well as a governmental component, where the ruler carries out various official duties (Flannery 1998). Standardized, multiroom temples likely are manifestations of a state religion staffed by a full-time specialized priesthood (Flannery 1998, Flannery & Marcus 1983b).

The state's ability to delegate partial authority is compatible with ambitious strategies of territorial expansion, including the conquest and long-term holding of distant territories. In chiefdoms, the lack of internal administrative specialization precludes effective delegation of partial authority, which means that the effective range of chiefly authority is more limited than that in a state; such limits to chiefly authority may lie in the vicinity of a half day of travel from the first-order center (Spencer 1990, 1998). In contrast, the state can transcend such limits and execute long-distance conquests, which may be evidenced by burned and abandoned villages, specialized forts and administrative outposts established by the conquering state, and enforced changes in the economic, social, and religious behaviors of subjugated peoples (Spencer & Redmond 1997, 2000). Some researchers argue that such predatory expansion plays a central role in the formation of states in the first place (Algaze 1993a; Carneiro 1970; Flannery 1999; Marcus 1992, 1998; Marcus & Flannery 1996, p. 157; Redmond 1983; Spencer 1982, 1998; Webster 1975).

Other investigators take a more benign view of the state, leading some scholars to recognize two contrasting theoretical frameworks: conflictive/coercive/predatory versus contractual/voluntaristic/benevolent (Carneiro 1970, Claessen & Skalník 1978b, Haas 1982, Service 1978). Still other researchers reject such efforts at general characterization, preferring to emphasize the differences rather than the similarities among state societies, and some doubt the very utility of the state as a concept (Crumley 1987, 1995; Gailey & Patterson 1987; Kohl 1984, 1987; Paynter 1989; Yoffee 1979, 1993). Issues such as these no doubt will continue to fester, but the best hope for their resolution lies in the comparative analysis of independent cases of primary state formation.

Primary state formation occurs when a first-generation state evolves in a context of nonstate societies, without contact with other preexisting states (Spencer 1998, Wright 1986). Few examples of true primary state formation exist, perhaps only six, as proposed by Service (1975): Egypt, Mesopotamia, the Indus River Valley, North China, Peru, and Mesoamerica. These cases offer a valuable opportunity to investigate the conditions and processes responsible for the pristine transformation of a society that has had no experience with state institutions into a functioning state. When the various cases of primary state formation are thoroughly documented, investigators can analyze the similarities and differences among the developmental trajectories. Such a comparative analysis should yield a better understanding of the state formation process and allow anthropologists to address whether the state as a form of political organization has certain fundamental and necessary features, regardless of historical and contextual differences among specific cases.

In a recent issue of this series, Stanish (2001) concludes that the earliest states in the Andean culture area were Moche, Wari, and Tiwanaku, which emerged during the first half of the first millennium CE; he draws attention to competition and war as major factors in these developments. In the present review, we examine the evidence relevant to early state formation from four areas in Mesoamerica (Figure 1), organizing the data according to three diagnostic criteria: (*a*) the emergence of a four-tier regional settlement-size hierarchy; (*b*) the appearance of royal palaces and specialized temples; and (*c*) the conquest/subjugation of distant territories. We attempt to discern which of the four cases was Mesoamerica's earliest state and how it developed from the nonstate societies that preceded it.

OAXACA

The hilltop site of Monte Albán was founded at the beginning of the Early Monte Albán I phase (500–300 BCE), and it became the capital of the early Zapotec state (Blanton 1978, Marcus & Flannery 1996). During the preceding Rosario

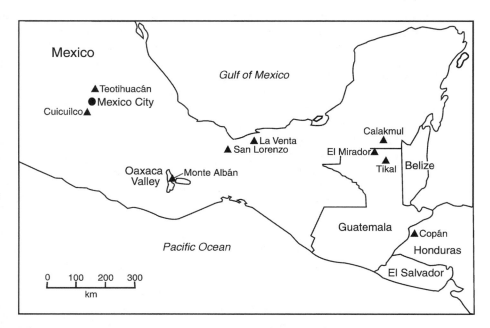

Figure 1   Map of Mesoamerica, showing places mentioned in the text.

phase (700–500 BCE), Monte Albán had not yet been established, and scholars generally agree that the three major branches of the Valley (Etla, Tlacolula, and Ocotlán-Zimatlán) were not politically unified but instead were occupied by at least three independent chiefly polities (Blanton et al. 1993, pp. 63–69; Marcus & Flannery 1996, pp. 123–26). By contrast, scholars have long recognized that by the Monte Albán II phase (100 BCE–200 CE) all branches of the Oaxaca Valley were integrated into a single polity, the early Zapotec state, under the rule of Monte Albán (Elson 2003, Flannery & Marcus 1983b). Noting that a four-tier settlement hierarchy, standardized temples and palaces, and the conquest of distant territories were absent in the Rosario phase but clearly established by the Monte Albán II phase, Flannery & Marcus (1983b) assert that this "throws the spotlight" on Monte Albán I (500–100 BCE) as the "crucial" period for the rise of the Zapotec state (p. 80).

Settlement Hierarchy

When Monte Albán was founded around 500 BCE, the Rosario phase chiefly center of San José Mogote (in the Etla subregion) was abandoned (Flannery & Marcus 1990). By contrast, the Tlacolula and Ocotlán-Zimatlán subregions continued to have impressive centers of their own throughout the Early Monte Albán I phase and the Late Monte Albán I phase (300–100 BCE), at Yegüih and San Martín Tilcajete, respectively (Figure 2). Moreover, these two centers grew to be larger than they were in the Rosario phase, which suggests that "they might still have been the paramount centers of rival polities" (Marcus & Flannery 1996, p. 163).

Our recent excavations at San Martín Tilcajete document the growth of that center from 25 ha in the Rosario phase, to 52.8 ha in the Early Monte Albán I phase, to 71.5 ha in the Late Monte Albán I phase (Spencer & Redmond 2001a). Feinman (1998, pp. 128–29) posits that the Tlacolula and Ocotlán-Zimatlán subregions were independent of the Monte Albán polity through the Late Monte Albán I phase. Marcus & Flannery (1996, p. 165) and Spencer & Redmond (2001a) argue that relations between the Etla-Central polity (dominated by Monte Albán) and the other two autonomous polities (Tlacolula and Ocotlán-Zimatlán) became increasingly competitive and hostile between the Early Monte Albán I and Late Monte Albán I phases. According to this rival polity model (Spencer & Redmond 2001a), all parts of the Oaxaca Valley did not become integrated into a single state polity under Monte Albán's control until Monte Albán II (Marcus & Flannery 1996, p. 165).

To assess the degree of hierarchy in settlement patterning, we use the data on site size (occupation area, in hectares) recovered by the Oaxaca Valley Settlement Pattern Survey (Kowalewski et al. 1989, Appendix I), using the methodology outlined in Spencer & Redmond (2003). In accordance with the rival polity model, we subdivide the Oaxaca Valley into its three subregions: Etla-Central, Tlacolula, and Ocotlán-Zimatlán (Spencer & Redmond 2001a) and generate histograms of the natural logarithm of site size. For the Rosario phase, the distribution of site

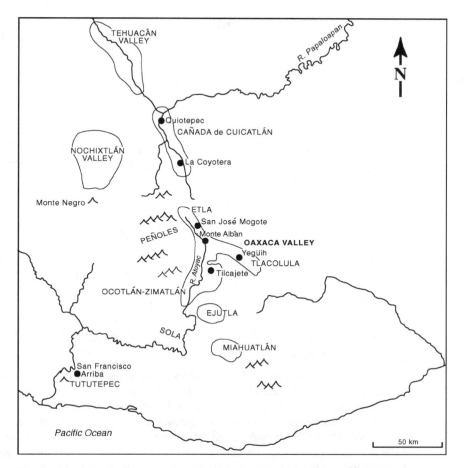

Figure 2   Map showing the Oaxaca Valley, its major subregions, and other surrounding regions; key archaeological sites are indicated.

size in the Etla subregion shows three modes (Figure 3a). During the Early Monte Albán I phase, there was a pronounced nucleation of population at Monte Albán, resulting in a distribution of site size for the Etla-Central subregion with just two clear modes (Figure 3b). By contrast, the histogram for the same subregion in the Late Monte Albán I phase shows four modes of site size (Figure 3c), which would be consistent with state organization at this time.

In the Ocotlán-Zimatlán subregion, three modes appear in the histogram for the Early Monte Albán I site size (Spencer & Redmond 2003, figure 10), whereas four modes can be discerned for the Late Monte Albán I phase (Figure 3d). In the Tlacolula subregion, there is a trimodal distribution of site size for the Early Monte Albán I phase (Spencer & Redmond 2003, figure 14) and minimally four

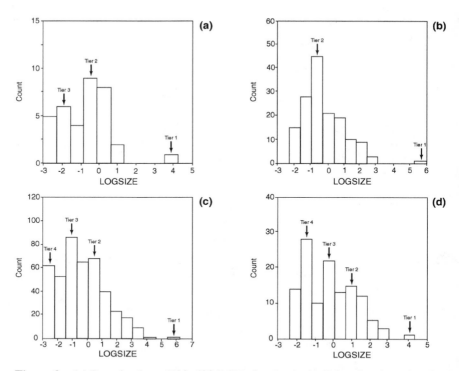

Figure 3 (*a*) Rosario phase (700–500 BCE) site size in the Etla subregion, showing three modes of site size, indicating a three-tier settlement hierarchy; (*b*) Early Monte Albán I phase (500–300 BCE) site size in the Etla-Central subregion, showing two modes of site size, indicating a two-tier settlement hierarchy; (*c*) Late Monte Albán I phase (300–100 BCE) site size in the Etla-Central subregion, showing four modes of site size, indicating a four-tier settlement hierarchy; (*d*) Late Monte Albán I phase (300–100 BCE) site size in the Ocotlán-Zimatlán subregion, showing four modes of site size, indicating a four-tier settlement hierarchy. LOGSIZE is the natural logarithm of site size in hectares; original data from Kowalewski et al. (1989, Appendix I).

modes for the Late Monte Albán I phase (Spencer & Redmond 2003, figure 15). We propose that the Tlacolula and Ocotlán-Zimatlán polities represent examples of secondary state formation during the Late Monte Albán I phase; each evolved a more complex administrative organization and corresponding settlement system as part of its overall strategy of resistance against Monte Albán (Spencer & Redmond 2003).

Palaces and Temples

During the Early Monte Albán I phase, the site of Monte Albán became the pre-eminent center in the Etla-Central subregion. The area of occupation reached an estimated 324 ha (Kowalewski et al. 1989, Appendix I). Because Monte Albán was heavily occupied for more than 1000 years, it has been difficult for archaeologists to recover information about the earliest constructions there. At least two buildings that were likely nonresidential or public in nature date to the Early Monte Albán I phase. One is represented by a sloping stone wall sitting on bedrock, at the bottom of a deep pit in the North Platform that Alfonso Caso excavated, in an area called the patio south of Mound A or PSA. (Flannery & Marcus 1983b). Some 300 m to the southwest lies the other public building that dates to Early Monte Albán I, the so-called *Edificio de los Danzantes*, a platform mound associated with a gallery of more than 300 carvings of slain captives, similar to the earlier carved stone at San José Mogote, and Stelae 12 and 13, which contain calendric and noncalendric hieroglyphs (Flannery & Marcus 1983c; Marcus 1976a, 1983).

During the Late Monte Albán I phase, the area of occupation at Monte Albán expanded to 442 ha. The Danzantes building apparently continued in use, and a new building was constructed above the previously mentioned Early Monte Albán I structure found in the PSA excavation. This Late Monte Albán I building, partly destroyed by later construction activities, had a vertical wall on which a serpent-like motif had been modeled in stucco (Acosta 1965, Flannery & Marcus 1983c). Also, within Mound K of System IV, on the western side of the Main Plaza, a construction exists that probably dates to the Late Monte Albán I phase; the excavated remains consist of a substantial sloping wall, several meters high, along with two rubble masonry columns (Acosta 1965, Flannery & Marcus 1983c).

Although archaeologists have excavated several Classic period (200–700 CE) palaces at Monte Albán, they found it difficult to determine whether earlier palaces were built at the site (Flannery 1983). A Late Monte Albán I or Monte Albán II palace may lie within a platform just north of Mound K and System IV. Measuring 50 m north-south by 20 m east-west, this platform reaches 2 m above the level of the Main Plaza (Winter 1994). Atop the platform are the remains of a large Classic period structure, but there are earlier building stages here as well, including a wall with large blocks that resembles the Late Monte Albán I construction within Mound K (Winter 1994, p. 19). Another building stage consists of a stuccoed, painted staircase flanked by walls that date to the Late Monte Albán I phase or, possibly, the Monte Albán II phase (Winter 1994, p. 19). Associated with this structure is a Monte Albán II tomb that Caso excavated (Caso et al. 1967, tabla VII).

Flannery (1983) suggests that the main royal palace at Monte Albán during the Classic period could have been the Patio Hundido construction on the North Platform. If so, the remains of an earlier palace could lie buried under—if not obliterated by—the massive construction of the North Platform. Because gaining access to early buildings at Monte Albán is difficult, Marcus & Flannery (1996) urge researchers to "look for other sites of the same period, where the overburden of later structures is not as heavy" (p. 165).

Recently, we carried out excavations at one of these "other sites," namely the Late Monte Albán I phase site of El Palenque (SMT-11b) at San Martín Tilcajete,

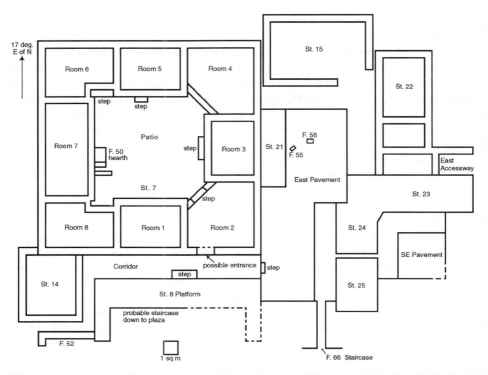

Figure 4   Schematic plan of the Area I palace complex at El Palenque, San Martín Tilcajete (SMT-11b). The palace complex covers 34 m x 25 m (850 m^2) and comprises nine structures as well as two paved areas; figure based on detailed field drawings by E. Redmond, C. Spencer, J. Sherman, C. Glew, L. Villamil, and C. Elson.

some 25 km south of Monte Albán (Figure 2). El Palenque was the first-order center of the Ocotlán-Zimatlán polity, which shows evidence of resisting incorporation by the Monte Albán state throughout the Monte Albán Late I phase (Spencer & Redmond 2001a, 2003). On the north side of the plaza at El Palenque, we exposed the well-preserved remains of a palace complex in our Excavation Area I (Figure 4). The Area I Palace comprises 9 structures and two open areas paved with flagstones, as well as corridors, staircases, and related features, all associated with Late Monte Albán I ceramics. The entire palace covers 34 × 25 m (850 m^2), and it has both residential and public or governmental components. The component labeled Structure 7 was probably residential in nature. Covering 16 × 16 m, it had stone foundations that supported walls of adobe bricks, some of which were still preserved. Eight rooms were arranged around an interior patio that measured 8 × 8 m. Inside the patio we located a multi-chambered hearth (Feature 50). The presence of grinding stones and other domestic debris attest to the largely residential nature of Structure 7. Across a corridor to the south lay Structure 8, a platform topped with flagstones that directly overlooked the plaza at El Palenque. To the east of Structure 7 was the East Pavement, a courtyard paved with flagstones, surrounded by several masonry constructions. Structure 21 was a low platform that overlooked the central part of the East Pavement, in which a large hearth (Feature 56) was located. Structure 15, on the north side of the East Pavement, contained evidence of food preparation, including butchering, on a large scale. We suspect that feasts were prepared in Structure 15 and perhaps cooked or kept warm in Feature 56. Delimiting the east side of the East Pavement were additional platforms (Structures 22–25), beyond which was the SE Pavement, marking the southeastern corner of the Area I Palace.

The initial construction of the Area I Palace is dated by charcoal embedded in the foundation of Structure 7. This sample (Beta-147540) yielded a conventional radiocarbon age of 2300 ± 80 BP (conventional radiocarbon date of 350 BCE ± 80), with a 2-Sigma calibrated range of 740–710 BCE and 530–180 BCE.

Two other charcoal samples from living floors pertain to the period of use of Structure 7. Beta-143354 (Room 6) produced a conventional radiocarbon age of 2110 ± 60 BP (conventional radiocarbon date of 160 BCE ± 60), with a 2-Sigma calibrated range of 360–280 BCE and 240 BCE–20 CE. Beta-143351 (corridor surface between Structure 7 and Structure 8) yielded a conventional radiocarbon age of 2080 ± 60 BP (conventional radiocarbon date of 130 BCE ± 60), with a 2-Sigma range of 350–310 BCE and 210 BCE–55 CE.

The latest radiocarbon date associated with Structure 7 came from the patio: Beta-143355, with a conventional radiocarbon age of 1970 ± 60 BP (conventional radiocarbon date of 20 BCE ± 60), and a 2-Sigma range of 100 BCE-140 CE. This charcoal sample was taken from a large deposit of charcoal, ash, and burned adobes, a deposit similar to other areas of burning in the Area I Palace. A major conflagration likely accompanied the abandonment of the Area I Palace in the first century BCE. In size and architectural form, this palace is similar to later Classic period Zapotec palaces at Monte Albán (Flannery 1983, 1998; Marcus & Flannery 1996, pp. 208–11). However, its Late Monte Albán I date makes the Area I Palace the earliest example of a palace thus far excavated in Oaxaca.

In Area G (Mound G)—on the eastern side of the El Palenque plaza—we excavated Structure 16, which consisted of two large contiguous rooms (one measuring 12.8 m by 2.35 m, and the other 9.8 m by 2.2 m), and two smaller rooms (measuring 3.4 m by 2.2 m and 2.75 m by 2.2 m), one at either end of the major rooms (Figure 5). All four rooms of Structure 16 (like those of Structure 7) had well-preserved stone foundations. Although Structure 16 is somewhat similar to the multiroom temples that investigators have excavated in Monte Albán II (and later) contexts at San José Mogote and Monte Albán (Marcus & Flannery 1996, p. 182), Structure 16 is associated with ceramics of the Late Monte Albán I phase. A radiocarbon sample (Beta-143353) was obtained from an ashy deposit on the NW Surface, probably associated with the burning that attended the structure's abandonment. Beta-143353 produced a conventional radiocarbon age of 1980 ±

St. 16

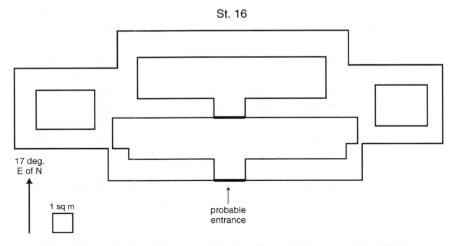

Figure 5   Schematic plan of Structure 16, Area G, a multiroom temple at El Palenque, San Martín Tilcajete (SMT-11b); figure based on detailed field drawings by E. Redmond, C. Elson, and A. Balkansky.

70 BP (conventional radiocarbon date of 30 BCE ± 70), with a 2-Sigma range of 165 BCE–155 CE; this date is very close to the latest date from Structure 7. Structure 16 was clearly in use during the Late Monte Albán I occupation of El Palenque and, like the Area I Palace complex, was burned and abandoned in the first century BCE, in the very early years of Monte Albán II.

In sum, the El Palenque excavations at Tilcajete have documented the existence of a palace and multiroom temple at the capital of what we regard as a secondary state in the Ocotlán-Zimatlán subregion during the Late Monte Albán I phase. Extrapolating from the Tilcajete data, we hypothesize that these key state institutions also must have existed by the Late Monte Albán I phase at Monte Albán itself. The testing of this hypothesis will require further excavation at Monte Albán, given the fragmentary nature of the current evidence there.

Conquest/Subjugation of Distant Territories

Archaeologists interpret the ~50 "conquest slab" inscriptions on Building J as referring to the taking and holding of territory through force (Caso 1947, Marcus 1980). Although many scholars assume that Building J and its inscriptions date to Monte Albán II, Caso (1938, p. 11) actually suggested that it was constructed in the preceding phase. Marcus (1976b, 1980) hypothesized that one of the conquered places referred to in the Building J inscriptions was the Cañada de Cuicatlán, a canyon traditionally inhabited by Cuicatec speakers, situated about 80 km north of Monte Albán, a distance much greater than a half-day of pedestrian travel (Figure 2).

In 1977–1978, we conducted a program of archaeological survey and excavations in the Cañada de Cuicatlán (Spencer & Redmond 1997). We recovered considerable evidence that the Cañada was conquered by Monte Albán at the onset of the Lomas phase (300 BCE) and remained in a subordinate, probably tributary, relationship until the end of that phase (200 CE), a time span that corresponds to the Late Monte Albán I and Monte Albán II phases combined. The evidence includes (*a*) a major settlement pattern disruption, including the abandonment of all Perdido phase (pre-300 BCE) occupations; (*b*) burning and other violence accompanying this abandonment, including the skeletal remains of a woman and an infant lying on the floor of an abandoned house; (*c*) the establishment of a large fortress at Quiotepec, on the northern edge of the conquered region; (*d*) the appearance of a ceramic boundary north of this fortress, which indicates that the Cañada was strongly linked to Monte Albán during the Lomas phase but no longer interacted freely with regions to the north; and (*e*) dramatic changes between the Perdido and Lomas phases in patterns of residence, economic activities, and ceremonial behavior at village sites south of the Quiotepec fortress, as documented by our excavations at La Coyotera (Redmond 1983; Spencer 1982; Spencer & Redmond 1997, 2001b, 2003).

A series of radiocarbon dates (Spencer & Redmond 2001b, figure 8) shows that the onset of the Lomas phase, and thus the onset of Zapotec conquest, corresponds to the beginning of Late Monte Albán I (300 BCE). Similarly, Balkansky (2002) argued that his data from the Sola Valley, about 75 km southwest of Monte Albán, indicate that this region also was brought under Monte Albán's control by Late Monte Albán I. Other regions were also annexed by Monte Albán, including Ejutla (Feinman & Nicholas 1990), Peñoles (Finsten 1996), Miahuatlán (Marcus & Flannery 1996, pp. 200–1), and perhaps the San Francisco Arriba area (Marcus & Flannery 1996, pp. 201–2) so that the area dominated by Monte Albán grew to some 20,000 km^2 by Monte Albán II times (Marcus 1992; Marcus & Flannery 1996, p. 206).

Other areas in Oaxaca remained independent of Monte Albán for varying lengths of time, often responding (as did Tilcajete) by developing into secondary states. Most of the Mixteca Alta northwest of the Oaxaca Valley seems never to have fallen under Monte Albán's domination but instead experienced a chain reaction of secondary state formation and urbanization during the Ramos phase (300 BCE–200 CE), the most likely trigger of which was Monte Albán's strategy of aggressive territorial expansion (Balkansky 1998a, 1998b; Balkansky et al. 2000).

Summary

For the Late Monte Albán I phase (300–100 BCE), we detect a four-tier regional settlement hierarchy in the Etla-Central subregion of the Oaxaca Valley, the core area most directly dominated by Monte Albán. At the El Palenque site (SMT-11b) near Tilcajete, the Structure 7/Area I Palace is dated by ceramics to the Late Monte Albán I phase, and radiocarbon dating suggests that its initial construction occurred around 300 BCE. The Structure 16 multiroom temple at El Palenque is dated by ceramics to the Late Monte Albán I phase. The conquest and domination of the Cañada de Cuicatlán is dated with ceramics to the Late Monte Albán I and Monte Albán II phases, and a series of radiocarbon dates puts the onset of this conquest at about 300 BCE. Thus, the archaeological evidence indicates that state organization existed in Oaxaca by the Late Monte Albán I phase, and two particular lines of evidence (the construction of the El Palenque palace and the initial conquest of the Cañada) imply that the state emerged by the beginning of this phase, or around 300 BCE. These data support the view that aggressive territorial expansion played a role very early in the process of Zapotec primary state formation (Spencer & Redmond 2001b). Finally, the rise of the Monte Albán state likely led to secondary state formation in certain nearby polities that managed to resist outright domination by Monte Albán.

THE SOUTHERN GULF COAST

Controversy surrounds the Olmec culture of the Southern Gulf Coast (Clark 1997; Diehl & Coe 1995; Flannery & Marcus 2000; Grove 1989a, 1997), but the issue of greatest concern for this review is whether the Early Preclassic San Lorenzo Olmec (1200–900 BCE) or the Middle Preclassic La Venta Olmec (800–400 BCE) show convincing evidence of state organization.

Settlement Hierarchy

The first-order center in the La Venta region was the site of La Venta itself, which according to González Lauck (1996, p. 75) originally covered some 200 ha, half of which has survived the impact of recent urbanization. Settlement pattern data collected by Rust from the La Venta region are consistent with a three-tier settlement hierarchy during the Late La Venta Period (800–500 BCE), the peak of Preclassic development in the area (Rust 1992, Rust & Sharer 1988). Rust (1992) concludes that the "overall social structure seems to be that of an advanced chiefdom in the process of evolving into an early stratified society, with La Venta identifiable as a temple town both administrating and surrounded by complex social groupings" (p. 126).

In the San Lorenzo region, settlement pattern surveys were conducted by Lunagómez (1995) and Symonds (1995). Symonds & Lunagómez (1997a, table 6.1; also, 1997b, figure 5.3) present a "working site typology" consisting of twelve types, which the authors define through a combination of factors, including nature of architectural modification, mounded architecture, and site area. Symonds & Lunagómez (1997a, p. 152) referred to this typology variously as a "temporary site typology" and a "preliminary site hierarchy," but there are substantial overlaps in the size ranges for most of the defined site types. What they have presented is a site typology, but it does not constitute a settlement hierarchy based on a site-size distribution, as we determined with the Oaxaca data. In a more recent paper, Symonds (2000) reduced the number of site types to seven by combining some of the previous categories, with San Lorenzo as the single example of a Type 7 site for the Early Preclassic (Symonds 2000, figure 8).

A map of the San Lorenzo site (Symonds 2000, figure 1) shows the limits of the site as estimated by Coe & Diehl (1980, map 1), as well as the larger occupation area determined by more recent survey (Lunagómez 1995). Using a Keuffel & Esser compensating polar planimeter, we obtained 50 ha for the smaller site area and 150 ha for the larger site area on Symonds' map (2000, figure 1). Although this smaller site area is very close to the 52.9-ha estimate that Coe (1981, p. 119) reported for San Lorenzo, the larger site area we obtained is much less than the 690-ha figure published recently by some researchers (Cyphers 1996, p. 67; Clark 1997, p. 216; Symonds 2000, p. 56). Grove (1997) suggests a possible explanation for this discrepancy: "Included in the 690-ha estimate is artifactual material that cannot be classified as to temporal period, and thus may represent areas of Classic and Postclassic occupation and activities" (p. 71). A site size of 690 ha would necessarily include many of the small sites in the vicinity of San Lorenzo that Symonds (2000, figure 8) and Symonds & Lunagómez (1997a, figure 6.3; 1997b, figure 5.4) reported as separate occupations (Coe & Diehl 1980, map 1; Flannery & Marcus 2000, p. 4, note 3). We conclude that the 690-ha figure for San Lorenzo should be viewed with skepticism.

Further difficulties are encountered if one tries to assess the Early Preclassic settlement hierarchy using the distribution of individual site sizes. Although Symonds' dissertation (1995) is cited as the source for the site-size estimates presumably used to create the overlapping size ranges for Early Preclassic sites in Symonds & Lunagómez (1997a, table 6.1; 1997b, figure 5.3), the site-area figures given for individual "outer hinterland" sites in Symonds (1995, Appendix C) represent total site areas and not occupation areas on a phase-by-phase basis. This is problematic because 85% of the sites with Early Preclassic occupation (and 100% of the 10-ha or larger sites with Early Preclassic occupation) also were inhabited during the Early Postclassic period (900–1100 CE) (Symonds 1995, Appendix C). Symonds (1995) acknowledged this finding when she observed that the Early Postclassic is the "period of greatest population growth and expansion" in the region (p. 663). In his description of "inner hinterland" sites, Lunagómez (1995) provided area estimates for most individual sites; but, like Symonds, he did not present occupation areas on a phase-by-phase basis for sites with multiple phases of occupation. Significantly, 12 of his 13 sites larger than 1 ha (including San Lorenzo itself) had Early Postclassic occupations. Considering the lack of data on the sizes of individual Early Preclassic occupations, we cannot realistically assess the evidence of a regional settlement-size hierarchy for that period.

Palaces and Temples

At Middle Preclassic La Venta, the "Great Pyramid," or Structure C-1, reached a height of 30 m and was associated with six monumental structures (González

Lauck 1996, p. 75–76). Just north of Structure C-1 is Complex A, the "ceremonial precinct" of La Venta (González Lauck 1996, p. 76). Excavations in this complex produced several well-known finds, including the burials of 2–3 young individuals who had been covered with red pigment and placed in a mortuary chamber accompanied by jade ornaments, stingray spines, and other offerings (Drucker et al. 1959, González Lauck 1996). Other discoveries in this area include four massive offerings of serpentine blocks and the arrangement of sixteen jade, serpentine, and sandstone figurines known as Offering 4. These finds, though representing impressive craftsmanship and labor, by themselves do not suggest a political organization more complex than a chiefdom (Flannery & Marcus 2000). There are no plans of standardized, multiroom temples at the site. The one structure at La Venta that could be a candidate for a palace is the Stirling Acropolis, but excavations thus far in this structure have been "insufficient to determine the precise nature, dating, and function of its construction" (González Lauck 1996, figure 1, p. 79).

At San Lorenzo, the nature of Early Preclassic architecture is not clear. The large mounds in a plaza-like arrangement at San Lorenzo (Coe & Diehl 1980, map 1) do not date to the Early Preclassic (Cyphers 1997a, p. 96; Grove 1997, p.77). Nor does it appear that the 200 low mounds surrounding the plaza area are Early Preclassic in date (Cyphers 1997a, p. 102). Cyphers (1996, p. 65; 1997a, p.101) reports the remains of a structure dating to the Early Preclassic that she designates the "Palacio Rojo" (or "Red Palace"). The remains consist of "a hematite-stained sand floor," along with the "use of stone, as in the *bancas* or benches, L-shaped stones usually about 1 m long which were embellishments in earthen and wooden constructions, possibly used as step coverings" (Cyphers 1997a, p. 101). The structure is associated with Monument 57, a basalt column, that may have served as a roof support, as well some limestone and bentonite slabs that may have been used in walls "because several were found in the collapsed debris" (Cyphers 1997a, p. 101). Photographs of the Palacio Rojo appear in Cyphers (1996, figure 3) and Cyphers (1997c, figure 4.6). The limited excavation exposure makes it difficult to evaluate the spatial extent or the function of this structure. Grove (1997, p. 77) suggests it could represent either an elite residence or a public building. Flannery & Marcus (2000) assert that the Palacio Rojo is "an easily remembered but misleading label since we lack a plan of the building, and what we do have looks nothing like a Mesoamerican palace" (p. 6, note 4). An elite residential function likely is represented by a construction atop the D4-7 mound; it measured 9 m × 12 m and had an apsidal shape defined by 20 postmolds (Cyphers 1997a, p. 101). As of this review, there is little architecture at San Lorenzo that can be dated to the Early Preclassic period, and what has been reported does not constitute convincing evidence of a palace or a standardized, multiroom temple.

Conquest/Subjugation of Distant Territories

Several researchers express doubt that the Olmec polities of San Lorenzo or La Venta ever executed conquests of distant regions, arguing instead that a model of interregional exchange of goods and ideas among developing chiefdoms is a better fit for the data from several Mesoamerican regions (Demarest 1989; Flannery 1968; Flannery & Marcus 1994, 2000; Grove 1989a,b, 1997; Hammond 1988; Marcus 1989). Flannery & Marcus (2000, p. 27) assert, furthermore, that the San Lorenzo Olmec played no leading role in such exchange networks; they note that excavations at San Lorenzo have produced relatively fewer examples of what some have called "Olmec" motifs than have excavations at the Oaxaca site of San José Mogote and the site of Tlapacoya in the Basin of Mexico.

By contrast, Clark (1997) maintains his belief not only in Olmec preeminence in exchange but also in interregional conquests by the Olmec, specifically during the eleventh century BCE of the Mazatán region on the Chiapas (Pacific) coast, some 280 km from San Lorenzo. Clark proposed that "formerly independent simple chiefdoms were consolidated into one complex chiefdom. . .the new Mazatán polity overtly signaled its connections to the heartland Olmec in a range of media, from domestic cooking vessels and figurines to public art" (p. 228). He points to a reduction in the consumption of foreign goods outside the regional center of Paso de la Amada, as well as a general population decline in the region, and asserts that "the data appear to indicate an aggressive takeover of the Mazatán region by their former trade allies, the Olmecs" (p. 228). Yet, the data he drew on are limited: There is no evidence of hostile intervention (e.g., no burned villages, no bodies left on house floors), and the only evidence offered for an Olmec presence in Mazatán is an increase in artifacts with Olmec traits, particularly at the regional center of Paso de la Amada (Clark 1997, p. 228). However, a recent study by Lesure (1998), another Mazatán researcher, raises questions about the significance of this change in artifact style. Lesure (1998) analyzed ceramic assemblages from Paso de la Amada that date to 1400–1000 BCE, paying particular attention to the pattern of appearance of a set of traits closely linked to the San Lorenzo Olmec. The results of his analysis provided some support for a model of symmetrical relations among societies of similar levels of complexity and somewhat less support for a model of asymmetrical relations whereby a less complex society emulates a more complex one (Lesure 1998, pp. 77–79). Lesure's analysis lends no support to the aggressive takeover model proposed by Clark (1997).

Summary

The environment of the Southern Gulf Coast admittedly makes it difficult to estimate occupation areas on a phase-by-phase basis. The current absence of such data prevents a quantitative analysis of the Early Preclassic settlement hierarchy in the San Lorenzo region. For the La Venta region, surveyors have reported a three-tier settlement hierarchy for the Middle Preclassic period. No convincing plans of palaces or standardized, multiroom temples have resulted from excavations at San Lorenzo or La Venta. There is no compelling evidence that the Olmecs of the Southern Gulf Coast carried out an aggressive takeover of any distant region. We conclude that the Formative period Olmecs are appropriately interpreted as chiefdoms, not states.

SOUTHEASTERN LOWLANDS

Marcus (1998, 2003) suggests that the Late Preclassic period in the Lowland Maya area (300 BCE–250 CE) was probably a time of competing chiefdoms, noting the evidence of "hereditary differences in rank, settlement hierarchies of two or three tiers, and sufficient interpolity raiding so that some sites have ditches, ramparts, palisades, and other defensive earthworks" (Marcus 1998, p. 61). Other Maya scholars argue that state organization appeared by the end of the Late Preclassic period, centered on the site of El Mirador (Matheny 1986, Sharer 1992).

Settlement Hierarchy

Sharer (1992, p. 131) argues that El Mirador occupied the top tier of a four-tier settlement hierarchy during the Late Preclassic, but the lack of detailed settlement pattern surveys in the El Mirador region precludes an evaluation of his assertion. Again, although we recognize that survey is difficult in the tropical lowland environment, we also maintain that site-size data are indispensable for assessing the complexity of regional settlement hierarchies.

Palaces and Temples

El Mirador has some impressively large platform mounds, though not all of them can be dated in their entirety to the Late Preclassic. The Tigre complex comprises an estimated 428,000 m^3 of construction material (Matheny 1986, p. 340). It likely was built in the second century BCE, although one should note that 44% of the excavated sherds were identifiable as Late Preclassic, 3% were Protoclassic, 6% were Classic, and 50% were classified as unknown (Matheny 1986, p. 339). Rivaling the Tigre Complex in bulk is the Danta Complex, which yielded considerable quantities of Classic period materials as well as Late Preclassic ceramics, leading Matheny (1986) to conclude the following: "Evidence gained in excavations and through analysis of the sherds recovered there indicates that the Late Classic may be the major period of construction" (p. 350). A second-century CE radiocarbon date was associated with the Pava Temple of the Danta Complex, though materials of both the Late Preclassic and Classic periods were found in excavations here. Matheny (1986) summed up as follows: "Evidence from the Pava Temple excavations indicates that the temple was constructed during the Late Preclassic period with occupation into A.D. times. Clearly only the stairs and central areas of the building were used in the Early Classic and the structures were not extensively modified at that time" (p. 347).

In the sector of the El Mirador site known as the Central Acropolis, excavations directed by Landeen (1986) found an elite residence that was "so large it may be best described as a kind of palace" (Matheny 1986, p. 344). Some rooms were located on a higher level to which one ascended by a stuccoed staircase; these upper rooms "apparently were residences that included sleeping platforms, formal doorways, a window in the principal room, benches inside the rooms, thick stuccoed surfaces on all stone structures, and outside trash deposits containing residues of burned bone, ash, broken pottery, and other bits of household debris" (Matheny 1986, pp. 344–45). Investigators assigned to the Late Preclassic period nearly all (98%) of the 3405 classifiable sherds associated with the structure (Landeen 1986, p. 106). Landeen also reported four radiocarbon dates (1986, Appendix B) with midpoints of 1900 BCE, 95 BCE, 10 CE, and 50 CE, the earliest of which she rejected as much too early (Landeen 1986, p. 57). A date of 100 BCE–100 CE would be reasonable for this excavated structure, which Landeen (1986) concluded was "the earliest documentation of Preclassic Maya palaces" (p. 106).

Conquest/Subjugation of Distant Territories

There is no evidence that El Mirador executed any campaigns of conquest in distant regions. El Mirador is connected by a causeway to Nakbe, another site with large constructions dating to the Middle Preclassic and Late Preclassic (Hansen 1998; Sharer 1992, p. 132). Although it is plausible that El Mirador exerted control over Nakbe during Late Preclassic times, it also is the case that Nakbe is too close to El Mirador (just 13 km) to qualify as a "distant" territory. Nakbe lies within a half-day of pedestrian travel from El Mirador, a distance compatible with the administrative capabilities of a chiefdom (Spencer 1990).

Summary

The evidence of state organization at El Mirador in the Late Preclassic period is tantalizing but inconclusive (Marcus 2003). The proposed palace in the Central Acropolis is associated with radiocarbon dates in the 100 BCE–100 CE range. The Pava Temple is associated with a second-century CE radiocarbon date. As of yet, there is no convincing evidence of a four-tier regional settlement hierarchy or the takeover of distant regions. Most areas of Southeastern Mesoamerica, particularly in the lowlands, have yet to see the kind of full-coverage surveys that yield phase-by-phase data on occupation areas for all the prehistoric sites in a region.

During the Early Classic period (250–500 CE) unambiguous Maya states appeared, characterized by "palaces, standardized two-room temples arranged on platforms in groups of three, royal tombs, and a four-tiered settlement hierarchy" (Marcus 1998, p. 61). The earliest palace construction at Calakmul has been dated to the beginning of the fifth century CE (Folan et al. 1995; Marcus 1998, p. 63). The earliest palace at Tikal is an Early Classic construction in the Central Acropolis. A vessel found in this palace bears a text referring to the palace as the house of the ruler Jaguar Paw, who reigned, according to another text, around the end of the fourth century CE (Marcus 1998, p. 65). Excavations in the Copán Acropolis have established that the earliest palace at this Maya capital was built around 430 CE (Sharer et al. 1999, p. 5).

THE BASIN OF MEXICO

There is no compelling evidence of state organization in the Basin of Mexico prior to the phase known variously as Tezoyuca-Patlachique at Teotihuacan (Cowgill 1997), Cuicuilco 6–7 at Cuicuilco (Muller 1990), the First Intermediate Phase Three in the Basin as a whole (Sanders et al. 1979), and the early portion of the Terminal Formative period as defined by Parsons (1971). The initial date of this period has undergone a shift in recent years. Sanders et al. (1979, p. 93) dated their First Intermediate Phase Three to 300–100 BCE and associated it with Tezoyuca and Patlachique phases, whereas Parsons (1971, table 5) had previously dated his Terminal Formative period to 250 BCE–150 CE and associated it with Tezoyuca, Patlachique, and Tzacualli phases combined. More recently, Cowgill (1992, p. 91; 1997, figure 1) gives 150 BCE as the initial date of the Patlachique phase, with the little-known Tezoyuca phase beginning perhaps as early as 200 BCE. In his scheme, the Patlachique phase gives way around BCE/CE to the Tzacualli phase, which lasts until 150 CE (Cowgill 1997, p. 133). On the basis of her analysis of excavated materials from Cuicuilco, Muller (1990, p. 55) dated the Cuicuilco 6 phase to 200–150 BCE and associated it with the Tezoyuca phase; she dated Cuicuilco 7 to 150–100 BCE and associated it with the Patlachique phase (Muller 1990, p. 61). Still more recently, Angulo (1998, pp. 106–8) cited the results of Manzanilla's excavations at Cuanalán (1985), which indicated that the Cuanalán phase at this site lasts until 100 BCE before giving way to the Patlachique phase. In sum, recent research would not support a beginning date for the time period known as Tezoyuca-Patlachique, First Intermediate Phase Three, or Cuicuilco 6–7 prior to 200–250 BCE, and there is some support for a starting date as late as 150–100 BCE.

Settlement Hierarchy

At Teotihuacan during the Tezoyuca-Patlachique phase, there were two foci of occupation covering a total of some 600–800 ha, with an estimated population of 20,000–40,000 (Cowgill 1992, figure 5.1; Sanders et al. 1979, p. 101). This is a considerable increase over the preceding Cuanalán phase, when there were just two villages in the Teotihuacan area, the larger covering some 15–30 ha (Cowgill 1992, p. 89). The extent of the contemporaneous occupation at Cuicuilco is difficult to determine because of the lava flows that cover the site, but Sanders et al. (1979) estimated it to be at least 400 ha, with a population of about 20,000; they noted, however, that "it is quite possible that the site may actually be significantly larger. The monumentality of the Phase Three (Tezoyuca-Patlachique) public architecture was without parallel in the entire Basin of Mexico, and only Teotihuacan equaled or exceeded it in size and population" (p. 99) Sanders et al. (1979) conclude that the Basin of Mexico at this time was not politically unified but was characterized by "high-level confrontation between Cuicuilco and Teotihuacan" (p. 103). Each center, they argue, was the focus of a cluster of sites that exhibited a four-tier settlement hierarchy (Sanders et al. 1979, p. 102). A histogram of site size for the Chalco-Xochimilco region, which was probably subordinate to Cuicuilco, manifests at least four modes for First Intermediate Phase Three (Sanders et al. 1979, table 5.7). By contrast, a settlement hierarchy of no more than three tiers can be detected for the preceding First Intermediate Phase Two or Ticomán-Cuanalán phase (Sanders et al. 1979, pp. 93, 98).

Palaces and Temples

By 200–300 CE, Teotihuacan had "the largest integrated complex of monumental structures in Mesoamerica" (Cowgill 1997, p. 130). Yet, the buildings that composed this complex (the Sun Pyramid, the Moon Pyramid, the Ciudadela, and others) were all constructed during the Tzacualli phase (1–150 CE) or later (Cowgill 1992, p. 97–114; 1997, p. 133). What Cowgill (1992) noted a decade ago remains true today: "We still know almost nothing of Patlachique phase structures at Teotihuacan" (p. 91).

At Cuicuilco, by contrast, several monumental or public buildings can be dated to the Cuicuilco 6–7 (Tezoyuca-Patlachique) period (Muller 1990). The Cuicuilco A sector of the site contains the famous round pyramid, composed of several construction stages that brought its height to 20 m and its diameter to 80 m by First Intermediate Phase Three; it is likely ceremonial in nature (Cummings 1933; Sanders et al. 1979, p. 99). Some 500 m west of the Cuicuilco A pyramid lies the Cuicuilco B sector. Here archaeologists have located at least 9 mounds and associated structures (Heizer & Bennyhoff 1958, 1972; Muller 1990, figure 1). Platform C is one of the excavated constructions in Cuicuilco B (Muller 1990, pp. 277–80). The uppermost construction layer of this platform was labeled Structure C′; it dates to Cuicuilco 6–7 and looks to us very much like a standard two-room temple (Muller 1990, figure 4, p. 279). Structure C′ was built directly above Structure C″, which dates to Cuicuilco 5 (Ticomán III) and looks like a one-room temple with a line of postmolds at the room's centerline (Muller 1990, p. 279, figure 4). A good candidate for a palace at Cuicuilco is Montículo 2, a platform measuring about 50 m on a side, on top of which was a large, multiroomed structure, only a small part of which has been excavated (Muller 1990, pp. 15–20, figures 1–2); indeed, this structure is referred to as the "Palacio" on the INAH (Instituto Nacional de Antropología e Historia) site maps posted at the site and in the on-site museum. Montículo 2 is situated in what may be an elite residential area in the southwestern corner of the Cuicuilco B sector. About 30–40 m east of Montículo 2 lies Montículo 1, which has the appearance of another residential construction, though not as elaborate as Montículo 2; in the open space between them, archaeologists found an extraordinary concentration of "tronco cónico" storage pits (Muller 1990, figure 2).

Conquest/Subjugation of Distant Territories

Some investigators argue that Cuicuilco and Teotihuacan "simultaneously sought to expand their spheres of influence" within the Basin of Mexico during First

Intermediate Phase Three (Sanders et al. 1979, p. 103). Settlement pattern changes at this time are thought to reflect a highly competitive and unstable situation. For example, in his discussion of Terminal Formative occupations in the Ixtapalapa area, Blanton (1970, p. 128) notes that "most Late Formative sites not in defendable positions were abandoned," whereas new sites were founded in hilltop locations suitable for defense. Although one site on the lakeshore (Tlapacoya) was not abandoned between the Late and Terminal Formative, it grew substantially, and Blanton (1970) proposed that "in the case of this community, nucleation was adopted as a defensive posture rather than movement to a high location" (p. 128). A concern for defense also may be reflected in the appearance of hilltop sites associated with Tezoyuca ceramics in the central and, especially, the northeastern part of the Basin; 6 of the 13 Tezoyuca hilltop sites were located on high terrain in the southern part of the Teotihuacan Valley, and three more were found on the southern edge of the Patlachique Range, which rises between the Teotihuacan Valley and the Texcoco Plain (Sanders et al. 1979, map 12). Sanders et al. (1979) suggested that "hostility and warfare were important enough to be major factors in selecting for settlement location in settings of maximum defensibility" (p. 105). The Tezoyuca phase sites are short-lived occupations, which Sanders et al. (1979, p. 105) saw as evidence that hostilities declined during the succeeding Patlachique phase. In contrast, Cowgill (1992, p. 92) noted that one of the two foci of Patlachique occupation at Teotihuacan was on the slopes of Cerro Colorado and Cerro Malinalco. He went on to propose, "Conceivably people moved to the hill slopes for better defense. No signs of Patlachique phase fortifications have ever been recognized, but the absence of fortifications need not mean that the defensive advantages of the location were unimportant" (Cowgill 1992, p. 93). The Tezoyuca-Patlachique site locations in the Teotihuacan Valley may reflect a concern for defense against aggression by Cuicuilco. Cuicuilco itself shows no evidence of a settlement shift at this time, though the extreme nucleation of population at the site could have served a defensive purpose.

There is no evidence that either Cuicuilco or Teotihuacan attempted to extend their control to any areas outside the Basin during the Tezoyuca-Patlachique phase. After 200–300 CE, Teotihuacan established a presence of some kind in some distant regions (Cowgill 1997, pp. 134–35), including Morelos (Hirth 1978), Hidalgo (Díaz Oyarzábal 1980), Veracruz (Santley 1989), and Guatemala (Kidder et al. 1946, Sanders and Michels 1977). By that time, however, Cuicuilco was no longer a major political force. The site was largely abandoned by the end of Tezoyuca-Patlachique phase (Muller 1990, pp. 229, 279), possibly as a result of an eruption of the Xitle volcano, which covered much of the site and its surroundings with a thick layer of lava (Sanders et al. 1979, p. 106).

Summary

There is evidence of a four-tier regional settlement hierarchy centered on the Cuicuilco site during the Tezoyuca-Patlachique, or Cuicuilco 6–7, phase (Sanders et al. 1979, p. 102, table 5.7), which according to recent research began no earlier than 200–150 BCE—and perhaps as late as 100 BCE—and lasted until about BCE/CE (Angulo 1998; Cowgill 1992, pp. 89–91; Cowgill 1997, figure 1; Muller 1990, p. 55, 61). Cuicuilco covered minimally 400 ha at this time (Sanders et al. 1979, p. 99) and contained at least 10 monumental public constructions, including Structure C′, a likely two-room temple, and Montículo 2, which was not extensively excavated but is thought by archaeologists to be a palace (Muller 1990, figure 1–2, 4). A settlement shift to defensible locations in many areas in the central and northeastern Basin may indicate that Cuicuilco was attempting to extend its political control through aggressive action over the entire Basin (including the Teotihuacan Valley, more than 60 km away) during the Tezoyuca-Patlachique phase; this possibility could be a fruitful topic for future research.

CONCLUSION

The archaeological data on primary state formation in Mesoamerica are less than ideal; more field research is needed. Yet, on the basis of the evidence in hand, we conclude that the strongest candidate for a primary state in Mesoamerica is the Monte Albán state, which emerged in the Late Monte Albán I phase (300–100 BCE). The lines of evidence associated with this development include (*a*) a clear, four-tier settlement hierarchy in the core region dominated by Monte Albán; (*b*) the appearance of at least two key institutional buildings (the palace and the multiroom temple) at the capital of an adjacent secondary state (and perhaps at Monte Albán itself, though this remains hypothetical, pending further excavation); and (*c*) the conquest and long-term subjugation by Monte Albán of distant regions, most clearly documented to date in the Cañada de Cuicatlán and the Sola Valley, both lying more than 70 km away from Monte Albán. Radiocarbon evidence indicates that the appearance of the palace and the conquest of the Cañada both occurred near the beginning of Late Monte Albán I (~300 BCE). No earlier case of state formation in Mesoamerica can be documented with the current evidence; indeed, the earliest possible signs of statehood in the Basin of Mexico (Cuicuilco) and the Southeastern Lowlands (El Mirador) are probably one to two centuries later than in Oaxaca.

The correspondence in time between the conquest of the Cañada and the appearance of state institutions in the Oaxaca Valley is consistent with the proposition that aggressive territorial expansion played a key role in the state formation process there. To carry out the initial conquest and the long-term control of distant territories, the political organization headquartered at Monte Albán needed to develop a powerful military and an internally specialized administration capable of managing distant tributary provinces through the effective delegation of authority. Tribute collected in conquered regions undoubtedly helped to finance this administrative transformation.

As a final point, we note that our view of the early Oaxaca state is similar to recent interpretations that Stanish (2001) and Algaze (1993a,b) offer of primary state formation in the Andes and Mesopotamia, respectively. All three cases appear to provide support for general theories that emphasize the coercive/predatory/expansionistic aspects of primary state formation.

ACKNOWLEDGMENTS

We thank Henry Wright, Joyce Marcus, and Jeffrey Parsons for their helpful comments as we worked on this review article. Bridget Thomas prepared the illustrations.

The *Annual Review of Anthropology* is online at http://anthro.annualreviews.org

LITERATURE CITED

Acosta JR. 1965. Preclassic and Classic architecture of Oaxaca. In *Handbook of Middle American Indians, Vol. 3: Archaeology of Southern Mesoamerica, Part 2*, ed. R Wauchope, GR Willey, pp. 814–36. Austin: Univ. Tex. Press

Algaze G. 1993a. Expansionary dynamics of some early pristine states. *Am. Anthropol.* 95:304–33

Algaze G. 1993b. *The Uruk World System: The Dynamics of Expansion of Early Mesopotamian Civilization.* Chicago: Univ. Chicago Press

Angulo J. 1998. El desarrollo sociopolítico como factor de cambio cronológico cultural. In *Los Ritmos de Cambio en Teotihuacán: Reflexiones y Discusiones de su Cronología*, ed. R Brambila, R Cabrera, pp. 103–28. México, DF: Inst. Nac. Antropol. Hist.

Balkansky AK. 1998a. Urbanism and early state formation in the Huamelulpan Valley of Southern Mexico. *Lat. Am. Antiq.* 9:37–67

Balkansky AK. 1998b. Origin and collapse of complex societies in Oaxaca (Mexico): evaluating the era from 1965 to the present. *J. World Prehist.* 12:451–93

Balkansky AK. 2002. *The Sola Valley and the Monte Albán State: A Study of Zapotec Imperial Expansion.* Ann Arbor: Mus. Anthropol., Univ. Mich. Mem. Mus. Anthropol. No. 36

Balkansky AK, Kowalewski SA, Pérez Rodríguez V, Pluckhahn TJ, Smith CA, et al.

2000. Archaeological survey in the Mixteca Alta of Oaxaca, Mexico. *J. Field Archaeol.* 27:365–89

Benson EP, de la Fuente B, eds. 1996. *Olmec Art of Ancient Mexico.* Washington, DC: Natl. Gallery Art

Blanton RE. 1970. *Prehispanic settlement patterns of the Ixtapalapa Peninsula Region, Mexico.* PhD diss. Univ. Mich. Ann Arbor: Univ. Microfilms. 2 vols.

Blanton RE. 1978. *Monte Albán: Settlement Patterns at the Ancient Zapotec Capital.* New York: Academic

Blanton RE, Kowalewski SA, Feinman GM, Finsten L. 1993. *Ancient Mesoamerica: A Comparison of Change in Three Regions.* Cambridge: Cambridge Univ. Press

Carneiro RL. 1970. A theory of the origin of the state. *Science* 169:733–38

Carneiro RL. 1981. The chiefdom: precursor of the state. In *The Transition to Statehood in the New World*, ed. GD Jones, RR Kautz, pp. 37–79. Cambridge: Cambridge Univ. Press

Caso A. 1938. *Exploraciones en Oaxaca: Quinta y Sexta Temporadas 1936–1937.* México, DF: Inst. Panamer. Geogr. Hist., Publ. 34

Caso A. 1947. Calendario y escritura de las antiguas culturas de Monte Albán. In *Obras Completas de Miguel Othón de Mendizábal.* México, DF. Vol. 1

Caso A, Bernal I, Acosta JR. 1967. *La Cerámica de Monte Albán.* México, DF: Inst. Nac.

Antropol. Mem. Inst. Nac. Antropol. Hist. No. 13

Claessen HJM, Skalník P, eds. 1978a. *The Early State*. The Hague: Mouton

Claessen HJM, Skalník P. 1978b. The early state: theories and hypotheses. See Claessen & Skalník 1978a, pp. 3–29

Clark JE. 1997. The arts of government in early Mesoamerica. *Annu. Rev. Anthropol.* 26:211–34

Coe MD. 1981. San Lorenzo Tenochtitlán. In *Handbook of Middle American Indians: Archaeology, Supp. 1*, ed. JA Sabloff, pp. 117–46. Austin: Univ. Tex. Press

Coe MD, Diehl RA. 1980. *In the Land of the Olmec, Vol. 1: The Archaeology of San Lorenzo Tenochtitlán*. Austin: Univ. Tex. Press

Cohen R. 1978. State origins: a reappraisal. See Claessen & Skalník 1978a, pp. 31–75

Cohen R, Service ER, eds. 1978. *Origins of the State: The Anthropology of Political Evolution*. Philadelphia: Inst. Study Hum. Issues

Cowgill GL. 1992. Toward a political history of Teotihuacan. In *Ideology and Precolumbian Civilizations*, ed. AA Demarest, GW Conrad, pp. 87–114. Santa Fe, NM: Sch. Am. Res. Press

Cowgill GL. 1997. State and society at Teotihuacan, Mexico. *Annu. Rev. Anthropol.* 26: 129–61

Crumley CL. 1987. A dialectical critique of hierarchy. See Patterson & Gailey 1987, pp. 155–69

Crumley CL. 1995. Heterarchy and the analysis of complex societies. In *Heterarchy and the Analysis of Complex Societies*, ed. R Ehrenreich, CL Crumley, JE Levy, pp. 1–5. Washington, DC: Am. Anthropol. Assoc. Archaeol. Pap. No. 6

Cummings B. 1933. Cuicuilco and the archaic culture of Mexico. *Univ. Ariz. Bull.* 4(8). Soc. Sci. Bull. 4.

Cyphers A. 1997a. Olmec architecture at San Lorenzo. See Stark & Arnold 1997, pp. 96–114

Cyphers A, ed. 1997b. *Población, Subsistencia y Medio Ambiente en San Lorenzo Tenochtitlán*. México, DF: Univ. Nac. Auton. México, Inst. Investig. Antropol.

Cyphers A. 1997c. La arquitectura Olmeca de San Lorenzo Tenochtitlán. See Cyphers 1997b, pp. 91–117

Cyphers Guillén A. 1996. Reconstructing Olmec life at San Lorenzo. See Benson & de la Fuente 1996, pp. 61–71

Danien EC, Sharer RJ, eds. 1992. *New Theories on the Ancient Maya*. Philadelphia: Univ. Mus., Univ. Penn. Univ. Monogr. 77

Demarest AA. 1989. The Olmec and the rise of civilization in eastern Mesoamerica. See Sharer & Grove 1989, pp. 303–44

Díaz Oyarzábal CL. 1980. *Chingú: Un Sitio Clásico del Área de Tula, Hidalgo*. México, DF: Inst. Nac. Antropol. Hist.

Diehl RA, Coe MD. 1995. Olmec archaeology. In *The Olmec World: Ritual and Rulership*, pp. 10–25. Princeton, NJ: Art Mus. Princeton

Drucker P, Heizer RF, Squier R. 1959. *Excavations at La Venta, Tabasco, 1955*. BAE Bull. 170. Washington, DC: Bur. Am. Ethnol.

Earle TK. 1987. Chiefdoms in archaeological and ethnohistorical perspective. *Annu. Rev. Anthropol.* 16:279–308

Elson CM. 2003. *Elites at Cerro Tilcajete: a secondary center in the Valley of Oaxaca, Mexico*. PhD diss. Univ. Mich. Ann Arbor

Feinman GM. 1998. Scale and social organization: perspectives on the archaic state. See Feinman & Marcus 1998, pp. 95–133

Feinman GM, Marcus J, eds. 1998. *Archaic States*. Santa Fe, NM: Sch. Am. Res. Press

Feinman GM, Nicholas LM. 1990. At the margins of the Monte Albán state: settlement patterns in the Ejutla Valley, Oaxaca. *Lat. Am. Antiq.* 1:216–46

Finsten L. 1996. Periphery and frontier in southern Mexico: the Mixtec Sierra in highland Oaxaca. In *Pre-Columbian World Systems*, ed. PN Peregrine, GM Feinman, pp. 77–95. Madison, WI: Prehistory Press. Monogr. World Archaeol. No. 26

Flannery KV. 1968. The Olmec and the Valley of Oaxaca: a model for interregional interaction in Formative times. In *Dumbarton Oaks Conference on the Olmec*, ed. EP Benson, pp. 79–117. Washington, DC: Dumbarton Oaks

Flannery KV. 1972. The cultural evolution of civilizations. *Annu. Rev. Ecol. Syst.* 3:399–426

Flannery KV. 1983. The legacy of the Early Urban Period: an ethnohistoric approach to Monte Albán's temples, residences, and royal tombs. See Flannery & Marcus 1983a, pp. 132–36

Flannery KV. 1995. Prehistoric social evolution. In *Research Frontiers in Anthropology*, ed. M Ember, pp. 1–26. Englewood Cliffs, NJ: Prentice-Hall

Flannery KV. 1998. The ground plans of archaic states. See Feinman & Marcus 1998, pp. 15–57

Flannery KV. 1999. Process and agency in early state formation. *Cambridge Archaeol. J.* 9(1):3–21

Flannery KV, Marcus J, eds. 1983a. *The Cloud People: Divergent Evolution of the Zapotec and Mixtec Civilizations.* New York: Academic

Flannery KV, Marcus J. 1983b. The origins of the state in Oaxaca: editors' introduction. See Flannery & Marcus 1983a, pp. 79–83

Flannery KV, Marcus J. 1983c. The earliest public buildings, tombs, and monuments at Monte Albán, with notes on the internal chronology of Period I. See Flannery & Marcus 1983a, pp. 87–91

Flannery KV, Marcus J. 1990. *Borrón y cuenta nueva*: setting Oaxaca's archaeological record straight. In *Debating Oaxaca Archaeology*, ed. J Marcus, pp. 17–69. Ann Arbor: Mus. Anthropol., Univ. Mich. Anthropol. Pap. No. 84

Flannery KV, Marcus J. 1994. *Early Formative Pottery of the Valley of Oaxaca, Mexico.* Ann Arbor: Mus. Anthropol., Univ. Mich. Mem. Mus. Anthropol. No. 27

Flannery KV, Marcus J. 2000. Formative Mexican chiefdoms and the myth of the "Mother Culture." *J. Anthropol. Archaeol.* 19:1–37

Folan WJ, Marcus J, Pincemin S, Domínguez Carrasco M, Fletcher L, Morales López A. 1995. Calakmul: new data from an ancient Maya city in Campeche, Mexico. *Lat. Am. Antiq.* 6:310–34

Gailey C, Patterson T. 1987. Power relations and state formation. See Patterson & Gailey 1987, pp. 1–16

González Lauck R. 1996. La Venta: an Olmec capital. See Benson & de la Fuente 1996, pp. 73–81

Grove DC. 1989a. Olmec: What's in a name? See Sharer & Grove 1989, pp. 8–14

Grove DC. 1989b. Chalcatzingo and its Olmec connection. See Sharer & Grove 1989, pp. 122–47

Grove DC. 1997. Olmec archaeology: a half century of research and its accomplishments. *J. World Prehist.* 11:51–101

Haas J. 1982. *The Evolution of the Prehistoric State.* New York: Columbia Univ. Press

Hammond N. 1988. Cultura hermana: reappraising the Olmec. *Q. Rev. Archaeol.* 9(4):1–4

Hansen RD. 1998. Continuity and disjunction: the Pre-Classic antecedents of Classic Maya architecture. In *Function and Meaning in Classic Maya Architecture*, ed. SD Houston, p. 49–122. Washington, DC: Dumbarton Oaks

Heizer RF, Bennyhoff JA. 1958. Archaeological investigation of Cuicuilco, Valley of Mexico, 1957. *Science* 127:232–33

Heizer RF, Bennyhoff JA. 1972. Archaeological excavations at Cuicuilco, Mexico, 1957. *Natl. Geogr. Soc. Res. Rep. 1955–1960*, pp. 93–104

Hirth KG. 1978. Teotihuacan regional population administration in eastern Morelos. *World Archaeol.* 9:320–33

Kidder AV, Jennings JD, Shook EM. 1946. *Excavations at Kaminaljuyu, Guatemala.* Washington, DC: Carnegie Inst. Wash., Publ. 561

Kohl P. 1984. Force, history and the evolutionist paradigm. In *Marxist Perspectives in Archaeology*, ed. M Spriggs, pp. 127–34. Cambridge: Cambridge Univ. Press

Kohl P. 1987. State formation: useful concept or idée fixe? See Patterson & Gailey 1987, pp. 27–34

Kowalewski SA, Feinman GM, Finsten L, Blanton RE, Nicholas LM. 1989. *Monte Albán's Hinterland, Part II: Prehispanic Settlement Patterns in Tlacolula, Etla, and Ocotlán, the Valley of Oaxaca, Mexico.* Ann Arbor: Mus. Anthropol., Univ. Mich. Mem. Mus. Anthropol. No. 23

Landeen ES. 1986. *Excavations on a Late Preclassic Plaza Unit at El Mirador, Petén, Guatemala.* MS thesis. Brigham Young Univ. Provo, UT

Lesure RG. 1998. Refining an Early Formative ceramic sequence from the Chiapas coast of Mexico. *Anc. Mesoam.* 9:67–81

Lunagómez R. 1995. Inner hinterland site descriptions. See Symonds 1995, Append. B

Manzanilla L. 1985. El sitio de Cuanalán en el marco de las comunidades pre-urbanas del valle de Teotihuacán. In *Mesoamérica y el Centro de México, Una Antología*, ed. J Monjarráz, E Pérez Rocha, R. Brambila, pp. 133–178. México, DF: Inst. Nac. Antropol. Hist.

Marcus J. 1976a. The origins of Mesoamerican writing. *Annu. Rev. Anthropol.* 5:35–67

Marcus J. 1976b. The iconography of militarism at Monte Albán and neighboring sites in the Valley of Oaxaca. In *The Origins of Religious Art and Iconography in Preclassic Mesoamerica*, ed. HB Nicholson, pp. 123–39. Los Angeles: Latin Am. Cent., Univ. Calif. Los Angeles

Marcus J. 1980. Zapotec writing. *Sci. Am.* 242:50–64

Marcus J. 1983. The first appearance of Zapotec writing and calendrics. See Flannery & Marcus 1983a, pp. 91–96

Marcus J. 1989. Zapotec chiefdoms and the nature of Formative religions. See Sharer & Grove 1989, pp. 148–97

Marcus J. 1992. Dynamic cycles of Mesoamerican states: political fluctuations in Mesoamerica. *Natl. Geogr. Res. Explor.* 8: 392–411

Marcus J. 1998. The peaks and valleys of ancient states: an extension of the dynamic model. See Feinman & Marcus 1998, pp. 59–94

Marcus J. 2003. Recent advances in Maya archaeology. *J. Archaeol. Res.* 11:71–148

Marcus J, Flannery KV. 1996. *Zapotec Civilization: How Urban Society Evolved in Mexico's Oaxaca Valley.* London: Thames & Hudson

Matheny RT. 1986. Investigations at El Mirador, Petén, Guatemala. *Natl. Geogr. Res.* 2:332–53

Muller F. 1990. *La Cerámica de Cuicuilco B: Un Rescate Arqueológico.* México, DF: Inst. Nac. Antropol. Hist.

Parsons JR. 1971. *Prehistoric Settlement Patterns in the Texcoco Region, Mexico.* Ann Arbor: Mus. Anthropol., Univ. Mich. Mem. Mus. Anthropol. No. 3

Patterson T, Gailey C, eds. 1987. *Power Relations and State Formation.* Washington, DC: Archaeol. Sect., Am. Anthropol. Assoc.

Paynter R. 1989. The archaeology of equality and inequality. *Annu. Rev. Anthropol.* 18:369–99

Redmond EM. 1983. *A Fuego y Sangre: Early Zapotec Imperialism in the Cuicatlán Cañada, Oaxaca.* Ann Arbor: Mus. Anthropol., Univ. Mich. Mem. Mus. Anthropol. No. 16

Rust WF. 1992. New ceremonial and settlement evidence at La Venta, and its relation to Preclassic Maya cultures. See Danien & Sharer 1992, pp. 123–29

Rust WF, Sharer RJ. 1988. Olmec settlement data from La Venta, Tabasco, Mexico. *Science* 242:102–4

Sanders WT. 1974. Chiefdom to state: political evolution at Kaminaljuyu, Guatemala. In *Reconstructing Complex Societies: An Archaeological Colloquium*, ed. CB Moore, pp. 97–116. Cambridge: Am. Sch. Orient. Res. Suppl. Bull. Am. Sch. Orient. Res., No. 20

Sanders WT, Michels JW, eds. 1977. *Teotihuacan and Kaminaljuyu.* University Park: Penn. State Univ. Press

Sanders WT, Parsons JR, Santley RS. 1979. *The Basin of Mexico: Ecological Processes in the Evolution of a Civilization.* New York: Academic

Santley RS. 1989. Obsidian working, long-distance exchange, and the Teotihuacan presence on the south Gulf Coast. In *Mesoamerica After the Decline of Teotihuacan, A.D. 700–900*, ed. RA Diehl, JC Berlo, pp. 131–51. Washington, DC: Dumbarton Oaks

Service ER. 1975. *Origins of the State and Civilization*. New York: Norton

Service ER. 1978. Classical and modern theories of the origins of government. See Cohen & Service 1978, pp. 21–34

Sharer RJ. 1992. The Preclassic origin of Lowland Maya States. See Danien & Sharer 1992, pp. 131–36

Sharer RJ, Grove DC, eds. 1989. *Regional Perspectives on the Olmec*. Cambridge: Cambridge Univ. Press

Sharer RJ, Traxler LP, Sedat DW, Bell EE, Canuto MA, Powell C. 1999. Early Classic architecture beneath the Copan Acropolis. *Anc. Mesoam.* 10:3–23

Spencer CS. 1982. *The Cuicatlán Cañada and Monte Albán: A Study of Primary State Formation*. New York: Academic

Spencer CS. 1990. On the tempo and mode of state formation: neoevolutionism reconsidered. *J. Anthropol. Archaeol.* 9:1–30

Spencer CS. 1998. A mathematical model of primary state formation. *Cult. Dyn.* 10:5–20

Spencer CS, Redmond EM. 1997. *Archaeology of the Cañada de Cuicatlán, Oaxaca*. New York: Am. Mus. Nat. Hist. Anthropol. Pap. No. 80

Spencer CS, Redmond EM. 2000. Lightning and jaguars: iconography, ideology, and politics in Formative Cuicatlán, Oaxaca. In *Cultural Evolution: Contemporary Viewpoints*, ed. GM Feinman, L Manzanilla, pp. 145–75. New York: Kluwer Academic/Plenum

Spencer CS, Redmond EM. 2001a. Multilevel selection and political evolution in the Valley of Oaxaca, 500–100 B.C. *J. Anthropol. Archaeol.* 20:195–229

Spencer CS, Redmond EM. 2001b. The chronology of conquest: implications of new radiocarbon analyses from the Cañada de Cuicatlán, Oaxaca. *Lat. Am. Antiq.* 12:182–202

Spencer CS, Redmond EM. 2003. Militarism, resistance, and early state development in Oaxaca, Mexico. *Soc. Evol. Hist.* 2(1):25–70

Stanish C. 2001. The origin of state societies in South America. *Annu. Rev. Anthropol.* 30:41–64

Stark BL, Arnold PJ III, eds. 1997. *Olmec to Aztec: Settlement Patterns in the Ancient Gulf Lowlands*. Tucson: Univ. Ariz. Press

Symonds S. 1995. *Settlement distribution and the development of cultural complexity in the Lower Coatzacoalcos Drainage, Veracruz, Mexico: an archaeological survey at San Lorenzo Tenochtitlán*. PhD diss. Vanderbilt Univ. Nashville, TN

Symonds S. 2000. The ancient landscape at San Lorenzo Tenochtitlán, Veracruz, Mexico: settlement and nature. In *Olmec Art and Archaeology in Mesoamerica*, ed. JE Clark, ME Pye, pp. 55–73. Washington, DC: Natl. Gallery Art

Symonds S, Lunagómez R. 1997a. Settlement system and population development at San Lorenzo. See Stark & Arnold 1997, pp. 144–73

Symonds S, Lunagómez R. 1997b. El sistema de asentamiento y el desarrollo de poblaciones en San Lorenzo Tenochtitlán, Veracruz. See Cyphers 1997b, pp. 275–302

Webster D. 1975. Warfare and the origin of the state: a reconsideration. *Am. Antiq.* 40:464–70

Winter M. 1994. El Proyecto Especial Monte Albán 1992–1994: antecedentes, intervenciones y perspectivas. In *Monte Albán: Estudios Recientes: Contribución No. 2 del Proyecto Especial Monte Albán 1992–1994*, ed. M Winter, pp. 1–24. Oaxaca, Mexico

Wright HT. 1977. Recent research on the origin of the state. *Annu. Rev. Anthropol.* 6:379–97

Wright HT. 1986. The evolution of civilizations. In *American Archaeology: Past and Future*, ed. D Meltzer, D Fowler, J Sabloff, pp. 323–65. Washington, DC: Smithsonian Inst. Press

Wright HT, Johnson GA. 1975. Population, exchange, and early state formation in southwestern Iran. *Am. Anthropol.* 77:267–89

Yoffee N. 1979. The decline and rise of Mesopotamian civilization: an ethnoarchaeological perspective on the evolution of social complexity. *Am. Antiq.* 44:5–35

Yoffee N. 1993. Too many chiefs? (or, safe texts for the '90s). In *Archaeological Theory: Who Sets the Agenda?*, ed. N Yoffee, A Sherratt, pp. 60–78. Cambridge: Cambridge Univ. Press

Annu. Rev. Anthropol. 2004. 33:201–22
doi: 10.1146/annurev.anthro.33.070203.143852

LANGUAGE BIRTH AND DEATH

Salikoko S. Mufwene

*Department of Linguistics, University of Chicago, Chicago,
Illinois 60637; email: s-mufwene@uchicago.edu*

Key Words ecology, exploitation colony, settlement colony, language
endangerment, "langue minorée"

■ **Abstract** Since the late 1980s, language endangerment and death have been discussed as if the phenomena had no connection at all with language birth. More recently
the phenomena have been associated almost exclusively with the intense and pervasive
economic globalization of same period, a process that some authors have reduced too
easily to the McDonaldization phenomenon. Moreover, the relation of globalization to
different forms of colonization has been poorly articulated. As a matter of fact, little of
the longer history of population movements and contacts since the dawn of agriculture
has been invoked in the literature on language endangerment to give some broader perspective on the mechanisms of language birth and death and on the ecological factors
that bear on how they proceed. This review aims to remedy these shortcomings in our
scholarship.

INTRODUCTION

Linguistics publications on language endangerment and death have increased since
Dorian's (1989) *Investigating Obsolescence* and more so since the 1992 publication of a special issue of *Language* (the Linguistic Society of America's jour-
nal) on the subject matter. Books alone include the following: Fishman (1991),
Robins & Uhlenbeck (1991), Brenzinger (1992, 1998), Hagège (1992, 2000),
Mühlhäusler (1996), Cantoni (1997), Dixon (1997), Grenoble & Whaley (1998),
Hazaël-Massieux (1999), Reyhner et al. (1999), Crystal (2000), Nettle & Romaine
(2000), Skutnab-Kangas (2000), Hinton & Hale (2001), Maffi (2001), Mufwene
(2001), Swaan (2001), Dalby (2002), Harmon (2002), Joseph et al. (2003), Maurais
& Morris (2003), and Phillipson (2003). Experts will undoubtedly notice some
omissions in this list, but one cannot help noticing the strong interest the subject
matter has aroused among linguists over the past two decades.

Research and publications on new language varieties have interested linguists
in a less dramatic way, despite the high visibility of Bickerton (1981, 1984),
Thomason & Kaufman (1988), and Chaudenson (1992, 2001). This asymmetry
may reflect the concern among linguists—stated in numerous publications—about
the increasing loss of linguistic materials that should inform them about typological variation. It also may be due to the following: Although genetic linguistics has

0084-6570/04/1021-0201$14.00

always been about speciation, researchers have typically focused on whether particular language varieties descend from the same ancestor and can thus be claimed to be genetically related—hence the central methodological role accorded to the comparative method. Linguists have not connected research on the development of creoles, pidgins, and indigenized varieties, which is obviously on the birth of new language varieties, to genetic linguistics. Thus, because of the way linguists think contact exerted an unusually major influence on these cases of language divergence, Thomason & Kaufman (1988), for instance, are more interested in showing how the development of creoles, pidgins, and the like deviates from what they see as the normal or usual kind of language change and speciation than in explaining the process of language birth itself.

Overall, the way that scholarship on language loss and birth has developed reflects in some ways the fact that genetic linguistics has assumed scenarios in which language contact has played an incidental, rather than catalytic, role. Such scenarios seem so artificial when one recognizes, for instance, that the diversification of Indo-European languages has been concurrent with the gradual dispersal of Indo-European populations in Europe and parts of Asia. The dispersal was a long migratory process during which these populations came in contact with non-Indo-Europeans. Because they did not relocate at the same pace, nor along the same routes, they often subsequently came in contact with each other. For instance, the Romans, speaking an Italic language, came in contact with the Celts, as would the Germanics some centuries later, though most of the Celts would already be Latinizing during that time. Little has been said about how languages vanished in Europe while Proto-Indo-European was speciating into so many modern languages.

Since the late 1980s, research on language loss has focused primarily on the indigenous languages of European ex-colonies and to some extent on minority languages of the European Union—languages such as Breton, Occitan, Basque, Sami, and Gaelic, which are still endangered by the official and dominant languages of their nations. The almost-exclusive association of language death and birth either with the emergence of modern European nation states united by single national languages or with Europe's colonization of most of the world since the sixteenth century has led to the illusion that both processes may be recent developments in the history of mankind.[1] The overemphasis on worldwide economic globalization as the primary cause of language loss has prevented any fruitful comparisons between, on the one hand, recent and current evolutions and, on the other, what must have occurred during the earliest political and economic hegemonies in the history of mankind. The closest thing to what I suggest can be found in Hagège (2000).

Although current research on language birth and death is well grounded in population contacts, the relevant literature does not highlight the fact that these

---

[1]Indeed there have been attempts to compare with "creolization" the development of Romance languages (e.g., Schlieben-Lange 1977) or that of Middle English (e.g., Bailey & Maroldt 1977), but such studies have been negatively criticized for good and bad reasons (e.g., Thomason & Kaufman 1988, regarding English).

processes usually have occurred under the same, or related, socioeconomic conditions identified by Mufwene (2001) as "ecological." For instance, the birth of creoles in the plantation settlement colonies of the Atlantic and Indian Oceans is a concomitant of language shift among the African populations who developed them. Likewise, the emergence of American English(es) is concomitant both of the gradual loss of especially continental European languages that came in contact with English in North America and of the restructuring of English varieties brought over from England (regardless of whether linguists factor in influence from the other languages).

In this review, I elaborate on these observations, focusing especially on the concern that scholars such as Nettle & Romaine (2000), Skutnab-Kangas (2000), and Maffi (2001) express about loss of "biodiversity" applied to the coexistence of languages. I historicize both colonization and economic globalization to show how they are related and provide differential ecologies for language birth and death. I highlight speakers as the unwitting agents of these phenomena, while also questioning the adequacy of terms such as language war, killer language, and linguicide.

My approach is generally the same as that taken in Mufwene (2001),[2] largely inspired by population genetics, with languages considered as populations of idiolects and, in respect to their evolutionary characteristics, as analogous to parasitic, viral species. Space limitations preclude justifying this position here. To suffice, the following assumptions are central to most of the discussion in the rest of this review: (*a*) languages are internally variable (between idiolects and between dialects); (*b*) they do not evolve in uniform ways, as changes may proceed faster or differently in one segment of a population of its speakers than they would in another; (*c*) the same language may thrive in one ecology but do poorly in another; (*d*) like biological species, their vitality depends on the ecology of their existence or usage; and (*e*) like viruses, language features may change several times in their lifetime. But we should start by articulating the meanings of language "birth" and "death" more explicitly.

THE MEANINGS OF BIRTH AND DEATH APPLIED TO LANGUAGES

The notions birth and death actually provide more arguments for treating languages as species. Languages are unlike organisms in the way they are born or die. As well noted by Chaudenson (1992, 2001, 2003) in the case of creoles, and Szulmajster

---

[2]Readers familiar with Harmon (1996) (with which I was not familiar until after completing this review) will notice several differences in our conceptions of the "linguistic species" and how he and I apply it to language evolution, as complementary as our positions are. For instance, my justifications here, as in Mufwene (2001), are quite different from his (which are also repeated in Harmon 2002).

(2000) regarding Yiddish, languages as communal phenomena cannot be issued birth or death certificates. The relevant processes are protracted, spanning several generations. The concept of "language birth" is in fact a misnomer of some sort. The birth involves no pregnancy and delivery stages, and the term refers to a stage (not a point in time!) in a divergence process during which a variety is acknowledged *post facto* as structurally different from its ancestor. For instance, no particular point in time can be associated with the emergence of creoles as separate vernaculars from the colonial European languages from which they evolved. Unlike in the case of organisms, but as in the case of species, language birth cannot be predicted. The recognition of separateness is made possible by a cumulative accretion of divergence features relative to an ancestor language, regardless of whether linguists consider contact with other languages.

Likewise, language death is a protracted change of state.[3] Used to describe community-level loss of competence in a language, it denotes a process that does not affect all speakers at the same time nor to the same extent. Under one conception of the process, it concerns the statistical assessment of the maintenance versus loss of competence in a language variety among its speakers. Total death is declared when no speakers are left of a particular language variety in a population that had used it.[4]

An important question nowadays has also been whether Latin—whose standard variety (Classical Latin) is still the lingua franca of the Vatican and whose vernacular, nonstandard variety (Vulgar Latin) has evolved into the Romance languages—is really a dead language (Hagège 2000)? If so, what is the most critical criterion to identify a language as dead? Is language death predicated on the presence of native speakers and on its transmission from one generation of speakers to another without the mediacy of the scholastic medium?[5] And in the case of the evolution

---

[3]To be sure, cases of sudden language death by genocide have been attested (see, e.g., Hagège 2000 and Nettle & Romaine 2000), but they are rare compared to the other cases most commonly discussed in the literature. They are not really part of natural evolution by competition and selection, as explained in the conclusions section below. They are not discussed in the present section.

[4]It is less clear whether a language is still alive, just moribund, or simply "in poor health" when it is used by semispeakers, individuals who claim they speak it but mix its vocabulary and grammar with another language system. Dorian's (1981) discussion of Scottish Gaelic has made such cases an important part of understanding language "obsolescence."

[5]Space limitations prevent the author from pursuing this issue here. Assessing the vitality of a language variety in relation to its association with native speakers would, for instance, entail questioning the legitimacy of identifying pidgins as languages. The status of makeshift languages such as Esperanto would also become problematic. Likewise, it would be misguided not to include the school system among the mechanisms of language transmission. Not doing so would make it difficult to account for the spread of major European lingua francas such as English and French around the world. It would also call for a reassessment of the status of Irish in Ireland as a natural language being passed by one generation to another.

of a language into a new variety, what is the relationship between language death and language birth? Can these processes be considered as two facets of the same process? Needless to say these are aspects of death that are untypical of organisms. More benefits from conceiving of languages as species or populations of idiolects become obvious below.

QUESTIONING SOME USUAL ACCOUNTS
OF LANGUAGE BIRTH AND DEATH

As noted above, the birth of new language varieties is central to creolistics, to the study of indigenized varieties of European languages, and to historical dialectology.[6] The list of titles is too long to include here, and any choice of a representative list would be biased. Consistent with the genetic linguistics tradition, few scholars are interested in the birth process itself, except that in the case of creoles and indigenized varieties, some linguists acknowledge language contact and the influence of non-European languages on the European targets as important ecological factors.

As in the case of creoles, the emergence of new dialects in former settlement colonies has not been correlated with the concurrent erosion and death of other European languages that did not become the official languages of the relevant colonies, for instance, French, Dutch, Danish, Norwegian, and German, among a host of others, in the United States. Works such as Haugen (1953) and Clyne (2003), to cite two chronological extremes, are based more on language obsolescence than on the emergence of new varieties of the dominant language. That language contact is seldom invoked to account for the divergence of these new, colonial dialects of European languages—which has implicitly contributed to making the development of creoles so curious—remains an intriguing matter. Linguists have generally overlooked the topic of their birth itself, which very well can be discussed in relation to that of indigenized varieties of the same languages (see, e.g., Thomason & Kaufman 1988, Thomason 2001, Winford 2003). One important exception to the above bias, insofar as the evolution of English is concerned, is the growing literature on Hiberno-English, as represented, for example, by Kallen (1997).

---

[6]The foci have been different in these research areas. Most creolists seek to demonstrate that creoles (and pidgins) are natural and as rule-governed as other languages, whereas students of indigenized varieties argue that these varieties are as legitimate offspring of English as the varieties said to be "native" and are spoken in former settlement colonies such as the Americas or Australia, where populations of European descent are now majorities. (Creoles are associated primarily with island and coastal plantation settlement colonies of the Atlantic and Indian Oceans, where populations of non-European descent are now majorities.) Historical dialectology focuses mostly on the nonstandard vernaculars of former settlement colonies, almost overlooking the fact that the varieties spoken today in their European metropoles are just as new.

More specifically, Thomason (2001) correctly notes that history provides several instances of language death. However, the linguistics literature of the past two decades on language endangerment has rarely included comparisons with older cases in human history. As noted above, the growing scholarship on the subject matter has focused on the recent and ongoing attrition of the indigenous languages of former European colonies. In the vast majority of cases, these languages (especially the indigenous languages of the Americas and Australia) certainly have played a marginal role in the evolution of the European varieties that either have driven them to extinction or are threatening them. Thus it would be unjustified to expect the relevant literature to have related the topic of language death with that of language birth. One can, in fact, expect similar scholarship about Europe to have related these processes with the experience of several European languages that have become *langues minorées*.[7] As described below, capturing these parallel evolutions would have enabled us to better understand why languages have been dying so rapidly since the nineteenth century.

The literature generally has invoked globalization to account for the loss or endangerment of several non-European languages. Unfortunately few have articulated what globalization means. This phenomenon has been confused too often with McDonaldization, i.e., the spread of McDonald stores around the world (see, e.g., Nettle & Romaine 2000). Likewise, the literature says nothing about whether globalization is novel and how it relates to colonization. This connection is critical because the related applied literature on the revitalization of endangered languages seldom refers to the ecology that would be most favorable to the revitalization process. Would commitment on the part of the relevant linguistic communities alone suffice? Or would any conditions other than the precolonial ones, under which most of these languages thrived, be supportive of the revitalization efforts?

The vitality of languages cannot be dissociated from the socioeconomic interests and activities of their speakers. Native Americans have not been shifting from their native vernaculars to those of the European colonists because they have lost pride in their traditions, and the Celts have not either in giving up their indigenous languages

---

[7]Hazaël-Massieux (2000) reports an important distinction made by French sociolinguists between *langue minoritaire* (minority language) and *langue minorée* (undervalued and/or marginalized language). The latter need not be spoken by a minority population. Like Haitian Creole, it may be spoken by the majority population of a polity but is relegated to ethnographically "low" communicative functions. If this view is taken literally, most indigenous languages in former European colonies fall into this category because they are not associated with the "high(er)" communicative functions of their polities. (See Pandharipande 2003 regarding such situations in India.) Consistent with seemingly precocious predictions that 50%–90% of the world's languages will have vanished by the end of the twenty-first century, the approach misleadingly suggests the same outlook onto the coexistence of languages of the powerless and of the powerful everywhere. However, the history of the world shows that languages of the powerless often have been more resilient, or demonstrated more vitality, than those of the powerful. *Pace* Fishman (2003), there is much more ecological complexity and variability that must be considered on this subject matter, as attempted, for instance, by Pandharipande (2003).

in favor of Vulgar Latin—and later, the Romance languages—or English. The reasons for these shifts cannot be (so) different from those that led numerous Europeans to give up their heritage languages in favor of the dominant ones in the Americas and Australia.

Because language loss and endangerment to date have not been uniformly catastrophic in different parts of the world, one asks whether globalization has been uniform. Why are Native American languages more endangered in North America, where English has been so dominant, than in Latin America? Does any correlation exist between this discrepancy and the fact that in the Americas creoles developed more in former French and English plantation colonies than in Portuguese and Spanish ones? Do the reasons for all these cases of language loss differ from those that caused the loss of African languages in the New World?

Like other populations, language shift among Native Americans seems to be an adaptive response to changing socioeconomic conditions, under which their heritage languages have been undervalued and marginalized. Native Americans recognize the economic value of the European colonial languages supported by the new, global-economy world order. This explanation is consistent also with why indigenous languages in former exploitation colonies of Africa and Asia have been losing grounds not to European colonial languages but to (new) indigenous vernaculars (former lingua francas) associated with new indigenous urban life, such as Swahili in much of East Africa, Town Bemba in Zambia, Lingala in parts of the Democratic Republic of Congo and of the Republic of Congo, Wolof in Senegal, Malay in Indonesia and Malaysia, and Hindi in India. Globalization has not affected former exploitation colonies in the same way it affected former settlement colonies. Several factors contribute to making these new indigenous languages more realistic targets than the European colonial ones, for instance, the high rate of illiteracy, the scarcity of jobs requiring command of European languages, the fact that other jobs are accessible with command of an indigenous lingua franca (which is acquired by oral interaction with speakers of the language), and the fact that an inspiring urban culture is expressed also in the same non-European lingua franca. Below I return to this topic.

Invoking lack of pride or prestige to account for the loss of minority languages and of the *langues minorées* fails to explain why the Romance languages evolved from Vulgar Latin (the nonstandard variety) rather than from Classical Latin; why, where Latin prevailed, it was not offset by Ancient Greek, despite the higher prestige of the latter even among the Roman elite; and why Sanskrit is dead, or dying, despite all the prestige it carries relative to other Indic languages. Other ecological factors exist also that we should endeavor to identify, for instance, why part of the western Roman Empire romanized but most of the eastern part did not, despite the extended presence of the Romans in the territory;[8] or why in areas of the same eastern part of the Roman Empire Arabic managed to impose itself as an

---

[8]To be sure, Romanian is an important exception, to which must be added Aromanian and Megleno-Romanian, spoken by the Vlah minorities of Albania, Macedonia, and Greece (Friedman 2001). As the names suggest, they are related to Romanian.

important language (at the expense of both Greek and Latin) but nothing like this happened in the western part of the Empire. Answers to such questions should help scholars understand what ecological factors are particularly conducive to language endangerment and death.

Efforts to revitalize some of the endangered languages have been devoted largely to developing writing systems for them and generating written literature. Noble as they are, most of these endeavors have also confused revitalization, which promotes usage of a language in its community, with preservation, which does nothing more than preserve texts in (and accounts of) a language basically as museum artifacts. Classical Latin and Ancient Greek, among others, are cited as dead languages, despite the abundant literature available in them. The absence of a writing system has not led to the extinction of nonstandard varieties of the same European languages that have endangered non-European languages, as stigmatized as the nonstandard varieties have been for centuries now.[9] In fact, the new Indo-European vernaculars spoken in European settlement colonies of the Americas and Australia have developed from the contact of many of these varieties among themselves—not of standard varieties. Such evolutions shows that lack of prestige does not equate with lack of vitality. Likewise, despite numerous predictions of their imminent death, unwritten nonstandard vernaculars such as Gullah and African American Vernacular English have shown much resilience (Mufwene 1994, 1997).[10]

A HISTORICAL PERSPECTIVE ON LANGUAGE BIRTH AND DEATH

The Recent Past

The correlation of language death with globalization as an economic network of production and consumption interdependencies is partly correct. However, it does not uniformly affect the whole world, especially when it is conceived of at the

---

[9]One should remember here that terms such as *patois* and *brogue* used in reference to nonstandard varieties of French and English, respectively—and the former also in reference to Celtic languages in rural France—have had negative connotations in part because they are generally unwritten. Earlier uses of the term jargon, associated also with some contact language varieties, have similar negative connotations of "unintelligible," "meaningless," or "gibberish."

[10]Since DeCamp's (1971) study, which repeats a hypothesis conjectured already by Schuchardt (1914) and Bloomfield (1933), several creoles have been assumed by linguists to die by a process misidentified as decreolization (Mufwene 1994, 2001). However, varieties such as Jamaican Creole (ironically the focus of DeCamp's own speculation) are not only still thriving but also developing more divergent varieties such as "Dread Talk" (Pollard 2000). Mufwene (1997) argues that Gullah may be dying for a reason independent of "decreolization" qua debasilectalization, e.g., the massive exodus of its speakers to the city, where the variety is given up not only because it is stigmatized but also because it is economically useless in the urban environment.

scale of multinational corporations that run the economies of the most industrial nations of North America, Western Europe, Japan, Australia, and some city-states such as Singapore and Hong Kong. One should bear in mind also that globalization as explained here can be very local, as in the case of many aspects of American industry such as food production. It often applies to regional organizations like the European Union and the Association of South East Asian Nations, in which partners set up privileged trade and/or production relations.

Globalization seems to have exerted the greatest impact on languages at mostly the local level, and the impact has been more disastrous to indigenous languages in former settlement colonies than to those in exploitation colonies. This differential evolution reflects the fact that in settlement colonies the European colonists sought to create new Europes outside their metropoles (Crosby 1986) from which they inherited the ideology of nation-states ideally unified by one single language. As the European populations became the majority in their new nations, they adopted a dominant or official language for branches of their government, in the emergent global industry, and in the school system. The chosen language gradually penetrated the private domains of citizens' lives to the point that it became the vernacular spoken by almost everybody.

To be sure, the shift from other European languages to the dominant one was not sudden, nor did it affect all populations and their respective members concurrently. The slaves everywhere were the first to lose their ancestral languages, not so much because they were forbidden to speak them or were always put in situations so multilingual that they could not do so, but because of the way the plantation societies developed from earlier homesteads. As explained by Chaudenson (1992, 2001), the latter, farm-size dwellings, in which the slaves were the minority and well-integrated into family units, did not favor the retention of African languages. This outcome of language competition resulted because creole children in these settings learned to speak the colonial European languages rather than the language of their African parents. Creole children were mixed and looked after together, regardless of race, while all the healthy adults worked together to develop the colonial economic infrastructure. Moreover, the African-born slaves typically did not form a critical mass to continue speaking their languages among themselves, even if someone who spoke the same language worked in the same or a nearby homestead.

As some of the homesteads became large plantations, in which African-born slaves would gradually become the majority, the creole and, later, the seasoned slaves speaking modified varieties of the colonial languages (be they creoles or other nonstandard varieties) became linguistic models, similar to how city-born children in Africa serve as models for rural-born children. This ethnographic state of affairs played a central role in favoring language shift, and therefore loss, in the settlement colonies. By the founder principle, the newcomers simply found it more practical to learn the vernacular spoken by the slaves who preceded them, even if they were lucky enough to find someone with whom they could speak a common African language in private. The same founder principle accounts for language shift and loss among post-Abolition indentured laborers from Africa and

Asia who gradually assimilated to the creole ex-slaves. Neither their initial social isolation nor their relative ethnolinguistic homogeneity could prevent the change of vernaculars. (See, e.g., Mohan & Zador 1986 and Bhatia 1988 regarding the Indian indentured laborers, Ferreira 1999 regarding the Portuguese, and Warner-Lewis 1996 regarding the Yoruba, all of these cases applying to Trinidad.) In fact, the stigmatization of the identured laborers by the Creoles must have exerted more pressure on them to shift from their heritage vernaculars to Creole. The pressure to avoid the stigma as "uncivilized" was additional to the basic necessity to use the local language to adapt linguistically to the new socioeconomic world order.

For the same reason of adaptation to a changing socioeconomic ecology, the European populations that spoke languages other than the dominant one gave up their ancestral vernaculars, quite gradually, in a process that would continue until the twentieth century. (See, e.g., Haugen 1953, regarding the Scandinavians, and Salmons 2003, regarding the Germans). The main reason for the protracted shift is that the Europeans, especially those who did not come as indentured servants, were nationally segregated (see, e.g., Fischer 1989) and could continue to use their ancestral languages as vernaculars within their ethnic communities. Not only are American cities nowadays still segregated into white and black neighborhoods, but also they have inherited from the pre–World War II period names such as Irish, Italian, and German neighborhoods as a legacy of the way Europeans were segregated even among themselves. While they lasted, the maintenance of these national identities and speakers' abilities within the relevant communities to run local business in their ancestral vernaculars (Salmons 2003)[11] only decelerated the language shift process.

These developments suggest that in losing their indigenous languages Native Americans have followed the evolutionary trajectory already taken by immigrants to their land, who were developing an economic system that made obselete the Native American one. Thus, ecological pressures for survival forced Native Americans to adapt to the new world order, which entailed some command of the local dominant European language to earn a living. The language shift proceeded faster where miscegenation with the newcomers was allowed. It was made possible otherwise by exodus to the city and other places for jobs. Basically language loss among Native Americans has been a concomitant process of Americanization in the sense of departure from their ancestral socioeconomic lifestyles to those belonging to the European immigrants.

The fact that fewer Native American languages have vanished in Latin America than in North America suggests that globalization has not proceeded at the same speed in settlement colonies. The differential evolution seems to reflect the kind of economy that the European settlers developed and/or the kind of physical

---

[11]Salmons (2003) reports that the Germans in Wisconsin owned parochial schools and published newspapers and other literature in their languages until the readership waned because an increasing number of community members were attracted by the larger, urban American global economy.

ecological challenges they faced in spreading from the Atlantic coast. For instance, the Amazon forest has been difficult and slow for the colonists to penetrate, and the Amazon is precisely where the highest concentration of Native American languages can be found today. It is not by accident that deforestation and the immediate impact of this exploitation on the indigenous population have awakened our awareness of language endangerment, on the model of species endangerment in macroecology. Deforestation has made obvious the fact that changes in the habitat and economic activities of a population bear on the vitality of its language and culture, as its members adapt to new lifestyles. More languages have died in North America because changes in its socioeconomic ecology have been more advanced and have affected its populations more pervasively. Basically the same explanation applies to the extensive loss of indigenous languages in Australia. The less marginalized the Natives are from the local global economy system, the more likely they are to lose their heritage.

This explanation does not apply to former exploitation colonies of Africa and Asia, where relatively fewer indigenous languages are threatened and where they are typically endangered not by the European colonial languages but by other indigenous languages. The latter have sometimes stood in the way of the demographic expansion of their European competitors, as in the case of Lingala in the Democratic Republic of Congo and Swahili in Tanzania. Numerous ecological reasons explain this differential development: (*a*) The European colonizers hardly intended to settle permanently in these continents, although many of them wound up doing so; (*b*) the European exploitation colony system hardly intended to share its languages with the indigenous populations, preferring to teach the colonial languages only to an elite class of auxiliaries that would serve as intermediaries between the colonizers and the colonized (see, e.g., Brutt-Griffler 2002a, 2002b); (*c*) unlike in the earlier cases that produced pidgins (such as in Nigeria, Cameroon, and Papua New Guinea), European languages were introduced in the exploitation colonies in the nineteenth century as lingua francas on the basis of scholastic inputs rather than as vernaculars naturalistically transmitted outside the school system; (*d*) despite the higher status they gained from Western-style education and association with the now-indigenized varieties of the European colonial languages, most of the elite have not severed ties with their ancestral traditions—they have continued to use their indigenous languages as vernaculars and/or as necessary lingua francas for communication with their less-affluent relatives and with the other members of their ethnic groups.

One must remember that while settlement colonization has gradually reduced—though it has not yet fully eliminated—ethnic identities and languages among populations of the new polities (especially among non-Europeans), exploitation colonization has retained them, thus preserving the function of most indigenous languages as markers of ethnic identity. Only the city, in Africa at least, has come close to reducing ethnic identities and languages, acting like sugar cane plantations and rice fields of the Atlantic and Indian Ocean settlement colonies, by being a contact setting in which ethnolinguistically heterogeneous populations interact regularly with each other in a common language that becomes their vernacular. The gradual obliteration of ethnic boundaries, caused in part by interethnic marriages, is an important factor in the loss of ethnic languages.[12]

Dialogue Between the Recent and Distant Pasts

Languages have been dying for a long time in human history (e.g., Hagège 2000, Mufwene 2001, Thomason 2001). Although linguists have correctly noted that language death has proceeded at an unprecedented pace during the last century, they have still not explained fully why languages die and what or who kills them. As shown above, language death has not been uniform in different parts of the world either. This nonuniformity also may have been the case in the distant past. It should thus be rewarding to establish a heuristic bridge between the distant and the recent pasts to learn what they can tell us about each other. As space is limited here, I focus briefly on language evolution in the western side of the Roman Empire, about which there is ample information on language evolution, and I focus on the Romance countries and the British Isles.

To be sure, the Romans do not seem to have colonized Europe and the rest of the Mediterranean world on the model of recent European exploitation or settlement colonies.[13] If anything, it was likely a combination of both styles, if we consider the army veterans who retired and became land owners in Gaul, for instance, though the economic exploitation of the colonies suggests more of the exploitation style (Bauer 1996). There is little evidence also that the Romans claimed full nation-wide geographical spaces as colonies. According to Polomé (1983), the Romans likely took more interest in developing trade and military centers, a practice that leads him to equate the Romanization of these colonies with urbanization. From

---

[12]Students of creolization in Hawaii should remember that sugar cane cultivation did not proceed here the same way it did in the Caribbean and Indian Oceans. Sugar cane cultivation in Hawaii involved no slavery, the indentured laborers came at different times from only a handful of ethnic groups (Chinese, Japanese, Portuguese, Korean, and Philippino), and they were not mixed on the plantations, where they lived in ethnically segregated houses and continued to speak their ancestral languages as vernaculars. Unlike in the other plantation settlement colonies, Hawaiian Creole English developed in the city, where there was more cross-ethnic interaction, and Hawaiian Pidgin English developed concurrently (not before) on the plantations (Roberts 1998). According to Chaudenson (1992, 2001) and Mufwene (2001), plantation settlement colonies elsewhere produced no ecological conditions favorable to the development of Pidgin either prior to or concurrently with the emergence of Creole. It is thus clear why ethnic distinctions and the related languages have survived among descendants of the indentured laborers in Hawaii but not among descendants of slaves in other settlement colonies (Mufwene 2004).

[13]Trade colonization is not worth considering here because the structure of the Empire seems to rule it out. Roman presence in the Empire was permanent, not sporadic. In recent history, trade colonies generally evolved into settlement or exploitation colonies, which suggests that the same evolution must have happened during Roman colonization. (See also Bauer 1996.)

the military and administrative domination point of view, they created networks of towns interconnected by good road and water transportation infrastructures, all ultimately leading to Rome.[14] The Romans formed alliances with local rulers, whom they coaxed to administer their territories in the Roman style, assisted with their Roman technical expertise (including military), and enticed to work in the economic interest of Rome (Garnsey & Saller 1987). These leaders were taught Classical Latin, their children were sent to Roman schools, they were granted Roman citizenship, and they could compete with the Romans themselves for offices as high as generalship, provincial governorship, and the Roman Senate. Some of them, such as Marcus Ulpius Traianus (born in Spain), Lucius Septimus Severus (born in North Africa), and Marcus Aurelius Antoninus Caesar (born in Gaul), even rose to become emperors.[15]

Indirect evidence that the Romans did not colonize Europe on the settlement model comes from the fact that they left the Western Empire in the fifth century. However, the local rulers, who had Romanized already, maintained Latin as the language of their administrations, while Vulgar Latin continued to be spoken among those who had interacted regularly with the legionaries, whose children conceived with indigenous women took advantage of their knowledge of the colonial language to access important offices. Missionaries and the intellectual elite continued to use Classical Latin, but linguistic evidence suggests that this standard and scholastic variety had little, if anything at all, to do with the development of the Romance languages.

More significant is that Roman colonies were not fully Latinized in the fifth century. When the Romans left, lower classes (the population majority) continued to use Celtic languages, especially in rural areas. According to Polomé (1983), the nonruling classes were largely multilingual in a Celtic language, Latin, and sometimes also Greek. This finding explains to some extent why it took up to the twentieth century before the indigenous population of France, for instance, would become fully francophone. The process of language shift was protracted and did not affect all segments of the population concurrently.[16]

---

[14]In a recent, still unpublished manuscript, Chaudenson emphasizes the role of waterways before the invention of trains, planes, and telecommunication in spreading languages outside their homelands. I return to the significance of geographical interconnectedness in economy below. Indeed, the Roman Empire's economic system instantiates some of the early stages of globalization.

[15]One must realize that Rome was too small to provide all the legionaries needed in the Roman army and the manpower necessary to staff its colonial administration. Latin was spread outside Rome largely by foreign mercenaries in the Roman legions, similar to how English is spreading today as a world lingua franca significantly by nonnative speakers using it and teaching it to others in their respective countries.

[16]Bauer (1996, pp. 32) argues that Gaulish (her generic term for Celtic language varieties spoken in Gaul) was already extinct by the seventh century, being replaced by nascent Romance vernaculars similar to Provençal and Occitan. Lodge (1993) presents a similar view. Breton, which was only moribund in the twentieth century, was brought to France

The fact that no Romance language developed at all in England—although Latin continued to be used there until the eighteenth century by the missionaries, by the intellectual elite, and in the Hanseatic trade—confirms not only the above hypothesis but also indirectly that the real shift to Latin as a vernacular for the masses of the populations in today's Romance countries took place only after the Romans had left. The challenge for linguists is to articulate the specific post-Roman socioeconomic dynamics that permitted the spread of Latin within the larger and overwhelming majority of commoner populations, the role of the growing number of towns and schools (noted by Bauer 1996 and Woolf 1998) notwithstanding. The protracted development of the Romance languages under the substrate influence of the Celtic languages is correlated with the gradual loss of the latter, as fewer and fewer children found it useful to acquire the Celtic languages and learned instead the derivatives of Latin now identified as Romance languages. Today the Celtic languages and other more indigenous languages similar to Basque, formerly spoken in the same territories, have vanished. If scholars wish to learn more about language vitality, more specifically how some languages die and some others survive, then it would help to identify the particular socioeconomic conditions that have helped Basque survive.

We could also explore why England, whose native populations during the Roman rule were also Celtic, has Anglicized (i.e., Germanicized) instead. If the use of Latin during the Roman rule proceeded in the same way in England as it did in continental Europe, then it is justified for scholars to assume that the Germanic colonizers (Jutes, Angles, and Saxons), who replaced the Romans, used their nonindigenous languages in their military and political institutions. It is difficult, however, to avoid asking, for the sake of comparison, why Iberia and Gaul continued to Romanize despite the later colonization of the former by the Arabs from the seventh to the fifteenth centuries and that of the latter by the Franks from the fifth to the ninth centuries.

Space limitations prevent me from addressing this question and other related ones in detail here. To suffice, these questions underscore the need to distinguish between different colonization styles and the different ways the colonizers/colonists interacted with the indigenous populations. It now seems necessary also to distinguish between different styles of settlement colonization. After all, the Franks did settle in Gaul and eventually mixed with the Celtic populations. Could it be that the Jutes, Angles, and Saxons had less respect for the Roman legacy than did the Franks, as suggested by Lodge (1993) and Bauer (1996)? The fact that fewer than a handful of their indigenous languages (notably Welsh and Irish) are still spoken

---

from England around the fifth century. Why its fate was different from that of the indigenous Celtic languages is not clear. Thus, the term *patois* often used in the history of France in reference to varieties considered unintelligible, chiefly to Parisians, must have applied to many such rural Romance varieties. Regardless of whether the Celtic languages had died by the seventh century, their death was gradual and the evolution of French into its present-day form was even more protracted. Latin was acquired by the masses of the population after the Romans had left.

today confirms the hypothesis that the insular Celts have Germanicized culturally and linguistically. Linguistic evidence suggests that the gradual shift must have occurred mostly after the languages of the Germanic colonizers mixed to produce Old English (see, e.g., Vennemann 2001, 2002), which ultimately evolved into modern English. In contrast, the Franks surrendered their Germanic traditions, embracing the language and religion of the indigenous rulers, Latin and Catholicism. More questions than I can address arise now about the differences in the ways the Germanics colonized the Celts north and south of the Channel. Whether the Arabs colonized Iberia on the model of the Franks or simply applied exploitation colonization is even less clear. Future scholarship should address such questions for linguistics to be better informed about the ecology of language death.

The above cases show also that language birth and death often proceed concurrently, though the balance sheet in almost all these territories likely has worked at the expense of the indigenous languages. This conclusion is plausible, especially when one does not consider the fact that the prevailing languages have evolved into several varieties and we know nothing about their future.[17] The histories of England, France, and Iberia show also that the colonizers/colonists are not always successful in imposing their languages. Like the colonization of Gaul by the Franks, the colonization of England by the Norse, the Danes, and the Norman French did not produce language shifts of any consequence in the history of this territory, except that the Anglicization of the Normans (Lüdtke 1995) led to the development of a standard English, which is largely influenced by French, though the influence of Latin as a scholarly language cannot be overlooked either. No German is spoken as a vernacular in France outside Alsace, and no Arabic is spoken as a vernacular in Spain or Portugal today, except among groups of recent immigrants. And yet today, Arabic is the vernacular of North Africa, which was colonized also by the Arabs in the seventh century. Does this mean that the Arabs applied different colonization styles in different parts of the world, thus perhaps applying a Roman-to-Frankish kind of exploitation colonization in Iberia, settlement colonization in North Africa, and some sort of trade colonization in South and East Asia? The linguistic consequences of Arabic colonization clearly vary in different parts of the world, with Arabic functioning mostly as a religious language east of the Middle East.

CONCLUSION

To summarize the review at this point without leaving out many other important considerations relevant to its subject matter is difficult. I use this section to survey some of them, connecting them indirectly to the above discussions. As noted

---

[17]At the worldwide scale we have no idea whether 1000 years from today the different varieties of English, for instance, still will be considered the same language. The fact that some of them already have been disfranchised as "indigenized" raises the question of whether some day they may not be considered separate languages all together in the same way that creoles already are.

in Mufwene (2001), parallelisms exist between language evolution in England since the Germanic colonization, on the one hand, and language evolution in North America since the European colonization, on the other hand. In both cases the invaders came to settle new homes (Crosby 1986). Oversimplifying things somewhat, note that in England the languages of the Germanics koinéized into a new variety now called English and gradually displaced the indigenous Celtic languages. In North America, as in other recent settlement colonies, the varieties brought from the major colonial metropole likewise koinéized into new colonial varieties and prevailed over the languages of both other European nations and indigenous populations. The Celtic languages have died as gradually as the Native American languages are dying now, regardless of the difference in speed.

Some similarities appear between former European exploitation colonies of Asia and Africa, on the one hand, and Southwestern Europe as a former constellation of Roman colonies, on the other. The most significant of these similarities may be the fact that in both cases the language of the former colonizer has (initially) been retained after independence as the language for the ethnographically high functions of their societies. From this finding arises the following question: Are the indigenized varieties of European languages likely to displace the indigenous languages in the same way as the indigenization of Latin has in the now-Romance countries?

This is really an open question because a great deal depends on how the economies of the former exploitation colonies fare and how the masses of the population are engaged in them. The emergence of an evolutionary path similar to that of the Romance countries seems possible in economically successful, though small, polities such as Singapore, where political leaders have promoted English as the main language for the overall population. However, one cannot ignore the different language evolution course followed by another successful city state, Hong Kong, where usage of English in the white-collar sector of the economy has had no negative impact on Cantonese. The demographic dominance of the Cantonese in Hong Kong, facilitated by the geographical proximity of Canton, makes this city an endogenous contact setting more favorable to the retention of its major indigenous language. Although the Chinese are an overwhelming majority in Singapore, they speak several Chinese varieties that are not necessarily mutually intelligible, and they are surrounded by Malay-speaking countries, a situation that makes the city an exogenous contact setting more likely to thrive with a colonial language. Unfortunately theories of evolution do not predict the future, and only the future will rule on these speculations.

For the vast majority of former exploitation colonies, one important factor bearing on the fate of the European languages is the concurrent development of indigenous lingua francas that function also as urban vernaculars of the overwhelming proletarian majorities. In kind, these nations share this particular evolutionary trajectory with former plantation settlement colonies, which were indeed ruled like exploitation colonies after the abolition of slavery and where creoles also are the primary vernaculars of their proletarian majorities. To the extent that creoles are considered separate languages by linguists, the economies of all these places have functioned in more than one language: the indigenized/local standard variety of the European language for the white-collar sector of the economy and an indigenous lingua franca or some variety of Creole (mesolectal or basilectal) for the other sectors of the economy. With the unemployment rate quite high and most of the available jobs limited to the nonwhite-collar sector, most of the populations have had no incentive to speak the European language, even if they learned it at school. The elite continue to speak some variety of Creole—as is obvious in Haiti (Dejean 1993) and in Jamaica (Mufwene 2003)—or any of the indigenous languages to remain in touch with less-fortunate members of their societies.[18] There is thus an ethnographic division of labor that does not make European languages a threat to indigenous ones. However, in the same way that, thanks to the urban lifestyle associated with it, the then-indigenizing Vulgar Latin of today's Romance countries was attractive to rural populations, the urban vernaculars are attractive to rural African populations in particular. (See also Pandharipande 2003 for a similar situation in India). Although one can argue that the prestige of urban lifestyle is having a negative impact on rural lifestyle, the notion of prestige itself, which has been invoked often as an important factor in language attrition, must be reconsidered in rather complex relative terms. Otherwise one would have expected European colonial languages to have given a fatal blow to the relevant indigenous vernaculars.

Although there are undoubtedly several endangered African and Asian languages, it is evident that language attrition is proceeding slower in Africa and Asia than it is in Europe and its former settlement colonies. Predictions of the imminent extinction of non-European languages around the world, as if the process were uniform everywhere, certainly must be reframed in a perspective that reflects the complexity of the present state of competition and selection among the world's languages.

We also must reassess the adequacy of terms such as "language war," "linguicide," and "killer language" in our academic discourse. These seem to be worse misnomers than the terms "competition" and "selection," which I prefer. The latter two terms concern values that speakers, as the immediate ecology of linguistic species (Mufwene 2001, 2003), assign to the languages in their community. These

---

[18]It is debatable whether the linguistic situation is that different in European countries and former settlement colonies where noncreole varieties of European languages have prevailed. Acrolectal varieties are used in the white-collar sector of the economy, whereas other varieties, including basilectal ones, are used in the other sectors. These nonstandard varieties are not endangered by their acrolectal counterparts. The few in this predicament, like the Ocracoke Brogue, are affected by neighboring nonstandard varieties (Wolfram & Schilling Estes 1995). Conservative, rural varieties of African American English (including Gullah) are influenced more by urban varieties of the same language than by white vernaculars (Bailey & Cukor-Avila 2005, Mufwene 1997, Wolfram & Thomas 2002). In general, non-European languages in former settlement colonies also may have been endangered by nonstandard vernaculars rather than by the standard varieties of the same languages.

values determine which particular language they find more useful to their lives and, conversely, which one they can afford not to speak and eventually do without. A major problem with the former terms is that they overshadow the agency of speakers as those who actually select and give up particular languages (although they are not necessarily aware of their acts), a choice that allows some to thrive and dooms others to extinction.

Languages do not engage in wars either, though they coexist in competition, like biological species. Languages are more endangered when populations speaking them interact peacefully with each other. As noted above, cases of language extinction associated with genocide remain a very small minority in the history of mankind. Moreover, in language competition, populations rarely engage in activities that endanger some languages in a concerted way, certainly unlike sport teams that anticipate some outcomes. Language endangerment is the cumulative outcome of individual practices of speakers, though communal patterns emerge from the ways their individual acts affect the vitality of their languages. The unplanned cumulation of individuals' practices into a communal behavior explains why language attrition and death are such protracted processes. They proceed in nonuniform ways in the relevant communities, affecting only subsets of the relevant population at a time.

We can learn one last thing from language endangerment in England and the Romance countries. It has everything to do with colonization and globalization, with the former interpreted as the political and economic domination of a population by another and the latter interpreted as an economic network in which the more powerful control production and consumption interdependencies. The two seem to go hand in hand but not in the same ways everywhere. Globalization proceeds faster and is more complex in the more recent than in the more distant cases of colonization and is faster and more pervasive in settlement colonies than in exploitation and trade colonies. Globalization cannot be confused with McDonaldization as the worldwide distribution of McDonald's and other fast-food restaurants as symbols of American lifestyle. McDonaldization, which is similar to the French terms *mondialisation* (universalization), is made possible by globalization but not the other way around. Moreover, as noted above, globalization is often local or regional. The smaller number of American fast-food restaurants and the shift of socioeconomic status associated with them in some former exploitation colonies, where one can be invited to McDonald's for a good dinner, is also an indication of the nonuniform way in which globalization has proceeded. Globalization has created economic inequities among the world's nations (Faraclas 2001, Stiglitz 2002, Blommaert 2003), and those inequities seem to be correlated with the uneven way in which language endangerment is proceeding.

I assume that primitive forms of colonization and globalization must have started with the domination of hunter gatherers by agriculturalists (see also Harmon 2002) and that these processes already had become more complex by the time the capitalist system had evolved in Europe, producing nation-states associated typically with single national languages and leading to the European colonization of the rest of the world over the past half millennium. Although political colonization is no longer in style, economic colonization has become more insidious and globalization much more complex, affecting former exploitation colonies differently from Europe and its former settlement colonies. From the language endangerment point of view, the settlement colonies are almost replicating the experience of Europe, where only 3% of the world languages are spoken today (Mayor & Bindé 2001). We have no clear picture of how language shift will proceed in most former exploitation colonies. However costly language endangerment is to typological research in linguistics, we cannot forget the fact the speakers shift languages as part of their adaptive responses to changing socioeconomic conditions (see also Pandharipande 2003).

Linguists concerned with rights of languages must ask themselves whether these rights prevail over the right of speakers to adapt competitively to their new socioeconomic ecologies. Advocates of the revitalization of endangered languages must tell us whether the enterprise is possible without restoring the previous socioeconomic ecologies that had sustained them. Like cultures, languages are dynamic, complex adaptive systems that cannot be considered independent of the adaptive needs of their speakers. In fact languages are constantly being shaped by those who speak them, precisely what the indigenization of European languages illustrates. Moreover, like features associated with them, languages and cultures at any given point in time are commodities with "market values"—"linguistic capitals" according to Bourdieu (1991)—which are subject to competition and selection. Speakers decide what is useful to them, and they determine history relative to their current needs without any foresight. Such has been history in population genetics, and such is it among humans, despite speakers' occasional consciousness of it. It is much easier to intervene in what affects our surroundings than in what affects ourselves in our spontaneous behavior.

ACKNOWLEDGMENTS

I am grateful to Cécile Vigouroux for useful editorial advice on my preliminary draft.

The *Annual Review of Anthropology* is online at http://anthro.annualreviews.org

LITERATURE CITED

Bailey C-JN, Maroldt K. 1977. The French lineage of English. In *Langues en Contact—Pidgins—Creoles—Languages in Contact*, ed. JM Meisel, pp. 21–53. Tübingen, Germany: Narr

Bailey G, Patricia C-A. 2005. *The Development of African-American Vernacular English*. Cambridge: Cambridge Univ. Press

Bauer Brigitte LM. 1996. Language loss in Gaul: socio-historical and linguistic factors in language conflict. *Southwest J. Ling.* 15:23–44

Bhatia TK. 1988. Trinidad Hindi: its genesis and generational profile. In *Language Transplanted: The Development of Overseas Hindi*, ed. RK Barz, J Siegel, pp. 179–96. Wiesbaden, Germany: Otto Harrassowitz

Bickerton D. 1981. *Roots of Language*. Ann Arbor, MI: Karoma

Bickerton D. 1984. The language bioprogram hypothesis. *Behav. Brain Sci.* 7.173–221

Blommaert J. 2003. A sociolinguistics of globalization. Commentary. *J. Socioling.* 7:607–23

Bloomfield L. 1933. *Language*. New York: Holt, Rinehart, & Winston

Bourdieu P. 1991. *Language and Symbolic Power*. Cambridge, MA: Harvard Univ. Press

Brenzinger M, ed. 1992. *Language Death: Factual and Theoretical Explorations with Special Reference to East Africa*. Berlin: Mouton de Gruyter

Brenzinger M, ed. 1998. *Endangered Languages in Africa*. Cologne, Germany: Rüdiger Köper Verlag

Brutt-Griffler J. 2002a. *World English: A Study of its Development*. Clevedon, UK: Multiling. Matters

Brutt-Griffler J. 2002b. Class, ethnicity, and language rights: an analysis of British colonial policy in Lesotho and Sri Lanka and some implications for language policy. *J. Lang. Identity Educ.* 1:207–34

Cantoni G, ed. 1997. *Stabilizing Indigenous Languages*. Flagstaff: North. Ariz. Univ. Cent. Excell. Educ.

Chaudenson R. 1992. *Des Îles, des Hommes, des Langues: Essais sur la Créolisation Linguistique et Culturelle*. Paris: L'Harmattan

Chaudenson R. 2001. *Creolization of Language and Culture*. London: Routledge

Chaudenson R. 2003. *La Créolisation: Théorie, Applications, Implications*. Paris: L'Harmattan

Clyne M. 2003. *Dynamics of Language Contact: English and Immigrant Languages*. Cambridge: Cambridge Univ. Press

Crosby AW. 1986. *Ecological Imperialism: The Biological Expansion of Europe, 900–1900*. Cambridge: Cambridge Univ. Press

Crystal D. 2000. *Language Death*. Cambridge: Cambridge Univ. Press

Dalby A. 2002. *Language in Danger*. New York: Columbia Univ. Press

DeCamp D. 1971. Toward a generative analysis of a post-creole speech continuum. In *Pidginization and Creolization of Language*, ed. D Hymes, pp. 349–70. Cambridge: Cambridge Univ. Press

Dejean Y. 1993. An overview of the language situation in Haiti. *Int. J. Sociol. Lang.* 102:73–83

Dixon RMW. 1997. *The Rise and Fall of Languages*. Cambridge: Cambridge Univ. Press

Dorian N. 1981. *Language Death: The Language Cycle of a Scottish Gaelic Dialect*. Philadelphia: Univ. Penn. Press

Dorian N, ed. 1989. *Investigating Obsolescence: Studies in Language Contraction and Death*. Cambridge: Cambridge Univ. Press

Faraclas N. 2001. *Globalization and the future of pidgin and creole languages*. Presented at the Meet. Soc. Pidgin Creole Ling., Coimbra, Portugal

Ferreira J-AS. 1999. *The Portuguese language in Trinidad and Tobago: a study of language shift and language death*. PhD thesis, Univ. West Indies, St. Augustine, Trinidad

Fischer DH. 1989. *Albion's Seed: Four British Folkways in America*. Oxford: Oxford Univ. Press

Fishman JA. 1991. *Reversing Language Shift: Theoretical and Empirical Foundations of Assistance to Threatened Languages*. Clevedon: Multiling. Matters

Fishman JA. 2003. Endangered minority languages: prospects for sociolinguistic research. *MOST J. Multicult. Soc.* Vol. 4

Friedman VA. 2001. The Vlah minority in Macedonia: language, identity, and standardization. In *Selected Papers in Slavic, Balkan, and Balkan Studies* (*Slavica Helsingiensa* 21), ed. J Nuoluoto, M Leiwo, J Halla-aho, pp. 26–50. Helsinki: Univ. Helsinki

Garnsey P, Richard S. 1987. *The Roman Empire: Economy, Society, and Culture*. Berkeley: Univ. Calif. Press

Grenoble LA, Lindsay JW, eds. 1998. *Endangered Languages: Current Issues and Future Prospects*. Cambridge: Cambridge Univ. Press

Hagège C. 1992. *Le Souffle de la Langue*. Paris: Odille Jacob

Hagège C. 2000. *Halte à la Mort des Langues*. Paris: Editions Odile Jacob

Harmon D. 1996. Losing species, losing languages, connections between biological and linguistic. *Southwest J. Ling.* 15:89–108

Harmon D. 2002. *In Light of our Differences: How Diversity in Nature and Culture Makes Us Human*. Washington, DC: Smithsonian Inst. Press

Haugen E. 1953. *The Norwegian Language in America: A Study in Bilingual Behavior*. Philadelphia: Univ. Penn. Press

Hazaël-Massieux M-C. 1999. *Les Créoles: L'Indispensable Survie*. Paris: Editions Entente

Hinton L, Ken H, eds. 2001. *The Green Book of Language Revitalization in Practice*. San Diego: Academic

Joseph B, Destafano J, Jacobs NG, Lehiste I, eds. 2003. *When Languages Collide: Perspectives on Language Conflict, Language Competition, and Language Coexistence*. Columbus: Ohio State Univ. Press

Kallen J, ed. 1997. *Focus on Ireland*. Amsterdam: John Benjamins

Lodge RA. 1993. *French: From Dialect to Standard*. London: Routledge

Lüdtke H. 1995. On the origin of Middle and Modern English. In *Linguistic Change Under Contact Conditions*, ed. J Fisiak, pp. 51–54. Berlin: Mouton

Maffi L, ed. 2001. *On Biocultural Diversity: Linking Language, Knowledge, and the Environment*. Washington, DC: Smithsonian Inst. Press

Maurais J, Michael AM, eds. 2003. *Languages in a Globalizing World*. Cambridge: Cambridge Univ. Press

Mayor F, Jérôme B. 2001. *The World Ahead: Our Future in the Making*. Paris: UNESCO; London/New York: Zed Books

Mohan P, Zador P. 1986. Discontinuity in a life cycle: the death of Trinidad Bhojpuri. *Language* 62:291–320

Mufwene SS. 1994. On decreolization: the case of Gullah. In *Language and the Social Construction of Identity in Creole Situations*, ed. M Morgan, pp. 63–99. Los Angeles: Cent. Afro-American Stud.

Mufwene SS. 1997. The ecology of Gullah's survival. *Am. Speech* 72:69–83

Mufwene SS. 2001. *The Ecology of Language Evolution*. Cambridge: Cambridge Univ. Press

Mufwene SS. 2003. Colonization, globalization, and the future of languages in the twenty-first century. *MOST J. Multicult. Soc.* Vol. 4

Mufwene SS. 2004. Multilingualism in linguistic history: creolization and indigenization. In *Handbook of Bilingualism*, ed. T Bhatia, W Ritchie, pp. 460–88. Malden, MA: Blackwell

Mühlhäusler P. 1996. *Linguistic Ecology: Language Change and Linguistic Imperialism in the Pacific Region*. London: Routledge

Nettle D, Romaine S. 2000. *Vanishing Voices: The Extinction of the World's Languages*. Oxford: Oxford Univ. Press

Pandharipande R. 2003. Minority matters: issues in minority languages in India. *MOST J. Multicult. Soc.* Vol. 4

Phillipson R. 2003. *English Only? Challenging Language Policy*. London: Routledge

Pollard V. 2000. *Dread Talk: The Language of Rastafari*. Mona, Jamaica: Univ. West Indies Press

Polomé EC. 1983. The linguistic situation in western provinces of the Roman Empire. *Principat* 29:509–53

Reyhner J, Cantoni G, St. Clair RN, Yazzie EP, eds. 1999. Revitalizing indigenous languages. Flagstaff: North. Ariz. Univ. Cent. Excell. Educ.

Roberts SJ. 1998. The role of diffusion in the genesis of Hawaiian Creole. *Language* 74:1–39

Robins RH, Uhlenbeck EM, eds. 1991. *Endangered Languages*. Oxford: Berg

Salmons J. 2003. The shift from German to English, World War I and the German-language press in Wisconsin. In *Menschen Zwischen Zwei Welten: Auswanderung, Ansiedlung, Akkulturation*, ed. WG Rädel, H

Schmahl, pp. 179–93. Trier, Germany: Wissenschaftlicher Verlag

Schlieben-Lange B. 1977. L'origine des langues romanes: un cas de créolisation ? In *Langues en Contact—Pidgins—Creoles—Languages in Contact*, ed. J Meisel, pp. 81–101. Tübingen, Germany: Gunter Narr

Schuchardt H. 1914. *Die Sprache der Saramakkaneger in Surinam*. Amsterdam: Johannes Muller

Skutnab-Kangas T. 2000. *Linguistic Genocide in Education–or World-Wide Diversity and Human Rights?* Mahwah, NJ: Lawrence Erlbaum

Stiglitz JE. 2002. *Globalization and its Discontents*. New York: Norton

Swaan A de. 2001. *Words of the World: The Global Language System*. Cambridge, UK: Polity Press

Szulmajster-Celnikier A. 2000. Un regard particulier sur le yidiche, l'ivrit et l'esperanto. *Cahiers Bernard Lazare* 204:15–19

Thomason SG. 2001. *Language Contact: An Introduction*. Washington, DC: Georgetown Univ. Press

Thomason SG, Terrence K. 1988. *Language Contact, Creolization, and Genetic Linguistics*. Berkeley: Univ. Calif. Press

Vennemann T. 2001. Atlantis Semitica: structural contact features in Celtic and English. In *Historical Linguistics 1999: Selected Papers from the 14th International Conference on Historical Linguistics, Vancouver, 9–13 August 1999*, ed. L Brinton, pp. 351–69. Amsterdam: John Benjamins

Vennemann T. 2002. On the rise of "Celtic" syntax in Middle English. In *Middle English from Tongue to Text: Selected Papers from the Third International Conference on Middle English*, ed. PJ Lucas, AM Lucas, pp. 203–34. Bern: Lang

Warner-Lewis M. 1996. *Trinidad Yoruba: From Mother Tongue to Memory*. Tuscaloosa: Univ. Ala. Press

Winford D. 2003. *Introduction to Contact Linguistics*. Malden, MA: Blackwell

Wolfram W, Erik RT. 2002. *The Development of African-American English*. Malden, MA: Blackwell

Wolfram W, Natalie S-E. 1995. Moribund dialects and the endangerment canon: the case of the Ocracoke Brogue. *Language* 71:696–721

Woolf G. 1998. *Becoming Roman: The Origins of Provincial Civilization in Gaul*. Cambridge: Cambridge Univ. Press

Annu. Rev. Anthropol. 2004. 33:223–50
doi: 10.1146/annurev.anthro.33.070203.143724
Copyright © 2004 by Annual Reviews. All rights reserved
First published online as a Review in Advance on May 14, 2004

THE ARCHAEOLOGY OF COMMUNICATION TECHNOLOGIES

Stephen D. Houston

*Department of Anthropology, Brown University, Providence,
Rhode Island 02912; email: Stephen_houston@brown.edu*

Key Words   writing, graphic notation, iconography, decipherment

■ **Abstract**   Accessing ancient meaning and sound from graphic notations is an immense challenge to archaeologists, whether with respect to marked objects, petrographs, or phonic writing. Two paths clear the way: the detection or reasoned reconstruction of "situation," how graphic notations were used in the past and in what social and cultural setting, and the process of "extraction," the hermeneutic scholarship that decodes such messages and establishes the relative plausibility of an interpretation. Situation is easier to study and extraction more likely to occur in cases of phonic writing, where varieties or types, physical inspection, decipherment, origins, and extinction permit multiple inroads into past sound and meaning.

INTRODUCTION

The ability to record thoughts and sounds goes far back in human antiquity, with image-making found as early as 30,000 BP (Conard 2003) and the possibility of systematic notations attested from about the same time (Marshack 1991, 1997). The detection of long-term patterns in such "technology" or "modes of graphic notation" is made difficult by the very age of the finds, a feature that prevents archaeologists from having any certainty of full samples or ready access to past mentalities. But scholars can hope for success in two ways. First, they can focus on "situation," the relationship between the graphic notation, whatever its nature, and the person intended to understand it (Harris 1995, p. 159). Interpretation is greatly assisted by tight chronological controls, such as those in place for the Upper Paleolithic images from Avdeevo, Russia (Gvozdover 1995, p. 52). Yet present-day observers still hover at some remove from this hermeneutic domain, uninvited guests in a system of communication designed for others; the very point of most notational systems is that not everyone can understand them (Gardner 1985, p. 47). The second approach is at once substantive and methodological, namely, "extraction," the means by which ancient thought and sound become accessible today.

0084-6570/04/1021-0223$14.00

Situation

"Situation" involves the many elements described by Basso in his influential piece on the ethnography of writing. "Situation" requires attention to "the status and role of attributes of participants, the form of the message, the code in which it is communicated. . . and the physical setting in which the message is encoded and decoded" (Basso 1989, p. 428). Even more distant are the emotions that messages are designed to communicate or trigger (Besnier 1995, Houston 2001). "Situation" is inherently sociological, referring to context, participants, and the relations between them. However, for all the current interest in practice theory and agency within archaeology (e.g., Dobres & Robb 2000), there is surprisingly little concern for how people learned to behave situationally while raised as children or trained as apprentices (Joyce 2000). The literature from classical studies is more informative in this regard and tends to emphasize the physically abusive and rote nature of learning, along with the arbitrary substance of what Bourdieu calls, in somewhat reductionist language, a "cultural consecration" of "cultivated disposition" that accentuates boundaries of class (Clarke 1972; Bourdieu 1993, p. 121; Morgan 1998; Tinney 1998; Vanstiphout 1979; Williams 1972).

To a notorious extent, early scripts around the world are full of gaps, rock art and prehistoric iconography even more so (Abélanet 1986; Bradley 1997; Clottes 2002; Lenik 2003; Schaafsma 1994; Stone & Künne 2003; Whitley 2000, 2001). To be activated, texts and images require a knowledgeable witness who can inject elements of meaning, context, and speech. Such training or steeping in practice and situated reception is culture- and history-bound, full of preparation and learned contingencies. Even international symbols, such as the "no-smoking" sign and sundry signals for managing automobiles, draw on graphic conventions descending from the geometry and pictorial conventions of Giotto and his successors (Edgerton 1991). The notion that graphic notations can exist prior to conditioning by language and culture is untenable, on the order of asserting that ideas have no relation to the language that frames them.

Extraction

"Extraction" can be as elusive as "situation." Most images are highly expansive, allowing all sorts of verbal interpolations by those commenting on them (Vastokas 2003). There is no one account, no one fixed response. The other problem with "extraction" is that mnemonic pictography, as practiced in much of North America and probably elsewhere, was idiosyncratic, "generally [serving] as reminders for individual use" (Taylor 1997, p. 284; Walker 1997). This claim can be taken too far: The so-called picture writing in North America was frequently directed toward maintaining traditional forms and memorized, often archaic, speech (Taylor 1997, p. 284). Still, the ability to "extract" can only degrade substantially from the gold standard set by makers and original users. In archaeological contexts, where few ancillary clues exist, this standard can seldom come within reach. Vastokas (2003) reminds us that extraction is made even more challenging by the esoteric nature of some graphic notations, their deliberate opacity clarified only for initiates. Rowlands (1993) and Bradley (2000) distinguish between "inscribed memory practices" and "incorporated memory practices," the former visible and repeated, the latter tending toward "opaque symbolism and secrecy" (van Dyke & Alcock 2003b, p. 4). But a categorical distinction between the two is surely misplaced, in that "opacity" can also occur in visible and repeated settings. Thus, scholars must settle for radically diminished powers of extraction and distinguish between what Taçon & Chippindale (1998, pp. 6–8) call "informed methods," drawing directly or indirectly on sources of insight supplied by the makers of the semasiographs, "formal methods" that rely only on our own ingenuity, and analogies drawn from comparable settings in other parts of the world. An analogical study would be Lewis-Williams' (2002a,b) use of shamanism to explain cave art in Europe, or the claim that entoptic, brain-based image making explains certain designs in settings as diverse as ethnographic Colombia and the ancient Maya (Haviland & Laguna de Haviland 1995, Price 2001, Reichel-Dolmatoff 1997). Informed methods are the most compelling in that they directly elucidate specific evidence. Their disadvantage is that they lie beyond reach for most prehistoric settings and the majority of graphs around the world. In contrast, ancient texts have the advantage of lending themselves directly to informed methods, in that they represent the self-conscious declarations of makers and users.

Arguments that rely on "extraction" are better made on a case-by-case basis, as judged by the quality and presentation of evidence. Vague or general claims often are unhelpful in their imprecision, as in Delporte's statement that "the 'mythology' of the 'Gravettian group' has to do with **woman**" (Delporte 1993, p. 256, bold-face in original) or Conkey's view, strikingly similar to the philosophical error of pathetic fallacy, that early imagery does not correspond to a "record" but is rather an "active, constructing, constituting agency, which does not express meaning, but produces it" (Conkey 1989). For Conkey (1987), meaning did not exist as "a single, inclusive, empirical entity or category of our inquiry," a claim that sits uncomfortably with the highly ordered, narratively encoded images of complex societies, such as the Moche of ancient South America (Donnan & McClelland 1979, 1999), the Olmec of Mexico (Taube 1995, 2000a), or the Classic Maya (Coe 1973). Furthermore, graphic notations accompanied by phonic texts are immeasurably easier to understand than are prehistoric petroglyphs. Macintosh, Morphy, and Davidson (Macintosh 1977; Morphy 1991; Davidson 1997, p. 127) may be correct that single, fixed meanings are difficult to corroborate for figures in Australian rock paintings. And perhaps Conkey is right that images did not have underlying intentions, ultimate objectives, or singular meanings that motivated their production. But Conkey, in asserting an interpretive opacity in Paleolithic images of early Europe, could not, by the very terms of her argument, address the presence or absence of such meanings. When considering the Paleolithic, an admission of interpretive fallibility may come not from the intrinsic indeterminancy of meaning but from the exiguous nature of Paleolithic data and the imprudence of applying "aesthetic tools of our own culture" to their study (White 2003, p. 220).

Situating and Extracting

The acts of situation and extraction require some notion of what to expect, what categories of information potentially exist in such notations. Gelb (1963, p. 11) sees these categories in evolutionary sequence. Meaning in the guise of sema-siographs came first, then sound signs or phonographs. But he was empirically mistaken: Notations of essentially different character do not replace one another in sequence but often occur together, in bundles or as separate marks, a point to be reemphasized later in this review. A good example of this "bundling" is Maya writing. It is phonic, in that it records sound, but it also contains ideas shown iconically, hieroglyphs grappling with one another, sprouting heads and bodies. As with all hieroglyphic systems, such as Egyptian (Davies 1987, p. 19), marks of this sort retain an existential tether to the world around them. They do so by their very property of representing visible and motile things. As a result, notations are not only records, standing for something else, be it meaning or sound. They also are fetishized entities taking on a life and intent of their own, sometimes with talis-manic or shamanic intent (Bierman 1998, Smalley et al. 1990). This very property is what, to judge from comparative evidence, accorded special status to makers of images and markers of meaning and sound (Kris & Kurz 1981) and in the past led to violent episodes of iconoclasm. Marvels of creativity, images can also be reviled as impious acts of creation that by right belong to God alone (Belting 1994, Besançon 2000). Gelb's "meaning signs" are also unlikely to detour completely around language, in that the sculpture of a particular deity or personage would almost certainly invoke an identifying name in the mind of the knowledgeable viewer. Images do not readily disengage from words, texts, and the behaviors they motivate (Mitchell 1986, pp. 42–46; Rappaport & Cummins 1998).

Two distinct systems of notation highlight the problems of situation and extrac-tion. The first are marks of quantification, in this instance the graphic manipulations of positive integers (Ascher 1991, Crump 1990, Mimica 1992). They can include everything from Muslim prayer beads (*subha*), a Maori genealogical staff, Melane-sian navigational charts, or a lunar calendar from the former Dahomey (Aveni 1985, pp. 264–65; Gaur 1992, p. 25; Ifrah 2000, pp. 11–19). Urton (1997, pp. 17–24) makes the point that, in anthropological terms, quantification cannot be divorced from the objects being numbered, the cultural setting of those objects, or the corporeal frames of reference that often undergird numbering. Mayan languages commonly use certain fixed elements to accompany quantifications of particular things, and the Classic-period records of ordinal numbers make obligatory use of a lexeme that may be related to the act of human arrival from some other location (*tal*). The uniform attribute of these quantifications is that, to be understood, they require other clues, either marks or signs of the items being enumerated, or mem-ories stored in the person accessing the numbers. In the latter, scholarly extraction becomes almost impossible, a problem that is especially challenging with respect to Andean knot records or khipu (Quilter & Urton 2002; Salomon 2001; Urton 1998, 2003) and string notations of the Salish in the American Northwest (Leechman

& Harrington 1921). The only hope is that such memories have become broadly distributed, thus achieving a more invariant, less idiosyncratic content. By their repetition and codification such meanings have higher chances of being accessed by scholars (Alcock 2002, Carruthers 1994), much less so when, as in Malanggan images from New Ireland or personal possessions from Indonesia, they touch on fine and irreproducible details of individual likeness and memory (Hoskins 1998, pp. 190–97; Küchler 2002, pp. 111–22).

The Malanggan leads us to the second category of notation, one that stands for a single thing or person. Such notations exist within "systems" insofar as they contrast with marks for similar entities. But they are not easily expandable and can operate only within the frame of reference for which they were intended. Examples of these, although little studied by anthropologists, are the "maker's" or "potter's" marks that existed in ancient Egypt, Minoan Crete, coastal Peru, Turkey, Medieval Europe, the Indus Valley, China, and many other locations (Alexander 1996, 1998; Gelb 1963, figure 15; Hastings & Moseley 1975; Keightley 1989, figure 11; Parpola 1994, figure 4.1; van den Brink 1992). These marks are regarded by some scholars as precursors to phonic writing, and yet that claim has no evidential basis. Instead, they were systematic marks devised in an ad hoc fashion to characterize goods, materials, authorship, and provenance in some locally recognizable manner. Much the same can probably be said about the so-called clan symbols of Shang and pre-Shang China (Keightley 1989, figure 16) or the poncho-like, "heraldic" elements discussed for Late Neolithic and Copper Age Iberia by Lillios (2002, 2003).

Writing

Situation and extraction are far easier to study and employ with early writing systems. Writing was a crucial advance in human development. It extended human memory and communicated detailed messages across space and time. In so doing, it transformed information from fleeting utterances to durable objects and broadened the scope of aesthetics through the invention of calligraphy and new literary genres (Coulmas 1989, pp. 11–14). The claims that writing did more—that it revolutionized thought (Goody & Watt 1963) and led to systematic oppression (Lévi-Strauss 1955, p. 344)—are more controversial. Investigators say that alphabets make "thinkers" out of "bards" (Havelock 1982, p. 11) and that writing in general furthered the exploitation of the unprivileged (Larsen 1988). Both assertions can be contested on empirical and theoretical grounds (Halverson 1992, Houston 1994a). Writing itself, the most momentous of all communication technologies in the deep past, must be considered first by defining writing (typology), then by examining methods of looking at script in archaeological contexts (epigraphy), the means by which we access the content of writing (decipherment), the beginnings (origins), operation (use), extinction of script (death), and the future of research in archaeological approaches to writing (prospects). Throughout this review, "script" and "writing" are used interchangeably. "Writing system" refers to a specific example of script and its organization and social setting.

Typology

Writing has both broad and narrow definitions. The broad view states that writing represents a system of orderly, permanent marks that record conventional ideas (Boone 1994, 1998). The more limited view, followed here, states that writing per se relates to language. The advantage of a broad definition is that it includes systems based on meaning (the semasiographic notations identified by Gelb) along with those that record sound and, by extension, language [glottographic systems (Sampson 1985, p. 29)]. The disadvantages are precisely the same, in that an overly inclusive definition obscures the very real trait that certain notations record language and others do not. The criticism that a narrow definition implies the superiority of glottographic over semasiographic systems has some validity, but even supposedly semasiographic notations, as in Mixtec and Aztec writing, contain a heavy glottographic component: They are, in fact, intricate packages of several different systems based on both sound and meaning. Moreover, the benefit of script is that it can communicate nonauditory but semantically rich information. Writing is not merely a reflection of language, nor is it always an incomplete form of language, although this incompleteness often happens to be the case. Consider the English terms "be" and "bee." The first serves a verbal function, and the second refers to a stinging insect. But there is no difference in sound. Script created a new means of communication operating on both phonic and semantic levels.

Boltz (1994, p. 19) created a method of showing how graphs or distinct marks carry other values. "G" for "graph" can appear in the following guises, with "P" standing for a phonetic aspect and "S" for a semantic aspect: [−P, −S], or random marks of little relevance here; [−P, +S], much like the skull and crossbones to indicate "death," "piracy," or "poison" (the indeterminacy is reduced by conventional understandings among those for whom the graph is intended); [+P, +S], word signs as occur in virtually all writing systems; and [+P, −S], a syllable, as in Mayan *ka* or *ta*. For Boltz, true writing is found only in the final two categories, those containing sound. In these categories the "G" can represent not a "graph" but a "grapheme," the irreducible, minimal unit of a writing system. An even-more-elaborate formulation is by Civil (1972), who proposes that all scripts can be understood according to three classes of graphic representation: phonological (sound), morpholexical (meaning), and syntactic (sequential) levels. All writing systems encode the first two classes by means of distinct graphemes. In logographic or word-sign writing, especially the varieties that record both phonological and morpholexical signs, there is great potential for interchange between the two forms of sign, a morpholexical grapheme alternating with one or more phonological graphemes.

Only with phonological graphemes can we unambiguously identify language. Scripts tending to phonological graphemes would produce the longest messages, if the easiest to decode; morpholexical would produce relatively short ones, if less flexible as records of language. Thus most writing systems include a combination of phonological and morpholexical elements. The syntactic grapheme is highly impractical. A purely syntactic script would have a near-infinite number of graphemes, and the inventory of signs would be so immense as to be unlearnable. The total number of signs reflects the nature of the writing system and provides a tool for decipherment in that it narrows the range of possibilities (Friedrich 1957, p. 152). Phonological scripts tend from the few dozen for alphabets, with an attested upper range of 74, to several hundred for syllables, and up to 50,000 morpholexical signs for the Kāngxi dictionary of Chinese. Nonetheless it is important to add that, with only a few exceptions, even morpholexical elements convey sound.

A descriptive typology of writing systems allows a more exact understanding of how graphemes encode sound and meaning. To some extent, such typologies permit the search for cross-cultural patterns but at the cost of implying evolutionary sequences between certain kinds of writing systems, especially as a teleological progression from the vagaries of logographic scripts to the fastidious phonography of alphabets. This search for cross-cultural regularities would be a grave mistake because it extracts writing systems from their cultural and historical settings (Trigger 1998) and underplays the supple flexibility of logosyllabic scripts. Another way of describing scripts focuses squarely on such settings. Certain writing systems are "open" in that they can be employed by any number of different groups; others are profoundly "closed" in that they exist only in close relation to particular languages and cultures (Houston 1994b). Mayan writing and Egyptian hieroglyphs could record, laboriously, the words and thoughts of other cultures, yet they either developed into radically different forms when transported to new settings, such as Egyptian script to the related Meroitic civilization, or failed to penetrate such settings at all. The Classic Maya had clear contact with other groups but tended to mark and "encyst" introduced graphemes, which seldom found any long-term purchase in their writing system. In contrast, cuneiform and the alphabet shifted with relative ease across linguistic and cultural boundaries, as did the set of conventions and representational strategies known generally as central Mexican script. Languages have "ethnolects" that correspond closely to particular communities. Likewise, "closed" writing systems can be seen as "ethnoscripts" shaped by cultural identities. Most of the scripts of eastern Mesoamerica were ethnoscripts, as were the Hebrew characters for Yiddish (a Germanic language), which marked Jewish identity in Europe.

Epigraphy

Inscriptions and other texts can be understood in two ways: as purveyors of content and as archaeological artifacts. The branch of archaeology that investigates inscriptions and other texts is "epigraphy," from the Greek word *epigraph ē*, meaning "inscription." It is a discipline with pronounced regionalisms, often within distinct traditions of philology. As yet there is no unitary approach to the problem of texts in archaeological settings, although the regional variants have much in common technically. All are concerned with the thorough recording, dissemination, and preservation of texts (Bodel 2001, Caminos & Fischer 1976, Gordon 1983,

Graham 1975, Keppie 1991, Sircar 1971, Salomon 1998, Woodhead 1992). The epigrapher's task, regardless of area, is to make the best possible records of ancient texts in a manner that does no harm (Houston 2000, p. 137). Earlier generations thought little of removing texts from archaeological contexts, sometimes in destructive ways. This practice is no longer acceptable. The two ethical variances for such removal is (*a*) if the text is in imminent danger of harm and (*b*) if it is small and portable. The other ethical need is that the texts also should be treated as artifacts, in which context is as important as content. This idea is particularly true where texts have an architectural setting or when archives are involved because physical disposition can reveal much about ancient processing of bureaucratic information (e.g., Bennet 1988).

One practice, increasingly outmoded, is direct recording, the use of molds, rubbings, and "squeezes" or papier maché to make a reproduction by direct contact with the surface. The advantages are clear (a more-or-less permanent record of an inscribed surface in all its texture and detail), as are the disadvantages (potential damage to the surface). Far preferable, although with its own limitations, is indirect recording by means of drawing, photography, and multispectral imaging. A drawing represents a second-order interpretation of the surface that is assisted immeasurably by "autopsy" or eyewitness inspection. Autopsy allows the epigrapher to use raking light and tactile scrutiny to wrest details from eroded texts. The beginner can handle well-preserved inscriptions; an eroded or fragmentary text requires far more experience. Such a rendering must anticipate not only present-day interests but record information of potential relevance to future generations (Bell 1987): What questions will be asked of the inscription today and tomorrow? Thus a perfect drawing is an unachievable goal, and the astute epigrapher must employ as many complementary images as possible to interpret an inscription.

Two new technologies hold much promise. The first combines digital multispectral technology with advances in computer science to record and process painted texts (Kamal et al. 1999). In the Maya region this technology—essentially the same as that used on satellites—has been taken to remote archaeological sites in increasingly smaller packages to document digital "cubes" of spectra far beyond the visible range. Work on the Classic Maya murals of Bonampak show that no amount of squinting or close-up study can penetrate underpaintings or obscured texts (Ware et al. 2002). With technological refinement, this technology will become more automatic, with the proviso that each archaeological setting presents unique problems of lighting and camera angles. A second technology—systematic laser measurements of three-dimensional surfaces—is theoretically possible and has been tested in engineering laboratories at Brigham Young University and at Harvard. Equipment remains too bulky and power-hungry, but this method would allow the indirect measurement of minute differences in carved surfaces. The epigrapher could manipulate and even reproduce inscriptions in other media. In no case can we assume that an inscription is permanently stabilized. Laser records preserve three-dimensional surfaces that will, with time, erode into illegibility.

Dissemination of texts continues to be urgent for ethical and practical reasons: ethically because hoarding data obstructs scholarship, practically because dissemination promotes it. Without access to raw material, epigraphers will simply retread established wisdom. The more traditional means of publication are in "corpora," of which the Corpus of Maya Hieroglyphic Inscriptions is a worthy example (Graham 1975). At their best, these sources publish drawings, a range of photographs with varied lighting, a record of archaeological context, and limited commentary. (Fuller commentary can slow distribution, as in the case of the Dead Sea scrolls.) It is inevitable that the Web will play an increasing role in epigraphy. Many rollouts of Maya vessels with texts are now available in the Kerr archive (http://www.famsi.org), and Robert Englund and his colleagues have placed a range of cuneiform texts on the Web (http://www.cdli.ucla.edu, the Cuneiform Digital Library Initiative).

Decipherment

If writing involves language, then decipherment is the full understanding of how a particular script records language—it is a special kind of extraction. It reverses the process by which an auditory world becomes concrete: Scholarly resourcefulness compels visible marks to release their sound and meaning. Decipherment is not the same as decoding or cryptography, which attempts to understand messages that have been intentionally obscured or disguised (Kahn 1996). Without decipherment, relatively little would be known about any number of ancient civilizations. Ignace Gelb (1975, p. 96) conceptualized this process according to a typology of circumstances, adapted here to include examples unfamiliar to Gelb: Type 0: known language and known writing (Phoenician words in Latin letters); Type I: unknown writing and known language (Linear B and Greek; Rongorongo; Isthmian in Mesoamerica?); Type II: known writing and unknown language (Etruscan); and Type III: unknown script and unknown language (Isthmian?, Linear A, Indus, Phaistos). Gelb's typology is useful for distinguishing between different kinds of decipherment, but it is defective in other respects: Type I is inherently an unstable category; Type 0 is really a matter of translation and code-switching, not decipherment; and, as Gelb acknowledged, Type II is less about decipherment than linguistic analysis. The fervent hope of decipherers, and sometimes their delusion (Fischer 1997), is that all constituents of Type III will eventually shift to Type 0.

Decipherment is both science and art, involving extremely close attention to patterning in scripts, a sharp degree of doubt about previous work coupled with a sense of productive leads such work provides, and a nose for the unexpected (Coe 1999). The stakes are high and the possibility of discomfiture is great. Decipherment can be seen as a grand enterprise, in which fundamental principles are unlocked, or as an incremental process in which logographs gradually yield their values (Houston et al. 2001, pp. 7–10). Pope (1999, pp. 186–91) lists other properties of decipherment: that it be thought doable; that spelling rules be discerned as quickly as possible and the full inventory of signs worked out (small numbers of signs hint at alphabets, large numbers at logosyllabic systems); that sets of substitutables be detected because these allow decipherers to cleave equivalences from contrastive elements; and that decipherers be prepared for the falsity of their preconceptions. Most decipherers are less dazzled by human brilliance than by the blinders that repeatedly prevent recognition of the obvious.

Decipherers need luck, but they can enhance their fortunes by having certain things in place (Coe 1995, Houston & Coe 2004). There must be a large and well-recorded set of texts, and there should be bilinguals that allow decipherers to travel from the known to the unknown, a well-understood cultural setting, and pictorial clues from images with texts. These features have allowed recent progress with Mayan script and yet, in their absence, profoundly hinder any attempts to understand the Indus or Isthmian writing systems (Houston 2000, p. 131; Houston & Coe 2004; Justeson & Kaufman 1993, Parpola 1994). A recent review of undeciphered scripts, ranging from Linear A to Indus and Zapotec scripts, underlines the difficulties: Each decipherment will require a different approach, plodding work, and, as often as not, collaborate effort (Robinson 2001). Optimism must be hedged by realism. Just because a problem exists does not mean that it can be solved.

Origins

The study of how writing began requires a clear definition of what writing is. As we see previously, that writing is a graphic device for recording language is a workable meaning. An account of how humans first discovered and systematically used such records is complex, of which four general questions stand out as the most important: (*a*) Was there only one place and time where writing began, or did it have multiple origins? (*b*) Did writing begin for a single reason or for many? (*c*) What kinds of information did early script record? (*d*) Are there any universal patterns to the origins and initial development of ancient scripts? Before answering these questions, one must draw an important distinction between "primary" and "secondary" origins. The first pertains to probable instances of writing systems that appeared de novo, as a result of local developments. The second relates to stimulus diffusion (a hard claim to prove or disprove since little more than a vague idea is being transmitted) and direct copying (such as the spread of the alphabet, as adjusted for new languages).

A subset of stimulus diffusion is the well-documented instances, often in colonial circumstances, in which a script both comes into existence under the influence of other scripts and yet avoids much borrowing from them. Examples include the Cherokee syllabary devised by Sequoyah (Walker & Sarbaugh 1993), or, in more extreme cases, the cues to shamanistic narratives and divinatory performance expressed in Naxi writing of Yunnan China (Jackson 1979, Rock 1963–1972), Yi script of southern Sichuan (Ramsey 1987, pp. 258–59), and Silas John script of the Western Apache (Basso & Anderson 1973). In part, these scripts maintain and preserve esoteric practices that underpin ethnic identities. As markers of social and religious difference, they contrast with the scripts of dominant or antagonistic groups. King Njoya of Bamum invented a script around 1903, but in doing so he could not bring himself to copy the script used by "disgusting" Hausa traders; he also wished to impress his colonial patrons, the Germans, by showing his ability to craft a writing system (Dalby 1968; Schmitt 1963, pp. 14–15; Tardits 1980, pp. 36–72). These writing systems also endure or expire according to the vitality of local practices. Both Naxi and Silas John lie close to extinction because the religious practitioners using them have grown old and found few followers.

According to Daniels, innovations represent "unsophisticated" examples of script creation, as the devisers are not versed in another, preexisting writing system; "sophisticated" examples include (*a*) the so-called "missionary scripts" fashioned by proselytes to spread Christianity (Daniels 1996, pp. 579–83) or (*b*) Hankul, the orderly, phonemically efficient script designed by King Seycong and his advisers to record Korean (Kim-Renaud 1996). However, Daniels' labels are value-laden and objectionable. The scripts admirably fulfilled the needs expected of them and were hardly "unsophisticated" in content and inspiration. By contrasting "sophisticated" and "unsophisticated" writing systems, Daniels also overlooks the colonial and conflictive conditions in which scripts like Cherokee and Bamum were created (Harbsmeier 1988, p. 261). Cherokee writing was supported in part by one dominant power (the U.S. Congress), and Bamum was actively discouraged by another (the French, after the expulsion of the Germans from the area following World War I). Yet, the point is that both scripts existed in relation to external forces, as part of what some would describe in current jargon as "counter-hegemonic discourse" (Williams & Chrisman 1994). By reshaping native practices, scripts held out the possibility—usually a vain one—of withstanding or coopting identities imposed or molded by outsiders. The invention of the Deseret alphabet for use by Mormons was explicitly conceived as part of a program to reform the world. Derived from Pitman shorthand, it was used by converts of different backgrounds, with the secondary benefit of marking and enhancing Mormon identity under threat from an advancing and often hostile wave of secular pressures affecting Mormon society in the second half of the nineteenth century (Watt 1994, pp. 139–40).

The first question (Was there only one origin or writing or several?) is no longer as controversial as it once was. Gelb (1963), whose *Study of Writing* influenced a generation of scholars, often in negative reaction to his more categorical declarations, asserted that "full or phonetic writing" most likely developed in Sumer and then spread abroad, if in ways that he regarded as uncertain or poorly documented, as for Chinese (p. 219). Some Sinologists regard Chinese as a probable derivative of Near Eastern scripts, but most scholars see no tangible evidence for this connection (Boltz 1986, 1994, 1999). The main arguments in favor of derivation are weak: that Shang, the earliest Chinese writing, postdates Near Eastern developments and that Shang wheat (*mai*) came ultimately from Western Asia. The first of these is thought to enhance the chances of copying and the second proves the existence of ancient contact (Chang 1980, pp. 148–49), yet neither provides direct evidence. Gelb's largest problem was with Mayan writing, which, given the circularity of his theory, had to be lumped with Dakota winter counts and Anatolian mason's marks (Gelb 1963, p. 51). The absurdity of this claim is now only too apparent, and there can be no doubt that several writing systems, in the fullest sense of the word, were invented independently. In fairness to Gelb, he did see the problem in more discriminating terms, as instances of vague stimulus diffusion embedded within distinct cultural and historical settings. Independent invention of syllabaries necessarily raises the issue of universals: Why did humans devise strikingly similar ways of recording sound and meaning? Is there a cognitive rationale that emanates from the innate features of the human brain? A development sure to take place in the coming century, with impact on the study of writing systems, is the exploration of common ground between the human and cognitive sciences (e.g., Boyer 1997, Sproat 2000). It is notable, for example, that most writing systems, however elaborate, hover around 500–1000 characters in common use, with a tendency in logosyllabic systems to the lower rather than the higher number. This quantity of signs may reflect general human limitations on graphic memory and the great difficulty of processing (recognizing and using) an unwieldy inventory of signs.

The second question (Why did writing begin and for what specific reasons?) is more controversial. One approach is technocratic, suggesting that, regardless of region, the first writing appeared for administrative or "utilitarian" reasons (Postgate et al. 1995, p. 478). This approach is best described as the "statist" view of writing because it is usually thought to develop concurrently with state systems of political organization; this matter would also touch on the third question, What kinds of information did early script record? A variant theory, especially as applied to Mesoamerica, construes the origins of writing as an attribute of complex polities whose rulers wish to control underlings and impress rivals by means of "propaganda" (Marcus 1992). Script was introduced to apportion labor and record tallies of goods and tribute or, in the propaganda variant, to justify hereditary inequality. The more complex the writing was, the more developed the state (Marcus 1992, p. 435). There is hardly any dispute about such bookkeeping functions for Mesopotamian cuneiform (Nissen et al. 1993, p. 11), but the argument becomes forced for other areas where sampling problems and perished records are held to explain the lack of uniform support for an administrative hypothesis (Postgate et al. 1995, p. 464). The problem of the Inka empire—a match for imperial Rome in extension and organizational brilliance—is that it supposedly did not have "full" writing and thus violated an important feature of early states. More recent appraisals remove this obstacle by underscoring the sophistication of the Inka khipu system of knotted cords, which employed elaborate numeration and semantic encoding, if in ways that remain poorly understood and perhaps inaccessible to recent scholarship (Locke 1923; Urton 1998, 2003). Early Andean states, such as that of Wari, engineered the first khipu, and, as in so many things, the Inka merely distilled and extended an older bureaucratic legacy (Conklin 1982).

A broader way of looking at script is simply to acknowledge that it came into existence for general reasons: (*a*) There was compelling local need for it to exist, whether for purposes of ceremonial and kingly display or the administration for nascent polities; (*b*) a preexisting system of orderly representation, be it Predynastic Egyptian painting, prehistoric seal impressions from Mesopotamia, Olmec iconography, or insignia from Neolithic China, provided a necessary predisposition to other kinds of orderly records (in this case, other kinds of language) (Collon 1990, p. 14). (This iconographic preadaptation makes more plausible the separate origins of Egyptian and Shang writings.) Such broader views accord with other trends in sociolinguistics, which sees literacy less as an "autonomous" technology with rigid, inevitable consequences than as an "ideological" system rooted in local power relations and cultural practices (Lewis 1999; Street 1993, p. 7). The propaganda theory has a superficial appeal because in Mesoamerica many surviving examples of early writing do concern royal personages. But this theory oversimplifies the ritual and supernatural focus of such writing and its individual trajectories of use, although, to be sure, it does acknowledge the need of elites to present and validate a certain point of view. The Postclassic Mixtec's highly elaborate writing can scarcely be said to issue from imposing kingdoms, nor can be Classic Mayan script, which came from relatively small polities (Grube 2000). A term like propaganda also invokes unwelcome anachronisms, as though recalling the machinations of Josef Goebbels or Stalin's brutish henchmen (Houston 2000, p. 169). Properly speaking, propaganda exists to counter other, threatening ideas of equal force. It is difficult to understand what those ideas could have been in pre-Hispanic Mesoamerica. As Webster suggests (personal communication), another word may be needed, even "advertising," to capture the dominant and dominating messages within self-interested declarations.

Another problem with the technocratic perspective is that it ignores our principal sources on script creation, those from ethnography. For reasons stated before, these examples of script invention cannot be viewed as illustrations of the first creations of writing (Harbsmeier 1988, p. 261), although it is not uncommon to see discussions of precursors to Shang script in terms of "primitive" Naxi writing (e.g., Xigui 2000, p. 10). Yet, to a disquieting extent, these inventions do situate the beginnings of writing in dreams and prophecy, as though innovations did not traditionally arise in considerations of efficiency but in revelatory visions, as in Alaska script, Bamum, and Ndjuka (Daniels 1996, pp. 583–84). Most ancient scripts were thought to originate as gifts from divinities (Senner 1989b, pp. 10–13). States make use of writing but they were not the sole inventors of writing, as this task could have been accomplished by a handful of part-time specialists (Monaghan & Hamann 1998, pp. 137–38). Innumerable scripts may well have been invented in the distant past (J. Monaghan, personal communication), but it took the creation of a durable script community—a social group committed to learning, using, and transmitting a writing system—to codify and perpetuate a script beyond its moment of revelatory creation (see below). Complex societies do not ensure the invention of writing, but they do enable its large-scale use and maintenance. Preexisting iconography bestows pictographic tools, emphasizes codification, and implies relatively broad currency. In turn, complex societies allow ventures in early writing to survive when their inventors die and their idiosyncratic experiments run the risk of passing away with them. The aniconic nature of the Inka khipu, which develops from a long-standing Andean emphasis on weaving as a means of expression, suggests a rare deviation from the iconographic principle that underlies other early scripts. It may be no coincidence that the one Andean area with systematic marks, in this instance probable maker's marks on construction adobes, exists in a region on coastal Peru with highly naturalistic iconography (Donnan & McClelland 1999, Hastings & Moseley 1975).

Another theory is the onomastic model, which relates to the urgent, culturally prescribed need to name things, people, and quantities (Stuart 2001). Preexisting numbering systems are folded into these emergent scripts so as to quantify such objects and people and to mesh them in social operations that control and distribute things of value and renown (Powell 1991, p. 182). This theory is more satisfying than is the administrative hypothesis because it focuses on what writing does rather than on its secondary functions. It involves a process by which the identities of persons and objects materialize in other forms, as enduring and easily identifiable proxies for concrete things and breathing people (Assmann 1994, pp. 17–18). The names are the means by which language intervenes in this process of replication and representation. By definition, hieroglyphic systems such as Egyptian and Mayan preserve this relation to their physical referents [naturally the Egyptian case is complicated by its acute digraphia and diglossia, as component scripts diverge in form and function and archaic language obtrudes at a later date (Parkinson 1999, pp. 48–49)]. This initial pictography is logical given that transient sounds are being described in terms of a solid, visual world (Robertson 2003). Other early scripts, such as archaic cuneiform and Shang writing, may begin this way but soon shift into a purely phonic and less-comprehensive forms of representation. Thus hieroglyphic systems often hitch to other forms of imagery (Baines 1989). As in Egyptian and Mayan, signs may even behave as animate beings, in a manner described as "animation" in unpublished work by S.D. Houston and D.S. Stuart or as the "emblematic mode" by Baines (1989, 1994; Fischer 1978; Taube 2000b). What probably keeps the parallel systems of script and imagery from merging is the link of writing to language. Imagery allows and even encourages different ways of looking at and traversing a scene; writing remains rooted in linear and sequential reading orders.

A final theory suggests that writing develops not only from state or ceremonial needs, but because certain languages are hospitable to their invention (Boltz 2000, 2001; Daniels 1988). The argument is that Sumerian, Chinese, and Mayan have morphemes that consist largely of single syllables. These morphemes can be easily transmitted by means of signs representing objects or creatures with monosyllabic names. The use of rebus—homophones with like sound but different meaning—permits the script to expand efficiently, recording sounds that are less easily linked to pictorial signs (the classic example is the English pronoun "I" indicated by the drawing of a human "eye"). Such a deterministic theory calls for skepticism. How are we to account for languages of monosyllabic nature that did not develop writing? There may well be a tendency for most signs, regardless of script, to record monosyllabic forms—certainly this was true of Mayan. But Mayan is not the earliest script in Mesoamerica (others are centuries older), nor can it be described as a monosyllabic family of languages. If anything, a deterministic theory inappropriately dislodges the problem of script origins from the ancient societies that created and nurtured early writing.

The fourth question (Are there universal features or tendencies in the invention of writing?) has already been addressed in part. Most primary inventions of writing took place within a preexisting system of iconography. In a word, they were hieroglyphic, if with the proviso that new, phonically laden signs may have contrasted deliberately with previous images by using a different inventory of graphs. Early writing also required a script community to survive: This infrastructure ensured transmission across generations and led toward codification and broad comprehensibility. The study of script origins is also one of the last refuges of unilineal evolution, the notion that human society must pass through certain stages on its way to, in this case, the acme of the alphabet, that most perfect of scripts, having first traversed logographs and syllables (Gelb 1963, p. 201). These claims are invalid on empirical evidence (Daniels 1990, p. 728). The alphabet, for example, was evidently invented only once and then spread quickly with the florescence of the ancient world economy: A single instance doth not a law make. But tendencies in development do exist. Most early scripts use word signs bundled with systems of numeration that probably had a different and far-more-ancient origin (Ifrah 2000, pp. 47–67; Schmandt-Besserat 1992, pp. 184–94). It is a common misconception that the packaging of different recording systems in one place (numbers with word signs) is a unitary phenomenon rather than the bundling of discrete strands (cf. Michalowski 1990), although, to be sure, the enormously complex systems of numeration in early cuneiform may have coalesced at approximately the same time as early script (J. Cooper, personal communication). The alphabetic preservation of numerical logographs ("6, 10") arises from efficient brevity but also may reflect long-standing divisions between graphic systems.

Focus on the word sign is crucial. To modify Boltz's terminology, a graph must first convey sound and meaning [+P, +S^1], followed logically by rebus [+P, +S^2] (Boltz 1994, p. 19). The sound remains approximately the same (at least as phonic semblances were understood by scribes), the meaning changes to that of an unrelated homophone (as denoted by the changing superscript), and yet the sign continues to express the material referent of the first meaning. From this process come signs that, in some contexts, eject meaning altogether, as in Mayan syllables (+P, −S), which were created by pruning consonants or semivowels from the ends of words. The extent to which writing necessarily involves large-scale use of rebus at an early date is uncertain. Rebus is present [**BAAH** for "image, corporeal body" but from "pocket gopher" (S.D. Houston & D.S. Stuart, unpublished studies; Houston & Stuart 1998)] in the earliest Mayan writing, yet it is hardly abundant or clearly detectable. A rich source for the expanded use of pictorial signs, rebus was probably not the crucial step per se. The key invention was the indelible attachment of [+P, +S] to graphs.

Another universal would seem to be the highly episodic nature of script invention. The most steadfast proponent of gradualistic views is Schmandt-Besserat (1992), who sees gradual accretions over millennia in accounting for the creation of cuneiform. This view is no longer held by many specialists (Michalowski 1990, 1993), at least not in the form espoused by Schmandt-Besserat and as first sketched by Amiet (1966). The date of script invention falls, regardless of region or time, within a short span, and plausibly no longer than a human lifetime. Often the lack of data for brief spans comes less from secure counter-evidence than from intrinsic problems of dating. Having hit on the idea of [+P, +S] graphs, a scribe could soon apply the principle more widely. The elaboration of signs would be even more probable with syllabic or alphabetic systems which must expand quickly to accommodate a full phonological inventory: Leaving vowel or consonant classes pending would not seem likely once the overall system had been conceived. The rapidity of such developments raises the possibility of what Gelb called the "men of genius" (1963, p. 199) who crafted these systems. [Nonetheless, Gelb may have been correct about writing as an exclusionary, gendered practice: The ancient involvement of women in literacy is noteworthy for its rarity and the development of female-associated scripts (Harris 1989, p. 24; Trigger 1998, p. 57).] Again, no amount of brilliance will count for much in the absence of societal impulses to propagate a particular writing system. But Gelb did have a point, and subsequent scholars have detected such "genius" in many contexts, particularly the origin of the Greek alphabet (Powell 1991, pp. 10–12). The novel theory that the alphabet was devised by an "adapter" to record hexameter poetry is less credible, as the earliest examples relate to a gift economy involving feasts and dedications (Morris 1986; Powell 1991, pp. 182–83; Thomas 1992, pp. 58–59). The poetic functions would seem entirely secondary, a means of phrasing but not a primary objective.

The episodic nature of script invention should not encourage the notion that scripts develop fully. This notion may have been true of largely phonic systems, such as the alphabet or various syllabaries, but does not explain the patterns in primary or early inventions. Early Egyptian, Mayan, cuneiform, and other scripts display a marked degree of undergrammaticalization: The earliest examples pay scant attention to the full intricacy of language, which instead tends to be profoundly underrepresented until some time later (Baines 2003; Cooper 2003; Englund 2003; Xigui 2000, p. 43). To put this another way, early writing favors discrete lexemes more than syntactic, morphological, and phonic complexity; this is seldom true of secondary inventions that overtly copy or react to other scripts. Early scripts are not documents that stand on their own, but instead they require further exegesis by readers or a sense of context that can be impossible to reconstruct. This may reflect several things, from an *aides mémoires* concept of writing, in which script merely assisted the overtaxed memories of proto-bureaucrats, to an orality that dominated modes of discourse and validated formal declarations (Clanchy 1979, pp. 211, 219; Trietler 1981). The onomastic emphasis of early runes suggest social, extrascript reasons for such limitations in primary inventions of script, insofar as inscribed objects in the runic system operated within redistributive economies predicated on gifting and prestation (Snædal 1994, pp. 9–11). There is no reason to believe that a script, once invented, immediately expanded to fill every conceivable function. This idea could be archly termed the laundry list perspective on early writing. Evidently, it did not apply to early runes, which appear to have had markedly restricted functions (Williams 2003). The laundry list view is anachronistic, transporting present-day uses of writing to wholly different contexts. Another possibility is that grammaticalization took place because of a progressive need to clarify messages intended for storage past the lifetime of a scribe, or as script function expanded into new genres that required such subtleties. Every writing system underwent changes and reforms well beyond the expectations of the first inventors. This fact makes it all the more important to avoid the "synoptic fallacy," the belief that a script in use over centuries or millennia can be understood as a synchronic phenomenon (Houston 2000, p. 144).

As a universal, it seems that initial stages of writing often display heterogeneity of sign use in ways that may diverge from later graphs (Baines 2003). For early Maya writing, this lack of codification and uniformity makes the first glyphs nearly impossible to understand. There is insufficient redundancy from text to text to give any confidence to decipherments, and the heterogeneity may reflect the workings of a poorly coalesced script community. A final general observation about script origins is that they occur in moments of societal change: the Olmec decline, the institution of expansive dynastic control in Egypt, city-state administration in Mesopotamia, the appearance of Shang civilization [admittedly a script that probably postdates its first occurrence on perishable media like bamboo (Xigui 2000 p. 43), although not by long (Bottéro 2003)]. Societal change was not so much a rupture with tradition as a space in which experimentation could flourish and find a purchase. The more dramatic leaps from logographic to phonic scripts frequently appear on the margins of areas where logosyllabic scripts reign. New cultural settings allow the expression of nontraditional forms (Trigger 1998, p. 57).

Situation

Writing systems not only supply content—the *topoi*, genres, dates, names, numbers, and events of interest to archaeologists—but also give glimpses into how script was used, how, in our terminology, script was situated. "Use" is a broad term that can be dissected further. Literary scholars speak of "textual communities" that learn, read, and interpret dominant texts, either oral or written, in much the same way (Stock 1990). Classical Greeks had a body of such texts, Homeric and otherwise, Medieval clerics had the Latin bible, and the Classic Maya had a rich set of myths and explanatory charters. These texts, following Halbwachs (1992, pp. 38–39, 51), allow the formation of joint identities and community feeling, which may adjust those texts in turn (Alcock 2002, pp. 24–25). An argument can be made that, in some periods, texts became "normativized" by achieving broad currency, consolidation, and relative uniformity. Han China is one such epoch, in which the memorization and study of texts represented a necessary step to wisdom, prestige, and authority (Connery 1998, pp. 7–18). The authority of texts had a centralizing function and implied the exclusion and devaluation of nonnormative texts. Such documents represented the discursive kernel of "high culture," the production and consumption of aesthetic items for the benefit of elites (Baines & Yoffee 1998, p. 235), with the understanding that "aesthetics" was not limited to elites but greatly refined by them as markers of distinction. In a very separate tradition, that of Yemeni muftis, the final and definitive book, the Quran, was also regarded as the first. From it derived a genealogy of texts that, as works of humans rather than of God, were seen as flawed but redeemable by demonstrable descent from authoritative texts (Messick 1993, pp. 16–23). Such texts interweave with oral transmission. At their inception they contain recitations by a Prophet who, according to doctrine, could neither read nor write, and they passed to later generations by means of oral readings and memorization.

A related notion is that of "script communities," which learn, read, and interpret writing systems (see above). Script communities cannot use a particular form of writing unless mechanisms are in place for transmitting this skill and interpreting content in a consistent fashion. This idea presupposes the institution of apprenticeship or more formal schooling. Without these, the script would become highly idiosyncratic, negligibly codified, and unreadable over time and distance. Script communities foster the application of regular reading strategies—left/right, right/left, boustrephedon (back-and-forth, like "ox-turning" furrows), linear and interrupted linear—that facilitate communication (Twyman 1982, 1985). Archaeologists should be able to find the material vestiges of such schools or workshops and the products of disciplined instruction.

A large question pertaining to the use of writing systems is how many people could use a script (Houston 1994a). Before the early modern period, regardless of region, literacy was relatively low, only improved by the intervention of the state in rural and primary education. The exclusionary nature of literacy therefore must be seen as inherently related to inequality and the restriction of privilege. The problem with this view is that, in many parts of the world, writing may have been a silent act, but reading was not: It could involve many people, even illiterates, and would necessitate a thorough digesting by oral interpretation (Chafe & Tannen 1987, p. 396). Conventionally, "literacy" combines writing and reading as one, when, in fact, these are separate acts: one mechanical and kinetic, the other a process of scanning and response. A study of writing is often far more possible than a history of reading. Yet, even reading can be performative, involving reading aloud and oral disquisitions in what Havelock called "recitation literacy" (Havelock 1982, p. 5). This background of oral narrative, now disappeared and essentially unretrievable, complicates our grasp of how script was used in the past. It also changes the extent to which, in contrast to speech, writing is seen as nondeictic, unconcerned with establishing spatial and temporal relations between referents, speaker, and listener. As cues for performance and as physical objects, sometimes in architectural settings, written texts interact with readers and listeners in ways that can be carefully crafted by the scribe. Such interactional properties are only slowly coming into archaeological focus (Houston 2000, p. 155).

Extinction

A well-studied topic in linguistics is the obsolescence and extinction of languages around the world. In recent years, this process of decline and death has accelerated rapidly. In Africa alone, about 200 languages now are on the verge of disappearing (Sasse 1992, p. 7). More is at stake than simply the loss of a particular vehicle for communicating sound and meaning. When a language dies, much of its cultural value goes with it, along with, at least potentially, the use of a language as an ethnic or group marker (Dorian 1981, 1989). In archaeological terms, the passing of Etruscan has made the interpretation of that civilization incalculably more difficult (Bonfante & Bonfante 1983), as has the death of Meroitic, another probable isolate with no clear linguistic relatives (Welsby 1996). Language death can occur in a situation where speakers disappear suddenly, often as a result of conflict, or when dominant forces vigorously suppress local languages. But the more usual example involves a process of gradual decay. Younger speakers shift from secure command of the language to progressively weaker understanding, eventually to little more than the recollection that such a language existed or the preservation of a few words (Campbell & Muntzel 1989, pp. 182–86). Proficiency may survive in sociolinguistic contexts of ritual or privilege—the so-called "latinate" pattern—or in precisely the opposite setting, where well-defined niches maintain a low-prestige language against pressures from a dominant one.

For many years imperfect speakers were hardly thought worthy of attention. This is still the case with script death, which has only just received comparative treatment (Houston et al. 2003). In many respects the concepts and terms of language obsolescence apply to the demise of writing. A script disappears because it no longer serves a purpose, having been stigmatized because of past associations, or because those proficient in its use have disappeared or have been exterminated, a frequent hazard in colonial situations. The questions are much the same, too: When is the use of script stable? When does it "tip" into obsolescence or experience "abrupt transmission failure" from writer to aspiring writer? What was the nature of the "abandoned script" and the "target script"? Does writing undergo simplification (loss of complexity) and reduction (defectivity) as it goes from semi-writers to terminal writers? And does the development of dialect roughly parallel the evolution of different variants of script?

Just as bilingualism induces conditions for the disappearance of less-favored languages, so it is necessary to introduce terms like biliteratism or even triliteratism, since scribes in one code were likely, as in well-attested examples from Mesoamerica, to adopt new codes when the functional and cultural setting of writing changed (Restall 1997, p. 267). However, biliteratism apparently serves as a condition for script death. The disappearance of writing in South Asia for a span of more than 1300 years is exceptional, and most instances of script death involve a parallel process of replacement. But biliteratism does not necessarily trigger the obsolescence of a writing system. The long-standing coexistence of Roman and runic script in Sweden shows that the linkage between script extinction and concurrent writing systems can be weak (Gustavson & Hallonquist 1994, p. 176). Much like language, when a script disappears the consequences reverberate strongly. The process is bidirectional: The debilitation of certain traditions and concepts undermines the use of particular writing systems, and the weakening of such systems undermines the traditions they convey and buttress. No script can be understood in isolation from the people who used it and their reasons for doing so. Yet, in other respects, script death must have followed a different path from language. All members of society speak or, barring pathology, have the ability to do so. Script instead tends to a pattern of restricted use (literacy) and application (genre and context) in most premodern societies. Speech must always survive because only the most exceptional and marked groups, such as monastic ones, can endure in absolute silence. Script will expire when the pressures that maintain it dissolve and a new set of values comes into play. No one factor is likely to lead to script extinction. Rather, script death results from a toxic combination of several causes, some external to the script community, others internal, concerning access to the script and the motivations to keep it (cf. Grenoble & Whaley 1998, pp. 52–54).

THE ARCHAEOLOGY OF COMMUNICATION TECHNOLOGIES

By focusing on "situation" and "extraction," scholars can achieve some idea of how graphic notations recorded thought and sound in distant times and places. Categorical statements of how and when situating and extracting should be done are only moderately useful. It is in specific cases that arguments seem compelling or not. The vast literature on petrographs around the world exemplifies the promise and pain of attempting a breakthrough to meaning. The relation of writing to archaeology is far reaching and so subtle and complex as to lie beyond the reach of a short review. Investigators increasingly opine that script exists in two modalities: as grist for comparative studies; and as cultural practices whose individual circumstances, histories, and practitioners cannot be ignored. The study of scripts also revolves around a paradox. Knowledge is deepening of particular systems of writing, often accessible to only a few specialists, alongside a collective need to look broadly at questions of mutual interest. Plainly, this paradox can be resolved by collaboration and the search for joint vocabulary and objectives. Fostering archaeological interest in writing systems, and reciprocal concern with archaeology among epigraphers and text-focused scholars, is a final issue. The material and textual worlds may represent different realities, but the fruitful tension between them opens paths of future growth in understanding the past.

ACKNOWLEDGMENTS

Many of the thoughts herein were refined during discussions with colleagues at a seminar, "The First Writing," which I organized at the Sundance Resort, Utah, in early spring of 2000. These colleagues included Bob Bagley, John Baines, Bill Boltz, Elizabeth Boone, Françoise Bottéro, Jerry Cooper, Bob Englund, Simon Martin, John Robertson, Gary Urton, and Henrik Williams. David Webster also provided sage advice, as did Jerry Cooper, in reading an earlier draft. Other thoughts came from a kind invitation by Katina Lillios to discuss papers in a session she organized at the 2003 meetings of the American Anthropological Association.

The *Annual Review of Anthropology* is online at http://anthro.annualreviews.org

LITERATURE CITED

Abélanet J. 1986. *Signes Sans Paroles: Cent Siècles d'Art Rupestre en Europe Occidentale.* Poitiers, France: Hachette

Alcock SE. 2002. *Archaeologies of the Greek Past: Landscape, Monuments, and Memories.* Cambridge: Cambridge Univ. Press

Alexander JS. 1996. Masons' marks and stone bonding. In *The Archaeology of Cathedrals,* ed. T Tatton-Brown, J Munby, pp. 219–36. Oxford: Oxford Univ. Comm. Arch.

Alexander JS. 1998. Southwell Minster choir: the evidence of the masons' marks. In *Southwell and Nottinghamshire: Medieval Art, Architecture, and Industry,* ed. JS Alexander, pp. 44–59. Leeds: Brit. Archaeol. Assoc.

Amiet P. 1966. Il y a 5000 ans les Elamites inventaient l'écriture. *Archaeologia* 12:20–22

Ascher M. 1991. *Ethnomathematics: A Multicultural View of Mathematical Ideas.* Pacific Grove, CA: Brooks/Cole

Assmann J. 1994. Ancient Egypt and the materiality of the sign. In *Materialities of Communication,* ed. HU Ludwig Pfeiffer, K Ludwig Pfeiffer, pp. 5–31. Stanford, CA: Stanford Univ. Press

Aveni AF. 1985. Non-western notational frameworks and the role of anthropology in our understanding of literacy. See Wrolstad & Fisher, pp. 252–80

Baines J. 1989. Communication and display: the integration of early Egyptian art and writing. *Antiquity* 63:471–82

Baines J. 1994. On the status and purposes of ancient Egyptian art. *Camb. Archaeol. J.* 4:67–94

Baines J. 2003. The earliest Egyptian writing: development, context, purpose. See Houston 2004. In press

Baines J, Yoffee N. 1998. Order, legitimacy, and wealth in ancient Egypt and Mesopotamia. In *Archaic States,* ed. GM Feinman, J Marcus, pp. 199–260. Santa Fe, NM: School Am. Res.

Basso KH. 1989. The ethnography of writing. In *Explorations in the Ethnography of Speaking,* ed. R Bauman, J Sherzer, pp. 425–32, 494–95. Cambridge: Cambridge Univ. Press

Basso K, Anderson N. 1973. A Western Apache writing system: the symbols of Silas John. *Science* 180:1013–22

Bell L. 1987. Philosophy of Egyptian epigraphy after sixty years: practical experience. In *Problems and Priorities in Egyptian Archaeology,* ed. J Assmann, G Burkard, V Davies, pp. 43–55. London: Kegan Paul

Belting H. 1994. *Likeness and Presence: A History of the Image Before the Era of Art.* Chicago, IL: Univ. Chicago Press

Bennet J. 1988. Approaches to the problem of combining Linear B textual data and archaeological data in the late Bronze Age Aegean. In *Problems in Greek Prehistory,* ed. EB French, KA Wardle, pp. 509–18. Bristol, UK: Bristol Class. Press

Besançon A. 2000. *The Forbidden Image: An*

Intellectual History of Iconoclasm. Chicago, IL: Univ. Chicago Press

Besnier N. 1995. *Literacy, Emotion, and Authority: Reading and Writing on a Polynesian Atoll.* Cambridge: Cambridge Univ. Press

Bierman I. 1998. *Writing Signs: The Fatimid Public Text.* Berkeley: Univ. Calif. Press

Bodel J. 2001. Epigraphy and the ancient historian. In *Epigraphic Evidence: Ancient History from Inscriptions*, ed. J Bodel, pp. 1–56. London: Routledge

Boltz WG. 1986. Early Chinese writing. *World Archaeol.* 17:420–36

Boltz WG. 1994. *The Origin and Early Development of the Chinese Writing System.* New Haven, CT: Amer. Orient. Soc.

Boltz WG. 1996. Early Chinese writing. In *The World's Writing Systems*, ed. PT Daniels, W Bright, pp. 191–99. New York/Oxford: Oxford Univ. Press

Boltz WG. 1999. Language and writing. In *The Cambridge History of Ancient China*, ed. M Loewe, EL Shaughnessy, pp. 74–123. Cambridge: Cambridge Univ. Press

Boltz WG. 2000. *Monosyllabicity and the Origin of the Chinese Script.* Preprint 143. Berlin: Max-Planck-Institut für Wissenschaftsgeschichte

Boltz WG. 2001. The invention of writing in China. *Oriens Extremis* 42:1–17

Bonfante G, Bonfante L. 1983. *The Etruscan Language: An Introduction.* Manchester, UK: Manchester Univ. Press

Boone EH. 1994. Introduction: writing and recording knowledge. In *Writing Without Words: Alternative Literacies in Mesoamerica and the Andes*, ed. EH Boone, WD Mignolo, pp. 3–26. Durham, NC: Duke Univ. Press

Boone EH. 1998. Pictorial documents and visual thinking in postconquest Mexico. In *Native Traditions in the Postconquest World*, ed. EH Boone, T Cummins, pp. 149–99. Washington, DC: Dumbarton Oaks

Bottéro F. 2004. Writing on shell and bone in Shang China. See Houston 2004. In press

Bourdieu P. 1993. *The Field of Cultural Production.* New York: Columbia Univ. Press

Boyer P. 1997. *The Naturalness of Religious Ideas: A Cognitive Theory of Religion.* Berkeley: Univ. Calif. Press

Bradley R. 1997. *Rock Art and the Prehistory of Europe: Signing the Land.* London: Routledge

Bradley R. 2000. *An Archaeology of Natural Places.* London: Routledge

Caminos R, Fischer HG. 1976. *Ancient Egyptian Epigraphy and Palaeography: The Recording of Inscriptions and Scenes in Tombs and Temples; Archaeological Aspects of Epigraphy and Palaeography.* New York: Metro. Mus. Art

Campbell L, Muntzel MC. 1989. The structural consequences of language death. In *Investigating Obsolescence: Studies in Language Contraction and Death*, ed. N Dorian, pp. 181–96. Cambridge: Cambridge Univ. Press

Carruthers M. 1994. *The Book of Memory: A Study of Memory in Material Culture.* Cambridge: Cambridge Univ. Press

Chafe W, Tannen D. 1987. The relation between written and spoken language. *Annu. Rev. Anthropol.* 16:383–407

Chang K-C. 1980. *Shang Civilization.* New Haven, CT: Yale Univ. Press

Civil M. 1972. The Sumerian writing system: some problems. *Orientalia* 42:21–34

Clanchy MT. 1979. *From Memory to Written Record: England 1066–1307.* Cambridge, MA: Harvard Univ. Press

Clarke ML. 1972. *Higher Education in the Ancient World.* London: Routledge Kegan Paul

Clottes J. 2002. *World Rock Art.* Malibu, CA: Getty Trust

Coe MD. 1973. *The Maya Scribe and His World.* New York: Grolier

Coe MD. 1995. On *not* breaking the Indus code. *Antiquity* 69:393–95

Coe MD. 1999. *Breaking the Maya Code.* London: Thames & Hudson. Rev. ed.

Collon D. 1990. *Interpreting the Past: Near Eastern Seals.* London: Br. Mus. Press

Conkey MW. 1987. New approaches in the search for meaning: a review of research in "paleolithic art." *J. Field Archaeol.* 14:413–30

Conkey MW. 1989. The structural analysis of paleolithic art. In *Archaeological Thought in America*, ed. CC Lamberg-Karlovsky, pp. 135–54. Cambridge: Cambridge Univ. Press

Conkey MW, Soffer O, Stratmann D, Jablonski NG, eds. 1997. *Beyond Art: Pleistocene Image and Symbol*. San Francisco: Mem. Calif. Acad. Sci. 23

Conklin WJ. 1982. The information of Middle Horizon quipus. In *Ethnoastronomy and Archaeoastronomy in the American Tropics*, ed. AF Aveni, G Urton, pp. 261–82. New York: Ann. New York Acad. Sci. 385

Conard NJ. 2003. Palaeolithic ivory sculptures from southwestern Germany and the origins of figurative art. *Nature* 426:830–32

Connery CL. 1998. *The Empire of the Text: Writing Authority in Early Imperial China*. Lanham, MD: Rowman & Littlefield

Cooper J. 2004. Babylonian beginnings: the origin of the cuneiform writing system in comparative perspective. See Houston 2004. In press

Coulmas F. 1989. *The Writing Systems of the World*. Oxford: Blackwell

Crump T. 1990. *The Anthropology of Numbers*. Cambridge: Cambridge Univ. Press

Dalby D. 1968. The indigenous scripts of West Africa and Surinam: their inspiration and design. *Afr. Lang. Stud.* 9:156–97

Daniels PT. 1988. The syllabic origin of writing and the segmental origin of the alphabet. In *The Linguistics of Literacy*, ed. P Downing, SD Limia, M Noonan, pp. 83–110. Amsterdam: Benjamins

Daniels PT. 1990. Fundamentals of grammatology. *J. Am. Orient. Soc.* 110(3):727–31

Daniels PT. 1996. The invention of writing. In *The World's Writing Systems*, ed. PT Daniels, W Bright, pp. 579–86. Oxford: Oxford Univ. Press

Davidson I. 1997. The power of pictures. See Conkey et al. 1997, pp. 125–59

Davies WV. 1987. *Reading the Past: Egyptian Hieroglyphs*. London: British Mus.

Delporte H. 1993. Gravettian female figurines: a regional survey. In *Before Lascaux: The Complex Record of the Early Upper Pale-olithic*, ed. H Knecht, A Pike-Tay, R White, pp. 243–57. Boca Raton, FL: CRC Press

Dobres M-A, Robb JE, ed. 2000. *Agency in Archaeology*. London: Routledge

Donnan C, McClelland D. 1979. *The Burial Theme in Moche Iconography*. Stud. Pre-Col. Art Archaeol. 21. Washington, DC: Dumbarton Oaks

Donnan C, McClelland D. 1999. *Moche Fineline Painting: Its Evolution and Artists*. Los Angeles, CA: Fowler Mus. Cult. Hist., UCLA

Dorian NC. 1981. *Language Death: The Life Cycle of a Scottish Gaelic Dialect*. Philadelphia: Univ. Penn. Press

Dorian NC, ed. 1989. *Investigating Obsolescence: Studies in Language Contraction and Death*. Cambridge: Cambridge Univ. Press

Edgerton SY, Jr. 1991. *The Heritage of Giotto's Geometry: Art and Science on the Eve of the Scientific Revolution*. Ithaca, NY: Cornell Univ. Press

Englund R. 2004. The state of decipherment of proto-Elamite. See Houston 2004. In press

Fischer HG. 1978. The evolution of composite hieroglyphs in ancient Egypt. *Metro. Mus. J.* 12:5–19

Fischer SR. 1997. *Glyphbreaker*. New York: Copernicus

Friedrich J. 1957. *Extinct Languages*. New York: Philos. Libr.

Gardner H. 1985. The development of symbolic literacy. See Wrolstad & Fisher 1985, pp. 39–56

Gaur A. 1992. *A History of Writing*. New York: Cross River Press

Gelb IJ. 1963. *A Study of Writing*. Chicago, IL: Univ. Chicago Press. 2nd ed.

Gelb IJ. 1975. Methods of decipherment. *J. Roy. Asiat. Soc. Gr. Brit. Irel.* 1:95–104

Gledhill J, Bender B, Larsen MT, eds. 1988. *State and Society: The Emergence and Development of Social Hierarchy, and Political Centralization*. London: Unwin Hyman

Goody J, Watt I. 1963. The consequences of literacy. *Comp. Stud. Soc. Hist.* 5(3):304–45

Gordon AE. 1983. *Illustrated Introduction to Latin Epigraphy*. Berkeley: Univ. Calif. Press

Graham I. 1975. *Corpus of Maya Hieroglyphic Inscriptions, Volume I.* Cambridge, MA: Peabody Mus. Harvard Univ

Grenoble L, Whaley LJ. 1998. Toward a typology of language endangerment. In *Endangered Languages: Language Loss and Community Response*, ed. LA Grenoble, LJ Whaley, pp. 22–54. Cambridge: Cambridge Univ. Press

Grube N. 2000. The city-states of the Maya. In *A Comparative Study of Thirty City-State Cultures*, ed. MH Hansen, pp. 547–65. København, Denmark: Det Kongelige Danske Videnskabernes Selskab

Gustavson H, Hallonquist S-G. 1994. Dalrunorna: en vidareutveckling av de medeltida runorna? In *Runmärkt från brev till klotter*, ed. S. Benneth, J Ferenius, H Gustavson, M. Åhlén, pp. 157–76. Stockholm: Carlssons

Gvozdover M. 1995. *Art of the Mammoth Hunters: The Finds from Avdeevo.* Oxbow Monogr. 49. Oxford: Oxbow

Halbwachs M. 1992. *On Collective Memory.* Chicago, IL: Univ. Chicago Press

Halverson J. 1992. Goody and the implosion of the literacy thesis. *Man* 27:301–17

Harbsmeier M. 1988. Inventions of writing. See Gledhill et al. 1988, pp. 252–76

Harris R. 1995. *Signs of Writing.* London: Routledge

Harris WV. 1989. *Ancient Literacy.* Cambridge, MA: Harvard Univ. Press

Hastings CM, Moseley ME. 1975. The adobes of Huaca del Sol and Huaca de la Luna. *Am. Antiq.* 40:196–203

Havelock EA. 1982. *The Literate Revolution in Greece and its Cultural Consequences.* Princeton, NJ: Princeton Univ. Press

Haviland WA, Laguna de Haviland A. 1995. Glimpses of the supernatural: altered states of consciousness and the graffiti of Tikal, Guatemala. *Lat. Am. Antiq.* 6(4):295–309

Hoskins J. 1998. *Biographical Objects: How Things Tell the Stories of People's Lives.* New York: Routledge

Houston SD. 1994a. Literacy among the Pre-Columbian Maya: a comparative perspective. In *Writing Without Words: Alternative Literacies in Mesoamerica and the Andes*, ed. EH Boone, WD Mignolo, pp. 27–49. Durham, NC: Duke Univ. Press

Houston SD. 1994b. Mesoamerican writing. In *The Encyclopedia of Language and Linguistics, Volume 5*, ed. RE Asher, JMY Simpson, pp. 2449–51. Oxford: Pergamon

Houston SD. 2000. Into the minds of ancients: advances in glyph studies. *J. World Prehist.* 14:121–201

Houston SD. 2001. Decorous bodies and disordered passions: representations of emotion among the Classic Maya. *World Archaeol.* 33(2):206–19

Houston SD, ed. 2004. *The First Writing.* Cambridge: Cambridge Univ. Press. In press

Houston SD, Coe MD. 2004. Has Isthmian writing been deciphered? *Mexicon.* 25(6):151–61

Houston SD, Baines J, Cooper J. 2003. Last writing: script obsolescence in Egypt, Mesopotamia, and Mesoamerica. *Comp. Stud. Soc. Hist.* 45(3):430–80

Houston SD, Chinchilla Mazariegos O, Stuart D, eds. 2001. *The Decipherment of Ancient Maya Writing.* Norman: Univ. Oklahoma Press

Houston SD, Stuart DS. 1998. The ancient Maya self: personhood and portraiture in the Classic period. *RES: Anthropol. Aesthet.* 33:73–101

Ifrah G. 2000. *The Universal History of Numbers, from Prehistory to the Invention of the Computer.* New York: Wiley

Jackson A. 1979. *Na-khi Religion: An Analytical Appraisal of the Na-khi Ritual Texts.* The Hague: Mouton

Joyce RA. 2000. Girling the girl and boying the boy: the production of adulthood in ancient Mesoamerica. *World Archaeol.* 31(3):473–83

Justeson JS, Kaufman T. 1993. A decipherment of Epi-Olmec hieroglyphic writing. *Science* 259:1703–11

Kahn D. 1996. *The Code-Breakers: The Comprehensive History of Secret Communication from Ancient Times to the Internet.* New York: Scribner

Kamal OS, Ware GA, Houston S, Chabries DM, Christiansen RW. 1999. Multispectral image processing for detail reconstruction and enhancement of Maya murals from La Pasadita, Guatemala. *J. Archaeol. Sci.* 26:1391–407

Keightley DN. 1989. The origins of writing in China: scripts and cultural contexts. See Senner 1989a, pp. 171–202

Keppie L. 1991. *Understanding Roman Inscriptions.* Baltimore, MD: Johns Hopkins Univ. Press

Kim-Reynaud YK, ed. 1996. *The Korean Writing System: Its History and Structure.* Honolulu: Univ. Hawaii Press

Kris E, Kurz O. 1981. *Legend, Myth and Magic in the Image of the Artist: A Historical Experiment.* New Haven, CT: Yale Univ. Press

Küchler S. 2002. *Malanggan: Art, Memory, and Sacrifice.* London: Berg

Larsen MT. 1988. Introduction: literacy and social complexity. See Gledhill et al. 1988, pp. 173–91

Leechman JD, Harrington MR. 1921. *String Records of the Northwest.* New York: Mus. Am. Indian

Lenik EJ. 2003. *Picture Rocks: American Indian Rock Art in the Northeast Woodlands.* Lebanon, NH: Univ. Press New England

Lévi-Strauss C. 1955. *Tristes tropiques.* Paris: Librairie Plon

Lewis ME. 1999. *Writing and Authority in Early China.* Albany: State Univ. N.Y. Press

Lewis-Williams D. 2002a. *A Cosmos in Stone: Interpreting Religion and Society Through Rock Art.* London: Rowman & Littlefield

Lewis-Williams D. 2002b. *The Mind in the Cave: Consciousness and the Origins of Art.* London: Thames & Hudson

Lillios K. 2002. Some new views of the engraved slate plaques of southwest Iberia. *Rev. Portug. Arqueol.* 5(2):135–51

Lillios K. 2003. Creating memory in prehistory: the engraved slate plaques of southwest Iberia. See Van Dyke & Alcock 2003a, pp. 128–50

Locke LL. 1923. *The Ancient Quipu or Peruvian Knot Record.* New York, NY: Am. Mus. Nat. Hist

Macintosh NWG. 1977. Beswick Creek Cave two decades later: a reappraisal. In *Form in Indigenous Art: Schematisation in the Art of Australian Aborigines and Prehistoric Europe*, ed. PJ Ucko, pp. 191–97. Canberra: Aust. Inst. Aborig. Stud.

Marcus J. 1992. *Mesoamerican Writing Systems: Propaganda, Myth, and History in Four Ancient Civilizations.* Princeton, NJ: Princeton Univ. Press

Marshack A. 1991. *The Roots of Civilization: The Cognitive Beginnings of Man's First Art, Symbol, and Notation.* Mount Kisco, NY: Moyer Bell

Marshack A. 1997. Paleolithic image making and symboling in Europe and the Middle East: a comparative review. See Conkey et al. 1997, pp. 53–91

Messick B. 1993. *The Calligraphic State: Textual Domination and History in a Muslim Society.* Berkeley: Univ. Calif. Press

Michalowski P. 1990. Early Mesopotamian communicative systems: art, literature, and writing. In *Investigating Artistic Environments in the Ancient Near East*, ed. AC Gunther, pp. 53–69. Washington, DC: Sackler Gallery

Michalowski P. 1993. Tokenism. *Am. Anthropol.* 95:996–99

Mimica J. 1992. *Intimations of Infinity: The Cultural Meanings of the Iqwaye Counting and Number System.* Oxford: Berg

Mitchell WJT. 1986. *Iconology: Image, Text, Ideology.* Chicago, IL: Univ. Chicago Press

Monaghan J, Hamman B. 1998. Reading as social practice and cultural construction. *Indiana J. Hisp. Lit.* 13:131–40

Morgan TJ. 1998. *Literate Education in the Hellenistic and Roman Worlds.* Cambridge: Cambridge Univ. Press

Morphy H. 1991. *Ancestral Connections: Art and an Aboriginal System of Knowledge.* Chicago, IL: Univ. Chicago Press

Morris I. 1986. Gift and commodity in Archaic Greece. *Man* 21:1–17

Nissen HJ, Damerow P, Englund RK. 1993. *Archaic Bookkeeping: Writing and Techniques of Economic Administration in the*

Ancient Near East. Chicago, IL: Univ. Chicago Press

Parkinson R. 1999. *Cracking Codes: The Rosetta Stone and Decipherment.* Berkeley: Univ. Calif. Press

Parpola A. 1994. *Deciphering the Indus script.* Cambridge: Cambridge Univ. Press

Pope M. 1999. *The Story of Decipherment from Egyptian Hieroglyphs to Maya Script.* Rev. ed. London: Thames & Hudson. Rev. ed.

Postgate N, Wang T, Wilkinson T. 1995. The evidence for early ceremonial writing: utilitarian or ceremonial? *Antiquity* 69:459–80

Powell BB. 1991. *Homer and the Origin of the Greek Alphabet.* Cambridge: Cambridge Univ. Press

Price N, ed. 2001. *The Archaeology of Shamanism.* London: Routledge

Quilter J, Urton G, eds. 2002. *Narrative Threads: Accounting and Recounting in Andean Khipu.* Austin: Univ. Tex. Press

Ramsey SR. 1987. *The Languages of China.* Princeton, NJ: Princeton Univ. Press

Rappaport J, Cummins T. 1998. Between images and writing: the ritual of the king's Quillca. *Col. Lat. Am. Rev.* 7(1):7–32

Reichel-Dolmatoff G. 1997. Drug induced optical sensations and their relationship to applied art among some Colombian Indians. In *Rainforest Shamans*, ed. G Reichel-Dolmatoff, pp. 243–60. Dartington, UK: Themis

Restall M. 1997. Heirs to the hieroglyphs: indigenous writing in colonial Mesoamerica. *Americas* 54:239–67

Robertson JS. 2004. The possibility and actuality of writing. See Houston 2004. In press

Robinson A. 2001. *Lost Languages: The Riddle of the World's Undeciphered Scripts.* New York: McGraw-Hill

Rock JFC. 1963–1972. *A Na-Khi–English Encyclopedic Dictionary.* Serie Orientale Roma 28. Rome: Instituto Italiano per il Medio ed Estremo Oriente

Rowlands M. 1993. The role of memory in the transmission of culture. *World Archaeol.* 25(2):141–51

Salomon F. 2001. How an Andean "writing without words" works. *Curr. Anthropol.* 42(1):1–27

Salomon R. 1998. *Indian Epigraphy: A Guide to the Study of Inscriptions in Sanskrit, Prakrit, and the Other Indo-Aryan Languages.* New York: Oxford Univ. Press

Sampson G. 1985. *Writing Systems: A Linguistic Introduction.* Stanford, CA: Stanford Univ. Press

Sasse H-J. 1992. Theory of language death. In *Language Death: Factual and Theoretical Explorations with Special Reference to East Africa*: ed. M Brenzinger, pp. 7–30. Berlin: Mouton de Gruyter

Schaafsma P. 1994. *The Rock Art of Utah: A Study from the Donald Scott Collection.* Salt Lake City: Univ. Utah Press

Schmandt-Besserat D. 1992. *Before Writing, Volume I: From Counting to Cuneiform.* Austin: Univ. Tex. Press

Schmitt A. 1963. *Die Bamum-Schrift.* Wiesbaden, Germany: O. Harrossowitz

Senner WM, ed. 1989a. *The Origins of Writing.* Lincoln: Univ. Neb. Press

Senner WM. 1989b. Theories and myths on the origins of writing: an historical overview. See Senner 1989a, pp. 1–26

Sircar DC. 1971. Introduction to Indian epigraphy and paleography. *J. Anc. Ind. Hist.* 4:72–136

Smalley WA, Vang CK, Yang GY. 1990. *Mother of Writing: The Origin and Development of Hmong Messianic Script.* Chicago, IL: Univ. Chicago Press

Snædal T. 1994. Vardagsliv och visdomsord: runorna i norden från urtid till nutid. In *Runmärkt från brev till klotter*, ed. S Benneth, J Ferenius, H Gustavson, M Åhlén. pp. 9–32. Stockholm: Carlssons

Sproat R. 2000. *A Computational Theory of Writing Systems.* Cambridge: Cambridge Univ. Press

Stock B. 1990. *Listening for the Text: On the Uses of the Past.* Philadelphia: Univ. Penn. Press

Stone A, Künne M. 2003. Rock art of Central America and Maya Mexico. In *Rock Art Studies, News of the World 2: Developments in*

Rock Art Research 1995–1999, ed PG Bahn, A Fossati, pp. 196–213. Oxford: Oxbow

Street BV. 1993. Introduction: the new literacy studies. In *Cross-Cultural Approaches to Literacy*, ed. BV Street, pp. 1–21. Cambridge: Cambridge Univ. Press

Stuart DS. 2001. *Proper names and the origins of literacy*. Work. Pap., Peabody Mus., Harvard Univ

Taçon PSC, Chippindale C. 1998. An archaeology of rock-art through informed methods and formal methods. In *The Archaeology of Rock-Art*, ed. C Chippindale, PSC Taçon, pp. 1–10. Cambridge: Cambridge Univ. Press

Tardits C. 1980. *Le Royaume Bamoum*. Paris: Armand Colin

Taube KA. 1995. The rainmakers: the Olmec and their contribution to Mesoamerican belief and ritual. In *The Olmec World*, ed. J Guthrie, pp. 83–103. Princeton, NJ: Art Mus. Princeton Univ.

Taube KA. 2000a. Lightning celts and corn fetishes: the Formative Olmec and the development of maize symbolism in Mesoamerica and the American Southwest. In *Olmec Art and Archaeology in Mesoamerica*, ed. JE Clark, ME Pye, pp. 296–337. Stud. Hist. Art 58. Washington, DC: Cent. Adv. Study Vis. Arts, Nat. Gallery Art

Taube KA. 2000b. *The Writing System of Ancient Teotihuacan*. Anc. Am. 1. Washington, DC: Cent. Anc. Am. Stud.

Taylor AR. 1997. Nonspeech communication systems. In *Handbook of Middle American Indians, Vol. 17: Languages*, ed. I Goddard, 275–89. Washington, DC: Smithsonian Inst.

Thomas R. 1992. *Literacy and Orality in Ancient Greece*. Cambridge: Cambridge Univ. Press

Tinney S. 1998. Texts, tablets, and teaching: scribal education in Nippur and Ur. *Expedition* 40(2):40–50

Trietler L. 1981. Oral, written, and literate process in the transmission of medieval music. *Speculum* 56(3):471–91

Trigger BG. 1998. Writing systems: a case study in cultural evolution. *Norw. Archaeol. Rev.* 31(1):39–62

Twyman M. 1982. The graphic presentation of language. *Inform. Design J.* 3:1–22

Twyman M. 1985. Articulating graphic language: a historical perspective. Wrolstad & Fisher 1985, pp. 188–251

Urton G. 1997. *The Social Life of Numbers: A Quechua Ontology of Numbers and Philosophy of Arithmetic*. Austin: Univ. Tex. Press

Urton G. 1998. From knots to narratives: reconstructing the art of historical record-keeping in the Andes from the Spanish transcriptions of Inka *khipus*. *Ethnohistory* 45:409–38

Urton G. 2003. *Signs of the Inka Khipu: Binary Coding in the Andean Knotted-String Records*. Austin: Univ. Tex. Press

Van den Brink ECM. 1992. Corpus and numerical evaluation of "Thinite" potmarks. In *The Followers of Horus: Studies Dedicated to Michael Allen Hoffman, 1944–1990*, ed. R Friedman, B Adams, pp. 265–96. Oxford: Oxbow Monogr. 20

Van Dyke RM, Alcock SE, ed. 2003a. *Archaeologies of Memory*. Oxford: Blackwell

Van Dyke, RM, Alcock SE. 2003b. Archaeologies of memory: an introduction. See Van Dyke & Alcock 2003a, pp. 1–13

Vanstiphout H. 1979. How did they learn Sumerian? *J. Cuneif. Stud.* 31:118–26

Vastokas J. 2003. *Beyond iconography: a contextual semiotics of Ojibwa pictography*. Presented at Annu. Meet. Am. Anthropol. Assoc., 102nd, Chicago

Walker WB. 1997. Native writing systems. In *Handbook of Middle American Indians, Vol. 17: Languages*, ed. I Goddard, pp. 158–84. Washington, DC: Smithsonian Inst.

Walker WB, Sarbaugh J. 1993. The early history of the Cherokee syllabary. *Ethnohistory* 40:70–94

Ware G, Miller M, Taube K, de la Fuente B. 2002. Infrared imaging of precolumbian murals at Bonampak, Chiapas, Mexico. *Antiquity* 76:325–26

Watt RG. 1994. The deseret alphabet. In *Utah History Encyclopedia*, ed. AK Powell, pp. 139–40. Salt Lake City: Univ. Utah Press

Welsby DA. 1996. *The Kingdom of Kush:*

The Napatan and Meroitic Empires. London: Brit. Mus. Press

White R. 2003. *Prehistoric Art: The Symbolic Journey of Humankind*. New York: Abrams

Whitley DS. 2000. *The Art of the Shaman: Rock Art of California*. Salt Lake City: Univ. Utah Press

Whitley DS. 2001. *Handbook of Rock Art Research*. London: Rowman & Littlefield

Williams H. 2004. Reasons for runes. See Houston 2004. In press

Williams P, Chrisman L, eds. 1994. *Colonial Discourse/Post-Colonial Theory*. New York: Columbia Univ. Press

Williams RJ. 1972. Scribal training in ancient Egypt. *J. Am. Orient. Soc.* 92(2):214–21

Woodhead AG. 1992. *The Study of Greek Inscriptions*. Norman: Univ. Oklahoma Press

Wrolstad ME, Fisher DF, eds. 1985. *Toward a New Understanding of Literacy*. New York: Praeger

Xigui Q. 2000. *Chinese Writing*. Berkeley: Inst. East Asian Stud., Univ. Calif.

Annu. Rev. Anthropol. 2004. 33:251–69
doi: 10.1146/annurev.anthro.33.070203.143749
First published online as a Review in Advance on May 14, 2004

HANG ON TO YOUR SELF: Of Bodies, Embodiment, and Selves

Steven Van Wolputte

*Department of Social and Cultural Anthropology, Katholieke Universiteit Leuven,
Tiensestraat 102, 3000 Leuven, Belgium; email: Steven.vanwolputte@ant.kuleuven.ac.be*

Key Words   subjectivity, intersubjectivity, corporeality, body symbolism,
vulnerability

■ **Abstract**   During the past twenty years the human body evolved from a rather
marginal social fact into a notion of central concern to current social and cultural
anthropology. But recent studies question the idea of the body as a given physical
entity. They focus on the experience or threat of finiteness, limitation, and vulnerability
and also raise doubts regarding the individuality of the self: Instead they emphasize
its fragmentary character and focus on the embodied uncertainties (such as hybridity
or irony) of human existence. In three main sections (respectively, on the social body,
embodiment, and subjectivity) this review eclectically explores an anthropological
debate that also betrays a more generalized and rising concern in Western society with
bodiliness and bodily appearance. From the discussion, the body emerges as a changing
relationship that, at the same time, unfolds as an ethical horizon—and challenge—for
the (un)making of self, identity, and belonging.

INTRODUCTION

We all have and we all are a body. This allusion to Merleau-Ponty's (1970) work is
probably one of the (if not the) most recurrent expressions—or perhaps clichés—in
the literature reviewed here. But even this certainty—that for many signified the last
objective stronghold against deconstructionism—is not so certain anymore. Under
the influence of, among others, disability studies and of feminist and postcolonial
scholarship, researchers have questioned the unity, neutrality, transparency, universality, and objectivity of the human organism (Grosz 1995b, Harraway 1991,
Ingstad & Whyte 1995); the supposed continuity, transcendence, and individuality
(indivisibility) of the self (see Battaglia 1995b, De Vos et al. 1985, Strathern 1988);
and the self-evidence of bodiliness and embodiment (Csordas 1994a, Geurts 2002,
Weiss 1999, Shildrick 2002).

This review focuses mainly on the literature of the past two decades. But it
does not pretend or intend to be an overview of bodies and selves in social and
cultural anthropology (see Csordas 1999; Farnell 1999, p. 346vv; Frank 1990;

0084-6570/04/1021-0251$14.00

Johnson 1985; Lock 1993; Morris 1994; Scheper-Hughes & Lock 1987; Synott 1993, pp. 7–37). Instead it sketches my own itinerary from the study of body symbolism to the uncertainties of embodiment as a crucial but precarious project of subjectivation: the incarnate subjectivity I refer to as the body-self.

Thus the review's scope is rather eclectic. To a varying degree it has been influenced by postcolonial criticism (see Fanon 1986; Mbembe 1992, 2002), Africanist anthropology (see Comaroff & Comaroff 1991, 1997; Devisch 1993; De Boeck 1996; Ranger 1993; Turner 1974; Werbner 1998), psychoanalysis (see Lichtenberg-Ettinger 1995, Grosz 1995b, Weiss 1999), feminism (Counihan 1999, Flax 1990, Haraway 1991), and (French) phenomenology and praxeology (Bourdieu 1977, 1980; Merleau-Ponty 1970; see also Jackson 1996; Csordas 1994a,b). I hope, then, to offer some sort of "social phenomenology"—to many a contradiction in terms—of which the basic premise is the idea that intersubjectivity is grounded in bodiliness or corporeality. This bodiliness, however, is that of the scarred and vulnerable body. It concerns, in the first instance, an intercorporeality (see Foster 1996).

To an important extent this perspective is also molded by my fieldwork in northwest Namibia, in an arid border region characterized by the memory of South African occupation and apartheid (1918–1990), civil war (1966–1988), and international conflict (1975–2002). Most people in this region practice a herding economy, and most refer to themselves as Himba and/or Herero. Among these herders, notions of selfhood do not refer to a psychological or biological core (ego-genes): As "bodiliness" also implies the bodies of the animals in one's herd, or the ancestors, selfhood in the first instance concerns a decentered (or ex-centric) subjectivity; it implies a body-self that originates in "outer" fields of meaning and extends in space and place, in material culture, in animals, and in the bodies of others (Van Wolputte 2004).

BODY AND SYMBOLISM

To an important extent, the history of the body (both as an object of study and as an analytical metaphor) in anthropology is a history of notions of self, person, and subject. This also means that the different bodies scholars care to distinguish and analyze reflect their concern with more encompassing social and political, or epistemological and methodological issues.

The Social Body

In social and cultural anthropology, the body was never completely absent, even if only for the fact that, implicitly, the bodiliness of the Other served as a principal marker of his or her Otherness (see De Kock 1996, McClintock 1996, Thomas 1994). But only in a few instances it gained explicit attention. Elias (1978a,b), for example, traced back the origin of the comportment and sentiment of Western civilization to its early medieval beginnings. He linked their history to the origin of the state in the centrifugal forces radiating from the feudal system in Europe. Mauss (1950, p. 379) formulated the idea that people are identified and distinguished by the way they "use" their bodies; this complex of bodily techniques he subsumed under the notion of habitus. Victor Turner (1974, pp. 55, 73–86; 1975, p. 55), in turn, amply demonstrated the bodily (or as he called it, "orectic") dimension of dominant symbols in Ndembu social life. And Douglas (1978) distinguished between the natural and the social body. Each body, she claims, is a physical entity but also is a representation; it is a medium of expression but one that is controlled and restricted by the social system. These two bodies constitute different realms of experience; they mirror the physical into the social and cause the physical to be experienced in social terms. The social body, hence, is a body of symbolic representation, a representational reality that "constrains the way the physical body is perceived" (Douglas 1978, p. 70); it refers "to the representational use of the body as a natural symbol with which to think about nature, society and culture" (Scheper-Hughes & Lock 1987, p. 7). Or, in the words of O'Neill (1985), "just as we think our society with our bodies so, too, we think our bodies with society" (p. 51). In the villages and former townships of northwestern Namibia, for instance, the animal body reflects the way people think about the human body and hence about society. So men will eat the hard parts of a sacrifice, and women and children the soft parts of the animal's body. Likewise, the way the herd is composed reflects dominant ideology regarding authority, power, gender, and seniority—regarding human relationships (see Van Wolputte 2002).

Body and Space

But Douglas' distinction, arguably, only reaffirmed the dualism of body and mind and the supremacy of the latter over the former. The 1975 Association of Social Anthropologists (ASA) conference on the anthropology of the body, for example, studied the human body as a privileged medium of expression and nonverbal communication (Blacking 1977). However, the conference responded to the need of a growing number of scholars to find a third term to mediate the conceptual gap between individual and aggregate, nature and culture, biology and sociology.

For some authors, this mediatrix was the human body. Terence Turner (1980, p. 140), for instance, demonstrates how among the Amazonian Kayapo the skin marks the boundary not only of the individual (as a biological and psychological entity) but also of the social self. Hence a social skin fashions the boundary not only between individual and other social actors, between the individual's presocial, individual drives and energies and its "internalized others," its social values, and norms, but also between groups of people, between social classes (also see Ahmed & Stacey 2001; Synott 1993).

Other writers prefer space as the third term to mediate (or interarticulate) social structure and individual agency. Hugh-Jones (1979), for example, documents in detail how spatial ordering "fits" the symbolic and social order; Moore (1996) interprets Marakwet spatial practice as the interface between ideology and history, text and context, or between actors' strategies and the "objective" social and economic conditions. She no longer considers space a reflection of social discourse. Instead, she views it as a social praxis riddled with contradiction and conflict, as much shaped by ruling ideology as it is by the practicalities (the material conditions) of everyday life. In these analyses of space the body is never far away; and some authors explicitly interpret space and time as closely related aspects of bodiliness that underpin the production of meaning (Casey 1996; Devisch 1993; Lovell 1998; see Low & Lawrence-Zúñiga 2003, pp. 2–5). Space is not a datum, but a relatum, a—bodily—relationship that for instance in Himbaland ("the land where Himba cattle graze") is associated with lineage membership, gender, and seniority, and with memory and history, ideology and hegemony, compliance but also subversion both toward local power-brokers and toward the postcolony (Lefebvre 1991).

For some scholars, space offers a way out of the subjectivism often associated with the study of the body. Jacobson-Widding (1991, pp. 15–23), for example, contrasts "body" and "space" as two different, though related, approaches to "meaning." Spatial models of the world operate according to a binary logic. They belong to the public, overt daytime realm and vehiculate a (dominant) symbolic order, a symbolic (hence logical understanding) of the world. Bodily (or triadic) models, in contrast, are part of the muted, covert, or inarticulate domain of ritual, myth, healing, and poetry. These models express (subjective) experience, phenomena, and agency, and not (objective) structures. These two logics coexist, though, and people continuously switch between body and space, dyadic and triadic models of thought.

Medical Anthropology and the Body Politic

By the mid-1980s a new subdiscipline that focused on the cultural, social, political, and historical dimensions of healing and health appeared. From this medical-anthropological perspective Scheper-Hughes & Lock (1987) launched their appeal to problematize the body in anthropology. For this purpose they distinguished three bodies, and three anthropological approaches, as well.

The individual (note this shift from the "natural") body is the domain of phenomenological analysis as it studies the "lived" or embodied experiences people have of their bodies. The social body, in contrast, relates to the ways the body (including its products: blood, milk, etc.) operates as a natural symbol, as a tool at hand to think and represent social relationships such as gender, kinship, and mode of production (see Featherstone et al. 1991). A third dimension states that power and control are embodied as well. This is the body politic: the human body as tool or weapon of domestication and disciplination and of identification, subjection, and resistance. These three bodies also constitute three levels of experience and analysis. What mediates between them, what according to the authors interarticulates nature, society, and individual, are emotions. As proto-symbols or proto-rituals emotions affect experience most immediately. Hence they can bridge the mind/body divide and bring the three bodies together (also see Lyon & Barbalet 1994).

Within this subdiscipline, scholars focused on the role and status of the body in local understandings and in so-called "traditional" healing (see Corin 1979, Koss-Chioino 1992) or on the way the body bridges or provokes the contradictions of the double bind (see Jacobson-Widding & Westerlund 1989, Taylor 1992). Influenced by Foucault, several authors questioned the social and cultural underpinnings of biomedicine and scrutinized the way the bodies of Self and Other were represented by Western ideology and technology (see, for example, Butchart 1998, Gilman 1988, Helman 1990). Alternatively, they analyzed how the body functions as the focus for disciplination strategies devised by the structures of dominance and bio-power of the West (for instance, Lyons 1992, Stalleybrass & Whyte 1986, Turner 1992, Vaughan 1991).

Others, following Bourdieu, studied the body as a medium and operator of social processes and political change. Munn (1986) concentrates on the bodily transformations effected by the circulation of Kula shells in Papua New Guinea; Jean Comaroff (1985a,b), in turn, studies how history and relations of power are mediated through social practice, notably through bodily symbolism. Just as the evangelization of the southern African interior puts central focus on the body, so do the Zionist churches of the South African Tshidi. In a context of apartheid and oppression, these churches address the experiential conflict of their members; they achieve healing through manipulating symbols so as to alter the state of the physical and social body. An outcome of a process of simultaneous reproduction and transformation, Zionist healing also implies a powerful social and political critique. It embodies a form of resistance that on the surface, however, and for obvious reasons, presents itself as apolitical. This kind of praxical and not discursive resistance may not directly confront the forces of domination: It defies the penetration of the hegemonic system into the structures of the natural world, of everyday life. Likewise, resistance against indirect rule in northwestern Namibia targeted in the first instance the state veterinarians and apartheid livestock policy. Through their animals rather than through armed rebellion people confined state power to certain, well-defined areas of life.

Studies such as these provide an unsettling critique of the Western civilizing mission. They reveal, among others, the striking parallels between the colonization of consciousness both in the colony and at home, and between the domestication of bodies whether female, laboring, or black (see Comaroff & Comaroff 1991, McClintock 1996).

Antibodies

In a provocative essay Terence Turner (1994) warns against those poststructuralist approaches that, not unlike Foucault himself, strongly oppose the bodily realm to the discursive exercise of power. Thus in equating bodiliness with the subjective experience of pleasure and pain they reduce it to individual sexuality and desire in order to, subsequently, neglect it (Brown 1988, Johnson 1987, Le Breton 1990, Martin 1992). This body, according to Turner, appears as distant, abstract, ahistorical, and self-contained as the Foucaultian concept of Power, of which it is the product and object (see Foucault 1986). This Foucaultian body concerns, ironically, a conceptual body, a disembodied subject. Turner (1994, p. 47) therefore coins it an antibody, a defensive organism that protects rather than questions mainstream Western philosophy and political thought by emphasizing the private and individualistic dimensions of bodiliness at the expense of its plural and relational aspects. Similar critiques (namely, that the turn toward the body remained embedded in a representationalist paradigm; that most scholars regarded the body solely as an outcome, and not as agent of social praxis; that bodiliness was reduced to physical properties; that all too often the body was considered an empty box or as a mere tool for the mind; and that the saliency of the body in contemporary debate reflected the centrality of a consumerist and medicalist representation of the body in social theory) were formulated by Benoist & Cathebras (1993), Csordas (1994b, p. 6), Devisch (1993, p. 43), Frank (1990), Jackson (1996, p. 2), Lyon & Barbalet (1994, p. 54), and Kirmayer (1992, p. 331). The body as understood by Turner (1994, p. 28) is, in the first instance, a relationship. It is both subjective and objective, meaningful and material, personal and social, and can be considered the "material infrastructure" of the production of selves, belonging, and identities.

EMBODIMENT AND PRAXIS

Bourdieu (1977, 1980) tried to answer similar questions when he argued that social action is governed by a hazy logic of approximation. This logic is operated by the habitus, the socially informed body, history turned into nature, or society embodied (Bourdieu 1977, p. 82; Mauss 1950, p. 368). It is subjective but not individual (because it is shared by members of the same social group or class), and it results in an immediate adhesion (*doxa*) to the world understood as "an endless circle of mutually reflecting metaphors" (Bourdieu 1977, p. 91). This unquestioned but not unquestionable acceptance of the world is a state of the body (Bourdieu 1980, p. 115). Bourdieu maintained that his approach moves from social facts to the process of the social facts' (re)production, from organism to embodiment. But his critics claim that he takes embodiment for granted and mistakes it for bodiliness (see, for example, Comaroff 1985a, p. 7; Lyon & Barthelet 1994, p. 50).

Body and Metaphor

Metaphor and metonymy also were forwarded as bodily alternatives to the "cognitive crystallography" of mainstream (post)structuralist approaches (Kirmayer 1992, p. 331; see Fernandez 1986; Jackson 1983). Some writers say these terms move beyond the symbolic order, beyond cognition and discourse. As Kirmayer

(1992, pp. 333, 337) shows, metaphors are extrarational and are tools not only to think, but especially to work with experience. They belong to the realm of praxis (and not of cognition) and suggest instead of conceive, elicit instead of define, or provoke instead of prescribe. At the same time, they are rooted in bodily (sensuous) experience, especially in the sense of touch that in more psychoanalytic approaches is put forward as the source of self (Anzieu 1985, see Brazelton 1990). And likewise, writers on this subject understand trauma and the violation of bodily boundaries as major sources of "unmaking" the self (see Scarry 1985, Favazza 1987).

Paraphrasing Winnicot (1989), metaphors are "the imaginative elaboration around bodily functions" (pp. 60, 205), and this bodiliness gives them a certain thickness and contiguity. However, their meaning is not bound by symbolic conventions (Devisch 1993, pp. 276–77); metaphors link one domain of experience to another, but this linking could both generate and cloud understanding—they do not have a mission (see Fernandez 1986, pp. 235–36). On the contrary, they create "an abundance of possible meanings" (De Boeck 1994, p. 468) and expand simultaneously in all directions. Nevertheless they produce effect, an efficacy that one can attribute to the fact that metaphors address both bodily and social experience (Kirmayer 1993, p. 184). Meaning is or can be bodily felt all over the world: For instance, Western pharmaceuticals convey a certain view of world and man; they (re)present a certain power and technology and metaphorize both the illness and a concrete way of addressing it. This not only accounts for their popularity but also in part explains why they work (Van der Geest & Whyte 1991, p. 353; see Helman 1990). Meanings are not only representational; they are or may be presentational also—embodied. Among the Himba, for instance, ancestors are embodied—remembered—by the particular diet of each patriclan; in the interdiction to mention one's fathers or husband by name; in the herd, in particular by the animals carrying their names; in the pastures and water holes claimed by the lineage and given by the ancestors' journey; in garments, hairstyle, and finery, or in the cooked butter with which women and men cover their bodies. Ancestors are intrinsically part of daily life and society.

Bodies and Embodiment

Emphasis on the body (and, arguably, embodiment) as the source of meaning is one of the things Merleau-Ponty and Bourdieu have in common (see Marcoulatos 2001). Advancing this point, Csordas (1990, p. 5) argues that the body should not be considered as an object but as the subject—the existential ground—of culture and that the latter should be studied by focusing on embodiment. In his study of healing among North American Charismatic Christians, for instance, Csordas (1994a) discusses glossolalia (speaking in tongues) as a ritual language that goes beyond or leaves behind the semantics of common language, that by most participants is experienced as inadequate to communicate with the divine. Speaking in tongues evokes (embodied) images that are further elaborated in vernacular speech—discursive thought—and participants in charismatic faith healing, typically and without effort switch back and forth between the two. Speaking in tongues creates belonging: As a verbal gesture it opens up the world of the sacred that, like ritual language, is a gift from God (Csordas 1990, pp. 25–26). Csordas also distinguishes, for example, between the demon as a cultural form or object, taking a place in an elaborate demonology that in itself is read as a moral statement, and behavior, thoughts or emotions—embodied distress—experienced as "out of control," as a "lived" manifestation of "evil" (Csordas 1994a, pp. 171–76).

Embodiment, says Csordas, is situated on the level of lived experience and not on that of discourse; embodiment is about "understanding" or "making sense" in a prereflexive or even presymbolic, but not precultural, way (Csordas 1990, p. 10). It precedes objectivation and representation and is intrinsically part of our being-in-the-world. As such it collapses the difference between subjective and objective, cognition and emotion, or mind and body (Csordas 1994a, p. 276).

Thus, for example, the garments and finery of members of the Herero "flags" (or social groupings) in Namibia and Botswana prove to be important markers and makers of individual and group identity. Scarfs, flags, and uniforms embody (and not merely represent) belonging; they make some body part of a larger social and moral community; as such they could (and can) forge the Herero into a political force during and after apartheid (Hendricksson 1996). Likewise, Africanist anthropology understands witchcraft or divination as an embodied epistemology, as knowledge-in-action that is the basis of social practice and world-making (De Boeck 1994, Peek 1991). Lan (1985), for instance, describes how spirit mediums in Zimbabwe effected political change and revolution by mobilizing the spirits of the royal ancestors—the bringers of rain and the original and legitimate owners of the land—for the independence struggle.

The occult, indeed, also manifests itself as a "lived" social and political commentary: Geschiere (1997, pp. 199, 212) documents how witchcraft practices embody a deeply rooted distrust toward the postcolony and its representatives. However, witchcraft discourse also is a tool to safeguard and fence off personal profits and political influence by the postcolonial elite. Witchcraft is ambiguous because power itself is experienced as such. In a similar vein, Mbembe (1992) forwards the body and embodiment as the playground of both oppression and resistance: Both the postcolonial state and its subjects indulge in a grotesque and obscene bodiliness that dissolves the boundaries between rulers and ruled, the powerful and powerless, the hegemonical and the counterhegemonical (see also Comaroff 1985b; Stallybrass & White 1986, pp. 138–48). Comaroff & Comaroff (1991, 1997) illustrate how these same ready-made dichotomies are challenged by microhistories and local experiences.

Ultimately, these highly contradictory and paradoxical processes of change, rupture, and transformation revolve around notions and experiences of space, time, body, self, and identity (see Fardon 1995, Werbner 1996). Boddy (1989), for example, studies female possession in the Zar cult in North Sudan as a form of embodied resistance or counterhegemonic practice. In the experience and performance of trance, women are brought into touch with their different selves and their non-selves, while the trance unlocks the dominant categories of gender, ethnicity, status, or religion (see also Comaroff 1985b). Hunt (1999), in turn, offers a microhistory of the medicalization of childbirth in the Democratic Republic of Congo and the way it effected the bodies of African women. In the first place, she focuses not on colonial discourse and on docile bodies, but on the way colonial power was mediated, translated, and transformed through obstetric practices and the female body (see also Whittaker 2001). And Counihan (1999) illustrates that in Sardinia and the United States the relation between gender and the production and consumption of food exemplifies cultural questions of power and control. Female identities are embodied in food practices; whereas thinness in dominant Western (and, increasingly, global) discourse is promoted as a symbol of self-control and power, however, the eating body may also manifest self-empowerment.

Embodiment and Intersubjectivity

These studies have in common the idea that the body unlocks a moral universe that often escapes social (symbolic) discourse. From this perspective, embodiment is not solely the source of self and subjectivity. Weiss (1999), for instance, explicitly forwards embodiment as a precondition for intersubjectivity, which she in the first instance conceives as an intercorporeality (see also Ahmed & Stacey 2001). This fundamental exchange between bodies is vested in the inherent multiplicity and indeterminacy of the body we have and are. Moreover, and paradoxically, this possibility of moving from one body (or body-image) to another may cause a more-or-less coherent sense of self to develop: This very flexibility and fluidity, this indeterminacy or metaphoric character of embodiment (see above), enables the self to engage in a wide variety of contexts and relationships (Weiss 1999, pp. 83, 166–167). In a similar vein, Grosz (1995b, pp. 32–36) notes that embodiment is made possible through the corporeality of the Other, how it originates in sources outside the self. In psychoanalysis as well feminist critics expose the centrality of the phallus and the fear of castration of the dominant patriarchic paradigm (see McClintock 1996). Lichtenberg-Ettinger (1995, pp. 15, 28), for instance, proposes the matrix (or womb) as an alternative, complementary way of entering the symbolic or imaginary realm. Against the fantasy of castration, she places the matrixial fantasy (Freud's *Mutterleibsphantasie*) that refers neither to absence nor to separation but to "relational difference in coemergence," to experience and subjectivation. In a sense, one can regard this matrix as complementary to the habitus: It is memory, not history, turned into nature (Bourdieu 1977, p. 82; see above).

This shift in social and cultural anthropology from symbol to metaphor, sign to signification, or meaning to sense marks the possibility of giving ambiguity and indeterminacy, nonfixity and indirection, irony and paradox, or contradiction and ambivalence (elements that do not fit the orthodox symbolic order) a place in anthropological theory and praxis. It also leads away from the dominant groups (in particular, the elders and ritual specialists in control of social discourse) in society. Moreover, it implies the abandonment of an almost exclusive focus on localized, bounded-off communities to more overarching or encompassing processes of globalization and marginalization, identity building, creolization, counterhegemony, commodification, or violence.

The shift brings with it also a renewed emphasis on the quotidian, on the daily experience (the doxa), of common people. But in postcolonial Africa, says Richard Werbner (1998), this "silent" experience of the world is, to an increasing extent, in crisis as daily life loses its taken-for-grantedness and the traces—the scars—left on the body and in the landscape continue to betray an often-untold history of violence and shattered identification (Devisch 1996). This crisis of the quotidian reveals also a crisis of memory. As memory practices—embodied memory—have become contested, so too the moral horizon along which self and subjectivity unfold has become insecure (see Battaglia 1995b; Das & Kleinman 2000, pp. 7–9; Scheper-Hughes 1992; Stoller 1994). That said, the quotidian is being bracketed by dissimulation: Daily upheaval and alienation are mastered by dissimulating them. Indeed, as Fernandez & Huber (2001, pp. 4, 18) remind us, ours is an age of irony (see also Strathern 1995). In this context, irony is a tool of the moral imagination, a way of questioning hegemony and fighting subordination (see Scott 1985). The question remains whether irony makes a material difference, or whether, ironically, it only perpetuates the existing (political, economic, etc.) discrepancies. In popular imagination, for example, the inhabitants of northwestern Namibia are described as natural-born conservatives. Most of them know that they are rewarded for behaving that way, i.e., "traditionally," in the past by the apartheid government and nowadays by the tourist industry in its quest for authenticity. Thus the irony appears: By mocking and subverting the Western stereotype of Otherness it is being confirmed and strengthened.

To the extent that each theory of meaning also implies a theory or critique of power (see Parkin 1982, p. xlvi; Arens & Karp 1989) the notion of power also has become dispersed or decentered; it is found to be polycentric and ambiguous, contradictory and uncertain. This subjunctivity is what I, following Flax's (1990, p. 222) lead, consider the material object of contemporary semantic anthropology: not to solve these contradictions, paradoxes, and uncertainties but to trace and expose them (Whyte 2002, p. 175). In this idea, the human body emerges as the meeting ground of both hegemony and counterhegemonic practices, power and defiance, authority and subversion. This body, though, extends far beyond the human organism, in space and time, in animals or in things (see Warnier 2004).

SELVES AND SUBJECTIVITY

Irony, parody, memory, moral imagination, and narrative—the list is incomplete—can be considered processes (and technologies) of self. Revolving around embodiment, they involve "individual" experience, but also, "always-already," imply intersubjectivity. Or, as Mead (1974) notes: "[W]e cannot be ourselves unless we are also members" (p. 163). He pointed out that a self is a social structure and process that arises in and from social experience, that it involves the body, and that the self—the generalized Other—is multiple or composite (Mead 1974, pp. 136–42; see Turner 1995). In northern Namibia, for example, selves—each with their own voices, memories, and history—are associated with different places and spaces (for example, with homestead and cattle post, village and town), periods of time (such as the rainy and dry seasons), or with different animals in the herd. They are exemplified by the garments and finery one wears. But one's dress also inscribes women and men in the history of the lineage, as aprons, bracelets, etc. are inherited and circulated through the lineage. These things forward an inter-corporeality that, at least in northern Namibia, implies not only the ancestors and one's descendants, but also the animals at the center of the homestead and of daily life.

Whereas psychological approaches place heavy emphasis on the antagonism between the "individual" and "collective" representations of self and the effects they have on the way selfhood is represented and experienced (see Sedikides & Brewer 2001), other investigators understand it as primarily the capacity for self-reflexivity and self-consciousness (De Vos et al. 1985), as a reflexive project (Giddens 1991), or as a tendency to organize and offer structure and continuity to experience (Morris 1994). And the more phenomenological approach of Csordas (1994a, p. 9) understands the self as an indeterminate process to engage or become oriented in the world; it is a whole of processes in which aspects of the world are thematized into different Gestalts and, next, represented (objectified) as a person with one or many identities. He portrays the self as indeterminate and inherently metaphorical; it appears through the interaction (embodiment) between bodily experience, cultural milieu, or world and habitus (see above; Csordas 1994a, p. 15). It is this incarnate subjectivity I refer to as the body-self (Langer 1989, p. 53; Merleau-Ponty 1970; see Anzieu 1985, Devisch 1993, Scheper-Hughes & Lock 1987, Winnicot 1989).

These authors draw attention to the self as an embodied and contextual, but also practical knowledge process [in the sense of "knowledge-at-hand" (Schütz 1962)]. This means that they do not focus on the question, "What is self?" Rather, they try to document how people create or maintain a sense of self and belonging and how this "becoming" is permeated with questions of hegemony and power (see Nast 1998, 96).

As Battaglia (1995a, pp. 3, 7) reminds us, the image of an unchanging and "universal" self is part of Western dominant ideology that associates individuality with modernization and a sociocentric personality with either traditionalism or nostalgia. Sökefeld (1999, p. 418), too, notes that the non-Western self is often conceptualized as the opposite of the bounded, autonomous, reflexive, and inde-pendent Western self and, consequently, that anthropology denies the possibility of self in the Other. It is therefore important to distinguish between, on the one hand, the self as an embodied process of self-making, of becoming (the body-self), and, on the other hand, the socially sanctioned self-image or representational Self. Dominant ideology could, for instance, promote a "transcendent self" or even the absence of self, a nonself (see De Vos et al. 1985). In this regard, Karp (1990, p. 90) points to what he terms "the paradox of agency." Studying Iteso spirit possession in Kenya he concludes that when agency is denied, as when the woman's body is taken over by the spirit, this female body becomes the most powerful locus of agency: By surrendering her self and body the "victim" suddenly finds herself in the center of power and once again in control of her life. Larsen (1998) makes a similar point by documenting how women and men in Zanzibar become identified (or localized) through their association with a spirit that, other than people, has a distinctive identity and a specific association with a place.

Fragmentation and Vulnerability

Directly and indirectly, studies such as these also question the unity and indivisibility (the atomic character) of the body-self. Whereas in the West multiple selves traditionally have been associated with pathologies such as schizophrenia or multiple personality disorder, the ethnographic record documents many instances where dominant ideology does promote a multiple Self (see Cohen 1998, pp. 12–13; Scheper-Hughes & Lock 1987, pp. 15–16). In Europe and North America as well, ideas and experiences regarding the in/dividual and self are subject to profound change.

Jameson (1991, p. 26) argues that the alienation and havoc brought about by late capitalism has resulted in a fragmented (and false) consciousness in the West. Postmodern culture (novels, movies, etc.), he says, testifies to this "schizophrenic" self characterized by information overload and the absence of an overarching narrative. According to him, this end of a coherent self or centered subject also means the end of individual expression and feelings and emotions. In a similar vein, Littlewood (1997) suggests that postmodernity and globalization have instigated an epidemic of multiple personality disorder in North America. The question he raises is whether this pluralism of the self reflects a new "idiom of distress," the pathology of postmodernism as informed and inspired by new information technologies and cyberspace; whether it embodies a new discourse on and model of self and subselves, an increasing fragmentation of self under the influence of the breakdown of the grand metanarratives; or, in contrast, a new technology to represent, incorporate, and master the Other in the form of serially accessed identities (or alters), a further step toward enhanced self-awareness.

This fragmentation (or dislocation, perhaps) of the self is illustrated by Strauss (1997, p. 369). She interviewed a number of Rhode Island (sub)urbanites in the wake of the closure of a major chemical plant and documents how people talk in different voices, with each voice referring to a set of metaphoric imagery and emotional valence. This fragmentation, though, is not total: According to Strauss, some integration is achieved through emotions, often associated with (the memory of) early life experiences. Ochs & Capps (1996, p. 22), in turn, put forward narrative as an important way to both evoke and partly integrate these fragmentary selves. They suggest that this fragmentation can take place along many axes, such as past and present, male and female, or public and private. And to an important extent this questioning of the self also implies the self of the ethnographer. For instance, in a challenging essay Rambo Ronai (1992, p. 122) points out the conflicts and fragmentation she experienced between her being a dancer, participant observer, student, wife, and author of the narrative (an "emotional striptease") that was meant to reassemble her self (also see Josephides 1997, p. 21; Kulich & Willson 1995). In the mountains of northern Namibia, too, this dividuality and fragmentation of the body-self may be partly and temporarily overcome during rituals and other emotionally charged events such as birth giving or death. This integration, however, is neither logical nor complete: It is associative, metaphoric, and "matrixial."

We all are Creoles of sorts: hybrid, divided, polyphonic, and parodic—a pastiche of our Selves. This contemporary body-self is fragmentary, often incoherent and inconsistent, precisely because it arises from contradictory and paradoxical experiences, social tensions, and conflicts that have one thing in common: They are real, that is, experienced. Therefore, the anthropology of the body focuses no longer on the abstract or ideal(ized) body, but on those moments during which the body and bodiliness are questioned and lose their self-evidence and on the experience or threat of finiteness, limitation, transience, and vulnerability. These embodied uncertainties do indeed challenge the autonomy of the in/dividual insofar as they no longer appear as a lack or deficiency, but instead as an existential characteristic of the human condition and as an ethical challenge (Shildrick 2002). It can thus be argued that it is through fragmentation that the sometimes violent rupture between experience and discourse, and objective and symbolic reality can be overcome, and a sense of belonging achieved.

CONCLUDING REMARKS

Is, as Jameson holds, a fragmentary or conflictual body-self particular to late capitalism, to postmodernism, or postcolonial disenchantment? Or are we dealing with a new academic paradigm and social discourse of self in the West? Does recognizing the existential eccentricity—the decentered subjectivity—and fragmentary character of the body-self mean it was not there before? And, to the extent that Western hegemony is based in and legitimated by the idea of an inalienable physical or psychological core, does not this mere recognition already jeopardize dominant modernist discourse and ideology (Weiss 1999, p. 168)? Haraway (1991), for example, stages the cyborg as a challenge to established power relations. The man/machine, as carnate hybridity, blends nature and civilization, organism and technology, male and female; thus the cyborg also is a parody to the themes and archetypes of modernist discourse. But is, as Moreiras (1999, p. 396) suggests, the political prize of this hybridity to resign to one's subaltern position vis-à-vis Euro-American hegemony and subjectivation?

In today's context the body is no longer given. On the one hand, it is a canvas on which major cultural, social, and political changes are projected. On the other hand, it is a (if not the) major focus and objective of these changes. In the West as elsewhere, traditional boundaries (between individual and society, public and private, nature and culture, masculine and feminine) have become insecure, but is the fear of change not something of all times and places? Distances have narrowed, and remoteness in space has evolved into a remoteness in time (Grosz 1995a, p. 49). For those who can afford it, the body is fully customizable and adaptable, whether through tattoos, piercings, branding, liposuction, or cosmetic surgery. And although identity is considered conterminous with lifestyle, a commodity to be purchased, dominant ideology promotes looking young and beautiful ("californication") as a way of being healthy, successful, and morally right (see Brodwin 2000).

I do not think this fragmentation and decentralization, or at least its recognition in the West, means that the West has lost its Self. On the contrary, in a context of globalization—a process of increasing compartmentalization—it asserts its hegemony stronger than ever before. This constitutes a fundamental paradox, namely that the awareness of fragmentation and multiplicity brings with it a stronger emphasis on an ideology that denies it. This political discourse has every interest in symbolically representing the person as indivisible and "one."

ACKNOWLEDGMENTS

I acknowledge the friendship and assistance of Mungandjo Kasanga. I also thank Rene Devisch, Filip De Boeck, and Peter Crossman for their suggestions and critical comments on earlier drafts. Of course, all mistakes and shortcomings are mine.

The *Annual Review of Anthropology* is online at http://anthro.annualreviews.org

LITERATURE CITED

Ahmed S, Stacey J. 2001. Introduction: dermographies. In *Thinking Through the Skin*, ed. S Ahmed, J Stacey, pp. 1–17. London: Routledge

Anzieu D. 1985. *Le Moi-Peau*. Paris: Dunod

Arens W, Karp I. 1989. Introduction. In *Creativity of Power: Cosmology and Action in African Societies*, ed. W Arens, I Karp, pp. xi–ixxx. Washington: Smithsonian Inst. Press

Battaglia D. 1995a. Problematizing the self: a thematic introduction. See Battaglia 1995b, pp. 1–15

Battaglia D, ed. 1995b. *Rhetorics of Self-Making*. Berkeley: Univ. Calif. Press

Benoist J, Cathebras P. 1993. The body: from an immateriality to another. *Soc. Sci. Med.* 36(7):857–66

Blacking J. 1977. Towards an anthropology of the body. In *The Anthropology of the Body. A.S.A. monograph 15*, ed. J Blacking, pp. 1–28. London: Academic

Boddy J. 1989. *Wombs and Alien Spirits: Women, Men, and the Zar Cult in Northern Sudan*. Madison: Univ. Wis. Press

Bourdieu P. 1977. *Esquisse d'Une Théorie*

de la Pratique. Précédé de Trois Études d'Ethnologie Kabyle. Genève: Dros

Bourdieu P. 1980. Le Sens Pratique. Paris: Editions Minuit

Brazelton TB. 1990. Touch as touchstone: summary of the round table. In Touch: the Foundation of Experience, ed. KA Barnard, TB Brazelton, pp. 561–66. Madison, CT: Int. Univ. Press

Brodwin PE, ed. 2000. Biotechnology and Culture. Bodies, Anxieties, Ethics. Bloomington, IN: Indiana Univ. Press

Brown P. 1988. The Body and Society. New York: Columbia Univ. Press

Butchart A. 1998. The Anatomy of Power. European Constructions of the African Body. London: Zed

Casey ES. 1996. How to get from space to place in a fairly short stretch of time. In Senses of Place, ed. S Feld, KH Basso, pp. 13–52. Santa Fe: Sch. Am. Res. Press

Cohen AP. 1998 [1994]. Self Consciousness. An Alternative Anthropology of Identity. London: Routledge

Comaroff J. 1985a. Body of Power, Spirit of Resistance. The Culture and History of a South African People. Chicago: Univ. Chicago Press

Comaroff J. 1985b. Bodily reform as historical practice: the semantics of resistance in modern South Africa. Int. J. Psychol. 20(4–5):541–68

Comaroff J, Comaroff JL. 1991. Of Revelation and Revolution, Volume One. Christianity, Colonialism and Consciousness in South Africa. Chicago: Univ. Chicago Press

Comaroff JL, Comaroff J. 1997. Of Revelation and Revolution, Volume Two. The Dialectics of Modernity on a South African Frontier. Chicago: Univ. Chicago Press

Corin E. 1979. A possession therapy in an urban setting: Zebola in Kinshasa. Soc. Sci. Med. 13B:327–38

Counihan CM. 1999. The Anthropology of Food and Body. Gender, Meaning, and Power. New York: Routledge

Csordas TJ. 1990. Embodiment as a paradigm for anthropology. Ethos 18:5–47

Csordas TJ. 1994a. The Sacred Self. A Cultural Phenomenology of Charismatic Healing. Berkeley: Univ. Calif. Press

Csordas TJ. 1994b. Introduction: the body as representation and being-in-the world. See Csordas 1994c, pp. 1–26

Csordas TJ, ed. 1994c. Embodiment and Experience. The Existential Ground of Culture and Self. Cambridge, UK: Cambridge Univ. Press

Csordas TJ. 1999. The body's career in anthropology. In Anthropological Theory Today, ed. H Moore, pp. 172–205. Cambridge, UK: Polity

Das V, Kleinman A. 2000. Introduction. In Violence and Subjectivity, ed. V Das, A Kleinman, M Ramphele, P Reynolds, pp. 1–18. Berkeley: Univ. Calif. Press

De Boeck F. 1994. Of trees and kings: politics and metaphor among the Aluund of Southwestern Zaire. Am. Ethnol. 21(3):451–73

De Boeck F. 1996. Postcolonialism, power and identity: local and global perspectives from Zaire. In Postcolonial Identities in Africa, ed. RP Werbner, TO Ranger, pp. 75–106. London: Zed

De Kock L. 1996. Civilising Barbarians. Missionary Narrative and African Textual Response in Nineteenth-Century South Africa. Johannesburg: Witwatersrand Univ. Press

Devisch R. 1993. Weaving the Threads of Life. The Khita Gyn-eco-logical Cult Among the Yaka. Chicago: Univ. Chicago Press

Devisch R. 1996. 'Pillaging Jesus': healing churches and the villagisation of Kinshasa. Africa 66(4):555–86

DeVos G, Marsella A, Hsu F. 1985. Introduction: approaches to culture and self. See Marsella et al. 1985, pp. 2–23

Douglas M. 1978 [1970]. Natural Symbols. New York: Praeger

Elias N. 1978a. The Civilizing Process 1: The History of Manners. Oxford: Blackwell

Elias N. 1978b. The Civilizing Process 2: State Formation and Civilization. Oxford: Blackwell

Fanon F. 1986 [1967]. Black Skin, White Masks. London: Pluto

Fardon R. 1995. Introduction: counterworks. In *Counterworks: Managing the Diversity of Knowledge*, ed. R Fardon, pp. 1–23. London: Routledge

Farnell B. 1999. Moving bodies, acting selves. *Annu. Rev. Anthropol.* 28:341–73

Favazza AR. 1987. *Bodies Under Siege: Self-Mutilation in Culture and Psychiatry*. Baltimore, MD: John Hopkins Univ. Press

Featherstone M, Hepworth M, Turner BS, eds. 1991. *The Body, Social Process and Cultural Theory*. London: Sage

Fernandez JW. 1986. *Persuasions and Performances. The Play of Tropes in Culture*. Bloomington: Indiana Univ. Press

Fernandez JW, Huber MT. 2001. Introduction: the anthropology of irony. In *Irony in Action. Anthropology, Practice and the Moral Imagination*, ed. JW Fernandez, MT Huber, pp. 1–40. Chicago: Univ. Chicago Press

Flax J. 1990. *Thinking Fragments. Psychoanalysis, Feminism and Postmodernism in the Contemporary West*. Berkeley: Univ. Calif. Press

Foster S, ed. 1996. *Corporealities: Dancing Knowledge, Culture and Power*. New York: Routledge

Foucault M. 1986. *The History of Sexuality, 3: The Care of the Self*. Transl. R Hurley. New York: Pantheon

Frank AW. 1990. Bringing bodies back in: a decade review. *Theory, Cult. Soc.* 7:131–62

Geschiere P. 1997. *The Modernity of Witchcraft. Politics and the Occult in Postcolonial Africa*. Charlottesville/London: Univ. Press Virginia

Geurts KL. 2002. *Culture and the Senses: Embodiment, Identity and Well-Being in an African Community. Ethnographic Studies in Intersubjectivity*. Berkeley: Univ. Calif. Press

Giddens A. 1991. *Modernity and Self Identity: Self and Society in the Late Modern Age*. Cambridge, UK: Polity

Gilman S. 1985. *Difference and Pathology: Stereotypes of Sexuality, Race and Madness*. New York: Ithaca

Grosz E. 1995a. Bodies-cities. In *Places Through the Body*, ed. H Nast, S Pile, pp. 42–51. Princeton: Princeton Arch. Press

Grosz E. 1995b. *Space, Time and Perversion: Essays on the Politics of Bodies*. New York: Routledge

Harraway D. 1991. *Simians, Cyborgs and Women: The Reinvention of Nature*. New York: Routledge

Helman CG. 1990 [1984]. *Culture, Health and Illness: An Introduction for Health Professionals*. London: Wright

Hendrickson H. 1996. Bodies and flags: the representation of Herero identity in colonial Namibia. In *Clothing and Difference. Embodied Identities in Colonial and Post-Colonial Africa*, ed. H Hendrickson, pp. 213–44. Durham, NC: Duke Univ. Press

Hugh-Jones C. 1979. *From the Milk River: Spatial and Temporal Processes in Northwest Amazonia*. Cambridge: Cambridge Univ. Press

Hunt NR. 1999. *A Colonial Lexicon of Birth Ritual, Medicalization and Mobility in the Congo. Body, Commodity, Text*. Durham, NC: Duke Univ. Press

Ingstad B, Whyte SR, eds. 1995. *Disability and Culture*. Berkeley: Univ. Calif. Press

Jackson M. 1983. Thinking through the body: an essay on understanding metaphor. *Soc. Anal.* 14:127–49

Jackson M. 1996. Introduction: phenomenology, radical empiricism and anthropological critique. In *Things as They Are: New Directions in Phenomenological Anthropology*, ed. M Jackson, pp. 1–50. Bloomington: Indiana Univ. Press

Jacobson-Widding A. 1991. Subjective body, objective space –an introduction. In *Body and Space. Symbolic Models of Unity and Division in African Cosmology and Experience*, ed. A Jacobson-Widding, pp. 15–50. Stockholm: Almqvist & Wicksell

Jacobson-Widding A, Westerlund D. 1989. *Culture, Experience and Pluralism. Essays on African Ideas of Illness and Healing. Acta Universalis Upssaliensis. Uppsula Studies in Cultural Anthropology 13*. Stockholm: Almqvist & Wichsel

Jameson F. 1997 [1991]. *Postmodernism, or, the Cultural Logic of Late Capitalism. Post Contemporary Interventions*. Durham, NC: Duke Univ. Press

Johnson M. 1987. *The Body in the Mind: The Bodily Basis of Meaning, Imagination and Reason*. Chicago: Univ. Chicago Press

Johnson M. 1985. The western concept of self. See Marsella et al. 1985, pp. 91–138

Josephides L. 1997. Representing the anthropologist's predicament. In *After Writing Culture. Epistemology and Praxis in Contemporary Anthropology. ASA Monographs 34*, ed. A James, J Hockey, A Dawson, pp. 16–33. London/New York: Routledge

Karp I. 1990. Power and capacity in Iteso rituals of possession. In *Personhood and Agency. The Experience of Self and Other in African Cultures. Uppsala Studies in Cultural Anthropology 14*, ed. M Jackson, I Karp, pp. 79–94. Stockholm: Almqvist och Wiksell

Kirmayer LJ. 1992. The body's insistence on meaning: metaphor as presentation in illness experience. *Med. Anthropol. Q.* 6(4):323–47

Kirmayer LJ. 1993. Healing and the invention of metaphor: the effectiveness of symbols revisited. *Cult. Med. Psychiatry* 17(2):161–95

Koss-Chioino J. 1992. *Women as Healers, Women as Patients. Mental Health Care and Traditional Healing in Puerto Rico*. Boulder/San Francisco/Oxford: Westview

Kulich D, Willson M, eds. 1995. *Taboo. Sex, Identity and Erotic Subjectivity in Anthropological Fieldwork*. London: Routledge

Lan D. 1985. *Guns and Rain. Guerillas and Spirit Mediums in Zimbabwe*. London: Currey

Langer MM. 1989. *Merleau-Ponty's Phenomenology of Perception. A Guide and Commentary*. Tallahassee: Fla. State Univ. Press

Larsen K. 1998. Spirit possession as historical narrative: the production of identity and locality in Zanzibar town. In *Locality and Belonging*, ed. N Lovell, pp. 125–146. London: Routledge

Le Breton D. 1990. *Anthropologie du Corps et Modernité*. Paris: Press. Univ. Fr.

Lefebvre H. 1991. *The Production of Space*. Oxford: Blackwell

Lichtenberg-Ettinger B. 1995. *The Matrixial Gaze*. Leeds, UK: Univ. Leeds, Dep. Fine Arts, Fem. Arts Hist. Netw.

Littlewood R. 1997. Agency and its vicissitudes: the pathologies of the future. *Transcult. Psychiatry* 34(1):78–90

Lock M. 1993. Cultivating the body: anthropology and epistemologies of bodily practice and knowledge. *Annu. Rev. Anthropol.* 22:133–55

Lovell N, ed. 1998. *Locality and Belonging*. London: Routledge

Low SM, Lawrence-Zúniga D, eds. 2003. *The Anthropology of Space and Place: Locating Culture. Blackwell Readers in Anthropology 4*. Oxford: Blackwell

Lyons M. 1992. *The Colonial Disease. A Social History of Sleeping Sickness in Northern Zaire, 1900–1940*. Cambridge: Cambridge Univ. Press

Lyon ML, Barbalet J-M. 1994. Society's body: emotion and the "somatization" of social theory. See Csordas 1994c, pp. 48–66

Marcoulatos I. 2001. Merleau-Ponty and Bourdieu on embodied significance. *J. Theory Soc. Behav.* 31(1):1–28

Marsella AJ, DeVos G, Hsu FLK, eds. 1985. *Culture and Self. Asian and Western Perspectives*. New York: Tavistock

Martin E. 1992. The end of the body? *Am. Ethnol.* 19:121–40

Mauss M. 1950. Les techniques du corps. In *Sociologie et Anthropologie*, ed. M Mauss, 363–86. Paris: Press. Univ. Fr.

Mbembe A. 1992. Provisional notes on the postcolony. *Africa* 62 (1):3–37

Mbembe A. 2002. African modes of self-writing. Transl. S Rendall. *Publ. Cult.* 14(1): 239–73

McClintock A. 1996. *Imperial Leather. Race, Gender, and Sexuality in the Colonial Contest*. New York: Routledge

Mead GH. 1974. *Mind Self and Society*. Chicago: Univ. Chicago Press

Merleau-Ponty M. 1970. *Phenomenology of Perception.* London: Routledge & Kegan Paul

Moore HL. 1996a. *Space, Text and gender. An Anthropological Study of the Marakwet of Kenya.* New York: Guilford

Moreiras A. 1999. Hybridity and double consciousness. *Cult. Stud.* 13 (3):373–407

Morris B. 1994. *Anthropology of the Self: The Individual in Cultural Perspective. Anthropology, Culture and Society.* London: Pluto

Munn N. 1986. *The Fame of Gawa. A Symbolic Study of Value Transformation in a Massim (Papua New Guuinea) Society.* Oxford: Oxford Univ. Press

Nast HJ. 1998. The body as "place": reflexivity and fieldwork in Kano, Nigeria. See Nast & Pile, pp. 93–115. London/New York: Routledge

Nast HJ, Pile S, eds. 1998. *Places Through the Body.* London: Routledge

O'Neill J. 1985. *Five Bodies: The Human Shape of Modern Society.* Ithaca/New York: Cornell Univ. Press

Ochs E, Capps L. 1996. Narrating the self. *Annu. Rev. Anthropol.* 25:19–43

Parkin D. 1982. *Semantic Anthropology. ASA Monograph 22.* London/New York: Academic

Peek PM, ed. 1991. *African Divination Systems: Ways of Knowing.* Bloomington: Indiana Univ. Press

Rambo Ronai C. 1992. The reflexive self through narrative: a night in the life of an erotic dancer/researcher. In *Investigating Subjectivity. Research on Lived Experience,* ed. C Ellis, MG Flaherty, pp. 102–24. London: Sage

Ranger T. 1993. The invention of tradition revisited. The case of colonial Africa. In *Legitimacy and the State in Twentieth-Century Africa. Essays in Honour of A.H.M. Kirk-Greene,* ed. T Ranger, O Vaughan, pp. 62–111. Houndsmill, UK: MacMillan

Scarry E. 1985. *The Body in Pain: The Making and Unmaking of the World.* New York: Oxford Univ. Press

Scheper-Hughes N. 1992. *Death Without Weeping: The Violence of Every Day Life in Brazil.* Berkeley: Univ. Calif. Press

Scheper-Hughes N, Lock MM. 1987. The mindful body: a prolegomenon to future work in medical anthropology. *Med. Anthropol. Q.* 1(1):6–41

Schütz A. 1962. *The Problem of Social Reality. Phaenomenologica 11. Collected Papers of Alfred Schütz,* ed. M Natanson. Nijhoff: The Hague

Scott J. 1985. *Weapons of the Weak.* New Heaven: Yale Univ. Press

Shildrick M. 2002. *Embodying the Monster. Encounters with the Vulnerable Self.* London: Sage

Sökefeld M. 1999. Debating self, identity and culture in anthropology. *Curr. Anthropol.* 40(4):417–47

Stallybrass P, White A. 1986. *The Politics and Poetics of Transgression.* London: Methuen

Stoller P. 1994. Embodying colonial memories. *Am. Anthropol.* 96(3):634–48

Strathern M. 1988. *The Gender of the Gift. Problems with Women and Problems with Society in Melanesia.* Berkeley: Univ. Calif. Press

Strathern M. 1995. Nostalgia and the new genetics. See Battaglia 1995b, pp. 97–120

Strauss C. 1997. Partly fragmented, partly integrated: an anthropological examination of "postmodern fragmented subjects." *Cult. Anthropol.* 12(3):362–404

Synott A. 1993. *The Body Social. Symbolism, Self and Society.* London: Routledge

Taylor CC. 1992. *Milk, Honey, Money. Changing Concepts in Rwandan Healing.* London: Routledge

Thomas N. 1994. *Colonialism's Culture. Anthropology, Travel and Government. A Study in Black and White.* Oxford: Polity

Turner BS. 1992. *Regulating Bodies: Essays in Medical Sociology.* London: Routledge

Turner T. 1994. Bodies and anti-bodies: flesh and fetish in contemporary social theory. See Csordas 1994c, pp. 27–47

Turner T. 1995. Social body and embodied subject: bodiliness, subjectivity and sociality among the Kayapo. *Cult. Anthropol.* 10:143–70

Turner TS. 1980. The social skin. In *Not Work Alone. A Cross-Cultural View of Activities Superfluous to Survival*, ed. J Cherfas, R Lewin, pp. 112–40. London: Temple Smith

Turner V. 1974 [1967]. *The Forest of Symbols. Aspects of Ndembu Ritual.* London: Cornell Univ. Press

Van der Geest S, Whyte SR. 1991. The charm of medicines: metaphors and metonyms. *Med. Anthropol. Q.* 5:345–67

Van Wolputte S. 2002. Coming of age and authority: milk as a source of power in Himbaland, Northern Namibia. In *Ageing in Africa. Sociolinguistic and Anthropological Approaches*, ed. S Makoni, K Stroeken, pp. 109–35. Aldershot, UK: Ashgate

Van Wolputte S. 2004. *Moving Bodies Spaces Selves. A Social Phenomenology of Praxis and Performance in a North-Namibian Setting.*Windhoek, Namibia: Gamsberg MacMillan. In press

Vaughan M. 1991. *Curing Their Ills. Colonial Power and African Illness.* Cambridge, UK: Polity

Warnier J-P. 2004. Introduction. Pour une praxéologie de la subjectivation politique. In *Matière à Politique. Le Pouvoir, les Corps et les Choses*, ed. J-F Bayart, J-P Warnier, pp. 7–31. Paris : Karthala

Weiss G. 1999. *Body Images. Embodiment as Intercorporeality.* New York: Routledge

Werbner R. 1996. Introduction: multiple identities, plural arenas. In *Postcolonial Identities in Africa*, ed. R Werbner, T Ranger, pp. 1–25. London: Zed

Werbner R. 1998. Beyond oblivion: confronting memory crisis. In *Memory and the Postcolony. African Anthropology and the Critique of Power*, ed. R Werbner, pp. 1–17. London: Zed

Whittaker A. 2001. Empowerment or control? Northeast Thai women and family planning. In *Borders of Being. Citizenship, Fertility, and Sexuality in Asia and the Pacific*, ed M Jolly, K Ram, pp. 203–31. Ann Arbor: Univ. Mich. Press

Whyte SR. 2002. Subjectivity and subjunctivity: hoping for health in Eastern Uganda. In *Postcolonial Subjectivities in Africa*, ed. R Werbner, pp. 171–90. London: Zed

Winnicot DWWC, Shepherd R, Davis ME. 1989. *Psycho-Analytic Explorations.* London: Karnac

Annu. Rev. Anthropol. 2004. 33:271–96
doi: 10.1146/annurev.anthro.33.070203.144024
Copyright © 2004 by Annual Reviews. All rights reserved
First published online as a Review in Advance on June 10, 2004

EARLY DISPERSALS OF *HOMO* FROM AFRICA

Susan C. Antón

Department of Anthropology, New York University, New York, NY 10003;
email: susan.anton@nyu.edu

Carl C. Swisher, III

Department of Geological Sciences, Rutgers University, Piscataway, NJ 08854;
email: cswish@rci.rutgers.edu

Key Words *H. erectus*, Indonesia, Georgia, Argon-Argon chronology

■ **Abstract** The worldwide distribution of our species, *Homo sapiens*, has its roots in the early Pleistocene epoch. However, evidence has been sufficient only in the past decade to overcome the conventional wisdom that hominins had been restricted to Africa until about 800,000 years ago. Indeed, the idea that hominin dispersal was technologically mediated, and thus must correlate with changes in stone tool technology seen at the Olduwan/Acheulean transition, has proven to be a persuasive hypothesis despite persistent claims for an early Pleistocene hominin presence outside Africa. We review multiple recent lines of evidence that suggest hominin dispersals from Africa in the earliest Pleistocene, if not the latest Pliocene, correlated with the appearance of hominins typically referred to as *Homo erectus* (*sensu lato*) who carried with them an Oldowan tool technology. Changes in body plan and foraging strategy are likely to ultimately underlie these dispersals.

INTRODUCTION

Until a decade ago, most evidence suggested that hominins had been restricted to Africa (and the Levant) until about 800,000 years ago (c.f., Pope 1983, Klein 1989, Langbroek & Roebroeks 2000). Investigators thought the earliest accepted Far East and Island Southeast Asian hominin sites were between 500 and 800 ka (Pope 1983). 'Ubeidiya, Israel represented the best evidence of 1 Ma or older hominins just outside Africa (Klein 1989, p. 204) but was widely attributed to, at best, short-term hominin forays outside Africa (Schick 1994). Thus, the earliest hominin dispersal from Africa was considered by paleoanthropologists to be relatively late in human evolution with hominins leaving Africa only with the assistance of Acheulean technology. Such a view has been dubbed the "short chronology" (e.g., Roebrooks 2001). Given the presumed timing of this dispersal, paleoanthropologists often assumed the dispersing hominin to be a late form of *Homo erectus.*

This short chronology contrasted with the opinion of many early workers in Asia who attributed the earliest hominin sites on Java to the early Pleistocene on geological grounds (e.g., von Koenigswald 1936, 1962; de Terra 1943) and to persistent, but isolated, voices that offered biogeographic, radiometric, or stratigraphic arguments for ages of 1.4 Ma or more for sites in the Levant and Indonesia (Jacob & Curtis 1971; Tchernov 1987, 1992; Franzen 1994). For most anthropologists, the data were simply too sparse and often insufficiently documented to make a strong case for early dispersals. Furthermore, the hominins in Java were too derived morphologically and too large brained to be compelling arguments of an early disperser.

In the past decade, a wealth of new data and sites have been offered supporting a "longer chronology" of hominin presence outside of Africa (e.g., Swisher et al. 1994; Larick et al. 2001; Gabunia et al. 2000a; Vekua et al. 2002). Although the precise age of the earliest occurrence varies among regions (and researchers), all regions have witnessed the accumulation of more robust evidence supporting an earlier occupation than that accepted just a decade ago. Although the precise age of many of these sites remains a controversial matter, the earliest occupation of Europe has increased to at least 800 ka, of Western Asia to 1.7 Ma, and of Indonesia to 1.6 or 1.8 Ma (Swisher et al. 1994; Carbonel et al. 1999; Gabunia et al. 2000a). Perhaps the most important, and least contested, of these sites in regard to establishing an age for the earliest African dispersals are the discoveries at Dmanisi, Republic of Georgia, dated to approximately 1.7 Ma; they are least contested both because of the combined radiometric, paleomagnetic, and biostratigraphic age estimates and because of the anatomy of the hominins discovered there.

Here we review multiple recent lines of evidence that support a longer chronology. Although scholars may quibble as to whether hominin dispersals from Africa began at 1.6 Ma or as early as 1.8 Ma, all data point to dispersal substantially prior to 800 ka, the conventional wisdom just a decade ago. These data correlate the first dispersal with the appearance of hominins typically referred to as *Homo erectus* (*sensu lato*) who carried with them an Oldowan tool technology. They do not speak to the number and longevity of these dispersals or to exactly how many forays of differential success there may have been (Dennell 2003). Nonetheless, after the late part of the early Pleistocene substantial areas of the Old World were no longer hominin-free. We discuss the possible underlying causes of such dispersal, including changes in body plan and inferred foraging strategy.

WHEN DID THEY LEAVE?: EARLY PLEISTOCENE HOMININ SITES OUTSIDE AFRICA (1.4–1.9 MA)

Throughout this text we adopt the use of a Plio-Pleistocene boundary that relatively coincides with the upper Olduvai Subchron–Matuyama Chron (Normal to Reverse) geomagnetic polarity transition, calibrated at ~1.78 Ma (e.g., Berggren et al. 1995). Therefore, the recognition of this boundary in the various regions becomes of

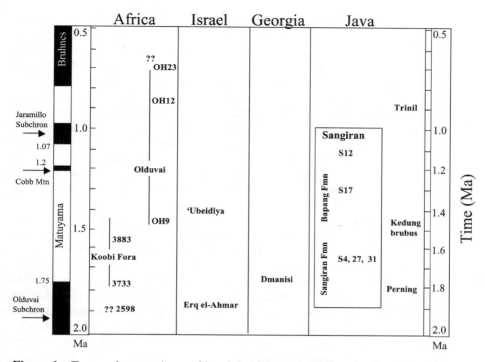

Figure 1 Temporal comparisons of hominins from early Pleistocene localities plotted by region and against the geomagnetic polarity time scale. Time is given in millions of years. Specimen numbers refer to fossil hominins.

utmost importance in the correlation and age assessment of these early hominins. Paleomagnetics, ^{40}Ar/^{39}Ar, and Fission-Track dating, as well as faunal correlations, currently provide the best critical means of assessing age.

Currently, the primary skeletal evidence for early Pleistocene hominins outside Africa comes from a single locality in the Republic of Georgia (~1.7 Ma) and from a series of localities in Indonesia (~1.6–1.8 Ma; Figure 1). Archaeological evidence and nonspecific hominin remains are also found in the Near East at 'Ubeidiya (~1.4 Ma) and archaeological remains alone at Erq el-Ahmar (~1.8–1.9 Ma).

Eurasia and the Neareast

Hominins were discovered by archaeologists in 1991 from a 16-m^2 area below a medieval village in Dmanisi, Republic of Georgia. Since 1991, four hominin crania and other hominin remains were retrieved from infillings, probably caused by soil piping, within the Pleistocene sediments (Gabunia et al. 2002a). Abundant faunal and archaeological remains were also retrieved from the infillings, overlying and underlying sediments.

Hominin fossils from Dmanisi are dated to ~1.7 Ma on the basis of various lines of evidence (Gabunia et al. 2000a,b). A maximum age of 1.78 Ma for the Dmanisi fossils is provided by the 1.8 Ma $^{40}Ar/^{39}Ar$ dates on the underlying Masavera Basalt and by the occurrence of the upper boundary (N-R) of the Olduvai Subchron as determined from paleomagnetics of the basalt and overlying fossil-bearing sediments. Inferred depositional rates of sediment and soil formation suggest deposition of the hominin-bearing strata quickly following cooling of the basalt flow. The reverse geomagnetic polarity of the hominin-bearing units directly above the 1.78-Ma Olduvai–Matuyama Boundary indicates a likely age range in the lower part of the mid-Matuyama chron. Although the site lacks an upper, radiometrically determined age limit, the presence of the rodents *Mimomys ostramosensis* and *M. tornensis* constrains the age of the site to the basal part of the mid-Matuyama between ~1.6 Ma and 1.78 Ma.

In Israel, the central Jordan valley is composed of a series of geological formations, two of which (Erq el-Ahmar and 'Ubeidiya) have yielded traces of hominins or hominin activity in the early Pleistocene (Bar-Yosef & Goren-Inbar 1993, Ron & Levi 2001). Both formations are underlain by the Cover Basalt that yielded K-Ar age estimates of 2.0 Ma or greater for its upper levels (Siedner & Horowitz 1974). The stratigraphically lowest of the Israeli hominin occupation levels, containing core and flake tools, occurs in the Erq el-Ahmar Formation in sediments of normal geomagnetic polarity. Given the age of the Cover Basalt, the presence of sediments of both normal and reverse polarity in the Erq el-Ahmar Formation, and the presence of an early Pleistocene fauna, the normal sediments in which the hominin tools are found are interpreted by geochronologists as representing the Olduvai Subchron (Ron & Levi 2001), dated elsewhere to 1.77–1.95 Ma (Berggren et al. 1995).

The 150-m 'Ubeidiya Formation has been the subject of systematic fieldwork for several decades (see Bar-Yosef & Goren-Inbar 1993). Strata of the 'Ubeidiya Formation stand nearly vertical and have yielded fossil faunas, abundant stone tool remains indicative of multiple occupations, and small fragments of hominin cranial vault bone and tooth. Initial age estimates suggested ages of 0.8–1.0 Ma based on pollen correlations (Horowitz 1989) and 1.8–2.0 Ma (Repenning & Fejfar 1982) based on outdated classifications of the fauna (Bar-Yosef & Goren-Inbar 1993). However, the 'Ubeidiya fauna lacks several extinct mollusk species present at Erq el-Ahmar (Tchernov 1987), suggesting a younger age for the 'Ubeidiya Formation. Systematic biostratigraphic analyses and comparisons with other Old World faunas suggest that the hominins and archaeology date to ~1.4 Ma (Tchernov 1987, 1992).

Far East

Although investigators propose the oldest occupation of China to have occured as early as 1.8 Ma (Huang et al. 1995), the mandible fragment from Longuppo is argued to be nonhominin and the associations of the isolated incisor have been questioned by some scholars (Schwartz & Tattersall 1996; Wolpoff 1999, p. 466;

Wu 1999). The first certain hominins from mainland Asia do not appear until about 1.15 Ma in Southern China at Gongwangling (Lantian; An et al. 1990) and are not discussed further here.

In contrast to these isolated occurrences, island Southeast Asia yields a relative abundance of fossil hominins with a record that is fairly continuous from the early- to middle Pleistocene. Hominins first appear ~1.8 Ma at Perning (Mojokerto) on Java, and shortly thereafter in the Sangiran Dome region (~1.66 Ma; Swisher et al. 1994), where there appears to have been a mostly continuous hominin presence up to about the Brunhes-Matuyama boundary (Figure 1; Table 1; Swisher et al. 1994, 1997; Larick et al. 2001).

The Sangiran area provides the most robust evidence for early dispersal into Indonesia because the ages are based on $^{40}Ar/^{39}Ar$ analyses on a series of tuffs located throughout the Sangiran section with multiple hominin fossils intercalated among them (Table 1). Fossil hominins occur in both the Sangiran (Pucangan) Formation and the overlying Bapang (Kabuh) Formation; however, the identity of the earliest dispersers rests with the hominins from the uppermost Sangiran Formation. The oldest hominin calvaria at Sangiran (e.g., Sangiran 4, 27, and 31) are associated with ages of >1.6 Ma on the basis of dates for tuffs of 1.66 Ma for the upper part of the Sangiran Formation and 1.58 Ma for the base of the Bapang (Kabuh) Formation (C. Swisher, unpublished data; Swisher et al. 1994, Antón & Swisher 2000). Fluorine analysis supports a derivation of Sangiran 4 from either the lower Bapang (Grenzbank zone) or upper part of the Sangiran (Pucangan) Formation (Matsu'ura 1982). Most sediments within the Sangiran (Pucangan) formation are of reverse geomagnetic polarity that, in conjunction with the chronology, have been attributed to the middle part of the Matuyama chron (Swisher et al. 1994). Preservational differences between fossils from the oldest strata (Sangiran Formation black clays that badly deform and telescope included bones) and younger, overlying strata (Bapang Formation cross-bedded sandstones that do not present deformed bones) indicate that hominins certainly are associated with the Sangiran Formation and thus with ages in excess of 1.6 Ma. Similar preservation of both Sangiran 27 and 31 supports their reported position in the upper Sangiran Formation, contrary to recent inferences by Larick and colleagues (2001).

In the following several paragraphs, we address in detail the challenges raised to this "long chronology." However, for the benefit of readers less familiar with geochronological techniques, we first "cut to the chase" by summarizing the major issues here. Challenges to the long chronology in Indonesia have been raised on the basis of biostratigraphic evidence, fission track ages, and paleomagnetic inference. Each of these indicators has specific issues detailed below. The Sangiran faunas are largely endemic to Java, thus offering little or no independent age information through correlation with Asian mainland faunas. Magnetostratigraphies on Java are of short duration and cannot be unambiguously correlated to the Geomagnetic Polarity Time Scale (GPTS). Thus, both the biostratigraphic and paleomagnetic calibrations are based on fission track dates from the Java sections themselves.

TABLE 1   Comparison of radiometric and other age estimates for the Sangiran Dome region

	Sample hominins	Faunas after de Vos	Biostrat Age de Vos calibrated to tektite	Microfossils (Ninkovich et al. 1982; Orchiston & Siesser 1978, 1982)	Ar/Ar Age (Semah et al. 2000)	Ar/Ar Age (Swisher et al. 1994, 1997)	Ar/Ar Age (Larick et al. 2001)	Polarity (Hyodo 2001)	Polarity (Semah et al. 2000)	GPTS (Geomagnetic Polarity Time Scale) at time of Ar/Ar ages
Notopuro Fmn						0.787 + 0.001		N		
Kabuh Fmn	Sangiran 10	Kedung brubus				1.09 ± 0.014	1.02 ± 0.06	N		Jaramillo subchron normal (N)
Upper tuff							1.27 ± 0.18	R		
Middle tuff	Sangiran 17		0.8 Ma				1.30 ± 0.12	R		Matuyama reversed (R)
Lower tuff		Trinil H.K.	1.0 Ma			1.47 ± 0.02	1.51 ± 0.08	R		
Lowest tuff	Sangiran 21					1.58 ± 0.02				
Grenzbank										
Sangiran Fmn	Sangiran 22, 27, 31	Ci Saat	1.2 Ma	1.6		1.66 ± 0.04	No data	N		Matuyama reversed (R)
T10		Satir	1.5 Ma			1.70 ± 0.003		R		
Diatomite T2				1.9–2.1		1.92 ± 0.08		Excursion		
Lower lahar					1.67, 1.97, or 2.3			R	N and R	
Kalibeng Fmn								N		

Arguably, the most convincing of the fission-track ages are those on Australasian tektites from Sangiran, dated reliably elsewhere to 790 ka. However, the stratigraphic positioning of these tektites, although once argued to be well-known, has been uncertain since the beginning of paleontological investigations at Sangiran. The tektite age thus offers no independent age calibration for either the biostratigraphy or the magnetostratigraphy. Thus the best age information for the Sangiran section comes from a series of stratigraphically consistent stratigraphic ^{40}Ar/^{39}Ar on primary volcanic layers and cross-correlated with previous microfossil age estimates.

Two recent critiques challenge all or part of these chronologies (Langbroek & Roebrooks 2000, Semah et al. 2000). Langbroek & Roebroeks (2000) suggest that all Javan hominin sites are younger than 1.0 Ma (see also Pope 1983). This critique relies heavily on the apparent stratigraphic position of Australiasian tektites in the middle part of the Bapang Formation, the occurrence of the Jaramillo in the upper part of the Sangiran Formation, and the Brunhes–Matuyama boundary in the overlying Bapang Formation.

Although the age of the Australiasian tektites is known with great accuracy on the basis of dates elsewhere (at 790 ka), their stratigraphic provenience at Sangiran is uncertain. Historically von Koenigswald and others thought the tektites came from sediment above the Bapang Formation. Arguments for a lower stratigraphic position, within the Bapang Formation, are largely based on the occurrence of a single, purportedly *in situ*, tektite found during trenching. The questionable stratigraphic placement of this tektite is noted by Antón (2002) and discussed by Larick et al. (2001), whose ages are also inconsistent with the proposed stratigraphic placement of the tektite and whose Indonesian coauthors, participants in the original field recovery of the tektite, have primary knowledge of the tektite's stratigraphic position (or lack thereof). It is relevant to note here that no *in situ* tektites have been recovered at Sangiran despite an increase in recent, systematic excavations in the middle part of the Bapang Formation (see Larick et al. 2001), as well as active searches dating back as early as von Koenigswald. It is of consequence that the age estimates assigned to the faunal sequences are also in part based on the stratigraphic placement of this tektite (see below).

The Langbroek critique also relies in part on older paleomagnetic data based entirely on alternating field (AF) rather than thermal demagnitization techniques (Semah 1982; Shimizu et al. 1985 in Watanabe & Kadar 1985). AF demagnitization cannot remove secondary magnetic overprints caused by secondary mineralizations, such as the formation of goethite. Consequently, it is difficult to trust normal, transitional, or intermediate polarities measured by AF demagnitization in sediments, such as those at Sangiran and Mojokerto, that are highly weathered and secondarily mineralized (see Hyodo 2001). Mixed or intermediate directions are considered the result of incomplete demagnetization and characterization of magnetic components residing in primary and secondary carriers. These types of data cannot be used to justify the occurrence of the Jaramillo in the Sangiran Formation. Similar problems may explain the preponderance of normal polarity directions in the upper part of the Sangiran section, as these strata increasingly show evidence of secondary oxidized mineralizations (Hyodo 2001). In these circumstances, such as those at Sangiran, calibration by radiometric dating provides the most robust means of evaluating these paleomagnetic measurements and correlating them to standard geologic time scales.

Unfortunately, the Langbroek critique ignores well-behaved ^{40}Ar/^{39}Ar analyses from multiple studies throughout the Sangiran section that are temporally consistent with their relative stratigraphic positions (Swisher 1997, Larick et al. 2001). Arguments for the reworking of volcanic materials from older deposits as a means to explain ^{40}Ar/^{39}Ar dates that some workers consider too old (e.g., Sémah et al. 2000; Hyodo 2002) cannot be justified given the excellant agreement between the dates and their relative stratigraphic position, as well as their occurrence in multiple sections throughout the Sangiran dome. These data are further supported by diatom and foraminiferal data from the Sangiran Formation that indicate an early Pleistocene age for the earliest hominin-bearing sediments on Java (Orchiston & Siesser 1978, 1982; Ninkovitch et al. 1982).

In another paleomagnetic and dating critique of the Sangiran Formation, Sémah and colleagues (2000) argue that the lowest part of the Sangiran Formation can be no older than ~1.7 Ma, on the basis of the geomagnetic polarity and ^{40}Ar/^{39}Ar age of the Lower Lahar of the Sangiran Formation (Table 1). In and of itself this conclusion does not necessarily conflict with the radiometric chronologies noted above. However, several inconsistencies exist in their data that make their interpretation difficult to understand. Sémah and colleagues report ^{40}Ar/^{39}Ar incremental heating of hornblendes from the Lower Lahar at Cenglik that resulted in a U-shaped release pattern, with a minimum saddle of 2.37 $\pm$ 0.06 Ma and an isochron age of 1.97 $\pm$ 0.06 Ma. A step-heating experiment on a single grain from the same site yielded a minimum age of 1.77 $\pm$ 0.08 Ma. They reject the bulk incremental heating age because the U-shaped spectra is considered indicative of excess argon; likewise the isochron age of 1.97 $\pm$ 0.06 Ma is rejected, although it should account for the excess argon, if present. Sémah and colleagues also obtained dates of 1.68 $\pm$ 0.02 Ma and 1.66 $\pm$ 0.04 mA on the basis of the total fusion of two single hornblende crystals from the lahar at the locality of Puren. According to their study, these analyses indicate that the lahar hornblendes are of a single, homogeneous population and that the older ages of the bulk sample are due to excess argon. Sémah and colleagues thus consider the best age for the Lower Lahar to be an average of the two single-grain dates from Puren (1.66 + 0.04 Ma) and the minimum age of 1.77 $\pm$ 0.08 Ma from Cengklik.

Although the younger total fusion dates may be reliable, as argued by Sémah and colleagues, they are difficult to evaluate. It is equally plausible that these data incorporate an amount of alteration, excess ^{36}Ar, or even ^{40}Ar loss that, if uncorrected, would result in ages that are too young. Without incremental heating of these hornblendes there is no way to be certain; however, their report of a ^{40}Ar/^{36}Ar isochron intercept of 274 (less than the expected 295 ^{40}Ar/^{36}Ar) for these data supports the idea that the single-grain ages may be too young.

For the bulk incremental heating experiment, the isochron should account for excess argon if present, making the isochron age of 1.97 ± 0.06 Ma an equally plausible age for the lahar. Alternatively the presence of older hornblende grains of similar composition could explain the results of the bulk experiment. Lahars are notorious for reworking older materials, a feature which makes them less-than-ideal candidates for radiometric dating. Essentially, we find these data too few and insufficient to reliably assess the age of the Lower Lahar.

Nonetheless, even if we accept the arguments by Sémah et al. for a $^{40}Ar/^{39}Ar$ age of 1.67 Ma for the lahar, it is difficult to rectify such an age with their geomagnetic polarity data. Sémah and colleagues (2001, as well as in their earlier work) state that the Lower Lahar gives different polarities at the two localities where measurements were made: normal for Cengklik and reverse for Puren. This finding then argues that the Lower Lahar strattles the upper Olduvai–Matuyama boundary, being of Olduvai age at Cengklik and Matuyama age at Puren. Two problems exist with this conclusion. First, it is highly unlikely, given the rapid emplacement of lahars, that the Lower Lahar, which all workers agree represents a single unit, records more than a single, true geomagnetic polarity. Given that geomagnetic polarity transitions are thought to encompass hundreds or thousands of years, whereas the deposition of lahars is more catastrophic, occurring in hours and days compared with years, it is more likely that spurious directions or secondary geomagnetic normal (present field) overprints have been incompletely removed during the laboratory demagnetization processes of these samples. Thus Sémah and colleagues have not adequately resolved the geomagnetic polarity of the lahar at the time of deposition from secondary magnetization directions. In support of this conclusion, Hyodo (2001) reports only reverse polarity in the lahar.

However, even if we assume that Sémah and colleagues correctly measured the upper Olduvai–Matuyama boundary, the age of this boundary, and thus the lahar, must be 1.78 Ma (Berggren et al. 1995), making their preferred $^{40}Ar/^{39}Ar$ age of 1.67 Ma for the Lower Lahar too young. Unpublished $^{40}Ar/^{39}Ar$ ages on two primary tuffs in the Sangiran Formation above the Lower Lahar give stratigraphically consistent ages of 1.7 Ma and 1.9 Ma, implying that the true age of the Lahar may be significantly older than that suggested by Sémah and others (Table 1) (C. Swisher, unpublished data). A preliminary $^{40}Ar/^{39}Ar$ age for the Lower Lahar of 2.08 Ma (C. Swisher, unpublished data) and a $^{40}Ar/^{39}Ar$ age of 1.9 ± 0.2 Ma reported by Bettis et al. (2004) further contradict age and implications for the Lower Lahar as drawn by Sémah and colleagues (2001).

Although these issues need to be addressed, an Olduvai–Matuyama boundary age (or, for that matter, an older age) for the Lower Lahar is not inconsistent with the findings of Swisher (1994, 1997) or Larick and coworkers (2001), or, for that matter, with Sémah's own normal polarity data.

For many years, biostratigraphic chronologies have been used to suggest that the first hominin colonization of Java occured no more than 1.0–1.3 Ma (e.g., Leinders et al. 1985, de Vos & Sondaar 1994, Sondaar et al. 1996). These authors agree that the earliest hominins at Sangiran occur in the upper Sangiran (Pucangan) Formation along with a limited fauna known as the Ci Saat fauna (see below). However, there are no reliable calibration points of a similar fauna elsewhere in Indonesia or on the Asian mainland, thus the fauna themselves do not offer an independent means of precise age assessment but ultimately must rely on radiometric dates on Java. The radiometric calibrations used for the biostratigraphy are based on the placement of the tektites and fission track ages (e.g., Suzuki et al. 1985 in Watanabe & Kadar 1985), the problems with which we have discussed above.

Dennell's (2003) recent review of the Indonesian age data likens the controversy between biostratigraphic and radiometric ages in Java to that over the KBS tuff at Koobi Fora Kenya and implies that the biostratigraphic indicators and previous paleomagnetic analyses, which have been used to argue for a hominin presence no older than 1.3 Ma, should be the more robust dataset and are the most consistent with the absence of early, mainland-Asian hominins. However, Dennell (2003) bases this conclusion on (*a*) the radiometric work of Sémah, which at best gives a lower age limit to the hominins not inconsistent with the ^{40}Ar/^{39}Ar chronologies of Larick et al. (2001) and Swisher et al. (1994); (*b*) the paleomagnetic work of Hyodo et al. (2002) that, independent of radiometric or other chronology, cannot indicate which period one is in, and that uses the biostratigraphy (which uses the tektite placement) and the suspect placement of the tektite as their radiometric calibration (Hyodo 2001, Hyodo et al. 2002); and (*c*) the biostratigraphic chronologies that use the same radiometric calibration that is in part dated by the tektite of uncertain provenience. All these lines of data are suspect. More important, all the above studies agree that the earliest hominins at Sangiran are from the Black clays of the Sangiran Formation and that none of them is inconsistent with the earliest hominins at Sangiran being greater than 1.0 Ma and probably 1.3 Ma.

Collectively, we conclude that the entire hominin-bearing section at Sangiran is greater than 1.0 Ma, a great departure from the accepted view just a decade ago. Further, a strong case can be made that the oldest of the Sangiran hominins is at least older than 1.5 Ma [i.e., the age for the base of the Bapang given by Larick et al. (2001), which unconformably overlies the Sangiran] and is likely older than 1.6 Ma. We find fault with the existing paleomagnetic, fission-track dating and biostratigraphies supporting a young age for Sangiran. One should note, however, that acceptance of this young chronology would require not simply reworking the volcanic elements of sediments at Sangiran but a systematic error in all ^{40}Ar/^{39}Ar dating of the Sangiran tuffs. Although anything is possible, ^{40}Ar/^{39}Ar dating currently provides us with the most accurate and reliable means of age calibration as witnessed by a plethora of such dated hominin sites in East Africa.

WHO DID THEY LEAVE WITH? FAUNAL COMMUNITIES OF EARLY PLEISTOCENE SITES

Near East and Eurasia

Tchernov (1987, 1992) argued that by at least 1.4 Ma, hominins were regular members of the faunal migrations that occurred when African ecological conditions expanded into the Levant. Whether movement within one's ecological niche rather than expansion outside of it can be considered a "true" dispersal event is debatable (Klein 1999). However, hominins were one of only a few African taxa to pass into the Levantine fauna, although a strong Ethiopian component was still retained in the 'Ubeidiya fauna (Table 2). The faunal assemblage at Dmanisi retains less

TABLE 2   Large mammal fauna from Early Pleistocene Hominin Sites

Dmanisi, Georgia Units A and B (Gabunia et al. 2000b)	'Ubeidiya, Israel Fi member (Tchernov 1987)	Sangiran Dome, Java Sangiran Formation— Upper Black Clays (Aziz 2001)
Ursus etruscus	*Ursus etruscus*	*Stegodon elephantoides*
Canis etruscus	*Canis cf. arnensis*	*Bubalus palaeokerabau*
Martes sp.	*Canis sp.*	*Bibos palaeosondaicus*
Megantereon megantereon	*Vulpes sp.*	*Homo erectus*
Homotherium crenatidens	*Lutra sp.*	
Panthera gombaszoegensis	*Vormela cf. peregusna*	From Equivalent aged Faunas elsewhere on Java (de Vos 1995, Sondaar et al. 1996)
Pachycrocuta perrieri	*Megantereon cf. cutridens*	
Archidiskodon meriodionalis	*Panthera gombaszaegensis*	
Dicerorhinus etruscus etruscus	*Lynx sp.*	*Panthera sp.*
Equus stenonsis	*Felis sp.*	*Stegodon trigonocephalus*
Gazella borbonica	*Crocuta crocuta*	*Hexaprotodon sivalensis*
Soergelia sp.	*Herpestes sp.*	*Sus stremmi*
Dmanisibos georgicus	*Mammuthus meridionalis*	Cervids
Eucladocerus aff. Senezensis	*Dicerorhinus e. etruscus*	Bovids
Cervidae cf. Arvernoceros	*Equus cf. tabeti*	Boselephini
Cervus perrieri	*Equus cf. caballus*	
Dama nesti	*Kolpochoerus olduvaiensis*	
Paleotragus sp.	*Sus strozzii*	
Homo ex. gr. erectus	*Hippopotamus behemoth*	
	Hippopotamus gorgops	
	Camelus sp.	
	Giraffidae	
	Praemegacerus verticornis	
	Cervidae	
	Bos sp.	
	Gazella cf. gazella	
	Gasellospira torticornis	
	Macaca sylvanus	
	Homo sp.	

of such a component, suggesting that hominins dispersed outside their African ecological niche. Only six of the Dmanisi taxa (including the hominins) are of African origin (Gabunia et al. 2000b), suggesting that Dmanisi represents a true hominin dispersal event.

Far East

The faunas associated with early hominins of Island Southeast Asia, although not as numerous or well studied as those mentioned above, are of Sino-Malayan and Siva-Malayan extract, thus representing an extensive hominin dispersal (Table 2). Faunal remains from the lower black clays of the Sangiran (Pucangan) formation at Sangiran, probably below that of the hominins, are somewhat impoverished (aka Satir Fauna of Sondaar et al. 1996), which likely suggests insularity due to sea-level rise. The fauna from the upper black clays at Sangiran, probably coincident with the earliest hominins, have been associated with the Ci Saat Fauna of Sondaar et al. (1996). At Sangiran the upper black clays yield open habitat bovids such as *Bubalus palaeokerabau* and *Bibos palaeosondaicus* (Table 2) (Aziz 2001). The Ci Saat fauna in other Javan localities includes some indicators of land connection including *Panthera* sp. in addition to taxa requiring lesser land connection (e.g., *Stegodon trigonocephalus* and *Hexaprotodon sivalensis*, among other taxa), possibly suggesting filtered dispersal from the mainland (de Vos 1985) in the early Pleistocene. Unlike the abundant faunas from the Bapang (Kabuh) formation, interpreting the significance of the Sangiran (Pucangan) fauna is difficult because it is based on relatively few specimens known from a restricted paleoenvironment. If faunas from the lower part of Kedungbrubus and Perning are temporal equivalants, as is indicated by the ^{40}Ar/^{39}Ar chronologies, then this early fauna is more diverse than indicated by the fossils from the "black clays" of Sangiran.

WHAT DID THEY TAKE WITH THEM? MATERIAL CULTURE AND BEHAVIOR

The early Pleistocene archaeological record of Africa is composed of Early Stone Age assemblages of the Oldowan and Developed Oldowan typified by core and flake technology. Some investigators argue that between 1.8 and 1.5 Ma this record begins to indicate a more complicated and diverse foraging strategy with greater utilization of marginal areas including dry uplands and areas further from standing water (Cachel & Harris 1998). Likewise others suggest that at this time a differential pattern focusing on both meat and marrow acquisition is evidenced in the faunal record with hominins accessing carcasses earlier than had previously been the case (Monahan 1996). The limited number of archaeological sites of this age outside Africa do not allow for the comparison of distributional patterns. However, the stone tool assemblages of early Pleistocene Koobi Fora and Olduvai Gorge afford comparisons to the material culture used by early Pleistocene hominins outside of Africa.

Near East and West Asia

The stone tool assemblage from Dmanisi is a core and flake industry similar to the Oldowan chopping-tool industry of East Africa (Nioradze & Justus 1998; Justus & Nioradze, personal communication; Gabunia et al. 2000c). All tools are produced from local raw materials with selection of finer grained materials (quartzite and basalt) for tool manufacturing. Justus & Nioradze (personal communication) argue that the Dmanisi tools were knapped elsewhere similar to the situation at sites such as HWK.E from lower Olduvai Gorge. However, Dmanisi differs from these assemblages by lacking spheroids and, to date, any evidence for hominin butchery of other vertebrates. Similarities have been noted also between Dmanisi assemblages and those recently retrieved from lake-edge contexts at 'Ubeidiya that have been interpreted as systematic tool abandonment at the point of food procurement (Shea & Bar-Yosef 1999).

The Jordan valley sites include core and flake technology and bifaces. The Erq el-Ahmar artifacts, which are similarly aged, or slightly older, than those at Dmanisi are likewise flake and core tools. The somewhat-younger 'Ubeidiya assemblages include flake and core tools in proportions most similar to a Developed Oldowan, as well as Acheulean influences including bifaces such as handaxes and picks, particularly in the upper levels of cycle FI (Bar-Yosef, Goren-Inbar 1993). The 'Ubeidiya tools include spheroids also, which are lacking at Dmanisi.

Far East

Early stone tool assemblages are rare in Indonesia and hominins and stone tools have yet to be found in association with one another. However, archaeologists have found some stone tools in the Grenzbank (boundary between the Sangiran and Bapang Formations) and in the Bapang Formation of the Sangiran Dome (Sémah et al. 1992, Simanjuntak 2001). Stone tools have been recovered also from the Upper Pleistocene deposits at Sambungmacan (Jacob et al. 1978). These tools typically represent either flakes or flaked cores, and retouched flakes represent a very small percentage of those recovered. Thus, although little behavioral data is afforded by these finds, one can parsimoniously conclude the *H. erectus* reached Java with an Oldowan-like tool kit.

WHO LEFT AFRICA? TAXONOMY OF HOMININS OUTSIDE AFRICA

Given an earliest Pleistocene age for the first hominins outside Africa, the first hominins to leave Africa could have been any species of early *Homo* or perhaps an australopithecine. Several authors suggest that a less-derived hominin than *H. erectus*, or a more primitive version of *H. erectus*, may have been the first to disperse from Africa, and thus multiple taxa may be found in the early non-African hominin faunas (e.g., Robinson 1953; Sartono 1981, Orban-Segebarth & Procureur

1983, Howell 1994, Tyler et al. 1995, Dennell 2003). Specific assertions that an australopithecine may be present in the early assemblages cannot be supported on the basis of current dentognathic evidence (Kramer 1994). However, the question of multiple taxa of *Homo* remains more problematic (e.g., Howell 1994). Thus, the morphological attributes of the earliest non-African hominins are of critical interest.

East African localities at Koobi Fora, Kenya, and Olduvai Gorge, Tanzania, provide the most abundant sources of early *Homo* skeletal material that may provide a source of dispersing hominins and appropriate comparisons for early Pleistocene hominins on other continents. Olduvai Gorge has yielded a number of early Pleistocene *Homo* fossils from Beds I and II (e.g., Leakey et al. 1964, Leakey 1971, Tobias 1991, Blumenschine et al. 2003). However, only one *H. erectus* specimen, Olduvai Hominid (OH) 9 from upper Bed II, dates to the early Pleistocene (≥ 1.47 Ma based on single crystal ^{40}Ar/^{39}Ar age determinations for the overlying tuff III-1; Manega 1993). Alternatively, numerous *H. erectus* fossils from the Turkana Basin, Kenya, range from possibly as much as 1.9 Ma to younger than 1.45 Ma (Wood 1991a, Brown & McDougall 1993, Walker & Leakey 1993, Leakey et al. 2003). The most remarkable of these are the relatively complete crania (KNM-ER 3733, 3883, and 42,700 at 1.78, 1.6, and 1.55 Ma, respectively) and the KNM-WT 15000 skeleton from West Turkana (~ 1.5 Ma). Earlier fragmentary Koobi Fora cranial remains, including the occipital fragment KNM-ER 2598 (1.88–1.9 Ma) and KNM-ER 3732 (1.89 Ma), and large-bodied postcranial remains (e.g., KNM-ER 3228 at 1.95 Ma) hint at an even earlier presence of *H. erectus*.

Early African members of *H. erectus* (e.g., KNM-ER 3733, 3883, KNM-WT 15000, and OH 9) are separable from earlier members of genus *Homo* on the basis of characteristics of the cranium including development of a supraorbital torus and posttoral gutter, an occipital torus (restricted in the African fossils to the middle third of the occipital), more angular cranial vaults, and occasionally cranial keeling along the sagittal (or metopic) suture (Table 3; Antón 2003). Early *H. erectus* also have somewhat enlarged cranial capacities; larger body sizes, based on postcranial remains; and elongated lower limbs (Table 4; McHenry and Coffing, 2000). However, it is relevant to note that recent discoveries at Ileret, Kenya, appear to extend the lower end of the size range of *H. erectus* (Leakey et al. 2003).

Hominins from Georgia

The Dmanisi material is particularly similar to African members of the species *H. erectus* (Gabunia & Vekua 1994; Rosas et al., 1998; Gabunia et al. 2000a,b; Vekua et al. 2002), and particularly to those from Kenya. Specific similarities include especially facial and dental characteristics (Antón 2003). However, the small cranial capacities (e.g., <700 cc) of recent discoveries (D2700) have again raised the specter of a pre-erectus disperser (Dennell 2003). These fossils, along with the 1.5 Ma KNM-ER 42700 from Ileret, question the relationship between

TABLE 3 Comparisons of some traits in earliest *H. erectus* and nonerectus *Homo*. SAG, sagittal; SOT, Supraorbital torus; SO, Supraorbital; MMR, Mesial marginal ridge

	Vault	Face	Dentition	Postcrania
Early Non-erectus *Homo*	500–700 cc vault rounded, keeling absent, thin-walled, mastoids in nuchal plane	No or small SOT No or restricted SO gutter	Broad molars Multi-rooted premolars	130–149 cm tall Variably platymeric
EARLIEST *H. erectus* East Africa (1.5–1.8 Ma, or more)	700–1067 cc Low and angular in sag view Broad posteriorly Moderate or no keeling Moderately thick walls	Moderate to large SOT Straight SO gutter Broad pyriform ap. Flat infraorbital Paranasal pillars Narrow extramolar sulcus Variable corpus height	Narrow, long molars No accessory cusps Low MMRs Multi/single-rooted premolars	147–173 cm tall platymeric femur (midshaft & higher) Thick cortical bone Acetabulocristal buttress strong
Georgia (~1.7 Ma)	650–780 cc Low and angular in sag view Broad posteriorly Incipient or no keeling Moderately thick walls	Moderate SOT Straight SO gutter Broad pyriform ap. Flat infraorbital Paranasal pillars Narrow extramolar sulcus	Broad, long molars Accessory cusps Low MMRs Single-rooted premolars	148 cm tall (from metatarsal)
Indonesia (>1.5–1.8 Ma)	908 cc Low and angular in sag view Broad posteriorly Marked keeling/tori Very thick walls	Massive SOT Broad pyriform ap. Convex infraorbital No paranasal pillars Tall mandibular corpus	Broad, long molars (very large) Accessory cusps High MMRs Multi/single-rooted premolars	?

TABLE 4 Long bone lengths, stature, and body-weight estimates[a]

Specimen	GeolAge Ma	Length (mm)	Midshaft AP (mm)	Midshaft ML (mm)	Stature (cm)	Weight (kg)
Femora		**Bicondylar**				
Early *Homo* Koobi Fora						
KNM-ER 1472	1.89	400	25.1	26.4	149	47
KNM-ER 1481	1.89	395	22.4	25.6	147	46
KNM-ER 3728	1.89	390	20.1	24.7	145	45
African *Homo erectus*						
KNM-ER 736	1.70	500	36.1	37.7	180	62
KNM-ER 737	1.60	440	27.1	32.4	160	52
KNM-ER 1808	1.69	480	—	—	173	59
KNM-ER 15000[b]	1.53	429 at death	24.5	24.3	159 at death	52
Third metatarsal		**Maximum**				
Dmanisi D2021	1.7	60	—	—	148	46

[a]Data are from H. McHenry (personal communication); McHenry & Coffing (2000); Walker & Leakey (1993); Gabunia et al. (2000c).
[b]To be conservative, subadult stature and body weights for KNM-WT 15,000 are used instead of the larger values projected had he lived to adulthood.

absolute size and shape-related features. Their interpretation is further complicated by the subadult age of both fossils; the sphen-occipital synchondrosis is unfused in D2700 (Vekua et al. 2002) and partially fused in KNM-ER 42700 (Leakey et al. 2003). KNM-ER 42700, despite its small size, exhibits classic *H. erectus* characters, including characters often thought to be limited to Asian *H. erectus* such as cranial keels (Leakey et al. 2003).

Alternatively, investigators have argued Dmanisi (D2700) to be very primitive in its anatomy and similar in its face to the Koobi Fora *H. habilis*, KNM-ER 1813 (Vekua et al. 2002). Though recognizing D2700's small size, the describers of D2700 are quite clear in their attribution of the fossil to *H. erectus* (Vekua et al. 2002); however, others have used D2700 to suggest *H. habilis* as a possible early disperser (Dennell 2003). Although the D2700 specimen is quite small, it has a wide cranial base and an open sphen-occipital synchondrosis coupled with a narrow face. These features suggest that the D2700 face had significant growth still to achieve, much of which would have been in width of the lateral face and in facial height. Thus, contra Dennell (2003), the appearance of the face in D2700 is not particularly useful in making arguments for a pre-erectus disperser. That said, the phyletic relationships among *H. erectus* and various possible nonerectus *Homo* taxa in Africa currently are quite muddled and require substantial revisitation (e.g., Stringer 1986, Wood & Collard 1999, Blumenschine et al. 2003).

As previously mentioned, the Dmanisi hominins are unexpectedly small for their cranial anatomy. On the basis of the metatarsal (D2021), the postcranial skeleton also appears to have been relatively small in comparison with African *H. erectus* (Gabunia et al. 2000c). A stature estimate of 1.48 m (SE = 65.4 mm) places the Dmanisi hominin at the small end of the female range for early African *H. erectus* (Table 4; Gabunia et al. 2000c) and more similar in size to the earlier, probably nonerectus, *Homo* from Koobi Fora that, owing to a lack of association with relevant cranial remains, are assigned only to *Homo* sp.

Hominins from Indonesia

Most previous work concludes that the earliest hominins in Indonesia are *H. erectus* (e.g., Rightmire 1993; Antón 1997, 2003; Grimaud-Hervé 2001). The very earliest Indonesian crania from the Sangiran (Pucangan) Formation are few in number and often badly deformed postmortem. The best preserved of these, Sangiran 4, exhibits morphology typical of Asian *H. erectus* (Table 3). Those crania dating to between 0.9 and 1.5 Ma are more numerous and less deformed and likewise exhibit morphology typical of Asian *H. erectus*. Estimates of size must rely on cranial robusticity and capacity, both of which are substantial in the earliest hominins. Cranial capacity is about 900 cc, and most of the earliest cranial and mandibular remains are, if anything, hyperrobust (Wolpoff 1999, Antón 2003). The entire Sangiran assemblage, however, shows substantial cranial size variation. Early Indonesian postcrania are currently unavailable for size estimates. Whereas some specific characters appear to unite earliest western Asian and Javan hominins, they each also show characters perhaps indicative of endemism and/or different source populations (Antón & Indriati 2002).

WHY DID THEY LEAVE? MODELS OF DISPERSAL

The early Pleistocene hominin dispersal(s) contrast the range retraction undergone by other k-selected apes throughout the Pliocene and recent times (Fleagle 1998). Thus hominins must have found a way around the usual restrictions placed on primates with their life-history variables (Cachel & Harris 1998, Jablonski et al. 2000, Antón et al. 2002). The foraging strategy associated with the Oldowan Industry and changes in body plan may have facilitated hominin dispersal (Shipman & Walker 1989, Leonard & Robertson 2000, Antón et al. 2002). Modeling the effects of these changes remains speculative but can draw from knowledge of the extant world in a number of ways.

Energetics, Body Size, and Home Range

Modeling the energetic requirements of ancient hominins begins with physical evidence of the fossil record including measures of brain size, body size, and proportions. Such models have been particularly useful in defining physiologically reasonable scenarios (Leonard & Robertson 2000, Sorensen & Leonard 2001).

TABLE 5   Estimated body weight and home range size for fossil hominins

Species	Avg Wt[a] (kg)	HR$_i$-Ape[b] (ha)	HR$_i$-Human[b] (ha)
A. afarensis	37.0	40	247
A. africanus	35.5	38	234
A. robustus	36.1	39	239
A. boisei	44.3	51	316
H. habilis	41.6	47	290
H. erectus	57.7	73	452
Large Koobi Fora early Homo	46.0	53	331
Dmanisi 2021	46.0	53	331
African H. erectus & Dmanisi	54.2	66	413
African H. erectus, Dmanisi, & Early Koobi Fora Homo	51.0	61	380
H. sapiens	59.5	76	471

[a]Average body weights for Australopithecines, *H. habilis*, *H. erectus*, and *H. sapiens* after McHenry (1992, 1994). Sample composition for body-weight estimates for Large Koobi Fora early *Homo*, Dmanisi 2021 African *H. erectus* and Dmanisi and African *H. erectus*, Dmanisi and Koobi Fora calculated from specimens and weights listed in Table 4.

[b]Home range estimates based on the equation $\log HR = 1.36(\log \text{Weight}) + 0.009(\text{Diet Quality}) - 2.01$, as derived by Leonard & Robertson (2000). Hr$_i$-Ape assumes a diet quality equal to the average for modern apes (DQ = 164), and for Hr$_i$-Human a diet quality at the low end of the range of modern tropical human foragers (DQ = 252).

The postcranial fossils of *H. erectus* are, in general, relatively larger than those of earlier hominins (e.g., McHenry 1992, 1994; Ruff & Walker 1993; Aiello & Wood 1994; Kappelman 1996; McHenry & Coffing 2000) (Tables 4, 5). Stature estimates range between 148 and 185 cm for known *H. erectus* specimens with related body-mass estimates of between 46 and 68 kg if all geographic areas and times are included (Antón 2003). In contrast, estimates for *H. habilis* (*sensu lato*) overlap with *Australopithecus* with a weight of less than 30 kg for a presumed female (OH 62; Johanson et al. 1987) and about 46 kg for a presumed male (KNM-ER 3735; Leakey et al. 1989), although sample sizes are extremely small. Body size increase itself is often considered a response to shifts in climate from moister to drier conditions and to more patchily distributed resources in East Africa around and slightly before the origin of *H. erectus* (e.g., Aiello & Key 2002, Antón et al. 2002).

Recent work allows the estimation of home range (HR) size from body-weight and diet-quality estimates and has suggested a substantial increase in HR size between early *Homo* and *H. erectus* (Table 5) (Leonard & Robertson 2000). However, as noted, apparently the range of body sizes is greater than paleoanthropologists have appreciated in the past. Large postcranial remains appear at Koobi Fora as early as 1.95 Ma (e.g., ilium KNM-ER 3228), whereas small *H. erectus* are present at Dmanisi and at Ileret Kenya (KNM-ER 42700 at 1.55 Ma; Leakey et al. 2003).

Recalculations of HR estimates, considering the recent discovery of smaller-bodied *H. erectus*, are reported in Table 5. These recalculations suggest that even if all of the largish postcrania older than 1.8 Ma are included in *H. erectus* (a step many are understandably unwilling to take; see Trinkaus 1984), average HR size is still larger in *H. erectus* than in earlier *Homo* (380 versus 290 ha, respectively). If only the Dmanisi remains are included with *H. erectus*, arguably a more reasonable position given cranial anatomy, then the differences between average *H. erectus* HR and that of earlier *Homo* are even more substantial (413 versus 290 ha, respectively).

Differences in estimated body and brain size between *H. erectus* and *Australopithecus* suggest substantially greater expenditures of total resting energy to maintain brain function in the former than in the latter (Leonard & Robertson 1992, 1994, 1996, 1997); approximately 17% of total resting energy (or about 260 Kcal) in *H. erectus* and only 11% in *Australopithecus* is devoted to brain support. These differences suggest that *H. erectus* must have had a more energy-rich diet than had earlier hominins. The smaller differences between early *Homo* and *H. erectus* as calculated above suggest similar, if less significant, foraging shifts.

Such an enriched diet might include animal meat and marrow (Walker et al. 1982, Shipman & Walker 1989, Leonard & Robertson 2000, Antón et al. 2002), honey (Skinner 1991; but see Skinner et al. 1995), or underground tubers (e.g., Wrangham et al. 1999). Underground tubers require fire to release their nutritional stores and thus may have been of limited use until well after the origin of *H. erectus*, given the scant evidence for early controlled fire (see Brain & Sillen 1988, Bellomo 1994). Alternatively, there is abundant archaeological evidence for meat consumption at hominin sites including butchered animal remains and associated stone tool assemblages (e.g., Leakey 1971, Shipman 1986, Blumenschine et al. 1994). The sporadic consumption of meat by some extant primates (Stanford 2001) and earlier hominins (de Heinzelin 1999) suggests that increasing reliance on animal resources was a feasible, although perhaps not an exclusive, means of increasing diet quality (Shipman & Walker 1989; Antón et al. 2001, 2002). Further support of meat consumption comes from tapeworm phylogenies that suggest the two most closely related, human-specific species (*Taenia saginata* and *T. asiatica*) diverged sometime betewwn 0.78 ka and 1.7 Ma (Hoberg et al. 2001), which suggests that a human host (*H. erectus*) was infected, presumably by consuming the flesh of an infected animal, during this time period.

Ancient Dispersals

Another line of recent work suggests that the geographic dispersal of *Homo* from Africa is intimately tied to the shifts in body size and foraging strategy discussed above. Estimates of the rate of hominin dispersal have been calculated using diffusion coefficients (*D*) based on site locations and ages from the fossil record (Leonard & Robertson 2000; Antón et al. 2001, 2002). A subset of these estimates are reported in Table 6. *D* values suggest rapid dispersal rates from Africa that contrast with ancient dispersals made by other primates. By analogy, ecological parameters that could have promoted the quick hominin dispersal include larger

TABLE 6   D values for extant mammals and calculated D values for fossil taxa

Species	Intrinsic rate of natural increase (r)	Time to occupy (t)	Area occupied[a] (z)	Diffusion coefficient[b] (D)
RECENT DISPERSALS[c]				
Enhydra lutris	0.06	various	various	13.5–54.7
Ondatra zibethicus	0.2–1.4	various	various	9.2–231
Sciurus carolinensis	0.82	various	various	0.4–18.5[c]
ANCIENT DISPERSALS				
Macaca sp. (Europe to Asia)	0.05	1.5 Ma–10 ka	3135	0.00,002–0.5
Theropithecus darti (to South Africa)	0.05	0.7 Ma–10 ka	2200	0.00,004–0.2
Homo erectus s.l. (to Indonesia)	0.01–0.015	200–10 ka	4380	0.01–4.8
Homo erectus s.l. (to Georgia)	0.01–0.015	100–10 ka	2665	0.02–1.8

[a]Z values are calculated as the square root of the linear distance between localities multiplied by a transect 1200 km wide.

[b]Diffusion coefficients calculated as $D^{1/2} = z \div (t)(2r^{1/2})$. Where z is the square root of area invaded, t is the time over which invasion occurred in years, and r is the intrinsic rate of increase of the species. See Antón et al. (2002) for further methodological details. Differences between modern and ancient dispersal rates relate to (*a*) the greater speed of dispersal in nonprimate, r-selected mammals such as squirrels and (*b*) time averaging inherent in paleo-samples.

[c]Data from Williamson (1996).

[d]Predicted values and observed historical spread are significantly lower than for other dispersing mammals, presumably because of ecological interaction between red and gray squirrels.

home-range sizes (Ehrlich 1989), a shift in foraging behavior (Ehrlich 1989, Shipman & Walker 1989, Leonard & Robertson 2000), and a somewhat slower pattern of dispersal than was the case for fossil carnivores (Antón et al. 2001, 2002). These parameters are similar to the shifts inferred above from increasing energetic requirements of increasing body and brain size, although they are based on independent datasets (Antón et al. 2001, 2002).

How Many Dispersals Were There?

The title of this review implies multiple early dispersals. Over the past decade increasing evidence has accumulated to suggest that hominins began dispersing from Africa in the early Pleistocene, a case we have summarized here. However, this evidence comes from only a few localities outside Africa. The tendency is to "connect the dots" between these localities with a single arrow and thus to imply that early dispersal was a single, unidirectional, always-successful event. From these few data points we try to sort out the types of hominins, nonhominin fauna, and toolkits that left Africa, as well as to discern the probable catalysts, if not the causes, of this dispersal. But this approach may lead us a bit astray.

Given modern mammalian dispersal and migration patterns it is likely that multiple dispersals of small groups occurred periodically, that the fossil hominins we currently know in the early Pleistocene outside of Africa come from slightly different source populations, that some of those that left stayed in localities whereas others moved further on, and that back migrations of genes or organisms were possible. It is also likely that, although the broad ecological parameters we outline, including shifts in body size and foraging strategy, were partly behind these dispersals, other less-logical or deliberate factors, such as curiosity, were involved as well. Certainly, if we look at the decision-making processes involved in modern human migrations we must also allow for any number of idiosyncratic causes leading to dispersal.

It is also plausible that the various pulses of dispersal were controlled in part by cyclic Pleistocene climate, waxing and waning between glacial and interglacial periods. Although less affected in equatorial regions, certain corridors or migratory paths may have been differentially affected owing to more northern latitude or elevation. Given the lack of sufficient hard data, these scenarios can only be speculative, being derived from temporal correlations with global Pleistocene climatic patterns. We are, however, unconvinced by Dennell's (2003) argument that the current early Pleistocene record of hominins outside Africa is any better read as "evidence of absence" (i.e., quite sporadic or episodic dispersal events) than it is as "absence of evidence" owing to insufficient investigation of early Pleistocene localities in large parts of the old world.

SUMMARY

In the past decade, a wealth of new data has supported a longer chronology of hominin presence outside Africa beginning at ~1.6–1.8 Ma (e.g., Swisher et al. 1994, Gabunia et al. 2000a, Larick et al. 2001, Vekua et al. 2002). Collectively, these data indicate an early Pleistocene date for the initial dispersal(s) from Africa of a hominin carrying a core and flake tool technology. The cranial anatomy of these hominins indicates that the source populations for these hominins were those of early African *H. erectus*. Although the resolution of the fossil record of the early ex-African sites could be interpreted as a single wave of dispersal, the anatomy of the hominin fossils outside of Africa and dispersing patterns of extant animals are suggestive of several source populations of *H. erectus* migrating at slightly different times. Nonetheless, increasing body size and home range size are likely responses to changing ecological conditions at the origin of *H. erectus* and are perhaps part of a web of "eco-morphological" factors that fueled the rapid expansion of *H. erectus* from Africa into Asia in the early Pleistocene.

ACKNOWLEDGMENTS

We are grateful to our many colleagues worldwide for access to specimens and field localities and for intriguing discussion. We are especially indebted to Drs. E. Indriati, T. Jacob, W.R. Leonard, F. Spoor, G. Scott, and G. Curtis.

The *Annual Review of Anthropology* is online at http://anthro.annualreviews.org

LITERATURE CITED

Aiello LC, Key C. 2002. Energetic consequences of being a *Homo erectus* female. *Am. J. Hum. Biol.* 14:551–65

Aiello LC, Wood BA. 1994. Cranial variables as predictors of hominin body mass. *Am. J. Phys. Anthropol.* 95:409–426

An Z, Gao W, Zhu Y, Kan X, Wang J, et al. 1990. Magnetostratigrapahic dates of Lantian *Homo erectus. Acta. Anthropol. Sinica* 9:1–7

Antón SC. 1997. Developmental age and taxonomic affinity of the Mojokerto child, Java, Indonesia. *Am. J. Phys. Anthropol.* 102:497–504

Antón SC. 2002. Evolutionary significance of cranial variation in Asian *Homo erectus. Am. J. Phys. Anthropol.* 118:301–323

Antón SC. 2003. A natural history of *Homo erectus. Yearb. Phys. Anthropol.* S37:126–70

Antón SC, Indriati E. 2002. Earliest Pleistocene *Homo* in Asia: comparisons of Dmanisi and Sangiran. *Am. J. Phys. Anthropol. Suppl.* 34:38

Antón SC, Aziz F, Zaim Y. 2001. Dispersal and migration in Plio-Pleistocene *Homo.* In *Humanity from African Naissance to Coming Millennia—Colloquia in Human Biology and Palaeoanthropology*, ed. PV Tobias, MA Raat, J Moggi-Cecchi, GA Doyle, pp. 97–108. Florence: Florence Univ. Press

Antón SC, Leonard WR, Robertson M. 2002. An ecomorphological model of the initial hominid dispersal from Africa. *J. Hum. Evol.* 43:773–85

Aziz F. 2001. New insight on the Pleistocene fauna of Sangiran and other hominid sites in Java. See Simanjuntak et al. 2001, pp. 260–71

Bar-Yosef O, Goren-Inbar N. 1993. *The lithic assemblages of 'Ubeidiya: a lower Paleolithic site in the Jordan Valley.* Hebrew Univ. Jerusalem, Monogr. 34

Bellomo RV. 1994. Methods of determining early hominid behavioral activities associated with the controlled use of fire at FxJj 20 Main, Koobi Fora, Kenya. *J. Hum. Evol.* 27:173–95

Berggren WA, Kent DV, Swisher III CC, Aubry M-P. 1995. A revised Cenozoic geochronology and chronostratigraphy. In *Geochronology, Time Scales and Global Stratigraphic Correlation*, ed. WA Berggren, DV Kent, M-P Aubry, J Hardenbol, pp. 129–212, Spec. Publ. No. 54. Tulsa OK: Society for Sedimentary Geology

Bettis III EA, Zaim Y, Larick RR, Ciochon RL, Suminto R, et al. 2004. Landscape development preceding Homo erectus immigration into Central Java, Indonesia: the Sangiran Formation Lower Lahar. *Palaeogeog. Palaeoclimat. Palaeoecol.* 206:115–31

Blumenschine RJ, Cavallo JA, Capaldo SD. 1994. Competition for carcasses and early hominid behavioral ecology: a case study and conceptual framework. *J. Hum. Evol.* 27:197–213

Blumenschine R, Peters C, Masao F, Clarke R, Deino A, et al. 2003. Late Pliocene *Homo* and hominid land use from western Olduvai Gorge, Tanzania. *Science* 299:1217–21

Brain CK, Sillen A. 1988. Evidence from the Swarkrans cave for the earliest use of fire. *Nature* 336:464–66

Brown P. 1994. Cranial vault thickness in Asian *Homo erectus* and *Homo sapiens.* In *100 Years of Pithecanthropus, the Homo erectus Problem*, ed. JL Franzen. *Courier Forsch Inst. Senckenberg* 171:33–46

Brown FH, McDougall I. 1993. Geological setting and age. In *The Nariokotome Homo erectus Skeleton*, ed. A Walker, R Leakey, pp. 9–20. Cambridge, MA: Harvard Univ. Press

Cachel S, Harris JWK. 1998. The lifeways of *Homo erectus* inferred from archaeology and evolutionary ecology: a perspective from East Africa. In *Early Human Behaviour in Global Context: The Rise and Diversity of the Lower Paleolithic Record*, ed.

MD Petraglia, R Korisettar, pp. 108–32. New York: Routledge

Carbonell E, Bermudez de Castro J, Arsuaga JL. 1999. Grand Dolina Stie: TD 6 Aurora Stratum (Burgos, Spain). *J. Hum. Evol.* 37:309–700

de Heinzelin J, Clark JD, White T, Hart W, Renne P, et al. 1999. Environment and behavior of 2.5 million year old Bouri hominids. *Science* 284:625–629

Dennell R. 2003. Dispersal and colonisation, long and short chronologies: How continuous is the Early Pleistocene record for hominids outside East Africa? *J. Hum. Evol.* 45:421–440

de Vos J. 1985. Faunal stratigraphy and correlation of the Indonesian hominid sites. In *Ancestors: The Hard Evidence*, ed. D Delson, pp. 215–20. New York: A.R. Liss, Inc.

de Vos J, Sondaar P. 1994. Dating honminid sites in Indonesia. *Science* 266:1726

Ehrlich PR. 1989. Attributes of invaders and the invading process: vertebrates. In *Biological Invasions: A Global Perspective*, ed. JA Drake, HA Mooney, F di Castri, RH Groves, FJ Kruger, M Rejmanek, M Williamson, pp. 315–28. New York: Wiley

Fleagle JG. 1998. *Primate Adaptation and Evolution*. Berkeley, CA: Academic. 2nd ed.

Foley RA, Lee PC. 1991. Ecology and energetics of encephalization in hominid evolution. *Philos. Trans. Soc. London B* 334:223–32

Gabunia L, Vekua A. 1995. A Plio-Pleistocene hominid from Dmanisi, East Georgia, Caucasus. *Nature* 373:509–12

Gabunia L, Vekua A, Lordkipanidze D, Swisher CC, Ferring R, et al. 2000a. Earliest Pleistocene cranial remains from Dmanisi, Republic of Georgia: taxonomy, geological setting, and age. *Science* 288:1019–25

Gabunia L, Vekua A, Lordkipanidze D. 2000b. The environmental contexts of early human occupation of Georgia (Transcaucasia). *J. Hum. Evol.* 38:785–802

Gabunia L, de Lumley M-A, Berillon G. 2000c. Morphologie et fonction du troisième métatarsien de Dmanissi, Géorgie orientale. In *Early Humans at the Gates of Europe*, ed. D Lordkipanidze, O Bar-Yosef, M Otte, pp. 29–41. Liège, Belgium: Etudes et Rech. Archéologiques, l'Univ. Liege

Gabunia L, Antón SC, Lordkipanidze D, Vekua A, Swisher CC, Justus A. 2001. Dmanisi and dispersal. *Evol. Anthropol.* 10:158–70

Grimaud-Hervé D. 2001. Taxonomic position of the Sangiran 31 hominid. See Simanjuntak et al. 2001, pp. 46–53

Hoberg EP, Alkire NL, de Querioz A, Jones A. 2001. Out of Africa: origins of the *Taenia* tapeworms in humans. *Proc. R. Soc. London B* 268:781–87

Horowitz A. 1989. Prehistoric cultures of Israel: correlation with the oxygen isotope scale. In *Investigations in South Levantine Prehistory*, ed. O Bar-Yosef, B Vandermeersch, Oxford: BAR Int. Ser.

Howell FC. 1994. A chronostratigraphic and taxonomic framework of the origins of modern humans. In *Origins of Anatomically Modern Humans*, ed. MH Nitecki, DV Nitecki, pp. 253–319. New York: Plenum

Huang W, Ciochon R, Yumin G, Larick R, Qiren F, et al. 1995. Early *Homo* and associated artefacts from Asia. *Nature* 378:275–78

Hyodo M. 2001. The Sangiran geomagnetic excursion and its chronological contribution to the Quaternary geology of Java. See Simanjuntak et al. 2001, pp. 320–36

Hyodo M, Nakaya H, Urabe A, Saegusa H, Shunrong X, et al. 2002. Paleomagnetic dates of hominid remains from Yuanmou, China and other Asian sites. *J. Hum. Evol.* 43:27–41

Jablonski N, Whitfort MJ, Roberts-Smith N, Quinqi X. 2000. The influence of life history and diet on the distribution of catarrhine primates during the Pleistocene in eastern Asia. *J. Hum. Evol.* 39:131–58

Jacob T, Curtis GH. 1971. Preliminary potassium-argon dating of early man in Java. *U.C. Berkeley, Arch. Res. Fac. Contrib.* 12:50

Jacob T, Soejono RP, Freeman LG, Brown FH. 1978. Stone tools from mid-Pleistocene sediments in Java. *Science* 202:885–87

Johanson DC, Masao FT, Eck GG, White TD, Walter RC, et al. 1987. New partial skeleton of *Homo habilis* from Olduvai Gorge, Tanzania. *Nature* 327:205–9

Kappelman J. 1996. The evolution of body mass and relative brain size in fossil hominids. *J. Hum. Evol.* 30:243–276

Klein RG. 1989. *The Human Career: Human Biological and Cultural Origins*. Chicago: Univ. Chicago Press

Klein RG. 1999. *The Human Career: Human Biological and Cultural Origins*. Chicago: Univ. Chicago Press. 2nd ed.

Kramer A. 1994. A critical analysis of claims for the existence of Southeast Asian Australopithecines. *J. Hum. Evol.* 26:3–21

Langbroek M, Roebroeks W. 2000. Extraterrestrial evidence on the age of the hominids from Java. *J. Hum. Evol.* 38:595–600

Larick R, Ciochon RL, Zaim Y, Sudijono S, Rizal Y, et al. 2001. Early Pleistocene ^{40}Ar/^{39}Ar ages for Bapang Formation hominins, Central Jawa, Indonesia. *Proc. Natl. Acad. Sci. USA* 98:4866–71

Leakey LSB, Tobias PV, Napier JR. 1964. A new species of the genus *Homo* from Olduvai Gorge. *Nature* 202:7–9

Leakey MD. 1971. *Olduvai Gorge: Excavations in Beds I and II 1960–1963*. Cambridge: Cambridge Univ. Press

Leakey MG, Spoor F, Brown FH, Gathogo PN, Leakey LN. 2003. A new hominin calvaria from Ileret (Kenya). *Am. J. Phys. Anthropol. Suppl.* 36:136

Leakey RE, Walker A, Ward CV, Grausz HM. 1989. A partial skeleton of a gracile hominid from the Upper Burgi Member of the Koobi Fora formation, East Lake Turkana, Kenya. In *Hominidae: Proceedings of the 2nd International Congress of Human Paleontology*, ed. G Giacobini, pp. 167–73. Milan: Editoriale Jaca Book

Leinders JJM, Aziz F, Sondaar PY, de Vos J. 1985. The age of the hominid bearing deposits of Java: state of the art. *Geologie en Mijnbouw* 64:167–173

Leonard WR, Robertson ML. 1992. Nutritional requirements and human evolution: a bioenergetics model. *Am. J. Hum. Biol.* 4:179–95

Leonard WR, Robertson ML. 1994. Evolutionary perspectives on human nutrition: the influence of brain and body size on diet and metabolism. *Am. J. Hum. Biol.* 6:77–88

Leonard WR, Robertson ML. 1996. On diet, energy metabolism and brain size in human evolution. *Curr. Anthropol.* 37:125–29

Leonard WR, Robertson ML. 1997. Comparative primate energetics and hominid evolution. *Am. J. Phys. Anthropol.* 102:265–81

Leonard WR, Robertson ML. 2000. Ecological correlates of home range variation in primates: implications for hominid evolution. In *On the Move: How and Why Animals Travel in Groups*, ed. S Boinski, P Garber, pp. 628–48. Chicago: Univ. Chicago Press

Manega PC. 1993. *Geochronology, geochemistry, and isotopic study of PlioPleistocene hominid sites and the Ngorongoro volcanic highlands in Northern Tanzania*. PhD thesis, Univ. Colorado

Matsu'ura S. 1982. A chronological framing for the Sangiran hominids: fundamental study by the fluorine dating method. *Bull. Natl. Sci. Mus Tokyo Ser. D* 8:1–53

McHenry HM. 1992. Body size and proportions in early hominids. *Am. J. Phys. Anthropol.* 87:407–31

McHenry HM. 1994. Behavioral ecological implications of early hominid body size. *J. Hum. Evol.* 27:77–87

McHenry HM, Coffing K. 2000. *Australopithecus* to *Homo*: transformations in body and mind. *Annu. Rev. Anthropol.* 29:125–46

Monahan CM. 1996. New zooarchaeological data from Bed II, Olduvai Goerge, Tanzania: implications for hominid behavior in the Early Pleistocene. *J. Hum. Evol.* 31:93–128

Ninkovitch D, Burckle LH, Opdyke ND. 1982. Palaeographic and geologic setting for early man in Java. In *The Ocean Floor*, ed. RA Scrutton, M Talwani, pp. 211–227. New York: Wiley

Nioradze M, Justus A. 1998. Stone tools of the ancient Palaeolithic site Dmanisi. In *Dmanisi I*, ed. J. Kopaliani, pp. 140–59. Tbilisi: Metsnieareba, Georgian Academy of Sciences, Centre for Archaeological Studies

Orban-Segebarth R, Procureur F. 1983. Tooth size of *Meganthropus palaeojavanicus*: an analysis of distances between some fossil hominids and a modern human population. *J. Hum. Evol.* 19:761–88

Pope GG. 1983. Evidence on the age of the Asian hominidae. *Proc. Natl. Acad. Sci. USA* 80:4988–92

Repenning CA, Fejfar O. 1982. Evidence for earlier date of Ubeidiya, Israel hominid site. *Nature* 299:344–47

Rightmire GP. 1993. *The Evolution of Homo erectus, Comparative Anatomical Studies of an Extinct Human Species.* New York: Cambridge Univ. Press

Robinson JT. 1953. Meganthropus, australopithecines and hominids. *Am. J. Phys. Anthropol.* 11:1–38

Roebroks W. 2001. Hominid behavior and the earliest occupation of Europe: an exploration. *J. Hum. Evol.* 41:437–61

Rosas A, Bermúdez de Castro JM. 1998. On the taxonomic affinity of the Dmanisi mandible (Georgia). *Am. J. Phys. Anthropol.* 107:145–62

Ruff CB, Walker A. 1993. Body size and body shape. In *The Nariokotome Homo erectus skeleton*, ed. A Walker and R Leakey. Cambridge, MA: Harvard University Press

Sartono S. 1981. Pre-*Homo erectus* population in Java, Indonesia. In *X Congreso Union Int. Ciencias Prehistoricas Protohistoricas*, pp. 47–86

Sartono S, Tyler DE, Krantz GS. 1995. A new '*Meganthropus*' mandible from Sangiran, Java: an announcement. In *Human Evolution in its Ecological Context Vol. 1, Evolution and Ecology of Homo erectus*, ed. JRF Bower, S Sartono, pp. 225–28. Leiden, Netherlands: Pithecanthropus Centen. Found.

Schick KD. 1994. The Movius line reconsidered: Perspectives on the earlier paleolithic of eastern Asia. In *Integrated Pathways to the Past, Festschrift in honour of F.C. Howell*, ed. R Corruccini and R Ciochon, pp. 569–596. New York: Prentice-Hall

Schwartz JH, Tattersall I. 1996. Whose teeth? *Nature* 381:201–2

Sémah F. 1982. Pliocene and Pleistocene geomagnetic reversals recorded in the Gemolong and Sangiran domes (Central Java): initial results. *Mod. Quat. Res. Southeast Asia* 7:151–164

Sémah F, Saleki H, Falguères C. 2000. Did early man reach Java during the late Pliocene? *J. Archaeol. Sci.* 27:763–69

Sémah F, Sémah A-M, Djubiantono T, Simanjuntak T. 1992. Did they also make stone tools? *J. Hum. Evol.* 23:439–66

Shea JJ, Bar-Yosef O. 1999. Lithic assemblages from the new (1988–1994) excavations at Ubeidiya: a preliminary report. *J. Israel Prehistoric Soc.* 28:5–20

Shipman P. 1986. Studies of hominid-faunal interactions at Olduvai Gorge. *J. Hum. Evol.* 15:691–706

Shipman P, Walker A. 1989. The costs of becoming a predator. *J. Hum. Evol.* 18:373–92

Siedner G, Horowitz A. 1974. Radiometric ages of Late Caeinozoic basalts from Northern Israel: chronostratigraphic implications. *Nature* 250:23–26

Simanjuntak T, Prasetyo B, Handini R, eds. 2001. *Sangiran: Man, Culture and Environment in Pleistocene Times.* Jakarta: Yayosan Obor Indonesia

Simanjuntak T. 2001. New insights on the tools of *Pithecanthropus*. See Simanjuntak et al. 2001, pp. 154–70

Skinner M. 1991. Bee brood consumption: an alternative explanation for hypervitaminosis A in KNM-ER 1808 (*Homo erectus*) from Koobi Fora, Kenya . *J. Hum. Evol.* 20:493–503

Skinner M, Jones R, Dunn R, 1995. Undetectability of vitamin A in bee brood. *Apidologie* 26:407–14

Sondaar P, Aziz F, van den Bergh GD, de Vos J. 1996. Faunal change and hominid evolution during Quaternary Java. *Geol. Res. Dev. Cent. Paleontol. Ser.* 8:1–10

Sorensen M, Leonard WR. 2001. Neandertal energetics and foraging efficiency. *J. Hum. Evol.* 40:483–95

Stanford CB. 2001. *The Hunting Apes*. Princeton, NJ: Princeton Univ. Press

Stringer CB. 1986. The credibility of *Homo habilis*. In *Major Topics in Primate and Human Evolution*, ed. BA Wood, LB Martin, P Andrews, pp. 266–94. New York: Liss

Swisher CC III. 1997. A revised geochronology for the PlioPleistocene hominid bearing strata from Sangiran, Java. *J. Hum. Evol.* 32:A23

Swisher CC III, Curtis GH, Jacob T, Getty AG, Suprijo A, Widiasmoro. 1994. Age of the earliest known hominids in Java, Indonesia. *Science* 263:118–21

Tchernov E. 1987. The age of the 'Ubeidiya Formation, an early Pleistocene hominid site in the Jordan Valley, Israel. *Israel J. Earth Sci.* 36:3–30

Tchernov E. 1992. Biochronology, paleoecology, and dispersal events of hominids in the southern Levant. In *The Evolution and Dispersal of Modern Humans in Asia*, ed. T Akazawa, K Aoki, T Kimura, pp. 149–88. Tokyo: Hokusen-Sha

Terra H de. 1943. Pleistocene geology and early man in Java. *Trans. Am. Philos. Soc.* 32:437–64

Tobias PV. 1991. *The Skulls Endocasts and Teeth of Homo habilis from Olduvai Gorge, Volume 4*. Cambridge: Cambridge Univ. Press

Trinkaus E. 1984. Does KNM-ER 1481 establish *Homo erectus* at 2.0 my B.P.? *Am. J. Phys. Anthropol.* 64:137–139

Tyler DE, Krantz GS, Sartono S. 1995. The taxonomic status of the "*Meganthropus*" cranial (Sangiran 31) and the '*Meganthropus*' occipital fragment III. In *Human Evolution in its Ecological Context Vol. 1, Evolution and Ecology of Homo erectus*, ed. JRF Bower, S Sartono, pp. 189–202. Leiden: Pithecanthropus Centen. Found.

Vekua A, Lordkipanidze D, Rightmire GP, Agusti J, Ferring R, et al. 2002. A new skull of early *Homo* from Dmanisi Georgia. *Science* 297:85–89

von Koenigswald GHR. 1936. Ein fossiler hominide aus dem Altpleistocän Ostjavas. *De Ingenieur in Ned-Indie* 8:149–58

von Koenigswald GHR. 1962. Das absolut alter des *Pithecanthropus erectus*. In *Evolution and Hominization*, ed. G Kurth, p. 113. Stuttgart: Verlag

Walker A, Leakey R, eds. 1993. *The Nariokotome Homo erectus skeleton*. Cambridge, MA: Harvard Univ. Press

Walker A, Zimmerman M, Leakey R. 1982. A possible case of hypervitaminosis A in *Homo erectus*. *Nature* 296:248–250

Watanabe N, Kadar D, eds. 1985. Quaternary geology of the hominid fossil bearing formations in Java. Bandung, Indonesia: Geol. Res. Dev. Cent., Spec. Publ. 4

Williamson M. 1996. *Biological Invasions*. New York: Chapman Hall

Wolpoff MH. 1999. *Paleoanthropology*. New York: McGraw Hill. 2nd ed.

Wood B. 1991. *Koobi Fora Research Project Volume 4, Hominid Cranial Remains*. Oxford: Clarendon

Wood B, Collard M. 1999. The Human Genus. *Science* 284:65–71

Wu X. 1999. Chinese human paleontological study in 20th century prospects. *Acta. Anthropol. Sinica* 18:165–75

Wrangham RW, Jones JH, Laden G, Pilbeam D, Conklin-Brittain N. 1999. The raw and the stolen: cooking and the ecology of human origins. *Curr. Anthropol.* 5:567–594

Annu. Rev. Anthropol. 2004. 33:297–317
doi: 10.1146/annurev.anthro.33.070203.143754
Copyright © 2004 by Annual Reviews. All rights reserved
First published online as a Review in Advance on June 10, 2004

THE BODY BEAUTIFUL: Symbolism and Agency in the Social World

Erica Reischer
Independent Scholar, Oakland, California; email: ericar@alumni.princeton.edu

Kathryn S. Koo
*Department of English, Saint Mary's College of California, Moraga, California 94575;
email: kkoo@stmarys-ca.edu*

Key Words beauty, embodiment, gender, femininity

■ **Abstract** The prominence of the body in popular culture has prompted intense academic interest in recent decades. Seeking to overturn a naturalistic approach to the body as a biological given, this broad literature redefines the body as a sociocultural and historical phenomenon. Within anthropology, two primary theoretical orientations toward the body have emerged: the body as "symbol" and the body as "agent." This review article provides an overview of these dominant theoretical approaches in the context of recent scholarship on body ideals and, in particular, the body beautiful. The review explores also the body beautiful as a primary site for the construction and performance of gender, and specifically of femininity, with examples drawn from the abundant literature on women's bodies.

INTRODUCTION

As the anthropological record amply demonstrates, bodies have been and continue to be reshaped in a myriad of culturally relevant ways. The evidence ranges from traditional practices of foot binding and neck elongation to more recent means of body modification through cosmetic surgery and scientifically sophisticated exercise regimes. Humans may be the only creatures that steadfastly refuse to let nature alone dictate their appearance. Indeed, our capacity for self-modification and adornment is a central and essential feature of our humanity, though the particular ways in which we alter our bodies are clearly a cultural phenomenon.

Bodies are modified for many reasons—for example, to register participation in a social group, to claim an identity in opposition to a social group, to signal a significant change in social status—but the overarching theme and primary end of most body work is the pursuit and attainment of beauty, however it may be defined. Among the tribes of the Kalahari Desert, shiny skin is considered an attractive feature, so much so that even in times of famine, the tribes choose to use precious animal fats as a skin emollient rather than as food (Turner 1980). In the West, cosmetics are a multibillion-dollar industry in the United States alone. A more extreme form of beautification, cosmetic surgery, once restricted to the elite, has in recent years enjoyed a much larger and more diverse clientele owing to its rapidly growing popularity and social acceptance. Statistics reveal that in the mid-1990s, 1 out of every 35 surgical procedures performed in the United States was performed for aesthetic reasons alone (Gilman 1999, p. 4). And the number of such procedures continues to rise.

Even our toys are undergoing "the knife" in the name of beauty. In 1997, Mattel's most famous toy, the Barbie doll, emerged from the factory operating room with a "wider waist, slimmer hips, and. . .a reduction of her legendary bustline" (*Wall Street Journal* 1997). This reconfiguration of the West's premiere icon of femininity after nearly forty years suggests that the image of femininity embodied by the original Barbie of the late 1950s has undergone a radical transformation of its own. Beauty, though highly subjective, is more than simply a matter of aesthetics or taste. Cultural ideals of beauty are also an index and expression of social values and beliefs—so much so that "the history of [society] is in large measure the history of women's beauty" (Jury & Jury 1986).

In the last few decades, the prominence of the body in popular culture has generated intense academic interest and activity. Instead of viewing the body as "an uninteresting prerequisite of human action" (Shilling 1993, p. 19), fields from across the disciplinary spectrum have turned their attention to the body as a central concern of social theory. Seeking to overturn a naturalistic approach to the body as biological given, this broad literature has redefined the body as a sociocultural and historical phenomenon (e.g., Bourdieu 1977, Elias 1978, Foucault 1979, Goffman 1968, Mauss 1973).

Within this rich and varied literature, two primary theoretical orientations toward the body, and the relationship between the body and society, have become prominent: the "symbolic body" and the "agentic body." The first and more prevalent perspective focuses on the representational or symbolic nature of the body as a conduit of social meaning, whereas the second highlights the role of the body as an active participant or agent in the social world. This chapter provides an overview of these dominant theoretical approaches, with an eye toward their varied, nuanced expressions in the context of recent anthropological scholarship on body ideals and, in particular, the body beautiful.

Because "beauty work" has historically been the province of women, examples of the body beautiful are drawn primarily from women's ideals of beauty. This is not to say, however, that male body ideals and the coding of masculinity through these ideals have been overlooked. Indeed, a number of recent works attest to the growing interest in the social and cultural production of the masculine. Connell (1995) has deployed feminist and queer theory in order to examine the highly constructed nature of Western masculinity. Bordo (1999), a prominent theorist on women and women's bodies, has considered the "double bind of masculinity" that has emerged in a culture that both celebrates male "primitive potency" and forbids male sexual aggression. Faludi (1999) surveys male disaffection in our contemporary culture (reflected in increased violence, resistance to feminism, extreme nationalism, etc.) as symptomatic of a growing crisis about the meaning of masculinity itself, a crisis that points to the "betrayal" of men by the very masculinist ideals that they are meant to embody. But beauty itself has been traditionally gendered as a female trait of desirability. This review focuses on beauty as read through women's bodies because, as one cultural historian has observed, beauty has historically been a "special category of women's experience" (Banner 1983, p. 9).

Authors across the disciplinary spectrum, including anthropology, sociology, psychology, and feminist studies, have written extensively on the body beautiful. Because it would be impossible to survey all the significant literature, this review focuses primarily on the key theoretical movements in the anthropological literature with an eye toward those theorists from other disciplines who provide a noteworthy addition, nuance, or complication to the cultural construction of beauty. This chapter is also bounded by geography. The growing number of studies concerned with the construction of beauty in non-Western contexts demands a specific framing of this chapter's investments. The West serves as the central focus of this study, whereas the regions of Saharan and sub-Saharan Africa serve as critical counterpoints to the West and its hegemonic cultural dominance. In the West, the condition of thinness has become such a widely accepted prerequisite of the body beautiful that it almost seems "natural" to assume that a thin body is aesthetically preferable to a corpulent one. But the celebration of female obesity in one Arab culture of Saharan Africa (Popenoe 2004) offers a revealing opposition to that ideal and further serves to illuminate the constructed nature of all notions of beauty.

Starting from the notion that the bodies we cultivate are ultimately indexes and expressions of the social world they inhabit, the chapter begins by exploring two main representational approaches: the body beautiful as an icon of social values and, less benignly, as a mechanism of social power and control. The discussion then turns to more recent theoretical perspectives that emphasize an active role for the body in the social world. These alternative conceptualizations highlight the body as a fundamental aspect of the acting self, and so recognize the capacity of embodied selves to appropriate the symbolic nature of the body to their own ends. Here, beauty becomes an embodied concept that is not simply an articulation of dominant cultural values but also a negotiation of them. In the merging of its symbolic and agentic capacities, then, the body beautiful may be read as a primary site for the social construction and performance of gender. The chapter concludes by integrating these theoretical views of the body in society that together suggest the capacity of the body to signify the social and to transform social reality.

THE SYMBOLIC BODY

Mary Douglas, in her groundbreaking work *Natural Symbols* (1970), was among the first to articulate the symbolic significance of the body. In this work, Douglas argues that "there is a strong tendency to replicate the social situation in symbolic form by drawing richly on bodily symbols in every possible dimension" (1970,

p. vii). Given this notion that the social situation is reproduced or "replicated" through bodily symbols, the body is viewed metaphorically as a text that can be "read" as a symbol or signifier of the social world that it inhabits. Although this notion of the body as a homologous reflection of social form has drawn criticism as scholarly conceptions of the body have become increasingly complex (see, for example, Comaroff 1985), Douglas's symbolic reading of the body stands as one of the defining works of the representational perspective.

If the body is, as Douglas argues, a "text" upon which social meanings are inscribed, then a common vocabulary, a common symbol set, is needed to decipher those meanings. Our bodies transmit a dizzying array of complex information about ourselves, with or without our intention, and we and other members of our culture tend to be expert at reading those culturally specific meanings almost instantaneously. But, whereas Americans would understand a ring worn on the third finger of a woman's left hand as a signifier of her status as a married woman, they are likely far less adept at deciphering the significance of a woman's white robes in India, which indicate widowhood. Even within a single culture, the message of the body is subject to change over time. Whereas in many Western cultures a large, plump body once connoted prosperity, health, and high social ranking, this same body now signifies quite the opposite: poverty, ill health, and low socioeconomic status.

Taking their cues from Douglas's reading of the body as the site of symbolic representation, many writers have observed that bodies have the potential to express core social values (Becker 1994, Bordo 1993, Brownell 1991, Crawford 1984, Glassner 1988, Ritenbaugh 1982). From this perspective, the quality of attractiveness that we find in the bodies around us is not insulated from cultural and cognitive processes; attractiveness is that which is found ideologically appealing within an overarching set of values. As Balsamo notes, "The body becomes. . .the site at which women, consciously or not, accept the meanings that circulate in popular culture about ideal beauty. . . . The female body comes to serve as a site of inscription, a billboard for the dominant cultural meanings that the female body is to have in postmodernity" (1996, p. 78).

Also characteristic of this perspective is Bordo's *Unbearable Weight: Feminism, Western Culture, and the Body* (1993) in which she argues that "the firm, developed body has become a symbol of correct *attitude*," suggesting "willpower, energy, control over infantile impulse, the ability to 'shape your life'" (1993, p. 195). Because in most Western cultures we generally take that which is communicated by the body to be a message about the self, Bordo notes that the size and shape of one's body has come to signify the moral state of the individual. For instance, one's body is a physical reflection of one's internal capacity for commitment and self-control. Bordo argues that our contemporary cultural abhorrence of fat, or loose flesh in general, is not about the aesthetics of physical size per se, but rather about changes in the social symbolism of body weight and size. Developing and displaying an ideal body type thus signals one's cooperative participation in a culturally meaningful system of values.

But feminist scholars such as Bordo view body ideals not simply as benign symbols of social values. Following the insights of Marx and Foucault, these feminist theorists also point to the ways in which body ideals serve as mechanisms of social power and control. For example, the slender body ideal symbolizes not only an aesthetic ideal but also the internal discipline that may be necessary to achieve it. As many critics have observed, the desire to demonstrate such discipline has manifested itself in the remarkable rise of eating disorders in recent decades (Bordo 1993, Callaghan 1994, Chernin 1981, Nichter & Nichter 1991, Orbach 1978, Wolf 1991, Vertinsky 1987). In their pursuit of this ideal, women have subjected themselves to extreme regimens of diet, exercise, and other forms of physical self-improvement, efforts that all too often become all consuming to the detriment of more socially relevant projects. Thus, the ideal gendered body does not merely remain in the realm of the symbolic; its power lies in its ability to directly influence behavior within the social domain.

Extending Crawford's (1984) observation that the contradictory economic mandates of production and consumption are reproduced at the site of the body, Bordo argues that personal body management is intimately connected with the management of the larger "social body" through consumer culture (1993, p. 199). Our market economy requires that we participate in regular cycles of control and release, as exemplified by our rotations between work and play, weekday and weekend. Control is required by capitalism so that production continues, and release is necessary so that the endless stream of products produced in a capitalist society is ultimately consumed. Capitalist ideology requires us to work hard eight hours a day or more and then feel entitled to an indulgent break from that disciplined regime, only to resume work again the next day. Consequently, the slender ideal is capitalist ideology embodied: It reminds us that we must know when to say when. But as Bordo notes, the fine balance between control and release can be elusive, given the contradictions that emerge between our discipline as producers and our desires as consumers. With increasing frequency, we bear witness to what happens when one aspect of our capitalist personality dominates the other: excessive discipline that results in anorexia, or excessive desire reflected in obesity. In the case of bulimia, the body becomes the site of both forms of excess (Bordo 1993, p. 201).

In her book *The Beauty Myth* (1991), Wolf notes that the rise of eating disorders in the 1980s coincided with the rise of women to positions of power and authority within the workplace. Their simultaneous rise was no accident, according to Wolf, as women were feeling the effects of a feminist backlash and the deployment of a "political weapon" (1991, p. 10) by male institutions of power: "the beauty myth." According to this myth, beauty is an objective attribute that all women necessarily want to embody. Representing fertility and evolutionary triumph, a beautiful woman is and always has been more desirable to men than are her peers. In debunking this myth, Wolf asserts that beauty is not a universal or natural category but rather a form of cultural "currency" used by male institutions to limit and control women's access to power. Within this economy, beauty is not merely a desirable asset but a "legitimate and necessary qualification for a woman's rise in power" (1991, p. 28). Through a rigorous reshaping of the body and a constant vigilance against the noticeable (and ultimately unavoidable) effects of aging, women might attain the beauty upon which their professional success depends. According to Wolf, a new "meritocracy" based on beauty has emerged in opposition to women's proven talents and capabilities in order to justify and maintain women's secondary status in the workplace.

If maintaining a "beautiful" body—carefully monitored and controlled in its size and appearance—is a symbol of cultural and social cooperation, then striving for a body in direct opposition to that ideal is tantamount to civil disobedience. In her study of compulsive overeating, Orbach (1978) argues that in a society where thinness is central to the normative construction of femininity, being fat is not an issue of self-control or willpower but instead represents an attempt to resist gender stereotypes. "Getting fat," Orbach writes, "is a very definite and purposeful act connected to women's social position" (1978, p. 31). Here, fat is not a sign of a woman's victimization by unattainable images of the body beautiful but rather is symbolic of her feminist rebellion against the dominant images of ideal womanhood that limit her ability to realize her own image. Orbach notes that excessive weight in the workplace can signify a revolt against the sexual objectification of the female worker, and indeed, may be an attempt to "neutralize" her sexual identity to gain power and respect in the work environment among her male peers. Overeating, then, may be seen as a direct attempt to symbolically overturn the limitations imposed on women.

Although obesity and anorexia are often viewed as separate disorders, Chernin (1981) views both as stemming from our cultural obsession with food and the body. Chernin argues that the anorexic girl and the obese woman both share "an unexpressed hostility, fear of sexuality, an uneasiness about what is expected of women in this culture" (1981, p. 73) that lead them to their respective behaviors toward food. Both disorders, Chernin asserts, participate in the symbolic in their reflection of women's anxieties about fulfilling the culturally constructed notion of the "acceptable body" (1981, p. 36). The obsessive overeater indulges in excessive amounts of food not to feed the hunger of the body, but to feed the "yearning for permission to enjoy the sensual aspects of the self" (1981, p. 15) that are forbidden to women in contemporary culture. In parallel but reverse fashion, the anorexic starves herself to deny the pleasures and the potential of the body. The anorexic takes to the extreme the long-standing dichotomy between body and mind. Thus, according to Chernin, the anorexic's disease is, above all, "an illness of self-division" that can only be understood as a "tragic splitting of body from mind" (1981, p. 47). It should not be surprising, then, that the opposition between celebration and denial of the female body gave rise to two "divergent movements" (1981, p. 99) that appeared in the same historical moment: the feminist movement of the 1960s, which envisioned new possibilities for women, and the simultaneous emergence of the new diet industry—heralded by the launching of an American cultural icon, Weight Watchers—that negated women's own potential to take charge of their lives, and by extension, their bodies.

Gremillion (2003) recently noted that even the clinical approach to "curing" anorexia is paradoxically a participant in the very cultural discourses—discourses of gender, individualism, and physical fitness—that contribute to the pathology of self-starvation in the first place. On the basis of her fieldwork in a state-of-the-art inpatient facility, Gremillion observes that the modern-day treatment of anorexia attempts to involve the patient in her own recovery by inviting her participation in the setting of her goal weight. But Gremillion argues that despite such attempts to include the patient in her own treatment plan, the standing power differential between the patient and the clinical staff results in the anorectic feeling that her identity and self-worth are inseparable from her medical statistics: her body weight and pulse rate. Ironically, the treatment for anorexia resurrects the same antagonisms between willpower and the body that it attempts to resolve. As Gremillion notes, "The psychiatric representation of the 'anorexic'—in particular, the anorexic body—as a pathologized object of therapeutic knowledge and practice recreates the culturally dominant idea that the female body is an obstacle in the making of fitness/health, and it also reinforces patients' perceived dependence on others even as they seek self-control" (2003, p. 47).

In her study of the hunger strike, Ellmann (1993) finds that the political prisoner who engages in the hunger strike and the female anorectic share more in common than their radically different agendas might initially indicate. Both the hunger striker and the anorectic have identified the body as a powerful "form of speech" (1993, p. 3) capable of articulating their respective discontents, the former using the body as a protest against an unjust political regime and the latter using the body as a protest against patriarchal structures of power. In both cases, the body enables the striker or the anorectic to symbolically circumvent and even transcend the conditions imposed upon it. Ellmann argues that although self-starvation was ultimately self-defeating for ten Northern Irish hunger strikers who died in a notorious detention camp for political prisoners in 1981, the symbolism conveyed by their wasted bodies was not. The hunger strike resulted in the public disgrace of the Thatcher administration amid worldwide publicity of the prisoners' plight. As Ellmann acutely argues, the body is central to personal and political expression, and when it is voluntarily starved and disciplined beyond its limits, it opens up a powerful symbolic territory for the articulation of dissent against forms of social or political oppression.

Since Orbach's and Chernin's linking of fat and feminist theory, social theorists have further interrogated the notion of fat as "transgression" by examining the ways in which the various discourses that have evolved around the corpulent body have attempted to "contain" and even "erase" that body (Braziel & LeBesco 2001). Further, scholars have paid increasing attention to the constructed nature of obesity, a condition that has most often been received as evidence of abnormality or pathological deviance without regard to the myriad number of influences— cultural, historical, political—that have shaped it (Braziel & LeBesco 2001). As a social construction, fat has thus become central to the shaping of identity politics. LeBesco attempts a "theoretical queering of fat politics" (2001, p. 77) in order to explore the political possibilities of a fat identity, an identity that has thus far been relegated to the extreme margins of the social order, while Mazer's study of a contemporary sideshow Fat Lady by the name of Helen Melon (Katy Dierlam in real life) reveals the ways in which the stereotype of the "smiling, fleshy woman in a baby-doll costume" has been problematized by her self-representation as an "appetite outlaw" and "sexual provocateur" (2001, p. 257), representations that challenge the very notion of the Fat Lady as spectacle and commodity.

In contrast to the majority of authors who focus their attention on adult notions of beauty, Mimi Nichter examines the ideal of the body beautiful as perceived by adolescent girls. In *Fat Talk* (2000), Nichter argues that the pervasive discourse among women and girls around the ideal of slenderness is a critical component of girls' socialization in two important ways. First, participation in "fat talk" facilitates the creation and maintenance of social relationships: It provides a means for girls (and women) to signal their membership in a group and to demonstrate a socially appropriate degree of humility (2000, p. 55). A second socializing function served by fat talk is the actual shaping of body ideals. While acknowledging the significant role of the media in dictating acceptable body ideals, Nichter contends that women and girls also play a critical role in their formation (2000, p. 183). Shaping these ideals are female peer groups and, most notably, according to Nichter, mothers and daughters, since dieting is often a shared activity between them; moreover, mothers are significant figures in the transmission of cultural messages about gender and femininity, constructions that are played out at the site of the body.

In analyzing images of adolescent beauty, Nichter also uncovers meaningful differences between ethnic groups. In contrast to "white girls" who engaged in frequent fat talk centered around a hegemonic ideal of youth and slenderness, the African American girls studied by Nichter demonstrated a "more fluid, flexible image of beauty" (2000, p. 178) that placed more emphasis on attitude and style than on body weight or size. Nichter relates this difference to an "ideology of egalitarianism" in the African American community that is reproduced at the site of the body: "In contrast to the more static image of beauty as bodily perfection found in white culture...that fosters envy and alienation, an egalitarian ethos is promoted, marked by mutual appreciation, cooperation, and approval of someone 'who's got it going on'" (2000, p. 178).

The ideal of the body beautiful—and how to attain that ideal—can also serve to illuminate significant cultural differences between and among Western countries that are often grouped together as one monolithic West. Stearns (1997) notes that despite basic similarities between the American and French histories of weight concern and control, the two countries' attitudes toward obesity and weight loss reveal important points of cultural divergence. Whereas in America obesity has been linked to moral degeneracy and social inadequacy, the same condition in France has not carried the same associations. Being fat, the French have long recognized, has serious consequences for one's health and one's appeal to the opposite sex, but it does not make one morally or ethically culpable (1997, pp. 202–10). In contrast, beauty in America has been so closely linked to character that a beautiful woman is necessarily one who has had the moral uprightness to achieve it (1997, pp. 202–3). To the French, beauty is an aesthetic quality and is therefore available to everyone, not just those with the moral rectitude to achieve it. According to Stearns, whereas the American dieter is haunted by the specter of social disgrace and moral failure, the French dieter is free to attempt individual bodily improvement without the presence of a "personal demon to exorcise" (1997, p. 210).

But the management of body size is only one area of reform. In the pursuit of body ideals that cannot be achieved by weight reduction alone, women in increasing numbers have turned to more radical means of body modification through cosmetic surgery. As Gilman (1998) argues, the rise of aesthetic surgery as a widely accepted practice reflects the popular belief in its ability not only to correct bodily deviance and deformation, but also to "cure" and "restore" the psyche that has been damaged by the body's stigmatization. The role of aesthetic surgery, then, is twofold: In curing the ills of the body, it can also cure the "unhappy" psyche. That aesthetic surgery is now a "form of psychotherapy" (1998, p. xi) points to the symbolic power of the body to reflect the status of the psyche itself. Gilman also notes the ways in which aesthetic surgery has historically been deployed to address and correct sexual and racial stigma, for example, the syphilitic nose that "marked the body as corrupt and dangerous" (1999, p. 49) and the racial nose of the "Jew," the "Irish," the "Oriental," and the "Black," which signaled difference from the Western ideal of beauty (1999, pp. 85–118).

Kaw's (1994) investigation of one specific surgical procedure among Asian American women points to the intersection between racial ideology and capitalist consumer culture. In an attempt to give their eyes a more "open appearance," Asian American women in increasing numbers are seeking the help of aesthetic surgeons to achieve a double eyelid, a fold above each eye that creates the appearance of a wider eye and reduces the look of "sleepiness," "dullness," and "passivity." As Kaw observes, Asian facial features have historically contributed to negative Asian stereotyping in this country: Asians' small, squinty eyes indicate a "childishness, narrow-mindedness, and a lack of leadership skills" (1994, p. 251), traits that continue to haunt Asian Americans in even the "positive" myth of the model minority. Interestingly, Kaw's subjects largely dismissed the notion that they were seeking the surgery in order to look more Caucasian, but they consistently recognized the socioeconomic advantages of having more open, and hence more alert-seeming, eyes; one such subject referred to the surgical procedure as nothing less than an "investment in your future" (1994, p. 254). As Kaw points out, "In the United States, where a capitalist work ethic values 'freshness,' 'a quick wit,' and assertiveness, many Asian American women are already disadvantaged at birth by virtue of their inherited physical features which society associates with dullness and passivity" (1994, p. 250). Although the Asian American women who participated in Kaw's subject group viewed their decision as a reflection of their own individuality and self-assertion, Kaw came to another conclusion: Their facial revisions reflected their internalization of society's negative portrayal of the Asian body (1994, p. 260).

For most feminist critics, the rise of cosmetic surgery as a viable and acceptable means of self-modification represents the ongoing oppression of women by the ideology of femininity and the cultural tyranny of beauty. But feminist critic Davis (1993) views cosmetic surgery not simply as a sign of women's victimization but rather as reflective of their engagement in a complex ideological dilemma, a dilemma "where women grapple actively and knowledgeably with opposing cultural discourse of femininity, beauty, and what should or should not be done about the female body" (p. 27). Contrary to the image of cosmetic surgery as an embrace of the coercive and oppressive demands of beauty within a capitalist consumer society, Davis finds that women who elect such surgery are acutely aware of the conflict between feminism and feminine ideology, and the decision itself may be more accurately described as an act of agency rather than as one of mere victimization. As Davis notes of one of her subjects, "Her decision is presented as a rational weighing of factors, and she emerges as an agent, exercising control over her life within a situation that is not entirely of her own making" (1993, p. 34).

In her history of American girlhood, Brumberg (1997) notes that the body has not always been the primary project and central focus of self-improvement that it is today. On the basis of her comparative readings of nineteenth- and twentieth-century diaries of adolescent girls, Brumberg finds that girls a century ago rarely focused their attention on their bodies as a means of bettering themselves or achieving personal distinction. On the contrary, the way to self-improvement was through minimizing the importance of the body and focusing instead on character development and performing good works for others. Today, good looks has clearly won out over good works (1997, pp. xx–xxii). With the help of a consumer industry that touts its ability to sanitize and perfect the human form, the body has now become the most significant and most preoccupying project of American girls because of its status as the "ultimate expression of the self" (1997, p. 97).

Although the work of Brumberg, Gilman, Bordo, and others is firmly rooted in the Western tradition that regards the body as the sign of individual selfhood, it is worth noting that the connection between body and self cannot be taken as a universal given. In contrast to the conception of the body as a message bearer about the "inhabiting" self, Becker (1994) notes that in Fiji the body is less a reflection of the self than it is a reflection of community. Becker claims that the Fijians do not see the body as a personal showcase but rather as a display of the nurturing or negligence of the larger community. The Fijian body is more of a collective achievement, and Fijians derive social prestige not from their own bodies but from the bodies of others with whom they are associated. Becker notes that this difference in the signifying potential of the body—that is, representing self versus others—is a function of culturally different notions of what it means to be a person and the relationship between self and body. In most Western cultures, this notion that the body "belongs" to the self is taken as hardly worth mentioning; from there, it is a short step to the idea that the body represents in some way the self's essence. In Fiji, however, the body is community property, not a product of the embodied self, but rather an artifact of social connectedness.

THE AGENTIC BODY

Although the body may serve as a powerful symbolic medium, the body is also endowed with the capacity to participate in the creation of social meaning. Arguing that the body's symbolic capacity to reflect the social world provides only a partial theoretical account of its significance in social theory, scholars more recently have conceived of the body as an active agent in the social world, on the grounds that our bodies inescapably mediate our relationship to the world around us. Drawing heavily on Merleau-Ponty's insight that "the body is our general medium for having a world" (1962, p. 146) and Bourdieu's (1977) notion that the body structures both how we act and how we perceive, theorists have pointed to the body as a fundamental aspect of the acting self, thus seeking to transcend the dichotomy of self as subject versus body as object in order to draw attention to the often overlooked role of the body in social action (e.g., Comaroff 1985; Comaroff & Comaroff 1992; Csordas 1990, 1993; Devische 1985; Frank 1991; Haraway 1991; Lock 1993; Scheper-Hughes & Lock 1987; Turner 1994; Wacquant 1995). Within this framework, a self that acts on the world necessarily does so through the medium of the body; accordingly, this approach is often referred to as "embodiment" (Csordas 1990).

To assert that the body is an agent is not to overlook that the body, as conceptualized in a dualistic Western philosophical tradition, is ultimately an object that in itself has neither subjectivity nor capacity for intentional action. However, the self is ultimately an embodied self, and the symbolic capacity of material bodies can thus be "employed" by this self so embodied as one way to act on the world. That is, bodies are not only constitutive of subjectivity, but also mediate the relationship between persons and the world: We meet the world through our bodies. Therefore, bodies necessarily participate in the agency of selves. This approach, and the term embodiment, which is often used to describe it, thus seek to create a new idiom for theorizing about the role of the body in the social world. Because the way we think about concepts or entities in themselves, or about the relationships between them, is highly influenced by the way we talk about them (Lakoff and Johnson 1980), a theory that seeks to reframe the way we conceive of the body in society must necessarily invoke different metaphors and alternate terms (such as embodiment, agency, etc.) by which the issue can be discussed. These terms thus metaphorically point to the central notion of the body as an active participant in the social domain. Thus, to say that the body is an "agent" or "subject" is not to assert that subjectivity is a feature of the body per se, but rather that bodies, because they are constitutive of subjectivity and also mediate the relationship between person and world, necessarily participate in the agency of the person.

Illustrative of this approach to the body is Csordas's (1993) work on religious and traditional healing practices that focus on shared empathy between healer and patient. On the basis of his theorization of "somatic modes of attention," which he defines as "culturally elaborated ways of attending to and with one's body in surroundings that include the embodied presence of others" (1993, p. 138),

Csordas argues that religious healing practices do not merely seek to confirm divine intervention. In their focus on bodily experience, these practices seek to create meaning through the intersubjectivity between supplicant and healer. The healer "anoints" his supplicant through the touch of hands and gains the "word of knowledge" about the supplicant's afflictions through sympathetically experienced pain. According to Csordas, healing shared between self and others offers up new ways of attending to an "embodied intersubjectivity" (1993, p. 146). Our attention to and with the body enables us also to redefine and reconceptualize our relationship to the categories of intuition, imagination, perception, and sensation.

Given its agency, the body necessarily plays a significant role in times of social, cultural, or political crisis. In a revolution, the established body ideal is one of the first things to be overturned or redefined in favor of a more ideologically appropriate replacement. In American history, for example, the 1960s slogan "Black is beautiful" served as the rallying call for the black power movement. The slogan was less about the attractiveness of a particular skin color than about the advancement of black consciousness and pride that was central to the civil rights movement. Such a perspective recognizes that "the body is not only a symbolic field for the reproduction of dominant values and conceptions; it is also a site for resistance to and transformation of those systems of meaning" (Crawford 1984, p. 95). In this capacity for "resistance" and "transformation," the body—because it is ultimately the basis for such an endeavor at the level of symbols—is conceptualized as agentic. Within this formulation, social actors appropriate and manipulate the body's symbolic capacities for their own ends, though this project is not necessarily a conscious endeavor. This perspective creates a powerful theoretical alliance, one in which the body is viewed as both "template and tool" (Comaroff & Comaroff 1992, p. 87).

Because the body is such a potent symbol, its form and appearance often are highly politicized, as Comaroff & Comaroff (1992) discovered in their ethnographic analyses of neocolonial settlements in South Africa. Indeed, body reform, according to these theorists, has always been critical to the project of empire-making:

> States old and new have built their esprit de corps by shaving, clothing, vaccinating, and counting their citizens, just as rising classes, ethnic groups, religious movements, and political associations tend to wear their self-awareness on their skin. For their part, conquerors and colonizers seem typically to feel a need to reverse prior corporeal signs, often making bodies into realms of contest. (1992, p. 41)

The body is at once a vehicle for the imposition of social, political, and economic forces onto individuals and groups and is a vehicle for resistance to these forces. Thus, the human frame "can never be a struggle-free zone, least of all when major historical shifts are under way" (Comaroff & Comaroff 1992, p. 40).

As Comaroff & Comaroff have shown, colonial power in Africa has historically focused on and circulated through the black body. Comaroff & Comaroff argue that the project of nineteenth-century British colonialism in Africa was inseparably linked to the rise of biomedical science that attempted to draw clear distinctions between what was perceived by the colonists to be the diseased and potentially contagious African body and the white, sanitized European body, which was then exposed to such sources of danger and disorder (1992, p. 216). In contrast to the dry and impermeable surface of the European body, the surface of the African body was "porous, dirty, and damp, one that 'gave off' contagion and odor to those with whom it came into contact" (1992, p. 225). As Comaroff & Comaroff have found, mid-nineteenth-century evangelists in Africa were as interested in bringing European methods of sanitation to the continent as they were in bringing Christianity to its peoples. Indeed, it was through the project of imposed sanitation that evangelists attempted to make "Protestant persons" (1992, p. 224) of their heathen charges.

But if the body is conceived as the means by which the colonialist project is enacted, it can also serve as the site of resistance to that project. In their ethnography of the South African frontier, Comaroff & Comaroff note that beauty itself can become the site of colonial contestation. Well aware of the power of European clothing to remake their people into something they were not, indigenous Tswana rulers took to embracing "fantastic fashions" (1992, p. 43) that both adopted and subverted the fashions of their colonizers. As Comaroff & Comaroff argue, "The Tswana 'style wars,' in which local leaders tried to fight off Western dress and architecture, were as much the site of colonial politics as were formal confrontations with government personnel or settler statesmen" (1992, p. 43). By subversively embracing the physical and cultural signs of British colonialism, South Africans found an alternative means of articulating their challenge to colonial oppression.

Thus far, to speak of "disciplining" the body has implied the willful work of self-deprivation in order to achieve a certain aesthetic and/or political ideal. In her study of the aesthetic of female fatness among the Azawagh Arabs of Niger, Popenoe (2004) found that bodily discipline can assume a far different form. Within this Islamic culture, fatness is considered such a beautiful and desirable trait in women that girls as young as five and six years old are forcibly fattened by an appointed female authority figure within the family. The force-feeding of young girls is intended to accelerate the process of sexual maturity because fatness is so closely associated with womanliness: The sooner a girl has assumed the contours and curves that come with corpulence, the sooner she is considered of a marriageable age (2004, pp. 44–45). By fattening, Muslim girls in this culture also hasten the fulfillment of their primary religious duty and purpose in life: to produce the next generation of the faithful (2004, p. 72).

Popenoe contends that in becoming fat, Azawagh Arab women actively cultivate an aesthetic of "softness, pliability, stillness, seatedness," which is in direct opposition to the aesthetic of men that valorizes "hardness, uprightness, mobility" (2004, p. 191). In the West, such an opposition typically translates into an imbalance of power between the genders, but Popenoe guards against such cultural transpositions by grounding her work in the specific Islamic context of this Moorish people. According to Islamic scripture, men and women are radically different kinds of beings that are best harmonized when opposed to one another. Differentiation between men and women in all aspects of life—in prayer, in work, in marriage—is not only to be respected but actively cultivated. Thus, the opposition between a woman's immobility within the home and a man's agility abroad is not to be taken as an automatic reflection of inequality, but rather as a sign of purposeful division. Indeed, whereas a Westerner might view a woman's getting fat as reflective of her failure to work and compete within the social marketplace, the Azawagh Arabs view a woman's getting fat as a form of labor itself (2004, p. 123). As Popenoe observes, "Female fatness among Azawagh Arabs is thus not only expressive and symbolic of fundamental cultural tenets, but also provides women with a powerful way of exercising agency in their own lives" (2004, p. 192).

By fattening and immobilizing herself, an Azawagh Arab woman simultaneously enhances her sexuality and sanctions her allure by becoming a powerful and culturally approved object of male desire. In her seeming inactivity and inertia within her tent, an Azawagh Arab woman nevertheless exerts a kind of "gravity" (2004, p. 195) in her social sphere, which serves to stabilize the transience and volatility of men's lives spent abroad in herding and trading. Immobility through fatness also serves as a powerful expression of a woman's self-control over her own sexual desires. By attaining a difficult body ideal, a woman proves herself able to control the dangers of her own desiring and thus proves willing to forego her own interests in favor of the interests of her society.

FEMININITY AND THE NEGOTIATION OF BEAUTY

What makes a woman a woman? The simplicity of the question belies the complexity of the answers that have been posited by theorists concerned with the categories of gender and sexual difference. Butler's (1990) assessment of gender as a cultural construction, and the body as a "variable boundary" that performs the cultural meanings of gender, has been central to the ongoing discussion of what constitutes a "feminine" identity. Although gender is often mistaken for natural category or biological fact, Butler argues that "the various acts of gender create the idea of gender, and without those acts, there would be no gender at all" (1990, p. 140). If gender is a series of repeated performances, then the distinctions of gender are dependent on the quality of its enactment by the body. As a result, the body has become the battleground for the policing of boundaries between men and women.

Grosz (1994) also attends to the question of sexual difference by turning to the body's vexed relationship with subjectivity. Overturning the long-established dichotomy between mind and body, Grosz approaches the corporality of the body itself as a "framework" for understanding sexual identity and subjectivity. To do so requires a rethinking of the "natural" body as having been socially constructed by the biological and medical discourses about the body, discourses that are commonly viewed as impervious to cultural or social bias (1994, p. x). According to Grosz, the body does not, in fact, belong to the realm of the "natural" but rather serves as "a neuralgic locus for the projection and living out of unreflective presumptions regarding the sexes and their different social, sexual, and biological roles" (1994, p. x). As such, bodies "cannot be adequately understood as ahistorical, precultural, or natural objects in any simple way; they are not only inscribed, marked, engraved, by social pressures external to them but are the products, the direct effects, of the very social constitution of nature itself" (1994, p. x).

But Butler's notion of gender as a performative category and Grosz's reading of subjectivity as grounded in the body are relatively recent approaches to the problem of defining women's experience. The ideologies that have defined woman's nature (what a woman is) and her competencies (what a woman can and should do) have historically relied on the physical materiality of the female body. This body and its "natural" physical characteristics "come to count as definitive emblems of female identity" (Balsamo 1996, p. 43) and both, in turn, support and legitimize the gendered structure of society. Similar to Lock's (1993) argument that even the "objective" sciences are culturally informed and constructed, Ludmilla Jordanova observes,

> Women's occupations were taken to be rooted in and a necessary consequence of their reproductive functions.... Women's destiny to bear and suckle children was taken to define their whole body and mind, and therefore their psychological capacities and social tasks. (1980, p. 49)

A significant correspondence, then, exists between women's bodies and their position in society, a connection largely mediated by social ideologies of gender because gender is a bodily "fact" that carries also social import and consequences. As Jordanova (1980) argues, social constructions of gender typically seek material grounding in the body, invoking these body-based "natural facts" to sustain their worldview. But these natural facts or "natural symbols" (Douglas 1970) grounded in the body actually "produce and are part of ideological systems; they disguise and justify the social artifice as a natural part of the unchangeable 'order of things'" (Devisch 1985, p. 409). In the nineteenth century, for instance, the archetypal feminine quality of softness became a physical metaphor for the construction of social views regarding both the nature of womanhood and the right and proper place of women in society (Jordanova 1980, p. 49). One prominent physician of the time wrote that "[women's] muscular feebleness inspires in [them] an instinctive disgust of strenuous exercise; it draws them towards amusements and sedentary occupations" (Cabanis 1956, p. 278; c.f., Jordanova 1980, p. 49).

In her social history of beauty, Banner (1983) notes early feminists' response to such culturally constructed notions of womanhood. Elizabeth Cady Stanton and Amelia Bloomer attempted to signal the beginning of a new era in women's consciousness by donning shorter skirts and pantaloons, which emancipated them from the traditional women's dress that confined their movement and activity. But the growing unpopularity and eventual demise of the "bloomer" within a few years of its introduction were, as Banner argues, due to its failure to address the more powerful symbolic appeal of women's fashion, that is, fashion as a means of cultivating a woman's ability to attract and hold the attention of men (1983, p. 100), still her primary concern in a culture that celebrated marriage as the goal of all women. According to Banner, the triumph of fashion over feminism as demonstrated in the demise of the bloomer was repeated again and again in American history. Indeed, Banner argues that even today we may witness the reenactment of this battle in the Miss America Pageant, a phenomenon that was first staged in 1921 and that has enjoyed popularity—and notoriety—ever since.

In her study of this long-standing cultural phenomenon, Banet-Weiser (1999) argues that today's beauty pageant is much more than a carefully rehearsed spectacle of femininity. As a "civic ritual," the beauty pageant participates in the realm of politics because it produces a national identity for its viewers through the mediation of ethnicity and femininity on the stage. Although beauty pageants have historically celebrated the "ideal female citizen" as incontrovertibly embodied by a white woman, the relatively recent phenomenon of nonwhite winners of beauty pageants demonstrates the function of beauty pageants as a mediation of race and ethnicity within national boundaries.

According to Banet-Weiser, the beauty pageant is caught in another crossroads: that between feminine objectification and feminine empowerment. Feminists have long argued that beauty pageants perpetuate the commodification of women as objects of display, which ultimately creates victims of its participants and profiteers of the spectacle's many stagers: producers, directors, and the audience at large. But Banet-Weiser argues that the beauty pageant has also become a "kind of feminist space where female identity is constructed by negotiating the contradictions of being socially constituted as 'just' a body while simultaneously producing oneself as an active thinking subject, indeed, a decidedly 'liberal' subject" (1999, p. 24). Indeed, the appropriation of a liberal feminist discourse in the self-presentation of contestants is now commonplace; Banet-Weiser notes that contestants now emphasize individual achievement and career ambitions, not homemaking and motherhood, as the means of asserting selfhood.

Other authors have explored the construction and negotiation of femininity and beauty in broader contexts, such as the workplace. As a whole, these studies highlight the central role of the body in supporting a vast symbolic system that enables individuals to situate themselves in relation to other social actors. For example, previous research that compares employed with unemployed women has found that women in the workforce evince less concern with their appearance than do their nonworking peers (Hayes & Ross 1986). Working women, the authors argue, have more direct access to capital and so are less likely to cultivate personal appearance as an indirect means of gaining resources, that is, through alliances with men.

But the notion that women cultivate their appearance chiefly in regard to men's preferences may be an oversimplification because this explanation overlooks other social and symbolic aspects of physical form. Researchers have found, for example, that women often idealize a different figure than their own estimate of what men would prefer (Fallon & Rozin 1985). The simple distinction between women working outside the home or not working outside the home seems less important, however, than the shifting nature of women's work as they enter positions and professions previously exclusive to men. Treating the secretary and the senior partner alike because they are both working women obscures significant differences in their social positioning and relationships with colleagues.

Recognizing this complexity and also addressing the issue of gender, Rodin (1993) contends that working women, particularly in certain kinds of occupations, may actually be more concerned with their physical appearance.

> Women who are successful in previously male-dominated professions often need both to minimize their female status and to retain it. [Since] physically attractive women are perceived as more feminine..., [L]ooking feminine, while displaying 'unfeminine' ambition and power, may serve to affirm a woman's identity to herself and others. (1993, p. 644)

Rodin thus speculates that "looking feminine"—generally synonymous with beauty, as Callaghan (1994) notes—tempers the impact of a woman's "unfeminine ambition," though this explanation somewhat takes for granted that what "looks feminine" changes considerably over time. What is notable about Rodin's perspective is her recognition of the contradictions that women in male-dominated occupations must frequently negotiate through the medium of the body. Paradoxically, they must be feminine yet not too feminine. As Rodin notes, they must display their femininity to compensate for their display of putatively "unfeminine" qualities associated with success in a "man's world."

The double bind between minimizing and yet affirming one's femininity in a gendered environment is explored also by Reischer (2000) in her study of the athletic/muscular body ideal that has emerged for women in contemporary American society. Like Rodin, Banet-Weiser, and others, Reischer shares the underlying notion that the body and its appearance are a prime site for negotiating women's position in a complex web of social meaning and value. Noting that other female body ideals, such as thinness, have historically waxed and waned in social prominence, she begins with the observation that late twentieth-century America is the first cultural moment in which muscles, a physical attribute once antithetical to femininity, have come to be associated with the body beautiful. Moreover, the emergence of this new image of beauty coincides—meaningfully, according to Reischer—with a major transformation in women's social position, particularly in the nature and meaning of women's work.

On the basis of both ethnographic and survey research with more than 200 women, Reischer's study has two key findings. First, it reveals that women of different cohorts or generations with respect to the modern women's movement—those who led or witnessed its legal and social reforms, and those who have been its primary beneficiaries—hold substantially different notions about the ideal female form. Younger women, those who largely came of age after the successes of feminist social reform, tend to idealize muscular female bodies significantly more than do their older counterparts. A second and more provocative finding is that women in differently gendered occupational environments (that is, male- versus female-dominated occupations) demonstrate measurably different sensibilities about their own and other female bodies. Specifically, women who work in male-dominated occupations tend to have a significantly more positive perception of muscular female bodies. Like Rodin, Reischer argues that women in male-dominated professions experience their bodies as central to workplace dynamics; they encounter a host of occupational pressures and challenges in their work environment—particularly around issues of appearance, reproduction, and sexuality—challenges that are largely related to these women's common experience of a paradoxical imperative to minimize their femininity even as they must also affirm it.

Departing from Bordo's (1993) notion of the muscular female body ideal as residing on a continuum with the slender body, Reischer argues that muscles participate in an entirely different symbolic category: Given the strong cultural signification of muscles as an emblem of masculinity, a muscular female body is qualitatively different from a slender one because it disrupts naturalized gender distinctions in a way that the slender body cannot. From this perspective, a muscular female physique embodies a new image of femininity that challenges naturalized social distinctions between men and women by acting on the social meanings grounded in the body. According to Reischer, by desiring to have muscles, women are seeking to embody social values associated with muscles and to demonstrate that muscles—which is to say strength, discipline, and other such socially valued qualities—are equally characteristic of women, within a revised definition of femininity that seeks to renegotiate its position with respect to masculinity, by acting on the social constructions grounded in the body.

In this dual capacity of women's bodies to both reflect and challenge their social positions, Reischer finds that even the limits and boundaries of idealized female muscularity index women's paradoxical position in the workforce and signal the deeply entrenched barriers to gender equality that women still experience. Although the cultivation and display of muscles is no longer exclusively a male perogative, women are clearly expected to do so in manifestly different ways than are men. As many feminist scholars note (e.g., Balsamo 1996, Bolin 1992, Haywood 1998, Mansfield & McGinn 1993), women must take caution not to develop muscles that are too large or well defined. As Mansfield & McGinn observe, "There is a great deal of difference between two kinds of female hard body image. [In contrast to] an acceptable hard body image such as that of Madonna. . .[there is] another hard body image which appears. . .more threatening: the image of the female bodybuilder, an image which goes far beyond that of the 'more athletic woman of today'" (1993, p. 54). For Reischer, this preservation of difference and distinction between gendered bodies reflects the barriers to income and status equality that women still confront in the workplace, despite their increasing presence in previously male-dominated professions; that is, the proverbial "glass ceiling" finds its analogue in the idealized shape of women's bodies. The body is thus a prime site for the contestation of social and individual power; it is the locus of both oppression and empowerment, simultaneously.

The Evolution of Beauty

Recent investigations of the body beautiful demonstrate the extraordinary capacity of the body not only to symbolize the social world, but also to participate actively in the creation of that world. Indeed, the two theoretical views of the body in society—as "artifact" and "agent"—are essentially complementary because the capacity of the body to signify the social also entails the power of the body to transform social reality (Comaroff & Comaroff 1992). Because cultural meanings and values reside in and on the material body, the body not only reflects these constructions but also has the capacity to challenge them. The body thus serves as a vehicle for social action even as it signifies social realities: Bodily (re)form both reflects and motivates processes of social reform. Responsive to the highly coded nature of beauty, women have learned to appropriate the body's symbolism to achieve their own ends. Women's bodies, and social constructions of the ideal female form, do more than reflect women's position in society: They offer a powerful means for negotiating, redefining, and reconceptualizing that position. However, these forms of resistance occur within overarching social structures that ultimately index existing power relations.

Despite our ability to theorize, analyze, and contextualize the underlying meaning of beauty in contemporary culture, we are no less enthralled by its display. To disavow beauty is ultimately to valorize its discursive power to define the "Good," the "Desirable," and even the "Ethical" and the "Moral." As much as we may find solace in the well-worn adages that "beauty is only skin deep" and "beauty is in the eye of the beholder," our daily experience in the social world, and even our own responses to the body beautiful, tell us otherwise. We are all beholders, and we are all looking far beyond the surface of the skin.

ACKNOWLEDGMENTS

The authors thank Michael Mascuch, Hertha D. Sweet Wong, and Jennifer Heung for their insightful critiques of this review in the final stages of its development. We also thank Jean Comaroff, Gilbert Herdt, and Richard Shweder.

The *Annual Review of Anthropology* is online at http://anthro.annualreviews.org

LITERATURE CITED

Balsamo A. 1996. *Technologies of the Gendered Body: Reading Cyborg Women.* Durham, NC: Duke Univ. Press

Banet-Weiser S. 1999. *The Most Beautiful Girl in the World: Beauty Pageants and National Identity.* Berkeley: Univ. Calif. Press

Banner L. 1983. *American Beauty.* New York: Knopf

Becker A. 1994. Nurturing and negligence: working on others' bodies in Fiji. See Csordas 1994, pp. 100–15

Bolin A. 1992. Vandalized vanity: feminine physiques betrayed and portrayed. In *Tattoo, Torture, Mutilation, and Adornment: The Denaturalization of the Body in Culture and Text,* ed. FE Mascia-Lees, P Sharpe, pp. 79–99. Albany: State Univ. NY Press

Bordo S. 1993. *Unbearable Weight: Feminism,*

Western Culture, and the Body. Berkeley: Univ. Calif. Press

Bordo S. 1999. *The Male Body: A New Look at Men in Public and in Private.* New York: Farrar, Straus and Giroux

Bourdieu P. 1977. *Outline of a Theory of Practice.* Cambridge: Cambridge Univ. Press

Braziel JE, LeBesco K, ed. 2001. *Bodies Out of Bounds: Fatness and Transgression.* Berkeley: Univ. Calif. Press

Brownell KD. 1991. Dieting and the search for the perfect body: where physiology and culture collide. *Behav. Therapy* 22:1–12

Brumberg JJ. 1997. *The Body Project: An Intimate History of American Girls.* New York: Random House

Butler J. 1990. *Gender Trouble: Feminism and the Subversion of Identity.* New York: Routledge

Callaghan KA, ed. 1994. *Ideals of Feminine Beauty: Philosophical, Social, and Cultural Dimensions.* Westport, CT: Greenwood Press

Chernin K. 1981. *The Obsession: Reflections on the Tyranny of Slenderness.* New York: Harper and Row

Comaroff J. 1985. *Body of Power, Spirit of Resistance.* Chicago: Univ. Chicago Press

Comaroff J, Comaroff J. 1992. *Ethnography and the Historical Imagination.* Boulder, CO: Westview Press

Connell RW. 1995. *Masculinities.* Berkeley: Univ. Calif. Press

Crawford R. 1984. A cultural account of "health": control, release, and the social body. In *Issues in the Political Economy of Health Care*, ed. JB McKinlay, pp. 60–103. New York: Tavistock

Csordas TJ. 1990. Embodiment as a paradigm for anthropology. *Ethos* 18:5–47

Csordas TJ. 1993. Somatic modes of attention. *Cult. Anthropol.* 8:135–56

Csordas TJ, ed. 1994. *Embodiment and Experience: The Existential Ground of Culture and Self.* Cambridge: Cambridge Univ. Press

Davis K. 1993. Cultural dopes and she-devils: cosmetic surgery as ideological dilemma. In *Negotiating at the Margins: The Gendered Discourses of Power and Resistance*, ed. S Fisher, K Davis, pp. 23–47. New Brunswick, NJ: Rutgers Univ. Press

Devisch R. 1985. Approaches to symbol and symptom in bodily space-time. *Int. J. Psychol.* 20:389–415

Douglas M. 1970. *Natural Symbols: Explorations in Cosmology.* New York: Pantheon Books

Elias N. 1978. *The Civilizing Process.* Oxford: Blackwell

Ellmann M. 1993. *The Hunger Artists: Starving, Writing, and Imprisonment.* Cambridge, MA: Harvard Univ. Press

Fallon AE, Rozin P. 1985. Sex differences in perceptions of desirable body shape. *J. Abnorm. Psychol.* 94:102–5

Faludi S. 1999. *Stiffed: The Betrayal of the American Man.* New York: Morrow

Foucault M. 1979. *Discipline and Punish: The Birth of the Prison*, trans. A. Sheridan. Harmondsworth: Penguin

Frank AW. 1991. For a sociology of the body: an analytical review. In *The Body: Social Process and Cultural Theory*, ed. M Featherstone, M. Hepworth, BS Turner, pp. 36–102. London: Sage

Gilman SL. 1998. *Creating Beauty To Cure the Soul.* Durham: Duke Univ. Press

Gilman SL. 1999. *Making the Body Beautiful: A Cultural History of Aesthetic Surgery.* Princeton, NJ: Princeton Univ. Press

Glassner B. 1988. *Bodies: Why We Look the Way We Do (and How We Feel About It).* New York: Putnam

Goffman E. 1968. *Stigma.* Harmondsworth: Penguin

Gremillion H. 2003. *Feeding Anorexia: Gender and Power at a Treatment Center.* Durham, NC: Duke Univ. Press

Grosz E. 1994. *Volatile Bodies: Toward a Corporeal Feminism.* Bloomington: Indiana Univ. Press

Haraway DJ. 1991. *Simians, Cyborgs, and Women: The Reinvention of Nature.* New York: Routledge

Hayes D, Ross CE. 1986. Body and mind: the effect of exercise, overweight, and physical health on psychological well-being. *J. Health Soc. Behav.* 27:387–400

Heywood L. 1998. *Bodymakers: A Cultural Anatomy of Women's Body Building.* New Brunswick, NJ: Rutgers Univ. Press

Jordanova LJ. 1980. Natural facts: a historical perspective on science and sexuality. In *Nature, Culture, and Gender,* ed. CP Mac Cormack, M Strathern, pp. 42–69. Cambridge: Cambridge Univ. Press

Jury M, Jury D. 1986. *Bizarre Rituals: Dances Sacred and Profane.* Documentary, 83 min.

Kaw E. 1994. "Opening" faces: the politics of cosmetic surgery and Asian American women. In *Many Mirrors: Body Image and Social Relations,* ed. N Sault, pp. 241–65. New Brunswick, NJ: Rutgers Univ. Press

LaKoff G, Johnson M. 1980. *Metaphors We Live By.* Chicago: Univ. Chicago Press

LeBesco K. 2001. Queering fat bodies/politics. In *Bodies Out of Bounds: Fatness and Transgression,* ed. JE Braziel, K LeBesco, pp. 74–87. Berkeley: Univ. Calif. Press

Lock M. 1993. Cultivating the body: anthropology and epistemologies of bodily practice and knowledge. *Annu. Rev. Anthropol.* 22:133–55

Mansfield A, McGinn B. 1993. Pumping irony: the muscular and the feminine. In *Body Matters: Essays on the Sociology of the Body,* ed. S Scott, D Morgan, pp. 49–68. London: Falmer Press

Mauss M. 1973. Techniques of the body. *Econ. Soc.* 21:70–88

Mazer S. 2001. "She's so fat...": facing the fat lady at Coney Island's sideshows by the seashore. In *Bodies Out of Bounds: Fatness and Transgression,* ed. JE Braziel, K LeBesco, pp. 257–76. Berkeley: Univ. Calif. Press

Nichter M. 2000. *Fat Talk: What Girls and Their Parents Say About Dieting.* Cambridge, MA: Harvard Univ. Press

Nichter M, Nichter M. 1991. Hype and weight. *Med. Anthropol.* 13:249–84

Orbach S. 1978. *Fat is a Feminist Issue.* New York: Paddington Press

Popenoe R. 2004. *Feeding Desire: Fatness, Beauty, and Sexuality Among a Saharan People.* London: Routledge

Reischer E. 2000. *Muscling in: the female body aesthetic and women's roles in contemporary American society.* PhD thesis. Univ. Chicago

Ritenbaugh C. 1982. Obesity as a culture-bound syndrome. *Cult. Med. Psychiatry* 6:347–61

Rodin J. 1993. Cultural and psychosocial determinants of weight concerns. *Ann. Intern. Med.* 119:643–45

Scheper-Hughes N, Lock M. 1987. The mindful body: a prolegomenon to future work in medical anthropology. *Med. Anthropol. Q.* 1:6–41

Shilling C. 1993. *The Body and Social Theory.* London: Sage

Stearns PN. 1997. *Fat History: Bodies and Beauty in the Modern West.* New York: New York Univ. Press

Turner T. 1980. The social skin. In *Not Work Alone: A Cross-Cultural View of Activities Superfluous to Survival,* ed. J Cherfas, R Lewin, pp. 112–40. Beverly Hills, CA: Sage

Turner T. 1994. Bodies and anti-bodies: flesh and fetish in contemporary social theory. See Csordas 1994, pp. 27–47.

Vertinsky P. 1987. Body shapes: the role of the medical establishment in informing female exercise and physical education in nineteenth-century North America. In *From 'Fair Sex' to Feminism: Sport and the Socialization of Women in the Industrial and Post-Industrial Eras,* ed. JA Mangan, RJ Park, pp. 256–81. London: Cass

Wacquant L. 1995. Pugs at work: bodily capital and bodily labour among professional boxers. *Body Soc.* 11:65–93

Wall Street Journal. Nov. 19, 1997. "Barbie Gets a Makeover."

Wolf N. 1991. *The Beauty Myth.* New York: Morrow

Annu. Rev. Anthropol. 2004. 33:319–44
doi: 10.1146/annurev.anthro.33.070203.143947
First published online as a Review in Advance on June 11, 2004

INSCRIBING THE BODY

Enid Schildkrout

*Division of Anthropology, American Museum of Natural History, New York,
New York 10024; email: eschild@amnh.org*

Key Words tattoo, scarification, art, skin, writing

■ **Abstract** Inscriptions on the body, especially tattoo, scarification, and body paint, have been part of ethnographic literature since before the birth of anthropology as a discipline. Anthropology's origins as the study of the exotic Other can be seen in the early descriptions of the body art of non-Western peoples. Anthropologists have generally focused on how the inscribed body serves as a marker of identity in terms of gender, age, and political status. More recently, scholars interested in this subject have looked also at issues of modernity, authenticity, and representation. The recent focus on the inscribed body responds to postmodern theory, the importance of body art in contemporary Western culture, reflections on the meaning of representations of the exotic, and an interest in the visible surface of the body as the interface between the individual and society. This article reviews recent literature in anthropology and related disciplines pertaining to the cultural construction of the inscribed body.

OVERVIEW: WRITING ON THE SKIN

As possibly the first, and certainly the most obvious, canvas upon which human differences can be written and read, skin has been a topic of continuous interest in anthropology and related disciplines from the earliest descriptions of exotic people to postmodern theorizing about the body in contemporary society. Skin, as a visible way of defining individual identity and cultural difference, is not only a highly elaborated preoccupation in many cultures; it is also the subject of wide-ranging and evolving scholarly discourse in the humanities and social sciences. Although my focus is mainly on the anthropological literature, it is impossible to ignore work in other fields. Today, archaeologists and historians are rewriting the history of the body using evidence from newly discovered ancient bodies, artworks, and texts. Discussions of contemporary "body work" (Benson 2000, p. 236) merge the perspectives of anthropology, sociology, psychology, cultural studies, philosophy, and gender studies, each discipline mapping onto the body its shifting theoretical preoccupations.

Much recent theorizing on the body is devoted to the idea of inscription. Derrida's focus on writing (1976, 1978), and Foucault's on the body as a text upon which social reality is inscribed (Csordas 1994, p.12; Mascia-Lee & Sharpe

0084-6570/04/1021-0319$14.00

(1992, p.147)), have led to many discussions of corporeal inscription and differing definitions and interpretations of what "inscription" and "body" actually mean. In much poststructuralist writing, the concepts of inscription and body are approached more in a metaphorical sense than in terms of the actual material modification of flesh through cutting, piercing, painting, or tattooing. Feminist scholarship, in particular, in its concern with the culturally constructed body and the embodied subject (Butler 1990; Braidotti 1996; Grosz 1994; Kristeva 1982, 1995; Lyon & Barbalet 1994), often uses the idea of inscription in this general sense. One notable exception is Fleming (2001), who acknowledges Derrida's broad notion of writing but focuses on the "ostentatious materiality" of writing in sixteenth-century England in graffiti, on monuments, buildings, pottery, and on tattooed bodies.

Reacting against the idea of the "disembodied" poststructuralist body, several writers have called for a greater focus on the body as subject and as material object, the body as "being-in-the-world" (Csordas 1994). Turner (1994, 1995) critiques theories of the disembodied poststructuralist body and argues for a renewed concern with subjectivity, the body as flesh, and personal agency. Brush (1998), discussing cosmetic surgery, writes: "If the body is—metaphorically—a site of inscription to various degrees for various theorists, then cosmetic surgery can be seen, at one level, as an example of the literal and explicit enactment of this process of inscription" (p. 24). Ahmed & Stacey (2001) explore "dermographics," the question of how the skin becomes, rather than simply is, meaningful in different cultural contexts. Jeffreys argues that contemporary body arts have to be seen in terms of their effects on real "flesh and blood" people; she argues for a human rights perspective rather than for either "the individualist explanations of self-mutilation offered by psychology" or "the liberal intellectualizing of postmodernists" (2000, p. 425). Taylor compares the relationship of tattooing to other art forms in contemporary Western culture and says that the tattoo renaissance as described by Rubin (1988) is more than a trivial fad precisely because of the powerful materiality of the body. In a world where virtual bodies seem to be everywhere, "body art represents a sustained effort to reverse the dematerialization of art by making the body matter" (Taylor 1995, p. 34).

These critiques of what Turner calls the "antibodies" of postmodernism and poststructuralism all point toward a renewed focus on literal bodily inscription. These practices, including tattooing, branding, and piercing, may be highly symbolic, but they are not metaphorical. They represent a kind of "border skirmishing" (Fleming 2001, p. 84) between selves and others and between social groups. They inevitably involve subjects who experience pain, pass through various kinds of ritual death and rebirth, and redefine the relationship between self and society through the skin.

It is not surprising, given this ambiguous terrain at the boundary between self and society, that skin has been a subject of theoretical interest by scholars in many disciplines. In psychoanalysis, because of its obvious concern with the individual, scholars have recognized the liminal quality of skin. Anzieu (1989), discussed at length in Gell (1993, pp. 28–38), writes about "the skin ego" as the interface between psyche and body, self and others. Prosser (2001, p. 53) and Fleming (2001, pp. 73–74) note that Freud also considered skin in conjunction with writing in his idea of the "mystic writing pad," referring to the way in which perceptions and memories are entangled inside and through the body's surface.

Corporeal Boundaries and Second Skins

In anthropology the study of the body as a boundary phenomena has a long history. Van Gennep (1909) described bodily transformations, often involving tattooing, scarification, or painting, within rites of passage. Lévi-Strauss (1963) discussed the body as a surface waiting for the imprintation of culture: "[T]he purpose of Maori tattooings is not only to imprint a drawing onto the flesh but also to stamp onto the mind all the traditions and philosophy of the group" (1963, p. 257). Douglas (1966), in exploring concepts of purity and danger, described the body as a boundary that can be used metaphorically to describe other socially significant classificatory systems. Turner (1980) first used the term "social skin" in his detailed discussion of how Kayapó culture was constructed and expressed through individual bodies. Using Bourdieu's (1977) "socially informed body," he explored Kayapó theories about "the nature of the human subject, the socialized body, and the relation between the two" (1995, p. 167). Kayapó body modifications, especially as performed in life-cycle rituals and everyday life, are part of the process of social production, creating a relationship between Kayapó subjects and the world in which they live (on Kayapó see also Conklin 1997, Verswijver 1992, Vidal & Verswijver 1992).

Gell (1993), in his monumental work on tattooing in Polynesia, referred to a "double skin folded over itself," mediating relations between persons, the sacred, and the present and the past. With tattoo, "the body multiplies; additional organs and subsidiary selves are created; spirits, ancestors, rulers and victims take up residence in an integument which begins to take on a life of its own" (p. 39). Tattooing, Gell wrote, is "simultaneously the exteriorization of the interior which is simultaneously the interiorization of the exterior" (pp. 38–39). Not only does the tattooed skin negotiate between the individual and society and between different social groups, but also mediates relations between persons and spirits, the human and the divine. Comparing Western and Melanesian ideas about skin and self, Benson (2000) describes anthropology's contribution to the study of contemporary Western body work in terms of how it elucidates the relationship between the surface of the body and the idea of the person, within specific cultural contexts.

To describe masks, wigs, body paint, and other impermanent forms of body art, anthropologists and art historians have often used the term second skin. Lévi-Strauss wrote about "mask cultures" (1963, p. 261), where masks replace tattoos as the mark of culture. Whether with tattoos, paint, or masks, the face is "predestined to be decorated, since it is only by means of decoration that the face receives its social dignity and mystical significance. Decoration is conceived for the face, but the face itself exists only through decoration." O'Hanlon (1992, p. 602) says that among the Wahgi in Papua New Guinea, a type of shoulder-length wig can be interpreted as a second skin, momentarily acknowledging the constitutive power of maternal kin at a festival otherwise given over to the celebration of agnatic values. He compares his use of the term second skin to the way in which scholars working in Australia have explained Aboriginal landscapes and paintings. Like skin, landscapes, revealed through "the Dreaming," are constituted by the act of inscription, what Biddle calls "ancestral imprintation" (Biddle 2003, p. 65; see also Gould 1990; Munn 1986; Myers 2002, pp. 36, 88–92). Similarly, Boas' descriptions of Northwest Coast masks, body paint, and tattoos (Jonaitis 1995; also discussed in Lévi-Strauss 1963, pp. 245–68) show an isomorphism among these forms, all of which involve effacing the boundaries between past and present, animal ancestors and human beings.

Following this line of analysis, there is no question that the topic of inscribing the body could lead us into a consideration of masked performances, ceremonial clothing, and many other kinds of transformations related to the body. Although I touch on these matters briefly, for the most part I restrict my discussion to the more literal practices of inscribing actual human flesh. Partly because of its universality in human culture, and its significance in defining cultural difference, this topic has a long history in anthropologic and ethnographic literature. Inscribed skin highlights an issue that has been central to anthropology since its inception: the question of boundaries between the individual and society, between societies, and between representations and experiences. In this review, I do not discuss the related and vitally important topic of the social construction of unmarked skin, particularly the idea of race. And because my focus is on the cultural readings of inscribed skin, I am not concerned with the fairly copious literature in psychology and medicine that treats bodily inscriptions as a manifestation of individual psychopathology.

Thus there remain three bodies of research relevant to this review. They all cross boundaries between disciplines in the social sciences and humanities. First, recent work has been done by historians, anthropologists, and literary scholars using historical sources, including early accounts of tattoo, newly discovered historic images, travel writing, and archaeological data. Second, recent ethnographic works exist on inscribed bodies outside Europe and North America, what one might label "new ethnography." Third, a body of literature addresses contemporary Western body modification. In the past three decades, Western body art has not only become a practice, and in some quarters a fashion, that has crossed social boundaries of class and gender, "high" culture and "low," but also it has been greatly influenced by "tribal" practices, past and present. The scholarly literature on contemporary body art focuses on issues of modernity, identity, hybridity, deviance, popular culture, gender, appropriation, authenticity, and globalization.

Whereas tattooing, branding, and piercing are technically distinct, and are used to express different kinds of identities in different social contexts, for the purposes of this review these topics are considered together. Among contemporary Western body art practitioners, important distinctions are made sometimes between people who focus on different practices, although all these techniques can be combined in the assertion of particular identities. Tattooing and scarification, or cicatrisation, as it is generally called in the European literature, are similar in that both involve the insertion of pigments under the skin to create permanent marks, either with pigment or texture, on the surface. Some authors, for example Gengenbach (2003) and Drewal (1988), use the term tattooing as a generic term for both, a practice I generally follow here. Branding is often associated with involuntary marking and the denial of personhood but has also been adopted in contemporary Western body culture as an assertion of group identity, for example in college fraternities. Piercing is not "inscription" in the literal sense of writing on the body, but in the contemporary Western context it too is often combined with tattooing as an assertion of neo-tribal identity. Historically, evidence of piercing is more abundant than that for tattooing because ornaments usually outlast bodies. In its engagement with objects used as ornaments, piercing is often used as the basis for displaying signs of status, but the act of piercing itself, like tattooing, branding, and scarification, is embedded in rituals of personal transformation.

THE AMBIVALENCE OF INSCRIBED SKIN

Before the Civil War, ads in North America for runaway slaves distinguished three kinds of body marking. A "Negro" runaway, if born and previously marked in Africa, would be said to have "country marks," in addition to scars from diseases, accidents, or beatings, and brands showing the name of the owner (Windley 1983). These advertisements broadly define the universe of body marking and the essential ambivalence so often found in association with corporeal inscriptions. On the one hand, these advertisements point us toward the understanding of the body as a site of where human beings become canvas for the inscription of political power; on the other hand, they raise the question of the agency of the individual in constructing a relationship between body and society.

The essential ambivalence of skin as a boundary is due, in part, to the possibility of individual agency subverting externally imposed inscriptions. Tattoos, scarifications, and brands can be imposed by authoritarian regimes in a symbolic denial of personhood. The brands and tattoos made by slave owners in ancient Greece and Rome (Gustafson 2000, Jones 2000) and in the southern United States (Windley 1983), Nazi concentration camp markings, and tattoos made as punishment in south Asia, Europe, Russia (Schrader 2000), and colonial East India (Anderson 2000), and in convict transports to Australia (Maxwell-Stewart & Duffield 2000) are inscriptions that are part of systems of control and surveillance. These are examples in which the Foucauldian model is enacted in a literal sense, although the evidence tells us little about how individuals may have reinterpreted these forms of subjugation and transformed them into signs of rebellion, as in Russia (Schrader 2000) or among Chicanos (Govenar 1988, Phillips 2001).

It has long been thought that in China tattooing was primarily used as a form of punishment. But Reed (2000) has analyzed early Chinese sources from the Zhou to the Ming dynasties, focusing especially on the work of a ninth-century writer Duan Chngshi, (c. 800–863), who described many different uses of tattooing in addition to the well-known stigmatizing use of tattoo on criminals and slaves. These literary sources reveal that early Chinese tattoos were extensive, often full-body tattoos, with elaborate pictorial imagery as well as written inscriptions. One policeman's entire body was covered with the poems of Bai Juyi (772–846).

In Brazil, on the Indian subcontinent, in Russia, and elsewhere, convicts marked by the penal authorities are known to reclaim their bodies by writing over the inscriptions or by displaying them in new social situations as a sign of resistance (Anderson 2000, p. 115; Govenar 1988; Schrader 2000). Penal and gang tattoos often represent a coalescence of socially imposed and voluntarily assumed marks, gaining some of their power from the fusion of subjection and resistance. Similarly, sex workers are said to reclaim their bodies through tattooing, using their tattoos to confront the fantasies that others project onto them [W. DeMichele (tattoo photographer), personal communication].

EARLY COMPARATIVE STUDIES

One of the earliest known comparative studies of body art around the world, John Bulwer's *Anthropometamorphosis* (1653), defined the descriptive terrain of this subject for the next three centuries. Body art, following Bulwer, at least in the popular imagination, became a way of describing the exotic uncivilized Other in comparison to the ideal civilized and Christian European. Bulwer, a Protestant doctor, based his diatribe against frivolity, especially on the part of women, on visual and written descriptions of body art that emerged from the first explorations of the new world. Writing a half century after Theodore de Bry published engravings of Indians from Virginia and Florida in 1590 (based on the drawings of Jacques Le Moyne de Morgues and John White), Bulwer compared the body art of exotic foreigners to the ideal of "natural" bodies made in God's image. Whereas the Egyptians, Indians, Brazilians, and Ethiopians might "slash and carbonade their bodies," Europeans also indulged their taste for fashion in "the slashing, pinking, and cutting of our Doublets." Bulwer riled against English women who applied pastes and patches to their faces, thereby falsifying what was made in God's image (Bulwer 1653, p. 537, cited in Rosencrans 2000, pp. 49–50; for more discussion of de Bry, White, and Le Moyne, see Fleming 2000, 2001, pp. 79–112; Hulton 1984).

If the idea that the unmarked body as a sign of God's work was linked to the Protestant reformation, the idea that body markings were a sign of savagery goes back even earlier. When de Bry published White's drawings of the inhabitants of Florida and Virginia, he also published White's depictions of the Picts, the ancient inhabitants of the British Isles. Known from Herodotus and other texts to have marked their bodies, these ancient Europeans could be compared to the tattooed natives of the Americas. White's depictions distanced the European body from its own past as well as from contemporary practices in early modern Europe. This is especially obvious in the image of the Pictish warrior holding a severed head, and the Botticelli-like Daughter of the Picts, a naked beauty covered in New World flowers and holding a sword.

THE INSCRIBED BODY IN HISTORY

Several important papers have demonstrated the volatility of body markings in Western Europe: their capacity to mean one thing in one period, and then shift as they move through space and time. The Greeks, Romans, and Celts used tattooing "for penal and property purposes" (Caplan 2000b, p.xvi; Gustafson 2000, Jones 2000). These meanings were inverted in early Christendom (Jones 2000) when pilgrims to the Holy Land and others adopted tattooing as signs of religious observance. On the basis of these rich historical studies, Caplan concludes that the history of European tattooing considerably antedates the age of exploration, whether reckoned from the Atlantic voyages of the sixteenth century or the Pacific expeditions of Captain Cook two centuries later (Caplan 2000b). The literature from the Greeks through medieval times shows that tattooing and body painting were variously used to mark outlaw status and nobility, insiders and outsiders, soldiers and slaves. Detailed studies, for example MacQuarrie's (2000, p. 41) on medieval Irish literature, show that not only is there evidence for tattooing as a cultural practice, but also that God's word and work were passed on through generations through tattoos inscribed on the bodies of Saints, like the stigmata on St. Francis of Assisi. These medieval texts continue a Biblical dichotomy between tattoos as "indicative of paganism, illiteracy, and criminality" and tattoos as connected to "literacy, Christianity and civilized culture" (MacQuarrie 2000, p. 42).

Despite the admonitions of churchmen and medical practitioners, tattooing was strongly associated with magical practices and widely used as medicine. Rosencrans (2000, p. 48) describes the self-inflicted tattoos of Simon Forman, a medical astrologer. By tattooing cosmological symbols on his own body, at precise astrologically calculated moments in the year 1609, Forman altered "both his flesh and his destiny." This "new magic," akin to alchemy, of the early modern period had its roots in the Renaissance: "In the sixteenth and seventeenth centuries, while Catholicism and Protestantism (in all of its various guises) clamoured for control of the Church of England, medieval popular magic quietly evolved into the 'new magic' of the renaissance" (Rosencrans 2000, p. 52). Marking the flesh with celestial inscriptions, used to cure and conjure, was an ongoing practice in the British Isles. These practices were not sanctioned by the church but occurred simultaneously with the importation of Jerusalem tattoos by pilgrims to the Holy Land.

Recent archaeological discoveries in Europe and central Asia support the idea that tattooing, far from being a nineteenth-century import into Europe, has a long, if not continuous, history on the continent. Actual bodies are obviously the best evidence of tattooing, and when the marks are legible, as in the case of the 5000-year-old Iceman from the Alps (Spindler 1994), a priestess of the goddess Hathor from Dynasty XI (2160–1994 B.C.) at Thebes (Bianchi 1988), Pazyryk horsemen and women from the sixth to the second century B.C. on the border between

China and Russia (Krutak 2004a, Polosmak 1994, Rudenko 1970), we can begin to decipher their meanings. In the case of the Pazyryk mummies, images of horses appear in textiles, in gold work, and on the skin. Skeletons of horses have been found in burials, suggesting the importance of the horse in the spiritual as well as the secular lives of these people. We can also infer medical uses of tattooing from tattooed and ochre-painted mummies on whose bodies correlations can be made between the placement of inscriptions and arthritic joints. Mallory & Mair (2000) describe such tattoos on the 3000–4000-year-old mummies found in western China.

Archaeologists and art historians have also found evidence of tattooing, piercing, and body shaping on artifacts. Recently discovered sculptures from the Jama-Coaque culture (Ecuador) from 500 B.C. to –500 A.D. reveal elaborate piercing on the face and torso of both men and women, whereas Maya figurines show elaborate body art associated with royalty (Baudez 2000). Thracian tattooing is revealed on painted vases dating from the fourth century A.D. (Zimmerman 1980). Krutak (2004b) and Griton (1988) use the illustrations in nineteenth-century explorers' accounts of their encounters with the peoples of Alaska, as does Kaeppler for Hawaii (1988, 2004), to reconstruct nineteenth-century piercing and tattooing practices. Selections from these historical accounts can be found in Gilbert (2001), a useful compendium of early writing on body art.

Even though the popular understanding of tattooing in Europe and North America dates the practice only to the late eighteenth-century Pacific voyages of Captain Cook (Guest 2000, Dye 1989, Thomas 2002), Caplan's study of tattooing in nineteenth-century Europe shows that in the early modern period, tattoos were widely used as occupational emblems, religious insignia, personal mementos, and insignia of patriotism and loyalty. Different local iconographies of tattooing can be identified, making it possible to distinguish tattoo traditions in Romania from those in Italy, Austria, or France. Caplan (2000, pp. 156–73) analyzes the European literature on tattoos and describes how criminologists, working from prison records, dominated the scientific discourse on tattooing in the nineteenth and early twentieth centuries. Although many people who were not criminals got tattoos, the criminological literature contributed to the popular understanding of tattooing as a form of negative deviant behavior (see also Gell 1993).

At the same time, sailors and merchants returning from the Pacific, as well as circus and carnival performers, increasingly got tattoos. Some fully tattooed people became celebrities, as did the tattooists who did the work. Despite the odd nobleman with a tattoo, this heterogeneous but generally lower-class population dominated the world of Western tattooing until the mid-twentieth century. Although tattooing steadily increased in popularity after the invention of the electric tattoo machine in the 1890s, it was not until the 1960s that the place of tattooing in popular culture radically shifted. As various kinds of social movements, from women's liberation, to punk, to neo-tribal, to Goth, used body art as a way of affirming identity, tattooing, piercing, and other forms of body modification crossed class boundaries, became common among people who would never before have considered it, and moved into the media as part of celebrity culture and fashion. By the turn of the millennium, tattoo became a fashion statement and had, in some quarters at least, become disassociated from the bikers, seamen, and carnival performers who once claimed it as their own. At the same time, the invocation of tribal culture by "modern primitives" and neo-tribals, gave new meaning to images of the primitive (deMello 1995a, 1995b, 2000; Hardy 1995b; McCabe 1997; Mifflin 1997).

REPRESENTATIONS OF THE EXOTIC OTHER

As images of people from Europe's colonies made their way into popular culture, representations of tattooing among the European underclass became conflated with the exotic bodies of Africans, Asians, and Native Americans. Much of this imagery was exhibited in world's fairs and sideshows (deMello 2000, pp. 44–70; Gilbert 2001, pp. 102–48; McCabe 1995; Oettermann 2000), settings where Western civilization asserted its hegemony by creating images of the non-Western Other (Cummings 2003). Tattooing and scarification, conflated with race, had been themes in descriptions of exotic peoples since the "age of exploration." Body art thus worked its way into Western thought as a major trope in identifying both non-Western peoples and the subaltern exotic within the West (Lutz & Collins 1993).

Coffee-table books displaying illustrated bodies from around the world (Fisher & Beckwith 1990, Gröning 1998, Rainier 1996) often emphasize the exotic and offer minimal analysis, yet they still serve as references for revival movements and contemporary practices. Performance artists and leaders of the "modern primitive" movement, such as the much-pierced and flayed Fakhir Musafar, who has been credited with inventing modern primitivism, draw on this archive to validate and explain their remade bodies (Vale & Juno 1989). This mass-market literature can be contrasted to more analytic work (Brain 1979, Ebin 1979, Burton 2001, Feher et al. 1989) that has attempted, in different ways, to compare the meaning of body art in different cultures.

Like museum collections of "salvaged objects," the published global body art archive, including both popular and academic literature, has become entangled in reclamation movements of various kinds. Pritchard (2000, 2001) discusses how Maori facial tattoo designs (*moko*) may be regarded as inalienable cultural property. Indeed, the Maori tattoo revival in New Zealand continues to be inspired by older works like Robley (1896) as well as newer publications like Simmons (1989) and Blackburn (1999). In the Marquesas (Allen & Gilbert 2001, pp. 55–66; Gell 1993, pp. 163–217), designs replicating the earliest known tattoos in the region are prominent in the contemporary tattoo revival and have become symbols of Marquesan identity. These designs would not be known were it not for the accounts of Von Langsdorff (1813-14), Handy (1922), and Von den Steinen (1928).

Body art, especially tattoos, but also body shaping, piercing, and scarification, have become major themes in discourses of modernity. They are, according to Cummings (2003), the visual component of Said's "Orientalism." Cummings notes the reliance on nonvisual text in both Said and Foucault and suggests that

Orientalism relied extensively on illustrations and descriptions of the body. Visual presentations of the exotic non-Western body are also important in the history of museums (Coombes 1994) and world's fairs (Rydell 1984, 1993), and in travel literature. Postcards showing lavishly tattooed and scarified bodies were sent around the world in the colonial period (Edwards 1992, Geary & Webb 1998). The 1999–2000 exhibition at The American Museum of Natural History, "Body Art: Marks of Identity" (http://www.amnh.org/exhibitions/bodyart/), for which I served as Curator, highlighted the issue of representations by displaying a wall of postcards to highlight the observer's gaze as part of the production of the exotic non-Western body (Schildkrout 2004).

ETHNOGRAPHIES OF INSCRIPTION

In anthropology, tattooing and other forms of "dermographics" have been of more than passing interest since the inception of the discipline. Boas described the masks, tattooing, and body painting of the Northwest Coast Indians (Jonaitis 1995). His analysis concerned the intersection of religion, masks, and tattoos, and also focused on a formal analysis of graphic design. Northwest Coast split representations also interested Lévi-Strauss (1963), who related them to competitive struggles to assert genealogical status. Gell again addressed the topic of "split representations" in his analysis of Marquesan art, showing that what appeared to Westerners to be three-dimensional sculpture can be understood in terms of two-dimensional skin (Gell 1998, pp. 193–96).

In the 1970s, many anthropologists began to analyze body art in detail, seeing it, as did Lévi-Strauss, as a microcosm of society. Turner's work on the Kayapó (1980), Faris' on the Nuba (1972, 1988), and A. Strathern & M. Strathern's on Mt. Hagen (1971, 1979) are all important ethnographies that interrogate the social significance of body decoration and the way in which body art creates identity for the individual and determines boundaries between groups. These authors described how, in different cultural contexts, temporary and permanent forms of body art are related to gender, the ancestors, spirits, warfare, and stratification, as well as to aesthetic ideas. All these anthropologists described societies where body art practices, at that moment in time, could be studied, for the most part, in isolation from national and global politics. In each of these areas, the next generation of anthropological fieldwork saw these same societies embedded in struggles for identity within national and global political and economic arenas. These same scholars and others, such as Knauft (2002), subsequently reexamined body art in Africa, South America, and the Pacific and situated these practices in wider sociopolitical arenas where tourism, mass media, and global politics had become part of the ethnographic landscape.

The decade following Turner's seminal work saw a number of art historians who were working in Africa and the Pacific turn their attention to body art. Cole, for example, called attention to what he termed the "vital arts" in East Africa

(1974). In the 1980s, Rubin convened a conference that led to the posthumous collection, *Marks of Civilization* (1988). Acknowledging that the "tattoo renaissance" in the United States, particularly on the West Coast, relied heavily on an engagement with non-Western cultures (Rubin 1988b, pp. 233–65), Rubin wanted to compare Western and non-Western practices. Expanding on Lévi-Strauss's idea that the marked body was a cultured body, the premise of *Marks of Civilization* was that tattooing and scarification around the world were universally associated with the idea of "civilization." Vogel (1988, pp. 97–106), writing about the Baule of Côte d'Ivoire, explicitly described Baule scarification as a sign of civilization, an idea that was subsequently contested by Gell (1993, pp. 17–18). The underlying premise of Rubin's edited work was that even where the underclass engaged in tattooing, as in Japan (McCallum 1988) or among Chicano gangs (Govenar 1988), the idea that tattooing and scarification could be considered "art" sublimated distinctions of class and caste under the rubric of "civilization." Roberts (1988, pp. 41–56) wrote that Tabwa "tegumentary inscriptions" reflected conceptions of the cosmos; Bohannan (1988, pp. 77–82) claimed that Tiv markings conferred membership in exclusive social groups; Berns, writing on the Ga'anda in Nigeria (1988, pp. 57–76), Griton on Alaska (1988, pp. 181–90), and Jonaitis (1988, pp. 191–206) on Tlingit labrets all described how gender was expressed and constructed through rituals of bodily inscription. Kaeppler (1988, pp. 157–70) and Gathercole (1988, pp. 171–78) discussed Hawaiian and Maori tattoo as expressions of genealogy, gender, and aesthetics, whereas Teilhet-Fiske (1988, pp. 135–40) and Rubin (pp. 141–54) dealt with the spiritual significance of tattoos in India. In *Marks of Civilization* these accounts of non-Western societies were juxtaposed with Sanders ethnography of Western tattoo studios (1988, pp. 219–32) and Rubin's study of the California tattoo community (pp. 233–65).

Gell's *Wrapping in Images: Tattooing in Polynesia* (1993) is the most ambitious study of tattoo in the anthropological literature. Gell attempts to interrogate the meaning of tattoo by doing a controlled comparison of societies with and without tattooing in Polynesia. Starting from Goldman's comparative study of stratification in Polynesia (1970), Gell sets out to do an "epidemiological" study of tattoo, relating it to stratification, mythology, ideas about the sacred, and virtually anything else where data is available. By exploring the relationship between tattooing, social and political hierarchy, and ideas of the sacred, Gell shows that there is no simple equivalency of status and tattooing. Tattooing creates and signifies difference (high or low) but is also a way of protecting the self and controlling the sacred. Gell concluded that tattooing was a "stigma of humanity" (p. 314): "[T]o be tattooed was always, in the final analysis, to interpose a barrier between a secular self and unmediated divinity" (p. 314). The gods were never tattooed in Polynesia, but people were, in an affirmation of personhood that played itself out differently in different societies. Whereas high-status persons might have tattoos, in the Marquesas their skins had to be removed at death in order for them to safely enter the realm of the gods. In contrast to Rubin, Gell concluded that the resonance between modern Western tattooing and traditional Polynesian tattooing was superficial. Whereas tattooing in Polynesia was "understood in the light of deeply entrenched cultural premises," Western tattooing is characteristically "unanchored." Gell's discussion of the cultural premises of tattooing in Polynesia is so extraordinarily rich, and his use of early sources and recent scholarship so comprehensive, that no serious consideration of tattooing can proceed without considering his work.

Gell was deeply interested in the anthropology of art, and, like some of the authors in *Marks of Civilization*, he looked at other media in relation to tattooing. In the Marquesas, art that was not on the body was still art of the body (1998, p. 168). Marquesan designs carved in wood do not represent real objects; like tattooing, they are ritual acts that offer protection. "The tattooing of, for example, an *etua* [godling] motif on the body was not a matter of representing an *etua* which existed (as a three-dimensional solid object) somewhere else. . . . The graphic act was a ritual performance that brought into being a protective spirit through the utterance of a 'legitimate' (stylistically coherent) graphic gesture" (1998, p. 191).

In the decade since *Wrapping in Images* appeared, many authors have revisited the subject of tattooing and body painting in non-Western societies. Drawing on Gell's wide use of sources and his theoretical overview, as well as on postmodern theorizing about the body, these authors interrogate the meaning of the body and the rituals and social contexts associated with marking the skin. Writing about the Warlpiri in Australia, Biddle shows how skin provides the medium through which women transform into the object world: Through marks on the skin women "'become' landscape, country, other species. . . . This fundamentally challenges and disrupts notions of 'the human body' and, in turn, it refigures the role of 'skin' inscription from the superficial to the constitutive in the production of cultural identities and differences" (Biddle 2001, p. 178). Warlpiri inscriptions (including modern acrylic paintings) are called *kuruwarri*—a "complex term meaning mark, trace, ancestral presence and/or essence, [and] birthmark or freckle" (p. 178). *Kuruwarri* are traces left over by ancestors and are read as a particular kind of text that constitutes a person in relation to the past, the ancestors, and the environment. Drawing on Derrida (1976, 1990) and Boone & Mignolo (1994), Biddle sees such writing "not as representation, not as that which refers, defers, to speech, sound or word, but rather as a force itself with effects" (p. 183).

Two recent studies in southern Africa consider how politics is inscribed on the body and how tattooing can be used as a means of empowerment (Gengenbach 2003) or as a means of social control (Auslander 1993). Drawing on Stoler's (1995) work on the colonial body, Gengenbach explores women's tattooing in Mozambique and shows how women in the twentieth century have used tattooing as a form of subversive resistance to colonial power. Tattooing, formerly associated with initiation and linked to kinship and marriage, was prohibited under Portuguese rule, but women in Mozambique continue to practice it. No longer closely linked to initiation and ethnicity, tattooing became a way in which women created networks and associations among themselves (Gengenbach 2003, pp. 109, 134), rewriting the "boundaries of difference" in society. Although tattoos were still considered by both men and women to be erotic, as others working in central Africa note

(Cameron 1995, Roberts & Roberts 1996), this was no longer their primary meaning. Women's tattoos expressed an engagement with the colonial economy by incorporating such images of modern objects as scissors and flower pots. These objects of modernity were felt to be possessed through their representations on the skin (2003, p. 115). Kaeppler (1988, 2004) describes a similar incorporation of exogenous objects in Hawaiian tattooing, but in that case tattoo was not a form of resistance but rather a continuation of an earlier tradition that was transformed as tattooed members of the upper class made claims to modernity.

Tattooing is also an element in contemporary witch-finding movements in Zambia. Auslander (1993) describes a witch finder who operated among the Ngoni people in Eastern Province, Zambia. Visiting villages in which witchcraft accusations had become common, this man used the apparatus of the coercive state and symbolism from modern medical practice to inoculate people against witchcraft by tattooing their bodies. He worked his way through rural communities persuading people to submit to bodily inspections with a mirror that was used to determine their vulnerability, according to a numerical scale. People were then inoculated by getting numbers tattooed on their arms. Auslander describes the fusion of symbols from Western medicine and bureaucratic data collection with practices of bodily inscription.

The search for protection also underlies the long tradition of tattooing in mainland southeast Asia, where both doctors and monks administer tattoos (McCabe 2003). Tannenbaum (1987) shows how the Therevada Buddhist Shan in Myanmar, southern China, and Thailand use tattoos that incorporate Khmer, Khom, or Burmese script. These tattoos are used for decoration and marking a man's maturity, for identification and controlling populations, and for protection. Shan tattoos also can be thought of as analogous to vaccinations in that they protect their bearers by causing supernatural beings and other people to "have loving kindness towards them" (p. 695). Verses from Buddhist teachings, *katha*, are written on the body; the operation itself involves recitations and the acceptance of various precepts such as refraining from killing, stealing, improper sexual behavior, lying, and intoxication. Tannenbaum analyzes various classes of tattoo in terms of the rituals involved in administering them, their purposes, and their intersection with gender, power, and religion. Through her study of tattooing, she shows how animist beliefs and state-sponsored Buddhism are integrated into a single moral universe.

THE BODY IN ART

Art historians and anthropologists working in Africa frequently refer to body markings in their descriptions of sculpture, textiles, wall painting, pottery, and woodcarving. Even though government prohibitions and missionary interventions all over Africa generally caused scarification and tattooing to cease, diminish, or become a form of subversion (Gengenbach 2003), evidence of past practices is preserved in art works that represent bodies or share the aesthetic of body art.

Women did the same body work on the things they made, such as textiles, pottery, and house painting, as on their bodies, whereas men carved scarification patterns on sculptures and inscribed them on metal. These markings are not simply for decoration but give the objects culturally appropriate meanings. In the Democratic Republic of the Congo, among the Mbuti as well as the Mangbetu and related groups, body painting and scarification motifs are also inscribed on bark cloth (Schildkrout & Keim 1990, Thompson 1991). Yoruba women use body art designs on resist-dyed indigo textiles (Drewal 1997), whereas Kuba women embroider raffia cloth (M. Adams 1978) with intricate geometric designs that also can be seen on sculptures and on actual bodies that were photographed during the colonial period. Ga'anda women in Nigeria make ritual beer pots that represent bodies and which are used by a groom to make substantial payments in beer to the bride's family. A new bride's house is built with architectural embellishments consisting of raised geometric designs covered in red ochre. These designs refer directly to the bodies of young female initiates. Here too body art was protective. Funeral ceremonies include ritual pottery incised with scarification marks. At the end of the ceremony the pots are smashed to allow the ancestral spirit to safely move on to the afterlife (Berns 1988, pp. 68–73).

In many African societies tattooing was formerly associated with marks of local identity as well as marks of elite status and membership in secret societies. Until the 1930s no male citizen in the Edo kingdom of Benin could exercise his perogative of membership in palace societies without tattoos (Nevadomsky & Aisien 1995). "As part of the cultural geography of the body, *iwu* [tattoos] mapped out ethnic terrain and transformed the self, inscribed male and female personhood, denoted stratification by pedigree, and delineated selected occupational roles" (p. 68). In the mid-twentieth century, tattooing ceased in this area and clothing and textile designs became important markers of social status and Edo identity, but tattoo designs (*ewe iwu*, tattoo designs on cloth) were placed on fabrics in a deliberate assertion of ethnicity. Although tattoos were "part of a cultural configuration that includes gender roles, status, hierarchy, medicine, and concepts of pollution and blood, the *ewu iwu* is more manipulatively a public recognition of political affiliation and loyalty" (p. 73).

Similarly in eastern Nigeria, Igbo scarification denoted age, gender, and political authority. As permanent body marking decreased, women continued painting designs, known as *uli* on the walls of their houses, on pottery, and on their bodies as temporary decoration during coming of age ceremonies (S. Adams 2002; Cole & Aniorkor 1984, pp. 39–46; Willis 1989).

In Australia, contemporary Aborigine acrylic painting on canvas cannot be understood without reference to body art. The medium changes but the messages on canvas, skin, and country (especially cave walls) are conflated (Biddle 2003, Gould 1990). So, too, in eastern Nigeria, contemporary artists, including male artists like Obiora Udechukwu, use the motifs of women's *uli* painting in their work (Ottenberg 2002). In a rare instance of a non-Western body artist becoming a Western celebrity, Setona (A.K.A. Fatma Ali Adam Uthman), a Sudanese woman living in Egypt, is an internationally acclaimed henna artist whose work adorns popular musicians, singers, and actors. Hassan (1998) discusses Setona, as well as the Iranian-born New York–based artist Shirin Neshat and the Moroccan modernist Farid Belkahia, in relation to issues of cultural appropriation. Henna has become a commodity in contemporary Western body art, but these artists use it to raise issues about gender, globalization, perceptions of the body, and "the culture of sex and desire" (Hassan 1998, p. 127). In New Zealand, where Maori tattooing has become associated with assertions of ethnicity and indigenous rights, a "theater of remembering" incorporated acts of real tattooing in a 1996 theatrical performance called *Tatau—Rites of Passage*. In this work, the New Zealand–based group Pacific Underground and the Australian-based Zeal Theater collaborated in a production that included actors, a tattoo artist, and a person being tattooed. The play was about a family of Samoan immigrants in New Zealand and the juxtaposition of gang tattoos and "authentic" tattooing as part of a coming-of-age ritual. Tattooing went on in public view during the performances to "explore the notion of ritual reincorporation. . . as a means of transcending diaspora and repairing the ruptures caused by it" (Balme & Carstensen 2001, p. 36). Tattooing here was not seen as specifically Maori or Samoan but rather as part of the creation of new pan-Pacific diasporic identities.

New Identities, Modernity, and Authenticity

Following the Stratherns' work on body decoration in Mt. Hagen (Strathern & Strathern 1971, A. Strathern 1977, M. Strathern 1979), others working in Oceania have continued to explore the changing ways in which body decoration expresses and constructs personal and cultural identity. Knauft (1989; 1999, pp. 21–89) has surveyed the importance of body paint, ornaments, masks, and wigs throughout colonial Melanesia in relation to "cycles of fertility, depletion, and regeneration" including the changes people confront in the physical environment, the individual body, and "the social and spiritual cycles through which interpersonal relationships grow, mature, and deteriorate" (1999, p. 84). O'Hanlon (1989, 1992) describes how Wahgi adornments articulate the inner realm of moral values with the outer world of politics and warfare, prestige, and protection. Wahgi people continually assess the moral qualities of others in terms of their appearance and take great pains expressing their own moral qualities through body ornamentation. Strathern & Strathern (1971, pp. 101–2) described how Highlanders associate black face paint with warfare, whereas Harrison (1993), working among the Avatip, describes how black paint carries with it the empowering spirit of the ancestors and effaces the person underneath, allowing the warrior to invoke a distinct moral code appropriate only to war.

Several scholars have looked at how body art is being used and transformed in the face of tourism, travel, and new technologies of communication (Timmer 2001). Movements of cultural identity within pluralistic states, the commoditization of body art, and the symbolic use of body art as political symbols by environmental and indigenous rights advocates are salient issues. Knauft, in discussing modernity in Papua New Guinea, describes how self-decoration is becoming less a means of symbolizing one's social relationship in the community and "more a fashion of de-contextualized bodily art among people who may not otherwise know each other" (2002, p. 226). Barker & Tietjen (1990) describe Maisin women's facial tattoo-ing in northeastern Papua New Guinea in the 1980s. Once associated with puberty ceremonies and gender distinctions, facial tattooing is now practiced as an individ-ualized assertion of ethnicity, maturity and femininity, cultural pride, and artistic ability. Body tattooing ceased during the second World War, but facial tattooing has taken on the expanded meaning of signaling ethnic identity. Maisin women pro-duce and sell *tapa* (bark-cloth) in urban centers where their tattoos identify them as Maisin. Through the association of their body art with a distinct local identity they add value to their labor in the context of a larger heterogeneous society.

O'Rourke's 1987 film, *Cannibal Tours*, shows American tourists putting on face paint and posing as "native" warriors as they cruise the Sepik River. Here, body painting symbolizes "native" identity, is marketed on souvenirs, and is used by the tourists, in their own performances, to mock both local people and themselves. Similarly Otto & Verloop (1996) describe the invention of the Asaro masked "mud-men" at an agricultural fair in the 1950s. A few individuals consciously created and continually adapt these legendary impersonations of Highlands New Guinea culture in performances for audiences of government administrators, tourists, tour operators, and other islanders. Today the mudman performance is a source of in-come for the Asaro but also has led to arguments over the origin and ownership of the body art represented in the tourist performance. Faris (1988, p. 39; 1982) describes the changes in Nuba body art subsequent to his fieldwork in the Sudan in the 1970s (Curling 1982, Faris 1972). In addition to the ravages of war and the pressures of Islam on the Nuba, Faris deplores the denigrating effects that tourism has had on Nuba body decoration, particularly following the publication of Reifenstahl's sensational and eroticized photographs (1974, 1976). Starting in the late 1970s, Nuba men began to perform for tourists by painting their bodies with meaningless designs that were calculated to bring in the most money from photographers, rather than with traditional designs that referred to their status in the age grade system and their eligibility for marriage.

Modernity is also a factor in the use of new materials in body decoration in Melanesia. Among the Massim there is an opposition between the dark wrinkled "bad" skin associated with age and death and soft bright "good" skin associated with youth, purity, and life. Myths and rituals involve casting off "bad" skin for "good." Liep describes how Johnson's baby powder has been "appropriated into a symbolic context of colours, smells and tactile qualities employed in a discourse of life and death, youth and old age, success and failure" (1994, p. 70). But whereas baby powder has been incorporated into "tradition," mainly because of its analogy with traditional materials, it has the added attraction for the Massim of partaking in modernity (p. 72). This idea is the inverse of Western neo-tribals or modern primitives using their skin to invoke the values of primitive societies.

Conklin (1997) describes how Amazonian Indians, responding to Western-ers' romantic conceptualizations of native peoples, selectively use internationally appealing components of Amazonian body art as "symbolic capital" (Bourdieu

1984) in national and international political arenas. Latching onto movements of contemporary environmental activism, the Wari', Kayapó, Nambiquara, and Awá activists incorporate into their self-representation, and disseminate through modern media, visual images of themselves looking like stereotyped "noble savages" bedecked in face paint and feathers but omit things like ornaments made of bones and canine incisors that might be objectionable to some Western viewers. Conklin (1997) explores the problems and paradoxes involved in these "neo-indigenous" self-representations. Although they have been useful in internationally based campaigns for indigenous and environmental rights, they have not fared as well in national politics where Indians have been accused of engaging in hypocritical political theater. These internationally oriented constructions of indigenous identity have also constricted some Indians' ability to determine their own ways of expressing authenticity (p. 728).

CONTEMPORARY TATTOO

When Rubin coined the term "tattoo renaissance" (Rubin 1988b, pp. 233–62) he referred to a shift in many aspects of Western tattooing (the nature of the people who created tattoos, involving a shift from tattooists to tattoo artists); a change in clientele (from sailors, bikers, and gang members to the middle and upper class); and a change in iconography (from the badge-like images based on repetitive premade designs known as "flash" to the customized full-body tattoo influenced by Polynesian and Japanese tattoo art). All these aspects of contemporary Western tattooing have received extensive treatment in the social sciences as well as in the vast literature produced by and for the tattoo community itself. DeMello argues that the attention given in recent years to the "tattoo renaissance" creates a misleading impression of historical evolution in the world of Western tattoo. By analyzing the popular discourse disseminated in tattoo magazines, cyberspace, tattoo shops, and conventions, she argues that many different communities exist, and they are often divided against each other (1995a, 2000, pp. 17–44).

Contacts between East and West long predate the "tattoo renaissance" identified by Rubin and others (Blanchard 1991, deMello 2000, Govenar 1984, Rosenblatt 1997). Until the 1960s most Western tattooing remained within a European aesthetic tradition (McCabe 1995, 1997). Within that tradition distinct subcultures can be identified, for example Chicano tattoo, skinheads, bikers, and prison tattoo. In the 1960s, however, a number of tattoo artists, many with fine-arts training, began to seriously study Polynesian graphic design and Japanese tattooing. Rubin describes how specific individuals like Phil Sparrow, Sailor Jerry (Norman Keith) Collins, Cliff Raven, and Don Ed Hardy revolutionized tattooing. Many of them studied with master tattooists from Japan, and they began traveling widely in Oceania, Europe, the Philippines, and Japan.

Although Westerners had long been interested in Pacific tattoos, the commercial and media success of these tattoo artists, and many others, shifted the way in which tattoo was perceived in the wider community (Tucker 1981). Tattooists began to incorporate into their work images from fine art, graphics from Japanese and Polynesia traditions, and new ways of using color and line. Instead of simply applying small badge-like designs on patches of skin, they began to work with the contours of the body. As more and more middle-class people were tattooed, and as artists with formal art training in other media entered the profession, tattoo gained new respectability. Among this middle-class clientele, custom work increasingly replaced flash, and people began to collect tattoos as works of art. Many women gravitated to these new kinds of tattooing (Atkinson 2002, deMello 1995b, Mifflin 1997). According to accounts in the press at the time, the fact that The American Museum of Natural History did a major exhibition on body art, incorporating into it not only images of non-Western body art but also Western tattooing and piercing, meant that this form of body art had finally reached the "mainstream" (Schildkrout 2004). Other exhibitions followed, for example one at The Victoria and Albert Museum. Mainstream museums and art institutions were now being asked to affirm the status of tattooing as an art form. And, in an *Amicus Curiae* brief submitted to the United States Supreme Court (Schildkrout 2002), I argue that a tattoo artist from South Carolina (one of only two states where tattooing was then banned) should be allowed to work on the basis of the protection of the First Amendment of the United States Constitution. This case hinged on the issue of free speech and the fact that tattooing could be considered a form of visual communication.

Whereas imagery from Japanese tattoo has been appropriated in the West (Hardy 1995b), a number of studies examine the incredibly rich history of tattooing in Japan. McCallum (1988) traces Japanese tattoo history back to 10,000 B.C. and describes the fascinating relationship between tattoo and the underworld in Japan in the nineteenth and twentieth centuries. In 1982, the photographer Sandi Fellman spent time in Tokyo photographing Japanese tattoo artists and subjects with a large-format Polaroid camera (Fellman 1986). Gilbert has recently published a translation of Kazuo Oguri's description of his apprenticeship as a tattooist. Gilbert (2001, pp. 77–87, and Kitamura & Kitamura 2001) describes the relationship between Japanese tattooing and the samurai tradition. Greenaway's 1996 film, *The Pillow Book*, is also a provocative contribution to the representation of Japanese tattooing. Set in contemporary Japan and Hong Kong, the film is an adaptation of a tenth-century Japanese literary classic, *The Pillow Book*, by a courtesan named Sei Shonagon. It explores the tangled connections between tattooing, writing, sex, homoeroticism, sado-masochism, and death.

NEW MODERNITIES

Contemporary Western tattooing, although increasingly mainstream in some respects, continues to redefine social boundaries, and in the process redefines itself. An extensive literature describes how various forms of "neo-primitive" body art are used to define emerging social groups and identities. Beginning with Vale & Juno's publication *Modern Primitives* (1989) segments of the New Age, Punk (Wojcik 1995), and modern primitive movement (Cummings 2001) adopted "extreme" forms of piercing, branding, and tattooing. "Extreme" is, of course, a relative and somewhat slippery term, but it is used in this literature for people who have extensive piercings, brands, and tattoos covering their bodies, and especially parts like the face and hands that cannot be concealed with clothing. This form of body modification is far removed from the kind of tattooing that Rubin described, as art, in his characterization of the tattoo renaissance. But as tattooing becomes more mainstream, those who turn to it to proclaim their outsider status obviously need to push the limits of acceptability.

Thus there is an on-going redefinition of body art in Western cultures (Atkinson 2001, 2003) and a continual discussion, particularly in the sociological literature, of the relationship between body art and deviance. Whereas anthropologists shy away from the concept of deviance because it so often carries embedded value judgments, sociologists tend to focus on it, even as they continually redefine it according to the subjective and objective situation of their subjects. Sanders (1989) approached the institution of tattooing as an aspect of negatively valued consumer culture, whereas Irwin (2001, 2003) describes how tattooing bridges the divide between positive and negative deviance, high and low culture: "Anti-heroes can be said to contribute to changing definitions of deviance, to evoke or confuse informal and formal social control mechanisms, and to dislodge or point to centers of power...[They] reinforce and challenge boundaries between social groups and between what is considered acceptable and unacceptable behavior" (2003, p. 54).

Many participants in the neo-primitive movement obviously cultivate "deviant" status, although deviancy is defined differently by different groups. Although obviously not everyone with piercings and tattoos defines themselves as deviant, those who do define themselves in this way make a commitment not only to "get a tattoo" or "get tattooed" but also to adopt a new lifestyle. Atkinson (2003) describes "straight edge tattooists" who associate their body art, especially piercing, with self-control and an abstemious lifestyle. Neo-primitives, bikers, and gang members, as well as prisoners, also cultivate "deviancy" as part of their identity (Bazan et al. 2002, Phillips 2001, Steward 1990). Deviancy is expressed both through the images people select in tattoos, and the degree to which they cover their bodies with tattoos, brands, and piercings.

Many authors are concerned with the personal journeys that individuals take as they redefine themselves through body art. Vail (1999) describes tattooing as a process of collecting, as well as of personal transformation: Tattoos "are like potato chips." Atkinson refers to a "flesh journey": "[T]he process of intentionally reconstructing the corporeal in order to symbolically represent and physically chronicle changes in one's identity, relationships, thoughts, or emotions over time ..." (2001, p. 118). Once they are part of a community whose identity is expressed through body art, people with a strong commitment to tattoos "socially construct the meanings of their particular styles of radical body modification and account for them using insider vocabularies" (Atkinson 2001, p. 140).

Much of this meaning-making involves notions about the primitive, about idealized non-Western cultures, and about alternative lifestyles inspired by these notions (Torgovnik 1997). This raises issues of authenticity, cultural appropriation, copyright, and the relationship between body art, media culture, and consumerism. In their lifestyles and on their bodies, these adherents of radical body alteration implicitly question standard definitions of modernity by using appropriated notions of the primitive, however imaginary, to do so. But focusing specifically on the discourse of Western tattoo, deMello raises the issue of class-based appropriation within the world of tattoo. She decries what she sees as the rewriting of the history of tattoo so that the bikers, sailors, and other members of the "underclass" are denied their rightful place in this history. By inventing a mythical new age and neo-tribal history, by moving from stigma to status (deMello 1995b, p. 49), tattooing has become not only "a means to symbolically undo the conquest of the primitive world" but also a way of denying authenticity to those who can actually claim authorship of tattooing in the West. This history belongs, according to deMello (and see also McCabe 1997), not to the middle class, not to the neo-primitives, not to the high-end tattoo artists, but rather to the bikers, sailors, circus performers, gang members, and prisoners who have been involved with tattoo since at least the nineteenth century and in some cases for centuries before.

SUMMARY

In my attempt to survey the diverse interdisciplinary literature on corporeal inscription several themes emerge. First, the body, as a canvas, is not only the site where culture is inscribed but also a place where the individual is defined and inserted into the cultural landscape. Tattoos, scars, brands, and piercings, when voluntarily assumed, are ways of writing one's autobiography on the surface of the body. These practices express belonging and exclusion, merge the past and the present, and, for the individual, define what Csordas (1994) has called "a way of being in the world" (p. 10). Second, bodily inscriptions are all about boundaries, a perennial theme in anthropology—between self and society, between groups, and between humans and divinity. Third, in this review I have focused on bodily inscriptions defined in a very real, material way, not as a metaphor as has been the tendency in poststructuralist discourse. But this approach also highlights the fact that the surface of the body has been the site of considerable theoretical interest since the beginning of anthropology. Skin is a surface onto which anthropology and related disciplines have projected their understandings of the relationship between psyche and society, the commonalities and differences between cultures, and even the meaning of art.

ACKNOWLEDGMENTS

Many people helped with this paper, beginning with my colleagues at The American Museum of Natural History, who worked with me on the exhibition, "Body Art: Marks of Identity." I am especially grateful to Ann Fitzgerald who collaborated on the exhibition and also carefully read a version of this paper. Michael O'Hanlon, Anne d'Alleva, and Victoria Ebin kindly pointed me to sources that

I might have overlooked, and innumerable colleagues including Sarah Adams, Elizabeth Cameron, Amanda Carlson, Herbert Cole, James Faris, Richard Gould, Karen Hansen, Donna Pido, Dale Rosengarten, Andrew Strathern, Pamela Stewart, and Susan Vogel shared their knowledge about various examples of body art. Special thanks go to Michelle Franke, Naomi Goodman, and Roxanne Rivera without whose bibliographical and technical help this article may never have been finished.

The *Annual Review of Anthropology* is online at http://anthro.annualreviews.org

LITERATURE CITED

Adams M. 1978. Kuba embroidered cloth. *Afr. Arts.* 12(1):24–39

Adams S. 2002. *Uli Di N'aka N'aka/Uli is from hand to hand: Igbo women's body and wall painting in southeastern Nigeria.* PhD thesis. Yale Univ.

Ahmed S, Stacey J, ed. 2001. *Thinking Through the Skin.* London/New York: Routledge

Allen T, Gilbert S. 2001. *The Marquesas. See Gilbert 2001*, pp. 55–66

Anderson C. 2000. Godna: inscribing Indian convicts in the nineteenth century. See Caplan 2000a, pp. 102–17

Anzieu D. 1989. *The Skin Ego.* New Haven, CT: Yale Univ. Press

Atkinson M. 2001. Flesh journeys: neo primitives and the contemporary rediscovery of radical body modification. *Deviant Behav. Interdiscipl. J.* 22:117–46

Atkinson M. 2002. Pretty in ink: conformity, resistance, and negotiation in women's tattooing. *Sex Roles* 47(5/6):219–35

Atkinson M. 2003. The civilizing of resistance: straightedge tattooing. *Deviant Behav. Interdiscipl. J.* 24:197–220

Auslander M. 1993. "Open the wombs!": the symbolic politics of modern Ngoni witchfinding. In *Modernity and Its Malcontents*, ed. J Comaroff, J Comaroff, pp. 167–92. Chicago: Univ. Chicago Press

Balme C, Carstensen A. 2001. Home fires: creating a Pacific theatre in the diaspora. *Theatre Res. Int.* 26(1):35–46

Barker J, Tietjen AM. 1990. Women's facial tattooing among the Maisin of Oro Province, Papua New Guinea: the changing significance of an ancient custom. *Oceania* 60(3):217–34

Baudez CF. 2000. The Maya king's body, mirror of the universe. *Anthropol. Aesthet.* 38:134–43

Bazan LE, Harris L, Lorentzen LA. 2002. Migrant gangs, religion and tattoo removal. *Peace Rev.* 14(4):379–83

Beckwith C, Fisher A. 1990. *African Ark.* New York: Abrams

Benson S. 2000. Inscriptions of the self: reflections on tattooing and piercing in contemporary Euro-America. See Caplan 2000a, pp. 234–54

Berns MC. 1988. Ga'anda scarification: a model for art and identity. See Rubin 1988a, pp. 57–76

Bianchi RS. 1988. Tattoo in ancient Egypt. See Rubin 1988a, pp. 21–28

Biddle J. 2001. Inscribing identity: skin as country in the Central Desert. See Ahmed & Stacey 2001, pp. 177–93

Biddle J. 2003. Country, skin, canvas: the intercorporeal art of Kathleen Petyarre. *Aust. N.Z. J. Art* 4(1):61–76

Blackburn M. 1999. *Tattoos From Paradise: Traditional Polynesian Patterns.* Atglen, PA: Schiffer

Blanchard M. 1991. Post-bourgeois tattoo: reflections on skin writing in late capitalist societies. *Vis. Anthropol. Rev.* 7(2):11–21

Bohannan P. 1988. Beauty and scarification amongst the Tiv. See Rubin 1988a, pp. 77–82

Boone EH, Mignolo WD, ed. 1994. *Writing Without Words: Alternative Literacies in*

Mesoamerica and the Andes. Durham, NC: Duke Univ. Press

Bourdieu P. 1977. *Outline of a Theory of Practice*. Cambridge: Cambridge Univ. Press

Bourdieu P. 1984. *Distinction: A Social Critique of Judgement and Taste*. Cambridge, MA: Harvard Univ. Press

Braidotti R. 1996. Cyberfeminism with a difference. *New Form.: J. Cult./Theory/Polit.* 29: 9–23. http://www.let.uu.nl/womens_studies/rosi/cyberfem.htm

Brain R. 1979. *The Decorated Body*. New York: Harper and Row

Brush P. 1998. Metaphors of inscription: discipline, plasticity and the rhetoric of choice. *Fem. Rev.* 58:22–43

Burton JW. 2001. *Culture and the Human Body: An Anthropological Perspective*. Prospect Heights, IL: Waveland

Butler J. 1990. *Gender Trouble: Feminism and the Subversion of Identity*. New York: Routledge

Cameron EL. 1995. *Negotiating Gender: Initiation Arts of "Mwadi" and "Mukanda" Among the Lunda and Luvale, Kabombo District, North-Western Province, Zambia*. PhD thesis. Univ. Calif. Los Angeles

Caplan J, ed. 2000a. *Written on the Body: The Tattoo in European and American History*, Princeton, NJ: Princeton Univ. Press

Caplan J. 2000b. 'National tattooing': traditions of tattooing in nineteenth-century Europe. See Caplan 2000a, pp. 156–73

Cole HM. 1974. Vital arts in northern Kenya. *Afr. Arts* 7(2):12–23, 78

Cole HM, Aniakor CC. 1984. *Igbo Arts: Community and Cosmos*. Los Angeles: Mus. Nat. Hist., Univ. Calif. Los Angeles

Conklin BA. 1997. Body paint, feathers and VCRs: aesthetics and authenticity in Amazonian activism. *Am. Ethnol.* 24(4):711–37

Coombes AE. 1994. *Reinventing Africa: Museums, Material Culture and popular Imagination in Late Victorian and Edwardian England*. New Haven: Yale Univ. Press

Csordas TJ, ed. 1994. *Embodiment and Experience: The Existential Ground of Culture and Self*. Cambridge: Cambridge Univ. Press

Cummings W. 2001. Modern primitivism: the recent history of civilization's discontents. In *Nature and Its Discontents from Virgin Land to Disney World: Reinterpretations of Freud's Civilization Thesis in the America(s) of Yesterday and Today*, ed. B Herzogenrath, pp. 115–33. Amsterdam: Editions Rodopi

Cummings W. 2003. Orientalism's corporeal dimensions. *J. Colon. Colon. Hist.* 4(2). http://muse.jhu.edu/journals/journal_of_colonialism_and_colonial_history/toc/cch4.2.htm

Curling C. 1982. *The South Eastern Nuba*. Film. BBC

DeMello M. 1995a. The carnivalesque body: women and tattoos. See Hardy 1995a, pp. 73–79

DeMello M. 1995b. 'Not just for bikers anymore': popular representations of American tattooing. *J. Popul. Cult.* 29(3):37–52

DeMello M. 2000. *Bodies of Inscription: A Cultural History of the Modern Tattoo Community*. Durham/London: Duke Univ. Press

Derrida J. 1976. *Of Grammatology*. Baltimore: Johns Hopkins Univ. Press

Derrida J. 1978. *Writing and Difference*. Chicago: Univ. Chicago Press

Derrida J. 1990. *Limited Inc*. Transl. S Weber, J Mehlman. Evanston, IL: Northwestern Univ. Press

Douglas M. 1966. *Purity and Danger: An Analysis of Concepts of Pollution and Taboo*. New York: Praeger

Drewal HJ. 1988. Beauty and being: aesthetics and ontology in Yoruba body art. See Rubin 1988a, pp. 83–96

Drewal HJ. 1997. Art or accident: Yoruba body artists and their deity Ogun. In *Africa's Ogun: Old World and New*, ed. S Barnes, pp. 235–60. Bloomington: Indiana Univ. Press

Dye I. 1989. The tattoos of early American seafarers. *Proc. Am. Philos. Soc.* 133:520–54

Ebin V. 1979. *The Body Decorated*. London: Thames and Hudson

Edwards E, ed. 1992. *Anthropology and Photography, 1860–1920*. New Haven: Yale Univ. Press

Faris JC. 1972. *Nuba Personal Art*. Toronto: Univ. Toronto Press

Faris J. 1988. Significance of difference in the male and female personal art of the Southeast Nuba. See Rubin 1988a, pp. 29–40

Feher M, Nadaff R, Tazi N, eds. 1989. *Fragments for a History of the Human Body*. New York: Urzone. 3 vols.

Fellman S. 1986. *The Japanese Tattoo*. New York: Abbeville

Fleming J. 2000. The renaissance tattoo. See Caplan 2000a, pp. 61–82

Fleming J. 2001. *Graffiti and the Writing Arts of Early Modern England*. Philadelphia: Univ. Penn. Press

Gathercole P. 1988. Contexts of Maori moko. See Rubin 1988a, pp. 171–77

Geary CM, Webb VL, eds. 1998. *Delivering Views: Distant Cultures in Early Postcards*. Washington, DC: Smithsonian Inst.

Gell A. 1993. *Wrapping in Images: Tattooing in Polynesia*. Oxford: Clarendon, Oxford Univ

Gell A. 1998. *Art and Agency: An Anthropological Theory*. Oxford: Clarendon

Gengenbach H. 2003. Boundaries of beauty: tattooed secrets of women's history in Magude District, Southern Mozambique. *J. Women Hist.* 14(4):106–41

Gilbert S. 2001. *Tattoo History: A Source Book*. New York: Juno Books

Goldman I. 1970. *Ancient Polynesian Society*. Chicago: Chicago Univ. Press

Gould RA. 1990. *Recovering the Past*. Albuquerque: Univ. N. M. Press

Govenar A. 1984. *Issues in the documentation of tattooing in the Western world*. PhD thesis. Univ. Tex., Dallas

Govenar A. 1988. The variable context of Chicano tattooing. See Rubin 1988a, pp. 209–18

Greenaway P. 1996. *The Pillow Book*. Film

Gritton J. 1988. Labrets and tattooing in Native Alaska. See Rubin 1988a, pp. 181–90

Gröning K. 1998. *Body Decoration: A World Survey of Body Art*. New York: Vendome Press

Grosz E. 1994. *Volatile Bodies, Toward a Corporeal Feminism*. Bloomington: Indiana Univ. Press

Guest H. 2000. Curiously marked: tattooing and gender difference in eighteenth-century British perceptions of the South Pacific. See Caplan 2000a, pp. 83–101

Gustafson M. 2000. The tattoo in the later Roman Empire and beyond. See Caplan 2000a, pp. 17–31

Handy W. 1922. *Tattooing in the Marquesas*. Honolulu: Bernice P. Bishop Mus.

Hardy DE, ed. 1995a. *Pierced Hearts and True Love: A Century of Drawings for Tattoos*. New York/Honolulu: Drawing Cent./Hardy Marks

Hardy DE. 1995b. Japanese tattooing: legacy and essence. See Hardy 1995a, pp. 58–71

Harrison S. 1993. *The Mask of War: Violence, Ritual and the Self in Melanesia*. New York: Manchester Univ. Press

Hassan SM. 1998. Henna mania: body painting as a fashion statement, from tradition to Madonna. In *The Art of African Fashion*, ed. E van der Plas, M Willemsen, pp. 103–28.: Africa World Press

Hulton P. 1984. *America 1585: The Complete Drawings of John White*. Chapel Hill, NC: Univ. N. C. Press

Irwin K. 2001. Legitimating the first tattoo: moral passage through informal interaction. *Symb. Interact.* 24(1):49–73

Irwin K. 2003. Saints and sinners: elite tattoo collectors and tattooists as positive and negative deviants. *Sociol. Spectrum* 23:27–57

Jeffreys S. 2000. 'Body art' and social status: cutting, tattooing and piercing from a feminist perspective. *Fem. Psychol.* 10(4):409–29

Jonaitis A. 1988. Women, marriage, mouths and feasting: the symbolism of Tlingit labrets. See Rubin 1988a, pp. 191–205

Jonaitis A, ed. 1995. *A Wealth of Thought: Franz Boas on Native American Art*. Seattle, WA: Univ. Wash. Press

Jones CP. 2000. Stigma and tattoo. See Caplan 2000a, pp. 1–16

Kaeppler AL. 1988. Hawaiian tattoo: a conjunction of genealogy and aesthetics. See Rubin 1988a, pp. 157–70

Kaeppler AL. 2004. Tattooed beauty: A Pacific case study. In *Anthropology Explored*, ed. RO

Selig, MR London, PA Kaupp. Washington DC: Smithsonian Books. 2nd ed.

Kitamura T, Kitamura KM. 2001. *Bushido: Legacies of the Japanese Tattoo*. Atglen, PA: Schiffer

Knauft BM. 1989. Bodily images in Melanesia: cultural substances and natural metaphors. See Feher et al. 1989, pp. 198–279

Knauft BM. 1999. *From Primitive to Post Colonial in Melanesia and Anthropology*. Ann Arbor: Univ. Mich. Press

Knauft BM. 2002. *Exchanging the Past: A Rainforest World of Before and After*. Chicago/London: Univ. Chicago Press

Kristeva J. 1982. *Powers of Horror*. Transl. Leon Roudiez. New York: Columbia Univ. Press

Kristeva J. 1995. *New Maladies of the Soul*. Transl. Ross Guberman. New York: Columbia Univ. Press

Krutak L. 2004a. *Tattoos of the Arctic*. http://www.vanishingtattoo.com/arctic_tattoos.htm

Krutak L. 2004b. *Piercing and Penetration: Body Arts of the Unangan, Alutiiq, and Chugach of Alaska*. http://www.vanishingtattoo.com/arctic_piercing.htm

Lévi-Strauss C. 1963. *Structural Anthropology*. New York: Basic Books

Liep J. 1994. Recontextualization of a consumer good: the ritual use of Johnson's baby powder in Melanesia. In *European Imagery and Colonial History in the Pacific*, ed. T Van Meijl, P van der Grijp. pp. 64–75. Saarbrucken, Germany: Entwicklungspolitik Breitenbach GmbH

Lutz CA, Collins JL. 1993. *Reading National Geographic*. Chicago: Univ. Chicago Press

Lyon ML, Barbalet JM. 1994. Society's body: emotion and the "somatization" of social theory. See Csordas 1994, pp 48–66

MacQuarrie CW. 2000. Insular Celtic tattooing: history, myth and metaphor. See Caplan 2000a, pp. 32–45

Mallory JP, Mair VH. 2000. *The Tarim Mummies: Ancient China and the Mystery of the Earliest Peoples from the West*. London: Thames & Hudson

Mascia-Lees FE, Sharpe P, eds. 1992. *Tattoo, Torture, Mutilation, and Adornment: The Denaturalization of the Body in Culture and Text*. Albany: State Univ. N. Y. Press

Maxwell-Stewart H, Duffield I. 2000. Skin deep devotions: religious tattoos and convict transportation to Australia. See Caplan 2000a, pp. 118–35

McCabe M. 1995. Coney Island tattoo: the growth of inclusive culture in the age of the machine. See Hardy 1995a, pp. 49–55

McCabe M. 1997. *New York City Tattoo: The Oral History of an Urban Art*. Honolulu: Hardy Marks

McCabe M. 2003. *Tattoos of Indochina: Magic, Devotion and Protection*. Atolen, PA: Schiffer

McCallum D. 1988. Historical and cultural dimensions of the tattoo in Japan. See Rubin 1988a, pp. 109–34

Mifflin M. 1997. *Bodies of Subversion: A Secret History of Women and Tattoo*. New York: Juno Books

Munn ND. 1986 1973. *Walbiri Iconography: Graphic Representation and Cultural Symbolism in a Central Australian Society*. Chicago: Univ. Chicago Press

Myers FR. 2002. *Painting Culture. The Making of an Aboriginal High Art*. Durham/London: Duke Univ. Press

Nevadomsky J, Aisien E. 1995. The clothing of political identity: costume and scarification in the Benin Kingdom. *Afr. Arts* 28(1):62–73, 100

Oettermann S. 2000. On display: tattooed entertainers in America and Germany. See Caplan 2000a, pp. 193–211

O'Hanlon M. 1989. *Reading the Skin: Adornment, Display and Society Among the Wahgi*. London: British Mus.

O'Hanlon M. 1992. Unstable images and second skins: artifacts, exegesis and assessments in the New Guinea Highlands. *MAN* 27(3):587–608

O'Rourke D. 1987. *Cannibal Tours*. Film. Direct Cinema

Ottenberg S. 2002. Sources and themes in the art of Obiora Udechukwu. *Afr. Arts* 35(2):30–45

Otto T, Verloop RJ. 1996. The Asaro mudmen: local property, public culture? *Contemp. Pac.* 8(2):349–86

Phillip SA. 2001. Gallo's body: decoration and damnation in the life of a Chicano gang member. *Ethnography* 2(3):357–88

Polosmak N. 1994. A mummy unearthed from the pastures of heaven. *Natl. Geogr.* 186(4): 80–103

Pritchard S. 2000. Essence, identity, signature: tattoos and cultural property. *Soc. Semiot.* 10(3):331–46

Pritchard S. 2001. An essential marking: Maori tattooing and the properties of identity. *Theor. Cult. Soc.* 18(4):27–45

Prosser J. 2001. Skin memories. See Ahmed & Stacey 2001, pp. 52–68

Rainier C. 1996. *Where Masks Still Dance: New Guinea.* New York: Little, Brown & Company

Reed CE. 2000. Tattoo in early China. *J. Am. Orient. Soc.* 120(3):360–77

Reifenstahl L. 1974. *Last of the Nuba.* New York: Harper Collins

Reifenstahl L. 1976. *The People of Kau.* New York: Harper Collins

Roberts AF. 1988. Tabwa tegumentary inscription. See Rubin 1988a, pp. 41–56

Roberts MN, Roberts AF, eds. 1996. *Memory: Luba Art & the Making of History* (catalog and exhibition). New York: Mus. Afr. Arts

Robley MG. 1896. *Moko; or Maori Tattooing.* London, UK: Chapman & Hall

Rosecrans JA. 2000. Wearing the universe: symbolic markings in early modern England. See Caplan 2000a, pp. 46–60

Rosenblatt D. 1997. The antisocial skin: structure, resistance and "modern primitive" adornment in the United States. *Cult. Anthropol.* 12(3):287–334

Rubin A, ed. 1988a. *Marks of Civilization: Artistic Transformations of the Human Body.* Los Angeles: Mus. Cult. Hist., Univ. Calif. Los Angeles

Rubin A. 1988b. Tattoo trends in Gujarat. See Rubin 1988a, pp. 141–53

Rudenko SI. 1970. *Frozen Tombs of Siberia: The Pazyryk Burials of Iron Age Horsemen,* pp. 110–114. Berkeley: Univ. Calif. Press

Rydell RW. 1984. *All the World's A Fair.* Chicago: Univ. Chicago Press

Rydell RW. 1993. *World of Fairs—The Century of Progress Expositions.* Chicago: Univ. Chicago Press

Sanders CR. 1989. *Customizing the Body: The Art and Culture of Tattooing.* Philadelphia: Temple Univ. Press

Schildkrout E. 2004. Body art as visual language. In *Anthropology Explored,* ed. RO Selig, MR London, PA Kaupp. Washington DC: Smithsonian Books. 2nd ed.

Schildkrout E. 2002. *In the Supreme Court of the United States, Ronald P. White, Petitioner v. State of South Carolina, Respondent. On Petition for Writ of Certiorari to the Supreme Court of South Carolina. Brief Amicus Curiae of Enid Schildkrout No. 01–1859.* New York: Counsel Press

Schildkrout E, Keim CA, eds. 1990. *African Reflections: Art from Northeastern Zaire.* Seattle/London: Univ. Wash. Press and New York: American Museum of Natural History

Schrader AM. 2000. Branding the other/ tattooing the self: bodily inscription among convicts in Russia and the Soviet Union. See Caplan 2000a, pp. 174–92

Simmons D. 1989. *Maori Tattoo.* Auckland, New Zealand: Bush Press

Spindler K. 1994. *The Man in the Ice: The Discovery of a 5,000-year-old Body Reveals the Secrets of the Stone Age.* New York: Harmony Books

Steward SM. 1990. *Bad Boys and Tough Tattoos: A Social History of the Tattoo with Gangs, Sailors, and Street-Corner Punks, 1950–1965.* Binghamton, NY/London: Harrington Park/Haworth

Stoler A. 1995. *Race and the Education of Desire: Foucault's History of Sexuality and the Colonial Order of Things.* Durham, NC: Duke Univ. Press

Strathern A. 1977. Why is shame on the skin? In *The Anthropology of the Body,* ed. J Blacking, pp. 99–110. London/New York: Academic

Strathern M. 1979. The self in self-decoration. *Oceania* 49:241–57

Strathern M, Strathern A. 1971. *Self-Decoration in Mount Hagen.* London: Gerald Duckworth

Tannenbaum N. 1987. Tattoos: invulnerability and power in Shan cosmology. *Am. Ethnol.* 14(4):693–711

Taylor MC. 1995. Skinscapes. See Hardy 1995a, pp. 29–45

Teilhet-Fisk J. 1988. The spiritual significance of Newar tattoos. See Rubin 1988a, pp. 135–39

Thomas N. 2002. *Skin Deep: A History of Tattooing.* Greenwich, UK: Natl. Maritime Mus.

Thompson RF, Bahuchet S. eds. 1991. *Pygmees?: Peintures sur Ecorce Battue des Mbuti (Haut-Zaire).* Paris: Musee Dapper

Timmer J. 2001. Huli wigmen engage tourists: self-adornment and ethnicity in the Papua New Guinea Highlands. *Pac. Tourism Rev.* 4: 121–35

Torgovnick M. 1997. *Primitive Passions: Men, Women, and the Quest for Ecstasy.* New York: Alfred A. Knopf

Tucker M. 1981. Tattoo: the state of the art. *Artforum* 19(9):42–47

Turner TS. 1980. The social skin. In *Not Work Alone: A Cross-Cultural View of Activities Superfluous to Survival,* ed. J Cherfas, R Lewin, pp. 112–40. Beverly Hills, CA: Sage

Turner T. 1994. Bodies and anti-bodies: flesh and fetish in contemporary social theory. See Csordas 1994, pp. 27–47

Turner T. 1995. Social body and embodied subject: bodiliness, subjectivity, and social-ity among the Kayapo. *Cult. Anthropol.* 10(2):143–53

Vail DA. 1999. Tattoos are like potato chips. . .you can't have just one: the process of becoming and being a collector. *Deviant Behav. Interdiscipl. J.* 20:253–73

Vale V, Junu A, ed. 1989. *Modern Primitives.* San Francisco: Research

Van Gennep A. 1909. *Les Rites de Passage.* Paris: É. Nourry

Vidal G, Verswijver G. 1992. Body painting among the Kaiapo: the concept of person and self. See Verswijver 1992, pp. 37–63

Verswijver G, ed. 1992. *Kaiapo, Amazonia: The Art of Body Decoration.* Tervuren, Gent: R. Mus. Centr. Afr.

Vogel S. 1988. Baule scarification: the mark of civilization. See Rubin 1988a, pp. 97–105

Von Den Steinen K. 1928. *Die Marquesaner und ihre Kunst.* Berlin, Germany: Dietrich-reimer

Von Langsdorff GH. 1813–14. *Voyages and travels in various parts of the world, during the years 1803, 1804, 1805, 1806, and 1807.* London: H. Colburn

Willis L. 1989. Uli painting and the Igbo world view. *Afr. Arts* 23(1):62–69

Windley LA, ed. 1983. *Runaway Slave Advertisements: A Documentary History from the 1730s to 1790,* Vol. 3. Westport, CT: Greenwood

Wojcik D. 1995. *Punk and Neo-Tribal Body Art.* Jackson: Univ. Press Miss.

Zimmerman K. 1980. Tatowierte Throakerinnen auf grieschischen vasenbildern. *Jahrbuch des Deutches Archaologische Instituts* 95:163–96

Annu. Rev. Anthropol. 2004. 33:345–67
doi: 10.1146/annurev.anthro.33.070203.143809
Copyright © 2004 by Annual Reviews. All rights reserved
First published online as a Review in Advance on June 11, 2004

CULTURE, GLOBALIZATION, MEDIATION

William Mazzarella

Department of Anthropology, University of Chicago, Chicago, Illinois 60637;
email: mazzarel@uchicago.edu

Key Words media, locality, communications, ethnography, essentialism

■ **Abstract** This chapter reviews the literature on media and globalization. It develops the argument that this literature foregrounds a problem that, ironically, it also largely disavows: namely, the question of mediation as a general foundation of social life. I explore the origins of this contradiction in the emergence of globalization studies out of earlier traditions in media and cultural studies. I suggest that the failure to move beyond this impasse has perpetuated a surprising and debilitating reliance on substantialist and essentialist models of culture, models that are both at odds with the critical thrust of globalization studies and fully complicit with the agendas of public and commercial bureaucracies. The review tracks the recurrence of such thinking in several key strands of globalization studies and proceeds to outline an alternative ethnographic and theoretical strategy on the basis of a general theory of media and mediation.

INTRODUCTION

This review explores the relation between the following propositions: (*a*) that the question of globalization should push anthropologists to think more carefully not simply about media but also, and more generally, about mediation as a constitutive process in social life; (*b*) that the cultural politics of globalization, inside and outside the academy, involve a contradictory relation to mediation, on the one hand foregrounding the mediated quality of our lives and on the other hand strenuously disavowing it; (*c*) that this tension becomes particularly visible in the puzzling contemporary status of the culture concept, half-abandoned in anthropological theory, celebrated everywhere else; and (*d*) that a critical ethnography of the cultural politics of globalization might usefully set its sights on those nodes of mediation where value is often produced and contested, more or less self-consciously, in the name of culture.

In the following text, I refer primarily to the literature on media and globalization. But my argument assumes a much broader concept of a medium, one that would allow anthropologists to theorize the intersection between, say, cinema and ritual performance as an intermedium relationship rather than a primarily media-culture relationship. I am particularly interested in an ambiguity that I think

0084-6570/04/1021-0345$14.00

characterizes all media, a tension that the condition of globalization has made particularly evident.

On one level, whether or not it is apprehended that way by its "users," a medium is a material framework, both enabling and constraining, for a given set of social practices. In this guise a medium is both dynamic and largely taken for granted. However, a medium is also a reflexive and reifying technology. It makes society imaginable and intelligible to itself in the form of external representations. Inseparable from the movement of social life and yet removed from it, a medium is thus at once obvious and strange, indispensable and uncanny, intimate and distant.

"Mediation" is a name that we might give to the processes by which a given social dispensation produces and reproduces itself in and through a particular set of media. Because of the structural ambiguity of media, the work of mediation is always potentially volatile. An obvious way of being in the world depends on certain everyday practices of mediation that can, with a slight shift of perspective, begin to appear arbitrary or externally imposed. To many, the moment of globalization appears as simply another installment of modernist disenchantment, as in Marx and Engels' famous phrase, "All that is solid melts into air." But in a subtler register it may also remind us that things were never quite as solid as they may have looked. These are very different analytical optics. On the one hand, an all-or-nothing confrontation between watertight cultural worlds and the poison of reflexivity. On the other, the recognition that meaning and value arise out of ongoing practices of mediation that are always at least half-conscious of the "close distance"—the blend of immersion and self-consciousness—that any cultural identification involves (Mazzarella 2003).

SOMETHING HAPPENED

In the late 1980s, just as the Cold War was running out of fuel and anthropologists were still reeling from the epistemic dislocation brought on by *Writing Culture*, something happened. As if on cue, a whole series of essays began appearing taking "globalization" as their object of inquiry. To some, no doubt, this was yet another nail in the coffin of a once-dignified discipline. To others, however, it spelled relief. Globalization studies made it possible, after all the hand wringing, to "do" relatively guilt-free ethnography again.

Why? This was partly an effect of the anthropology of globalization shifting the ontological burden back onto our informants. The ethnographic critique of the 1980s had called into question our habitual practices of representing culture. By the early 1990s, many anthropologists, responding to the globalist provocation, found a path back to ethnography by studying what Appadurai (1996) has called "the production of locality"—that is, our informants' habitual (and not-so-habitual) practices of representing culture. Drs. Clifford, Marcus, and Fischer had prescribed greater reflexivity. But in an age of globalizing media and markets, it turned out that reflexivity, and how best to manage it, was as much a concern for our informants as it was for us (Ginsburg et al. 2002).

Already manifest in the emergence of such new domains of inquiry as "public culture" (Appadurai & Breckenridge 1988, 1995; Pinney 2001), on one level this concern indexed a heightened self-consciousness about the relationship between media and culture. One pressing challenge was to understand the staggeringly complex interaction between different media in the reproduction of social experience. Another challenge emerged from the slightly bemused recognition that while the culture concept was undergoing an apparently terminal crisis in anthropology the rest of the world was lustily discovering it.

The world after globalization is one in which culture is everywhere, and everywhere at issue—except, it seems, in the avant-garde of anthropological theory. Appadurai writes of a new generalized "culturalism," Poster (2001) begins a book by declaring that "Culture has become a problem for everyone" (p. 1), and Tomlinson (1997) announces that "the globalization process is revealing both political and conceptual problems at the core of our assumptions about what a 'culture' actually is" (p. 133; Hall 1997). Sometimes this new culturalism is expressly political: an idiom through which to make claims, locally and transnationally, on scarce resources and shortening attention spans (Ginsburg et al. 2002, Povinelli 2002, Wilk 2002). Elsewhere, it is theorized as symptomatic of a new "linguistic," "symbolic," or "postmodern" phase of world capitalism (Featherstone 1991, Harvey 1990, Jameson 1991, Lyotard 1985, Poster 2001), where profit is realized from the sale of signs and experiences as much as out of more conventionally defined products. Meanwhile, other social sciences less encumbered by the burden of culture have, during this same period, optimistically latched onto the concept in response to the sense that globalization must be understood, at least in part, in terms of the management of meaning-that-matters (du Gay et al. 1997, Eyerman 1999, Friese & Wagner 1999, Hall 1997).

The culture concept's newfound popularity often displays the kind of essentialist or substantialist tendency that drove many anthropologists in the 1980s and 1990s to disown the concept or at least to insist on a radical revision of its analytical status (Gupta & Ferguson 1997; compare discussions in Kuper 1999 and Ortner 1999). Its contemporary global careers manifest a curious tension: a simultaneous foregrounding and denial of the social processes of mediation that anything that we might recognize as "culture" necessarily involves. On the one hand, the mediated quality of culture has never been so obvious. On the other hand, and in response to a sense that this recognition constitutes a kind of crisis of value, the culture-mongers in commercial, nongovernmental, and state bureaucracies are desperately trying to recuperate the aura of authenticity that the word still popularly evokes. As I show here, even many critical academic projects that are in other ways dexterously attentive to the politics of mediation nevertheless seem unable to shake the substantialist habit.

Electronic audiovisual media enjoy, as many scholars point out, an overdetermined relationship to the discourse of cultural globalization. They are at once its infrastructural means and its privileged signs (Barker 1997, Jameson 1991, Hardt & Negri 2001). Whereas the benefits of media are loudly foregrounded in mainstream debates—"let's wire the world!"—mediation itself is frequently denied. This denial occurs because the idea of mediation implies distance, intervention, and displacement. It thus undercuts the romance of authentic, intuitive identification, which, in turn, is the ideological guarantee that both capitalism and politics are driven by the interests of the consumer-citizen, not the corporation-party.

Marketing and politics, those rigorous machines of mediation, both proclaim cultural sensitivity as the salve for modernist alienation and use it to link the grandest institutional ambitions with the most intimate habits of the heart. Many of our most widely noted "critical" divinations of the present, for example Hardt & Negri's (2001) recent *Empire*, recognize and deplore this motivated disavowal of mediation as characteristic of the contemporary workings of power. But instead of taking mediation as the object of critical analysis, they compound the problem by demonizing it as the death-dealing, freeze-frame technology of those whose global sway depends on "fixing" the dynamic, productive, and im-mediate (their word is "immanent") energies of the "multitude." By romanticizing the emergent and the im-mediate, this neo-vitalist position tends too briskly to dismiss given social formations as always already foreclosed. This is clearly an impossible point of departure for an ethnographer because the critical value of fieldwork depends on an understanding of social process as an ongoing mediation of the virtual and the actual, of potentiality and determination.

Contrary to a widespread belief that globalization-talk has meant the end of "good" anthropology, I believe that it holds the potential to revitalize the discipline, precisely as a mode of critically informed empirical inquiry, an inquiry that is attentive to the specific social conditions or mediations out of which particular representations (including "culture") emerge in our informants' lives and work. And such an anthropology would track the ways that these representations, once in circulation, recursively help to remediate these social conditions. In so doing, it would capture the dialectical doubleness of mediation—its close distance—in the flow of practice, not just as an analytical problem.

To make my case below, I begin by going back to the inaugural provocations of globalization studies, the moment at which what I have ironically come to think of as The Formula was first proclaimed. I trace the intellectual conjuncture out of which The Formula emerged, the better to understand the persistence in contemporary anthropology of the central contradiction to which I allude above: the simultaneous awareness and disavowal of the problem of mediation. I survey the manifestation of this contradiction in several recurrent narratives in globalization studies, including the ideas of "the resurgence of the local," "cultural proximity," and "hybridity." Finally, I develop some general thoughts on mediation and media as objects of ethnographic inquiry, along with a brief argument about why I think anthropologists are particularly well situated to move us beyond the current intellectual impasse.

THE FORMULA: ORIGINS AND IMPASSES

In a chorus of voices speaking many dialects, the heralds of globalization studies announced a deceptively simple Formula. The Formula registered a sense of disorientation, the dizziness of inhabiting a world in which familiar relationships of scale, as well as taken-for-granted hierarchies of general and particular, were coming unstuck.

Robertson spoke, palindromically, of a "twofold process of the particularization of the universal and the universalization of the particular" (Jameson & Miyoshi 1998, p. xi). Appadurai (1996), for his part, remarked that "the central problem in today's global interactions is the tension between cultural homogenization and cultural heterogenization" (p. 32; for other variations, see Featherstone 1990; Hannerz 1992, 1996; Miller 1995; Straubhaar 1997).

But what tools might be required for an ethnography of such processes and tensions? One thing seemed clear: The successive critical models of the 1970s and the 1980s—cultural imperialism and active audiences, respectively—needed a kind of theoretical *Aufhebung* for the 1990s. Whereas previous models of cultural dynamics had tended to posit uniformity and difference as existing in a kind of zero-sum struggle (occasionally moderated by concepts such as syncretism), globalization studies saw them as poised in a kind of volatile, perhaps dialectical, coconstitution.

A brief genealogy might help to clarify the stakes. In the 1960s and 1970s, the critics of cultural imperialism took aim at the happy one-world pieties of the postwar global modernization project, interpreting them as the ideological discourse of Euro-American geopolitical domination (Boyd-Barrett 1977; Burton & Franco 1978; Dorfman & Mattelart 1975; Galtung 1979; Lee 1980; Nordenstreng & Varis 1974; Schiller 1976, 1989; Nordenstreng & Schiller 1993; Sarti 1981). In many cases, they also traced back the conceptual and technical infrastructures of contemporary media systems to the compulsions and requirements of nineteenth-century European imperialism (Hendy 2000, Herman & McChesney 1997, Lau 2003, Mattelart 1994, Shohat & Stam 1994, Sreberny-Mohammadi et al. 1997).

Drawing on the more romantic tendencies of the early Marx and his subsequent interpreters, the cultural imperialism thesis combined a critique of Western-led commodification with a celebration of the organic integrity and cultural density of societies that were peripheral to the world system. Neo-imperialist culture, pale and sickly despite its world-conquering thrust, was vampirically dependent on extracting the lifeblood—first the labor and raw materials, later the symbolic content—of thriving local communities. Thus "authentic" culture was attenuated and depleted, alienated from its organic connection to the timeless authority of tradition, remaining only as a vulnerable, deracinated husk in need of (often rather paternalistic) nurturance and protection. Meanwhile, global culture was too thin, too brittle, and too inauthentic for proper affective commitment and identification, those pillars of civil society (Meyrowitz 1985, Smith 1991). Even after the United

Nations Educational, Scientific, and Cultural Organization (UNESCO)-sponsored New World Information and Communication Order (NWICO) collapsed in the mid-1980s, European states continued to draw on these assumptions during the General Agreement on Tariffs and Trade (GATT) and World Trade Organization (WTO) negotiations of the 1990s, arguing that culture constituted a unique (and uniquely vulnerable) kind of resource that needed to be protected from the predations of the market (Garcia Canclini 2001; Hamelink 1983, 1994).

By the 1980s, scholars were roundly and rightly deconstructing the cultural imperialism model on several counts: its overemphasis on macrolevel determinants of social change, its tendency to conflate economic power with social and cultural effects, its assumption of a passive and helpless audience, and its fetishization of endangered "authentic" cultures (Garofalo 1993; Golding & Harris 1997; Harindranath 2003; Tomlinson 1991, 1999). A new wave of media studies busied itself with studying the micropolitics of reception, highlighting the unpredictable ways in which local needs and inclinations refracted the would-be hegemonic discourse of national or transnational media content (Ang 1985, Fiske 1987, Gillespie 1995, Liebes & Katz 1990, Silj et al. 1988, Wasko et al. 2001). And of course the *topos* of the active audience, with its localism and its kitchen-sink heroism, found a ready audience among anthropologists, particularly in combination with the parallel ascendance of "everyday life" as a vantage point for critical theory (de Certeau 1984, Highmore 2001, Lefebvre 1992).

The limitations of the active audience/popular pleasures position soon, in turn, became too evident to ignore (Ang 2003 [1990], Gripsrud 1989, Miller 1998, Modleski 1986, Morley 2003 [1993], Morris 1988, Schudson 1987). If the cultural imperialism thesis had underplayed the complexity of reception, then the active audience model was blind in the other direction. By overemphasizing the cultural and political integrity of the average suburban living room it ran the risk of turning the ethnography of media into a celebration of banal differences and pyrrhic insurrectionary acts. And by locating the site of politics and complexity at the level of the family den, it diverted critical attention away from the complex of institutions, mediations, and interests that used to be known as the culture industries. The ironic upshot was that reception studies actually helped to perpetuate the image of a monolithic, seamlessly functioning capitalist culture-machine, kept from achieving total hegemony only by the mischievous "agency" of what used to be called the masses. Consequently, the local—whether the village or the living room—tended to be reconfirmed in its structural integrity, "appropriating" what it desired from the surrounding world.

It was out of an increasingly desperate sense of the intransigence and inertia of these binaries—power and resistance, structure and agency, macro and micro, political economy and culture—that the programmatic Formula of globalization studies emerged. But The Formula also represented an attempt to integrate the poststructuralism that anthropologists had imported from the humanities with the continuing challenge of empirical ethnographic study. That being the case, it is perhaps not surprising that the most visible internal differences in the literature on globalization concerned the relative weight to be given to institutional determinations versus the indeterminacies of translation and mediation.

Appadurai (1996), for example, highlights the disorienting "disjunctures" between conceptual entities—economy, politics, culture, etc.—whose stability and mutual determinations previous models had confidently assumed. For many scholars, globalization entailed the supplanting of both the ideological polarities of the Cold War and modernist hierarchies of command and control by decentralized, multipolar networks of complexity, chaos, and emergence. This current of globalization theory resonated with the extraordinary, seemingly anarchic, explosion of the Internet in the 1990s, and consequently also found common intellectual ground with many cybertheorists in the antifoundationalist philosophy of Deleuze and Guattari and their heirs (Deleuze & Guattari 1987, Guattari 1995, Hardt & Negri 2000, Massumi 2002).

Other scholars, however, saw in the cultural politics of globalization the consolidation of structures of knowledge and institutional practices that served to organize cultural production in relatively predictable ways. Wilk (1995), for example, speaks of the dissemination of "common structures of difference"; Hannerz (1990) surmises that what we might call a "world culture [. . .] is marked by an *organization of diversity* rather than by a replication of uniformity" (p. 237, emphasis in original). Valuable interventions explored the relation between putatively "global culture" and the practical requirements of identifiable professional elites (Featherstone 1996; Hannerz 1992, 1996, 2004; Sklair 1991; Turner 1990). And the literature on "global cities" was an important corrective to the ideological tendency to speak as if global capitalism has, in this so-called information age, become weightless and dematerialized (Castells 1989, Dear & Flusty 1999, Sassen 2001, Scott 2002, Soja 2000, Thrift 1996). In these writings, globalization was essentially a matter of the attempted global extension of a modernist dynamic of coordination, administration, and equivalence.

Both strands had identified something fundamental. The prophets of indeterminacy noted the heightened sense of disjuncture felt by many at this historical moment, as the rapid spread of novel technologies had upset and displaced long-naturalized relations between center and periphery, form and content. Those who discerned "common structures of difference" were, for their part, responding to the fact that these novel technologies and relations nevertheless often remain closely tied to professional, political, and economic interests that had important stakes in mobilizing and regulating global media. These interests, even as they capitalized on the proliferation of "cultural difference," also demanded that such cultural difference be rendered manageable as content within globally reproducible (and thus marketable) forms and genres.

The tension between these two lines of inquiry manifested itself as an apparent incommensurability, an analytic lacuna that might be expressed as follows: There is no simple correlation between the spatiality of cultural production and the production of cultural space. That is, a detailed understanding of the political economy and scalar management of the global media business will tell us much about media ownership patterns, structures of influence, and the movement of capital. But it will tell us less about the relation between these structures and movements, on the one hand, and the densely particular assemblages of practice and meaning that they depend on and reproduce, on the other.

Always troubling, this impasse has been aggravated by the need to come to terms with a world where the so-called logic of commodification more than ever depends on semiosis, and semiotic processes are in turn increasingly inseparable from the political economy of mass communications. As ethnographers, we need strategies that will allow us not so much to worry the impasse as a conceptual problem but rather to capture its dynamics as a practical challenge in the lives and work of our informants. One way of doing this is to focus ethnographically on what one might call nodes of mediation. These are the sites at which the compulsions of institutional determination and the rich, volatile play of sense come into always provisional alignment in the service of (and always, in part, against the grain of) a vast range of social projects, from the grass roots to corporate boardrooms.

The urgency of developing such strategies can perhaps best be shown by considering some of the problems that continue to haunt many contemporary studies of globalization and media.

LOCALITY, PROXIMITY, HYBRIDITY

Since The Formula was announced, it has become virtually de rigueur to insist that, contrary to longstanding expectations of McWorld-style homogenization, globalization has in fact led to a revalorization of the local. There is, of course, a kind of prima facie obviousness to the idea that we value that which we know from the everyday rounds of our lives. Mauss (1990) argued that valuables are generally "a class of goods more closely linked to the soil" (p. 10). On the other side of the coin, the postcolonial "allure of the foreign" (Orlove 1997) is often taken as a symptom of cultural self-alienation, especially on the part of what dependency theorists used to call comprador classes.

But the narrative of local revival begs a couple of questions. First, what spatial or scalar level is denoted by this "local"? The nation remains, of course, an important unit of representation, legislation, and collective address: the nation-form as commodity form and media public (Abu-Lughod 1993, 1995; Davila 1997; Foster 2002; Guss 1996; Mankekar 1999; Mazzarella 2003; Miller 1997; Moeran 1996b; Morley 1992; Rajagopal 2001; Scannell 1996). The nation remains popular partly because it is a readily available and generally intelligible unit of scalar mediation. Much of the mediating work deliberately performed by public and commercial bureaucracies still involves achieving at least provisional commensurations between the nation-form and, on the one hand, transnational imaginaries and relationships and, on the other, regional commitments and interests. Of course, and this point is discussed at greater length below, the relative emphasis given to different scalar levels is in part a function of the particular medium being used—of its formal properties as well as the historical contingencies of its development in a particular place.

The second question is more directly focused on the problem of cultural substantialism; it addresses how we imagine the ontological relationship between the entities that we call "the local" and "the media." Accounts and analyses often imply that media are something that happen to or are imposed on already-constituted local worlds. The local, in this view, is composed of a certain set of cultural values and practices to which media must then adapt, in order to find an audience. The media are then commonly understood to "impact" the local world in a number of beneficial and/or deleterious ways. But rarely is it acknowledged that mediation, and its attendant cultural politics, necessarily precedes the arrival of what we commonly recognize as "media": that, in fact, local worlds are necessarily already the outcome of more or less stable, more or less local, social technologies of mediation.

Most discussions of culture and media include an obligatory nod to the fact that media "produce and reproduce dominant ideas." And yet many of these analyses nevertheless continue to presuppose that such ideas actually ontologically precede the media that supposedly produce and reproduce them. This is particularly the case when these ideas are taken to belong to a domain of social life that is understood to be in some sense "deep," such as culture. For example, Lee et al. (2002) discuss the production of local relevance in global television reporting along these lines, concluding with a routine invocation of sociological/anthropological authority: "[M]ass media stand at the forefront of institutional venues through which each national community acts out its shared experiences and the underlying cultural premises" (p. 4). Global events are "selectively domesticated [. . .] in tandem with core social values. Global news must be filtered through the domestic system of commonsense knowledge (Berger & Luckman 1967) or 'local knowledge' (Geertz 1993)" (p. 4, references in original).

In this kind of argument, culture and media are not in fact seen as coconstitutive. Instead, "underlying cultural premises" and "the domestic system of commonsense knowledge" are reconfirmed as always already preexisting the intervention of the media. But what are the mediations through which these "underlying cultural premises" are constituted? And which new kinds of mediation are required to link these existing social mediatory practices to the transnational circulation of spectacular news reportage? It may very well be interesting and important for us, as anthropologists, to theorize the kinds of shifts that occur in the self-understandings and practices of a particular social group when, for example, a "traditional" ritual is performed especially for television cameras. But we must also remember that the ritual is itself already a medium, with its own distinctive mechanisms and possibilities of objectification and translation. The problem, then, is less the meeting of "culture" and "media," and more the intersection of two or more systems of mediation.

Making things worse, and against its own best insights, the discourse of globalization often tends toward an exaggerated sense of novelty that easily gives rise to the implication that commercial satellite television and the Internet have suddenly made ordinary people cognitively and affectively dependent on external processes of mediation, whereas previously stable and locally rooted "schemas" have sufficed to make sense of the world (Graber 1984, Gurevitch 1991). Even the most reflexive analyses remain curiously dependent on this anchor of authenticity. John Durham Peters (1997), in the context of a volume dedicated to questioning the naturalized boundaries of culture, spends a provocative article exploring the mediated, or as he puts it "bifocal," structure of experience. And still he chooses to conclude with a sentiment that fully reinstates the pathos of the local-under-fire: "We must take a gamble on the ongoing relevance of the lifeworld, however perforated it may be by the system" (p. 92).

The point is not simply academic. Rather, the substantialist understanding of culture and locality, embedded as it is in the bureaucratic imagination, is indispensable to the functioning of power. In the culture industries, it helps to maintain the fiction that media and marketing are merely "responding" to the already-constituted desires of audiences—even as many decisions are actually made on a hunch basis by a surprisingly small group of people worldwide (Havens 2003, Sinclair et al. 1996, Tinic 2003). Multiculturalist strategies of governmentality attempt at once to incite and to contain the conviction that "cultural identity" might be a legitimate basis for political claims (Benhabib 2002, Gutmann 1994, Kymlicka 2001, Young 2002). At the same time and for the same reasons, cultural substantialism is just as likely to appear as a weapon of the weak (Gupta 1998, Miller 1994, Povinelli 2002, Spivak 1988). It is, then, hardly radical to suggest that if we, as anthropologists, want any critical purchase on these phenomena, we need to be doubly attuned to the potential complicity between the substantialist current in our discipline and its appearance in the discourses and practices of our informants.

Take, for example, the study of the local adaptation of globally circulating types of entertainment and information: soap operas, talk shows, and news (Abu-Lughod 1995, Allen 1995, Barker 1997, Boyd-Barrett 1997, Das 1995, Hannerz 2004, Jeffrey 2000, Mattelart 1994, McMillin 2003, Miller 1998, Rajagopal 1993, Ståhlberg 2002, Tinic 2003, Wilk 1995), or consumer brands and their advertising (Davila 1997, Foster 2002, Kemper 2001, Mazzarella 2003, Miller 1997, Moeran 1996a, Watson 1997). As any ethnographer of the global media will have found, the "organic intellectuals" internal to these industries will often deploy substantialist models of culture to explain, and to attempt to predict, what works where. We might call the basic idea cultural proximity. This notion is frequently found imported, without noticeable modification, from the desks of corporate media planners to those of media theorists at major universities. The key proposition, deceptively simple, is that "like attracts like." This then becomes the explanation for apparently fortuitous cultural "fits." So, for instance, the Japanese TV series *Oshin* does well in Iran, of all places, "because its values of perseverance and long suffering were compatible with cultural codes prevalent in what might appear a distinctly different society" (Mowlana & Rad, cited in Lechner & Boli 2000, p. 305).

In this line of thought, the object is to identify correspondences at more or less manifest levels, between two reified cultures.

Another, more interesting, variation on the idea of cultural proximity introduces a note of ambivalence. Here, the power and attraction of particular forms of media depend on their close distance, that is, their ability to appeal at once to the intimately quotidian and the compellingly distant. Many regionally powerful centers of media production and dissemination have, it seems, been able to withstand the pressure of Hollywood by offering an aspirational idiom desirable precisely by virtue of its non-American modernity: Mexico and Brazil for Latin America, India for South Asia, Egypt for the Arab Middle East, Hong Kong and Taiwan for ethnically Chinese East Asia, etc. (Barker 1997, Ching 2000, Iwabuchi 2001, Liechty 2002, Shohat & Stam 1996, Shohat & Stam 2003, Yang 1997). Indeed, close distance–based strategies have been responsible, at a national level, for some of the classic examples of the resurgence of the local. McMillin's (2003) description of the formula that guided production at Channel V, India's (Hong Kong–based, Bombay-produced) alternative to Music Television (MTV), is exemplary: "Producers knew that 'an all-English veejay [video jockey] [brought] abysmal ratings while an all-vernacular veejay [was] not hip enough for a country that generally worship[ed] English—Hinglish, Gujlish, Tamlish, Anythinglish'" (p. 344).

Of course, just as evolutionary theorists can divine adaptive advantages in just about any given social phenomenon, so the mysterious correspondences of cultural proximity can be discerned, *post facto*, in almost any conceivable culture/media relationship. The reliance on substantialist models of culture and cultural correspondence ultimately becomes a strategy for avoiding the questions that really need to be asked. These questions require us to confront culture as, at one and the same time, ideology and social process, as something continuously made and remade through constantly shifting relations, practices, and technologies of mediation. The answers we may reach will not be much good for modeling or mapping. But they will give us a much better sense of the complex cultural politics of what is happening when, for instance, Hausa youth in northern Nigeria find in Hindi films a resonant-yet-removed idiom through which to explore and elaborate sexuality and romance (Larkin 1997). Moreover, as opposed to the self-fulfilling teleology of culture-as-destiny, such projects are likely to foreground the often provisional and unstable translational politics of transnational media encounters, what Boellstorff (2003) terms "dubbing culture," meaning made out of tenuous, glancing, fragmentary, and half-understood engagements.

The spectre of "hybridity" inevitably rears its head in this connection. Therefore, let me emphasize that I am by no means advocating a celebration of complexity (or indeed "diversity") for its own sake. In the early years of globalization studies (and even now in mainstream discourse) the invocation of complexity often seemed designed to allow a kind of joyous explanatory abdication. This was the realm of the "charming" juxtaposition of the traditional and the modern, or the kind of studiedly casual demotic multiculturalism for which Dick Hebdige's JoJo of Balsall Heath became an early and subsequently rather overextended poster boy (Hannerz 1996,

Hebdige 1981, Inda & Rosaldo 2001). As West & Sanders (2003) complain, "It is far too commonplace, in this literature, to speak in ill-supported generalities—to conjure evocative images of people, things and ideas found in surprising new places" (p. 10).

What makes systematic critical analysis more urgent is that these figures, although apparently radical in their will to unsettle, are in fact fully consonant with disturbingly conservative political and intellectual agendas. As Hutnyk (2000) reminds us, "Hybridity and difference sell; the market remains intact" (p. 36). Indeed, celebratory discourses of hybridity often depend on precisely the cultural substantialism that they disavow (Friedman 1999). The grimly repetitive publicity formula of Tibetan monks with cellphones or computers in remote yet colorful Indian villages leans on the historicist categories of Eurocentric modernity for its effect even as it appears to trouble it (Chakrabarty 2000). And our delight in ethnographic reports of remote islanders finding, in a Coke bottle, a convenient ritual representation of the female torso mixes this questionable, overdetermined enchantment with a comforting reassurance about the pragmatically adaptive integrity of "traditional" lifeways (also see Taussig 1993).

What is lost in both the affirmation of local integrity and the celebration of freewheeling hybridity is any sustained understanding of the grounded actuality of cultural politics. By taking given social processes of mediation as the practical loci of politics, we also see that these processes are the points at which institutional overdetermination and the indeterminacies of translation cohabit, all the time and everywhere. Rather than hanker for im-mediacy—understood either as ethnological nostalgia or as the vitalist romance of emergent potentiality/difference—we need, ethnographically speaking, to attend to the places of mediation, the places at which we come to be who we are through the detour of something alien to ourselves, the places at which we recognize that difference is at once constitutive of social reproduction and its most intimate enemy.

MEDIATION AND MEDIA

As anthropologists of media and globalization, we confront a world in which cynicism about the social functions of the media and romanticism about the authenticity and value of culture are equally widespread. These two phenomena are, moreover, related, and their interrelationship arises, in part, out of the profound ambivalence that a heightened self-consciousness about the mediated quality of our lives has produced.

Our everyday understanding of mediation involves notions such as harmonization and the resolution of differences, often through the intervention of an apparently neutral third term. This neutrality is an ideological or discursive effect, but a powerful one; it has important social consequences for the credibility, legitimacy, and, indeed, the seeming naturalness (or im-mediacy) of a given type of mediation. All mediation involves the appearance of an ontological separation between form and content. This appearance, in turn, makes possible the apparently impartial authority that modern institutions rely on. And it helps to support the ideological proposition that media are simply formal, neutral tools that may be applied to any situation.

At the same time, however, mediation is a matter of the greatest intimacy. It is the process by which the self recognizes itself by returning to itself, renewed and once removed. I separate the prefix "re-" here to signal a paradox. On the one hand, reflexive social entities (selves, societies, cultures) are fundamentally constituted (and not just reconstituted) through mediation. On the other hand, as Derrida and other scholars suggest, this constitutive mediation also always produces a fiction of premediated existence. Hence the term identity, a concept that expresses this recursive doubling, this simultaneous intimacy and distance. And hence, also, the persistent plausibility—against all the evidence, as it were—of substantialist ideas of culture and origin.

All mediation, then, involves a dual relation: a relation of simultaneous self-distancing and self-recognition. In the words of the now-most-unfashionable theorist of the media, McLuhan (1994), "All media are active metaphors in their power to translate experience into new forms. The spoken word was the first technology by which man was able to let go of his environment in order to grasp it in a new way" (p. 57). We "let go" in order to see ourselves differently, to be able to do new things in a reconstituted world. Peters' (1997) concept of media as practices and technologies of "social envisioning" (p. 79) usefully captures the fact that media (in his account not only television, radio, press, and cinema but also statistics, accounting, mapping, and census taking) make society imaginable to itself. Because they are so intimately tied to the very possibility of imagining and inhabiting our social worlds in particular ways, these mediations are also commonly naturalized. That is, discursive and affective constructs like a "society," a "nation," or a "culture" depend, for their apparent self-evidence, on mediations and contingencies that they must ultimately deny.

An important feature of the moment of globalization, as registered in social theory, is a sudden and vertiginous self-consciousness of many of these mediations and, by the same token, a heightened awareness of the contingency and the brittleness of our social worlds. It is as if the disenchantment of tradition that has so often been described as a leitmotif of the experience of modernity were spatialized and generalized to encompass not only our relation to our pasts, but also now the differences that served to distinguish geocultural selves from others. In its cruder alarmist and affirmative versions, the discourse of globalization tends toward both a compulsive fixation on the problem of cultural authenticity (even, as we have seen, in the guise of hybridity) and a fetishization of media per se as utopian or apocalyptic technologies. In a more critical register, however, it encourages us to reopen the problem of mediation, to explore the practices and predicaments that constitute our worlds via particular media.

Ironically, the iconization of a medium is in part a result of its embedding in social process, an embedding which retrospectively acquires the appearance of necessity. The formal and material properties of a medium arise out of and crystallize a socially and historically determinate field of possibilities. Having emerged, the medium then recursively remediates each new social context to which it becomes relevant, often at great spatial and temporal removes from its origins. Insofar as it requires and enables particular social relations, a medium starts to appear definitive of certain socio-historical forms—colonialism, nationalism, transnationalism. This process should not be confused with technological determinism. For example, to speak of the complicity of a particular medium with nationalism does not mean that the existence of the medium necessarily "leads to" nationalism in any simple sense. Rather, we are registering the historical effect of mediation: that neither of the social relationships and institutional histories that we recognize in turn as nationalism and a particular medium are any longer fully intelligible or recognizable to us in isolation from each other (for discussions of the relation between nationalist imaginaries/publics and various media see Anderson 1983, Fair 2003, Garcia Canclini 2001, Ginsburg et al. 2002, Hendy 2000, Hilmes 2003, Mankekar 1999, Rajagopal 2001, Schwoch 2003, Urla 1997).

At an early point in the development of a medium, this overidentification between particular media and particular social forms often appears as utopian or dystopian prophecy. Later, once a medium has grown functionally inseparable from a form of life, it appears as a kind of forgetting. Consequently, and ironically, the first step that any critique has to take is one of abstraction: an attempt to remember the potentialities of a medium away from the social routines that it has come to define. At this level it is useful to insist that media do have formal properties and that these properties condition their social potentials, the alternative social lives that they may yet live.

Any given medium enables and constrains the control and dissemination of information in particular ways. Different media offer different communicational structures: broadcast or closed circuit, far-flung or face-to-face, one-to-one, one-to-many, or many-to-many. The price, availability, and complexity of hardware combined with the extent to which content may be modified or re-created by users at different locations in the social field of circulation will condition the extent to which a given medium becomes the focus for "alternative" or "radical" uses and mobilizations. For example, in contrast to typically national media, certain kinds of mass media technologies—particularly those with relatively low user overhead, such as radio, video, and the Internet—frequently offer opportunities to address very specialized audiences, either in the form of outlaw or dissident programming, indigenous radio, or—in a more dispersed spatial mode—diasporic and/or exilic production (Browne 1990, Hendy 2000, King & Woods 2001, Llorens 1991, Marks 2000, McLagan 2002, Naficy 1993, O'Connor 1990, Schein 2002, Urla 1997).

The importance of, at a very literal level, controlling broadcast facilities is obvious from the priority given, in contemporary political coups, to seizing radio and television stations. But once the seizure has been effected, more complex questions arise about the relative interplay between intimacy, interactivity, and anonymity in a given medium. Radio, for example, is often taken to be a medium both intimate and amenable to disguise; hence Radio España Independiente, which purported to be the regional voice of the Pyrenees but was in fact Soviet-based and backed (Hendy 2000). The diffused structure of the Internet provides a powerful political alternative to control over centralized state media apparatuses—witness the Zapatistas' ability to mobilize worldwide support for their rebellion in the mid-1990s. But the Internet's' combination of real-time interactivity and anonymity also enables both the transgressive-liberatory thrills of ethnic and sexual "passing" in multiple user dimensions (MUDs), MUD object-oriented dimensions (MOOs), and chat groups, and the agonies of identity theft and other forms of cybercrime (Bell & Kennedy 2000, Castells 2001, Herman & Swiss 2000, Kolko 2003, Levy 2000, Lunenfeld 2000, Nakamura 2002, Turkle 1997).

The possible social lives of media are further conditioned by their radically different "lexes," that is, the structure of reading that a particular medium requires and allows: still images versus moving pictures, audio-visual versus silent, textual versus visual, the sensory intensity of a 15-second commercial versus the stately unfolding of a 3-hour epic film. McLuhan (1994) remarks of the relation between the patterns of sociality and the sensory properties of media: "The use of any kind of medium or extension of man alters the patterns of interdependence among people, as it alters the ratio among our senses" (p. 90). From the Frankfurt School onward, the question of our sensory engagement with media has been at the center of debates over their social implications and effects. For example, television and video enable more decentralized diffusion and viewing than does the highly concentrated experience of the cinema; however, the insertion of television into everyday life is also likely to be more low-key, leading, perhaps, to more distracted forms of engagement (Mankekar 1999; McCarthy 2001; Rajagopal 2001; Silverstone 1994; Williams 1974, 1999).

Ethnographic approaches to mediation are potentially powerful because they do not have to rely primarily on speculative abstraction to render visible those potentialities that are constitutive of, and yet disavowed in, any social order. Given a well-chosen field site, an anthropologist has access, as events unfold, to the precarious relationship between determination and indeterminacy that structures mediation in the flow of social practice. Nonethnographic critical theorists of the media may strive to rescue or redeem these potentialities by projecting them into a radical future or mourning them in a receding past. But anthropologists enjoy the empirical benefits of being in the thick of it while not succumbing to the plain empiricism that characterizes instrumental and applied analyses of culture, globalization, and mediation.

There is of course an important anthropological tradition of attending to "failed" mediations, to the points at which cultural difference precludes translation. Scholars who have worked in ethnographic film production, for instance, have been particularly attentive not only to the more-or-less creative appropriation of media technologies and narratives by communities new to electronic media or, indeed, to writing, but also to the possibility of radical incommensurability. Aboriginal songs or stories that last for hours or even days may not be suited to radio broadcast;

modes of knowledge inscription may not allow for the alienation between writer and reader characteristic of mass-produced print; conventions of representation and viewing may not translate into the formal conventions of the cinema (Browne 1990; Ginsburg 1994a,b, 2000, 2002; Langton 1993; McDougall 2002; Michaels 1986, 1994; Smith & Ward 2000a; Turner 1992, 2002; Zimmerman et al. 2000).

An important distinction between postglobalization anthropologists of the media and many of their forebears in the study of ethnographic film and indigenous media is the recognition that difference can no longer simply be understood as a function of culture. Difference is no longer so much a measure of the distance between two or more bounded cultural worlds; rather, we may now understand it as a potentiality, a space of indeterminacy inherent to all processes of mediation, and therefore inherent to the social process per se.

Globalization studies, contrary to superficial objections, announce neither the end of culture nor the end of difference. Rather, they remind us that culture is an effect of social processes of mediation, that these processes of mediation always grapple with internal indeterminacies as well as external provocations, and that social actors—consciously or unconsciously—try to manage or fix these indeterminacies and provocations by means of reified schemes of cultural identity and cultural difference. That such a "fixing" is at once both necessary and impossible is one of the ground rules of cultural politics.

CONCLUSION

Half a generation ago, the theorists of globalization noted that we had reached a kind of watershed, a moment in our apprehension of the world as a totality that was characterized both by unprecedented connection and by incomparable complexity. Skeptics, for their part, complained that there was nothing new about globalization. Both camps were right, and both were wrong. The power of the globalist provocation was, in a sense, that it finally required us rigorously to confront and to theorize what we had "known" all along. *Writing Culture* and the critique of representation tackled the cult of immediacy in ethnographic writing, that is to say the disavowal of the mediating work done by means of naturalized literary devices. Globalization studies turned this critical awareness outward, onto the practices of our informants, refashioning it as a methodological tool.

Substantially, this review has been largely a discussion of projects and problems emerging out of the anthropology of the media as currently constituted, particularly vis-à-vis the problematic of globalization. But of course my intention has been to suggest that the question of mediation is a far more general one, one that touches on the very fundamentals of social process. Indeed, we should be careful not to choose only overdetermined nodes of mediation as sites from which to explore these issues. These are the sites where mediation is, as it were, out in the open— part of the explicit discourse and self-imagination of a type of institution, a class of people. But this is of course only the tip of the iceberg. If, in fact, mediation is a dynamic principle at the root of all social life, then, having developed ways of theorizing it, we should move toward exploring its conditions and outcomes in social projects and movements that may not recognize themselves in those terms.

Similarly, although the discourse on globalization has foregrounded the question of the relation between the local and the global, this relation could usefully, I think, be read as a variation on the larger theme of close distance. Mediation produces and reproduces certain configurations of close-distance, mediated self-understandings that depend on the routing of the personal through the impersonal, the near through the far, and the self through the other. Close distance is therefore a figure for the dialectic of engagement and alienation inherent in all cultural politics. Again, this is not simply a theoretical or even just an existential issue, although it is both of these. Rather, documenting the play of close distance can be a useful way into an analysis of social projects of value across the board: the half-managed dialectics of desire and distance, engagement and fear that structure all our attempts to wring meaning, value, and permanence out of the contingencies of our lives.

The *Annual Review of Anthropology* is online at http://anthro.annualreviews.org

LITERATURE CITED

Abu-Lughod L. 1993. Finding a place for Islam: Egyptian television serials and the national interest. *Public Cult.* 5(3):493–513

Abu-Lughod L. 1995. The objects of soap opera: Egyptian television and the cultural politics of modernity. In *Worlds Apart: Modernity Through the Prism of the Local*, ed. D Miller, pp. 190–210. London: Routledge

Allen R, ed. 1995. *To Be Continued...Soap Opera Around the World*. London: Routledge

Anderson B. 1983. *Imagined Communities: Reflections on the Origin and Spread of Nationalism*. London: Verso

Ang I. 1985. *Watching Dallas: Soap Opera and the Melodramatic Imagination*. London: Routledge

Ang I. 2003[1990]. Culture and communication: towards an ethnographic critique of media consumption in the transnational media system. See Parks & Kumar 2003, pp. 363–75

Appadurai A. 1996. *Modernity At Large: Cultural Dimensions of Globalization*. Minneapolis: Univ. Minn. Press

Appadurai A, Breckenridge C. 1988. Why public culture? *Public Cult.* 1(1):5–9

Appadurai A, Breckenridge C. 1995. Public modernity in India. In *Consuming Modernity: Public Culture in a South Asian World*, ed. C Breckenridge, pp. 1–15. Minneapolis: Univ. Minn. Press

Askew K, Wilk R, eds. 2002. *The Anthropology of Media: A Reader*. Oxford: Blackwell

Barker C. 1997. *Global Television: An Introduction*. Oxford: Blackwell

Bell D, Kennedy B, eds. 2000. *The Cybercultures Reader*. London: Routledge

Benhabib S. 2002. *The Claims of Culture: Equality and Diversity in the Global Era*. Princeton, NJ: Princeton Univ. Press

Boellstorff T. 2003. 'I knew it was me:' mass media, 'globalization' and lesbian and gay Indonesians. In *Mobile Cultures: New Media in Queer Asia*, ed. C Berry, F Martin, A Yue, pp. 21–51. Durham, NC: Duke Univ. Press

Boyd-Barrett O. 1977. Media imperialism: towards an international framework for an analysis of media systems. In *Mass Communication and Society*, ed. J Curran, M Gurevitch, J Woollacott, pp. 116–35. London: Edward Arnold

Browne D. 1990. Aboriginal radio in Australia:

from Dream Time to prime time? *J. Commun.* 40 (1):111–20

Burton J, Franco J. 1978. Culture and imperialism. *Lat. Am. Perspect.* 5(1):2–12

Castells M. 1989. *The Informational City: Information Technology, Economic Restructuring and the Urban-Regional Process.* Oxford: Blackwell

Castells M. 2001. *The Internet Galaxy: Reflections on the Internet, Business and Society.* New York: Oxford Univ. Press

Chakrabarty D. 2000. *Provincializing Europe.* Princeton, NJ: Princeton Univ. Press

Ching L. 2000. Globalizing the regional, regionalizing the global: mass culture and Asianism in the age of late capital. *Public Cult.* 12(1):233–58

Das V. 1995. On soap opera: What kind of anthropological object is it? In *Worlds Apart: Modernity Through the Prism of the Local,* ed. D Miller, pp. 169–89. London: Routledge

Davila A. 1997. *Sponsored Identities: Cultural Politics in Puerto Rico.* Philadelphia, PA: Temple Univ. Press

Dear M, Flusty S. 1999. The postmodern urban condition. In *Spaces of Culture: City-Nation-World,* ed. M Featherstone, S Lash, pp. 64–85. London: Sage

de Certeau M. 1984. *The Practice of Everyday Life.* Berkeley, CA: Univ. Calif. Press

Deleuze G, Guattari F. 1987. *A Thousand Plateaus: Capitalism and Schizophrenia.* Minneapolis: Univ. Minn. Press

Dorfman A, Mattelart A. 1975. *How to Read Donald Duck: Imperialist Ideology in the Disney Comic.* New York: Int. Gen.

du Gay P, Hall S, Janes L, Mackay H, Negus K. 1997. *Doing Cultural Studies: The Story of the Sony Walkman.* London: Sage

Eyerman P. 1999. Moving culture. In *Spaces of Culture: City-Nation-World,* ed. M Featherstone, S Lash, pp. 116–37. London: Sage

Fair JE. 2003. *Francophonie* and the national airwaves: a history of television in Senegal. See Parks & Kumar 2003, pp. 189–210

Featherstone M. 1991. *Consumer Culture and Postmodernism.* London: Sage

Featherstone M. 1996. Localism, globalism and cultural identity. In *Local/Global: Cultural Production and the Transnational Imaginary,* ed. R Wilson, W Dissanayake, pp. 46–77. Durham, NC: Duke Univ. Press

Featherstone M, ed. 1990. *Global Culture: Nationalism, Globalization and Modernity.* London: Sage

Featherstone M, Lash S, eds. 1999. *Spaces of Culture: City-Nation-World.* London: Sage

Fiske J. 1987. *Television Culture.* London: Methuen

Fiske J. 2003[1993]. Act globally, think locally. See Parks & Kumar 2003, pp. 277–85

Foster R. 2002. *Materializing the Nation: Commodities, Consumption and Media in Papua New Guinea.* Bloomington: Indiana Univ. Press

Friedman J. 1999. The hybridization of roots and the abhorrence of the bush. See Featherstone & Lash 1999, pp. 230–56

Friese H, Wagner P. 1999. Not all that is solid melts into air: modernity and contingency. See Featherstone & Lash 1999, pp. 101–15

Galtung J. 1979. A structural theory of imperialism. In *Transnational Corporations and World Order: Readings in International Political Economy,* ed. G Modleski, pp. 155–71. San Francisco: Freeman

Garcia Canclini N. 2001. *Consumers and Citizens: Globalization and Multicultural Conflicts.* Minneapolis: Univ. Minn. Press

Garofalo R. 1993. Whose world, what beat: the transnational music industry, identity and cultural imperialism. *World Music* 35(2):16–22

Gillespie M. 1995. *Television, Ethnicity and Cultural Change.* London: Routledge

Ginsburg F. 1994a. Culture/media: a mild polemic. *Anthropol. Today* 10(2):5–15

Ginsburg F. 1994b. Embedded aesthetics: creating a discursive space for indigenous media. *Cult. Anthropol.* 9(3):365–82

Ginsburg F. 2000. Resources of hope: learning from the local in a transnational era. See Smith & Ward 2000b, pp. 27–47

Ginsburg F. 2002. Mediating culture: indigenous media, ethnographic film and the production of identity. See Askew & Wilk 2002, pp. 187–209

Ginsburg F, Abu-Lughod L, Larkin B, eds. 2002. *Media Worlds: Anthropology On New Terrain*. Berkeley, CA: Univ. Calif. Press

Golding P, Harris P, eds. 1997. *Beyond Cultural Imperialism: Globalization, Communication and the New International Order*. London: Sage

Graber D. 1984. *Processing the News*. New York: Longman

Gripsrud J. 1989. 'High culture' revisited. *Cult. Stud.* 3(2):194–207

Guattari F. 1995. *Chaosmosis: An Ethico-Aesthetic Paradigm*. Bloomington: Indiana Univ. Press

Gupta A. 1998. *Postcolonial Developments: Agriculture in the Making of Modern India*. Durham, NC: Duke Univ. Press

Gupta A, Ferguson J. 1997. Culture, power, place: ethnography at the end of an era. In *Culture, Power, Place: Explorations in Critical Anthropology*, ed. A Gupta, J Ferguson, pp. 1–29. Durham, NC: Duke Univ. Press

Gurevitch M. 1991. The globalization of electronic journalism. In *Mass Media and Society*, ed. J Curran, M Gurevitch, pp. 204–24. London: Edward Arnold

Guss D. 1996. 'Full speed ahead with Venezuela:' the tobacco industry, nationalism, and the business of popular culture. *Public Cult.* 9(1):33–54

Gutmann A, ed. 1994. *Multiculturalism*. Princeton, NJ: Princeton Univ. Press

Hall S. 1997. The centrality of culture: notes on the cultural revolutions of our time. In *Media and Cultural Regulation*, ed. K Thompson, pp. 208–38. London: Sage

Hall S, ed. 1997. *Representation: Cultural Representations and Signifying Practices*. London: Sage

Hamelink C. 1983. *Cultural Autonomy in Global Communications*. New York: Longman

Hamelink C. 1994. *The Politics of World Communication*. London: Sage

Hannerz U. 1990. Cosmopolitans and locals in world culture. See Featherstone 1990, pp. 237–51

Hannerz U. 1992. *Cultural Complexity: Studies in the Social Organization of Meaning*. New York: Columbia Univ. Press

Hannerz U. 1996. *Transnational Connections: Culture, People, Places*. London: Routledge

Hannerz U. 2004. *Foreign News: Exploring the World of Foreign Correspondents*. Chicago: Univ. Chicago Press

Hardt M, Negri A. 2001. *Empire*. Cambridge, MA: Harvard Univ. Press

Harindranath R. 2003. Reviving 'cultural imperialism:' international audiences, global capitalism and the transnational elite. See Parks & Kumar 2003, pp. 155–68

Harvey D. 1990. *The Condition of Postmodernity: An Inquiry into the Origins of Cultural Change*. Oxford: Blackwell Publishers

Havens T. 2003. African American television in an age of globalization. See Parks & Kumar 2003, pp. 423–38

Hebdige D. 1981. *Subculture: The Meaning of Style*. London: Routledge

Hendy D. 2000. *Radio in the Global Age*. Cambridge: Polity Press

Herman A, Swiss T, eds. 2000. *The World Wide Web and Contemporary Cultural Theory: Magic, Metaphor, Power*. London: Routledge

Herman S, McChesney R. 1997. *The Global Media: The New Missionaries of Corporate Capitalism*. London: Cassell

Highmore B. 2001. *Everyday Life and Cultural Theory*. London: Routledge

Hilmes M. 2003. Who we are, who we are not: battle of the global paradigms. See Parks & Kumar 2003, pp. 53–73

Hutnyk J. 2000. *Critique of Exotica: Music, Politics and the Culture Industry*. London: Pluto

Inda JX, Rosaldo R, eds. 2001. *The Anthropology of Globalization: A Reader*. Oxford: Blackwell

Iwabuchi K. 2001. Becoming 'culturally proximate:' the a/scent of Japanese idol dramas in Taiwan. In *Asian Media Productions*, ed.

B Moeran, pp. 54–74. Honolulu: Univ. Hawai'i Press

Jameson F. 1991. *Postmodernism, or, the Cultural Logic of Late Capitalism.* Durham, NC: Duke Univ. Press

Jameson F, Miyoshi M, eds. 1998. *The Cultures of Globalization.* Durham, NC: Duke Univ. Press

Jeffrey R. 2000. *India's Newspaper Revolution: Capitalism, Politics and the Indian-Language Press, 1977–1999.* New York: St Martin's Press

Kemper S. 2001. *Buying and Believing: Sri Lankan Advertising and Consumers in a Transnational World.* Chicago: Univ. Chicago Press

King R, Wood N, eds. 2001. *Media and Migration: Constructions of Mobility and Difference.* London: Routledge

Kolko B, ed. 2003. *Virtual Publics: Policy and Community in an Electronic Age.* New York: Columbia Univ. Press

Kuper A. 1999. *Culture: The Anthropologist's Account.* Cambridge, MA: Harvard Univ. Press

Kymlicka W. 2001. *Politics In the Vernacular: Nationalism, Multiculturalism and Citizenship.* New York: Oxford Univ. Press

Langton M. 1993. *Well, I Heard It On the Radio and I Saw It On the Television.* Sydney: Aust. Film Comm.

Larkin B. 1997. Indian films and Nigerian lovers: media and the creation of parallel modernities. *Africa* 67(3):406–39

Lau J, ed. 2003. *Multiple Modernities: Cinemas and Popular Media in Transcultural East Asia.* Philadelphia: Temple Univ. Press

Lechner F, Boli J, eds. 2000. *The Globalization Reader.* Oxford: Blackwell

Lee CC. 1980. *Media Imperialism Reconsidered: The Homogenizing of Television Culture.* London: Sage

Lee CC, Chan JM, Pan Z, So C, eds. 2002. *Global Media Spectacle: News War Over Hong Kong.* Albany: SUNY Press

Lefebvre H. 1992. *Critique of Everyday Life: An Introduction.* New York: Verso

Levy P. 2000. *Collective Intelligence: Mankind's Emerging World in Cyberspace.* Cambridge, MA: Perseus

Liebes T, Katz E. 1990. *The Export of Meaning: Cross-Cultural Readings of Dallas.* New York: Oxford Univ. Press

Liechty M. 2002. *Suitably Modern: Making Middle-Class Culture in a New Consumer Society.* Princeton, NJ: Princeton Univ. Press

Llorens JA. 1991. Andean voices on Lima airwaves: highland migrants and radio broadcasting in Peru. *Stud. Lat. Am. Popul. Cult.* 10:177–89

Lunenfeld P, ed. 2000. *The Digital Dialectic: New Essays on New Media.* Cambridge, MA: MIT Press

Lyotard J-F. 1985. *The Postmodern Condition: A Report on Knowledge.* Minneapolis: Univ. Minn. Press

Mankekar P. 1999. *Screening Culture, Viewing Politics: An Ethnography of Television, Womanhood and Nation in Postcolonial India.* Durham, NC: Duke Univ. Press

Marks L. 2000. *The Skin of the Film: Intercultural Cinema, Embodiment, and the Senses.* Durham, NC: Duke Univ. Press

Massumi B. 2002. *Parables for the Virtual: Movement, Affect, Sensation.* Durham, NC: Duke Univ. Press

Mattelart A. 1994. *Mapping World Communication: War, Progress, Culture.* Minneapolis: Univ. Minn. Press

Mauss M. 1990. *The Gift.* New York: Norton

Mazzarella W. 2003. *Shoveling Smoke: Advertising and Globalization in Contemporary India.* Durham, NC: Duke Univ. Press

McCarthy A. 2001. *Ambient Television: Visual Culture and Public Space.* Durham, NC: Duke Univ. Press

McDougall D. 2002. Complicities of style. See Askew & Wilk 2002, pp. 148–60

McLagan M. 2002. Spectacles of difference: cultural activism and the mass mediation of Tibet. See Ginsberg et al. 2002, pp. 90–111

McLuhan M. 1994. *Understanding Media: The Extensions of Man.* Cambridge, MA: MIT Press.

McMillin D. 2003. Marriages are made on television: globalization and national identity in

India. See Parks & Kumar 2003, pp. 341–59

Meyrowitz D. 1985. *No Sense of Place: The Impact of Electronic Media on Social Behavior.* New York: Oxford Univ. Press

Michaels E. 1986. *The Aboriginal Invention of Television in Central Australia: 1982–86.* Canberra: Aust. Inst. Aborig. Stud.

Michaels E. 1994. *Bad Aboriginal Art: Tradition, Media and Technological Horizons.* Minneapolis: Univ. Minn. Press

Miller D. 1997. *Capitalism: An Ethnographic Approach.* Oxford: Berg

Miller D, ed. 1995. *Worlds Apart: Modernity Through the Prism of the Local.* London: Routledge

Miller T. 1994. *The Well-Tempered Self: Citizenship, Culture and the Postmodern Subject.* Baltimore, MD: Johns Hopkins Univ. Press

Miller T. 1998. *Technologies of Truth: Cultural Citizenship and the Popular Media.* Minneapolis: Univ. Minn. Press

Modleski T. 1986. Introduction. In *Studies in Entertainment: Critical Approaches to Mass Culture*, ed. T Modleski, pp. ix–xix. Bloomington: Indiana Univ. Press

Moeran B. 1996a. *A Japanese Advertising Agency.* Honolulu: Univ. Hawai'i Press

Moeran B. 1996b. The Orient strikes back: advertising and imaging in Japan. *Theory Cult. Soc.* 13(3):77–112

Morley D. 1992. *Family Television: Cultural Power and Domestic Leisure.* London: Comedia

Morley D. 2003[1993]. Where the global meets the local: notes from the sitting room. See Parks & Kumar 2003, pp. 286–302

Morris M. 1988. Banality in cultural studies. *Block* 14:15–25

Naficy H. 1993. *The Making of Exile Cultures: Iranian Television in Los Angeles.* Minneapolis: Univ. Minn. Press

Nakamura L. 2002. *Cybertypes: Race, Ethnicity and Identity on the Internet.* London: Routledge

Nordenstreng K, Schiller H, eds. 1993. *Beyond National Sovereignty: International Communication in the 1990s.* Norwood, NJ: Ablex

Nordenstreng K, Varis T. 1974. *Television Traffic: A One Way Street.* Paris: UNESCO

O'Connor A. 1990. The miners' radio stations in Bolivia: a culture of resistance. *J. Commun.* 40(1):102–10

Orlove B, ed. 1997. *The Allure of the Foreign: Imported Goods in Postcolonial Latin America.* Ann Arbor, MI: Univ. Mich. Press

Ortner S, ed. 1999. *The Fate of 'Culture:' Geertz and Beyond.* Berkeley: Univ. Calif. Press

Parks L, Kumar S, eds. 2003. *Planet TV: A Global Television Reader.* New York: NYU Press

Peters JD. 1997. Seeing bifocally: media, place, culture. In *Culture, Power, Place: Explorations in Critical Anthropology*, ed. A Gupta, J Ferguson, pp. 75–92. Durham, NC: Duke Univ. Press

Pinney C. 2001. Introduction: public, popular and other cultures. In *Pleasure and the Nation: The History, Politics, and Consumption of Public Culture in India*, ed. R Dwyer, C Pinney, pp. 1–34. New Delhi: Oxford Univ. Press

Poster M. 2001. *What's the Matter With the Internet?* Minneapolis: Univ. Minn. Press

Povinelli E. 2002. *The Cunning of Recognition: Indigenous Alterities and the Making of Australian Multiculturalism.* Durham, NC: Duke Univ. Press

Rajagopal A. 1993. The rise of national programming: the case of Indian television. *Media Cult. Soc.* 15(1):91–112

Rajagopal A. 2001. *Politics After Television: Hindu Nationalism and the Reshaping of the Indian Public.* Cambridge: Cambridge Univ. Press

Sarti I. 1981. Communication and cultural dependency. In *Communication and Social Structure*, ed. E McAnany, J Schnitman, N Janus, pp. 317–34. New York: Praeger

Sassen S. 2001. *The Global City: New York, London, Tokyo.* Princeton, NJ: Princeton Univ. Press. 2nd ed.

Scannell P. 1996. *Radio, Television and Everyday Life.* Oxford: Blackwell

Schein L. 2002. Mapping Hmong media in

diasporic space. See Ginsberg et al. 2002, pp. 229–44

Schiller H. 1976. *Communication and Cultural Domination*. White Plains, NY: Int. Arts Sci. Press

Schiller H. 1989. *Culture, Inc.: The Corporate Takeover of American Expression*. New York: Oxford Univ. Press

Schudson M. 1987. The new validation of popular culture: sense and sentimentality in academia. *Crit. Stud. Mass Commun.* 4(1): 51–68

Schwoch J. 2003. Television, Chechnya and national identity after the Cold War. See Parks & Kumar 2003, pp. 226–42

Scott A, ed. 2002. *Global City-Regions: Trends, Theory, Policy*. New York: Oxford Univ. Press

Shohat E, Stam R. 1994. *Unthinking Eurocentrism: Multiculturalism and the Media*. London: Routledge

Shohat E, Stam R. 1996. From the Imperial family and the transnational imaginary: media spectatorship in the age of globalization. In *Global/Local: Cultural Production and the Transnational Imaginary*, ed. R Wilson, W Dissanayake, pp. 145–70. Durham, NC: Duke Univ.

Shohat E, Stam R, eds. 2003. *Multiculturalism, Postcoloniality and Transnational Media*. Piscataway, NJ: Rutgers Univ. Press

Silj A, Alvarado M. 1988. *East of Dallas: The European Challenge to American Television*. London: Br. Film Inst.

Silverstone R. 1994. *Television and Everyday Life*. London: Routledge

Sinclair J, Jacka E, Cunningham S, eds. 1996. *New Patterns in Global Television: Peripheral Vision*. New York: Oxford Univ. Press

Sklair L. 1991. *Sociology of the Global System*. London: Harvester Wheatsheaf

Smith A. 1991. *National Identity*. Reno: Univ. Nev. Press

Smith C, Ward G. 2000a. Globalization and indigenous peoples: threat or empowerment? See Smith & Ward 2000b, pp. 1–24

Smith C, Ward G, eds. 2000b. *Indigenous Cultures in an Interconnected World*. Vancouver: Univ. B. C. Press

Soja E. 2000. *Postmetropolis: Critical Studies of Cities and Regions*. Oxford: Blackwell

Spivak GC. 1988. Subaltern studies: deconstructing historiography. In *Selected Subaltern Studies*, ed. R Guha, GC Spivak, pp. 3–32. New York: Oxford Univ. Press

Sreberny-Mohammadi A, Winseck D, McKenna J, Boyd-Barrett O, eds. 1997. *Media in Global Context*. London: Edward Arnold

Straubhaar J. 1997. Distinguishing the global, regional and national levels of world television. In *Media in Global Context*, ed. A Sreberny-Mohammadi, D Winseck, J McKenna, O Boyd-Barrett, pp. 284–98. London: Edward Arnold

Ståhlberg P. 2002. *Lucknow Daily: How a Hindi Newspaper Constructs Society*. Stockholm: Stockholm Stud. Soc. Anthropol.

Taussig M. 1993. *Mimesis and Alterity: A Particular History of the Senses*. London: Routledge

Thrift N. 1996. *Spatial Formations*. London: Sage

Tinic S. 2003. Going global: international coproductions and the disappearing domestic audience in Canada. See Parks & Kumar 2003, pp. 169–85

Tomlinson J. 1991. *Cultural Imperialism*. Baltimore, MD: Johns Hopkins Press

Tomlinson J. 1997. Internationalism, globalization and cultural imperialism. In *Media and Cultural Regulation*, ed. K Thompson, pp. 118–53. London: Sage

Tomlinson J. 1999. *Globalization and Culture*. Chicago: Univ. Chicago Press

Tucker R, ed. 1978. *The Marx-Engels Reader*, 2nd edition, p. 476. New York: Norton

Turkle S. 1997. *Life On the Screen*. New York: Simon and Schuster

Turner B. 1990. *Theories of Modernity and Postmodernity*. London: Sage

Turner T. 1992. Defiant images: the Kayapo appropriation of video. *Anthropol. Today* 8(6):5–16

Turner T. 2002. Representation, politics and

cultural imagination in indigenous video: general points and Kayapo examples. See Ginsburg et al. 2002, pp. 75–89

Urla J. 1997. Outlaw language: creating alternative public spheres in Basque free radio. In *The Politics of Culture in the Shadow of Capital*, ed. L Lowe, D Lloyd, pp. 280–99. Durham, NC: Duke Univ. Press

Wasko J, Phillips M, Meehan E. 2001. *Dazzled By Disney?* London: Leicester Univ. Press

Watson J, ed. 1997. *Golden Arches East: McDonald's in East Asia*. Stanford, CA: Stanford Univ. Press

West H, Sanders T. 2003. Power revealed and concealed in the new world order. In *Transparency and Conspiracy: Ethnographies of Suspicion in the New World Order*, ed. H West, T Sanders, pp. 1–37. Durham, NC: Duke Univ. Press

Wilk R. 1995. Learning to be local in Belize: global structures of common difference. In *Worlds Apart: Modernity Through the Prism of the Local*, ed. D Miller, pp. 110–33. London: Routledge

Wilk R. 2002. 'It's destroying a whole generation:' television and moral discourse in Belize. See Askew & Wilk 2002, pp. 286–98

Williams R. 1974. *Television: Technology and Cultural Form*. New York: Schocken

Williams R. 1999. *Raymond Williams on Television: Selected Writings*. London: Routledge

Yang M. 1997. Mass media and transnational subjectivity in Shanghai: notes on (re) cosmopolitanism in a Chinese metropolis. In *Ungrounded Empires: The Cultural Politics of Modern Chinese Transnationalism*, ed. A Ong, D Nonini, pp. 287–319. London: Routledge

Young IM. 2002. *Inclusion and Democracy*. New York: Oxford Univ. Press

Zimmerman L, Bruguier L, Zimmerman K. 2000. Cyberspace smoke signals: new technologies and Native American ethnicity. See Smith & Ward 2000b, pp. 69–86

Annu. Rev. Anthropol. 2004. 33:369–92
doi: 10.1146/annurev.anthro.33.070203.143805
Copyright © 2004 by Annual Reviews. All rights reserved
First published online as a Review in Advance on June 11, 2004

THE WORLD IN DRESS: Anthropological Perspectives on Clothing, Fashion, and Culture

Karen Tranberg Hansen

*Department of Anthropology, Northwestern University, Evanston,
Illinois 60208-1310; email: kth462@northwestern.edu*

Key Words   dressed body, material culture, consumption, clothing practice, style diversification

■ **Abstract**   Clothing research has attracted renewed interest in anthropology over the past two decades, experiencing a florescence that had been kept within bounds by reigning theoretical paradigms. The works have been influenced by general explanatory shifts in anthropology, which inform disparate bodies of clothing research that otherwise have little unity. The most noticeable trend is a preoccupation with agency, practice, and performance that considers the dressed body as both subject in, and object of, dress practice. The turn to consumption as a site and process of meaning making is evident also in clothing research. Dress has been analyzed, by and large, as representing something else rather than something in its own right, although new efforts to reengage materiality suggest that this approach is changing. Little work has been done on clothing production issues, though some scholars examine the significance of dress in the context of the entire economic circuit and the unequal relationships between its actors.

INTRODUCTION

A rich literature on dress has appeared across the scientific and popular board in recent years. Active and creative engagements with apparel extend across disciplines into museum exhibitions where fashion is displayed as art. Several encyclopedias on clothing and fashion are forthcoming. The new wealth of academic scholarship includes articles, monographs, and edited collections with regional or topical foci. *Fashion Theory*, a new interdisciplinary journal, complements the scholarship of *Costume*, the journal of the Costume Society in the United Kingdom, and *Dress*, the journal of the Costume Society of America. Berg is publishing a new book series, *Dress, Body, and Culture*. Highly profiled international conferences on themes ranging from clothing and imperialism to fashion and consumption showcase dress scholarship.

Anthropology contributes to this growing body of research by giving new life to the study of clothing, which for a long time received only passing attention.

0084-6570/04/1021-0369$14.00

Reigning theoretical paradigms are to blame for much of this neglect, making clothes an accessory in symbolic, structural, or semiotic explanations. As a result, any serious engagement with clothing itself has almost vanished. Since the late 1980s, anthropologists have set a new research agenda on clothing, placing the body surface at center stage. The chief inspirations for this shift are readily identifiable. Rather than defining culture in the foundational sense of comprising the shreds and patches of a specifically bounded society, we now view culture processually as created through agency, practice, and performance. Conventional physical space and place delimitations have given way to understandings of globalization as a process in which the local and the global interact. The single most important medium through which these processes have been examined is consumption, conceived not only as markets and economic actors but as cultural processes that construct identity.

Clothing research is not a separately identifiable part of anthropology; it shares the general reorientation of the discipline and incorporates many frameworks and concerns from other disciplines that also study the dressed body. Museum-based research on textiles and cloth overlaps anthropological studies of dress, complicating disciplinary distinctions. Anthropologists are inspired by interdisciplinary scholarship on textiles and dress, dress/costume history, design/art history, and social and economic history. Works on representation and textual analysis in cultural and media studies also provide stimulus. Compared to these disciplines, anthropology's hallmark has always been its holistic and contextual approach to the cross-cultural study of clothes and their symbolic and cultural meanings. Excellent overviews (Eicher 2000, Taylor 2002), Schneider's (1987) *ARA* review on the anthropology of cloth, and Weiner & Schneider's *Cloth and the Human Experience* (1989) set the precedent for this review.

The questions the new scholarship on clothing is addressing are shaped by the paradigmatic shift from social structure to agency and practice. Some works view dress as a set of competing discourses, linked to the operation of power, that construct the body and its presentation. Aside from these general observations, there is little congruence across these bodies of scholarship. Some works pursue historical questions about changes in dress practice brought about by a variety of encounters including colonialism and Westernization. Much recent dress research explores the effects of globalization. The research barely touches high-end clothing, except in works on clothing designed for export and on third-world middle-class efforts to construct class through consumer culture. Although many works focus on clothing consumption, some scholars seek to link production and consumption when examining the significance of dress. Taken together, these new works demonstrate that fashion no longer is an exclusive property of the West. Contemporary fashions are created rapidly and in great volume from Latin America, Africa, and Asia, redefining both consumption and fashion itself in the process and propelling multidirectional style shifts across the globe.

This review considers a selection of anthropological research on dress since the publication of important works mentioned above from the late 1980s. Primarily discussing works that fall outside the West's conventional fashion canon, I focus on scholarship in which dress is central, omitting works that address clothing in passing and largely considering English-language sources.[1] Throughout the review, I pay deliberate attention to what people wear. The entries by which I organize the review define the scope both topically and conceptually in terms I clarify shortly. The regional focus in the first part of the review identifies processes that play out similarly and differently in specific regional contexts, highlighting distinct concerns of regional scholarship. The next part of the review presents a number of crosscutting themes that command distinct literatures. I bypass several dress issues that appear briefly in the regional overviews but that have not attracted much substantive work.

FROM CLOTHING AND CULTURE TO DRESS AND FASHION

Several terms with overlapping meanings appear in the works reviewed here: clothing, costume, dress, garment, apparel, and fashion. My choice to use dress is strategic, made in an effort to be inclusive and to avoid the ambiguities surrounding distinctions between cloth and clothing that arise when textiles shift from folded cloth to wrapped garments. In adopting the term dress, I follow Eicher & Roach-Higgins (1992) who view it as an "assemblage of body modifications and/or supplements," a definition that reckons both with the strategic effects entailed in the material properties of dress and their expressive abilities. Even then, I continue using the terms clothing/clothes and dress interchangeably but in the inclusive sense of dress just defined. I avoid the term costume used in dress scholarship for ensembles coordinated for masquerades, theatrical parts, dress from distinct historical periods, and native, indigenous clothing styles. The term rarely appears in the works reviewed here save from Latin America in reference to ethnic or regional dress. I speak of garments when referring to specific items of clothing and apparel when addressing issues concerning manufactured garments. Last but not least, I use fashion to frame this review because it is at the heart of widespread contemporary preoccupations with clothing and is central to the most exciting new scholarship on dress.

When examining other people's clothes as fashion, anthropologists have to come to terms with several long-standing scholarly concerns that have marginalized

---

[1]Important works on dress in cultural studies, popular culture, folklore, ethnology, psychology, and marketing fall beyond my scope. I have not considered works on dress and subcultural style, including gay and lesbian studies, a subject on which cultural and media studies are in the forefront. Most clothing research, including by anthropologists, focuses on young adults and adult populations, rarely examining the dress practices of children or the elderly. For reasons of space, I omit many interesting works on individual garments (e.g., Arthur 1999, 2000; Brydon 1998; Colchester 2003b; Foster & Johnson 2003; Kelly 2003).

research on dress. One is the trivializing of consumers', especially Western women's, interest in clothes, an antifashion tendency that devalues the significance of dress as a cultural and economic phenomenon. Today this tendency is less of an issue as many women and men study dress and as negotiations over gender boundaries through dress practice form part of the research agenda.

The second concern is the distinction between fashion in the West and the "traditional" clothing of much of the rest of the world drawn by scholars who explain fashion's origin in terms of the development of the capitalist production system in the West. "Traditional" dress was never a cultural "heritage issue" in anthropology but was always a changing practice, remaking itself in interaction with other dress styles, with garments of Western commercial manufacture and the West's fashion system. Globalization in the era of hypercommunication is creating a new "world in dress," breaking down conventional fashion boundaries. Understanding fashion as a global phenomenon is further supported by shifts in the organization of garment production across the globe as well as by the vast economic significance of garment production in world trade.

The third concern arises from the lingering effects of trickle-down theories that have restrained our understanding of the sources and currents of dress inspirations. Bourdieu's (1984) class-based explanatory model of differentiation may be criticized in this vein for accentuating distinctions between mass and high culture. Polhemus (1994) acknowledges influences on style adoption from the bottom up. Dress influences travel in all directions, across class lines, between urban and rural areas, and around the globe. A proliferation of styles is simultaneously available, facilitating eclectic mixing if not idiosyncratic dress presentations (Polhemus 1996). Examining stylistic choice as a complex and heterogeneous process, contemporary anthropological work has moved beyond the idea of emulation to embrace notions of bricolage, hybridity, and creolization. Clarifying these dynamics and the power differentials that shape them is at the heart of today's anthropological study of dress.

What is it about the dressed body that has prompted so much recent anthropological scholarship to approach it as a site of convergence for transnational, global, urban, and local forces? Because it both touches the body and faces outward toward others, dress has a dual quality, as Turner (1993 [1980]) noted when he coined the notion the social skin. This two-sided quality invites us to explore both the individual and collective identities that the dressed body enables. The subjective and social experiences of dress are not always mutually supportive but may contradict one another or collide. The contingent dynamic between these two experiences of dress gives rise to considerable ambiguity, ambivalence, and, therefore, uncertainty and debate over dress. Dress readily becomes a flash point of conflicting values, fueling contests in historical encounters, in interactions across class, between genders and generations, and in recent global cultural and economic exchanges.

Some recent scholarship has revived a past era's concerns with clothing as material culture but adds a new twist to highlight the efficacy of surfaces. Refocusing our attention on materiality as a surface that constitutes social relations and states of being, Miller (1994) and his colleagues explore how material properties affect what people do with cloth and clothing (Küchler & Miller 2005). Because clothes are so eminently malleable, we shape them to construct our appearance. There is an experiential dimension to the power of clothing, both in its wearing and viewing (O'Connor 2005). Our lived experience with clothes, how we feel about them, hinges on how others evaluate our crafted appearances, and this experience in turn is influenced by the situation and the structure of the wider context (Woodward 2005). In this view, clothing, body, and performance come together in dress as embodied practice.

While clothes are among our most personal possessions, they are also an important consumption good. Their worldwide production, export, and import circuits have altered the availability of apparel both on high streets in the West and in open-air urban markets in the third world. This accessibility not only facilitates individualism but also pushes the diversification of tastes in numerous directions, turning local consumers into arbiters of stylistic innovations that are contributing to the breakdown of fashion's Western hegemony.

LATIN AMERICA

The rich cloth traditions of Mesoamerica and the Andes loom large in contemporary anthropological scholarship on clothing in Latin America. These works examine the changing dynamics of indigenous dress in more detail than the clothing practices of the large wave of European immigrants at the turn of the twentieth century or the contemporary fashion scene (Root 2004). The cultural dress icons are women's indigenous dress consisting of a variety of pre-Columbian elements: *pollera* (full pleated skirt) and *vestido* (factory-made dress). *De pollera* also connotes identity as Indian or *cholo* (urban Indian) and *de vestido* as *mestiza* or white. There is no straightforward correspondence between dress and ethnicity, and much of the region's new scholarship demonstrates considerable temporal and situational variations in dress practice.

Latin American dress has changed through selective incorporation of influences that have continually redefined individual and local identities against the backdrop of this region's changing political regimes and opportunities in the global arena. In Guatemala, *traje*, Maya dress, is central to the identity of Maya people. Hendrickson (1995) traces the cultural biography of *traje*, examining the elements of dress that come together into complete garments and changes made to it over time. Although defining local Maya identity, *traje* is worn also in parades, queen contests, and in the tourist and export business, making it part of a larger politics.

Dress is a complex ethnic marker among the Sakaka, an Andean group in northern Bolivia (Zorn 2004b). Viewing dress styles as genres, Zorn identifies six variations of Indian "ethnic" dress. These variations shift from pre-Columbian and Spanish peasant-derived, long, pleated dresses with embroidery, *polleras*, shawls, and felt hats to "new traditional" styles for women and hand-woven pants, vests, and jackets with embroidery, factory-made shirts, ponchos, and white felt hats for men. The new styles have elaborate embroidery and are constructed almost entirely of factory-made inputs. Financed largely by incomes from migration, these dress styles comprise a distinctive indigenous fashion system, a self-conscious choice in the face of white and *mestizo* control of the Bolivian state. Femenìas (2004a) discusses how rural Peruvians from Caylloma province shift their identification as Indians, whites, and *mestizos* through locally produced garments called *bordados*. *Bordados* are garments with brightly colored embroidery for which a tourist market has developed. Most artisans are also vendors, and at some point they may become merchants. Both ethnicity and dress practice are situational as vendors wear *pollera* or dress in *bordado* to trade on ethnicity. In another work, Zorn (2004a) examines transformations of cloth production and the effects of its recent commoditization for the tourist market among the Taquile, an Andean group living on two islands on the Peruvian side of Lake Titicaca. Taquileans have been relatively successful at controlling, and thus benefiting from, tourism. Presenting themselves in Indian dress is part of their cultural strategy (2004a).

The Otavalo of Equador are well known for their relatively successful local harnessing of economic and social capital from textile and clothing sales and music performances in the international tourist arena. Otavalho entrepreneurs dress in "Indian" costumes for musical performances. Discussing the specific meanings of such dress choices, Meisch (2002) describes the development of a pan-Otavalo dress. This dress style contains archaic elements, such as the dress whites and ponchos that young men wear only on special occasions. As old styles disappear, the new styles become defined as indigenous. Men's dress is changing more rapidly than women's, and different generations are wearing slightly different dress. Rather than adopting the clothing styles of the local dominant group, young Otavalenos leapfrog local dress styles.

Contests fueled by women's dress mediate cross-class interaction between Aymara-speaking migrants who are live-in servants in *cholo pacenos* (racially and culturally mixed, urban) and "white" elite households or work as street vendors in La Paz, Bolivia (Gill 1993). The *cholo pacenas* cultivate *de pollera* styles of expensive materials, adorned with jewels to distance themselves from the less ostentatious *pollera* of their workers with whom they may share cultural backgrounds. Upper-class employers like to see their Aymara servants in *pollera*. Many of the migrant workers like to dress in *vestido*. It is less costly, avoids the stigma of being Aymara, and gives workers a sense of freedom while they are away from the controlling influence of their employers.

AFRICA

Scholarship on dress in Africa revolves around the enduring appeal and transformations of cloth/clothing; the effects on dress and identity of colonization, modernity, and globalization; and dress issues in the diaspora. Diverse local dress practices have changed in complex ways in interaction with Islam and Christianity. In their examination of these processes, the disciplines of anthropology and history overlap considerably. Africa presents two broad dress cultures based on the draping of cloth in West, Central, and parts of East Africa, and tailored Western-styled attires in much of the rest of East Africa and Southern Africa. The dress icons are the *boubou* (loose gown worn by women and men); cloth wrapper and head tie; and Western-styled dress. In response to local, regional, and external influences, the boundaries of these styles are shifting across the continent and beyond.

Renne's (1996) ethnography of Buna cloth in Nigeria examines culture and history of a specific part of Yorubaland, where distinct categories of women and men wear differently colored and patterned cloths. Young women dress in black cloth at marriage, hunters wear black-and-white-striped shirts, and chiefs don red masquerade cloth with magnificent patterns. White is the color of spiritual relations. The associative power of these dress practices persists as part of everyday life along with factory-produced imported cloth and tailored clothing. As in much of the rest of West Africa, Buna cloths outlive their owners and are handed down. West African cloths are commodities with social lives in Perani & Wolff's work (1999) on cloth and dress as patronage in Hausa, Nupe, and Yoruba cloth traditions in Nigeria. Technologies of cloth production and artistic concerns converge in this study of several types of cloth, the effects of conversion to Islam on the cloth trade, the impact of British colonialism, and the coming of factory-produced yarn. They also discuss the fashionable Yoruba dress world in which lurex yarns entered strip-cloth weaving to produce the popular *shain-shain* styles of the 1990s. The cloth/clothes dynamic in Nigeria continues to shift, most recently in response to structural adjustment programs that reduce overall purchasing power. Denzer (2002) examines how the reforms affected the demand for custom-made clothing. Tailors continued producing traditional garments for ceremonial occasions but had fewer requests for Western fashions.

Comaroff & Comaroff (1997) view clothing as central to missionary conversion in the early nineteenth century in Bechuanaland, a frontier region between colonial Botswana and South Africa. The struggle for souls entailed dressing African bodies in European clothes to cover their nudity and managing these bodies through new hygiene regimes. European clothes were a popular prestige good preceding the arrival of missionaries; converts accepted the clothes eagerly and wore them as they saw fit, expressing their personal desires in a new culture of consumption that the missionaries could not fully control. Martin (1994) offers urban vistas of vibrant and rapidly changing styles that the culturally diverse African townspeople integrated into their dress in Brazzaville during the French colonial period. This colonial cosmopolis was an historical crossroad of trade and exchange where ostentatious body display accentuated long-held cultural ideas that connected dress and social status.

Because of the contingent meanings of the dressed body, clothing readily becomes a contested issue (Allman 2004a). Recent works focus on dress to examine struggles over class, gender, and generation (Byfield 2004, Fair 2004, Moorman 2004), investigating attempts to create "national dress" before and after independence (Allman 2004b, De Jorio 2002). Tensions over "proper dress" arising from the popularity of miniskirts continue after independence, revolving around issues of national culture (Ivaska 2004), revolution (Burgess 2002), and gender and sexual dynamics (Hansen 2004). Several works examine the incorporation of European styles and fabrics into the local dress universe, such as the smocked *Sotho* dress (James 1996) and the *Herero* long dress (Hendrickson 1994), that serve as visible markers for "traditional" dress in southern Africa. While dressing "our way" is part of the embodied experience of the long dress, the shared sensibility of wearing it is also a means of establishing connections (Durham 1995, 1999).

The symbolic interplay of bodies and changing social experiences devolves on dress in different ways. Masquelier (1996) offers vivid insight into the power of clothing to define identity in Muslim Mawri communities in Southern Niger, where spirits of the *bori* cult choose their hosts and mediums embody spirit identities by the clothes they wear. Renne's (2000) new research on style interaction in Yoruba ecclesiastical dress demonstrates how hand-woven textiles connect cloth and body, asserting an African identity that is also Roman Catholic. In Cherubim and Seraphim churches (African Independent Churches) (Renne 2004), church leaders' visions and dreams inspire creativity in clothing designs, tailored by church members to reflect aesthetic aspects of belief and practice. Wearing visionary garments, almost as a souvenir from another world, church leaders emphasize their otherworldly connections and supernatural abilities in material terms.

Dressing differently than cultural norms prescribe may provoke politically charged reactions, as Bastian (1996) describes for southeastern Nigerian women's adoption of the Hausa-style tunic on top of wrappers or trousers. Experimenting with elite dress from the Muslim north that politicians and businessmen took up in the wake of the 1970s oil boom, women created their own dress practice, as did young male tailors who used colors, fabrics, and accessories to subvert the dress aesthetic associated with chiefly rank in their hierarchically, male-dominated society. Such clothing practices cross not only gender and class/rank lines but also continental divides as in the striking displays of brand-named Parisian garments by the Congolese *sapeurs* who traveled between Congo and Paris to earn money to purchase clothes (Gandoulou 1989). Friedman's analysis (1994b) of Gandoulou's work connects this region's historical preoccupation with body display to the contemporary *sapeurs'* extravagant experimentation with imported clothes. *La sape* is French slang for elegant and fashionable clothing. Although the *la sape* has precursors in urban popular culture, it keeps incorporating new elements. Today, *la sape* has spread beyond the two Congos to francophone West Africa and the diaspora, involving both young women and men. Recent work explains *la sape* as a contest over equality and participation in a world over which young people have little control (Gondola 1999, Scheld 2001).

Persisting ideas of dressing well have inspired work in Gambia and Senegal on *sanse*, a Wolof noun for finery and a verb for dressing up in elaborately tailored gowns requiring many lengths of expensive woven cloth or imported damask, costly accessories, cosmetics and perfume, and last but not least, a particular demeanor (Heath 1992, Mustafa 1998). The cut, decorative styling, and embellishments have changed, incorporating influences from many directions including neighboring West African countries, Islamic North Africa, India, and France. Derived from the French verb *changer*, *sanse* alludes to the numerous changes of clothing women undergo at dress-up events.

Linking social identity and wealth, *sanse* marks difference. Yet women of lesser means challenge its sartorial dominance by wearing dress imitations made from factory printed cloth. Analyzing *sanse* as a language of dress, Heath (1992) explains women's dress practice as a dialogue between dominant and subordinate voices. Playing into a vibrant clothing scene, *sanse* arbitrates changing external dress influences. This process creates a sartorial ecumene most pronounced in urban settings where global flows and media are active in creating hybrid styles (Mustafa 1998). On Dakar's lively fashion scene today, everyone wants to look good including youth who go for *la sape*, and yet they dress in elegant gowns on Muslim holidays and at life-cycle events (Scheld 2001). Constant style changes have turned tailoring into an entrepreneurial niche for women as haute couture designers and small-scale tailors. Incorporating influences from magazines, music videos, and street scenes, their custom-made clothes blend cultures from within Africa and beyond, with both new and secondhand clothing serving as resources (Grabski 2002).

Conventional analytical dichotomies of traditional/modern, African/Western, and local/global fall short in capturing the many diverse influences on contemporary style dynamics in Africa and African-inspired dress diasporas in the West. The African dress diaspora includes couturiers from Mali and Senegal in Paris, producers and marketers of Afrocentric fashions in the United States, tourists, and many others (Ross 1998; Rovine 2001). Approaching such processes as a circuit, with three interconnected sites—Dakar in Senegal, Nairobi in Kenya, and Los Angeles—Rabine (2002) analyzes African fashion as a semiotic system. She suggests that economic and symbolic exchange come together in African fashion production, textile printing, and dyeing, imbuing the products with meaning. She is particularly concerned with the subordinate position of artisanal production in a global economic system fueled by mass production. Because they are more interested in creativity and aesthetics than in standardization and uniformity, African artisans do not enter this system easily.

SOUTH ASIA

Dress scholarship on the subcontinent of India includes historically oriented work on negotiations over dress both by colonizers and the colonized and on the interplay of imperialism and nationalism in matters of dress choice. There is detailed work on historical changes in Indian dress in terms of regional, caste, and class differences. Other works include attention to high fashion and contemporary style challenges. A growing body of work considers dress choices in the South Asian diaspora and their effects on clothing consumption within India. The dress icon is the sari, variations of the draped and wrapped women's garment long prevalent in South Asia. It coexists with the *shalwar kamiz* and with Western dress styles in a relationship that is modified across the region's changing political history in interaction with regional, national, and international styles.

Tarlo (1996) offers rich insights into clothing choices over the past 100 years in India. Both men's and women's dress consisted of cloth folded in specific ways around the body. Throughout the colonial period there was tension between wearing cut and tailored dress and draped styles of clothing. More men than women adopted, and then rejected, different types of European clothing. Dress became a public issue in the 1920s when Ghandi promoted the use of homemade cloth in an effort to restore both individual spirituality and public patriotism but achieved little success especially from the Indian elite and village women. Tarlo describes how members of different castes dealt with dress issues, including "untouchables" who had the least to lose by changing dress. She also examines the ethnic fashion revival in the boutiques of Hauz Khas, a shopping center in Delhi for Indian designer clothes, art, and furnishings.

Banerjee & Miller (2003) take up discussion of the sari where Tarlo stopped, emphasizing the complex personal and social relationships Indian women have with their clothes and examining individual life experiences with saris from youth to adulthood into old age and hierarchical interactions between women and their maids. A special feature of this work is its attention to the sari's materiality and the consequences of this draped garment for the act of wearing it, especially the strategic possibilities of the *pallu*, the end of the sari that drapes over the shoulder. They examine shopping for saris and consider esthetics, design, manufacture, preferences for silk and cotton versus synthetics, and the effects of the visual media on the "modern" sari. Acknowledging the popularity of the *shalwar kamiz*, they suggest that the sari's dominant status as an expression of cultural identity may decline over the long term. Even then, they see the two dress forms as complementary in representing contemporary Indian dress.

Nepal, which did not allow foreigners into the country until 1816 after the Anglo-Indian war, is an interesting contrast to India because it imported foreign goods without foreign interpreters. The elite eagerly embraced a selection of European goods, including clothes. During the transformation process from city-state to nation, these changing modes of elite distinction served to construct class. So does fashion today in the aspirations of middle-class Nepali consumers (Liechty 2003).

Questions about cultural identity and belonging are salient in South Asian communities around the world. The *shalwar kamiz* has become a widespread alternative to the sari among young East Asian women in the United Kingdom, Canada, and the United States (Khan 1993, Raghuram 2003). Asian women entrepreneurs have begun to manufacture *shalwar kamizes* that now have become a common sight in public in the West (Bhachu 2004). Much more straightforward to wear than the sari, it also has considerable appeal to non-Indian women.

EAST AND SOUTHEAST ASIA

East and Southeast Asia's diverse societies have several dress icons, among them the *sarong* in Indonesia, the *qipao* in China and Vietnam where it is known a *ao dai*, and the *kimono* in Japan. Dress scholarship has focused on changes in clothing practices through complex socioeconomic and political transformations set into motion by shifting local and Western economic and military dominance and, more recently, by processes of globalization.

Indonesian dress is a product of the changing relationship between indigenous, Muslim, and Western influences (Schulte Nordholt 1997). Islam arrived much earlier than did Christianity (van Dijk 1997). Western dress entered with Dutch East India Company rule and was appropriated differently by urban women and men. Revolutionary youth activists dressed in a variety of uniforms (Sekimoto 1997). Incorporating Indonesia's rich textile traditions, "ethnic" dress persists, transformed, reconfigured, if not reinvented in a combination of woven cloths, into dress consisting of a sarong wrapped around the lower body with matching shoulder cloth slung over a blouse (Niessen 2003). They coexist with Western-styled dress, which some urban middle-class women take courses to learn to wear in attempts to control their own appearance and propriety. Whereas some women feel good in Western-styled dress, others are putting on the fitted head covering they associate with being faithful Muslims (Jones 2003).

Dalby's study (1993) of the kimono focuses on the interplay of local and European styles of dress. Describing the changing forms of garments that gave shape to the modern kimono, she examines the kimono as work wear, fashion item, and art form. She explores how this wrapped, geometrically constructed garment faced competition from the West's cut, tailored, and stitched garments, gradually giving way to imported styles after the 1860s. Wearing Western-styled clothing in their everyday lives today, most Japanese use the kimono for special occasions.

Only lately have dress scholars begun exploring how Chinese people experienced the dress edicts and production restrictions under the cultural revolution (Chen 2003, Wilson 1999). In efforts to include China's diverse population into the new socialist body politics, reform campaigns sought to alter dress styles and practices. The effects varied across regions as Friedman (2004) demonstrates for the socialist denouncement of women's distinctive dress, headpieces, and hairstyles in Hui'an in southeastern China. But in the new market economy, such dress styles are extolled as ethnic in a process that is reworking notions of citizenship.

The chief focus in this region's anthropological dress scholarship is on the unfolding dynamics of power and directional influences on fashion and design in the process of globalization (Niessen et al. 2003). Across the region, governments are promoting textile and garment production for export. The emerging fashion industry in China in the 1970s and 1980s combined dress elements from many of China's ethnic groups and Western styles with specific focus on the *qipao*. Designers in Hong Kong and Taiwan used the *qipao* also as a strategy of conscious Orientalizing (Li 1998). The *ao dai* in Vietnam is considered the national costume, even if it is of hybrid origin and achieved its current form only in the 1970s. Leshkowich (2003) describes the flourishing entrepreneurship to which the *ao dai*'s popularity has given rise as women design, produce, and market both locally and overseas. The Orientalizing strategy may place designers in a bind as Skov (2003) shows, comparing young Hong Kong designers who create garments with "Chinese" motifs with those who try to work in a genuinely international style but have little success. By contrast, Japan has become both a player in the global fashion network centered in Paris and a fashion center for East Asia. Yohi Yamamoto and Rei Kawakubo's success on the Paris fashion scene in the 1980s had little to do with "traditional" Japanese clothing and more with their design sensibilities and Japan's international prominence in the textile and apparel industry. Their styles are an oppositional gesture, according to Kondo (1992), contesting hegemonic European and American aesthetic conventions, an attempt at counter-Orientalism.

Dress scholarship on Asia qualifies the historical opposition between East and West in many ways (Steele & Major 1999). Yet the East/West divide persists with new twists in the present with the global fashion scene incorporating diverse elements of East Asian dress and immigrants in the West wearing "traditional" dress on a variety of occasions. While Niessen and their contributors (2003) challenge stereotypes of Asian style as passive and traditional, they analyze the globalization of Asian fashions as an Orientalizing phenomenon that construes a feminine Asia and a masculine West. When "Asian chic" fashions travel from Europe and North America to Asia, designers and consumers are ambivalent about the mixed effects of self-Orientalization. Comparing reactions to "Asian chic" gone local in Vietnam and Indonesia, Leshkowicz & Jones (2003) use a performance model to explain the outcomes as strategies for garnering symbolic and material power or as a demeaning trend that accentuates ethnic stereotypes.

Kimono-, *qipao-*, and *sarong-*influenced clothes continue to be worn locally and globally. Analyzing these design and dress practices as a self-exoticization of Asia hides a major part of contemporary Asian wardrobes from view, in effect limiting our understanding of the world of dress. In post-Mao's China, as elsewhere in the region, urban residents wear suits and dresses, polos and T-shirts, jeans and skirts, and high heels and sneakers. Gender, age, and class position probably serve as the main differentiating factors. Although anthropological studies of consumption have noted the widespread localization of Western dress, few have substantively addressed the significance of Western dress styles in Asia. Tobin (1992) refers to the process as a domestication of the West, a formulation that retains agency with local actors rather than by making them slaves of the foreign. Print, visual media, and the culture industry (Skov & Moeran 1995) are contributing to this process that has particular appeal to youth. Socialization into cultural norms of conformity has made uniforms important in many areas of everyday life from schools to government offices in Japan (McVeigh 2000). Reacting to wearing uniforms, young Japanese buy "cute" things and fashion conscious youth use "cuteness" as a dress and adornment strategy to counter the norms of uniformity (Kinsella 1995).

THE PACIFIC

Most of the recent work on clothing from this region is a product of collaborative research between anthropologists and art historians in a British project using museum collections to examine historical and contemporary interactions with cloth and clothing across the Pacific Islands (Colchester 2003a, Küchler & Were 2004). Rather than assigning the status of dress icon to any single garment or dress practice, in this region we might consider animacity as iconic. Pacific islanders perceive clothing as efficacious.

The Clothing the Pacific project has addressed many of the same themes as scholarship on other regions, yet it stands apart from it by challenging our thinking of how materiality comes to matter. When clothes are not considered to be signs or representations of social relations, what then do they do, asks Keane (2004), discussing the indexical and iconic qualities that he argues are rendering clothing "effective."

Attributing a transformative potential to fibrous surfaces, this scholarship views materiality as powerful in its own right. Throughout the region, this efficacy transforms clothing by shifting motifs onto new surfaces, decomposing and reassembling materials that prompt recognition and identification by association. A translation results so that even when they do not dress bodies, cloth and clothing contribute to new ways of thinking and being.

Some of these works describe the cultural and ritual significance of dressed bodies and their adornment by gender and status/rank relations and the mutual vexations dress caused Europeans and Pacific islanders in early encounters. They include an analysis of constructions of nakedness, dress, and morality in early European voyagers' descriptions of Tahitian women stripping (Tcherkezoff 2003), and of the stunning cultural synthesis in Samoan Christians' bark cloth "ponchos" (Thomas 2003), which not only expressed new ideas of modesty but in fact made modesty possible by providing new ways to cover bodies. Missionaries delighted in Pacific Islanders' adoption of clothing, seeing it as a sign of religious conversion in the new moral economy of mind and body. But understanding clothing as a product of conversion masks its attraction as a new material medium of ritual efficacy. In Vanuatu, the design and cut of the missionary-inspired Mother Hubbard dress inspired island-specific variations with links to grass skirts and pandanus textiles. This dress form has come close to being considered national dress and is associated with notions of proper womanhood (Bolton 2003).

Efficacy arising from differently constructed surfaces has driven innovation and transformations of what Pacific Islanders did with clothing, creating new styles and designs. Methods of surface construction work out differently across the region with selective appropriations of the patterns from printed calico in Melanesia and the cutting and shredding of cloth for restitching into quilts in Eastern Polynesia. In Melanesia, missionaries saw the eager adoption of printed calico as an outward sign of conversion. Melanesians interpreted these patterns with reference to systems and ideas about empowered bodies. Patterned calico became an agent of translation, enabling people to establish connections between existing systems and ideas and new ways of being (Were 2005). In Eastern Polynesia, women's groups linked to religious denominations meet regularly to work on quilts. Such quilts condense women's biographical and personal attachments. Kept in trunks to be given away at weddings, birthdays, and funerals, a woman's quilts reappear when she dies, to be wrapped around her body and accompany her into her grave. Cultural value is created, not by the consumption of quilts, but by their divestment into biographical relations and markers of time (Küchler 2003).

THE VEIL

Few other dress items have been as burdened with cultural signification as the veil, the icon for the practice of covering women's heads and bodies, which varies both temporally and spatially across the world's Islamic societies. Many other regional appellations refer to veiling, among them *hijab*, *chador*, *burqah*, and *bui-bui*. Because of its visibility, the veil is the emblem of Muslim identity and the difference in Orientalizing approaches both in scholarship and popular media, serving as the symbol par excellence of women's subordination. Most scholarship on Islamic dress examines women's clothing even though socioeconomic changes and Islamic revival have changed Muslim men's dress as well. Muslim women do not veil everywhere nor all the time. In much of West Africa, Muslim women manipulate the layers of their voluminous robes to present themselves modestly in public. Anthropology's cross-cultural record includes such variations as men's face veiling and women's headdress among the nomadic Tuareg in Niger (Rasmussen 1991).

The 1970s' and 1980s' scholarship qualified the connection between veiling and women's subordination by demonstrating the veil's diverse uses and women's individual experiences with this dress practice in different parts of the Muslim world. Scholarship of the past two decades has expanded the empirical and theoretical scope. In these new works, politics and religion are weighing down heavily on women's dressed bodies as Islamic dress continues to be reframed by events that affect clothing practices locally and abroad.

Past and present in Turkey, dress has been indentured to political ideology according to White (1999). In the 1970s, some young women began challenging the ban on wearing headscarves to university. Blue headscarves and long coats symbolized dissent as well as alignment with the Islamic political party. *Testettür* fashion of long coats and long silk headscarves has become political chic. Both the hardening and blurring of Turkey's Islamicist/secular divide is evident in the increasing differentiation within "Islamic fashion." Providing long-term historical and comparative background, El Guindi's (1999) study of contemporary Egypt discusses how *hijab* became the object and symbol for a new Islamic consciousness and activism. Because this urban style of veiling differs from earlier practices, some considered it a "new" veiling. Middle- and upper-class women have gradually begun veiling.

Such processes have prompted questions about women's agency and resistance. Examining the accentuation of veiling in Malaysia, Ong (1990) explored the revival of practices associated with Islam. Through clothing, including full *purdah*, which historically is alien to Malay culture, the reformist groups introduced rigid divisions between men's public and women's private roles, attacking the new freedoms young village women experienced as factory workers in free trade zones. As consumers in their own right, wanting to wear jeans and other Western-styled garments, these young women challenged household and community claims on their sexuality and income. University students and middle-class women who took up veiling sought to uphold men's authority, constructing the role of women to preserve an Islamic Malay community. In Java where veiling is neither deeply rooted nor encouraged by the majority, Brenner (1996) explored why Islamic dress had become a common sight by the end of the 1980s. Veiling, she suggests, distances the past and envisions a more perfect future where women can refashion themselves according to their own images of modern Islamic womanhood.

Anthropological concerns with context help to reveal agency as in Abu-Lughod's (1990) discussion of Beduins settled in permanent communities in Egypt where women are subject to surveillance whenever they step out. Young women desire nylon lingerie, cosmetics, and perfumes. Brides display them proudly with their trousseaus. Attracted to the kind of sexualized femininity associated with the market economy's consumerism, these young women become enmeshed in new sets of power relations that they do not readily resist. Similar ambiguities are at the heart of Fuglesang's (1992) discussion of young Muslim women's testing the boundaries of respectability in Lamu, an island off the Kenyan coast, in elaborate dress performances in private settings. Preoccupied with appearance, hairstyle, clothes, and their own local fashions, women dress up for each other. On the day after a wedding, the new bride displays herself in all her finery for her women guests who wear the latest "local" fashion, often inspired by designs on Indian film or syndicated American television shows. Such private events form the trend-setting world of aesthetics and fashion where young women experiment with what it means to be modern and Muslim.

BEAUTY PAGEANTS

The dressed body in beauty pageants constitutes a rich site for dress research on representation, gender construction, performance, and politics. While beauty contests demonstrate the proliferation of Western styles and influences, they are also setting into motion complicated negotiations between local and global norms of beauty, gender, and sexuality (Cohen et al. 1996). In these events, body and dress feed into and subvert world fashion trends.

Dress is central to beauty contests' construction of gender on local, national, and international stages, at times prompting controversy. Queen rallies in Liberia in the early 1980s (Moran 1996) were fund-raising events for development by local constituencies rather than sponsored by the central government. The fashion show followed the Western model of a beauty contest, including revealing outfits such as shorts and swimsuits that were considered quite daring. The winning queens represented different ethnic groups, termed tribes in Liberia, thus mapping the country's political tensions on to women's bodies. Beauty pageants construe an idealized femininity in nationalist projects such as in a Maya queen contest where contestants dressed in *traje* to represent an "authentic" Guatemalan past (McAllister 1996). In Belize's history of national pageants, beauty contests became a tool for articulating different political positions in the country's changing political climate (Wilk 1996). The typical format had contestants entering in "ethnic" costume, sometimes not their own. The swimsuit competition relegated ethnicity to the background, pushing sexuality to the fore. At the end, contestants dressed in expensive formal wear, performing the new nation.

Much of the work on beauty pageants examines local tensions arising over this global phenomenon. Young women from across Mali competed at the 1994 "Miss ORTM" (Office de la Radio et Television du Mali) (Schulz 2000). They paraded in three costumes, two tailored of identical fabric by the same dressmaker: one in the style of everyday dress made from cotton print, and the other from imported cotton fabric with damask weave. They were free to choose the third dress. Participants and spectators did not agree about whether the contest celebrated national identity, local culture, or even African beauty. Still the ORTM contest served as a springboard for Mali's participation in international pageants where the local standard of full-bodied beauty was aligned with that of the slender girl. Beauty pageants represent and contest idealized notions of gender and sexuality as Cohen (1996) shows for a male and female beauty contest in the British Virgin Islands that manifested very distinct gender "styles." In the Mr. Personality and Ms. Glamorous contest all contestants competed in casual and evening wear; only women competed in sports and business wear, while men competed in talent demonstration and bathing suit modeling, highlighting their ability, drive, and power.

Beauty contests are performative. The Miss Galaxy beauty contest (Besnier 2002) at the completion of the Heilala Festival after the crowning of a female beauty queen on Tonga island is a glamorous show of fashion and bodies by transgendered males who assemble outfits from scratch into flamboyant gowns, diminutive miniskirts, and eye-catching accessories. The contest presents a selective adoption of Western-styled clothing, language (English), names, and performance that temporarily dislocates contestants from local society at the same time as they remain in place both geographically and socially. Transvestite beauty pageants in the southern Philippines (Johnson 1996) also fuel debate over local identities in the face of selective appropriations of desirable yet potentially threatening global influences. These contests began with parades of "ethnic attire" or "national costume" in which contestants were presented, for example, as Miss Germany or Miss Canada; the parades were followed by competitions in cocktail dress, summer and sports wear, swim wear, and evening gowns; and the pageants ended with question and answer periods to assess the contestants' intelligence. As performance events, beauty contests provide an occasion for transvestite men to negotiate images of cosmopolitan femininity with which they test the local boundaries of gender identity.

SECONDHAND CLOTHING

In much of the West today, secondhand clothing makes up fringe, or niche, markets, whereas in many third-world countries secondhand clothing imported from the West is an important clothing source. In secondhand clothing consumption, desire confronts emulation in processes recent scholarship examines from a variety of perspectives (Palmer & Clark 2004). Secondhand clothing has been studied as a consumption site where gender, appearance, and identity are constructed through dress. Most work on secondhand clothing in the West investigates the incorporation of accessories and specific garments into youth wardrobes (McRobbie 1988). Today in Germany, the 1960s style scene of movies, music, and material culture is popular with young people who dress in garments from the 1960s or in self-made clothes constructed from old patterns (Jenss 2004). This retro style attributes history and authenticity to garments that wearers experience as unique and personal.

Dress practices developing around the consumption of imported secondhand clothing in the third world are the subject of works in Zambia, the Philippines, and India. Many economists would be inclined to view the growth of the secondhand clothing market in Zambia as a response to economic decline. Such an account misses the opportunities this vast import offers consumers to construct themselves through dress. Tracing the flow of secondhand clothing from the point of donation in the West, through its sorting and export, to its local distribution and consumption in Zambia, Hansen (2000a) accounts for the incorporation of secondhand clothing as desirable apparel into a gendered dress universe informed by a local cultural economy of judgment and style. Far from emulating the West's fashions, secondhand clothing practices implicate clothing-conscious consumers in efforts to change their lives for the better.

Secondhand clothing only recently became readily available in Ifugao in northern Luzon in the Philippines, some of it shipped directly to Philippine ports and some arriving via Hong Kong. In Ifugao, this translocal trade circulates through channels that are rooted in local cultural scripts (Milgram 2004), guided by notions of personalized associations that women traders operationalize in their business activities. In narratives about secondhand clothing, retailers, vendors, and consumers draw connections between people and clothes that constantly change. Such tales domesticate the logic of the market and the meaning of this global commodity in terms of local norms of status and values, and in so doing, they transform these norms. Combining secondhand garments into styles that display knowledge of wider clothing practice or subvert their received meanings, traders and consumers effect a creolization of this imported commodity to serve their personal and community identities.

Norris's work (2003) on clothing recycling in India shifts the research emphasis on clothing from consumption to the materiality of cloth as a strategic resource for the unmaking and remaking of persons and identities. Unlike Zambia, India prohibits the import of secondhand clothing. It permits the import of woolen fibers among which are "mutilated hosiery," a trade term for wool garments shredded by machines in the West prior to export. Tracing the flow between India and the West, Norris examines two processes. One is the import of "mutilated" fabrics; their sorting into color ranges; their shredding, carding, spinning; and their reappearance as threads used for blankets, knitting yarn, and wool fabrics for local consumption and export. The other process is domestic recycling of Indian clothing by barter, hand-me-downs, donations, and resale. She examines Indian women's wardrobes in detail, their changes over the life course, and the disposal of garments onto India's secondhand clothing market.

PRODUCTION ISSUES

Complex global flows redefine north/south boundaries, localizing the significance of imported goods like secondhand clothing and many other items of apparel, for example the Sebago moccasin produced in the United States, and copied in China and Morocco, so popular with youth in Dakar, Senegal (Scheld 2003), and the Barbie doll indigenized in Maya costume in Mexico (MacDougall 2003). Inspired by interdisciplinary scholarship on commodity chains and systems of provision, these works use clothing to highlight some of the close interconnections in the global economy. By establishing links between specific global economic domains and clothing recycling in India, Norris (2004) revealed an informal economy that turned used garments into industrial rags, reassembled fabrics for interior decoration, and manufactured Indian fashions for tourists. As a result, an export supply chain emerged, formalizing what had begun as an informal trade.

The focus on consumption and dress practice in much of the clothing research by anthropologists hides the exploitative social relations of production so evident in garment manufacturing for export from third-world countries as well as in the West's metropolitan sweatshops. These processes have a literature of their own that is more concerned with unfair labor practices in gender and age terms than with dress. Some anthropological works on artisanal textile and clothing production for the international tourist market (Femenìas 2004b), sometimes organized by fair trade principles (Grimes & Milgram 2000, Nash 1993), have investigated local and regional efforts to redirect the unequal terms of the global garment-production industry. The effect of such programs on the global apparel market's inherent production inequalities is limited even if they, in the short term, have positive local ramifications on livelihoods. Such production issues introduce new versions of "ethnic clothing" (Hepburn 2000) in a world of dress that knows few boundaries.

THE WORLD IN DRESS

Clothing matters differently across the world's major regions. Aside from examining the effects on dress practice of grand-scale processes such as colonization and globalization, regional scholarship differs in emphasis. Works from Latin America focus on "indigenous dress" and its transformations, Africanist dress scholarship stresses the importance of dressing well and its significance for dress-style dynamics in contemporary clothing encounters, and South Asian scholarship examines the changing cultural importance of the sari in its interaction with other dress practices. East and Southeast Asian research explores multiple influences on local fashion and the export and import of "Asian chic" styles, and clothing research in the Pacific poses new questions about the efficacy of material surfaces. The regionally specific preoccupations with dress are evident in dress diasporas that domesticate elements of regional dress on global terms. Challenging us to shift perspective, the recent anthropological scholarship on dress outside of the West's established fashion canon opens up new vistas for dress scholarship in general.

Having turned distinct cultural dress icons into framing devices for my regional discussions, I must acknowledge the larger relationship in which their continuously shifting forms interact. This is the world of fashion dominated by the economic power of the West, even if the West no longer fully controls the creative inspirations. When arguing that anthropology's dress world is a world of fashion, I refer to fashion in several interactive senses including and extending beyond the West's fashion system: "Ethnic" dress is dynamic and changing; it even has fads. People everywhere want "the latest" by whatever changing definitions of local preference. Widespread desire "to move with fashion" and be "in style" now (Hansen 2000b) makes notions of fashion and style converge on the dressed body, directing our attention to the combination of garments that construct identity on the surface, and in so doing, objectify it (Miller 1994). This is how dress becomes implicated in life projects, and why there is nothing quite like it in anthropology to enrich our cross-cultural understanding.

ACKNOWLEDGMENTS

This review is inspired by the pioneering works by Joanne Eicher, whom I thank for her readiness to share her vast knowledge about dress. Ten years of teaching a freshman seminar on clothing and culture challenged me to engage dress scholarship with young critics. I thank Joanne Eicher, LaRay Denzer, and Elisha Renne for their constructive suggestions and advice on this manuscript. Numerous colleagues cited in this review made their new works available to me, and I thank them all. Lindsay Sakraida, my research assistant, provided bibliographical support. I am grateful to Northwestern University's Residential College System for making Ms. Sakraida's work possible.

The *Annual Review of Anthropology* is online at http://anthro.annualreviews.org

LITERATURE CITED

Abu-Lughod L. 1990. The romance of resistance: tracing transformations of power through Beduin women. *Am. Anthropol.* 17(1):41–55

Allman J, ed. 2004a. *Fashioning Power: Clothing, Politics and African Identities.* Bloomington: Indiana Univ. Press

Allman J. 2004b. "Let your fashion be in line with our Ghanaian Costume": nation, gender and the politics of clothing in Nkrumaha's Ghana. See Allman 2004a, pp. 144–65

Arthur LB, ed. 1999. *Religion, Dress and the Body.* Oxford: Berg

Arthur LB, ed. 2000. *Undressing Religion: Commitment and Conversion from a Cross-Cultural Perspective.* Oxford: Berg

Banerjee M, Miller D. 2003. *The Sari.* Oxford: Berg

Barnes R, Eicher JB, eds. 1992. *Dress and Gender: Making and Meaning.* Oxford: Berg

Bastian ML. 1996. Female *"Alhajis"* and entrepreneurial fashions: flexible identities in southeastern Nigeria. See Hendrickson 1996, pp. 97–132

Besnier N. 2002. Transgenderism, locality, and the Miss Galaxy beauty pageant in Tonga. *Am. Ethnol.* 29(3):534–66

Bhachu P. 2004. *Dangerous Designs: Asian Women Fashion the Diaspora Economies.* New York: Routledge

Bolton L. 2003. Gender, status and introduced clothing in Vanuatu. See Colchester 2003a, pp. 119–40

Bourdieu P. 1984. *Distinction: A Social Critique of the Judgment of Taste.* Transl. R. Nice. Cambridge, MA: Harvard Univ. Press

Brenner S. 1996. Restructuring self and society: Javanese Muslim women and "the veil." *Am. Ethnol.* 23(4):673–97

Brydon A. 1998. Sensible shoes. See Brydon & Niessen 1998, pp. 1–22

Brydon A, Niessen S, eds. 1998. *Consuming Fashion: Adorning the Transnational Body.* Oxford: Berg

Burgess T. 2002. Cinema, bell bottoms, and miniskirts: struggles over youth and citizenship in revolutionary Zanzibar. *Int. J. Afr. Hist. Stud.* 35(2/3):287–313

Byfield J. 2004. Dress and politics in post world war II Abeokuta (Western Nigeria). See Allman 2004a, pp. 31–49

Chen TM. 2003. Proletarian white and working bodies in Mao's China. *Positions* 11(2):361–93

Cohen CB. 1996. Contestants in a contested domain: staging identities in the British Virgin Islands. See Cohen et al. 1996, pp. 125–46

Cohen CB, Wilk R, Stoeltje B, eds. 1996. *Beauty Queens on the Global State: Gender, Contests, and Power.* New York: Routledge

Colchester C, ed. 2003a. *Clothing the Pacific.* Oxford: Berg

Colchester C. 2003b. T-shirts, translation and humour: on the nature of wearer-perceiver relationships in South Auckland. See Colchester 2003a, pp. 167–92

Comaroff JL, Comaroff J. 1997. Fashioning the colonial subject. In *Of Revelation and Revolution. Vol. II. The Dialectics of Modernity on a South African Frontier,* ed. JL Comaroff, J Comaroff, pp. 218–73. Chicago: Univ. Chicago Press

Dalby L. 1993. *Kimono: Fashioning Culture.* New Haven, CT: Yale Univ. Press

De Jorio R. 2002. Gendered museum, guided he(tour)topias: women and social memory in Mali. *Polar* 25(2):50-72

Denzer L. 2002. High fashion and fluctuating fortunes: the Nigerian garment industry under structural adjustment. In *Money Struggles and City Life: Devaluation in Ibadan and Other Urban Centers in Southern Nigeria, 1986–1996,* eds. J Guyer, L Denzer, A Agbade, pp. 93–114. Portsmouth NH: Heinemann

Durham D. 1995. The lady in the logo: tribal dress and Western culture in a Southern

African community. See Eicher 1995, pp. 183–94

Durham D. 1999. The predicament of dress: polvalency and the ironies of cultural identity. *Am. Ethnol.* 26(2):389–411

Eicher JB, ed. 1995. *Dress and Ethnicity: Change Across Space and Time.* Oxford: Berg

Eicher JB. 2000. The anthropology of dress. *Dress* 27:59–70

Eicher JB, Roach-Higgins ME, eds. 1992. Definition and classification of dress: implications for analysis of gender roles. See Barnes & Eicher 1992, pp. 8–28

El Guindi F. 1999. *Veil: Modesty, Privacy and Resistance.* Oxford: Berg

Fair l. 2004. Remaking fashion in the Paris of the Indean Ocean: dress, performance and the cultural construction of a cosmopolitan Zanzibari identity. See Allman 2004a, pp. 13–30

Femenìas B. 2004. *Gender and the Boundaries of Dress in Contemporary Peru.* Austin: Univ. Tex. Press

Femenìas B. 2004a. "Why do Gringos like black?": mourning, tourism, and changing fashions in Peru. See Root 2004b. In press

Foster HB, Johnson DC, eds. 2003. *Wedding Dress Across Cultures.* Oxford: Berg

Friedman J, ed. 1994a. *Consumption and Identity.* Chur: Harwood

Friedman J. 1994b. The political economy of elegance: an African cult of beauty. See Friedman 1994a, pp. 167–88

Friedman S. 2004. Embodying civility: civilizing processes and symbolic citizenship in southeastern China. *J. Asian Stud.* 63(3)

Fuglesang M. 1992. No longer ghosts: women's notions of "development" and "modernity" in Lamu town, Kenya. In *Kam-Ap or Take-Off,* ed. G Dahl, A Rabo, pp. 123–57. Stockholm: Stockholm Stud. Soc. Anthropol.

Gandoulou JL. 1989. *Dandies á bacongo: Le culte de l'élegance dans la societé congolaise contemporaine.* Paris: L'Harmattan

Gill L. 1993. "Proper women" and city pleasures: gender, class, and contested meanings in La Paz. *Am. Ethnol.* 20(1):72–88

Gondola CD. 1999. Dream and drama: the search for elegance among Congolese youth. *Afr. Stud. Rev.* 42(1):23–44

Grabski J. 2002. Making fashion in the city: a case study of tailors and designers in downtown Dakar. Presented at symposium on The Cultured Body: African Fashion and Body Arts, University of Iowa, Iowa City, Iowa

Grimes KM, Milgram LB, eds. 2000. *Artisans and Cooperatives: Developing Alternative Trade for the Global Economy.* Tucson: Univ. Ariz. Press

Hansen KT. 2000a. *Salaula: The World of Secondhand Clothing and Zambia.* Chicago: Univ. Chicago Press

Hansen KT. 2000b. Other people's clothes? The international second-hand clothing trade and dress practices in Zambia. *Fashion Theory* 4(3):245–74

Hansen KT. 2004. Dressing dangerously: miniskirts, gender relations and sexuality in Zambia. See Allman 2004a, pp. 166–88

Heath D. 1992. Fashion, anti-fashion, and heteroglossia in urban Senegal. *Am. Ethnol.* 19(1):19–33

Hendrickson H. 1994. The 'long' dress and the construction of Herero identities in Southern Africa. *Afr. Stud.* 53(2):25–54

Hendrickson C. 1995. *Weaving Identities: Construction of Dress and Self in a Highland Guatemalan Town.* Austin: Univ. Tex. Press

Hendrickson H, ed. 1996. *Clothing and Difference: Embodied Identities in Colonial and Post-Colonial Africa.* Durham: Duke Univ. Press

Hepburn S. 2000. The cloth of barbaric pagans: tourism, identity, and modernity in Nepal. *Fashion Theory* 4(3):275–300

Ivaska A. 2004. Anti-militants meet modern Misses: urban style, gender and the politics of "National Culture" in 1960s Dar es Salaam, Tanzania. See Allman 2004a, pp. 102–24

James D. 1996. "I dress in this fashion": transformations in Sotho dress and women's lives in a Sekhukhuneland village, South Africa. See Hendrickson 1996, pp. 34–65

Jenss H. 2004. Sixties dress only! The

consumption of the past in youth cultural retro-scene. See Palmer & Clark 2004. In press

Johnson M. 1996. Negotiating style and mediating beauty: transvestite (*Gay/Bantut*) beauty contests in the Southern Philippines. See Cohen et al. 1996, pp. 89–104

Jones C. 2003. Dress for *sukses*: fashioning femininity and nationality in urban Indonesia. See Niessen et al. 2003, pp. 185–214

Keane W. 2004. The hazards of new clothes: what signs make possible. See Küchler and Were 2004. In press

Kelly M. 2003. Projecting an image and expressing identity: T-shirts in Hawaii. *Fashion Theory* 7(2):191–212

Khan N. 1993. Asian women's dress: from burqah to bloggs–changing clothes for changing times. In *Chic Thrills: A Fashion Reader*, ed. J Ash, E Wilson, pp. 61–74. Berkeley: Univ. Calif. Press

Kinsella S. 1995. Cuties in Japan. In *Women, Media and Consumption in Japan*, ed. L Skov, B Moeran, pp. 220–55. Honolulu: Univ. Hawaii Press

Kondo D. 1992. The aesthetics and politics of Japanese identity in the fashion industry. In *Re-Made in Japan: Everyday Life and Consumer Taste in a Changing Society*, ed. J Tobin, pp. 176–203. New Haven: Yale Univ. Press

Küchler S. 2003. The poncho and quilt: material Christianity in the Cook Islands. See Colchester 2003a, pp. 97–116

Küchler S, Miller D, eds. 2005. *Clothing as Material Culture*. Oxford: Berg. In press

Küchler S, Were G, eds. 2004. *The Art of Clothing: A Pacific Experience*. London: Univ. Coll. London Press

Leshkowich AM. 2003. The *Ao Dai* goes global: how international influences and female entrepreneurs have shaped Vietnam's "National Costume." See Niessen et al. 2003, pp. 79–116

Leskhowicz AM, Jones C. 2003. What happens when Asian chic becomes chic in Asia? *Fashion Theory* 7(3/4):281–300

Li X. 1998. Fashioning the body in post-Mao China. See Brydon & Niessen 1998, pp. 71–89

Liechty M. 2003. *Suitably Modern: Making Middle-Class Culture in a New Consumer Society*. Princeton, NJ: Princeton Univ. Press

MacDougall JP. 2003. Transnational commodities as local cultural icons: Barbie dolls in Mexico. *J. Popul. Cult.* 37(2):257–75

Martin P. 1994. Contesting clothes in colonial Brazzaville. *J. Afr. Hist.* 35(3):401–26

Masquelier A. 1996. Mediating threads: clothing and the texture of spirit/medium relations in *Bori* (Southern Niger). See Hendrickson 1996, pp. 66–94

McAllister C. 1996. Authenticity and Guatemala's Maya queen. See Cohen et al. 1996, pp. 105–24

McRobbie A. 1988. Second-hand dresses and the role of the ragmarket. In *Zoot Suits and Second-Hand Dresses*, ed. A McRobbie, pp. 23–49. Boston: Unwin Hyman

McVeigh BJ. 2000. *Wearing Ideology: State, Schooling and Self-Presentation in Japan*. Oxford: Berg

Milgram LB. 2004. "Ukay-ukay" chick: tales of fashion and trade in secondhand clothing in the Philippine Cordillera. See Palmer & Clark 2004. In press

Miller D. 1994. Style and ontology. In *Consumption and Identity*. See Friedman 1994a, pp. 71–96

Meisch LA. 2002. *Andean Entrepreneurs: Otavalo Merchants and Musicians in the Global Arena*. Austin: Univ. Tex. Press

Moorman M. 2004. Putting on a pano and dancing like our grandparents: nation and dress in late colonial Luanda. See Allman 2004a, pp. 84–103

Moran M. 1996. Carrying the queen: identity and nationalism in a Liberian queen rally. See Cohen et al. 1996, pp. 147–60

Mustafa HN. 1998. Sartorial ecumenes: African styles in a social and economic context. See van der Plas & Willemsen 1998, pp. 13–48

Nash J, ed. 1993. *Crafts in the World Market: The Impact of Global Exchanges on Middle American Artisans*. Albany: State Univ. New York Press

Niessen S. 2003. Three scenarios from Batak clothing history: designing participation in the global fashion trajectory. See Niessen et al. 2003, pp. 49–78

Niessen S, Leshkowich AM, Jones C, eds. 2003. *Re-Orienting Fashion: The Globalization of Asian Dress*. Oxford: Berg

Norris KL. 2003. *The life-cycle of clothing: recycling and the efficacy of materiality in contemporary urban India*. PhD thesis. Univ. Coll. London

Norris KL. 2004. Creative entrepreneurs: the recycling of second hand Indian clothing. See Palmer & Clark 2004. In press

O'Connor K. 2005. Lycra, girdles and leggings: the immaterial culture of social change. See Küchler & Miller 2005. In press

Ong A. 1990. State versus Islam: Malay families, women's bodies, and the body politic in Malaysia. *Am. Ethnol.* 17(2):258–76

Palmer A, Clark H, eds. 2004. *Old Clothes, New Looks: Second-Hand Fashion*. Oxford: Berg. In press

Perani J, Wollf NH. 1999. *Cloth, Dress and Art Patronage in Africa*. Oxford: Berg

Polhemus T. 1994. *Streetstyle: From Sidewalk to Catwalk*. New York: Thames & Hudson

Polhemus T. 1996. *Style Surfing: What to Wear in the 3rd Millennium*. London: Thames & Hudson

Rabine LW. 2002. *The Global Circulation of African Fashion*. Oxford: Berg

Rasmussen S. 1991. Veiled self, transparent meanings: Tuareg headdress as social expression. *Ethnology* 30:101–17

Rraghuram P. 2003. Fashioning the South Indian diaspora: production and consumption tales. In *South Asian Women in the Diaspora*, ed. N Puwar, P Raghurman, pp. 21–42. Oxford: Berg

Renne EP. 1996. *Cloth That Does not Die: The Meaning of Cloth in Bunu Social Life*. Seattle: Univ. Wash. Press

Renne EP. 2000. Cloth and conversion: Yoruba textiles and ecclesiastical dress. See Arthur 2000, pp. 7–24

Renne EP. 2004. Visions of sacred textiles in a Yoruba Aladura Church. In *Yoruba Religious Textiles in Southwestern Nigeria*, ed. EP Renne, T Agbaje-Williams. Ibadan, Nigeria: Book Builders. In press

Root RA, ed. 2004. *The Latin American Fashion Reader*. Oxford: Berg. In press

Ross DH. 1998. *Wrapped in Pride: Ghanaian Kente and African American Identity*. Los Angeles: Univ. Calif. Los Angeles, Fowler Mus. Cult. Hist. Textile Ser. No. 2

Rovine VL. 2001. *Bogolan: Shaping Culture Through Cloth in Contemporary Mali*. Washington, DC: Smithsonian Inst. Press

Scheld S. 2001. *The production and consumption of* La Sape: *researching fashion fever and writing teen fashion magazines in Dakar, Senegal*. Presented at Colloq. Women's Stud. Dept., Coll. Univ. NY, New York

Scheld S. 2003. The city in a shoe: redefining urban Africa through Sebago footwear consumption. *City Soc.* 15(1):109–30

Schneider J. 1987. The anthropology of cloth. *Annu. Rev. Anthropol.* 16:409–48

Schulte Nordholt H, ed. 1997. *Outward Appearances: Dressing State and Society in Indonesia*. Leiden: KITLV Press

Schulz DE. 2000. Mesmerizing *Missis*, nationalist awakenings: beauty pageants and the public controversy over "Malian" womanhood. *Paideuma* 46:111–35

Sekimoto T. 1997. Uniforms and concrete walls: dressing the village under the New Order in the 1970s and 1980s. See Schulte Nordholt 1997, pp. 307–38

Skov L. 2003. Fashion-nation: a Japanese globalization experience and a Hong Kong dilemma. See Niessen et al. 2003, pp. 215–42

Skov L, Moeran B, eds. 1995. *Women, Media and Consumption in Japan*. Honolulu: Univ. Hawaii Press

Steele V, Major J, eds. 1999. *China Chic: East Meets West*. New Haven, CT: Yale Univ. Press

Tarlo E. 1996. *Clothing Matters: Dress and Identity in India*. Chicago: Univ. Chicago Press

Taylor L. 2002. Ethnographical approaches. In *The Study of Dress History*, pp. 193–241. Manchester, UK: Manchester Univ. Press

Tcherkezoff S. 2003. On cloth, gifts and nudity: regarding some European misunderstandings during early encounters in Polynesia. See Colchester 2003a, pp. 51–75

Thomas N. 2003. The case of the misplaced ponchos: speculations concerning the history of cloth in Polynesia. See Colchester 2003, pp. 79–96

Tobin J, ed. 1992. *Re-Made in Japan: Everyday Life and Consumer Taste in a Changing Society*. New Haven, CT: Yale Univ. Press

Turner T. 1993 [1980]. The social skin. In *Reading the Social Body*, ed. CB Burroughs, J Ehrenreich, pp. 15–39. Iowa City: Univ. Iowa Press

van der Plas E, Willemsen M, eds. 1998. *The Art of African Fashion*. Prins Klaus Fund, the Netherlands. Trenton, NJ: Africa World Press

Van Dijk K. 1997. Sarongs, jubbahs, and trousers. See Schulte Nordholt 1997, pp. 39–84

Weiner A, Schneider J, eds. 1989. *Cloth and the Human Experience*. Washington, DC: Smithsonian Inst. Press

Were G. 2005. Patterns, efficacy and enterprise: on printed calico in Melanesia. See Küchler & Miller 2005. In press

White J. 1999. Islamic chic. In *Istanbul: Between the Global and the Local*, ed. C. Keyder, pp. 77–91. Lanham, MD: Rowman & Littlelfield

Wilk R. 1996. Connections and contradictions: from the Crooked Cashew Queen to Miss World Belize. See Cohen et al. 1996, pp. 217–32

Wilson V. 1999. Dress and the cultural revolution. See Steele & Major 1999, pp. 167–86

Woodward S. 2005. Looking good: feeling right–aesthetics of the self. See Küchler & Miller 2005. In press

Zorn E. 2004a. *Weaving a Future: Tourism, Cloth, and Culture on an Andean Island*. Iowa City: Univ. Iowa Press

Zorn E. 2004b. Dressed to kill: the embroidered fashion industry of the Ritual Battle Fighters in Highland Bolivia. See Root 2004. In press

Annu. Rev. Anthropol. 2004. 33:393–418
doi: 10.1146/annurev.anthro.33.070203.144000
Copyright © 2004 by Annual Reviews. All rights reserved
First published online as a Review in Advance on June 16, 2004

SOCIAL STATUS AND HEALTH IN HUMANS AND OTHER ANIMALS

Robert M. Sapolsky

Departments of Biological Sciences, Neurology, and Neurological Sciences,
Stanford University, Stanford, California 94305-5020; Institute of Primate Research,
National Museums of Kenya, Karen, Nairobi, Kenya; email: sapolsky@stanford.edu

Key Words   stress, nonhuman primates, socioeconomic status, glucocorticoids, psychoneuroimmunology

■ **Abstract**   Dominance hierarchies exist in numerous social species, and rank in such hierarchies can dramatically influence the quality of an individual's life. Rank can dramatically influence also the health of an individual, particularly with respect to stress-related disease. This chapter reviews first the nature of stress, the stress-response and stress-related disease, as well as the varieties of hierarchical systems in animals. I then review the literature derived from nonhuman species concerning the connections between rank and functioning of the adrenocortical, cardiovascular, reproductive, and immune systems. As shown here, the relationship is anything but monolithic. Finally, I consider whether rank is a relevant concept in humans and argue that socioeconomic status (SES) is the nearest human approximation to social rank and that SES dramatically influences health.

INTRODUCTION

Most of us were subjected in ninth-grade biology to a barely remembered concept that forms a cornerstone of physiology. This is the idea of homeostasis, in which various physiological endpoints—blood pressure, heart rate, body temperature, and so on—are at their optimal levels. [The term allostasis has been introduced to update the homeostatic concept. The older term implies a single optimal set point for any measure, maintained by local regulatory mechanisms, whereas allostasis encompasses the fact that regulation is organism wide and that optimal set points are constantly in flux (Schulkin 2003).]

Regardless of the term used, maintaining physiologic balance is essential to health. A stressor is any physical or psychological factor that perturbs or threatens to perturb homeostasis, and stress is the state of homeostatic imbalance. The body reestablishes homeostasis by marshalling neural and endocrine adaptations that collectively constitute the stress-response.

The environment produces endless means of perturbing homeostasis. Evading a predator, pursuing a prey, a sustained drought, or the harassments of social subordination all challenge homeostasis and mobilize the stress-response. Such mobilization can be life-saving; yet, a central point of this chapter is that excessive activation of the stress-response increases the risk of various stress-related diseases.

Naturally, there is considerable interindividual variation in how readily stress-related disease occurs. This arises from variation in (*a*) the amount of stressors an organism is exposed to (frequency, duration, and severity); (*b*) the adaptiveness of the stress-response mobilized (whether it is activated only in response to legitimate stressors, as well as the speed and magnitude of its activation and recovery); and (*c*) the sources of coping available.

Here, I review one source of variability among social animals: How does the rank of an individual in a social hierarchy influence the pattern of stressors to which it is exposed, the nature of the physiological stress-response it mobilizes, and its sources of coping? And thus, how does social rank influence patterns of stress-related disease?

Taking into consideration nonhuman species, with an emphasis on primates, I first outline the natures of the stress-response, stress-related disease, coping, and dominance hierarchies in social organisms. I review the relationship between social rank and stress-related physiology (recognizing that few readers are or wish to be physiologists). I then consider some critical factors that modulate the rank/physiology relationship. Finally, I consider whether rank/stress physiology relations are relevant to humans.

THE STRESS-RESPONSE AND ITS PATHOGENIC POTENTIAL

The Adaptive Nature of the Stress-Response

Why is it adaptive for the body to mobilize the same stress-response in the face of markedly differing stressors (e.g., evading a predator while injured as opposed to pursuing a prey while starving) (reviewed in McEwen 2002, Sapolsky 2004)? Despite obvious variability, most physical stressors place some similar demands on the body. Critically, coping with any acute physical stressor demands transfer of energy from storage sites to exercising muscle. Such transfer should be as rapid as possible, accomplished by increased blood pressure and heart rate. Furthermore, long-term building projects that are not essential to immediate survival are inhibited until more auspicious times. Such triaging includes inhibiting digestion, growth, tissue repair, and reproduction. Immune defenses are enhanced, pain perception is blunted, cognition is enhanced, and sensory thresholds are sharpened.

Activating some neural and endocrine systems, and inhibiting others, accomplishes these adaptations. The initial wave of activation occurs within seconds; the sympathetic nervous system is stimulated to release epinephrine (adrenaline) from the adrenal glands and norepinephrine (noradrenaline) from nerve endings throughout the body. Within minutes, glucocorticoids (such as hydrocortisone or cortisol) are secreted from the adrenals as the final step of a cascade beginning in the hypothalamus. This triggers the release of a pituitary hormone that, in turn, stimulates the adrenals. Although there is stress-induced secretion of other hormones (e.g., glucagons, beta-endorphin, prolactin), the bulk of the stress-response is mediated by glucocorticoids and the sympathetic catecholamines (i.e., epinephrine and norepinephrine).

The primary neuroendocrine axis inhibited during stress is the parasympathetic nervous system, which works in opposition to the sympathetic system. The secretion of insulin, various digestive hormones, growth hormone, and reproductive hormones are also inhibited.

Collectively, these adaptations are essential for surviving an acute physical stressor. The precise pattern of stress-hormone secretion varies somewhat with each stressor (e.g., some stressors are dominated by catecholamine secretion, others by glucocorticoid secretion). Nonetheless, all stressors mobilize a broadly similar stress-response.

The importance of the stress-response is best demonstrated by diseases in which it fails (e.g., Addison's or Shy Drager's diseases, in which there is impaired secretion of glucocorticoids and sympathetic catecholamines, respectively). Such maladies, if untreated, can prove fatal when an individual attempts something physically taxing.

Chronic Stress and the Emergence of Stress-Related Disease

Despite the adaptiveness of the stress-response, chronic stress can be pathogenic. At one time, it was erroneously believed that chronic stress "exhausts" the stress-response (i.e., the adrenals become depleted of epinephrine and glucocorticoids, the pancreas is depleted of glucagon, and so on). However, the pathologies of chronic stress emerge because the stress-response, if chronically activated, can become as damaging as the stressor itself.

Thus, if energy is constantly mobilized, it is never stored, which produces muscle atrophy, fatigue, and an increased risk of insulin-resistant (adult-onset) diabetes. And, although hypertension is vital to sustaining a sprint from a predator, chronic hypertension damages blood vessels and, when combined with the metabolic stress-response, predisposes these vessels toward atherosclerosis.

Deferring digestion, growth, repair, and reproduction during an acute stressor is adaptive but, if chronic, increases the risk of peptic ulcers, irritable bowel syndrome, impaired growth and tissue repair, irregular ovulatory cycles, and erectile dysfunction. Furthermore, the stimulation of immunity in response to stress soon gives way to immune suppression and impaired defenses against infectious disease. Finally, although short-term stress enhances cognition, chronic stress disrupts it and impairs synaptic plasticity as well as the birth of new neurons, atrophies dendritic processes in neurons, and increases the incidence of neuron death.

These findings constitute a double-edged sword: In the face of a typical mammalian stressor (i.e., a brief physical challenge), the stress-response is essential. However, during chronic stress, the stress-response is pathogenic. This fact is particularly relevant to socially complex species such as primates that generate chronic stress for purely psychological reasons.

Psychological Stress

As noted, the stress-response can be mobilized in anticipation of a homeostatic perturbation (reviewed in Levine et al. 1989). If that perturbation does occur, the anticipatory stress-response is adaptive. But if the threat is imagined, the costly and disruptive stress-response will have been mobilized for no reason. Critically, humans and other cognitively sophisticated species may mobilize the stress-response for purely psychological or social reasons, in the absence of a threat to homeostasis, which explains our proclivity toward stress-related disease. Such psychological stressors may be local and ongoing events with no physiological reality (e.g., the stressfulness of public speaking), or they may be displaced in space and time (e.g., war on another continent or contemplation of one's eventual death). Obviously, social subordination often may involve physical stressors, but there can be a surfeit of psychological stressors as well. Thus, I review the components of psychological stressors.

LACK OF PREDICTABILITY   A stress-response is more likely when an organism lacks predictive information about a stressor. This has been demonstrated in studies in which two rats received identical patterns of intermittent shocks. However, one rat was given a warning (e.g., a bell) five seconds before each shock and, as a result, was less likely to mobilize a stress-response or develop a stress-related disease than was the yoked control rat.

LACK OF CONTROL   The importance of a sense of control was shown by a similar pairing of rats. In this case, one rat was trained previously in an active avoidance task (e.g., lever pressing) that decreased the likelihood of shock. In the experimental situation, the lever was disconnected (i.e., was a placebo). Nevertheless, lever pressing gave the rat a sense of control, thereby decreasing its risk of stress-related disease.

LACK OF OUTLETS FOR FRUSTRATION   In this situation, two rats received identical shocks, but one had access to a source of distraction or displacement (food, a running wheel, a bar of wood to gnaw on), which prevented a stress-response. Importantly (and unfortunately), the ability to aggressively attack another individual is a highly effective coping outlet. Such "displacement aggression" is common among primates, including humans.

THE INTERPRETATION OF THE STRESSOR   A severe abdominal pain can be a source of anxiety, which will likely elicit a stress-response. However, if the pain indicates that a drug is effectively killing cells of a liver tumor, this same pain might elicit euphoria. Thus, the interpretation of an external stressor can influence the physiological response to it. An experimental demonstration of this effect might involve a rat receiving 10 shocks in the first hour and 20 in the second, while a second rat receives 50 shocks in the first hour, followed by 20 in the second. Thus, the first rat receives a total of 30 shocks and the second receives 70. Nevertheless, at the end of the second hour, the second rat will have the smaller stress-response, because the second rat's circumstances improved over time, whereas the first rat's worsened.

LACK OF SOCIAL SUPPORT   Numerous studies demonstrate the capacity of social support to blunt the stress-response in the face of numerous homeostatic challenges.

SOCIAL RANK AND ITS RELATIONSHIP TO STRESS

Over the years, notions about the nature of dominance hierarchies among animals have varied. At one extreme, some investigators have considered rank as defining an animal's life, equating it with reproductive success and Darwinian fitness. In contrast, some have questioned whether hierarchy is meaningful to an animal or whether it is a construct imposed by humans (i.e., an animal merely categorizes conspecifics as dominate or subordinate to it, rather than assigning an ordinal rank) (Rowell 1974). Most investigators would agree that a hierarchy is meaningful to animals within it and that it is an emergent property of the group rather than the mere aggregation of individual dyadic relations (Chase et al. 2002); however, rank is not necessarily synonymous with Darwinian fitness (e.g., Bercovitch 1993).

Various criteria have been used to determine rank. Some investigators have based rankings on outcomes of agonistic interactions. At the other extreme, some have derived hierarchies from subtle attentional fields (patterns of eye contact and avoidance of eye contact among group members). Rankings based on the unequal distribution of contested resources have been most common.

Hierarchical structure varies among species. For example, hierarchies can be (*a*) gender-specific or involve both sexes; (*b*) hereditary or labile; (*c*) linear or contain circularities (i.e., A > B > C > A); or (*d*) situational, with rank fluctuating as a function of the resource contested or the presence of allies. There also is variability according to what sorts of stressors accompany a particular rank. I now consider the stressors associated with subordination in hierarchies in which subordination is a state imposed forcefully from above. As discussed in Why Are There Inconsistencies in These Data?, below, there are dramatic exceptions to this picture.

It is easy to imagine that subordination can produce an excess of physical stressors. Subordinate animals may have to work harder for calories, or be calorically deprived. If a member of a prey species, subordinate animals are more likely to be exposed to predators [by being forced into the periphery in variations on the Geometry of the Selfish Herd (Hamilton 1971)]. Subordinate animals also are more likely to be the subjects of unprovoked displacement aggression.

Subordination also carries numerous psychological stressors. Each physical stressor just noted also involves a lack of control and predictability. Moreover, subordinate animals have relatively few coping outlets (e.g., being able to displace aggressive frustration onto someone with lower ranking) and fewer means of social support (e.g., social grooming). Thus, within the classical picture of a dominance hierarchy, subordinate animals are likely to suffer excessive physical and psychological stressors (but see section below for exceptions to this pattern).

STRESS/RANK CORRELATES IN INDIVIDUAL PHYSIOLOGICAL SYSTEMS

I now review the relationship between rank and functioning of some physiological systems relevant to the stress-response. The many correlations cited raise the question of whether rank drives physiology, vice versa, or neither. Many studies have employed one of two designs that allow insight into this question. In the first version, animals are initially singly housed, and physiological measures are taken before and after group formation. Thus, one can determine whether a specific physiological profile preceded or emerged only after the animal's rank was established (e.g., Morgan et al. 2000). In the second, social groups are reorganized intermittently, producing circumstances in which an animal is dominant in one group but subordinate in another. Here we try to answer whether physiological measures precede or follow the rank changes. Overwhelmingly, the distinctive physiological correlates of a particular rank emerge after the rank is achieved, suggesting that behavior drives physiology more than physiology drives behavior.

Rank, the Adrenocortical Axis, and Circulating Levels of Glucocorticoids

As noted, the two workhorses of the stress-response are the sympathetic nervous system and the release of glucocorticoids by the adrenocortical axis. These two branches typify the double-edged nature of the stress-response, in that glucocorticoids and catecholamines are essential for surviving an acute physical stressor, but are pathogenic when secreted in excess (reviewed in Sapolsky et al. 2000).

Thus, one can outline readily the ideal secretory profile of their hormones. First, under basal, nonstressed conditions, there should be minimal secretion; such basal secretion should be unchanged by a purely psychological stressor. Next, a true homeostatic challenge should provoke rapid and massive secretion. Finally, recovery should occur rapidly following stressor termination.

It is difficult to obtain accurate catecholamine measures, because these levels change within seconds. However, glucocorticoid levels change over 1–2 min, allowing extensive study of the relationship between social rank and glucocorticoid profile; these findings generally suggest that the optimal glucocorticoid profile, as outlined, is a characteristic of dominant individuals. In contrast, subordinate animals tend toward a pathogenic profile of elevated basal glucocorticoid levels (or the enlarged adrenals that support such basal hypersecretion), a sluggish stress-response, and a delayed recovery poststress. Facets of this profile have been observed in mice (Davis & Christian 1957, Southwick & Bland 1959, Vessey 1964, Bronson & Eleftheriou 1964, Louch & Higginbotham 1967, Archer 1970, Popova & Naumenko 1972, Leshner & Polish 1979, Raab et al. 1986, Schuhr 1987, Barnard et al. 1993, Avitsur et al. 2001), rats (Barnett 1955, Korte et al. 1990, Dijkstra et al. 1992, de Goeij et al. 1992, McKittrick 1995, Blanchard et al. 1995), hamsters (Huhman et al. 1992), guinea pigs (Sachser & Prove 1986), wolves (Fox & Andrews 1973), rabbits (Farabollini 1987), pigs (Fernandez et al. 1994, McGlone et al. 1993), sugar gliders (Mallick et al. 1994), fascicularis macaques (Adams et al. 1985, Adams et al. 1987), talapoins (Keverne et al. 1982), olive baboons (Sapolsky 1990), squirrel monkeys (Manogue et al. 1975), tree shrews (Fuchs et al. 1993, 2001; Fuchs & Flugge 1995; Magarinos et al. 1996) and lemurs (Schilling & Perret 1987).

It seems reasonable that subordination is linked with elevated basal levels of glucocorticoids, given the stressors of low rank. But why should subordination be associated with a sluggish turning on and off of the stress-response? An explanation for the former is not readily available; however, there appears to be a link between basal hypersecretion and sluggish termination of glucocorticoid secretion poststress. The adrenocortical axis operates by negative feedback regulation, in which glucocorticoids inhibit the brain from triggering subsequent glucocorticoid secretion (akin to how heat, detected by a sensor in a thermostat, decreases the likelihood of the subsequent generation of heat). If glucocorticoid levels are chronically elevated, the brain's sensitivity to the hormone becomes blunted (via a down-regulatory decrease in the number of glucocorticoid receptors). As a result, the brain becomes less responsive to a glucocorticoid negative feedback signal, and sluggish in terminating glucocorticoid secretion poststress (reviewed in Sapolsky & Plotsky 1990).

Among wild baboons, subordinate animals have been found to have both excessive basal secretion of glucocorticoids and a blunted response to glucocorticoid negative feedback signals. Studies have uncovered regulatory changes at the levels of the brain, pituitary, and adrenals which explain this subordinate profile. Although the details of these findings are not relevant to the present review, the pattern of changes in a subordinate baboon was identical to what occurs in humans with major depression (in which there is often basal glucocorticoid hypersecretion and negative feedback resistance) (Sapolsky 1990). Cognitive psychologists traditionally have described depression as a state of learned helplessness; this formulation might describe as well the psychological state of a subordinate baboon.

Despite the finding of basal hypersecretion of glucocorticoids among subordinates, exceptions have been reported among rats (Blanchard et al. 1995), macaques (Chamove & Bowman 1976; van Schaik 1991; Gust et al. 1991, 1993; Bercovitch & Clark 1995), squirrel monkeys (Coe et al. 1979, Mendoza et al. 1979, Steklis 1986), marmosets (Saltzman 1994), talapoin monkeys (Keverne et al. 1982), lemurs (Cavigelli 1999), wild dogs and dwarf mongooses (Creel et al. 1996), and wolves (McLeod et al. 1996). Below, possible resolutions of these contradictions are considered.

Rank, Cardiovascular Function, and Cardiovascular Disease

The link between stress and physiology is rarely as clear as in cardiovascular function, simply because heart rate changes noticeably in response to stressors. It has been known for decades that chronic stress increases the risk of cardiovascular disease through well-understood underlying mechanisms. These include the following: (*a*) The increase of blood pressure and heart rate via activation of the sympathetic nervous system in turn increases the risk of mechanical damage to blood vessels. (*b*) Once such damage occurs, circulating lipids and cholesterol can infiltrate into the injury site, promoting atherosclerotic plaque formation. Stress exacerbates this process by increasing circulating lipids and by decreasing levels of "good" (HDL) cholesterol, which opposes plaque formation. (*c*) Stress causes circulating platelets to aggregate at injury sites, worsening plaque formation. (*d*) Estrogen can protect blood vessels from damage, and as reviewed below, stress suppresses estrogen levels (this holds true despite the complex and controversial recent findings regarding the effects of postmenopausal estrogen replacement on cardiovascular disease). (*e*) Once coronary arteries are damaged, stress causes them to constrict (as opposed to stress-induced dilation in healthy arteries), producing myocardial ischemia during stress.

Social stress can adversely affect cardiovascular function in rodents (Henry 1977), nonhuman primates (Strawn et al. 1991, Manuck et al. 1995), and humans (Williams 1989). This leads us to ask, does cardiovascular function vary with social rank? Social subordination has been associated with elevated resting blood pressure in laboratory rats, rabbits (Eisermann 1992), baboons (Cherkovich & Tatoyan 1973, Sapolsky & Share 1994), and macaques (Kaplan & Manuck 1989). This hypertension is typically secondary to elevated sympathetic activity or, less often, to elevated glucocorticoid levels. Moreover, social subordination in Old World primates of both sexes (Sapolsky & Mott 1987, Kaplan et al. 1995) has been associated with lower levels of HDL cholesterol and/or higher levels of "bad" (LDL and VLDL) cholesterol. Additionally, when macaques were fed an atherogenic diet, it was subordinate animals of both sexes who were more prone to atherosclerosis in coronary blood vessels (Kaplan et al. 1982, Herd et al. 1987, Shively & Clarkson 1994, Manuck et al. 1995), an effect mediated by the sympathetic nervous system (Kaplan & Manuck 1989). Moreover, stress-induced suppression of estrogen levels in subordinate females also contributed to vascular damage (Kaplan et al. 1995).

Thus, social subordination can increase cardiovascular disease risk. Although most of these studies involved captive animals in highly manipulated social groups (as well as, in the case cited, requiring a high-fat diet), some studies have utilized wild primates (Sapolsky & Mott 1987, Sapolsky & Share 1994), suggesting an ethological validity to this stress/disease link.

Rank and the Reproductive System

FEMALES   Stress can disrupt the reproductive axis of females in numerous species through well-delineated mechanisms involving excesses of glucocorticoids, prolactin, and beta-endorphin working at the levels of the hypothalamus, pituitary, ovaries, and uterus. Such suppression can involve (*a*) lower levels of reproductive hormones, (*b*) later onset of puberty, (*c*) lower fertility rates and longer interbirth intervals, (*d*) higher miscarriage rates, and (*e*) earlier onset of a senescent decline in fertility.

Is reproductive physiology suppressed in subordinate females of various species, relative to dominant animals? Numerous studies support this picture (but see Packer et al. 1995 for one partial exception and Altmann et al. 1995 for criticisms of it). For example, among macaques living in groups with linear dominance hierarchies, subordinate females were subject to the highest rates of aggression, had the lowest rates of contact and grooming, and had elevated basal glucocorticoid levels. Critically, subordinate females had a higher rate of anovulatory cycles, with suppressed estradiol and progesterone levels. In the most severe instances, hormone levels were as low as in ovariectomized animals (Shively & Clarkson 1994).

Such reproductive suppression among subordinate animals could be due to at least four mechanisms: (*a*) "social contraception" (i.e., direct stressful harassment by dominant animals), (*b*) fewer calories, (*c*) more work required for calories, and (*d*) constitutional biology giving rise to both lower rank and impaired gonadal function. Although support for all four mechanisms has been found, the macaque studies just discussed eliminate all but social contraception. This is because these captive animals had equal access to food (eliminating *b* and *c*), and because group membership was occasionally reorganized, often producing very different rankings in different hierarchies (eliminating *d*).

When a rank/physiology relationship occurs (for example, between subordination and low estrogen levels), it is critical to ask whether the estrogen levels are low enough to impair fertility. This question has rarely been answered in these studies, because reports have tended to contain either physiological data (such as hormone levels) or demographic data (such as interbirth intervals or age at first conception), but not both.

An additional caveat: When subordination in a species is associated with reproductive suppression, it need not be the result of stress. For example, New World monkeys such as tarmarins and marmosets live in groups of a pair-bonded dominant pair and four to six subordinates. Only the dominant pair breeds, and subordinate females do not ovulate. However, this is not caused by stress; subordinate females do not have elevated levels of any key stress hormones, and have glucocorticoid levels even lower than dominant females. Moreover, subordinate females are not subject to high rates of aggression, and typically are younger sisters of the breeding female, waiting their turn to breed and helping to raise their nieces and nephews (Abbott et al. 1998). Thus, subordination is not always synonymous with stress.

MALES   Stress suppresses gonadal function in males just as it does in females. This suppression takes the form primarily of low levels of circulating testosterone, due to the actions of stress hormones at the levels of the brain, pituitary, and testes. Thus, it is not surprising that social subordination has been associated with suppressed testosterone levels in laboratory rodents. However, no such consistent relationship has been found in nonhuman primates (the sources of this confusion are considered below).

Amid these inconsistencies regarding basal testosterone levels, studies of wild baboons have suggested that the response of testosterone levels to stress varies with rank. Specifically, with the onset of a stressor, testosterone levels promptly declined in subordinate males, but transiently rose in dominant ones (reviewed in Sapolsky 1991) (due most likely to rank-related differences in sympathetic nervous system function and testicular blood flow).

When rank-related differences in testosterone levels do occur, are levels sufficiently suppressed in subordinates to impair reproductive physiology and fertility? Although often assumed, this has rarely been found to be the case. With the exception that rapid changes in testosterone levels may have altered muscle physiology (Tsai & Sapolsky 1996), fluctuations of testosterone levels within the normal range have been found to have remarkably few effects on reproductive physiology or on reproductive or aggressive behavior (in contrast, levels below or above the normal range, due to castration or pharmacological androgen abuse, respectively, do alter these endpoints). When a behavior/testosterone correlation was observed, it was typically the behavior that drove the hormonal change, rather than the other way around.

A variant of this revisionism has emerged from research on orangutans. Adult male orangutans occur in two morphs: A robust, mature form involves well-developed secondary sexual characteristics, whereas a gracile, juvenile form suggests an adult animal in an arrested periadolescent state. Typically, there is only one mature male in a region of orangutans in the wild or in a captive group, and when the mature male is removed, the largest juvenile develops over the coming months into a mature male.

One may speculate that the juvenile form is stress-related, with a dominant male stressing subordinates (via direct interactions or, as is more likely in the rain forest with these solitary animals, via long calls or pheromonal markings) into reproductive suppression and arrested development. However, this is not the case; juveniles do not have elevated levels of glucocorticoids or other stress hormones, nor do they have suppressed levels of reproductive hormones (instead, from an endocrine standpoint, the most stressed males are ones transitioning to mature status). Furthermore, "arrested" males are fertile and occasionally reproduce, typically through forced copulation. This evidence of reproductive success, when coupled with the low injury rate, low metabolic demands, and foraging ease of juveniles, suggests that this is not stress-induced pathology, but an alternative male strategy (Maggioncalda et al. 1999, 2000, 2002).

Finally, stress does not always suppress the testicular axis. Consider a male with an opportunity to mate following challenging and stressful male-male competition.

It would be maladaptive if the stress of that competition impaired fertility, or if impaired fertility occurred in males that mate only once a lifetime (e.g., in semelparous species in which mating is followed by programmed cell death), in species with a narrow breeding season, or in species in which, because of the transience of dominance, individuals may have only a short window of opportunity for mating. In all these circumstances, the testicular axis becomes resistant to the suppressive effects of stress (reviewed in Wingfield & Sapolsky 2003).

Thus, there has been little evidence to support the widely held assumptions that among males, social dominance is synonymous with aggression and high testosterone levels, and that subordination is synonymous with testicular suppression.

Rank and the Immune System

The first evidence to link stress and immunity, discovered in the 1930s by the pioneering stress physiologist, Hans Selye, was that chronic stress suppressed immunity. Since then, psychoneuroimmune studies have uncovered the physiological, cellular, and molecular mechanisms mediating this process, with much of the attention revolving around the immunosuppressive actions of glucocorticoids (which underlie the clinical use of glucocorticoid steroids to suppress organ rejection after transplantion, or to inhibit an overactive immune system during an autoimmune disease).

One might assume then that chronic stress-induced suppression of immunity would lead to increased risk or severity of infectious diseases. However, it has been difficult to demonstrate this under physiological circumstances. One reason for this is that such studies have relied on severe stressors, or on artificially induced diseases (such as the transplantation of a tumor into the rat), limiting the relevance of these findings to more naturalistic stressors and pathogens. A second reason is that profound immunosuppression–far greater than that achieved with the most severe stressors–is needed to compromise defenses against more serious infectious diseases.

A third reason emerged with the recent development of more sensitive immune assays. These have prompted the recognition (as noted above) that during the first hour or two of the stress-response, immunity is stimulated, rather than suppressed, and that the slower immunosuppressive effects of glucocorticoids constitute recovery from the stress-response (Dhabhar & McEwen 2001). Why is such a recovery necessary (as opposed to maintaining the immune system at a heightened level of surveillance)? Such hyperactivity is costly; and, furthermore, immune hyperactivity increases the risk of inadvertently developing an immune response to something benign (i.e., something in the environment producing an allergy, or a part of the body producing an autoimmune disease) (Munck et al. 1984).

Despite these qualifiers, stressors, including social stressors, have been found to increase the risk of the common cold and mononucleosis, and to reactivate latent viruses such as the herpes simplex virus (e.g., Cohen et al. 1991, Ader et al. 2001). However, the relationship between stress and more serious infectious diseases is less clear. For example, although social stress (in the form of frequent changes of group composition) increased the mortality rate among monkeys infected with simian immunosuppressive virus (Capitano et al. 1998), stress seemed to accelerate the decline in immune function in only a subset of AIDS patients with certain psychosocial characteristics (Cole & Kemeny 2001). In addition, there is ample evidence of a lack of connection between stress and risk of nearly all types of cancers.

Given this picture of immune function during stress, one can make a number of tentative predictions about rank-related differences. Assuming that subordinate organisms are subject to more stressors, subordination might involve (*a*) suppression of the immune system basally, (*b*) greater risk of infectious diseases, (*c*) impairment of the transient activation of the immune response immediately following a stressor, and (*d*) an accelerated reversal of that activation.

No studies, to my knowledge, have examined *c* or *d*. There is, however, ample evidence for *a*. For example, subordinate laboratory rodents have impaired immune responses to various immune challenges (Vessey 1964, Ito et al. 1983, Raab et al. 1986, Fleshner et al. 1989, Devoino et al. 1993), and their immune cells, when cultured in petri dishes, are impaired in their responses to in vitro challenges (Raab et al. 1986, Ito et al. 1983, Fleshner et al. 1989). Similarly, subordination is associated with fewer circulating lymphocytes (or fewer key subsets of them) in pigs (McGlone et al. 1993), rhesus monkeys (Gust et al. 1993), and wild baboons (Sapolsky 1993).

There are exceptions to this rank/immunity link, however. The previous section notes that it would make little sense for the stressor of reproductive competition to suppress reproduction. Similarly, if the stressors of subordination included high rates of challenges to immunity, it would be particularly maladaptive to be immunosuppressed. Similarly, although subordination has been associated generally with immune suppression in mice, when such subordination involved frequent wounds, the immune system developed a resistance to the immunosuppressive effects of glucocorticoids (Avitsur et al. 2001).

When subordination is accompanied by immunosuppression, does this translate into a greater risk of infectious disease? Not surprisingly, given the complications discussed, there has been no consensus on this matter. On the one hand, subordination increases the risk of succumbing to a leukemia-causing virus in mice (Ebbesen et al. 1991), or of developing a respiratory infection when exposed to a cold-causing virus in macaques (Cohen et al. 1997). On the other hand, dominant rodents and primates have the most severe parasitic infections (Hausfater & Watson 1976; Barnard et al. 1993, 1994), and dominant chimps have the highest rates of respiratory infections (Masataka 1990).

The link between stress and increased risk of infectious disease is one of the weaker links in stress pathophysiology. It is not surprising, then, that the link between social subordination and increased risk of infectious disease is also quite weak.

To summarize, there have been numerous reports that socially subordinate animals have elevated basal glucocorticoid levels, hypertension, increased risk of cardiovascular disease, and, in females, reproductive dysfunction. The evidence of links between social subordination and reproductive dysfunction among males, and of sufficient immune suppression which seriously compromises disease resistance has been far weaker. However, despite the solid evidence that social subordination is more predisposing toward pathophysiology in the realm of adrenocortical, ovarian, and cardiovascular function, there have been many exceptions to that pattern. I now consider some factors that give rise to these exceptions.

WHY ARE THERE INCONSISTENCIES IN THESE DATA? MODIFIERS OF RANK/PHYSIOLOGY RELATIONSHIPS

Throughout this review, a picture has been developing in which socially subordinate animals are subject to a disproportionate share of physical and psychological stressors and show the physiological indices of chronic stress. However, social subordination may not always be disproportionately stressful (as shown with marmosets and tamarins). Moreover, as is clear from the literature reviewed, subordination is not always associated with the physiological indices of stress. I now review some of the modifiers underlying these exceptions.

What Does Rank Mean in a Particular Species?

In the stereotypical picture of a hierarchy, dominant individuals impose resource inequities on subordinates through force or threats of force. This scenario is typical of most Old World primates. Among such species, enforcement may arise from psychological rather than physical means, since dominant individuals rarely had the highest rates of aggression (Altmann et al. 1995, Blanchard et al. 1995).

Yet, in cooperative breeding species, subordination is not enforced from above and does not involve a disproportionate share of stressors. Thus, subordination was not associated with elevated glucocorticoid levels among cooperatively breeding species such as marmosets and tamarins (Abbott et al. 1998), white-browed sparrows, Florida scrub jays, naked mole-rats, dwarf mongooses, and wild dogs (Faulkes & Abbott 1996, Creel et al. 1996, Creel 2001). Therefore, there is a social context in which rank occurs, and this may differ by species.

This insight extends beyond comparing cooperative and noncooperative breeders. Other qualitative features of dominance also vary among species, such as whether dominant animals constantly need to aggressively reassert their dominance, whether alternative strategies to dominance are available (such as the arrested juvenile stage of orangutans), and so on.

This variation was studied systematically in a meta-analysis of the dozen or so primate species x gender cases for which data have been published concerning the relationship between rank and basal glucocorticoid levels. Across the examples, levels in subordinate individuals ranged from approximately one-half those of dominant animals (marmosets) to 50% higher than dominants (male baboons, female talapoins). Experts on the behavior of each species were recruited to answer a scaled questionnaire regarding quality of life for dominant and subordinate individuals (i.e., In this species, does aggression play a big role in maintaining dominance? How unequally divided are resources? Do subordinate animals have kin present in the group? How often do ranks change?). The relationship between rank and basal glucocorticoid levels was more heavily affected by the quality of life of subordinate animals than that of dominant ones. Specifically, the best predictors of elevated basal glucocorticoid levels among subordinate individuals (or low basal levels among dominant individuals) were (*a*) high rates of harassment by dominant animals and (*b*) few coping outlets for subordinate animals (Abbott et al. 2003).

What Does Rank Mean in a Particular Population?

In addition to interspecific variation in qualitative features of dominance, there is also intraspecific variation, and the physiological correlates of rank vary systematically with this. For example, the elevated basal glucocorticoid levels typically seen among subordinate female macaques or subordinate male baboons were not observed in troops that happened to have low rates of aggression and high rates of affiliative support (Gust et al. 1993, Wallner 1996, Sapolsky & Share 2004). Moreover, in the baboon study, subordination in a typical troop also involved physiological indices of anxiety (specifically, elevated signaling by endogenous benzodiazepines, anxiety-reducing compounds whose synthetic versions include Valium and Librium), but these did not occur in the less aggressive, more affiliative troop (Sapolsky & Share 2004).

Stable Versus Unstable Dominance Hierarchies

Within any given dyad, dominance interactions can strongly reinforce the status quo. Thus, individual number 5 in a hierarchy may win 90% of interactions with individual number 6, but lose 90% of them to number 4. In a stable hierarchy, interactions up and down the rankings typically reinforce the status quo this strongly.

In contrast, if number 5 wins only 51% of interactions with number 6, their relationship is unstable, and their relative positions of dominance may soon switch. On rare occasions, dominance relations throughout an entire hierarchy become destabilized, albeit not necessarily to this extent. The instabilities tend to be somewhat local (i.e., the animal destined to be number 3 when the hierarchy stabilizes wins nearly all interactions with the animal destined to be number 20; it is the interactions with the future numbers 1, 2, 4, and 5 that are unstable). Among wild populations, instability can arise because of the death, immigration, or emigration of a key individual, or the formation or dissolution of a key coalition. In captive populations, instability is characteristic of the first months after a social group is formed.

As mentioned above, in species in which subordination is enforced from above, it is the dominant individuals who have the fewest stressors. However, this is true only in stable hierarchies. In unstable ones, competition and instability center on the higher ranks, with dominant individuals experiencing the most physical stressors and the greatest sense of loss of control and predictability.

It is not surprising, therefore, that the advantages of dominance, as measured by stress-related physiology, disappear during periods of hierarchical instability. At such times, high rank was no longer associated with lower basal glucocorticoid levels (Keverne et al. 1982 for talapoin monkeys, Coe et al. 1979, Mendoza et al. 1979 for squirrel monkeys, Chamove & Bowman 1976, Gust et al. 1991 for rhesus monkeys, Sapolsky 1993 for wild baboons). Furthermore, dominant males were most likely to develop coronary artery atherosclerosis (Manuck et al. 1995 for macaques), to be immunosuppressed, and to have the highest incidence of respiratory infections (Masataka 1990 for chimpanzees). Moreover, in unstable hierarchies, dominant males have the highest testosterone levels (Sackser & Prove 1986 for guinea pigs, Rose et al. 1971 for macaques, Eberhart & Keverne 1979 for talapoins, Coe et al. 1979, Mendoza et al. 1979 for squirrel monkeys, Sapolsky 1993 for baboons).

What Is the Personal Experience of Rank in One's Species and Population?

The qualitative features of rank not only vary on the inter- and intraspecies level, but also translate on a basic level into very different individual experiences, which influence physiology accordingly. For example, among wild female baboons, the more often an individual was harassed by a particularly aggressive male, the more immunosuppressed she became (Sapolsky 1993). Similarly, among macaques, the less social contact an animal had, the more immunosuppressed it became (Boccia et al. 1997).

Even in a stable hierarchy, there will be pockets of instability (e.g., numbers 8 and 9 may be in the process of switching ranks). One might predict that higher rates of such unstable interactions would be associated with higher glucocorticoid levels (insofar as instability generates a milieu of low predictability). In a study of wild male baboons, this was found to be the case for unstable interactions with animals directly below a subject in the hierarchy; in contrast, no correlation with glucocorticoid levels occurred with the rate of unstable interactions with the individuals above the subject in the hierarchy (Sapolsky 1992). This is logical: Unstable interactions with immediate subordinates indicate that they are gaining on an individual, clearly a cause of stress. In contrast, unstable interactions with higher-ups are not signs of stress, but of impending career advancement. In such cases, the stress-reducing effects of the perception of improving circumstances outweighs the stressful effects of unpredictability in the situation.

Personality as a Filter for the Experience of Rank

It is not anthropomorphic to discuss personality and temperament among animals (i.e., stable affective styles that bias how the individual responds to stimuli) (Clark

& Boinski 1995). Part of the variability in the rank/stress physiology relationship reflects the intervening variable of personality. Studies of both captive macaques (Suomi 1987) and wild baboons (Sapolsky & Ray 1989, Ray & Sapolsky 1992) indicated a "hot reactor" personality style. These are animals whose ongoing behaviors are disrupted easily by novelty, who have trouble distinguishing neutral from threatening stimuli, and who tend to lack effective coping outlets for stress (such as seeking social affiliation). This style bears a striking resemblance to the Type A profile in humans, in which neutral stimuli are atypically interpreted as threatening (Williams 1989). Strikingly, after controlling for rank, such individuals were found to have elevated basal glucocorticoid levels (Suomi 1987, Sapolsky & Ray 1989, Ray & Sapolsky 1992, Virgin & Sapolsky 1997) and an increased risk for atherosclerosis (Manuck et al. 1983, 1989). Moreover, these traits remained stable over time in these individuals, and arose from both genetic (Scanlon et al. 1985) and developmental (Clark & Boinski 1995) influences.

Summary

As discussed above, the social rank of an animal influences stress-related physiology. However, there is no monolithic rank/physiology relationship, either across or within species. In many circumstances, social subordination involves exposure to high rates of physical and psychological stressors, a tendency toward chronic activation of the stress-response, and an increased risk of stress-related diseases. Nonetheless, there are numerous exceptions to this profile, depending upon the social context in which rank occurs and the personality with which the individual reacts to that rank and context.

HUMANS, RANKS, AND HIERARCHY

In discussing relationships between rank and stress-related disease and physiology in humans, one must question whether humans have meaningful ranks and hierarchies. This is important for a number of reasons: (*a*) As exemplified by contemporary hunter-gatherer societies, much of human history probably has been spent in fairly egalitarian groups. (*b*) Humans belong to multiple hierarchies and tend to value most the one in which they rank highest. Consider, for example, the mailroom clerk who is also the best player on the company's softball team. The place in the former hierarchy may be dismissed as "just a job," whereas the latter may be emphasized and become a source of considerable self-esteem. (*c*) Humans readily alter the psychological meaning of a rank. Consider a novice runner who manages to complete a marathon, finishing 1000th, versus the anticipated winner who faded to number 5. Despite the differences in the formal ranking, the former is likely to be more pleased than is the latter.

Thus, although some studies have examined rank/physiology correlates in humans (e.g., the endocrine responses in winners versus losers of a wrestling match), there are many reasons to question the relevance of such studies to understanding human health. However, a reasonable argument can be made for one realm of human experience in which hierarchical ranking is meaningful in the context of stress and health: socioeconomic status (SES).

Socioeconomic Status and Health

Data stretching back centuries demonstrate that each step down the SES ladder increases the morbidity and mortality for numerous diseases. This gradient, documented in all industrialized societies, is considerable, with mortality rates due to some diseases differing by an order of magnitude between the highest and lowest echelons of SES ladders (reviewed in Syme & Berkman 1976, Adler et al. 1993, Evans et al. 1994, Wilkinson 2000).

In theory, health can both influence and be influenced by SES. Although there is evidence for poor health causing a downward SES spiral, prospective studies have amply documented that SES can precede health status and be highly predictive of it.

How does SES influence health (and is stress relevant)? Generally speaking, there have been psychosocial and nonpsychosocial explanations offered. Although the latter most readily come to mind, they do not begin to explain the SES/health gradient.

Health Care Access, Lifestyle Risk Factors, and Protective Factors

To those oriented toward nonpsychosocial explanations of how SES influences health, the most obvious explanation is the fact that poverty limits access to health care. This is certainly the case in the United States, where poorer people have fewer preventative checkups, longer waits for medical procedures, less access to new experimental procedures, and so on. However, health care access alone does not explain the existence of an SES/health gradient: (*a*) This gradient occurs in countries with socialized medicine and has even worsened during the time when universal health care was instituted. (*b*) The SES gradient is indeed a variable slope: Rather than there being a threshold of poverty below which health care access (and health) declines precipitously, health declines with every step in the SES gradient, starting at the wealthiest and progressing through the middle class. (*c*) A gradient exists for diseases whose incidences are unchanged by access to preventative health care (e.g., juvenile diabetes or rheumatoid arthritis) (reviewed in Pincus & Callahan 1995, Wilkinson 2000).

These findings have shifted the focus from nonpsychosocial explanations to differential exposure to risk factors and protective factors. As one descends the SES slope, the incidence of smoking, drinking to excess, obesity, sedentary lifestyles, poor diets, proximity to toxic dumps, and so on all increase. Moreover, lower SES also translates into fewer protective factors (e.g., fewer safe parks, fewer health club memberships). However, careful multivariate studies indicate that the major risk and protective factors account for only approximately one third of the SES gradient.

Psychosocial Factors and Stress

Most researchers view psychosocial factors related to stress as major mediators of the SES/health relationship. In addition to the insufficiency of the most notable nonpsychosocial explanations, indirect support for psychosocial factors includes the following: (*a*) The poor have an excess of physical and psychological stressors (Marmot & Feeny 2000); (*b*) studies report an SES gradient related to basal glucocorticoid levels (Kristnson et al. 1997, Lupien et al. 2000); and (*c*) the strongest SES gradients occur for diseases with the greatest sensitivity to stress, such as heart disease, diabetes, metabolic syndrome, and psychiatric disorders (Wilkinson 2000).

The case for stress-related psychosocial factors has become more direct. To appreciate this, one must consider a truism: Given food, shelter, and safety sufficient to sustain health, if everyone is poor, then no one is. In modern societies, it is never the case that everyone is equally (non)poor. This paves the way for a key point about the gradient, namely that poor health is not so much the outcome of being poor, but of feeling poor, that is, feeling poorer than others. Therefore, poverty, rather than being an absolute measure, is a subjective assessment that is mired in invidiousness.

This conclusion has been demonstrated in studies that assess subjective SES (subjects were shown a picture of a ladder with ten rungs and asked to indicate where they place themselves in their society in terms of "how they are doing"). Remarkably, subjective SES was as good or better a predictor than objective SES of stress-related health outcomes (cardiovascular and metabolic measures, glucocorticoid levels). Ongoing work in this area examines how local is the community within which one makes comparisons. The media's global village allows one to make SES comparisons with vastly larger numbers of people than in traditional human experience (Adler & Ostrove 1999, Adler et al. 2000, Singh-Manoux et al. 2003, Goodman et al. 2003).

The importance of subjective SES is reinforced by more top-down economic health literature. Intrinsic to the idea that the SES/health gradient reflects feeling poorer than others is that there are societal mechanisms that make some feel poorer than others. Numerous studies have shown that poverty in a community is not as strong a predictor of crime as is poverty amid plenty, i.e., income inequality. In the United States, at both the state and metropolitan level, the higher the degree of income inequality, the worse the health, the higher the mortality rates, and the steeper the SES/health gradient (independent of the absolute level of wealth) (Wilkinson 2000). This relationship seems not to hold as strongly, if at all, in more economically egalitarian European countries (Lynch et al. 2004).

This is a critical observation, but it could arise from a subtle confound. Suppose that in a society, the bad health of the poor is more sensitive to SES factors than is the good health of the wealthy. If income were made more equal through the transfer of wealth, this would produce a small health decline for the few wealthy and a large health improvement for the numerous poor. Although this would result in an overall improvement in health, it would be irrelevant to these psychosocial considerations. However, the finding that health is better for all strata of SES in more economically equitable communities rules out this confound (Evans 2002).

How do a subjective sense of low SES and living in an environment of income inequality adversely impact health? Amid the proposed routes, the most intriguing concerns the concept of "social capital." Although the term's definition is still evolving, it refers to salutary features of a community that transcend the level of individuals or individual networks. These features reflect trust, reciprocity, lack of hostility and cynicism, group participation, and a collective sense of efficacy. Thus, for example, social capital is high in a community with lots of volunteerism, in which doors rarely are locked, and in which people belong to effective unions and tenant organizations (most studies assay social capital with two measures, the response of people to statements such as, "Would most people take advantage of you if they got a chance, or would they be fair?," and the number of organizations people belong to).

A fascinating and robust literature has revealed two key findings: (*a*) As income inequality rises in a community, not only does crime increase, but levels of social capital also decline (Kawachi et al. 1999, Kawachi & Putnam 2001). This inverse relationship can be viewed as inevitable, in that social capital is, by definition, about reciprocity and symmetry of relationships, whereas income inequality, by definition, is about hierarchy and asymmetry (Wilkinson 2000). (*b*) Path analyses indicate that the links between income inequality, poor health, and high mortality rates are mediated predominately by the decline in social capital (Kawachi & Kennedy 2002).

Collectively, this literature makes some critical points: First, once basic needs are met, poverty alone is not as predictive of poor health as is poverty amid plenty. Second, when there is considerable poverty amid plenty (i.e., high income inequality), people tend to decrease their investment in (and expectations of) the community, thereby reducing everyone's quality of life. This decline results in more psychological stressors (because of a reduced collective sense of efficacy and control, greater need for vigilance amid increased crime, and so on) and less social support. Finally, amid the adverse community-wide consequences of income inequality and low social capital, the wealthy have disproportionate opportunities (both financial and otherwise) to obtain private means of stress-reduction, further decreasing their incentive to invest in public, community-wide means. An inevitable result of such a "secession of the wealthy" is the production of "private affluence and public squalor," which steepens the SES gradients of stress and poor health (Evans 2002).

This is a far cry from the initial assumption that the SES/health gradient is primarily about poor people having too little money to afford health care. This point has been made by the economist Robert Evans, who observed that, "Most graduate students have had the experience of having very little money, but not of poverty. They are very different things" (Evans 2002).

CONCLUSIONS

The first half of this review focuses on the relationship between social rank and either stress-related physiology or stress-related disease in nonhuman species. Although there is considerable support for a picture of social subordination involving an excess of stress and stress-related pathology, this finding is not universal among social species, and the rank/health relationship can be modified dramatically by an array of factors ranging from individual temperament to nonhuman culture. Findings such as these amply confirm the subtlety and complexity of behavior and social systems among animals other than humans.

Some related issues are then discussed in relation to humans. The transition from nonhuman to human subjects typically involves an increase in the subtleties and complexities considered. In many ways, this is the opposite of what occurs when switching from the subject of nonhuman rank and health to that of human SES and health. In contrast to the modifiers and qualifiers in the nonhuman realm, the most striking quality of the human SES/health gradient is its imperviousness. Do socially subordinate animals suffer a disproportionate share of poor health? The answer can only be, "Often, but certainly not as a rule." Do poor humans suffer a disproportionate share of poor health? The answer must be a robust, Yes—regardless of gender, age, or race; with or without universal healthcare; in culturally homogeneous societies or one's rife with ethnic tensions; and under governments with socialist or capitalist credos.

The developments of class, stratification, and poverty are fairly recent in hominid history. What these findings suggest is that nothing in the world of nonhuman sociality involves such an utterly, psychologically permeating sense of subordination as does the human invention of poverty.

ACKNOWLEDGMENTS

Funds for the original research described were provided by the Harry Frank Guggenheim Foundation and the Templeton Foundation. Manuscript assistance was provided by Stephen Bezruchka, Ichiro Kawachi and Lisa Pereira.

The *Annual Review of Anthropology* is online at http://anthro.annualreviews.org

LITERATURE CITED

Abbott D, Saltman W, Schultz-Darken N, Tannenbaum P. 1998. Adaptations to subordinate status in female marmoset monkeys. *Comp. Biochem. Physiol. C Pharmacol. Toxicol. Endocrinol.* 119:261–74

Abbott D, Keverne E, Bercovith F, Shively C, Mendoza S, et al. 2003. Are subordinates always stressed? A comparative analysis of rank differences in cortisol levels among primates. *Horm. Behav.* 43:67–82

Adams M, Kaplan J, Koritnik D, Clarkson T. 1985. Ovariectomy, social status, and atherosclerosis in cynomolgus monkeys. *Arteriosclerosis* 5:192–200

Adams M, Kaplan J, Koritnik D. 1987. Psychosocial influences on ovarian endocrine and ovulatory function in Macadca fascicularis. *Physiol. Behav.* 35:935–40

Ader R, Felton D, Cohen N. 2001. *Psychoneuroimmunology.* San Diego: Academic. 3rd ed.

Adler N, Boyce T, Chesney M, Folkman S, Syme S. 1993. Socioeconomic inequalities in health: no easy solution. *J. Am. Med. Assoc.* 269:3140–45

Adler N, Epel E, Castellazzo G, Ickovics J. 2000. Relationship of subjective and objective social status with psychological and physiological functioning: preliminary data in healthy white women. *Health Psychol.* 19:586–92

Adler N, Ostrove J. 1999. SES and health: what we know and what we don't. *Ann. N.Y. Acad. Sci.* 896:3–15

Altmann J, Sapolsky R, Licht P. 1995. Baboon fertility and social status. *Nature* 377:688–90

Archer J. 1970. Effects of aggressive behavior on the adrenal cortex in laboratory mice. *J. Mammal.* 51: 327–32

Avitsur R, Stark J, Sheridan J. 2001. Social stress induces glucocorticoid resistance in subordinate animals. *Horm. Behav.* 39:247–57

Barnard C, Behnke J, Sewell J. 1993. Social behavior, stress and susceptibility to infection in house mice: effects of duration of grouping and aggressive behavior prior to infection on susceptibility of Babesia microti. *Parasitology* 107:183–92

Barnard C, Behnke J, Sewell J. 1994. Social behaviour and susceptibility to infection in house mice: effects of group size, aggressive behavior and status-related hormonal responses prior to infection on resistance to Babesia microti. *Parasitology* 108:487–96

Barnett S. 1955. Competition among wild rats. *Nature* 175:126–277

Bercovitch F. 1993. Dominance rank and reproductive maturation in male rhesus macaques (Macaca mulatta). *J. Reprod. Fertil.* 99:113–20

Bercovitch F, Clarke A. 1995. Dominance rank, cortisol concentrations, and reproductive maturation in male rhesus macaques. *Physiol. Behav.* 58:215–21

Blanchard DC, Spencer RL, Weiss SM, Blanchard RJ, McEwen B, Sakai RR. 1995. Visible burrow system as a model of chronic social stress: behavioral and neuroendocrine correlates. *Psychoneuroendocrinology* 20:117–34

Boccia M, Scanlon J, Laudenslager M, Berger C, Hijazi A, Reite M. 1997. Juvenile friends, behavior, and immune responses to separation in bonnet macaque infants. *Physiol. Behav.* 61:191–98

Bronson F, Eleftheriou B. 1964. Chronic physiologic effects of fighting on mice. *Gen. Comp. Endocrinol.* 15:9–14

Capitano J, Mendoza S, Lerche N, Mason W. 1998. Social stress results in altered glucocorticoid regulation and shorter survival in SIV syndrome. *Proc. Natl. Acad. Sci. USA* 95:4714–19

Cavigelli S. 1999. Behavioural patterns associated with faecal cortisol levels in free-ranging female ring-tailed lemurs, Lemur catta. *Anim. Behav.* 57:935–44

Chamove A, Bowman R. 1976. Rank, rhesus social behavior, and stress. *Folia Primatol.* 26:57–66

Chase I, Tovey C, Spangler-Martin D, Manfredonia M. 2002. Individual differences versus social dynamics in the formation of animal dominance hierarchies. *Proc. Natl. Acad. Sci. USA* 99:5744–49

Cherkovich G, Tatoyan S. 1973. Heart rate (radiotelemetrical registration) in macaques and baboons according to dominant-submissive rank in a group. *Folia Primatol.* 20:265–73

Clarke A, Boinski S. 1995. Temperament in nonhuman primates. *Am. J. Primatol.* 37:103–14

Coe C, Mendoza S, Levine S. 1979. Social status constrains the stress response in the squirrel monkey. *Physiol. Behav.* 23:633–38

Cohen S, Line S, Manuck S, Rabin B, Heise E, Kaplan J. 1997. Chronic social stress, social status and susceptibility to upper respiratory infections in nonhuman primates. *Psychosom. Med.* 59:213–21

Cohen S, Tyrrell D, Smith A. 1991. Psychological stress and susceptibility to the common cold. *New Engl. J. Med.* 325:606–12

Cole S, Kemeny M. 2001. Psychosocial influences on the progression of HIV infection. See Adler et al. 2001, p. 583

Creel S. 2001. Social dominance and stress hormones. *Trends Ecol. Evol.* 16:491–96

Creel S, Creel N, Monfort S. 1996. Social stress and dominance. *Nature* 379:212–13

Davis D, Christian J. 1957. Relation of adrenal weight to social rank of mice. *Proc. Soc. Exp. Biol. Med.* 94:728–31

de Goeij D, Dijkstra H, Tilders F. 1992. Chronic psychosocial stress enhances vasopressin, but not corticotropin-releasing factor, in the external zone of the median eminence of male rats: relationships to subordinate status. *Endocrinology* 131:847–53

Devoino L, Alperina E, Kudryavtseva N, Popova N. 1993. Immune responses in male mice with aggressive and submissive behavior patterns: strain differences. *Brain Behav. Immun.* 7:91–96

Dhabhar F, McEwen B. 2001. Bidirectional effects of stress and glucocorticoid hormones on immune function: possible explanation for paradoxical observations. See Adler et al. 2001, pp. 301–2

Dijkstra H, Tilders F, Hiehle M, Smelik P. 1992. Hormonal reactions to fighting in rat colonies: prolactin rises during defence, not during offence. *Physiol. Behav.* 51:961–68

Ebbesen P, Villadsen J, Villadsen H, Heller K. 1991. Effect of subordinance, lack of social hierarchy, and restricted feeding on murine survival and virus leukemia. *Exp. Gerontol.* 26:479–86

Eberhart J, Keverne E. 1979. Influences of the dominance hierarchy on LH, testosterone and prolactin in male talapoin monkeys. *J. Endocrinol.* 83:42–43

Eisermann K. 1992. Long-term heart rate responses to social stress in wild European rabbits: predominant effect of rank position. *Physiol. Behav.* 52:33–36

Evans R. 2002. *Interpreting and addressing inequalities in health: from Black to Acheson to Blair to...?* London: OHE

Evans R, Barer M, Marmor T. 1994. *Why Are Some People Healthy and Others Not? The Determinants of Health of Populations.* New York: de Gruyter

Farabollini F. 1987. Behavioral and endocrine aspects of dominance and submission in male rabbits. *Aggress. Behav.* 13:247–56

Faulkes C, Abbott D. 1996. The physiology of a reproductive dictatorship: regulation of male and female reproduction by a single breeding female in colonies of naked mole-rats. In *Cooperative Breeding in Mammals*, ed. N Solomon, J French, pp. 302–34. Cambridge: Cambridge Univ. Press

Fernandez X, Meunier-Salaun M, Mormede P. 1994. Agonistic behavior, plasma stress hormones, and metabolites in response to dyadic encounters in domestic pigs: interrelationships and effect of dominance status. *Physiol. Behav.* 56:841–47

Fleshner M, Laudenslager M, Simons M, Maier S. 1989. Reduced serum antibodies associated with social defeat in rats. *Physiol. Behav.* 45:1183–87

Fox M, Andrews R. 1973. Physiologic and biochemical correlates of individual differences in behavior of wolf cubs. *Behaviour* 46:129–40

Fuchs E, Flugge G. 1995. Modulation of binding sites of CRH by chronic psychosocial stress. *Psychoneuroendocrinology* 20:33–51

Fuchs E, Flugge G, Ohl F, Lucassen P, Vollmann-Honsdorf G, Michaelis T. 2001. Psychosocial stress, glucocorticoids, and structural alterations in the tree shrew hippocampus. *Physiol. Behav.* 73:285–91

Fuchs E, Johren O, Flugge G. 1993. Psychosocial conflict in the tree shrew: effects on sympathoadrenal activity and blood pressure. *Psychoneuroendocrinology* 18:557–65

Goodman E, Adler N, Daniels S, Morrison J, Slap G, Dolan L. 2003. Impact of objective and subjective social status on obesity in a biracial cohort of adolescents. *Obes. Res.* 11:1018–26

Gust D, Gordon T, Hambright K, Wilson M.

1993. Relationship between social factors and pituitary-adrenocortical activity in female rhesus monkeys (Macaca mulatta). *Horm. Behav.* 27:318–31

Gust D, Gordon T, Wilson M, Ahmed-Ansari A, Brodie A, McClure H. 1991. Formation of a new social group of unfamiliar female rhesus monkeys affects the immune and pituitary adrenocortical system. *Brain Behav. Immun.* 5:296–307

Hamilton WD. 1971. Geometry for the selfish herd. *J. Theor. Biol.* 31:295–311

Hausfater G, Watson D. 1976. Social and reproductive correlates of parasite ova emissions by baboons. *Nature* 262:688–89

Henry J. 1977. *Stress, Health, and the Social Environment.* New York: Springer-Verlag

Herd J, Falkner B, Anderson D, Kosta P, Dembroski T. 1987. Psychophysiologic factors in hypertension. *Circulation* 76:189–194

Huhman K, Moore T, Mougey E, Meyerhoff J. 1992. Hormonal responses to fighting in hamsters: separation of physical and psychological causes. *Physiol. Behav.* 51:1083–86

Ito Y, Mine K, Ago Y. 1983. Attack stress and IgE antibody production in rats. *Pharmacol. Biochem. Behav.* 19:883–86

Kaplan J, Adams M, Anthony M, Morgan T, Manuck S, Clarkson T. 1995. Dominant social status and contraceptive hormone treatment inhibit atherogenesis in premenopausal monkeys. *Arterioscler. Thromb. Vasc. Biol.* 15:2094–100

Kaplan J, Manuck S. 1989. The effect of propranolol on social interactions among adult male cynomolgus monkeys (Macaca fascicularis) housed in disrupted social groupings. *Psychosom. Med.* 51:449–62

Kaplan J, Manuck S, Clarkson T. 1982. Social status, environment and atherosclerosis in cynomolgus monkeys. *Arteriosclerosis* 2:359–68

Kawachi I, Kennedy B. 2002. *The Health of Nations: Why Inequality is Harmful to Your Health.* New York: New Press

Kawachi I, Kennedy B, Wilkinson R. 1999. Crime: social disorganization and relative deprivation. *Soc. Sci. Med.* 48:719–31

Kawachi I, Putnam R. 2001. Firearm prevalence and social capital. *Ann. Epidemiol.* 11:484–90

Keverne E, Meller R, Eberhart J. 1982. Dominance and subordination: concepts or physiological states? In *Advanced Views in Primate Biology,* ed. V Chiarelli, J Corruccini, pp. 81–94. New York: Springer-Verlag

Korte S, Smit J, Bouws G, Koolhaas J, Bohus B. 1990. Behavioral and neuroendocrine response to psychosocial stress in male rats: the effects of the 5-HT 1A agonist ipsapirone. *Horm. Behav.* 24:554–67

Kristenson et al. 1997. Antioxidant state and mortality from coronary heart disease in Lithuanian and Swedish men. *Br. Med. J.* 314:629–33

Leshner A, Polish J. 1979. Hormonal control of submissiveness in mice: irrelevance of the androgens and relevance of the pituitary-adrenal hormones. *Physiol. Behav.* 22:531–34

Levine S, Wiener S, Coe C. 1989. The psychoneuroendocrinology of stress: a psychobiological perspective. In *Psychoendocrinology,* ed. S Levine, F Brush, pp. 341–47. New York: Academic

Louch C, Higginbotham M. 1967. The relation between social rank and plasma corticosterone levels in mice. *Gen. Comp. Endocrinol.* 8:441–44

Lupien S, King S, Meaney M, McEwen B. 2000. Child's stress hormone levels correlate with mother's socioeconomic status and depressive state. *Biol. Psychiatry* 48:976–80

Lynch J, Smith G, Harper S, Hillemeier M, Ross N, et al. 2004. Is income inequality a determinant of population health? Part 1. A systematic review. *Milbank Q.* In press

Magarinos A, McEwen B, Flugge G, Fuchs E. 1996. Chronic psychosocial stress causes apical dendritic atrophy of hippocampal CA3 pyramidal neurons in subordinate tree shrews. *J. Neurosci.* 16:3534–40

Maggioncalda A, Czekala N, Sapolsky R. 2000. Growth hormone and thyroid stimulating hormone concentrations in captive male orangutans: implications for understanding developmental arrest. *Am. J. Primatol.* 50:67–76

Maggioncalda A, Czekala N, Sapolsky R. 2002. Male orangutan subadulthood: a new twist in the relationship between chronic stress and developmental arrest. *Am. J. Phys. Anthropol.* 118:25–32

Maggioncalda A, Sapolsky R, Czekala N. 1999. Reproductive hormone profiles in captive male orangutans: implications for understanding developmental arrest. *Am. J. Phys. Anthropol.* 109:19–32

Mallick J, Stoddart D, Jones I, Bradley A. 1994. Behavioral and endocrinological correlates of social status in the male sugar glider (Petaurus breviceps Marsupialia: Petauridae). *Physiol. Behav.* 55:1131–34

Manogue K, Leshner A, Candland D. 1975. Dominance status and adrenocortical reactivity to stress in squirrel monkeys (Saimiri sciureus). *Primates* 16:457–63

Manuck S, Kaplan J, Adams M. 1989. Behaviorally elicited heart rate reactivity and atherosclerosis in female cynomolgus monkeys (Macaca fascicularis). *Psychosom. Med.* 51:306–18

Manuck S, Kaplan J, Clarkson T. 1983. Behaviorally induced heart rate reactivity and atherosclerosis in cynomolgus monkeys. *Psychosom. Med.* 45:95–108

Manuck S, Marsland A, Kaplan J, Williams J. 1995. The pathogenicity of behavior and its neuroendocrine mediation: an example from coronary artery disease. *Psychosom. Med.* 57:275–83

Marmot M, Feeney A. 2000. Health and socioeconomic status. In *Encyclopedia of Stress*, Vol. 2, ed. G Fink, p. 313. New York: Academic

Masataka N. 1990. Dominance and immunity in chimpanzees (Pan troglodytes). *Ethology* 85:147–55

McEwen B. 2002. *The End of Stress.* New York: Joseph Henry

McGlone JJ, Salak JL, Lumpkin EA, Nicholson RI, Gibson M, Norman RL. 1993. Shipping stress and social status effects on pig performance, plasma cortisol, natural killer cell activity, and leukocyte numbers. *J. Anim. Sci.* 71: 888–96

McKittrick C. 1995. Serotonin receptor binding in a colony model of chronic social stress. *Biol. Psychiatry* 37:383–93

McLeod P, Moger W, Ryon J, Gadbois S, Fentress J. 1996. The relation between urinary cortisol levels and social behaviour in captive timber wolves. *Can. J. Zool.* 74:209–16

Mendoza S, Coe C, Lowe E, Levine S. 1979. The physiological response to group formation in adult male squirrel monkeys. *Psychoneuroendocrinology* 3:221–29

Morgan D, Grant KA, Prioleau OA, Nader SH, Kaplan JR, Nader MA. 2000. Predictors of social status in cynomolgus monkeys (Macaca fascicularis) after group formation. *Am. J. Primatol.* 52:115–31

Munck A, Guyre P, Holbrook N. 1984. Physiological actions of glucocorticoids in stress and their relation to pharmacological actions. *Endocr. Rev.* 5:25–44 Review

Packer C, Collins D, Sindimwo A, Goodall J. 1995. Reproductive constraints on aggressive competition in female baboons. *Nature* 373:60–63

Pincus T, Callahan L. 1995. What explains the association between socioeconomic status and health: primarily access to medical care or mind-body variables? *Advances* 11:4–11

Popova N, Naumenko E. 1972. Dominance relation and the pituitary-adrenal system in rats. *Anim. Behav.* 20:108–11

Raab A, Dantzer R, Michaud B, Mormede R, Taghzouti K, et al. 1986. Behavioural, physiological and immunological consequences of social status and aggression in chronically coexisting resident-intruder dyads of male rats. *Physiol. Behav.* 36:223–28

Ray J, Sapolsky R. 1992. Styles of male social behavior and their endocrine correlates among high-ranking baboons. *Am. J. Primatol.* 28:231–50

Rose R, Holaday J, Bernstein I. 1971. Plasma testosterone, dominance rank and aggressive behavior in male rhesus monkeys. *Nature* 231:366–68

Rowell T. 1974. The concept of social dominance. *Behav. Biol.* 11:131–54

Sachser N, Prove E. 1986. Social status and plasma-testosterone-titers in male guinea pigs. *Ethology* 71:103–14

Saltzman W. 1994. Social and reproductive influences on plasma cortisol in female marmoset monkeys. *Physiol. Behav.* 56:801–10

Sapolsky R. 1990. Adrenocortical function, social rank and personality among wild baboons. *Biol. Psychiatry* 28:862–78

Sapolsky R. 1991. Testicular function, social rank and personality among wild baboons. *Psychoneuroendocrinology* 16:281–93

Sapolsky R. 1992. Cortisol concentrations and the social significance of rank instability among wild baboons. *Psychoneuroendocrinology* 17:701–9

Sapolsky R. 1993. Endocrinology alfresco: psychoendocrine studies of wild baboons. *Recent Prog. Horm. Res.* 48:437–68 Review

Sapolsky R. 2004. *Why Zebras Don't Get Ulcers: A Guide to Stress, Stress-Related Diseases and Coping.* New York: Holt. 3rd ed.

Sapolsky R, Mott G. 1987. Social subordinance in a wild primate is associated with suppressed HDL-cholesterol concentrations. *Endocrinology* 121:1605–10

Sapolsky R, Plotsky P. 1990. Hypercortisolism and its possible neural bases. *Biol. Psychiatry* 27:937–52

Sapolsky R, Ray J. 1989. Styles of dominance and their physiological correlates among wild baboons. *Am. J. Primatol.* 18:1–13

Sapolsky R, Share L. 1994. Rank-related differences in cardiovascular function among wild baboons: role of sensitivity to glucocorticoids. *Am. J. Primatol.* 32:261–70

Sapolsky R, Share L. 2004. A pacific culture among wild baboons, its emergence and transmission. *Publ. Lib. Sci.* 2:E106–11

Sapolsky RM, Romero LM, Munck AU. 2000. How do glucocorticosteroids influence stress responses? Integrating permissive, suppressive, stimulatory and preparative actions. *Endocr. Rev.* 21:55–89

Scanlon J, Sutton S, Maclin R, Suomi S. 1985. The heritability of social dominance in laboratory reared rhesus monkeys. *Am. J. Primatol.* 8:363–71

Schilling A, Perret M. 1987. Chemical signals and reproductive capacity in a male prosimian primate (Microcebus murinus). *Chem. Senses* 12:143–57

Schuhr B. 1987. Social structure and plasma corticosterone level in female albino mice. *Physiol. Behav.* 40:689–93

Schulkin J. 2003. Allostasis: a neural behavioral perspective. *Horm. Behav.* 43:21–27

Shively C, Clarkson T. 1994. Social status and coronary artery atherosclerosis in female monkeys. *Arterioscler. Thromb.* 14:721–26

Shively C, Kaplan J. 1984. Effects of social factors on adrenal weight and related physiology of Macaca fascicularis. *Physiol. Behav.* 33:777–82

Singh-Manoux A, Adler N, Marmot MG. 2003. Subjective social status: its determinants and its association with measures of ill-health in the Whitehall II study. *Soc. Sci. Med.* 56:1321–33

Southwick C, Bland V. 1959. Effect of population density on adrenal glands and reproductive organs of CFW mice. *Am. J. Physiol.* 197:111–14

Steklis H. 1986. Biochemical and hormonal correlates of dominance and social behavior in all-male groups of squirrel monkeys (Saimiri sciureus). *Am. J. Primatol.* 11:133–40

Strawn W, Bondjers G, Kaplan J. 1991. Endothelial dysfunction in response to psychosocial stress in monkeys. *Circ. Res.* 68:1270–79

Suomi S. 1987. Genetic and maternal contributions to individual differences in rhesus monkey biobehavioral development. In *Perinatal Development: A Psychobiological Perspective*, ed. N Krasnegor, E Blass, M Hofer, W Smotherman, pp. 397–419. New York: Academic

Syme S, Berkman L. 1976. Social class, susceptibility and sickness. *Am. J. Epidemiol.* 104:1–8 Review

Tsai L, Sapolsky R. 1996. Rapid stimulatory effects of testosterone upon myotubule metabolism and hexose transport, as assessed by silicon microphysiometry. *Aggress. Behav.* 22:357–65

Van Schaik C. 1991. A pilot study of the social correlates of levels of urinary cortisol, prolactin, and testosterone in wild long-tailed macaques (Macaca fascicularis). *Primates* 32:345–51

Vessey S. 1964. Effect of grouping on levels of circulating antibodies in mice. *Proc. Soc. Exp. Biol. Med.* 115:252–55

Virgin CE, Sapolsky R. 1997. Styles of male social behavior and their endocrine correlates among low-ranking baboons. *Am. J. Primatol.* 42:25–39

Wallner B. 1996. Female post estrous anogenital swelling and male-female interactions in barbary macaque. In *The Integrative Neurobiology of Affiliation*, ed. C Carter, B Kirkpatrick, I Lederhendler, p. 45. New York: NY Acad. Sci.

Wilkinson R. 2000. *Mind the Gap: Hierarchies, Health and Human Evolution.* London: Weidenfeld & Nicolson

Williams R. 1989. *The Trusting Heart: Great News About Type A Behavior.* New York: Random House

Wingfield J, Sapolsky R. 2003. Reproduction and resistance to stress: when and how. *J. Neuroendocrinol.* 15:711–24

Annu. Rev. Anthropol. 2004. 33:419–45
doi: 10.1146/annurev.anthro.33.070203.143706
Copyright © 2004 by Annual Reviews. All rights reserved
First published online as a Review in Advance on June 16, 2004

ANTHROPOLOGY AND CIRCUMCISION

Eric K. Silverman

*Department of Sociology/Anthropology, DePauw University, Greencastle,
Indiana 46135; email: erics@depauw.edu*

Key Words   gender, body, cultural relativism

■ **Abstract**   This chapter reviews the anthropology of male and female circumcision over the past century. After surveying classic sociocultural and psychodynamic interpretations of male circumcision, I shift to the biblical and Jewish rite, focusing on gender symbolism and counter-hegemonic practice within European-Christian society. The chapter then reviews the relationship between male circumcision in sub-Saharan Africa and reduced rates of HIV. Next, I address female circumcision, focusing again on symbolism but especially on highly impassioned debates over cultural relativism and human rights, medical complications, criticism and imperialism, and female agency versus brute patriarchy. What are the moral, political, and scientific obligations of anthropology to a cultural practice that is increasingly vilified in Western popular culture and jurisprudence? Should anthropology advocate eradication, contextualize Western opposition, or critique one's own bodily practices? Finally, I critically analyze the growing movement to ban the medical and ritual circumcision of infant boys in the West.

INTRODUCTION

"Foreskins are facts," writes Boon (1999), "cultural facts." Indeed, the male prepuce is a serious fact, whether wretched or praised, severed or stolen, cultural or biological, depending on your perspective. The sheer facticity of women's genital cuttings (pricks, excisions, and infibulations) is even more apparent, and controversial. For some, circumcision is all about culture, a symbolic message concerning personhood, gender, cosmology, status, and community inscribed in the body. For others, circumcision is an incontrovertible reality of biology and human rights that requires anthropology to transcend and often condemn culture.

Male and female circumcision is a topic of enduring anthropological interest, beginning with Frazer (1904). Today, impassioned debate about the plight of women in the developing world suggests that the moral worth of anthropology often seems to hang on foreskins and genital cuttings. Debates between pluralism and imperialism, analysis and activism, relativism and rights, are both urgent and irreducible.

Male and female circumcisions occur variously throughout the traditional cultures of sub-Saharan and North Africa, the Muslim Middle East, the Jewish diaspora, Aboriginal Australia, the Pacific Islands, Southeast Asia, and elsewhere.

These practices are less common in the indigenous cultures of North America and Europe. The female rite, in particular, as a result of transnational movements and refugees, is now clashing with Western law from California to Paris. At the same time, Western activists and governments impose notions of somatic integrity onto the bodies and states of others, thus reproducing colonialism or, depending again on your perspective, enabling human rights.

The study of circumcision, one of the most disputed issues in contemporary anthropology, challenges cultural relativism, universalism, modernization, and advocacy. International debates over male and female circumcision focus on health care, AIDS, development, the United Nations, ethics, and law, and frequently draw on the "data" of anthropology. At the same time, anthropologists often are criticized for allowing their moral commitment to pluralism to eclipse what should be a more fundamental duty to defend basic human rights. The very existence of these debates, as well as the rhetorical strategies employed in them, demand anthropological analysis.

This review surveys the anthropology of male and female circumcision from multiple angles. Given the global scope of these rites, no essay could possibly include all instances, themes, and sources, anthropological or otherwise. With the proliferation of on-line databases and myriad Internet sites, readers can readily search for additional materials. My task is necessarily selective: I seek to highlight significant issues and perspectives that have been recognized but largely neglected by anthropology.

I begin by discussing male circumcision, reviewing classic studies that analyze the symbolic, political, historical, and psychodynamic aspects of the rite. I then discuss dilemmas pertaining to Jewish circumcision, after which I shift to recent research investigating links between male circumcision and efforts to curtail the spread of HIV in sub-Saharan Africa. Next, I discuss female circumcision, focusing on gender, medical harm, agency, and relativism. I also examine local arguments in favor of the rite, and especially the moral stances of anthropologists who engage this pressing topic. Finally, I review recent debates over routine medical and ritual male circumcision in the West—angry debates with sweeping claims that anthropologists have yet to investigate. In the end, I suggest that male and female circumcision is a topic that might help anthropology redefine its sense of moral purpose.

MALE CIRCUMCISION

The derisive description of male circumcision (abbreviated MC) as a cross-cultural oddity is a venerable Western tradition, extending back to Hellenistic and Roman authors such as Strabo, Herodotus, Martial, and Tacitus.[1] In addition to MC, anthropologists have gazed also on a wide range of male genital practices that captivate students, popular audiences, and (let's face it) ourselves: Aboriginal

---

[1]Puzzlingly, virtually all cultures that practice some form of circumcision view the uncircumcised with disgust, and vice versa—more so than, say, the unbearded.

Australian subincision (Ashley-Montagu 1937, Singer & DeSole 1967), supercision (Firth 1936, Rubel et al. 1971), Melanesian urethral incision and penile purgations (Hogbin 1970, Lewis 1980), phallocrypts or penis sheaths (Ucko 1969), penis inserts (Brown et al. 1988), and so forth. The anthropology of MC and all penile practices is fraught with the ethnocentric perils of revulsion, admiration, and exoticism. Even the very idea that there is a cross-cultural category worthy of comparison called male circumcision is now challenged (Boon 1999).

A spate of anthropological accounts of MC rites was published from the 1880s through the early decades of the twentieth century (Aufinger 1941, Brewster 1919, Brown 1921, Jensen 1933, Speiser 1944, Spencer & Gillen 1899). Scores of reports appeared in the *Journal of the Royal Anthropological Institute, Man, Africa, Anthropos, Anthropologie, Bulletins et Mémoires de la Société d'Anthropologie de Paris*, etc. (On-line bibliographic databases make these references readily identifiable.) Early anthropologists seemed reluctant to engage the public in a debate about these rites, preferring instead the dispassionate discourses of science. But this is no longer the case, as we shall see.

Conventional Accounts

Van Gennep (1909) classed circumcision with other transitional cuttings, marks, and separations of childhood. Foreskins resemble hair and teeth. The rite often is sacrificial (Loeb 1923). Most classic accounts of MC, focusing on Africa, probed common symbolic themes: enhancement of masculine virility and fecundity, arboreal fertility, complementary opposition between men and women, preparation for marriage and adult sexuality, and the hardening of boys for warfare (Crosse-Upcott 1959; Gluckman 1949; La Fontaine 1985; Spencer 1965; Tucker 1949; Turner 1962, 1967; White 1953).[2] The traditional male rite, stressed Paige & Paige (1981), always precedes marriage. It typically entails physical brutality, seclusion, testing, esoteric knowledge, death and rebirth imagery, name changes, dance, masked costumes, and dietary and sexual taboos (Beidelman 1964, 1965; Hambly 1935; Heald 1986; Holdredge & Young 1927). The rite fuses Islam with local traditions (Miner 1942), mediates intergroup relations (Turnbull 1957), and integrates the sociocultural system (Ngxamngxa 1971). For the most part, the idea of male or female circumcision evoked little moral disquiet. It was one of those phenomena, like cross-cousin marriage, that required cool analytic attention.

Of course, generalizations are difficult. Usually, boys are expected to endure circumcision stoically—but not so the Ngindo (Crosse-Upcott 1959, p. 176) and Tiv (Bohannan 1954, p. 4). Although men generally do the cutting, high-ranking boys in a Melanesian society are circumcised by women (Todd 1934).

Gender and ideology often are central to MC. The Merina rite on Madagascar, richly analyzed by Bloch (1986), transfers fertility between generations, shifts boys

---

[2]The fate of severed foreskins—gulped, saved, buried—also merits review (see Brauer 1942, pp. 17–38; Gluckman 1949, p. 155; Patai 1983b, p. 358, 1983c, p. 283).

from mothers to men, and associates males with timeless, entombed ancestors and descent groups rather than with houses and women. The rite sustains an ideology that "women, sex, birth, and nature" can be "violently conquered" by men. At the same time, the Merina ceremony admits its limitations by assenting to the vital role of women in human life.

Bloch (1986, 1992) also focused on politics, tracing the historical relationship between large-scale circumcision ceremonies and state conquest. Paige & Paige's (1981) encyclopedic, cross-cultural survey of MC reduced the rite to a political oath in potentially fissile, patrilineal societies. A father demonstrates loyalty by entrusting his son's reproductive potential to elder kinsmen and the "fraternal-interest group." Although the rite often renews group unity (Mercier 1951), it may also enable political realignments (Levine 1959).

Turner's famous analysis of Ndembu circumcision rites elucidated the nuances of symbolic classification (1962, 1967; see also Beidelman 1964, McWilliam 1994). de Heusch (1985, ch. 6) presented a structuralist relationship between the bloods of circumcision, sacrifice, menstruation, and castration in Dogon myth. And Lévi-Strauss (1988; cf. Mills 1961) provocatively juxtaposed the circumcised removal of the natural biblical prepuce with the Bororo encasement of the penis in a cultural sheath.

Among the noncircumcising Kayapo of central Brazil, penis sheaths certify men's entitlement to enter into sexual relations and marriage (Turner 1995). But, although the sheath signifies an erection, public displays of the glans are considered shameful. The sheath obscures what it celebrates (Gell 1971). The same dynamic occurs in "circum-incision" on Malekula (Layard 1942, ch. 18). The prepuce is removed to expose the glans, which is covered by a pandanus wrapper. A cultural foreskin, associated with men (but plaited by women), replaces the natural, feminine prepuce (Layard 1942).

In sum, a series of themes and approaches emerges from classic accounts of MC in the anthropological literature: symbolism, politics, aggressive manhood, history, structuralist inversions, and the nature-culture dichotomy.

The Psychodynamic Phallus

Layard's (1942) underappreciated study recognized the homoerotic dimensions of circumcision, something most other anthropologists oddly seem to miss. Indeed, classic texts on MC generally understood the rite to engender singular—not contrary—meanings pinned typically to dominant ideologies.

Often, however, MC is a dialogical rite that both sustains and subverts its own intended symbolism. In terminology and gesture, the rite frequently flirts with castration (Bohannan 1954, p. 3; Cansever 1965).[3] Egyptian adults, reported Ammar (1954, p. 123), may threaten to recircumcise children! Yet MC is also not

---

[3]In addition to hair and teeth, foreskins double as heads (Turner 1962, p. 170) and eyes (Beidelman 1965, p. 146; Boyarin 1992).

castrative: The rite almost always unleashes male fecundity, leaving a "heroically scarred" penis (Paul 1990, pp. 328–29) to teach boys that "masculinity is safe" (Levy 1973, p. 373; Ozturk 1973).

Or is it? The adolescent rite may plague boys (and adult men) with unresolved anxieties surrounding the social significance of sexuality (Kennedy 1970, pp. 183–87). Circumcised masculinity, too, I stress, often circumscribes males within a maternal or uterine yearning. The rite is phallic and feminizing. It crafts a parturient phallus.[4]

Many anthropologists, as I mentioned, have probed the psychological and psychoanalytic dimensions of circumcision (Ammar 1954; Burridge 1969; Graber 1981; Heald 1986, 1994; Hiatt 1994; Ottenberg 1988; Róheim 1942, 1945; Rosen 1988; Walter 1988). Several well-known papers drew on the Human Relations Area Files (HRAF) to correlate globally pubertal rites such as circumcision with mother-child sleeping patterns, absent fathers, postpartum sex taboos, solidarity, sex differentiation, residence and marriage patterns, sociocultural complexity, and so forth (Barry & Schlegel 1980; Burton & Whiting 1961; Graber 1981; Harrington 1968; Kitahara 1974, 1976; Paige & Paige 1981; Whiting et al. 1958; Young 1965).[5]

The work of Róheim represents a classic yet underappreciated psychodynamic-symbolic perspective on circumcision. For him, "separation from the mother is represented as a separation of a part of the body from the whole" (1942, p. 366). The removal of the foreskin, too, symbolizes the birth of the boy (Róheim 1945, p. 71; see also Turner 1962). Yet circumcision, which detaches Aboriginal boys from motherhood, also attaches them to potent paternal symbols such as bullroarers (albeit symbols bedecked with uterine insignia). Circumcision rebirths boys into manhood, identifies them with mothers, and reenacts birth (Warner 1958/1937, pp. 127–31; Meek 1885/1931, p. 357). In addition, as Róheim (and Mehta 1996) emphasized, the physical act of circumcision, carving unity into duality, mirrors the psychosocial movement of boys from the youthful mother-child dyad to the adult pairings of father-son, man-ancestor, and husband-wife. Circumcision dramatizes unease over separation-individuation through a symbolism that affirms yet blurs the normative boundaries between masculinity and motherhood.

Let me illustrate this idea with reference to biblical and rabbinic circumcision. Often, MC ritually reenacts birth as a type of couvade (Silverman 2003; relatedly, Crosse-Upcott 1959, pp. 173–74; La Fontaine 1972).[6] The rite creates a form of manhood that is modeled after, and yet in opposition to, uterine fertility, parturition, menstruation, and motherhood (see also Turner 1962). In my analysis, biblical

---

[4]For nineteenth century ethnology, Protestant Bible dictionaries, and Lacan's Phallus, see Carpenter (1988).

[5]The electronic Human Relations Area Files (eHRAF) contain a wealth of information on circumcision in several classic cultures I do not discuss, such as Dogon and Maasai.

[6]The classic statement is Bettleheim's (1954), despite his erroneous contention that infant circumcision expresses only oedipal tension, not male envy.

culture and rabbinic Judaism construed the blood of circumcision as a positive male transformation of negative menstrual blood (Silverman 2003; see also Delaney 1991). Within these two allied cultural formations, this paradox contributed to a valid construction of normative, heterosexual manhood (Boyarin 1997). But, from the perspective of hegemonic Euro-Christian notions of gender, Jewish manhood was invalid, illegitimate, and diminished, little better (and often worse) than the other significant category of European Others, women.[7] Circumcision in Judaism (and Ancient Israel) emulates menstruation to invest men with the ability to reproduce the community. Despite a denuded phallus (as it were) circumcised Jews within Judaism remain whole men. In the eyes of non-Jews, however, the rite is further proof that Jewish males are less than true men. That is, the rite constructs an emasculated rather than an alternative form of masculinity. In this regard, it seems reasonable to propose that the blood of circumcision likely contributed to the long-standing belief that Jewish men menstruated. Here, however, male menstruation was linked not to the masculine reproduction of culture, but to divine punishment for betraying Christ. Because the rite so powerfully cuts into the core of Western cultural notions of embodied selfhood and disembodied salvation, MC remains deeply dissonant within dominant Western traditions.

Many theorists argued that circumcision expresses the father's anxieties as projected onto his son (Graber 1981, Róheim 1945, Rosen 1988). This interpretation inverts the common Freudian analysis that circumcision is a castrative reaction by fathers to youthful licentiousness, or a warning against moral trespass (Hiatt 1994, p. 177; see also Raum 1940, pp. 310–11; Róheim 1945, pp. 73–74).

Crapanzano (1981) brilliantly analyzed Muslim MC in Morocco.[8] The rite, because of the financial burden of sponsoring a ceremony, exacerbates father-son tensions, as it does elsewhere (Heald 1994). More significantly, Crapanzano argued that the rite presents only the illusion of passage from dependence to adulthood. Instead, circumcision is a "rite of return" that in various ways, some even erotic, renews the mother-child bond and equates the boy with women and infants. The rite commemorates nontransition by cutting an absence, gap, or negation into the boy's body.

After circumcision, Moroccan boys believe themselves emasculated, a castration they attribute to their mothers. Sometimes the cut boy is placed on his mother's naked back. She then dances, and sweating causes a sting on her son's penis that adult men recall with horror. The Moroccan rite, according to Crapanzano, also allows adult men to relive their own circumcision through their sons. I add to this assertion that the ceremony might also permit men a vicarious experience of taboo intimacy with motherhood (see also Heald 1994). After the circumcision and the

---

[7]As a truncated penis, reports Gilman (1993, pp. 38–39), the clitoris in *fin de siècle* Vienna was called the "Jew"; female masturbation was "playing the Jew."

[8]Muslim circumcision often resembles marriage (Geertz 1960, ch. 5; Kennedy 1970, pp. 176–77). Removing the foreskin parallels bridal defloration (Delaney 1991, p. 86; Mehta 1996, p. 220).

boy's painful union with his mother's body, she puts him to bed, and the adult men sleep with prostitutes. The Moroccan rite thus seems to express ambivalently—neither thwarting nor actualizing—oedipal conflicts.

Genesis, Gender, and Jews

Few anthropologists have explored biblical circumcision (e.g., Genesis 17), which "cuts" God's covenant into the male body partly to establish Abrahamic monotheism. Goldberg (1996, p. 27) contended that the timing of this rite—in infancy—stressed the importance of the family and women for socialization. By contrast, puberty rites signal an educational shift away from the family to non-coresident men. Goldberg (1996, p. 31) and Prewitt (1990) also situated the biblical rite in a pattern of affinal and agnatic alliances. For Delaney (1998, 2001), Abrahamic circumcision created a notion of paternity that, even today, erased legal and moral motherhood. Although painful to boys, the rite was (and remains) a form of violence mainly directed at women and mothers.

Paul (1996), from a psychoanalytic perspective, anchored biblical circumcision to the oedipal dimensions of generational succession. As mentioned above, I interpret the rite as an expression of male envy of female fertility (Silverman 2003, n.d.). The physical act of circumcision—dividing a single body into two parts—parallels the structure of the Genesis 1 cosmogony, the Genesis 2 creation of woman from the body of an androgynous yet male creature, and the formation of society in the Hebrew Bible.

Many scholars in Jewish Studies borrowed from anthropology to analyze the biblical rite. They drew on the ethnography of Middle Eastern and African pastoral societies (Morgenstern 1966, Eilberg-Schwartz 1990), and structuralism (Hoffman 1996, Kunin 1996). Further afield, scholars often have mined anthropology for insights into the Jewish rite (e.g., Daly 1950, Weiss 1966).

For contemporary Jews, Boyarin & Boyarin (1995) argued, circumcision marks the male body, like the presence of a skullcap (yarmulke), as ethnically distinctive within a diasporic setting. Jewish circumcision, mandated by tradition, resists the ideology of the "self-made man." The rite also challenges the Hellenistic ideal of the naturally whole body that achieved hegemony through the spread of Pauline Christianity (Boyarin 1994). Finally, the Jewish gesture is counterphallic, cutting an image of manhood that is distinctive and contrary to dominant notions of male identity by incorporating desirable qualities associated with women into an ideal of masculinity (Boyarin 1997).

Bilu (2000) compared circumcision among the Israeli ultraorthodox to a first haircutting ceremony.[9] The ritual trimming, as a type of adolescent weaning, reenacts infant circumcision so that, this time, the boy is able to remember the ritual messages (Bilu 2000). The haircutting ceremony, like circumcision, snips boys from

---

[9]Accounts of non-European Jewish circumcision practices include Brauer (1942, 1947) and Patai (1983a).

femininity and motherhood, and tethers them to adult men who, through feeding and care, nurture youth. Bilu (2000) also identified themes of cutting and division throughout traditional Jewish culture, including menstruation, charity, and food.

To the Jewish mystical and classic rabbis, circumcision inscribed God's name into the body of men (Wolfson 2002). Today, Jewish circumcision is at the center of increasing controversy. The bodily rite has become a text for contested inscriptions of gender, power, sexuality, and ethnic particularism. Reform Judaism emerged in the late nineteenth century to integrate the religion into the Enlightenment tenets of modernity, emphasizing individual autonomy and scientific rationality. Today, many nontraditional Jews question the necessity of circumcision, advocating either the abolishment of the rite or comparable ceremonies (liturgical mainly, but including one call for hymenal pricks) that hallow the birth of girls (see Goldberg 2003, Hoffman 1996, Silverman n.d.). To some, these revisions ensure a viable future for Judaism as a worthy, moral ethnicity. To others, Jewish arguments against the covenantal cut unwittingly yield to Pauline hegemony and transform the obligations of tradition into an optional, contractual relationship.

For traditional Judaism, no less than for many Melanesian and African cosmologies, male and female bodies require postpartum refinements to attain proper wholeness. Although an anathema to most Western sensibilities, the body is not everywhere complete upon birth. Many foes of the Jewish rite understand circumcision to be antisexual. But the canonical rabbis argued otherwise: Jewish circumcision celebrates sexuality and bodily experience by marking the covenant in flesh. For the most part, however, anthropologists have neglected to study the impassioned debate over MC in Judaism, a debate that resonates with the same issues as disputes over female circumcision.

Male Circumcision and HIV

Until recently, anthropologists have said little about the medical aspects of male circumcision, infant or adolescent (e.g., Meintjes 1998).[10] The relationship between MC and various diseases, especially cancer and syphilis, has punctuated the debate—both pro and con—over Jewish circumcision. To Western culture since the Letters of Paul, the circumcised Jew represents the preeminent bodily symbol of dangerous Difference. Sometimes his foreskinlessness points to enviable hygiene; at other times, it threatens non-Jews with fearful, often contagious, infirmities. This is well known.

Less well known is the fact that several anthropologists are now investigating links between MC and the epidemiology of AIDS, especially in Africa. Much of this research suggests that MC may inhibit the spread of HIV and other sexually transmitted diseases. The fragile foreskin is susceptible to minute scratches and tears. It also contains specialized cells (e.g., Langerhans) that join readily with HIV and other pathogens (Auvert et al. 2001, Quigley et al. 2001, Bailey et al. 2001,

---

[10]For evolutionary views of MC and infibulation, see Gallo (1992a), Immerman & Mackey (1997, 1998), Rowanchilde (1996).

Halperin & Bailey 1999, Moses et al. 1998, USAID/AIDSMark 2003; cf. Siegfried et al. 2003). Cultural anthropologists might identify here echoes of the attribution of medical benefits to the Jewish rite. The circumcised penis yet again is the site of hygienic marvels, this time on the body of Africans. Medical anthropologists, however, should find the evidence compelling. Some anthropologists have suggested the introduction of MC, or its reintroduction after missionary curtailment, to stem the AIDS epidemic, in cooperation with local authorities and medical practitioners (Bailey et al. 2002, Halperin 2000; see also Soori et al. 1997). Research on the relationship beween MC and HIV is ongoing, and new studies, both pro-circumcision and con-, appear almost weekly, mainly in medical journals.

Of course, MC techniques vary greatly (Brown et al. 2001), thus complicating the matter. Moreover, no anthropologist has advocated MC as a "natural condom" (Bonner 2001, Lagarde et al. 2003). Just the opposite: There is persistent concern that MC might substitute, tragically, for other efforts (as in Papua New Guinea; see Jenkins & Alpersi 1996), such as condom use and behavioral modifications (for "dry sex," see Halperin 1999). Yet opponents of medical MC (addressed below) are appalled at the idea of performing surgical interventions instead of altering social practices (Hodges et al. 2002). As in the case of female circumcision, however, the matter is not simply a debate within the Western medical-ethical community. Africans themselves are participating increasingly in discussions about MC and AIDS. In the main, they seem to endorse the proposal (Bailey et al. 2002, Kebaabetswe et al. 2003).

Another factor may be at work here. In many African cultures, MC was problematic for Christian missionaries (e.g., Beidelman 1997). The rite represented the "dark" ways of the sinful past. But MC also received biblical backing from both Abraham and Christ. In one fascinating case from Papua New Guinea, MC (actually, supercision) was introduced after World War II by health orderlies, and so became associated locally with the hygienic practices of Europeans and modernity (Kempf 2002). The rite, linked to Christ's Crucifixion and Christian purification, became integrated into male initiation in the 1950s and 1960s. By removing the sinful, dark foreskin, MC enables the Ngaing to maintain tradition while integrating into modernity and contesting European domination. Other anthropologists who work in traditionally non-circumcizing areas of Melanesia anecdotally report on men who underwent the rite to emulate Europeans, especially American GIs during World World II. In one location, members of the South Seas Evangelical Church, who see themselves as a lost tribe of Israel, recently initiated circumcision. Here and elsewhere, MC intersects in complex ways with the past, modernity, hygiene, medicine, and the religious entanglements of colonialism.

FEMALE CIRCUMCISION

Female circumcision has emerged as one of the central moral topics of contemporary anthropology (Kratz 1999, Shell-Duncan & Hernlund 2000). No area of the discipline seems so entwined with ethical claims, activism, and the participation of governmental and nongovernmental organizations. Today, few anthropologists would dare merely to describe clitoridectomy (e.g., Mayer 1952) or to defend it boldly as Kenyatta (1959, pp. 153–54) famously did. But, as Kenyatta's oft-invoked apology for the practice demonstrates, all statements about the topic are embedded in complex colonial and postcolonial histories (Browne 1991, Natsoulas 1998, Thomas 2003). Terminological shifts and disputes are nothing new in anthropology. But few quarrels are as morally and politically loaded as that between proponents of the terms female circumcision (which dilutes the horror), female genital mutilation (or FGM, which evokes only horror),[11] and female genital cutting (which is neutral; see Walley 1997).

There is a broad spectrum of female circumcision (abbreviated here FC). So-called symbolic circumcision entails a slight prick of the clitoris or, in some communities, the application of red color or some other, nonintrusive gesture that responds to concerns over actual cutting. More dramatic are two other practices: removal of the clitoral prepuce, called "sunna circumcision" (a term controversially derived from Islam), which reduces the clitoris entirely; and excision or clitoridectomy. (Sunna circumcision compares best with MC.) These procedures correspond to the World Health Organization (WHO) Types I and II. Most dramatic is pharaonic circumcision. This practice removes the external genitalia (prepuce, clitoris, labia minora, and all or part of the labia majora) and then, through infibulation, stitches together the vagina, leaving only a tiny opening for drops of urine and menstrual blood (WHO Type III). A final, rare form of FC is introcision, or the cutting away of the external genitalia (WHO Type IV, which includes unclassified forms of the procedure).

African FC occurs to a great extent in association with Islam. In fairness, canonical Islamic texts offer little justification for the practice. But this theological point seems more significant to educated Muslim opponents of the rite and to its Western foes than to local women who frequently tie their Islamic identity as women to the practice of the rite (Johnson 2000).

Feminizing the Female

In the past two decades, anthropologists have offered many important studies of FC (e.g., Ahmadu 2000, Boddy 1996, Gruenbaum 2001, Hayes 1975, Shell-Duncan & Hernlund 2000, van der Kwaak 1992). These works examined the symbolism of the rite, often drawing on recent ideas in gender theory. A common rationale for Muslim FC echoed, despite the lack of historical connections, the rabbinic view of the male prepuce as repulsive: Uncircumcised female genitals are unclean and impure. Worse, they may grow like a penis (Gordon 1991; Inhorn & Buss 1993, p. 232; van der Kwaak 1992, p. 781). This view suggests that FC feminizes a woman's otherwise androgynous genitalia, and thus corresponds to MC, since uncircumcised foreskins often are said to resemble female genitals (Turner 1962,

---

[11]The term male genital mutilation (MGM) is obscure, except among opponents of the rite.

p. 161; 1967, pp. 265–74). FC and MC, then, commonly transform cross-sexed youth into wholly male and female persons (Talle 1993). But there is a key difference. MC, as we saw, often creates feminine men. But no FC rite, as far as I know, masculinizes the vulva.

MC in Northern Sudan, argued Boddy (1982, 1989), exposes the male reproductive organ (relatedly, see Beidelman 1964, 1965). The foreskin is a penile "veil." This phallic exposure represents male privilege to venture into the outside, nondomestic world.[12] Women enclose their genitals through excision and infibulation. The female rite thus corresponds to confinement within the village. This bodily enclosure also "sews" a woman into an agnatic group so that, later, she is opened by her husband (Talle 1993). Here again, MC and FC create or carve single-sexed bodies.

Another localized explanation for FC is that women develop less reason than men, and so are more prone to carnal desires. FC constrains woman's sexuality, which is sometimes associated with the wild bush (Beidelman 1965; Muller 1993, 2002 for "pseudoexcision"). The rite is less about enhancing male sexual pleasure, as is commonly averred, and more about preparing a woman for motherhood by retaining her inner, fertile moisture.

To repeat, anthropologists such as Boddy (1982) have shown that FC persists precisely because the rite is embedded in culturally salient idioms of purity, embodiment, sexuality, fertility, and "enclosedness." The local meaning of FC expands well beyond stereotypical notions of male coital satisfaction.

Is FC Medically Harmful?

Perhaps the greatest complicating factor in the moral evaluation of FC by anthropology is that these rites are largely practiced—and advocated—by women. But isn't FC medically harmful to women? The anthropological response is equivocal. Medical complications such as infertility do occur (Gordon 1991, Gruenbaum 1982, Inhorn & Buss 1993, Larson 2002).[13] Still, several anthropologists deemed that these perils have been overly—if not unjustly—magnified in the popular imagination, because this view of FC portrays Africans, especially African women, as passive victims of their own ignorance and of patriarchy, wholly wounded in body and spirit, devoid of any possible joy, erotic or otherwise. In effect, this view of FC offers the West justification for intervention and, more subtly, assertions of cultural superiority. Anthropologists increasingly contest the view of African women as mutilated and imprisoned by a physiological mar of their own making (Ahmadu 2000, Gruenbaum 1996, Walley 1997; cf. Balk 2000). In turn, these anthropologists are themselves contested. Obermeyer (1999) concluded that most accounts of the medical, sexual, and reproductive horrors of FC are lacking in

---

[12]A boy's grandmother wore his foreskin as a ring (Boddy 1982, p. 688), a practice similar to that of a medieval female mystic who wedded Christ with the Holy Prepuce (Bynum 1987, pp. 174–75).

[13]Jackson et al. (2003) discussed inconsistencies in self-reporting.

scientific evidence (see also Stewart et al. 2002). Mackie (2003) strongly refuted this claim, prompting an accusation of selective reading (Obermeyer 2003). At stake in this debate is the relationship between anthropology and advocacy. In addition, a meta-debate is taking place over the definition of valid data in regard to this emotionally charged issue.

Because FC seems so horrifying, one could argue that it might be best to suspend the standards that define rigorous empirical science so that we can attend to the sheer anguish. The issue is humanistic. But, because FC is a physiological and medical issue, too, one could also argue that all legitimate claims must be supported by the highest standards of empirical research. The issue is now one of science. Therein, I suggest, lies much of the methodological quandary.

How to Respond?

The ethical dimensions of FC in anthropology are bitterly disputed. Most anthropologists who study FC do not condone the rite. But they temper their criticism in order to advocate on behalf of subjected women while not reproducing stereotypes that continue to silence African and Muslim women. We often read that, despite FC, Africans are not ignorant, are not in need of Western salvation, and are not immobilized psychologically by brute patriarchy. Moreover, the accusatory finger is often pointed at us: Clitoridectomy was not uncommon in Victorian England and America (Sheehan 1981), and the practice still persists, or did so until recently, on the fringes of Western medicine.[14] Furthermore, many African and Muslim women are appalled at our standards of beauty, honor, and dignity.

A telling exchange of views followed Gordon (1991), who positioned FC just outside the limits of relativist acceptance (see also Salmon 1997). What about our own treatment of women's bodies?, asked Boddy (1991). Moreover, to condemn the rite often seems like a vacuous gesture, a mere classroom exercise. And what right have we to criticize them? Morsy (1991) excoriated the "Western civilizational project" that underlies opposition to FC. [In fairness, most anthropologists believe that all efforts to curtail FC ultimately must arise from local women (Gruenbaum 1982).] Scheper-Hughes (1991) commented on the (unjustified, in her view) practice of MC in the United States.[15] For these anthropologists, criticism against FC is misguided at best and racist at worst.

Yet some anthropologists strongly object to FC. van der Kwaak (1992) dismissed appeals to cultural relativism and, although acknowledging the validity of local beliefs, endorsed eradication. Oboler (2001) objected to FC primarily because of lack of consent, as do most opponents of routine neonatal MC (see below).

---

[14]Dr. William Burt of Akron, Ohio, the so-called "Love Doctor," surgically altered scores of clitorises of both consenting and nonconsenting women to enhance, not stifle, their sexual pleasure, and even published a book in 1975, *Love Surgery*. His practice ended in 1989.

[15]In the past, anthropologists often defended MC against colonial, missionary, and European sensibilities as moral, not carnal (e.g., Browne 1913, p. 140; Mayer 1971; Tucker 1949, p. 59). Today, anthropology more often is ambivalent (Heald 1986).

Many women who experience or suffer FC did not grant informed consent and were culturally unable to do so.

Shweder (2000, 2002) argued that the extraordinary moral outrage evoked by the very idea of FC stymies true pluralism, because "seeing the cultural point and getting the scientific facts straight is where tolerance begins." For him, one fact is clear: That FC seems beyond discussion is precisely the reason why the issue warrants anthropological skepticism. How should we respond? With ambivalence, perhaps.

Agency, Not Patriarchy

Alice Walker's celebrated book, *Possessing the Secret of Joy*, and her more recent film and literary collaboration *Warrior Marks* significantly raised public awareness of FC. To most anthropologists, though, these works seem somewhat naive. Worse, they may reproduce antiquated, even racist, images of Africa as a Hobbesian place of savage brutality in need of American healing (Babatunde 1998, James 1998).

Western responses to FC today emerge typically from visceral reactions, not from informed knowledge as defined by the sensibilities and canons of anthropology (Gruenbaum 1996). Consequently, critics of FC portray circumcised women as ignorant, hapless, traumatized victims of a brutal patriarchy. This characterization denies to many African women the capacity for agency, decision making, and legitimate consciousness (Abusharaf 2001, Hayes 1975, Walley 1997). African and Muslim cultures are oppressive and insane; Western culture is ennobling and free. They are enslaved to an evil, irrational tradition; we transcend tradition through rationality. They subsume individuality within the collectivity; we applaud the person who stands above the crowd. Therefore, as a consequence of a type of moral manifest destiny, we must change them.

However, for many African women, FC and its attendant meanings "are means whereby the limitations of ascribed inferiority are overcome . . . they use, perhaps unconsciously, perhaps strategically, what we in the West might prefer to consider instruments of their oppression as means to assert their value" (Boddy 1989, p. 345; see also Omorodion 1991, Skinner 1988). Rites we see as horribly demeaning are a form of symbolic capital to alleged victims, gaining them access to custom, community, virtue, and morality. FC even allows some women to contest, not accede to, patriarchy, and to define, not erode, their self-worth.

For critics, FC betokens a lack of power and control. But some instances of FC give local women a sense of control so that they can become socially relevant actors in a highly gendered world (Abusharaf 2001, Kratz 1994). By cutting off undesirable sexuality, FC allows women the inner psychological strength to manipulate their husbands who, in various Islamic settings, lack any such control over their own sexuality. FC violates no human rights, claimed the Sudanese women studied by Abusharaf (2001). To them, the rite was deeply meaningful, in part because they understood the human whose rights we are discussing in vastly different terms. Although FC rites are often painful, Walley (1997, p. 422) pointed out that women who undergo the rite may attribute significant social meanings to their ability to endure it. We may shudder at the thought of FC, but they viewed the pain as something to be endured, not avoided, because it fostered positive transformations of the self (Johnson 2000).[16]

However much Westerners might yearn to save and enlighten African women—neglecting, typically, to ask whether they want this salvation—the means of our assistance unwittingly might exacerbate the muteness of the circumcised subaltern. The clash between moral universes is particularly acute for women in the African and Islamic diaspora who wish to continue the rite (Gallo 1992b, Johnsdotter 2002). Moreover, the current obsession in the West with addressing FC seems routinely to detract from far more pressing and lethal forms of everyday oppression such as lack of land, food, and clean water, not to mention war, drought, and international isolation (Abusharaf 1998; Gruenbaum 1996; Mandara 2000, p. 104; Omorodion & Myers 1989). It is always easier to oppose their rites than our wrongs.

Circumcision and History, Theirs and Ours

I have alluded repeatedly to the importance of history in understanding the meanings of different forms of male and female circumcision. Rarely, however, do anthropologists embed the rite in wider changes of bodily practices associated with colonialism, diaspora, and modernity (cf. Comaroff 1985). Middleton (1997) presented an insightful exception. A Madagascar people who once practiced circumcision in order "to have a history" have forgone the rite to recollect a more recent history of "impotence and defeat." This discontinuation of MC was a conscious practice, not a passive acquiescence to colonialism. By making taboo circumcision and other ancestral activities, absence becomes a form of omnipresent memory.[17]

Is it possible that many women practice FC today for a similar reason? Perhaps the rite is a response to modernity and the lack of memory that the modernist project implies. At the very least, many Third World women do not see eye-to-eye with First World feminists on FC. To them, our opposition is part of a long history of colonialism. Perhaps FC resists certain aspects of modernity, or helps transform modernity from a monolithic conception into a vernacular reality that both accedes to and yet defies the Western assumptions of the world system and development.

As Parker (1999) demonstrated, most Western accounts of FC tell us far more about our own historically embedded sexual anxieties and subjectivities. Beginning in the mid-twentieth century, female selfhood entailed the capacity to experience orgasm (and, for the male, the ability to make this happen). From this point of view, the salience of FC in anthropology and wider public discourses is about our history, not their practices. In this regard, it is noteworthy that anthropologists

---

[16]The ritual role of bodily pain remains undertheorized (but see Whitehouse 2000).
[17]Jewish, especially mystical, traditions inscribed memory in the space once occupied by the foreskin, a notion captivating to Derrida (Wolfson 2002).

troubled by uncritical condemnations of FC almost never refer to an obvious aspect of Western history: the long-standing rhetoric against Jewish circumcision. Critics of Jewish particularism since the medieval era—actually, since the letters of Paul—have painted Jewish circumcision with the same colors of barbarism and ignorance that now so frequently taint Africans and Muslims (Gilman 1999, Lyons 1981).[18] To the extent that European objections to Jewish circumcision often are rooted in the bodily assumptions of Pauline-Hellenistic Christianity, opposition to FC may be seen as a similar form of bodily imperialism. (To this, some foes will respond, So what?) Moreover, opposition to FC tends to arise from unstated culture-specific and historical notions of citizenship, statehood, individualism, and intrinsic rights (Droz 2000). For many Westerners, a woman's vagina (and a man's foreskin) is the individual's intrinsic property. But this individualism clashes with cultural epistemologies in which foreskins and pudenda have importance that expands beyond the individual's rights (Talle 1993).

To further complicate the picture, young girls in at least one traditionally non-circumcising region of Africa (southern Chad) now practice FC for reasons that are unclear but seem linked with notions of modernity, not primitivism (Leonard 2000a). There, FC is a "fashion statement, a fad, something that is fun, rebellious, and cool" (Leonard 2000b, p. 190). When Leonard continued to query a woman about this novel rite, she was scolded: "You are looking too hard—there is nothing."

So, What to Do?

Anthropologists suggest a number of practical ways of reducing or challenging FC. Oboler (2001) drew on Mackie's (1996) analogy with Chinese antifootbinding societies to propose the formation of anti-FGM associations. These groups could foster local marriage "markets" for women in regions where the rite is linked to male matrimonial desire. This way, women who decline FC could still marry. Because medical complications are uncommon in some areas, over-reaction might be detrimental. Rather, the introduction of "correct information about negative consequences...in general education programmes" should suffice (Myers et al. 1985).[19] And, although some anthropologists have defended legal bans as providing moral support to public education campaigns (Oboler 2001), others have suggested that the illegality of FC might drive the procedure underground, thus increasing potential harm. Instead, FC would be best ameliorated through medicalization (Shell-Duncan 2001; see also Browne 1991). However, this argument may prove as unsavory to opponents of FC as recent developments in penile nerve blocks are to foes of routine MC: It simply makes a bad practice acceptable (Mandara 2000, pp. 103–4). No position about FC lacks moral and immoral implications.

---

[18]One also might recall the fearful bodily image of the licentious African woman, marred by an enlarged clitoris (the so-called "Hottentot apron") that cautioned Victorian women against succumbing to sexual excess.

[19]For examples of public campaigns against FC, see Creel et al. (2001), El-Gibaly et al. (2002), Gosselin (2000), and Hernlund (2000).

Fuambai Ahmadu, a Sierra Leonean raised in the United States, while pursuing an Anthropology PhD, returned to her natal Kono village to undergo FC (Ahmadu 2000). Ahmadu's circumcision initiation into the "secret women's society" failed to dampen her sexuality. She discovered also that Kono women derive considerable empowerment from the rite. Through "supernatural" associations, they can assert legitimate ritual leadership, thus arresting the possibility of male hegemony. Ahmadu maintained that the experiences of Kono women with FC contradict the Western assertion that the rite is a devastating violation of African women.

Ahmadu spoke, if not for all African woman, at least to a point many African voices have raised in the recent anthropological literature. Although some African women have opposed FC, others view Western opposition to the rite as another form of colonial domination. For this reason, many anthropologists have drawn attention to debates within cultures that practice FC (Gruenbaum 1996), listening carefully to women, and not criminalizing them (Abusharaf 2001). In other words, ruptures within official cultural ideologies present opportunities for Western critics to engage circumcised rites, wrongs, and rights.

OPPOSITION TO MALE CIRCUMCISION AS AN ANTHROPOLOGICAL PROBLEM

Opposition to FC is well known and common. Less obvious to anthropologists is an equally vociferous, diverse movement that opposes the routine medical and ritual circumcision of infant boys in the West (e.g., Denniston et al. 1997, 1999; Goldman 1997). The number and acronymic flamboyance of these activist groups are staggering, even occasionally absurd and self-mocking. But these groups are serious, and it would be incorrect to dismiss them as the fringe. They are fast moving to the center of legal, medical, and moral discourse. And they are both very angry and very aggressive.

A partial list of anti-MC groups includes NOCIRC (National Organization of Circumcision Resources), INTACT (Infants Need to Avoid Circumcision Trauma), UNCIRC (Uncircumcising Information and Resources Center), D.O.C. (Doctors Opposing Circumcision), NOHARMM (National Organization to Halt the Abuse and Routine Mutilation of Males), MUSIC (Musicians United to Stop Involuntary Circumcision), Boys Too (as in "Boys Too Deserve the Same Protection as Girls"), Mothers Against Circumcision, OUCH (Outlaw Unnecessary Circumcision in Hospitals), S.I.C. Society (Stop Infant Circumcision Society), Nurses for the Rights of the Child, ARC (Attorneys for the Rights of the Child), and In Memory of the Sexually Mutilated Child. Nearly all these organizations maintain elaborate Web sites which are worth viewing, regardless of one's position.

Much of the anti-MC movement draws moral support from the origins of the medical rite in late-nineteenth-century Victorian America. Then, the health of bodies and the body politic were believed to hinge on an economy of sexual desire and "vital" nervous energy. Also prominent was widespread concern with moral-physical hygiene, fueled in part by the arrival of new immigrants. Male circumcision emerged as a routine medical practice from specific historical anxieties. This procedure insured against youthful masturbation, a scourge then thought to spawn a host of psychological, social, and physiological ailments (Gollaher 2000). Here, as elsewhere, culture was scripted in a bodily idiom.

To contemporary opponents of MC (who prefer the term "prointact" or "genital integrity"), recent medical justifications for the rite are little different than those proffered in the late nineteenth century. Moreover, foes of MC today attribute a broad range of social and psychological ailments to infant MC, including, post-traumatic stress disorder, low self-esteem, depression, inferiority, envy of "intact men," rage, resentment, hate, fear, diminished body image, guilt, and obsession with penis size. Circumcised men express, in the uniquely modern American practice of public confession, their intimate experiences with sexual dysfunction, poor relationships, and feelings of parental betrayal, violation, victimization, power-lessness, distrust, shame, abuse, deformity, and alienation. Circumcised men who oppose MC have often likened the procedure to rape and maternal abandonment. Consequently, it is often said that circumcised men are more likely to abuse and rape women. Others have asserted that circumcision made them gay.

Many circumcision foes, emboldened by studies of genuine childhood neglect and abuse, have attributed a host of societal woes to the trauma of male circumcision—alcoholism, drug addiction, violence, teenage suicide, low productivity, theft, and divorce. Having lost their errogenously sensitive foreskin, circumcisied men are driven to "unnatural" sexual practices such as fellatio and "deep" intercourse. Goldman (1997), who received a radiant endorsement from a noted anthropologist (Montagu 1995), shockingly proposed that the trauma of infant circumcision sometimes results in Sudden Infant Death Syndrome (SIDS) as a form of "infant suicide." MC illustrates the insidious power of matriarchy, since mothers allow their sons to be cut, as well as the insidious power of patriarchy that rips helpless infants from their mothers' loving arms. We all suffer: The social implications of MC result in fiscal burdens through rising medical costs and taxes to fund crime prevention, prisons, law enforcement, and welfare programs.

But all is not lost for the emotionally disabled, sexually stilted, foreskinless man. Men now can restore their foreskins, and join self-help groups such as NORM (National Organization of Restoring Men; http://www.norm.org), formerly known as RECAP ("RECover A Penis"), and BUFF (Brothers United for Future Fore-skins). Non-surgical restoration methods include stretching the existing skin over the glans with various devices such as lead fishing weights, steel balls, weighted cones, external catheters, infant bottle nipples, and several commercial devices (e.g., VacuTrac, Foreballs, and Tug Ahoy).

Circumcisers, as they are called after the cognate term "abortionist," are routinely derided as perverts, sadists, and Nazis. Circumcised men deny their own "primal wounding." Denial leads to repetition-compulsion. Hence, cut physicians sadistically cut defenseless infants (and women) to reenact their own trauma. So outraged are circumcised men by the sight of the foreskinned penis that they inflict this torture on the very babies they father!

Many opponents of routine medical and religious MC have mobilized the same moral and legal arguments as are used in opposition to FC, including notions of consent and appeals to international treaties such as the U.N. Convention on the Rights of the Child, the U.N. Convention Against Torture, and the European Convention on Human Rights. Indeed, a common refrain has been that the global concern with FC neglects the equally harmful effects of MC, thus further attesting to the broad societal denigration of the male body and psyche. According to this view, it is an easy step from cutting off foreskins to cutting away men's emotions and sending them off to war.

FC is now illegal in the United States. In 1996, Congress passed the "Federal Prohibition of Female Genital Mutilation Act" (S.1030), initiated by Representative Pat Schroeder. Many legal challenges to MC in US courts appeal on this basis to the equal protection clause of the fourteenth Amendment.

I propose that, for many opponents of the procedure, MC is a potent symbol of anxieties that are not linked directly to the penis. Rather, the lost foreskin symbolizes a series of modern losses arising from historically specific anxieties (Silverman 2000). These anxieties concern the lost effectiveness of the political, economic, and judicial processes; pluralism; violence; contested notions of masculinity, motherhood, sexuality, and gender; the medicalization of birth; vulnerability before technological advances; notions of personhood similar to those raised in the abortion debate; and the hypercapitalist commodification of the body. Opposition to MC, widely hailed by the mythopoetic men's movement, also has revealed an enduring and disturbing antisemitism (Silverman n.d.).

I have devoted considerable space to discussing the anti-MC movement, not because I find it morally compelling or equivalent to the debate over FC, but because I believe the growing opposition to MC is a fascinating, occasionally deeply disturbing cultural phenomenon which is unknown to most anthropologists, but surely is worthy of sustained investigation.

CONCLUSION

Because FC—both the rite and the popular discourse—is so important to the public, it deserves further anthropological investigation. As I have tried to make clear, it cannot be assumed that strong opposition to circumcision occurs only in the case of FC. But opponents of MC have received virtually no anthropological attention.

Anthropology should redouble its efforts to compile further ethnographic and historical research on circumcision, to fine-tune relevant methodologies such as gender theory and ritual theory, to investigate the relationship between circumcision and HIV, and to embed the opposition to all forms of circumcision in the contemporary cultural milieu. Indeed, I have argued that the fact that the practice of circumcision is or is not a topic of study is no less an object of anthropological concern than is the practice itself.

Circumcision offers anthropology an opportunity to examine our sense of who we are as a discipline that remains tethered to a Western tradition that aspires to pluralism, yet refuses to cede certain long-standing (if not God-given) tenets of the body and self. We can reflect on what is going on in our own cultural systems, and we can rethink how we want to engage morally such vital issues as human rights and cultural relativism. To the extent that many of us are ensconced within the relative safety of the classroom or book-lined office, the topic of circumcision also offers us an opportunity to escape the claim that we are, or might become, irrelevant.

All too frequently, public, legislative, and even scholarly opinions about MC and FC lack the measured, nuanced, careful understanding that most of us value as the signature of the anthropological project. Often, it seems nonanthropologists are not interested in what we have to say, or how we say it.

One has the nagging suspicion that, in the end, the topic of circumcision presents anthropology with something of an identity crisis. Well-intentioned folks such as Pat Schroeder and Alice Walker successfully oppose FC on the basis of little anthropological knowledge. If anthropologists merely agree with them, what unique insight do we have to offer? If we disagree, who will pay attention to us?

As the wider world debates FC and MC, it behooves us to enter the fray to justify anthropology as a unique, legitimate, and serious endeavor. We had better have something important to say. I think we do, and I think it can be found in the sources I have here reviewed. But does the rest of the world agree? I am not sure.

The *Annual Review of Anthropology* is online at http://anthro.annualreviews.org

LITERATURE CITED

Abusharaf RM. 1998. Unmasking tradition: a Sudanese anthropologist confronts female "circumcision" and its terrible tenacity. *Sciences* 38:22–28

Abusharaf RM. 2001. Virtuous cuts: female genital circumcision in an African ontology. *Differences* 12:112–40

Ahmadu F. 2000. Rites and wrongs: an insider/outsider reflects on power and excision. See Shell-Duncan & Hernlund 2000, pp. 283–312

Ammar H. 1954. *Growing Up in an Egyptian Village*. London: Routledge & Kegan Paul

Ashley-Montagu MF. 1937. The origin of subincision in Australia. *Oceania* 8:193–207

Aufinger A. 1941. Einige ethnographische notizen zur beschneidung in Neuguinea. *Ethnos* 6:25–39

Auvert B, Buve A, Lagarde E, Kahindo M, Chege J, et al. 2001. Male circumcision and HIV infection in four cities in sub-Saharan Africa. *AIDS* 15:S31–40

Babatunde E. 1998. *Women's Rites Versus Women's Rights: A Study of Circumcision Among the Ketu Yoruba of Southwestern Nigeria*. Trenton, NJ: Africa World Press

Bailey R, Muga R, Poulussen R, Abicht H. 2002. The acceptability of male circumcision to reduce HIV infections in Nyanza province, Kenya. *AIDS Care* 14:27–40

Bailey RC, Plummer FA, Moses S. 2001. Male circumcision and HIV prevention: current knowledge and future research directions. *Lancet Infect. Dis.* 1:223–31

Balk D. 2000. To marry and bear children: the demographic consequences of infibulation in

Sudan. See Shell-Duncan & Hernlund 2000, pp. 55–71

Barry H III, Schlegel A. 1980. Early childhood precursors of adolescent initiation ceremonies. *Ethos* 8:132–45

Beidelman TO. 1964. Pig (guluwe): an essay on Ngulu sexual symbolism and ceremony. *Southwest. J. Anthropol.* 20:359–92

Beidelman TO. 1965. Notes on boys' initiation among the Ngulu of East Africa. *Man* 65:143–47

Beidelman TO. 1997. *The Cool Knife: Imagery of Gender, Sexuality, and Moral Education in Kaguru Initiation Ritual.* Washington, DC: Smithsonian Inst. Press

Bettelheim B. 1954. *Symbolic Wounds: Puberty Rites and the Envious Male.* Glencoe, IL: Free Press

Bilu Y. 2000. Circumcision, the first haircut and the Torah: ritual and male identity among the Ultraorthodox community of contemporary Israel. In *Imagined Masculinities: Male Identity and Culture in the Modern Middle East,* ed. M Ghoussoub, E Sinclair-Webb, pp. 33–63. London: Saqi Books

Bloch M. 1986. *From Blessing to Violence: History and Deology in the Circumcision Ritual of the Merina of Madagascar.* Cambridge: Cambridge Univ. Press

Bloch M. 1992. *Prey Into Hunter: The Politics of Religious Experience.* Cambridge: Cambridge Univ. Press

Boddy J. 1982. Womb as oasis: The symbolic context of pharaonic circumcision in rural Northern Sudan. *Am. Ethnol.* 9:682–98

Boddy J. 1989. *Wombs and Alien Spirits: Women, Men and the Zar Cult in Northern Sudan.* Madison: Univ. Wisc. Press

Boddy J. 1991. Body Politics: continuing the anticircumcision crusade. *Med. Anthropol. Q.* 5:15–17

Boddy J. 1996. Violence embodied? Circumcision, gender politics, and Cultural aesthetics. In *Rethinking Violence Against Women,* ed. RE Dobash, RP Dobash, pp. 77–110. Thousand Oaks, CA: Sage

Bohannan P. 1954. Circumcision among the Tiv. *Man* 54:2–6

Bonner K. 2001. Male circumcision as an HIV control strategy: not a 'natural condom'. *Reproduc. Health Matters* 9:143–55

Boon JA. 1999. Circumcision/uncircumcision: an essay amidst the history of a difficult description. In *Implicit Understandings: Observing, Reporting, and Reflecting on the Encounters Between Europeans and Other Peoples in the Early Modern Era,* ed. SB Schwartz, pp. 556–85. Cambridge: Cambridge Univ. Press

Boyarin D. 1992. "This we know to be the carnal Israel": circumcision and the erotic life of God and Israel. *Crit. Inq.* 18:474–502

Boyarin D. 1994. *A Radical Jew: Paul and the Politics of Identity.* Berkeley: Univ. Calif. Press

Boyarin D. 1997. *Unheroic Conduct: The Rise of Heterosexuality and the Invention of the Jewish Man.* Berkeley: Univ. Calif. Press

Boyarin J, Boyarin D. 1995. Self-exposure as theory: the double-mark of the male Jew. In *Rhetorics of Self-Making,* ed. D Battaglia, pp. 16–42. Berkeley: Univ. Calif. Press

Brauer E. 1942. The Jews of Afghanistan: an anthropological report. *Jew. Soc. Stud.* 4:121–38

Brauer E. 1947. *The Jews of Kurdistan.* Transl. R Patai, 1993. Detroit: Wayne State Univ. Press (From Hebrew)

Brewster AB. 1919. Circumcision in Noikoro, Noemalu and Mboumbudho. *J. R. Anthropol. Inst.* 49:309–16

Brown DE, Edwards JW, Moore RP. 1988. *The Penis Inserts of Southeast Asia: An Annotated Bibliography with an Overview and Comparative Perspectives.* Occ. Pap. 15, C. South Southeast Asia Stud., Univ. Calif., Berkeley

Brown JE, Micheni KD, Grant EM, Mwenda JM, Muthiri FM, Grant AR. 2001. Varieties of male circumcision: a study from Kenya. *Sex. Transm. Dis.* 28:608–12

Brown JT. 1921. Circumcision rites of the Becwana tribes. *J. R. Anthropol. Inst.* 51:419–27

Browne DL. 1991. Christian missionaries,

Western feminists, and the Kikuyu clitoridectomy controversy. In *Politics of Culture*, ed. B Williams, pp. 243–42. Washington, DC: Smithsonian Inst. Press

Browne GStJO. 1913. Circumcision ceremonies among the Amwimbe. *Man* 13:137–40

Burridge K. 1969. *Tangu Traditions: A Study of the Way of Life, Mythology, and Developing Experience of a New Guinea People*. Oxford: Clarendon Press

Burton RV, Whiting JWM. 1961. The absent father and cross-sex identity. *Merrill-Palmer Q. Behav. Develop.* 7:85–95

Bynum CW. 1987. *Holy Feast and Holy Fast: The Religious Significance of Food to Medieval Women*. Berkeley: Univ. Calif. Press

Cansever G. 1965. Psychological effects of circumcision. *Br. J. Psychol.* 38:321–31

Carpenter MW. 1988. "A bit of her flesh": circumcision and "the signification of the phallus" in *Daniel Deronda. Genders* 1:1–23

Comaroff J. 1985. *Body of Power, Spirit of Resistance: The Culture and History of a South African Power*. Chicago: Univ. Chicago Press

Crapanzano V. 1981. Rite of return. *Psychoanal. Stud. Soc.* 9:15–36

Creel E. 2001. *Abandoning Female Genital Cutting: Prevalence, Attitudes, and Efforts to End the Practice*. Washington, DC: Popul. Ref. Bur. http://www.prb.org/pdf/AbandoningFGC_Eng.pdf

Crosse-Upcott ARW. 1959. Male circumcision among the Ngindo. *J. R. Anthropol. Inst.* 89:169–89

Daly CD. 1950. The psycho-biological origins of circumcision. *Int. J. Psychoanal.* 31:217–36

de Heusch L. 1985. *Sacrifice in Africa: A Structuralist Approach*. Bloomington: Indiana Univ. Press

Delaney C. 1991. *The Seed and the Soil: Gender and Cosmology in Turkish Village Society*. Berkeley: Univ. Calif. Press

Delaney C. 1998. *Abraham on Trial: The Social Legacy of Biblical Myth*. Princeton, NJ: Princeton Univ. Press

Delaney C. 2001. Cutting the ties that bind: the sacrifice of Abraham and patriarchal kinship. In *Relative Values: Reconfiguring Kinship Studies*, ed. S Franklin, S McKinnon, pp. 445–67. Durham, NC: Duke Univ. Press

Denniston GC, Hodges FM, Milos MF, ed. 1999. *Male and Female Circumcision: Medical, Legal, and Ethical Considerations in Pediatric Practice*. New York: Kluwer Academic/Plenum

Denniston GC, Milos MF, ed. 1997. *Sexual Mutilations: A Human Tragedy*. New York: Plenum

Droz Y. 2000. Circoncision féminine et masculine en pays kikuyu. *Cahiers d'Études Africaines* 158:215–40

Eilberg-Schwartz H. 1990. *The Savage in Judaism: An Anthropology of Israelite Religion and Ancient Judaism*. Bloomington: Indiana Univ. Press

El-Gibaly O, Ibrahim B, Mensch BS, Clark WH. 2002. The decline of female circumcision in Egypt: evidence and interpretation. *Soc. Sci. Med.* 54:205–20

Firth R. 1936. *We, the Tikopia: Kinship in Primitive Polynesia*. Boston: Beacon

Frazer JG. 1904. The origins of circumcision. *Indep. Rev.* 4:204–18

Gallo PG. 1992a. The origin of infibulation in Somalia: an ethological hypothesis. *Ethnol. Sociobiol.* 13:253–65

Gallo PG. 1992b. Les mutilationes genitales feminines des Africains en Italie. *Rivista di Antropologia* 70:175–83

Geertz C. 1960. *The Religion of Java*. Glencoe, IL: Free Press

Gell AF. 1971. Penis sheathing and ritual status in a West Sepik village. *Man* 6:165–81

Gilman SL. 1991. *The Jew's Body*. New York: Routledge

Gilman SL. 1993. *Freud, Race, and Gender*. Princeton: Princeton Univ. Press

Gilman SL. 1999. "Barbaric" rituals? In *Is Multiculturalism Bad for Women?*, ed. J Cohen, M Howard, MC Nussbaum, pp. 53–58. Princeton, NJ: Princeton Univ Press

Gluckman M. 1949. The role of the sexes in Wiko circumcision ceremonies. In

Social Structure: Studies Presented to A.R. Radcliffe-Brown, ed. M Fortes, pp. 145–67. Oxford: Clarendon

Goldberg HE. 1996. Cambridge in the land of Canaan: descent, alliance, circumcision, and instruction in the Bible. J. Anc. Near E. Soc. 24:9–34

Goldberg HE. 2003. Jewish Passages: Cycles of Jewish Life. Berkeley: Univ. Calif. Press

Goldman R. 1997. Circumcision: The Hidden Trauma. Boston: Vanguard

Gollaher D. 2000. Circumcision: A History of the World's Most Controversial Surgery. New York: Basic Books

Gordon D. 1991. Female circumcision and genital operations in Egypt and the Sudan: a dilemma for medical anthropology. Med. Anthropol. Q. 5:3–14

Gosselin C. 2000. Handing over the knife: Numu women and the campaign against excision in Mali. See Shell-Duncan & Hernlund 2000, pp. 193–214

Graber RB. 1981. A psychocultural theory of male genital mutilation. J. Psychoanal. Anthropol. 4:413–34

Gruenbaum E. 1982. The movement against clitoridectomy and infibulation in Sudan: public health policy and the women's movement. Med. Anthropol. Newsl. 13:4–12

Gruenbaum E. 1996. The cultural debate over female circumcision: the Sudanese are arguing this one out for themselves. Med. Anthropol. Q. 10:455–75

Gruenbaum E. 2001. The Female Circumcision Controversy: An Anthropological Perspective. Philadelphia: Temple Univ. Press

Halperin DT. 1999. Dry sex practices and HIV infection in the Dominican Republic and Haiti. Sex. Transm. Infect. 75:445–46

Halperin DT. 2000. Cut and dry: reviving male circumcision and introducing dry sex prevention in South Africa and Botswana. Presented at Annu. Meet. Am. Anthropol. Assoc., 99th, San Francisco

Halperin DT, Bailey RC. 1999. Male circumcision and HIV infection: 10 years and counting. Lancet 354:1813–15

Hambly WD. 1935. Tribal initiation of boys in Angola. Am. Anthropol. 37:36–40

Harrington C. 1968. Sexual differentiation in socialization and some male genital mutilations. Am. Anthropol. 70:951–56

Hayes RO. 1975. Female genital mutilation, fertility control, women's roles, and the patrilineal in modern Sudan: a functional analysis. Am. Ethnol. 2:617–33

Heald S. 1986. The ritual use of violence: circumcision among the Gisu of Uganda. In The Anthropology of Violence, ed. D Riches, pp. 70–85. London: Basil Blackwell

Heald S. 1994. Every man a hero: Oedipal themes in Gisu circumcision. In Anthropology and Psychoanalysis: An Encounter Through Cultures, ed. S Heald, A Deluz, pp. 184–209. London: Routledge

Hernlund Y. 2000. Cutting without ritual and ritual without cutting: Female "circumcision" and the re-ritualization of initiation in the Gambia. See Shell-Duncan & Hernlund 2000, pp. 235–52

Hiatt LR. 1994. Indulgent fathers and collective male violence. In Anthropology and Psychoanalysis: An Encounter Through Cultures, eds. S Heald and A Deluz, pp. 171–83. London: Routledge

Hodges FM, Svoboda JS, Van Howe RS. 2002. Prophylactic interventions on children: balancing human rights with public health. J. Med. Ethics 28:10–16

Hoffman LA. 1996. Covenant of Blood: Circumcision and Gender in Rabbinic Judaism. Chicago: Univ. Chicago Press

Hogbin I. 1970. The Island of Menstruating Men: Religion in Wogeo, New Guinea. Scranton: Chandler

Holdredge CP, Young K. 1927. Circumcision rites among the Bajok. Am. Anthropol. 29:661–69

Immerman RS, Mackey WC. 1997. A biocultural analysis of circumcision. Soc. Biol. 44:265–75

Immerman RS, Mackey WC. 1998. A proposed relationship between circumcision and neural reorganization. J. Genet. Psychol. 159:367–378

Inhorn MC, Buss KA. 1993. Infertility, infection, and iatrogenesis in Egypt: the anthropological epidemiology of blocked tubes. *Med. Anthropol.* 15:217–44

Jackson EF, Akweongo P, Sakeah E, Hodgson A, Asuru R, Phillips JF. 2003. *Women's Denial of Having Experienced Female Genital Cutting in Northern Ghana: Explanatory Factors and Consequences for Analysis of Survey Data.* New York: Popul. Counc. http://www.popcouncil.org/pdfs/wp/178.pdf

James SM. 1998. Shades of othering: reflections on female circumcision/genital mutilation. *Signs* 23:1031–48

Jenkins C, Alpersi M. 1996. Urbanization, youth and sexuality: insights for an AIDS campaign for youth in Papua New Guinea. *PNG Med. J.* 39:248–51

Jensen AE. 1933. *Beschneidung und Reifezeremonien bei Naturvöölkern.* Stuttgart: Strecker und Schrööder

Johnsdotter S. 2002. *Created by God: How Somalis in Swedish Exile Reassess the Practice of Female Circumcision.* Lund: Lund Monogr. Soc. Anthropol.

Johnson MC. 2000. Becoming a Muslim, becoming a person: female "circumcision," religious identity, and personhood in Guinea-Bissau. See Shell-Duncan & Hernlund 2000, pp. 215–33

Kebaabetswe P, Lockman S, Mogwe S, Mandevu R, Thior I, et al. 2003. Male circumcision: an acceptable strategy for HIV prevention in Botswana. *Sex. Transm. Infect.* 79:214–19

Kempf W. 2002. The politics of incorporation: masculinity, spatiality and modernity among the Ngaing of Papua New Guinea. *Oceania* 73:56–78

Kennedy JG. 1970. Circumcision and excision in Egyptian Nubia. *Man* (NS) 5:175–91

Kenyatta J. 1959. *Facing Mount Kenya: The Tribal Life of the Gikuyu.* London: Secker & Warburg

Kitahara M. 1974. Living quarter arrangements in polygyny and circumcision and segregation of males at puberty. *Ethnology* 13:401–13

Kitahara M. 1976. A cross-cultural test of the Freudian theory of circumcision. *Int. J. Psychoanal. Psychother.* 5:535–46

Kratz C. 1994. *Affecting Performance: Meaning, Movement, and Experience in Okiek Women's Initiation.* Washington, DC: Smithsonian Inst. Press

Kratz C. 1999. Contexts, controversies, dilemmas: teaching circumcision. In *Great Ideas for Teaching About Africa*, ed. ML Bastian, JL Parpart, pp. 103–18. Boulder: Lynne Rienner

Kunin SD. 1996. The bridegroom of blood: a Structuralist analysis. *J. Stud. O. T.* 70:3–16

La Fontaine JS. 1972. Ritualization of women's life-crises in Bugisu. In *The Interpretation of Ritual: Essays in Honour of A.I. Richards*, ed. JS La Fontaine, pp. 159–86. London: Tavistock

La Fontaine JS. 1985. *Initiation.* Manchester: Manchester Univ. Press

Lagarde E, Dirk T, Puren A, Reathe RT, Bertran A. 2003. Acceptability of male circumcision as a tool for preventing HIV infection in a highly infected community in South Africa. *AIDS* 17:89–95

Larsen U. 2002. The effects of type of female circumcision on infertility and fertility in Sudan. *J. Biosoc. Sci.* 34:363–77

Layard J. 1942. *Stone Men of Malekula.* London: Chatto & Windus

Leonard L. 2000a. 'We did it for pleasure only': hearing alternative tales of female circumcision. *Qual. Inq.* 6:212–28

Leonard L. 2000b. Adopting female "circumcision" in Southern Chad: the experience of Myabé. See Shell-Duncan & Hernlund 2000, pp. 167–91

Levine RA. 1959. An attempt to change the Gusii initiation cycle. *Man* 59:117–20

Lévi-Strauss C. 1988. Exode sur *Exode. L'Homme* 28:13–23

Levy RI. 1973. *Tahitians: Mind and Experience in the Society Islands.* Chicago: Univ. Chicago Press

Lewis G. 1980. *Day of Shining Red: An Essay on Understanding Ritual.* Cambridge: Cambridge Univ. Press

Loeb EM. 1923. *The Blood Sacrifice Complex.* Am. Anthropol. Assoc. Memoir, No. 30

Lyons H. 1981. Anthropologists, moralities, and relativities: the problem of genital mutilations. *Can. Rev. Sociol. Anthropol.* 18:499–518

Mackie G. 1996. Ending footbinding and infibulation: a convention account. *Am. Sociol. Rev.* 61:999–1017

Mackie G. 2003. Female genital cutting: a harmless procedure? *Med. Anthropol. Q.* 17:135–58

Mandara MU. 2000. Female genital cutting in Nigeria: views of Nigerian doctors on the medicalization debate. See Shell-Duncan & Hernlund 2000, pp. 95–107

Mayer P. 1952. Gusii initiation ceremonies. *J. R. Anthropol. Instit. of G. B. Ireland* 83:9–36

Mayer P. 1971. 'Traditional' manhood initiation in an industrial city: the African view. In *Man: Anthropological Essays Presented to O.F. Raum,* ed. EJ De Jager, pp. 7–18. Cape Town: C. Struik

McWilliam A. 1994. Case studies in dual classification as process: childbirth, headhunting and circumcision in West Timor. *Oceania* 65:59–74

Meek CK. 1931. *Tribal Studies in Northern Nigeria.* 2 vols. London: Paul, Trench, Trubner (Originally 1885)

Mehta D. 1996. Circumcision, body and community. *Contrib. Indian Sociol.* 30:215–43

Meintjes G. 1998. *Manhood at a Price: Socio-Medical Perspectives on Xhosa Traditional Circumcision.* Grahamstown, South Africa: Inst. Soc. Eco. Res., Rhodes Univ.

Mercier P. 1951. The social role of circumcision among the Besorube. *Am. Anthropol.* 53:326–37

Middleton K. 1997. Circumcision, death, and strangers. *J. Rel. Africa* 27:341–73

Mills AR. 1961. Ritual circumcision on Tanna, New Hebrides. *Man* 61:185

Miner H. 1942. Songhoi circumcision. *Am. Anthropol.* 44:621–37

Montagu A. 1995. Mutilated humanity. *Humanist* 55:12–15

Morgenstern J. 1966. *Rites of Birth, Marriage,*

Death, and Kindred Occasions Among the Semites.* Cincinnati: Hebrew Union Coll. Press

Morsy SA. 1991. Safeguarding women's bodies: the white man's burden medicalized. *Med. Anthropol. Q.* 5:19–23

Moses S, Bailey RC, Ronald AR. 1998. Male circumcision: assessment of health benefits and risks. *Sex. Transm. Infect.* 74:368–373

Muller J-C. 1993. Les deux fois circoncis et les presque excisees: le cas des Dii de l'Adamaoua (Nord Cameroun). *Cahiers d'Etudes Africaines* 33:531–44

Muller J-C. 2002. *Les Rites Initiatiques des Dii de l'Adamaoua (Cameroun).* Nanterre: Société d'Ethnologie

Myers RA, Omorodion FI, Isenalumhe AE, Akenzua GI. 1985. Circumcision: its nature and practice among some ethnic groups in Southern Nigeria. *Soc. Sci. Med.* 21:581–88

Natsoulas T. 1998. The politicization of the ban on female circumcision and the rise of the independent school movement in Kenya: the KCA, the missions and government, 1929–1932. *J. Asian Afr. Stud.* 33:137–58

Ngxamngxa ANN. 1971. The function of circumcision among Xhosa-speaking tribes in historical perspective. In *Man: Anthropological Essays Presented to O.F. Raum,* ed. EJ De Jager, pp. 183–204. Cape Town: C. Struik

Obermeyer CM. 1999. Female genital surgeries: the known, the unknown, and the unknowable. *Med. Anthropol. Q.* 13:79–106

Obermeyer CM. 2003. The health consequences of female circumcision: science, advocacy, and standards of evidence. *Med. Anthropol. Q.* 17:394–412

Oboler RS. 2001. Law and persuasion in the elimination of female genital mutilation. *Hum. Org.* 60:311–18

Omorodion FI, Myers RA. 1989. Reasons for female circumcision among some ethnic groups in Bendel State, Nigeria. *Afr. Stud. Monogr.* 9:197–207

Omorodion FI. 1991. Nature and practice of female circumcision among the Ubiaja people of Bendel State, Nigeria. *W. Afr. J. Archaeol.* 21:172–86

Ottenberg S. 1988. Oedipus, gender and social solidarity: a case study of male childhood and initiation. *Ethos* 16:326–52

Ozturk OM. 1973. Ritual circumcision and castration anxiety. *Psychiatry* 36:49–60

Paige KE, Paige JM. 1981. *The Politics of Reproductive Ritual*. Berkeley: Univ. Calif. Press

Parker M. 1999. Female circumcision and cultures of sexuality. In *Culture and Global Change*, ed. T Skelton, T Allen, pp. 201–11. London: Routledge

Patai R. 1983a. *On Jewish Folklore*. Detroit: Wayne State Univ. Press

Patai R. 1983b. Jewish birth customs. See Patai 1983a, pp. 337–43 (From Hebrew 1944–1965)

Patai R. 1983c. Sephardi folkore. See Patai 1983a, pp. 279–287 (Orig. unabridged 1960)

Paul RA. 1990. Bettelheim's contribution to anthropology. *Psychoanal. Stud. Soc.* 15:311–34

Paul RA. 1996. *Moses and Civilization: The Meaning Behind Freud's Myth*. New Haven, CT: Yale Univ. Press

Prewitt TJ. 1990. *The Elusive Covenant: A Structural-Semiotic Reading of Genesis*. Bloomington: Indiana Univ. Press

Quigley MA, Weiss HA, Hayes RJ. 2001. Male circumcision as a measure to control HIV infection and other sexually transmitted diseases. *Curr. Opin. Infect. Dis.* 14:71–75

Raum OF. 1940. *Chaga Childhood: A Description of Indigenous Education in an East African Tribe*. London: Int. Inst. Afr. Lang. Cult.

Róheim G. 1942. Transition rites. *Psychoanal. Q.* 11:336–74

Róheim G. 1945. *The Eternal Ones of the Dream: A Psychoanalytic Interpretation of Australian Myth and Ritual*. New York: Int. Universities Press

Róheim R. 1949. The symbolism of subincision. *Am. Imago* 6:321–28

Rosen LN. 1988. Male adolescent initiation rituals: Whiting's hypothesis revisited. *Psychoanal. Stud. Soc.* 12:135–55

Rowanchilde R. 1996. Male genital modifica-

tion: a sexual-selection interpretation. *Hum. Nat.* 7:189–215

Rubel AJ, Liu WT, Brandewie E. 1971. Genital mutilation and adult role behavior among lowland Christian Filipinos of Cebu. *Am. Anthropol.* 73:806–10

Salmon MH. 1997. Ethnical considerations in anthropology and archaeology, or relativism and justice for all. *J. Anthropol. Res.* 53:47–63

Scheper-Hughes N. 1991. Virgin territory: the male discovery of the clitoris. *Med. Anthropol. Q.* 5:25–28

Shapiro W. 1989. The theoretical importance of pseudo-procreative symbolism. *Psychoanal. Stud. Soc.* 14:71–88

Sheehan E. 1981. Victorian clitoridectomy: Isaac Baker Brown and his harmless operative procedure. *Med. Anthropol. Newsl.* 12:9–15

Shell-Duncan BK. 2001. The medicalization of female "circumcision": harm reduction or promotion of a dangerous practice? *Soc. Sci. Med.* 52:1013–28

Shell-Duncan B, Hernlund Y, eds. 2000. *Female "Circumcision" in Africa: Culture, Controversy, and Change*. Boulder: Lynne Rienner

Shweder RA. 2000. What about "female genital mutilation"? And why understanding culture matters in the first place. *Daedalus* 129:209–32

Shweder RA. 2002. What about "female genital mutilation"? And why understanding culture matters in the first place. In *Engaging Cultural Differences: The Multicultural Challenge in Liberal Democracies*, ed. RA Shweder, M Minow, HR Markus, pp. 216–51. New York: Russell Sage

Siegfried N, Muller M, Volmink J, Deeks J, Egger M, et al. 2003. Male circumcision for prevention of heterosexual acquisition of HIV in men (Cochrane Review). *The Cochrane Library,* Issue 4. Chichester, UK: Wiley

Silverman EK. 2000. *Anti anti-circumcision: a symbolic critique of the male circumcision controversy*. Presented at the Annu. Meet. Am. Anthropol. Assoc., 99th, San Francisco

Silverman EK. 2003. The cut of wholeness:

psychoanalytic interpretations of biblical circumcision. In *The Covenant of Circumcision: New Perspectives on an Ancient Jewish Rite*, ed. EW Mark, pp. 43–57. Hanover: Brandeis Univ. Press

Silverman EK. n.d. *Circumcision and Its Discontents: Jewish Circumcision from Abraham to America*. Lanham: Rowman & Littlefield

Singer P, DeSole DE. 1967. The Australian subincision ceremony reconsidered: vaginal envy or Kangaroo bifid penis envy. *Am. Anthropol.* 69:355–58

Skinner EP. 1988. Female circumcision in Africa: the dialectics of equality. In *Dialectics and Gender: Anthropological Approaches*, ed. RR Randolph, DM Schneider, pp. 195–210. *Boulder: Westview*

Soori N, Boerma JT, Robert W, Mark U. 1997. The popularization of male circumcision in Africa: changing practices among the Sukuma of Tanzania. *Afr. Anthropol.* 4:68–79

Speiser F. 1944. Uber die Beschneidung in der Südsee. *Acta Tropica* 1:9–29

Spencer B, Gillen FJ. 1899. *The Native Tribes of Central Australia*. London: Macmillan

Spencer P. 1965. *The Samburu: A Study of Gerontocracy in a Nomadic Tribe*. London: Routledge & Kegan Paul

Stewart H, Morison L, White R. 2002. Determinants of coital frequency among married women in Central African Republic: the role of female genital cutting. *J. Biosocial Sci.* 34:525–39

Talle A. 1993. Transforming women into 'pure' agnates: aspects of female infibulation in Somalia. In *Carved Flesh/Cast Selves: Gender Symbols and Social Practices*, ed. V Broch-Due, I Rudie, T Bleie, pp. 83–106. Oxford: Berg

Thomas LM. 2003. *Politics of the Womb: Women, Reproduction, and the State in Kenya*. Berkeley: Univ. Calif. Press

Todd JA. 1934. Report on research in South-West New Britain. *Oceania* 5:80–101, 193–213

Tucker JT. 1949. Initiation ceremonies for Luimbi boys. *Africa* 19:53–60

Turnbull CM. 1957. Initiation among the BaMbuti pygmies of the Central Ituri. *J. R. Anthropol. Inst.* 87:191–216

Turner T. 1995. Social body and embodied subject: bodiliness, subjectivity, and sociality among the Kayapo. *Cult. Anthropol.* 10:143–70

Turner V. 1962. Three symbols of passage in Ndembu circumcision ritual. In *Essays on the Ritual of Social Relations*, ed. M Gluckman. pp. 124–73. Manchester: Manchester Univ. Press

Turner V. 1967. Mukanda: the rite of circumcision. In *The Forest of Symbols: Aspects of Ndembu Ritual*, pp. 151–279. Ithaca: Cornell Univ. Press

Ucko PJ. 1969. Penis sheaths: a comparative study. *Proc. R. Anthropol. Inst. 1969*, pp. 27–67

USAID/AIDSMark. 2003. *Male Circumcision: Current Epidemiological and Field Evidence; Program and Policy Implications for HIV Prevention and Reproductive Health*. Conference Report. Washington, DC: USAID. http://www.rho.org/men+rh_% 209–02/menrh_mc_conf_report(rev).pdf

van der Kwaak A. 1992. Female circumcision and gender identity: a questionable alliance? *Soc. Sci. Med.* 35:777–87

Van Gennep A. 1960 [1909]. *Rites of Passage*. Transl. MB Vizedom, GL Caffe. Chicago: Univ. Chicago Press. (From French)

Walley CJ. 1997. Search for "voices": feminism, anthropology, and the global debate over female genital operations. *Cult. Anthropol.* 12:405–38

Walter MAHB. 1988. The fetal and natal origins of circumcision and other birth symbols. In *Choice and Morality in Anthropological Perspective: Essays in Honor of Derek Freeman*, ed. GN Appell, TN Madan, pp. 213–37. Albany: State Univ. NY Press

Warner WL. 1958. *A Black Civilization: A Social Study of an Australian Tribe*. New York: Harper. Rev. ed.

Weiss C. 1966. Motives for male circumcision among preliterate and literate peoples. *J. Sex Res.* 2:69–88

Weiss HA, Quigley MA, Hayes RJ. 2000. Male circumcision and risk of HIV infection in sub-Saharan Africa: a systematic review and meta-analysis. *AIDS* 14:2361–70

White CMN. 1953. Notes on the circumcision rites of the Balovale tribes. *Afr. Stud.* 12:41–56

Whitehouse H. 2000. *Arguments and Icons: Divergent Modes of Religiosity*. Oxford: Oxford Univ. Press

Whiting JWM, Kluckhohn R, Anthony A. 1958. The function of male initiation ceremonies at puberty. In *Readings in Social Psychology*, ed. EE Maccoby, TM Newcomb, EL Hartley, pp. 359–70. New York: Henry Holt. 3rd ed.

Wolfson ER. 2002. Assaulting the border: Kabbalistic traces in the margins of Derrida. *J. Am. Acad. Rel.* 70:475–514

Young FW. 1965. *Initiation Ceremonies: A Cross-Cultural Study of Status Dramatization*. Indianapolis: Bobbs-Merrill

Annu. Rev. Anthropol. 2004. 33:447–74
doi: 10.1146/annurev.anthro.33.070203.143835
Copyright © 2004 by Annual Reviews. All rights reserved
First published online as a Review in Advance on June 17, 2004

CHRISTIANITY IN AFRICA: From African Independent to Pentecostal-Charismatic Churches

Birgit Meyer

Research Centre Religion and Society, University of Amsterdam, Amsterdam,
The Netherlands; email: b.meyer@uva.nl

Key Words African Independent Churches, Pentecostalism, Africanization, globalization, public sphere

■ **Abstract** Taking as a point of departure Fernandez's survey (1978), this review seeks to show how research on African Independent Churches (AICs) has been reconfigured by new approaches to the anthropology of Christianity in Africa, in general, and the recent salient popularity of Pentecostal-Charismatic Churches (PCCs) in particular. If the adjectives "African" and "Independent" were once employed as markers of authentic, indigenous interpretations of Christianity, these terms proved to be increasingly problematic to capture the rise, spread, and phenomenal appeal of PCCs in Africa. Identifying three discursive frames—Christianity and "traditional religion," Africa and "the wider world," religion and politics—which organize(d) research on AICs and PCCs in the course of the past 25 years, this chapter critically reviews discussions about "Africanization," globalization and modernity, and the role of religion in the public sphere in postcolonial African societies.

INTRODUCTION

Ever since African Independent Churches became a central research focus for anthropologists in the 1960s, these churches have not only formed fascinating research locations but also have been major sites for more general theoretical reflection and innovation in anthropology. Classical works published in the 1960s and 1970s (e.g., Fabian 1971, Jules-Rosette 1975, Peel 1968, Sundkler 1961 [1948]) showed how African Independent Churches or movements instigated the development of alternatives to the then still dominant structural-functionalist paradigm, which failed to address "social change" in a theoretically adequate way (see also Fabian 1981). As this vast interdisciplinary research field has been surveyed up to the mid-1980s (Fernandez 1978, Ranger 1986; see also Jules-Rosette 1994), this review is confined to the past 25 years. It does not aim to present a comprehensive survey but seeks to highlight some major trends from an anthropological perspective. In this period, the study of African Independent Churches (AICs), or, as some prefer to call them, African Indigenous Churches (e.g., Appiah-Kubi 1981) or

0084-6570/04/1021-0447$14.00

African Initiated Churches (Anderson 2001), has been considerably reconfigured, empirically as well as theoretically. Nothing can better evoke what is at stake than the salience of the contrast between the familiar image of African prophets from Zionist, Nazarite, or Aladura churches, dressed in white gowns, carrying crosses, and going to pray in the bush, and the flamboyant leaders of the new mega-churches, who dress in the latest (African) fashion, drive nothing less than a Mercedez Benz, participate in the global Pentecostal jetset, broadcast the message through flashy TV and radio programs, and preach the Prosperity Gospel to their deprived and hitherto-hopeless born-again followers at home and in the diaspora (Marshall-Fratani 2001). Although it would be too simple to assume that the latter simply replaced the former, the emergence of these new figures suggests that the appropriation of Christianity in Africa has entered a new phase. If in the 1980s Independent Churches were found to be attractive, by African Christians as well as researchers, above all because they seemed to offer a more "authentic," Africanized version of Christianity than do the presumably Western-oriented mainline churches, current Pentecostal-Charismatic Churches (PCCs) appear to derive their mass appeal at least partly from propagating a "complete break with the past" (Meyer 1998a, Engelke 2004). Dissociating themselves from both mainline churches and African Independent, or as they call them, "Spiritual" Churches, the new PCCs promise to link up their born-again believers with global circuits. Although PCCs gain an ever-increasing number of followers, also from the older AICs, anthropologists—and, for that matter, missiologists and African theologians—have only recently and reluctantly started to study them. This hesitance, of course, stems from the fact that anthropologists, by the nature of their discipline, were usually attracted by cultural difference and authenticity, whereas religious scholars had a strong interest in Africanization or "inculturation." PCCs, with their intensive links to transnational circuits, in particular to American televangelists, and their enthusiastic drive to proselytize nonbelievers (researchers included), were difficult to accept as viable objects of study.

This chapter seeks to highlight not only the shift from AICs to PCCs as new foci of empirical study but also the conceptual transformations to which it gave rise. In the first section, I show how anthropologists' understanding of AICs changed in relation to new approaches in the study of Christianity in Africa. I argue that PCCs' spectacular rise raises important theoretical questions and renders the adjectives "African" and "Independent" increasingly problematic. Three subsequent sections place particular emphasis on discursive contexts that have been major frames organizing research in the period under review: (*a*) the relationship between Christianity and "traditional religion" and the question of Africanization; (*b*) the relationship between Africa and "the wider world" and the question of globalization; and (*c*) the relationship between religion and politics and the question of religion in the public sphere. My main concern is to show how these frames have been reconfigured in the period under review, and in particular by current research on PCCs, and to indicate fruitful avenues for further research.

RECONFIGURATIONS: FROM AFRICAN INDEPENDENT
TO PENTECOSTAL-CHARISMATIC CHURCHES

Fernandez's earlier overview (1978) in the *Annual Review of Anthropology* marks the transition in the study of AICs or movements from a focus on typologies and taxonomies and crisis cults to a more critical-reflexive and ethnographic approach. Critiquing earlier socio-structural as well as the Marxist-inspired approaches that were en vogue in the 1970s (e.g., Van Binsbergen 1977, 1981), Fernandez argued that researchers' analytical terms and concepts tended to impose Western categories on rather than revealing much about these movements: "My point is, and I think it is a very anthropological one, our real enlightenment lies not in the application of imageless ideas exported from the West, but in beginning with African images and by careful method learning what they imply—what is embedded in them" (Fernandez 1978, p. 215). Calling for the study of these movements at a grassroots level, he expressed his support of the "new historiography" represented by Terence Ranger cum suis (Ranger & Kimambo 1972). He sought to stimulate anthropologists to study African religious imaginations by striving to discern their inherent "argument of images," that is, the way in which people face deprivation and achieve revitalization by redeploying "primary images of body and household, field and forest life" (Fernandez 1978, p. 228). His own work on the emergence of the syncretist Bwiti religion among the Fang (Gabon) (1982, see also 1986) is a magisterial example of this approach, which had a major impact on subsequent research and was a matter of much debate (Fernandez 1990; Schoffeleers 1986; Werbner 1985, 1990).

If Fernandez made a strong plea for semantic or symbolic ethnography to replace social-structuralist approaches, in the Introduction to their influential collection Van Binsbergen & Schoffeleers (1985) argued for the necessity to integrate both of these as a precondition for a better understanding of religious movements in Africa. As the contributions to their collection clearly document, since the mid-1980s both strands have certainly come closer together. This quest for integration also stood central in two ground-breaking monographs: Jean Comaroff's *Body of Power, Spirit of Resistance* (1985) and Karen Fields's *Revival and Rebellion in Colonial Central Africa* (1985). Both works, in their own manner, offer insight into African religious practices and symbolic universes on the basis of detailed empirical research and explore the relationship between religion and politics in a new imaginative way, without reducing the former to the latter or maintaining a Durkheimian view of religion as underpinning societal order (see also Werbner 1985). Examining the ways in which the British colonial administration perceived outbreaks of Watchtower activities in Malawi and Zambia in the first three decades of the twentieth century as a major political threat, Fields showed how baptism, speaking in tongues, prophecy, and healing actually operated as effective political tools. Her work challenges the often-implicit distinction between religion and the secular, which assumes that politics and religion essentially belong to separate spheres, and it shows that such a separation did not exist in colonial Central

Africa, colonial officials' claims to the contrary notwithstanding. Questioning the very basis on which the (in practice untenable) distinction between religion and politics thrives, Fields was able to show that religion was a continuously contested part of the ideology of colonial modernity. Similarly, in her exploration of Tshidi's material and symbolic struggle in the South African–Botswana borderland to act on the global and national forces that shape their lives, Comaroff argued for the necessity to focus on colonial encounters between Western and local forces. She thus integrated "what Fernandez calls the imageless concepts of mode of production, class formation and underdevelopment with a profound exploration of the argument of images in Tshidi Zionism" (Ranger 1986, p. 12). Although she only engaged with Fernandez's approach in passing (Comaroff 1985, p. 170), she clearly moved beyond his rather narrow understanding of ethnography as being geared to African cultural and symbolic repertoires and the essentializing opposition between Africa and the West on which it thrives. In so doing she laid the base for her and John Comaroff's later work (1991, 1997), which reframed the project of ethnography as not merely a thorough study of the Other but as a detailed investigation of the zones of contact between Africa and the West. Central to this investigation stand the material, social, and cultural possibilities and constraints articulated in the "long conversations" between Western missionaries, traders, and administrators and local people, which took off in colonial times and have continued ever since.

The studies by Fields and Comaroff also signal a growing awareness of the need to situate AICs in a broader historical, social, and cultural frame. As Ranger explained in his sophisticated overview, the treatment of Independent churches, missionary Christianity, and traditional religion in isolation from each other was "artificial and distorting" (1986, p. 49). He stresses that the study of AICs tended to draw too strong a contrast with traditional religion, and to misrepresent the former as the sole suitable laboratory for social change, whereas the latter was perceived as static and hence merely a nostalgic point of reference doomed to disappear (Ranger 1993). Ranger also argues that an exclusive focus on AICs implies a far too rigid contrast between presumably more "authentic" AICs and Westernized mainline churches perceived as the ideological superstructure of colonialism and hence as familiar and not worthy of anthropological study (Ranger 1987). This contrast, he shows, was challenged by the fact that religious revival movements occurred in mainline churches at the grassroots level (e.g., MacGaffey 1983), whereas AICs experienced processes of institutionalization and routinization, in the course of which "pastors" started to assume a more important role than did the prophets who had initially broken away from mission churches (e.g., Probst 1989).

The realization that it is fruitful for anthropologists to focus on Christianity, or even religion, in Africa as a dynamic field, in which so-called AICs, mission, or mainline churches and traditional religion are in ongoing exchange, conflict, and dialogue with each other, changed the ways in which anthropology and African theology constructed their research object. In the aftermath of a large conference organized in Jos (Nigeria) in 1975, which resulted in the famous *Christianity in*

Independent Africa (Fasholé-Luke et al. 1978), the scope of research gradually broadened from the study of AICs to the history and anthropology of Christianity in Africa [e.g., James & Johnson 1988, Spear & Kimambu 1999; see also Hastings' (2000) perceptive overview]. Most notable in the field of history are the accounts by Hastings (1979, 1995), Isichei (1995), and Sundkler & Steed (2000), which take as a point of departure African agency (see also Gray 1990, Maxwell 1997, Salaome 1996). As mission or mainline churches were no longer considered solely the domain of theologians and missiologists (Beidelman 1982, Etherington 1983), they became a new study object for anthropologists and historians (Comaroff & Comaroff 1991, 1997; Etherington 1996; Landau 1995; Meyer 1999; Peel 1990, 1995; Pels 1999; Ross & Bredecamp 1995; Ter Haar 1992). These historical-anthropological works do not take for granted the mission of Western-derived churches, but instead explore them with the same historical and ethnographic vigor as so-called AICs. The question of how to account for African evangelists' own narratives and agency without neglecting the Western part in the encounter nor reinscribing colonial power claims to the history of Christianity in Africa gave rise to much debate (Peel 1995, Comaroff & Comaroff 1997).

Although many anthropological studies focus on plural religious fields, taking into account dissenting voices and conflicts (Middleton 1983, Schoffeleers 1985, 1994; Werbner 1989; Maxwell 1999a; Meyer 1999), most publications still concentrate on a single movement or organization (see Spear & Kimambo 1999, Blakely et al. 1994). A more elaborate engagement with Islam as part of these fields is still very scarce (but see Peel 2003, Sanneh 1996), though this shortcoming has been signaled by several authors (Maxwell 1997, p. 147; Hastings 2000, p. 42). Strangely, the term Independent remains current even after scholars broadened their research focus and questioned the usefulness of the opposition between Western missionary concepts and practices and their indigenous appropriation in AICs. Maxwell (1999b) notes that Christian independency, originally a colonial term to designate Christian movements lacking white supervision, does not make sense in the postcolonial era. The use of a supposedly neutral terminology, initially employed to mark the difference between "authentic" AICs and "foreign" mission churches, fails to acknowledge the interrelatedness of these supposedly different kinds of organizations.

The study of AICs was reconfigured not only by researchers' awareness that these churches were part of a broader field, but also by the salient popularity of new PCCs from the 1970s onward. Initially, these African-founded, yet globally oriented, PCCs were not regarded as suitable objects of anthropological study because of their presumed link with Western conservatives and fundamentalists. This link intrigued Gifford (1987, 1991), prompting him to conduct his early research on the influence of European and American evangelists on PCCs in Southern Africa (see also Arntsen 1997). According to the latest edition of the World Christian Encyclopedia (Barrett 2001, see also Anderson 2001), in 2000 there were 83 million Independents and 126 million Pentecostal-charismatics in Africa. Although these categories partially overlap, the figures exceed earlier projections by far. If

Christianity appears to be on the wane in (Northern) Europe (and thus seemed to offer a prime case in favor of the secularization thesis), a new global brand of Pentecostalism thrives in Africa, Latin America, and Asia (Corten 1997, Droogers 2001, Freston 1998, Jenkins 2002, Lehman 2001, Martin 2002, Poewe 1994).

The Wold Christian Encyclopedia's confusion about the use of categories such as AIC and PCC shows how difficult it is to capture with adequate terms the diversity of Christianity in Africa. If for good conceptual reasons (Fabian 1981) anthropologists pleaded to use "movement" rather than "church," African Christians seemed to prefer the latter term, presumably because of its more solid, official connotations. In describing themselves and others, they tend to adopt categories such as mission or mainline church, AIC or PCC. AICs, in particular, increasingly came under attack by the fast-growing PCCs (both in terms of membership and sheer number), which were founded by and organized around the personality of a charismatic African leader and remained institutionally independent from, though they had strong links to, Western Pentecostal churches. To view the popularity of Pentecostalism as an entirely new phenomenon would be mistaken. Although Pentecostal churches, such as the Assemblies of God or the Apostolic Church, played a role in the African Christian scene since the 1920s, scholars did not draw a strong distinction between these churches and AICs until around 1990. Southern African AICs especially developed typical Pentecostal features such as glossolalia (Daneel 1970, Sundkler 1961) and scholars took them as paradigmatic of African Pentecostalism (Cox 1994a,b). At the same time, many AICs straddled the typological divide and recast themselves as Pentecostal churches (Meyer 1999, Maxwell 2001, Ukah 2003a). What is new is the fact that the hitherto blurred typological distinction between AICs and Pentecostal churches became increasingly polarized in the course of PCCs' massive expansion.

Therefore, scholars should not take for granted these classifications, but instead understand them as part and parcel of a politics of self-representation. Pentecostal rhetoric about the disappearance of AICs notwithstanding, these churches persist and attract followers and researchers (Adogame 2000, Dozon 1995). Especially in South Africa, Zionist Churches still have a mass appeal (M. Fraehm-Arp, unpublished manuscript; Gunnner 2002; Kiernan 1992, 1994; Niehaus et al. 2001), although growth of PCCs is on the rise (M. Fraehm Arp, P. Germond & I. Niehaus, personal communication)—an issue that calls for detailed future research. More in general, quite similar to AICs, PCCs stress the importance of the Holy Spirit above biblical doctrines and provide room for prophetism, dreams and visions, speaking in tongues, prayer healing, and deliverance from evil spirits. The attraction of charismatic Pentecostalism throughout Africa is not confined to PCCs, but also materializes in prayer groups in the confines of established Protestant Churches, the charismatic renewal in the Roman Catholic Church, and nondenominational fellowships that born-again Christians attend without leaving their churches (Asamoah-Gyadu 1997, Ayuk 2002, Meyer 1999, Ojo 1988, Ter Haar 1992, Milingo 1984). Therefore, a crude distinction between AICs, PCCs, and mainline churches is as problematic as the earlier "taxonomic games" distinguishing types of AICs, which has been critiqued by Fernandez (1978) and Fabian (1981). Nevertheless, the PCCs of the 1990s are characterized by a distinct form, in terms of scale, organization, theology, and religious practice, and this distinct form warrants investigators seeing them as a new phenomenon (Corten & Marshall Fratani 2001; M. Fraehm-Arp, unpublished manuscript; Gifford 1998). Although they should not be approached as a monolithic entity—fission seems to be intrinsic to Pentecostalism and hence a broad spectrum of PCCs with differences in doctrinal emphasis and style exists throughout Africa (Martin 2002, p. 176)—they clearly share a number of significant family resemblances.

Because there has been little systematic, comparative research on PCCs in different African countries (but see Gifford 1998), it is not easy for anthropologists to explain why PCCs arose earlier and on a more massive scale in British ex-colonies, such as Ghana and Nigeria. The rise of PCCs depends at least in part on a plural religious arena and the existence of AICs, against which PCCs define themselves. Important historical factors to be considered concern differences between religious cultures in Anglophone and Francophone ex-colonies and the extent to which states endorse or reject religious pluralism (Barrett 1968), as well as the predominance of Islam. Conversely, the fact that PCCs eventually did become increasingly popular in several francophone countries such as Togo, Benin, and Cameroon, whose Catholic elites for long distrusted Pentecostalism for "tending to draw its adherents into a mainly Protestant, U.S.-oriented, anglosphere" (J. Peel, personal correspondence), also calls for explanation. As Konings (2003) suggests in accounting for the long-term absence and yet the recent rise of PCCs in Cameroon (2003), political liberalization, resulting from implementation of International Monetary Fund–instigated forms of good governance and democratization, forms a key condition for PCCs' successful manifestation and massive mobilization of followers (see also Laurent 2001a, Mayrargue 2001).

What is distinctly new about PCCs is their propagation of the Prosperity Gospel and their strong global inclination. Their names, which often refer to the church's aspired "international" or "global" (out)reach, highlight PCCs' aim to develop and maintain international branches in other African countries and the West, and to deploy notions of identity and belonging that deliberately reach beyond Africa. In this sense, PCCs are a global phenomenon that calls for comparison with similar churches in other parts of the world, most notably South America. As is shown in more detail below, much current research on PCCs explores the personal, cultural, political, social, and economic dimensions of being born-again, as well as the ways in which the upsurge of these churches is related to the crisis of the postcolonial nation-state, transnationalism and diasporic culture, the rise of neo-liberal "millennial capitalism" (Comaroff & Comaroff 2001), and mass-mediated popular culture.

If Fernandez (1978) could still state that religious movements (in any case those like Bwiti), though giving "evidence of a successful adaptation to the modern world," "remain community enterprises within, resisting modernization in the capitalist sense" (p. 217), obviously current Pentecostal-Charismatic Churches do not engage in this type of resistance and, on the contrary, even seem to eagerly embrace capitalism. Such empirical shifts demand new theory and, against the backdrop of the fact that many churches act on a transnational scale, new methods. Thus, within a span of 25 years, Fernandez's plea to turn to African imagery as a prerequisite for a true understanding of AICs collided with the realization that the condition for understanding Pentecostalism's appeal and impact lies in moving beyond, or at least problematizing, "African" and "Independent" as taken-for-granted categories (Appiah 1992, Mudimbe 1988). Whereas Fernandez's point to conduct an ethnographic study of African religious imaginations may have been well taken at the time, it proved to be problematic in the long run because of the rather essentializing understanding of the attribute "African" on which it depends. The seemingly "un-African," globally inclined PCCs challenge the usefulness of the notion of "African" as a marker of cultural difference and call for a reformulation of the major discursive contexts through which AICs have been approached.

CHRISTIANITY AND "TRADITIONAL RELIGION"

A major discursive context framing research on AICs focuses on the relationship between Christianity and "traditional religion." As intimated in the Introduction, for a long time the research interests of anthropologists, missiologists, and African theologians converged on the issue of Africanization, and this convergence opened up a space for interdisciplinary debate, above all in the *Journal of Religion in Africa*. Although there has never been an agreement among scholars as well as religious practitioners about the appropriate nomenclature (terms like Inculturation, Indigenization, Contextualization, Africanization, or African theology were all in circulation), the key concern was the search for an "authentic African expression of Christianity" (Mbiti 1980, Ojo 1988, Wijsen 2000). Phrases such as *Traditional Religion and Christianity: Continuities and Conflicts* (the title of the second part of the collection *Christianity in Africa* by Fasholé-Luke et al. 1978) pinpoint a particular discursive context that informed both religious scholars' seemingly irresolvable question, "how to be Christians and Africans at the same time," (Appiah-Kubi 1981, Baëta 1968, Mugambi 1996, Sindima 1994) and anthropologists' understanding of AICs as the backbones of African authenticity [or even as "surrogate tribes," as Fabian (1980) put it critically]. The dualism of these reified categories, Christianity and traditional religion, has been criticized increasingly for its inherent, unquestioned assumptions, which misrepresent African religious traditions as static, mission churches as alien(ating), and AICs as syncretically mixing elements from both yet ultimately rooted in and geared toward traditional culture. Such a view not only neglects African agency in processes of conversion in the context of mission churches, but also is unable to acknowledge the extent to which AICs actually oppose(d) traditional notions and practices and incorporate(d) key notions "from outside," as has been documented in many older anthropological studies of AICs (without, however, being sufficiently theorized). Ranger (1987) argues that "we should see mission churches as much less alien and independent churches as much less 'African'" (p. 31) and acknowledge the extent to which AICs derive inspiration from revivalist movements within mission churches and in the context of European and North American Pentecostalism (see also Maxwell 1997, Ojo 1988).

Recently, the notion of Africanization has been problematized. In my historical and ethnographic work on local appropriations of Christianity among the Ewe in Ghana I have sought to point out (Meyer 1992, 1999) that it is a mistake to view Africanization as solely confined to AICs or to design it "from above" into new theological programs (as was the case with the then acting moderator of the Evangelical Presbyterian Church where I conducted my research). Africanization, understood as appropriation of Christianity at the grassroots level, has been an integral component of the spread of missionary Christianity from the outset. This "[A]fricanization from below" came about through processes of both translation into the vernacular (Sanneh 1991) and the diabolization of Ewe religion (and its construction as "heathendom"), thereby merging nineteenth-century popular missionary Christianity and local religious practices and ideas. Old gods and spirits, and also witchcraft, continued to exist as Christian demons under the auspices of the devil. Hence, in addition to investigating African ideas about God or the positive convergence of African and Christian notions, I argued for the need for scholars to consider also the negative incorporation of the spiritual entities in African religious traditions into the image of the Christian devil as part and parcel of local appropriations. In this way, the "old" and forbidden, from which Christians were required to distance themselves, remained available, albeit in a new form (see also Droz 1997).

Hence it makes little sense to use Africanization in a singular manner and reserve it for the AICs, as was the tendency among anthropologists, or affirm the need for Africanization in theology, as was, and still is, the tendency among many African theologians and missiologists (e.g., Bediako 1995, but see Onyinah 2002). Such a broad understanding of Africanization, as not simply entailing a positive incorporation of tradition or its revival (often referred to with the biblical trope of "old wine in new skins"), pinpoints the necessity for scholars to revise the view of AICs as the sole sites of successful, "syncretic" combinations of traditional religious and Christian elements.[1] It means also that an understanding of tradition in terms of more or less incorporable elements belonging to the past was found to be much too static. Nevertheless in the period under review here, it seems that a sophisticated treatment of African religious traditions in relation to Christianity is still relatively scarce (but see MacGaffey 1983; Maxwell 1999a; Peel 1992, 2003; Schoffeleers 1994; Werbner 1989). This lack may be due to the fact that,

---

[1]Much more could be said about the politics of use of the term syncretism, which was often employed by representatives of mainline churches in a pejorative manner, so as to designate AIC Christian understandings as impure and deviant. Conversely, anthropologists tended to celebrate syncretism as an achieved synthesis of foreign and indigenous elements (for a useful critical discussion see Stewart & Shaw 1994).

from a Christian perspective, local traditions are often viewed in a temporalizing perspective, which denies traditional religion its "coevalness" (Fabian 1983) with Christianity, allegedly the religion of modernity par excellence (Meyer 1998a, Steegstra 2004). For a long time, scholars have rather uncritically reproduced this temporalizing device, thus still echoing Sundkler's (1961) view of AICs "as the bridge over which Africans are brought back to heathendom" (p. 297).

More general debates about the "invention" or "imagination of tradition" (Hobsbawm & Ranger 1983), which stressed that tradition is not simply a matter of the past and hence ultimately opposed to modernity, but an essential part of discourses of modernity, shaped the research of scholars of Christianity in Africa. They started to approach traditional beliefs and practices no longer as a given but as actively produced in particular arenas, by colonial and postcolonial state officials, artists striving for rehabilitation of the African Cultural Heritage and Christian churches or movements. Investigators argued that far from simply alienating African converts from their own culture, missionaries and African evangelists produced reified notions of indigenous culture, which affirmed cultural difference and the imagination of distinct tribal or ethnic identities (Meyer 2002a, Peel 2003, Steegstra 2002, Vail 1989). Conversely, those cultural agents who refer to tradition as a desirable point of reference and basis of cultural pride are often involved in a project of secularizing traditional rituals, thereby turning them into "harmless culture" (Peel 1994, p. 163)

PCCs' rather merciless attitude toward local cultural traditions and rejection of village culture has caused many researchers to ponder these churches' stances toward local religious traditions. Certainly those churches fiercely opposing local traditions may be much more indebted to traditional ways of thinking than cultural agents celebrating tradition as cultural heritage (Peel 1994; see also Coe 2000, Hall 1999, Meyer 1999, Steegstra 2004). Although charismatics tend to critique mainline churches for seeking to accommodate local culture through Africanization, they dismiss "Spiritual Churches" for drawing on occult forces, making use of allegedly idolatric elements such as candles and incense, and thus linking up with the "powers of darkness" (Sackey 2001). Tying into popular narratives (often put into circulation by nineteenth-century missionaries and African evangelists) about the devil as the head of all the demons who were once cast out from heaven and settled in Africa, many PCCs devote much room to deliverance from the satanic forces, which possess members and are held to cause material and psychic problems in the sphere of health and wealth. In such semipublic or private meetings, Pentecostal pastors and members of the "prayer force" seek to cast out demons by calling on the Holy Spirit to turn the demonically possessed into born-again Christians (Asamoah-Gyadu 1997, p. 23 and subsequent pages; Laurent 2001b; Meyer 1999, p. 155 and and subsequent pages; for a detailed description from an insider perspective see Onyina 2002, pp. 122–25). Such deliverance sessions happen both in African rural and urban settings (in prayer camps or churches) as well as in PCCs catering to the needs of (often illegal) African immigrants in the diaspora (Van Dijk 1997, 2002). In a sense, they offer a version of African Christianity that does not make it necessary to (secretly) seek for help outside the confines of the church. Being born-again is perceived as a radical rupture not only from one's personal sinful past, but also from the wider family and village of origin (Engelke 2004; Laurent 2001; Marshall-Fratani 1998; Meyer 1998a, 1999; Van Dijk 1992, 1998). Thus, while at first sight these churches appeared as heavily antitraditional, closer investigation reveals that this attribute is problematic, as PCCs take seriously spiritual forces to a much larger extent than do mainline churches, which tend to regard such beliefs as superstitious (albeit on the level of their theologically trained leaders, not at the grassroots level).

The fact that PCCs affirm a negative, inversed image of traditional gods and spirits and allow for spirit possession in the context of deliverance pinpoints the extent to which Christianity and local religious traditions are interrelated. In a sense, PCCs' ongoing concern with deliverance shows the very impossibility of their self-ascribed project to break with what Pentecostals discursively construct as the "forces of the past." Claims to the ultimate power of the Holy Spirit notwithstanding, the despised evil spirits seem to be alive and kicking. Against this backdrop it has become clear that, despite the need for analysis on the level of believers' ideas, it would be much too simple for researchers to remain within PCCs' own self-descriptions and take at face value the claim that they lead believers away from their local background. This notion must be analyzed as a conversion narrative, rather than as an achieved state (Engelke 2004). Pentecostal-charismatic practice ultimately affirms the impossibility for born-again Christians to escape from forces grounded in and emanating from the local. In this sense, PCCs, while speaking to desires to link up with the wider world and escape the constraints of poverty, also articulate Christianity in relation to local concerns.

Whereas, up until now PCCs have mainly referred to local cultural and religious traditions through diabolization or demonization, signs indicate a more positive appreciation of these traditions in charismatic circles. Pentecostal African theologians recently started to reconcile African religious traditions and Christianity in a postmodern synthesis (e.g., Onyinah 2002). For example, the charismatic leader of the International Central Gospel Church [headquartered in Accra, Ghana (Gifford 1994, 1998, 2003; De Witte 2003), yet opening branches all over Africa] seeks to develop the notion of African pride (Otabil 1992, see also Larbi 2001). Also the emergence of new Gospel Music groups that deliberately incorporate traditional signs and symbols into their lyrics and performance suggests that the rather negative attitude toward tradition may be changing (M. de Witte, personal communication). The question is, of course, what to make of this revival of tradition (if it gets through at all). I would suggest that rather than viewing this apparent revival as a return to the "authentic," and thus relapse into the resilient yet false temporalizing device that locates authenticity and tradition in the past, it may be more useful to understand it as a new practice of signification in which tradition features as a cultural style (see also Ferguson 1999, p. 96). In any case, as anthropologists have successfully deconstructed the modernization perspective, on which the view of tradition as a matter of the past ultimately depended, it has become difficult, though all the more challenging, to find an appropriate conceptual space for the authentic or the traditional. This is one of the major tasks researchers will face in the future.

AFRICA AND "THE WIDER WORLD"

Whereas the notion of Africanization, thriving in the interface of anthropology and religious studies, ceased to be the main drive behind anthropological research, globalization and modernity became the buzz words in the 1990s. This new focus opened up new venues for interdisciplinary exchange with sociologists of religion (Lehman 2001, Martin 2002), and opened up possibilities for debates about PCCs across the limits of area studies (Coleman 2002, Corten & Marshall-Fratani 2001, Corten & Mary 2001, Poewe 1994). Of course, the question as to how Africans related to the "modern world" already informed earlier studies of AICs. Much research in the 1960s and 1970s was conducted from a perspective of modernization, which saw indigenous culture as ultimately doomed to disappear with ongoing Westernization and secularization. Whether classified as escapist "crisis cults" or as creative Independent movements, AICs were regarded as indicators of the extent to which Africans still found themselves between traditional and modern society. This perspective, with its reference points of "traditional religion" and "new nation-state," was indebted to "a notion of society as a normally stable arrangement of structures, roles and institutions" that regarded religious enthusiasm as ultimately disturbing, at least conceptually if not politically (Fabian 1981 [1991], p. 114). AICs were held to cope with modernization, be it by offering the capacity to "explain, predict and control" the larger macrocosm into which Africans were drawn by colonialism through conversion to the High God (Horton 1975), or by enabling revitalization through a symbolic experience of "returning to the whole" (Fernandez 1982). Horton's intellectualist approach is problematic because it regards the individual quest for knowledge as the prime drive behind and explanation for conversion, thereby neglecting the metaphoric richness of religious thought and action, the emotive appeal of the sacred, and the power of more structural political-economic processes. Fernandez's position, as outlined above, draws too strong a contrast between African images and the forces of colonialism and modernization.

Anthropology's (re)turn to modernity and globalization in the 1990s is a complex and contested matter, which far exceeds African studies and cannot be addressed here (see Appadurai 1996, Inda & Rosaldo 2002, Kearney 1995). Researchers of PCCs were pushed to rethink modernity in the context of globalization above all because, on the one hand, they were puzzled by these churches' transnational organizational structure and the outspoken links made between being born-again and going global, and, on the other hand, by the way in which believers' life worlds were shaped by contradictions between political, social, and economic aspirations and possibilities arising from Africa's partial participation in the global economy. The key challenge was to develop a conceptual framework that would allow for a more sophisticated understanding of the complicated relationship between modern and traditional, or global and local; thus it became urgent to discover how these seeming oppositions, though called on in PCCs' practice, are actually entangled. It was certainly not a question of returning to the modernization perspective, although researchers, in their eagerness to make sense of PCCs' self-descriptions, may occasionally find themselves relapse into this old discourse. The main concern was to address modernity not from within the paradigm of modernization, but as a critique thereof. Taking as a point of departure critiques of anthropology's bounded notions of culture that question a view of the local as a primal category (Appadurai 1996; Fabian 1991, Ch. 10; Gupta & Ferguson 1997) and the realization that cultural specificity, rather than being opposed to globalization, is an essential component of globalization's dialectics of flow and closure (Clifford 1988, Meyer & Geschiere 1999), many anthropologists ventured into ethnographies of modernity. This endeavor, characterized by a dialectical understanding of the relationship between theory and empirical research, seeks to explore how people's encounters with colonialism, missions, or the capitalist market economy take a different shape in different localities. Hence one finds the emphasis on multiple modernities situated at different times and places, rather than on one single teleological structure (Comaroff & Comaroff 1993, Geschiere 1997). Given the characteristics of PCCs, the framework of ethnographies of modernity was perceived as appealing. In any case, "modernity" proved to be a powerful point of reference, and is also good to disagree with (Englund & Leach 2000, see below).

Many PCCs present themselves as ultimate embodiments of modernity. Building huge churches to accommodate thousands of believers, making use of elaborate technology to organize mass-scale sermons and appearances on TV and radio, organizing spectacular crusades throughout the country—often parading foreign speakers—so as to convert nominal Christians, Muslims, and supporters of traditional religions, creating possibilities for high-quality Gospel Music, and instigating trend-setting modes of dress all create an image of successful mastery of the modern world (de Witte 2003, personal observation; Droz 2001; Hackett 1998). PCCs owe at least part of their wealth to the fact that they successfully oblige members to pay tithes (10% of their income). To help believers advance, some PCCs offer a small loan to needy members, which should enable them to engage in trade and become financially independent—an aim desirable not only to the person in question but also to the church, as it eventually yields higher donations. Many PCCs represent prosperity as a God-given blessing and resent the mainline churches for legitimizing poverty by referring to Jesus Christ as a poor man (Marshall-Fratani 1998, Maxwell 1998, Meyer 1997). The figure of the charismatic pastor—with such stars as Nicolas Duncan-Williams and Mensah Otabil (Ghana), Nevers Mumba (Zambia), and most important, Benson Idahosa (Nigeria) as paradigmatic figures—dressed in exquisite garments and driving a posh car pinpoints that prosperity and being born-again are held to be two sides of the same coin.

The question of how to relate religious content to social-economic issues and class has been addressed by many researchers, thus linking up with the sociology of Pentecostalism in Latin America developed by Martin (1990, 2002) and Freston (1998). These churches had tremendous appeal especially for young people, who seek to eschew gerontocratic hierarchies and aspire to progress in life (the upwardly mobile), yet think (realistically, perhaps) that this goal can be achieved only through a God-given miracle. Indeed, "Your miracle is on the way" is a popular slogan, to be seen on church advertisements, car stickers, and shops all over Africa, which embodies the power of the still unfulfilled, yet resilient "expectations of modernity," which are frustrated by daily experiences of disconnectedness and marginalization (Ferguson 1999). However, the Prosperity Gospel also risks becoming subverted by its own appeal, in particular if the promise of wealth on which it thrives fails to materialize among believers (Maxwell 1998, p. 366 and subsequent pages). Numerous scandals show many times over that power and wealth may seduce even the staunchest born-again pastor to go astray (a favorite topic of especially Nigerian video-movies). Smith showed that charismatic Pentecostalism not only tends to reproduce the structures of inequality against which it positions itself (see also Marshall 1998), but also stands "dangerously close to the world of witchcraft," and, while critiquing the possibly evil, occult sources of wealth, is easily suspected to draw on those (Smith 2001). In Owerri (Nigeria) witchcraft suspicions regarding the wealth of flashy born-again pastors led to public riots, in which the church premises and pastors' residences were destroyed. More research needs to be conducted to assess the way in which the Prosperity Gospel is at once PCCs' main attraction and, as the promise in the long run fails to materialize among most ordinary believers, its main weakness.

Despite PCCs' strive for prosperity, the achievement of wealth is moralized by distinguishing between divine and occult sources of wealth, often by referring to traditional ideas concerning the nexus of wealth and morality (Droz 2001). Because the modern world is represented as thriving on temptation (Marshall-Fratani 1998, Meyer 2002b), PCCs appear to alert believers of being wary not to lose themselves in crude consumptive behavior and to use wisely the money they earn. People should avoid drinking alcohol, leading a loose moral life, and, in the case of men, squandering money with "cheap girls." They offer elaborate lessons on marriage, which young couples prior to their wedding must attend, and special hours for marriage counseling. Though the issue of gender appears to be pertinent, little research has been conducted in this regard (but see Mate 2002). The ideal is a moral self, not misled by the glitzy world of consumer capitalism nor misguided by the outmoded world of tradition, but instead filled with the Holy Spirit. Although there is likely much overlap between the Protestant modes of conduct that Max Weber found to be typical of early Protestantism, the strong emphasis on becoming prosperous and showing off wealth distinguishes PCCs from early modern Protestantism. Because the devil is supposed to operate not only through blood ties linking people to their extended family, in particular, and local culture, in general, but also at the heart of modernity in the sphere of consumption, the prospect of prosperity is made to depend on deliverance. Occult forces, embodied by the Spirit of Poverty, may block the accumulation of capital; seductive powers, as embodied by Mami Water, may induce them to squander their money on petty things such as cosmetics, perfumes, and sweets, whereas witchcraft and ancestral spirits may prevent them from prospering in life (Bastian 1997; Meyer 1998a,b; Ukah 2003b; see also Ellis & Ter Haar 1998, p. 183 and subsequent pages.). Linking up with ongoing debates about the "modernity of witchcraft" in African studies (Cziekawy & Geschiere 1998, Geschiere 1997, Moore & Sanders 2001), PCCs' witchcraft discourses express the contractions of modernity, its malcontents and promises (Comaroff & Comaroff 1993), and the moral panics to which it gives rise (Marshall 1991).

As the (prospective) born-again person is PCCs' point of departure to change the world, much research has focused on Pentecostal notions of the self, the way in which members are enticed to write new scripts for their lives. In my own work I tried to show that, as deliverance was understood as "cutting blood ties" (thus preventing jealous family members and demanding spirits to intrude a person), the invasion of the Holy Spirit through whom this severing occurred could be understood as a symbolic creation of a modern individual subject (1999). Although many charismatics are suspicious of the extended family and "the witches in the village" is a recurrent trope in many sermons, the extent to which PCCs stimulate the genesis of new forms of communality, which may act as a surrogate family, should not be neglected (as emphasized by Van Dijk 1997, 2002; see also Englund & Leach 2000, p. 235). As Marshall-Fratani (2001) argues, "it is not so much the individualism of Pentecostal conversion which leads to the creation of modern subjects, but the ways in which its projection on a global scale of images, discourses and ideas about renewal, change and salvation opens up possibilities for local actors to incorporate these into their daily lives" (2001, p. 80; see also Marshall-Fratani & Peclard 2002). Calling on believers as brothers and sisters in Christ, contemporary PCCs incite imaginations of community that surpass the space of the ethnic group or the nation as these imaginations are delocalized. This stance materializes in widely available (cassette and video) sermons, music, and literature that circulate in global Pentecostal networks and entice the constitution of a new public of born-again believers with a strong global outlook (Ellis & Ter Haar 1998). It also plays an important role in the diaspora, where many Africans do not have a staying permit and yet are entitled to be married in the church, thereby surpassing national identity politics (Van Dijk 2002). As Martin (2002) put it, "Charismatic Christianity is the portable identity of people in diaspora" (p. 145). So far, however, anthropologists have done little to develop more adequate research methodologies taking into account the transnational dimension of PCCs. They are still mainly studied at one particular location in Africa. One notable exception is Rijk van Dijk, who has researched Pentecostal networks stretching over Europe and Africa and conducted multi-sited fieldwork in Accra, The Hague, and Botswana (1997, 2002, nd.).

Although the research presented so far in this section may suggest that PCCs' practices translate smoothly into the notions of modernity and globalization, their use has also triggered debate. Englund & Leach (2000) have criticized anthropological fieldwork on PCCs for being "organized by the meta-narrative of modernity," which draws them into a Western perspective that ultimately fails to capture what actually goes on in these churches. In order to avoid misrepresentation, they advocate "to subscribe to a tradition of realist ethnography in which fieldwork as lived experience is indispensable for the production of anthropological knowledge" (p. 229). Presenting the case of Pentecostals in Chinsapo (Malawi), Englund & Leach offer valuable ethnographic material (see also Englund 1996), which indeed cautions not to disregard the particularities of different localities at the expense of sweeping generalizations about PCCs' attitude toward modernity. Although this is not the place to discuss these authors' intervention in any detail (but see the comments on their piece in *Current Anthropology*), I would like to briefly address the relationship they propose between ethnography and theory. Their plea resonates quite well with Fernandez's opposition of African imaginations and imageless Western concepts. The problem with such a view, as I try to point out above, is that it is based on an understanding of "African" or, as Englund & Leach call it, "local" as ontologically prior to and distinct from "the wider world" (see also Gupta 2000), and thus as impossible to capture by imageless theoretical frameworks, be it structural-functionalism, Marxism, or modernity. Given that the main reason for turning to modernity (and globalization), as outlined above, was the quest to better grasp how the supposedly "African" or local relates to foreign or global forces without relying on essentializing reifications, Englund & Leach's theoretical intervention does not have much to offer.

The need to move beyond this position, which has been haunting African studies—and certainly research on Christianity in Africa—for decades, has been asserted by the French political scientist Jean-François Bayart. In his reflections (2000) on "extraversion," he seeks to surpass the "sterile distinction between the internal dimension of African societies and their insertion in the international system" (p. 234; see also 1993). Insisting that Africa, in its own way, is a player in the process of globalization (rather than being merely disconnected), he investigates how initially foreign, colonial forces subjected Africans by constituting them as subjects. Building on Foucault's insights, Bayart argues that subjectivation, in both senses of the term, occurs most successfully through a noncoercive use of power, as, for instance, was the case with missions that played a key role in generating a new type of person characterized by new internalized modes of conduct perceived as irredeemably constitutive of one's identity. For Bayart, appropriation is the prime strategy of extraversion; but in his opinion it is not a question of "new wine in old skins," as was the case in the discursive context of Christianity and traditional religion. Instead, the appropriators themselves change in the process of appropriating new matters through external links. Here external and internal are not absolute but dialectical categories that continuously erase each other (and this, in the end, makes it difficult to say what exactly is African about strategies of extraversion, as Bayart still seems to claim). Extraversion, understood in this way, should not however be viewed as innocently creative and positive; rather, as Bayart shows, through appropriation and other strategies of extraversion, Africans also participate(d) dramatically in their own submission, resulting in political turmoil, war, and despair, and the adoption of alternative strategies such as trickery and brute coercion. Against the backdrop of this complex argumentation, which can only be evoked here, it becomes clear that essentialist differences between Africa and the world or the local and the global are impossible to maintain. Accounting for both structural constraints and creative appropriation, the notion of extraversion also allows scholars to reconcile an emphasis on narrativity and agency (Peel 1995), with attention paid to the "long conversation" initiated by the dynamics of newly emerging power structures (Comaroff & Comaroff 1991).

The usefulness of Bayart's approach to the study of Christianity in general (see Peel 2003) and PCCs in particular is obvious. Gifford (1998), for example, observes: "[F]or all the talk within African circles of localisation, inculturalisation, Africanisation or indigenisation, external links have become more important than ever" (p. 308). Extraversion being both a practice in place to incorporate external material and spiritual matters and a method of surviving, "Africa's newest Christianity, while in many ways reinforcing traditional beliefs, also serves [. . .] as one of Africa's best remaining ways of opting *into* the global order" (p. 321). Corten & Marshall-Fratani (2001), Maxwell (2000) and, somewhat surprisingly against the backdrop of his earlier stance, Englund (2003) have drawn similar conclusions. There is a danger, though, of overemphasizing the creative and positive aspects of extraversion, which would bring the notion disturbingly close to earlier approaches toward Africanization in the sense of tradition-oriented wholeness and harmony. In many respects, the study of PCCs has little eye for the possibly disorienting, unsettling, and destructive implications of born-again Christianity, the contradictions on which it thrives and the disappointments it generates (but see Behrend 1999, Marshall-Fratani 2001, Smith 2001). This omission may have to do with the fact that the anthropology of religion as a whole still seems to be very much biased toward an understanding of religion as stabilizing above all, in that it offers modes of orientation and control and a secure place to feel at home.

RELIGION AND THE PUBLIC SPHERE

If the two discursive contexts presented so far struggled, albeit in different ways, with the question of the relationship between Africa and the world, the last—and still less developed—discursive context to be presented here is organized along somewhat different faultlines: the relationship between Christianity and politics, or, in more general terms, religion and the secular. The question of AICs' political dimension having been a key concern for a long time, debates on the relationship between religion and politics tend to downplay one at the expense of the other (Ranger 1986). Whereas some scholars saw AICs as proto-nationalist organizations, others regarded them as inferior to political activity. Yet, Ranger (1986) noted, "few can study these movements without feeling that even if they were not unequivocally anticolonial they constituted a form of politics" (p. 6). This feeling that religion and politics were entangled in a more complicated way than would suggest their straightforward distinction and the academic division of labor associated with it (religious studies and political science) continued to inform debates about questions of resistance and domination. In these debates the understanding of resistance, and for that matter politics, was broadened so as to encompass the sphere of everyday life. Comaroff (1985), for instance, presented Tshidi Zionism under apartheid as constructing a "systematic counterculture, a modus operandi explicitly associated with those estranged from the centers of power and communication" (p. 191). Because afflicted people served as metonyms for the whole group, healing and deliverance from evil spirits was not merely individual, but rather involved collective restorative work. That Zionist churches did not stimulate overt collective political action was, Comaroff reasoned, due to a lack of opportunity to protest openly. Therefore, the powerless protested within the domain of everyday practice. Although Zionism could only mediate societal contradictions, but not transcend them, it did not turn Tshidi into docile servants of Apartheid, but instead enabled them to express symbolic resistance against the system. Schoffeleers (1991), building on similar data, argued that this understanding of resistance extended the notion beyond recognition. He presented the Zionist churches, and for that matter healing churches in general, as instilling political quiescence in their members—a position which evoked much disagreement (Gunner 2002, p. 6 and subsequent pages). Research on the relation between the symbolic and the political in AICs stretched "the semantics of the political" (Gunner 2002, p. 7) and developed into more complex reflections on processes of domination and control, in terms of Gramsci's notion of hegemony (see Comaroff & Comaroff 1991) or Bayart's notion of extraversion.

In my view, the relation between religion and politics is much more complicated than is highlighted in debates about the kind and extent of AICs' resistance. Scholars recognized that, power being always "rooted in the fusion of the secular and sacred worlds" (Akyeampong 1996, p. 167), it was impossible to disentangle religion and politics. Yet at the same time they reflected on religion and politics in a modern framework, which stressed that both belonged to separate spheres. In retrospect, one can observe that the master narrative of secularization, which, if implicitly, informed theorizing about AICs' politics, collided with the pressing realization that secularization made little sense with regard to the empirical context under study. Fields's (1985) study, mentioned previously, was crucial in highlighting this contradiction by showing that even in the colonial administration, a modern site par excellence, it was impossible to contain Christianity in a private realm. It went disturbingly public.

If research on AICs' politics has mainly explored symbolic forms of resistance, the new PCCs of the 1990s, often emerging in conjunction with processes of democratization and liberalization, urged researchers to pose new questions about Christianity's public role (e.g., Gifford 1998, Haynes 1996). Gifford's (1998) pioneering work on Christianity's public role in Ghana, Uganda, Zambia, and Cameroon articulates the paradox at stake: "In the West Christianity, while arguably a key source of modernity, has declined in its public significance as modern society has taken shape. In Africa it may be that Christianity is assuming an increasing significance in the creation of a modern, pluralistic African society" (p. 20). Important factors explaining Christianity's—not only PCCs'—public role are the precarious role of the African postcolonial state, with its run-down structures of governance and failure to achieve legitimacy, and its loosening grip on "civil society" as a result of IMF's pressure for "good governance" and "democratization." PCCs, in particular, owe their appeal to the fact that they easily link up with popular world views, which assert the power of invisible forces to impinge on the visual realm and thus readily match Pentecostalism's emphasis on evil spirits and deliverance.

The question of how to appreciate PCCs' politics is a matter of debate. Whereas, for instance, the political scientist Haynes (1996) sees PCCs as catering to the real needs of the people and countering the woes of modernization, Gifford is more reserved. Critiqued by mainline churches for their irrational outlook and political opportunism, PCCs easily "walk the corridors of power" (Gifford 1998, p. 341) and align themselves with the government, as numerous examples given by Gifford show. Conversely, those in power may parade their born-again identity, as was the case for Zambia's president Chiluba or Benin's president Kérékou. Nevertheless, here too, it is problematic to generalize, as different charismatic pastors adopt different stances toward politics and the government (as, for example, the case of the Ghanaian Mensah Otabil, who was a fierce critic of the Rawlings government, shows, whereas other charismatics aligned themselves with Rawlings) and PCCs' members' attitudes toward politics has hardly been subject to research. Recently, the question of PCCs' attitude toward democracy has become a new research focus which, for instance, materialized in a program funded by the Pew Foundation "Evangelicals and Politics in Africa, Asia and Latin America," with Ranger acting as the head of the African dimension of the program (Ranger 2003). The link between anthropological and political science approaches in research on PCCs and the recontextualization of this research in a global frame is laudable. Yet, an all-too-easy slippage into the discursive frameworks of democracy and civil society—the current catch words of global development circuits—needs to be resisted because these notions are often employed in a Eurocentric and normative way that is not helpful in understanding politics in Africa.

The most important feature of Gifford's analysis is the suggestion to investigate PCCs' popularity against the backdrop of the shifting role of the state in Africa. Whereas in the era of one-part dictatorial regimes (aptly analyzed by Mbembe 2001) the state sought to contain Christianity outside the public realm (and often fiercely resented mainline churches' criticisms leveled against its politics), the situation changed significantly with the onset of democratization and liberalization, when politicians (to be) voted into power depended on the consent of their often largely born-again constituencies. In such a situation, becoming Pentecostal may be a seductive political strategy, although, as Phiri (2003) has shown, declaring Zambia a Christian nation was of no help for the born-again president Chiluba to stay in power. It is fruitful to proceed along these lines in the future because the rise of particular PCCs and their public role can be understood only in reference to the reconfiguration of the political field in general, and the state in particular (Marshall-Fratani 1998). Capturing the entanglement of religion and politics requires an analysis in which attention to religious content and its political positioning converge, as argued (as well as demonstrated) by Ellis & Ter Haar (1998) in their perceptive analysis of the political implications of religious tracts as part and parcel of power struggles that straddle the boundary between the visible and invisible world as easily as that between religion and politics, or fantasy and reality (though, by calling attention to the religious dimension, they paradoxically reaffirm the understanding of religion as a separate sphere, which they put into question). The important and marked public role of PCCs testifies to the fact that the master narrative of secularization, which claims an intrinsic link between modernization and the decline of the public importance of religion, is inadequate to understand PCCs' attraction and impact on the political as well as personal level.

What is likely at stake is the way in which charismatic movements impinge on the imagination of communities, once the privileged sphere of the nation-state (Anderson 1991). Although our world is a world of nation-states, current African politics shows the incapacity of postcolonial states to bind the citizens into the vision of the nation. The constant occurrence of wars and terror in Africa—presented as a seemingly natural feature that does not even call for explanation in much press footage—pinpoints that the state seems to reach its limits in the face of both small-scale autochthonous incentives and transnational movements such as political Islam or PCCs. Recently the role of PCCs in the formulation of alternative imaginations of community has become a research topic. In this context, the blurring of distinctions between politics and religion is addressed in relation to the emergence of new modes of communication and debate in the public realm. Many PCCs (as well as Islamist movements) have been found to appropriate keenly new electronic media that have become easily accessible and, in a context of media deregulation, allow for an active part to play in identity politics (Marshall-Fratani 1998, Meyer 2004). In addition to the question of how newly available media technologies impinge on and possibly transform existing practices of mediation between the divine and the human world (Bastian 2001, Hackett 1998; see also Lyons 1990, Lyons & Lyons 1991, de Witte 2003), investigators also pay attention to the political and cultural implications of PCCs' new public voice. This is a question not only of politics in a more narrow sense, but also of the way in which PCCs contribute to the emergence of a new, more Christian public culture. Interesting in this context is the question of how, as a result of PCCs' popularity, public culture assumes a strong Pentecostal touch, yet also evokes strong opposition from other camps, such as neo-traditionalists (who increasingly tend to adopt the same media formats as PCCs) and Muslims (Meyer 2004).

In the future, there is a need not only for more comparative work between PCCs in Africa and other continents, but above all for more grounded investigations of the different voices in a particular arena, taking into account Islam, neo-traditional movements, and charismatic Christianity. An important issue concerns the way in which religions play into current identity politics, as they thrive in the limits of the state, by adopting new media practices that enable them to assume a public voice. Of particular interest is the question of how far, despite mutual disagreement and animosities, different religions actually tend to adopt similar formats of public articulation and religious mediation [as the striking similarities between the charismatic Muslim leader Haidara in Mali (Schulz 2003) and Mensah Otabil (de Witte 2003, Gifford 2003) suggest].

Ultimately, the need for anthropologists to pay attention to the shifting role and place of religion in Africa, which motivates much current research, also calls for a critical investigation of the notion of religion itself. As Asad (1993) argues, an understanding of religion in terms of "inner belief" is historically situated in Western Christianity and can thus not be applied simply to different religious traditions that may, for example, place much more emphasis on ritual and materiality (the often-reported misunderstandings between missionaries and Africans about the material outcome of conversion are telling in this regard). Much research on PCCs, however, refers to the religious dimension in terms of a deeply seated inner belief that constitutes the, in a sense, ungraspable power of religion, thereby reaffirming a definition of religion as a separate sphere (e.g., Ellis & Ter Haar 1998, Englund 2003, Hackett 1986). Although it is important to pay attention to PCCs' power to evoke deeply felt emotions and to mediate experiences of the supernatural, a universal definition of religion must be resisted. As Martin (2002) argues, for instance, certain features such as the strong notions of the "mobile self" and the "portability of charismatic identity" raise the question of whether Pentecostalism represents "postmodern religion" par excellence.

CONCLUDING REMARKS

The main aim of this review has been to show how the shift from AICs, as prime focus of study, to PCCs in the 1990s impinged on three discursive frames that shaped, yet were transformed by, the study of Christianity in Africa. Echoing a more general trend in anthropology (and cultural studies), also in the field surveyed here, researchers' relative certainties about the classifications and categories in use—as well as their usefulness—gave way to, albeit contested, processes of de-essentializing such notions as African, authentic, or local, detemporalizing tradition, deconstructing modernization, multiplying modernity, blurring the boundary between religion and politics, and even deuniversalizing religion. Of course, as I have tried to argue, these deconstructions happened for good reasons as, in a sense, the object of study itself seemed to demand these conceptual "liquidations" to be understood as part and parcel of a wider world. And yet, paradoxically, researchers' growing uneasiness about fixed categories and qualifications does not seem to be paralleled in the world they study. The openings facilitated by the acceleration of flows of people, goods, and ideas, the intensification of global links across national borders, and the compression of time and space seem to call into being new boundaries. Attempts to de-exoticize Africa and grasp its entanglement with "the wider world" notwithstanding, it is equally clear that many Africans experience being marginalized and "forgotten." The mass appeal of PCCs can be explained, at least in part, against this backdrop. Adopting a strategy of extraversion, which deliberately develops external links and promises connection with the world, PCCs nevertheless have to address a politics of identity and belonging, in which fixed markers govern processes of in- and exclusion, both in Africa and the diaspora. The challenge for the future is not only to understand what charismatic religion can and, equally importantly, cannot do in such configurations, but also to grasp the power of identity without naturalizing it, to deconstruct reifications without neglecting their power. The call for solid ethnography is as pertinent as ever.

ACKNOWLEDGMENTS

Many thanks to John Peel and my colleagues at the Research Centre Religion and Society and the Department of Anthropology (University of Amsterdam): Gerd Baumann, Peter Geschiere, Mattijs van de Port, Peter van Rooden, and Jojada Verrips for their perceptive, stimulating, and constructive comments on earlier versions of this review.

The *Annual Review of Anthropology* is online at http://anthro.annualreviews.org

LITERATURE CITED

Adogame A. 2000. Aiye Loja, orun nile—The appropriation of ritual space-time in the cosmology of the celestial church of Christ. *J. Relig. Afr.* 30(1):3–29

Akyeampong E. 1996. *Drink, Power, and Cultural Change. A Social History of Alcohol in Ghana, c.1800 to Recent Times.* Oxford: Currey

Anderson AH. 2001. Types and butterflies: African initiated churches and European typologies. *Int. Bull. Mission. Res.* 25:107–13

Anderson B. 1991. *Imagined Communities: Reflections on the Origins and Spread of Nationalism.* London: Verso. Rev. ed.

Appadurai A. 1996. *Modernity at Large. Cultural Dimensions of Globalization.* Minneapolis/London: Univ. Minn. Press

Appiah KA. 1992. *In My Father's House: Africa in the Philosophy of Culture.* New York/Oxford: Oxford Univ. Press

Appiah-Kubi K. 1981. *Man Cures, God Heals. Religion and Medical Practice Among the Akans of Ghana.* Totwa, NY: Allaheld, Osmun & Co

Arntsen H. 1997. *The Battle of the Mind.* IMK-Rep. No. 26. Oslo: Dep. Media Commun., Univ. Oslo

Asad T. 1993. *Genealogies of Religion: Discipline and Reasons of Power in Christianity and Islam.* Berkeley: Univ. Calif. Press

Asamoah-Gyadu K. 1997. 'Missionaries without robes': lay charismatic fellowships and the evangelization of Ghana. *Pneuma* 19(2): 167–88

Ayuk AA. 2002. The pentecostal transformation of Nigerian church life. *Asian J. Pentecostal Stud.* 5(2):189–204

Baëta CG, ed. 1968. *Christianity in tropical Africa.* Presented at 7th Int. Afr. Semin., Univ. Ghana, April 1965. London: Oxford Univ. Press

Barrett DB. 1968. *Schism and Renewal in Africa*. Oxford: Oxford Univ. Press

Barrett DB, ed. 2001. *World Christian Encyclopedia: A Comparative Study of Churches and Religions in the Modern World*. 2 Vols. Oxford: Oxford Univ. Press

Bastian ML. 1997. Married in the water: spirit kin and other afflictions of modernity in southeastern Nigeria. *J. Relig. Afr.* 27(2): 116–34

Bastian ML. 2001. Vulture men, campus cultists and teenaged witches. Modern magics in Nigerian popular media. In *Magical Interpretations, Material Realities. Modernity, Witchcraft and the Occult in Postcolonial Africa*, ed. HL Moore, T Sanders, pp. 71–96. London/New York: Routledge

Bayart JF. 1993. *The State in Africa. The Politics of the Belly*. Harlow: Longman

Bayart JF. 2000. Africa in the world: a history of extraversion. *Afr. Aff.* 99:217–67

Bediako K. 1995. *Christianity in Africa. The Renewal of a Non-Western Religion*. Edinburgh: Edinburgh Univ. Press

Behrend H. 1999. *Alice Lakwena and the Holy Spirit: War in Northern Uganda 1985–97*. Oxford: Currey

Beidelman TO. 1982. *Colonial Evangelism. A Socio-Historical Study of an East African Mission at the Grassroots*. Bloomington: Indiana Univ. Press

Blakely TD, Van Beek WEA, Thompson DL, eds. 1994. *Religion in Africa: Experience and Expression*. Oxford: Currey

Clifford J. 1988. *The Predicament of Culture: Twentieth Century Ethnography, Literature and Art*. Cambridge, MA: Harvard Univ. Press

Coe C. 2000. *'Not just drumming and dancing.' The production of national culture in Ghana's schools*. Diss. Univ. Penn., Philadelphia

Coleman S, ed. 2002. The Faith movement: a global religious culture. *Cult. Relig.* 3(2):1–128. Special issue

Comaroff J. 1985. *Body of Power, Spirit of Resistance: The Culture and History of a South African People*. Chicago: Univ. Chicago Press

Comaroff J, Comaroff J. 1991. *Of Revelation and Revolution: Christianity, Colonialism, and Consciousness in South Africa*, Vol. 1. Chicago: Univ. Chicago Press

Comaroff J, Comaroff J. 1997. *Revelation and Revolution: The Dialectics of Modernity on a South African Frontier*, Vol. 2. Chicago: Univ. Chicago Press

Comaroff J, Comaroff J, eds. 1993. *Modernity and Its Malcontents*. Chicago: Univ. Chicago Press

Comaroff J, Comaroff J, eds. 2001. *Millenial Capitalism and the Culture of Neoliberalism*. Durham, NC: Duke Univ. Press

Corten A. 1997. The growth of the literature on Afro-American, Latin American and African pentecostalism. *J. Contemp. Relig.* 12(3):311–34

Corten A, Marshall-Fratani R, eds. 2001. *Between Babel and Pentecost: Transnational Pentecostalism in Africa and Latin America*. Bloomington: Indiana Univ. Press

Corten A, Mary A, eds. 2001. *Imaginaires politiques et pentecôtisme: Afrique/Amérique du Sud*. Paris: Karthala

Cox H. 1994a. Healers and ecologists: Pentecostalism in Africa. *Christ. Century* 111(32): 1042–46

Cox H. 1994b. *Fire from Heaven: The Rise of Pentecostal Spirituality and the Shaping of Religion in the Twenty-First Century*. Cambridge, MA: Da Capo Press

Cziekawy D, Geschiere P, eds. 1998. Containing witchcraft: conflicting scenarios in postcolonial Africa. *Afr. Stud. Rev.* 41(3):1–209. Special issue

Daneel I. 1970. *Zionism and Faith-healing in Rhodesia: Aspects of African Independent Churches*. The Hague: Mouton

de Witte M. 2003. Altar Media's *Living Word*: televised charismatic Christianity in Ghana. *J. Relig. Afr.* 33(2):172–202

Dozon J-P. 1995. *La Cause des Prophètes. Politique et Religion en Afrique Contemporaine*. Paris: Seuil

Droogers A. 2001. Globalisation and

Pentecostal success. See Corten & Marshall-Fratani 2001, pp. 41–61

Droz Y. 1997. Si Dieu veut ... ou suppôts de Satan; incertitudes, millénarisme et sorcellerie parmi les migrants kikuyus. *Cahiers d'Etudes Africaines* 145:85–114

Droz Y. 2001. Des origines vernaculaires du réveil pentecôtiste kenyan: conversion, guérison, mobilité social et politique. See Corten & Mary 2001, pp. 81–101

Ellis S, Ter Haar E. 1998. Religion and politics in Sub-Saharan Africa. *J. Mod. Afr. Stud.* 36(2):175–201

Engelke M. 2004. Discontinuity and the discourse of conversion. *J. Relig. Afr.* 34(1–2):82–109

Englund H. 1996. Witchcraft, modernity, and the person: the morality of accumulation in Central Malawi. *Crit. Anthropol.* 16:257–79

Englund H. 2003. Christian independency and global membership: Pentecostal extraversions in Malawi. *J. Relig. Afr.* 33(1):83–111

Englund H, Leach J. 2000. Ethnography and the meta-narratives of modernity. *Curr. Anthropol.* 41(2):225–48

Etherington N. 1983. Missionaries and the intellectual history in Africa. *Itinerario* 7:116–43

Etherington N. 1996. Recent trends in the historiography of Christianity in Southern Africa. *J. South. Afr. Stud.* 22(2):201–19

Fabian J. 1971. *Jamaa: A Religious Movement in Katanga.* Evanston, IL: Northwestern Univ. Press

Fabian J. 1981. Six thesis regarding the anthropology of African religious movements. *Religion* 11:109–26

Fabian J. 1983. *Time and the Other. How Anthropology Makes Its Object.* New York: Columbia Univ. Press

Fabian J. 1991. *Time and the Work of Anthropology. Critical Essays.* Chur: Harwood Acad.

Fasholé-Luke E, Gray R, Hastings A, Tasie G, eds. 1978. *Christianity in Independent Africa.* London: Collings

Ferguson J. 1999. *Expectations of Modernity. Myths and Meanings of Urban Life on the Zambian Copperbelt.* Berkeley/Los Angeles: Univ. Calif. Press

Fernandez JW. 1978. African religious movements. *Annu. Rev. Anthropol.* 7:195–234

Fernandez JW. 1982. *Bwiti: An Ethnography of the Religious Imagination in Africa.* Princeton, NJ: Princeton Univ. Press

Fernandez JW. 1986. The argument of images and the experiences of returning to the whole. In *The Anthropology of Experience*, ed. V Turner, E Bruner, pp. 159–87. Urbana: Univ. Ill. Press

Fernandez JW. 1990. The body in Bwiti. Variations on a theme by Richard Werbner. *J. Relig. Afr.* 20(1):92–111

Fields K. 1985. *Revival and Rebellion in Colonial Central Africa.* Princeton, NJ: Princeton Univ. Press

Freston P. 1998. Evangelicals and politics: a comparison between Africa and Latin America. *J. Contemp. Relig.* 13(1):37–49

Geschiere P. 1997. *The Modernity of Witchcraft. Politics and the Occult in Postcolonial Africa.* Charlottesville: Univ. Press Va.

Gifford P. 1987. "Africa shall be saved": an appraisal of Reinhardt Bonnke's pan-African crusade. *J. Relig. Afr.* 27(1):63–92

Gifford P. 1991. *The New Crusaders: Christianity and the New Right in Southern Africa.* London: Pluto

Gifford P. 1994. Ghana's Charismatic churches. *J. Relig. Afr.* 24(3):241–65

Gifford P. 1998. *African Christianity. Its Public Role.* London: Hurst

Gifford P. 2003. *Ghana's New Christianity: Pentecostalism in a Globalising African Economy.* London: Hurst

Gray R. 1990. *Black Christians and White Missionaries.* New Haven: Yale Univ. Press

Gunner E. 2002. *The Man of Heaven and the Beautiful Ones of God. Umuntu Wasezulwini Nabantu Abahle Bakankulunkulu. Writings from Ibandla lamaNazaretha, a South African Church.* Leiden: Brill

Gupta A. 2000. Comment on Englund & Leach. *Curr. Anthropol.* 41(2):240–41

Gupta A, Ferguson J, eds. 1997. *Anthropological Locations: Boundaries and Grounds of a Field Science.* Berkeley: Univ. Calif. Press

Hackett RIJ. 1986. African new religious movements. *Afr. Stud. Rev.* 29(3):141–46

Hackett RIJ. 1998. Charismatic/Pentecostal appropriation of media technologies in Nigeria and Ghana. *J. Relig. Afr.* 28(3):1–19

Hall P. 1999. *Unity and faith: the negotiation of social and religious identities in Calabar.* Diss. Univ. Edinburgh

Hastings A. 1979. *A History of African Christianity 1950–1975.* Cambridge: Cambridge Univ. Press

Hastings A. 1995. *The Church in Africa, 1450–1950.* Oxford: Clarendon

Hastings A. 2000. African Christian studies, 1967–1999: reflections of an editor. *J. Relig. Afr.* 30(1):30–45

Haynes J. 1996. *Religion and Politics in Africa.* London: Zed Books

Hobsbawm E, Ranger TO, eds. 1983. *The Invention of Tradition.* Cambridge: Cambridge Univ. Press

Horton R. 1975. On the rationality of conversion: Part I & II. *Africa* 45(3):219–35, (4) 373–99

Inda JX, Rosaldo R, eds. 2002. *The Anthropology of Globalization. A Reader.* Malden, Oxford: Blackwell

Isichei E. 1995. *A History of Christianity in Africa. From Antiquity to the Present.* London: SPCK

James W, Johnson DH, eds. 1988. *Vernacular Christianity: Essays in the Social Anthropology of Religion Presented to Godfrey Lienhardt.* New York: Barber

Jenkins P. 2002. *The Next Christendom: the Coming of Global Christianity.* New York: Oxford Univ. Press

Jules-Rosette B. 1975. *African Apostles: Ritual and Conversion in the Church of John Maranke.* Ithaca: Cornell Univ. Press

Jules-Rosette B. 1994. The future of African theologies—situating new religious movements in an epistemological setting. *Soc. Compass* 41(1):46–95

Kearney M. 1995. The local and the global: the anthropology of globalization and trans-

nationalism. *Annu. Rev. Anthropol.* 24:547–65

Kiernan J. 1992. The herder and the rustler: deciphering the affinity between Zulu diviner and Zionist prophet. *Afr. Stud.* 51(1):231–42

Kiernan J. 1994. Variation on a Christian theme: the healing synthesis of Zulu Zionism. In *Syncretism/Anti-Syncretism. The Politics of Religious Synthesis,* pp. 59–84. London: Routlege

Konings P. 2003. Religious revival in the Roman Catholic Church and the authochthony-allochthony conflict in Cameroon. *Africa* 73(1):31–56

Landau PS. 1995. *The Realm of the Word. Language, Gender, and Christianity in a Southern African Kingdom.* London: Currey

Larbi EK. 2001. *Pentecostalism. The Eddies of Ghanaian Christianity.* Accra: Centre Pentecostal Charism. Stud.

Laurent P-J. 2001a. Transnationalism and local transformations. The example of the church of Assemblies of God of Burkina Faso. See Corten & Marshall-Fratani 2001, pp. 256–73

Laurent P-J. 2001b. The faith-healers of the Assemblies of God in Burkina Faso: taking responsibility for diseases related to "living together." *Soc. Comp.* 48(3):333–51

Lehman D. 2001. Charisma and possession in Africa and Brazil. *Theory Cult. Soc.* 18(5):45–74

Lyons AP. 1990. The television and the shrine. Towards an anthropology of mass communications. *Vis. Anthropol.* 3:429–56

Lyons AP, Lyons HD. 1991. Religion and the mass media in Nigeria. In *Religion and Society in Nigeria,* ed. J Olupona, pp. 97–128. Ibadan, Nigeria: Spectrum

MacGaffey W. 1983. *Modern Congo Prophets.* Bloomington: Indiana Univ. Press

Marshall R. 1991. Power in the name of Jesus. *Rev. Afr. Polit. Econ.* 52:21–38

Marshall R. 1998. God is not a democrat: Pentecostalism and democratization in Nigeria. In *The Christian Churches and the Democratisation of Africa,* ed. P Gifford, pp. 139–60. New York: Brill

Marshall-Fratani R. 1998. Mediating the global and the local in Nigerian Pentecostalism. *J. Relig. Afr.* 28(3):278–315

Marshall-Fratani R. 2001. Prospérité miraculeuse: les pasteurs pentecôtistes et lárgent de dieu au Nigeria. *Polit. Afr.* 82:24–44

Marshall-Fratani R, Peclard D, eds. 2002. Sujects de dieu. *Polit. Afr.* 87: 1–161. Special issue

Martin D. 1990. *Tongues of Fire.* Oxford: Blackwell

Martin D. 2002. *Pentecostalism: The World Their Parish.* Oxford: Blackwell

Mate R. 2002. Wombs as God's laboratories: Pentecostal discourses of feminity in Zimbabwe. *Africa* 72(4):549–68

Maxwell D. 1997. New perspectives on the history of African Christianity. *J. South. Afr. Stud.* 23(1):141–48

Maxwell D. 1998. Delivered from the spirit of poverty?: Pentecostalism, prosperity and modernity in Zimbabwe. *J. Relig. Afr.* 28(3): 350–73

Maxwell D. 1999a. *Christians and Chiefs in Zimbabwe: A Socal History of the Hwesa People, 1870–1990s.* Edinburgh: Edinburgh Univ. Press

Maxwell D. 1999b. Historicizing Christian independency: the southern African Pentecostal movement, 1908–50. *J. Afr. Hist.* 40(2):243–64

Maxwell D. 2000. "Catch the cockerel before dawn": Pentecostalism and politics in postcolonial Zimbabwe. *Africa* 70(2):247–77

Maxwell D. 2001. "Sacred history": traditions and texts in the making of a southern African transnational religious movement. *Comp. Stud. Soc. Hist.* 43(3):502–24

Mayrargue C. 2001. The expansion of Pentecostalism in Benin: individual rationales and transnational dynamics. See Corten & Marshall-Fratani 2001, pp. 274–92

Mbiti J. 1980. The encounter of Christian faith and African religion. *Christ. Century* 97(Aug. 27):817–20

Mbembe A. 2001. *On the Postcolony.* Berkeley: Univ. Calif. Press

Meyer B. 1992. 'If you are a devil you are a witch and, if you are a witch you are a devil.' The integration of 'Pagan' ideas into the Conceptual Universe of Ewe Christians in Southeastern Ghana. *J. Relig. Afr.* 22(2):98–132

Meyer B. 1997. Christian mind and worldly matters. Religion and materiality in nineteenth-century Gold Coast. *J. Mater. Cult.* 2(3):311–37

Meyer B. 1998a. "Make a complete break with the past." Memory and post-colonial modernity in Ghanaian Pentecostalist discourse. *J. Relig. Afr.* 27(3):316–49

Meyer B. 1998b. Commodities and the power of prayer. Pentecostalist attitudes towards Consumption in contemporary Ghana. In *Globalization and Identity. Dialectics of Flow and Closure Development and Change*, ed. B Meyer, P Geschiere, 29(4):751–77. Oxford: Blackwell

Meyer B. 1999. *Translating the Devil. Religion and Modernity Among the Ewe in Ghana.* Edinburgh: Edinburgh Univ. Press

Meyer B. 2002a. Christianity and the Ewe nation: German Pietist missionaries, Ewe converts and the politics of culture. *J. Relig. Afr.* 32(2):167–99

Meyer B. 2002b. Pentecostalism, prosperity and popular cinema in Ghana. *Cult. Relig.* 3(1):67–87

Meyer B. 2004. 'Praise the Lord.' Popular cinema and pentecostalite style in Ghana's New Public Sphere. *Am. Ethnol.* 31(1):1–19

Meyer B, Geschiere P, eds. 1999. *Globalization and Identity. Dialectics of Flow and Closure.* Oxford: Blackwell

Middleton J. 1983. One hundred and fifty years of Christianity in a Ghanaian town. *Africa* 53(3):2–19

Milingo E. 1984. *The World in Between: Christian Healing and the Struggle for Spiritual Survival*, ed. M Macmillan. London: Hurst

Moore HL, Sanders T, eds. 2001. *Magical Interpretations, Material Realities. Modernity, Witchcraft and the Occult in Postcolonial Africa.* London: Routledge

Mudimbe VY. 1988. *The Invention of Africa. Gnosis, Philosophy, and the Order of Knowledge.* Bloomington: Indiana Univ. Press

Mugambi JNK. 1996. African churches in social transformation. *J. Int. Aff.* 50(1):194–220

Niehaus I, Mohlala E, Shokane K. 2001. *Witchcraft, Power and Politics. Exploring the Occult in the South African Lowveld.* London: Pluto Press

Ojo M. 1988. The contextual significance of the charismatic movements in Western Nigeria. *Africa* 57(2):175–92

Onyinah O. 2002. Deliverance as a way of confronting witchcraft in modern Africa: Ghana as a case history. *Asian J. Pentecostal Stud.* 5(1):107–34

Otabil M. 1992. *Beyond the Rivers of Ethiopia: A Biblical Revelation on God's Purpose for the Black Race.* Accra: Altar Int.

Peel JDY. 1968. *Aladura: A Religious Movement Among the Yoruba.* London: Oxford Univ. Press

Peel JDY. 1990. The pastor and the *babalawo*: the interaction of religions in nineteenth-century Yorubaland. *Africa* 60(3):338–69

Peel JDY. 1994. Historicity and pluralism in some recent studies of Yoruba religion. Review article. *Africa* 64(1):150–66

Peel JDY. 1995. 'For who hath despised the day of small things?' Missionary narratives and historical anthropology. *Comp. Stud. Soc. Hist.* 37(3):581–607

Peel JDY. 2003. *Religious Encounter and the Making of the Yoruba.* Bloomington: Indiana Univ. Press

Pels P. 1999. *The Microphysics of Crisis. Contacts Between Catholic Missionaries and Waluguru in Late Colonial Tanganyika.* Chur: Harwood Acad.

Phiri I. 2003. President Frederick J.T. Chiluba of Zambia: the Christian nation and democracy. *J. Relig. Afr.* 33(4):401–28

Poewe K, ed. 1994. *Charismatic Christianity as Global Culture.* Columbia: Univ. S.C. Press

Probst P. 1989. The letter and the spirit: literacy and religious authority in the history of the Aladura movement in Western Nigeria. *Africa* 59(4):478–495

Ranger TO. 1986. Religious movements and politics in Sub-Saharan Africa. *Afr. Stud. Rev.* 29(2):1–69

Ranger TO. 1987. Religion, development and African Christian Identity. In *Religion, Development and African Identity*, ed. K Holst Petersen, pp. 29–57. Uppsala: Scand. Inst. Afr. Stud.

Ranger TO. 1993. The local and the global in Southern African religious history. In *Conversion to Christianity. Historical and Anthropological Perspectives on a Great Transformation*, ed. RW Hefner, pp. 65–98. Berkeley/Los Angeles: Univ. Calif. Press

Ranger TO. 2003. Evangelical Christianity and democracy in Africa: a continental comparison. *J. Relig. Afr.* 33(1):112–17

Ranger TO, Kinambo IN, eds. 1972. *The Historical Study of African Religion.* London: Heineman Educ.

Ross R, Bredekamp H, eds. 1995. *Missions and Christianity in South African History.* Johannesburg: Univ. Witwatersrand Press

Sackey B. 2001. Charismatics, independents, and missions: church proliferation in Ghana. *Cult. Relig.* 2(1):41–59

Salaome F. 1996. A history of Christianity in Africa. Review article. *Afr. Stud. Rev.* 39(3): 179–85

Sanneh L. 1991. *Translating the Message: The Missionary Impact on Culture.* Maryknoll, NY: Orbis Books

Sanneh L. 1996. *Piety and Power: Muslims and Christians in West Africa.* Maryknoll, NY: Orbis Books

Schoffeleers M. 1985. *Pentecostalism and Neo-Traditionalism: The Religious Polarization of a Rural District in Southern Malawi.* Amsterdam: Free Univ. Press

Schoffeleers M. 1986. Review of Bwiti by J Fernandez. *Africa* 56(3):352–56

Schoffeleers M. 1991. Ritual healing and political acquiescence; the case of Zionist churches in Southern Africa. *Africa* 61(2):1–25

Schoffeleers M. 1994. *River of Blood: the Genesis of a Martyr Cult in Southern Malawi, c. A.D. 1600.* Madison: Univ. Wis. Press

Schulz D. 2003. Charisma and brotherhood revisited: mass-mediated forms of spirituality in urban Mali. *J. Relig. Afr.* 33(2):146–71

Sindima HJ. 1994. *Drums of Redemption. An Introduction to African Christianity*. Westport, CT: Greenwood Press

Smith DJ. 2001. 'The arrow of God.' Pentecostalism, inequality, and the supernatural in South-Eastern Nigeria. *Africa* 71(4):587–613

Spear T, Kimambo IN, eds. 1999. *East African Expressions of Christianity*. Oxford: Currey

Steegstra M. 2002. 'A mighty obstacle to the gospel': Basel missionaries, Krobo women, and conflicting ideas about gender and sexuality. *J. Relig. Afr.* 32(2):200–30

Steegstra M. 2004. *Resilient rituals*. Diss. Univ. Nijmegen

Stewart C, Shaw R, eds. 1994. *Syncretism/Anti-Syncretism. The Politics of Religious Synthesis*. London: Routledge

Sundkler B. 1961 [1948]. *Bantu Prophets in South Africa*. London: Oxford Univ. Press

Sundkler B, Steed C. 2000. *History of the Church in Africa*. Cambridge: Cambridge Univ. Press

Ter Haar G. 1992. *Spirit of Africa: The Healing Ministry of Archbishop Milingo of Zambia*. London: Hurst

Ukah AFK. 2003a. *Redeemed Christian Church of God, Nigeria. Local identities and gobal processes in African Pentecostalism*. PhD thesis. Univ. Bayreuth, Bayreuth

Ukah AFK. 2003b. Advertising God: Nigerian Christian video-films and the power of consumer culture. *J. Relig. Afr.* 33(2):203–31

Vail L, ed. 1989. *The Creation of Tribalism in Southern Africa*. London/Currey/Berkeley: Univ. Calif. Press

Van Binsbergen WMJ. 1977. Religious innovation and political conflict in Zambia. A contribution to the interpretation of the Lumpa Rising. In *African Perspectives 1976/2 Religious Innovation in Modern African Society*, ed. WMJ van Binsbergen, R Buitenhuis, pp. 101–35. Leiden: Afr. Stud.

Van Binsbergen WMJ. 1981. *Religious Change in Zambia: Exploratory Studies*. London: Routledge & Kegan Paul

Van Binsbergen WMJ, Schoffeleers JM. 1985. Introduction. In *Theoretical Explorations in African Religion*, ed. WMJ van Binsbergen, JM Schoffeleers, pp. 1–49. London: Routledge & Kegan Paul

Van Dijk R. 1992. *Young Malawian Puritans: Young Puritan Preachers in a Present-day African Urban Environment*. Utrecht: ISOR

Van Dijk R. 1997. From camp to encompassment: discourses of transsubjectivity in the Ghanaian Pentecostal diaspora. *J. Relig. Afr.* 27(2):135–60

Van Dijk R. 1998. Fundamentalism, cultural memory and the state. Contested representations of time in postcolonial Malawi. In *Memory and the Postcolony: African Anthropology and the Critique of Power*, ed. R Werbner, pp. 155–81. London: ZED Books

Van Dijk R. 2002. The soul is the stranger: Ghanaian Pentecostalism and the diasporic contestation of 'flow' and 'individuality'. *Cult. Relig.* 3(1):49–66

Van Dijk R. (nd). Transnational images of Pentecostal healing: comparative examples from Malawi and Botswana

Werbner RP. 1985. The argument of images: From Zion to the wilderness in African churches. See Van Binsbergen & Schoffeleers 1985, pp. 253–86

Werbner RP. 1989. *Ritual Passage, Sacred Journey: the Process and Organization of Religious Movement*. Manchester: Manchester Univ. Press

Werbner RP. 1990. Bwiti in reflection: on the fugue of gender. *J. Relig. Afr.* 20(1):63–91

Wijsen F. 2000. Popular Christianity in East Africa: inculturation or syncretism? *Exchange* 29(1):37–60

Annu. Rev. Anthropol. 2004. 33:475–98
doi: 10.1146/annurev.anthro.33.070203.143758
Copyright © 2004 by Annual Reviews. All rights reserved

THINKING ABOUT CANNIBALISM

Shirley Lindenbaum

*Department of Anthropology, City University of New York, New York,
New York 10016-4309; email: lindenbaum@mindspring.com*

Key Words exoticism, primitivism, anthropological theory, savage/civilized
opposition, the modern Western and postmodern self

■ **Abstract**   The discourse of cannibalism, which began in the encounter between
Europe and the Americas, became a defining feature of the colonial experience in the
New World, especially in the Pacific. The idea of exoticism, like that of the primitive,
is also a Western construct linked to the exploring/conquering/cataloguing impulse of
colonialism. We now live in a world where those we once called exotic live among us,
defining their own identities, precluding our ability to define ourselves in opposition
to "others" and to represent our own culture as universal. This chapter reviews anthropological approaches to cannibalism and suggests that we may now be in a position
to exorcise the stigma associated with the notion of the primitive. If we reflect on the
reality of cannibal practices among ourselves as well as others, we can contribute to
dislodging the savage/civilized opposition that was once essential to the formation of
the modern Western self and Western forms of knowledge.

INTRODUCTION

Few topics have attracted more attention in recent years than that of corporeality
(Cottom 2001, p. xi). Following a shift in perspective in the human sciences in the
1970s, which gave closer attention to bodily representation, the "body" became a
source of creative tension in anthropology. The body had long been "good to think"
(Lévi-Strauss 1963, p. 89). Decentering the physical body of the basic sciences and
questions concerning the epistemological assumptions entailed in the production
of natural facts radicalized and relativized our perspective on such recalcitrant
dichotomies as nature/culture, self/other, and mind/body. The shift in perspective
is also said to have incited increased reflexivity in the anthropological study of
bodily practices (Lock 1993, p. 134).

At first glance it may seem that a similar story can be told about body eating.
For many years the history and analysis of cannibalism was written from within
a European or Western tradition little concerned with issues of power and representation. Renewed interest in the practice followed in part from Arens (1979)
provocative suggestion that institutionalized cannibalism never existed because
centuries of reports about cannibalism were not based on reliable eyewitness

0084-6570/04/1021-0475$14.00

evidence. In light of this criticism, many anthropologists reevaluated their data, and more nuanced studies became available from Papua New Guinea (Brown & Tuzin 1983; Knauft 1985, 1993, 2002; Goldman 1999), South America (Conklin 2001), China (Sutton 1995), Africa (Ellis 1999; Geschiere 1998; Guille-Escuret 1998, 2000), and Fiji (Sahlins 2003). Noting the ethnocentricity of the criticism, some anthropologists called for reflection on our own horror of the practice and for the topic to be discussed in ways that avoid resort to denial or euphemism (Gardner 1999, Ernst 1999). Brady (1982) also pointed to the strict positivism and naturalism of the criticism and proposed a return to the search for meaning in the accounts of actors in cannibal cosmologies, dramas, and rituals.

At the same time, the turn toward representation in the late 1980s gave new life to studies of cannibalism as a colonizing trope and stratagem. Cannibalism is said to be one of the most important topics in cultural criticism today, one which pierces to the very heart of current discussions of difference and identity (Kilgour 2001, p. vii). Kilgour's (1990) anatomy of metaphors of incorporation, which examines the relationship between cannibalism and our dominant Western mode of producing meaning through strategies of exclusion, paved the way for current readings of cannibalism as a metaphor in colonial discourse. Representation of the cannibal as the cultural "other" was soon to be a theme for a wide array of studies (Lestringant 1997, Barker et al. 1998, Creed & Hoorn 2001, Guest 2001, McAvoy & Walter 2002).

By the 1990s a full counter-narrative had emerged. Cannibalism was viewed as a calumny used by colonizers to justify their predatory behavior. Postcolonial studies proposed "that the figure of the cannibal was created to support the cultural cannibalism of colonialism through the projection of Western imperialist appetites onto cultures they then subsumed" (Kilgour 2001, p. vii). The idea that some accounts of cannibalism by missionaries, administrators, and adventurers, as well as the allegations of neighboring groups, might be seen as derogatory or ethnic stereotypes, was an idea worth serious consideration. Like many counter-narratives, however, it is in danger of oversimplifying the story it seeks to overturn. The idea continues to appeal to sceptics who view cannibalism as a mere product of the European imagination, a tool of Empire, with its origins in the disturbed human psyche (Hulme 1998, p. 3). From the time of Montaigne to the present, the image of the cannibal is said to have had a tendency to overrun its own borders until nothing coherent, nothing literal, is left either of the behavior, or the flesh that is its nominal object (Lestringant 1997, p. 8; Cottom 2001, p. xvii). Just as the body is in danger of slipping from our grasp (Lock 1993), the cannibal of discourse is becoming more spectre than substance.

Our desire to think about cannibalism has a long history in a wide range of studies in history, philosophy, psychoanalytic theory, and literature. In the fifth century B.C., Herodotus (1973) wrote about anthropophagi, said to be living beyond the light of Greek civilization. In the sixteenth century, Montaigne introduced us to man eating in the New World, and in the twentieth century, psychoanalysts proposed that cannibal images were projections of unconscious desires in early childhood

(Freud 1913, Klein 1975). In literature, Defoe, de Sade, Melville, Flaubert, Conrad, Harris, and other scholars provided readers with the frisson of pleasure to be experienced in different images of cannibal transgression.

TYPOLOGIES OF CANNIBALISM

The word cannibal is said to be a legacy of Columbus' second voyage to the Caribbean in 1493. Referring originally to the Caribs in the Antilles who were identified as eaters of human flesh, the term was subsequently extended as a descriptive term for flesh eaters in other populations (Hulme 1992, p. 16). The discourse of cannibalism, which began with the encounter between Europe and the Americas, was to become a defining feature of colonial encounters in the New World, and especially the Pacific, during which the image of the "noble savage" suffered progressive degradation. As a prime symbol or signifier of "barbarism" the cannibal was central to the construction of the cultural "other," and to Enlightenment notions of refinement, modernity, and Western civilization. The resilience of the conceptual opposition of the "savage other" and the "civilized self" is a question to which I return later.

Even among sceptics, cannibalism is acknowledged in several forms. Survival cannibalism and cannibalism as psychopathology are most frequently noted. Survival cannibalism, the consumption of others under conditions of starvation such as shipwreck, military siege, and famine, in which persons normally averse to the idea are driven by the will to live, applies to such well-known cases as that of the Donner Party. Caught in the Sierra Nevada mountains in 1846 during a brutal winter storm, the survivors resorted to eating those who had died, as well as two Indian scouts sent to save the expedition. In a similar case, Alferd Packer confessed to eating members of his small band of fellow travelers caught in a mountain blizzard in Colorado in 1883 (see Conklin 2001, pp. 87–88). More recently, several survivors of the Uruguayan rugby team, whose plane crashed in the Andes in 1972, spoke about the experience for television, and an early case of cannibalism was the subject of Edgar Allan Poe's "The Narrative of Gordon Pym" (1946 [1938]), based on the explorer's confession published in the *Southern Literary Magazine* in 1837. Scholars have also documented the eating of human flesh during conditions of famine in France during the 1570s (Rawson 2001, p. 25), in China between 1958 and 1962 (Becker 1999), and in Cambodia in the late 1970s (*N.Y. Times* 1979, Kristof 1993). The evolutionary underpinnings of cannibalism as a survival strategy, said to have been practiced since prehistoric times, is the subject of *The Cannibal Within* (Petrinovich 2000).

The current surge of interest in cannibalism has also fed salacious newspaper and television reports of cannibalism as psychopathology, aberrant behavior considered to be an indicator of severe personality disorder or psychosis. Recent cases include a Japanese student at the Sorbonne who in 1981 murdered and ate his Dutch girlfriend. Considered mentally incompetent to stand trial in France, Mr. Sagawa returned to Japan where he spent a year in hospital. His serialized novel of the crime and his role as a talk show commentator have resulted in his celebrity status as a "bunkajin," a person of culture with expertise in a specific area (*South China Morning Post* 2000). More recent cases include that of Albert Fentress, a former school teacher who spent 20 years in psychiatric hospitals for killing and eating a Poughkeepsie student (LeDuff 1999), and a 41-year-old German software technician, prosecuted for killing and eating a man he met through a Web site where he solicited "young, well-built men aged 18 to 30 to slaughter" (Landler 2003). Other cases of cannibalism as psychopathology can be found on the Web (one can use http://www.google.com to search for cannibalism as psychopathology).

The many anthropological attempts to create a typology for the diversity of literal cannibalism (Farb & Armelagos 1980, Sanday 1986, Brady 1996, Goldman 1999, Conklin 2001, Tuzin 2001) have resulted in such well-accepted categories as endocannibalism, the volitional eating of someone from within the group, and exocannibalism, eating someone from outside the group. (See Viveiros de Castro 1992, p. 258–59 for a concept of cannibalism in South America which is neither "endo" nor "exo.") Endocannibalism usually occurs in the form of funerary or mortuary consumption, in which all or part of the body is ingested as an act of affection (Glasse 1963, 1967; Lindenbaum 1979; Conklin 2001), or for group renewal and reproduction (Gillison 1983, Meigs 1984). Exocannibalism as an act of aggression, often in the context of warfare, has been reported from the Americas, the South Pacific, and Africa. Recent accounts include the Wari of Amazonia, who practice both forms (Conklin 2001, p. xxiii), along the south coast of New Guinea (where it is associated with head hunting), in the middle Sepik region and much of the Solomon Islands (see Knauft 1999, p. 103), as well as among inland groups in the Strickland-Bosavi region of New Guinea's Southern Highlands Province (Ernst 1999, p. 144). We also have well-documented accounts of officially sanctioned aggressive cannibalism from Guangxi, China, during the Cultural Revolution in the late 1960s (Yi 1993, Sutton 1995), and more recently by soldiers in the Congo (Bergner 2003).

The many typologies of cannibalism describe a wide diversity of behaviors that shade into Western medical and dietary regimes. Medicinal cannibalism, for example, the ingestion of human tissue, has been documented in European medical literature since at least the first century A.D. Pliny said that drinking human blood was a cure for epilepsy. In addition to blood, Europeans ingested human tissue, usually that of an executed criminal, as a supposed medicine or tonic (Gordon-Grube 1988). Medicinal ingestion involving human flesh, blood, heart, skull, bone marrow, and other body parts was widely practiced throughout Europe from the sixteenth to the eighteenth centuries. Human flesh obtained from "mummy shops," where the remains of an embalmed, dried, or otherwise prepared human body that had ideally met with sudden, violent death, was considered to be a "universal panacea" by the Parcelsians who, in contrast to the Galenists, promoted the use of a variety of body substances. Samuel Johnson's 1785 dictionary of English includes a description for preparing mummy, indicating that it was still being sold at that date, and it was still available in 1909 from a reputable German pharmaceutical company (pp. 405–9).

Advances in medicine are said to have created technological cannibalism in the global traffic in human organs, as well as in the potential for human cloning.

Cadaver-derived drugs from pituitary glands for the production of human growth hormones (for enhanced body building and for clinically stunted children) were used extensively in England from the late 1960s to early 1980s, a practice that came under scrutiny during the epidemic of mad cow disease.

Auto-cannibalism (or autophagy) refers to the act of eating parts of oneself: hair, nail clippings, mucous, excrement, and placenta, but also instances in which individuals under torture or other duress partake of their living flesh, raw or cooked (Favazza 1987, Bergner 2003). Placentophagy, in which the mother eats her newborn baby's placenta (as was the case among the Fore in precolonial times), became popular in the United States with the spread of the home-birth movement in the 1970s. In the American context, the placenta is often shared among close family members. Some vegetarians are enthusiastic about eating placenta because they do not classify the placenta as meat. For those who avoid meat out of compassion for animal suffering, placenta is said to be the meat of life, the only "unkilled" meat available (Janszen 1980).

Just as the home-birth movement provided a niche for placentophagy, consuming the ashes of a loved one became feasible in the United States as professional services for the cremated body of the deceased were no longer felt to be obligatory (C. Baird, personal communication). Bone ash cannibalism has been reported also in South America among the Amahuaca (Dole 1974) and the Yanomami (Lizot 1976).

Sacrificial cannibalism, in which the victim is treated with solicitude and honor as a prelude to sacrifice to the gods, is a widely reported form of aggression. Aztec cannibalism in fifteenth-century Mexico (Harner 1977), as well as nineteenth-century Fijian practices (Sahlins 1983), belong in this category. The Christian ritual of the Eucharist is its symbolic extension. Tannahill (1975, pp. 27–28) suggests that the biblical pattern of sacrifice from "probably human, through animal, through monetary, to its symbolic form of fasting and prayer" is a sequence found in other countries and religions.

Innocent cannibalism, a category in Tuzin's (2001) refined inventory, occurs when a person is unaware that he or she is eating human flesh. In Greek legend, Atreus punishes his brother Thyestes for seducing his wife by tricking him into eating his own children (Tuzin 2001). The unwitting ingestion of human flesh is also a theme in popular entertainment. *Sweeney Todd* (http://www.crimelibrary.com/serial9/sweeney) is based on the case of a murderous barber and a baker, his partner in crime, who dispose of bodies by baking them into pies. It is also a theme in *Motel Hell* (http://classic-horror.com/reviews/motelhell.html), in which a farmer makes smoked meats composed of individuals he considers to be contributing undesirable elements to the gene pool.

As Tuzin (2001, p. 2) wisely notes, types of cannibalism vary not only according to motive and circumstance, but also the diversity is so great that it tends to overwhelm the common feature of ingestion and confound efforts to understand the practice as a unitary phenomenon (Wike 1984, Lestringant 1997). The problem of coming to terms with such diversity is so great that it might be better to talk about "cannibalisms." Moreover, cannibal typologies remain lodged within categories emerging from our own culture and institutions. How anthropology might provide an adequate account of the many forms of cannibalism is a topic I address also at the end of the review.

CANNIBALISM AND ANTHROPOLOGICAL THEORY

A review of anthropological approaches to cannibalism takes us on a walk through the history of theory in the human sciences. Cannibalism, similar to incest, aggression, the nuclear family, and other phenomena of universal human import, appears to be a concept on which to exercise certain theoretical programs (Tuzin & Brown 1983, pp. 2–3). Montaigne's (1581) essay on cannibalism is often cited as a precursor to the development of later ideologies of cultural relativism (Goldman 1999). Modern accounts might begin in the 1930s with Malinowski's functional analyses of the way the institutions of society fit together and reinforce one another, a stance he took in recognizing the value of African culture "even to the point of defending such traditional practices as witchcraft and cannibalism" (Stocking 1991, p. 56). Evans-Pritchard's own investigations (1937), as well as his evaluation of other accounts of cannibalism in the Zande region (1955, 1956), led him to believe cannibalism was based on a desire for meat. He also thought that there were ethnic and geographical variations and that was probably not a regular practice.

The functionalist concerns of British anthropology in the late 1950s led scholars to examine cannibalism in Highland New Guinea in the context of relationships among social structure, sorcery, politics, and warfare (Berndt 1962). In the 1970s the practice was sometimes presented in an evolutionary frame as a cultural trait reflecting a stage in humanity's social and moral development (Tannahill 1975).

Aspects of functionalism, found compelling through the 1970s, prompted anthropologists to suggest that the consumption of human flesh was of nutritional benefit for some populations in New Guinea, and to the further suggestion that an ecological explanation may apply to tropical peoples living at low-medium population densities exploiting a diverse range of animal foods (Dornstreich & Morren 1974). A materialist explanation was also said to account for the ritual slaughter and consumption of war captives by the Aztecs in fifteenth-century Mexico during times of famine and shortage of animal protein (Harris 1977, 1985), and to support the proposition that human flesh provided incentives for warriors and helped to sustain the power of elites. The Aztec case provoked a heated debate about population levels and ecological conditions in the valley of Mexico (Ortiz de Montellano 1978), eliciting Sahlins' (1979, p. 53) criticism of the bourgeois grounding of such Western-oriented materialist explanations.

Sahlins (1978) observations about Aztec cannibalism provide a clue to the theoretical shift taking place during 1970s and 1980s toward matters of cultural belief, cosmology, and ritual. The "practical function of institutions," he said, "is never adequate to explain their cultural structure" (p. 45). Essays and monographs began to reflect this shift toward symbolism, ritual, and cosmology (Wagner 1967, Lindenbaum 1983, MacCormack 1983, Poole 1983, Tuzin 1983, Meigs 1984, Knauft 1985). Psychological analyses indebted to Freud were also a feature of this period (Sagan 1974; Tannahill 1975; Gillison 1983, 1986; Sanday 1986).

By the 1980s, following 50 years of theoretical engagement with the topic, global theorizing about cannibal practices was judged to be decidedly premature. Anthropologists were said to be notably uninformed about cannibalistic ideas and practices in specific cultural settings, and a volume of essays was offered in the hope of "advancing our knowledge and cultural understanding of this aspect of human fact and fantasy" (Tuzin & Brown 1983, pp. 3–4).

During the 1990s, anthropologists continued to document the diversity of bodily practices and beliefs in particular locations, asking in each instance what it meant for those who practiced it. By this time a consensus of opinion had formed among anthropologists working in Melanesia (Goldman 1999; Knauft 1999, p. 103), South America (Conklin 2001, p. 13), and in some instances in Africa and China that institutionalized cannibalism was practiced by some peoples in the past. The focus of scholarly attention turned instead to the mirrored reflections of both fact and fantasy to be found in diverse behaviors and beliefs (Goldman 1999). Reluctant to deny the "reality" of cannibal practices prior to contact, Geschiere (1998) looked at the ways in which the rubber boom in South Cameroon and the brutal confrontation between the Germans and the Makka shaped the imaginary of cannibalism for all concerned. (Compare Guille-Escuret 1998 for discussion of Central Africa; Ellis 1999, p. 265 on Liberia; and a sensationalist report from the Congo by Bergner 2003.) In China, Sutton (1995, p. 169) looked beyond the ideology of politically sanctioned cannibalism during the cultural revolution to the cultural factors underwriting and justifying the practice. Verrips (1991) suggested that cannibal themes in recent movies, books, and music, as well as in foods named after human body parts, provide substitutes and imaginary satisfaction for cannibalistic tendencies in societies where the Eucharist has lost much of its sway. The substitution of newer for older forms of sublimation thus harnesses in culturally appropriate ways the deep-seated desire (and accompanying anxiety) of humans to eat their own kind (p. 50).

Refinements of natural selection theory in the 1960s and 1970s encouraged evolutionary biologists to tackle what they viewed as the "vile or unsavory behaviors performed by animals," such as "rape, slavery, infanticide, mate-desertion and cannibalism" (Mock 1992, p. 1969). The paradigm was shifting from the view that traits evolve mainly for the good of the population or species, to the idea that phenotypic traits, including behavior patterns, evolved because of net benefit to the individual's inclusive fitness. As in the other sciences, the topic of cannibalism had become a more-or-less respectable area for investigation. Attention turned to the taxonomic diversity and evolutionary significance of intraspecific predation, and to the proximate cues underlying cannibalistic acts, their genetic basis, and the impact of cannibal practices on population and community structure (Mock 1992).

During the 1980s archaeologists also turned to the "darker side of humanity" to examine violence, slavery, and cannibalism, displacing an earlier focus on nationalism and gender. Some scholars are persuaded that cannibalism occurred in the prehistoric American Southwest, on the basis of reports of human myoglobin detected in a cooking pot, as well as the chemical residue of human flesh found in fossilized human feces (Marlar et al. 2000). Other archaeologists dispute these findings as well as evidence of bone damage patterns, which they believe is better explained by ritualized violence associated with the persecution and execution of witches (Ogilvie & Hilton 2000). Walker (2001) provides a summary of the debate and notes that cannibalism seems to have been widespread in both the Old and New Worlds. Recent accounts of cannibalism among early hominids in Spain (Wilford 2003) are expected to enhance our ability to explain prehistoric practices by establishing a pattern across time and space.

At the turn of the twenty-first century, the topic of cannibalism continues to lend itself to explanatory trends in the human sciences. Anthropologists have come to appreciate the dangers of framing cultural difference in historical terms, ignoring the extent to which various social and cultural forms and practices encountered in the present are themselves the products of modern social, political, and cultural processes. Modern transformations of behavior and practice are now seen to involve the constant creation of new expressions of cultural difference, as well as redefinitions of alternate beliefs and practices (O'Brien & Roseberry 1991). Studies have moved from examining cultural isolates to documenting the historical processes by which people in distant locations were becoming "alternatively modern" (Knauft 2002). Knauft's early-1980s ethnography of Gebusi social life in New Guinea, for example, provides a rich menu of all-night dances, elaborate initiation ceremonies, and a dramatic array of sorcery inquests and divinations that had led in preceding decades to the execution and cannibalism of up to one third of the adult population. When he returned in 1998, fundamentalist Christianity, schooling for children, and the marketing of garden produce had effected changes so great that indigenous dances and initiations were mostly limited to remote villages, spirit mediumship was defunct, and sorcery inquests and cannibalism no longer occurred (Knauft 2002, p. 107). Ethnographic attention to "vernacular or alternative modernities" seemed one way to counter the legacy of the Enlightenment concept of "modernity" and the social science discourse of "the West and the Rest" (Hall 1992).

As indicated earlier, the topic of cannibalism has recently provided lifeblood for postcolonial and cultural studies. Although some aspects of postmodernism had earlier filtered into cultural anthropology, the topic of cannibalism did not seem to lend itself to a postmodern pastiche of genres, voices, and identities. Taussig's (1987) study of terror and healing in Colombia is, perhaps, an exception, as is Tom Harrison's (1937) little-known work *Savage Civilisation*, an exercise in postmodernism before its time. Harrison's boastful talk of hobnobbing with cannibals in Vanuatu and headhunters in the Borneo bush, as well as criticism of his data collection methods that seemed but an accumulation of disconnected observations, may have deflected attention from this protopostmodern creation of a plural text, its questioning of ethnographic authority, recognition of the need for reflexivity, and its irreducibly literary nature (MacClancy 2002).

As Geertz (1995) observes, cultural anthropology draws the greater part of its vitality from the controversies that animate it. Between 1992 and 2003, Obeyesekere and Sahlins have been engaged in a high-profile debate concerning how scholars should understand non-Western cultures. Obeyesekere (1992) considers that people's beliefs and actions have practical function in people's lives and should be understood along psychological lines. If we pay attention to the dialogical nature of cannibalistic discourse in the logs and journals of Cook's voyages, he suggests, we see that they reveal more about the relations between Europeans and Savages than about the nature of Savage anthropophagy (pp. 630–31). The British and the Maori, both fascinated by cannibal behaviors, shared the "dark bond of cannibalism" (p. 638). The British fascination is said to have provoked the exaggerated behavior of the Maori in the relish with which they consumed the roasted human flesh that the British offered them (p. 638). A historical account of this scene (Thomas 2003, p. 214) similarly considers the Maori performance to be a response to the sailors' manifest preoccupation with the topic and was intended to produce shock. (Compare Dening 1980, p. 287 on the "performance" and shock value of cannibalism in the South Pacific).

In contrast to Obeyesekere, Sahlins (1983) takes the view that there are distinct cultures and that they should be understood along structuralist lines. The cultural sense of cannibalism is the concept of it as set by its place in a total cultural scheme, which gives it a differential value in relationship to other categories or concepts. The project to recuperate Fijian cannibalism thus amounts virtually to the recuperation of the culture. It was "a complex phenomenon whose myriad attributes were acquired by its relations to a great variety of material, political, linguistic, ritual, supernatural elements of society" (Sahlins 2003, p. 4). Sahlins rejects Obeyesekere's suggestion that "cannibalism" be used to refer only to a British discourse about the practice, distinguishing it from the older term anthropophagy for the sacrifical practices of Polynesian peoples.

The echo of Lévi-Strauss in Sahlins' analysis is present also in recent French essays, where cannibalism is still "good to think." Going beyond the narrow view of anthropophagy merely as human consumption, cannibal metaphors are said to speak about different social, cultural, and religious realities. The creativity of the metaphor establishes connections among objects in different contexts: between eating human flesh and relations of kinship and alliance, as well as notions of identity and difference, savagery, animality, the excessive use of power, and the operations of the law. The figure of the cannibal allows authors in different epochs to think reflectively about other ways of life and different ways of being human (Kilani

2001/2002). Cultural views and representations of bodily aggression associated with sorcery, warfare anthropophagy, corporal punishment, and sacrifice are also said to reveal significant connections between the body and order and disorder in cosmic and social life (Godelier & Panoff 1998). Helen Clastres (1972) suggests that the objective of Tupi warfare, in which the Tupi killed and devoured brothers-in-law, was carried out not to capture women, but as an expression of a yearning for a world without affines and dependency on others. Lemonnier's (1992) account of the striking homogeneity of forms of bodily aggression among different Anga groups leads him to suggest transformation (in a historical and structural sense) of an older cultural system common to them all.

The Spanish ethnographer Viveiros de Castro (1992) also adopts a Lévi-Straussian stance in his analyis of cannibalism among the Arawete of eastern Amazonia. The theme of divine cannibalism, central to the Arawete definition of the human condition, is treated as part of the complex of Tupi-Guarani ritual anthropophagy. Tupinamba cannibalism has no privileged level of explication but is an element in a complex system that cannot be reduced to a simple function. It consists "in an interrelation of several explanatory levels" (p. 274).

Curiously, all the major positions on cannibalism maintained today are said to have been well represented by the eighteenth century (Cottom 2001, p. 145). Expressions of doubt can be found in John Atkins' [1735] narrative of exploration, in which he argues that cannibalism was simply unthinkable, and in the report of William Wales, the astronomer assigned to the Resolution on Cook's second voyage (pp. 138–39). That cannibalism was an act with an audience in mind, intended to induce terror, was proposed by a thirteenth-century Dominican friar (concerning the Mongols), by Léry in the sixteenth century (about the Tupi), and in 1778 by John Carver (about the Iriquois) (Sanborn 1998, p. 61). Jean de Léry also cites cases of famine cannibalism in France in 1573, when mothers ate their children (Lestringant 1997, p. 74). Lévi-Strauss' suggestion (1964, p. 386) that certain of our own customs might seem barbarous to an observer from a different society was prefigured in Montaigne's 1562 encounter with the Brazilians in Rouen. The notion that the conqueror is as savage as the savages appears in Book 1 of the *Iliad*, in Plato's *Republic*, and in Aristotle's *Politics*. It recurs in the response of some early Christians about their Roman prosecutors who called the Christians cannibals because of the Eucharistic rite (the Christians said that the Romans, who roasted their victims at the stake, were the true cannibals), and the preoccupation with the notion of the "savage in all of us" includes Plato's reflections on the tyrant whose brutalities are equivalent to cannibal barbarism (Rawson 1997, p. 6). The cannibal within every human being was also the judgment of a contributor to the *Encyclopédie* [1751–1765] edited by Diderot (Cottom 2001, p. 160).

Cannibalism as metaphor also has a long history in philosophy and literature (Lestringant 1997, Rawson 2001). Montaigne, de Pauw, Swift, Diderot, Rousseau, Bougainville, de Sade, Flaubert, and Jules Verne each drew on the topic to speak about the social realities of their time. Stepping into metaphor is said to be a traditional maneuver whereby troubling insinuations about cannibalism can be considered without being taken for real (Rawson 2001, pp. 25–33).

THE SEMANTICS OF TRANSGRESSIVE CONSUMPTION

Shrinking from literalism is also an artifact of a selective focus on aggressive exo-cannibalism, overlooking endocannibalism, which lacks the same symbolic charge (Guille-Escuret 1998, p. 120). Reflecting a Western "cannibal phobia" (Guille-Escuret 2000, p. 186), the notion of cannibalism is described as "repugnant" (Arens), a "dark bond" (Obeyesekere), "vile and unsavory" (evolutionary biology), casting a "dark shadow" (Sartore), and one that displays the "darker side of humanity" (archaeology). Setting aside for the moment the racist and at times gendered inflection of the language, cannibalism in Western eyes is viewed as a transgressive form of consumption. The Western encounter with savage transgression provided an opportunity to test and explore fundamental boundaries in the home culture. The nature of transgressive consumption, however, is seen in a different light at different times.

Marco Polo's ecstatic description of the natural wonders of Quilon portrayed difference as a source of pleasure and delight. For late-thirteenth-century authors, the wonders of the East had overwhelmingly positive associations. They found much to blame, such as idolatry and occasionally the alleged cannibalism of the peoples they described, but the exotic races were too remote and strange to present a conceptual or political threat. At its most transgressive state, cannibal behavior served to satirize courtly and aristocratic culture, but it did not appear scandalous or pathological. The thirteenth-century and fourteenth-century topographical literature embraced exoticism, finding expression in the topos of the relativity of the marvellous (Daston & Park 1998, p. 34).

The Renaissance image of the heroic cannibal adopted by Montaigne as well as by the first missionaries to the New World, which was linked to the aristocratic values of magnanimity and chivalry, would soon be challenged by the greed of the conquistadors and the excessive zeal of missionaries (Lestringant 1997, p. 7). The earliest images of cannibalism for European eyes, however, were provided by the illustrators of de Bry's *Great Voyages* [1590–1634]. For these seventeenth-century Protestant engravers, cannibalism, although not condoned, was not a theological sin but a form of immoderate eating. The Tupinambas were thus judged to be pagans and savages for committing one or another of the four kinds of gluttony: excess frequency (eating before need); quality (seeking delicacies for pleasure); quantity (consuming immoderate amounts); or table manners (eating with avidity) (Bucher 1981, p. 51). Renaissance views of cannibalism also held it to be "natural" because the four humors make human flesh tasty to humans who are made of the same stuff (Shapin 2002, p. 21).

The literal ingestion of human flesh not surprisingly evoked the Eucharist, its sublimated variant. Debate over the Eucharist, fraught with cannibal associations since the earliest days of the Christian Church, became a major point of polemical contest in Reformation Europe (Rawson 1997, p. 4). Carried to the New World, the sins of immoderate consumption were extended to the excesses of Spanish colonization. The analogy between the sacrament and New World anthropophagy allowed Calvinists to compare Catholics to the Outeca, bad cannibals who ate their victims raw, an allusion to the sanguinary sacrifice of the Catholic mass. The Tupinamba, who cooked their enemies after death, and who provided hospitality to strangers, were the good cannibals, who, like good Protestants, invited worshippers to gather round the communal table in devotions that were open to the whole group (Rawson 1997). The trope of the good and the bad cannibal (the noble and ignoble savage) would reappear and become transformed with French and British adventures in the Pacific, which settled on new images of transgression and desire.

Political and economic conditions in seventeenth-century Europe also provided the context for dwelling on images of gourmandizing excess. Poverty and unrest stemming from the decline of the wool trade allowed Protestant and Republican authors to focus on the sins of appetite associated with unreformed religion. Morality plays depict monks and priests as gluttonous lechers: The Spanish were the tyrants consuming other nations to satisfy their Babylonian, Roman Catholic, and absolutist ambitions (Healy 2002, p. 179). The theme of sensual and gourmandizing excess retains its political resonance in judgments about contemporary tyrants. Reports of Emperor Bokassa of the Central African Empire eating humans for breakfast, often in a flaming brandy sauce, is a way of speaking about the illegitimate use of power in Africa in cultures where the language of "eating" is used as a metaphor for power and accumulation (Bayart 1993, White 2003).

During the eighteenth century, the theme of cannibalism retains its transgressive edge for European audiences but begins to acquire new meaning. With the opening of the human body, Enlightenment thinking is said to have taken a visceral turn. "Disgusting questions of incorporation, assimilation, and digestion" were vital to the philosophical self-images of the Enlightenment (Cottom 2001, p. xii). A rhetoric of visceral embodiment and metamorphosis is threaded through the philosophical discourses of the era. Metamorphosis provided the issue around which nature was conceived. and which, in a pre-Darwinian era, the relation between sameness and difference could be articulated. The self-contradictory, self-consuming figure of the cannibal, confounding the distinction between self and other, stood for all the uncertainties in the Enlightenment conception of the world (Cottom 2001, p. xiv).

In the context of increasing overseas trade, religious proselytization, and imperial expansion, some eighteenth-century writers began to explore the perverse attractiveness of the image of the cannibal in order to reflect on certain features of their own societies (Cottom 2001, p. 153). Defoe (1719) portrays the cannibal as a nexus of ambiguous desire. Robinson Crusoe is attracted to the idea of eating human flesh and to being eaten, illustrating the way in which the bourgeois subject was being defined by the exclusion of what is marked as dirty, repulsive, or contaminating, an exclusion that bears the imprint of desire (Stallybrass & White 1986).

The ambivalence of cannibal transgression perhaps reached its extreme in de Sade's (1797) description of his characters gorging on wines, liqueurs, shit, semen, and bits of human flesh. His critique of colonial exploitation is perhaps undone by his own exploitation of cannibal eroticism. Flaubert's 1862 novel *Salammbo* was also designed to flout the conventions of the literary world and vilify the bourgeoisie. Set in Carthage in the fourth century B.C., *Salammbo* is a story of cannibalism, torrid eroticism, the din of battles, and the sacrifice of children, written in what he calls his "cannibal style," transgressive writing about a transgressive topic. At a dinner to launch the book he is said to have offered his guests "human flesh, brain of bourgeois and tigress clitorises sauteed in rhinoceros butter" (Slater 2001, pp. 4–5).

In the postmodern world the idea of the cannibal has been emptied of the urbane irony present in Swift's (1729) *Modest Proposal* in which he argued that the sale of small Irish children for human consumption would rescue the economy, please the Irish nation, prevent the children of the poor from being a burden to their parents, work in favor of marriage, put a stop to abortions, and make men as fond of their pregnant wives as they were of their mares in foal, cows in calf, or sows ready to farrow, no longer beating them for fear of miscarriage. Contemporary performances of "immoderate eating" for profit and entertainment have also lost the moral edge and political resonance we associate with early forms of transgressive consumption. Competitions in the United States and Japan, in which people eat as much of a given food as possible in a set time, receive television coverage and attract a wide audience (Hesser 2002, Ballard 2003), as does the sight of Americans eating beetles and other culturally questionable substances (Ogunnaike 2003). No longer regarded as a sin of gluttony or a platform for ridiculing bourgeois behaviors, popular enactments of immoderate eating merely play with the borders of modern sensibilities. When Tobias Schneebaum consumed human flesh while living with the Amarakaire in Peru, he crossed the boundary and was judged by many Americans to have descended into primitivism, illustrating the resilience of the taboo, since cannibalism is not a crime in the United States. The event is recorded in Schneebaum's 1969 autobiography and retold in the film *Keep the River on Your Right* (see Zalewski 2001). Schneebaum's experiment with transgressive consumption ran afoul of a European discourse on cannibalism, highly developed in the nineteenth century (Obeyesekere 1992, p. 641), and which depended on the opposed concepts of the primitive other and the civilized self.

FROM PAGAN TO PRIMITIVE IN THE PACIFIC

During the eighteenth century a significant change was taking place in the way native inhabitants of new worlds came to be understood and described. Renaissance perceptions of difference had been religious rather than racial or national. The intruders were described not as Spaniards, Europeans, or whites, but Christians, and the Indian was not a savage of any particular type, but a naked pagan, available to be converted. The shift away from religiously framed difference entailed new models for constructing otherness couched in a narrative of natural history. Humanitarian and appreciative assessments of dissimilarity (as well as some negative judgments) were displaced from the late Enlightenment onward by a more uniform, intolerant, and less subtle denigration of physical inferiority and moral fault (Thomas 1994, pp. 77–79). The decisive move in Enlightenment thinking away from mythological, religious, and other "causes" of social evolution to material causes recast the history of mankind in a single continuum, with societies ranked lower or higher on the same scale. This Enlightenment discourse about social progress depended on the discursive figures of the "noble" and "ignoble savage," formulated in terms of "the West and the Rest," and provided the language in which "modernity" first came to be defined (Hall 1992, pp. 312–14). Cannibalism was to become the prime symbol or signifier of "barbarism" for a language of naturalized typification and essentialized difference that would harden in the negative racism of the nineteenth century (Thomas 1994, p. 79).

The image of the noble savage had attained sociological status with Rousseau's account of simple, unsophisticated people living in a state of nature, unfettered by laws, government, property, or social divisions. This state of paradise was discovered anew with French and British exploration of the Pacific. Bougainville's reports from Tahiti ("I thought myself transported into the Garden of Eden") seemed to fulfill this preoccupation with an image that provided a vehicle for criticism of over-refinement, religious hypocrisy, and social inequalities in the West (Hall 1992, p. 311). When Cook arrived in Tahiti in 1769, the same idyll of a sexual paradise and ideas of innocence were repeated again (p. 302), and early paintings of Cook's death in Hawaii portrayed both Cook and the natives who killed him in the "heroic" mold (p. 310). When Cook brought the Tahitian Omai to Europe in 1774, his tattoos fascinated London society, sparking a tattooing vogue among the English aristocracy. The noble savage was still alive when Kabris, a French seaman shipwrecked and tattooed in the Marquesas, was rescued and taken to St. Petersburg, where his tattoos were admired at the Court of the Tzar. When he reached France in 1817, however, his tattoos were no longer viewed with wonder and delight. Now marked as a savage, the tattooed Kabris found employment only in Bordeaux's Cabinet of Illusions and in fairs where he had become "a monster in a menagerie of anatomical and morbid curiosities" (Le Fur 2001, pp. 38–41).

During the nineteenth century, missionaries in the Pacific began to denounce the tattoo as an unpardonable mockery of the divine work. By 1875 Cesare Lambroso had outlined his theories concerning heredity and criminal behavior ("L'homme criminel"), noting the tendency for criminal offenders to be tattooed, the sign of pathology (Boulay 2001, p. 110). For Pierre Marie Dumoutier, the phrenologist on Dumont D'Urville's 1837–1840 expedition to the South Seas, the intricate designs tattooed on the skin of high-ranking and common people in the Marquesas were judged by the yardstick of their supposed barbarity. They represented the outward marks of a society of cruelty, which refused to allow the "natural" expressions of human nature (Rochette 2003).

By the end of the eighteenth century, as maritime exploration turned its focus to the scientific classification of animal and human species (Boulay 2001, p. 32), and with the death and disappearance of the navigator Defresne (killed and eaten by the Maori), the disappearance of De Lange and La Pérouse, and the death of Cook in 1779, the idealized image of the noble savage was no longer tenable. The stereotype of the noble savage had always contained within it its mirror opposite, the ignoble savage. In this new location, the dualism became gendered in the form of the beautiful, enticing siren and the malicious, bestial cannibal, a distinction that, as colonial intentions became more focused, would be extended to civilized, white Polynesians and savage, black Melanesians. In the South Pacific, the Western sense of self had produced another fantasy of longing and transgression: a world of sirens without men and cannibals without women (Boulay 2001, p. 114).

The construction of the stereotype of the South Seas savage took place on many fronts. Beginning in London in 1851 and ending in 1931 in Paris, international exibitions proclaimed the superiority of Western civilization. Visitors to the 1889 Paris exhibition were invited to view the skulls of primitive men organized by the exhibition's director of anthropology, illustrating the ladder of races with whites at the summit. One hundred "kanaks" were imported from New Caledonia for the 1931 Paris exhibit, where they were installed in the Bois de Boulogne, a park for exotic plants and animals. Newspapers ran stories about two sensational attractions: wild cannibals and 1000 crocodiles. The "kanaks" were subsequently exhibited as savage cannibals and polygnists in a number of German towns, although most of the Polynesians were practicing Catholics (Le Fur 2001, pp. 44–45).

The image of the primitive savage was also a creation directed at young minds. A pedagogical discourse on the antipodes was developed in nineteenth-century French atlases and encyclopedias designed for children. A 1910 history book for primary schools still noted that barbarians are people who do not know how to cultivate the earth, have no metal nor schools, and are ignorant. In addition, they do not know how to nourish, clothe, or house themselves properly, they are always quarelling with one another, and they have no understanding of justice. They are the reverse of all that is civilized. Jules Verne's novels, in which children survive a terrible confrontation with Pacific cannibals, represent a genre of adventure stories reflecting these views. Between 1880 and 1910 his contemporary, Louis Boussenard, published more than 50 similar adventure books: *Le Tour du Monde d'un Gamin de Paris* (1880) and *Aventures d'un Gamin de Paris en Océanie* (1890) were among the most popular (Boulay 2001, pp. 146–62).

Nineteenth-century missionary literature was particularly skillful at creating an image of primitivism. Called on to explain the existence of savagery in divine creation, the ecclesiastics proposed that the long migration of the sons of Ham from the banks of the Euphrates, passing through India, had come to rest in Melanesia. Thus, one finds among the blacks in Africa, Asia, and Oceania "loathsome vices. . .and cannibalism in all its hideous subtleties" (Boulay 2001, pp. 104–9). Such nineteenth-century romanticism, which dwelt on an image of the heroic missionary marching toward the supreme sacrifice, perhaps destined to impress mission donors, continued well into the twentieth century (e.g., Dupeyrat's 1954 autobiography *Savage Papua: A Missionary Among Cannibals*). The discovery of gold in Papua New Guinea extended the life of similar tales of personal encounters with savage cannibals (Booth 1929, Demaitre 1936).

Airbrushed out of these mythologies of heroic adventure are the complexities of interethnic encounter and sexual confrontation, as well as the more gruesome story of conflict, violence, and dispossession (Thomas 1994, p. 76; Rawson 2001, p. 150). To justify political intervention and colonization, however, the literature on adventure by the end of the nineteenth century had settled on the Fijian King Thakombau (for the English) and chief Bourarate de Hienghene, the "king" of New Caledonia (for the French) to represent the abominations of anthropophagy (Boulay 2001, p. 60).

THE END OF EXOTICISM

The idea of exoticism, like the notion of the primitive, is a Western construct linked to the exploring/conquering/cataloging impulse from the late fifteenth century to the present, a concept now undermined by changing historical and material conditions. From the beginning of the sixteenth century, the Tupinamba of Brazil quickly came to represent the extreme of exoticism in the European imagination (Guille-Escuret 2000, p. 195). More than a lyrical celebration of things tropical, the concept of exoticism was a particular way of introducing the "foreign" to the West. The generic representation of otherness found in Western texts allowed subjects of a dominant culture to counter that culture in the very process of returning to it (Célestin 1996, p. 3). The factors that form its basis are found in a predominantly French literature representing colonial exploration and the discovery of new territories (p. 23). Montaigne, for example, presents the exotic as a viable alternative to the "civilized" world. He considers the absence of laws among the Tupinambas to be more desirable than their proliferation in France, a decentering of the assumptions of his world through the use of the exotic (Célestin 1990).

We now live in a postmodern world in which those we once called exotic live among us. Writers from formerly exoticized locations define their own identities as they find exoticism in the streets of Paris or New York. We are said to have reached the limits of exoticism in a world in which cultural differences have become so diffuse and shifting. When the exotic becomes part of "home," we experience a break in the clear opposition between the Western self and the exotic other and in the ability of the West to represent its own culture as universal (Célestin 1996, pp. 16–18).

International flows of capital have also conflated the idea of "inside" and "outside," of center and periphery. In the West, we have become consumers of the products of our own exported capital. Exotic goods arrive in our markets as kitsch, leached of local meanings. Hotels in the Pacific offer for sale skulls that hint at the "mana" of the savage victor who has appropriated this important body part, and France Telecom promotes the "tatoo," a small reception device worn as a bracelet for elite consumers to "stay in contact with your tribe" (Boulay 2001, p. 177). Ethnic fusion in dance, dress, music, art, and cuisine undermine the political valence of "exoticism," which had coincided with the high point of colonial expansion (Célestin 1996, p. 19). The once-seductive siren of the Pacific, now revived to promote tourism to Polynesia, has lost much of her ideological presence.

THE END OF PRIMITIVISM?

The image of colonized peoples, however, depended on the idea of the "primitive" as well as the "exotic." Primitivism, like exoticism, formed part of the larger conceptual framework that produced a history of "mankind" on the basis of a single continuum divided into a series of stages. Although exoticism may have reached something of an endpoint (Célestin 1996, p. 3) and we are said to be witnesses to the end of "serious academic exploration of exoticism" (Goldman 1999, p. 3), this is not the case with primitivism. Sometimes conflated, the "primitive" and the "exotic" are not the same. Exoticism has more to do with difference and strangeness rather than with an antithetical relation to modernity. The primitive, in contrast, assumes some kind of originary, socially simple and natural character (Thomas 1994, p. 173). The figure of the "cannibal," an icon of primitivism, retains much of its ideological force.

As this review suggests, however, we are at a turning point in thinking about cannibalism. The common factor in the history of cannibal allegations is the combination of denial in ourselves and attribution of it to those we wish to defame, conquer, and civilize. In these so-called egalitarian times, and in the current atmosphere of postcolonial guilt and imperial self-inculpation, denial about ourselves has been extended to denial on behalf of those we wish to rehabilitate and acknowledge as our equals (Rawson 1997, p. 3).

The literal figure of the cannibal has recently reappeared, however, even flourished, in both non-Western and Western settings. Anthropologists working in the Americas, Africa, and Melanesia now acknowledge that institutionalized cannibalism occurred in some places at some times. Archaeologists and evolutionary biologists are taking cannibalism seriously. We have evidence of the incorporation of human body parts in Western medicinal and technological procedures, as well as in some birth and mortuary rituals. The possibility that cannibalism was a widespread practice among early humans was suggested recently by a British team of investigators studying a common polymorphism in the human prion protein gene (PRNP) known to confer resistance to prion diseases. Studies among the Fore of Papua New Guinea showed that in marked contrast to younger Fore who had not eaten human flesh, and who were thus not exposed to the prion-causing kuru, the protective gene was most prevalent among Fore women over 50 years of age who had participated in multiple mortuary ceremonies, and who had survived the kuru epidemic that devastated the population from the 1920s to the 1950s. The spread of prion-related disease triggered by endocannibalism, it is suggested, could have increased pressure to develop the protective polymorphism. This same genetic variation is said to protect against a variant of Creutzfeldt-Jacob disease, the human form of mad cow disease in Britain (Mead et al. 2003).

The suggestion that cannibalism might have been a widespread practice among early humans provides a welcome opportunity to move from double denial to double acknowledgment, freeing us from fabricating conceptions about ourselves that depend on defaming others. A willingness to accept the idea of cannibalism as a widespread practice is impelled by the urge, common to both camps, to close the conceptual space dividing the West from the Rest.

How might we write about cannibalism today? In recent years, some anthropologists have called on their colleagues to provide information they have about the practice. Reticence not only damages the ethnographic project by failing to document the varieties of ways of being human; it has done nothing to modify popular stereotypes and racially defamatory discourses and gives weight to the bourgeois tendency to universalize its own standards of behavior (Ernst 1999). Acknowledging the possibility that cannibalism has been part of the human record, including our own, could perhaps meet Brady's call (1982) for philosophical housecleaning around the complexities of getting to know cannibals. We are encouraged also to take seriously the notion that anthropology is one of the moral disciplines whose characteristic modality is not only the study of their objects but also an ethically relevant engagement with them (Gardner 1999).

An anthropology of cannibalism that steps beyond metaphors about our own behaviors could unsettle dominant Western systems of knowledge, said to be lacking in recent literature on the topic (Ernst 1999, p. 155). Even Montaigne, who we rightly honor for his ethical exploration of cannibalism not weighed down by the need to make moral judgment, suppresses the fact that cannibal acts about which he must have known occurred during the religious wars in France. An especially famous case occurred in the Protestant city of Sancerre, and several other instances were reported about the public sale and consumption of parts of mutilated Huguenots in Paris, Lyon, and Auxerre, events witnessed and reported by Léry in 1574, before Montaigne published his essay (Rawson 2001, pp. 25–26).

The task of writing about cannibalism will not be left to anthropologists alone. People in Papua New Guinea have recently expressed their views about the practice. During a number of court trials held in the 1960s and 1970s, villagers brought to court to face the charge of cannibalism, which they did not contest, were acquitted. In 1971, for example, an Australian judge acquitted seven men from Western Papua because cannibalism was "not improper or indecent in the community to which the charged men belonged," and there was at that time no specific charge in Territory law (Courier-Mail 1971). By 1978, however, another judge convicted 3 men of "improperly interfering with a body," but he admitted he labored under the disability of not being a Papua New Guinean by birth. Recently appointed to the Papua New Guinean national court, the judge made it clear, however, that cannibalism was now contrary to the new Papua New Guinea national constitution, which guaranteed certain basic human rights (Baker 1978, Smales 1978).

Papua New Guinea writers have also addressed the issue. Douglas Waiko interviewed elderly men from the Binandere community in Northern Papua, who recalled with pride their own practices of "cannibalism, raiding and the like" (Waiko 1970). In 1995, Buluna discussed famous cases of cannibalism in the Milne Bay area with people who provided detailed descriptions of the protocol associated with the treatment and consumption of victims, and of the accompanying elaborate feasting and dancing (Buluna 1995).

The topic also received recent attention in the national parliament. In 1972, a member from the Eastern Highlands informed the House of Assembly that he had eaten human flesh and requested that education be extended to his area so his children would not continue to do the same thing (*Sun* 1972). Greater publicity was given to Prime Minister Skate's remarks following an insensitive joke about cannibalism by Prince Philip of Britain during his 1998 visit to Papua New Guinea. Mr. Skate said he was saddened by suggestions that cannibalism is still practiced in Papua New Guinea. Two months later, however, at a ceremony celebrating the opening of a school in the Gulf province, the Prime Minister cautioned oil industry representatives present at the ceremony that should they decide to abandon Papua New Guinea, he would readily lead his people back to the days when his ancestors killed and ate a white man (Goldman 1999, p. 20).

Skate's invocation of cannibalism as a sign of strength, self-reliance, and possibly a threat to outsiders could be compared to the heroic phase (1920–1930) of Brazilian "modernismo," when intellectuals and artists self-consciously adopted a primitivist identity in an attempt to promote an aesthetic revolution commensurate with modernity. Andrade's *Revista de Antropofagia* used anthropophagy as a metaphor for the cosmopolitan enterprise of absorbing foreign and native cultures as the means to construe a unique Brazilian identity. Adopting a cannibal identity transformed a taboo into a totem and redefined anthropophagic primitivism as a positive value—a witty and self-reflective critique of colonialism (Bellei 1998).

The Enlightenment sciences of man provided the framework within which modern social science and the idea of "modernity" were formulated. The discourse of the West and the Rest is still at work in some of the conceptual categories, stark oppositions, and theoretical dualisms of contemporary social thought (Hall 1992, p. 313). The figure of the cannibal, long used to establish difference and construct racial boundaries, can now be called on in projects to deconstruct them (Kilgour 1998, p. 242). The stigma of savagery and primitivism, it seems, is best countered when we forgo our attachment to metaphor to describe our own behaviors and reflect on the reality of cannibal activities among ourselves as well as others. We are then in a position to dislodge the savage/civilized dualism, once essential to the formation of a modern Western identity and Western forms of knowledge, as we fashion a new understanding of our postmodern selves.

The *Annual Review of Anthropology* is online at http://anthro.annualreviews.org

LITERATURE CITED

Arens W. 1979. *The Man-Eating Myth: Anthropology and Anthropophagy*. New York: Oxford Univ. Press

Baker M. 1978. Jungle law tangle. *Age* Sept. 1

Ballard C. 2003. That stomach is going to make you money some day. *NY Times Mag.* Aug. 31, pp. 24–27

Barker F, Hulme P, Iversen M, eds. 1998. *Cannibalism and the Colonial World*. Cambridge: Cambridge Univ. Press

Bayart J-F. 1993. *The State in Africa: The Politics of the Belly*. London: Longman

Becker J. 1999. *Hungry Ghosts. Mao's Secret Famine*. New York: Holt

Bellei SLP. 1998. Brazilian anthropophagy revisited. See Barker et al. 1998, pp. 87–109

Bergner D. 2003. The most unconventional weapon. *NY Times* Oct. 26, pp. 48–53

Berndt R. 1962. *Excess and Restraint. Social Control Among a New Guinea Mountain People*. Chicago: Univ. Chicago Press

Booth DR. 1929. *Mountains Gold and Cannibals*. London: Palmer

Boulay R. 2001. *Essays in Kannibals and Vahinés. Imagerie des mers du Sud*. Paris: Ed. Reun. Mus. Natx.

Brady I. 1982. The myth-eating man. *Am. Anthropol.* 84:595–610

Brady I. 1996. Cannibalism. In *The Encyclopedia of Cultural Anthropology*, ed. D Levinson, M Ember, pp. 163–67. New York: Holt

Brown P, Tuzin D, eds. 1983. *The Ethnography of Cannibalism*. Washington, DC: Soc. Psychol. Anthropol.

Bucher B. 1981. *Icon and Conquest. A Structural Analysis of the Illustrations Of de Bry's GREAT VOYAGES*. Chicago: Chicago Univ. Press

Buluna M. 1995. Having the neighbours for dinner. *East. Star* May 1, pp. 12–13

Célestin R. 1990. Montaigne and the cannibals: toward a redefinition of exoticism. *Cult. Anthropol.* 5(3):292–313

Célestin R. 1996. *From Cannibals to Radicals. Figures and Limits of Exoticism*. Minneapolis: Univ. Minn. Press

Clastres H. 1972. Les beaux-frères enemis: a propos du cannibalisme Tupinamba. *Nouv. Rev. Psychanal.* 6:71–82

Conklin BA. 2001. *Consuming Grief. Compassionate Cannibalism in an Amazonian Society*. Austin: Univ. Tex. Press

Cottom D. 2001. *Cannibals and Philosophers. Bodies of Enlightenment*. Baltimore, MD: Johns Hopkins Univ. Press

Creed B, Hoorn J. 2001. *Body Trade. Captivity, Cannibalism and Colonialism in the Pacific*. New York: Routledge

Daston L, Park K. 1998. *Wonders and the Order of Nature, 1150–1750*. Cambridge: MIT Press

Defoe D. 1981 [1719]. *The Life and Adventures of Robinson Crusoe*. Harmondsworth, UK: Penguin

Demaitre E. 1936. *New Guinea Gold. Cannibals and Gold-seekers in New Guinea*. Boston: Houghton Mifflin

Dening G. 1980. *Islands and Beaches. Discourse on a Silent Land. Marquesas 1774–1880*. Honolulu: Univ. Hawaii Press

Dole GE. 1974. Endocannibalism among the Amahuaca Indians. In *Native South Americans: Ethnology of the Least Known Continent*, ed. P Lyon, pp. 302–8. Boston: Little, Brown and Co.

Dornstreich MD, Morren EB. 1974. Does New Guinea cannibalism have nutritional value? *Hum. Ecol.* 2:1–12

Dupeyrat A. 1954. *Savage Papua. A Missionary Among Cannibals*. New York: Dutton

Ellis S. 1999. *The Mask of Anarchy. The Destruction of Liberia and the Religious Dimension of an African Civil War*. New York: N.Y. Univ. Press

Ernst TM. 1999. Onabasulu cannibalism and the moral agents of misfortune. See Goldman 1999, pp. 43–159

Evans-Pritchard EE. 1955. Review. *Africa* 25(2):202–3

Evans-Pritchard EE. 1956. Cannibalism: a Zande text. *Africa* 26:73–74

Evans-Pritchard EE. 1958 [1937]. *Witchcraft, Oracles and Magic Among the Azande*. Oxford: Clarendon Press

Farb P, Armelagos G. 1980. *Consuming Passions. The Anthropology of Eating*. Boston: Houghton Mifflin

Favazza AR. 1987. *Bodies Under Siege. Self-Mutilation in Culture and Psychiatry*. Baltimore: Johns Hopkins Univ. Press

Flaubert G. 1997 [1862]. *Salammbo*. London: Penguin Classics

Freud S. 1953 [1913]. *Totem and Taboo. Standard Edition of the Collected Works of Sigmund Freud*. London: Hogarth Press

Gardner D. 1999. Anthropophagy, myth, and the subtle ways of ethnocentrism. See Goldman 1999, pp. 27–50

Geertz C. 1995. Culture war. *N.Y. Rev. Books* Nov. 30, pp. 4–6

Geschiere P. 1998. Rubber and cannibalism. Pap. Semin. *Fantasy Spaces—The Power of Images in a Globalizing World*, ed. B Meyer, B. Thoden van Velzen, Amsterdam

Gillison G. 1983. Cannibalism among women in the Eastern Highlands of Papua New Guinea. See Brown & Tuzin 1983, pp. 33–50

Glasse R. 1963. *Cannibalism in the Kuru Region*. Territ. Papua New Guinea: Dep. Public Health

Glasse R. 1967. Cannibalism in the Kuru Region of New Guinea. Trans. *N.Y. Acad. Sci.* Ser. 11, 29(6):748–54

Godelier M, Panoff M, eds. 1998. *Le Corps Humain Supplicié, Possédé, Cannibalisé*. Amsterdam: Overseas Publ.

Goldman LR, ed. 1999. *The Anthropology of Cannibalism*. Westport, CT: Bergen & Garvey

Gordon-Grube KI. 1988. Anthropophagy in post-Renaissance Europe: the tradition of medical cannibalism. *Am. Anthropol.* 90(2): 405–9

Guest K, ed. 2001. *Eating Their Words*. Albany: State Univ. N.Y. Press

Guille-Escuret G. 1998. Le corps du delit et l'exoticisme artificiel: a propos de l'anthropophagie guerriere en forêt centrafricaine. In *Le Corps Humain*, ed. M Godelier, M Panoff, pp. 109–35. Amsterdam: Overseas Publ.

Guille-Escuret G. 2000. Epistemologie du témoignage. *L'Homme* 153:183–205

Hall S, ed. 1992. *Formations of Modernity*. Cambridge, UK. Polity Press

Harner M. 1977. The ecological basis for Aztec sacrifice. *Am. Ethnol.* 4:117–35

Harris M. 1977. *Cannibalism and Kings*. New York: Random House

Harris M. 1985. *The Sacred Cow and the Abominable Pig*. New York: Random House

Harrison T. 1937. *Savage Civilization*. New York: Knopf

Healy M. 2002. Monstrous tyrannical appetites: "& what wonderfull monsters have there now lately ben borne in Englande." In Consuming Narratives, ed. LH McAvoy, T Walters, pp. 157–69. Cardiff: Univ. Wales Press

Herodotus. 1973. *History Books 7 – 9. Introduction by Reginald Walter Macan*. New York: Arno Press

Hesser A. 2002. Big eaters, sure, but this is absurd. *N.Y. Times*, Oct. 30, pp. F1, F5

Hulme P. 1992. *Colonial Encounters. Europe and the Native Caribbean 1492–1797*. London: Routledge

Hulme P. 1998. Introduction. The cannibal scene. See Barker et al. 1998, pp. 1–38

Janszen K. 1980. Meat of life. *Sci. Digest* Nov/Dec:78–81

Kilani M. 2001/2002. Cannibalisme et metaphore de l'humain. *Gradhiva* 30/31:31–55

Kilgour M. 1990. *From Communion to Cannibalism. An Anatomy of Metaphors of Incorporation*. Princeton, NJ: Princeton Univ. Press

Kilgour M. 1998. The function of cannibalism at the present time. See Barker et al. 1998, pp. 238–59

Kilgour M. 2001. Foreward. In *Eating Their Words. Cannibalism and the Boundaries of Identity*, ed. K Guest, pp. vii–viii. Albany: State Univ. N.Y. Press

Klein M. 1975 [1932]. *The Psycho-Analysis of Children*. Transl. A Strachey. New York: Dell

Knauft M. 1985. *Good Company and Violence. Sorcery and Social Action in a Lowland New Guinea Society*. Berkeley: Univ. Calif. Press

Knauft M. 1993. *South Coast New Guinea Cultures: History, Comparison, Dialectic*. Cambridge: Cambridge Univ. Press

Knauft M. 1999. *From Primitive to Postcolonial in Melanesia and Anthropology*. Ann Arbor: Univ. Mich. Press

Knauft M. 2002. *Critically Modern Alternatives, Alterities, Anthropologies*. Bloomington: Indiana Univ. Press

Kristof N. 1993. A tale of red guards and cannibals. *N.Y. Times*, Jan. 6, p. A8

Landler M. 2003. Eating people is wrong! But is it homicide? Court to rule. *N.Y. Times*, Dec. 26, p. A4

LeDuff C. 1999. Jury decides hospitalized killer can go free. *N.Y. Times*, April 21, p. B1

Le Fur Y. 2001. How can one be Oceanian? The display of Polynesian "Cannibals" in France. In *Body Trade. Captivity, Cannibalism and Colonialism*, ed. B Creed, J Hoorn, pp. 36–46. New York: Routledge

Lemonnier P. 1992. Couper-coller. Attaques corporelles et cannibalisme ches Les Anga de Novelle-Guinee. *Terrain* 18:87–94

Lestringant F. 1997. *Cannibals. The Discovery and Representation of the Cannibal from Columbus to Jules Verne*. Berkeley: Univ. Calif. Press

Lévi-Strauss C. 1963. *Totemism*. Transl. R Needham. Boston: Beacon

Lévi-Strauss C. 1964. *Tristes Tropiques. An Anthropological Study of Primitive Societies in Brazil*. New York: Antheneum

Lindenbaum S. 1979. *Kuru Sorcery. Disease and Danger in the New Guinea Highlands*. Palo Alto, CA: Mayfield

Lindenbaum S. 1983. Cannibalism: symbolic production and consumption. See Brown & Tuzin, pp. 94–106

Lizot J. 1976. *Le Cercle des Feux: Faits et Dits des Indiens Yanomami*. Paris: Seuil

Lock M. 1993. Cultivating the body: anthropology and epistemologies of bodily practice and knowledge. *Annu. Rev. Anthropol.* 22:133–200

MacClancy J. 2002. Cage me a Harrison. *Times Lit. Supp.* Aug. 16, pp. 3–4

MacCormack CP. 1983. Human leopards and crocodiles: political meanings of categorical anomalies. See Brown & Tuzin, pp. 51–60

Marlar RA, Leonard BL, Billman BR, Lambert PM, Marlar JE. 2000. Biochemical evidence of cannibalism at a prehistoric Puebloan site in southwestern Colorado. *Nature* 407:74–78

McAvoy LH, Walters T, eds. 2002. *Consuming Narratives. Gender and Monstrous Appetite in the Middle Ages and the Renaissance*. Cardiff: Univ. Wales Press

Mead S, Stumpf MPH, Whitfield J, Beck JA, Poulter M, et al. 2003. Balancing selection at the prion protein gene consistent with prehistoric Kurulike epidemics. *Science* 300:640–43

Meigs AS. 1984. *Food, Sex, and Pollution: A New Guinea Religion*. New Brunswick, NJ: Rutgers Univ. Press

Mock D. 1992. Dining respectably. *Science* 258:1969–70

Montaigne M. 1964 [1581]. *Selected Essays*. Boston, Houghton Mifflin. *N.Y. Times*. 1979. A Cambodian reporter tells of his ordeal. Oct. 12, p. 10

Obeyesekere G. 1992. "British cannibals": contemplation of an event in the death and resurrection of James Cook, explorer. *Crit. Inq.* 18:630–54

O'Brien J, Roseberry W. 1991. *Golden Ages, Dark Ages. Imagining the Past in Anthropology and History*. Berkeley: Univ. Calif. Press

Ogilvie MD, Hilton CE. 2000. Ritualized villence in the prehistoric American Southwest. *Int. J. Osteoarchaeol.* 10(1):27–48

Ogunnaike L. 2003. For green, the "yuck" stops here. *Int. Herald Trib.* July 4, p. 20

Ortiz de Montellano BR. 1978. Aztec cannibalism: an ecological necessity? *Science* 200:511–617

Petrinovich L. 2000. *The Cannibal Within*. New York: Aldine De Gruyter

Poe AE. 1946 [1938]. *The Complete Works 1809–1849*. New York: Knopf

Poole FP. 1983. Cannibals, tricksters, and witches: anthropophagic images among Bimin-Kuskusmin. See Brown & Tuzin 1983, pp. 6–32

Rawson C. 1997. The horror, the holy horror. *Times Lit. Suppl.* Oct. 31, pp. 3–5

Rawson C. 2001. *God, Gulliver, and Genocide. Barbarism and the European Imagination, 1492–1945.* Oxford: Oxford Univ. Press

Rochette M. 2003. Durmont d'Urville's phrenologist: Dumoutier and the aesthetics of races. *J. Pac. Hist.* 38(2):251–68

Sade de Marquis. 1966 [1797]. *The History of Juliette.* Paris: Cercle du Livres Précieux. Vol. 8/9 Oevres Completes

Sagan E. 1974. *Cannibalism: Human Aggression and Cultural Form.* New York: Harper and Row

Sahlins M. 1978. Culture as protein and profit. *N.Y. Rev. Books* Nov. 23, pp. 45–53

Sahlins M. 1979. Cannibals and kings: an exchange. *N.Y. Rev. Books* June 28, pp. 52–53

Sahlins M. 1983. Raw women, cooked men, and other "great things" of the Fiji Islands. See Brown & Tuzin 1983, pp. 72–93

Sahlins M. 2003. Artificially maintained controversies. *Anthropol. Today*, 19(3):3–5

Sanborn G. 1998. *The Sign of the Cannibal.* Durham: Duke Univ. Press

Sanday PR. 1986. *Divine Hunger. Cannibalism as a Cultural System Cambridge.* Cambridge: Cambridge Univ. Press

Sartore RL. 1994. *Humans Eating Humans. The Dark Shadow of Cannibalism.* Notre Dame, IN: Cross Cult. Publ.

Shapin S. 2002. Barbecue of the vanities. *London Rev. Books* 24(16):21–23

Slater M. 2001. Recluse at work. Gustave Flaubert and the dedication to writing. *Times Lit. Suppl.* Oct. 12, pp. 4–5

Smales A. 1978. Three jailed for Cannibalism. *Sun* Aug. 23

South China Morning Post. 2000. Cannibalism in the news. April 19.

Stallybrass P, White A. 1986. *The Politics and Poetics of Transgression.* Ithaca, NY: Cornell Univ. Press

Stocking GW. 1991. Colonial situations. *Hist. Anthropol.* 7:56

Sun. 1972. I was a cannibal, MP says. Sept. 29

Sutton DS. 1995. Consuming counterrevolution: the ritual and culture of cannibalism in Wuxuan, Guangxi, China, May to July 1968. *Comp. Stud. Soc. Hist.* 37:136–73

Swift J. 1729 [1949 (1933)]. *Satires and Personal Writings,* ed. WA Eddy. London: Oxford Univ. Press

Tannahill R. 1975. *Flesh and Blood. A History of the Cannibal Complex.* New York: Stein and Day

Taussig M. 1987. *Shamanism, Colonialism, and the Wild Man. A Study in Terror and Healing.* Chicago: Univ. Chicago Press

Thomas N. 1994. *Colonialism's Culture. Anthropology, Travel and Government.* Princeton, NJ: Princeton Univ. Press

Thomas N. 2003. *Cook. The Extraordinary Voyages of Captain Cook.* New York: Walker

Tuzin D. 1983. Cannibalism and Arapesh cosmology: a wartime incident with the Japanese. See Brown & Tuzin 1983, pp. 61–72

Tuzin D. 2001. Cannibalism. In *International Encyclopedia of the Social & Behavioral Sciences,* Vol. 3, ed. N Smelser, PB Baltes, pp. 1452–54. Amsterdam: Elsevier Sci.

Tuzin D, Brown P, eds. 1983. Editors' preface. See Brown & Tuzin 1983, pp. 1–5

Verrips J. 1991. 'Ik kan je wel opvreten.' En(i)ge notities over het thema kannibalisme in westerse samenlevingen. *Etnofoor* 1V(1):19–50

Viveiros de Castro E. 1992. *From the Enemy's Point of View.* Chicago: Univ. Chicago Press

Wagner R. 1967. *The Curse of Souw: The Principles of Daribi Clan Definition and Alliance.* Chicago: Chicago Univ. Press

Waiko JD. 1970. A payback murder. The green bloodbath. *J. Papua New Guinea Soc.* 4(2):27–35

Walker PL. 2001. A bioarchaeological perspective on the history of violence. *Annu. Rev. Anthropol.* 30:573–96

White L. 2003. Human sacrifice, structural

adjustment and African studies: a review. *Soc. Study Contemp. Hist. Soc.* 45(3):632–39

Wike J. 1984. A reevaluation of Northwest Coast cannibalism. In *The Tsimshian and Their Neighbors of the North Pacific Coast*, ed. J Miller, C Eastman, pp. 239–54. Seattle: Univ. Wash. Press

Wilford JN. 2003. First Europeans bring a mystery to New York. *N.Y. Times* Jan. 10, p. E41

Yi Z. 1993. *Scarlet Memorial. Tales of Cannibalism in Modern China*. Transl. TP Sym. Boulder, CO: Westview Press

Zalewkski D. 2001. Once, in the jungle. *N.Y. Times Mag.* March 25:54–57

Annu. Rev. Anthropol. 2004. 33:499–523
doi: 10.1146/annurev.anthro.32.061002.093129

ANTHROPOLOGY IN AREA STUDIES

Jane I. Guyer

*Department of Anthropology, Johns Hopkins University, Macaulay Hall,
Baltimore, Maryland 21218; email: jiguyer@jhu.edu*

Key Words   intellectual history, race, governmentality, American universities

■ **Abstract**   After 1989, the interpretation of a complex set of disputes and exigencies settled into a conventional narrative of paradigm shift, in which the intellectual past became essentialized as "traditional area studies" and "classic anthropology." This approach obscures the processes of engagement (including dispute) by which disciplinary change occurred. The Area Studies[1] engagement with interdisciplinary colleagues and voices from the "area" has been critically important over several decades. Necessarily, the intellectual terms for addressing other interlocutors about regional conditions and events have differed according to the experience of the area in changing universalist politics and analysis. The area/anthropology intersection is examined for Africa (where race is basic to disputes), Latin America (where the place of culture and race in political economic arguments is central), and Europe (where culture and nation are at issue). During the 1990s a collective approach to areas emerged. Anthropologists, and particularly scholars of Asia, played a major role. The varied angles from different areas are linked by a broadly shared concern with the formation of emergent political communities and with themes of governmentality. Although the wider circulation of these ideas is promising, does it risk losing the grounding and accountability that Area Studies imposed (like it or not)? The events of September 11, 2001 and those that followed have made starkly clear the poverty and the dangers of essentialism, and the importance of focusing on the loci from which terms of argumentation in relation to power arise. Middle Eastern Studies is briefly discussed as "epicenter" for defining such an approach.

INTRODUCTION

Both advocates and critics present Area Studies[1] as more volatile than the social science disciplines of which they are mainly comprised; Area Studies seems more prone to intense controversies. A new confrontation arose in mid-2003 over

---

[1]Where Area Studies is capitalized I refer to institutionalized programs and centers with substantial resources for which the federally funded National Resource Centers are the archetype. Many other kinds of more modest and differently organized area programs exist, instituted to meet student demand or local interest, and on the basis of their own definition of area or culture. When referring to this whole domain, area studies is not capitalized. Most critique refers to the formalized programs.

0084-6570/04/1021-0499$14.00

the university-based, federally funded Title VI National Resource Centers in the context of the September 11, 2001 events, the War on Terror, and the U.S. and Coalition Forces invasion of Iraq. Between my acceptance of the invitation to write this review in the spring of 2001 and the present, the force of these world events has challenged me to craft this chapter to reflect my own institutional experience with, and theoretical conviction about, volatility, controversy, and the force of events. Several comprehensive reviews of Area Studies (Cumings 2002, Smelser & Baltes 2001[2]), specific areas (Guyer 1996, Haugerud 1997, Miyoshi & Harootunian 2002), and from an anthropological standpoint (Lee 2001, Szanton 2001) have already been published. Viewing the world from the 1990s, these accounts tend to frame an intellectual trajectory in terms of epochs. My account follows more closely, in form and in content, the antiessentialist project in my own work. I reposition and revalorize history and controversy as at the heart of the complex intersection of anthropology and Area Studies and point to the multifaceted emergence of a collective focus on reason(ing) in relation to power.

In the 40 years between the foundation of interdisciplinary Area Studies centers in American universities after World War II and the end of the Cold War in 1989, the basic Area Studies structure did not change significantly. With the United States assuming a unique role in the world after 1989—as hegemon, imperialist power, or liberator of market and democratic forces (depending on the theorist)—the pressures built up for an institutional reconfiguration of research about the rest of the world. Understandably, those who advocated change had recourse to retrospective homogenization of the field across space and time. Explaining his decision to decommission the Area Studies committees of the Social Science Research Council (SSRC) after 24 years, President Kenneth Prewitt made the case thus: "Now free from the bi-polar perspective of the cold war and increasingly aware of the multiple migrations and intersections of people, ideas, institutions, technologies and commodities, scholars are confronting the inadequacy of world 'areas' as bounded systems of social relations and cultural categories" (1996, p. 1).

The experience and the scholarship, however, had been more varied and less coherent than such a sketch conveyed. The capitalist/communist divide crosscut "area" geography all across the globe as, for example, Kissinger's domino policy directly linked withdrawal from Vietnam with interventions in Angola and Chile in the early 1970s. Fundamental changes in the energy and money markets across the world followed rapidly, ushering in the vast problem of Third World debt. Intellectual orientations were also less neatly reducible to structures in the first instance and fluidities in the second. Structuralism of various theoretical sorts accommodated

---

[2]*The International Encyclopedia of the Social and Behavioral Sciences* includes fifteen articles on Area and International Studies: on specific areas (Eastern Europe, Western Europe, South Asia, Southeast Asia); disciplines (archeology, cultural studies, economics, international relations, law, linguistics, political economy, sociology); and characteristics of the field (institutional arrangements, intellectual trends, stakeholders).

historical agency—struggle, resistance, practice, "social organization"—long before the newly "free" moment of the late 1980s. And in that moment, the "cultural turn" meant that anthropology tended to turn first to shifting patterns of movement [Appadurai's (1990) "scapes"] rather than to the deliberation and action through which these new geographies were being produced. So area-based scholars who had addressed world issues and grappled with dependency theory simply did not recognize Prewitt's depiction of what they had been doing for two decades or more (Watts 1997, p. 186; for a similar point on globalization, see Mintz 1998).

Giving greater space here to events, contestations, and paradoxes highlights a quality of disciplinary scholarship that I believe has emanated particularly from its area engagements. Long-term commitment to place, however place is conceptualized, imposes empirical grounding and accountability on all abstractive practices that detach the elements of analysis from their antecedents and implications in people's radically different ongoing experiences in the world. Area institutions demand sustained attention to discussions beyond the discipline itself: in other disciplines, in the intellectual and artistic worlds of the regions, and with respect to locally meaningful events. This openness—whether actively sought or more painfully demanded—entails a kind of "reality testing" through which the commensurability (Povinelli 2001) of different angles on the present and the adequacy of concepts and arguments are exposed and explored. It creates public spheres beyond *in camera* conversations among disciplinary colleagues. Openness to a variety of nondisciplinary, nonacademic arguments is rarely a function of disciplines themselves for two reasons. The temporalities of the world often breach disciplinary prescriptions for intellectual "progress," intervening by what economists call external shocks. But more profoundly, attending to shocks demands implicit or explicit judgment about the truth value of different accounts of them, in ways that test the repertoires of argumentation. This is rocky ground, but not *terra incognita* if one looks past the retrospective homogenizations of the 1990s.

Three kinds of debates arise around and within Area Studies: (*a*) challenges to the whole practice on the grounds that it fosters particularism: ideological, theoretical or just plain parochial and clientelistic; (*b*) engagements with area-specific issues; and (*c*) attempts to use an "area" base to address what may be new universalities of condition, experience, and disciplinary approach.[3] These debates structure this review. What are Area Studies and Anthropology for this purpose? Lambert (2001) makes the important point that "Area studies is not the only intellectual format for the study of single countries and world regions" (p. 689). Culture areas, linked multisites (Marcus 1998), and multilevel locations (Gupta & Ferguson 1997,

---

[3]Possible examples include transnational forms (the indigenous movement, the World Social Forum, international banking, or management of the HIV/AIDS epidemic); parallel correspondences (global urbanization, insurgent youth politics, or the power of new media); linked dynamics (global inequalities, marginalization, and citizenship regimes); and recurrent incoherences (advocacy of simultaneous nation building and state downsizing, legal rationalism and apocalyptic religion).

Tsing 2000) are such alternative frameworks for area knowledge within the discipline of anthropology. The Area Studies formulation—multidisciplinary, explicitly geopolitical, and therefore more susceptible to shocks—engages anthropologists in quite different intellectual encounters. So a brief history of anthropologists' involvement in Area Studies is useful, in its own right and as an introduction to the confrontations of the 1990s.

AREAS AND DISCIPLINES

The Institutional Context

Except for the few academic departments devoted to areas of the world, Area Studies programs have been a struggle intermittently to establish and maintain because they depend on collaboration. For Title VI programs, government, philanthropy, and individual university administrations all contribute. Federal funding supports fellowships, library, staff, and some ongoing activities but not faculty salaries. Only by leveraging university-level interest can an Area Studies Center influence disciplinary hiring. Foundation funding requires competitive proposal submission. So initiatives depend heavily on disciplinary profile and dynamism (see Biddle 2003), and therefore involve faculty in ways that are quite indeterminate at any one time and place.

Another indeterminacy for anthropologists' involvement in Area Studies has been the definition of "area." Anthropology addressed a world that had been subdivided first into three categories—the modern west (sociology, political science, economics), the literate non-West (oriental studies), and the nonliterate non-West (anthropology)—and then into Boasian culture areas (Greenberg 1971). Important anthropological areas such as Australia, New Guinea, the Pacific Islands, Native America, nomadic Inner Asia, and the Mediterranean world had no counterpart at all in Area Studies. The most prominent anthropologist to spearhead an Area Studies center, Melville J. Herskovits, tried unsuccessfully to expand African Studies at Northwestern University to include the entire Afro-American Atlantic on which his Boasian research career had been based (Guyer 1998). In yet other areas very few anthropologists were doing research at all, the Soviet Union being the most important.

The expansion of the discipline in the 1960s and 1970s gave anthropologists a greater presence in Area Studies programs.[4] This heyday for anthropology coincided, however, with a decline in foundation support and even a threat to the whole system in the early 1980s with the Reagan administration's plans to eliminate the Department of Education, founded by President Carter and made the home of the Title VI programs (Merkx 2001). Senior scholars eventually saved it, only to

---

[4]By 1980, anthropology doctoral students accounted for 41% of SSRC international research fellowships, up from 10% in 1965 (Haugerud & Cadge 2000, p. 80).

see it threatened again by the 1994 Republican Congress. The main innovation of these years was the foundation of a new federal program for international studies, the controversial National Security Education Program, which some Area Studies programs postponed applying to until it moved out of the Department of Defense. This configuration, with level funding, remains in place to the present.

Meanwhile, there had been sharp and persistent reductions in political science and economics participation in Area Studies, starting in the 1970s. In the 1990s, a new SSRC predissertation fellowship was targeted at students in the quantitative social sciences: economics, political science, sociology, and psychology. But over the ten years of its life, it failed to overcome the active discouragement of academic advisers in these disciplines (Haugerud & Cadge 2000, p. 17). Between 1990 and 1995, one third of all SSRC dissertation fellowships were in history and 20% in anthropology (Worcester 1996:11)

Nevertheless, public and academic interest in the composition of a diversifying America and a mobile world meant that demand for area and ethnic studies programs intensified in the 1990s. Szanton (2001, p. 693) writes that there are now at least 500 area studies centers in the United States, that is, four times as many as are funded under Title VI. "(A)lmost half of universities and colleges in the U.S. offer curricular concentrations focused on one or other world area" (Lambert 2001, p. 687). The genie of area/ethnic studies is definitively out of the federal funding and large foundation bottle. It now inhabits what McCann (2002, p. 35) calls a "polycentric landscape." The effort to "internationalize" the American university (Biddle 2003) now spans heterogeneous organizations and complex mixes of universalism, diversity, and critique.

In their final year of operation, SSRC area committees showed the variety of area definitions as they had evolved in name and practice. Japan and Korea, supported by funding from the region, was "race-nation without further explanation," as Harootunian (2002, p. 158) argues. Africa was a continent, provoking race/culture disputes about criteria for inclusion of North Africa and the world diaspora in the definition of "Africa." The Middle East was a historic region but with unclear boundaries. The Soviet Union and Successor States was a new conceptualization of the Cold War "area." Western Europe and Eastern Europe were separately constituted, but membership in the European Union was blurring the distinction. Latin America faced the inclusion of the Caribbean, especially as Black Atlantic scholarship was including the islands in a four-"area" ecumene (Africa, Europe, and Latin and North America), with continuing expansions into Asia. South and Southeast Asia remained less contentious, except for the new concept of Pacific Rim. This march away from any political or comparative theoretical coherence made it clear that Area Studies institutions were more arena than agenda, and that the humanities were taking an increasingly important role in defining the debates.

When the polyglot pragmatisms of intellectual ventures that were stretched thin over an impossibly huge and varied mandate finally crossed a certain threshold of institutional tolerance at the funding foundations, the crisis broke across a much broader front than simply definitions of geography. For the polemic purpose of clearing the deck, two intellectual fictions were retrospectively invented: "traditional area studies" and "classic anthropology."

The Invention of Traditional Area Studies and Classic Anthropology

Already by the 1970s, several major works from the margins of Western disciplines had charged that the specialized study of mutually exclusive "areas" necessarily elided the global history of imperialism (Amin 1974, Fanon 1963, Rodney 1972). By the time I first worked for an Area Studies institution—as a member of the Joint Committee on African Studies of the SSRC/American Council of Learned Societies (ACLS) (1981–1986)—our committee was responding in some measure to these critiques. We were working on peasant economies, feminism, vernacular literatures, and world religions. In anthropology, Wolf published *Europe and the People Without History* (1982), and Mintz (1985) traced the world history of sugar. The political geographies at work here can be critiqued (see Coronil 1997), but they were no longer the bounded territories of the conventionalized Area Studies map.

From our vantage point then, Appadurai's key article of 1986 that launched the idea of anthropological theory harboring area-specific "gatekeeping concepts"—such as lineage and segment in Africa and hierarchy in India (1986, p. 357)—evoked an academic world well on the wane. He identified "theoretical metonyms": allowing a single part to stand for a whole society or culture, and imposing a "copyright" on ideas to be borrowed at an intellectual price (1986, p. 358). We were inclined to be skeptical. Our own struggle over gatekeeping at that time was more literal: the confrontation over exclusion launched by African and African American scholars at the African Studies Association Meetings in Montreal in 1969, which was squarely readdressed in the ASA meetings only as late as 1985 (Amory 1997, Zeleza 1997). In many respects this struggle continues, particularly in the recuperation of an occluded African and African American intellectual history (Yelvington 2001).

Our skepticism about metomyny turned out to be misplaced. This sense of a connection between area knowledge and intellectual "gatekeeping" has not dissipated over the years. Rather it has focused and refocused, from one conceptual border to another: between areas, between locals and diasporas (Yanagisako 2002 for Japanese), and between dominant and subordinate voices (Trouillot 1995). Then, during the 1990s, coindexing all these critiques and attaching them to a unified intellectual past seemed plausible. "Traditional area studies" and "classic anthropology" were created, largely occluding the fact that some of the challenges to which the new directions purported to respond had arisen over time and often within area arenas themselves.

The arguments from the SSRC were very influential. To expand on Prewitt's view, it is "conceptually useful to draw a distinction between traditional area studies, on the one hand, and area-based knowledge on the other. . . . Traditional area studies is primarily knowledge about an area." He credits this kind of work with "a level of insight, subtlety, creativity, and self-reflection that would not have been imaginable when area studies programs were first established." By contrast "area based knowledge starts with knowledge about an area, but then applies that knowledge to processes, trends, and phenomena that transcend any given area...processes that link...events that, although geographically distant, are culturally, economically, strategically, or ecologically quite near" (1996, p. 2). This latter, however, precisely describes the careers and arguments of Fanon (1963), Amin (1974), and Rodney (1972), more than 20 years earlier.

Marcus (1998) wrote a comparably sympathetic but definitively retrospective review of "stable disciplinary practices in place for the past fifty years" (p. 233) within anthropology. He linked these practices to "making a contribution to the world ethnographic archive divided into distinct culture areas...each with a distinctive history of anthropological discourse..." (1998, p. 233), a practice from which we were now emerging. There is an elision of history here that is consequential. The metonymic rhetoric whereby "the critique of the 1980s" was what undermined "agreed upon functionalist topics such as kinship, ritual, religion etc....and the "Notes and Queries" inventory that defined classic ethnography" (p. 246) presents these shifts as if they had all happened contemporaneously [although elsewhere he does acknowledge theoretical variety in the processes (Marcus 1998)]. The past is telescoped and radically pruned to support this interpretation. In fact, *Notes and Queries* was first published in 1874 and put out of print in the 1950s. The functionalism that had shaped its 1920s editions was already being rethought by theorists working in processual and historical terms in the 1960s (see Gluckman 1968). Marcus endorses, then, Prewitt's narrative of rupture, with all its implications for a misleadingly selective account of the past.

Subsequent analyses advocate a yet more extreme "totalization of what went before in order to move beyond it" (Miyoshi & Harootunian 2002, p. 14) by those who see the continuation of orientalism within postcolonial scholarship, especially in Asian Studies, up to the present. The theme in this collection is provocative but ultimately falls into the same quagmires as it finds the opposition mired in. For example, Harootunian accuses modernization theory of failing to recognize difference and history, and yet in the very next sentence claims that the modernization approach has "dominated research agendas related to area studies" from the 1950s to the present, that is, all area studies and all decades, no difference and no history. It's hard to know exactly what the authors consider moribund here (p. 173): tedious career scholars, directionless programs, neglected areas, arrogant disciplines, or some vast encompassing malaise of everything.

This advocacy of rupture intersected contingently with other intellectual and political shifts. Having detoured out of Area Studies, political scientists became highly critical of the entire idiographic approach that they saw enshrined there. Bates (1997), a long-time African Studies scholar, rejected an area approach and suggested that rational choice theory "provides a framework which transforms ethnography and narratives into theory-driven claims amenable to refutation...," assuming that only by this kind of transformation could we answer the question "what has the study of area contributed to the broader discipline?" (pp. 169–70).[5]

In the face of the rational choice insurgence, anthropologists mounted a defense of area approaches, even though privileging area knowledge co-existed awkwardly with the "paradigm shift" that was otherwise in motion. One reason was to preserve the concept of culture by extending it to the areas already claimed by rational choice theory—contemporary North America and Europe—as a way of "parochializing" them (Szanton 2001), or of reweaving the threads of a radical tradition that rejected the ahistorical divisions of the world in the first place (di Leonardo 1998). Anthropologists invaded new area meetings. In 1994, at the Conference of Europeanists, "there were at least as many anthropologists as political scientists. . . .[talking] about the cultural construction of consumerism, the contestation of public symbols, and the reconstruction of national memories," leading the reviewer to conclude that "European anthropology is the success story of the past decade" (Hall 1996, pp. 4–5, 14). Anthropologists moved back into China, experimenting with designations of a more inclusive area, such as "eastern Asia" (Brook & Luong 1997) to include the People's Republic, overseas Chinese, Vietnam, Malaysia, and Korea. Anthropologists were also central to the Ford Foundation project entitled *Crossing Borders* (1999) to "revitalize" Area Studies by experimenting with the definition of area, encompassing new disciplinary collaborations, bridging area and ethnic programs, and promoting language study in new ways. Perhaps most surprising, almost all of the area subdivisions of the American Anthropological Association were founded in the late 1980s and 1990s.[6]

A second reason for revived area commitment is the surge in the study of nation and identity, with the crucial critical perspective of gender studies now demanding political and ethical grounding. The past involvement of particular anthropologists or subfields in national level U.S. politics would demand a comprehensive history of its own (see Escobar 1995). In the 1990s, however, the discipline moved broadly into the study of ethnicity and governmentality and thereby necessarily into area arenas. In a shifted political and theoretical world, we are not so far from the 1960s (Watts 2001) or even the 1950s (Fischer 1999, p. 472) in the sense of listening to new voices on critical world events.

It is from this complex vantage point—variety of practice, involvement worldwide, humanities theoretical orientation, and surge in studies of political community—that anthropologists face the renewed critiques of federally funded Area

---

[5]Since then his views have shifted again. He is quoted in a recent article as saying "Africa makes us look stupid. It makes us realize that our assumptions require re-examination and reformulation," and studying Africa can "challenge the fundamentals in a lot of fields in very productive ways" (Arenson 2003, p. A19).

[6]Subdivisions include specifically Society for Latin American Anthropology (1969), Society for the Anthropology of Europe (1988), Society for Africanist Anthropology (1993), Society for the Anthropology of North America (1994), Middle East Section (1996), Melanesia Interest Group (1999), and East Asian Studies (2000).

Studies, by supporters of the Bush administration's policies in the Middle East (Kurtz 2003). Rhetorical metonymy is at work again, lumping everything under the "signature" feature of postcoloniality (Goldberg 2003). If, as I have argued, a continuing theme of Area Studies is less essentialized cultures than localized engagements, then we ourselves need to recognize and valorize this. It still crosscuts disciplinary style in ways that will be crucial for anthropology's current work on emergent political community and the powers of reasoning in the post-1989 and post–September 11th world.

AREAS AND ARGUMENTS

Reexamining the lived experience of Area Studies raises some issues for which the theory lags behind the practice. The Area Studies configuration—sustained interdisciplinarity, obligation to engage with intellectuals and artists from the "area," attention to events as they arise—necessarily brings anthropologists (and others) into arguments about criteria of judgment in complex fields of action. Emergent and interstitial realities in the present raise unavoidable problems of theoretical and ethical placement (Fischer 1999), as they intersect in often surprising ways with persistent categories and metaphors such as race, class/inequality, and gender. The policy social sciences pitch in immediately, either from current theoretical models or from the license to experiment that is offered by defining events as "crises." Although critical and exploratory by disciplinary orientation, anthropology in an Area Studies context cannot take an opposite position, withdrawing into reference to culture, autonomy, or memory/history, and deferring judgment—by default—to relativity, freedom, or the "bar of history." Analytical judgments, in situ, are ultimately ethical and political judgments about antecedents and implications (causes and effects) and—like it or not—others in the same arena will assign their own "responsibility." Experience of this kind of triangulation of truths has necessarily been different from region to region because judgment of truth is grounded in different experience and participations. I explore the different groundedness of what I see as common grand concerns in African, Latin American, and European Studies, turning later to emerging convergences, particularly through Asian and Middle Eastern Studies.

Africa

In academic African and Diaspora Studies, counteracting conventional Western "knowledge" framed in terms of race (or cognate concepts) has remained an unfulfilled ideal for a hundred years. An epochal intellectual history of American Area Studies and anthropology masks this specificity. "Race" has been chipped away at, in the face of recurrent critiques whose implications for scholarship have shifted over time. But it has not disappeared. Only last year, Trouillot (2003) argued that anthropology has even been complicit in its persistence by using the concept of culture to be "a shortcut for too many things" (p. 116), including most prominently the results of racism and political domination. In African Studies, the main tactic for addressing the problem of racial interpretation has been through creation of a history: in response to Hegel's (1956 [1837]) famous statement that Africa lay "beyond the day of history...enveloped in the dark mantle of night," permanently lacking the consciousness of freedom of "Spirit" and therefore the capacity for "universality" (p. 91). Hegel's criteria for judgment and the terms of his depiction of Africa set the stage for what is now an almost immovable Western metanarrative of primitivity.[7] (See also Apter 1999.[8])

To invest Africa with a history of its past was the polemic purpose of *Black Folks Then and Now* (Du Bois 1939) and *The Myth of the Negro Past* (Herskovits 1941). Comparative anthropology, meanwhile, was deeply invested for theoretical reasons in classification according to the "ethnographic present." It was outside attacks that shifted the framing in the 1960s: by African intellectuals, Marxist theorists, and historians. The most trenchant initiatives focused on theoretical framing as it affected method. Historian Vansina's particular target was the Malinowskian concept of the "mythical charter," which delegitimated his only plausible "archive"—oral history—as a reliable source of evidence of the past (Vansina 1965). His skepticism about hasty theorization persists among scholars who see the empirical challenge about the African past as still largely before us (Kriger 1999, Zeleza 1996). Economic historians dismissed anthropological substantivism as "Merrie Africa" (Hopkins 1973). Or they simply showed how much could be done about the history of domination through creative methods and theoretical imagination (Cooper 1977).

The idea that beyond creating a history the entire analytical repertoire would need unpacking, historicizing, and politicizing was stunning when philosopher Valentin Mudimbe launched it in such an original fashion in 1985, in an article that prefigured his enormously influential book *The Invention of Africa* (1988). He argued that terms came from the missionary imagination dating from the late fifteenth century, an imagination he later (Mudimbe 1994) depicted as, in any case, more enriched by long-term engagement with African peoples, in their own languages, than was typical of anthropologists in the professionalized post-war era. It was a question not only of amplifying a past but of rethinking erstwhile stable-seeming phenomena, whose fixity clearly traces a long genealogy that passes directly through Hegel: famine (Watts 1983), "fetishism" (Pietz 1985), the landscape itself (Fairhead & Leach 1996, Richards 1996).

One significant answer from anthropology has been to revive the empirical effort on culture and knowledge by relating them to historical experience. Philosopher

---

[7]I can hardly bear to insert in the text, nor leave out all together, reference to the addiction of commentators of all kinds to the imagery of Joseph Conrad's *Heart of Darkness*, which precisely reorders Hegel's categories in his own original narrative form.

[8]Apter 1999 has addressed many of the same issues. Moore (1994) has explored theoretical achievements. I highlight here the kind of confrontation and response that moved these issues forward, according to my own experience with them.

Hallen (2000) argues against "the ubiquitous paradigm of the prereflective, symbolic character of traditional cultures (that) channels anthropological approaches to Africa" (p. 147). An array of more recent works takes a knowledge-based approach to practices for which Africa has been considered particularly original: conceptions of power (McGaffey 2000), healing (Davis 2000), the sensorium (Geurts 2002), reproductive regimes (Bledsoe 2002), witchcraft (Geschiere 1997, Shaw 2002), and the practice of secrecy (Ferme 2001). The convergence toward the topic of reason—another racially marked category of Western thinking—has great potential. And yet these topics tend also to be shaped by the same intellectual geneology. In the meantime, the frontier of experience and commentary keeps moving, with the public arena often applying concepts of race to new contexts.

In the 1980s, the antiapartheid struggle, the wars in Mozambique and Angola, instability and poverty associated with structural adjustment policies, and the rising threat of HIV/AIDS became both subjects and benchmarks to judge the salience and adequacy of theory and method. In the 1990s, the genocide in Rwanda, the rapid rise of religious intensity, transitions to democracy, the existence of child soldiers in Sierra Leone and Liberia, and explosive cultural creativity in the African Diaspora added topics that tested critical thinking about the implicit subtexts of our accounts. Interchanges became more deeply acrimonious. Mamdani (1990) argued that American African Studies lacked sufficient immersion in African struggles. Mafeje (1998) called for the total demise of anthropology in Africa. The policy disciplines leaped to judgment on African rulers with concepts such as "neopatrimonial government," with all the pathologizing implications this entails for both past and present, and with little reference to the western support given to dictators under Cold War politics. Cutting across the rising polarization between apologists and critics of one theoretical subtext or another, and exasperated with racial indexing on both sides, Mbembe launched a scathing critique of what he saw as African scholars' exploitation of the experience of racial victimization to mask mediocre work and ignorance of the broader intellectual archive. Intense controversy followed, taken up in the pages of *Public Culture* (2003), where Mbembe later proposed to address current disasters through a different concept, that of "necropolitics."

Some scholars have simply abandoned African Studies because they find the ethical/racial issues just too debilitating or paralyzing.[9] Staying on in African anthropology entails repositioning. Comaroff & Comaroff (1991) derive a problematic of practice from hegemonic missionary and colonial processes. Other approaches take empirical categories or topics as points of departure, such as food, music, youth, or environment, and trace outward to antecedents, implications, and comparisons. An interdisciplinary, international group of scholars looks at the chronicity of turbulence as one potential temporal and political context for logical placing of popular economic experience (Guyer et al. 2002). Yet others make fundamental contributions under the oldest of anthropological rubrics—diversity

---

[9]See the Chronicle of Higher Education debate (Postel 2003).

and commonality—now focused on repertoires for creative composition, in life, and in art (Barber 2001). Finally, there is a broad interest in people's own redomestication of the racist past (Coombes 2003) and their own search for concealed or willfully misrepresented truths. The South African Truth and Reconciliation Commission reminds us that in any racialized situation, establishing a truth, and not just alternative representations, does matter.

The aforementioned studies are all work-in-progress. To achieve a broader sense of theoretical place, issues that have for decades (and necessarily) indexed ultimately to race need to be brought into new philosophical and macrohistorical/comparative perspectives. The Latin American struggles over indigeneity and legality are different but historically convergent.

Latin America

The history/anthropology interface is less salient for anthropology in Latin America, and the epistemological dimension is less prominent because the scholarship answers to different historical experience. Owing to the prominence of Latin American scholars in developing dependency theory, the most important disciplinary interface for anthropologists was with political science and political economy. Local communities were seen more or less from the outset as components of national life and as "peasants" (e.g., Tax 1953). Latin American studies was at the forefront of thinking about land distribution and management, regional economic systems (Smith 1976), stratification, and leveling mechanisms. It was only under the pressure of political repression and social movements in the late 1960s that the racial aspects of political economy began to demand attention and culture was inserted as a source of political thought and action. From an activist standpoint, African and Diasporic thinking (e.g., Fanon 1963) offered one resource, alongside other antiracial thinking following World War II (see Messer 1993), for Native Americans to face racial constructions and to create the specifically American concept of indigeneity.

The state is crucial to both the recognition of race/culture and the representation of race as indigeneity. There is a fairly long history to indigenous claims (Niezen 2003). However, it was the insurgent national development plans of Latin American military governments from the 1960s that drew anthropologists' attention to a new phase in the dispossession of Native Americans. The earliest academic initiatives to defend communities ravaged by resource extraction and "national integration" strategies were taken by the Barbados group of Latin American anthropologists in 1969. Cultural Survival, now one of the most important nongovernmental organizations working on indigenous rights, was founded by Harvard anthropologists in 1972. Davis's *Victims of the Miracle* was published in 1977. The devastation of the Guatemalan state's insurgency into the Maya Highlands, peaking between 1979 and 1984 but not settled until 1995, provoked an intense round of new work by anthropologists (Warren 1993, 1998) elucidating further the identity element in otherwise-construed class/region/ideology divisions. The political-economy theoretical grounding is never lost, however. Scholars such as

Nash (1979) and Taussig (1980) pioneered the cultural analysis of state/capital intervention. In the 1990s, the political study of Afro-Latin movements was added and theoretically linked back again to the intellectual history of the African Diaspora (Hanchard 1994, Gordon 1998).

The fuller development of the mutual critique among anthropology, political science, political economy, and activism emerged particularly powerfully in the 1980s, attendant on democratization within nations on one hand and the rise of international environmental and indigenous movements on the other. Political scientists took up the question of indigeneity and multiculturalism (van Cott 1994). As Hale's (1997) and Paley's (2002) reviews show, the anthropological engagement with the creation of new political communities through active organization in formally democratic contexts was particularly strong in the Latin American literature. This line of inquiry can only continue. The year 2003 saw the toppling of the Bolivian government by a popular movement based substantially in indigenous communities that opposed the tactics of coca elimination under the U.S. drug policy (Rohter 2003). Similar exasperation is growing in Peru (Rojas-Perez 2003). The legal concept of indigeneity begins to migrate from Native Americans to other minorities, for example, Africa-descended communities of Brazil and Colombia (Ng'weno 2002). The goals for which identity is mobilized by groups themselves—rights to land and to livelihood—place the issues squarely within a powerful continuing tradition of the political economy of competition over resource control.

Indigeneity has encouraged greater attention in Latin American anthropology than African anthropology to the state itself as the locus for contestation over the ambiguities of class/race/regional/indigenous identities in relation to citizenship (Hale 1997). The Latin American state has been powerful enough to manipulate this conceptual slippage, although not powerful enough (apparently) to clarify it. Castro-Leiva & Pagden (2001) suggest that Latin American republicanism is driven by internal contradictions about "the moral basis for all forms of political life" (p. 179) in the tension between the communitarianism of ancient republicanism and the liberal individualism of the modern. Lomnitz's (2001) analysis of the symbolism of the Mexican state makes a parallel point that "internal economic and cultural fragmentation made. . .[s]traightforward identification between the state and society. . .impossible" (p. 136). He shows that "indigenismo" has been an elite, Catholic/Aztec, spiritual argument, ill at ease with modernizing materialism and also—one must assume—with the insurgent modernist claims of the present-day Aztec and Maya peoples. Their lives on the persistently ambiguous margins created by this fluidity of national theory and associated institutions constitute a new domain of anthropological work (Das & Poole 2004). In Brazil, significant numbers of anthropologists have been recruited to actually mediate these marginalities through their participation in legal processes.

In a population whose differentiations follow complex overlays of class, region, language/culture, and race, these issues are discussed and debated by Latin American intellectuals and marginalized citizens themselves, in those terms and with respect to immediate issues of resource control. It is mainly the actors, with some mediation by outsiders, who have spearheaded the remarkable expansion in the legal rights of "indigenous peoples" all over the world (Niezen 2003). African peoples are now involved: not only the obvious categories of Mbuti, San, and other hunter gatherers, but also and surprisingly "nomads" such as the Tuareg, longtime traders across the Sahara from the Mediterranean. Local community opposition to extractive industries is also linked now to worldwide movements. The creative novelty of the movement itself, its success in the United Nations institutions, and its ability to capture and manipulate its own definitions of "indigenous," mean that the epistemological/essentialist issues faced by African and Diaspora studies are addressed here through excavating the historical/political process of legality. This innovative approach to national and international constitutionality makes of Latin American anthropology a particularly powerful resource for new analyses of national and international legal process.

Europe

After 1989 Europe became charismatic almost in the old sense of the "exotic" frontier. Its reconstitution during the 1990s was a thematic counterpoint to the impact of neoliberal globalization elsewhere. Whereas one branch of anthropology turned to conceptualizing flows and diasporas that bypass or supersede old institutions and structures, the anthropology of the newly configured and expanding European community picked up enormous momentum precisely by problematizing the recreation of those structures. Under the pre-1989 Area Studies format, Europe was divided into East, West, and the Soviet Union, and anthropologists were a very minor contingent in all three contexts. European anthropology moved rapidly from studies of the margins to analysis of mainstream culture. To do so, they created some of the classic area institutions: organizations, journals, review papers, and an intellectual pedigree around the anthropology of Europe. In their own accounts of their origins, Europeanists emphasize the ruptures in their work (often within a single career): from exotic margins to centers, from cultures of honor and shame to national identities (Parman 1998).

The surprising impression is given that anthropologists surged into a relative intellectual vacuum, at least in American scholarship. The rational choice wings of political science and economics were not much more seriously active in Europe than in the non-Western world ["the study of Europe has been peripheral to the discipline of economics in America" (Hall 1996, p. 16)]. Anthropologists wrote as if their topic was largely uninhabited territory, at least in terms of critical thinking (see Asad 2002 on Muslims in Europe), and other scholars seemed to accept the novelty of an anthropological imagination. The opposition was rather muted: At worst "[t]his book. . .is an extraordinary mishmash. . .." (Littlewood 1996 of Goddard et al. 1994), or puzzled by the apparent willingness "to relegate anthropology to a mere subheading of political science" (Sutton 1996 of Goddard et al. 1994).

With the anthropological push, concepts within European studies were moved correspondingly from aggregate populations to a "citizen's Europe" (Sutton 1996 of Goddard et al. 1994) The topics of Europeanist conferences changed to include panels devoted to "the study of social or collective identity...the cultural construction of consumerism, the contestation of public symbols, and the reconstruction of national memories" (Hall 1996, pp. 4–5). The discipline oriented toward the construction of legitimacy, in its broadest sense, to include identity definition, recognition, communication, and acceptance of a common framework of accountability and trust, therefore both political and cultural. It focused on organizations such as mafias (Humphrey 2002) and financial institutions (Verdery 1996) as well as the state. Although an anthropology of the state—as a contingent, historical, and variable set of institutions—predates 1989, more research and debate has been devoted to the relationship between formalization and emergent social/cultural phenomena in recent Europeanist anthropology than anywhere else. Study of a specifically cultural underpinning to European unity focused first on the state-people relationship in particular European states. Herzfeld's writings on bureaucratic indifference (1992) and cultural intimacy (1997) are particularly important. Cultural themes have been extrapolated to larger fields by Borneman (1997) and to some degree disputed by Llobera (2003), arguing that national and European identity are not the same type of discursive practice and are therefore overlaid rather than merged.

Clearly one of the important implications of anthropology taking on Europe in these terms has been the revival of interest in Western political philosophy: not as the universal intellectual history of modernity but as the local intellectual history of class/race/historically-specific groups. Europe is itself seen in a postcolonial situation, facing at home the long-term implications of having compromised its own proclaimed universalism abroad with respect to citizenship, gender, and human rights. Constitutionality moves into central discussion. Foucault has been particularly important in providing anthropologists with a framework for the new work on Europe, in part because his work already submits Europe to an anthropological imagination and in part because of the sheer intellectual power of his thinking on governmentality.[10]

The ethnographic and philosophical inspection of liberal democracy "at home," however, would not be engaged in the same terms were it not for the direct confrontations between states and immigrant minorities in the political arenas of Europe (Carter 1997, Wikan 2002). The moral ambiguity of both the state and the "alternative" organizations poses very starkly the question of subtext judgments in area and anthropological scholarship. Immigrant minorities in Europe are unable to take refuge in indigeneity. Often discriminated against, sometimes adrift of the law, and yet utterly needed by the liberal economy, they inhabit a life space that tests liberal constitutionality and provokes new questions for an anthropology

---

[10]His theory of the shift in governmentality from liberal to reflexive as a historical epochal change (see Dean 1999) inspires both enthusiasm for theoretical acuity about process and great concern for eurocentrism of the larger (implied) claim that these are universal shifts. Correspondingly, one sees the analytical relevance of "risk" for the West, but the substantive experience is much more acute elsewhere.

of "reason" (Rabinow 1996) and political community in constitutional orders. The stakes here are as high as the issues are difficult.

CONVERGENCES: CIRCULATIONS AND CENTERS

Area Studies anthropology has been converging around certain related issues— racial/indigenous/minority/class/gender identities, history and experience, reasoning and rationality, political communities and legality—but from different standpoints and with quite different emphases, largely owing to area accountability. In the 1990s, a kind of "collective Area Studies," about the emergent linkages and universalities of globalization, began to take shape in which anthropologists and historians of Asia were particularly active.

Collective Area Studies in the 1990s

Limitations of space (and knowledge) prevent me from continuing in this same vein through all the areas. However, the fact that certain connective interventions have been particularly promoted in Asian scholarship allows me to address those areas here. Asia and the Middle East always straddled, or escaped from, the other salient categorization of the Cold War era: the first, second, and third worlds. In the "development" era, it was the main area of the world that actually was developing. The political experience of South Asia also straddles configurations elsewhere in the world: postcolonial but still national, with political fragments as well as social classes; cosmopolitan national intellectual traditions with a profusion of religious, linguistic, and regional community dynamics; and self-conscious civil and political societies (Chatterjee 2001). Subaltern studies made the modes of addressing these partly shared characteristics an intellectual resource for the critical study of state-society dynamics elsewhere. Guha sees the "subjection (of officialdom) to doubt" and the insertion of multiple alterities into the nationalist narrative to be a generational phenomenon of the 1970s. Twenty years after the end of colonial rule, failure of nationalist promises led to the "clash of doubt and self-doubt, interrogation and response" (Guha 1997, p. xiii). The basic theoretical shift was political, to seeing the colonial state as dominant but not hegemonic. This shift opened up for study "manifold diversities that it has been beyond the oversimplified elitist interpretation to cope with" (Guha 1997, p. xvi), such as, for example, the actions of the masses as distinct from elites in anticolonial movements. Subaltern scholars show how the actions of the masses mobilized idioms of struggle "derived from their communitarian experience of working and living together" (p. xviii) and not from any education in "modern" political concepts. Grounded in evidence of political conditions and community experience, subaltern studies historians mobilized evidence and argument to make judgments about nationalist scholarship as unable to "cope."

The intellectual issues resonated elsewhere. As in Africa, there were arguments that needed to be declared simply wrong or inadequate. As in Latin America, the rationality of law needed addressing. As in Europe, class needed to be loosened up to include other bases for identification and argumentation. By virtue of addressing ethnicity and nationalism from within, South Asian studies opened up the question of "native anthropology," "anthropologies of the South," and South-South connections.

Anthropology in Southeast Asian studies presents itself quite differently, rather as a series of imaginative interventions with specific contributions on cultural and religious complexity. Scholars commit less to historical reconstruction than in either Africa or South Asia. "The field has not been so weighted down by the heritage of Orientalist scholarship as some other area studies nor so madly driven by the prestige of international policy-making" (Tsing in SSRC 1999, p. 15). A historian even regrets "the overwhelming dominance of presentism" (Andaya in SSRC 1999, p. 17). Tsing argues that this freedom produced a "[t]heoretically informed quirkiness," "creative refusal of orthodoxy" (SSRC, p. 15) that used "regional diversity in a creative, positive manner...[which] has saved the field from getting so deeply inside nationalist historiography that one cannot see beyond its categories—another big trap for area studies." Attention to a kind of "lateral" diversity, "at once territorially porous, internally diverse, and inherently hybrid" (Steedly in SSRC 1999, p. 13), takes precedence over detailed accounts of historical emergence (although see Geertz 1964). Hefner's (e.g., 2001) impressive corpus on religion and politics is focused analytically on coexistence in the present. Topics resonate with other areas: ethnic diversity and state violence, world religions, economic growth, extractive industries, and environmental destruction.

A further element developing out of Asian studies is a certain futurism that is particularly evident with respect to East Asia. Since the 1980s, no area of the non-Western world other than East Asia has claimed, as do Brook & Luong, that "it seems inevitable that Eastern Asian cultures will shape, even remake, capitalism into a system of production and consumption beyond its original definition, letting it become something that is more genuinely universal than the European version" (Brook & Luong 1997, pp. 12, 20). The possibility of even imagining this scenario puts East Asian dynamics out as one possible benchmark for the cutting edge of world change and "parochializes" Europe probably more trenchantly than can internal critique or reframing from the margins. As a consequence, new Asian work revisits empirically and theoretically the European historical and contemporary processes of enchantment and disenchantment, rationality and culture, technologies and institutions (Hertz 1998, Lee 2001, Miyazaki 2003).

Anthropologists in all these Asian areas have been particularly active in rethinking American Area Studies in the 1990s. As a participant in initiatives to unify Area Studies under a new collective approach, Lee clearly grounds his arguments in the East Asian experience of complexity and futurism. "[T]he velocity, scale, and form of these [globalization] processes and circulations challenge virtually all existing narratives of culture, place and identity and the intellectual and academic frameworks used to study them. ...Circulation is a cultural process with its own forms of abstraction" (Lee 2001, p. 661). He places at the "cutting edge" a practice of Area Studies that operates like an "imagined community," participating in the circulations of both its objects and its arguments, decentered from the Euro-American academy.

This collective movement builds in exciting ways on area knowledge, both substantive and analytical. The question here is, how does the circulating work of an imagined community retain the contestability and accountability of the Area Studies arenas from which it arose? Does it thereby "abstract" itself from the triangulation of truths? These are real questions, not rhetorical ones. I am reminded of a local commentary on a cosmopolitan conference that I attended entitled *Globalization and the Social Sciences in Africa.* ". . .[M]any of the participants. . .have been in similar gatherings on numerous occasions. . . which meant that there was little critical engagement on crucial issues. . .[such as] poverty, tyranny and exploitation. . ." (Nieftagodien 1999, p. 60; on other "frustrations" about academic abstraction/distraction see Graeber 2002).

The Middle East: "Epicenter"?

The precisely located and inescapable moral and political geography of the current Middle East is a dramatic counterpoint to circulation and abstraction, where accountability issues are unavoidable and deeply consequential. In the Middle East, questions that arose in other areas [How is indigeneity conceptualized? How does the concept of culture become a sliding signifier for race, religion and political conviction (Trouillot 2003)? How do economics and culture interact (Lee 2001)?] bring the discipline face to face with challenges that go beyond where we now stand.

The Middle East has always been recalcitrant not just to theory but "area" as well. It may be its unique historical, symbolic, financial, and political centrality for at least half of the global population that has made the Middle East conceptually marginal in comparative Area Studies: It fails to be a comparative case. Using the idea of the Middle East instead as a conceptual triangulation point in the creation of a new polarization within Western civilization, between the United States and Europe, Borneman (2003a,b) has recently suggested that the region is the "new epicenter of world power" (p. 487). He raises a question for the newly reconfigured intersection of Area Studies and anthropology more broadly, namely how current disciplinary practices of documenting "pluralization, voicing, and . . .fluidity" help to address the encompassing questions of "relative significance and hierarchy" (Borneman 2003b, p. 507).

Borneman does not seem (to me) to provide an answer. The Middle East as real place and people, rather than imaginative topos, does not enter much into the debate about his paper (*Am. Ethnol.* 2003). And yet "voice" and speaking/writing for themselves have been at the heart of the region's life and of its legacy to the world, as reflected in particular attention by anthropologists to the powers of language (Abu Lughod 1986, Fischer & Abedi 1990, Gilsenan 1997, Haeri 2003, Said 1978). Political scientist Chaudhry (1994) depicts this view negatively:

"Middle East studies charted a spartan path from the Orientalism of the 1960s to the postmodernism of the 1990s. In the process, political economy approaches were deconstructed before they took shape" (p. 41). She regrets that the regional scholarship somehow fails to achieve "the mysterious alchemy through which world regions escape the confines of area studies and achieve legitimate status in general debates. . ." (p. 42). Mitchell (2003) argues with Chaudhry that comparativism can never make this leap because it simply produces a debilitating array of exceptions. He argues that Area Studies is at least as intellectually tenable as the disciplines. The sense that Middle East studies itself has also been a straightjacket—defining the scholarship but not elevating it in the process—is suggested by anthropologist Navaro-Yashin (2002) to be due to Arab and Muslim essentialism. Indexing everything to Arab culture and Muslim religion leaves out of the equation "hybrid identities, diasporic existences, minorities, and marginal communities. . ... It also assumes and reconstructs a necessary difference with Iran, Turkey, Sudan, Israel, and Europe, among other important spaces in the region" (p. 74).

The most striking singularity of the new Middle East scholarship, and what may make it an intellectual "epicenter," seems to me to be its principled framing of contingency, the creation of events. This idea is best captured by Mitchell's (2002) argument that "[c]apitalism. . .has no single logic, no essence" (p. 303) in relation to modern Egypt, also reflected in the present originality of Turkish public life. Conjunctures are multiple and—above all for my argument here—argued through and mediated situationally. This condition is widespread; I have addressed "formalities" (in the plural) as distinct from a coherent "formal sector" in Africa (Guyer 2004). But in the Middle East both the traditions of reasoning and the kinds of power are projected onto the big screen, even the global screen. Possibly nowhere else are forms of argumentation so culturally/historically resonant and the political-economic stakes so high. And the present situation itself enforces for the discipline the imperative of addressing reason/rationality/negotiation and intervention as intrinsic and inescapable practices of our own and not topics or tools "out there" to be addressed or applied in some optative fashion.

CONCLUSION

The rhetoric of intellectual rupture of the 1990s was an effort, in part, to shift metaphors for our own activities: from (in)groups to networks, and now to nodes (topical, geographical). Redrawing the geography of the world can be one tangible way of mediating a much more complex intellectual transformation. I think, however, that what actually happens, or can happen, in Area Studies is rather closer than is the discipline to meeting Trouillot's (2003) requirement that we take the "risk" of making "an explicit effort to reassess the epistemological status of the native voice in ethnography, to recognize its competency" (p. 136). For him, the first step is to suspend the concept of culture, which now gets in the way. There are many initiatives in this direction within the area literatures. Exploiting and exporting them would mean taking a larger systematic step into ethnographies of argumentation on the one hand and more detailed analysis of the situations to which people's competence is applied on the other hand. The simple truth is that we do not generally make such changes just by reflexivity, disciplinary "normal science," or changed organizational blueprints. We do it because we are challenged, criticized, shamed, or inspired by "another" to whom we are absolutely committed to keep listening. It is not inevitable that Area Studies should foster such engagements, but their forms of accountability can facilitate it. The question of whether the kinds of engagement and accountability we find crucial for the twenty-first century can be fostered by the specific institutions we already have would take me beyond this review. But ruling them out as passé fails to recognize the interventions that those outside the discipline—colleagues and "the people"—have been able to make through the area arenas. And it fails to acknowledge how profoundly anthropologists have been challenged and changed by the imperatives of Area Studies engagements.

ACKNOWLEDGMENTS

I am grateful to many people over the years for stimulating, in one way or another, the ideas expressed here. They include, most recently, colleagues and students at the Program of African Studies, Northwestern University (1994–2001); Sheila Biddle and the advisory panel on her *Internationalization of the Universities* project; the advisory group, staff, and all participants in the Ford Foundation *Crossing Borders* project; and Ron Kassimir and Craig Calhoun who organized a very fruitful discussion for me with the international staff at the Social Science Research Council. For their helpful and insightful comments on the particular form the ideas take in this review, I thank Shelton Davis and colleagues in the Department of Anthropology at Johns Hopkins University: Sara Berry, Niloofar Haeri, Ruby Lal, and Deborah Poole. Michael Watts was characteristically generous with time and thought at a crucial point. Christopher Kolb gave valued research support.

The *Annual Review of Anthropology* is online at http://anthro.annualreviews.org

LITERATURE CITED

Abu Lughod L. 1986. *Veiled Sentiments: Honor and Poetry in a Bedouin Society*. Berkeley: Univ. Calif. Press

Amin S. 1974. *Accumulation on a World Scale: A Critique of the Theory of Underdevelopment*. New York: Mon. Rev. Press

Amory D. 1997. African studies as American institution. In *Anthropological Locations: Boundaries and Ground of a Field Science*, ed. A Gupta & J Ferguson, pp. 102–116. Berkeley: Univ. of California Press *Am. Ethnol*. 2003. Forum. 30(4):487–507

Appadurai A. 1986. Theory in Anthropology: Center and Periphery. *Comparative Studies in Society and History* 28:356–61

Appadurai A. 1990. Disjuncture and difference in the global cultural economy. *Public Cult.* 2:1–14

Apter A. 1999. Africa, empire and anthropology: a philological exploration of anthropology's heart of darkness. *Annu. Rev. Anthropol.* 28:577–98

Arenson KW. 2003. A growing appetite for African studies. *New York Times* Nov. 12, A19

Asad T. 2002. Muslims and European identity: Can Europe represent Islam? In *The Idea of Europe. From Antiquity to the European Union*, ed. A Pagden, pp. 209–27. Washington, DC/Cambridge: Woodrow Wilson Cent. Press/Cambridge Univ. Press

Barber K. 2001. *The Generation of Plays: Yorùbá Popular Life in Theater.* Bloomington: Univ. Indiana Press

Bates RH. 1997. Area studies and the disciplines: a useful controversy? *PS: Polit. Sci. Polit.* 30(2):166–69

Biddle S. 2003. *Internationalization: Rhetoric or Reality?* New York: Am. Counc. Learned Soc. Occas. Pap. Ser.

Bledsoe CH. 2002. *Contingent Lives. Fertility, Time and Aging in West Africa.* Chicago: Univ. Chicago Press

Borneman J. 2003a. Is the United States Europe's Other? *Am. Ethnol.* 30(4):487–92

Borneman J. 2003b. Someone won the war! *Am. Ethnol.* 30(4):504–5

Borneman J. 1997. *Settling Accounts: Violence, Justice, and Accountability in Postsocialist Europe.* Princeton, NJ: Princeton Univ. Press

Brook T, Luong HV, eds. 1997. *Culture and Economy. The Shaping of Capitalism in Eastern Asia.* Ann Arbor: Univ. Mich. Press

Carter D. 1997. *States of Grace: Senegalese in Italy and the New European Immigration.* Minneapolis: Univ. Minn. Press

Castro-Leiva L, Pagden A. 2001. Civil society and the fate of the Modern Republics of Latin America. In *Civil Society. History and Possibilities*, ed. S Kaviraj, S Khilnani, pp. 179–203. Cambridge: Cambridge Univ. Press

Chatterjee P. 2001. On civil and political society in post-colonial democracies. In *Civil Society. History and Possibilities*, ed. S Kaviraj, S Khilnani, pp. 165–78. Cambridge: Cambridge Univ. Press

Chaudhry KA. 1994. The Middle East and the political economy of development. *Items* 48(2–3):41–49

Comaroff J, Comaroff JL. 1991. *Of Revelation and Revolution.* Chicago: Univ. Chicago Press

Coombes AE. 2003. *History After Apartheid. Visual Culture and Public Memory in a Democratic South Africa.* Durham/London: Duke Univ. Press

Cooper F. 1977. *Plantation Slavery on the East Coast of Africa.* New Haven: Yale Univ. Press

Coronil F. 1997. Beyond occidentalism: toward nonimperial geohistorical categories. *Cult. Anthropol.* 11:51–87

Cumings B. 2002. Boundary displacement; the State, the foundations, and area studies during and after the Cold War. In *Learning Places. The Afterlives of Area Studies*, ed. M Miyoshi, H Harootunian, pp. 261–302. Durham/London: Duke Univ. Press

Das V, Poole D, eds. 2004. *Anthropology in the Margins of the State.* Santa Fe, NM: Sch. Am. Res. Press

Davis CO. 2000. *Death in Abeyance: Illness and Therapy among the Tabwa of Central Africa.* Edinburgh: Edinburgh Univ. Press

Davis SH. 1977. *Victims of the Miracle: Development and the Indians of Brazil.* Cambridge/New York: Cambridge Univ. Press

Dean M. 1999. *Governmentality. Power and Rule in Modern Society.* London: Sage

di Leonardo M. 1998. *Exotics at Home. Anthropologies, Others, American Modernity.* Chicago: Chicago Univ. Press

Du Bois WEB. 1939. *Black Folk, Then and Now; An Essay in the History and Sociology of The Negro Race.* New York: Holt

Escobar A. 1995. *Encountering Development. The Making and Unmaking of the Third World.* Princeton: Princeton Univ. Press

Fairhead J, Leach M. 1996. *Misreading the African Landscape. Society and Ecology in a Forest-Savanna Mosaic.* Cambridge: Cambridge Univ. Press

Fanon F. 1963. *The Wretched of the Earth.* Transl. C Farrington. New York: Grove Weidenfeld

Ferme 2001. *The Underneath of Things. Violence, History and the Everyday in Sierra Leone.* Berkeley/Los Angeles/London: Univ. Calif. Press

Fischer MMJ. 1999. Emergent forms of life: anthropologies of late or postmodernities. *Annu. Rev. Anthropol.* 28:455–78

Fischer MMJ, Abedi M. 1990. *Debating Muslims. Cultural Dialogues in Postmodernity And Tradition.* Madison, WI: Univ. Wisc. Press

Ford Found. 1999. *Crossing Borders. Revitalizing Area Studies.* New York: Ford Found.

Geschiere P. 1997. *The Modernity of Witchcraft. Politics and the Occult in Postcolonial Africa.* Charlottesville: Univ. Press Va.

Geurts KL. 2002. *Culture and the Senses. Bodily Ways of Knowing in an African Community.* Berkeley/Los Angeles/London: Univ. Calif. Press

Gilsenan M. 1997. *Lords of the Lebanese Marches: Violence and Narrative in Arab Society.* London: Tauris

Gluckman M. 1968. The utility of the equilibrium model in social anthropology. *Am. Anthropol.* 70(2):219–37

Goddard V, Llobera J, Shore C. 1994. *The Anthropology of Europe: Identity and Boundaries in Conflict.* Oxford: Berg

Goldberg M. 2003. Neo-cons enlist congress in the assault on Middle East studies. *Salon.com* Nov. 6

Gordon ET. 1998. *Disparate Diasporas: Identity and Politics in an African Nicaraguan Community.* Austin: Univ. Tex. Press

Graeber D. 2002. The anthropology of globalization (with notes on Neomedievalism, and the end of the Chinese model of the nation-state). *Am. Anthropol.* 104(4):1223–27

Greenberg J. 1971. Interdisciplinary perspectives in African Linguistic research. Presidential address to the African Studies Association. In *Language, Culture and Communication*, ed. J Greenberg (selected and introduced by AS Dil), pp. 228–248. Stanford, CA: Stanford Univ. Press

Guha R. 1997. Introduction. In *A Subaltern Studies Reader 1986–1995*, ed. R Guha, pp. ix–xxii. Minneapolis/London: Univ. Minn. Press

Gupta A, Ferguson J. 1997. *Anthropological Locations. Boundaries and Grounds of a Field Science.* Berkeley/Los Angeles/London: Univ. Calif. Press

Guyer JI. 1998. Perspectives on the beginning. *PAS News Events* 8(3):2, 4

Guyer JI. 2004. *Marginal Gains. Monetary Transactions in Atlantic Africa.* Chicago: Univ. Chicago Press

Guyer JI, Denzer L, Agbaje A, eds. 2002. *Money Struggles and City Life. Devaluation in Ibadan and Other Urban Centers in Southern Nigeria, 1986–1996.* Portsmouth, NH: Heinemann

Haeri N. 2003. *Sacred Language, Ordinary People: Dilemmas of Culture and Politics in Egypt.* New York: Palgrave Macmillan

Hale CR. 1997. Cultural politics of identity in Latin America. *Annu. Rev. Anthropol.* 26:567–90

Hall PA. 1996. *The State of European Studies.* New York: Counc. Eur. Stud./Soc. Sci. Res. Counc.

Hallen B. 2000. *The Good, the Bad and the Beautiful, Discourse about Values in Yoruba Culture.* Bloomington, IN: Indiana Univ. Press

Hanchard M. 1994. *Orpheus and Power: The Movimento Negro of Rio de Janeiro and São Paulo, Brazil 1945–1988.* Princeton, NJ: Princeton Univ. Press

Haugerud A, ed. 1997. The future of regional studies. *Afr. Today* 44(2). Special issue

Haugerud A, Cadge W. 2000. *The Social Sciences and Area Studies. An Evaluation of the SSRC's International Predissertation Fellowship Program, 1991–2000.* New York: Ford Found.

Harootunian W. 2002. Postcoloniality's unconscious/area studies desire. In *Learning Places. The Afterlives of Area Studies*, ed. M Miyoshi, HD Harootunian, pp. 150–74. Durham/London: Duke Univ. Press

Hefner R, ed. 2001. *The Politics of Multiculturalism. Pluralism and Citizenship in*

Malaysia, Singapore, and Indonesia. Honolulu: Univ. Hawai'i Press

Hegel GWF. 1837/1956. *The Philosophy of History.* Transl. G Sibree. New York: Dover

Herskovits MJ. 1941. *The Myth of the Negro Past.* Boston: Beacon

Hertz E. 1998. *The Trading Crowd: An Ethnography of the Shanghai Stock Market.* Cambridge: Cambridge Univ. Press

Herzfeld M. 1992. *The Social Production of Indifference. Exploring the Symbolic Roots of Western Bueaucracy.* Oxford: Berg

Herzfeld M. 1997. *Cultural Intimacy. Social Poetics in the Nation-State.* New York/London: Routledge

Hopkins AG. 1973. *An Economic History of West Africa.* New York: Columbia Univ. Press

Humphrey C. 2002. *The Unmaking of Soviet Life: Everyday Economies After Socialism.* Ithaca: Cornell Univ. Press

Kriger CE. 1999. *Pride of Men. Ironworking in Nineteenth Century West Central Africa.* Portsmouth, NH: Heinemann

Kurtz S. 2003. Statement before the Subcommittee on Select Education, Committee on Education and the Workforce, US House Represent. June 19

Lambert RD. 2001. Area and international studies in the United States: institutional arrangements. See Smelser & Baltes 2001, pp. 686–92. Amsterdam: Elsevier. Vol. 2

Lee B. 2001. Areas and international studies: cultural studies. See Smelser & Baltes 2001, pp. 657–62

Littlewood P. 1996. Review of Goddard et al. *Urban Stud.* 33(2):389–91

Llobera J. 2003. The concept of Europe as an idee-force. *Crit. Anthropol.* 23(2):155–74

Lomnitz C. 2001. Elusive Property: the personification of Mexican national sovereignty. In *The Empire of Things,* ed. F Myers, pp. 119–138. Santa Fe, NM: Sch. Am. Res. Press

MacGaffey W. 2000. *Kongo Political Culture. The Conceptual Challenge of the Particular.* Bloomington, IN: Indiana Univ. Press

Mafeje A. 1998. Anthropology and independent Africans: suicide or end of an era? *Afr. Sociol. Rev.* 2(1):1–43

Mamdani M. 1990. A glimpse at African Studies. *CODESRIA Bull.* 2:7–11

Marcus G. 1998. *Ethnography Through Thick and Thin.* Princeton, NJ: Princeton Univ. Press

Mbembe A. 2002. African Modes of Self-writing. *Public Cult.* 14:239–73

Mbembe A. 2003. Necropolitics. *Public Cult.* 15(1):11–40

McCann JC. 2002. Title VI and African Studies; prospects in a polycentric academic landscape. *Afr. Issues* 30(2):30–36

Merkx GW. 2001. Area and international studies in the Unites States: stakeholders. See Smelser & Baltes 2001, pp. 699–707. Amsterdam: Elsevier

Messer E. 1993. Anthropology and human rights. *Annu. Rev. Anthropol.* 22:221–49

Mintz SW. 1985. *Sweetness and Power. The Place of Sugar in Modern History.* New York: Viking Penguin

Mintz SW. 1998. The localization of anthropological practice. From area studies to transnationalism. *Crit. Anthropol.* 18(2):117–33

Mitchell T. 2002. *Rule of Experts. Egypt, Techno-Politics, Modernity.* Berkeley/Los Angeles/London. Univ. Calif. Press

Mitchell T. 2003. The Middle East in the past and future of social science. In *The Politics of Knowledge: Area Studies and the Disciplines,* ed. D Szanton. Berkeley: Univ. Calif. Press/Univ. Calif. Int. Area Stud. Digit. Collect. Ed. vol. 3. http://repositories.cdlib.org/uciaspubs/editedvolumes/3/3

Miyazaki H. 2003. The temporalities of the Market. *Am. Anth.* 105(2):255–265

Miyoshi M, Harootunian HD, eds. 2002. *Learning Places. The Afterlives of Area Studies.* Durham/London: Duke Univ. Press

Moore SF. 1994. *Anthropology and Africa. Changing Perspectives on a Changing Scene.* Charlottesville: Va. Univ. Press

Mudimbe VY. 1985. African Gnosis: philosophy and the order of knowledge. An introduction. *Afr. Stud. Rev.* 28(2/3):149–233

Mudimbe VY. 1988. *The Invention of Africa: Gnosis, Philosophy, and the Order of Knowledge*. Bloomington: Indiana Univ. Press

Mudimbe VY. 1994. *The Idea of Africa*. Bloomington: Indiana Univ. Press

Nash J. 1979. *We Eat the Mines and the Mines Eat Us: Dependency and Exploitation in Bolivian Tin Mines*. New York: Columbia Univ. Press

Navaro-Yashin Y. 2002. *Faces of the State. Secularism and Public Life in Turkey*. Princeton, NJ: Princeton Univ. Press

Ng'weno B. 2002. *The state in question. Afro-Colombians, ethnic territories and governing in the Andes*. PhD. diss., Johns Hopkins Univ., Univ. Microfilms, Ann Arbor, MI

Nieftagodien N. 1999. Globalization and social sciences in Africa. Conference note. *CODESRIA Bull.* 1,2:56–60

Niezen R. 2003. *The Origins of Indigenism. Human Rights and the Politics of Identity*. Berkeley/Los Angeles/London: Univ. Calif. Press

Paley J. 2002. Toward an anthropology of democracy. *Annu. Rev. Anthropol.* 31:469–96

Parman S, ed. 1998. *Europe in the Anthropological Imagination*. Upper Saddle River, NJ: Prentice Hall

Pietz W. 1985. The problem of the fetish. Part 1. *Res* 9:5–17

Poole D. 2004. Between threat and guarantee: justice and community in the margins of the Peruvian state. In *Anthropology in the Margins of the State*, ed. V Das, D Poole, pp. 35–66. Santa Fe, NM: Sch. Am. Res. Press

Povinelli EA. 2001. Radical worlds: the anthropology of incommensurability and inconceivability. *Annu. Rev. Anthropol.* 30:319–34

Prewitt K. 1996. Presidential items. *Items* 50(1):15–18

Rabinow P. 1996. *Essays on the Anthropology of Reason*. Princeton, NJ: Princeton Univ. Press

Richards P. 1996. *Fighting for the Rainforest. War, Youth and Resources in Sierra Leone*. Oxford/Portsmouth, NH: Currey/Heinemann

Rodney W. 1972. *How Europe Underdeveloped Africa*. London/Dar es Salaam: Bogle-L'Ouverture/Tanzania Publ. House

Rohter L. 2003. Bolivian leader's ouster seen as earning on US drug policy. *N.Y. Times* A1, p. 1

Rojas-Perez I. 2003. *The push for zero coca: democratic transition and counternarcotics policy in Peru*. Wash. Off. Lat. Am.: Drug War Monit. Brief. Ser. 2(1)

Said E. 1978. *Orientalism*. New York: Pantheon

Shaw R. 2002. *Memories of the Slave Trade*. Chicago: Univ. Chicago Press

Smelser NJ, Baltes PJ, eds. 2001. *International Encyclopedia of the Social and Behavioral Sciences*. Amsterdam: Elsevier. Vol. 2

Smith C, ed. 1976. *Regional Analysis*. New York: Academic

Soc. Sci. Res. Counc. 1999. *Weighing the Balance. Southeast Asian Studies Ten Years After*. New York: Soc. Sci. Res. Counc.

Szanton DL. 2001. Area and international studies in the United States: intellectual trends. See Smelser & Baltes, pp. 692–99

Sutton D. 1996. Review of Goddard et al. *Am. Ethnol.* 23(3):652–53

Taussig MT. 1980. *The Devil and Commodity Fetishism in South America*. Chapel Hill: Univ. N.C. Press

Tax S. 1953/1963. *Penny Capitalism: A Guatemalan Indian Economy*. Chicago: Univ. Chicago Press

Trouillot M-R. 1995. *Silencing the Past: Power and the Production of History*. Boston, MA: Beacon Press

Trouillot M-R. 2003. *Global Transformations. Anthropology and the Modern World*. New York: Macmillan/Palgrave

Tsing A. 2000. Inside the economy of appearances. *Public Cult.* 12(1):115–44

Van Cott DL. 1994. *Indigenous Peoples and Democracy in Latin America*. New York: St. Martins/Inter-Am. Dialogue

Vansina J. 1965. *Oral Tradition: A Study in Historical Methodology*. Chicago: Aldine

Verdery K. 1996. *What Was Socialism and What Comes Next?* Princeton, NJ: Princeton Univ. Press

Warren KB. 1993. Interpreting la Violencia in Guatemala: shapes of Mayan silence and resistance. In *The Violence Within Cultural and Political Opposition in Divided Nations*, ed. KB Warren, pp. 25–56. Boulder: Westview

Warren KB. 1998. *Indigenous Movements and Their Critics: Pan-Maya Activism in Guatemala*. Princeton, NJ: Princeton Univ. Press

Watts MJ. 1983. *Silent Violence: Food, Famine, and Peasantry in Northern Nigeria*. Berkeley: Univ. Calif. Press

Watts MJ. 1997. African studies at the fin de diecle: Is it really the Fin? *Afr. Today* 26(1): 185–92

Watts MJ. 2001. 1968 and all that .... *Prog. Hum. Geogr.* 25(2):157–88

Wikan U. 2002. *Generous Betrayal. Politics of Culture in the New Europe*. Chicago: Univ. Chicago Press

Wolf ER. 1982. *Europe and the People Without History*. Berkeley/Los Angeles/London: Univ. Calif. Press

Worcester KW. 1996. Survey of international field research fellowships, 1990–1995. *Items* 50(1):8–14

Yanagisako S. 2002. Asian exclusion acts. In *Learning Places. The Afterlives of Area Studies*, ed. M Miyoshi, HD Harootunian, pp. 175–89. Durham/London: Duke Univ. Press

Yelvington KA. 2001. The anthropology of Afro-Latin America and the Caribbean: diasporic dimensions. *Annu. Rev. Anthropol.* 30:227–60

Zeleza PT. 1996. *A Modern Economic History of Africa. Vol 1: The Nineteenth Century*. Dakar: CODESRIA

Zeleza PT. 1997. *Manufacturing African Studies and Crises*. Dakar: CODESRIA

Postel D. 2003. Out of Africa. A pioneer of African Studies explains why he left the field, and provokes a firestorm of debate within it. *Chron. High. Educ.* March 28

Annu. Rev. Anthropol. 2004. 33:525–49
doi: 10.1146/annurev.anthro.32.061002.093248
Copyright © 2004 by Annual Reviews. All rights reserved
First published online as a Review in Advance on July 16, 2004

ORIGINS AND DEVELOPMENT OF URBANISM:
Archaeological Perspectives

George L. Cowgill

Department of Anthropology, Arizona State University, Tempe, Arizona 85287-2402;
email: cowgill@asu.edu

Key Words   cities, early states, practice, self-organization, city-states

■ **Abstract**   I survey recent literature about early cities in the regional traditions of Southwest Asia, Egypt, South Asia, China, Mesoamerica, Andean South America, Sub-Saharan Africa, Greece, and Rome. Major themes include the importance of theorizing individuals and their practices, interests, and emotions; the extent to which the first cities were deliberately created rather than merely emerging as by-products of increasing sociopolitical complexity; internal structure of cities and the interplay of top-down planning and bottom-up self-organization; social, economic, and political relations between cities and their hinterlands; interactions of cities with their physical environments; and the difficult "city-state" concept. Some axes or dimensions for describing settlements are proposed as better than typological concepts.

INTRODUCTION

I address this chapter to the broad community of archaeologists, anthropologists, historians, sociologists, and other scholars interested in the origins and development of urbanism. When I use terms such as "we," it is to this group I refer, and phrases such as "of interest" mean of interest to many members of this group.

Work on ancient urbanism is influenced by the legacy of concepts, attitudes, and assumptions of earlier writers such as Weber, Childe, Wheatley, and Mumford, and by geographers such as Von Thünen, Christaller, Lösch, Berry, and C. Smith. Adams' (1966) comparative study of Mesopotamian and Central Mexican urbanism provides a key foundation for further work, and scholars still often refer to Fox (1977). These and other "classics" remain important, but I concentrate on more recent publications, mostly since Blanton's (1976) review and mostly those in English, in which earlier publications are cited amply. I discuss regions outside Mesoamerica as an outsider, and even within Mesoamerica my coverage is uneven. However, I hope to provide guidance for specialists in all areas and many disciplines. I emphasize Southwest Asia, Egypt, South Asia, China, Mesoamerica, Andean South America, Sub-Saharan Africa, Greece, and Rome. I omit Southeast Asian, Medieval European, and other cities, as well as most settlements in less

0084-6570/04/1021-0525$14.00   **525** complex polities, only for lack of time and space; these are also highly useful for students of urbanism.

In the 1980s and early 1990s there was much excavation and survey involving sites described as "urban," but interest focused more on the origins and development of complex polities or states, especially in their political, economic, and technological aspects, and the notion of "urban society" often seemed little more than an appendage to the concept of "the state." Relatively few archaeological publications directly addressed urbanism as a theoretical topic. Notable exceptions include Kolata (1983), Marcus (1983), and Sanders & Santley (1983). Recently we have seen an upsurge of attention to theoretical and conceptual issues about the nature of premodern cities and their social and physical contexts. This is a welcome trend that is likely to continue.

KEY DEFINITIONS AND CONCEPTS

"City," "urban site," "urban society," and "urbanization" are often undertheorized, and it is easy to find publications that leave these terms undefined and assume that we all know what they mean. Often a site is simply labeled a city or a society is called urban without the author explaining why. It is also common to see "urban society" and "the state" conflated, as if no states ever existed without cities and as if cities never existed without states. Fox (1977, p. 24) asserts that cities are found only in societies that are organized as states. Probably many would still agree with this, but others argue that one or the other sometimes occurred without the other. M.L. Smith (2003b), for example, claims that there were cities in Early Historic India before real states arose, whereas others question whether the early Egyptian state was very urbanized. One can define both "city" and "state" in ways that make their co-occurrence tautological, but it is better to frame the matter more broadly, as issues concerning the relations among kinds of settlements (or kinds of systems of settlements) and forms of political, economic, social, and religious institutions and practices, as well as technologies and natural environments.

It is notoriously difficult to agree on a cross-culturally applicable definition of "the" city, but we cannot do without definitions altogether. One mischievous property of the English language is that routine use of the definite article encourages us to speak unthinkingly of "the" city and "the" state. This leads us toward reification and essentialization of categories and creates unnecessary conceptual difficulties. It is far better to think of "cities" or "a" city, but never of "the" city.

No single criterion, such as sheer size or use of writing, is adequate, and it seems best to use a somewhat fuzzy core concept rather than to try to establish criteria that will clearly demarcate all cities from all noncities. I vaguely define a city as a permanent settlement within the larger territory occupied by a society considered home by a significant number of residents whose activities, roles, practices, experiences, identities, and attitudes differ significantly from those of other members of the society who identify most closely with "rural" lands outside such settlements.

All settlements have catchment areas, but only cities have hinterlands. Inhabitants of cities may have interests and even additional dwellings in the countryside, and rural people may visit cities for many purposes—the distinction is, above all, one of identities (cf. Emberling 2003). Unless we also consider size, this definition could include the larger settlements in many relatively small societies whose political institutions are not highly developed. Quite so, this definitional problem is why it is useful to think of urbanism as a cluster of variables that can be measured (if only roughly) on ordinal or interval scales, rather than as a discrete category.

There may or may not be terminological or jural distinctions between city and countryside in specific cases, but there is always a physical contrast between a relatively large and concentrated settlement or closely spaced settlement cluster and a less densely occupied hinterland. This contrast is true, to some degree, even for low-density settlements such as those in the Maya Lowlands and parts of Africa. Also, cities are typically political, economic, and religious centers for a surrounding territory and loci for wider ranges of specialized production and services than are found elsewhere in the region.

I use "urban" as an adjective pertaining to city-ness and "rural" for places, entities, and practices outside of cities. Societies without cities can be called nonurban, but not rural, because rural has meaning only as a sector within societies that also have an urban sector. I use "urbanization" to denote the creation of cities by a society that formerly lacked urban settlements (in contrast to some usages in which urbanization refers to processes by which individuals from the rural sector make a transition to the urban sector). An urban society is simply a society with cities. That is, it has places that are the physical settings for urban activities, practices, experiences, and functions. "Urbanism" denotes the prevalence of urban places in a society.

Many argue that the differences between urban and other kinds of settlements or societies are qualitative as well as quantitative. This may be true. Nevertheless, we have better conceptual tools if we think of multiple properties (i.e., variables or axes) along which rough measurements can be made. This enables us to think of degrees and kinds of urbanization. Ideas about abrupt changes in specific historical trajectories or qualitative differences between cases then become hypotheses to be tested empirically, rather than prior assumptions that restrict our thought.

Sometimes there is only a single urban settlement within the territory of a society or polity. I discuss the thorny concept of "city-state" in a later section. I avoid the term "territorial state." I use "regional" polity to refer to those polities large enough to encompass substantial parts of one or more natural regions, typically with more than one urban settlement. Polities span a continuum from small to large. Often there are several cities in a region, rankable in terms of their size and/or significance. A city that is clearly preeminent, at least politically, is a "capital city." A capital city that is far larger than any other single settlement within its region is a "primate city."

Although size and sociopolitical complexity alone are not adequate criteria for city-ness, some general notions about size and complexity are useful. Settlements or societies with no more than a few hundred members cannot sustain the degrees of specialization and sociopolitical power that we are accustomed to thinking of as urban. Populations of a least a few thousand seem a necessary, if not sufficient, requirement for a settlement or a society to be urban.

MAJOR ISSUES

My selection of the most interesting issues is personal, and I say little or nothing about many topics of interest. To my mind, the most important recent development is increasing recognition that ancient cities, like all other ancient and modern sociocultural phenomena, and no matter what the spatiotemporal scale of analysis, cannot be well understood without taking explicit account of individuals—their practices, perceptions, experiences, attitudes, values, calculations, and emotions. Emphatically, this is not to say that the search for regularities in larger-scale or longer-term phenomena should be discontinued. Indeed, connecting individuals with polities, institutions, and other larger entities is among the most challenging and potentially rewarding tasks that confront us. It is difficult to make well-warranted inferences about individuals in societies where contemporary texts are scanty or absent. Nevertheless, these difficulties are not all insurmountable. Even when we cannot track particular persons, we must constantly think about how individuals could plausibly have given rise to the larger-scale phenomena observable without texts.

Many scholars have thought of increasing urbanism as simply a by-product or even an unintended consequence of the creation of increasingly large and complex political systems. It has long been recognized that politically and/or economically powerful persons often sponsor monumental architecture as an expression of their power. Some (notably A. Smith 2003) now go further and view civic-ceremonial buildings and layouts themselves as active instruments for shaping behavior, attitudes, and emotions—as parts of the means by which power is both legitimized and enacted. At issue is the extent to which early cities did not simply "happen" as consequences of technological, political, and economic innovations, but instead were actively and intentionally created.

Whether or not there ever were highly urban settlements in the absence of state-like polities, or statelike polities that wholly lacked highly urban settlements, marked differences can be found in degrees and kinds of urbanism among different early complex societies. What were the associations of kinds of cities with specific political forms? How large and strong can polities become if no settlements are very urban, and how urban can settlements become if polities are small and weak? It is as unproductive to try too hard to fit all cases into a single kind of historical trajectory as it is to avoid comparison altogether. We need richer accounts, based on better data, that do justice to the uniqueness of specific cases but also are alert to significant resemblances among different cases.

Other major topics include structure within cities and top-down planning versus grassroots self-organization; social, economic, and political relations between cities and their hinterlands; interactions of cities with their physical environments (including issues of sustainability); and the roles of religion and other ideology in the emergence or creation of cities.

Before discussing these issues in detail, I briefly review recent literature about early urban occurrences in various major world regions.

WHAT, WHEN, WHERE?

Multiregional Studies

The book edited by ML Smith (2003a) emphasizes the social construction of ancient cities. Contributors provide examples from Mesoamerica, Mesopotamia, Peru, South Asia, Africa, and China. The volume edited by Nichols & Charlton (1997) concentrates on what they define as city-states. Numerous reviewers have found their definition of city-state problematic, especially in being excessively broad (it includes everything from Teotihuacan—a regional state or possibly a hegemonic empire—to the numerous small polities in the Basin of Mexico in the 1300s). Nevertheless, their book contains numerous valuable case studies from Mesoamerica, Mesopotamia, Egypt, South Asia, China, Greece, Okinawa, and Peru. Hansen (2000) provides studies of some 30 cases that may meet his definition of city-state. Contributors represent the Near East, Greece, Italy, barbarian and medieval Europe, the Arabian Peninsula, China, South Asia, Southeast Asia, Sub-Saharan Africa, and Mesoamerica. A recent supplement (Hansen 2002) adds six more cases from Mesopotamia, Anatolia, Syria, Mesoamerica, South Asia, and Europe. Both of Hansen's works (2000, 2002) and the Nichols & Charlton (1997) volume emphasize state at least as much as city, but all three include much useful data for studies of urbanism. Storey's (2004) edited volume focuses on demography but is informative about many other aspects of early cities in Greece, the Roman Republic and Empire, the Levant, China, Korea, Bolivia, Mesoamerica, Southeast Asia, Africa, Medieval Denmark, and even eighteenth- to nineteenth-century New York. Several Old World regions are also represented in Gates (2003).

The book on empires edited by Alcock et al. (2001) includes useful data on urbanism, as does Feinman & Marcus' (1998) edited volume on early states, and Trigger's (2003) volume on early civilizations. The volume on communities edited by Canuto & Yeager (2000) includes some cities. The early section of Southall (1998) on ancient cities makes little use of recent research and tends to treat traditional Marxist categories as givens into which cases are fitted, rather than as concepts deserving further research and refinement. Hall (1998) may be of considerable value for the past few centuries but says little about the earliest cities.

Southwest Asia

Van De Mieroop (1997) is a good general book on Mesopotamian cities, though it does not cover the most recent discoveries. Pre-Pottery Neolithic A (PPNA) Jericho (c. 10,000–8500 B.C.) in the Jordan Valley and Çatal Höyük in Anatolia (c. 7000–6000 B.C.) have been claimed as the world's first cities, but Emberling (2003),

Van De Mieroop (1997, pp. 26–27), and A. Smith (2003) briskly dismiss these claims. Çatal Höyük was an exceptionally large settlement for its time, but it unreasonably stretches the concept of city to label either Çatal Höyük or PPNA Jericho urban. By the Ubaid period (c. 5500–3800 B.C.) settlements in southern Mesopotamia have a better claim to be precursors of cities (Stein & Rothman 1994). Emberling (2003) sees a rather sudden rise of fully urban settlements in southern Mesopotamia c. 3500 B.C. at sites such as Uruk and a nearly contemporary appearance in northern Mesopotamia at Tell Brak. Rothman (2001) provides much new data on the late prehistoric Uruk period of the fourth millennium B.C. Many regional specialists doubt Marcus' (1998) claim for a large regional state at this early date, as well as Algaze's (1993) argument for a major political expansion from the south into northern Mesopotamia. There were strong and varied southern presences in the north at this time, but their political and economic nature is debated. Clearly there was a great deal of regional interaction well before the better-documented literate societies of the third millennium. However, Stein (1999, 2002) argues that it is inappropriate to try to apply "world systems" concepts to these phenomena, and he proposes instead a "trade diaspora" model. Data from Hudson & Levine (1999) are important for later periods.

Publications describing quite different urban trajectories in the Levant include Falconer & Savage (1995), Herzog (1997), Schwartz & Falconer (1994), and Fleming (2004).

Marcus (1998) minimizes differences between Egypt and Mesopotamia, but most regional specialists are impressed by differences as well as similarities. In Mesopotamia a large natural and cultural region was occupied for most of the time from the fourth through the second millennium by numerous small autonomous polities that can reasonably be called city-states. Periods of wider political integration were short-lived. In contrast, Egypt was politically unified for much of this time, and periods of political fragmentation generally appear to have been times of trouble. That Egypt was a more sharply bounded natural region, and its districts more closely interconnected by the Nile, whereas the subregions of Mesopotamia were less effectively linked by the Tigris and Euphrates, may partly explain this difference. Nevertheless, differences in traditions of political institutions, practices, and concepts were probably important also.

Egypt

Egypt in the late Predynastic (c. 3600–3050 B.C.), Early Dynastic (3050–2700 B.C.), and Old Kingdom (2700–2160 B.C.) was not as devoid of cities as once thought. Very little is known of settlements during this interval, and some, especially Memphis, may have been of considerable size. Most, however, seem to have covered no more than 10–20 ha, and they very likely were not highly urbanized. More striking is the early and relatively rapid development of a sizable regional state in the Early Dynastic. Throughout Egypt's history, political unification has been the normal state of affairs. Many late Predynastic regional centers seem to have actually become smaller in the Early Dynastic, at least partly because they became more compact, but probably also because, with political unification, they became less important. New Kingdom Amarna was large but atypical (Kemp 2000). Other useful recent publications include Baines (2003), Bard (1997), Brewer & Teeter (1999), Kemp (1989), Lacovara (1997), O'Connor (1998), and Wilkinson (1999).

Sub-Saharan Africa

Recent work, especially that reported by R. McIntosh (1991, 1998), S.K. McIntosh (1991; 1999a,b), and McIntosh & McIntosh (1993) has emphasized historical trajectories interestingly different from those commonly used in comparative studies of political and urban development.

South Asia

The Indus Valley (or Harappan) civilization (c. 2600–1900 B.C.) remains enigmatic and perhaps unusually different from all other early civilizations, so much so that Possehl (1998) even questions whether its political organization should be termed a state. However that may be, its largest settlements were surely urban to a significant extent. Kenoyer (1998), Possehl (2002), J. McIntosh (2001), and Ratnagar (2001) are recent books on Harappan civilization. Other recent publications include Jansen (1980, 1989), Kenoyer (1991, 1997), Miller (2000), and Possehl (1997).

Also of interest are major settlements of the Early Historic period (ca. 600 B.C. to the early centuries A.D.). Publications include Allchin (1995), Chakrabarti (1995), Champakalakshmi (1996), Sinopoli (2001), M.L. Smith (2003b), and Spodek & Srinavasan (1993). For coverage of the historic medieval city of Vijayanagara, see Fritz et al. (1984), Mack (2002), Morrison (2001), and Sinopoli (2003).

China

For decades we have had fascinating data on the frequently huge prehistoric and early historic cities of the Shang, Western Chou, Spring and Autumn, and Warring States periods (c. 1500–221 B.C.), especially through the English-language publications of the late K.-C. Chang and studies such as Boyd (1962), on architecture and town planning, and Wheatley (1971); however, scholars aware of what regional settlement-pattern studies in other parts of the world have accomplished have been frustrated by the absence of comparable data from China. This lack of data is now changing, largely owing to the efforts of Feinman, Underhill, and others (Underhill et al. 1998, 2002). Much further work has been done on urban sites themselves, both in the traditional heartland of northern China and in other regions (Shen 1994, Yates 1997). Major sources for later imperial China are Skinner (1977) and Steinhardt (1990).

Mesoamerica

Sanders et al. (2003) presents papers (with parallel texts in Spanish and English) from the first two of a projected series of six international conferences on urbanism in Mesoamerica, sponsored by the Instituto Nacional de Antropología e Historia and Pennsylvania State University. Areas represented include western Mexico, the central Mexican highlands, northern and central Veracruz, the Mixteca and nearby parts of Guerrero and Oaxaca, and the Maya Lowlands. There are also chapters on West Africa and Medieval France. Regional synthesis chapters in Adams & MacLeod (2000) include data on Mesoamerican urban settlements. M.E. Smith (2004) reviews Late Postclassic (c. A.D. 1250–1520) Mesoamerican city sizes.

The best-known indications of early complex societies in Mesoamerica are "Olmec" sites such as San Lorenzo, in the hot and moist southern Gulf of Mexico lowlands, perhaps as early as 1200 bc (uncalibrated ^{14}C dates), although a degree of complexity is also present as early or earlier at sites in the Pacific lowlands of Chiapas and Guatemala. The extent to which these societies are "chiefdoms" or "states" and their main settlements "urban" is debated interminably. Better data are needed, but the most important requirement is to outgrow typological approaches and focus instead on degrees and kinds of urbanism. Among other things, doing so should make it easier to explore possible quantum leaps.

Monte Albán, in the highland Valley of Oaxaca, was a major settlement by 300 B.C. or earlier, the center of a polity that soon controlled the Valley and beyond (Blanton et al. 1993, Marcus & Flannery 1996). Blanton et al. (1999, p. 53) estimate a population of 5000 by 500–300 B.C., and 17,000 by 100 B.C. In the Southern Maya Lowlands, Nakbe and El Mirador were major sites with huge pyramids by this time, several centuries earlier than previously thought. For the Central Mexican highlands, Sanders et al. (1979) remains the best overall publication on settlement history in the c. 5000-km^2 Basin of Mexico. However, although this publication is based on surveys that were relatively complete and systematic, these surveys were not extremely intensive and were without benefit of the most recent data on ceramic chronology, so their results must be interpreted with caution. Really large settlements seem a little later than those found in Oaxaca, although little is known of Cholula, just east of the Basin, which may have become fairly urban quite early. In the southern Basin, Cuicuilco is poorly known because it was covered by several meters of nearly impenetrable lava (quite a different matter than volcanic ash) early in the first millennium A.D. Sanders et al. (1979, pp. 97–99) estimate that by 300 B.C. it had a population of 5000–10,000, and by 100 B.C. it may have covered over 400 ha, with a population of c. 20,000. Cuicuilco was soon overtaken by Teotihuacan, in the northeastern part of the Basin, which probably began very rapid growth in the first century B.C. (Cowgill 1997, 2000a, 2003; Millon 1981, 1988, 1992). Teotihuacan was by no means without urban predecessors in Mesoamerica, and it should not be thought of as a "pristine" city. Millon's (1973) exceptionally detailed surface survey and the fact that materials of all periods of occupation are well represented on the surface, means that, even in the absence of deciphered texts, in some ways we know more about Teotihuacan than any other ancient city. By c. A.D. 200 it covered around 2000 ha, with a population estimated by Millon as 100,000–200,000, although I presently think it may have been no more than 80,000–100,000. Even so, it was exceptionally large in both area and population compared to early cities in most parts of the world, except probably China. Part of the reason may be differences in survey methods. Millon (1973) began by exploring the perimeter, defining city boundaries by a strip at least 300-m wide without evidence of Teotihuacan-period occupation. Work on ancient cities elsewhere has often concentrated on central parts, and it may be that total areas of occupation, especially those beyond city walls, have been underestimated in many cases. Another reason for Teotihuacan's large population may be that settlements elsewhere in the Basin were rather few and mostly small. Depopulation of the countryside was not as extreme as once thought, but a high proportion of Teotihuacan's food producers must have resided within the city. Survey data have been supplemented by few excavations in Teotihuacan's rural hinterland, but work in progress at small sites near the city by T.H. Charlton and C. Otis Charlton is beginning to remedy this situation. More data are also becoming available from Azcapotzalco and Cerro Portezuelo, moderate-sized regional centers 30–50 km from the city.

Aside from residential districts, the civic-ceremonial central part of Teotihuacan was itself exceptionally large, some 150–250 ha, with pyramids approaching those of Old Kingdom Egypt, though they were made of earth and rubble with calcareous concrete outer surfaces, rather than cut stone.

Teotihuacan was probably in decline in the 500s; some time in the 600s, major civic-ceremonial structures were burned, and there were sharp changes in the ceramic tradition and areas of densest settlement, probably reflecting a sizable incursion of newcomers. A period of political fragmentation ensued, followed by a regional state centered on the city of Tula, just northwest of the Basin of Mexico. Though overshadowed by Teotihuacan before it and by Aztec cities later, Tula was more substantial than often represented, covering up to 1400 ha and with a population reasonably estimated as c. 60,000. Mastache et al. (2002) is a recent summary of knowledge about that city and its hinterland. The dissolution of the Tula regional state was followed by another episode of political fragmentation and small polities in Central Mexico. Early in the 1400s the city of Tenochtitlan, in coalition with Texcoco and Tlacopan, launched a series of wars that conquered other Basin polities, absorbed its sister city, Tlatelolco, and by the late 1400s had created an empire (now called Aztec) that dominated much of Mesoamerica except for West Mexico (where the Tarascan state successfully resisted Aztec expansion), the Maya area, and most other groups east of the Isthmus of Tehuantepec. Combined use of textual and archaeological data has made the fifteenth- to sixteenth-century Basin of Mexico one of the best-studied instances of urbanism in the ancient world outside of Greece and Rome, although many issues are unresolved and much remains to be learned.

For the Maya Lowlands, especially important publications include Chase et al. (1990) and Houston et al. (2003).

Andean South America

Kolata (1983, 1997) are important works on Andean urbanism. Some Andeanists view Andean states as not highly urbanized, although a number of settlements certainly qualify as cities, including Wari, Tiwanaku, and Cuzco in the highlands, and Galindo and Chan Chan on the north coast of Peru. Stanish (2001a,b; C. Stanish, personal communication) argues that urbanization was limited because Andean states tended to depend on staple financing rather than wealth financing, and price-fixing market institutions were weakly developed. However, his idea that the largest Andean cities were smaller than in most other early states may depend on his acceptance of quite high estimates for some early cities in other regions and on limited use of Mesopotamian data, where fourth- and even third-millennium cities appear, by Mesoamerican standards, surprisingly small in both area and population. Von Hagen & Morris (1998, pp. 220–27) list several Andean settlements covering areas from 150 to more than 600 ha, and at least some seem to have had high density. Bawden (1996) suggests that big cities such as Galindo were an aberration from the Peruvian north coast cultural tradition and were supported by coercion rather than legitimated by appeal to tradition, and for that reason they were ultimately unsuccessful.

Greece and Rome

Whatever the case in the past, a significant number of classical scholars are paying attention to anthropological theory, and there are serious efforts to connect dirt archaeology and text-based historical studies. A sampling of important publications includes Allison (1999), Andreau (1999), Branigan (2001), Cahill (2002), Garnsey (1998), Hopkins (1978), Morley (1996), Morris (1997), Owens (1991), Parkins (1997), Parkins & Smith (1998), Rich & Wallace Hadrill (1991), Storey (2004), and Zanker (1998). For the city of Rome, Stambaugh (1988) is a highly readable introduction that pays attention to attitudes, intentions behind built aspects of environments, and ideation in general.

I turn now from regional summaries to consideration of a few topics of interest.

CITIES AS CREATIONS

Scholars often assume that places with urban qualities simply arose as natural responses to various forms of political and/or economic centralization by which people were, in Childe's famous words, "persuaded or compelled" to congregate in considerable numbers in certain places, together with large and impressive structures and arrays of structures intended to express and further legitimize the authority of powerful political, religious, and/or military leaders. Increasingly powerful

political leaders intentionally planned their courts to be large and impressive, religious leaders oversaw construction of increasingly impressive temples, or both,
while the dwellings of those who staffed these planned cores or otherwise served
the rulers simply aggregated around the peripheries, with no particular planning
or supervision. In this view, other features of the earliest urban places arose either
as unintended consequences of these new kinds of settlements or as responses to
these unintended consequences. However, investigators increasingly are thinking
harder about links between kinds of early polities and kinds of settlements or
communities. Perhaps many cities did simply come into being as unintended consequences of sociopolitical and technological developments. But many of the first
cities (some would argue all) may have been intentionally created in their entirety
to serve the interests of powerful individuals or groups. In theoretical terms, the
idea of cities as inventions is appealing, but much remains to be done to develop
this notion. If cities were created, why were they created, by whom, and for whom?

If the first cities were deliberately created, it is likely that they were new kinds of
settlements that arose abruptly, rather than old kinds of settlements that gradually
grew so large that they became qualitatively as well as quantitatively different.
Did people merely find themselves in new kinds of settlements, calling forth new
practices and new institutions? If there were multiple paths toward the first cities
do these paths lead to different types of cities?

There is some empirical support for the former view, in some cases. Emberling
(2003) observes thresholds and quantum leaps in the history of settlement size and
complexity in Mesopotamia, and A. Balkansky (personal communication) notes
this in Oaxaca also. The extent to which urbanism develops gradually or by abrupt
steps should be explored in other regional traditions. Fletcher (1995) argues for
thresholds, but I am uncomfortable with his high level of abstraction. In Greece
and elsewhere, many cities seem to have been formed abruptly through the process
called synoecism: bringing together the inhabitants of a cluster of separate villages
into a single larger and more complex settlement. Attarian (2003) suggests something similar in north-coastal Peru. This should not be confused with the modern
phenomenon of cities growing so large that they create contiguous metropolitan
zones that encompass formerly physically separate settlements (which typically
preserve their legal distinctness).

In other cases, urban settlements remained quite dispersed, with multiple population concentrations. This is what McIntosh (1999b) describes for the Inland
Niger Delta, which is perhaps somewhat similar to the "capital zones" described
by Stark (1999) for south central Veracruz in Mesoamerica and Maya "green
cities" (Graham 1999). Even Harappan cities are described as having multiple nuclei (Kenoyer 1998), although they seem fairly compact. Do urban sites lacking a
clear single central nucleus imply a relatively weak central political authority or
multiple hierarchies? Compactness is surely strongly influenced by land prices,
and where investment in costly strong defensive walls is thought necessary there
is an obvious incentive to minimize the walled area. The contrast between single
and multiple nuclei is another matter.

A. Smith's (2003) generally well-taken critique of neo-evolutionist approaches of the 1960s and 1970s emphasizes alleged inattention to space, whereas I blame excessive abstraction in general and inattention to individual practice. We both see excessive reification of sociopolitical types, compression of variation within these types, and, above all, too little sense of how things actually worked in specific cases. Smith addresses four central topics: ties among polities, links between regimes and their subjects, interactions between elites and grassroots organizations, and ties among the different institutions within the governing apparatus of a polity; he organizes his case studies around the concepts of experience, perception, and imagination. He is concerned with early complex polities in general, rather than cities as such, but he has much to say about early urbanism, which he sees as dramatically variable. He argues that built environments are not passive settings for action or expressions of power, but instead are active instruments for legitimizing and constituting authority, and legitimate authority in turn is a key basis for political and other kinds of power. Throughout this work, he emphasizes the concept of practice. Another recent publication in this vein is Blake (2002).

Betz (2002) goes further yet to argue that the first cities were inventions designed in their entirety as new kinds of settlement intended to attract people by the qualities of the cities' built features. She makes extensive use of neurological, psychological, city-planning, and other literature unfamiliar to most archaeologists. Miksic (1999), at an opposite extreme from Betz, writes, "Rather than desiring to live in cities, it is likely that many people in ancient times avoided them as far as possible" (p. 170). In any case, Betz raises issues and concepts that provide important insights. We must attend to environmental settings, technologies of production and transport, and political and economic considerations, but we miss something important if we do not also think hard about the likely new experiences, attitudes, and emotions generated by life in cities. It is also important to recognize that, for the first time, other segments of societies began to have the experience of not living in a city.

In thinking about cities as possibly having been creations, we should distinguish among "pristine" and mature and "planted" cities. Many think the term pristine is problematic, but it is a good term for settlements that exhibit a degree of urbanness previously unknown and unheard of in the local tradition, which means that occupants have neither a prior model to emulate nor prior experience with the consequences of urbanism. Over time, pristine cities mature and acquire features not previously present, often as responses or accommodations to earlier features. By planted cities I mean those created by people who did have some prior experience with urban life. Many of these cities were colonies derived from parent communities (notably among the Greeks). Other cities were special-purpose settlements; garrisons, ports, and other trading centers; and places for mining and other extraction of localized resources. In all cases, previous knowledge was available. Existing cities might be emulated, or the new city might be seen as an opportunity to avoid problems perceived to stem from features of older cities. Sometimes, as apparently in Greece, new forms could in turn provide models for parent settlements. Special-purpose settlements, of course, often called for special features such as extensive fortifications for garrisons and harbors and storage facilities for trading centers.

Another important concept is "public amenity." This idea covers diverse features, including fountains, reservoirs, and aqueducts for water supply; systems of waste disposal such as drains and sewers; paved streets; places of worship; marketplaces; public baths; theaters and other facilities for recreation and public assemblies; provision for marginal and disabled persons (including medical facilities); fortifications and places of refuge; as well as institutions for maintaining public order and distributions of food or other material benefits to some sectors of the population. To what extent, in various traditions, were certain of these amenities already present in the earliest cities? Whatever the extent to which some amenities were present from the beginning, many were added or enhanced later in the history of established cities and can well be thought of as "embellishments" and their sponsors as "benefactors." In historically documented cases I see two principal kinds of benefactors: rulers (often distant in regional states or empires) and local dignitaries. Rulers can play the role of benefactor to enhance their prestige and authority, and they may also sponsor features that promote or impede specific attitudes and practices, thus using these material elements as active tools of power. Motives of local dignitaries are perhaps more mixed and variable; often they sponsor amenities to enhance their prestige in competition with other locals; and this can serve their own aspirations for a greater share in local power. In other cases, local dignitaries are expected to sponsor amenities simply to maintain their legitimacy, or a political superior may demand such sponsorship as what is, in effect, a form of taxation, even if phrased as a voluntary contribution. In Greece and Rome the variations in such practices over time and space are interesting.

Some amenities may be created at a grassroots level by nonelite elements of society, typically modest and on a neighborhood scale.

Cities as Cosmograms or Sacred Centers

In some regions, the clear close adherence of many cities to an overall plan, contemporary texts, or both, provide overwhelming evidence for meaningful overall planning, although the reasons and the meanings behind the planning may not be obvious. Greek and Roman texts, for example, advocate certain orientations as simply more healthful or more agreeable. It is much more difficult to decide whether less-close or less-pervasive spatial ordering is meaningful. Appearances of vague ordering may be only coincidental, or the ordering may be real but mean nothing more than a general idea that certain arrangements are more fitting and proper than are others. In some times and places people have thought it best that a Christian church should face eastward, but this preference was not always followed; as far as I know there was never any idea that anything essential was lost by a church's being oriented otherwise. It may be thought adequate to embody a very precise mental model by physical features (built or natural) that relate only very approximately to the mental model. Carl et al. (2000) debate these issues for many parts of the world.

There is good evidence that the layouts of many cities in East and Southeast Asia were designed to be cosmograms, or at least to physically embody some important religious concepts, as argued by Wheatley (1971) and many others. However, the use of city layouts to express such concepts is less clear in other parts of the world, and there seems to be great variation. Kemp (2000), for example, discounts cosmic aspects to planning in New Kingdom Egypt, and he reminds us that one should approach each case with skepticism, remembering how easily one can deceive oneself with coincidences that seem too good to be merely accidental. In Mesoamerica, Teotihuacan shows overwhelming evidence for such a high degree of planning that it must have been meaningful, although the precise meanings are debated (Cowgill 2000b, Sugiyama 1993). The situation in the Maya area is less clear. M.E. Smith (2003) and Ashmore & Sabloff (2002, 2003) debate the degree of planning and argue over what counts as excessive subjectivity in detection and interpretation of meaningful spatial patterning.

Even when cities were not laid out to reflect cosmograms or other sacred principles, many were regarded as sacred centers. Most, or probably all, of the earliest cities had physically prominent places of worship. But it is unclear that the attraction of sacred places was more than occasionally a cause of emergence of pristine cities. At least in Greece and Early Historic South Asia (M.L. Smith 2003b) many shrines and pilgrimage centers were in hinterlands, and not in cities. In these cases one might say cities arose or were created at the places where they were located in spite of sacred centers being elsewhere within their regions.

URBAN ANATOMY: BOTTOM UP AND TOP DOWN

In considering structure within cities, three sectors should be distinguished: the central political authority (which, in the case of a regional state or empire, may be located outside the city); lesser elites, such as religious communities, prosperous merchants, regional governors, and local hereditary nobles; and nonelite residents (grass roots). Amenities may be provided by any of these levels, and at least the upper two may explicitly shape physical features and impose specific practices. Other structured aspects, however, may arise from practices at any of these levels without explicit planning, through self-organizing processes.

Studies of ancient urban neighborhoods often find that they are rather heterogeneous, at least in socioeconomic status. Better put, modern cities seem unusually segregated by socioeconomic status. Much work has been done on identifying and characterizing neighborhoods in Teotihuacan, most recently by Robertson (1999, 2004) who has used sophisticated computer and spatial mathematical methods applied to data from Millon's Mapping Project. He confirms and adds detail to Millon's earlier suggestion that neighborhoods were relatively heterogeneous internally. He goes beyond that to identify districts with different mixes of high- and low-status occupants. In broad terms, neighborhoods with higher proportions of high-status occupants are more prevalent toward the center of the city, but to say this is to oversimplify more complex spatial patterns. He also sees a tendency for neighborhoods to become less heterogeneous over time, and he suggests that this may have led to increasing social tensions within Teotihuacan. Studies of craft specialization (summarized by Cowgill 2000a) find some specialists clustered in compact neighborhoods and others probably more dispersed, with both attached specialists and others likely organized on a household or neighborhood level.

For the Mesopotamian city of Nippur, Stone (1987, 1995), aided by texts, has provided especially interesting data on neighborhoods and spatial organization of the city. Keith (2003) discusses urban neighborhoods in the Old Babylonian period of the early second millennium B.C., and Stone & Zimansky (1992) address the anatomy of Mashkan-shapir. Bawden (1996, p. 86) observes considerable variation in North Coastal Perú; Late Moche Galindo (c. A.D. 700) was highly segregated into walled districts, whereas earlier Gallinazo and later Chimú settlements do not exhibit this rigid differentiation.

There is also a good deal of information on the anatomy of some cities of Classical Antiquity, notably Olynthus (Cahill 2002), and including, not surprisingly, Pompeii. But, even at Pompeii, there are limits to the "Pompeii premise," and interpretations are not as easy as one might think (Allison 1999).

Early cities, however, may be rather segregated ethnically. Ethnic enclaves are readily apparent at Teotihuacan, for example (Cowgill 2000a).

CITIES AND THEIR SETTINGS

In even the largest ancient cities no locale was more than a short walk from the countryside. Even at Teotihuacan, considered hyperlarge by many, few people could have lived more than 2 km (in a straight line) from the settlement margins, only a few minutes' brisk walk. Of course, movement in ancient cities was often restricted by cultural and legal impediments for various categories of residents, and in some cities there were also physical barriers to movement. Nevertheless, no one was nearly as physically remote from rural places as are many occupants of modern cities. Furthermore, in all but the most compact parts of ancient cities, some spaces within the settlement likely were used for agricultural production. This was even more true for less-compact urban settlements such as those in lowland Mesoamerica, parts of Africa, and elsewhere.

There was likely considerable variation in jural relations between cities and their hinterlands. In sixteenth-century Mesoamerica generally it seems no legal distinction and even no clear terminological distinction were made. In Greece the term *polis* applies both to a major settlement and to the polity associated with the settlement—a source of some ambiguity in interpreting ancient texts. Yet there is also a word for the countryside (*chora*), and texts very explicitly discuss the merits of holding land in both town and country; Greeks were perfectly aware of the difference, and it is hard to believe that Mesoamericans were not also highly aware of it.

In contrast, in medieval and later Europe there were often sharp legal distinctions between town and country. In cases where texts are lacking, how can we discern the legal and conceptual limits of cities? Even massive walls do not fully suffice: There can be large agricultural areas within the walls, or substantial housing outside them, which may or may not have been regarded as part of the city proper. We are confronted by a difficult task.

Literature on ecological and environmental aspects of relations between ancient cities and their hinterlands is growing. Not the least appeal of these topics is that they have potential relevance to present-day concerns that is readily grasped in anthropologically unsophisticated quarters, thereby providing access to funding on a scale unavailable for many other topics of research. Issues include the environmental impacts of cities, their long-term sustainability, technologies of provisioning ancient cities (e.g., Garnsey 1988, Morley 1996, Zeder 2003), and the extent to which ancient cities were more or less healthful than their hinterlands were (Miksic 1999, Storey 2004).

Environmental disasters have sometimes played critical roles in the demise of cities and polities, but it is easy to overdo such explanations, and we should never exclude consideration of other sources of change. Monocausal explanations in terms of environmental disasters sometimes tacitly assume that states and cities would be immortal as long as they weren't destroyed by external phenomena.

"Consumer" Cities?

Students of Greek and Roman cities debate the extent to which some of the cities some of the time may have been more than just "consumer" cities, as thought by Weber and Moses Finley. At issue is the extent of entrepreneurial spirit and practices and the degree to which activities in cities generated wealth, as well as consuming wealth generated in the countryside. This topic is related to, but not to be confused with, the formalist/substantivist debate of Polanyi and others. Recent publications include Rich & Wallace-Hadrill (1991), Parkins (1997), and Parkins & Smith (1998). The current state of this debate seems to be that Weber and Finley overestimated the differences between earlier cities and the cities of medieval Europe, with their relatively high degree of political autonomy and strongly entrepreneurial spirit. Entrepreneurial activities and attitudes were by no means insignificant in all early cities. The differences were not always as great as Fox's (1977) contrast between "administrative" and "mercantile" cities would suggest. Nevertheless, many scholars think this calls for modification of Weber and Finley's ideas rather than sweeping rejection, and new concepts to replace theirs have not been proposed.

Until the industrial revolution that started in the late 1700s was well underway, rights to income from large and diversified agrarian holdings were not only the most prestigious source of wealth everywhere, but also, as a rule, the least risky and often the most profitable. Debate about the Weber/Finley model is not so much about relations between cities and their hinterlands as about the extent to which prevalent attitudes and political, legal, and economic institutions hindered or promoted development of nonagrarian sectors of the economies of various ancient and more recent societies. The general thrust of recent work on Mesopotamia, Rome, and the Late Postclassic Basin of Mexico suggests that there was somewhat more entrepreneurship and development in nonagrarian sectors than Weber, Finley, and many other scholars have thought, yet perhaps significantly less than in Early Modern Western Europe. However, a great deal remains to be learned about the economies of these and other early complex societies, and there may well have been considerable variation among them and over time. Also, material culture and technological knowledge must not be neglected. It is not clear to me that, for example, the Roman empire might have developed an industrial revolution early on if only institutions and attitudes had been more conducive to it. There was significant cumulative technological progress in the world between the 300s and the 1300s, and this is a factor that should not be dismissed.

The combination of textual and archaeological data enables specialists on Greece and Rome to argue about issues concerning internal social, economic, and physical aspects of cities and their interactions with their surroundings on a level that can scarcely be approached anywhere else in the ancient world. Nevertheless, classical scholars are searching for new concepts and models, and it is likely that their search will be aided by data and concepts from other regions. The consumer city concept is also debated for Mesopotamia (e.g., Van De Mieroop 1997). Archaeological, ethnohistoric, and archival work on Aztec society may be approaching a similar degree of development. Although controversy continues, a reasonable amount of evidence can be debated. Major recent publications include Berdan et al. (1996), Charlton et al. (2000), Hodge (1984), Hodge & Smith (1994), Nichols et al. (2002), M.E. Smith (2000), and papers in Sanders et al. (2003).

CITIES AND POLITIES

Possehl (1998) questions whether Harappan polities qualify as states. For the later Early Historic Period of South Asia, M.L. Smith (2003b) argues for cities without states, though Sinopoli (2001) takes a more moderate view. Such controversies may be irresolvable and not very productive as long as we stick with "cities" and "states" as typological boxes. It is more effective to frame the matter as issues concerning the relations between (*a*) types of settlements (or types of systems of settlements); (*b*) environmental circumstances and available technologies; and (*c*) types of political, social, economic, and religious institutions and practices. Is preexistence of certain types within any one of these categories a necessary condition for creation or spontaneous emergence of certain types within another category? Sufficient as well as necessary? If neither quite sufficient or necessary, is such preexistence at least conducive to change in another category? Were some types of early polity more prone to urbanism than were others? One issue here is the roles of environmental/technological constraints relative to institutions, practices, and ideas about what is desirable. Balkansky (2002, pp. 10–13) offers an especially insightful discussion of these issues for the Mesoamerican city of Monte Albán and the Monte Albán state, summarizing the views and theoretical assumptions of various researchers, emphasizing the importance of diverse analytical scales (including macroregional), and making concrete suggestions about how different models can be empirically tested.

"City-States"

Concepts and definitions vary widely. One axis of differentiation is whether emphasis is more on the "state" aspect or the "city" aspect. The label unhappily invites us to confound kinds of polities and kinds of settlements. Trigger (2003) argues that there was a sharp contrast between city-states and regional states. His argument is useful in that it recognizes diversity among early polities and aptly questions whether either type consistently preceded the other, but I doubt whether all early states really fit neatly into one or the other of Trigger's two types. A small polity may or may not be highly urbanized, and a highly urbanized settlement may or may not be the capital of a large polity. When emphasis is mostly on the state, it would be better to use a term such as "little state" or "statelet" to refer to polities small enough that the central authority does not need to delegate much decision-making authority to persons located outside the center. When a polity is large enough that, given environmental circumstances and prevailing technology, appointees of the central authority or local dignitaries have a significant degree of autonomy, a whole new series of practices and interests come into play, especially struggles for still greater autonomy by the locals and resistance to these struggles from the center (e.g., Cowgill 1988). A chronic problem for small states is avoiding domination or incorporation by neighbors; for large states the problem is more one of avoiding fragmentation.

Fox (1977) emphasizes the city aspect, and for him city-states are limited to "mercantile" cities that have carried their relative independence from encompassing regional states to the logical extreme where the regional state, at least for practical purposes, no longer exists. Many find Fox's concept too narrow. One common denominator is that we are thinking of sets of polities whose citizens have both a strong identification with their specific city and awareness of strong cultural similarities with neighboring polities in the same general region. But we need to go beyond that common denominator if we are to make the concept very useful. I suggest it is best to focus on regions rather than settlements. The phenomenon of interest is that some regions, in environmental and technological terms, might have been politically integrated but, during significant periods, were not. This approach moves us away from the problematic notion of an isolated city-state, and it underscores the point that regions, or macroregions, rather than individual settlements, are, for many purposes, better units of study (Balkansky 2002).

ALTERNATIVES TO TYPOLOGIES

Fox's (1977) typology of cities, "regal-ritual," "administrative," and "mercantile," remains useful up to a point, but these categories are too broad and encompass too much variation. Rather than subdivide them into more categories, however, it would be better to specify more variables (axes, dimensions) on which specific cases can be located in a multivariate space. Area and population are two obvious examples. Because it is difficult to estimate these figures very accurately, they should be presented with confidence intervals and sensible rounding (e.g., c. 15,000 ± 5000, rather than 14,847) and illustrated by versions of box-and-whisker plots in which the boxes might span a 67% confidence interval and the whiskers a 95% interval. Other variables, often only rankable on ordinal scales or even less quantifiable, might include sharpness of physical edges of settlement (including walls, which may or may not be transgressed by the settlement); investment in fortifications; extent of top-down planning; degree of spatial segmentation (physically distinct districts); scale of civic-ceremonial structures and configurations; durability of civic-ceremonial, residential, and other built features; division of labor (the extent to which households produce goods and services intended for consumption by other households); and prevalence of various kinds of amenities (as discussed previously). These variables occur to me as relevant to some of the issues discussed above. Other topics will suggest other variables. An important goal is to identify variables that have broad applicability across different regional traditions. This offers the possibility of developing knowledge bases that do not homogenize local variability too much, yet are suitable for cross-cultural comparisons.

PROBLEMS IN IDENTIFYING TIERS IN REGIONAL SITE HIERARCHIES

A considerable literature has been built up around the premise that the number of distinct tiers in a regional site hierarchy is diagnostic of distinct levels of sociopolitical integration (e.g., Flannery 1998). This premise appeals to some archaeologists because it implies that if the number of tiers can be satisfactorily ascertained one can simply read off from it the type of society—"chiefdom," "state," etc. More complex societies do tend to have wider ranges of site sizes. But both conceptual and methodological problems abound. There is no space to discuss them adequately here; I hope to do so in another publication.

METHODS AND FUTURE WORK

It is impractical to excavate more than small parts of large cities. This fact calls for sophistication in excavation research design, selection, and sampling, informed by theoretical issues to be tested, supplemented by systematic survey and, where feasible, remote-sensing techniques to detect subsurface features. We need a balance between surveys and excavations in hinterlands and in cities themselves: Neither can be understood without the other. "Complete coverage" is a phrase that masks great differences in survey intensity. Excavations as well as surveys are needed in hinterlands. Computer applications such as geographic information systems and databases have much to offer, if used appropriately. Regional and macroregional knowledge bases require overcoming problems of integrating disparate databases created by multiple projects. Interdisciplinary approaches are needed, including not only natural sciences and geography but also history and psychology.

One central task for the future is to improve our ability to use the built environment to validly infer the social phenomena of which the built environment is both outcome and shaper. Ethnographic and historical analogies are important, with the usual proviso that we must take pains to avoid overgeneralizing from too few or inappropriate cases. Flannery (1998) offers some steps in this direction, but we need to go much further in testing assumptions, assembling accurate data, and refining concepts.

ACKNOWLEDGMENTS

I thank Geoff Emberling, Jonathan Mark Kenoyer, Philip Kohl, Ian Morris, Carla Sinopoli, Michael Smith, Monica Smith, Charles Stanish, Glenn Storey, Kristin Sullivan, Marc Van De Mieroop, Barbara Stark, David Wengrow, and Norman Yoffee for suggesting important publications, providing access to unpublished material, and giving useful advice.

The *Annual Review of Anthropology* is online at http://anthro.annualreviews.org

LITERATURE CITED

Adams REW, MacLeod M, eds. 2000. *The Cambridge History of the Native Peoples of the Americas, Volume II: Mesoamerica, Part 1: Archaeology.* Cambridge: Cambridge Univ. Press

Adams RMcC. 1966. *The Evolution of Urban Society: Early Mesopotamia and Prehispanic Mexico.* Chicago: Aldine

Alcock SE, D'Altroy TN, Morrison KD, Sinopoli CM, eds. 2001. *Empires: Perspectives from Archaeology and History.* Cambridge: Cambridge Univ. Press

Algaze G. 1993. *The Uruk World-System.* Chicago: Univ. Chicago Press

Allchin FR, ed. 1995. *The Archaeology of Early Historic South Asia: The Emergence of Cities and States.* Cambridge: Cambridge Univ. Press

Allison PM, ed. 1999. *The Archaeology of Household Activities.* London: Routledge

Andreau J. 1999. *Banking and Business in the Roman World.* Cambridge: Cambridge Univ. Press

Ashmore W, Sabloff JA. 2002. Spatial orders in Maya civic plans. *Lat. Am. Antiq.* 13:201–15

Ashmore W, Sabloff JA. 2003. Interpreting ancient Maya civic plans: reply to Smith. *Lat. Am. Antiq.* 14(2):229–36

Attarian CJ. 2003. Cities as a place of ethnogenesis: urban growth and civilization in the Chicama Valley, Peru. See ML Smith 2003a, pp. 184–211

Bacus EA, Lucero LJ, eds. 1999. *Complex Polities in the Ancient Tropical World.* Arlington, VA: Am. Anthropol. Assoc.

Baines J. 2003. In *Culture Through Objects: Ancient Near Eastern Studies in Honour of P.R.S. Moorey*, ed. TM Potts, M Roaf, D Stein. Oakville, CT: David Brown

Balkansky AK. 2002. *The Sola Valley and the Monte Albán State: A Study of Zapotec*

Imperial Expansion. Ann Arbor: Mus. Anthropol., Univ. Mich.

Bard K. 1997. Urbanism and the rise of complex society and the early state in Egypt. In *Emergence and Change in Early Urban Societies,* ed. L Manzanilla, pp. 59–86. New York: Plenum Press

Bawden G. 1996. *The Moche.* Oxford: Blackwell

Berdan FF, Blanton RE, Boone EH, Hodge MG, Smith ME, Umberger E. 1996. *Aztec Imperial Strategies.* Washington, DC: Dumbarton Oaks

Betz VM. 2002. *The city as invention: an environmental psychological approach to the origins of urban life.* PhD thesis. Ariz. State Univ., Tempe

Blake E. 2002. Spatiality past and present: an interview with Edward Soja. *J. Soc. Archaeol.* 2(2):139–58

Blanton RE. 1976. Anthropological studies of cities. *Annu. Rev. Anthropol.* 5:249–64

Blanton RE, Feinman GM, Kowalewski SA, Nicholas LM. 1999. *Ancient Oaxaca: The Monte Albán State.* Cambridge: Cambridge Univ. Press

Blanton RE, Kowalewski SA, Feinman GM, Finsten LM. 1993. *Ancient Mesoamerica: A Comparison of Change in Three Regions.* Cambridge: Cambridge Univ. Press. 2nd ed.

Boyd A. 1962. *Chinese Architecture and Town Planning 1500 B.C.-A.D. 1911.* London: Alec Tiranti

Branigan K, ed. 2001. *Urbanism in the Aegean Bronze Age.* Sheffield, UK: Sheffield Acad.

Brewer DJ, Teeter E. 1999. *Egypt and the Egyptians.* Cambridge: Cambridge Univ. Press

Cahill N. 2002. *Household and City Organization at Olynthus.* New Haven, CT: Yale Univ. Press

Canuto MA, Yaeger J, eds. 2000. *The Archaeology of Communities: A New World Perspective.* New York: Routledge

Carl P, Kemp B, Laurence R, Coningham R, Higham C, Cowgill GL. 2000. Were cities built as images? *Cambridge Archaeol. J.* 10(2):327–65

Chakrabarti DK. 1995. *The Archaeology of Ancient Indian Cities.* Delhi/London: Oxford Univ. Press

Champakalakshmi R. 1996. *Trade, Ideology, and Urbanization: South India 300 BC to AD 1300.* Delhi/New York: Oxford Univ. Press

Charlton TH, Nichols DL, Otis Charlton C. 2000. Otumba and its neighbors: ex oriente lux. *Anc. Mesoam.* 11(2):247–65

Chase AF, Chase DS, Haviland WA. 1990. The Classic Maya city: reconsidering the Mesoamerican urban tradition. *Am. Anthropol.* 92:499–506

Cowgill GL. 1988. Onward and upward with collapse. In *The Collapse of Ancient States and Civilizations,* ed. N Yoffee, GL Cowgill, pp. 244–76. Tucson: Univ. Ariz. Press

Cowgill GL. 1997. State and society at Teotihuacan, Mexico. *Annu. Rev. Anthropol.* 26: 129–61

Cowgill GL. 2000a. The Central Mexican Highlands from the rise of Teotihuacan to the decline of Tula. See Adams & MacLeod 2000, pp. 250–317

Cowgill GL. 2000b. Intentionality and meaning in the layout of Teotihuacan, Mexico. See Carl et al. 2000, pp. 358–61

Cowgill GL. 2003. Teotihuacan: cosmic glories and mundane needs. See ML Smith 2003a, pp. 37–55

Emberling G. 2003. Urban social transformations and the problem of the "first city": new research from Mesopotamia. See ML Smith 2003a, pp. 254–68

Falconer SE, Savage SH. 1995. Heartlands and hinterlands: alternative trajectories of early urbanization in Mesopotamia and the southern Levant. *Am. Antiq.* 60(1):37–58

Feinman G, Marcus J, eds. 1998. *Archaic States.* Santa Fe, NM: SAR Press

Flannery KV. 1998. The ground plans of archaic states. See Feinman & Marcus 1998, pp. 15–57

Fleming DE. 2004. *Democracy's Ancient Ancestors: Mari and Early Collective Governance.* Cambridge: Cambridge Univ. Press

Fletcher R. 1995. *The Limits of Settlement*

Growth: A Theoretical Outline. Cambridge: Cambridge Univ. Press

Fox RG. 1977. *Urban Anthropology: Cities in Their Cultural Settings.* Englewood Cliffs, NJ: Prentice-Hall

Fritz JM, Michell G, Nagaraja Rao MS. 1984. *Where Kings and Gods Meet: The Royal Centre of Vijayanagara, India.* Tucson: Univ. Ariz. Press

Garnsey P. 1988. *Famine and Food Supply in the Graeco-Roman World.* Cambridge: Cambridge Univ. Press

Gates C. 2003. *Ancient Cities: The Archaeology of Urban Life in the Ancient Near East and Egypt, Greece, and Rome.* New York: Routledge

Graham E. 1999. Stone cities, green cities. See Bacus & Lucero 1999, pp. 185–94

Hall P. 1998. *Cities in Civilization.* London: Weidenfeld & Nicolson

Hansen MH, ed. 2000. *A Comparative Study of Thirty City-State Cultures.* Copenhagen: R. Dan. Acad. Sci. Lett.

Hansen MH, ed. 2002. *A Comparative Study of Six City-State Cultures.* Copenhagen: R. Dan. Acad. Sci. Lett.

Herzog Z. 1997. *Archaeology of the City: Urban Planning in Ancient Israel and its Social Implications.* Tel Aviv: Emery and Claire Yass Univ. Press

Hodge MG. 1984. *Aztec City-States.* Ann Arbor: Univ. Mich. Mus. Anthropol.

Hodge MG, Smith ME, eds. 1984. *Economies and Polities in the Aztec Realm.* Albany: Inst. Mesoam. Stud., State Univ. N.Y.

Hopkins K. 1978. Economic growth and towns in classical antiquity. In *Towns and Societies,* ed. P Abrams, EA Wrigley, pp. 35–77. Cambridge: Cambridge Univ. Press

Houston S, Escobedo H, Child M, Golden C, Muñoz R. 2003. The moral community: Maya settlement transformation at Piedras Negras, Guatemala. See ML Smith 2003a, pp. 212–53

Hudson M, Levine BA, eds. *Urbanization and Land Ownership in the Ancient Near East.* Cambridge, MA: Peabody Mus., Harvard Univ.

Jansen M. 1980. Public spaces in the urban settlements of the Harappa culture. *Art Archaeol. Res. Pap.* 17:11–19

Jansen M. 1989. Some problems regarding the *forma urbis* Mohenjo-Daro. In *South Asian Archaeology 1985,* ed. K Frifelt, P Sorenson, pp. 247–54. London: Curzon Press

Keith K. 2003. The spatial patterns of everyday life in Old Babylonian neighborhoods. See ML Smith 2003a, pp. 56–80

Kemp BJ. 1989. *Ancient Egypt: Anatomy of a Civilization.* New York: Routledge

Kemp BJ. 2000. Bricks and metaphor. See Carl et al. 2000, pp. 335–46

Kenoyer JM. 1991. The Indus Valley tradition of Pakistan and western India. *J. World Hist.* 5(4):331–85

Kenoyer JM. 1997. Early city-states in South Asia: comparing the Harappan phase and the Early Historic period. See Nichols & Charlton 1997, pp. 51–70

Kenoyer JM. 1998. *Ancient Cities of the Indus Valley Civilization.* Oxford: Oxford Univ. Press

Kolata AL. 1983. Chan Chan and Cuzco: on the nature of the ancient Andean city. In *Civilization in the Ancient Americas: Essays in Honor of Gordon R. Willey,* ed. RM Leventhal, AL Kolata, pp. 345–72. Albuquerque/Cambridge, MA: Univ. N.M. Press/Peabody Mus., Harvard Univ.

Kolata AL. 1997. Of kings and capitals: principles of authority and the nature of cities in the native Andean state. See Nichols & Charlton 1997, pp. 245–54

Lacovara P. 1997. *The New Kingdom Royal City.* New York: Kegan Paul

Mack A. 2002. *Spiritual Journey, Imperial City: Pilgrimage to the Temples of Vijayanagara.* New Delhi: Vedams

Marcus J. 1983. On the nature of the Mesoamerican city. See Vogt & Leventhal 1983, pp. 195–242

Marcus J. 1998. The peaks and valleys of ancient states: an extension of the dynamic model. See Feinman & Marcus 1998, pp. 59–94

Marcus J, Flannery KV. 1996. *Zapotec*

Civilization: How Urban Society Evolved in Mexico's Oaxaca Valley. New York: Thames & Hudson

Mastache AG, Cobean RH, Healan DM. 2002. *Ancient Tollan: Tula and the Toltec Heartland.* Boulder: Univ. Press Colo.

McIntosh J. 2001. *A Peaceful Realm: The Rise and Fall of the Indus Civilization.* Boulder, CO: Westview Press

McIntosh RJ. 1991. Early urban clusters in China and Africa: the arbitration of social ambiguity. *J. Field Archaeol.* 18:199–212

McIntosh RJ. 1998. *The Peoples of the Middle Niger.* Oxford: Blackwell

McIntosh SK, ed. 1999a. *Beyond Chiefdoms: Pathways to Complexity in Africa.* Cambridge: Cambridge Univ. Press

McIntosh SK. 1999b. Floodplains and the development of complex society: comparative perspectives from the West African semi-arid tropics. See Bacus & Lucero 1999, pp. 151–61

McIntosh SK, McIntosh RJ. 1993. Cities without citadels: understanding urban origins along the middle Niger. In *The Archaeology of Africa: Food, Metals, and Towns,* ed. CT Shaw, P Sinclair, B Andah, A Okpako, pp. 622–41. London: Routledge

Miksic JN. 1999. Water, urbanization, and disease in ancient Indonesia. See Bacus & Lucero 1999, pp. 167–84

Miller HML. 2000. Reassessing the urban structure of Harappa: evidence from craft production distribution. In *South Asian Archaeology 1997: Volume 1,* ed. M Taddei, G De Marco, pp. 77–100. Rome: Istituto Italiano per l'Africa e l'Oriente

Millon R. 1973. *The Teotihuacan Map. Part 1: Text.* Austin: Univ. Tex. Press

Millon R. 1981. Teotihuacan: city, state, and civilization. In *Supplement to the Handbook of Middle American Indians, Volume One: Archaeology,* ed. VR Bricker, JA Sabloff, pp. 198–243. Austin: Univ. Tex. Press

Millon R. 1988. The last years of Teotihuacan dominance. In *The Collapse of Ancient States and Civilizations,* ed. N Yoffee, GL Cowgill, pp. 102–64. Tucson: Univ. Ariz. Press

Millon R. 1992. Teotihuacan studies: from 1950 to 1990 and beyond. In *Art, Ideology, and the City of Teotihuacan,* ed. JC Berlo, pp. 339–429. Washington, DC: Dumbarton Oaks

Morley N. 1996. *Metropolis and Hinterland: The City of Rome and the Italian Economy 200 B.C. – A.D. 200.* Cambridge: Cambridge Univ. Press

Morris I. 1997. An archaeology of equalities? The Greek city-states. See Nichols & Charlton 1997, pp. 91–105

Morrison KD. 2001. Coercion, resistance, and hierarchy: local processes and imperial strategies in the Vijayanagara empire. See Alcock et al. 2001, pp. 252–78

Nichols DL, Brumfiel EM, Neff H, Hodge M, Charlton TH, Glascock MD. 2002. Neutrons, markets, cities, and empires: a 1000-year perspective on ceramic production and distribution in the postclassic Basin of Mexico. *J. Anthropol. Archaeol.* 21(1):25–82

Nichols DL, Charlton TH, eds. 1997. *The Archaeology of City-States: Cross-Cultural Approaches.* Washington, DC: Smithsonian Inst. Press

O'Connor D. 1998. *City and Cosmos in Ancient Egypt.* London: Athlone Press

Owens EJ. 1991. *The City in the Greek and Roman World.* New York: Routledge

Parkins HM, ed. 1997. *Roman Urbanism: Beyond the Consumer City.* New York: Routledge

Parkins HM, Smith C, eds. 1998. *Trade, Traders, and the Ancient City.* New York: Routledge

Possehl G. 1997. The transformation of the Indus civilization. *J. World Prehist.* 11(4):425–72

Possehl G. 1998. Sociocultural complexity without the state: the Indus civilization. See Feinman & Marcus 1998, pp. 261–91

Possehl G. 2002. *The Indus Civilization: A Contemporary Perspective.* Blue Ridge Summit, PA: AltaMira Press

Ratnagar S. 2001. *Understanding Harappa.* Abhiramapuram, Chennai, India: Tulika

Rich J, Wallace-Hadrill A, eds. 1991. *City and*

Country in the Ancient World. New York: Routledge

Robertson IG. 1999. Spatial and multivariate analysis, random sampling error, and analytical noise: empirical bayesian methods at Teotihuacan, Mexico. *Am. Antiq.* 64(1):137–52

Robertson IG. 2004. *Mapping the Social Landscape of an Early City: Teotihuacan, Mexico.* Tucson: Univ. Ariz. Press. In press

Rothman MS, ed. 2001. *Uruk Mesopotamia and Its Neighbors: Cross-Cultural Interactions in the Era of State Formation.* Santa Fe, NM: SAR Press

Sanders WT, Mastache AG, Cobean RH, eds. 2003. *Urbanism in Mesoamerica.* Mexico City/University Park: Instituto Nacional de Antropología e Historia/Penn. State Univ

Sanders WT, Parson JR, Santley RS. 1979. *The Basin of Mexico: Ecological Processes in the Evolution of a Civilization.* New York: Academic

Sanders WT, Santley RS. 1983. A tale of three cities: energetics and urbanization in pre-Hispanic Central Mexico. See Vogt & Leventhal 1983, pp. 243–91

Schwartz GM, Falconer SE, eds. 1994. *Archaeological Views from the Countryside: Village Communities in Early Complex Societies.* Washington, DC: Smithsonian Inst. Press

Shen C. 1994. Early urbanization in the Eastern Zhou in China (770–221 BC): an archaeological view. *Antiquity* 68:724–44

Sinopoli CM. 2001. On the edge of empire: form and substance in the Satavahana Dynasty. See Alcock et al. 2001, pp. 155–78

Sinopoli CM. 2003. *The Political Economy of Craft Production: Crafting Empire in South India, c. 1350–1650.* Cambridge: Cambridge Univ. Press

Skinner GW, ed. 1977. *The City in Late Imperial China.* Stanford, CA: Stanford Univ. Press

Smith AT. 2003. *The Political Landscape: Constellations of Authority in Early Complex Polities.* Berkeley: Univ. Calif. Press

Smith ME. 2000. Aztec city-states. See Hansen 2000, pp. 581–95

Smith ME. 2003. Can we read cosmology in ancient Maya city plans? Comment on Ashmore and Smith. *Lat. Am. Antiq.* 14(2):221–28

Smith ME. 2004. City size in late postclassic Mesoamerica. *J. Urban Hist.* In press

Smith ML, ed. 2003a. *The Social Construction of Ancient Cities.* Washington, DC: Smithsonian Inst. Press

Smith ML. 2003b. Early walled cities of the Indian subcontinent as "small worlds." See ML Smith 2003a, pp. 269–89

Southall A. 1998. *The City in Time and Space: From Birth to Apocalypse.* Cambridge: Cambridge Univ. Press

Spodek H, Srinavasan DM, eds. 1993. *Urban Form and Meaning in South Asia: The Shaping of Cities from Prehistoric to Precolonial Times.* Washington, DC: Natl. Gallery Art

Stambaugh JE. 1988. *The Ancient Roman City.* Baltimore: Johns Hopkins Univ. Press

Stanish C. 2001a. The origin of state societies in South America. *Annu. Rev. Anthropol.* 30:41–64

Stanish C. 2001b. Regional research on the Inca. *J. Archaeol. Res.* 9(3):213–41

Stark BL. 1999. Formal architectural complexes in south-central Veracruz, Mexico: a capital zone? *J. Field Archaeol.* 26:197–225

Stein GJ. 1999. *Rethinking World-Systems: Diasporas, Colonies, and Interaction in Uruk Mesopotamia.* Tucson: Univ. Ariz. Press

Stein GJ. 2002. From passive periphery to active agents: emerging perspectives in the archaeology of interregional interaction. *Am. Anthropol.* 104(3):903–16

Stein GJ, Rothman MS, eds. 1994. *Chiefdoms and Early States in the Near East.* Madison, WI: Prehistory Press

Steinhardt NS. 1990. *Chinese Imperial City Planning.* Honolulu: Univ. Hawaii Press

Stone EC. 1987. *Nippur Neighborhoods.* Chicago: Univ. Chicago Press

Stone EC. 1995. The development of cities in ancient Mesopotamia. In *Civilizations of the*

Ancient Near East, ed. JM Sasson, pp. 235–48. New York: Scribner

Stone EC, Zimansky P. 1992. Mashkan-shapir and the anatomy of an Old Babylonian city. *Biblic. Archaeol.* 55:21–18

Storey GR. 2004. *From Mbanza to Metropolis: A Cross-Cultural Sampling of Preindustrial Urban Population Issues.* Tuscaloosa: Univ. Ala. Press. In press

Sugiyama S. 1993. Worldview materialized in Teotihuacan, Mexico. *Latin Am. Antiq.* 4(2):103–29

Trigger B. 2003. *Understanding Early Civilizations: A Comparative Study.* Cambridge: Cambridge University Press

Underhill AP, Feinman GM, Nicholas L, Bennett G, Cai F, et al. 1998. Systematic, regional survey in SE Shandong province, China. *J. Field Archaeol.* 25(4):453–74

Underhill AP, Feinman GM, Nicholas LM, Bennett G, Fang H, et al. 2002. Regional survey and the development of complex societies in southeastern Shandong, China. *Antiquity* 76(293):745–55

Van De Mieroop M. 1997. *The Ancient Mesopotamian City.* Oxford: Oxford Univ. Press

Vogt EZ, Leventhal RM, eds. 1983. *Prehistoric Settlement Patterns: Essays in Honor of Gordon R. Willey.* Albuquerque/Cambridge, MA: Univ. N.M. Press/Peabody Mus., Harvard Univ.

Von Hagen A, Morris C. 1998. *The Cities of the Ancient Andes.* New York: Thames & Hudson

Wheatley P. 1971. *The Pivot of the Four Quarters: A Preliminary Enquiry into the Origins and Character of the Ancient Chinese City.* Chicago: Aldine

Wilkinson TAH. 1999. *Early Dynastic Egypt.* New York: Routledge

Yates RDS. 1997. The city-state in ancient China. See Nichols & Charlton 1997, pp. 71–90

Zanker P. 1998. *Pompeii: Public and Private Life.* Cambridge, MA: Harvard Univ. Press

Zeder M. 2003. Food and provisioning in urban societies: a view from northern Mesopotamia. See ML Smith 2003a, pp. 156–83

Annu. Rev. Anthropol. 2004. 33:551–83
doi: 10.1146/annurev.anthro.33.070203.143932
Copyright © 2004 by Annual Reviews. All rights reserved

THE PEOPLING OF THE NEW WORLD:
Perspectives from Molecular Anthropology

Theodore G. Schurr

*Department of Anthropology, University of Pennsylvania, Philadelphia,
Pennsylvania 19104-6398; email: tgschurr@sas.upenn.edu*

Key Words mtDNA, Y chromosome, Americas, migrations, Siberia

■ **Abstract** A number of important insights into the peopling of the New World
have been gained through molecular genetic studies of Siberian and Native American
populations. These data indicate that the initial migration of ancestral Amerindian
originated in south-central Siberia and entered the New World between 20,000–14,000
calendar years before present (cal yr BP). These early immigrants probably followed
a coastal route into the New World, where they expanded into all continental regions.
A second migration that may have come from the same Siberian region entered the
Americas somewhat later, possibly using an interior route, and genetically contributed
to indigenous populations from North and Central America. In addition, Beringian
populations moved into northern North America after the last glacial maximum (LGM)
and gave rise to Aleuts, Eskimos, and Na-Dené Indians.

INTRODUCTION

The past decade has been an enormously productive period for research into questions concerning the peopling of the Americas. During this time, investigators
from all subfields of anthropology and from many different laboratories across the
world have focused their attention on determining who the First Americans were.
Like their intellectual predecessors before them, these researchers have attempted
to elucidate when ancestral Native Americans first arrived in the New World, how
many population expansions or migrations were involved in this colonization process, and where in Asia/Eurasia these ancestral groups came from. Their efforts
have yielded new insights into the origins of Native Americans, while also raising
a number of additional and intriguing questions about Native American prehistory.

Until relatively recently, the dominant explanation for the colonization of the
Americas was the Clovis First model. According to this model, human populations
first entered the Americas around 12,900 calendar years before present (cal yr BP),
after the last glacial maximum (LGM) (24,000–13,050 cal yr BP). They entered
from the Beringian landmass and followed an ice-free corridor that had opened
in northern North America into the interior of the continent, where they rapidly

expanded into the uninhabited areas of the Americas (Haynes 1992, 1993; Fiedel 1999; Meltzer 1997; Meltzer et al. 1997; Fagan 2000). These early pioneers were thought to be part of a cultural tradition that employed large, sophisticated bifacial points for big game hunting. Because no older Paleoindian sites had been discovered or confirmed, and because all other lithic traditions in the Americas seemed to derive from the Clovis culture, many archeologists believed that the Clovis points demarcated the earliest occupancy of the Americas by modern human groups.

However, recent archeological data have brought the Clovis First model into question. The Meadowcroft site in Pennsylvania (Adovasio et al. 1998, 2000), the Cactus Hill site in Virginia (McAvoy et al. 2000, McAvoy & McAvoy 1997), the Topper site in South Carolina (Goodyear 1999), several sites in Texas (Collins 2002), and other locations in North America (Dixon 2001, 2002) have all been dated to between 16,000–14,250 cal yr BP, times that are older than those associated with Clovis lithic sites in North America (12,900–12,550 cal yr BP). Similarly, a growing number of sites in South America, including the well-publicized Monte Verde site in southern Chile (Dillehay 1989, 1997, 1999; Dillehay et al. 1992; Keefer et al. 1998; Roosevelt et al. 1996, 2002; Sandweiss et al. 1998), are at least the same age, if not older, than Clovis sites in North America. These South American sites have yielded lithic and other cultural materials that do not appear to have been created by Clovis peoples. Their existence implies that ancestral Native Americans arrived in the New World earlier than 13,000 cal yr BP, and hence, began settling the Americas prior to the emergence of the Clovis lithic tradition in North America.

The date at which ancestral Native Americans arrived in the New World from Siberia has also come under increasing scrutiny. A problem for migration models involving very early expansion times (before the LGM) has been that these estimates approached the dates for the oldest known human occupation sites in southeastern Siberia (40,000–30,000 cal yr BP) and were older than the archeological sites in northeastern Siberia (18,000–22,000 cal yr BP) (Goebel & Aksenov 1995, Goebel 1999, Goebel et al. 2001, Hoeffecker et al. 1993, Waters et al. 1997). However, a recent study of the Yana River site has indicated that humans were living in the Arctic by ∼30,000 years ago, well before the LGM (Pitulko et al. 2004). This date, as well as the fact that human groups were able to adapt to cold climates at that time, suggests that an entry from eastern Siberia shortly before the LGM might not be as implausible as once thought.

Furthermore, data from a variety of geological, archeological, and paleontological studies are now questioning the idea of an ice-free corridor in North America at the time of the emergence of the Clovis lithic tradition. These data suggest that there were no connections between Beringia and areas south of the Wisconsin and Laurentide glaciers in northern North America until ∼12,550 cal yr BP (Clague et al. 1987, Jackson & Duk-Rodkin 1996). Likewise, no animal bones have been recovered from the ice-free corridor between 21,000–11,500 years BP (until 13,050 cal yr BP) (Burns 1996). Thus, it appears that glacial ice sheets blocked the movement of human groups from Beringia through the interior of

North America between ∼24,000–13,000 cal yr BP (Fedje 2002, Heaton & Grady 2003, Mathewes 1989).

Given these facts, if the earliest immigrants to the Americas arrived during the LGM, then they must have followed a coastal route into the New World. This possibility had been put forward previously on the basis of geological and linguistic evidence (Fladmark 1979, 1983; Gruhn 1987, 1992). Computer simulations of a colonization process by interior and coastal routes using demographic data from hunter-gatherer groups have also suggested that the patterns of genetic diversity in Amerindian populations are more consistent with a coastal model that allowed an earlier and rapid expansion into the Southern hemisphere (Fix 2002).

However, until recently, geological evidence for the deglaciation of the Northwest Coast of North America, hence, the availability of this region as a migratory route, had been equivocal. Current studies now indicate that human occupation of these areas was possible between 16,800–14,850 cal yr BP (Blaise et al. 1990, Bobrowsky et al. 1990, Fedje 2002, Fedje & Christiansen 1999, Hetherington & Reid 2003, Jackson & Duk-Rodkin 1996, Josenhans et al. 1997, Mandryk et al. 2001, Mann & Hamilton 1995). Therefore, immigrant groups could have made use of the glacial refugia during their movements down the coast of western North America via watercraft. Once deglaciation took place around 13,000–11,000 cal yr BP, human populations would then have been free to expand into North America from the Beringia platform, as well as expand north from regions below the ice sheets.

Studies of craniometric variation in human remains from the Americas have also shed light on the biological history of these regions. These data have revealed biological differences between the earliest settlers of the Americas, the Paleoindians, and populations dating from the Archaic Period (7000 cal yr BP) to modern times (Brace et al. 2001, Jantz & Owsley 2001, Ross et al. 2002). The Paleoindian individuals show a much wider range of variation in their craniofacial features compared to later Native Americans, and they show almost no overlap in these features with these latter groups. Such differences suggest that the Paleoindians and subsequent Amerindian populations may have arisen from two temporally distinct migrations that originated in different parts of Asia. However, not all researchers think that these differences reflect two migrations and instead assert that these craniofacial differences resulted from the effects of genetic drift and adaptation over the past 10,000 years (Powell & Neves 1999). Even so, many of these Paleoindian crania, including the 9300-year-old Kennewick Man skeleton (Chatters 2001), seem to bear some resemblance to those of ancient Eurasian/East Asian populations (Brace et al. 2001; Hanihara et al. 2003, 2004).

These lines of evidence set the stage for a discussion of the molecular genetic data from Siberian and Native American populations and their implications for the peopling of the New World. In the majority of recent molecular studies, researchers have analyzed two uniparentally inherited genetic systems, the mitochondrial DNA (mtDNA) and nonrecombining portion of the Y chromosome (NRY). The mtDNA and NRY possess a series of different markers that define or identify specific genetic

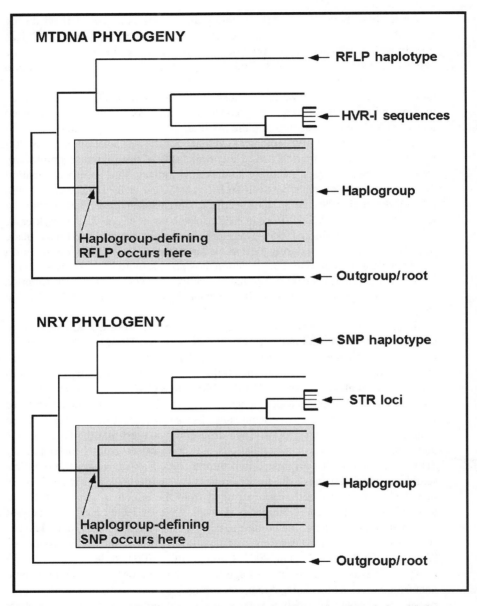

Figure 1 Mitochondrial DNA and NRY phylogenies illustrating the relationship between different kinds of mutations used in phylogenetic reconstructions.

lineages present in human populations (Figure 1). By analyzing the sequence variation in them, one can identify the maternal and paternal lineages present within populations, characterize the extent of diversity within them, and ascertain the manner in which they have been spread into neighboring groups. Other genetic loci also have been used to explore Native American origins and affinities, but they are not discussed here (Crawford et al. 1998, Rothhammer et al. 1997, Salzano 2002, Schurr 2004c).

This paper reviews the findings of molecular genetic studies of Native American and Siberian populations and explores their implications for the peopling of the New World. Several specific issues are addressed, including (*a*) the nature of genetic diversity in Native Americans and Siberians, (*b*) the timing of the initial colonization of the New World, (*c*) the number of expansions that entered the Americas, and (*d*) the source area for ancestral Native Americans. In addition, the population history of Native American tribes after the initial colonization, and the consequences of contact with Europeans since the late fifteenth century, are discussed briefly.

GENETIC DIVERSITY OF NATIVE AMERICAN POPULATIONS

mtDNA Diversity in Siberia and the Americas

Much is now known about the maternal genetic lineages present in Native American populations. Their mtDNAs belong to five founding haplogroups, which have been designated A–D and X (Brown et al. 1998; Forster et al. 1996; Schurr et al. 1990; Torroni et al. 1992, 1993a,c). Each of these maternal lineages is distinguished by a unique combination of restriction fragment length polymorphisms (RFLPs) and hypervariable region I (HVR-I) sequence polymorphisms, as well as coding region mutations (Kivisild et al. 2002, Yao et al. 2002). Together, they encompass 96%–100% of the mitochondrial haplotypes in modern indigenous populations of the New World (Schurr 2002, and references therein).

There are also several major geographic trends in the distribution of the founding mtDNA lineages in the Americas. First, haplogroups A–D are observed in Amerindian populations from North, Central, and South America (Schurr 2002, and references therein) (Figure 2, see color insert). These trends also have been detected in the three Native American linguistic groups (Amerind, Na-Dené, Eskimo-Aleut) proposed by Greenberg et al. (1986) and Greenberg (1987). Investigators interpret these findings as indicating that all four mtDNA lineages were present in the original migration(s) to the New World (Kolman et al. 1996; Merriwether et al. 1994, 1995; Stone & Stoneking 1998). However, Na-Dené Indians and Eskimo-Aleuts show a different haplogroup profile than do Amerindians, one consisting largely of haplogroup A and D mtDNAs, and may have lacked haplogroup B, and possibly haplogroup C, in their original genetic makeup (Rubicz et al. 2003; Saillard et al. 2000; Shields et al. 1993; Starikovskaya et al. 1998; Torroni et al.

1992, 1993a; Ward et al. 1993). For this reason, they may represent a different expansion into North America than that giving rise to Amerindians.

At a continental level, the five founding haplogroups are differentially distributed in the New World. Among Amerindians, haplogroup A decreases in frequency from north to south, whereas haplogroups C and D generally increase in the same direction. However, haplogroup B shows no similar clinal distribution, other than being virtually absent in northern North America (Lorenz & Smith 1996, 1997; Schurr et al. 1990; Torroni et al. 1992, 1993a, 1994a,c). Haplogroup B does appear at high frequencies in both the Southwest United States and the Andean region, probably because of recent population expansions (Malhi et al. 2001; Merriwether et al. 1994, 1995). By contrast, haplogroup X is found nearly exclusively in North America (Bolnick & Smith 2003; Brown et al. 1998; Malhi et al. 2001; Scozzari et al. 1997; Smith et al. 1999; Torroni et al. 1992, 1993a), with only trace frequencies of this mtDNA lineage possibly being seen elsewhere (Ribiero-dos-Santos et al. 1996). These distributions probably reflect the original pattern of settlement of the Americas, as well as the subsequent genetic differentiation of populations within certain geographic regions.

Although mtDNAs from haplogroups A–D commonly occur together in single populations, many tribes lack haplotypes from at least one of these haplogroups (Batista et al. 1995; Easton et al. 1996; Ginther et al. 1993; Lorenz & Smith 1996, 1997; Kolman et al. 1996; Kolman & Bermingham 1997; Rickards et al. 1999, Scozzari et al. 1997; Torroni et al. 1992, 1993a, 1994a,c). This is especially true for Central American populations, which essentially have only haplogroup A and B mtDNAs (Batista et al. 1995; Gonzalez-Oliver et al. 2004; Kolman et al. 1996; Kolman & Bermingham 1997; Melton et al. 2004; Santos et al. 1994; Torroni et al. 1993a, 1994c). Various studies have also revealed a high frequency of "private haplotypes" in individual populations or groups of related Amerindian tribes (e.g., Lorenz & Smith 1997; Malhi et al. 2001; Torroni et al. 1993a). These patterns reflect the role that genetic drift and founder effects have played in the stochastic extinction and fixation of mtDNA haplotypes in Native American populations.

A number of haplotypes not clearly belonging to these five maternal lineages have been also detected in different Native American groups (Bailliet et al. 1994; Easton et al. 1996; Lorenz & Smith 1996, 1997; Merriwether et al. 1994, 1995; Ribiero-dos-Santos et al. 1996; Rickards et al. 1999; SE Santos et al. 1996; Smith et al. 1999; Torroni et al. 1993a; Ward et al. 1991). These "other" mtDNAs have often been considered additional founding haplotypes or haplogroups in New World populations. However, most have since been shown to be derivatives of haplogroups A–D that have lost diagnostic mutations (Schurr 2002, 2004a; Schurr & Wallace 1999). The remainder appears to have been contributed to indigenous groups through nonnative admixture (see below). In addition, the "other" mtDNAs detected in archeological samples (e.g., Hauswirth et al. 1994, Parr et al. 1996, Ribiero-dos-Santos et al. 1996) may have resulted from contamination with modern mtDNAs, or were insufficiently analyzed to make a determination of their haplogroup status.

Y Chromosome Diversity in Siberia and the Americas

To characterize NRY variation in Native Americans, researchers have employed a number of different single nucleotide polymorphisms (SNPs) and short tandem repeat (STR) loci to define the paternal lineages present within them (Bianchi et al. 1997, 1998; Hammer et al. 1997; Karafet et al. 1997, 1999; Lell et al. 1997, 2002; Pena et al. 1995; Underhill et al. 1996, 1997, 2000, 2001). However, these research groups have not consistently used the same combination of genetic markers in their studies, which leads to alternative and sometimes confusing nomenclatures for NRY haplotypes and haplogroups. A recent synthesis of these data has resulted in a consensus nomenclature based on known SNPs [Y Chromosome Consortium (YCC) 2002], and it is used in this review. This system identifies an NRY haplogroup by a letter and the primary SNP that defines it (e.g., G-M201).

A variety of NRY haplogroups are present in Native American populations, with most of these also being present in Siberia (Figure 3). These haplogroups include Q-M3, R1a1-M17, P-M45, F-M89, and C-M130. Two of them, Q-M3 and P-M45, represent the majority of Native American Y chromosomes. Q-M3 haplotypes appear at significant frequencies in all Native American populations and are distributed in an increasing north-to-south cline within the New World (Bianchi et al. 1996, Karafet et al. 1997, 1999; Lell et al. 1997, 2002; Santos et al. 1999; Underhill et al. 1996, 1997) (Figure 4, see color insert). In addition, the STR data from Q-M3 haplotypes reveal significant differences in haplotype distributions between North, Central, and South American populations (Bianchi et al. 1996, 1998; Karafet et al. 1999; Lell et al. 1997, 2002; Ruiz-Linares et al. 1999; Santos et al. 1996b, 1999). These data point to different population histories in the two major continental regions of the New World, a pattern also seen in the gamma globulin (GM), major histocompatibility locus antigen (HLA), and nuclear genetic data from Native American groups (Erlich et al. 1997, Rothhammer et al. 1997, Schanfield et al. 1992).

P-M45 haplotypes also are widely distributed among Native American populations and represent approximately 30% of their Y chromosomes (Lell et al. 2002,

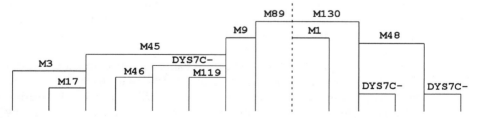

Figure 3   An NRY phylogeny that illustrates the relationships among the SNPs that define different paternal haplogroups in world populations. This is an abbreviated version of the phylogenies appearing in Underhill et al. (2001) or YCC (2002).

Ruiz-Linares et al. 1999, Santos et al. 1999). Phylogenetic analysis has revealed two distinct sets of P-M45 haplotypes in Native American populations. One of these (M45a) is more broadly distributed in populations from North, Central, and South America, whereas the second (M45b) appears in only North and Central American groups (Bortolini et al. 2003, Lell et al. 2002).

The remaining NRY haplotypes belong to one of several different haplogroups and constitute only 5% of Native American Y chromosomes. For the most part, these haplotypes have limited distribution, being present only in North and Central America. For example, C-M130 haplotypes have been detected only in Na-Dené-speaking Tanana, Navajo, and Chipewayans, and the Amerindian Cheyenne (Bergen et al. 1999, Bortolini et al. 2003, Karafet et al. 1999, Lell et al. 2002). In addition, R1a1-M17 haplotypes have been observed only in the Guaymi (Ngöbe), a Chibchan-speaking tribe from Costa Rica (Lell et al. 2002). The limited distribution of these minor haplogroups suggests that they were brought to the New World as part of a secondary expansion of ancient Asian populations.

TIMING OF THE INITIAL MIGRATION TO THE NEW WORLD

Although there is relatively little controversy now about the number and type of founding haplogroups in the New World, the ages of these maternal and paternal lineages continues to be debated. Early studies of RFLP variation in Native American mtDNAs produced time depths for haplogroups A, C, D, and X of between 35,000–20,000 cal yr BP (Torroni et al. 1992, 1993a, 1994a,c). Investigators viewed these estimates as reflecting the genetic diversity that had accumulated in the American branches of these mtDNA lineages, and hence, the time at which modern humans first entered the Americas. Additional support for these findings came from the fact that Native American and Siberian populations did not appear to share any specific haplotypes (Schurr et al. 1999, Starikovskaya et al. 1998, Torroni et al. 1993b). By contrast, Brown et al. (1998) estimates the age for haplogroup B in the New World at 17,000–13,000 cal yr BP, which suggests that haplogroup B was brought to the Americas in a later and separate migration from the earlier one(s) bringing the other four maternal lineages. The age of haplogroup X was identical to that of haplogroup B when estimated from RFLP haplotype data, although it increased when estimated from HVS-I sequence data (Brown et al. 1998).

Subsequent analyses of HVS-I sequence variation in Native Americans argued against the great antiquity of these haplogroups. They showed that haplogroups A, B, and C had roughly the same extent of genetic diversification in North America, and that haplogroup B could possibly have been present in the New World by 30,000–20,000 cal BP (Bonatto & Salzano 1997, Forster et al. 1996, Lorenz & Smith 1997, Stone & Stoneking 1998). The older date also implied that haplogroup B arrived in the Americas around the same time as did haplogroups A, C, and

D. In fact, most HVS-I studies have provided ages for the four major founding haplogroups that range between 35,000–15,000 cal BP, with the earliest dates being 14,000–12,000 cal BP (Shields et al. 1993). A recent analysis of mtDNA coding region sequences in Native American populations has also provided dates for haplogroups A–D of between 20,000–15,000 cal BP (Silva et al. 2002). Thus, most studies now favor an entry time for these mtDNA lineages that is intermediate between the earliest estimates and the dates associated with the Clovis lithic sites in North America.

Two related issues about haplogroup ages have arisen in this debate. The first issue centers on the question of whether haplogroup age estimates actually reveal the timing of human expansion(s) into the New World. Because the genetic divergence or coalescence of genetic lineages does not necessarily correspond to the timing of population splits, some scholars suggest that the older dates instead reflect the emergence of these mtDNA lineages in Asia rather than their entry into the Americas (Bonatto & Salzano 1997, Merriwether et al. 1995, Shields et al. 1993, Ward et al. 1993). On the other hand, only the founding RFLP haplotypes for haplogroups A–D and X have been shown to be present in both Siberia and the Americas (Brown et al. 1998; Schurr et al. 1999; Torroni et al. 1992, 1993a). Thus, the temporal split between the ancestral Amerindian population and its Asian precursor would appear to mirror the split in the branches of each respective haplogroup in each geographic region.

The second issue is the number of founding haplotypes that were brought with each founding haplogroup. The number of founders present in a genetic lineage will affect estimates of its age because a certain amount of the diversity present in that lineage will have accumulated from each founding type. If a haplogroup had more than one founding haplotype, then its age or entry time would need to be estimated from the diversity of haplotypes accumulating from each of its founding haplotypes. Otherwise, the estimated ages made under the assumption of a single founder might inflate the antiquity of these genetic lineages in the Americas. For Native Americans, the presence of more than one founding haplotype would imply that the ages of haplogroups A–D should be less than 30,000–25,000 cal BP, and that the colonization date for the Americas is more consistent with a late-entry, or Clovis-first migration model.

As noted above, there appears to be only one founding haplotype each for haplogroups A–D and X, on the basis of RFLP data (Brown et al. 1998; Schurr et al. 1999; Torroni et al. 1992, 1993a, 1994a,c). These founder haplotypes are the most widely distributed mtDNAs in the Americas and are central to the diversification of their respective haplogroups. However, other investigators have suggested that more than one founding haplotype from haplogroups A–D were among the original set of Native American mtDNAs (Bailliet et al. 1994; Easton et al. 1996; Merriwether et al. 1994, 1995; Rickards et al. 1999; SE Santos et al. 1996). Unfortunately, none of these studies provide additional RFLP or HVR-I sequence data to demonstrate that these are actually the same founding haplotypes defined in other studies (Schurr 2004b, Schurr & Wallace 1999).

In comparison, more than one founder HVS-I sequence from some of these haplogroups may have been brought to the Americas, with these being identical to ones present in Asian and Siberian populations (Malhi et al. 2001, Schurr et al. 1999, Torroni et al. 1993a). However, it is difficult to distinguish founding HVS-I sequences from derivatives that have lost or gained key polymorphisms that delineate American from Asian motifs. A major contributor to this problem is the fact that recurrent mutations typically occur in the mtDNA control region (Gurven 2000, Stoneking 2000). Thus, additional coding region data must be obtained from these same mtDNAs to clearly define their putative status as founder haplotypes.

A recent attempt to date the entry of ancestral Native Americans employed the mismatch analysis of mtDNA RFLP haplotypes from Amerindian populations (Schurr & Sherry 2004). This method extracts demographic information from DNA sequences that reveals episodes of population expansion and growth that can be dated using known mutation rates (Rogers & Harpending 1992, Sherry et al. 1994). This analysis distinguished between the initial expansion of these haplogroups in Siberia or Eurasia (25,000–18,000 cal yr BP) and their expansion in the New World (18,000–12,000 cal yr BP). The shape of the mismatch curve for all Native American haplogroups was generally unimodal, implying that there was an initial major expansion into the Americas. However, the mismatch curves for individual Native American tribes were often bimodal, which suggests that they had experienced at least two episodes of expansion since their ancestral populations first came to the New World.

Another intriguing line of evidence concerning the antiquity of these haplogroups comes from ancient DNA studies. On the basis of current analyses of ancient Holocene skeletal materials from North America, only haplogroups B, C, D, and X, and not haplogroup A (Smith et al. 2000a) have been identified definitively in these remains. These observations tentatively suggested that haplogroup A, rather than haplogroup B, arrived in the New World later than the other four founding mtDNA lineages. This interpretation receives some support from the higher frequencies of haplogroup A in North and Central American populations compared with South American populations. However, the aggregate mtDNA data from modern Native American populations do not support this view, nor do ancient DNA studies of other human populations in the Americas (e.g., Merriwether et al. 1994; Monsalve et al. 1996, 2002; Ribiero dos Santos et al. 1996). Thus, additional skeletal samples dating from before 7000 cal yr BP must be analyzed for genetic variation to clarify these preliminary findings.

Antiquity of Y Chromosome Haplogroups in Siberia and the Americas

The methods for dating NRY haplogroups have employed both the SNPs that define them and the STR loci that occur on each Y chromosome. Because SNPs are rare, if not unique, evolutionary events, it is difficult for investigators to estimate when they evolved in a particular paternal lineage using only this kind of data.

To get around this problem, Underhill et al. (2001) used an average mutation rate estimated from SNP variation in three NRY genes (Thomson et al. 2000) to date the various branches (haplogroups) of their phylogeny. This estimate of 1.24×10^{-9} produced an age of ~59,000 cal BP for the major expansion of modern humans out of Africa. Using this date for the most recent common ancestor (MRCA) of their SNP phylogeny, Underhill et al. (2000) estimated an average evolution rate of 1 SNP per every 6900 years. With this rate, it is possible to tentatively date the major branches of the NRY phylogeny, as well as other points of SNP haplotype diversification.

An alternative strategy for dating the ages of NRY haplogroups is to analyze variation in the faster-evolving STR loci that co-occur on each SNP haplotype. In this case, the extent of allelic diversity of a set of STR loci are measured and averaged over all loci, with the average then being multiplied by an STR mutation rate to determine the actual age of the NRY lineage. Recent mutation rates have been estimated across multiple generations of males (meiotic transmissions) in human families. Although these rates vary somewhat depending on the type of STR used for the estimates (di-, tri-, tetra-), most studies have found that the average mutation rate of NRY STRs is around 2.80×10^{-3} per generation (Bianchi et al. 1998; Heyer et al. 1997; Kayser et al. 1997, 2000; Thomson et al. 2000). This rate can be used to date both the major SNP haplogroups and their smaller branches, which have arisen more recently in evolutionary time.

Considerable effort has been made to estimate the age of Q-M3 haplotypes because they appear to signal the initial entry of ancestral populations into the New World. Using the SNP mutation rate from Underhill et al. (2000), one obtains an age for haplogroup Q-M3 of ~13,800 cal yr BP (Schurr 2004b). The estimates made with STR mutation rates are somewhat broader, ranging from 30,000–7600 cal BP (Bianchi et al. 1998, Forster et al. 2000, Hammer et al. 1998, Karafet et al. 1999, Underhill et al. 1996). Together, these analyses tend to favor a later entry of the Q-M3 lineage into the New World, or perhaps the time at which it evolved and expanded in the Americas.

Recent efforts to date the NRY haplotypes in Native American populations have utilized a newly identified SNP called Q-M242 (Bortolini et al. 2003, Seielstad et al. 2003). The Q-M242 marker occurred within haplogroup P-M45 in Central Asia prior to the emergence of the Q-M3 SNP and the expansion of its haplotypes in the Americas. For this reason, the Q-242 marker appears to demarcate the initial human entry into the Americas somewhat more precisely than does the Q-M3 marker. Using a standard STR mutation rate, Bortolini et al. (2003) and Seielstad et al. (2003) have estimated its entry time at ~18,000–15,000 cal yr BP.

The P-M45 lineage is considerably older than the Q-M3/Q-M242 lineage, which derives from it. Using the SNP mutation rate from Underhill et al. (2000), P-M45 haplotypes were estimated to be at least 30,000 years old (Schurr 2004b). This degree of antiquity is also reflected by their widespread distribution in Siberia and Eurasia (Lell et al. 2002, Underhill et al. 2000). As noted above, the P-M45 lineage has been present in Siberia long enough to diversify into different subgroups. Its antiquity is indicated by the presence of two different sets of NRY haplotypes in Native Americans: a central Siberian set (P-M45a) that is present in all Native American populations, and an eastern Siberian set (P-M45b) that appears only in Native Americans from North and Central America (Lell et al. 2002).

Researchers have also estimated the ages of several other NRY lineages present in Siberia and the Americas. One of the older lineages in Siberia, K-M9, has been dated at >50,000 cal yr BP (Karafet et al. 1999, Underhill et al. 2000). The antiquity of the K-M9 lineage is consistent with the presence of this SNP in a sizeable majority of Siberian Y chromosomes (Karafet et al. 1999, Lell et al. 2002, Santos et al. 1999, Underhill et al. 2000). An older SNP in the Eurasian branch of the NRY phylogeny, F-89, can be dated to ~62,000 cal BP. F-89 predates the occurrence of the K-M9 lineage because it appears in all haplotypes bearing the latter mutation. Its age also likely reflects the time at which modern human populations began expanding out of East Africa because it demarcates the majority of all non-African NRY haplotypes in the Old World.

The C-M130 lineage is somewhat younger than the F-M89 or K-M9 lineages, having been dated at ~30,000–25,000 cal BP (Karafet et al. 1999, Underhill et al. 2000). This date is generally consistent with the broad distribution of C-M130 in East Asia, where it appears to have originated, and with its considerable haplotypic diversity in eastern Siberian and East Asian populations (Lell et al. 2002, Su et al. 1999). In fact, the C-M130 lineage is quite widespread, being found in India, Australia, Papua New Guinea, and Melanesia (Underhill et al. 2000, 2001, Su et al. 1999), and may be more ancient than previously estimated because researchers associate it with the earliest expansions into East Asia.

The estimated age of haplogroup R1a1-M17 is also intriguing. Using the SNP evolution rate from Underhill et al. (2000), one obtains an age of 13,800 cal yr BP for this lineage, which falls toward the end of the LGM. These haplotypes also constitute a distinct branch within R1a and are not especially common in Siberian populations, although they do occur across a broad geographic area (Lell et al. 2002). Such data suggest that R1a1-M17 haplotypes did not emerge in Siberia until after the Americas had already been settled, and they, along with C-M130 and P-M45b haplotypes, were brought to the New World through a secondary expansion of ancient Asian populations (Lell et al. 2002).

NUMBER OF MIGRATIONS TO THE NEW WORLD

One of the most hotly debated issues concerning the peopling of the Americas has been about the number of migrations that reached the New World and gave rise to ancestral Native Americans. On the basis of nonmolecular data, this number has ranged from one to eight or more, depending on the data set being examined (craniometric, dental, blood group markers, GM allotypes, HLA haplotypes). There is general agreement that the Eskimo-Aleuts and Na-Dené Indians represent the last significant population expansion into the New World. However, investigators still

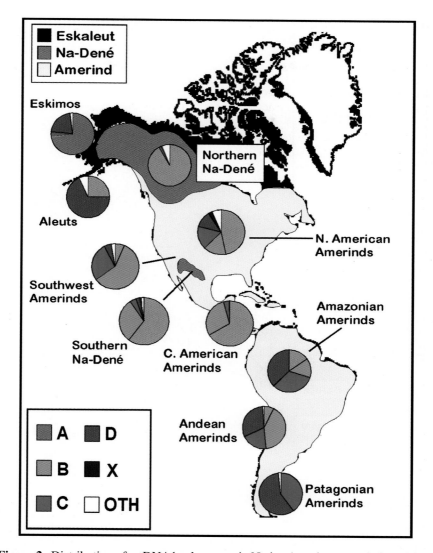

Figure 2 Distribution of mtDNA haplogroups in Native American populations. The key for Native American language groups is indicated in the upper left-hand corner of the figure, whereas the color key for the haplogroups is indicated in the lower left-hand corner. The OTH category represents "other" mtDNAs that do not belong to haplogroups A–D and X, i.e., they come from African or European populations. The frequencies shown for different parts of the Americas represent summaries of mtDNA diversity across broad geographic areas and may not reflect the regional diversity occurring at more local levels. Data for individual populations can be found in the references listed in the Literature Cited.

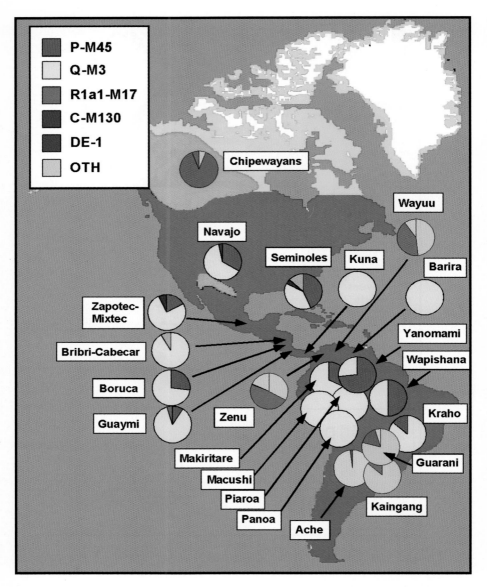

Figure 4   Distribution of NRY haplogroups in Native American populations. The color key for the haplogroups is indicated in the upper left-hand corner. The OTH category represents NRY haplotypes that do belong to "other" haplogroups, i.e., those contributed by African or European populations. The data shown here were taken from Lell et al. (2002) and Bortolini et al. (2003). For the Bortolini et al. (2003) data, the Q-M242 frequencies were added to the P-M45 frequency totals to make the distributions equivalent to those appearing in Lell et al. (2002), who did not screen their samples for the M242 SNP.

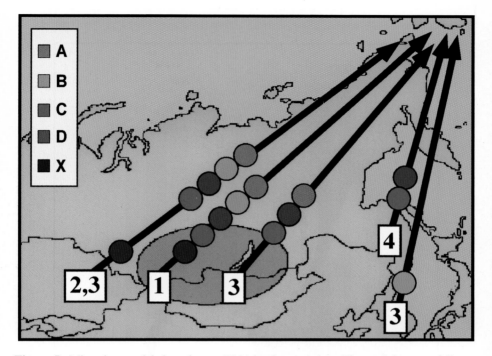

Figure 5 Migration models based on mtDNA haplogroup data. The models are as follows: (1) haplogroups A–D and X were brought together in single migration from central Siberia; (2) haplogroups A–D came with the initial migration, and haplogroup X represents a separate migration; (3) haplogroups A, C, and D were part of the initial migration, with haplogroups B and X representing separate migrations from different regions of Siberia/East Asia; (4) haplogroups C and D may have been reintroduced into the Americas as part of a secondary expansion of ancestral groups. Currently, the data support some form of model 1 or 2.

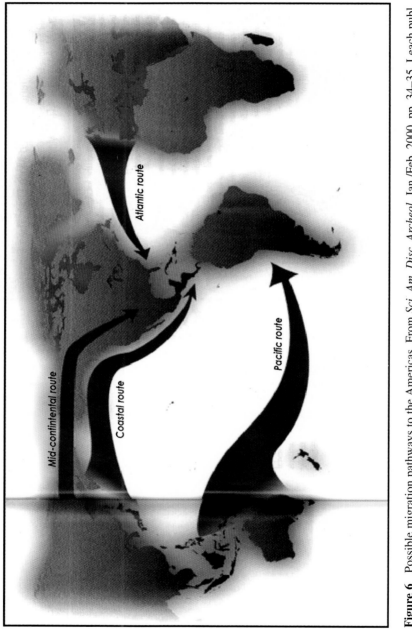

Figure 6 Possible migration pathways to the Americas. From *Sci. Am. Disc. Archeol.* Jan./Feb. 2000, pp. 34–35. Leach publ. Group Ltd.

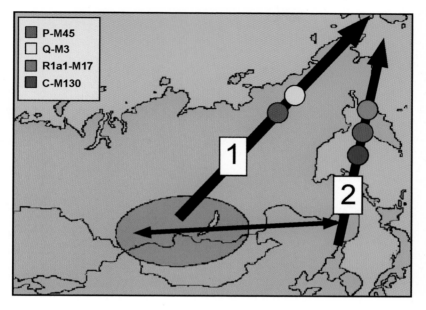

Figure 7 Migration model based on NRY haplogroup data. This model involves the following stages: (1) Haplogroups P-M45 and Q-M3 (M242) were initially brought to the Americas from central Siberia; alternatively, Q-M3 arose in the Americas shortly after human populations arrived there; (2) a secondary expansion from either central or eastern Siberia brought additional P-M45 haplotypes, along with those from C-M130 and R1a1-M17.

do not agree on the number of population movements that generated the genetic diversity in Amerindian groups, although a growing consensus for a single major expansion is developing.

Number of Migrations Based on mtDNA Haplogroup Data

Over the past decade, several different models for the peopling of the New World have been proposed on the basis of mtDNA data. Many researchers have asserted that haplogroups A–D were brought to the New World in a single migratory event (Figure 5, see color insert). This view is based on the fact that all four of them are present throughout the Americas (Forster et al. 1996; Kolman et al. 1996; Merriwether et al. 1995, 1996) and on statistical analyses of their HVR-I sequences that indicates similar levels of diversity in each mtDNA lineage (Bonatto & Salzano 1997, Silva et al. 2002, Stone & Stoneking 1998). According to this view, the pattern of genetic variation seen in modern Native American groups is largely attributed to in situ differentiation and population movements occurring after the initial colonization of the New World, rather than as a consequence of sequential expansions.

Other investigators have argued for the occurrence of two or more migrations to the Americas. In one such model, ancestral Amerindian populations brought haplogroup A, C, and D mtDNAs from Siberia during the initial colonization(s) of the New World, whereas haplogroup B possibly represented a second independent migration. This view was based on the facts that haplogroup B appeared to be younger than the other founding lineages, was absent from most of northern Asia from East Asia to the Americas, and was widely distributed in East and South-east Asia (Derenko et al. 2000; Schurr 2003; Schurr et al. 1999; Starikovskaya et al. 1998; Torroni et al. 1993a,b). However, evidence indicating similar levels of diversity in haplogroups A–D in the Americas weakens this interpretation.

In contrast, haplogroup X may represent a separate migration from somewhere in Eurasia. It is absent in nearly all indigenous Siberian populations except Altaian groups (Derenko et al. 2000, 2001; Schurr 2003; Schurr et al. 1998, 2000, 2004d; Schurr & Wallace 2003; Starikovskaya et al. 1998; Torroni et al. 1993b) and appears only in North American Amerindian populations (Bolnick 2004; Bolnick et al. 2003; Brown et al. 1998; Huoponen et al. 1997; Malhi et al. 2001, 2003; Scozzari et al. 1997; Smith et al. 1999; Torroni et al. 1992, 1993a). Its estimated age in Eurasia ranges from 35,000–20,000 cal yr BP (Richards et al. 1998, 2000), and its age in the Americas is somewhat younger (30,000–13,000 cal yr BP) (Brown et al. 1998, Reidla et al. 2003).

Haplogroup X is most strongly associated with the expansion of Algonquian-speaking populations (Bolnick & Smith 2003, Malhi et al. 2001, Schultz et al. 2001, Smith et al. 1999), although it seems to have arrived in North America prior to this time. It may have been brought to the Americas with ancestral Na-Dené Indians and subsequently disseminated into Amerindian populations through contact between these groups. Such a scenario is suggested by the distribution of the albumin Naskapi variant in native North American populations (Smith et al.

2000b). However, at present, there are insufficient genetic data from Na-Dené Indian groups to test this hypothesis.

An alternative scenario is that haplogroup X was contributed to the Native American gene pool by ancient European peoples (Stanford 1999, 2000) (Figure 6, see color insert). According to this model, bearers of the Solutrean culture left Western Europe during the LGM (18,000–16,000 cal yr BP) and navigated their way across the Atlantic Ocean along the existing ice sheet until reaching North America. Once settled, their descendants eventually developed the Clovis lithic technology that spread across North America between 13,500–12,100 cal yr BP. This process would explain the lack of an obvious Siberian precursor to the Clovis lithic culture (Boldurian & Cotter 1999, Goebel 1999, Haynes 1982), the European appearance of these projectile points (Stanford & Bradley 2000), and the greater antiquity, density, and diversity of fluted points in the American Southeast (Anderson 2004).

However, this scenario is problematic for several reasons. First, the apparent homology between the Clovis and the Solutrean lithic traditions may be circumstantial, the reflection of parallel innovations in lithic manufacturing. In addition, it is not entirely certain that Solutrean groups in Iberia were coastally adapted people, as the archeological record suggests they hunted mostly wild horses, red deer, and reindeer (Klein 1999, Strauss 2000). In fact, Strauss (2000) views the Solutrean culture as having arisen in response to the climatic changes of the LGM, and its restricted geographic distribution as evidence of a human refugium in southwestern Europe. Furthermore, there is no clear reason why this trans-Atlantic migration would involve a haplogroup (X) that typically comprises no more than 2% of the mtDNAs in modern European populations to the exclusion of another such as haplogroup H, which represents ~40% of mtDNAs in all of these groups (Comas et al. 1997, 1998; Macaulay et al. 1999; Richards et al. 1998, 2000; Sajantila et al. 1995; Torroni et al. 1994b, 1996). Thus, at best, current mtDNA data provide modest support for an ancient Solutrean migration to the New World.

It remains possible that haplogroups A–D were introduced into the Americas more than once in separate expansion events. This scenario receives tentative support from the fact that, in addition to the consensus founder haplotypes for these haplogroups, there are other HVS-I sequences shared between Asian/Siberian and Native American populations that could potentially be additional founder mtDNAs (see above). These putative founder haplotypes are not widespread in Asia and the Americas, but they appear in populations living in the vicinity of the hypothesized source area or migration route for ancestral Native Americans (Malhi et al. 2002, 2003; Schurr et al. 2000; Schurr & Wallace 1999). However, additional HVR-I sequence and coding region sequence data from both Siberian and Native American populations will be needed to confirm this interpretation.

Some scholars have suggested also that expanding Austronesian speakers, the ancestors of modern Polynesians, genetically contributed to the founding Amerindian populations of South America (Lum et al. 1994, 1998; Rickards et al. 1999). This idea was suggested by the sharing of certain linguistic and cultural features between Polynesians and Andean populations, as well as the finding that agriculture foodstuffs cultivated in South America also were present in Polynesia. In addition, genetic data from Andean Indians do not clearly show the presence of haplogroup B mtDNAs possessing the Polynesian motif, something that would be expected if there was any significant maternal gene flow between Austronesian speakers and Andean Indian groups (Bonatto et al. 1996). In addition, a recent NRY study of the Polynesian slave trade suggests that the shared paternal haplotypes and cultural contacts between these cultures were a consequence of South American Indians being enslaved, not the result of a trans-Pacific voyage to the New World (Hurles et al. 2003). Thus, the existing genetic data do not support ancient contacts between Polynesia and South America.

Number of Migrations Based on NRY Haplogroup Data

To date, researchers have identified six major paternal SNP haplogroups that are shared between Siberian and the American populations (DE-M1, Q-M3, R1a1-M17, P-M45, N3-M46, and C-M130). Only two of these, P-M45 and Q-M3, were part of the initial peopling of the New World, either through single (Bianchi et al. 1998, Santos et al. 1999, Underhill et al. 1996) or multiple (Bortolini et al. 2003, Karafet et al. 1999, Lell et al. 2002) migrations (Figure 7, see color insert). The Q-M3 haplogroup is the most frequent paternal lineage in Native American populations and is widely distributed throughout the New World (Bianchi et al. 1998, Bortolini et al. 2003, Karafet et al. 1999, Lell et al. 2002). In addition, the ancestral P-M45a haplogroup, the direct ancestor to the Q-M3 lineage, has the widest geographic distribution of all of those present in the Americas, occurring in populations from central Siberia to South America (Bortolini et al. 2003, Lell et al. 2002).

A second and later expansion(s) of human groups from Beringia appears to have brought a different set of P-M45 haplotypes to the Americas. These P-M45b haplotypes show a different array of STR alleles than do the Q-M3/P-M45a haplotypes that arrived in the initial expansion into the New World, and they also possess the M173 SNP. This second set of P-M45b haplotypes is also shared between eastern Siberian and North and Central American groups but is absent in those groups from central Siberia and South America (Lell et al. 2002). This secondary expansion may also have contributed the R1a1-M17 and C-M130 haplotypes to Amerindian populations. On the basis of their distribution in Siberia, P-M45b and C-M130 haplotypes were suggested to have come from the Amur River region (Karafet et al. 1999, Lell et al. 2002).

Bortolini et al. (2003) supports the proposal that there were two major expansions of NRY haplogroups into the New World. However, they interpret these data as showing that both NRY migrations came from southern/central Siberia to the Americas. In their view, the interpretation that the second migration came from the Amur River region is inconsistent with the generally high frequency of haplogroup K-M9 in eastern Siberia and its absence in the Americas. In addition, they detected shared ancestry in Central Asia for some of the initial migrants to Europe and the Americas. In either case, south-central Siberia appears to have played a major role in the peopling of the New World, as well as the expansion of many indigenous groups into different parts of Siberia itself.

Expansion of Circumarctic Peoples

Recent work has provided new information about the expansion of Native American populations from the circumarctic region. All circumarctic populations have primarily haplogroup A mtDNAs that possess the 16192T mutation, with these haplotypes being absent in Amerindian groups. This is also true of the Navajo and Apache tribes of the American Southwest, who arose out of a southern expansion of Na-Dené groups some 500–1000 years ago (Budowle et al. 2002; Lorenz & Smith 1996; Malhi et al. 2001; Torroni et al. 1992, 1993a). The dating of the 16192T branch of haplogroup A suggests that the populations ancestral to the Aleuts, Eskimos, and Na-Dené Indians emerged between 13,120–10,000 cal yr BP (Rubicz et al. 2003, Starikovskaya et al. 1998). These circumarctic groups share only certain founding haplotypes from haplogroups A and D, and have become genetically differentiated from each other, as evidenced by the presence of population-specific sublineages within them (Derbeneva et al. 2002b, Rubicz et al. 2003, Schurr et al. 1999, Starikovskaya et al. 1998). The most recent expansion across the Canadian Arctic by the Inuit or Thule people took place between 4000–1000 cal yr BP and reached Greenland by around 1000 A.D. (Saillard et al. 2000).

Ancient DNA studies of archeological populations of the Canadian Arctic also have added new information about the colonization of this region. Ongoing analyses of mtDNA variation in the Dorset, Sadlermuit, and Thule populations suggest that these groups expanded into this region in a sequential fashion. The earliest settlers, the Dorset, who date to 1250 BP, had predominantly haplogroup D mtDNAs. The related Sadlermuit culture showed roughly similar frequencies of haplogroups A and D, whereas the later Thule people had exclusively haplogroup A mtDNAs (O'Rourke et al. 2000b). This series of cultural expansions is further supported by stable isotope work, which shows dietary differences between the Dorset and Thule peoples based on their consumption of marine and terrestrial species (Hayes et al. 2003).

Molecular studies also are providing a more complete picture of the settlement of the Aleutian Islands. Similar to other circumarctic groups, Aleuts have only haplogroup A and D mtDNAs (Derbeneva et al. 2002b, Merriwether et al. 1994, Rubicz et al. 2003). However, unlike Eskimos and Na-Dené Indians, Aleuts have predominantly haplogroup D mtDNAs. Although sharing several haplotypes with other circumarctic groups, Aleuts have mostly unique HVS-I sequences, including those belonging to two distinct sublineages of A and D. These Aleut-specific sublineages have been dated to 6540 and 6035 years BP, respectively, with these estimates being generally congruent with the earliest archeological dates for the colonization of the Aleutian archipelago (Rubicz et al. 2003). In addition, Aleuts lack haplogroup A mtDNAs, with the 16265G mutations that are specific to Eskimo populations (Saillard et al. 2000, Shields et al. 1993, Starikovskaya et al. 1998), as well as mtDNAs with the 16331G mutations that are specific to Na-Dené Indian groups (Shields et al. 1993; Starikovskaya et al. 1998; Torroni et al. 1992, 1993). Overall, Aleuts are genetically closer to Chukotkan groups (Chukchi and Siberian Yupik) rather than to Alaskan Eskimos, Native Americans, or Kamchatkan populations (Koryaks and Itel'men) (Rubicz et al. 2003).

With regard to Na-Dené Indians, some scholars suggest, on the basis of linguistic data, that Na-Dené and Yeniseian (Kets) speakers have a common phylogenetic origin (Greenberg 1987, Greenberg et al. 1986, Ruhlen 1994). This idea receives some support from the presence of certain NRY haplogroups thought to be ancestral to those in northern Native American populations, including Na-Dené Indians, in Kets and Sel'kups, as well as in Altaian groups (Bianchi et al. 1998, Bortolini et al. 2003, Karafet et al. 2001, Santos et al. 1999). However, the mtDNA haplogroup profiles for Kets and Na-Dené Indians are quite different from each other, with Kets having largely haplogroups C, F, and U mtDNAs and Athapaskan Indians having mostly haplogroup A mtDNAs (Derbeneva et al. 2002b; Schurr & Wallace 1999, 2003; Shields et al. 1993; Torroni et al. 1992, 1993a). In fact, when genetic data from indigenous Siberian and Native American populations were analyzed, the Na-Dené Indians clustered with other Native American populations, whereas the Kets genetically resembled surrounding Siberian groups (Rubicz et al. 2002). Whether this discrepant pattern is related to the differential distribution of male- and female-mediated haplotypes in the Americas during its colonization remains to be determined.

REGIONAL POPULATION HISTORIES

As ancestral Native American populations expanded into the New World, they began colonizing the new environments they encountered. This process has been modeled using the patterns of genetic diversity present in these groups. According to one model, ancestral groups settled at particular locations very early in the colonization process and remained in those areas since that time. This pattern would lead to significant biological and cultural continuity between the ancient groups and their modern antecedents. Alternatively, the genetic composition of ancient populations occupying the same geographic region as extant groups might not be the same because population relocations, mergers of adjacent tribes, genetic drift, or other stochastic processes could have altered patterns of biological diversity in them over time. In this case, there would likely be reduced biological continuity between ancient and modern Native American groups.

Malhi et al. (2002) suggest that the initial colonization process involved the prehistoric spread of small bands of people from west to east across the North American continent. This idea is supported by the greater diversity of language families along the west coast of North America compared to that in its interior regions (Gruhn 1987, 1992; Nichols 1990, 1994). A similar colonization process took place in South America but probably involved a bidirectional settlement pattern using both Andean and Amazonian routes (Keyeux et al. 2002, Salzano & Callegari-Jacques 1988, Tarazona-Santos et al. 2001). Under this scenario, the colonizing groups would have initially experienced significant drift effects because of their relative isolation from one another but would have remained part of the same gene pool owing to gene flow across the region. Relatively soon after occupying these regions, however, native populations underwent a tribalization process, with this stage being marked by a significant reduction in gene flow among them (Salzano & Callegari-Jacques 1988, Malhi et al. 2002, Torroni et al. 1993a). This transition may be seen at archeological sites from the Archaic Period, where evidence for the specialization and intensification of local resource use appears (Dillehay 1999, Fiedel 1999, Fagan 2000, Roosevelt et al. 1996). The increased population growth and sedentarization of these groups that accompanied these changes would have reduced the effects of genetic drift in these populations and increased gene flow within local groups, thereby contributing to the formation of regional gene pools (Malhi et al. 2002).

In large part, the ancient DNA (aDNA) data support this perspective. They indicate that Amerindian populations, or groups of related populations, maintained their genetic integrity within a particular region for thousands of years, once becoming genetically distinct from surrounding groups (O'Rourke et al. 2000a,b). Patterns of continuity are seen in the American Southwest between Anasazi and modern Puebloan groups (Carlyle et al. 2000, Parr et al. 1996), ancient Tainos and modern Puerto Ricans whose ancestors trace to Carib Indian populations (Martinez-Crusado et al. 2001, Lalueza-Fox et al. 2001), and ancient and modern populations from southern Chile and Patagonia (Fox 1996, Lalueza et al. 1997, Moraga et al. 2000). By contrast, the expansion of Numic peoples in the Great Basin led to genetic discontinuity between ancient and historical populations from that region (Kaestle & Smith 2001). There are also intriguing differences in haplogroup frequencies between ancient and modern Maya populations (González-Oliver et al. 2001; Torroni et al. 1992, 1993a). Ongoing studies of ancient populations in Peru, Chile, and Argentina should also illuminate the relationships between ancient and modern groups in those regions (Adachi et al. 2004, Cabana & Merriwether 2000; McKenney et al. 2000; Williams et al. 2000).

Molecular data have also helped to reveal regional patterns of population settlement and movement in the Americas. In the southeastern United States, there are significant differences in mtDNA haplotype diversity between Muskogean and Iroquian groups (Bolnick & Smith 2003). This difference is attributable to the Iroquoian Cherokee having moved to the U.S. Southeast from the Great Lakes region in the recent past. All these populations show reduced genetic diversity, which probably reflects a genetic bottleneck related to their historical population decline (Bolnick & Smith 2003). Algonquian speakers are also known to have expanded into the Great Lakes region ~2500–3000 years ago, which is reflected by the high frequencies of haplogroup X there, and show affinities with Siouan-speaking populations of the northern United States (Malhi et al. 2001, Schultz et al. 2001, Shook 2004). In addition, aDNA studies of Hopewell and Adena remains have revealed ties between these archeological populations from the Ohio Valley and Great Lakes tribes (Mills 2003).

Another region that has been the focus of numerous genetic studies, the U.S. Southwest, is also one of the most genetically diverse regions of North America, largely because of the number of population expansions it has experienced throughout its long history. Interestingly, the tribal haplogroup frequencies in the southwest United States are structured more by the archeological traditions in the area than by the linguistic affiliation of its extant groups (Malhi et al. 2002, 2003). Although the Uto-Aztecan languages prevalent in the region are thought to have arisen in northern Mexico, there is no evidence of maternal gene flow north from Mexico to the U.S. Southwest. This finding suggests that males disseminated Uto-Aztecan languages north into the U.S. Southwest (Malhi et al. 2002, 2003). Further evidence for the expansion of haplogroup B mtDNAs in the Southwest exists (Torroni et al. 1993a; Lorenz & Smith 1996, 1997; Malhi et al. 2002), probably in association with maize agriculture. This recent re-expansion of haplogroup B might explain its lower age estimate relative to those of the other four founding lineages (e.g., Torroni et al. 1993a), as most of its haplotypes would be derived recently, and hence, limited in genetic diversity.

Overall, the extent of language and gene association varies from region to region in the Americas. In the Pacific Northwest, there is only a modest association between language and genes (Shields et al. 1993; Ward et al. 1991, 1993). Lorenz & Smith (1997) later observed a general concordance between genetic and linguistic diversity in many North American populations. However, Hunley & Long (2004) recently showed that, within North America, there is a weak correlation between patterns of linguistic and mtDNA variation in Native American groups. Conversely, the linguistically related Chibchan-speaking populations of Costa Rica share a number of mtDNA haplotypes in common (Batista et al. 1995; Kolman et al. 1995; Kolman & Bermingham 1997; Torroni et al. 1993a, 1994c). There is a similar correspondence between mtDNA haplogroup frequencies and linguistic affiliations in Bolivian Amerindian tribes speaking Andean, Equatorial-Tucanoan, and Ge-Pano-Carib languages (Bert et al. 2001). In fact, when Fagundes et al. (2002) reanalyzed genetic data from a number of loci in South American Indian tribes, they found that mtDNA variation correlated significantly with language when geography was held constant. Thus, differences exist in language-gene covariance between the continental regions of the Americas.

Various investigators are also using molecular approaches to explore the kinship and population affinities of individuals buried at archeological sites or mound complexes in different parts of the Americas. This approach was taken at the Norris Farms site in the Illinois Valley, where patterns of haplotypic diversity were detailed in different burials around the cemetery (Stone & Stoneking 1998). Studies of human remains from the Mochica and Middle Sican cultures in Peru have also revealed genetic differences between these cultures, as well as between high-status males and the lower-status males and females who were sacrificed and buried with them in mound tombs (Shimada et al. 2004a,b). Researchers are also undertaking similar kinds of comparisons between ancient Aztec and Toltec individuals and those from living indigenous groups of central Mexico (Kemp et al. 2004). These kinds of studies will help elucidate the interactions between ancient populations of Mesoamerican and the Andean regions and the population structure and diversity of state-level societies in the Americas.

POST-CONTACT AMERICAS

The entry of Europeans into the New World brought about a number of significant changes for Native American populations. For one thing, warfare and epidemic disease killed huge numbers of individuals from various tribal populations, sometimes leading to the extinction of particular ethnic groups. This demographic decline likely led to a reduction in the genetic diversity of these populations, as well as the formation of new populations from the remnants of tribes affected by colonizing Europeans and their microbes (Crawford 1998, Thornton & Marsh-Thornton 1981, Ubelaker 1988). Increasing interactions with peoples of European descent, as well as the introduction of African slaves from the sixteenth through the nineteenth centuries, generated many mestizo populations in different parts of the Americas. As a consequence of these events, the indigenous American gene pool has been substantially remodeled over the past 500 years.

Admixture can be seen in several forms, depending on the genetic system being used. Previous work utilized classical blood group markers and immune system genes to assess admixture levels. Current molecular genetic studies screen populations for markers defining West Eurasian H-K and T-X and African L1-L3 (Chen et al. 1995, 2000) mtDNA haplogroups, and those defining European and African M1, K-M9, M173, and other non-native NRY haplogroups (Hammer et al. 1997, 1998; Underhill et al. 1999, 2001; YCC 2002).

On the basis of these molecular data, differences exist in the extent of non-native gene flow in different parts of the Americas. Several mtDNA studies have revealed low levels of European maternal gene flow into North American Indian populations in the form of West Eurasian haplogroup H, J, and K mtDNAs (Scozzari et al. 1997, Smith et al. 1999, Torroni et al. 1993a). Evidence of European paternal gene flow has also been seen in studies of blood group markers and NRY variation in these populations (Bolnick 2004, Huoponen et al. 1997, Kaspirin et al. 1987, Pollitzer et al. 1962). In fact, nearly 60% of Greenlandic Inuit Y chromosomes may have European origins, with these most likely coming from Norse settlers who were assimilated into Inuit groups some 500 years ago (Bosch et al. 2003).

Not surprisingly, many rural and urban mestizo groups show differing degrees of female and male genetic contributions from non-native populations, with most European genotypes being introduced by males. These differences reflect a historically documented colonial policy of European males taking indigenous mates as part of the settlement process in various parts of the Americas (Alves-Silva et al. 2000, Bortolini et al. 1997, Bravi et al. 1997, Carvajal-Carmona et al. 2000, Mesa et al. 2000, Rodas et al. 2003, Rodriguez-Delfin et al. 1997). One can see similar patterns in North America with Mexican Americans, with the extent of Native American ancestry varying depending on their geographic location in the United States (e.g., Merriwether et al. 1997). For these populations, there is usually a much greater Native American maternal and greater European paternal contribution to their genetic makeup.

Likewise, investigators have observed African admixture in a number of Native American groups. Haplogroup L mtDNAs have been detected in several tribal populations from the American Southeast (Huoponen et al. 1997, Smith et al. 1999). In addition, several Central American populations have African-derived DE-M1 NRY haplotypes, including the Mixe from southern Mexico (Karafet et al. 1999, Lell et al. 1997). Generally speaking, Mexico shows regional patterns of genetic variation that reflect its history of colonial settlement. European genetic influence is stronger in the northern part of the country, African influence is stronger along coastal areas, and Amerindian influence is stronger in the central/southeast region (Gorodezky et al. 2001, Green et al. 2000).

A study of the Garifuna (Black Caribs) further confirms the complex history of Mesoamerica and the Caribbean. The majority of Garifuna mtDNA haplotypes are African in origin, but some belong to haplogroups B, C, and D (Monsalve & Hagelberg 1997). These Amerindian mtDNAs likely originated with Arawak and Carib Indians who lived in this region prior to the entry of Europeans. The mixed ancestry of the Garifuna people is also evident in their nuclear gene data, which show a stronger African than European or Amerindian genetic component (Crawford 1986; Crawford et al. 1981, 1982).

Overall, Caribbean populations show a pattern of genetic variation similar to that of the Garifuna, as seen in Cubans (Torroni et al. 1995) and Puerto Ricans (Martinez-Crusado et al. 2001). However, the relative contributions of maternal and paternal genotypes by African, European, and Amerindian populations vary from island to island. These patterns reflect the distinct history of prehistoric settlement and later European colonization of the Caribbean region.

SUMMARY

Both mtDNA and NRY data now provide an initial entry time of ancestral Native Americans of between 20,000–15,000 cal yr BP. This date favors a relatively late expansion of the First Americans, which, while being more consistent with current archeological data from the New World, supports a pre-Clovis entry time. Because these dates fall in the middle of the LGM, before the earliest time at which an ice-free corridor was available for passage by modern human populations, the colonizing groups must have used a coastal route during their initial movement into North America.

The early immigrants apparently brought with them to the Americas mtDNA haplogroups A–D (maybe X) and NRY haplogroups P-M45a and Q-242/M3 haplotypes, with these being dispersed throughout the continental areas of the New World. A subsequent expansion may have brought mtDNA haplogroup X (maybe more A–D haplotypes) and contributed NRY haplogroups P-M45b, C-M130, and R1a1-M17 to Native American populations, with these being disseminated in only North and Central America. This expansion may have coincided with the opening of the ice-free corridor around 12,550 cal yr BP.

A somewhat later expansion likely involved the ancestors of modern circum-arctic populations, such as the Yupik and Inupik Eskimos, Aleuts, and Na-Dené Indians. These populations show some similarities to Amerindians living south of Canada, which suggests that their founders may have shared a common ancestral population with Amerindians. However, they have since become distinct from Amerindians in terms of the types and frequencies of genetic haplotypes and lineages they possess.

The *Annual Review of Anthropology* is online at http://anthro.annualreviews.org

LITERATURE CITED

Adachi N, Shinoda K, Shimada I. 2004. Mitochondrial DNA analysis of the ancient Peruvian highlanders. *Am. J. Phys. Anthropol. Suppl.* 123(38):50 (Abstr.)

Adovasio JM, Pedler DR, Donahue J, Stuckenrath R. 1998. Two decades of debate on Meadowcroft Rockshelter. *North Am. Archaeol.* 19(4):317–41

Alves-Silva J, Santos MD, Guimarães PEM, Ferreira ACS, Bandelt H-J, et al. 2000. The ancestry of Brazilian mtDNA lineages. *Am. J. Hum. Genet.* 67(2):444–61

Anderson D. 2004. Paleoindian occupations in the Southeastern United States. In *New Perspecives on the First Americans*, ed. BT Lepper, R Bonnichsen, pp. 119–28. Corvallis: Cent. Study First Am., Tex. A&M Univ.

Bailliet G, Rothhammer F, Carnese FR, Bravi CM, Bianchi NO, et al. 1994. Founder mitochondrial haplotypes in Amerindian populations. *Am. J. Hum. Genet.* 54:27–33

Batista O, Kolman CJ, Bermingham E. 1995. Mitochondrial DNA diversity in the Kuna Amerinds of Panama. *Hum. Mol. Genet.* 4: 921–29

Bergen AW, Wang C-Y, Tsai J, Jefferson K, Dey C, et al. 1999. An Asian-Native American paternal lineage identified by RPS4Y resequencing and microsatellite haplotyping. *Ann. Hum. Genet.* 63:63–80

Bert F, Corella A, Gené M, Perez-Perez A, Turbon D. 2001. Major mitochondrial DNA haplotype heterogeneity in highland and lowland Amerindian populations from Bolivia. *Hum. Biol.* 73:1–16

Bianchi NO, Bailliet G, Bravi CM, Carnese RF, Rothhammer F, et al. 1997. Origin of Amerindian Y chromosomes as inferred by the analysis of six polymorphic markers. *Am. J. Phys. Anthropol.* 102:79–89

Bianchi NO, Catanesi CI, Bailliet G, Martinez-Marignac VL, Bravi CM, et al. 1998. Characterization of ancestral and derived Y-chromosome haplotypes of New World native populations. *Am. J. Hum. Genet.* 63: 1862–71

Blaise B, Clague JJ, Matthewes RW. 1990. Time of maximum Late Wisconsin glaciation, west coast of Canada. *Q. Res.* 34:282–95

Bobrowsky PT, Catto NR, Brink JW, Spurling BE, Gibson TH, Rutter NW. 1990. Archeological geology of sites of western and northwestern Canada. *Centennial Special Vol. 4,* pp. 87–122. Boulder, CO: Geol. Soc. Am.

Boldurian AT, Cotter JL. 1999. *Clovis Revisited.* Philadelphia: Univ. Penn. Mus. Press

Bolnick DA. 2004. Using Y-chromosome and mtDNA variation to reconstruct eastern North American population history. *Am. J. Phys. Anthropol. Suppl.* 123(38):65 (Abstr.)

Bolnick DA, Smith DG. 2003. Unexpected patterns of mitochondrial DNA variation among Native Americans from the southeastern United States. *Am. J. Phys. Anthropol.* 122: 336–54

Bonatto SL, Redd AJ, Salzano FM, Stoneking M. 1996. Lack of ancient Polynesian-Amerindian contact. *Am. J. Hum. Genet.* 59(1):253–58

Bonatto SL, Salzano FM. 1997. Diversity and age of the four major mtDNA haplogroups, and their implications for the peopling of the New World. *Am. J. Hum. Genet.* 61:1413–23

Bortolini C, Zago MA, Salzano FM, Silva-Junior WA, Bonatto SL, et al. 1997. Evolutionary and anthropological implications of mitochondrial DNA variation in African Brazilian populations. *Hum. Biol.* 69:141–59

Bortolini M-C, Salzano FM, Thomas MG, Stuart S, Nasanen SPK, et al. 2003. Y-chromosome evidence for differing ancient demographic histories in the Americas. *Am. J. Hum. Genet.* 73:524–39

Bosch E, Calafell F, Rosser ZH, Norby S, Lynnerup L, et al. 2003. High level of male-biased Scandinavian admixture in Greenlandic Inuit shown by Y-chromosomal analysis. *Hum. Genet.* 112:353–63

Brace CL, Nelson AR, Seguchi N, Oe H, Sering L, et al. 2001. Old World sources of the first New World human inhabitants: a comparative craniofacial view. *Proc. Natl. Acad. Sci. USA* 98:10017–22

Bravi CM, Sans M, Bailliet G, Martinez-Marignac VL, Portas M, et al. 1997. Characterization of mitochondrial DNA and Y-chromosome haplotypes in a Uruguayan population of African ancestry. *Hum. Biol.* 69:641–52

Brown MD, Hosseini SH, Torroni A, Bandelt H-J, Allen JC, et al. 1998. mtDNA haplogroup X: an ancient link between Europe/Western Asia and North America? *Am. J. Hum. Genet.* 63:1852–61

Budowle B, Allard MW, Fisher CL, Isenberg AR, Monson KL, et al. 2002. HVI and HVII mitochondrial DNA data in Apaches and Navajos. *Int. J. Legal. Med.* 116(4):212–15

Burns JA. 1996. Vertebrate paleontology and the alleged ice-free corridor: the meat of the matter. *Quat. Int.* 32:107–12

Cabana GS, Merriwether DA. 2000. *Prehistoric population relationships in Azapa Valley, Chile.* Presented at Annu. Meet. Am. Anthropol. Assoc., 99th, San Francisco

Carlyle SW, Parr RL, Hayes MG, O'Rourke DH. 2000. Context of maternal lineages in the Greater Southwest. *Am. J. Phys. Anthropol.* 113:85–101

Carvajal-Carmona LG, Soto ID, Pineda N, Ortiz-Barrientos D, Duque C, et al. 2000. Strong Amerind/white sex bias and a possible Sephardic contribution among the founders of a population in northwest Colombia. *Am. J. Hum. Genet.* 67:1287–95

Chatters JC. 2001. *Ancient Encounters: Kennewick Man and the First Americans.* New York: Simon & Shuster

Chen Y-S, Olckers A, Schurr TG, Kogelnik AM, Huoponen K, Wallace DC. 2000. Mitochondrial DNA variation in the South. African Kung and Khwe and their genetic relationships to other African populations. *Am. J. Hum. Genet.* 66:1362–83

Chen Y-S, Torroni A, Excoffier L, Santachi AS, Wallace DC. 1995. Analysis of mtDNA variation in African populations reveals the most ancient of all human continent-specific haplogroups. *Am. J.Hum. Genet.* 57:133–49

Clague JJ, et al. 1989. Quaternary geology of the Canadian Cordillera. In *Quaternary Geology of Canada and Greenland*, ed. RJ Fulton, pp. 17–96. Ottawa: Geol. Soc. Can.

Collins MB. 2002. The Gault site, Texas, and Clovis research. *Athena Rev.* 3(2):31–41

Comas D, Calafell F, Mateu E, Perezlezaun A, Bosche E, Bertranpetit J. 1997. Mitochondrial DNA variation and the origin of the Europeans. *Hum. Genet.* 99:443–49

Crawford MH. 1986. Origin and maintenance of genetic variation on Black Carib populations of St. Vincent and Central America. In *Genetic Variation and Its Maintenance in Tropical Populations*, ed. DF Roberts, G De Stefano, pp. 157–79. Cambridge, UK: Cambridge Univ. Press

Crawford MH. 1998. *The Origins of Native Americans*. Cambridge, UK: Cambridge Univ. Press

Crawford MH, Dykes DD, Skradsky K, Polesky HF. 1982. Blood group, serum protein, and red cell enzyme polymorphisms, and admixture among the Black Caribs and Creoles of Central America and the Caribbean. In *Developments in Anthropological Genetics*. Vol. III: *Black Caribs: A Case Study of Biocultural Adaptation*, ed. MH Crawford, pp. 303–33. New York: Plenum

Crawford MH, Gonzalez NL, Schanfield MS, Dykes DD, Skradski K, Polesky HF. 1981. The Black Caribs (Garifuna) of Livingston, Guatemala: Genetic markers and admixture estimates. *Hum. Biol.* 53:87–103

Derbeneva OA, Starikovskaya EB, Volodko NV, Wallace DC, Sukernik RI. 2002a. Mitochondrial DNA variation in Kets and Nganasans and the early peopling of Northern Eurasia. *Genetika* 38(11):1554–60

Derbeneva OA, Sukernik RI, Volodko NV, Hosseini SH, Lott MT, Wallace DC. 2002b. Analysis of mitochondrial DNA diversity in the Aleuts of the Commander Islands, and its implications for the genetic history of Beringia. *Am. J. Hum. Genet.* 71:415–21

Derenko MV, Malyarchuk BA, Dambueva IK, Shaikhaev GO, Dorzhu CM, et al. 2000. Mitochondrial DNA variation in two south Siberian aboriginal populations: implications for the genetic history of North Asia. *Hum. Biol.* 72(6):945–73

Dillehay TD. 1989. *Monte Verde: A Late Pleistocene Settlement in Chile*. Washington, DC: Smithson. Inst. Press

Dillehay TD. 1997. *Monte Verde: A Late Pleistocene Settlement in Chile*. Vol. 2: *The Archeological Context*. Washington, DC: Smithson. Inst. Press

Dillehay TD. 1999. The late Pleistocene cultures of South America. *Evol. Anthropol.* 7(6):206–16

Dillehay TD, Calderón GA, Politis G, Beltrão M. 1992. Earliest hunters and gatherers of South America. *J. World Prehist.* 6:145–204

Dixon EJ. 2002. How and when did people come to North America? *Athena Rev.* 3(2): 23–27

Easton RD, Merriwether DA, Crews DE, Ferrell RE 1996. mtDNA variation in the Yanomami: evidence for additional New World founding lineages. *Am. J. Hum. Genet.* 59:213–25

Erlich HA, Mack SJ, Bergstrom T, Gyllensten UB. 1997. HLA Class II alleles in Amerindian populations: implications for the evolution of HLA polymorphisms and the colonization of the New World. *Hereditas* 127:19–24

Fagan BM. 2000. *Ancient North America: The Archaeology of a Continent*. New York: Thames & Hudson

Fagundes NJR, Bonatto SL, Callegari-Jacques SM, Salzano FM. 2002. Genetic, geographic, and linguistic variation among South American Indians: possible sex influence. *Am. J. Phys. Anthropol.* 117:68–78

Fedje D. 2002. The early post-glacial history of the northern Northwest Coast: a view from Haida Gwaii and Hecate Strait. *Athena Rev.* 3(2):28–30

Fedje DW, Christensen T. 1999. Modeling paleoshorelines and locating early Holocene coastal sites in Haida Gwai. *Am. Antiq.* 64(4):635–52

Fiedel SJ. 1999. Older than we thought: implications of corrected dates for Paleoindians. *Am. Antiq.* 64:95–115

Fix AG. 2002. Colonization models and initial genetic diversity in the Americas. *Hum. Biol.* 74(1):1–10

Fladmark KR. 1979. Routes: alternative migration corridors for early man in North America. *Am. Antiq.* 44:55–69

Fladmark KR. 1983. Times and places: environmental correlates of Mid-to-Late Wisconsin human population expansion in North America. In *Early Man in the New World*, ed. R Shutler, pp. 13–42. Beverly Hills, CA: Sage

Forster P, Harding R, Torroni A, Bandelt H-J. 1996. Origin and evolution of Native American mtDNA variation: a reappraisal. *Am. J. Hum. Genet.* 59:935–45

Forster P, Röhl A, Lünnermann P, Brinkmann C,

Zerjal T, et al. 2000. A short tandem repeat-based phylogeny for the human Y chromosome. *Am. J. Hum. Genet.* 67:182–96

Fox CL. 1996. Mitochondrial DNA haplogroups in four tribes from Tierra del Fuego-Patagonia: inferences about the peopling of the Americas. *Hum. Biol.* 68:855–71

Ginther C, Corach D, Penacino GA, Rey JA, Carnese FR, et al. 1993. Genetic variation among the Mapuche Indians from the Patagonian region of Argentina: mitochondrial DNA sequence variation and allele frequencies of several nuclear genes. In *DNA Fingerprinting: State of the Science*, ed. SDJ Pena, R Chakraborty, JT Epplan, AJ Jefferies, pp. 211–19. Basel: Berkhauser-Verlag

Goebel T. 1999. Pleistocene human colonization of Siberia and peopling of the Americas: an ecological approach. *Evol. Anthropol.* 8(6):208–27

Goebel T, Aksenov M. 1995. Accelerator radiocarbon dating of the initial Upper Paleolithic in southeast Siberia. *Antiquity* 69:349–57

Goebel T, Waters MR, Meshcherin MN. 2001. Masterov Kliuch and the early Upper Palaeolithic of the Transbaikal, Siberia. *Asian Perspect.* 39(1–2):47–70

González-Oliver A, Ascunce MS, Mulligan CJ. 2004. Comparison of Y-chromosome and mitochondrial genetic diversity in Panamanian Amerinds. *Am. J. Phys. Anthropol. Suppl.* 123(38):102 (Abstr.)

González-Oliver A, Marquez-Morfin L, Jimenez JC, Torre-Blanco A. 2001. Founding Amerindian mitochondrial DNA lineages in ancient Maya from Xcaret, Quintana Roo. *Am. J. Phys. Anthropol.* 116(3):230–35

Goodyear AC III. 1999. The Early Holocene occupation of the Southeastern United States: a geogarcheological summary. In *Ice Peoples of North America*, ed. R. Bonnichsen, KL Turnmire, pp. 432–81. Corvallis, Tex.: Cent. Study First Am.

Gorodezky C, Alaez C, Vazquez-Garcia MN, de la Rosa G, Infante E, et al. 2001. The genetic structure of Mexican mestizos of different locations: tracking back their origins through MHC genes, blood group systems, and microsatellites. *Hum. Immunol.* 62:979–91

Green LD, Derr JN, Knight A. 2000. mtDNA affinities of the peoples of north-central Mexico. *Am. J. Hum. Genet.* 66:989–98

Greenberg JH. 1987. *Language in the Americas*. Stanford, CA: Stanford Univ. Press

Gruhn R. 1987. On the settlement of the Americas: South American evidence for an expanded time frame. *Curr. Anthropol.* 28:363–64

Gruhn R. 1992. Linguistic evidence in support to the coastal route of the earliest entry into the New World. *Man* 23:77–100

Gurven M. 2000. How can we distinguish between mutational 'hot spots' and 'old sites' in human DNA samples? *Hum. Biol.* 72:455–71

Hammer MF, Karafet T, Rasanayagam A, Wood ET, Altheide TK, et al. 1998. Out of Africa and back again: nested cladistic analysis of human Y chromosome variation. *Mol. Biol. Evol.* 15:427–41

Hammer MF, Spurdle AB, Karafet T, Bonner MR, Wood ET, et al. 1997. The geographic distribution of human Y chromosome variation. *Genetics* 145:787–805

Hanihara T, Ishida H, Dodo Y. 2003. Characterization of biological diversity through analysis of discrete cranial traits. *Am. J. Phys. Anthropol.* 121(3)195–292

Hanihara T, Kawano M, Ishida H. 2004. Craniofacial variation of prehistoric and recent populations from Far East, Oceania, and New World: model-free and model-bound approach. *Am. J. Phys. Anthropol. Suppl.* 123(38):108 (Abstr.)

Hauswirth WW, Dickel CD, Rowold RJ, Hauswirth MA. 1994. Inter- and intrapopulation studies of ancient humans. *Experientia* 50:585–91

Hayes MG, Coltrain JB, O'Rourke DH. 2003. Molecular archaeology of the Dorset, Thule, and Sadlermiut: ancestor-descendant relationships in Eastern North American arctic prehistory. In *The Dorset Culture: 75 Years After Jenness*, ed. P Sutherland. Hull,

Quebec: Mercury Ser., Archaeol. Surv. Can., Can. Mus. Civiliz. In press

Haynes CV Jr. 1992. Contributions of radiocarbon dating to the geochronology of the peopling of the New World. In *Radiocarbon After Four Decades*, ed. RE Taylor, A Long, RS Kra, pp. 355–74. New York: Springer-Verlag

Haynes CV Jr. 1993. Clovis-Folsom geochronology and climatic change. In *From Kosteniki to Clovis*, ed. O Soffer, ND Praslov, pp. 219–326. New York: Plenum

Haynes CV Jr. 1982. Were Clovis progenitors in Beringia? In *Paleoecology of Beringia*, ed. DM Hopkins, JV Matthews Jr, CW Schweger, SB Young, pp. 383–98. New York: Academic

Heaton TH, Grady F. 2003. The Late Wisconsin vertebrate history of Prince of Wales Island, southeast Alaska. In *Vertebrate Paleontology of Late Cenozoic Cave Deposits in North America*, ed. BW Schubert, JI Mead, RW Graham, pp. 17–53. Bloomington: Indiana Univ. Press

Hetherington R, Reid RGB. 2003. Malacological insights into the marine ecology and changing climate of the late Pleistocene–early Holocene Queen Charlotte Islands archipelago, western Canada, and implications for early peoples. *Can. J. Zool.* 81: 626–61

Heyer E, Puymirat J, Dieltjes P, Bakker E, De Knijff P. 1997. Estimating Y chromosome specific mutation frequencies using deep rooted pedigrees. *Hum. Mol. Genet.* 6: 799–803

Hoeffecker JF, Powers WR, Goebel T. 1993. The colonization of Beringia and the peopling of the New World. *Science* 259:46–53

Hunley K, Long JC. 2004. Does Greenberg's linguistic classification predict patterns of New World genetic diversity? *Am. J. Phys. Anthropol. Suppl.* 123(38):117 (Abstr.)

Huoponen K, Torroni A, Wickman PR, Sellitto D, Gurley DS, et al. 1997. Mitochondrial and Y chromosome-specific polymorphisms in the Seminole tribe of Florida. *Eur. J. Hum. Genet.* 5:25–34

Hurles ME, Maund E, Nicholson J, Bosch E, Renfrew C, et al. 2003. Native American Y chromosomes in Polynesia: the genetic impact of the Polynesian slave trade. *Am. J. Hum. Genet.* 72(5):1282–87

Jackson LE Jr, Duk-Rodkin A. 1996. Quaternary geology of the ice-free corridor: glacial controls on the peopling of the New World. In *Prehistoric Mongoloid Dispersals*, ed. T Akazawa, EJE Szathmary, pp. 214–27. Oxford, UK: Oxford Univ. Press

Jantz RL, Owsley DW. 2001. Variation among early North American crania. *Am. J. Phys. Anthropol.* 114(2):146–55

Josenhans H, Fedje D, Pienitz R, Southon J. 1997. Early humans and rapidly changing Holocene sea levels in the Queen Charlotte Islands-Hecate Strait, British Columbia, Canada. *Science* 277:71–74

Kaestle FA, Smith DG. 2001. Ancient mitochondrial DNA evidence for prehistoric population movement: the Numic expansion. *Am. J. Phys. Anthropol.* 115(1):1–12

Karafet T, Xu L, Du R, Wang W, Feng S, et al. 2001. Paternal population history of East Asia: sources, patterns, and microevolutionary processes. *Am. J. Hum. Genet.* 69:615–28

Karafet TM, Zegura SL, Posukh O, Osipova L, Bergen A, et al. 1999. Ancestral Asian source(s) of New World Y-chromosome founder haplotypes. *Am. J. Hum. Genet.* 64: 817–31

Karafet TM, Zegura SL, Vuturo-Brady J, Posukh O, Osipova L, et al. 1997. Y-Chromosome markers and trans-Bering Strait dispersals. *Am. J. Phys. Anthropol.* 102:301–14

Kaspirin DO, Crow M, McClintock C, Lawson J. 1987. Blood types of the Native Americans of Oklahoma. *Am. J. Phys. Anthropol.* 73:1–8

Kayser M, Caglià C, Corach D, Fretwell N, Gehrig C, et al. 1997. Evaluation of Y-chromosomal STRs: a multicenter study. *Int. J. Legal. Med.* 110:125–33

Kayser M, Roewer L, Hedman M, Henke L, Henke J, et al. 2000. Characteristics and frequency of germline mutations at microsatellite loci from the human Y chromosome, as revealed by direct observation in father/son pairs. *Am. J. Hum. Genet.* 66:1580–88

Keefer DK, deFrance SD, Moseley ME, Richardson JB III, Satterlee DR, Day-Lewis A. 1998. Early maritime economy and El Niño events at Quebrada Tachuay, Peru. *Science* 281:1833–35

Kemp BM, Resendez A, Román-Berrelleza JA, Malhi RS, Smith DG. 2004. An analysis of ancient mtDNA from Tlateloco: pre-Columbian relations and the spread of Uto-Aztecan. In *Biomolecular Archaeology: Genetic Approaches to the Past*, ed. D Reed. Carbondale, IL. In press

Keyeux G, Rodas C, Gelvez N, Carter D. 2002. Possible migration routes into South America deduced from mitochondrial DNA studies in Colombian Amerindian populations. *Hum. Biol.* 74(2):211–33

Kivisild T, Tolk H-V, Parik J, Wang Y, Papiha SS, et al. 2002. The emerging limbs and twigs of the East Asian mtDNA tree. *Mol. Biol. Evol.* 19(10):1737–51

Klein RG. 1999. *The Human Career: Human Biological and Cultural Origins.* Chicago, IL: Univ. Chicago Press

Kolman CJ, Bermingham E. 1997. Mitochondrial and nuclear DNA diversity in the Choco and Chibcha Amerinds of Panama. *Genetics* 147:1289–302

Kolman CJ, Bermingham E, Cooke R, Ward RH, Arias TD, Guionneau-Sinclair F. 1995. Reduced mtDNA diversity of the Ngöbé Amerinds of Panamá. *Genetics* 140:275–83

Kolman CJ, Sambuughin N, Bermingham E. 1996. Mitochondrial DNA analysis of Mongolian populations and implications for the origin of New World founders. *Genetics* 142:1321–34

Lalueza C. 1996. Mitochondrial DNA haplogroups in four tribes from Tierra del Fuego-Patagonia: inferences about the peopling of the Americas. *Hum. Biol.* 68:855–71

Lalueza C, Pérez-Pérez A, Prats E, Cornudella L, Turbon D. 1997. Lack of founding Amerindian mitochondrial DNA lineages in extinct aborigines from Tierra del Fuego-Patagonia. *Hum.Mol. Genet.* 6(1):41–46

Lalueza-Fox C, Calderon FL, Calafell F, Morera B, Bertranpetit J. 2001. MtDNA from extinct Tainos and the peopling of the Caribbean. *Ann. Hum. Genet.* 65:137–51

Lell JT, Brown MD, Schurr TG, Sukernik RI, Starikovskaya YB, et al. 1997. Y chromosome polymorphisms in Native American and Siberian populations: identification of founding Native American Y chromosome haplotypes. *Hum. Genet.* 100:536–43

Lell JT, Sukernik RI, Starikovskaya YB, Su B, Jin L, et al. 2002. The dual origin and Siberian affinities of Native American Y chromosomes. *Am. J. Hum. Genet.* 70:192–206

Lorenz JG, Smith DG. 1996. Distribution of four founding mtDNA haplogroups among native North Americans. *Am. J. Phys. Anthropol.* 101:307–23

Lorenz JG, Smith DG. 1997. Distribution of sequence variations in the mtDNA control region of native North Americans. *Hum. Biol.* 69:749–76

Lum JK, Cann RL, Martinson JJ, Jorde LB. 1998. Mitochondrial and nuclear genetic relationships among Pacific Island and Asian populations. *Am. J. Hum. Genet.* 63(2):613–24

Lum JK, Rickards O, Ching C, Cann RL. 1994. Polynesian mitochondrial DNAs reveal three deep maternal lineage clusters. *Hum. Biol.* 66:567–90

Macaulay V, Richards V, Hickey E, Vega E, Cruciani F, et al. 1999. The emerging tree of West Eurasian mtDNAs: a synthesis of control-region sequences and RFLPs. *Am. J. Hum. Genet.* 64:232–49

Malhi RS, Eshleman JA, Greenberg JA, Weiss DA, Shook BAS, et al. 2002. The structure of diversity within New World mitochondrial DNA haplogroups: implications for the prehistory of North America. *Am. J. Hum. Genet.* 70:905–19

Malhi RS, Mortensen HM, Eshleman JA, Kemp BM, Lorenz JG, et al. 2003. Native American mtDNA prehistory in the American Southwest. *Am. J. Phys. Anthropol.* 120:108–24

Malhi RS, Schultz BA, Smith DG. 2001. Distribution of mitochondrial lineages among

Native American tribes of northeastern North America. *Hum. Biol.* 73:17–55

Mandryk CAS, Josenhans H, Fedje DW, Mathewes RW. 2001. Late Quaternary paleoenvironments of northwestern North America: Implications for inland versus coastal migration routes. *Q. Sci. Rev.* 20:301–14

Mann DH, Hamilton TD. 1995. Late Pleistocene and Holocene paleoenvironments of the North Pacific coast. *Q. Sci. Rev.* 14:449–71

Martinez-Crusado JC, Toro-Labrador G, Ho-Fung H. 2001. Mitochondrial DNA analysis reveals substantial Native American ancestry in Puerto Rico. *Hum. Biol.* 73(4):491–511

Mathewes RW. 1989. Paleobotany of the Queen Charlotte Islands. In *The Outer Shores*, ed. G Scudder, N Gessler, pp. 75–90. Skidgate: Queen Charlotte Mus. Press

McAvoy JM, Baker JC, Feathers JK, Hodges RL, McWeeney LJ, et al. 2000. *Summary of research at the Cactus Hill Archeological Site 40SX02, Sussex County, Virginia.* Rep. Natl. Geogr. Soc. in compliance with stipulations of Grant #6345–98

McAvoy JM, McAvoy LD. 1997. *Archeological investigations of Site 40SX02, Cactus Hill, Sussex County, Virginia.* Va. Dep. Hist. Resourc., Res. Rep. Ser. 8, Richmond

McKenney K, Rasmussen P, Castaneda J. 2000. *Mitochondrial and nuclear DNA analysis of Inca mummies from Argentina.* Presented at Annu. Meet. Am. Anthropol. Assoc., 99th, San Francisco

Melton PE, Papiha SS, Briceno I, Bernal J, Devor R. 2004. *mtDNA variation in Chibchan speaking groups from Sierra Nevada de Marta, northwest Colombia.* Presented at Annu. Meet. Hum. Biol. Assoc., 29th, Tampa

Meltzer DJ. 1997. Monte Verde and the Pleistocene peopling of the Americas. *Science* 276:754–55

Meltzer DJ, Grayson DK, Ardila G, Barker AW, Dincauze DF, et al. 1997. On the Pleistocene antiquity of Monte Verde, southern Chile. *Am. Antiq.* 62:659–63

Merriwether DA, Hall WW, Vahlne A, Ferrell RE. 1996. mtDNA variation indicates

Mongolia may have been the source for the founding population for the New World. *Am. J.Hum. Genet.* 59:204–12

Merriwether DA, Huston S, Iyengar S, Hamman R, Norris JM, et al. 1997. Mitochondrial versus nuclear admixture estimates demonstrate a past history of directional mating. *Am. J. Phys.Anthropol.* 102(2):153–59

Merriwether DA, Rothhammer F, Ferrell RE. 1994. Genetic variation in the New World: ancient teeth, bone, and tissue as sources of DNA. *Experientia* 50:592–601

Merriwether DA, Rothhammer F, Ferrell RE. 1995. Distribution of the four-founding lineage haplotypes in Native Americans suggests a single wave of migration for the New World. *Am. J. Phys. Anthropol.* 98:411–30

Mesa NR, Mondragon MC, Soto ID, Parra MV, Duque C, et al. 2000. Autosomal, mtDNA, and Y-chromosome diversity in Amerinds: Pre- and Post-Colombian patterns of gene flow in South America. *Am. J. Hum. Genet.* 67:1277–86

Mills LA. 2003. *Mitochondrial DNA analysis of the Ohio Hopewell of the Hopewell Mound Group.* PhD Diss. Dep. Anthropol., Ohio State Univ.

Monsalve JV, Hagelberg E. 1997. Mitochondrial DNA polymorphisms in Carib people of Belize. *Proc. R. Soc. London Ser. B* 264:1217–24

Monsalve MV, Cardenas F, Guhl F, Delaney AD, Devine DV. 1996. Phylogenetic analysis of mtDNA lineages in South American mummies. *Ann. Hum. Genet.* 60:293–303

Monsalve MV, Stone AC, Lewis CM, Rempel A, Richards M, et al. 2002. Molecular analysis of the Kwaday Dan Ts'finchi ancient remains found in a glacier in Canada. *Am. J. Phys. Anthropol.* 119(3):288–91

Moraga ML, Rocco P, Miquel JF, Nervi F, Llop E, et al. 2000. Mitochondrial DNA polymorphisms in Chilean aboriginal populations: implications for the peopling of the Southern Cone of the continent. *Am. J. Phys. Anthropol.* 113:19–29

Nichols J. 1990. Linguistic diversity and the

first settlement of the New World. *Language* 66:475–521

Nichols J. 1994. The spread of language around the Pacific rim. *Evol. Anthropol.* 1:206–15

O'Rourke DH, Hayes MG, Carlyle SW. 2000a. Ancient DNA studies in physical anthropology. *Annu. Rev. Anthropol.* 29:217–42

O'Rourke DH, Hayes MG, Carlyle SW. 2000b. Spatial and temporal stability of mtDNA haplogroup frequencies in native North America. *Hum. Biol.* 72:15–34

Parr RL, Carlyle SW, O'Rourke DH. 1996. Ancient DNA analysis of Fremont Amerindians of the Great Salt Lake Wetlands. *Am. J. Phys. Anthropol.* 99:507–18

Pena SDJ, Santos FR, Bianchi NO, Bravi CM, Carnese FR, et al. 1995. A major founder Y-chromosome haplotype in Amerindians. *Nat. Genet.* 11:15–16

Pitulko VV, Nikolsky PA, Girya EY, Basilyan AE, Tumskoy VE, et al. 2004. The Yana RHS site: humans in the Arctic before the last glacial maximum. *Science* 303:52–56

Pollitzer WS, Hartmann RC, Moore H, Rosenfield RE, Smith H, et al. 1962. Blood types of the Cherokee Indians *Am. J. Phys. Anthropol.* 20(1):33–43

Powell JF, Neves WA. 1999. Craniofacial morphology of the First Americans: pattern and process in the peopling of the New World. *Yrbk. Phys. Anthropol.* 42:153–88

Reidla M, Kivisild T, Metuspalu E, Kuldma K, Kambets K, et al. 2003. Origin and diffusion of mtDNA haplogroup X. *Am. J. Hum. Genet.* 73(6):1178–90

Ribiero dos Santos AK, Santos SE, Machado AL, Guapindaia V, Zago MA. 1996. Heterogeneity of mitochondrial DNA haplotypes in Pre-Columbian natives of the Amazon region. *Am. J.Phys. Anthropol.* 101:29–37

Richards M, Macaulay V, Hickey E, Vega E, Sykes B, et al. 2000. Tracing European founder lineages in the near eastern MtDNA pool. *Am. J. Hum. Genet.* 67:1251–76

Richards M, Macaulay VA, Bandelt H-J, Sykes BC. 1998. Phylogeography of mitochondrial DNA in western Europe. *Ann. Hum. Genet.* 62:241–60

Rickards O, Martiñez-Labarga C, Lum JK, De Stefano GF, Cann RL. 1999. mtDNA history of the Cayapa Amerinds of Ecuador: detection of additional founding lineages for the Native American populations. *Am. J. Hum. Genet.* 65:519–30

Rodas C, Gelvez N, Keyeux G. 2003. Mitochondrial DNA studies show asymmetrical Amerindian admixture in Afro-Colombian and Mestizo populations. *Hum. Biol.* 75(1): 13–30

Rodriguez-Delfin L, Santos SEB, Zagos MA. 1997. Diversity of the human Y chromosome of South American Amerindians: a comparison with Blacks, Whites and Japanese from Brazil. *Ann. Hum. Genet.* 61:439–48

Rogers AR, Harpending H. 1992. Population growth makes waves in the distribution of pairwise genetic differences. *Mol. Biol. Evol.* 9:552–69

Roosevelt AC, Douglas J, Brown L. 2002. The migrations and adaptations of the first Americans: Clovis and pre-Clovis viewed from South America. In *The First Americans: The Pleistocene Colonization of the New World*, ed. NG Jablonski, pp. 159–235. San Francisco: Calif. Univ. Press

Roosevelt AC, da Costa ML, Machado CL, Michab M, Mercier N, et al. 1996. Paleoindian cave dwellers in the Amazon: the peopling of the Americas. *Science* 272:373–84

Ross AH, Ubelaker DH, Falsetti AB. 2002. Craniometric variation in the Americas. *Hum. Biol.* 74(6):807–18

Rothhammer F, Silva C, Callegari-Jacques SM, Llope E, Salzano FM. 1997. Gradients of HLA diversity in South American Indians. *Ann. Hum. Biol.* 24:197–208

Rubicz R, Melvin KL, Crawford MH. 2002. Genetic evidence for the phylogenetic relationship between Na-Dene and Yeniseian speakers. *Hum. Biol.* 74(6):743–60

Rubicz R, Schurr TG, Babb PL, Crawford MH. 2003. Mitochondrial DNA diversity in modern Aleuts, and their genetic relationship with other circumarctic populations. *Hum. Biol.* 75(6):809–35

Ruhlen M. 1994. *The Origin of Language: Tracing the Evolution of the Mother Tongue.* New York: Wiley

Ruiz-Linares A, Ortiz-Barrientos D, Figueroa M, Mesa N, Munera JG, et al. 1999. Microsatellites provide evidence for Y chromosome diversity among the founders of the New World. *Proc. Natl.Acad. Sci. USA* 96: 6312–17

Saillard J, Forster P, Lynnerup N, Bandelt H-J, Norby S. 2000. mtDNA variation among Greenland Eskimos: the edge of the Beringian expansion. *Am. J. Hum. Genet.* 67: 718–26

Sajantila A, Lahermo P, Anttinen T, Lukka M, Sistonen P, et al. 1995. Genes and languages in Europe: an analysis of mitochondrial lineages. *Genome Res.* 5:42–52

Salzano FM. 2002. Molecular variability in Amerindians: widespread but uneven information. *Ann. Acad. Bras. Cienc.* 74(2):223–63

Salzano FM, Callegari-Jacques SM. 1988. *South American Indians: A Case Study in Evolution.* Oxford, UK: Clarendon

Sandweiss DH, McInnis H, Burger RL, Cano A, Ojeda B, et al. 1998. Quebrada Jaguay: early South American maritime adaptations. *Science* 281:1830–32

Santos FR, Pandya A, Tyler-Smith C, Pena SDJ, Schanfield M, et al. 1999. The central Siberian origin for Native American Y-chromosomes. *Am. J. Hum. Genet.* 64:619–28

Santos FR, Rodriguez-Delfin L, Pena SD, Moore J, Weiss KM. 1996. North and South Amerindians may have the same major founder Y chromosome haplotype. *Am. J. Hum. Genet.* 58:1369–70

Santos MR, Ward RH, Barrantes R. 1994. mtDNA variation in the Chibcha Amerindian Huetar from Costa Rica. *Hum. Biol.* 66:963–77

Santos SE, Ribeiro-dos-Santos AK, Meyer D, Zago MA. 1996. Multiple founder haplotypes of mitochondrial DNA in Amerindians revealed by RFLP and sequencing. *Ann. Hum. Genet.* 60:305–19

Schultz BA, Malhi RS, Smith DG. 2001. Examining the Proto-Algonquian migration: analysis of mtDNA. In *Proc. 32nd Algonquian Conf.*, ed. JD Nichols, A Ogg, pp. 470–92. Ottawa, ON: Carleton Univ. Press

Schurr TG. 2002. A molecular anthropological view of the peopling of the Americas. *Athena Rev.* 3(2):59–77

Schurr TG. 2003. Molecular genetic diversity of Siberian populations: implications for ancient DNA studies of archeological populations from the Cis-Baikal region. In *Prehistoric Foragers of the Cis-Baikal, Siberia: Proc. 1st Conf. Baikal Archaeol. Project*, ed. A Weber, H McKenzie, pp. 155–86. Edmonton: Can. Circumpolar Inst.

Schurr TG. 2004a. An anthropological genetic view of the peopling of the Americas. In *The Settlement of the American Continents: A Multidisciplinary Approach to Human Biogeography*, ed. GA Clark, CM Barton, D Yesner, G Pearson. Tucson: Ariz. State Univ. Press. In press

Schurr TG. 2004b. Genetic diversity in Siberians and Native Americans suggests an early migration to the New World. In *Entering America: Northeast Asia and Beringia Before the Last Glacial Maximum*, ed. D Madsen. Salt Lake City: Univ. Utah Press. In press

Schurr TG. 2004c. Tracking genes through time and space: changing perspectives on New World origins. In *Paleoamerican Origins: Moving Beyond Clovis*, ed. R Bonnichsen, B Lepper, DG Steele, D Stanford, JA Harris, CN Warren, R Gruhn, pp. 169–90. College Station: Cent. Study First Am./Texas A & M Univ.

Schurr TG, Ballinger SW, Gan Y-Y, Hodge JA, Merriwether DA, et al. 1990. Amerindian mitochondrial DNAs have rare Asian variants at high frequencies, suggesting they derived from four primary maternal lineages. *Am. J. Hum. Genet.* 46:613–23

Schurr TG, Sherry ST. 2004. Mitochondrial DNA and Y chromosome diversity and the peopling of the Americas. *Am. J. Hum. Biol.* 16:1–18

Schurr TG, Starikovskaya YB, Sukernik RI, Torroni A, Wallace DC. 2000. Mitochondrial

DNA diversity in lower Amur River populations, and its implications for the genetic history of the North Pacific and the New World. *Am. J. Phys. Anthropol. Suppl.* 30:274–75 (Abstr.)

Schurr TG, Sukernik RI, Starikovskaya YB, Wallace DC. 1999. Mitochondrial DNA variation in Koryaks and Itel'men: Population replacement in the Okhotsk Bering Sea region during the Neolithic. *Am. J. Phys. Anthropol.* 108:1–39

Schurr TG, Wallace DC. 1999. MtDNA variation in Native Americans and Siberians and its implications for the peopling of the New World. In *Who Were the First Americans: Proc. 58th Annu. Biol. Colloq., Oregon State Univ.*, ed. R Bonnichsen, pp. 41–77. Corvallis, OR: Cent. Study First Am.

Schurr TG, Wallace DC. 2003. Genetic prehistory of Paleoasiatic-speaking peoples of northeastern Siberia and their links to Native American populations. In *Constructing Cultures Then and Now: Celebrating Franz Boas and the Jesup North Pacific Expedition*, ed. L Kendall, I Krupnik, pp. 239–58. Baltimore, MD: Smithson. Inst. Press

Schurr TG, Zhadanov SI, Osipova LP. 2004d. mtDNA variation in indigenous Altaians, and their genetic relationships with Siberian and Mongolian populations. *Am. J. Phys. Anthropol. Suppl.* 123(38):176 (Abstr.)

Scozzari R, Cruciani F, Santolamazza P, Sellitto D, Cole DEC, et al. 1997. mtDNA and Y-chromosome-specific polymorphisms in modern Ojibwa: implications about the origin of their gene pool. *Am. J. Hum. Genet.* 60: 241–44

Seielstad M, Yuldasheva N, Singh N, Underhill P, Oefner P, et al. 2003. A novel Y-chromosome variant puts an upper limit on the timing of the first entry into the Americas. *Am. J. Hum. Genet.* 73(3):700–5

Schanfield MS. 1992. Immunoglobulin allotypes (GM and KM) indicate multiple founding populations of Native Americans: evidence of at least four migrations to the New World. *Hum. Biol.* 64:381–402

Sherry ST, Rogers AR, Harpending H, Soodyall H, Jenkins T, Stoneking M. 1994. Mismatch distributions of mtDNA reveal recent human population expansions. *Hum. Biol.* 66:761–75

Shields GF, Schmiechen AM, Frazier BL, Redd A, Voevoda MI, et al. 1993. mtDNA sequences suggest a recent evolutionary divergence for Beringian and northern North American populations. *Am. J. Hum. Genet.* 53:549–62

Shimada I, Shinoda K, Bourget S, Corruccini RS, Watanabe H. 2004a. MtDNA analysis of Mochica and Sicán populations of pre-Hispanic Peru. In *Biomolecular Archaeology Genetic Approaches to the Past*, ed. D Reed. Carbondale, IL: Cent. Archaeol. Investig., South. Ill. Univ. In press

Shimada I, Shinoda K, Farnum J, et al. 2004b. An integrated analysis of pre-Hispanic mortuary practices: a Middle Sicán case study. *Curr. Anthropol.* 45(3). In press

Shook BA. 2004. Detecting relationships in the Great Lakes region using ancient mtDNA. *Am. J. Phys. Anthropol. Suppl.* 123(38):181 (Abstr.)

Silva WA, Bonatto SL, Holanda AJ, Ribeiro-dos-Santos AK, Paixao BM, et al. 2002. Mitochondrial genome diversity of Native Americans supports a single early entry of founder populations into America. *Am. J. Hum. Genet.* 71:187–92

Smith DG, Malhi RS, Eshleman J, Lorenz JG, Kaestle FA. 1999. Distribution of haplogroup X among native North Americans. *Am. J. Phys. Anthropol.* 110:271–84

Smith DG, Malhi RS, Eshleman JA, Schultz BA. 2000. *A study of mtDNA of Early Holocene North American Skeletons.* Presented at Annu. Meet. Am. Anthropol. Assoc., 99th, San Francisco

Stanford D. 1999. *Iberia, not Siberia.* Presented at Clovis and Beyond Conf., Santa Fe, NM

Stanford D. 2000. *Trans-Atlantic crossing for Clovis.* http://www.mnh.si.edu/arctic/arctic/html/dennis_stanford.html

Stanford D, Bradley B. 2000. The Solutrean solution. *Sci. Am. Discov. Archeol.* 2:54–55

Starikovskaya YB, Sukernik RI, Schurr TG,

Kogelnik AM, Wallace DC. 1998. Mitochondrial DNA diversity in Chukchi and Siberian Eskimos: implications for the genetic prehistory of ancient Beringia. *Am. J. Hum. Genet.* 63:1473–91

Stone AC, Stoneking M. 1998. mtDNA analysis of a prehistoric Oneota population: implications for the peopling of the New World. *Am. J. Hum. Genet.* 62:1153–70

Stoneking M. 2000. Hypervariable sites in the mtDNA control region are mutational hotspots. *Am. J. Hum. Genet.* 67:1029–32

Strauss LG. 2000. A quarter-century of research on the Solutrean of Vasco-Cantabria, Iberia and beyond. *J. Archeol. Res.* 56(1):39–58

Su B, Xiao J, Underhill P, Deka R, Zhang W, et al. 1999. Y-chromosome evidence for a northward migration of modern humans into eastern Asia during the last Ice Age. *Am. J. Hum. Genet.* 65:1718–24

Tarazona-Santos E, Carvalho-Silva DR, Pettener D, Luiselli D, De Stefano GF, et al. 2001. Genetic differentiation in South Amerindians is related to environmental and cultural diversity: Evidence from the Y chromosome. *Am. J. Hum. Genet.* 68:1485–96

Thomson R, Pritchard JK, Shen PD, Oefner PJ, Feldman MW, et al. 2000. Recent common ancestry of human Y chromosomes: Evidence from DNA sequence data. *Proc. Natl. Acad. Sci. USA* 97:7360–65

Thornton R, Marsh-Thornton J. 1981. Estimating prehistoric American Indian population size for United States area: implications of the nineteenth century decline and nadir. *Am. J. Phys. Anthropol.* 55:47–53

Torroni A, Brown MD, Lott MT, Newman NJ, Wallace DC, et al. 1995. African, Native American and European mitochondrial DNAs in Cubans from the Pinar del Rio Province and implications for the recent epidemic neuropathy in Cuba. *Hum. Mutat.* 5:310–17

Torroni A, Chen Y-S, Semino O, Santachiara-Beneceretti AS, Scott CR, et al. 1994a. MtDNA and Y-chromosome polymorphisms in four Native American populations from southern Mexico. *Am. J. Hum. Genet.* 54:303–18

Torroni A, Huoponen K, Francalacci P, Petrozzi M, Morelli L, et al. 1996. Classification of European mtDNAs from an analysis of three European populations. *Genetics* 144:1835–50

Torroni A, Lott MT, Cabell MF, Chen Y-S, Lavergne L, Wallace DC. 1994b. mtDNA and the origin of Caucasians: identification of ancient Caucasian-specific haplogroups, one of which is prone to a recurrent somatic duplication in the D-loop region. *Am. J. Hum. Genet.* 55:760–76

Torroni A, Neel JV, Barrantes R, Schurr TG, Wallace DC. 1994c. A mitochondrial DNA "clock" for the Amerinds and its implications for timing their entry into North America. *Proc. Natl. Acad. Sci. USA* 91:1158–62

Torroni A, Schurr TG, Cabell MF, Brown MD, Neel JV, et al. 1993a. Asian affinities and the continental radiation of the four founding Native American mtDNAs. *Am. J. Hum. Genet.* 53:563–90

Torroni A, Schurr TG, Yang C-C, Szathmary EJ, Williams RC, et al. 1992. Native American mitochondrial DNA analysis indicates that the Amerind and the Na-Dene populations were founded by two independent migrations. *Genetics* 130:153–62

Torroni A, Sukernik RI, Schurr TG, Starikovskaya YB, Cabell MF, et al. 1993b. mtDNA variation of aboriginal Siberians reveals distinct genetic affinities with Native Americans. *Am. J. Hum. Genet.* 53:591–608

Ubelaker DH. 1988. North American Indian population size, 1500 to 1985. *Am. J. Phys. Anthropol.* 77:289–94

Underhill PA, Jin L, Lin AA, Mehdi SQ, Jenkins T, et al. 1997. Detection of numerous Y chromosome biallelic polymorphisms by denaturing high performance liquid chromatography. *Genome Res.* 7:996–1005

Underhill PA, Jin L, Zemans R, Oefner PJ, Cavalli-Sforza LL. 1996. A pre-Columbian

Y chromosome-specific transition and its implications for human evolutionary history. *Proc. Natl. Acad. Sci. USA* 93:196–200

Underhill PA, Passarino G, Lin AA, Shen P, Mirazón Lahr M, et al. 2001. The phylogeography of Y chromosome binary haplotypes and the origins of modern human populations. *Am. Hum. Genet.* 65:43–62

Underhill PA, Shen P, Lin AA, Jin L, Passarino G, et al. 2000. Y chromosome sequence variation and the history of human populations. *Nat. Genet.* 26:358–61

Ward RH, Frazier BL, Dew-Jager K, Paabo S. 1991. Extensive mitochondrial diversity within a single Amerindian tribe. *Proc. Natl. Acad. Sci. USA* 88:8720–24

Ward RH, Redd A, Valencia D, Franzier B, Paabo S. 1993. Genetic and linguistic differentiation in the Americas. *Proc. Natl. Acad. Sci. USA* 90:10063–67

Waters MR, Forman SL, Pierson JM. 1997. Diring Yuriakh: a Lower Paleolithic site in central Siberia. *Science* 275:1281–84

Williams SR, Cansino V, Wise K. 2000. *Genetic variation at Kilometer 4, a Preceramic site on the far south coast of Peru.* Presented at Annu. Meet. Am. Anthropol. Assoc., 99th, San Francisco

Yao Y-G, Kong Q-P, Bandelt H-J, Kivisild T, Zhang YP. 2002. Phylogeographic differentiation of mitochondrial DNA in Han Chinese. *Am. J. Hum. Genet.* 70:635–51

Y Chromosome Consortium. 2002. A nomenclature system for the tree of human Y-chromosomal binary haplogroups. *Genome Res.* 12:339–48

Annu. Rev. Anthropol. 2004. 33:585–623
doi: 10.1146/annurev.anthro.33.070203.143955
Copyright © 2004 by Annual Reviews. All rights reserved
First published online as a Review in Advance on June 21, 2004

THE EVOLUTION OF HUMAN SKIN AND SKIN COLOR

Nina G. Jablonski

*Department of Anthropology, California Academy of Sciences, San Francisco,
California 98103; email: njablonski@calacademy.org*

Key Words pigmentation, melanin, UV radiation, thermoregulation, race

■ **Abstract** Humans skin is the most visible aspect of the human phenotype. It is distinguished mainly by its naked appearance, greatly enhanced abilities to dissipate body heat through sweating, and the great range of genetically determined skin colors present within a single species. Many aspects of the evolution of human skin and skin color can be reconstructed using comparative anatomy, physiology, and genomics. Enhancement of thermal sweating was a key innovation in human evolution that allowed maintenance of homeostasis (including constant brain temperature) during sustained physical activity in hot environments. Dark skin evolved *pari passu* with the loss of body hair and was the original state for the genus *Homo*. Melanin pigmentation is adaptive and has been maintained by natural selection. Because of its evolutionary lability, skin color phenotype is useless as a unique marker of genetic identity. In recent prehistory, humans became adept at protecting themselves from the environment through clothing and shelter, thus reducing the scope for the action of natural selection on human skin.

INTRODUCTION

When humans visualize a body, they see mostly skin. The skin is the body's direct interface with the physical environment, conveying a state of health and personal identity. The skin comprises a sheet-like investiture that protects the body from attack by physical, chemical, and microbial agents. It is the organ that regulates body temperature through control of surface blood flow and sweating and detects critical information about the ambient environment and objects touched. The largest and most massive of the organs of the body, the skin of the average adult human exceeds 2 m² yet is generally no thicker than 2 mm (Odland 1991). The skin also provides a forum for advertising. It provides information about a person's age, health, and some aspects of ancestry, and furnishes a placard upon which further information is placed through temporary and permanent decoration.

Research on the evolution of human skin and skin color has not been commensurate with the importance of skin in human evolution. Skin is generally not preserved in the fossil record and so details of its evolution can be gained only from

0084-6570/04/1021-0585$14.00

comparative anatomical and physiological evidence. Skin has also been overlooked as a topic of research interest in anthropology and human biology in recent decades because of the social sensitivity surrounding discussions of skin color and because of the use and misuse of skin color in biological and social concepts of race.

The goal of this review is to provide a comprehensive yet economical survey of the biology, evolution, and culture of human skin and skin color, with an emphasis on new research—especially on the evolution of skin color. The review begins with an overview of the basic biology of skin itself, followed by discussions of the evolution of skin and skin color, and of skin color and race.

THE STRUCTURE AND FUNCTIONS OF HUMAN SKIN

The skin serves as an effective physical barrier because its laminar structure renders it relatively resistant to abrasion, puncture, and percutaneous absorption, and because its immune cells mount a first line of defense against pathogens coming in contact with the body. Lacking adequate protection from hair, human skin has undergone numerous adaptive structural changes that give it strength, resilience, and sensitivity (Montagna 1981). The skin of humans, like that of all tetrapods, acts as a sun shield to protect the body from most solar UV radiation (UVR) and is the locus for the initiation of the important, UVR-driven process of vitamin D production in the body.

Epidermis

The laminar structure of human skin comprises two major tissue layers, a thinner outer layer, the epidermis, and a thicker and more internally complex inner layer, the dermis (Figure 1). The epidermis is a stratified keratinizing epithelium with a smooth, abrasion-resistant surface that is interrupted only by hair follicles and the pores of sweat glands. The barrier properties of the skin are predicated on the integrity of the stratum corneum (Elias et al. 2003, Taylor 2002). Keratinocytes are the principal cell type found in epidermis and are composed largely of filamentous proteins known as keratins, which are imbedded in an amorphous matrix. The skin's elasticity and resistance to physical and chemical attack can be attributed to the high elastic modulus and unique amino acid composition of the keratinized layer of the epidermis (Marks 1991, Odland 1991). The epidermis also contains populations of three types of immigrant dendritic cells: melanocytes, Langerhans cells, and Merkel cells. Melanocytes produce the skin's primary pigment, melanin, and are discussed in greater detail below. Langerhans cells are specialized cells of the immune system that present and respond to antigens coming in contact with the skin, and Merkel cells are associated with nerve terminals that together function as slow-adapting mechanoreceptors for touch; they are most common on the glabrous skin of the fingertips (Chu et al. 2003, Kripke & Applegate 1991, Lynn 1991, Odland 1991). The epidermis is subdivided into four layers from deep to superficial: the stratum basale (the germinative layer of keratinocytes), the

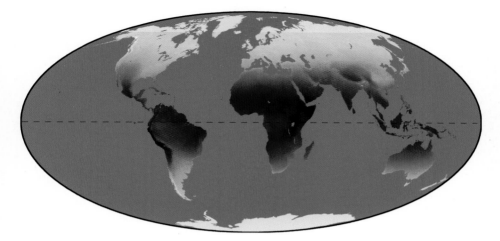

Figure 3 Human skin coloration as predicted from multiple regression formulae. See text for discussion.

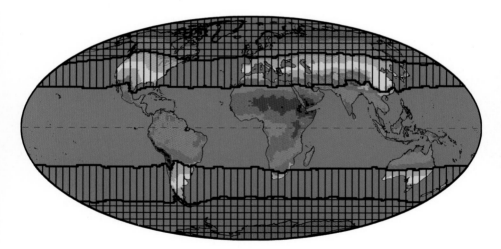

Figure 5 The potential for synthesizing vitamin D_3 in the skin relative to levels of annual average UVMED. The highest UVMED levels are indicated in deep violet, with incrementally lower levels indicated in shades of red, orange, yellow, green, and gray. Zone 1 (*area without hachure enclosing the tropics*) represents the region with adequate UVR throughout the year to catalyze vitamin D_3 synthesis. Zone 2 (*vertical hachure*) represents the area in which there is insufficient UVR during at least one month of the year to produce vitamin D_3. Zone 3 (*cross-hatched area*) represents the region in which there is insufficient UVR averaged over the entire year to photosynthesize vitamin D_3. See text for further description.

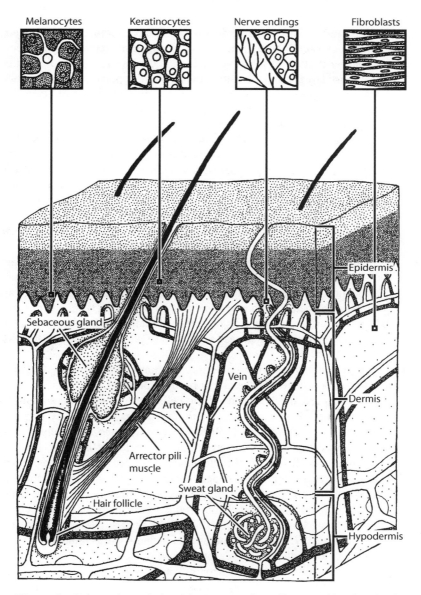

Figure 1   Schematic rendering of a cross-section of human skin, showing its laminar structure, main cell types, and appendages.

stratum spinosum, the stratum granulosum, and the stratum corneum. The stratum corneum consists of flattened, nonviable keratinocytes. In darkly pigmented or heavily tanned individuals, these keratinocytes contain specks of melanin "dust" (Kollias 1995a). The stratum corneum acts as a barrier to the unrestrained passage of water and solutes through the skin, defends against invasion by microorganisms and the penetration of toxic substances, and protects against most mechanical injury caused by friction, abrasion, pricks, or arthropod bites (Marks 1991). These functions are successfully served despite the epidermis being in a constant state of turnover, as the outermost cornified cells of the stratum corneum are shed as they are replaced from below.

Differences between human groups in epidermal structure and thickness have been reported, but most studies of this topic have been based on small samples with poorly controlled experimental designs, as reviewed elsewhere (Taylor 2002). Considerable variation in epidermal thickness exists within human populations and is likely related to age and history of sun exposure. The stratum corneum of darkly pigmented or heavily tanned people is more compact and consists of more cornified cell layers than that of lightly pigmented people; these characteristics enhance the barrier protection functions of the skin (Taylor 2002).

In all primates, the epidermis of the volar surfaces of the hands and feet exhibit well-developed epidermal ridges or dermatoglyphics, which impart greater resistance against friction and help to insure secure purchase on locomotor substrates and on objects being gripped or manipulated. Dermatoglyphics are also found on the ventral surfaces of the tails of prehensile-tailed New World monkeys and on the knuckle pads of chimpanzees and gorillas (Ellis & Montagna 1962, Montagna 1971).

The melanocytes of the epidermis warrant close attention because of their role in the production of the skin's primary pigment or chromophore, melanin. Melanocytes are specialized dendritic cells that reside in the stratum basale of the epidermis and in the matrix portion of the hair bulb. They originate in the neural crest as melanoblasts proliferate and migrate to the epidermis during the eighteenth week of embryonic development (Rawles 1948). Melanocytes produce melanins in specialized cytoplasmic organelles called melanosomes, which vary in size and degree of aggregation depending on skin type and pigmentation (Figure 2) (Szabo et al. 1969). The density of melanocytes varies over the surface of the body, and the number of active (melanin-producing) melanocytes varies with age and can be increased by exposure to UVR (Halaban et al. 2003, Jimbow et al. 1991, Quevedo et al. 1975). The total number of melanocytes is relatively invariant from one person to another, however, and is not related to variation between human groups in skin pigmentation (Fitzpatrick et al. 1961, Jimbow et al. 1991, Robins 1991, Young & Sheehan 2001). MacKintosh, following Wasserman, has recently advanced the hypothesis that melanocytes, melanosomes, and melanin together function as part of the immune system against invading microorganisms and that the more darkly pigmented skins of the indigenous peoples of the tropics have evolved primarily to serve this function (MacKintosh 2001; Wassermann 1965b, 1974).

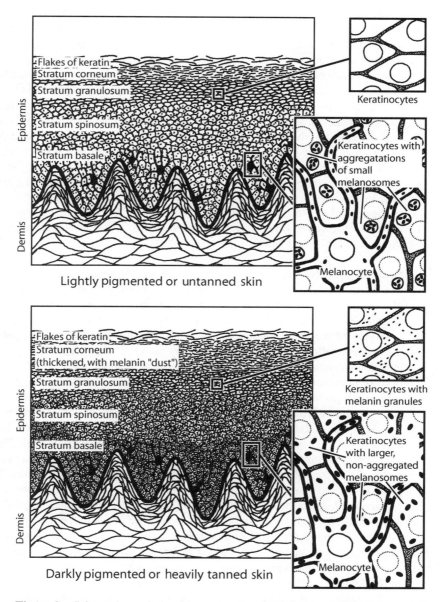

Figure 2   Schematic rendering of cross-sections of lightly and darkly pigmented human skin, showing differences in stratum corneum structure and in the size and aggregation of melanin-containing melanosomes.

Melanocytes project their dendrites into keratinocytes where they then transfer mature melanosomes (Figure 2). Melanosomes are ellipsoidal, membrane-bound organelles containing melanin. After melanosomes have been transferred to keratinocytes, they become aggregated and surrounded by a membrane in a melanosome complex (Jimbow et al. 1991, Szabo et al. 1969). In darkly pigmented skin, melanosomes are large and are not clumped in aggregations, whereas in lightly pigmented skin these organelles are smaller and aggregated (Szabo et al. 1969). Intensity of skin coloration is determined by many factors: (*a*) The total number of melanosomes in the keratinocytes and melanocytes, and their degree of dispersion; (*b*) the rate of melanin production (melanogenesis); (*c*) the degree of melanization of melanosomes; (*e*) the rate of transport and type of incorporation of melanosomes into keratinocytes; (*f*) the degradation of melanosomes within the keratinocytes; and (*g*) a person's chronological age because the number of metabolically active melanocytes decreases over time (Halaban et al. 2003, Jimbow et al. 1976, Ortonne 1990, Parker 1981). Larger melanosomes break down more slowly in keratinocytes and contribute to higher levels of pigmentation (Sulaimon & Kitchell 2003).

MELANIN PIGMENTATION AND ITS MEASUREMENT   Human skin derives most of its pigmentation from melanin, an extremely dense, virtually insoluble, high molecular weight polymer that is attached to a structural protein (Jimbow et al. 1991, Ortonne 2002, Parker 1981, Sulaimon & Kitchell 2003). Human skin contains the two types of melanin found in all mammals, the brownish-black eumelanin and the reddish-yellow pheomelanin (Thody et al. 1991). Higher concentrations of eumelanin characterize darker skin phenotypes including tanned skin. Concentrations of pheomelanin in the skin vary considerably from individual to individual within any given human group, but pheomelanin-rich skin phenotypes are more common among red-haired northern Europeans, as well as East Asians and Native Americans (Rana et al. 1999, Thody et al. 1991). Melanin is synthesized by oxidation of tyrosine via the enzyme tyrosinase (Fitzpatrick et al. 1950, Jimbow et al. 1976, Ortonne 2002). Eumelanins and pheomelanins arise from a common metabolic pathway in which dopaquinone is the key intermediate (Ortonne 2002). As is discussed in greater detail below, production of melanins is regulated by pigmentation genes, hormones, and UVR (Fitzpatrick & Ortonne 2003, Sulaimon & Kitchell 2003, Thody & Smith 1977). A balance of many regulatory factors is essential for normal pigment production in the melanocyte, and derangements of these factors can lead to anomalies of cutaneous pigmentation such as albinism piebald spotting, and various types of hyperpigmentation (Robins 1991, Sulaimon & Kitchell 2003, Thody & Smith 1977).

The optical and chemical properties of melanins have been studied in detail (Ito 2003, Kollias et al. 1991, Ortonne 2002, Prota 1992c), but detailed chemical characterization of the compounds has been difficult to obtain because melanin polymers are composed of many different units connected through strong carbon-carbon bonds (Ito 2003). The optical properties of natural melanin in vivo are related to its abilities to absorb, scatter, and reflect light of different wavelengths (Kollias et al. 1991, Ortonne 2002). The melanins in human skin are a heterogeneous mixture of melanin polymers, precursors, and metabolites, characterized by a continuous absorption capacity in the UV range and exponentially declining absorption capacity from the UV to the visible range (Kollias 1995b, Sarna & Swartz 1998). Natural protection against sunburning (photoprotection) is due to the absorption and scattering of UVR by melanin (Kaidbey et al. 1979; Kollias 1995a,b). Both processes are influenced by the density and distribution of melanosomes within keratinocytes (Figure 2), with the larger, singly dispersed and heavily melanized melanosomes of darkly pigmented skin absorbing more energy than the smaller, less dense, and lightly melanized melanosomes of lightly pigmented skin (Kaidbey et al. 1979).

Melanin was long considered to act as a passive screening filter against UVR, but it is by no means inert (Fitzpatrick et al. 1961). Photodegradation (photolysis) and/or oxidative polymerization of melanin may occur when it absorbs photons (Ortonne 2002). Recent evidence indicates that the photoprotective role of melanin in darkly pigmented skin may be augmented by its ability to scavenge oxygen-derived radicals (reactive oxygen species), such as superoxide anion and hydrogen peroxide, which are cytotoxic compounds generated by the interaction of UV photons with membrane lipids and other cellular components (Ortonne 2002, Prota 1992c, Sulaimon & Kitchell 2003, Young & Sheehan 2001). At the physiological level, the protective role of melanin pigmentation against UVR exposure derives from its ability to prevent direct and indirect (oxidative) damage to DNA at wavelengths where it is most vulnerable (Cleaver & Crowley 2002, Kielbassa et al. 1997, Shea & Parrish 1991).

Melanin pigmentation in human skin is considered as either constitutive skin color or facultative skin color (Quevedo et al. 1975). Constitutive skin color is the amount of genetically determined cutaneous melanin pigmentation that is generated without any influence of solar radiation (Jimbow et al. 1976, Quevedo et al. 1975). Facultative skin color or "tan" constitutes the short-lived, immediate, and delayed tanning reactions elicited by exposure to UVR (Jimbow et al. 1991, 1976; Quevedo et al. 1975). Lighter constitutive pigmentation is associated with a higher sunburn response, a lower tanning response, and a greater susceptibility to skin cancers (Kollias et al. 1991, Sturm 2002, Wagner et al. 2002).

Objective and reproducible assessment of melanin pigmentation has long been a goal of anthropology and dermatology. In anthropology, verbal descriptions of skin colors ("white," "yellow," "black," "brown," and "red") were replaced by color-matching methods during the early twentieth century (Olivier 1960, von Luschan 1897). The most popular of these methods was the von Luschan scale, based on the use of colored tablets or tiles of different colors and hues with which the colors of unexposed skin were matched. These and similar matching methods could not be consistently reproduced, however, and were swiftly abandoned when reflectance spectrophotometry was introduced in the early 1950s (Lasker

1954, Wassermann 1974). Reflectance spectrophotometry remains the method of choice for the objective study of skin pigmentation, color definition, and the spectral reflectance curves of skin because the incident light used and the distance between the light source and the subject are invariable and because subjective factors inherent in the visual matching methods are excluded (Wassermann 1974). All instrumental approaches to skin color evaluation depend on the illumination of the skin site by a standard light source at a fixed relative angle that minimizes the reflected light from the stratum corneum. The detector collects light re-emitted by the skin site from a particular angle and with a chosen color filter (Kollias 1995a). Because of the importance of assessing constitutive skin color on a part of the body that is not routinely exposed to sun, the inner (medial) surface of the upper arm has long been the standard reference site for studies of skin color. Portable reflectance spectrophotometers came into use with Weiner's (1951) study, with two types of instruments being commonly employed in anthropology during the latter part of the twentieth century. The instrument manufactured by the Evans Electroselenium Company (EEL) has been the most widely used, especially in studies of the skin colors of Old World peoples (Wassermann 1974), whereas that made by the Photovolt Corporation was more widely used in studies of New World peoples. Unfortunately, the skin reflectance measurements obtained by these two instruments are not directly comparable, requiring conversion formulae to make them so (Lees & Byard 1978). Research is now underway that may make possible the conversion of skin color assessments made by von Luschan color tablets to values comparable with those derived from reflectance spectrophotometry (M. Henneberg, personal communication).

In clinical medicine, constitutive skin color and skin sensitivity has been classified commonly according to skin phototypes or sun-reactive skin types, from Type I (very sensitive, easily burned, with little or no potential for tanning) to Type VI (insensitive, never burns, and deeply pigmented) (Fitzpatrick 1988, Fitzpatrick & Ortonne 2003, Jimbow et al. 1991). Skin type does not correspond well to constitutive skin color, however, and has limited applicability with respect to the responses of moderately or deeply pigmented skin (Kollias et al. 1991, Prota 1992c, Taylor 2002, Wagner et al. 2002, Westerhof et al. 1990). Despite these limitations, skin phototyping has been widely embraced by many clinicians because assessments can be made without instrumentation. In recent years, highly sensitive diffuse reflectance spectrophotometers such as the DermaSpectrometer and the Datacolor International Microflash as well as chromaticity meters have been used increasingly to measure skin pigmentation and skin response to UVR (Kollias 1995a, Wagner et al. 2002).

The photoprotective benefits of melanin have been assessed using several different measures including minimal erythemal dose (MED), DNA damage, and incidence of skin cancer (Kollias et al. 1991). The MED represents the minimum amount of UVR necessary to bring about a slight visible reddening of lightly pigmented skin. It is the easiest and most common method of assessing skin reactions to UVR but is difficult to determine for deeply pigmented individuals in whom visual redness is difficult to assess (Kaidbey et al. 1979, Ortonne 2002, Shono et al. 1985).

Exposure of human skin to UVR results in a profound alteration of the metabolism, structure, and function of epidermal cells. These activities include increased activation of melanocytes, augmentation of melanosome production, an increase in the size of melanosome complexes incorporated within keratinocytes, and initiation of vitamin D synthesis (Parker 1981, Prota 1992a, Urbach 2001). The erythema response or sunburn reaction is related to constitutive skin color: Dark-skinned individuals can tolerate longer sun exposure than light-skinned individuals can. The skin of individuals with dark constitutive pigmentation exhibits a sun protection factor (SPF) of 10–15, whereas that of moderately pigmented people (e.g., from the circum-Mediterranean) achieves an SPF of only 2.5 (Kaidbey et al. 1979, Kollias et al. 1991, Ortonne 2002). In vitro studies of the reactions of human melanocytes to UVR have shown that heavily pigmented melanocytes have a greater capacity to resume cell division after irradiation with short wavelength UVR (UVB) than do their lightly pigmented counterparts, which suggests that they suffered less damage to their DNA (Barker et al. 1995). In contrast, UVB damages the immune system of the skin regardless of constitutive pigmentation by depleting both heavily and lightly pigmented skin of Langerhans cells (Cleaver & Crowley 2002, Kripke & Applegate 1991). The protective role of melanin in connection with skin cancer thus derives from its role in preventing damage to DNA in the first place, not in protecting against damage to the cutaneous immune system (Vermeer et al. 1991). Tanning or facultative pigmentation induced by UVR is photoprotective to some degree against the deleterious effects of further UVR exposure, but it does not significantly increase the SPF of individuals with light constitutive pigmentation or protect the DNA of their skin from UVR-induced damage (Kaidbey et al. 1979, Ortonne 2002). Although repeated exposure of tanned skin to UVR increases the number of metabolically active melanocytes and the intensity of melanogenesis (Lock-Anderson et al. 1998), the increased concentration of melanin in the tanned skin of inherently lightly pigmented people does not approach the photoprotection conferred by natural melanin in intrinsically darker-skinned people (Kaidbey et al. 1979). Individuals with lightly to moderately pigmented skin, who are repeatedly exposed to UVR, experience premature aging (photoaging) of the skin, which is characterized by wrinkling and anomalies of pigmentation (Chung 2001, Fisher et al. 2002, Kollias et al. 1991). This process is initiated by the photochemical generation of reactive oxygen species causing degradation of structural proteins in the dermis that confer strength and resiliency to the skin (Fisher et al. 2002).

Dermis

The dermis is a thick, dense fibroelastic connective tissue composed of collagen fibers, elastic fibers, and an interfibrillar gel composed of glycosaminoglycans, salts, and water. The primary cells of the dermis are collagen-rich fibroblasts. Collagen, which constitutes 77% of the fat-free dry weight of skin, largely accounts for the tensile strength of the skin's fabric and for some of the ability of the dermis to scatter visible light (Kollias 1995a, Shea & Parrish 1991). Interwoven with the collagen is a network of abundant elastic fibers that restore the skin to its normal configuration after stretching. The dermis is equally thick in people with dark or light constitutive pigmentation (Taylor 2002).

The dermis encloses a widely ramifying network of blood vessels, an extensive nerve network, sweat glands, and a pilosebaceous complex of hair follicles and sebaceous glands (Figure 1). Of these, only the sweat glands are addressed in detail in this review because of their importance in thermoregulation.

The rich vascular supply of the skin is responsible for supplying the needs of the sweat glands, hair follicles, and rapidly multiplying epidermal cells in the stratum basale. The density of cutaneous blood vessels varies throughout the body's surface and is related to temperature and blood pressure regulation and the relative amounts of intermittent physical pressure different parts of the body must withstand, with the highest concentrations found in the skin covering the head, nipples, palms, soles, and ischial tuberosities (Edwards & Duntley 1939). The perineal skin of female macaques, baboons, and chimpanzees is richly suffused with blood vessels (Montagna 1967, Montagna 1971) that create large sexual swellings advertising the female's state of reproductive receptivity and lifetime reproductive potential (Domb & Pagel 2001). The oxygenated and deoxygenated forms of hemoglobin carried in the skin's blood vessels are some of the skin's main pigments, with a person's skin color determined mainly by the skin's melanin and hemoglobin content (Edwards & Duntley 1939). The erythema or strongly red appearance of the skin caused by exposure to UVR is the result of increases in the number and diameter of vascular capillaries through which blood is flowing and an increase in the blood flow through each capillary (Kollias 1995a). Sunburned skin feels hot to the touch because of the increased vascularization of the skin and the inflammatory response mounted by the skin as it works to repair UVR-induced damage (Ryan 1991, Shea & Parrish 1991).

The nerve supply of the skin is highly complex because the skin is a major sensory surface that contains varied types of receptors sending signals to the central nervous system about the external environment and the internal state of the skin (Chu et al. 2003, Lynn 1991). These receptors include two types of temperature sensors, diverse mechanoreceptors associated with both hairy and glabrous skin, and an important group of cutaneous sensory cells (nociceptive afferents) specialized for the detection of tissue-threatening stimuli or the presence of injury or inflammation (Lynn 1991). The glabrous skin of the hands and feet of primates is densely packed with sensory nerve endings that permit highly sensitive tactile discrimination and exquisite differentiation of temperature and texture (Chu et al. 2003, Lynn 1991, Martin 1990). These attributes greatly enhance the manipulative functions of these appendages, especially the hand (Martin 1990).

Numerous hairs, which grow from hair follicles located in the dermis, are associated with mechanoreceptors and sebaceous glands. Hair performs a range of functions from insulation, to protection against the sun, enhancement of cutaneous sensation to communication of emotion (through piloerection), and ornamentation (Lavker et al. 2003; Montagna 1967, 1971; Wheeler 1984, 1985). Humans are unique among primates in possessing effectively naked skin, except on the scalp, the male chin, the axilla, and the groin. Although human skin bears millions of hairs, most of them are so small as to be nearly invisible (Montagna 1981).

SWEAT GLANDS   Human dermis contains two main types of sweat glands, eccrine and apocrine. The former are widely distributed throughout the surface of the body, whereas the latter are concentrated in the axilla, perineum, and external auditory canal. Eccrine glands are tubular in form (Figure 1) and lie in the outer portion of the dermis. They produce copious amounts of dilute, watery fluid expressed to the surface of the skin through an individual pore. Humans have two to four million eccrine glands on the surface of their bodies, with an average distribution ranging from $\sim$150–340/cm^2 (Folk & Semken 1991, Goldsmith 2003). Both apocrine and eccrine sweat glands are stimulated by the sympathetic division of the autonomic nervous system and produce sweat in response to thermal stimulation (thermal sweating). In contrast, the eccrine glands of the palms and soles respond only to emotional stimuli, whereas those of the face and axilla respond to both (Folk & Semken 1991, Zihlman & Cohn 1988).

Considerable attention has been placed on comparisons of the quantity, structure, and function of sweat glands between human groups. The number of strictly controlled comparisons between members of different populations after equivalent periods of deliberate acclimatization is quite small (Weiner 1977). The results of most rigorous comparative study of sweat gland densities in humans (Knip 1977) indicate that only small differences in the total number and average density of sweat glands exist between disparate human populations. As yet it has proven virtually impossible to design studies that can determine conclusively whether differences in sweating performance between human groups are due to genetic influences or environmental adaptations.

The Skin in Thermoregulation

Dissipation of heat is the function that most conspicuously distinguishes human skin from that of all other animals (Montagna 1981). The reasons for the evolution of this unique capacity are discussed in the following section. Humans encounter heat stress more or less year round in equatorial areas and for varying lengths of time in the rest of the world except for circumpolar and alpine environments. Heat stress is exacerbated by prolonged or rigorous exercise. Maintenance of homeostasis requires that the body's core temperature remain close to a neutral point, which varies from about 36.8 to 37.2°C, in order to permit uninterrupted functioning of the temperature-sensitive cells of the human central nervous system. If the rates of production or loss of heat are excessively out of balance, core temperature can quickly increase or decrease to dangerous levels (Kraning 1991, Wenger 2003).

Temperature regulation in humans includes involuntary (physiologic) and voluntary (behavioral) activity (Wenger 2003). Voluntary temperature regulation involves the conscious actions taken by people to maintain thermal comfort, including the seeking of shade and shelter, and the wearing or shedding of clothing.

Involuntary temperature regulation in the skin has been studied in great detail in the past 50 years by both physiologists and anthropologists, and only a superficial summary of this corpus of work is presented here. Regulation of temperature by the skin is accomplished through its roles in (a) perceiving and transmitting its own temperature to the central nervous system; (b) regulating heat transfer between the body's core and the skin through the cutaneous circulation; (c) serving as a superficial casing through which body heat is conducted from the vascular layers to the surface; (d) acting as an interface for the loss or gain of heat to or from the environment by radiation, convection, or conduction; and (e) acting as a surface for the spreading of sweat necessary for evaporative cooling (Frisancho 1981, Kraning 1991). The relative role of the four avenues of heat loss (radiation, convection, conduction, and evaporation) depends on the interaction of the ambient temperature and humidity (Chaplin et al. 1994; Frisancho 1981; Wenger 2003; Wheeler 1984, 1991b). The ability of sweat glands to respond to heat stress is adversely affected by sunburn (Pandolf et al. 1992). Protection of the integrity of sweat glands against damage caused by UVR, therefore, has been of great importance during the long course of human habitation of the tropics.

Experimental studies and simulations undertaken to determine how thermal homeostasis is maintained under the stressful environmental conditions of the tropics have shown that heat loss is maximized in people with a high ratio of skin surface area to body weight, such as Nilotic tribespeople, the Kung San, and Australian Aborigines (Frisancho 1981; Wheeler 1991a,b, 1992). This relationship supports Allen's Rule in mammals, which states that mammals living in cold regions will minimize the size and surface area of their extremities, whereas those inhabiting hot areas will increase the relative size of appendages.

The Role of the Skin in Vitamin D Biosynthesis

Synthesis of vitamin D in the skin of vertebrates is the only unanimously agreed positive effect of UVR exposure. Vitamin D_3 is the form of vitamin D that is synthesized by vertebrates, whereas vitamin D_2 is the primary form found in plants (Holick 2003). Vitamin D_3 is more accurately characterized as a prosteroid hormone than as a vitamin because, in mammals, it is derived from a cholesterol-like precursor (7-dehydrocholesterol) found in the skin (Holick 2003). Vitamin D is a unique natural product thought to have first occurred on Earth as a photosynthetic product in marine phytoplankton more than 750 mya (Holick 1995). Although the physiological role of vitamin D in plants and invertebrates is not clear, vitamin D was essential for the evolution of terrestrial vertebrates (Holick 1991, 1995).

Holick has reasoned that early tetrapods depended on vitamin D for the efficient use of scarce dietary calcium to preserve their rigid calcified skeletons (Holick 1995). Vitamin D can be synthesized only by a photochemical process, so early tetrapods could only satisfy their body's vitamin D requirements by exposing themselves to sunlight to photosynthesize vitamin D in their own skin or by ingesting foods containing vitamin D (Holick 1995).

Vitamin D_3 synthesized in the skin requires successive hydroxylations in the liver and kidney to be converted to its biologically active form, 1α, 25-dihydroxy-vitamin D_3 (Holick 1991, Jones et al. 1998). This functionally active form is important for the regulation of calcium and phosphorus metabolism, skeletal development and mineralization, the regulation of normal cell growth, and the inhibition of cancer cell growth (Holick 1991, 2001). The production of vitamin D_3 is optimally stimulated by UVR wavelengths of 295–300 nm, in the UVB range (MacLaughlin et al. 1982). High-energy UVB photons penetrate the skin and are absorbed by the 7-dehydrocholesterol in the keratinocytes of the epidermis (especially of the strata basale and spinosum) and fibroblasts of the dermis, catalyzing the formation of previtamin D_3 (Holick 2001, Webb et al. 1988). Once formed in the skin, previtamin D_3 can undergo isomerization to vitamin D_3 at body temperature and then undergo further chemical conversions to 1α, 25-dihydroxyvitamin D_3. The conversion of previtamin D_3 or vitamin D_3 to the functionally active form is rate-limited, however. In the presence of biologically sufficient amounts of 1α, 25-dihydroxyvitamin D_3 in the circulation, previtamin D_3 and vitamin D_3 are transformed by UVA or UVB into a variety of inert byproducts, thus averting overproduction of the biologically active form and subsequent "vitamin D intoxication" (Holick 2001, Holick et al. 1981). This finding disproves the hypothesis that dark constitutive skin pigmentation evolved in the tropics as an adaptation to protect against the overproduction of 1α, 25-dihydroxyvitamin D_3 (Loomis 1967).

Melanin pigments are highly effective at absorbing and scattering the UVB wavelengths that catalyze vitamin D_3 synthesis. Thus, high concentrations of melanin in the skin result in a decrease in the efficiency of conversion of 7-dehydrocholesterol to previtamin D_3; pigmentation slows but does not prevent cutaneous production of the vitamin (Holick et al. 1981, Webb et al. 1988). Individuals with very deep constitutive pigmentation often require 10 to 20 times longer exposure to sunlight than those of lighter pigmentation in order to promote an adequate synthesis of vitamin D_3 (Holick et al. 1981). This finding explains why dark-skinned individuals living at high latitudes with low levels of environmental UVB are at greater risk of vitamin D_3–deficiency diseases than are light-skinned people (Clemens et al. 1982, Holick 2001, Mitra & Bell 1997). The evolutionary significance of this observation is discussed further below. The photoconversion of 7-dehydrocholesterol to previtamin D_3 in the skin is also adversely affected by increasing age (Holick 1995), the wearing of clothing (Matsuoka et al. 1992), and by the use of topical sunscreens, which block the UVB wavelengths responsible for both sunburn and vitamin D_3 production (Holick 1997, Webb et al. 1988).

THE EVOLUTION OF MODERN HUMAN SKIN

Reconstruction of the evolution of human skin relies on evidence provided by comparative anatomy and physiology, as well as study of the evolution of the genes and gene complexes that determine the function and pigmentation of skin. Using basic principles of historical morphology, one can reconstruct the major steps in the evolution of human skin by utilizing a well-established phylogeny to examine historical transformations of structure and function (Jablonski & Chaplin 2000). This method leads to the reconstruction of the probable appearance of the skin in the last common ancestor of the human and chimpanzee lineages as being lightly pigmented and covered with dark hair, like most catarrhine primates today (Jablonski & Chaplin 2000).

The skin of modern humans is distinguished from that of other primates mainly by its naked appearance, its greatly enhanced abilities to dissipate body heat through sweating, and by the great range of genetically determined skin colors present within a single species. Most investigators have considered these attributes to be adaptations forged by natural selection.

The Evolution of the Thermoregulatory Properties of Human Skin

Human skin is not hairless, but—as discussed above—the hairs over most of the body's surface are so fine and present at a sufficiently low density that the skin appears essentially naked. Explanations for the evolution of human hairlessness have been many, varied, and often highly creative. The most cogent explanations are based on the importance of a functionally naked skin in maintaining body temperature in hot environments.

Many animals, including primates, which live in hot environments, have heavy coats of insulating fur or feathers. In the heat caused by strong sunlight, such insulation reduces environmental heat gain (Folk & Semken 1991, Walsberg 1988). This is the case even for black coats, which absorb short-wave radiation near or at the surface of the fur and reradiate large amounts of long-wave radiation before it reaches the skin (Dmi'el et al. 1980). The effectiveness of fur insulation in reducing environmental heat gain is lessened by sweating. The most efficient evaporative cooling occurs at the skin's surface; in heavily furred animals, water vapor is transferred through the fur to the atmosphere (Folk & Semken 1991). If the fur is wet from sweating, however, maximum evaporation occurs at the surface of the fur, and heat from the blood vessels cannot be transferred as efficiently to the site of evaporation (Folk & Semken 1991). Under these circumstances, much more water must be used for evaporative cooling. Thermal sweating as a method of cooling becomes more important as environmental temperatures rise or as activity levels increase because the lower gradient between core and environmental temperatures restricts the amount of heat loss that can be achieved by radiation, convection, and conduction (Frisancho 1981, Wheeler 1991b). Removal of excess heat is, therefore, greatly facilitated by the loss of body hair because it increases thermal conductance and permits additional heat loss through sweating (Wheeler 1985, Zihlman & Cohn 1988).

A strong case can be made for the evolutionary loss of apocrine sweat glands in humans because these sweat glands are most common in heavily furred animals (Folk & Semken 1991). The African apes exhibit a ratio of approximately 40% apocrine sweat glands to 60% eccrine; the great preponderance of eccrine sweat glands in modern humans probably evolved under the strong influence of natural selection, following the loss of the apocrine component to sweating (Folk & Semken 1991, Montagna 1981, Zihlman & Cohn 1988). This process was probably propelled by increases in body size and activity levels associated with modern limb proportions and striding bipedalism, which occurred in the transition from the primitive hominins of the late Miocene to the genus *Homo* of the Plio-Pleistocene (Chaplin et al. 1994; Folk & Semken 1991; Jablonski & Chaplin 2000; Montagna 1981; Schwartz & Rosenblum 1981; Wheeler 1984, 1996).

The importance of body cooling through the skin in modern humans has been emphasized repeatedly by both physiologists and anthropologists because of the primacy of preventing hyperthermia and attendant damage to the central nervous system (Cabanac & Caputa 1979, Falk 1990, Wheeler 1984, Zihlman & Cohn 1988). The temperature of the brain closely follows arterial temperature, requiring that the temperature of the circulating blood be carefully regulated (Nelson & Nunneley 1998). This process became increasingly important as activity levels and brain size increased in the genus *Homo* through the Pleistocene. Simulations and experimental studies have confirmed that maintenance of stable core temperature under conditions of increased environmental heat load or exercise is best accomplished via recruitment of a whole-body cooling system, involving cooling of peripheral blood vessels through sweating (Desruelle & Candas 2000, Nelson & Nunneley 1998). A recently mooted hypothesis that human hairlessness evolved late in human evolution as a result of the adoption of clothing and the need to reduce the load of external parasites (Pagel & Bodmer 2003) finds no support in light of the overwhelming evidence of the importance of hairlessness in thermal sweating and whole-body cooling in maintaining stable core temperature and homeostasis.

The Evolution of Human Skin Pigmentation

RECONSTRUCTION OF SKIN COLOR IN EARLY *HOMO*   The early members of the genus *Homo* from the late Pliocene and Early Pleistocene of Africa exhibited larger bodies, relatively larger brains, and relative longer lower limbs than did their australopithecine predecessors (McHenry & Berger 1998; Ruff et al. 1993, 1997). The higher activity levels and larger day ranges reconstructed for them (Wheeler 1991a, 1992) would have required that their skin be functionally naked and endowed with a high density of eccrine sweat glands in order to facilitate heat loss (Jablonski & Chaplin 2000, Wheeler 1984). This situation created a new physiological challenge for human skin: protection of a naked integument against

UVR. Dense hairy coats protect the skin of mammals from UVR-induced damage to the skin because the hairs themselves absorb or reflect most short-wavelength solar radiation. In mammals with sparse coats of hair, however, 3%–5% of incident UVR is transmitted to the skin (Walsberg 1988). Nonhuman mammals that are active in hot, sunny environments exhibit sparse coats because they facilitate passive heat loss; they also display highly melanized skin on their exposed (dorsal) surfaces to effectively block the UVR transmitted to the skin (Walsberg 1988). This evidence clearly indicates that hair loss in the human lineage was coupled with increased melanization of the skin as activity levels in hot environments increased. The early members of the genus *Homo*, the ancestral stock from which all later humans evolved, were, thus, darkly pigmented (Jablonski & Chaplin 2000). This interpretation has recently been supported by genetic evidence demonstrating that strong levels of natural selection acted about 1.2 mya to produce darkly pigmented skin in early members of the genus *Homo* (Rogers et al. 2004).

Heavily pigmented skin does not, in fact, perceptibly increase the body's heat load under conditions of intense solar radiation (Baker 1958, Walsberg 1988). This is because for half of the solar radiation reaching the Earth's surface—in the infrared—there is essentially no difference in absorption between dark and light skin (Baker 1958, Daniels 1964). This evidence negates the claim by Blum (1961) and others (Morison 1985) that heavily melanized pigmentation in humans could not be adaptive in the hot tropics because of the increased heat load caused by greater amounts of absorbed solar radiation.

SKIN PIGMENTATION IN MODERN HUMAN POPULATIONS   Many of the accounts of travelers and explorers from the fifteenth century onward include reports of the skin color of the peoples they encountered. As natural historians and human geographers—mostly from Europe—ventured into Asia, Africa, Australia, and the Americas and began to study the indigenous human populations in detail, maps depicting the worldwide distribution of human skin color were slowly assembled. The best known of these maps is that composed by the Italian geographer Renato Biasutti, which was based on the von Luschan skin color scale. This map has gained broad circulation in several widely distributed publications (Barsh 2003, Lewontin 1995, Roberts 1977, Walter 1971), despite the fact that, for areas with no data, Biasutti simply filled in the map by extrapolation from findings obtained in other areas (Robins 1991). A more accurate and exhaustive compilation of the skin colors of indigenous peoples based only on published skin reflectance measurements is now available (Jablonski & Chaplin 2000). Both maps show similar trends, with darkly pigmented peoples found near the Equator and incrementally lighter ones found closer to the Poles. A larger percentage of people with dark skin is found in the Southern Hemisphere as compared with the Northern Hemisphere (Relethford 1997) because of a latitudinal bias in the distribution of land masses (Chaplin & Jablonski 1998).

The data compiled by Jablonski and Chaplin also provide conclusive evidence of sexual dimorphism previously observed in human skin pigmentation (Frost

1988, van den Berghe & Frost 1986), with females being consistently lighter than males in all populations studied (Jablonski & Chaplin 2000).

One of the major problems encountered in assembling data on the distribution of human skin color in indigenous populations is determining exactly what an indigenous population represents. For most anthropologists and human geographers, an arbitrary cutoff date of 1500 has been adopted to distinguish native or indigenous peoples from immigrant populations. This date is reasonable with respect to the inauguration of the modern era of European colonization but fails to recognize the several major movements of human groups within continents (such as the so-called Bantu expansion within Africa) that occurred before 1500. These movements, along with European colonization and the increasingly rapid and distant migrations of human populations through time, have fundamentally altered the human landscape established in prehistoric times. This has made the interpretation of geographically and biologically significant trends in human populations much more difficult.

ENVIRONMENTAL CORRELATES OF HUMAN SKIN COLOR   The skin pigmentation of indigenous human populations shows remarkable regularity in its geographic distribution. Darker skins occur in more tropical regions and lighter skins in temperate, although the gradient is less intense in the New World as compared to the Old World. Even within Africa, the continent with the largest equatorial land mass, there is considerable heterogeneity of skin color, with the deepest colors occurring not in the lowest latitudes but in the open grasslands (Chaplin 2001, Roberts 1977). The strong latitudinal signal in skin color led most early workers to conclude that skin pigmentation represented an adaptation to sunlight or other solar-driven phenomena such as temperature. Walter (1958, 1971) was the first researcher to suggest that the pigmentation gradient observed was linked to the intensity of UVR, and he established this relationship by calculation of correlation coefficients between skin color (as measured on the von Luschan scale) and estimated UVR. The relationship between skin color and environment was further explored by studies in which the relationship of skin color, as measured by reflectance spectrometry, to latitude, temperature, and humidity was studied by correlation and regression analyses (Roberts 1977, Roberts & Kahlon 1976). These analyses showed the dominant association of skin reflectance with latitude, which was then deduced to be an effect related to the intensity of UVR (Roberts 1977, Roberts & Kahlon 1976).

In recent years, studies of the relationships between morphological and physiological variation and attributes of the physical environment have been advanced by the availability of remotely sensed data on levels of UVR, total solar radiation, temperature, humidity, precipitation, and other environmental variables at the Earth's surface. These data, which were not widely available to workers before 1990, have permitted correlation, regression, and other analyses of skin reflectance to be conducted against actual measurements, rather than estimates, of environmental variables (Chaplin 2001, 2004; Jablonski & Chaplin 2000).

Using data on the minimal erythemal dose of UVR (UVMED) at the Earth's surface collected by the NASA TOMS 7 satellite, Jablonski & Chaplin were able to establish a conclusive correlation between latitude and annual average UVMED, and thence between annual average UVMED and skin reflectance (Jablonski & Chaplin 2000). This publication was followed by a study in which the influence of minimum, maximum, and seasonal levels of UVR, as well as other directly measured environmental variables, relative to skin reflectance were studied (Chaplin 2001, Chaplin 2004). This study showed that skin reflectance was correlated with autumn levels of UVMED, and that skin reflectance could be almost fully modeled as a linear effect of this variable alone (Chaplin 2001, 2004). This study also showed that the relationship between summer levels of UVMED and skin reflectance appeared to reach a threshold past which higher levels of UVR were not correlated with incrementally lower skin reflectance (darker pigmentation) (Chaplin 2001, 2004).

Low reflectance values for human skin (dark pigmentation) are primarily a function of UVMED (Jablonski & Chaplin 2000), with regression analysis demonstrating that autumn UVMED levels have the strongest effect. This indicates that skin color is more strongly correlated with UVA, which is consistently higher throughout the year at all latitudes, than with UVB (Chaplin 2001, 2004). Maximum UVMED had the next most significant effect (Chaplin 2001, 2004). Winter levels of precipitation have the opposite effect, being positively correlated with high reflectance values (light pigmentation) (Chaplin 2001, 2004). Multiple regression formulae relating skin reflectance to these environmental parameters can then be used to derive a map of predicted human skin colors, with the colors shown being realistic approximations of the true color of skin (Chaplin 2001, 2004) (Figure 3, see color insert). This map depicts an idealized situation in which humans worldwide are assumed to have inhabited their respective regions for the same lengths of time, and have followed similar cultural practices that could affect skin color (e.g., diet, activity schedules, use of clothing and shelter).

NATURAL SELECTION AND THE EVOLUTION OF HUMAN SKIN PIGMENTATION   The geographical distribution of human skin colors has invited many explanations, most of which have claimed melanin pigmentation to be an adaptation to some attribute of the physical environment that varies primarily by latitude. Ever since the harmful effects of UVR began to be appreciated by scientists, explanations for the evolution of deeply melanized skin have centered on the importance of resistance to sunburn, solar degeneration, and skin cancer (Daniels et al. 1972). Equally popular has been the vitamin D hypothesis, which stated that lightly pigmented skins were necessary outside of the tropics in order to permit vitamin D biosynthesis in the skin by low levels of UVR, whereas darkly pigmented skin afforded protection against production of toxic doses of vitamin D in equatorial regions (Loomis 1967). Lightly pigmented skin has also been explained as an adaptation to resist cold injury, on the basis of experimental and epidemiological data that have documented more severe injuries incurred by pigmented skin exposed to freezing conditions (Post et al. 1975, Steegmann 1967). Other explanations have imputed highly melanized skin as providing effective concealment in habitats such as tropical forests with differing light intensities and environmental illumination (Cowles 1959, Morison 1985), and still others have reasoned that tropical diseases and parasites rather than tropical climate were the major selective forces leading to the evolution of differential pigmentation in humans (MacKintosh 2001; Wassermann 1981, 1965a).

Although adaptive explanations for human pigmentation have dominated the literature, others have downplayed or discounted the role of adaptation by natural selection. Some workers have emphasized the role of sexual selection, especially by way of explaining the lighter constitutive pigmentation of females relative to males (Aoki 2002, Frost 1988). Deol claimed that differences in skin color between human populations were the pleiotropic byproducts of natural selection on other functions of pigmentation genes (Deol 1975). Others have simply discouraged the "amusing pastime" of adaptive reconstruction in the absence of data on the differential survival and reproduction of varying skin pigmentation phenotypes (Blum 1961, Lewontin 1995). Adaptive explanations "for" any given phenotypic trait require demonstration that the trait increases the real or probable reproductive success of the organism. Although such evidence is often difficult to muster in the case of traits borne by long-lived mammals, it is incumbent that adaptive reconstructions be tethered by this responsibility.

In the past, adaptive explanations for different levels of melanin pigmentation in human skin have suffered from an inability to demonstrate probable or real differences in survivorship and reproduction of different skin color phenotypes under the same environmental conditions. Blum introduced this mode of critical appraisal of competing hypotheses when he drew attention to the fact that dark skin pigmentation could not have evolved primarily as adaptive protection against skin cancer because such cancers rarely cause death during peak reproductive years (Blum 1961, Jablonski & Chaplin 2000). Other adaptive explanations for light or dark skin pigmentation (e.g., protection against cold injury; camouflage) have similarly failed to demonstrate real or probable increases in reproductive success as a result of possession of these phenotypes.

MELANIN AS A REGULATOR OF THE PENETRATION OF UVR INTO THE SKIN Recently, Jablonski & Chaplin (2000) published a new adaptive hypothesis for the evolution of human skin pigmentation stating that melanin pigmentation evolved to regulate the penetration of UVR into the skin in order to prevent the photolysis of photo-labile compounds while permitting the photosynthesis of others. This hypothesis was based on two equally important observations: (*a*) that the B vitamin folate is destroyed by long wavelength UVR (UVA), and that folate deficiencies can markedly reduce individual reproductive success by adversely affecting cell division; and (*b*) that vitamin D_3 is synthesized in the skin by short wavelength UVR (UVB) and that severe vitamin D deficiencies adversely affect reproductive success by interfering with normal calcium metabolism (Jablonski & Chaplin

2000). Natural selection has produced two opposing clines of skin pigmentation. The first is a cline of photoprotection that grades from darkly pigmented skin at the Equator to lightly pigmented skin near the Poles. The second is a cline of vitamin D_3 photosynthesis that grades from lightly pigmented near the Poles to darkly pigmented at the Equator. In the middle of the two clines we find peoples with enhanced abilities to develop facultative pigmentation according to seasonal UVR levels.

THE FOLATE HYPOTHESIS   The potential importance of dark skin pigmentation in protecting folate from UVR-induced photolysis was first recognized upon discovery that folate undergoes photolysis in vitro when subjected to UVA (360 nm) and that serum folate levels of human subjects dramatically declined when humans underwent long-term exposure (minimum of 3 months) to the same wavelength, for 30–60 min once or twice a week (Branda & Eaton 1978). The potential significance of the finding to the evolution of human skin pigmentation was echoed later, but a causal mechanism was not mooted (Zihlman & Cohn 1988).

Few nutrients compare with folate (folic acid) for its impact on health. Adequate folate status is vital for the synthesis, repair, and expression of DNA, and therefore for all processes involved in cell division and homeostasis (Kesavan et al. 2003, Lucock et al. 2003, Suh et al. 2001). The subtle influence of folate on the cell's genomic machinery has led to the realization that even marginal folate deficiencies may have significance in developmental disorders and degenerative diseases associated with high morbidity and mortality (Lucock et al. 2003). Now that folate deficiency is widely acknowledged as a risk factor for neural tube defects, recurrent early pregnancy loss, and other complications of pregnancy, the maintenance of adequate folate status in women of reproductive age has become a primary public health concern (Bower & Stanley 1989, Fleming & Copp 1998, Minns 1996, Suh et al. 2001). Folate's importance in spermatogenesis also highlights its important role in maintaining male reproductive competence (Cosentino et al. 1990, Mathur et al. 1977).

The recognition of folate's pivotal roles in DNA synthesis and repair—and thus most processes associated with reproductive success in both sexes—has underlined the importance of protecting the body's folate stores from physical or chemical degradation. Because folate is susceptible to oxidative damage as a result of exposure to UVR and ionizing radiation (Branda & Eaton 1978, Hirakawa et al. 2002, Kesavan et al. 2003), the primary evolutionary function of melanin in regions receiving high annual UVR is to protect folate from photodegradation (Jablonski & Chaplin 2000). Photolysis of folate has been experimentally demonstrated at 340 nm and 312 nm, in the UVA and near-UVA wavelengths (Hirakawa et al. 2002, Lucock et al. 2003). With skin reflectance being most closely correlated with autumn levels of UVMED dominated by UVA, one can conclude that the longer wavelengths of UVR, which are capable of penetrating deep into the dermis of the skin, have been the most important agents of natural selection in connection with the evolution of skin pigmentation (Chaplin 2001) (Figure 4). The results of

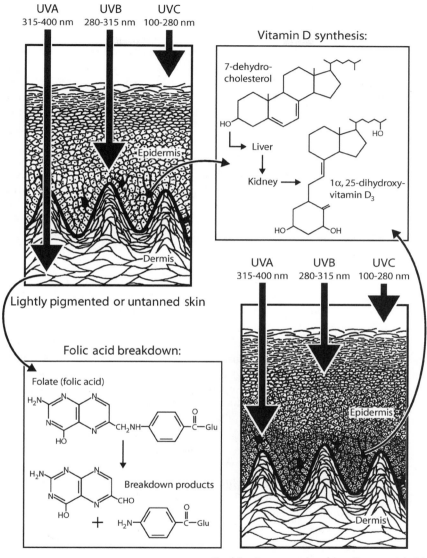

Figure 4 The effects of UV radiation on the skin. Different wavelengths of UVR penetrate to different thicknesses in the skin, with UVA penetrating more deeply than UVB. UVC generally does not penetrate the Earth's atmosphere.

a recent study (Gambichler et al. 2001) did not confirm the photolytic effect of UVA on serum folate levels in a small number of human volunteers. This finding runs counter to the results of previous in vivo and in vitro studies demonstrating profound photodegradation of folate upon exposure to UVR (Hirakawa et al. 2002, Lucock et al. 2003) and to X- and γ-irradiation (Kesavan et al. 2003). A true and statistically robust test of the folate hypothesis would require a case-control study involving a large number of human volunteers experiencing long-term (once or twice a week for a minimum of three months) exposure to UVR, with measurement of more labile folate species such as specific red cell folate coenzymes (Lucock et al. 2003).

SKIN PIGMENTATION AND VITAMIN D BIOSYNTHESIS   In the millennia prior to about 1.6 mya, the earliest members of the genus *Homo* appear to have been restricted in their distribution to the high-UVR regimes of equatorial Africa. Under these environmental conditions, possession of highly melanized skin was critical for survival. As populations of early *Homo* moved both northward and southward, they began to experience different schedules and intensities of UVR exposure.

UVR levels at the Earth's surface are affected by latitude, altitude, season, moisture content, cloud cover, the depth of the ozone column, orbital parameters, and other factors (Hitchcock 2001, Madronich et al. 1998). Short wavelength UVR (UVB, 280–315 nm) is more effectively absorbed by atmospheric ozone than are longer wavelengths (UVA, 315–400). Thus, as one moves away from the Equator and the angle of solar elevation decreases, the thickness of the atmosphere (including the ozone layer), through which sunlight must pass, increases. This results in a greater attenuation of UVR, especially of UVB, by scattering and absorption by ozone, and consequently very low levels of UVB in high-latitude ecosystems (Caldwell et al. 1998). Very small increments or decrements of UVB lead to substantial biological effects (Madronich et al. 1998); thus, it is highly biologically significant that regions north and south of 50° latitude receive only tiny doses of UVB, and only then at the peak of summer (Caldwell et al. 1998, Chaplin 2001, Johnson et al. 1976, Neer 1985).

As discussed earlier, deeply melanized skin confers excellent protection against the deleterious effects of UVR, but it also greatly slows the process of vitamin D_3 synthesis in the skin. As hominins moved out of the tropics, their exposure to UVR—especially to vitamin D–inducing UVB—was dramatically reduced. Levels of UVR at the Earth's surface are not thought to have been appreciably different in the Pleistocene as compared to today because similar conditions of solar emissivity and orbital parameters existed at the time, and similar levels of UVR have been reconstructed from biological proxies (Rozema et al. 2002). Even before remotely sensed data on UVB levels outside of the tropics were available, theorists surmised that early humans living in high latitudes with deeply pigmented skin would have not been able to produce sufficient vitamin D_3 in their skin to meet their physiological demands and that strong selective pressure for depigmentation of the skin had been exerted in order to facilitate photosynthesis of vitamin D_3 (Loomis 1967, Murray 1934, Neer 1975).

Using known values of UVMED at the Earth's surface (Herman & Celarier 1996) and the precise dosage of UVB necessary to catalyze vitamin D synthesis in human skin at a specific latitude (Webb et al. 1988), researchers can calculate the worldwide potential for vitamin D_3 synthesis for lightly pigmented skin (Jablonski & Chaplin 2000) (Figure 5, see color insert). Zone 1 (shown without hachure in Figure 5) corresponds closely to the tropics and represents an area in which there is adequate UVR throughout the year to catalyze vitamin D_3 synthesis in the skin (Jablonski & Chaplin 2000). Zone 2 (area covered by vertical hachure in Figure 5) represents the region in which there is insufficient UVR during at least one month of the year to produce vitamin D_3, and Zone 3 (cross-hatched area of Figure 5) represents that in which there is insufficient UVR, as averaged over the entire year, to photosynthesize vitamin D_3 in the skin (Jablonski & Chaplin 2000). The configuration of vitamin D synthesis zones for darkly pigmented skin differs markedly from this depiction, with Zone 1 being greatly reduced in area, and Zones 2 and 3 significantly expanded because of the attenuation of UVB absorption by dark melanin pigmentation and concomitant prolongation of the length of UVB exposure required for vitamin D_3 biosynthesis (Jablonski & Chaplin 2000). This analysis clearly demonstrates the profound impact of constitutive pigmentation on the potential for vitamin D_3 synthesis in the skin. An empirical demonstration of this was recently provided by a school population of darkly pigmented and albino children in South Africa, in which the former group of children required a significantly higher dietary intake of vitamin D_3 to attain the same levels of vitamin D_3 and plasma calcium than did the albinos (Cornish et al. 2000). The importance of the synthesis and physiological activity of vitamin D have been further born out by studies of the worldwide polymorphism in the vitamin D–binding protein (or group-specific component, Gc) that show a clear relationship between the frequency of specific Gc alleles and levels of sunlight (OMIM 2003).

Vitamin D_3 insufficiency and deficiency can exert sinister effects on the body throughout life and have the demonstrated potential to reduce fitness when they afflict children and adolescents. The most serious and notorious of the vitamin D_3–deficiency diseases is rickets, caused by a failure of mineralization in the cartilaginous matrix of developing bones as a result of calcium and phosphate malabsorption (Shaw 2003, Wharton & Bishop 2003). Comprehensive clinical descriptions of rickets (Bereket 2003, Holick 1995, Shaw 2003, Wharton & Bishop 2003) catalog the devastating osseous and nonosseous effects of the disease on children and adolescents, including the delayed closure of fontanelles, bowing of the lower limb bones, and narrowing of the pelvic outlet in females, which can cause obstructed labor and a high incidence of infant and maternal morbidity and mortality. Vitamin D_3 deficiency in adults produce osteomalacia, a softening of the bone matrix, but inadequate vitamin D_3 status in pregnant women contributes to hypocalcemia and rickets in their babies (Wharton & Bishop 2003). The deleterious effects of vitamin D_3 deficiency encompass a suite of problems affecting evolutionary fitness, including those involving the formation and maintenance of the skeleton, control of normal cell growth, inhibition of cancerous cell growth, and maintenance of normal immune system function (Grant 2002; Holick 1991, 2001; Wharton & Bishop 2003). An important, but little reported consequence of vitamin D deficiency in laboratory mice and rats is a marked reduction in female fertility and female reproductive failure apparently due to failure of vitamin D to interact normally with its receptor on the ovary (Jones et al. 1998).

An abundance of clinical and epidemiological evidence now supports the argument that depigmentation of the skin evolved in humans living outside of the tropics because of the importance of maintaining adequate vitamin D_3 production in the skin for as long as possible throughout the year. Alterations in the function of the vitamin D endocrine system in darkly pigmented people as a consequence of diminished exposure to sunlight result in vitamin D_3 insufficiency and deficiency, as recently reviewed elsewhere (Mitra & Bell 1997, Wharton & Bishop 2003). These problems potentially afflict dark-skinned people who have migrated to or who inhabit UVB-poor regions (e.g., northern Europe, the northern United States, or Canada) or darkly pigmented people living in sunny regions who habitually stay indoors or consistently wear concealing clothing when outdoors (Atiq et al. 1998, Bereket 2003, Brunvand & Haug 1993, Fogelman et al. 1995, Fonseca et al. 1984, Gessner et al. 1997, Hodgkin et al. 1973, Holick 1995, Wharton & Bishop 2003). In these populations, vitamin D_3 deficiency is exacerbated by breast feeding because of the low concentration of vitamin D_3 in human breast milk (Gessner et al. 1997, Shaw 2003, Wharton & Bishop 2003).

Vitamin D_3 insufficiency and deficiency also afflict lightly pigmented people who are not exposed to sufficient sunlight because of occupation, advanced age, or hospitalization, or people who consistently wear protective clothing or sunscreen when outdoors (Holick 1995, 1997, 2001; Thomas et al. 1998). Rickets (known to many as the English disease) was, in fact, first recognized as a disease of light-skinned children living in dark, multistoried structures devoid of sunlight (Holick 1991, 1995).

Brace (1963) argues that depigmentation of human skin occurred not as the result of active selection for lighter pigmentation, but because of the relief of selective pressure on pigmentary systems as humans populated increasingly high latitudes where dark pigmentation was no longer required as a shield against UVR. This structural reduction hypothesis is based on the "probable mutation effect" whereby mutations in the genes controlling melanin pigmentation would accumulate, leading to reduction of or failure to produce melanin (Brace 1963). A recent variation on this argument states that where natural selection for dark skin is sufficiently weak, a sexual preference for lighter skin could have driven the evolution of light skin (Aoki 2002, Ihara & Aoki 1999) (see below also). These arguments find limited support today with respect to the evolution of human skin coloration in light of the impressive body of recent clinical evidence cited above that attests to the many and highly significant functions of vitamin D_3 in humans, which directly impact human health and reproductive competence.

Strong natural selection for vitamin D_3 production in human skin was likely a powerful factor influencing the evolution of skin pigmentation in human populations at high latitudes. Preliminary study of the distribution of paleontological and archaeological sites for the genus *Homo* in relationship to the vitamin D_3 synthesis zones described above indicates that year-round hominin habitation of Zone 3, i.e., latitudes generally higher than 50°, occurred only after human populations had developed the technological competence to harvest fish, marine mammals, or other sources of food [such as reindeer lichen, or reindeer meat, organs, or milk (Bjorn & Wang 2000)] rich in vitamin D_3 (N. Jablonski, G. Chaplin & D. Tyler, manuscript in preparation). This capability is associated almost primarily with Upper Paleolithic peoples, living approximately 15,000–10,000 years ago, who are known to have made extensive use of fish hooks, fish traps, nets, harpoons, and other implements for the harvesting of marine animals.

SEXUAL DIMORPHISM IN HUMAN SKIN COLOR   The observation that females exhibit lighter skin pigmentation than do males in all populations examined (Jablonski & Chaplin 2000, van den Berghe & Frost 1986) has invited speculation that the phenomenon may be due to infantile mimicry, sexual selection, or a combination of both factors (Aoki 2002, Frost 1988, Ihara & Aoki 1999, van den Berghe & Frost 1986). These hypotheses are based on the observations that the attraction of human infants and human females is partly due to their lighter pigmentation, and that lighter-colored adult females are perceived as more feminine than are darker females, and therefore are preferred as partners (Frost 1988). Jablonski & Chaplin (2000) have advanced the idea that sexual dimorphism in skin pigmentation is primarily due to natural selection, on the basis of the need of females to maximize cutaneous vitamin D_3 production in order to meet their absolutely higher calcium requirements of pregnancy and lactation. Also, darker pigmentation may have been the object of natural selection in males because of the importance of maintaining optimal levels of folate in order to safeguard sperm production, a process dependent on folate for DNA synthesis (G. Chaplin, personal communication). Sexual selection is thus considered to have played a role in increasing the disparity in skin color between the sexes in some societies through preference for more lightly pigmented females, but this was not its ultimate cause (Jablonski & Chaplin 2000).

TANNING AND BLEACHING   The temporary development of increased melanin pigmentation through exposure to UVR is called facultative pigmentation or tanning. Individuals with very light constitutive pigmentation (skin phototypes I and II) never tan or tan minimally, whereas those with moderate to dark constitutive pigmentation (phototypes V and VI) tan profusely (Taylor 2002). Considerable variation in tanning potential exists even between people with ostensibly very similar levels of constitutive pigmentation (Lee & Lasker 1959). Tanning develops in two stages (immediate and delayed) over the course of several hours or days, depending on the wavelength and duration of UVR exposure (Ortonne 1990). Exposure to UVA causes tanning to develop quickly (Ortonne 1990), possibly as an adaptation to protect against photodegradation of essential biomolecules. Facultative pigmentation is probably most important in areas such as the circum-Mediterranean that receive low levels of UVB but receive moderate levels of UVA that cause photodegradation of folate, DNA, and vitamin D_3.

The practice of recreational tanning has been eschewed by health care workers in the past 20 years because of the explosion in skin cancer rates due to increased UVR exposure. A tanned skin is still viewed by many as fashionable or as a sign of well-being, however, and this positive image has spurred the development of a simulated tanning industry in Europe, the Americas, and Australia (Brown 2001, Randle 1997).

In many countries, however, tanned or dark skin does not connote membership in a fashionable class, and the possession of light skin—especially among women—was and still is viewed as highly desirable and indicative of higher social standing. In many Asian countries, most women practice sun avoidance diligently. In other countries where constitutive pigmentation is darker, skin-bleaching agents (including potent topical corticosteroids and hydroquinone formulations) have become popular (Taylor 2002).

THE MULTIFACTORIAL DETERMINATION OF SKIN PIGMENTATION IN MODERN HUMANS   The evolution of skin pigmentation in humans has been determined by many factors (Figure 6). By far the most important of these is the UVR regime of the environment because intensity of UVR has been the main selective factor influencing the evolution of melanin pigmentation in the skin. Through time, the number of factors influencing the evolution of human skin pigmentation has increased, and culture clearly has reduced the scope for the action of natural selection on human skin. Cultural behaviors such as the wearing of clothes and the utilization of shelter have become more common through time and have affected the evolution of skin pigmentation in some populations because of their effects of reducing an individual's UVR exposure. Related to this phenomenon is the length of time that a population has inhabited an area with a particular UVR regime and the latitudinal distance traversed from the ancestral to the new homeland. There is certainly a considerable lag time between the time of settlement of an area and time that a population reaches its "optimum" skin color for the UVR conditions of the area. The length of that lag period for any population is not known but would depend on the intensity of natural selection exerted on the population by environmental influences. In early prehistory, humans possessed a simpler material culture, spent considerable time accumulating food, and had fewer cultural trappings to buffer themselves against the environment. Under these conditions, natural selection would have promoted mainly biological adaptations to the environment—including changes in skin coloration, body proportions, and regulation of thermal cooling. With increasing cultural competence over time, cultural solutions to the environmental challenges of sun, heat, and cold became preeminent. The oft-cited example of the skin colors of the native populations of equatorial South America is worth revisiting in this connection. These populations have long been recognized

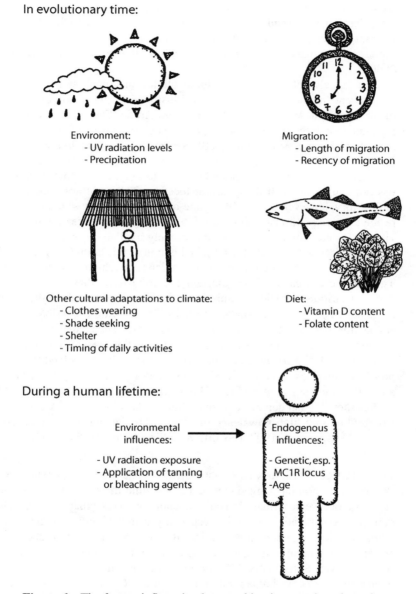

Figure 6 The factors influencing human skin pigmentation, through evolutionary time and during the course of a human lifetime.

as being more lightly pigmented than are their counterparts at similar latitudes and altitudes in the Old World (Frisancho 1981, Jablonski & Chaplin 2000). This fact is almost certainly due to the recency of populations' migration into South America from Asia (within the past 10,000–15,000 years) and the fact that the immigrant populations into South America possessed many cultural behaviors and accoutrements that protected them from high UVR exposure (Jablonski & Chaplin 2000).

Diet has also played a part in the evolution of human skin pigmentation in very recent human history, as is well illustrated by the Eskimo-Aleut peoples of the northeast Asian and North American Arctic. Eskimo-Aleuts exhibit skin pigmentation darker than would be predicted on the basis of the UVMED in their habitats (Jablonski & Chaplin 2000). Several factors have likely contributed to this phenomenon, including the relative recency of their migration to the far north from a lower-latitude Asian homeland and its implication that their skin color has not caught up with their current location. This is almost certainly not the entire story, however. The UVR regime of the latitudes in which Eskimo-Aleuts reside comprises almost exclusively UVA throughout the year, with virtually no vitamin D–inducing UVB except for extremely small doses in the summer months (Chaplin 2001, Johnson et al. 1976). Habitation of this latitude (Figure 5, Zone 3) by humans would be impossible without reliance on a highly vitamin D–rich diet. The major components of the aboriginal Eskimo-Aleut diet—marine mammals, fish, and caribou—provide vitamin D_3 in abundance. Much of the dietary vitamin D_3 is stored in body fat (Mawer et al. 1972), denoting a possible evolutionary connection between the development of generous subcutaneous fat stores and vitamin D_3 storage in these populations. With selection pressure on depigmentation apparently relaxed because of diet, Eskimo-Aleuts have evolved darker skin to protect themselves from high levels of UVA as a result of direct solar irradiation and reflection from snow and ice. This scenario is supported by epidemiological studies showing that departure from traditional diets in Eskimo-Aleut populations has resulted in a high prevalence of vitamin D_3–deficiency diseases, especially rickets (Gessner et al. 1997, Haworth & Dilling 1986, Moffatt 1995).

THE GENETICS OF HUMAN SKIN COLORATION   The study of genetics of human skin pigmentation has lagged considerably behind the study of the diversity and causation of diverse human skin color phenotypes. This situation is now changing rapidly as comparative genomics, especially detailed studies of the genes regulating coat color pigmentation in mice (Barsh 1996, Sturm et al. 2001), begin to permit identification of the genes responsible for the pigmentation of human hair, skin, and eyes. Sixty of the 127 currently recognized pigmentation genes in the mouse appear to have human orthologs (Bennett 2003).

Human skin pigmentation has long been considered a polygenic trait that follows a quasi-Mendelian pattern of inheritance (Brues 1975, Byard 1981, Byard & Lees 1981), with a few major genes of dramatic effect and additional modifier genes (Sturm et al. 2001). Because pigmentation is a trait determined by the synchronized interaction of various genes with the environment (John et al. 2003), determination of the relative roles of variant genes and varying environments has proven extremely challenging (Sturm et al. 1998). Classical genetic studies of in-heritance of human skin coloration have shed little light on the molecular basis of skin color variation, beyond showing that interbreeding between light and dark skin color phenotypes produces offspring of intermediate pigmentation (Robins 1991; Sturm et al. 1998, 2001). As a result of recent advances in the understand-ing of the chemistry and enzymology of the biosynthesis of melanins, the genetic regulation of the many steps in melanin production is now beginning to be under-stood. Among the numerous mutations affecting melanocyte function in human populations are the *P*-gene and members of the *TYRP* and *SILV* gene families, which direct the assembly and maturation of melansomes within melanocytes (Sturm et al. 2001). Investigation of the influence of these genes on skin pigmen-tation phenotypes is just beginning (Akey et al. 2001), however, and it remains to be demonstrated whether polymorphism in these gene systems correlates with pigmentary differences between populations.

To date, the greatest scholarly attention has been focused on the melanocortin-1 receptor (*MC1R*) gene, which is the human homologue of the *Agouti* locus that in mice regulates the production of the eumelanin and pheomelanin pigments of the coat (Barsh 1996, Rana et al. 1999). In humans, the synthesis of eumelanin is stimulated by the binding of α-melanotropin (α-melanocyte-stimulating hormone) to the functional *MC1R* expressed on melanocytes (Scott et al. 2002). The *MC1R* appears to be one of the major genes involved in the determination of human hair and skin pigmentation, with *MC1R* polymorphisms in northern European popula-tions associated with red hair and fair skin, reduced tanning ability, and high risk of melanoma and nonmelanoma skin cancer (Healy et al. 2001, Scott et al. 2002, Smith et al. 1998). The *MC1R* locus is characterized by high levels of polymor-phism in light-skinned individuals outside of Africa and lower levels of variation in dark-skinned individuals within Africa (John et al. 2003, Rana et al. 1999). This is opposite the pattern observed in most other loci, where Africans are most polymorphic (Shriver et al. 1997). The observed pattern of variation in the *MC1R* suggests that different selective pressures among individuals with dark and light skin have shaped the genetic variation at this locus, with functional constraints operating to limit variation in African populations (John et al. 2003). The numer-ous *MC1R* polymorphisms in light-skinned individuals were originally thought to denote relaxation of selection for production of eumelanin outside of tropical latitudes (Harding et al. 2000). A reinterpretation of these data indicates, however, that adaptive evolution for sun-resistant *MC1R* alleles began when humans first became hairless in tropical Africa, and that human movement into the less sunny climes of Eurasia favored any mutant *MC1R* allele that did not produce dark skin (Rogers et al. 2004). Recent study of the *MC1R* promoter function casts doubt on the relaxation hypothesis and suggests instead the possible action of purifying or diversifying selection on some *MC1R* variants in Asian and Europeans (Makova et al. 2001). A study comparing populations in southern Africa of Bantu-language speakers and San people showed some variation in *MC1R* sequences, but investigators concluded that although some MC1R mutants are tolerated in Africa, this gene has been the object of purifying selection and has played an important role in the maintenance of dark pigmentation in Africans (John et al. 2003). The presence of higher levels of *MC1R* variation in dark-skinned populations subjected to lower levels of UVR in southern Africa (as compared to equatorial Africa) supports the notion that number and kinds of *MC1R* variants are strongly influenced by purifying selection (John et al. 2003). Further genetic studies of more African populations are needed to determine if the great diversity of skin color observed in populations in sub-Saharan Africa (Relethford 2000) can be related to specific patterns of *MC1R* or other polymorphisms that evolved in response to the region's considerable heterogeneity of UVR and precipitation regimes (Chaplin 2001).

The study of the genetics of human skin pigmentation is still in infancy, and much remains to be learned about the levels, effects, and interactions of polymorphisms in the loci influencing skin color phenotype. The production of eumelanin is under strong functional constraint as a result of natural selection in regions of the world with high levels of UVR (Sturm et al. 2001), and there is increasing evidence that at least *MC1R* variation is an adaptive response to selection for different alleles in different environments (Makova et al. 2001, Sturm et al. 2001). From what is known of the timing and nature of movements of groups of early *Homo* species and of *Homo sapiens* in prehistory, it appears that populations of humans have moved in and out of regions with different UVR regimes over the course of thousands of years. This finding would suggest that natural selection would have favored the evolution of dark and light skin pigmentation in disparate places at different times, resulting in the independent evolution of dark and light skin phenotypes and possibly involving recurrent episodes of repigmentation and depigmentation (Jablonski & Chaplin 2000). This phenomenon would have been pronounced in the early history of the genus *Homo* (including the early history of *Homo sapiens*) when cultural buffers against the environment were less effective and sophisticated.

SKIN COLOR AND RACE   Skin color is the most obvious visible attribute of the human body. It has been the primary characteristic used to classify people into purportedly genetically distinct geographic groups or "races." The biological basis of skin pigmentation in humans, however, strongly argues against its use as a diagnostic classificatory trait. Critical examination of the distribution of skin color phenotypes in humans leads to the conclusion that skin pigmentation is adaptive, and its evolution in specific populations has been strongly influenced by the environmental conditions (the UVR regimes, in particular) of specific places. Highly adaptive phenotypic characteristics of organisms are of little use in classification because they are subject to homoplasy (parallelism or convergent evolution) and are extremely labile. Emerging genetic evidence indicates that the evolution of pigmentation genes has been driven by purifying and diversifying selection working to produce adaptive responses in different environments (Makova et al. 2001,

Rogers et al. 2004, Sturm et al. 2001). This evidence indicates that similar skin colors have evolved independently in human populations inhabiting similar environments. Darkly or lightly pigmented skin, therefore, provides evidence only about the nature of the past environments in which people have lived, rendering skin pigmentation useless as a marker for membership in a unique group or "race."

The continued social importance of skin color in human affairs reflects a high degree of sensitivity to skin color, brought about by historic and complex cultural attitudes toward skin colors (Ehrlich & Feldman 1969, Lewontin 1995, Parra et al. 2003). The apparent existence of a difference between so-called human races and subgroups is predicated on an exaggerated perception and heightened sensitivity to a visually obvious attribute of human appearance. The enormity of this bias is revealed when the small amounts of actual genetic variation within purported racial groups are revealed (Lewontin 1995, Marks 2002). Overall, human populations are remarkably similar to one another, with the greatest fraction of human variation being accounted for by differences between individuals (Lewontin 1972, 1995; Marks 2002). This collective evidence militates that the concept of biological race be abandoned and publicly disavowed (Lewontin 1995, Marks 2002, Muir 1993). Race thus emerges as a cultural construct devoid of explanatory power and destructive of human and social relations (Lewontin 1972, 1995; Muir 1993).

PROSPECTUS

The past decade has witnessed a tremendous advance in the understanding of the evolution of human skin and especially skin color, largely as a result of two phenomena. First is availability of remotely sensed environmental data that permit hypotheses about the adaptive value of properties of skin to be thoroughly tested. Second is the proliferation of studies of the molecular genetics of the skin color that are permitting new insight into the origins of skin color phenotypes and the mechanisms by which they have evolved. Growth is anticipated in both of these areas, and great potential exists for their interaction, in particular for the testing of hypotheses of adaptation through the simultaneous and detailed study of patterns of phenotypic, genotypic, and environmental variation, such as has been done in the study of butterfly pigmentation (Watt et al. 2003). The study of the evolution of human skin and skin color will also be advanced by the documentation of differential survival of well-defined phenotypes and genotypes in different environmental regimes through the use of epidemiological data, as has been undertaken recently in the study of geographic patterns of melanoma (Garland et al. 2003).

Continued study of the evolution of human skin and skin color is important not only to our realization of a more complete picture of human evolution, but also it is important because the skin is involved in so many aspects of human well-being. Many humans now live in regions far distant from their ancestral homelands, but they retain a covering of skin adapted to remote Pleistocene conditions. As is evidenced by modern rates of skin cancer and vitamin D deficiencies, human behavior and culture are not perfect buffers against the effects of these major translocations. An appreciation of the many roles of skin will improve human health and attitudes toward diversity and will promote the fundamental understanding of why it is that people look the way they do.

ACKNOWLEDGMENTS

Conversations and discussions with many colleagues in the months and years leading up to the writing of this review greatly enriched the content of this paper. These include Walter Alvarez, Carol Boggs, Carol Bower, C. Loring Brace, Jim Cleaver, Paul Ehrlich, Roberto Frisancho, Cedric Garland, Maciej Henneberg, the late Gabriel Lasker, Charles Oxnard, Bill Nye, Lynn Rothschild, Donald Tyler, and Ward Watt. I thank Rachel Wolf for helping to assemble references. Figures 1, 2, 3, and 6 were produced by Jennifer Kane, whom I thank for her skillful renderings and patient revisions. I thank George Chaplin for producing Figures 4 and 5, and for more than ten years worth of challenging and inspiring discussions on the evolution of human skin and skin coloration. The spatial analyses and maps summarized here were made possible by generous donations of geographical information systems software to the California Academy of Sciences from Charles Convis and the Conservation Program of the Environmental Systems Research Institute (ESRI).

The *Annual Review of Anthropology* is online at http://anthro.annualreviews.org

LITERATURE CITED

Akey JM, Wang H, Xiong M, Wu H, Liu W, et al. 2001. Interaction between the melanocortin-1 receptor and P genes contributes to inter-individual variation in skin pigmentation phenotypes in a Tibetan population. *Hum. Genet.* 108:516–20

Aoki K. 2002. Sexual selection as a cause of human skin colour variation: Darwin's hypothesis revisited. *Ann. Hum. Biol.* 29:589–608

Atiq M, Suria A, Qamaruddin Nizami S, Ahmed I. 1998. Maternal vitamin-D deficiency in Pakistan. *Acta Obstet. Gynecol. Scand.* 77:970–73

Baker PT. 1958. Racial differences in heat tolerance. *Am. J. Phys. Anthropol.* 16:287–305

Barker D, Dixon K, Medrano EE, Smalara D, Im S, et al. 1995. Comparison of the responses of human melanocytes with different melanin contents to ultraviolet B irradiation. *Cancer Res.* 55:4041–46

Barsh G. 1996. The genetics of pigmentation:

from fancy genes to complex traits. *Trends Genet.* 12:299–305

Barsh GS. 2003. What controls variation in human skin color? *Public Libr. Sci. Biol.* Oct. 1(1):E27

Bennett DC. 2003. IL-12. The colours of mice and men—100 genes and beyond? *Pigment Cell Res.* 16:576–77

Bereket A. 2003. Rickets in developing countries. In *Vitamin D and Rickets*, ed. Z Hochberg, pp. 220–32. Basel: Karger

Bjorn LO, Wang T. 2000. Vitamin D in an ecological context. *Int. J. Circumpolar. Health* 59:26–32

Blum HF. 1961. Does the melanin pigment of human skin have adaptive value? *Q. Rev. Biol.* 36:50–63

Bower C, Stanley FJ. 1989. Dietary folate as a risk factor for neural-tube defects: evidence from a case-control study in Western Australia. *Med. J. Aust.* 150:613–19

Brace CL. 1963. Structural reduction in evolution. *Am. Nat.* 97:39–49

Branda RF, Eaton JW. 1978. Skin color and nutrient photolysis: an evolutionary hypothesis. *Science* 201:625–26

Brown DA. 2001. Skin pigmentation enhancers. See Goldsmith 1991, pp. 637–75

Brues AM. 1975. Rethinking human pigmentation. *Am. J. Phys. Anthropol.* 43:387–92

Brunvand L, Haug E. 1993. Vitamin D deficiency amongst Pakistani women in Oslo. *Acta Obstet. Gynecol. Scand.* 72:264–68

Byard PJ. 1981. Quantitative genetics of human skin color. *Yearb. Phys. Anthropol.* 24:123–37

Byard PJ, Lees FC. 1981. Estimating the number of loci determining skin colour in a hybrid population. *Ann. Hum. Biol.* 8:49–58

Cabanac M, Caputa M. 1979. Natural selective cooling of the human brain: evidence of its occurrence and magnitude. *J. Physiol.* 286:255–64

Caldwell MM, Bjorn LO, Bornman JF, Flint SD, Kulandaivelu G, et al. 1998. Effects of increased solar ultraviolet radiation on terrestrial ecosystems. *J. Photochem. Photobiol. B.* 46:40–52

Chaplin G. 2001. *The geographic distribution of environmental factors influencing human skin colouration.* M.Sc. thesis, Manchester Metropolitan Univ.

Chaplin G. 2004. Geographical distribution of environmental factors influencing skin coloration. *Am. J. Phys. Anthropol.* 123:In press

Chaplin G, Jablonski NG. 1998. Hemispheric difference in human skin color. *Am. J. Phys. Anthropol.* 107:221–24

Chaplin G, Jablonski NG, Cable NT. 1994. Physiology, thermoregulation and bipedalism. *J. Hum. Evol.* 27:497–510

Chu DH, Haake AR, Holbrook K, Loomis CA. 2003. The structure and development of skin. See Freedberg et al. 2003, pp. 58–88

Chung JH. 2001. The effects of sunlight on the skin of Asians. See Goldsmith 1991, pp. 69–90

Cleaver JE, Crowley E. 2002. UV damage, DNA repair and skin carcinogenesis. *Front. Biosci.* 7:1024–43

Clemens TL, Henderson SL, Adams JS, Holick MF. 1982. Increased skin pigment reduces the capacity of skin to synthesise vitamin D_3. *Lancet* 1:74–76

Cornish DA, Maluleke V, Mhlanga T. 2000. An investigation into a possible relationship between vitamin D, parathyroid hormone, calcium and magnesium in a normally pigmented and an albino rural black population in the Northern Province of South Africa. *BioFactors* 11:35–38

Cosentino MJ, Pakyz RE, Fried J. 1990. Pyrimethamine: an approach to the development of a male contraceptive. *Proc. Natl. Acad. Sci. USA* 87:1431–35

Cowles RB. 1959. Some ecological factors bearing on the origin and evolution of pigment in the human skin. *Am. Nat.* 93:283–93

Daniels F. 1964. Man and radiant energy: solar radiation. In *Adaptation to the Environment*, ed. DB Dill, EF Adolph, CG Wilber, pp. 969–85. Washington, DC: Am. Physiol. Soc.

Daniels F, Post PW, Johnson BE. 1972. Theories of the role of pigment in the evolution of human races. In *Pigmentation: Its Genesis and Biologic Control*, ed. V Riley, pp. 13–22. New York: Appleton-Century-Crofts

Deol MS. 1975. Racial differences in pigmentation and natural selection. *Ann. Hum. Genet. London* 38:501–3

Desruelle AV, Candas V. 2000. Thermoregulatory effects of three different types of head cooling in humans during a mild hyperthermia. *Eur. J. Appl. Physiol.* 81:33–39

Dmi'el R, Prevulotzky A, Shkolnik A. 1980. Is a black coat in the desert a means of saving metabolic energy? *Nature* 283:761–62

Domb LG, Pagel M. 2001. Sexual swellings advertise female quality in wild baboons. *Nature* 410:204–6

Edwards EA, Duntley Q. 1939. The pigments and color of living human skin. *Am. J. Anat.* 65:1–33

Ehrlich PR, Feldman SS. 1969. *The Race Bomb: Skin Color, Prejudice, and Intelligence.* New

York: Quadrangle/N.Y. Times Book Co. 207 pp.

Elias PM, Feingold KR, Fluhr JW. 2003. Skin as an organ of protection. See Freedberg et al. 2003, pp. 107–18

Ellis RA, Montagna W. 1962. The skin of primates. VI. The skin of the gorilla (*Gorilla gorilla*). *Am. J. Phys. Anthropol.* 20:79–93

Falk D. 1990. Brain evolution in *Homo*: the "radiator" theory. *Behav. Brain Sci.* 13:333–81

Feldman D, Glorieux FH, Pike JW, eds. 1997. *Vitamin D*. San Diego: Academic

Fisher GJ, Kang S, Varani J, Bata-Csorgo Z, Yinsheng W, et al. 2002. Mechanisms of photoaging and chronological skin aging. *Arch. Dermatol.* 138:1462–70

Fitzpatrick TB. 1988. The validity and practicality of sun reactive skin type I through VI. *Arch. Dermatol.* 124:869–71

Fitzpatrick TB, Becker SW Jr, Lerner AB, Montgomery H. 1950. Tyrosinase in human skin: demonstration of its presence and of its role in human melanin formation. *Science* 112:223–25

Fitzpatrick TB, Seiji M, McGugan AD. 1961. Melanin pigmentation. *New Engl. J. Med.* 265:328–32

Fitzpatrick TR, Ortonne J-P. 2003. Normal skin color and general considerations of pigmentary disorders. See Freedberg et al. 2003, pp. 819–25

Fleming A, Copp AJ. 1998. Embryonic folate metabolism and mouse neural tube defects. *Science* 280:2107–9

Fogelman Y, Rakover Y, Luboshitsky R. 1995. High prevalence of vitamin D deficiency among Ethiopian women immigrants to Israel: exacerbation during pregnancy and lactation. *Isr. J. Med. Sci.* 31:221–24

Folk GEJ, Semken HAJ. 1991. The evolution of sweat glands. *Int. J. Biometeor.* 35:180–86

Fonseca V, Tongia R, El-Hazmi M, Abu-Aisha H. 1984. Exposure to sunlight and vitamin D deficiency in Saudi Arabian women. *Postgrad. Med. J.* 60:589–91

Freedberg IM, Eisen AZ, Wolff K, Austen FK, Goldsmith LA, Katz SI, eds. 2003. *Fitz-patrick's Dermatology in General Medicine*. New York: McGraw-Hill

Frisancho AR. 1981. *Human Adaptation: A Functional Interpretation*. Ann Arbor: Univ. Mich. Press. 209 pp.

Frost P. 1988. Human skin color: a possible relationship between its sexual dimorphism and its social perception. *Perspect. Biol. Med.* 32:38–59

Gambichler T, Sauermann K, Bader A, Altmeyer P, Hoffmann K. 2001. Serum folate levels after UVA exposure: a two-group parallel randomised controlled trial. *BMC Dermatol.* 1(1):8

Garland CF, Garland FC, Gorham ED. 2003. Epidemiologic evidence for different roles of ultraviolet A and B radiation in melanoma mortality rates. *Ann. Epidemiol.* 13:395–404

Gessner BD, deSchweinitz E, Petersen KM, Lewandowski C. 1997. Nutritional rickets among breast-fed black and Alaska native children. *Alaska Med.* 39:72–87

Giacomoni PU, ed. 2001. *Sun Protection in Man*. Amsterdam: Elsevier

Goldsmith LA, ed. 1991. *Physiology, Biochemistry, and Molecular Biology of the Skin*. New York: Oxford Univ. Press

Goldsmith LA. 2003. Biology of eccrine and apocrine sweat glands. See Freedberg et al. 2003, pp. 99–106

Grant WB. 2002. An estimate of premature cancer mortality in the U.S. due to inadequate doses of solar ultraviolet-B radiation. *Cancer* 94:1867–75

Halaban R, Hebert DN, Fisher DE. 2003. Biology of melanocytes. See Freedberg et al. 2003, pp. 127–47

Harding RM, Healy E, Ray AJ, Ellis NS, Flanagan N, et al. 2000. Evidence for variable selective pressures at MC1R. *Am. J. Hum. Genet.* 66:1351–61

Haworth JC, Dilling LA. 1986. Vitamin-D-deficient rickets in Manitoba, 1972–84. *Can. Med. Assoc. J.* 134:237–41

Healy E, Jordan SA, Budd PS, Suffolk R, Rees JL, Jackson IJ. 2001. Functional variation of MCR1 alleles from red-haired individuals. *Hum. Mol. Genet.* 10:2397–402

Herman J, Celarier E. 1996. TOMS Version 7 UV-erythemal exposure: 1978–1993. Data developed by NASA Goddard Space Flight Cent. Ozone Process. Team

Hirakawa K, Suzuki H, Oikawa S, Kawanishi S. 2002. Sequence-specific DNA damage induced by ultraviolet A-irradiated folic acid via its photolysis product. *Arch. Biochem. Biophys.* 410:261–28

Hitchcock RT. 2001. *Ultraviolet Radiation.* Fairfax, VA: Am. Ind. Hyg. Assoc. 49 pp.

Hodgkin P, Kay GH, Hine PM, Lumb GA, Stanbury SW. 1973. Vitamin-D deficiency in Asians at home and in Britain. *Lancet* 2:167–72

Holick MF. 1991. Photobiology, physiology, and clinical applications for vitamin D. See Goldsmith 1991, pp. 928–56

Holick MF. 1995. Environmental factors that influence the cutaneous production of vitamin D. *Am. J. Clin. Nutr.* 61:638S–45

Holick MF. 1997. Photobiology of vitamin D. See Feldman et al. 1997, pp. 33–39

Holick MF. 2001. A perspective on the beneficial effects of moderate exposure to sunlight: bone health, cancer prevention, mental health and well being. See Goldsmith 1991, pp. 11–37

Holick MF. 2003. Vitamin D: a millenium perspective. *J. Cell Biochem.* 88:296–307

Holick MF, MacLaughlin JA, Doppelt SH. 1981. Regulation of cutaneous previtamin D_3 photosynthesis in man: Skin pigment is not an essential regulator. *Science* 211:590–93

Ihara Y, Aoki K. 1999. Sexual selection by male choice in monogamous and polygynous human populations. *Theor. Popul. Biol.* 55:77–93

Ito S. 2003. A chemist's view of melanogenesis. *Pigment Cell Res.* 16:230–36

Jablonski NG, Chaplin G. 2000. The evolution of skin coloration. *J. Hum. Evol.* 39:57–106

Jimbow K, Fitzpatrick TB, Wick MM. 1991. Biochemistry and physiology of melanin pigmentation. See Goldsmith 1991, pp. 873–909

Jimbow K, Quevedo WC Jr, Fitzpatrick TB, Szabo G. 1976. Some aspects of melanin biol-

ogy: 1950–1975. *J. Invest. Dermatol.* 67:72–89

John PR, Makova K, Li WH, Jenkins T, Ramsay M. 2003. DNA polymorphism and selection at the melanocortin-1 receptor gene in normally pigmented southern African individuals. *Ann. N.Y. Acad. Sci.* 994:299–306

Johnson FS, Mo T, Green AES. 1976. Average latitudinal variation in ultraviolet radiation at the Earth's surface. *Photochem. Photobiol.* 23:179–88

Jones G, Strungnell SA, DeLuca HF. 1998. Current understanding of the molecular actions of vitamin D. *Physiol. Rev.* 78:1193–231

Kaidbey KH, Agin PP, Sayre RM, Kligman AM. 1979. Photoprotection by melanin—a comparison of black and Caucasian skin. *Am. Acad. Dermatol.* 1:249–60

Kesavan V, Pote MS, Batra V, Viswanathan G. 2003. Increased folate catabolism following total body y-irradiation in mice. *J. Radiat. Res.* 44:141–44

Kielbassa C, Roza L, Epe B. 1997. Wavelength dependence of oxidative DNA damage induced by UV and visible light. *Carcinogenesis* 18:811–16

Knip AS. 1977. Ethnic studies on sweat gland counts. In *Physiological Variation and its Genetic Basis*, ed. JS Weiner, pp. 113–23. London: Taylor & Francis

Kollias N. 1995a. The physical basis of skin color and its evaluation. *Clin. Dermatol.* 13:361–67

Kollias N. 1995b. The spectroscopy of human melanin in pigmentation. In *Melanin: Its Role in Human Photoprotection*, ed. L Zeise, MR Chedekel, TB Fitzpatrick, pp. 11–22. Overland Park: Valdenmar

Kollias N, Sayre RM, Zeise L, Chedekel MR. 1991. Photoprotection by melanin. *J. Photochem. Photobiol. B.* 9:135–60

Kraning KK. 1991. Temperature regulation and the skin. See Goldsmith 1991, pp. 1085–95

Kripke ML, Applegate LA. 1991. Alterations in the immune response by ultraviolet radiation. See Goldsmith 1991, pp. 1222–39

Lasker GW. 1954. Seasonal changes in skin color. *Am. J. Phys. Anthropol.* 12:553–38

Lavker RM, Bertolino A, Freedberg IM, Sun T-T. 2003. Biology of hair follicles. See Freedberg et al. 2003, pp. 148–58

Lee MMC, Lasker GW. 1959. The sun-tanning potential of human skin. *Hum. Biol.* 31:252–60

Lees FC, Byard PJ. 1978. Skin colorimetry in Belize. I. Conversion formulae. *Am. J. Phys. Anthropol.* 48:515–22

Lewontin RC. 1972. The apportionment of human diversity. *Evol. Biol.* 6:381–98

Lewontin RC. 1995. *Human Diversity*: Freeman

Lock-Anderson J, Knudstorp ND, Wulf HC. 1998. Faculative skin pigmentation in caucasians: an objective biological indicator of lifetime exposure to ultraviolet radiation? *Br. J. Dermatol.* 138:826–32

Loomis WF. 1967. Skin-pigment regulation of vitamin-D biosynthesis in man. *Science* 157:501–6

Lucock M, Yates Z, Glanville T, Leeming R, Simpson N, Daskalakis I. 2003. A critical role for B-vitamin nutrition in human development and evolutionary biology. *Nutr. Res.* 23:1463–75

Lynn B. 1991. Cutaneous sensation. See Goldsmith 1991, pp. 779–815

MacKintosh JA. 2001. The antimicrobial properties of melanocytes, melanosomes and melanin and the evolution of black skin. *J. Theor. Biol.* 211:101–13

MacLaughlin JA, Anderson RR, Holick MF. 1982. Spectral character of sunlight modulates photosynthesis of previtamin D_3 and its photoisomers in human skin. *Science* 216:1001–3

Madronich S, McKenzie RL, Bjorn LO, Caldwell MM. 1998. Changes in biologically active ultraviolet radiation reaching the Earth's surface. *J. Photochem. Photobiol. B.* 46:5–19

Makova K, Ramsay M, Jenkins T, Li W-H. 2001. Human DNA sequence variation in a 6.6-kb region containing the melanocortin 1 receptor promoter. *Genetics* 158:1253–68

Marks J. 2002. *What It Means to be 98% Chimpanzee: Apes, People, and Their Genes.* Berkeley: Univ. Calif. Press. 312 pp.

Marks R. 1991. Mechanical properties of the skin. See Goldsmith 1991

Martin RD. 1990. *Primate Origins and Evolution: A Phylogenetic Perspective.* Princeton, NJ: Princeton Univ. Press. 804 pp.

Mathur U, Datta SL, Mathur BB. 1977. The effect of aminopterin-induced folic acid deficiency on spermatogenesis. *Fertil. Steril.* 28:1356–60

Matsuoka LY, Wortsman J, Dannenberg MJ, Hollis BW, Lu Z, Holick MF. 1992. Clothing prevents ultraviolet-B radiation-dependent photosynthesis of vitamin D_3. *J. Clin. Endocrinol. Metabol.* 75:1099–103

Mawer EB, Backhouse J, Holman CA, Lumb GA, Stanbury SW. 1972. The distribution and storage of vitamin D and its metabolites in human tissues. *Clin. Sci.* 43:413–31

McHenry HM, Berger LR. 1998. Body proportions in *Australopithecus afarensis* and *A. africanus* and the origin of the genus *Homo. J. Hum. Evol.* 35:1–22

Minns RA. 1996. Folic acid and neural tube defects. *Spinal Cord* 34:460–65

Mitra D, Bell NH. 1997. Racial, geographic, genetic, and body habitus effects on vitamin D metabolism. See Feldman et al. 1997, pp. 521–32

Moffatt MEK. 1995. Current status of nutritional deficiencies in Canadian Aboriginal people. *Can. J. Physiol. Pharmacol.* 73:754–58

Montagna W. 1967. Comparative anatomy and physiology of the skin. *Arch. Dermatol.* 96:357–63

Montagna W. 1971. Cutaneous comparative biology. *Arch. Dermatol.* 104:577–91

Montagna W. 1981. The consequences of having a naked skin. *Birth Defects: Orig. Artic. Ser.* 17:1–7

Morison WL. 1985. What is the function of melanin? *Arch. Dermatol.* 121:1160–63

Muir DE. 1993. Race: the mythic root of racism. *Sociol. Inq.* 63:339–50

Murray FG. 1934. Pigmentation, sunlight, and nutritional disease. *Am. Anthropol.* 36:438–45

Neer RM. 1975. The evolutionary significance of vitamin D, skin pigment, and ultraviolet light. *Am. J. Phys. Anthropol.* 43:409–16

Neer RM. 1985. Environmental light: effects of vitamin D synthesis and calcium metabolism in humans. *Ann. N.Y. Acad. Sci.* 453:14–20

Nelson DA, Nunneley SA. 1998. Brain temperature and limits on transcranial cooling in humans: quantitative modeling results. *Eur. J. Appl. Physiol.* 78:353–59

Odland GF. 1991. Structure of the skin. See Goldsmith 1991, pp. 3–62

Olivier G. 1960. *Pratique Anthropolgique.* Paris: Vigot Fréres

Online Mendelian Inheritance in Man. 2003. *139200 group-specific component; GC. In *Online Mendelian Inheritance in Man.* Bethesda, MD: Natl. Cent. Biotechnol. Inf.

Ortonne J-P. 1990. Pigmentary changes of the ageing skin. *Br. J. Dermatol.* 122:21–28

Ortonne J-P. 2002. Photoprotective properties of skin melanin. *Br. J. Dermatol.* 146:7–10

Pagel M, Bodmer W. 2003. A naked ape would have fewer parasites. *Proc. R. Soc. London B* 270:S117–19

Pandolf KG, Gange RW, Latzka WA, Blank IH, Kraning KK, Gonzalez RR. 1992. Human thermoregulatory responses during heat exposure after artificially induced sunburn. *Am. J. Physiol.* 262:R610–16

Parker F. 1981. The biology of pigmentation. *Birth Defects* 17:79–91

Parra FC, Amado RC, Lambertucci JR, Rocha J, Antunes CM, Pena SDJ. 2003. Color and genomic ancestry in Brazilians. *Proc. Natl. Acad. Sci. USA* 100:177–82

Post PW, Daniels F Jr, Binford RT Jr. 1975. Cold injury and the evolution of "white" skin. *Hum. Biol.* 47:65–80

Prota G. 1992a. Melanin-producing cells. See Prota 1992b, pp. 14–33

Prota G, ed. 1992b. *Melanins and Melanogenesis.* San Diego: Academic

Prota G. 1992c. Photobiology and photochemistry of melanogenesis. See Prota 1992b, pp. 208–24

Quevedo WC Jr, Fitzpatrick TB, Pathak MA. 1975. Role of light in human skin color variation. *Am. J. Phys. Anthropol.* 43:393–408

Rana BK, Hewett-Emmett D, Jin L, Chang BH, Sambuughin N, et al. 1999. High polymorphism at the human melanocortin 1 receptor locus. *Genetics* 151:1547–57

Randle HW. 1997. Suntanning: differences in perceptions throughout history. *Mayo Clin. Proc.* 72:461–66

Rawles ME. 1948. Origin of melanophores and their role in development of color patterns in vertebrates. *Physiol. Res.* 28:383–408

Relethford JH. 1997. Hemispheric difference in human skin color. *Am. J. Phys. Anthropol.* 104:449–57

Relethford JH. 2000. Human skin color diversity is highest in sub-Saharan African populations. *Hum. Biol.* 72:771–80

Roberts DF. 1977. Human pigmentation: its geographical and racial distribution and biological significance. *J. Soc. Cosmet. Chem.* 28:329–42

Roberts DF, Kahlon DPS. 1976. Environmental correlations of skin colour. *Ann. Hum. Biol.* 3:11–22

Robins AH. 1991. *Biological Perspectives on Human Pigmentation.* Cambridge: Cambridge Univ. Press. 253 pp.

Rogers AR, Iltis D, Wooding S. 2004. Genetic variation at the MC1R locus and the time since loss of human body hair. *Curr. Anthropol.* 45:105–7

Rozema J, van Geel B, Bjorn LO, Lean J, Madronich S. 2002. Toward solving the UV puzzle. *Science* 296:1621–22

Ruff CB, Trinkaus E, Holliday TW. 1997. Body mass and encephalization in Pleistocene *Homo.* *Nature* 387:173–76

Ruff CB, Trinkaus E, Walker A, Larsen CS. 1993. Postcranial robusticity in *Homo.* I: Temporal trends and mechanical interpretation. *Am. J. Anthropol.* 91:21–53

Ryan TJ. 1991. Cutaneous circulation. See Goldsmith 1991, pp. 1019–84

Sarna T, Swartz HM. 1998. The physical properties of melanins. In *The Pigmentary System: Physiology and Pathophysiology*, ed. JJ

Nordlund, RE Boissey, VJ Hearing, pp. 333–57. New York: Oxford Univ. Press

Schwartz GG, Rosenblum LA. 1981. Allometry of primate hair density and the evolution of human hairlessness. *Am. J. Phys. Anthropol.* 55:9–12

Scott MC, Suzuki I, Abdel-Malek ZA. 2002. Regulation of the human melanocortin 1 receptor expression in epidermal melanocytes by paracrine and endocrine factors and by ultraviolet radiation. *Pigment Cell Res.* 15: 433–39

Shaw NJ. 2003. Vitamin D deficiency rickets. In *Vitamin D and Rickets*, ed. Z Hochberg, pp. 93–104. Basel: Karger

Shea CR, Parrish JA. 1991. Nonionizing radiation and the skin. See Goldsmith 1991, pp. 910–27

Shono S, Imura M, Ota M, Ono S, Toda K. 1985. The relationship of skin color, UVB-induced erythema, and melanogenesis. *J. Invest. Dermatol.* 84:265–67

Shriver MD, Jin L, Ferrell RE, Deka R. 1997. Microsatellite data support an early population expansion in Africa. *Genome Res.* 7: 586–89

Smith RM, Healy E, Siddiqui S. 1998. Melanocortin 1 receptor variants in an Irish population. *J. Invest. Dermatol.* 111:119–22

Steegmann AT Jr. 1967. Frostbite of the human face as a selective force. *Hum. Biol.* 39:131–44

Sturm RA. 2002. Skin colour and skin cancer—*MC1R*, the genetic link. *Melanoma Res.* 12:405–16

Sturm RA, Fox NF, Ramsay M. 1998. Human pigmentation genetics: the difference is only skin deep. *BioEssays* 20:712–21

Sturm RA, Teasdale RD, Fox NF. 2001. Human pigmentation genes: identification, structure and consequences of polymorphic variation. *Gene* 277:49–62

Suh JR, Herbig AK, Stover PJ. 2001. New perspectives on folate catabolsim. *Annu. Rev. Nutr.* 21:255–82

Sulaimon SS, Kitchell BE. 2003. The biology of melanocytes. *Vet. Dermatol.* 14:57–65

Szabo G, Gerald AB, Pathak MA, Fitzpatrick TB. 1969. Racial differences in the fate of melanosomes in human epidermis. *Nature* 222:1081–82

Taylor SC. 2002. Skin of color: biology, structure, function, and implications for dermatologic disease. *J. Am. Acad. Dermatol.* 46:S41–62

Thody AJ, Higgins EM, Wakamatsu K, Ito S, Burchill SA, Marks JM. 1991. Pheomelanin as well as eumelanin is present in human epidermis. *J. Invest. Dermatol.* 97:340–44

Thody AJ, Smith AG. 1977. Hormones and skin pigmentation in the mammal. *Int. J. Dermatol.* 16:657–64

Thomas MK, Lloyd-Jones DM, Thadhani RI, Shaw AC, Deraska DJ, et al. 1998. Hypovitaminosis D in medical inpatients. *New Engl. J. Med.* 338:777–83

Urbach F. 2001. The negative effects of solar radiation: a clinical overview. See Goldsmith 1991, pp. 39–67

van den Berghe PL, Frost P. 1986. Skin color preference, sexual dimorphism and sexual selection: a case of gene-culture coevolution? *Ethnic Rac. Stud.* 9:87–113

Vermeer M, Schmieder GJ, Yoshikawa T, van den Berg J-W, Metzman MS, et al. 1991. Effects of ultraviolet B light on cutaneous immune responses of humans with deeply pigmented skin. *J. Invest. Dermatol.* 97:729–34

von Luschan F. 1897. *Beitrage zur Volkerkunde der Deutschen Schutzgebieten.* Berlin: Deutsche Buchgemeinschaft

Wagner JK, Parra EJ, Norton HL, Jovel C, Shriver MD. 2002. Skin responses to ultraviolet radiation: effects of constitutive pigmentation, sex, and ancestry. *Pigment Cell Res.* 15:385–90

Walsberg GE. 1988. Consequences of skin color and fur properties for solar heat gain and ultraviolet irradiance in two mammals. *J. Comp. Physiol. B* 158:213–21

Walter H. 1958. Der zusammenhang von hautfarbenverteilung und intensitat der ultravioletten strahlung. *Homo* 9:1–13

Walter H. 1971. Remarks on the environmental adaptation of man. *Humangenetik* 13:85–97

Wassermann GD. 1981. On the nature of the theory of evolution. *Philos. Sci.* 48:416–37

Wassermann HP. 1965a. The circulation of melanin—its clinical and physiological significance. *S. Afr. Med. J.* 39:711–16

Wassermann HP. 1965b. Human pigmentation and environmental adaptation. *Arch. Environ. Health* 11:691–94

Wassermann HP. 1974. *Ethnic Pigmentation.* New York: Blackwell Sci. 284 pp.

Watt WB, Wheat CW, Meyer EH, Martin J-F. 2003. Adaptation at specific loci. VII. Natural selection, dispersal and the diversity of molecular-functional variation patterns among butterfly species complexes (*Colias*: Lepidoptera, Pieridae). *Mol. Ecol.* 12:1265–75

Webb AR, Kline L, Holick MF. 1988. Influence of season and latitude on the cutaneous synthesis of vitamin D_3: Exposure to winter sunlight in Boston and Edmonton will not promote vitamin D_3 synthesis in human skin. *J. Clin. Endocrinol. Metabol.* 67:373–78

Weiner JS. 1951. A spectrophotometer for measurement of skin colour. *Man* 51:152–53

Weiner JS. 1977. Variation in sweating. In *Physiological Variation and its Genetic Basis*, ed. JS Weiner, pp. 125–37. London: Taylor & Francis

Wenger BC. 2003. Thermoregulation. See Freedberg et al. 2003, pp. 119–26

Westerhof W, Estevez-Uscanga O, Meens J, Kammeyer A, Durocq M, Cario I. 1990. The relation between constitutional skin color and photosensitivity estimated from UV-induced erythema and pigmentation dose-response curves. *J. Invest. Dermatol.* 94:812–16

Wharton B, Bishop N. 2003. Rickets. *Lancet* 362:1389–400

Wheeler PE. 1984. The evolution of bipedality and loss of functional body hair in hominids. *J. Hum. Evol.* 13:91–98

Wheeler PE. 1985. The loss of functional body hair in man: the influence of thermal environment, body form and bipedality. *J. Hum. Evol.* 14:23–28

Wheeler PE. 1991a. The influence of bipedalism on the energy and water budgets of early hominids. *J. Hum. Evol.* 21:117–36

Wheeler PE. 1991b. The thermoregulatory advantages of hominid bipedalism in open equatorial environments: the contribution of increased convective heat loss and cutaneous evaporative cooling. *J. Hum. Evol.* 21:107–15

Wheeler PE. 1992. The thermoregulatory advantages of large body size for hominids foraging in savannah environments. *J. Hum. Evol.* 23:351–62

Wheeler PE. 1996. The environmental context of functional body hair loss in hominids (a reply to Amaral, 1996). *J. Hum. Evol.* 30:367–71

Young AR, Sheehan J. 2001. UV-induced pigmentation in human skin. See Goldsmith 1991, pp. 357–75

Zihlman AL, Cohn BA. 1988. The adaptive response of human skin to the Savanna. 3:397–409

Annu. Rev. Anthropol. 2004. 33:625–49
doi: 10.1146/annurev.anthro.33.070203.144008

TALK AND INTERACTION AMONG CHILDREN AND THE CO-CONSTRUCTION OF PEER GROUPS AND PEER CULTURE

Amy Kyratzis

*Gervitz Graduate School of Education, University of California, Santa Barbara,
California 93106; email: Kyratzis@education.ucsb.edu*

Key Words   peer talk, strategic language, identity, language socialization, social
organization

■ **Abstract**   According to recent interpretive approaches to the study of children's
socialization, meaning creation is an active process by which children playfully transform and actively resist cultural categories, and where language is viewed as social
action that helps shape reality (Gaskins et al. 1992). Four ways in which children's
peer talk establishes and maintains peer culture are considered: (*a*) how children elaborate games and codes (and ritualize the basis of inclusion in the peer group) through
peer talk, (*b*) how conflict talk functions to elaborate peer culture, (*c*) how identities
as peer group phenomena are talked into being through peer talk, and (*d*) how adult
culture is resisted through peer talk. Agentive goals of children's peer culture, and
the role of language in achieving them, are discussed in each section. I conclude that
sociolinguistics gives researchers a way to think about social competence as sets of linguistic practices (e.g., positionings, voicings, participation framework manipulations)
that children enact.

INTRODUCTION

This chapter reviews studies in sociology, sociolinguistics, and linguistic anthropology that examine children talking to, and socializing, other children in everyday
activities in their peer and friendship groups. The studies reviewed view children's
talk as strategic, accomplishing social action in peer culture.

The study of children's peer talk evolved through several phases that attributed
to children's language an increasingly important role in their own socialization
(Cook-Gumperz & Kyratzis 2001). The first was the discourse-centered approach
presented in Ervin-Tripp and Mitchell-Kernan's (1977) edited collection *Child
Discourse*. These studies and the many that followed (Garvey & Berninger 1981,
McTear 1985, Ochs & Schieffelin 1979) shifted focus from the child's ability to
approximate adult norms of grammar in elicited settings to the child's acquisition
of communicative competence, the social knowledge that underlies situationally

0084-6570/04/1021-0625$14.00

appropriate speech in naturalistic activities (Hymes 1962). The focus on social competence set the stage for the second approach to children's discourse, "language socialization" (Ochs & Schieffelin 1984, Schieffelin & Ochs 1986), which examined how children came to be participating members of a culture through participation in its language routines. The view of children as active agents in their own cultural learning through their use of language set the stage for the third approach, which shifted focus to "the child as a member of a culture that was different from that of the adult world" (Cook-Gumperz & Kyratzis 2001, p. 591).

With this third approach, children's peer talk became a locus for study of the children's cultural production (Cook-Gumperz & Corsaro 1986, Corsaro 1985, Gaskins et al. 1992, Goodwin 1980). Adult-based models of socialization view children as passively "reproducing" adult culture. However, according to recent interpretive approaches to the study of children's socialization, meaning creation and "interpretive reproduction" (Gaskins et al. 1992, p. 7) are active processes by which children, in their negotiations with other children, "take a variety of stances toward cultural resources—acceding to...playfully transforming, actively resisting (Gaskins et al. 1992, p. 11)." Children are not merely unformed adults (Schwartzman 2001); they reformulate social categories (e.g., friendship, gender) appropriated from the adult culture in ways that are sensitive to context (Thorne 1993, 2001) and reflective of children's personalities and momentary goals and agendas in the culture of peers, goals often related to entry into, and achieving power within, peer groups (Corsaro 1985, 1997; Goodwin 2001; Hirschfeld 2002; Paley 1992; Thorne 2001).

Studies in this third approach are the focus of this review. The approach is marked by two defining features. First, language is viewed as having in a role in children's cultural production (see Corsaro & Eder 1990, and Hoyle & Adger 1998a for prior reviews). Approaches that treat language as social action view language as helping create reality, not merely reflect it (Ahearn 2001, Gaskins et al. 1992, Gumperz 1994, Gumperz & Levinson 1996). Second, a rich, agentive view is taken of children's peer cultures. Detailed sociological and anthropological studies of peer social life in friendship and peer groups are looked to to help researchers discern what children seek to accomplish socially in the peer group. Further studies in the sociolinguistic and linguistic anthropological traditions record children, via audio and video, in peer and friendship groups (with attempts to minimize adult presence where possible—see Ervin-Tripp 2000 for discussion of these issues) to study how language allows them to accomplish these goals. To address these issues, I first consider the definition of peer cultures, which came out of these studies. I then consider four ways in which language and peer talk can help in the establishment and maintenance of peer culture: (a) how children elaborate games and ritualize the basis of inclusion through peer talk; (b) how conflict talk functions to elaborate peer culture; (c) how identities function as peer-group phenomena and how they are talked into being through peer talk; and (d) how adult culture is resisted through peer talk. For each area of talk influence, agentive goals of children's peer interactions and the role of language and communicative competence in accomplishing these goals are outlined. The studies consider children and preadolescents aged, for the most part, between ~2 and ~13 years. However, a few studies of adolescents (aged 14–18 years) are included in the review also.

DEFINITION OF PEER CULTURES

Peer cultures are "a stable set of activities or routines, artifacts, values, and concerns that children produce and share in interaction with peers" (Corsaro & Eder 1990, p. 197; and Corsaro 1997 for prior reviews). The concerns of children's peer cultures include (*a*) constructing a gender identity (Adler & Adler 1998, Corsaro 1997, Eckert 2000) for participating in peer groups and practice communities; (*b*) for adolescents, as they experience considerable embarrassment exploring romantic relationships (Eder 1991), relationships between the genders; (*c*) resisting adult culture—as children attend day care and school settings and increasingly participate in peer groups, they form a group identity strengthened by resisting adults and adult values (Corsaro 1985, Corsaro & Eder 1990, Eder 1998); and (*d*) for children growing up in societies where dominant and minority languages are in contact, reconstructing ethnicities to index peer group affiliation (e.g., Rampton 1995).

This chapter argues that there are two additional major concerns: (*e*) inclusion and power in the peer group. A central value of children's peer cultures is "doing things together," and "the protection of interactive space" (Corsaro 1997). Once children share an activity and bond with a peer, they seek to protect it against intrusion from others (Corsaro 1997, p. 124). Uninvolved children seek to gain entry, developing a complex set of "access strategies" (Corsaro 1997, p. 124). For example, Corsaro described a preschool girl, Debbie, who observed for a time two girls playing together at putting sand in cupcake trays, then undertook several access rituals to join their play, including attempting to get hold of one of their teacups, invoking the notion "friends," and producing a variant of the play ("I'm making coffee") (Corsaro 1979, pp. 320–21). When a child's access to play becomes an enduring quality of a specific relationship, then it is viewed as inclusion.

Corsaro (1997, p. 154, 159) acknowledges "differentiation" as a concern of children's peer cultures but claims that stable hierarchies and exclusion were not observable among the Italian and American preschoolers he studied. Corsaro & Eder (1990) argued that peer status comes into play during adolescence. However, recent approaches view power and hierarchy as central concerns of children's peer cultures across many cultures of the world and across many ages (Adler & Adler 1998; Berentzen 1984; Ervin-Tripp et al. 1990; Evaldsson 2002; Goodwin 1990a, 1998, 2002a,b; Kyratzis & Guo 2001; Kyratzis et al. 2001; Paley 1992). Peer exclusion is observable in many contexts, including normally developing peers reacting, under certain circumstances, with censure and rejection to children with language disabilities in school (Ochs et al. 2001). For these reasons, in this chapter, power is viewed as a central concern of children's peer cultures from early on. I turn now to a consideration of four ways in which language and peer talk contribute to the establishment and maintenance of peer cultures.

HOW CHILDREN ELABORATE GAMES AND CODES
(AND RITUALIZE THE BASIS FOR INCLUSION)
THROUGH PEER TALK

Researchers studying children's social worlds have noted that children articulate their own games, songs, and rituals not derived from adult cultural forms (Hirschfeld 2002, Opie & Opie 1960) and have emphasized that the rituals and speech events that children organize themselves should be studied (Ervin-Tripp & Mitchell-Kernan 1977b, Hoyle & Adger 1998a). Katriel (1987), on the basis of her work observing the sharing ritual ("*xibidum*") used among Israeli children, suggests that the ritual's significance resides in how it realizes and reflects the goals of children's peer cultures, particularly inclusion and exclusion in the peer group and the group's affirmation and independence from the adult world (Katriel 1987, p. 319). In fact, invoking adult norms (e.g., "no eating from mouth to mouth") is severely ridiculed by the children because it impedes this affirmation (Katriel 1987, p. 318). Studies documenting how the games and codes that children develop provide linguistic resources for organizing participation are reviewed in this section. The second sub-section reviews studies documenting communicative competence in organizing games.

The Relationship Between Games and Social Order

Berentzen's (1984) ethnographic longitudinal study of peer social life in a preschool classroom in Norway found that the social order that evolved, organized around gender dichotomies, arose as a solution to the central question of peer social life in this classroom, belonging, or "Can I play?" Among boys, the leaders were usually the ones who started a game or activity. Boys looked for possibilities for "showing strength, courage and speed" (Berentzen 1984, p. 100). The boys that wanted to be included "make suggestions they feel others (particularly the boys who control the game) will like" (Berentzen 1984, p. 59).

Girls in this classroom articulated a series of moves to strengthen alliances, including praising and inviting each other home and conforming to another's attempts to elaborate a game, and two girls could indicate a relationship by excluding a third party (Berentzen 1984, p. 77). Girls try to have the right things (e.g., dolls) and "secrets" (104) to enhance the possibility for forming alliances. "A girl's current alliance partner is praised, while all the other girls are criticized. Style of behavior and use of idioms were criticized" (Berentzen 1984, p. 80). Games and codes of behavior evolved in keeping with how they could attract partners and allow inclusion. It is the special meanings that the children create in these pretend games that give them power to attract partners and create involvement. When one of two preschool girls intiated a play theme with the other ("Pretend you-we-we wanted to get married, right?"), this game attracted a third girl, who wanted to join the play (Sheldon 1996, p. 62). However, the making of groups involves both displaying alignment with, as well as excluding, other children. Preschool children reported that they would be especially reluctant to let nonfriends into a game of play if the game were particularly "special" (Paley 1992). Pretend play provides rich affordances to accomplish exclusion through the pretend frame (Sheldon 1992, 1996), minimizing responsibility, as when the two preschool girls described above postponed the entry of the third's by saying "but not yet" to the third's proposal that she was the baby brother growing in the mommy's (one of the other girls') tummy and that it was time for him to be born (Sheldon 1996, p. 63).

The Role of Language in Organizing and Producing Variants of Games

Because games are the ritualization of inclusion on the child's own terms, the central issue for children becomes, how can I start a game that will draw other children, or how can I fit into and elaborate a game that others have started? The complexities of accomplishing and negotiating pretend games have been described by Cook-Gumperz (1995), Goodwin (1993), Goldman (1998), Nelson & Seidman (1984), Sheldon (1992, 1996), Whelan (1995), and other researchers. Goodwin (1993) noted that "[p]retend play differs from other domains of play in that children enact vocal and nonvocal scripts appropriate to their relative positions in a pretend reality. . . this accomplished through the skillful managing of staged identities, artful uses of a repertoire of voices, and careful attention to the framing of interaction" (p. 160). For example, when one child states that she is the mom and another child is the daughter, she includes the other child in a game, thereby indexing a bond. She, however, also gets to control the behavior of the other through appropriating the authoritative register associated with the mom role, as well as by managing the other's staged identities (Goodwin 1993). She also renders as "programmatically relevant" (Sacks 1992) other family roles; games (e.g., "family") specify a category set of players, which "provides an adequate set of categories for referring to personnel" (Sacks 1992, p. 498). It is this potential of defining a category set of players (Sacks 1992), as well as of defining the ways in which the staged identities talk to one another (Goodwin 1993), that games have that renders them ideally suited to organizing participation rights in the game and hierarchical relationships among players.

Children strive to maintain the definition of the situation as play, and what the specific definition of the frame is (Goodwin 1993, Whelan 1995). They also strive to index its egalitarian, cooperative nature through the use of future-oriented proposals and tag questions rather than directives (Garvey & Kramer 1989, Goldman 1998, Goodwin 1990a, Kyratzis 1999).

Narratives produced during pretend play have different "voices" that need indexing with distinctive marking (Cook-Gumperz 1995, Gee & Savasir 1986, Heath 1984, Kyratzis 1999, Wolf & Hicks 1989). The narrative voice consists of statements that set the frame for what will happen in the play. It is distinguished by special lexical features ("and," "because") and a measured reading tone (Cook-Gumperz 1995, p. 413). These statements are sometimes marked with "pretend" but can be keyed through other devices (e.g., the past tense, the simple present) (Blum-Kulka et al. 2005, Cook-Gumperz 1995, Cook-Gumperz & Kyratzis 2001, Kyratzis 1999). Stage-managing voices are used when children are negotiating background detail (Cook-Gumperz 1995, Wolf & Hicks 1989). The voice quality has "often a tone of urgency" (Cook-Gumperz 1995, p. 413).

An important way in which children display their alignment to one another is to align to one anothers' character voices in role play (Hoyle 1998). Voices are indexed through contextualization devices (Cook-Gumperz 1995, Kyratzis 1999) and specialized register features (Hoyle 1998). These features indicate "the manner in which children enact their recognition of the relationship between language and identity...their intersubjectively shared understandings of how roles present as distinct 'voicings'" (Goldman 1998, p. 146). For example, a portrayal of "doctor" by a Huli child might be projected as "a deep gruff voice—and partly on his interspersed injections of pidgin words as markers of role authenticity and integrity" (Goldman 1998, p. 155). Children even correct one another for their understandings of voicings. They switch into, out of, and among different character voices implicitly and paralinguistically (Cook-Gumperz & Gumperz 1978; Goldman 1998; Kyratzis 1999, 2001)." In the way they do these voicings, and the relative willingness they display to "prestigiously emulate" (Goldman 1998, p. 172) different roles such as white administrator, mother, doctor, anthropologist, and anthropologist's assistant, children construct their own understandings of the adult world. In role play, sportscasters are portrayed as hurried-through devices such as the simple present and syntactic reduction (Ferguson 1983, Hoyle 1998) and doctors as highly authoritative through discourse markers and the collusive "we" form [e.g., "So. Mmph. Now we will see then" (Aronsson & Thorell 2002, p. 289; Andersen 1990)]. Mothers are portrayed as speaking with bald directives, and older children and group leaders are consistently allocated the Mom role (Goodwin 1993, Kyratzis et al. 2001). Patwa-English-speaking preschoolers in Dominica, West Indies, through using Patwa (despite Patwa being sanctioned by adults) to voice adult authoritative roles, such as bus driver, may be "transforming the associations with the languages through using them in their play" (Paugh 2005, p. 23), thereby issuing their own construals of power relationships among languages in contact (see also De Leon 2002). "Children's subtle observation of the background features of adult speech is never revealed so fully as in their role play" (Ervin-Tripp 1996, p. 33). Children emulate powerful adult roles, privileged to speak with high-status control act forms, to achieve their own power in the peer group (Goodwin 1993, Kyratzis et al. 2001, Paugh 2005).

Pretend games are major speech events for forming alliances with peers. We need to consider other speech events. Sound or word play (with rounds structure) is a major venue for preschoolers and toddlers (Garvey 1974), as are competitive story-telling rounds (Ervin-Tripp & Kuntay 1996). Youngsters show adeptness at turn-taking, responding quickly, building on and topping their partners, capitalizing on rhythmic patterning (Brenneis & Lein 1977), and using dramatic effects and humorous substitutions (Katz 2004). For older children, collaborative story telling, humorous stories, and gossip talk fulfill these roles (Cheshire 2000; Coates 1994, 1997; Ervin-Tripp & Lampert 1992; Evaldsson 2002; Goetz & Shatz 1999; Goodwin 1990a; Gottman 1986; Sanford & Eder 1984). How children index these speech events to one another is a major forum for sociolinguistic investigation

(Blum-Kulka et al. 2005, Ervin-Tripp 1996, Hoyle & Adger 1998a). We also need to examine the linguistic strategies by which children create alignment and involvement and build a sense of group with peers within these speech events. Several studies consider children's use of the following features: repetition and sing-song intonation in jokes, songs, and sound play, including the ritualized Italian children's sing-song chant, the *cantilena* (Cook-Gumperz 1995, Corsaro & Rizzo 1990, Garvey 1974); and playful recyclings and parodic imitations of teachers' authoritative discourse, which even minimal users of a second language can use to render joint commentary on classroom interactions (Cekaite & Aronsson 2005). Other linguistic devices for alignment and involvement include making affiliative references, such as references to friendship (Corsaro 1985); finishing each other's sentences and latching (Eder 1993, Greenwood 1998, Heath 1998, Hoyle 1998, Tannen 1990), teasing to build solidarity (Corsaro 1997, Eder 1993); repeating joking abuse to build solidarity and defuse differences (Rampton 1995); using reported dialogue in conversation to instantiate the particular and enable listeners "to create their understanding by drawing on their own history of associations" (Tannen 1989, p. 133); and initiating group-affirming moves such as copying each other's work, rendering invitations to birthday parties and stay-overs, giving compliments, and using other affiliative strategies (Berentzen 1984, Cook-Gumperz & Szymanski 2001). Through these speech events that children index themselves linguistically, they reflect on their world together and ritualize the basis for inclusion in the peer group on their own terms.

CONFLICT TALK AND THE ELABORATION OF PEER CULTURE

In an earlier review of children's disputes, Corsaro & Rizzo (1990) noted that there were many positive functions of conflicts in children's peer interactions and that although conflicts involve strategies such as justification (Eisenberg & Garvey 1981), their goal is not resolution (see Genishi & DiPaulo 1982, Maynard 1985). Recent studies focus on the complex moment-to-moment interactional processes by which such talk events as gossip talk, teasing, and conflict in games, as used in close peer groups of children, provide resources for "construct[ing] and reconstruct[ing] their social organization on an ongoing basis" (Goodwin 1990b, p. 33) as well as for "staging identities . . . and sanctioning deviant behaviors" (Evaldsson 2002, p. 201). Studies examining these processes, and the specific linguistic means by which they are carried out, are examined in this section.

How Conflict Talk Elaborates Peer Group Norms and Peer Group Social Organization

An influential study was Goodwin's (1990a) ethnographic observation of 9- to 13-year-old African American children in their Philadelphia neighborhood peer groups. In frequent gossip disputes and dispute stories, children replayed past experiences during which they animated the voices of themselves and others, thereby staging their own and peers' identities, reflecting on one anothers' characters and negotiating their social organization.

Further studies examined how gossip talk functions in peer groups. Gossip talk can consolidate the views of the group (Eckert 1993, p. 40). Those who construct versions of events to which the peer group ascribes are positioned as leaders (Eckert 1993). Those in the peer group who, during gossip events, displayed "proficiency in repeatedly (a) depicting the deviant character of others and (b) soliciting audience support for particular versions of events positioned them as leaders...(these boys) legitimate their power while subordinating the interests of others" (Evaldsson 2002, p. 219). Displaying expertise and opposing others' claims to expertise, then, play a role in negotiating peer group status. In an adolescent friendship group of nerd girls, displays of intelligence were central, and therefore members' claims to knowledge were often disputed (Bucholtz 1999a). Nerdiness is a contested domain by virtue of establishing "who counts as a nerd" (Bucholtz 1999a, p. 220).

Teasing is another (partly) confrontational interaction used to negotiate the norms of the peer group. Teasing is a way of managing jealousy and bringing out differences about sensitive topics in the peer group short of direct confrontation (Eder 1991, 1993) The correct stances of the peer group toward heterosexual behavior (e.g., asking boys out, wearing make-up) and ethnic relations can be negotiated and displayed in these moves (Eder 1991, Rampton 1995). Teasing and other humorous genres establish who is in the know, who can stand their ground on sensitive topics, and the group's social organization. For groups of adolescent girls in middle school, two humorous behaviors indexed marginalized or nongroup members: telling humorous stories that depicted group norms violations (e.g., about make-up), and practical jokes (Sanford & Eder 1984, p. 241).

Rule-based games provide another venue for elaboration of norms within the peer group and are a contested domain. "Physically skilled girls...strengthened their authority...by repeatedly a) deciding on positions first, b) defining the ways of throwing, and c) commenting on one another's game performances" (Evaldsson 2004). Games provide their own internal criteria for evaluating members' performances. In games such as hopscotch, four-square, and jumprope, girls can be observed to sanction each other and hold each other accountable to rules and standards of the peer group (Hughes 1993; Goodwin 1995, 1998). The social and moral order that children evolve together within games gives cohesion to the group and sets boundaries. "Spatial considerations are crucial....Hopscotch is a 'situated activity system [Goffman 1961]' involving a physical environment...and procedures for moving within it" (Goodwin 1999, p. 393). Children do not passively follow rules; they actively "treat rules as resources to be probed and played with" (Goodwin 1998, p. 25).

For younger, preschool-aged children, conflicts serve some of the same purposes. African American Midwestern preschoolers in Head-Start "constructed social identities, cultivated friendships, and both maintained and transformed the social order of the peer culture" (Corsaro & Maynard 1996, p. 163) through conflict. Among working-class preschoolers of African American and of Italian descent, performance aspects of disputes, including format-tying, are emphasized, and they provide opportunities for differentiating group members, although this is not the case for American middle-class preschoolers (Corsaro & Rizzo 1990, Corsaro & Maynard 1996). It is not clear whether younger children's disputes provide resources for elaboration of group norms and sanctioning of group members' behavior as rich as those described for older children's. Rizzo (1989) argues that American children argue over friendship expectations. Sanctioning about behavioral norms has been documented in disputes of Italian (Corsaro & Rizzo 1990), Norwegian (Berentzen 1984), Taiwanese (Farris 1991) and Mainland Chinese middle-class preschoolers—"when are you going to stop steaming it, huh?" (Kyratzis & Guo 2001, p. 56). There are further comparative differences. In cultures of the world where children care for young siblings, hierarchies within peer groups may be less open for negotiation. Children socialized in empathic relationships such as the nurturing elder-sister (_ade_) role, described by Schieffelin (1990) for the Kaluli of New Guinea, or in apprenticeship models, which emphasize the helping of younger children (such as those described for Zinacantec Maya children—see Maynard 2002), may be less aggressive toward peers.

COMMUNICATIVE COMPETENCE IN CONFLICT TALK   Because the major goal of stories told during conflicts (Goodwin 1990a, Shuman 1986) is social organization, how then is social organization accomplished through the talk itself? "Through a multiplicity of voices (Goffman 1974), the teller of the story and her hearers animate principal figures in the story and offer commentary upon the unfolding actions and the characters" (Goodwin 1990b, p. 34). In the he-said, she-said story below told to Julia, Bea animates the voice of Kerry, reporting Kerry as having described Julia as acting stupid. Kerry's voice is animated with a whiny high-pitched tone "enacting Kerry's distaste" (Goodwin 1990b, p. 49; see Example 1) for Julia. In contrast, later in the telling, Bea portrays herself as having defended Julia and is effective in drawing a commitment from Julia to confront Kerry in the future.

Example 1   He-said, she-said story

26. Bea: *She* said, *She* said that um, (0.6)

27.   that (0.8) if that *girl* wasn't

28.   there = *You* know that girl that always

29.   makes those funny jokes, *h Sh'aid if

30.   that *girl* wasn't there *you* wouldn't be

31.   *ac*tin (0.4) a:ll *stu*pid like that.

(Goodwin 1990b, pp. 48–49)

Further social and linguistic aspects of communicative competence in conflict talk include culturally and gender-appropriate conflict management styles

(Eder 1990; Farris 1991, 2000; Goodwin 1995, 1998, 1999; Kyratzis & Guo 2001; Nakamura 2001a; see Goodwin 2003 for a review). Chinese and Taiwanese middle-class girls as well as African American and Latina working-class girls in the United States learn to use bald directives and direct forms of conflict management, whereas American and Japanese middle-class girls use more mitigated forms (Farris 1991; Goodwin 1995, 1998; Kyratzis & Guo 2001; Nakamura 2001a; Sheldon 1992, 1996). Knowing when to mitigate agency is also a factor in Hawaiian children's use of the talk-story (Watson-Gegeo & Boggs 1977). There are many stylized aspects of conflict Italian *discussione* involves highly complex strategies including interruption devices, predisagreements, emphasis markers, and format tying; these features are not employed by American nursery-school children (Corsaro & Rizzo 1990). Format tying in ritual insult as practiced by preschool-aged African American children involves the ability to link into partners' speech and use their own words against them (Corsaro & Maynard 1996; Goodwin 1990a, Goodwin & Goodwin 1987). Communicative competence can also be seen in children's knowledge of how to rally support from others. African American working-class girls' he-said-she-said reports are highly artful in their ability to elicit commitments to courses of action in the future and in their ability to transform disputes into large public events (Goodwin & Goodwin 1987, p. 231). An effective strategy in game disputes is to align to the verbal and physical format of partners' moves, contrasting positions (Evaldsson 2004). Aggravated directives, insults and threats, shored up by embodied and verbalized accounts of positions, and pitch leaps (Goodwin et al. 2002c) create powerful moral stances (Evaldsson 2004; Goodwin 1995, 1998). An effective strategy in teasing exchanges is the use of direct speech and voicing of others in caricature (Goodwin 1990a, Heath 1998); this process requires production formats of animator and principal (Goffman 1974) to be differentiated from one another (Cromdal & Aronsson 2000). Ritual insulting among working-class adolescent girls has rules attached—the themes are often about sexual and romantic behavior and the target is required to respond in a playful manner (Eder 1990). These studies hint at the complex social and linguistic skills involved in peers' participation in teasing and dispute.

Communicative competence can also be seen in social aspects of teasing and conflict events, for example, children's knowledge of who to engage in conflict. In the ritualized conflict event, the "brogez" (time-out), Israeli children knew to engage only those close enough to their own status for a status change to be possible (Katriel 1985). Communicative competence can be seen in the grammatical marking of conflict moves. Children learn to utilize quasi-modal forms, including "hafta" to mark second-turn moves in a conflict (Gerhardt 1990) and "so" to mark concluding positions (Sprott 1992).

Finally, communicative competence can be seen in how children manipulate categories from the adult culture ("nice," "mean," "friendship," and gender, ethnicity, and class) (Berentzen 1984; Corsaro 1985; Goodwin, 2002a,b; Hughes 1993). Building relationships with some peers necessarily entails opposing others, which is how everyday concepts appropriated from the adult culture such as "nice," "mean" (Hughes 1993), "play" and "pretend" (e.g., "we'll just pretend that we are with her," Berentzen 1984, p. 78), gender, and class (Goodwin 2001, 2002a,b) come to take on specialized and sometimes paradoxical meanings in the ways in which children use them in conflict negotiations.

HOW CHILDREN CONSTRUCT VALUED IDENTITIES OF THE PEER GROUP THROUGH PEER TALK

The studies in this section consider identities as peer group phenomena, documenting how children appropriate gender ideologies from the adult culture to use as a basis for organizing their peer social groups in classrooms and schools. The second sub-section considers the role of language in the constitution of peer group identities.

Children Appropriate Gender Ideologies from the Adult Culture to Organize Peer Social Structure at School

Preschoolers appropriate gender categories to organize classroom social structure (Berentzen 1984, Kyratzis 2001, Nicolopoulou 2002). Elementary- and middle-school-age children appropriate gender categories to organize the social structure (Eder et al. 1995) or "clique structure" that is the "dominant feature of. . .their social world" (Adler & Adler 1998, p. 56) at school. Clique boundaries are carefully monitored, and violating norms of the peer group provides grounds for ridicule and expulsion from the peer group.

Girls and boys "constructed idealized images of masculinity and femininity" (Adler et al. 1992, p. 169), serving as grist for the mill of these clique negotiations. Girls derived status from clothes, appearance, grooming, friendship ties (Adler & Adler 1998, p. 195) and the correlates of socioeconomic status (material possessions and leisure pursuits). "Boys. . .were accorded popularity and respect. . .for traits such as toughness, troublemaking, domination, coolness, and interpersonal bragging and sparring skills" (Adler & Adler 1998, p. 196). The gatekeepers were expert at using the dominant gender ideology as a basis for marginalization. "They manipulated others in the group to establish their central position and to dominate the definition of the group's boundaries" (Adler & Adler 1998, p. 49). Weak boys, and girls who were lacking in the accoutrements of high socioeconomic status and attractiveness (e.g., overweight girls), were derided by the ringleaders and rendered the subjects of gossip, rumor, and en face derision (Adler & Adler 1998; Eder et al. 1995, pp. 113–14).

The impetus to utilize gender displays to participate groups at school becomes even stronger as children leave the smaller, intimate friendship clusters of elementary school and junior high and enter high school. Peers monitor their value in the social market (Eckert 1989, 2000). Despite these pressures, contexts may differ in the extent to which children separate by gender (Whiting

& Edwards 1988) and monitor each other for displays of gender (Ervin-Tripp 1978, 2001). Thorne (1993) observed girls and boys to engage in games that emphasized gender boundaries (boys chasing girls and vice versa) in large public settings. However, several studies document contextual variation in gender-associated displays (e.g., Farris 2000, Kyratzis 2001, Kyratzis & Guo 2001, Thorne 1993). The display of mitigated speech by girls, or girls-against-boys, boundary-marking behavior by both girls and boys, was not in evidence in all-female interactions among girls with high levels of physical game skill (Evaldsson 2004, Goodwin 1998), in cross-sex games in which boys sought to learn to play a game in which girls held expertise (Goodwin 2001), and in less public (neighborhood) settings with mixed age groupings of children (Thorne 1993). To understand how children agentively utilize gender as an organizing social category for their peer interactions, one must pay close attention to its fluctuating significance for children's social lives (Thorne 1993, p. 61), especially in terms of power (Thorne 1993), as well as to individual differences (Bucholtz 1999b, Thorne 2001).

Communicative Competence in Displaying Valued Identities of the Peer Group

Communicative competence in negotiating gender identities of the peer group is seen in deploying norms of the peer group during peer disputes, for example, singling out a girl for collusive commentary on the basis of the fact that she "put themselves above them" (Goodwin 2002a, p. 401). Children need to know how to deploy these norms proficiently, obtaining positive category affiliations for oneself while avoiding negative ones (Evaldsson 2002). To position themselves as having "done well" (Eckert 1993, p. 37) in the competitive social marketplace, girls portray themselves as having boyfriends and knowing popular boys. They effectively manipulate the groups' consensus on views. Girls have to know how to use lunchtime discussion, which "frequently provided ways of differentiating group members with respect to access to privileges of the upper middle class" (Goodwin 2002a, p. 400), to their own advantage, using specific illustrations to manipulate positions (Eckert 1993, p. 41). In addition to knowing the important symbols of consumer culture, girls use format tying to prior utterances to achieve maximal topping effect (Goodwin 2002a, p. 401). Part of jockeying for status entails the exclusion of certain members of the group; to do this, girls have to effectively cast negative category affiliations (e.g., shopping at Goodwill) on tag-a-long members while gaining audience alignment (Goodwin 2002b).

Communicative competence is also seen in the use of linguistic and paralinguistic cues of contextualization that cue the speaker as having the "right" emotional and assertive stances with regard to approved norms of gender identity for the culture in question. In her recent review of gender (and culture) in children's peer interactions, Goodwin (2003) concluded that "[d]espite the fact that simple polarized depictions of gender groups cannot be established, there are differences in the criteria each gender uses for making distinctions among group members as well as procedures for achieving social organization" (p. 234). These differences are documented in several studies (Berentzen 1984, Danby & Baker 2001, Farris 1991, 2000, Kyratzis & Ervin-Tripp 1999, Maltz & Borker 1982, Sachs 1987). For example, Sheldon (1996) observed that preschool girls used a range of strategies, termed double-voice discourse, to mitigate the assertive (i.e., self-oriented) aspect of many of their control moves, thereby emphasizing group harmony. Boys used more heavy-handed dispute tactics, including physical intimidation and threats (Sheldon 1990). Japanese girls spent considerable time setting up and negotiating the roles to be assumed, whereas boys lunged into the pretend play right away, often lapsing into fights that disrupted it. Boys used forms to mark self-assertion and commands, whereas for girls, commands were rare and requests were mitigated and polite ("I wonder if you would try this for me") (Nakamura 2001a). In terms of emotion talk, preschool boys enact rough, aggressive themes in play ("smashers") and themes of terror that involve them in enacting aggressive stances through cues of contextualization, including bald and terse commands, building on each other's in-role threats, and physical action ("smash this girl!") (Danby & Baker 2001, Farris 1991, Kyratzis 2001). Girls, in contrast, used effusive emotional language with hyperbole ("you draw me a hundred million pictures all day") and emotion labels ("but we *love* you") (Kyratzis 2001). In Example 2, below, two preschool girls, Judy and Ethel, despite having just had a dispute about who will be the mama, use effusive language, including expressions of concern ("cause you might get some in your eye"), references to sharing ("can *I have some lotion?"), offers ("I'm gonna get you some"), hyperbole ("brighter," "lighter"), and high, plaintive pitch throughout the excerpt, as cues of contextualization, depicting themselves as caring and likable.

Example 2   Effusive language used by girls' group in 'Sun Lotion' play

J = Judy, E = Ethel, B = Betty

1. E: yeah// can *I have some lotion?

2. J: no// *i'm gonna get you some// [stroking Ethel's face with the stick]

3. E: why?

4. J: 'cause you might get some in your eyes//

5. ─────

6. J: there's the (sprite)// my smile looks brighter// doesn't it? Bright means *lighter//

(Adapted from Kyratzis 2001, pp. 382–83)

Preschool and school-aged peers "do gender" through manipulation of stylistic features and contextualization cues in play. Adolescents, on the other hand, utilize more reflective genres, framing speech events such as gossip, teasing, humor, and collaborative stories that allow them to display valued identities of the peer group (Coates 1994; Cheshire 2000; Eckert 1993; Eder 1991, 1993; Ervin-Tripp &

Lampert 1992) as well as new adult-like roles (Emihovich 1998, Heath 1998). "Adolescence is a time when humorous play activities are an essential part of peer culture. Through play, children transform the familiar into something novel and create their own culture" (Eder 1993, p. 17). "Note exchanging as utilized among adolescent girls displays identities; notes containing effusive and vivid declarations of heterosexual desire may serve to display authors' heterosexuality and maturing femininity among their peers" (Cahill 2001, p. 83). Swearing and telling sexual jokes may display tellers' sophistication (Sanford & Eder 1984). Children can construct themselves as heterosexual beings through the way in which they use language in collaborative stories. How can self-construction be accomplished through narrative? Narratives have a point of view. Some of the major perspectival options afforded through narrative are how the narrative allows the teller to position characters with respect to story worlds, thereby positioning the characters and the teller herself with respect to broader moral issues (Bamberg 1997, Bamberg & Barcinski 2003, Ochs & Capps 1996). Cheshire (2000) described white working-class British adolescent boys displaying themselves as tough through telling stories about smoking, standing up to their fathers, throwing knives, etc. Participation frameworks of conversational stories as told in friendship groups could be manipulated in ways that help communicate gender identities (e.g., males interrupting, challenging, and insulting a teller to project masculinity; Cheshire 2000). Portrayals of others as deviant during gossip talk fall along gendered lines (e.g., portraying a boy as having cried or acted cowardly; Evaldsson 2002, Goodwin 1990a). Younger adolescent males positioned themselves in opposition to females, whereas older adolescent males positioned themselves with being heterosexual and girlfriend experienced (Bamberg & Barcinski 2003).

Adolescent girls struggle with competing possible subjectivities in the collaborative stories they tell in friendship group talk (Coates 1994, 1997). They use syntactic devices to construct a "discourse of repression," representing themselves as affected, nonagentive beings through the use of stative verbs ("was," "had," "got"), through negative words (e.g., "horrible"; Coates 1997, p. 303), and through lexical terms allying with a patriarchal discourse (e.g., "premenstrual tension"). Girls also construct themselves alternatively, as heterosexual feminine subjects (Coates 1997, p. 296), through their choice of vocabulary ("hunk").

HOW ADULT CULTURE IS RESISTED THROUGH PEER TALK

Children seek to have control over the "confusions" raised by the adult world, as well as the limitations and constraints imposed by it (Corsaro & Eder 1990, p. 205; Corsaro 1997). In play and talk among themselves, children have been observed to mock, reflect on, and resist the existing social order (Schwartzman 1976). For young children, resisting rules of a specific social organization (classroom clean-up time) (Corsaro 1985) and scatological references (Nakamura 2001b) are key venues to resist adult norms and establish preschoolers' sense of group. Preschoolers also resist through role play; girls playing privately among themselves display oppositional feminine identities (boiling babies) (Cook-Gumperz 2001), and girls playing with boys can take on superhero roles (Fernie et al. 1993).

Preadolescent and adolescent teens resist dominant ideologies of the adult culture, including gender, through mocking and animating others during collaborative stories with friends. Animating a speaker and using his/her own words against them provides a powerful means of disaligning both with the person and with their moral views, while providing a means of creating alignments with copresent collaborators in the story telling (Eder 1998, Goodwin 1990a, Heath 1998). Adolescent males mock tough coaches to render commentary on society's view "that males should be skillfull athletes" (Eder 1998, p. 90). Adolescent females utilized animations of adults' speech to resist adult views positing that "normative behavior for girls consists of being cooperative and acting like 'ladies'" (Eder 1998, p. 87) and resisted growing concerns with attractiveness by mocking the idea of make-up (Eder et al. 1995, p. 112). Investigators observed young adolescent girls challenging each other's repressive discourse (e.g., through accusations of being "prudish"), resisting heterosocial pressures of media images, and opposing sexual harassment by boys (Coates 1994, p. 120). "Injections of direct discourse within an account resemble verbal caricatures of the original speakers" (Heath 1998, p. 232). Other people's voices can be stylized as silly, stupid, old fashioned, oppressive, and unenlightened to implicitly evoke them in particular ways (e.g., as defending patriarchal standards, speaking dialect, etc.) (Kotthoff 2005; see also Ervin-Tripp & Lampert 1992). Young migrant Turkish adolescent girls in Germany stylized the dialects of various social groups (e.g., "Gasterbeiterdeutsch" or "migrant workers' German") to render commentary among themselves (Kallmeyer & Keim 2003).

In today's globalized economy, children grow up in societies where majority and minority languages are in contact with each other. Adolescents' "cultural production of ethnicities" (Rampton 1999, p. 482), and their uses of language relevant to "the production, maintenance and/or change of social structure" (Rampton 1999, p. 496) have recently been examined in studies of language crossing, where speakers use language forms associated with other ethnic groups. Minimal uses of Caribbean Creole by white adolescents in South London were acceptable and served as a means of peer group renegotiation of broader societal racial relations (Hewitt 1986). In the peer culture of a multiracial, urban high school in Great Britain (Rampton 1995), crossing referred to uses of Panjabi by monolingual Afro-Caribbean and Anglo youth, to uses of Creole by monolingual Anglos and Panjabis, and to uses of Stylized Indian English by all three groups (p. 4). Panjabi crossing, for example, was used in highly structured games for ritualized insult and joking abuse. These uses were usually well received by adolescents of Indian and Pakistani descent. Concomitantly, Stylized Asian English was used by adolescent students to white teachers, symbolically, to draw parallels between adult control over youth and the school's marginalization of ESL learners (Rampton 1996). These peer-language uses contribute to "enunciation of interethnic youth, class, and neighborhood community" (Rampton 1995, p. 4), or in other words, minimized interethnic differences.

Peers among themselves, reflect on, react to, and resist values of the adult society through the languages and speaking styles they embrace and evoke and the ways that they use code switching (Zentella 1997). For example, code switching to get the conversational floor, rather than switching to index contrasts between in-group/out-group meanings characteristic of their parents' generation, indexes 7- to 10-year-old Turkish-Danish bilingual students' opposition to adult norms and affiliation with a bilingual youth peer group (Jorgensen 1999, p. 249). However, youth responses and language uses do not always entail inclusive forms (see for example Bucholtz 1999c). Negative attitudes toward immigrant Mexican American Northern Californian students' code-switching varieties in the schooling community led to polarization of attitudes among the Latinas at a Northern California high school. The teenage girls organized themselves into two ideological orientations toward speaking Spanish and code switching, the polar extremes of which were represented by two gangs, the Nortenas and Surenas (Mendoza-Denton 1994). Quichua-Spanish-speaking children used extensive format tying in peer play dialogues, but only in Spanish; the children refused to use Quichua among themselves, despite Quichua being used by parents to children (Rindstedt & Aronsson 2002). African American students at "Capitol High" in Washington, D.C., used various linguistic means to "adopt temporarily, but refuse to claim as their own, the discourse sanctioned by the academy" (Fordham 1998, p. 208). Youth ideological responses to dominant language ideologies, and creative youth uses of linguistic means to accomplish ideological stances, are important to consider.

CONCLUSIONS

Children socialize one another, constructing their own norms and valued identities of the peer group. These social meaning systems evolve over time as solutions to the central problems of power and inclusion. Language is key, having an influence in the four domains considered (i.e., elaboration of games, group norms elaboration, identity-construction, resistance). Specific linguistic devices that children use to realize these goals include (a) indexing and keying pretend play and speech events; (b) indexing character voices and speaking styles; (c) positioning morally via narrative and argument; (d) manipulating participation frameworks during narratives, conflicts, and other speech events to forge alignments and rally an audience; and (e) constructing their own variants of speaking styles to display allegiance to a broader youth culture.

Peer talk is essential for elaborating peer culture in the five ways described. These five ways point to four broader domains of influence of language and peer talk on peer culture. Peer talk is essential for the negotiation of children's status within and inclusion in the peer group, and therefore for building relationships and developing social competence. Child development researchers recognize the need for children to understand peers' thought processes to cooperatively play with them (Dunn & Cutting 1999), and that peer relationships are an important motivational forum for the development of social competence (Coie et al. 1990, Dunn 1996, Hartup 1996). Sociolinguistics, however, gives us a way to think about social competence, not as knowledge that resides in the heads of children but as sets of linguistic practices (e.g., voicings, stylizations, positionings) that children actually enact. These processes are constituted in language and difficult to capture on Lickert scales of "competence" or "likability." Nor are the performances that we see in ethnographic studies of children's peer groups fully consistent with descriptions from sociometric studies—the deferent, cooperative, conforming, helpful child painted positively in the popularity studies (see, e.g., Coie et al. 1990 for a review) is not the assertive leader who emerges from ethnographic fieldwork and who is often involved in doing "not nice" things (e.g., opposing others, painting them as deviant, allocating them unflattering roles), and this is no less true of girls than of boys (Goodwin 2002a).

Peer (and sibling) talk are essential for cognitive (e.g., Rogoff 1998) and language development, including pragmatic development (see also Blum-Kulka & Snow 2005). Like other cultural and ethnographic approaches to development (Gaskins et al. 1992, Rogoff 1998, Schieffelin & Ochs 1986), the agentive approach to children's peer cultures outlined here views the outcome of development in terms of the values and goals of the members of the culture. What children learn is tied to what they are trying to accomplish in terms of identity- and social organization–forming work. Language is a major arena for development because it is through language that identities and social organization are constituted. Take the case of narrative. The connected discourse skills of young children are impressive (Blum-Kulka et al. 2005). However, narrative, speech stylization, and pragmatic skills do not develop in a vacuum. They are deployed by children strategically as resources to help them organize their social worlds. With its rich opportunities for positioning through its evaluative dimension, through its dramaturgical (character speech stylization) opportunities, and through its potential for arrangements of participation frameworks, narrative affords children a rich repertoire of resources to utilize in their exploration of possible identities, as well as in their own construction of the hierarchical social organization of their peer group. The need to belong to and organize social groups leads children to make great strides in pragmatic development, learning to manipulate features of style and story to accomplish particular social ends.

Peer talk is an essential device for displaying identities and ideologies and for resisting them. Children index their moral stances, who they are (at least for the moment), and what they believe in, through narrative, as a device of positioning, through character voicing, the primary way for children to enact their understanding of the relationship between language and identity. What better way is there to index how a female should behave than to voice appropriate emotional and assertive stances through cues of contextualization? What better way is there to render commentary on how adults do things than to mock them by animating their voices and using their own words against them, rallying an audience to this display? How can one better display the valued identities of the peer group than by telling a story that instantiates how the self lived up to these norms? What better way is there to display one's attitude toward a language variety than to mock a child who uses it, or give a speaker of it a low-status role in pretend play? The identity one ultimately displays oneself to have—morally assertive versus deferent and conforming, racist versus not racist, affiliating with a liberal subjectivity or a repressive one, member of a community of speakers versus not a member—these moral, ideological, and emotional stances are mainly enacted through embodied, linguistic, and paralinguistic means.

Peer talk is essential for second-language learning (see Blum-Kulka & Snow 2005 for a similar point). The games of childhood are key scaffolds for second-language learning (Ervin-Tripp 1986). To enter a peer group, children rally whatever resources are at hand to contribute to the elaboration of games. However, also important is the ideological orientation toward the languages in contact, itself constructed by child peers among themselves, through crossing and defining their own speaking styles.

The sociolinguistic and linguistic anthropology studies reviewed document that children, from an early age, manipulate a broad range of linguistic features, using them to enact power, establish positive footing with peers, and articulate norms of the peer group. Developmental differences in sophistication of genres (Blum-Kulka et al. 2005) and linguistic features used (e.g., younger children rely more on prosody, whereas older children rely on grammatical and lexical forms; Hoyle & Adger 1998a) are evident; however, from an early age, even as young as the preschool period, children show facility in using these features. By understanding how the linguistic forms that children use are suited to the social goals that they are seeking to accomplish in their peer social worlds, we can understand their communicative and social competence.

The *Annual Review of Anthropology* is online at http://anthro.annualreviews.org

LITERATURE CITED

Adler PA, Kless S, Adler P. 1992. Socialization to gender roles: popularity among elementary school boys and girls. *Sociol. Educ.* 65:169–87

Adler PA, Adler P. 1998. *Peer Power: Preadolescent Culture and Identity*. New Brunswick: Rutgers Univ. Press

Ahearn L. 2001. Language and agency. *Annu. Rev. Anthropol.* 30:109–37

Andersen ES. 1990. *Speaking with Style: The Sociolinguistic Skills of Children*. London: Routledge

Aronsson K, Thorell M. 2002. Voice and collusion in adult-child talk: towards an architecture of intersubjectivity. In *Talking to Adults: The Contribution of Multi-Party Discourse to Language Acquisition*, ed. S Blum-Kulka, CE Snow, pp. 277–93. Mahwah, NJ: Erlbaum

Bamberg M. 1997. Positioning between structure and performance. *J. Narrat. Life Hist.* 7:335–42

Bamberg M, Barcinski M. 2003. *Developing a (male) sense of a (heterosexual) self: position strategies in 10-, 12-, and 14-year-olds on the topic of girls and sexuality.* Symp. Annu. Meet. Jean Piaget Soc., 33rd, Chicago

Berentzen S. 1984. *Children Constructing Their Social World: An Analysis of Gender Constrast in Children's Interaction in a Nursery School.* Bergen, Norway: Bergen Occas. Pap. Soc. Anthropol., No. 36., Univ. Bergen, Dep. Soc. Anthropol.

Blum-Kulka S, Huck-Taglicht D, Avni H. 2005. The social and discursive spectrum of peer talk. *Discourse Studies.* In press

Blum-Kulka S, Snow C. 2005. The potential for peer talk. *Discourse Studies.* In press

Bucholtz M. 1999a. "Why be normal?" Language and identity practices in a community of nerd girls. *Lang. Soc.* 28:203–23

Bucholtz M. 1999b. Bad examples: transgression and progress in language and gender studies. In *Reinventing Identities: The Gendered Self in Discourse*, ed. M Bucholtz, AC Liang, LA Sutton pp. 123–44. Oxford: Oxford Univ. Press

Bucholtz M. 1999c. You da man: narrating the racial other in the production of white masculinity. *J. Socioling.* 3/4:443–60

Cahill S. 2001. Notably gendered relations: relationship work in early adolescents' notes. In *Gender in Interaction*, ed. B Baron, H Kothoff, pp. 75–97. Amsterdam: Benjamins

Cekaite A, Aronsson K. 2005. Repetition and joking in children's second language conversations: playful recyclings in an immersion classroom. *Discourse Stud.* In press

Cheshire J. 2000. The telling or the tale? Narratives and gender in adolescent friendship networks. *J. Socioling.* 4:234–62

Coates J. 1994. Discourse, gender, and subjectivity: the talk of teenage girls. In *Cultural Performances: Proceedings of the Third Annual Berkeley Women and Language Conference*, ed. M Bucholtz, AC Liang, L Sutton, C Hines, pp. 116–31. Berkeley: Berkeley Women Lang. Group

Coates J. 1997. Competing discourses of femininity. In *Communicating Gender in Context*, ed. H Kotthoff, R Wodak, pp. 285–313. Amsterdam: Benjamins

Coie JD, Dodge K, Kupersmidt JP. 1990. Peer group behavior and social status. In *Peer Rejection in Childhood*, ed. SR Asher, JD Coie, pp. 17–59. New York: Cambridge Univ. Press

Cook-Gumperz J. 1995. Reproducing the discourse of mothering: how gendered talk makes gendered lives. In *Gender Articulated: Language and the Socially Constructed Self*, ed. K Hall, M Bucholtz, pp. 401–419. London: Routledge

Cook-Gumperz J. 2001. The interactional accomplishment of gender and girls' oppositional stances: young children between nursery school and family life. In *Gender in Interaction*, ed. B Baron, H Kothoff, pp. 41–74. Amsterdam/Philadelphia: Benjamins

Cook-Gumperz J, Corsaro W. 1986. Introduction. In *Children's Worlds, Children's Language*, ed. J Cook-Gumperz, W Corsaro, J Streeck, pp. 1–16. Berlin: Mouton de Gruyter

Cook-Gumperz J, Gumperz JJ. 1978. Context in children's speech. In *The Development of Communication*, ed. N Waterson, C Snow, pp. 3–23. New York: Wiley

Cook-Gumperz J, Kyratzis A. 2001. Child discourse. In *A Handbook of Discourse Analysis*, ed. D Schiffrin, D Tannen, H Hamilton, pp. 590–611. Oxford: Blackwell

Cook-Gumperz J, Szymanski M. 2001. Classroom families: cooperating or competing—girls' and boys' interactional styles in a bilingual classroom. *Res. Lang. Soc. Interact.* 34: 107–30

Corsaro W. 1979. "We're friends, right?": children's use of access rituals in a nursery school. *Lang. Soc.* 8:315–36

Corsaro W. 1985. *Friendship and Peer Culture in the Early Years.* Norwood, NJ: Ablex

Corsaro W. 1997. *The Sociology of Childhood.* Thousand Oaks, CA: Pine Forge

Corsaro W, Eder D. 1990. Children's peer cultures. *Annu. Rev. Sociol.* 16:197–220

Corsaro W, Maynard DW. 1996. Format tying in discussion and argumentation among Italian and American children. See Slobin et al. 1996, pp. 157–74

Corsaro W, Rizzo T. 1990. Disputes in the

peer culture of American and Italian nursery school children. In *Conflict Talk: Sociolinguistic Investigations of Arguments in Conversations*, ed. AD Grimshaw, pp. 21–66. New York: Cambridge Univ. Press

Cromdal J, Aronsson K. 2000. Footing in bilingual play. *J. Socioling.* 4(3):435–57

Danby S, Baker CD. 2001. Escalating terror: Communicative strategies in a preschool classroom dispute. *Early Educ. Dev.* 12:343–57

De Leon L. 2002. Soldiers and curers: Mayan children's play in contemporary Chiapas. In *Children Socializing Children Through Language: New Perspectives on Agency, Play, and Identities.* Presented at Annu. Meet. Am. Assoc. Anthropol., New Orleans

Dunn J, Cutting AL. 1999. Understanding others, and individual differences in friendship interactions in young children. *Soc. Dev.* 8: 201–19

Dunn J. 1996. Arguing with siblings, friends, and mothers: developments in relationships and understanding. See Slobin et al. 1996, pp. 191–203

Eckert P. 1989. *Jocks and Burnouts: Social Categories and Identity in the High School.* New York: Teach. Coll. Press

Eckert P. 1993. Cooperative competition in adolescent "girl talk". See Tannen 1993, pp. 32–61

Eckert P. 2000. *Linguistic Variation as Social Practice: The Linguistic Construction of Identity in Belten High.* Malden, MA: Blackwell

Eder D. 1990. Serious and playful disputes: variation in conflict talk among female adolescents. In *Conflict Talk: Sociolinguistic Investigations of Arguments in Conversations*, ed. AD Grimshaw, pp. 67–84. New York: Cambridge Univ. Press

Eder D. 1991. The role of teasing in adolescent peer group culture. In *Sociological Studies of Child Development*, ed. SA Cahill, pp. 181–97. London: JAI Press. Vol. 4

Eder D. 1993. "Go get ya a French!" Romantic and sexual teasing among adolescent girls. See Tannen 1993, pp. 17–30

Eder D. 1998. Developing adolescent peer culture through collaborative narration. See Hoyle & Adger 1998b, pp. 82–94

Eder D, Evans CC, Parker S. 1995. *School Talk: Gender and Adolescent Culture.* New Brunswick, NJ: Rutgers Univ. Press

Eisenberg A, Garvey K. 1981. Children's use of verbal strategies in resolving conflicts. *Discourse Process.* 4:149–70

Emihovich C. 1998. Bodytalk: discourses of sexuality among adolescent African-American girls. See Hoyle & Adger 1998b, pp. 68–94

Ervin-Tripp SM. 1978. 'What do women sociolinguists want?' Prospects for a research field. *Int. J. Sociol. Lang.* 17:17–28

Ervin-Tripp SM. 1986. Activity structure as scaffolding for children's second language learning. In *Children's Worlds and Children's Language*, ed. W Corsaro, J Cook-Gumperz, J Streeck, pp. 327–58. Berlin: Mouton de Gruyter. Vol. 1

Ervin-Tripp SM. 1996. Context in language. See Slobin et al. 1996, pp. 21–36

Ervin-Tripp SM. 2000. Studying conversation: how to get natural peer interaction. In *Methods for Studying Language Production*, ed. L Menn, NB Ratner, pp. 195–214. Mahwah, NJ: Erlbaum

Ervin-Tripp SM. 2001. The place of gender in developmental pragmatics: cultural factors. In *Gender Construction in Children's Interactions: A Cultural Perspective* (Spec. Issue). *Res. Lang. Soc. Interact.* 34(1):131–47

Ervin-Tripp SM, Guo J, Lampert M. 1990. Politeness and persuasion in children's control acts. *J. Pragmat.* 14:195–219

Ervin-Tripp SM, Kuntay A. 1996. The occasioning and structure of conversational stories. In *Conversation: Cognitive, Communicative, and Social Perspectives*, ed. T Givon, pp. 133–66. Amsterdam: John Benjamins

Ervin-Tripp SM, Mitchell-Kernan C. 1977a. *Child Discourse.* New York: Academic

Ervin-Tripp SM, Mitchell-Kernan C. 1977b. Introduction. See Ervin-Tripp & Mitchell-Kernan 1977a, pp. 1–23

Ervin-Tripp SM, Lampert M. 1992. Gender differences in the construction of humorous talk. In *Locating Power: Proceedings of the Second Berkeley Women and Language Conference 2*, ed. K Hall, M Bucholtz, B Moonwomon, pp. 108–17. Berkeley, CA: Berkeley Women Lang. Group

Evaldsson A-C. 2002. Boys' gossip telling: staging identities and indexing (unacceptable) masculine behavior. *Text* 22(2):199–225

Evaldsson A-C. 2004. Shifting moral stances: morality and gender in same-sex and cross-sex game interaction. *Res. Lang. Soc. Interact.* 37(3):In press

Farris CS. 1991. The gender of child discourse: same-sex peer socialization through language use in a Taiwanese preschool. *J. Ling. Anthropol.* 2:198–224

Farris CS. 2000. Cross-sex peer conflict and the discursive production of gender in a Chinese preschool in Taiwan. *J. Pragmat.* 32:539–68

Fernie D, Davies B, Kantor R, McMurray P. 1993. Becoming a person in the preschool: creating integrated gender, school culture, and peer culture positionings. *Qualitat. Stud. Educ.* 6:95–110

Ferguson C. 1983. Sportscaster talk: syntactic aspects of register variation. *Lang. Soc.* 12:153–72

Fordham S. 1998. Speaking standard English from nine to three. See Hoyle & Adger 1998b, pp. 205–16

Garvey C. 1974. Some properties of social play. *Merrill-Palmer Q.* 20:163–80

Garvey C. 1984. *Children's Talk.* London: Fontana

Garvey C, Berninger G. 1981. Timing and turn-taking in children's conversations. *Discourse Process.* 4:27–57

Garvey C, Kramer TL. 1989. The language of social pretend play. *Dev. Rev.* 9:364–82

Gaskins S, Miller PJ, Corsaro WA. 1992. Theoretical and methodological perspectives in the interpretive study of children. In *Interpretive Approaches to Children's Socialization*, ed. WA Corsaro, PJ Miller, pp. 5–24. *New*

Directions for Child Development (Ser.), No. 58. San Francisco: Jossey-Bass

Gee J, Savasir J. 1986. On the use of will and gonna: towards a description of activity types for child language. *Discourse Process.* 8:143–76

Genishi C, DiPaulo M. 1982. Learning through argument in preschool. In *Communicating in the Classroom*. New York: Academic

Gerhardt J. 1990. The relation of language to context in children's speech: the role of hafta in structuring 3-year-olds' discourse. *Pap. Pragmat.* 4:1–56

Goetz M, Shatz M. 1999. When and how peers give reasons: justifications in the talk of middle school children. *J. Child Lang.* 26:721–48

Goffman E. 1961. *Encounters. Two Studies in the Sociology of Interaction*. Indianapolis: Bobs-Merrill

Goffman E. 1974. *Frame Analysis: An Essay on the Organization of Experience*. New York: Harper & Row

Goldman LR. 1998. *Child's Play: Myth, Mimesis, and Make-Believe*. New York: Oxford Univ. Press

Goodwin MH. 1980. Directive-response speech sequences in girls' and boys' task activities. In *Women and Language in Literature and Society*, ed. S McConnell-Ginet, R Borker, N Furman, pp. 157–73. New York: Praeger

Goodwin MH. 1990a. *He-Said-She-Said: Talk as Social Organization Among Black Children*. Bloomington: Indiana Univ. Press

Goodwin MH. 1990b. Tactical uses of stories: participation frameworks within girls' and boys' disputes. *Discourse Process.* 13:33–71

Goodwin MH. 1993. Accomplishing social organization multi-modality in girls' play: patterns of competition and cooperation in an African-American working class girls' group. In *Feminist Theory and Folklore*, ed. ST Hollis, L Pershing, MJ Young, pp. 149–65. Urbana: Univ. Ill. Press

Goodwin MH. 1995. Co-construction in girls' Hopscotch. *Res. Lang. Soc. Interact.* 28:261–82

Goodwin MH. 1998. Games of stance: conflict and footing in Hopscotch. See Hoyle & Adger 1998b, pp. 23–46

Goodwin MH. 1999. Constructing opposition within girls' games. In *Reinventing Identities: The Gendered Self in Discourse*, ed. M Bucholtz, AC Liang, LA Sutton, pp. 388–409. Oxford: Oxford Univ. Press

Goodwin MH. 2001. Organizing participation in cross-sex jump rope: situating gender differences within longitudinal studies of activities. *Res. Lang. Soc. Interact.* 34(1):75–106

Goodwin MH. 2002a. Exclusion in girls' peer groups: ethnographic analysis of language practices on the playground. *Hum. Dev.* 45:392–415

Goodwin MH. 2002b. Building power asymmetries in girls' interactions. *Discourse Soc.* 13(6):715–30

Goodwin MH, Goodwin C, Yaeger-Dror M. 2002c. Multi-modality in girls' game disputes. *J. Pragmat.* 34:1621–49

Goodwin MH. 2003. Gender, ethnicity, and class in children's peer interactions. In *Handbook of Language and Gender*, ed. J Holmes, M Meyerhoff, pp. 229–51. Oxford: Blackwell

Goodwin MH, Goodwin C. 1987. Children's arguing. In *Language, Gender, and Sex in Comparative Perspective*, ed. SU Philips, S Steele, C Tanz, pp. 157–73. New York: Praeger

Gottman JM. 1986. The observation of social process. In *Conversations of Friends: Speculations on Affective Development*, ed. JM Gottman, JG Parker, pp. 51–100. Cambridge: Cambridge Univ. Press

Greenwood A. 1998. Niceness, meanness, and discourse norms. See Hoyle & Adger 1998b, pp. 68–81

Gumperz JJ. 1994. Contextualization and understanding. *In Rethinking Context: Language as an Interactive Phenomenon*, ed. A Duranti, C Goodwin, pp. 229–52. Cambridge: Cambridge Univ. Press

Gumperz JJ, Levinson SC, eds. 1996. *Rethinking Linguistic Relativity*. Cambridge: Cambridge Univ. Press

Hartup WW. 1996. Cooperation, close relationships, and cognitive development. In *The Company They Keep: Friendship in Childhood and Adolescence*, ed. WM Bukowski, AF Newcomb, WA Hartup, pp. 213–37. New York: Cambridge Univ. Press

Heath SB. 1984. Taking a cross-cultural look at narrative. *Top. Lang. Disord.* 7:84–94

Heath SB. 1998. Working through language. See Hoyle & Adger 1998b, pp. 217–40

Hewitt R. 1986. *White Talk, Black Talk: Inter-Racial Friendship and Communication Amongst Adolescents*. Cambridge: Cambridge Univ. Press

Hirschfeld LA. 2002. Why don't anthropologists like children? *Am. Anthropol.* 104:611–27

Hoyle SM. 1998. Register and footing in role play. See Hoyle & Adger 1998b, pp. 47–67

Hoyle SM, Adger CT. 1998a. Introduction. See Hoyle & Adger 1998b, pp. 3–21

Hoyle SM, Adger CT, ed. 1998b. *Kids Talk: Strategic Language Use in Later Childhood*. Oxford: Oxford Univ. Press

Hughes LA. 1993. 'You have to do it with style': girls' games and girls' gaming. In *Feminist Theory and the Study of Folklore*, ed. ST Hollis, L Pershing, MJ Young, pp. 130–48. Urbana: Univ. Ill. Press

Hymes D. 1962. The ethnography of speaking. In *Anthropology and Human Behavior*, ed. T Gladwin, W Sturtevant, pp. 15–53. Washington, DC: Anthropol. Soc. Wash.

Jorgensen JN. 1999. Children's acquisition of code-switching for power-wielding. In *Code-Switching in Conversation: Language, Interaction, and Identity*, ed. P Auer, pp. 237–58. London: Routledge

Kallmeyer W, Keim I. 2003. Communicative social style and social identity. In *Language and Style Indexing Social Identities*. Presented at Int. Pragmat. Conf., 8th, Toronto, Canada

Katriel T. 1985. Brogez: ritual and strategy in Israeli children's conflicts. *Lang. Soc.* 16:467–90

Katriel T. 1987. "Bexibudim!" Ritualized

sharing among Israeli children. *Lang. Soc.* 16:305–20

Katz J. 2005. Building peer relationships in talk: toddlers' peer conversations in child-care. *Discourse Stud.* In press

Kotthoff H. 2005. Conversational mocking and the stylization of a progressive self and a traditional other. In *Social Identity and Communicative Styles: An Alternative Approach to Linguistic Variability*, ed. P Auer, W Kallmeyer. New York: Mouton de Gruyter. In press

Kyratzis A. 1999. Narrative identity: preschoolers' self-construction through narrative in same-sex friendship group dramatic play. *Narrat. Inq.* 9:427–55

Kyratzis A. 2001. Emotion talk in preschool same-sex friendship groups: fluidity over time and context. In *Language Socialization and Children's Entry into Schooling* (Spec. issue), ed. N Budwig. *Early Educ. Dev.* (Ser.) 12:359–91

Kyratzis A, Ervin-Tripp SM. 1999. The development of discourse markers in peer interaction. *J. Pragmat.* 31:1321–38

Kyratzis A, Guo J. 2001. Preschool girls' and boys' verbal conflict strategies in the U.S. and China: cross-cultural and contextual considerations. In *Gender Construction in Children's Interactions: A Cultural Perspective* (Spec. issue), ed. A Kyratzis. *Res. Lang. Soc. Interact.* 34(1):45–73

Kyratzis A, Marx T, Wade ER. 2001. Preschoolers' communicative competence: register shift in the marking of power in different contexts of friendship group talk. In *Early Pragmatic Development* (Spec. issue), ed. H Marcos. *First Lang.* 21:387–431

Maltz DN, Borker RA. 1982. A cultural approach to male-female miscommunication. In *Language and Social Identity*, ed. JJ Gumperz, pp. 196–216. Cambridge: Cambridge Univ. Press

Maynard AE. 2002. Cultural teaching: the development of teaching skills in Zinacantec Maya sibling interactions. *Child Dev.* 73(3):969–82

Maynard DW. 1985. On the functions of social conflict among children. *Am. Sociol. Rev.* 50:207–23

McTear M. 1985. *Children's Conversations.* Oxford: Basic Blackwell

Mendoza-Denton N. 1994. Language attitudes and gang affiliation among California Latina girls. In *Cultural Performances: Proceedings of the Third Annual Berkeley Women and Language Conference*, ed. M Bucholtz, AC Liang, L Sutton, C Hines, pp. 478–86. Berkeley: Berkeley Women Lang. Group

Nakamura K. 2001a. Gender and language use in Japanese preschool children. *Res. Lang. Soc. Interact.* 34(1):15–44

Nakamura K. 2001b. Peers and language: the acquisition of "male" speech forms and conversational style by Japanese boys. In *Research on Child Language Acquisition: Proceedings of the 8th Conference of the International Association for the Study of Child Language*, ed. M Almgren, A Barrena, M Ezeizabarrena, I Idiazabal, B MacWhinney, pp. 504–20. Somerville, MA: Cascadilla Press

Nelson K, Seidman S. 1984. Playing with scripts. In *Symbolic Play: The Development of Social Understanding*, ed. I Bretherton, pp. 45–71. New York: Academic

Nicolopoulou A. 2002. Peer group culture and narrative development. In *Talking to Adults: The Contribution of Multi-party Discourse to Language Acquisition*, ed. S Blum-Kulka, CE Snow, pp. 117–52. Mahwah, NJ: Erlbaum

Ochs E, Capps L. 1996. Narrating the self. *Annu. Rev. Anthropol.* 25:19–43

Ochs E, Kremer-Sadlik T, Solomon O, Sirota KG. 2001. Inclusion as social practice: views of children with autism. *Soc. Dev.* 10(3): 399–419

Ochs E, Schieffelin BB. 1979. *Developmental Pragmatics.* New York: Academic

Ochs E, Schieffelin BB 1984. Language acquisition and socialization: three developmental stories and their implications. In *Culture Theory: Essays on Mind, Self, and Emotion*, ed. RA Shweder, RA LeVine. Cambridge: Cambridge Univ. Press

Opie I, Opie P. 1960. *The Lore and Language of Schoolchildren.* Oxford: Claredon Press

Paley V. 1992. *You Can't Say You Can't Play.* Cambridge: Harvard Univ. Press

Paugh AL. 2005. Multilingual play: children's codeswitching, role play, and agency in Dominica, West Indies. *Lang. Soc.* In press

Rampton B. 1995. *Crossing: Language and Ethnicity Among Adolescents.* London: Longman

Rampton B. 1996. Youth, race, and resistance: a sociolinguistic perspective. *Ling. Educ.* 8:159–73

Rampton B. 1999. Deutsch in Inner London and the animation of an instructed foreign language. *J. Socioling.* 3/4:480–504

Rindstedt C, Aronsson K. 2002. Growing up monolingual in a bilingual community: the Quichua revitalization paradox. *Lang. Soc.* 31:721–42

Rogoff B. 1998. Cognition as a collaborative process. In *Handbook of Child Psychology, 5th Edition*, eds. D Kuhn, RS Siegler, pp. 679–744. New York: Wiley

Rizzo T. 1989. *Friendship Development Among Children in School.* Norwood, NJ: Ablex

Sachs J. 1987. Preschool girls' and boys' language use in pretend play. In *Language, Gender, and Sex in Comparative Perspective*, ed. SU Phillips, S Steele, C Tanz, pp. 178–88. Cambridge: Cambridge Univ. Press

Sacks H. 1992. On some formal properties of children's games. In *Lectures on Conversation*, ed. G Jefferson, pp. 489–506. Oxford: Basil Blackwell. Vol. 1

Sanford S, Eder D. 1984. Adolescent humor during peer interaction. *Soc. Psychol. Q.* 47: 283–300

Schieffelin BB, Ochs E. 1986. *Language Socialization Across Cultures.* Cambridge: Cambridge Univ. Press

Schieffelin BB. 1990. *The Give and Take of Everyday Life: Language Socialization in Kaluli Children.* Cambridge: Cambridge Univ. Press

Schwartzman HB. 1976. An anthropological study of children's play. *Annu. Rev. Anthropol.* 5:239–328

Schwartzman HB. 2001. Introduction. In *Children and Anthropology: Perspectives for the 21st Century*, ed. HB Schwartzman, pp. 1–13. Westport: Bergin and Garvey

Sheldon A. 1990. Pickle fights: gendered talk in preschool disputes. *Discourse Process.* 13: 5–31

Sheldon A. 1992. Conflict talk: sociolinguistic challenges to self-assertion and how young girls meet them. *Merrill-Palmer Q.* 38:95–117

Sheldon A. 1996. You can be the baby brother but you aren't born yet: preschool girls' negotiation for power and access in pretend play. In *Constituting Gender Through Talk in Childhood: Conversations in Parent-Child, Peer, and Sibling Relationships* (Spec. issue), ed. A Sheldon. *Res. Lang. Soc. Interact.* 29:57–80

Slobin DI, Gerhardt J, Kyratzis A, Guo J, eds. 1996. *Social Interaction, Social Context, and Language: Essays in Honor of Susan Ervin-Tripp.* Mahwah, NJ: Erlbaum

Sprott RA. 1992. Children's use of discourse markers in disputes: form-function relations and discourse in child language. *Discourse Process.* 15:423–39

Shuman A. 1986. *Storytelling Rights: The Uses of Oral and Written Texts by Urban Adolescents.* Cambridge: Cambridge Univ. Press

Tannen D. 1989. *Talking Voices: Repetition, Dialogue, and Imagery in Conversational Discourse.* Studies in Interactional Sociolinguistics 6 (Ser.). Cambridge: Cambridge Univ. Press

Tannen D. 1990. Gender differences in topical coherence: creating involvement in best friends' talk. *Discourse Process.* 13(1):73–90

Tannen D, ed. 1993. *Gender and Conversational Interaction.* Oxford: Oxford Univ. Press

Thorne B. 1993. *Gender Play: Girls and Boys in School.* New Brunswick, NJ: Rutgers Univ. Press

Thorne B. 2001. Gender and interaction: widening the conceptual scope. In *Gender in Interaction: Perspectives on Femininity and*

Masculinity in Ethnography and Discourse, ed. B Baron, H Kotthoff, pp. 75–97. Amsterdam: John Benjamins

Watson-Gegeo KA, Boggs ST. 1977. From verbal play to talk story: the role of routines in speech events among Hawaiian children. See Ervin-Tripp & Mitchell-Kernan 1977a, pp. 67–90

Whalen MR. 1995. Working toward play: complexity in children's fantasy activities. *Lang. Soc.* 24:315–47

Whiting BB, Edwards CP. 1988. *Children of Different Worlds: The Formation of Social Behavior.* Cambridge, MA: Harvard Univ. Press

Wolf D, Hicks D. 1989. The voices within narratives: the development of intertextuality in young children's stories. *Discourse Process.* 12:329–53

Zentella AC. 1997. *Growing Up Bilingual: Puerto Rican Children in New York.* Oxford: Blackwell

Subject Index

A

Africa
Area Studies of, 507–10
See also Eastern Africa,
Tropical Sub-Saharan
Africa, Western Africa
African Independent
Churches, 447–68
shift to
Pentecostal-Charismatic
Churches in Africa from,
447–68
Allostasis, 393
American Council of Learned
Societies (ACLS), 504
Ancient state economies,
73–94
archaeology of, 73–94
commercialization in, 73,
78–80
degree of, 78–80
economic change, 92–93
exchange in, 81, 83–85
production in, 81–83
agriculture, 81–82
craft production, 82–83
scale of, 85–87
trade in, 83–85
types of states, 80–81
Americas
migrations to, 551–72
circumarctic peoples
and, 566–67
molecular genetic data
from Siberia and Native
American populations
and, 551–72
number of, 562–67
timing of initial, 558
molecular genetic data
from Siberia and Native

American populations,
553–72
mitochondrial DNA
(mtDNA), 551, 553–72
nonrecombining portion
of Y chromosome
(NRY), 553–72
peopling of, 551–72
Clovis First model of,
551–52
craniometric variation in
human remains and,
553
molecular perspectives
of, 551–72
Amerindian
See Native American
populations
Anthropological archaeology,
76–78
Archaeological political
economy, 77–78, 87–93
economic change, 92–93
identification of
commercial exchange,
87–90
money, 90–91
metallist and chartalist
views, 90–91
property and labor, 91–92
Area Studies, 499–518
areas and disciplines,
502–7
areas in which theory lags
behind practice, 507–14
Africa and Diaspora
studies, 507–10
Europe, 512–14
Latin America, 510–12
convergences
collective Area Studies

in 1990s, 514–16
Middle East, 516–17
kinds of debates that arise
around and within, 501
"traditional area studies"
and "classic
anthropology," 499,
504–7
invention of, 504–7

B

Beauty, 297–315
constructed nature of
notions of, 299
evolution of, 315
femininity and negotiation
of, 310–15
Beauty pageants, 311–12,
383–85
gender identity and,
383–85
Biodiversity
language diversity and, 22
Bioethics, 13–16
diversity and uniqueness
and, 14–16
genetic counseling and,
15–16
informed consent, 15–16
Nuffield Report, 13–14
Biomedicine
diversity and, 14
pharmacogenetics and,
14–16
turn-of-the-century, 1,
13–16
uniqueness and, 14
Body
agentic, 297–98, 307–310
body reform and, 308
template and tool, 308

651

CUMULATIVE INDEXES

CONTRIBUTING AUTHORS, VOLUMES 25–33

CHAPTER TITLES, VOLUMES 25–33

Overviews

Archaeology

International Anthropology and Regional Studies

Sociocultural Anthropology

Theme I: Aids

Theme I: The Body as a Public Surface

Theme I: Capitalism and the Reinvention of Anthropolgy

Theme II: New Technologies of Communication

ANNUAL REVIEWS
Intelligent Synthesis of the Scientific Literature

Annual Reviews – Your Starting Point for Research Online
http://arjournals.annualreviews.org

- Over 900 Annual Reviews volumes—more than 25,000 critical, authoritative review articles in 31 disciplines spanning the Biomedical, Physical, and Social sciences—available online, including all Annual Reviews back volumes, dating to 1932
- Current individual subscriptions include seamless online access to full-text articles, PDFs, Reviews in Advance (as much as 6 months ahead of print publication), bibliographies, and other supplementary material in the current volume and the prior 4 years' volumes
- All articles are fully supplemented, searchable, and downloadable—see http://anthro.annualreviews.org
- Access links to the reviewed references (when available online)
- Site features include customized alerting services, citation tracking, and saved searches

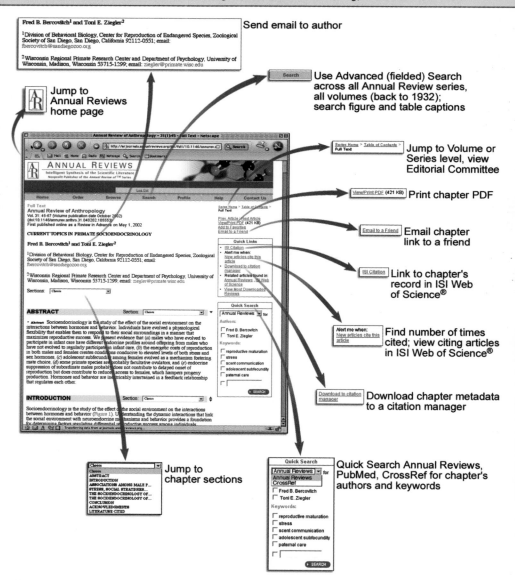

Send email to author

Use Advanced (fielded) Search across all Annual Review series, all volumes (back to 1932); search figure and table captions

Jump to Annual Reviews home page

Jump to Volume or Series level, view Editorial Committee

Print chapter PDF

Email chapter link to a friend

Link to chapter's record in ISI Web of Science®

Find number of times cited; view citing articles in ISI Web of Science®

Download chapter metadata to a citation manager

Jump to chapter sections

Quick Search Annual Reviews, PubMed, CrossRef for chapter's authors and keywords